UNITED STATES SUPREME COURT DECISIONS:

An Index to Excerpts, Reprints, and Discussions

second edition

by

Nancy Anderman Guenther

THE SCARECROW PRESS, INC.
METUCHEN, N.J., & LONDON
1983

Library of Congress Cataloging in Publication Data

Guenther, Nancy Anderman, 1949–
  United States Supreme Court decisions.

    Bibliography: p.
    Includes index.
    1. Law reports, digests, etc.--United
States--Indexes. 2. United States. Supreme
Court. I. Title.
KF101.6.G83 1983   348.73'413   82-10518
ISBN 0-8108-1578-8   347.30841

CONTENTS

iii

PREFACE

The objective of this publication is to provide students a means of locating reprints, excerpts, and discussions of Supreme Court decisions available in publications printed from 1960 to 1980 that are generally accessible to undergraduate students. The bibliography includes all works indexed in the first edition. For those works for which new editions have been located, the older edition has been omitted and replaced by the newer edition. Only those works that could be located for examination are included in this book.

The book list was compiled through a search of the Cumulative Book Index; a search of library collections in the Philadelphia area; and attention to the bibliographies of books examined. Periodical indexes searched included the following: Readers' Guide to Periodical Literature, Social Science Index, General Science Index, Business Periodicals Index, Education Index, and Public Affairs Information Service Bulletin.

Please note that the Index to Legal Periodicals is not included; nor are any newspapers. Index to Legal Periodicals was considered beyond the scope of this work, since it is more appropriate for graduate studies. Students needing relevant information in newspapers should be aided by the inclusion in this book of dates of Supreme Court decisions.

The content of the items examined varied in the extent to which they covered Supreme Court decisions:

1. citation of a case while discussing a topic or another case;

2. discussions of history, content, and impact of specific decisions;

3. excerpts or reprints of the decisions, the intent being to provide the essential portions of the opinion.

No attempt is made to index every mention of each decision (no. 1 above), nor is there an attempt to index cases for which the Supreme Court issued no opinion. In indexing the discussions of opinions (no. 2 above), every effort was made to include pages of discussion whether or not the case was named on each page. For this reason, this index and the indexes of the individual books cited will not always agree.

References to reprints of opinions (no. 3) have been starred (*) to distinguish them from discussions. The objective here is to indicate those sources that intend to present the major components of the opinion. It is not the intent of this index to indicate every quotation of a justice's opinion.

Every attempt has been made to minimize errors during the preparation of this index. It seems probable, however, that some have slipped through. The author would appreciate being informed of errors, as well as suggestions for improvement, that come to light as a result of using this reference tool.

ACKNOWLEDGMENTS

I wish to thank Lorraine Shade and her counterparts in other Inter-library Loan offices for their efforts in making accessible the many volumes needed for the completion of this work.

A special thanks to my family, especially my husband, Karl, and my son, Andrew, for allowing me the time to write this book.

N. A. G.

INSTRUCTIONS FOR USE

This work is divided into five basic sections:

1. A bibliography of the books indexed;
2. A bibliography of periodical titles;
3. A chronological listing of the court decisions located; each with a citation and date and a listing of the books and pages where found. Relevant periodical articles are also listed under each decision.

For example, searching Case Number 2 (located on page 47), a reprint of Georgia v. Brailsford, decided in 1792, will be found in Justices of the Supreme Court, volume 1, page 159. A discussion or explanation of the case will be found in Charles Haines' book, The Role of the Supreme Court in American Government and Politics, volume 1, page 123. The complete decision will be found in 2 Dallas 402 (volume 2, page 402 of the original reports prepared by Dallas).

A star (*) in front of a listing (e. g. before Justices [Friedman] described in the example above) indicates that the item is an excerpt or reprint of the case. Absence of a star indicates discussion of the decision.

A number in parentheses following a periodical citation indicates the number of Supreme Court opinions discussed in that particular periodical article.

4. An alphabetical listing of the parties involved in each case, including, where possible, any known popular names for cases.
5. A subject index to the topics discussed in the various cases and the federal statutes that were important to the cases.

If the U.S. Reports citation or the date is known for a desired case, the user can go directly to Section 3. By comparing

vii

short titles with Section 1, the user can determine which sources contain the case for which he is searching. A question concerning abbreviated periodical titles may be answered by checking the list of abbreviations on page 46.

Those searching by case name or by subject will need to begin with Section 4 or 5 respectively. In either instance, the reference will be from that section to the appropriate case entry number in Section 3.

Adam	Adam Clayton Powell and the Supreme Court. Kent M. Weeks. New York: Dunellen, 1971.
Admin Law (Gellhorn)	Administrative Law; cases and comments. Walter Gellhorn, Clark Byse and Peter L. Strauss. 7th ed. Mineola, N. Y.: Foundation Press, 1979.
Admin Law (Schwartz)	Administrative Law; a casebook. Bernard Schwartz. Boston: Little, Brown, 1977.
Advertising	Advertising and Free Speech. Allen Hyman and M. Bruce Johnson, eds. Lexington, Mass.: Heath and Co., 1977.
Affair	An Affair with Freedom; Justice William J. Brennan. Stephen J. Friedman, ed. New York: Atheneum, 1967.
Against	Against the Law; tho Nixon Court and Criminal Justice. Leonard Levy. New York: Harper and Row, 1974.
Ages	Ages of American Law. Grant Gilmore. New Haven, Conn.: Yale University Press, 1977.
Am Consttn (Kelly)	The American Constitution; its origins and development. 5th ed. Alfred H. Kelly and Winfred Harbison. New York: Norton, 1976.
Am Consttn (Lockhart)	The American Constitution; cases, comments, questions. 4th ed. William Lockhart, Yale Kamisar, and Jesse Choper. St. Paul: West Publishing Co., 1975.
Am Consttnl Issues	American Constitutional Issues. Charles H. Pritchett. New York: McGraw-Hill, 1962.
Am Consttnl Law (Bartholomew)	American Constitutional Law. 2nd ed. Paul C. Bartholomew. Totowa, N. J.: Littlefield, Adams, 1978. 2 vols.
Am Consttnl Law (Mason)	American Constitutional Law; Introductory essays and selected cases. 6th ed. Alpheus T.

1

Mason. Englewood Cliffs, N.J.: Prentice-
Hall, 1978.

Am Consttnl Law (Saye)

American Constitutional Law; Text and cases.
2nd ed. Albert Saye. St. Paul: West Publishing Co., 1979.

Am Consttnl Law (Shapiro)

American Constitutional Law.   5th ed.   Martin
Shapiro and Rocco Tresolini. New York:
Macmillan, 1979.

Am Consttnl Law Reader

American Constitutional Law Reader.   Robert
B. McKay. New York: Oceana, 1958.

Am Govt

American Government; Readings and cases.
6th ed. Peter Woll. Boston: Little, Brown,
1978.

Am Indian

The American Indian and the United States; a
Documentary History. Wilcomb E. Washburn.
New York: Random House, 1973. 4 vols.

Am Land Planning

American Land Planning Law; cases and materials. Norman Williams. New Brunswick,
N.J.: Rutgers--Center for Urban Policy Research, 1978. 2 vols.

Am Landmark

American Landmark Legislation; primary materials. Irving B. Sloan, ed. Dobbs Ferry,
New York: Oceana Publications, 1976-79.
10 vols.

Am Poltcl System

American Political System.   Bernard Brown.
Rev. ed. Homewood, Ill.: Dorsey, 1971.

Am Politics

American Politics and the Constitution.   Thomas
G. Walker. North Scituate, Mass.: Duxbury
Press, 1978.

Am Primer

American Primer. Daniel Boorstin. Chicago:
University of Chicago Press, 1966.

Am Spirit

The American Spirit. 4th ed. Thomas A.
Bailey. Lexington, Mass.: Heath and Co.,
1978.

Am Testament

American Testament; Fifty Great Documents
of American History. Irwin Glusker. New
York: American Heritage, 1971.

Anatomy

The Anatomy of a Constitutional Law Case.
Alan F. Westin. New York: Macmillan,
1958.

Annals

Annals of America. Mortimer Adler. Chicago:
Encyclopaedia Britannica, 1968. 20 vols.

Antecedents

Antecedents and Beginnings to 1801. Julius

Goebel, Jr. (History of the Supreme Court of the United States, v. 1.) New York: Macmillan, 1971.

Antitrust (Posner)

Antitrust; Cases, Economic Notes and other Materials. Richard A. Posner. St. Paul: West Publishing Co., 1974.

Antitrust Analysis

Antitrust Analysis; Problems, Text, Cases. 2nd ed. Phillip Areeda. Boston: Little, Brown, 1974.

Anxiety

Anxiety and Affluence; 1945-1965. Ernest May. New York: McGraw-Hill, 1966.

Apportionment

The Apportionment Cases. Richard C. Cortner. Knoxville, Tenn.: University of Tennessee, 1970.

Arbitration

Arbitration and Collective Bargaining; Conflict Resolution in labor relations. Paul Prasow and Edward Peters. New York: McGraw-Hill, 1970.

Argument

Argument; the Oral Argument before the Supreme Court in Brown v. Board of Education of Topeka, 1952-55. Leon Friedman, ed. New York: Chelsea House, 1969.

Arrest (Berry)

Arrest, search and seizure. Calvin W. Berry. Charlottesville, Va.: Michie, 1973.

Arrest (Waddington)

Arrest, Search and Seizure. Lawrence C. Waddington. Beverly Hills, Cal.: Glencoe Press, 1974.

Authority

Authority to Control the School Program. Tyll Van Geel. Lexington, Mass.: Heath and Co., 1976.

Bakke (Dreyfuss)

Bakke Case; the Politics of Inequality. Joel Dreyfuss and Charles Lawrence III. New York: Harcourt Brace Jovanovich, 1979.

Bakke (Sindler)

Bakke, De Funis and Minority Admissions; the Quest for Equal Opportunity. Allan P. Sindler. New York: Longman, 1978.

Basic Business

Basic Business Law. Len Young Smith and G. Gale Roberson. St. Paul: West Publishing Co., 1977.

Basic Cases

Basic Cases in Constitutional Law. Duane Lockard and Walter F. Murphy. New York: Macmillan, 1980.

Basic Corporation

Basic Corporation Law; Materials, Cases, Text. Detlow F. Vagts. Mineola, N.Y.: Foundation Press, 1979.

Basic Criminal   Basic Criminal Procedure. 4th ed. Yale
                        Kamisar, Wayne R. LaFave, and Jerold Israel.
                        St. Paul: West Publishing Co. , 1974.

Basic Documents   Basic Documents in American History. Rich-
                        ard B. Morris. Princeton, N. J. : Van Nos-
                        trand, 1965. (Reprinted by: Huntingdon, N. Y. :
                        Krieger, 1980.)

Basic History   A Basic History of the United States Supreme
                        Court. Bernard Schwartz. Huntingdon, N. Y. :
                        Krieger, 1979. (Reprint of: 1968 ed. Prince-
                        ton: Van Nostrand.)

Basic Text   Basic Text on Labor Law, Unionization and
                        Collective Bargaining. Robert A. Gorman.
                        St. Paul: West Publishing Co. , 1976.

Bible   The Bible, Religion and the Public Schools.
                        3rd ed. Donald E. Boles. Ames: Iowa State
                        University Press, 1965.

Bill (Cohen)   Bill of Rights; Constitutional Law for Under-
                        graduates. William Cohen and John Kaplan.
                        Mineola, N. Y. : Foundation Press, 1976.

Bill (Konvitz)   Bill of Rights Reader; Leading Constitutional
                        Cases. 5th ed. Milton R. Konvitz. Ithaca,
                        N. Y. : Cornell University Press, 1973.

Biography   A Biography of the Constitution of the United
                        States; Its Origin, Formation, Adoption, Inter-
                        pretation. 2nd ed. Broadus Mitchell and
                        Louise P. Mitchell. New York: Oxford Uni-
                        versity Press, 1975.

Black   Black Ballots; Voting Rights in the South, 1944-
                        1969. Steven F. Lawson. New York: Colum-
                        bia University Press, 1976.

Brethren   The Brethren; Inside the Supreme Court. Bob
                        Woodward and Scott Armstrong. New York:
                        Simon and Schuster, 1979.

Business   Business Law Text. 3rd ed. Jordan L. Paust
                        and Robert D. Upp. St. Paul: West Publish-
                        ing Co. , 1979.

Busing   Busing; The Political and Judicial Process.
                        James Bolner. New York: Praeger, 1974.

By These Words   By These Words. Paul Angle. New York:
                        Rand McNally, 1966, c1954.

By What Right   By What Right? a Commentary on the Supreme
                        Court's Power to Revise the Constitution.
                        Louis Lusky. Charlottesville, Va. : Michie,
                        1975.

CQ Guide

Congressional Quarterly's Guide to the United States Supreme Court. Elder Witt, ed. Washington, D. C. : Congressional Quarterly, Inc. , 1979.

Cases Admiralty

Cases and Materials on Admiralty. Nicholas J. Healy and David J. Sharpe. St. Paul: West Publishing Co. , 1974.

Cases Antitrust Law

Cases and Materials on Antitrust Law. Harlan Blake and Robert Pitofsky. Brooklyn, N. Y. : Foundation Press, 1967.

Cases Antitrust Policy

Cases in Antitrust Policy. Paul W. Cook. New York: Holt, Rinehart, and Winston, 1964.

Cases Civil Liberties

Cases in Civil Liberties. 3rd ed. Robert F. Cushman. New York: Appleton-Century-Crofts, 1979.

Cases Civil Procedure

Cases and other Materials on Civil Procedure. Austin W. Scott and Robert B. Kent. Boston: Little, Brown, 1967.

Cases Consttnl Law (Cushman)

Cases in Constitutional Law. 5th ed. Robert F. Cushman. New York: Appleton-Century-Crofts, 1979.

Cases Consttnl Law (Gunther)

Cases and Materials on Constitutional Law. 10th ed. Gerald Gunther. Mineola, N. Y. : Foundation Press, 1980.

Cases Consttnl Law (Rosenblum)

Cases on Constitutional Law; Political Roles of the Supreme Court. Victor Rosenblum and A. Diderick Castberg. Homewood, Ill. : Dorsey, 1973.

Cases Consttnl Rights

Cases and Materials on Constitutional Rights and Liberties. 4th ed. William Lockhart, Yale Kamisar, and Jesse Choper. St. Paul: West Publishing Co. , 1975.

Cases Copyright (Kaplan)

Cases on Copyright, Unfair Competition and Other Topics. 2nd ed. Benjamin Kaplan and Ralph S. Brown. Mineola, N. Y. : Foundation Press, 1974.

Cases Copyright (Nimmer)

Cases and Materials on Copyright and Other Aspects of Law Pertaining to Literary, Musical and Artistic Works. 2nd ed. Melville B. Nimmer. St. Paul: West Publishing Co. , 1979.

Cases Criml Justice

Cases and Materials on Criminal Justice Administration. Frank W. Miller. Mineola, N. Y. : Foundation Press, 1976.

Cases Criml Law (Hall)

Cases and Readings on Criminal Law and

Procedure. 3rd ed. Jerome Hall. Indianapolis: Bobbs-Merrill, 1976.

Cases Criml Law (Inbau)

Cases and Comments on Criminal Law. Fred
E. Inbau, James R. Thompson, and Andre A.
Moenssens. Mineola, N. Y. : Foundation Press,
1979.

Cases Criml Law
(Perkins)

Cases and Materials on Criminal Law and Procedure. 5th ed. Rollin M. Perkins and Ronald
N. Boyce. Mineola, N. Y. : Foundation Press,
1977.

Cases Domestic

Cases and Other Materials on Domestic Relations. 3rd ed. Walter Wadlington and Monrad
G. Paulsen. Mineola, N. Y. : Foundation Press,
1978.

Cases Drug

Cases, Text and Materials on Drug Abuse and
the Law. Gerald F. Uelmen and Victor G.
Haddox. St. Paul: West Publishing Co. , 1974.

Cases Electronic

Cases and Materials on Electronic Mass Media:
Radio Television and Cable. 2nd ed. William
K. Jones. Mineola, N. Y. : Foundation Press,
1979.

Cases Employment

Cases and Materials on the Employment Rela-
tion. Wex S. Malone, Marcus L. Plant, and
Joseph W. Little. St. Paul: West Publishing
Co. , 1974.

Cases Environmental Law
(Gray)

Cases and Materials on Environmental Law.
2nd ed. Oscar Gray. Washington, D. C. :
Bureau of National Affairs, 1973.

Cases Environmental Law
(Hanks)

Cases and Materials on Environmental Law and
Policy. Eva H. Hanks, A. Dan Tarlock, and
John L. Hanks. St. Paul: West Publishing
Co. , 1974.

Cases Equity

Cases and Materials on Equity. 5th ed. Zechariah Chaffee and Edward Domenic Re.
Brooklyn, N. Y. : Foundation Press, 1975.

Cases Evidence

Cases and Materials on Evidence. 6th ed.
John M. Maguire and others. Mineola, N. Y. :
Foundation Press, 1973.

Cases Federal Courts

Cases and Materials on Federal Courts. 6th
ed. Charles T. McCormick, James H. Chad-
bourn, and Charles Alan Wright. Mineola,
N. Y. : Foundation Press, 1976.

Cases Food

Cases and Materials on Food and Drug Law;
a Study in Consumer Legislation. 2nd ed.
Thomas W. Christopher and William Goodrich.
New York: Commerce Clearing House. 1973.

Cases Individual	Cases and Materials on Individual Rights in Constitutional Law. Gerald Gunther. 2nd ed. Mineola, N.Y.: Foundation Press, 1976.
Cases Labor (Cox)	Cases and Materials on Labor Law. 7th ed. Archibald Cox and Derek C. Bok. Mineola, N.Y.: Foundation Press, 1969.
Cases Labor (Handler)	Cases and Materials on Labor Law. Milton Handler and Paul Hays. 4th ed. St. Paul: West Publishing Co., 1963.
Cases Labor (Leslie)	Cases and Materials on Labor Law; Process and Policy. Douglas L. Leslie. Boston: Little, Brown, 1979.
Cases Labor (Oberer)	Cases and Materials on Labor Law, Collective Bargaining in a Free Society. Walter Oberer. 2nd ed. St. Paul: West Publishing Co., 1979.
Cases Labor (Stern)	Cases in Labor Law. Duke Nordlinger Stern and Joseph P. Yaney. Columbus, Ohio: Grid, 1977.
Cases Land	Cases and Materials on Land Use. Jacob Henry Beuscher, Robert R. Wright, and Morton Gitelman. 2nd ed. St. Paul: West Publishing Co., 1976.
Cases Law and Poverty	Cases and Materials on Law and Poverty. George Cooper and others. St. Paul: West Publishing Co., 1973.
Cases Law of Wills	Cases and Text on the Law of Wills. 2nd ed. W. Barton Leach. Boston: Little, Brown, 1960.
Cases Modern	Cases and Materials on Modern Juvenile Justice. Sanford J. Fox. St. Paul: West Publishing Co., 1972.
Cases Pleading	Cases and Materials on Pleading and Procedure; State and Federal. David W. Louisell and Geoffrey C. Hazard. Mineola, N.Y.; Foundation Press, 1979.
Cases Professional	Cases and Materials on Professional Responsibility. 3rd ed. Maynard E. Pirsig and Kenneth F. Kirwin. St. Paul: West Publishing Co., 1976.
Cases Property (Casner)	Cases and Text on Property. A. James Casner and W. Barton Leach. Boston: Little, Brown, 1969.
Cases Property (Donahue)	Cases and Materials on Property; an Introduction to the Concept and the Institution. Charles Donahue and others. St. Paul: West Publishing Co., 1974.

Cases Regulated	Cases and Materials on Regulated Industries. 2nd ed. William K. Jones. Mineola, N.Y.: Foundation Press, 1976.
Cases Regulation	Cases and Materials on the Regulation of International Trade and Investment. Carl H. Fulda and Warren F. Schwartz. Mineola, N.Y.: Foundation Press, 1970.
Cases Trade	Cases and Materials on Trade Regulation. Milton Handler. Mineola, N.Y.: Foundation Press, 1967.
Cases Workmen	Cases and Materials on Workmen's Compensation. Wex Malone and Marcus Plant. St. Paul: West Publishing Co., 1963.
Censorship	Censorship; Government and Obscenity. Terrence J. Murphy. Baltimore: Helicon, 1963.
Censorship Landmarks	Censorship Landmarks. Edward De Grazia. New York: R.R. Bowker Co., 1969.
Century	A Century of Civil Rights. Milton R. Konvitz. New York: Columbia University Press, 1961.
Changing	Changing America and the Supreme Court. Barbara Habenstreit. New York: Messner, 1974.
Church and State	Church and State in the United States. Anson P. Stokes and Leo Pfeffer. New York: Harper and Row, 1964. (Reprinted: 1975 ed. Westport, Conn.: Greenwood.)
Church State and Freedom	Church, State and Freedom. Rev. ed. Leo Pfeffer. Boston: Beacon, 1967.
Civil Liberties (Barker)	Civil Liberties and the Constitution. 3rd ed. Lucius Barker. Englewood Cliffs, N.J.: Prentice-Hall, 1978.
Civil Liberties (Kauper)	Civil Liberties and the Constitution. Paul Kauper. Ann Arbor: University of Michigan Press, 1966, © 1962.
Civil Liberties (Stone)	Civil Liberties and Civil Rights. Victor J. Stone, ed. Urbana: University of Illinois Press, 1977.
Civil Liberties (Sweet)	Civil Liberties in America; a Casebook. Esther C. Sweet. Princeton, N.J.: Van Nostrand, 1966.
Civil Liberties (Wasby)	Civil Liberties; Policy and Policy Making. Stephen Wasby. Lexington, Mass.: Lexington Books, 1976.
Civil Procedure (Carrington)	Civil Procedure; Cases and Comments on the

vol. 2, Journalistic Freedom.   Joseph J. Hemmer.   Metuchen, N. J. :   Scarecrow, 1979-80.

Communications Law   Communications Law Explosion.   New York:
                          Practising Law Institute, 1973.

Communism   Communism, the Courts and the Constitution.
                          Allen Guttmann.   Lexington, Mass. :   Heath
                          and Co. , 1964.

Comparative   Comparative Constitutional Law;   Cases and
                          Commentaries.   Walter F. Murphy and Joseph
                          Tanenhaus.   New York: St. Martin's Press,
                          1977.

Competition   Competition and Public Policy; Cases in Anti-
                          trust.   H. Lee Fusilier and Jerome C. Dar-
                          nell.   Englewood Cliffs, N. J. :   Prentice-Hall,
                          1971.

Compliance   Compliance and the Law; a Multidisciplinary
                          Approach.   Samuel Krislow and others, eds.
                          Beverly Hills, Cal. :   Sage Publications, 1972.

Compulsory   Compulsory Education and the Amish; the Right
                          Not to be Modern.   Albert N. Keim.   Boston:
                          Beacon Press, 1975.

Conceived   Conceived in Liberty.   E. Sandoz.   North
                          Scituate, Mass. :   Duxbury Press, 1978.

Conflict   A Conflict of Loyalties; the Case for Selective
                          Conscientious Objection.   James Finn, ed.
                          New York: Pegasus, 1968.

Congress Against   Congress Against the Court.   Adam C. Breck-
                          enridge.   Lincoln: University of Nebraska
                          Press, 1970.

Congress and the Court   Congress and the Court; a Case Study in the
                          American Political Process.   Walter F. Mur-
                          phy.   Chicago: University of Chicago Press,
                          1962.

Congress Investigates   Congress Investigates; a Documented History,
                          1792-1974.   Arthur M. Schlesinger, Jr. and
                          Roger Bruns.   New York: Chelsea House,
                          1975.   5 vols.

Congress Versus   Congress Versus the Supreme Court.   Charles
                          Herman Pritchett.   Minneapolis: University of
                          Minnesota Press, 1961.   (Reprinted 1973 by
                          Da Capo Press.)

Conscience   Conscience in America; a Documentary History
                          of Conscientious Objection in America, 1757-
                          1967.   Lillian Schlissel.   New York: Dutton,
                          1968.

Conservative	Conservative Crisis and Rule of Law; Attitudes of Bar and Bench, 1887-1895. Arnold M. Paul. Ithaca, N.Y.: Cornell University Press, 1960. (Reprinted 1969 by Harper and Row.)
Consttn (Barber)	The Constitution and the Delegation of Congressional Power. Sotirias A. Barber. Chicago: University of Chicago Press, 1975.
Consttn (Hirschfield)	The Constitution and the Court; the Development of the Basic Law Through Judicial Interpretation. Robert S. Hirschfield. New York: Random House, 1962.
Consttn (Konvitz)	The Constitution and Civil Rights. Milton R. Konvitz. New York: Farrar, Straus and Giroux, 1977. (Reprint of 1946 ed.)
Consttn (Mendelson)	The Constitution and the Supreme Court. Wallace Mendelson. New York: Dodd, Mead, 1965.
Consttn (Morris)	The Constitution and American Education. 2nd ed. Arval A. Morris. St. Paul: West Publishing Co., 1980.
Consttn (Pollak)	Constitution and the Supreme Court; a Documentary History. Louis H. Pollak. Cleveland, Ohio: World Publishing Co., 1966. 2 vols.
Consttn (Swindler)	The Constitution and Chief Justice Marshall. William F. Swindler. New York: Dodd, Mead, 1978.
Consttn (Wilcox)	The Constitution and the Conduct of Foreign Policy. Francis O. Wilcox and Richard Frank. New York: Praeger, 1976.
Consttnl Aspects	Constitutional Aspects of Watergate; Documents and Materials. A. Stephen Boyan, ed. Dobbs Ferry, N.Y.: Oceana Publications, 1976. 4 vols.
Consttnl Bricolage	Constitutional Bricolage. Gerald Garvey. Princeton, N.J.: Princeton University Press, 1971.
Consttnl Cases	Constitutional Cases in American Government. Walter F. Berns. New York: Crowell, 1963.
Consttnl Counterrevolution	Constitutional Counterrevolution? The Warren Court and the Burger Court; Judicial Policy Making in Modern America. Richard Y. Funston. New York: Schenkman, 1977.
Consttnl Criml (Marks)	Constitutional Criminal Procedure. Thomas C. Marks and J. T. Reilly. North Scituate, Mass.: Duxbury, 1979.

Consttnl Criml (Scarboro)	Constitutional Criminal Procedure; Cases, Questions and Notes. James E. Scarboro and James B. White. Mineola, N. Y.: Foundation Press, 1977.
Consttnl Decisions	Constitutional Decisions in American Government. Rocco J. Tresolini. New York: Macmillan, 1965.
Consttnl Decisions of Marshall	Constitutional Decisions of John Marshall. Joseph P. Cotton, Jr. New York: Da Capo Press, 1969. 2 vols.
Consttnl Law (Barrett)	Constitutional Law; Cases and Materials. 5th ed. Edward L. Barrett. Mineola, N. Y.: Foundation Press, 1977.
Consttnl Law (Barron)	Constitutional Law; Principles and Policy. Jerome A. Barron and C. Thomas Dienes. Indianapolis: Bobbs-Merrill, 1975.
Consttnl Law (Cortner)	Constitutional Law and Politics; Three Arizona Case-Studies. Richard C. Cortner and Clifford M. Lytle. Tucson: University of Arizona Press, 1971.
Consttnl Law (Felkenes)	Constitutional Law for Criminal Justice. George T. Felkenes. Englewood Cliffs, N. J.: Prentice-Hall, 1978.
Consttnl Law (Freund)	Constitutional Law; Cases and other Problems. 4th ed. Paul A. Freund and others. Boston: Little, Brown, 1977.
Consttnl Law (Grossman)	Constitutional Law and Judicial Policy Making. 2nd ed. Joel B. Grossman and Richard S. Wells. New York: Wiley, 1980.
Consttnl Law (Kauper)	Constitutional Law; Cases and Materials. 4th ed. Paul G. Kauper. Boston: Little, Brown, 1972.
Consttnl Law (Klein)	Constitutional Law for Criminal Justice Professionals. Irving J. Klein. North Scituate, Mass.: Duxbury Press, 1980.
Consttnl Law (Lockhart)	Constitutional Law; Cases--Comments--Questions. 5th ed. William Lockhart, Yale Kamisar, and Jesse H. Choper. St. Paul: West Publishing Co., 1980.
Consttnl Law (Maddex)	Constitutional Law; Cases and Comments. 2nd ed. James L. Maddex. St. Paul: West Publishing Co., 1979.
Consttnl Law (Schmidhauser)	Constitutional Law in the Political Process. John R. Schmidhauser. Chicago: Rand McNally, 1963.

Courts   The Courts and Higher Education. John Bru-
                                bacher. San Francisco: Jossey-Bass, 1971.

Courts, Judges   Courts, Judges and Politics; an Introduction to
                                the Judicial Process. 3rd ed. Walter F.
                                Murphy and C. Herman Pritchett. New York:
                                Random House, 1979.

Criminal Evidence   Criminal Evidence; Principles, Cases and Read-
                                ings. Thomas J. Gardner. St. Paul: West
                                Publishing Co. , 1978.

Criminal Justice (Galloway)   Criminal Justice and the Burger Court. John
                                Galloway, ed. New York: Facts on File, 1978.

Criminal Justice (Kaplan)   Criminal Justice; Introductory Cases and Ma-
                                terials. 2nd ed. John Kaplan. Mineola, N. Y. :
                                Foundation Press, 1978.

Criminal Justice (Way)   Criminal Justice and the American Constitu-
                                tion. H. Frank Way. North Scituate, Mass. :
                                Duxbury Press, 1980.

Criminal Law (Dix)   Criminal Law. George E. Dix and M. Michael
                                Sharlot. 2nd ed. St. Paul: West Publishing
                                Co. , 1979.

Criminal Law (Felkenes)   Criminal Law and Procedure: Text and Cases.
                                George T. Felkenes. Englewood Cliffs, N. J. :
                                Prentice-Hall, 1976.

Criminal Law (Kadish)   Criminal Law and Its Processes; Cases and
                                Materials. 3rd ed. Sanford H. Kadish and
                                Monrad G. Paulsen. Boston: Little, Brown,
                                1975.

Criminal Law (Wells)   Criminal Law. Kenneth M. Wells and Paul B.
                                Weston. Santa Monica, Cal. : Goodyear Pub-
                                lishing Co. , 1978.

Criminal Law (Young)   Criminal Law: Codes and Cases. R. Bruce
                                Young. New York: McGraw-Hill, 1972.

Criminal Law Revolution   Criminal Law Revolution and Its Aftermath,
                                1960-1971. Washington, D. C. : Bureau of
                                National Affairs, 1972.

Criminal Procedure (Lewis)   Criminal Procedure; the Supreme Court's
                                View--Cases. Peter W. Lewis, ed. St. Paul:
                                West Publishing Co. , 1979.

Criminal Procedure (Wells)   Criminal Procedure and Trial Practice. Ken-
                                neth M. Wells and Paul B. Weston. Englewood
                                Cliffs, N. J. : Prentice-Hall, 1977.

Crisis   A Crisis for the American Press. John Hohen-
                                berg. New York: Columbia University Press,
                                1978.

sions on Race and the Schools. Leno A. Graglia. Ithaca, N.Y.: Cornell University Press,
1976.

Discriminating

Discriminating Against Discrimination; Prefer-
ential Admissions and the De Funis Case.
Robert M. O'Neil. Bloomington: Indiana University Press, 1975.

Discrimination

Discrimination and Civil Rights; Cases, Text
and Materials. Norman Dorsen. Boston:
Little, Brown, 1969.

Dispassionate

Dispassionate Justice; a Synthesis of the Judicial Opinions of Robert H. Jackson. Glendon
Schubert. New York: Bobbs-Merrill, 1969.

Dissent

Dissent in the Supreme Court; a Chronology.
Percival E. Jackson. Norman: University of
Oklahoma Press, 1969.

Documentary

Documentary History of Banking and Currency.
Herman Krooss. New York: Chelsea House,
1969. 4 vols.

Documents History

Documents of American History. 9th ed.
Henry S. Commager. New York: Appleton-
Century-Crofts, 1973.

Documents Indian

Documents of United States Indian Policy.
Francis P. Prucha. Lincoln: University of
Nebraska Press, 1975.

Double (Miller)

Double Jeopardy and the Federal System.
Leonard G. Miller. Chicago: University of
Chicago, 1968.

Double (Sigler)

Double Jeopardy; the Development of a Legal
and Social Policy. Jay A. Sigler. Ithaca,
N.Y.: Cornell University Press, 1969.

Douglas

Douglas Opinions. Vern Countryman, ed.
New York: Random House, 1977.

Dred Scott Case

The Dred Scott Case; its Significance in American Law and Politics. Don E. Fehrenbacher.
New York: Oxford University Press, 1978.

Dred Scott Decision

Dred Scott Decision; Law or Politics. Stanley
I. Kutler, ed. Boston: Houghton Mifflin,
1967.

Dred Scott's Case

Dred Scott's Case. Vincent Charles Hopkins.
New York: Russell & Russell, 1967.

Dynamics

Dynamics of Compliance: Supreme Court Decision Making from a New Perspective. Richard M. Johnson. Evanston, Ill.: Northwestern
University Press, 1967.

Westport, Conn. : Greenwood Press, 1975.
(Reprint of 1938 ed. by Liveright Publishing
Corp.)

Essentials

Essentials of School Law.   Robert L. Drury
and Kenneth C. Ray.   New York: Appleton-
Century-Crofts, 1967.

Evolution

Evolution of a Judicial Philosophy: Selected
Opinions and Papers of Justice John M. Harlan.
David L. Shapiro, ed.   Cambridge, Mass.:
Harvard University Press, 1969.

Exclusionary

Exclusionary Injustice; the Problem of Illegally
Obtained Evidence.   Steven R. Schlesinger.
New York: Dekker, 1977.

Executive Privilege

Executive Privilege; a Constitutional Myth.
Raoul Berger.   Cambridge, Mass. : Harvard
University Press, 1974.

Expanding Liberties

Expanding Liberties; Freedom's Gains in Post-
war America.   Milton R. Konvitz.   New York:
Viking, 1966.   (Reprinted 1976 by Greenwood
Press.)

Family

The Family and the Law; Problems for Decision
in the Family Law Process.   Joseph Goldstein
and Jay Katz.   New York: Free Press, 1965.

Federal Censorship

Federal Censorship; Obscenity in the Mail.
James C. Paul and Murray L. Schwartz.
New York: Free Press, 1961.   (Reprinted
1977 by Greenwood.)

Federal Courts

The Federal Courts and the Federal System.
2nd ed.   Paul M. Bator and others.   Mineola,
N. Y. : Foundation Press, 1973.

Federal System

The Federal System in Constitutional Law.
Charles Herman Pritchett.   Englewood Cliffs,
N. J. : Prentice-Hall, 1978.

Felix Frankfurter (Baker)

Felix Frankfurter.   Liva Baker.   New York:
Coward-McCann, 1969.

Felix Frankfurter
(Mendelson)

Felix Frankfurter; the Judge.   Wallace Mendelson.   New York: Reynal, 1964.

Felix Frankfurter
(Phillips)

Felix Frankfurter Reminisces.   Harlan B.
Phillips.   New York: Reynal, 1960.   (Reprinted 1978 by Greenwood.)

Felix Frankfurter
(Thomas)

Felix Frankfurter: Scholar on the Bench.
Helen S. Thomas.   Baltimore: Johns Hopkins,
1960.

First Amendment (Berns)

The First Amendment and the Future of Amer-

ican Democracy.   Walter Berns.   New York:
Basic Books, 1976.

First Amendment (Franklin)   The First Amendment and the Fourth Estate;
Communications Law for Undergraduates.   Marc
Franklin and Ruth Franklin.   Mineola, N. Y. :
Foundation Press, 1977.

First Amendment (Konvitz)   First Amendment Freedoms; Selected Cases on
Freedom of Religion, Speech, Press, Assembly.
Milton R. Konvitz.   Ithaca, N. Y. :   Cornell,
1963.

First Amendment   First Amendment; the History of Religious
(Marnell)   Freedom in America.   William Marnell.   New
York: Doubleday, 1966, © 1964.

Foreign Affairs   Foreign Affairs and the Constitution.   Louis
Henkin.   New York: Norton, 1975, © 1972.

Franklin D. Roosevelt   Franklin D. Roosevelt and the Supreme Court.
Rev. ed.   Alfred H. Cope.   Lexington, Mass. :
Heath, 1969.

Free Enterprise   Free Enterprise and Economic Organization;
Antitrust Regulatory Controls.   Louis B.
Schwartz.   4th ed.   Mineola, N. Y. :   Founda-
tion Press, 1972.

Free Speech (Kurland)   Free Speech and Association; the Supreme
Court and the First Amendment.   Philip B.
Kurland, ed.   Chicago: University of Chicago
Press, 1975.

Free Speech (Summers)   Free Speech and Political Protest.   Marvin
Summers, ed.   Boston: Heath, 1967.

Freedom and Protection   Freedom and Protection; the Bill of Rights.
Andrew D. Weinberger.   Westport, Conn. :
Greenwood, 1972.

Freedom and Reform   Freedom and Reform; Essays in Honor of
Henry Steele Commager.   Harold M. Hyman
and Leonard W. Levy, eds.   New York:
Harper, 1967.

Freedom and the Court   Freedom and the Court; Civil Rights and Liberties in the United States.   3rd ed.   Henry
Julian Abraham.   New York: Oxford, 1977.

Freedom of Speech   Freedom of Speech.   Franklyn S. Haiman.
(Haiman)   Skokie, Ill. : National Textbook Co. , in con-
junction with the American Civil Liberties
Union, 1976.

Freedom of Speech   Freedom of Speech and Press in America.
(Hudon)   Edward G. Hudon.   Washington, D. C. :   Public
Affairs Press, 1963.

Freedom of Speech   Freedom of Speech; the Supreme Court and
   (Shapiro)   Judicial Review.   Martin Shapiro.   Englewood
                           Cliffs, N. J. : Prentice-Hall, 1966.

Freedom of the Press   Freedom of the Press for Whom?   The Right
   (Barron)   of Access to Mass Media.   Jerome A. Barron.
                           Bloomington: Indiana University Press, 1973.

Freedom of the Press   Freedom of the Press from Hamilton to the
   (Nelson)   Warren Court.   Harold Nelson.   Indianapolis:
                           Bobbs-Merrill, 1967.

Freedom of the Press   Freedom of the Press vs. Public Access.
   (Schmidt)   Benno C. Schmidt.   New York: Praeger, 1976.

Freedom Reader   Freedom Reader.   2nd ed.   Edwin S. Newman.
                           Dobbs Ferry, N. Y. : Oceana, 1963.

Freedom Spent   Freedom Spent.   Richard Harris.   Boston:
                           Little, Brown, 1976.

Freedom vs. National   Freedom vs. National Security.   Morton Hal-
   Security   perin and Daniel Hoffman.   New York: Chel-
                           sea House, 1977.

From Brown   From Brown to Bakke; the Supreme Court and
                           School Integration: 1954-1978.   J. Harvis
                           Wilkinson.   New York: Oxford University
                           Press, 1979.

From Confederation   From Confederation to Nation; the American
                           Constitution, 1835-1877.   Bernard Schwartz.
                           Baltimore: Johns Hopkins, 1973.

From the Diaries   From the Diaries of Felix Frankfurter.   Joseph
                           P. Lash, ed.   New York: Norton, 1975.

Frontiers   Frontiers of Civil Liberties.   Norman Dorsen.
                           New York: Pantheon Books, 1968.

Garden   The Garden and the Wilderness: Religion and
                           Government in American Constitutional History.
                           Mark DeWolfe Howe.   Chicago: University of
                           Chicago Press, 1965.

Gideon's Trumpet   Gideon's Trumpet.   Anthony Lewis.   New York:
                           Random House, 1964.

God   God Save This Honorable Court.   Louis M.
                           Kohlmeier, Jr.   New York: Scribner, 1972.

Gomillion   Gomillion versus Lightfoot.   Bernard Taper.
                           New York: McGraw-Hill, 1962.

Good Guys   The Good Guys, the Bad Guys and the First
                           Amendment; Free Speech vs. Fairness in
                           Broadcasting.   Fred Friendly.   New York:
                           Random House, 1976.

Government | Government by Judiciary; the Transformation of the Fourteenth Amendment. Raoul Berger. Cambridge, Mass.: Harvard University Press, 1977.

Government and Business | Government and Business. 3rd ed. Ronald Anderson. Cincinnati, Ohio: South-Western, 1966.

Government Regulation | Government Regulation of Business. Robert H. Bowie, Eugene V. Rostow, and Robert Bork. Brooklyn, N. Y.: Foundation Press, 1963.

Great Events American | Great Events from History; American Series. Frank Magill, ed. Englewood Cliffs, N. J.: Salem Press, 1975.

Great Events Worldwide | Great Events from History; Worldwide Twentieth Century Series. Frank Magill, ed. Englewood Cliffs, N. J.: Salem Press, 1980.

Great Reversals | The Great Reversals; Tales of the Supreme Court. Morris L. Ernst. New York: Weybright and Talley, 1973.

Great School Bus | The Great School Bus Controversy. Nicolas Mills. New York: Teachers College, Columbia University, 1973.

Growth | Growth of Presidential Power; a Documented History. William M. Goldsmith. New York: Chelsea House, 1974. 3 vols.

Guarantee | The Guarantee Clause of the United States Constitution. William M. Wiecek. Ithaca, N. Y.: Cornell, 1972.

Handbook | Handbook of Free Speech and Free Press. Jerome Barron and C. Thomas Dienes. Boston: Little, Brown, 1979.

Handbook Politics | Handbook of Politics. Edward McPherson. New York: Da Capo Press, 1972. Reprint of volumes originally published 1872-1894. 12 vols. in 4.

Historic Decisions | Historic Decisions of the Supreme Court. 2nd ed. Carl Brent Swisher. New York: Van Nostrand, 1969.

Historic Documents (year) | Historic Documents 1972-79. Washington, D. C.: Congressional Quarterly, Inc., 1973-1980.

History of the Supreme Court of the United States;
   v. 1, see: Antecedents and Beginnings to 1801.
   v. 5, see: The Taney Period, 1836-64.
   v. 6, pt. 1, see: Reconstruction and Reunion, 1864-88.

Hugo Black (Dunne) | Hugo Black and the Judicial Revolution. Gerald T. Dunne. New York: Simon and Schuster. 1977.

Hugo Black (Hamilton)   Hugo Black and the Bill of Rights. Hugo Black
                               Symposium in American History edited by Vir-
                               ginia Van der Veer Hamilton. University:
                               University of Alabama Press, 1978.

Hugo Black (Strickland)   Hugo Black and the Supreme Court; a Sympos-
                               ium. Stephen Parks Strickland. Indianapolis:
                               Bobbs-Merrill, 1967.

Impact (Becker)   The Impact of Supreme Court Decisions. Theo-
                               dore Becker, ed. New York: Oxford, 1969.

Impact (Wasby)   The Impact of the United States Supreme Court;
                               some Perspectives. Stephen Wasby. Home-
                               wood, Ill. : Dorsey Press, 1970.

Impeachment   Impeachment; the Constitutional Problems.
                               Raoul Berger. Cambridge, Mass. : Harvard
                               University Press, 1973.

In His Own Image   In His Own Image; the Supreme Court in Rich-
                               ard Nixon's America. James F. Simon. New
                               York: McKay, 1973.

Individual   Individual and Group Privacy. Edward J.
                               Blaustein. New Brunswick, N. J. : Transaction
                               Books, 1978.

Injunctions   Injunctions. Owen M. Fiss. Mineola, N. Y. :
                               Foundation Press, 1972.

Inquiring   The Inquiring Mind. Zechariah Chaffee. New
                               York: Da Capo Press, 1974. (Reprint of 1928
                               ed. by Harcourt, Brace and Co.)

Integration   Integration vs. Segregation. Hubert H. Hum-
                               phrey. New York: Crowell, 1964. (Also
                               published under title: School Desegregation,
                               Documents and Commentaries.)

Introduction (Cataldo)   Introduction to Law and the Legal Process.
                               3rd ed. Bernard Cataldo and others. New
                               York: Wiley, 1980.

Introduction (Mashaw)   Introduction to the American Public Law Sys-
                               tem; Cases and Materials. Jerry L. Mashaw
                               and Richard A. Merrill. St. Paul: West
                               Publishing Co. , 1975.

It Is So Ordered   It Is So Ordered; the Supreme Court Rules on
                               School Segregation. Daniel M. Berman. New
                               York: Norton, 1966.

John Marshall (Baker)   John Marshall; a life in law. Leonard Baker.
                               New York: Macmillan, 1974.

John Marshall (Konefsky)   John Marshall and Alexander Hamilton; Archi-
                               tects of the American Constitution. Samuel J.
                               Konefsky. New York: Macmillan, 1964.

John Marshall's Defense   John Marshall's Defense of McCulloch v. Maryland. Gerald Gunther, ed. Stanford, Cal.:
Stanford University Press, 1969.

Joseph Story   Joseph Story and the American Constitution; a
Study in Political and Legal Thought. James
McClellan. Norman: University of Oklahoma,
1971.

Judicial Crises   Judicial Crises; the Supreme Court in a Changing America. Richard Funston. New York:
Schenkman Pub., 1974.

Judicial Excerpts   Judicial Excerpts Governing Students and Teachers. Edward C. Bolmeier. Charlottesville,
Va.: Michie Co., 1977.

Judiciary (Abraham)   The Judiciary; the Supreme Court in the Gov-
ernmental Process. 5th ed. Henry J. Abra-
ham. Boston: Allyn and Bacon, 1980.

Judiciary (Roche)   The Judiciary. John P. Roche and Leonard
W. Levy. New York: Harcourt, Brace and
World, 1964.

Jurisprudence   The Jurisprudence of John Marshall. Robert
K. Faulkner. Princeton, N.J.: Princeton University Press, 1968. (Reprinted 1980 by Greenwood.)

Justice   Justice and the Supreme Court. Rocco J.
Tresolini. Philadelphia: Lippincott, 1963.

Justice Daniel   Justice Daniel Dissenting; a Biography of Peter
V. Daniel, 1784-1860. John P. Frank. Cam-
bridge, Mass.: Harvard University Press,
1964.

Justice Frankfurter   Justice Frankfurter and Civil Liberties. Clyde
E. Jacobs. New York: Da Capo Press, 1974.
(Reprint of 1961 ed. by University of California
Press.)

Justice Hugo Black   Justice Hugo Black and the First Amendment.
Everette E. Dennis, Donald M. Gillmor, and
David L. Grey, eds. Ames: Iowa State Uni-
versity Press, 1978.

Justice Joseph Story   Justice Joseph Story and the Rise of the Supreme Court. Gerald T. Dunne. New York:
Simon and Schuster, 1970.

Justice Rutledge   Justice Rutledge and the Bright Constellation.
Fowler V. Harper. Indianapolis: Bobbs-
Merrill, 1965.

Justice Without Trial   Justice Without Trial; Law Enforcement in
Democratic Society. 2nd ed. Jerome H.
Skolnick. New York: Wiley, 1975.

| Justices (Friedman) | The Justices of the United States Supreme Court, 1789-1978, Their Lives and Major Opinions. Leon Friedman and Fred L. Israel. New York: Chelsea House, 1969-78. 5 vols. |

Justices Black and Frank-   Justices Black and Frankfurter; Conflict in the
   furter   Court. 2nd ed. Wallace Mendelson. Chicago:
                                   University of Chicago Press, 1966.

Juvenile Offender   Juvenile Offender and the Law; a Symposium.
                                   Dan Hopson and others. New York: Da Capo
                                   Press, 1971, © 1968.

Labor Law (Herman)   Labor Law; Cases, Test and Legislation. E.
                                   Edward Herman and Gordon S. Skinner. New
                                   York: Random House, 1972.

Labor Law (Meltzer)   Labor Law; Cases, Materials and Problems.
                                   Bernard D. Meltzer. Boston: Little, Brown,
                                   1970.

Labor Law (Twomey)   Labor Law and Legislation. 6th ed. David P.
                                   Twomey. Cincinnati: South-Western, 1980.

Labor Relations (Edwards)   Labor Relations Law in the Public Sector;
                                   Cases and Materials. Harry T. Edwards, R.
                                   Theodore Clark, and Charles B. Craver. 2nd
                                   ed. Indianapolis: Bobbs-Merrill, 1979.

Labor Relations (Getman)   Labor Relations; Law, Practice and Policy.
                                   Julius G. Getman. Mineola, N.Y.: Founda-
                                   tion Press, 1978.

Labor Relations (Group   Labor Relations and the Law. Labor Law
   Trust)   Group Trust. 3rd ed. Boston: Little, Brown,
                                   1965.

Labor Relations (Taylor)   Labor Relations Law. Benjamin J. Taylor and
                                   Fred Witney. 3rd ed. Englewood Cliffs, N.J.:
                                   Prentice-Hall, 1979.

Land Ownership   Land Ownership and Use. 2nd ed. Curtis J.
                                   Berger. Boston: Little, Brown, 1975.

Land-use   Land-use Planning; a Casebook on the Use,
                                   Misuse and Re-use of Urban Land. 3rd ed.
                                   Charles M. Haar. Boston: Little, Brown,
                                   1977.

Landmark Decisions   Landmark Supreme Court Decisions on Public
                                   School Issues. Edward C. Bolmeier. Char-
                                   lottesville, Va.: Michie, 1973.

Law and Education   Law and Education; Contemporary Issues and
                                   Court Decisions. H. C. Hudgins and Richard
                                   S. Vacca. Charlottesville, Va.: Michie, 1979.

Law and Politics   Law and Politics in the Supreme Court; New

Approaches to Political Jurisprudence.   Martin
Shapiro. New York: Free Press, 1964.

Law and Public Education   Law and Public Education; Cases and Materials.
(Goldstein)   Stephen R. Goldstein. Indianapolis: Bobbs-
                             Merrill, 1974.

Law and Public Education   Law and Public Education, with Cases.   Robert
(Hamilton)   R. Hamilton and Paul R. Mort. 2nd ed.
                             Brooklyn, N.Y. : Foundation Press, 1959.

Law Enforcement   Law Enforcement and Justice. Stanley N.
                             Worton. Rochelle Park, N.J. : Hayden Books,
                             1977.

Law Indian   Law and the American Indian. Monroe Price.
                             Indianapolis: Bobbs-Merrill, 1973.

Law Lawyers   Law, Lawyers and Social Change. Harold W.
                             Horowitz and Kenneth Karst. Indianapolis:
                             Bobbs-Merrill, 1969.

Law of Arrest (Creamer)   The Law of Arrest, Search and Seizure. 3rd
                             ed. J. Shane Creamer. New York: Holt,
                             Rinehart and Winston, 1980.

Law of Arrest (Markle)   The Law of Arrest and Search and Seizure; a
                             State Attorney's Guide for the Prosecution and/
                             or the Law Enforcement Officer. Arnold
                             Markle. Springfield, Ill. : Thomas, 1974.

Law of Evidence   Law of Evidence for Police. 2nd ed. Irving
                             J. Klein. St. Paul: West Publishing Co. ,
                             1978.

Law of Mass   Law of Mass Communications; Freedom and
                             Control of Print and Broadcast Media. 3rd ed.
                             Harold L. Nelson and Dwight L. Teeter. Min-
                             eola, N.Y. : Foundation Press, 1978.

Law of Obscenity   The Law of Obscenity. Frederick F. Schauer.
                             Washington, D.C. : Bureau of National Affairs,
                             1976.

Law of Public Education   The Law of Public Education. 2nd ed. E.
                             Edmund Reutter and Robert R. Hamilton.
                             Mineola, N.Y. : Foundation Press, 1976.

Law Power   Law, Power and Personal Freedom. Lionel
                             H. Frankel. St. Paul: West Publishing Co. ,
                             1975.

Law Sup Ct   The Law, the Supreme Court and the People's
                             Rights. Rev. ed. Ann Fagan Ginger. Wood-
                             bury, N.Y. : Barrons Educational Series, 1974.

Leading Consttnl Cases   Leading Constitutional Cases on Criminal Jus-
                             tice. Lloyd L. Weinreb. Mineola, N.Y. :
                             Foundation Press, 1978.

Leading Consttnl Decisions   Leading Constitutional Decisions.   15th ed.
                               Robert F. Cushman.   Englewood Cliffs, N. J. :
                               Prentice-Hall, 1977.

Least Dangerous   The Least Dangerous Branch; the Supreme
                               Court at the Bar of Politics.   Alexander M.
                               Bickel.   New York: Bobbs-Merrill, 1962.

Legacy   The Legacy of Holmes and Brandeis; a Study
                               in the Influence of Ideas.   Samuel J. Konefsky.
                               New York: Macmillan, 1956.   (Reprinted 1974
                               by Da Capo.)

Legal Aspects   Legal Aspects of Technology Utilization.   Rich-
                               ard I. Miller.   Lexington, Mass. : Heath and
                               Co. , 1974.

Legal Environment   Legal Environment of Business.   Robert Neil
                               Corley and others.   4th ed.   New York: Mc-
                               Graw-Hill, 1977.

Legal Foundations   Legal Foundations of Land Use Planning; Text-
                               book/Casebook and Materials on Planning Law.
                               Jerome G. Rose.   New Brunswick, N. J. : Rut-
                               gers--Center for Urban Policy Research, 1979.

Legal Problems   Legal Problems of the Poor; Cases and Ma-
                               terials.   Arthur L. Berney and others.   Bos-
                               ton: Little, Brown, 1975.

Legal Regulation   Legal Regulation of the Competitive Process;
                               Cases Materials and Notes on Unfair Business
                               Practices, Trademarks, Copyrights and Patents.
                               Edmund W. Kitch and Harvey S. Perlman.   2nd
                               ed.   Mineola, N. Y. : Foundation Press, 1979.

Legislative (Hetzel)   Legislative Law and Process.   Otto J. Hetzel.
                               Indianapolis: Bobbs-Merrill, 1980.

Legislative (Linde)   Legislative and Administrative Progress.   Hans
                               A. Linde and George Bunn.   Mineola, N. Y. :
                               Foundation Press, 1976.

Liberty   Liberty and Justice.   Rev. ed.   James M.
                               Smith and Paul L. Murphy.   New York: Knopf,
                               1965-1968.   2 vols.

Literary Censorship   Literary Censorship; Principles, Cases, Prob-
                               lems.   Kingsley Widmer and Eleanor Widmer.
                               San Francisco, Cal. : Wadsworth, 1961.

Literature   Literature, Obscenity and Law.   Felice Flanery
                               Lewis.   Carbondale: Southern Illinois Univer-
                               sity Press, 1976.

Making   The Making of Justice; the Supreme Court in
                               Action.   James E. Clayton.   New York: Dut-
                               ton, 1964.

Managing	Managing Our Urban Environment; Cases, Text and Problems. 2nd ed. Daniel Mandelker. Indianapolis: Bobbs-Merrill, 1971.
Marshall	Marshall versus Jefferson; the Political Background of Marbury v. Madison. Donald O. Dewey. New York: Knopf, 1970.
Mass Communication	Mass Communication Law; Cases and Comments. 3rd ed. Donald M. Gillmor and Jerome A. Barron. St. Paul: West Publishing Co., 1979.
Mass Media (Clark)	Mass Media and the Law; Freedom and Restraint. David G. Clark and Earl R. Hutchinson. New York: Wiley-Interscience, 1970.
Mass Media (Devol)	Mass Media and the Supreme Court; the Legacy of the Warren Years. 2nd ed. Kenneth G. Devol. New York: Hastings House, 1976.
Mass Media (Francois)	Mass Media Law and Regulation. 2nd ed. William E. Francois. Columbus, Ohio: Grid, Inc., 1978.
Materials Consttnl Law	Materials in Constitutional Law; Part 1: The Federal Judiciary. Sherman L. Cohn. Washington, D.C.: Lerner Law Book Co., 1968.
Materials Law	Materials and Cases on the Law of the Employment Relation. Alfred W. Blumrosen. New Brunswick, N.J.: Rutgers, the State University, 1962. 2 vols.
Materials Legislation	Materials and Problems on Legislation. Julius Cohen. 2nd ed. Indianapolis: Bobbs-Merrill, 1969.
Materials Reorganization	Materials on Reorganization, Recapitalization and Insolvency. Walter J. Blum and Stanley A. Kaplan. Boston: Little, Brown, 1969.
Media Access	Media Access; Your Rights to Express Your Views on Radio and Television. Andrew O. Shapiro. Boston: Little, Brown, 1976.
Media and the First Amendment	Media and the First Amendment in a Free Society. Amherst: University of Massachusetts Press, 1973.
Memoirs	The Memoirs of Earl Warren. Earl Warren. Garden City, N.Y.: Doubleday and Co., 1977.
Milestones	Milestones; 200 Years of American Law; Milestones in Our Legal History. Jethro K. Lieberman. St. Paul: West Publishing, 1976.
Milligan Case	The Milligan Case. Samuel Klaus, ed. New York: Da Capo Press, 1970. (Reprint of 1929 ed. by Knopf.)

Mr. Justice Frankfurter	Mr. Justice Frankfurter and the Constitution. Philip B. Kurland. Chicago: University of Chicago, 1971.
Mr. Justice Jackson	Mr. Justice Jackson; Four Lectures in his Honor. Charles Desmond and others. New York: Columbia University, 1969.
Mr. Justice Murphy (Howard)	Mr. Justice Murphy; a political biography. J. Woodford Howard. Princeton, N. J.: Princeton University Press, 1968.
Mr. Justice Murphy (Norris)	Mr. Justice Murphy and the Bill of Rights. Harold Norris, ed. Dobbs Ferry, N. Y.: Oceana Publications, 1965.
Modern Business	Modern Business Law. Thomas Dunfee and others. Columbus, Ohio: Grid, 1979.
Modern Consttnl Law	Modern Constitutional Law; Commentary and Case Studies. Richard C. Cortner and Clifford M. Lytle. New York: Free Press, 1971.
Modern Criml Procedure	Modern Criminal Procedure and Basic Criminal Procedure, Supplement. Yale Kamisar, Wayne LaFave, and Jerold Israel. St. Paul: West Publishing Co., 1980.
Modern Social Legislation	Modern Social Legislation. Stefan A. Riesenfeld and Richard C. Maxwell. Brooklyn, N. Y.: Foundation Press, 1950.
Modern Supreme Court	The Modern Supreme Court. Robert G. McCloskey. Cambridge, Mass.: Harvard University Press, 1972.
Monetary Decisions	Monetary Decisions of the Supreme Court. Gerald T. Dunne. New Brunswick, N. J.: Rutgers University Press, 1960.
Morrison R. Waite	Morrison R. Waite; the Triumph of Character. C. Peter Magrath. New York: Macmillan, 1963.
Movies	Movies, Censorship and the Law. Ira H. Carmen. Ann Arbor: University of Michigan, 1966.
Nature	Nature and Functions of Law. 4th ed. Harold J. Berman and William R. Greiner. Mineola, N. Y.: Foundation Press, 1980.
Negro (Kalven)	The Negro and the First Amendment. Harry Kalven. Chicago: University of Chicago, 1966, c1965.
Negro (Franklin)	The Negro in Twentieth Century America; a Reader on the Struggle for Civil Rights. John

H. Franklin and Isidore Starr.   New York:
Vintage Books, 1967.

New Dimensions
New Dimensions of Freedom in America.
Frederick Wirt and Willis Hawley.   San Fran-
cisco, Cal.:   Chandler, 1969.

Obscenity (Bosmajian)
Obscenity and Freedom of Expression.   Haig
Bosmajian.   New York: Burt Franklin and Co.,
1976.

Obscenity (Clor)
Obscenity and Public Morality; Censorship in a
Liberal Society.   Harry M. Clor.   Chicago:
University of Chicago Press, 1969.

Obscenity (Friedman)
Obscenity; the Complete Oral Arguments Before
the Supreme Court in the Major Obscenity
Cases.   Leon Friedman.   New York: Chelsea
House, 1970.

Obscenity (Sunderland)
Obscenity; the Court, the Congress and the
President's Commission.   Lane V. Sunderland.
Washington, D. C.:   American Enterprise Insti-
tute, 1974.

O'er the Ramparts
O'er the Ramparts They Watched.   Victor E.
Blackwell.   New York: Carlton, 1976.

One Man's Stand
One Man's Stand for Freedom; Justice Black
and the Bill of Rights.   Irving Dilliard, ed.
New York: Knopf, 1963.

One Woman's Fight
One Woman's Fight.   Rev. ed.   Vashti C.
McCollum.   Boston: Beacon Press, 1961.

Papers
The Papers and the Papers.   Sanford J. Ungar.
New York: Dutton and Co., 1972.

Patent
Patent Enforcement, Misuse and Antitrust;
Cases and Materials.   Henry Shur.   Washing-
ton, D. C.:   Lerner Law Book Co., 1967.

Pentagon Papers
The Pentagon Papers and the Courts.   Martin
Shapiro.   San Francisco, Cal.:   Chandler,
1972.

Perspective
Perspective.   Charles Rembar.   New York:
Arbor House, 1975.

Perspectives (Black)
Perspectives in Constitutional Law.   Charles
L. Black, Jr.   Englewood Cliffs, N. J.:
Prentice-Hall, 1970.

Petitioners
The Petitioners; the Story of the Supreme
Court of the United States and the Negro.
Loren Miller.   Cleveland, Ohio: World Pub-
lishing Co., 1966.

Police
The Police, the Judiciary and the Criminal.

	2nd ed. Vivian A. Leonard. Springfield, Ill.: Thomas, 1975.
Political Rights	Political and Civil Rights in the United States; a Collection of Legal and Related Materials. Thomas I. Emerson, David Haber, and Norman Dorsen. 3rd ed. Boston: Little, Brown, 1967. 2 vols.
Political Thicket	The Political Thicket; Reapportionment and Constitutional Democracy. Royce Hanson. Englewood Cliffs, N. J.: Prentice-Hall, 1966.
Politics	The Politics of Civil Liberties. Jonathan D. Casper. New York: Harper and Row, 1972.
Pornography	Pornography, Obscenity and the Law. Lester Sobel. New York: Facts on File, 1979.
Poverty	Poverty, Inequality and the Law; Cases, Commentary, Analyses. Barbara Brudno. St. Paul: West Publishing Co., 1976.
Power	Power and Balance; an Introduction to American Constitutional Government. Ira H. Carmen. New York: Harcourt Brace Jovanovich, 1978.
Practice	The Practice of Collective Bargaining. Edwin F. Beal and Edward D. Wickersham. 3rd ed. Homewood, Ill.: Irwin, 1967.
Prayer	Prayer in the Public Schools; Law and Attitude Change. William K. Muir, Jr. Chicago: University of Chicago, 1967. (Published in 1973 with title: Law and Attitude Change.)
Prejudice	Prejudice, War and the Constitution. Jacobus ten Brock, Edward N. Barnhart, and Floyd W. Matson. Berkeley: University of California Press, 1975, © 1954.
Presidential Power	Presidential Power and the Constitution; Essays. Edward S. Corwin. Ithaca, N. Y.: Cornell, 1976.
Press Freedoms	Press Freedoms Under Pressure. Twentieth Century Fund Task Force on the Government and the Press. New York: Twentieth Century Fund, 1972.
Principles Arrest	Principles and Cases of the Law of Arrest, Search and Seizure. Thomas J. Gardner. New York: McGraw-Hill, 1974.
Principles Freedom	Principles and Practice of Freedom of Speech. Haig A. Bosmajian. Boston: Houghton Mifflin, 1971.
Principles Proof	Principles of Evidence and Proof. 3rd ed.

Development; Cases and Materials. Donald G.
Hagman. St. Paul: West Publishing Co.,
1973.

Public School Law   Public School Law; Cases and Materials. Kern
                             Alexander, Ray Corns, and Walter McCann.
                             St. Paul: West Publishing Co., 1969.

Public Schools   Public Schools and Religion; the Legal Context.
                             Sam Duker. New York: Harper and Row,
                             1966.

Quarrels   Quarrels That Have Shaped the Constitution.
                             John Garraty, ed. New York: Harper and
                             Row, 1964.

Quest   The Quest for Equality; the Constitution, Con-
                             gress and the Supreme Court. Robert J. Har-
                             ris. Westport, Conn.: Greenwood Press,
                             1977. (Reprint of 1960 ed. by Louisiana State
                             University Press, Baton Rouge.)

Race   Race, Racism and American Law. Derrick A.
                             Bell. Boston: Little, Brown, 1973.

Racial Equality   Racial Equality. Laughlin McDonald. Skokie,
                             Ill.: National Textbook Co., 1977.

Radio   Radio, Television and the Administration of
                             Justice. Association of the Bar of the City
                             of New York, Special Committee on Radio and
                             Television. New York: Columbia University,
                             1965.

Ransom   Ransom; a Critique of the American Bail Sys-
                             tem. Ronald L. Goldfarb. New York: Harper
                             and Row, 1965.

Rationing   The Rationing of Justice; Constitutional Rights
                             and the Criminal Process. Arnold S. Trebach.
                             New Brunswick, N.J.: Rutgers University
                             Press, 1964.

Readings American   Readings in American Government. 5th ed.
                             Henry Malcolm MacDonald. New York: Cro-
                             well, 1968.

Readings Law   Readings in Law and Psychiatry. Rev. ed.
                             Richard Allen and others. Baltimore: Johns
                             Hopkins, 1975.

Reapportionment (Baker)   The Reapportionment Revolution; Representation,
                             Political Power and the Supreme Court. Gordon
                             Baker. New York: Random House, 1966.

Reapportionment (McKay)   Reapportionment; the Law and Politics of Equal
                             Representation. Robert B. McKay. New York:
                             Twentieth Century Fund, 1965.

Reconstruction	Reconstruction and Reunion, 1864-88. Charles Fairman. (History of the Supreme Court of the United States, v. 6, pt. 1) New York: Macmillan, 1971.
Religion (Blanchard)	Religion and the Schools; the Great Controversy. Paul Blanchard. Boston: Beacon Press, 1963.
Religion (Drinan)	Religion, the Courts and Public Policy. Robert F. Drinan. New York: McGraw-Hill, 1963. (Reprinted 1978 by Greenwood Press.)
Religion (Fellman)	Religion in American Public Law. David Fellman. Boston: Boston University Press, 1965.
Religion (Katz)	Religion and American Constitutions. Wilber G. Katz. Evanston, Ill.: Northwestern, 1964.
Religion (Kauper)	Religion and the Constitution. Paul G. Kauper. Baton Rouge: Louisiana State University Press, 1964.
Religion (Kurland)	Religion and the Law; of Church and State and the Supreme Court. Philip Kurland. Chicago: Aldine Publishing Co., 1962.
Religion (School Administrators)	Religion in the Public Schools. American Association of School Administrators. Commission of Religion in the Public Schools. Washington, D.C., 1964.
Religious Freedom (Arnold)	Religious Freedom on Trial. Otto Carroll Arnold. Valley Forge, Pa.: Judson Press, 1978.
Religious Freedom (Pfeffer)	Religious Freedom. Leo Pfeffer. Skokie, Ill.: National Textbook, 1977.
Religious Liberty	Religious Liberty and Conscience; a Constitutional Inquiry. Milton Konvitz. New York: Viking, 1968.
Render	Render unto Caesar; the Flag-Salute Controversy. David R. Manwaring. Chicago: University of Chicago, 1962.
Reverse	Reverse Discrimination. Barry R. Gross, ed. Buffalo, N.Y.: Prometheus Books, 1977.
Right of Assembly	The Right of Assembly and Association. Glenn Abernathy. Columbia: University of South Carolina Press, 1961.
Right to Counsel	Right to Counsel in Criminal Cases; the Mandate of Argersinger v. Hamlin. Sheldon Krantz and others. Cambridge, Mass.: Ballinger, 1976.
Right to Privacy	Right to Privacy; Essays and Cases. P. Allen

Dionisopoulos and Craig R. Ducat. St. Paul:
West Publishing Co., 1976.

Right to Treatment   Right to Treatment for Mental Patients. Stuart
                                      Golann and William J. Fremouw, eds. New
                                      York: Irvington, 1976.

Rights (Shattuck)   Rights of Privacy. John H. F. Shattuck.
                                      Skokie, Ill.: National Textbook Co., 1977.

Rights of the People   The Rights of the People; the Major Decisions
                                      of the Warren Court. Elaine and Walter Good-
                                      man. New York: Farrar, Straus and Giroux,
                                      1971.

Rise   The Rise of the Guardian Democracy; the Su-
                                      preme Court's Role in Voting Rights Disputes,
                                      1845-1969. Ward E. Y. Elliott. Cambridge,
                                      Mass.: Harvard University Press, 1974.

Role (Cox)   The Role of the Supreme Court in American
                                      Government. Archibald Cox. New York: Ox-
                                      ford, 1976.

Role (Haines)   The Role of the Supreme Court in American
                                      Government and Politics. Charles Grove Haines
                                      and Foster H. Sherwood. New York: Da Capo
                                      Press, 1973. 2 vols. (Reprint of 1944-57 ed.
                                      by University of California.)

School Bus   The School Bus Law; a Case Study in Education,
                                      Religion and Politics. Theodore Powell. Mid-
                                      dletown, Conn.: Wesleyan University Press,
                                      1960.

School in the Legal   The School in the Legal Structure. Edward C.
  Structure   Bolmeier. 2nd ed. Cincinnati: W. H. Ander-
                                      son, 1973.

School Law (Alexander)   School Law. Kern Alexander. St. Paul: West
                                      Publishing Co., 1980.

School Law (Remmlein)   School Law. Madaline K. Remmlein. Danville,
                                      Ill.: The Interstate Printers and Publishers,
                                      Inc., 1962.

School Prayer (Dolbeare)   The School Prayer Decisions; from Court Pol-
                                      icy to Local Practice. Kenneth M. Dolbeare
                                      and Philip Hammond. Chicago: University of
                                      Chicago, 1971.

School Prayers (Lauboch)   School Prayers; Congress, the Courts and the
                                      Public. John H. Lauboch. Washington, D.C.:
                                      Public Affairs Press, 1969.

Schools (Hogan)   The Schools, the Courts and the Public Interest.
                                      John C. Hogan. Lexington, Mass.: Heath and
                                      Co., 1974.

Scottsboro	Scottsboro, a Tragedy of the American South. Rev. ed. Dan T. Carter. Baton Rouge: Louisiana State University Press, 1979.
Search and Seizure	Search and Seizure and the Supreme Court; a Study in Constitutional Interpretation. Jacob W. Landynski. Baltimore: Johns Hopkins University Press, 1966.
Search for Meaning	Search for Meaning. Richard Marshall. Philadelphia: Lippincott, 1973.
Selected Antitrust Cases	Selected Antitrust Cases; Landmark Decisions. 5th ed. Irwin M. Stelzer. Homewood, Ill.: Irwin, 1976.
Self-inflicted Wound	The Self-inflicted Wound. Fred P. Graham. New York: Macmillan, 1970.
Sex Discrimination 1975	Sex Discrimination and the Law; Cases and Remedies. Barbara Babcock and others. Boston: Little, Brown, 1975.
Sex Discrimination 1978	Sex Discrimination and the Law; Causes and Remedies. 1978 supplement. Wendy Webster Williams. Boston: Little, Brown, 1978.
Sex Litigation	Sex Litigation and the Public Schools. Edward C. Bolmeier. Charlottesville, Va.: Michie, 1975.
Sex Roles	Sex Roles in Law and Society; Cases and Materials. Leo Kanowitz. Albuquerque: University of New Mexico, 1973.
Shaping	The Shaping of the American Tradition. Louis Hacker. New York: Columbia University Press, 1947. (Reprinted 1968.)
Significant Decisions (Year)	Significant Decisions of the Supreme Court; 1969/70 Term--1978/79 Term. Paul C. Bartholomew. Bruce E. Fein. Washington, D.C.: American Enterprise Institute, 1970-80. 10 vols.
Simple Justice	Simple Justice; the History of Brown v. Board of Education and Black America's Struggle for Equality. Richard Kluger. New York: Knopf, 1975. 2 vols.
Social Forces	Social Forces and the Law; a Guide for the Businessman and the Citizen. Ronald A. Anderson. Cincinnati: Southern Publishing Co., 1969.
Sources American Republic	Sources of the American Republic; a Documentary History of Politics, Society and Thought. Marvin Meyers, Alexander Kern, and John G.

Cawelti.   Chicago: Scott, Foresman, 1961.
2 vols.

Sources Antislavery

The Sources of Antislavery Constitutionalism
in America, 1760-1848.   William M. Wiecek.
Ithaca, N.Y.:   Cornell University Press, 1977.

Sovereign Prerogative

The Sovereign Prerogative; the Supreme Court
and the Quest for Law.   Eugene V. Rostow.
New Haven, Conn.:   Yale University, 1962.

Spirit

The Spirit and the Letter; the Struggle for
Rights in America.   Bernice Kohn Hunt.   New
York: Viking, 1974.

Statutory History Civil
    Rights

Statutory History of the United States; Civil
Rights.   Bernard Schwartz.   New York: Chelsea House, 1970.

Statutory History Eco-
    nomic

Statutory History of the United States; the Economic Regulation of Business and Industry.
Bernard Schwartz.   New York: Chelsea House,
1973.   5 vols.

Statutory History Income

Statutory History of the United States; Income
Security.   Robert B. Stevens.   New York:
Chelsea House, 1970.

Statutory History Labor

Statutory History of the United States; Labor
Organization.   Robert F. Koretz.   New York:
Chelsea House, 1970.

Steamboat

The Steamboat Monopoly; Gibbons v. Ogden,
1824.   Maurice G. Baxter.   New York: Knopf,
1972.

Struggle

The Struggle for Racial Equality; a Documentary Record.   Henry Steele Commager, ed.
New York: Harper & Row, 1967.

Sup Ct (Forte)

The Supreme Court.   David F. Forte.   New
York: Franklin Watts, 1979.

Sup Ct (Freund)

The Supreme Court of the United States; its
Business, Purposes, and Performance.   Paul
A. Freund.   Cleveland, Ohio: World Publish-
ing Co., 1961.   Reprinted 1972 by Peter Smith.

Sup Ct (Mason)

The Supreme Court; Palladium of Freedom.
Alpheus T. Mason.   Ann Arbor: University
of Michigan, 1962.

Sup Ct (Mendelson)

The Supreme Court; Law and Discretion.
Wallace Mendelson.   Indianapolis: Bobbs-
Merrill, 1967.

Sup Ct (North)

The Supreme Court; Judicial Process and Judicial Politics.   Arthur A. North.   New York:
Appleton-Century-Crofts, 1966.   (Also published

under title: The Supreme Court and the Judicial Process, 1964.)

Sup Ct (Sheldon)   The Supreme Court; Politicians in Robes.
                           Charles H. Sheldon. Beverly Hills, Cal.:
                           Glencoe Press, 1970.

Sup Ct and Agencies   Supreme Court and Administrative Agencies.
                           Martin M. Shapiro. New York: Free Press,
                           1968.

Sup Ct and American   Supreme Court and American Capitalism.
Capitalism   Arthur S. Miller. New York: Free Press,
                           1968.

Sup Ct and American   Supreme Court and American Economic Life.
Economic Life   Benjamin M. Ziegler. Evanston, Ill.: Row,
                           Peterson, 1962.

Sup Ct and Am Govt   The Supreme Court and American Government;
                           a Casebook. John H. Vanderzell. New York:
                           Crowell, 1968.

Sup Ct and Commander in   The Supreme Court and the Commander in
Chief   Chief. Clinton L. Rossiter. Ithaca, N.Y.:
                           Cornell, 1976.

Sup Ct and Commerce   The Supreme Court and the Commerce Clause,
                           1937-1970. Paul R. Benson. New York:
                           Dunellen, 1970.

Sup Ct and Confessions   Supreme Court and Confessions of Guilt. Otis
                           H. Stephens. Knoxville: University of Ten-
                           nessee, 1973.

Sup Ct and Consttn   The Supreme Court and the Constitution; Read-
                           ings in American Constitutional History. Stan-
                           ley I. Kutler. Boston: Houghton Mifflin, 1969.

Sup Ct and Criml   The Supreme Court and the Criminal Process;
Process   Cases and Comments. Peter W. Lewis and
                           Kenneth D. Peoples. Philadelphia: Saunders,
                           1978. (First seven chapters printed under
                           title: Constitutional Rights of the Accused,
                           1979.)

Sup Ct and Education   The Supreme Court and Education. 3rd ed.
                           David Fellman. New York: Teachers College
                           Press, 1976.

Sup Ct and Electoral   The Supreme Court and the Electoral Process.
Process   Richard Claude. Baltimore: Johns Hopkins,
                           1970.

Sup Ct and Labor   The Supreme Court and Labor-Management Re-
                           lations Law. Alvin L. Goldman. Lexington,
                           Mass.: Heath, 1976.

Sup Ct and News   The Supreme Court and the News Media. David

L. Gray, Evanston, Ill.: Northwestern University
Press, 1968.

Sup Ct and Patents

The Supreme Court and Patents and Monopolies.
Philip Kurland, ed.   Chicago: University of
Chicago, 1976.

Sup Ct and Poltcl
Freedom

The Supreme Court and Political Freedom.
Samuel Krislow.   New York: Free Press, 1968.

Sup Ct and Poltcl
Questions

The Supreme Court and "Political Questions";
a study in Judicial Evasion.   Phillipa Strum.
University: University of Alabama Press, 1974.

Sup Ct and Public Policy

The Supreme Court and Public Policy.   Martin
M. Shapiro.   Glenview, Ill.:   Scott, Foresman,
1969.

KF
4783
.M65

Sup Ct and Religion

The Supreme Court and Religion.   Richard E.
Morgan.   New York: Free Press, 1974.

Sup Ct and Rights

Supreme Court and the Rights of the Accused.
John Galloway.   New York: Facts on File,
1973.

Sup Ct and Uses

The Supreme Court and the Uses of History.
Charles A. Miller.   Cambridge, Mass.:   Harvard University Press, 1969.

Sup Ct as Policy-Maker

Supreme Court as Policy-maker; Three Studies
on the Impact of Judicial Decisions.   David H.
Everson, comp.   2nd ed.   Carbondale: Southern
Illinois University, 1972.

Sup Ct Decision Making

Supreme Court Decision Making.   David W.
Rohde and Harold J. Spaeth.   San Francisco,
Cal.:   Freeman, 1976.

Sup Ct from Taft

The Supreme Court from Taft to Burger.   3rd
ed.   Alpheus Thomas Mason.   Baton Rouge:
Louisiana State University Press, 1979.   (Original title: The Supreme Court from Taft to
Warren.)

Sup Ct in Am History

Supreme Court in American History; Ten Great
Decisions; The People, the Times, and the Is-
sues.   Marjorie G. Fribourg.   Philadelphia:
Macrae Smith, 1965.

Sup Ct in Crisis

Supreme Court in Crisis; a History of Conflict.
Robert J. Steamer.   Amherst: University of
Massachusetts, 1971.

Sup Ct in Free Society

The Supreme Court in a Free Society.   Alpheus
T. Mason and William M. Beaney.   New York:
Norton, 1968.

Sup Ct Obscenity

Supreme Court Obscenity Decisions.   San Diego,
Cal.:   Greenleaf Classics, 1973.

Sup Ct on Freedom	Supreme Court on Freedom of the Press. William Hachten. Ames: Iowa State University Press, 1968.
Sup Ct on Trial	The Supreme Court on Trial. Charles S. Hyneman. Westport, Conn.: Greenwood Press, 1974. (Reprint of 1963 ed. by Atherton Press.)
Sup Ct Review (year)	Supreme Court Review, 1960-1979. Philip B. Kurland, ed. Chicago: University of Chicago, 1960-1980.
Sup Ct Speaks	The Supreme Court Speaks. Jerre S. Williams. Freeport, N.Y.: Books for Libraries Press, 1970, © 1956.
Sup Ct Under Marshall	The Supreme Court Under Marshall and Taney. R. Kent Newmyer. New York: Crowell, 1968.
System	The System of Freedom of Expression. Thomas I. Emerson. New York: Random House, 1970.
Taking	Taking Rights Seriously. Ronald M. Dworkin. Cambridge, Mass.: Harvard University Press, 1977.
Taney	The Taney Period, 1836-64. Carl B. Swisher. (History of the Supreme Court of the United States, v. 5.) New York: Macmillan, 1974.
Teacher	The Teacher and School Law; Cases and Materials in the Legal Foundations of Education. Edward E. Loveless and Frank R. Krajewski. Danville, Ill.: Interstate, 1974.
Teaching Materials	Teaching Materials on Criminal Procedure. Jerry L. Dowling. St. Paul: West Publishing Co., 1976.
Ten Years	Ten Years of Prelude; the Story of Integration since the Supreme Court's 1954 Decision. Benjamin Muse. New York: Viking, 1964.
Text Administrative Law	Text, Cases, Problems on Administrative Law, Regulation of Enterprise, and Individual Liberties. Edwin Wallace Tucker. St. Paul: West Publishing Co., 1975.
Text Antitrust	Text, Cases and Materials on Antitrust Fundamentals. 2nd ed. George C. Thompson and G. P. Brady. St. Paul: West Publishing Co., 1974.
Text Consttnl Aspects	Text, Cases and Materials on Constitutional Aspects of Sex-Based Discrimination. Ruth B. Ginsburg. St. Paul: West Publishing Co., 1974.
Text Legal Regulation	Text, Cases, Problems on Legal Regulation of

Environment.   Edwin W. Tucker.   St. Paul:
West Publishing Co. , 1972.

Text Sex-Based Dis-   Text, Cases and Materials on Sex-Based Dis-
    crimination   crimination.   Kenneth M. Davidson, Ruth Gins-
                         burg, and Herma Kay. St. Paul: West Pub-
                         lishing Co. , 1974.

Text Social Issues   Text, Cases, Problems on the Adjudication of
                         Social Issues.   Edwin Wallace Tucker.   2nd ed.
                         St. Paul: West Publishing Co. , 1977.

These Liberties   These Liberties; Case Studies in Civil Rights.
                         Rocco J. Tresolini.   Philadelphia: Lippincott,
                         1968.

Thin Disguise   The Thin Disguise.   Otto Olsen.   New York:
                         Humanities Press, 1967.

Third Branch   The Third Branch of Government; Eight Cases
                         in Constitutional Politics.   C. Herman Prit-
                         chett and Alan F. Westin.   New York: Har-
                         court, Brace and World, 1963.

This Honorable Court   This Honorable Court; a History of the United
                         States Supreme Court.   Leo Pfeffer.   Boston:
                         Beacon Press, 1965.   (Reprinted 1978 by Oc-
                         tagon.)

To Preserve   To Preserve These Rights; Remedies for the
                         Victims of Constitutional Deprivations.   Robert
                         L. Spurrier.   Port Washington, N. Y. : Kennikat
                         Press, 1977.

Transformation   Transformation of American Law, 1780-1860.
                         Morton J. Horwitz.   Cambridge: Harvard Uni-
                         versity Press, 1977.

Tropic   Tropic of Cancer on Trial; a Case History of
                         Censorship.   E. R. Hutcheson.   New York:
                         Grove Press, 1968.

Truman   Truman and the Steel Seizure Case; the Limits
                         of Presidential Power.   Maeva Marcus.   New
                         York: Columbia University Press, 1977.

Two Swords   Two Swords; Commentaries and Cases in Re-
                         ligion and Education.   Donald Boles.   Ames:
                         Iowa State University Press, 1967.

Ultimate Tyranny   The Ultimate Tyranny; the Majority over the
                         Majority.   Eugene J. McCarthy.   New York:
                         Harcourt Brace Jovanovich, 1980.

U. S. Prison Law   United States Prison Law; Sentencing to Prison,
                         Prison Conditions and Release; the Court De-
                         cisions.   Sol Rubin.   Dobbs Ferry, N. Y. :
                         Oceana Publications, 1975-80.   6 vols.

dicial Process. Walter F. Murphy. New York: Random House, 1965.

Without Fear

Without Fear or Favor; a Biography of Chief Justice Roger Brooke Taney. Walker Lewis. Boston: Houghton Mifflin, 1965.

Woman

Woman and the Law. Eve Cary and Kathleen W. Peratis. Skokie, Ill.: National Textbook Co., 1977.

Yazoo

Yazoo--Law and Politics in the New Republic; the Case of Fletcher v. Peck. C. Peter Magrath. Providence, R.I.: Brown University Press, 1966.

SECTION 2:

PERIODICAL TITLES CITED

AAUP Bulletin (American Association of University Professors)
ALA Bulletin (American Library Association)
Academe
Advertising Age
Aging
America
American Academy of Political and Social Science. Annals
American Behavioral Scientist
American City
American City and County
American Druggist
American Education
American Forests
American Heritage
American Historical Review
American Journal of International Law
American Journal of Orthopsychiatry
American Journal of Psychiatry
American Libraries
American Political Science Review
American Politics Quarterly
American Psychologist
American Quarterly
American Scholar
American School and University
American School Board Journal
American Teacher Magazine
Architectural Record
Art in America
Atlantic
Aviation Week

Bankers Magazine (Boston)
Banking
Darron's
Bests Review
Bioscience
Black Enterprise
Black Scholar

Boston College Environmental Affairs Law Review
Burrough Clearing House
Business History Review
Business Horizons
Business Insurance
Business Week

CLU Journal (Chartered Life Underwriters)
CPA Journal (Certified Public Accountants)
CTA Journal (California Teachers Association)
Catholic World
Center Magazine
Change
Chemical and Engineering News
Chemical Marketing Reporter
Chemical Week
Child Welfare
Children
Children Today
Christian Century
Christianity and Crisis
Christianity Today
Chronicle of Higher Education
Civil Liberties Review
Civil Rights Digest
Civil Service Journal
Civil War History
Clearing House
College and University Business
College Student Journal
Columbia Journalism Review
Commentary
Commerce America
Commonweal
Compact
Conference Board Record
Congressional Digest
Consumer Reports
Contemporary Drug Problems
Controller

Credit and Financial Management
Crime and Delinquency
Crisis
Current
Current History

Drug Topics

ETC (Et cetera)
Ebony
Economist
Editor and Publisher
Education
Education and Urban Society
Education Digest
Educational Administration Quar-
   terly
Educational Forum
Educational Horizons
Educational Leadership
Educational Record
Educational Researcher
Educational Theory
Electrical World
Electronic News
Engineering News-Record
English Journal
Environment
Environmental Affairs
Esquire
Ethics

FDA Consumer (Food and Drug
   Administration)
Family Planning Perspectives
Farm Journal
First World
Fleet Owner
Fortune
Freedomways

Geographical Review
Georgia Historical Quarterly
Good Housekeeping
Graduate Woman

Harper's Magazine
Harvard Business Review
Harvard Educational Review
High School Journal
Historian
History Today
Horizon
House and Home

Illinois Education
Industrial Distributor
Industrial Research and Development
Industry Week
Institutional Investor
Instructor
Integrated Education
Intellect
International Journal of Offender
   Therapy
International Migration Review
Iron Age

Job Safety and Health
Journal of Accountancy
Journal of Advertising
Journal of Aesthetic Education
Journal of American History
Journal of American Studies (Great
   Britain)
Journal of Broadcasting
Journal of College Student Personnel
Journal of Communication
Journal of Criminal Law and Crim-
   inology
Journal of Criminal Law, Criminol-
   ogy and Police Science
Journal of Educational Measurement
Journal of Educational Sociology
Journal of Law and Economics
Journal of Marketing
Journal of Negro Education
Journal of Negro History
Journal of Police Science and Ad-
   ministration
Journal of Politics
Journal of Purchasing and Materials
   Management
Journal of Retailing
Journal of Risk and Insurance
Journal of School Health
Journal of Taxation
Journalism Quarterly

Labor History
Labor Law Journal
Language Learning
Law and Contemporary Problems
Law and Society Review
Liberal Education
Library Journal
Life
Lithopinion
Living Wilderness
Look

MH
MSU Business Topics (Michigan
  State University)
McCalls
Maclean's
Management Record
Merchandising
Merchandising Week
Michigan Education Journal
Midwest Quarterly
Modern Age
Momentum
Monthly Labor Review
Mortgage Banker
Ms.
Music Educators Journal

NASPA Journal (National Associa-
  tion of Student Personnel Ad-
  ministrators)
NASSP Bulletin (National Associa-
  tion of Secondary School Prin-
  cipals)
NCEA Bulletin (National Catholic
  Education Association)
NEA Journal (National Education
  Association)
NEA Research Bulletin (National
  Education Association)
NOLPE School Law Journal (Na-
  tional Organization on Legal
  Problems of Education)
NPN (National Petroleum News)
Nation
National Association of College
  Admissions Counselors. Jour-
  nal
National Civic Review
National Elementary Principal
National Parks and Conservation
  Magazine
National Real Estate Investor
National Review
National Tax Journal
National Underwriter
Nation's Business
Nation's Cities
Nation's Schools
Nation's Schools and Colleges
Negro Education Review
Negro History Bulletin
New Republic
New Statesman
New Times (Boulder, Colo.)
New York
New York Review of Books
New York State Education
New York Times Book Review

New York Times Magazine
New Yorker
Newsweek
North American Review
North Carolina Education

Ohio Schools
Oil and Gas Journal
Oil Paint and Drug Report
Outdoor Life
Overview

PTA Magazine
Parents' Magazine
Peabody Journal of Education
Pennsylvania School Journal
People
Personnel
Personnel and Guidance Journal
Personnel Journal
Personnel Psychology
Phi Delta Kappan
Phylon
Planning
Policy Studies Journal
Political Science Quarterly
Political Studies
Politics Today
Population and Development Review
Practical Accountant
Professional Builder and Apartment
  Business
Progressive
Progressive Grocer
Psychology Today
Public Administration Review
Public Interest
Public Opinion Quarterly
Public Personnel Management
Public Relations Journal
Public Relations Quarterly
Public Utilities Fortnightly
Public Welfare
Publishers Weekly
Purchasing

Quarterly Journal of Economics
Quarterly Journal of Speech

Railway Age
Reader's Digest
Real Estate Appraiser
Redbook
Religion in Life
Religious Education

Reporter
Research Management
Retirement Living
Review of Politics
Rolling Stone

SLJ (School Library Journal)
Saturday Evening Post
Saturday Review
School and Society
School Life
School Management
School Review
Science
Science News
Science Teacher
Scientific American
Senior Scholastic
Seventeen
Social Education
Social Policy
Social Problems
Social Science Quarterly
Social Service Review
Social Studies
Social Work
Society
Southern Speech Communication
    Journal
Sponsor
State Government
Steel
Supervision

TIP (Theory into Practice)
Taxes
Teachers College Record
Technology Review
Thought
Time
Times Educational Supplement (London)
Times Higher Education Supplement (London)
Today's Education
Trial
Trusts and Estates

USA Today
U. S. News and World Report
Urban Education

Viewpoints, Bulletin of the School of Education, Indiana University
Vital Speeches of the Day

Washington Monthly
Western Political Quarterly
Wilson Library Bulletin
Wilson Quarterly (Woodrow Wilson International Center for Scholars)
Writer's Digest

Young Children

LIST OF ABBREVIATIONS

Admin	Administration	J	Journal (of)
Adv	Advertising	Mag	Magazine
Am	American	Mgt	Management
Assoc	Association	Natl	National
Bd	Board	Natns	Nation's
Bul	Bulletin	Poltcl	Political
Bus	Business	Poltcs	Politics
Chem	Chemical	Pub	Publisher(s)
Col	College	Q	Quarterly
Cont	Contemporary	R	Review
Criml	Criminal	Rec	Record
Crimlgy	Criminology	Rep	Report
Dig	Digest	Res	Research
Eductn	Education	Sat	Saturday
Eductnl	Educational	Sch	School
Eng	Engineering	Sci	Science
Govt	Government	Socl	Social
Ind	Industrial	Tech	Technology
Intl	International	Wk	Week

SECTION 3:

UNITED STATES SUPREME COURT DECISIONS

1. United States v. Worrall   1798   2 Dallas 384
   Role (Haines) v. 1, 159-160
   *Teaching Materials 4-7

2. Georgia v. Brailsford   1792   2 Dallas 402
   *Justices (Friedman) v. 1, 159
   Role (Haines) v. 1, 123

3. Hayburn's Case   1792   2 Dallas 409
   *Federal Courts 85-89
   Role (Haines) 128-130
   Sup Ct (Mason) 74
   Sup Ct Review 1973 131-132, 135-139

4. Chisholm v. Georgia   1793   2 Dallas 419
   *Am Consttnl Law (Mason) 148-153
   Antecedents 726, 728-734
   CQ Guide 303-304
   *Documents History v. 1, 160-162
   Freedom Spent 442-444
   *Justices (Friedman) v. 1, 23-29, 71-73, 97-105, 116-118, 133-145
   *Liberty v. 1, 85-86
   Role (Haines) v. 1, 133-136
   Sup Ct (Mason) 75-76
   *Sup Ct and Consttn 3-6
   Sup Ct in Free Society 75
   This Honorable Court 50-52
   To Preserve 41-42
   PERIODICALS:
       "Chisholm v. Georgia: background and settlement," Doyle Mathis.
       J Am History 54: 19-29 June '67.

5. Glass v. the Sloop Betsey   1794   3 Dallas 6
   Antecedents 689, 760-765
   *Justices (Friedman) v. 1, 29-30
   Role (Haines) v. 1, 143-144

6. Bingham v. Cabbot   1795   3 Dallas 19
   Antecedents 689-690

7. Penhallow v. Doane's Administrators   1795   3 Dallas 54
   Antecedents 708-710, 766-770
   Role (Haines) v. 1, 139-140

47

8. Talbot v. Janson   Aug 22, 1795   3 Dallas 133
    Antecedents 710-711, 770-775
    *Justices (Friedman) v. 1, 54, 178-182

9. Hylton v. United States   1796   3 Dallas 171
    Am Consttn (Kelly) 181-182
    *Am Consttnl Law (Bartholomew) v. 1, 144-146
    *Am Consttnl Law (Mason) 317-318
    *Am Consttnl Law (Saye) 152-154
    Antecedents 682, 778-782
    *Cases Consttnl Law (Cushman) 139-141
    Conservative 166-168
    Great Reversals 70-74
    John Marshall (Baker) 391
    *Justices (Friedman) v. 1, 175-178
    Role (Haines) v. 1, 147-148
    Sup Ct (Mason) 75
    *Sup Ct and Consttn 20-22
    Sup Ct in Free Society 129-130

10. Hills v. Ross   1795   3 Dallas 184
    Antecedents 691-695

11. Ware v. Hylton   1796   3 Dallas 199
    Am Consttn (Kelly) 180
    Antecedents 748-754
    CQ Guide 304
    Foreign Affairs 260-261
    John Marshall (Baker) 157-163
    *Justices (Friedman) v. 1, 73-75, 199-213
    *Liberty v. 1, 97-98
    Role (Haines) v. 1, 141-143
    *Sup Ct and Consttn 17-19
    This Honorable Court 59-60

12. Cotton v. Wallace   1796   3 Dallas 302
    Antecedents 711-713

13. Arcambel v. Wiseman   1796   3 Dallas 306
    Antecedents 716-717

14. Moodie v. The Ship Phoebe Anne   1796   3 Dallas 319
    *Justices (Friedman) v. 1, 236

15. Grayson v. Virginia   1796   3 Dallas 320
    Antecedents 725

16. Wiscart v. Dauchy   1796   3 Dallas 321
    Antecedents 699-702
    *Justices (Friedman) v. 1, 237-239

17. Del Col v. Arnold   1796   3 Dallas 333
    Antecedents 713-715
    *Cases Admiralty 77-78

18. Jennings and Venner v. Arcambal   1797   3 Dallas 336
    and The Brig Perseverance
    Antecedents 702-704, 718

19. Brown v. Van Braam Houchgueest   1797   3 Dallas 344
    Antecedents 719-720

20. Bingham v. Cabot   1797   3 Dallas 382
    Antecedents 683-684

21. Calder v. Bull   1798   3 Dallas 386
    Am Consttn (Kelly) 183
    *Am Consttn (Lockhart) 350-352
    *Am Consttnl Law (Bartholomew) 1-3
    *Am Consttnl Law (Mason) 374-377
    *Am Consttnl Law (Saye) 233-234
    Antecedents 704-705, 782-784
    *Cases Civil Liberties 2-4
    *Cases Consttnl Law (Cushman) 232-234
    *Cases Consttnl Rights 110-112
    *Cases Criml Law (Hall) 30-32
    Conceived 31-32
    *Consttnl Law (Barrett) 568-569
    *Consttnl Law (Lockhart) 421-422
    Defendants 99-100
    Felix Frankfurter (Mendelson) 2
    Government 251-252
    *Justices (Friedman) v. 1, 214-219
    Role (Haines) v. 1, 154-157
    *Sources Antislavery 289-290
    *Sup Ct (Mendelson) 41-47
    *Sup Ct and Consttn 13-16
    *Teaching Materials 9-11

22. Wilson v. Daniel   1798   3 Dallas 401
    Antecedents 680-681
    Great Reversals 17-18
    Role (Haines) v. 1, 157-158

23. New York v. Connecticut   1799   4 Dallas 1
    Role (Haines) v. 2, 251-254

24. Turner v. Bank of North America   1799   4 Dallas 8
    *Materials Consttnl Law 25-26

25. Cooper v. Telfair   1800   4 Dallas 14
    Antecedents 705-707
    Felix Frankfurter (Mendelson) 2-3

26. Bas v. Tingy   1800   4 Dallas 37
    *Justices (Friedman) v. 1, 280-281
    Role (Haines) v. 1, 158

27. Talbot v. Seeman   1801   1 Cranch 1
    John Marshall (Baker) 364-366
    Role (Haines) v. 1, 226

28. Wilson v. Mason   1801   1 Cranch 45
    Mason v. Wilson
    John Marshall (Baker) 366-369
    Role (Haines) v. 1, 265

29. United States v. Schooner Peggy   1801   1 Cranch 103
     John Marshall (Baker) 369-370
     Role (Haines) v. 1, 226-227

30. Marbury v. Madison   Feb 24, 1803   1 Cranch 137
     Am Consttn (Kelly) 214-219
     *Am Consttn (Lockhart) 1-7
     *Am Consttnl Issues 18-22
     *Am Consttnl Law (Bartholomew) v. 1, 2-5
     *Am Consttnl Law (Mason) 38-41
     *Am Consttnl Law (Saye) 15-20
     *Am Consttnl Law (Shapiro) 81-85
     *Am Consttnl Law Reader 13-20
     *Am Govt 529-533
     Am Politics 4-9
     *Annals v. 4, 165-170
     *Basic Cases 1-6
     *Basic Documents 83-88
     Basic History 18-21
     *Basic History 104-109
     Biography 246-251
     By What Right 70-73
     CQ Guide 69-71, 236, 707-708
     *Cases Consttnl Law (Cushman) 3-6
     *Cases Consttnl Law (Gunther) 2-12
     *Cases Consttnl Law (Rosenblum) 12-17
     *Cases Consttnl Rights 1-7
     *Cases Individual 3-12
     Changing 32-35
     *Comparative 108-110
     Conceived 13-18
     Congress 9-11
     *Consttn (Hirschfield) 12-17
     *Consttn (Mendelson) 5-9
     *Consttn (Pollak) 176-185
     Consttn (Swindler) 24-33
     *Consttn (Swindler) 125-143
     *Consttnl Cases 153-162
     *Consttnl Decisions 9-15
     *Consttnl Decisions of Marshall v. 1, 7-43
     *Consttnl Law (Barrett) 18-26
     *Consttnl Law (Barron) 1-10
     *Consttnl Law (Felkenes) 15-23
     *Consttnl Law (Freund) 3-9
     *Consttnl Law (Grossman) 88-94
     *Consttnl Law (Kauper) 1-6
     *Consttnl Law (Lockhart) 1-8
     *Consttnl Law (Schmidhauser) 55-58
     *Consttnl Politics 181-188
     *Consttnlism 56-59
     *Courts, Judges 16-19
     *Desegregation (Ziegler) 23-26
     *Documents History v. 1, 191-195
     Dred Scott Case 222-224
     Executive Privilege 185-187
     *Federal Courts 74-81
     *Federal System 33-36
     *Government and Business 18-20
     Great Events American v. 1, 437-442

*Historic Decisions 7-12
John Marshall (Baker) 394-413
John Marshall (Konefsky) 81-91
*Judiciary (Roche) 27-35
Jurisprudence 201-202
*Justices (Friedman) v. 1, 305-316
*Leading Consttnl Decisions 1-10
Least Dangerous 1-12
*Liberty v. 1, 111-115
Marshall.
Milestones 67-89
Power 32-34
*Processes 50-66
Quarrels 1-14
*Readings American 365-371
Role (Cox) 9-16
Role (Haines) v. 1, 245-250, 253-257
*Role (Haines) 250-253
*Social Forces 342-343
Sup Ct (Forte) 20-23
Sup Ct (Mason) 80-83
*Sup Ct and Am Economic Life 9-15
*Sup Ct and Am Govt 11-17
*Sup Ct and Consttn 25-31
Sup Ct in Am History 15-28
Sup Ct in Crisis 35-36
Sup Ct in Free Society 8-9
Sup Ct on Trial 74-76, 95-102
Sup Ct Speaks 6-10
Sup Ct under Marshall 28-32
This Honorable Court 66-67, 79-84
PERIODICALS:
"Marbury v. Madison; the case of the 'missing' commissions," John
    A. Garrity. Am Heritage 14: 6-9, 84-86, 88-89 June '63.

31. Mandeville and Jameson v. Riddle and   1803   1 Cranch 290
    Co.
    Transformation 221

32. Stuart v. Laird   1803   1 Cranch 299
    John Marshall (Baker) 380-381

33. Capron v. Van Noorden   1804   2 Cranch 126
    *Civil Procedure (Cound) 20

34. Little v. Barreme   1804   2 Cranch 170
    John Marshall (Baker) 519
    Presidential Power 127
    Role (Haines) v. 1, 266

35. Adams v. Woods   1804   2 Cranch 336
    John Marshall (Baker) 518

36. United States v. Fisher, Assignees of   1804   2 Cranch 358
    Blight
    *Consttnl Decisions of Marshall v. 1, 46-63

37. Hepburn and Dundas v. Ellzey   1804   2 Cranch 445
    *Consttnl Decisions of Marshall v. 1, 65-67

38. Huidekoper's Lessee v. Douglass   1805   3 Cranch 1
    Role (Haines) v. 1, 268-269
    Sup Ct under Marshall 70

39. Hallet and Bowne v. Jenks   1805   3 Cranch 210
    John Marshall (Baker) 545

40. Strawbridge v. Curtiss   1806   3 Cranch 267
    *Cases Federal Courts 176-177
    *Elements Civil 210-211
    *Federal Courts 1064
    Great Reversals 29-30

41. Scott v. Negro London   1806   3 Cranch 324
    John Marshall (Baker) 725
    Petitioners 30-31

42. Ex parte Burford   1806   3 Cranch 448
    John Marshall (Baker) 542-543

43. Ex parte Bollman   1807   4 Cranch 75
    Ex parte Swarthwout
    *Consttn (Swindler) 162-169
    *Consttnl Decisions of Marshall v. 1, 69-95
    Dissent 27
    John Marshall (Baker) 456-457
    Jurisprudence 278-280
    Role (Haines) v. 1, 280-282
    Sup Ct Review 1962 160-162

44. Rose v. Himely   1808   4 Cranch 241
    Dissent 26
    Great Reversals 3-4

45. Croudson v. Leonard   1808   4 Cranch 434
    Role (Haines) v. 1, 269

46. United States v. Burr   1807   4 Cranch 469
    *Consttnl Decisions of Marshall v. 1, 100-203

47. Hope Insurance Co. v. Boardman   1809   5 Cranch 57
    *Consttnl Decisions of Marshall v. 1, 206

48. Bank of United States v. Deveaux   1809   5 Cranch 61
    *Consttnl Decisions of Marshall v. 1, 207-216
    Great Reversals 30-32
    John Marshall (Baker) 589-590
    Taney 459

49. United States v. Judge Peters   1809   5 Cranch 115
    CQ Guide 304-305
    *Consttnl Decisions of Marshall v. 1, 219-227
    John Marshall (Konefsky) 91-93
    Role (Haines) v. 1, 270-273
    Sup Ct in Crisis 40-41
    Sup Ct under Marshall 35

50. Hodgson and Thompson v. Bowerbank   1809   5 Cranch 303
    *Cases Federal Courts 5-6

58. Mima Queen v. Hepburn   Feb 13, 1813   7 Cranch 290
    John Marshall (Baker) 726-727
    Jurisprudence 49-50

59. Cargo of the Brig Aurora Burnside v. Feb 26, 1813   7 Cranch 382
    United States
    Consttn (Barber) 53-59

60. Schooner Hoppet and Cargo v. United   Feb 27, 1813   7 Cranch 389
    States
    John Marshall (Baker) 543

61. Riggs v. Lindsay   1813   7 Cranch 500
    *Justices (Friedman) v. 1, 401-403

62. Fairfax's Devisee v. Hunter's Lessee Mar 15, 1813   7 Cranch 603
    Dissent 32
    John Marshall (Baker) 573-580
    Joseph Story 241-242
    Justice Joseph Story 115-116
    This Honorable Court 101-102

63. Clementson v. Williams   Feb 19, 1814   8 Cranch 72
    John Marshall (Baker) 543-544

64. Brown v. United States   Mar 2, 1814   8 Cranch 110
    John Marshall (Baker) 555-556
    Joseph Story 264

65. The Venus   Mar 12, 1814   8 Cranch 253
    John Marshall (Baker) 545-546

66. Terrett v. Taylor   Feb 17, 1815   9 Cranch 43
    Church and State 104-105
    Freedom and the Court 325
    John Marshall (Baker) 654-656
    Joseph Story 129-130, 197-198
    Role (Haines) v. 1, 335-336
    Sup Ct and Religion 37-38

67. Town of Pawlett v. Clark   Mar 10, 1815   9 Cranch 292
    Joseph Story 198-199

68. The Nereide   Mar 11, 1815   9 Cranch 388
    Dissent 31-32

69. New Orleans v. Winter   1816   1 Wheaton 91
    *Consttnl Decisions of Marshall v. 1, 264-265

70. Preston v. Browder   1816   1 Wheaton 115
    *Justices (Friedman) v. 1, 413-414

71. Martin v. Hunter's Lessee   1816   1 Wheaton 304
    Am Consttn (Kelly) 269
    *Am Consttnl Law Reader 20-30
    Basic History 21-22
    *Cases Consttnl Law (Cushman) 129-133
    Cases Consttnl Law (Gunther) 36-44
    *Consttn (Swindler) 293-297

*Consttnl Law (Barrett) 32-35
*Consttnl Law (Barron) 27-34
Consttnl Law (Felkenes) 23-26
*Consttnl Law (Freund) 20-26
*Consttnl Law (Grossman) 107-112
*Consttnl Law (Kauper) 84-92
*Consttnl Law (Lockhart) 31-34
*Courts, Judges 98-100
*Federal Courts 442-455
*Federal System 303-305
Impact (Wasby) 198
John Marshall (Konefsky) 94
Joseph Story 240, 243-248
*Judiciary (Roche) 35-43
Justice Joseph Story 133-136
*Justices (Friedman) v. 1, 454-468
*Liberty v. 1, 127-129
Right to Privacy 340-349
Sovereign Prerogative 36-37
*Sup Ct and Consttn 36-40
Sup Ct in Crisis 42
Sup Ct Speaks 14-28
This Honorable Court 102

72. United States v. Coolidge   1816   1 Wheaton 415
    *Federal Courts 1263-1264
    Joseph Story 170-178
    This Honorable Court 128-129

73. Slocum v. Mayberry   1817   2 Wheaton 1
    *Consttnl Decisions of Marshall v. 1, 267-271
    John Marshall (Baker) 550

74. The Argo   1817   2 Wheaton 288
    John Marshall (Baker) 544

75. Gelston v. Hoyt   1818   3 Wheaton 246
    Role (Haines) v. 1, 350-351

76. United States v. Bevans   1818   3 Wheaton 337
    *Consttnl Decisions of Marshall v. 1, 274-280
    Daniel 39-40
    John Marshall (Baker) 581-582

77. United States v. Palmer   1818   3 Wheaton 610
    John Marshall (Baker) 542

78. Sturges v. Crowninshield   1819   4 Wheaton 122
    Am Consttn (Kelly) 265-266
    *Consttnl Decisions of Marshall v. 1, 282-299
    Daniel 111-112
    Elements Judicial 60
    Impact (Wasby) 107
    John Marshall (Baker) 582-586
    John Marshall (Konefsky) 131-137
    Role (Haines) v. 1, 368-369
    This Honorable Court 109-110

79. M'Millan v. M'Neill   1819   4 Wheaton 209
    Daniel 112

80. M'Culloch v. Maryland   Mar 7, 1819   4 Wheaton 316
     Am Consttn (Kelly) 272-275
     *Am Consttn (Lockhart) 111-118
     *Am Consttnl Issues 79-85
     *Am Consttnl Law (Bartholomew) v. 1, 31-35
     *Am Consttnl Law (Mason) 153-164
     *Am Consttnl Law (Saye) 130-133
     *Am Consttnl Law (Shapiro) 124-128
     *Am Consttnl Law Reader 48-61
     *Am Govt 76-79
     Am Politics 24-29
     *Am Primer 239-254
     *Am Spirit v. 1, 220-221
     Am Spirit v. 1, 221-222; reprinted from Niles' Weekly Register 16
        (1819), 41, 43.
     *Am Testament 78-84
     *Annals v. 4, 530-539
     *Basic Cases 25-34
     Basic History 24-25
     Biography 268-284
     By What Right 80-81
     CQ Guide 15, 329, 708-709
     *Cases Consttnl Law (Cushman) 122-129
     *Cases Consttnl Law (Gunther) 79-92
     *Cases Consttnl Law (Rosenblum) 237-242
     Changing 40-44
     *Comparative 168-172
     *Consttn (Hirschfield) 225-235
     *Consttn (Mendelson) 185-191, 220-223
     *Consttn (Pollak) 213-220
     Consttn (Swindler) 66-76
     *Consttn (Swindler) 305-323
     *Consttnl Decisions 48-54
     *Consttnl Decisions of Marshall v. 1, 307-345
     *Consttnl Law (Barrett) 168-176
     *Consttnl Law (Barron) 144-156
     *Consttnl Law (Felkenes) 45-49
     *Consttnl Law (Freund) 154-162
     *Consttnl Law (Grossman) 113-121
     *Consttnl Law (Kauper) 107-117, 452-457
     *Consttnl Law (Lockhart) 78-87
     *Consttnl Politics 269-274
     Daniel 170-178
     Dissent 34
     *Documentary 482-503
     *Documents History v. 1, 213-220
     Dred Scott Case 220
     Executive Privilege 96-97
     *Federal System 209-212
     Government 375-378
     *Government and Business 7-9
     Great Events American v. 1, 564-569
     *Historic Decisions 23-34
     Impact (Wasby) 104-105
     John Marshall (Baker) 588-603
     John Marshall (Konefsky) 165-191
     John Marshall's Defense.
     *John Marshall's Defense 23-51
     Jurisprudence 102-103

Justice Joseph Story 177-178
Justices (Friedman) v. 1, 328-340
*Leading Consttnl Decisions 70-84
*Liberty v. 1, 131-134
Milestones 117-131
Monetary Decisions 28-32
Perspectives (Black) 21-22
*Processes 173-185, 190-194
Quarrels 30-48
*Readings American 62-68
Right to Privacy v. 1, 353-357
*Social Forces 355-357
Sup Ct (Forte) 29-30, 47
*Sup Ct and Am Govt 41-54
*Sup Ct and Consttn 50-60
Sup Ct in Am History 30-44
Sup Ct in Crisis 36-37
Sup Ct in Free Society 76
Sup Ct Speaks 32-50
Sup Ct under Marshall 40-45
This Honorable Court 110-113

81. The General Smith   1819   4 Wheaton 438
     *Cases Admiralty 228-230

82. Dartmouth College v. Woodward   Feb 2, 1819   4 Wheaton 518
     Am Consttn (Kelly) 263-264
     *Am Consttnl Law (Bartholomew) v. 2, 188-190
     *Am Consttnl Law (Mason) 378-382
     *Am Consttnl Law (Shapiro) 213-216
     *Annals v. 4, 522-528
     Biography 202-200
     CQ Guide 311-312, 708
     *Cases Civil Liberties 11-17
     *Cases Consttnl Law (Cushman) 241-247
     Changing 47-50
     *Consttn (Mendelson) 242-245
     Consttn (Swindler) 56-65
     *Consttn (Swindler) 253-292
     *Consttnl Decisions 100-105
     *Consttnl Decisions of Marshall v. 1, 351-382
     *Consttnl Law (Barrett) 574-575
     Courts 78-81
     Daniel 65-109
     *Documents History v. 1, 220-223
     Education (Lapati) 150-151
     *Education (Spurock) 17-24
     *Historic Decisions 16-22
     John Marshall (Baker) 652-671
     John Marshall (Konefsky) 146-164
     Joseph Story 199-210
     Justice Joseph Story 165-168, 179-184
     *Justices (Friedman) v. 1, 341-351
     *Liberty v. 1, 143-144
     Milestones 91-115
     Quarrels 15-29
     Role (Haines) v. 1, 379-419
     *Sup Ct and Am Economic Life 27-32
     *Sup Ct and Consttn 72-78

Sup Ct in Am History 45-56
Sup Ct in Free Society 199-200
Sup Ct under Marshall 77-79
This Honorable Court 107-109
PERIODICALS:
"Corporate heart," Sheldon Novick. Environment 17: 18-20, 25-31
   Dec '75.
"Dartmouth College v. Woodward; It is ... a small college ... yet,
   there are those who love it," Richard N. Current. Am Heritage
   14: 10-15, 81-84 Aug '63.

83. Houston v. Moore   1820   5 Wheaton 1
    Double Jeopardy (Miller) 10-16
    Joseph Story 268-269

84. United States v. Wiltberger   1820   5 Wheaton 76
    *Cases Criml Law (Hall) 17-18

85. United States v. Smith   1820   5 Wheaton 153
    *Cases Criml Law (Inbau) 180-185

86. Loughborough v. Blake   1820   5 Wheaton 317
    *Consttnl Decisions of Marshall v. 1, 384-392

87. Owings v. Speed   1820   5 Wheaton 420
    *Consttnl Decisions of Marshall v. 1, 393-397

88. Conn v. Pennsylvania   1820   5 Wheaton 426
    John Marshall (Baker) 548

89. United States v. Lancaster   1820   5 Wheaton 434
    John Marshall (Baker) 548

90. Farmers and Mechanics Bank of   1821   6 Wheaton 131
    Pennsylvania v. Smith
    *Consttnl Decisions of Marshall v. 1, 399

91. Anderson v. Dunn   1821   6 Wheaton 204
    *Justices (Friedman) v. 1, 374-377

92. Cohens v. Virginia   1821   6 Wheaton 264
    Am Consttn (Kelly) 270-272
    *Am Consttnl Law (Mason) 164-171
    *Am Consttnl Law (Shapiro) 128-134
    *Annals v. 5, 1-3
    Basic History 22
    Biography 285-286
    CQ Guide 306
    Cases Consttnl Law (Gunther) 44-46
    *Consttn (Mendelson) 41-44
    *Consttn (Swindler) 323-329
    *Consttnl Decisions of Marshall v. 1, 402-462
    *Documents History v. 1, 228-232
    Freedom Spent 444-445
    John Marshall (Baker) 620-622
    John Marshall (Konefsky) 93, 97-107
    Justice Joseph Story 210-212
    *Liberty v. 1, 129-130
    Role (Haines) v. 1, 427-443

*Sup Ct and Consttn 41-49
Sup Ct in Crisis 43-44
Sup Ct in Free Society 15-17, 77
Sup Ct under Marshall 47-48
This Honorable Court 102-104

93. Watts v. Lindsey's Heirs   1822   7 Wheaton 158
    *Justices (Friedman) v. 1, 414-416

94. Green v. Biddle   1823   8 Wheaton 1
    Am Consttn (Kelly) 264-265
    Joseph Story 211-212
    Justice Joseph Story 209-210
    Right to Privacy v. 2, 464-469
    Sup Ct in Crisis 44
    Sup Ct under Marshall 69-70
    This Honorable Court 104-105

95. Johnson & Graham's Lessee v. M'Intosh 1823   8 Wheaton 543
    *Am Indian v. 4, 2537-2553
    *Cases Property (Donahue) 235-240
    *Consttnl Decisions of Marshall v. 2, 2-35
    Daniel 143
    *Documents Indian 35-37
    John Marshall (Baker) 732
    Jurisprudence 52-56
    *Law Indian 359-365

90. Gibbons v. Ogden   Mar 2, 1824   9 Wheaton 1
    Am Consttn (Kelly) 277-280
    *Am Consttn (Lockhart) 125-128
    *Am Consttnl Issues 123-130
    *Am Consttnl Law (Bartholomew) 197-199
    *Am Consttnl Law (Mason) 209-217
    *Am Consttnl Law (Saye) 134-136
    *Am Consttnl Law (Shapiro) 233-238
    *Am Consttnl Law Reader 61-69
    *Annals v. 5, 128-133
    *Basic Cases 35-41
    Basic History 25-26
    CQ Guide 83-84, 315-316, 709
    *Cases Consttnl Law (Cushman) 171-175
    *Cases Consttnl Law (Gunther) 114-117, 259-262
    Changing 44-47
    Commerce 5-12
    *Comparative 173-176
    *Consttn (Mendelson) 85-90
    *Consttn (Pollak) 243-247
    Consttn (Swindler) 77-85
    *Consttn (Swindler) 356-382
    *Consttnl Decisions 106-114
    *Consttnl Decisions of Marshall v. 2, 38-83
    *Consttnl Law (Barrett) 180-188
    *Consttnl Law (Barron) 162-165, 245-248
    *Consttnl Law (Felkenes) 73-78
    *Consttnl Law (Freund) 164-173
    *Consttnl Law (Grossman) 329-334
    *Consttnl Law (Kauper) 120-124, 316-321
    *Consttnl Law (Lockhart) 97-101

*Consttnl Politics 369-375
Daniel 196-207
*Documents History v. 1, 238-242
*Federal System 224-229
*Government and Business 273-274
Great Events American v. 1, 600-606
*Historic Decisions 35-40
Impact (Wasby) 105-106
John Marshall (Baker) 673-687
John Marshall (Konefsky) 193-212
Jurisprudence 84-85, 108-110
Justice Joseph Story 213-214, 225
*Justices (Friedman) v. 1, 316-328, 378-383
*Leading Consttnl Decisions 98-107
*Liberty 145-148
Perspectives (Black) 22-23
Quarrels 49-61
*Readings American 531-536
Role (Haines) v. 1, 488-494
*Sources American Republic v. 1, 254-257
Steamboat.
*Sup Ct and American Economic Life 32-41
Sup Ct and Commerce 9-25
*Sup Ct and Consttn 90-96
Sup Ct in Am History 58-73
Sup Ct in Crisis 37-38
Sup Ct in Free Society 77-78, 106-108
Sup Ct on Trial 142-146
Sup Ct Review 1975 152-153
Sup Ct Review 1977 239, 242-246
*Sup Ct Speaks 54-61
Sup Ct under Marshall 49-52
This Honorable Court 114-115
PERIODICALS:
"Gibbons v. Ogden; the steamboat's charter of freedom," George
Dangerfield. Am Heritage 14: 38-43, 78-80 Oct '63.

97. The St. Jago de Cuba   1824   9 Wheaton 409
     *Cases Admiralty 248-250

98. United States v. Perez   1824   9 Wheaton 579
     *Criminal Justice (Way) 274

99. Osborn v. President, Directors and 1824   9 Wheaton 738
     Co. of the Bank of the United
     States
     Am Consttn (Kelly) 275-276
     Biography 286-287
     *Cases Federal Courts 102-108
     *Consttnl Decisions of Marshall v. 2, 87-142
     Daniel 178-181
     *Federal Courts 850-859
     John Marshall (Baker) 691-695
     Justice Joseph Story 226-227
     *Materials Consttnl Law 99-107
     Monetary Decisions 33-35
     Quarrels 30-48
     Role (Haines) v. 1, 471-476
     Sup Ct under Marshall 48-49

100. Bank of the United States v. Planters'   1824   9 Wheaton 904
        Bank of Georgia
     *Consttnl Decisions of Marshall v. 2, 144-150
     Daniel 179-181

101. Wayman v. Southard   1825   10 Wheaton 1
     Consttn (Barber) 63-72
     Role (Haines) v. 1, 469-470

102. Elmendorf v. Taylor   1825   10 Wheaton 152
     Role (Haines) v. 1, 471

103. The Steamboat Thomas Jefferson   1825   10 Wheaton 428
     *Cases Admiralty 154-155
     Great Reversals 22-23
     Justice Daniel 222-223

104. Marianna Flora   1826   11 Wheaton 1
     Justice Joseph Story 255-256

105. Etting v. President, Directors and   1826   11 Wheaton 59
        Co. of the Bank of the United
        States
     Daniel 183-184

106. Martin v. Mott   1827   12 Wheaton 19
     *Documents History v. 1, 246-247
     Joseph Story 266
     *Liberty 121-122
     Sup Ct and Commander in Chief 14-17

107. President, Directors and Co. of the   1827   12 Wheaton 64
        Bank of the United States
     Daniel 184-185
     Role (Haines) v. 1, 580

108. Ogden v. Saunders   1827   12 Wheaton 213
     Am Consttn (Kelly) 266-267
     *Consttnl Decisions of Marshall v. 2, 177-213
     Daniel 112-119
     John Marshall (Baker) 695-700
     John Marshall (Konefsky) 138-141
     Justice Joseph Story 260-263
     *Justices (Friedman) v. 1, 258-266, 523-532
     Role (Haines) v. 1, 526-532
     *Sup Ct and Consttn 79-86
     Sup Ct under Marshall 86

109. Mason v. Haile   1827   12 Wheaton 370
     Daniel 145-146

110. Brown v. Maryland   1827   12 Wheaton 419
     Am Consttn (Kelly) 280
     *Am Consttn (Lockhart) 289-290
     *Am Consttnl Law (Bartholomew) v. 1, 202-204
     *Am Consttnl Law (Mason) 220-224
     *Am Consttnl Law (Saye) 190-192
     CQ Guide 329-330
     *Cases Consttnl Law (Cushman) 179-182

*Consttn (Mendelson) 211-215
*Consttnl Cases 229-246
*Consttnl Decisions of Marshall v. 2, 153-173
*Consttnl Law (Barron) 293-298
*Consttnl Law (Freund) 185-188
*Consttnl Law (Kauper) 362-369
*Consttnl Law (Lockhart) 414-415
*Consttnl Law (Morris) 189-191
John Marshall (Baker) 688-691
John Marshall (Konefsky) 213-225
*Liberty 148-149
Role (Haines) v. 1, 533-535
*Sup Ct and American Economic Life 41-47
Sup Ct and Commerce 25
Sup Ct in Free Society 108
Sup Ct under Marshall 52
This Honorable Court 116

111. The Antelope   1827   12 Wheaton 546
      *Justices (Friedman) v. 1, 519-523
      Petitioners 32-34

112. Ramsay v. Allegre   1827   12 Wheaton 611
      Justice Joseph Story 263-265

113. American Insurance Co. v. 356 Bales 1828   1 Peters 511
         of Cotton, Canter, claimant
      *Am Consttnl Law (Bartholomew) v. 1, 140-142
      *Consttnl Decisions of Marshall v. 2, 216-227
      *Documents History v. 1, 248-249
      Dred Scott Case 144, 372-373
      *Liberty 117-118

114. Pennock v. Dialogue   1829   2 Peters 1
      Daniel 153

115. Van Ness v. Pacard   1829   2 Peters 137
      Joseph Story 168-169
      Transformation 55-56

116. Boyce v. Anderson   1829   2 Peters 150
      John Marshall (Baker) 728-729
      This Honorable Court 141

117. Wilson v. Black Bird Creek Marsh   1829   2 Peters 245
         Company
      Am Consttn (Kelly) 280-281
      CQ Guide 316
      *Cases Consttnl Law (Gunther) 263-264
      *Consttn (Pollak) 257-258
      *Consttnl Decisions of Marshall v. 2, 230-233
      *Consttnl Law (Barrett) 191-192
      *Consttnl Law (Freund) 174
      John Marshall (Konefsky) 225-227
      Jurisprudence 110-111
      Role (Haines) v. 1, 581-582
      Sup Ct and Commerce 25
      *Sup Ct and Consttn 97-98
      Sup Ct in Free Society 110

118. Foster and Elam v. Neilson   1829   2 Peters 253
     *Consttnl Decisions of Marshall v. 2, 235-260
     Daniel 53
     Great Reversals 20-21

119. Satterlee v. Matthewson   1829   2 Peters 380
     Role (Haines) v. 1, 582-583

120. Weston v. City Council of Charleston   1829   2 Peters 449
     *Consttnl Decisions of Marshall v. 2, 265-274
     Jurisprudence 93-94
     Role (Haines) v. 1, 584-588

121. Wilkinson v. Leland   1829   2 Peters 627
     Daniel 146-147
     Joseph Story 213-215
     Role (Haines) v. 1, 583-584
     Sup Ct in Free Society 201-202

122. LeGrand v. Darnall   1829   2 Peters 664
     *Justices (Friedman) v. 1, 430-432

123. Craig, Moore and Moore v. Missouri   1830   4 Peters 410
     *Consttnl Decisions of Marshall v. 2, 279-298
     *Documents History v. 1, 252-253
     Monetary Decisions 37-40
     Role (Haines) v. 1, 590-593
     This Honorable Court 116-117

124. Providence Bank v. Billings and Pittman 1830   4 Peters 514
     CQ Guide 313
     *Consttnl Decisions of Marshall v. 2, 300-308
     Role (Haines) v. 1, 588-580
     *Sup Ct and Consttn 87-89

125. Cherokee Nation v. Georgia   1831   5 Peters 1
     Am Consttn (Kelly) 180-181
     *Am Indian v. 4, 2554-2602
     *Annals v. 5, 427-430
     CQ Guide 17, 307, 709
     *Consttnl Decisions of Marshall v. 2, 312-320
     Dissent 39-40
     *Documents History v. 1, 255-258
     *Documents Indian 58-60
     Dred Scott's Case 117
     John Marshall (Baker) 734-740
     Jurisprudence 56-58
     Justice Joseph Story 295-298
     *Justices (Friedman) v. 1, 493-509
     *Law Indian 33-35
     Role (Haines) v. 1, 598-600

126. Doe ex dem. Patterson v. Winn   1831   5 Peters 233
     Joseph Story 169-170

127. Fisher v. Cockerell   1831   5 Peters 248
     *Consttnl Decisions of Marshall v. 2, 322-333
     Role (Haines) v. 1, 607-608

128. New Jersey v. New York   1831   5 Peters 284
      Role (Haines) v. 2, 254-261

129. Worcester v. Georgia   1832   6 Peters 515
      *Am Indian v. 4, 2603-2648
      *Consttnl Decisions of Marshall v. 2, 337-377
      *Documents History v. 1, 258-259
      *Documents Indian 60-62
      Impact (Wasby) 216
      John Marshall (Baker) 740-746
      *Law Indian 40-44
      Role (Haines) v. 1, 600-604

130. United States v. Arrendondo   1832   6 Peters 691
      Daniel 144-145

131. United States v. Percheman   1833   7 Peters 51
      *Cases Property (Donahue) 243-248
      Great Reversals 21-22

132. United States v. Wilson   1833   7 Peters 150
      CQ Guide 224

133. Barron v. Mayor and City Council   1833   7 Peters 243
      of Baltimore
      *Am Consttnl Law (Bartholomew) v. 2, 9-10
      *Am Consttnl Law (Saye) 253-254
      *Am Consttnl Law (Shapiro) 134-135
      Am Politics 49-50
      CQ Guide 374-375
      *Cases Civil Liberties 18-20
      *Cases Consttnl Law (Cushman) 248-250
      *Cases Consttnl Law (Gunther) 460-462
      *Cases Individual 85-87
      *Civil Liberties (Sweet) 9-10
      *Civil Rights (Abernathy) 1977 23-25
      *Consttnl Decisions of Marshall v. 2, 379-386
      *Consttnl Law (Barrett) 565-567
      *Consttnl Law (Kauper) 512-515
      *Consttnl Law (Klein) 103-105
      *Consttnl Politics 414-416
      Dred Scott Case 520-521
      Freedom and the Court 34-35
      John Marshall (Baker) 762-763
      Judiciary (Abraham) 71-72
      *Leading Consttnl Decisions 160-164
      Role (Haines) v. 1, 608-609
      Sup Ct (North) 72-73
      *Sup Ct and American Economic Life 47-51
      *Sup Ct and Consttn 60-62

134. Wheaton v. Peters   1834   8 Peters 591
      *Cases Copyright (Kaplan) 24-39
      Daniel 148-152
      Justice Joseph Story 324-328

135. Mitchel v. United States   1835   9 Peters 711
      Daniel 145

136. Hagan v. Lucas   1836   10 Peters 400
     Role (Haines) v. 2, 27-28

137. Ewing v. Burnet   1837   11 Peters 41
     *Cases Property (Casner) 57-61
     *Cases Property (Donahue) 106-107

138. United States v. The Ship Garonne   1837   11 Peters 73
     United States v. The Ship Fortune
     Taney 534-535

139. Mayor, Aldermen and Commonalty of   1837   11 Peters 102
     the City of New York v. Miln
     Am Consttn (Kelly) 328
     CQ Guide 323
     Commerce 124-126
     Consttnl Bricolage 94
     Daniel 208-209
     Dissent 43
     From Confederation 13-14
     Great Reversals 130-131
     *Justices (Friedman) v. 1, 728-734
     Role (Haines) v. 2, 43-49
     Sup Ct and Commerce 25-26
     *Sup Ct and Consttn 126-129
     Sup Ct in Free Society 80-81, 112
     Sup Ct under Marshall 102-103
     Taney 360-365
     This Honorable Court 126-127
     Without Fear 295-298

140. Briscoe v. President and Directors of 1837   11 Peters 257
     the Bank of Kentucky
     Am Consttn (Kelly) 323-324
     Consttnl Bricolage 93
     From Confederation 12
     Joseph Story 257-258
     *Liberty 177-178
     Monetary Decisions 40-42
     Obscenity (Clor) 100-101
     Role (Haines) v. 2, 48-52
     Without Fear 307-308

141. Charles River Bridge v. Warren   1837   11 Peters 420
     Bridge
     Am Consttn (Kelly) 324-325
     *Am Consttnl Law (Mason) 383-387
     *Am Consttnl Law (Saye) 240-241
     *Am Consttnl Law (Shapiro) 216-220
     *Annals v. 6, 326-332
     Basic History 30-31
     *Basic History 117-121
     Biography 266-267
     CQ Guide 313
     Changing 58-59
     Consttnl Bricolage 91-92
     Daniel 119-135
     *Documents History v. 1, 285-287
     Dred Scott Case 229-230

From Confederation 8-12
*Historic Decisions 41-47
Impact (Wasby) 107
Joseph Story 215-226
Justice Joseph Story 357-359, 360-363
*Justices (Friedman) v. 1, 656-666
*Liberty 175-177
Privilege.
Quarrels 62-76
Role (Haines) v. 2, 28-43
*Sup Ct (Mendelson) 55-64
*Sup Ct and American Economic Life 51-59
*Sup Ct and Consttn 114-119
Sup Ct in Crisis 61-62
Sup Ct in Free Society 203-204
Sup Ct under Marshall 95-97
Taney 74-93
This Honorable Court 123-125
Transformation 46-47, 130-134
Without Fear 281-290

142. United States v. Coombs   1838   12 Peters 72
     Joseph Story 255-256
     Role (Haines) v. 2, 328-329

143. Kendall v. United States ex rel. Stokes   1838   12 Peters 524
     CQ Guide 230
     From Confederation 61-63
     Justice Joseph Story 374-375
     Presidential Power 91-94
     Sup Ct and Poltcl Questions 136-137
     Taney 158-164
     Without Fear 320-321

144. Rhode Island v. Massachusetts   1838   12 Peters 657
     Justice Joseph Story 374, 375-377
     Role (Haines) v. 2, 261-268
     Taney 513-514

145. Ex parte Hennen   1839   13 Peters 225
     Role (Haines) v. 2, 321-323

146. Wilcox v. Jackson ex dem. M'Connel   1839   13 Peters 498
     Taney 755-756

147. Bank of Augusta v. Earle   1839   13 Peters 519
     Bank of United States v. Primrose
     New Orleans and Carrollton Railroad
         Co. v. Earle
     Am Consttn (Kelly) 326-327
     Daniel 185-192
     Exclusionary 292-293
     From Confederation 23-25
     Justice Joseph Story 390-391
     *Justices (Friedman) v. 1, 705-713, 786-792
     *Liberty 179-180
     Monetary Decisions 43-44
     Role (Haines) v. 2, 60-76
     *Sup Ct and American Economic Life 59-61

*Sup Ct and Consttn 139-141
Sup Ct under Marshall 98-99
Taney 115-121

148. Commercial and Railroad Bank of Vicksburg v. Slocumb, Richards and Co. Taney 460	1840	14 Peters 60
149. Rhode Island v. Massachusetts Role (Haines) v. 2, 269-271	1840	14 Peters 210
150. Decatur v. Paulding Role (Haines) v. 2, 302-305 Sup Ct and Poltcl Questions 138 Taney 167-168	1840	14 Peters 497
151. United States v. Gratiot Role (Haines) v. 2, 217-218	1840	14 Peters 526
152. Holmes v. Jennison Foreign Affairs 231-233 *Justices (Friedman) v. 1, 581-598 Role (Haines) v. 2, 206-217 Taney 176-177 Without Fear 302-303	1840	14 Peters 540
153. Gaines v. Relf Taney 756-759	1841	15 Peters 9
154. United States v. Dickson Role (Haines) v. 2, 305-306	1841	15 Peters 141
155. Groves v. Slaughter Brown v. Slaughter Commerce 66-72 Daniel 209-213 Dissent 55 Justice Joseph Story 395-396, 397 Petitioners 44-47 Role (Haines) v. 2, 110-118 Sup Ct in Crisis 68 Taney 365-370 This Honorable Court 141-144 Without Fear 321-323	1841	15 Peters 449
156. United States v. Schooner Amistad *Civil Rights (Blaustein) 103-110 God 25-26 Justice Joseph Story 396 Petitioners 44 Role (Haines) v. 2, 98-109 Sup Ct under Marshall 124 Taney 189-194 This Honorable Court 144-145 Without Fear 337-346	1841	15 Peters 518
157. Swift v. Tyson Ages 30-35	1842	16 Peters 1

*Cases Civil Procedure 274-276
*Cases Federal Courts 573-577
Daniel 154-156
*Federal Courts 691-694
Hugo Black 182-183
Joseph Story 180-189
Justice Joseph Story 405-407
Justices (Friedman) v. 1, 468-472
Role (Haines) v. 2, 317-320
Sup Ct Review 1972 111
Taney 327-331
This Honorable Court 129, 323-324
Transformation 245, 249-252

158. United States v. Eliason   1842   16 Peters 291
      Taney 171

159. Dobbins v. Commissioners of Erie   1842   16 Peters 435
      County
      Role (Haines) v. 2, 219-221

160. Prigg v. Pennsylvania   1842   16 Peters 539
      Am Consttn (Kelly) 338-340
      By What Right 93-94
      *Consttnl Law (Freund) 757-759
      Dissent 56
      *Documents History v. 1, 292-295
      Dred Scott Case 42-46
      From Confederation 100-102
      Joseph Story 261-262
      Justice Daniel 177-180
      Justice Joseph Story 399-402
      *Liberty 191-193
      Petitioners 48-50
      Role (Haines) v. 2, 121-128
      *Sup Ct and Consttn 145-149
      Sup Ct in Crisis 69
      Sup Ct under Marshall 124-125
      Taney 535-547
      This Honorable Court 145-146
      Without Fear 367-368
      PERIODICALS:
      "Prigg v. Pennsylvania and northern state courts: anti-slavery use
      of a pro-slavery decision," Paul Finkelman. Civil War History
      25: 5-35 Mar '79.

161. Jewell v. Jewell   1843   1 Howard 219
      Justice Daniel 262-263

162. Bronson v. Kinzie   1843   1 Howard 311
      Role (Haines) v. 2, 340-342
      Taney 148-149
      Without Fear 294

163. Vidal v. Mayor, Alderman and Citizens   1844   2 Howard 127
      of Philadelphia, Executors of
      Girard
      Church and State 105-106
      Daniel 156-168

Dissent 49-50
Education (Lapati) 152-153
Education (Spurock) 66-70
Joseph Story 130-132
Justice Joseph Story 417-419
Sup Ct and Religion 39

164.	Louisville, Cincinnati and Charleston Railroad Co. v. Letson Great Reversals 34-36 *Justices (Friedman) v. 1, 626-632 Role (Haines) v. 2, 76-82 *Sup Ct and Consttn 142-144 Taney 461-464 Without Fear 293	1844	2 Howard 497
165.	Gaines v. Chew Taney 759-760	1844	2 Howard 619
166.	Bank of the United States v. United States Taney 124-125 Without Fear 308-312	1844	2 Howard 711
167.	Kendall v. Stokes Role (Haines) v. 2, 301-302 Taney 166	1845	3 Howard 87
168.	Ex parte Dorr Dissent 59 Role (Haines) v. 2, 311-313 Taney 515-518 This Honorable Court 133-134	1045	3 Howard 103
169.	Searight v. Stokes Justice Daniel 213-215 *Justices (Friedman) v. 1, 806-810 Taney 399-400	1845	3 Howard 151
170.	Pollard's Lessee v. Hagan *Justices (Friedman) v. 1, 778-786 Role (Haines) v. 2, 218 Taney 751-753	1845	3 Howard 212
171.	Cary v. Curtis Joseph Story 267-268 *Materials Consttnl Law 27-28 Role (Haines) v. 2, 324-325	1845	3 Howard 236
172.	Permoli v. Municipality No. 1 of New Orleans Church and State 100-107 Expanding Liberties 3-4 First Amendment (Marnell) 131-132	1845	3 Howard 589
173.	Gantly's Lessee v. Ewing Role (Haines) v. 2, 342	1845	3 Howard 707
174.	Rhode Island v. Massachusetts	1846	4 Howard 591

Daniel 54-58
Role (Haines) v. 2, 271-273

175. Rowan v. Runnels   1847   5 Howard 134
     Role (Haines) v. 2, 118-120

176. In re Metzger   1847   5 Howard 176
     Taney 177-179

177. Jones v. Van Zandt   1847   5 Howard 215
     *Justices (Friedman) v. 2, 864-869
     Role (Haines) v. 2, 129-132
     Taney 548-554
     This Honorable Court 147
     Without Fear 364-366

178. Cook v. Moffat   1847   5 Howard 295
     Role (Haines) v. 2, 342-347
     Taney 153

179. Fox v. Ohio   1847   5 Howard 410
     Criminal Law (Wells) 131
     Double (Miller) 17-24

180. Waring v. Clarke   1847   5 Howard 441
     *Cases Admiralty 16-18
     Daniel 49-50
     Role (Haines) v. 2, 329-331
     Taney 436-439

181. Thurlow v. Massachusetts   1847   5 Howard 504
     Fletcher v. Rhode Island
     Pierce v. New Hampshire
     "License Cases"
     Am Consttn (Kelly) 328-329
     Commerce 126-135
     Consttnl Law (Barrett) 192-193
     Daniel 213-217
     Great Reversals 190-192
     *Justices (Friedman) v. 1, 696-705, 750-759
     Role (Haines) v. 2, 142-152
     Sup Ct and Commerce 26
     Sup Ct under Marshall 103-104
     Taney 371-377

182. Brashear v. Mason   1848   6 Howard 92
     Sup Ct and Poltcl Questions 138-139

183. Planters' Bank of Mississippi v. Sharp   1848   6 Howard 301
     Baldwin v. Payne
     Daniel 135-136
     Justice Daniel 202-204
     *Justices (Friedman) v. 1, 696-705, 750-759
     Role (Haines) v. 2, 360-363
     Taney 472-473

184. New Jersey Steam Navigation Co. v. 1848   6 Howard 344
     Merchants' Bank of Boston
     "Lexington Case"

Daniel 43-49, 50-52
Taney 439-442

185. Houston v. City Bank of New Orleans   1848   6 Howard 486
     Taney 145-146

186. West River Bridge Co. v. Dix   1848   6 Howard 507
     West River Bridge Co. v. Towns of
       Brattleboro and Dummerston
     Daniel 136-140
     Justice Daniel 207-212
     *Justices (Friedman) v. 1, 810-814
     Role (Haines) v. 2, 349-351
     Taney 471

187. Patterson v. Gaines   1848   6 Howard 550
     Taney 760-762

188. Luther v. Borden   1849   7 Howard 1
     *Am Consttnl Law (Bartholomew) v. 1, 14-16
     *Am Consttnl Law (Mason) 50-53
     *Am Consttnl Law (Shapiro) 86-89
     *Cases Consttnl Law (Cushman) 13-16
     *Cases Consttnl Law (Rosenblum) 118-124
     Consttnl Counterrevolution 21-22
     Daniel 58-64
     Dred Scott Case 232-233
     From Confederation 31-33
     Guarantee 111-129
     Impeachment 107-108
     Law and Politics 182-184
     Power 39
     Rise 44-54
     Role (Haines) v. 2, 310-317
     Sup Ct (Freund) 147-148
     Sup Ct and Commander in Chief 14-17
     *Sup Ct and Consttn 101-105
     Sup Ct and Poltcl Questions 16-21
     Taney 518-527
     This Honorable Court 134-135
     Without Fear 325-336

189. United States v. Chicago   1849   7 Howard 185
     Taney 756

190. Smith v. Turner   1849   7 Howard 283
     Norris v. Boston
     "Passenger Cases"
     Am Consttn (Kelly) 329-330
     Commerce 136-139
     Daniel 218-224
     Justice Daniel 192 104
     Petitioners 52-53
     Role (Haines) v. 2, 152-172
     Sup Ct and Commerce 26
     *Sup Ct and Consttn 130-134
     Sup Ct in Free Society 112-113
     Sup Ct under Marshall 104-105
     Taney 382-391
     Without Fear 298-300

191. Peck v. Jenness   1849   7 Howard 612
     Role (Haines) v. 2, 200, 204-206
     Taney 145

192. Missouri v. Iowa   1849   7 Howard 660
     Role (Haines) v. 2, 277-278

193. Taylor v. Taylor   1850   8 Howard 183
     Justice Daniel 264-265

194. Lord v. Veazie   1850   8 Howard 251
     *Nature 56-60

195. Sheldon v. Sill   1850   8 Howard 441
     *Cases Federal Courts 6-8
     *Consttnl Law (Freund) 136-137
     *Federal Courts 309-310
     *Materials Consttnl Law 30-32

196. Perrine v. Chesapeake and Delaware 1850   9 Howard 172
     Canal Co.
     Taney 471-472

197. Withers v. Greene   1850   9 Howard 213
     Transformation 224

198. United States v. Marigold   1850   9 Howard 560
     Double (Miller) 24-27
     Role (Haines) v. 2, 186-189

199. Fleming v. Page   1850   9 Howard 603
     Role (Haines) v. 2, 306-308

200. Strader v. Graham   1850   10 Howard 82
     "Minstrels Case"
     Dred Scott Case 260-262
     Justice Daniel 247-248
     Role (Haines) v. 2, 136-138
     Taney 556-558
     This Honorable Court 149-150
     Without Fear 371-373

201. Woodruff v. Trapnall   1850   10 Howard 190
     Role (Haines) v. 2, 363-366

202. Barnard v. Adams   1850   10 Howard 270
     *Cases Admiralty 608-611

203. Gayler v. Wilder   1850   10 Howard 477
     Justice Daniel 270-271
     Legal Regulation 915-917
     Taney 510-511

204. Hotchkiss v. Greenwood   1850   11 Howard 248
     Sup Ct and Agencies 159, 163-164
     Sup Ct Review 1966 309-315

205. Florida v. Georgia   1850   11 Howard 293
     Role (Haines) v. 2, 278-280

206. Randon v. Toby   1850   11 Howard 493
         Taney 352-353

207. Hogg v. Emerson   1850   11 Howard 587
         Justice Daniel 272-273

208. Cooley v. Board of Wardens of Port   1851   12 Howard 299
         of Philadelphia
       Am Consttn (Kelly) 330
       *Am Consttn (Lockhart) 239-240
       *Am Consttnl Law (Bartholomew) v. 1, 205-206
       *Am Consttnl Law (Mason) 217-220
       *Am Consttnl Law (Saye) 173-174
       *Am Consttnl Law (Shapiro) 238-241
        CQ Guide 21, 317-318
       *Cases Admiralty 714-718
       *Cases Consttnl Law (Cushman) 176-179
       *Cases Consttnl Law (Gunther) 266-268
       *Consttn (Mendelson) 196-199
       *Consttnl Law (Barrett) 194-197
       *Consttnl Law (Barron) 252-255
       *Consttnl Law (Freund) 175-178
       *Consttnl Law (Grossman) 334-337
       *Consttnl Law (Kauper) 322-327
       *Consttnl Law (Lockhart) 280-282
       *Consttnl Politics 376-380
        Daniel 224-225
       *Federal System 329-333
        From Confederation 19-22
       *Historic Decisions 48-53
        Justice Daniel 195-197
       *Justices (Friedman) v. 2, 909-915
       *Liberty v. 1, 180-182
       *Processes 207-214
       *Role (Haines) v. 2, 172-176
       *Sup Ct and American Economic Life 62-67
        Sup Ct and Commerce 26-29
       *Sup Ct and Consttn 135-138
        Sup Ct in Free Society 113-114
        Sup Ct Review 1975 154-155
        Sup Ct under Marshall 105-107
        Taney 404-406
        This Honorable Court 129-130
        Without Fear 300

209. Propeller Genesee Chief v. Fitzhugh   1851   12 Howard 443
        From Confederation 35-36
        Great Reversals 25-27
        Justice Daniel 223-224
        Role (Haines) v. 2, 331-333
       *Sup Ct and Consttn 105-109
        Taney 442-446
        Without Fear 303-306

210. Fretz v. Bull   1851   12 Howard 466
         Taney 446

211. Gaines v. Relf   1851   12 Howard 472
         Taney 763-766

212. United States v. Ferreira   1851   13 Howard 40
      Role (Haines) v. 2, 325-327

213. Richmond, Fredericksburg and Potomac   1851   13 Howard 71
      Railroad Co. v. Louisa Railroad Co.
      Role (Haines) v. 2, 353

214. Mitchell v. Harmony   1851   13 Howard 115
      Role (Haines) v. 2, 308-310
      Taney 172-173

215. Pennsylvania v. Wheeling and Belmont   1851   13 Howard 518
      Bridge Co.
      Am Consttn (Kelly) 330-331
      *Consttnl Law (Freund) 178-184
      Justice Daniel 198-199
      Role (Haines) v. 2, 176-186
      Without Fear 323-325

216. Moore v. Illinois   1852   14 Howard 13
      Double (Miller) 27-31
      Justice Daniel 249-250
      Role (Haines) v. 2, 133-134
      Taney 588-589

217. Kennett v. Chambers   1852   14 Howard 38
      Taney 201-203

218. Rundle v. Delaware and Raritan   1852   14 Howard 80
      Canal Co.
      Taney 465-466

219. In re Kaine   1852   14 Howard 103
      Taney 180-182

220. Board of Trustees of Vincennes   1852   14 Howard 268
      University v. Indiana
      Role (Haines) v. 2, 354-356

221. Veazie v. Moor   1852   14 Howard 568
      Role (Haines) v. 2, 189-190

222. O'Reilly v. Morse   1853   15 Howard 62
      *Legal Regulation 798-804
      Taney 498-504

223. Northern Indiana Railroad Co. v.   1853   15 Howard 233
      Michigan Central Railroad Co.
      Justice Daniel 232-233

224. Curran v. Arkansas   1853   15 Howard 304
      Role (Haines) v. 2, 367-369

225. Marshall v. Baltimore and Ohio   1853   16 Howard 314
      Railroad
      Justice Daniel 204-205
      Role (Haines) v. 2, 83-89
      Taney 466-469

226. Piqua Branch of the State Bank of   1853   16 Howard 369
     Ohio v. Knoop
     *Justices (Friedman) v. 1, 759-766
     Role (Haines) v. 2, 376-382
     Sup Ct in Crisis 62-63
     Taney 475-476

227. Ohio Life Insurance and Trust Co. v.   1853   16 Howard 416
     Debolt
     Dissent 51-52
     Role (Haines) v. 2, 372-376
     *Sup Ct and Consttn 120-123
     Taney 476-477

228. Deshler v. Dodge   1853   16 Howard 622
     Taney 479

229. Shields v. Barrow   Feb 30, 1855 17 Howard 130
     *Elements Civil 452-454

230. United States ex rel Goodrich v.   Feb 6, 1855   17 Howard 284
     Guthrie
     Taney 169-171

231. Bogart v. The Steamboat John Jay   1854   17 Howard 399
     *Cases Admiralty 290-291

232. Fremont v. United States   Mar 10, 1855 17 Howard 542
     Justice Daniel 268
     Taney 770-780

233. Ward v. Peck   Feb 26, 1856 18 Howard 267
     *Cases Admiralty 208-210

234. Den, Murray's Lessee v. Hoboken   Feb 19, 1856 18 Howard 272
     Land and Improvement Co.
     CQ Guide 524
     *Consttnl Law (Barrett) 588-589
     Role (Haines) v. 2, 334-336
     Sup Ct in Free Society 215

235. Ex parte Wells   Apr 9, 1856   18 Howard 307
     CQ Guide 226

236. Dodge v. Woolsey   Apr 8, 1856   18 Howard 331
     *Justices (Friedman) v. 1, 612-626; v. 2, 940-950
     Role (Haines) v. 2, 386-389
     *Sup Ct and Consttn 124-125
     Taney 480-482

237. Pennsylvania v. Wheeling and Belmont   Apr 21, 1856 18 Howard 421
     Bridge Co.
     Taney 415-418

238. Seymour v. McCormick   Jan 7, 1857   19 Howard 96
     Taney 505-507

239. Dred Scott v. Sanford   Mar 6, 1857   19 Howard 393
     Am Consttn (Kelly) 361-367

*Am Consttnl Law (Mason) 46-50
*Am Consttnl Law (Shapiro) 135-140
*Am Spirit v. 1, 400-401
Am Spirit v. 1, 401-402--reprint of Southside (Va.) Democrat, in
    The Liberator (Boston), April 3, 1857.
Am Spirit v. 1, 402-403--reprint of Christian Watchman and Re-
    flector (Boston) in The Liberator (Boston), March 27, 1857.
*Annals v. 8, 440-449
*Basic Documents 117-120
Basic History 35-36
Biography 288-299
CQ Guide 22, 135-138, 710-711
*Cases Consttnl Law (Rosenblum) 73-85
*Consttn (Mendelson) 516-519
*Consttn (Pollak) v. 2, 212-219
Changing 61-62
*Civil Rights (Bardolph) 17-19
Civil Rights (Blaustein) 146-158
*Civil Rights (Blaustein) 158-169
Civil Rights (Konvitz) 132-133
Congress 29-31
Consttnl Bricolage 95-98
*Consttnl Cases 327-349
*Consttnl Law (Barrett) 589-591
*Consttnl Law (Freund) 729-733
*Democracy 89-99
*Desegregation (Ziegler) 37-42
Dissent 56-57
*Documents History v. 1, 339-345
Dred Scott Case.
Dred Scott Decision.
*Dred Scott Decision, 9-43
Dred Scott's Case.
From Confederation 107-130
God 27-29
Great Events American v. 2, 900-905
Great Reversals 45-46
*Historic Decisions 54-60
Justice 13-15
Justice Daniel 250-257
*Justices (Friedman) v. 1, 547-567, 666-696; v. 2, 833-839, 915-
    924, 950-960
*Law Lawyers 84-98
*Liberty v. 1, 203-207
Milestones 135-161
Petitioners 59-81
Power 43-44
Quarrels 77-89
*Race 2-21
*Racial Equality 4-6
Role (Haines) v. 2, 393-435
*Search for Meaning 112-115
*Sup Ct and Consttn 150-157
Sup Ct in Crisis 72-78
Sup Ct on Trial 77
*Sup Ct Speaks 68-79
Sup Ct under Marshall 119-120, 131-143
Taney 592-630

This Honorable Court 151-155
Without Fear 382-429
PERIODICALS:
"Dred Scott Decision 1857," Louis C. Kleber. History Today 22:
    873-878 Dec '72.
"Dred Scott v. Sandford; Black Pawn on a Field of Peril," Bruce
    Catton. Am Heritage 15: 66-71, 90-91 Dec '63.
"Was the Dred Scott Case Valid?" Walter Ehrlich. J Am History
    55: 256-265 Sep '68.

240. Dynes v. Hoover   Feb 1, 1858   20 Howard 65
     *Cases Criml Law (Inbau) 151-152

241. Jackson v. Steamboat Magnolia   Apr 13, 1858   20 Howard 296
     Taney 449-450

242. McCormick v. Talcott   Apr 22, 1858   20 Howard 402
     Taney 507-509

243. United States v. Fossat   Apr 30, 1858   20 Howard 413
     Taney 786-788

244. McFaul v. Ramsey   May 18, 1858   20 Howard 523
     Taney 353-354

245. The Propeller Niagara v. Cordes Jan 4, 1859   21 Howard 7
     The Propeller Niagara v. Sexton
     *Cases Admiralty 464-466

246. Ableman v. Booth   Mar 7, 1859   21 Howard 506
     United States v. Booth
     Am Consttn (Kelly) 356
     Basic History 33-34
     CQ Guide 360
     *Documents History v. 1, 358-361
     From Confederation 28
     *Liberty v. 1, 193-194
     Petitioners 51-52
     Role (Haines) v. 2, 224-242
     *Sup Ct and Consttn 110-113
     *Sup Ct Speaks 81-88
     Taney 653-664
     Without Fear 433-440

247. Board of Commissioners of Knox County Mar 11, 1859   21 Howard 539
        v. Aspinwall
     Reconstruction 931-933

248. Barber v. Barber   Mar 11, 1859   21 Howard 582
     Justice Daniel 216-217

249. Springfield Township of Franklin Jan 3, 1860   22 Howard 56
        County v. Quick
     Digest 2-3
     Education (Spurlock) 28-31

250. Richardson v. Goddard   Jan 16, 1860   23 Howard 28
     Religion (Kurland) 97

251. Alabama v. Georgia   May 1, 1860   23 Howard 505
      Role (Haines) v. 2, 280-281

252. Kentucky v. Dennison   Mar 14, 1861   24 Howard 66
      *Am Consttnl Law (Bartholomew) v. 1, 55
      Role (Haines) v. 2, 135-136
      Sup Ct and Poltcl Questions 132-134
      Taney 686-690
      Without Fear 440-441

253. Palmer v. United States   Jan 7, 1861   24 Howard 125
      Taney 784-785

254. Suydam v. Williamson   Mar 14, 1861   24 Howard 427
      Great Reversals 42-44

255. Gaines v. Hennen   Mar 14, 1861   24 Howard 553
      Taney 767-771

256. Jefferson Branch Bank of State of   Mar 17, 1862   1 Black 436
      Ohio, at Steubenville v. Skelly
      Role (Haines) v. 2, 389

257. Ex parte Gordon   Feb 17, 1862   1 Black 503
      Taney 704-707

258. Mississippi and Missouri Railroad   Jan 20, 1863   2 Black 485
      Co. v. Ward
      *Cases Federal Courts 228-229

259. New York ex rel. Bank of Commerce   Mar 10, 1863   2 Black 620
      v. Commissioner of Taxes for
      City of New York
      Taney 939-940

260. Preciat v. United States   Mar 10, 1863   2 Black 635
      Currie v. United States
      Miller v. United States
      Currie v. United States
      "Prize Cases"
      *Am Consttnl Law (Bartholomew) v. 1, 118-119
      *Am Consttnl Law (Mason) 102-106
      *Am Consttnl Law (Saye) 110-112
      Am Consttnl Law (Shapiro) 172-173
      Basic History 36-37
      CQ Guide 126, 187-189
      *Consttn (Hirschfield) 136-142
      *Consttn (Mendelson) 56-58
      *Consttnl Law (Barrett) 502-504
      *Consttnl Law (Kauper) 285-289
      Dissent 62
      *Federal System 155-157
      From Confederation 134-137
      *Historic Decisions 61-64
      *Justices (Friedman) v. 2, 884-892
      *Liberty v. 1, 229-230
      *Processes 431-434
      Role (Haines) v. 2, 469-480
      Sup Ct and Commander in Chief 68-77

*Sup Ct and Consttn 161-164
*Sup Ct Speaks 90-96
Sup Ct under Marshall 145-146
Taney 884-899
Without Fear 456-458

261. Mercer County v. Hackett   Jan 18, 1864   1 Wallace 83
     Reconstruction 944-945

262. Gelpcke v. Dubuque   Jan 11, 1864   1 Wallace 175
     Reconstruction 924, 935-939
     Sup Ct Review 1972 112-113
     Taney 335-338

263. Ex parte Vallandigham   Feb 15, 1864   1 Wallace 243
     Role (Haines) v. 2, 481-487
     Sup Ct and Commander in Chief 28-30
     Sup Ct Review 1962 168-169
     Taney 925-930

264. Von Hostrup v. Madison (City)   Jan 11, 1864   1 Wallace 291
     Reconstruction 944-946

265. Meyer and Stucken v. City of Muscatine Feb 1, 1864   1 Wallace 384
     Reconstruction 946-947

266. Roosevelt v. Meyer   Dec 21, 1863   1 Wallace 512
     Great Reversals 47-48

267. United States v. Gomez   Apr 18, 1864   1 Wallace 690
     Taney 802-805

268. Hathorn v. Calef   Jan 16, 1865   2 Wallace 10
     Reconstruction 45-46

269. Drury v. Foster   Jan 23, 1865   2 Wallace 24
     Reconstruction 33-34

270. Ex parte Dugan   Feb 27, 1865   2 Wallace 134
     Ex parte Hogan
     Reconstruction 55-58

271. The Circassian   Jan 30, 1865   2 Wallace 135
     Hunter v. United States
     Reconstruction 37-38

272. Marine Bank of Chicago v. Fulton Jan 23, 1865   2 Wallace 252
        County Bank
     Reconstruction 33

273. The Slavers (Kate)   Mar 8, 1865   2 Wallace 350
     The Brig Kate v. United States
     Reconstruction 39

274. Mrs. Alexander's Cotton   Mar 10 1865   2 Wallace 404
     United States v. Alexander
     Reconstruction 38-39

275. Tobey v. Leonard   Feb 13, 1865   2 Wallace 423
     Reconstruction 34-35

276. Pacific Mail Steamship Co. v.   Jan 30, 1865   2 Wallace 450
     Joliffe
     Reconstruction 50-51

277. Gordon v. United States   Mar 10, 1865   2 Wallace 561
     Reconstruction 52-54
     Role (Haines) v. 2, 327-328

278. Fossat v. United States   Apr 4, 1864   2 Wallace 649
     Taney 798-800

279. Blackburn v. Crawford's Lessee   Mar 5, 1866   3 Wallace 175
     Reconstruction 75-76

280. Daniels v. Chicago and Rock Island   Mar 26, 1866   3 Wallace 250
     Railroad Co.
     Reconstruction 138-140

281. Newell v. Norton   Apr 3, 1866   3 Wallace 257
     Reconstruction 135-136

282. The Bermuda   Mar 12, 1866   3 Wallace 514
     Haigh v. United States
     Blakely v. United States
     Fraser, Trenholm and Co. v.
     United States
     Reconstruction 40-41

283. Van Allen v. the Assessors   Mar 26, 1866   3 Wallace 573
     Churchill v. Utica
     Williams v. Nolan
     Van Allen v. Nolan
     Reconstruction 46-49

284. The Reform   Jan 29, 1866   3 Wallace 617
     United States v. Schooner Reform
     Reconstruction 142

285. United States v. Scott   Mar 19, 1866   3 Wallace 642
     Reconstruction 140-141

286. United States v. Murphy   Mar 19, 1866   3 Wallace 649
     Reconstruction 140-141

287. Ex parte Milligan   Dec 17, 1866   4 Wallace 2
     Am Consttn (Kelly) 417-419
     *Am Consttnl Law (Mason) 675-679
     *Am Consttnl Law (Shapiro) 173-177
     Am Politics 178-183
     *Annals v. 10, 31-36
     *Basic Cases 7-13
     Basic History 39
     *By These Words 371-384
     CQ Guide 189-190
     *Cases Consttnl Law (Cushman) 73-78
     *Cases Consttnl Rights 1218-1220
     *Comparative 666-669
     Congress 36-38

*Consttn (Mendelson) 166-170
*Consttnl Aspects v. 4, 493-515
*Consttnl Law (Barrett) 545-548
*Consttnl Law (Felkenes) 110-113
*Consttnl Law (Freund) 1050-1054
*Consttnl Law (Kauper) 292-298
*Courts Judges 349-352
 Dissent 64
*Documents History v. 1, 472-476
*Due Process 187-189
*Federal System 158-161
*Historic Decisions 65-71
*Justices (Friedman) v. 2, 1054-1065
*Leading Consttnl Decisions 140-152
*Liberty v. 1, 235-237
 Milligan Case.
*Milligan Case 225-250
 O'er the Ramparts 192-196
 Power 173-174
 Prejudice 227-231
 Quarrels 90-108
 Reconstruction 143-144, 185-222
 Sup Ct and Commander in Chief 30-39
*Sup Ct and Consttn 164-169
 Sup Ct in Am History 74-90
 Sup Ct in Crisis 102-103
*Sup Ct Speaks 99-104
 This Honorable Court 172-174

288. Cummings v. Missouri   Jan 14, 1867   4 Wallace 277
      "Test Oath Case"
       Defendants 87
       Dissent 67
       Reconstruction 240 244
      *Sup Ct and Consttn 170-174
      *Sup Ct Speaks 107-113

289. Ex parte Garland   Jan 14, 1867   4 Wallace 333
      "Test Oath Case"
      *Am Consttnl Law (Bartholomew) v. 1, 107-109
       CQ Guide 224-226
       Defendants 87
       Dissent 67
      *Documents History v. 1, 477-478
      *Liberty v. 2, 258-260
       Petitioners 89-90
       Reconstruction 58-59, 134, 240-244

290. The Moses Taylor v. Hammons   Feb 4, 1867   4 Wallace 411
      *Cases Admiralty 64-67

291. Mississippi v. Johnson   Apr 15, 1867   4 Wallace 475
       Am Consttn (Kelly) 451
      *Am Consttnl Law (Bartholomew) v. 1, 133-135
       Am Consttnl Law (Shapiro) 177-178
      *Comparative 140-141
      *Documents History v. 1, 478-479
      *Federal System 121-122

*Historic Decisions 72-74
*Liberty v. 2, 260-261
Reconstruction 378-383
*Sup Ct and Consttn 174-176
Sup Ct and Poltcl Questions 134-136
Watergate 122-124

292.	The Springbok The Bark Springbok v. United States Reconstruction 41-42	Jan 3, 1867	5 Wallace 1
293.	The Peterhoff The Steamer Peterhoff v. United States Reconstruction 42	Apr 15, 1867	5 Wallace 28
294.	Campbell v. Kenosha Reconstruction 1025-1027	Apr 29, 1867	5 Wallace 194
295.	The Grey Jacket The Steamer Grey Jacket v. United States Reconstruction 248-250	May 6, 1867	5 Wallace 342
296.	Merchants' Insurance Co. v. Ritchie Reconstruction 252	Feb 18, 1867	5 Wallace 541
297.	Thompson v. Riggs Reconstruction 701	May 16, 1867	5 Wallace 663
298.	Crandall v. Nevada *Consttnl Law (Freund) 339-341 *Consttnl Law (Kauper) 568-571 Perspectives (Black) 81 *Processes 260-262 Reconstruction 1302-1307	Mar 16, 1868	6 Wallace 35
299.	Georgia v. Stanton Mississippi v. Stanton Reconstruction 384-396	Feb 10, 1868	6 Wallace 50
300.	Reichert v. Felps Reconstruction 1429-1430	Mar 16, 1868	6 Wallace 160
301.	Georgia v. Grant Reconstruction 434-437, 470-471	Mar 16, 1868	6 Wallace 241
302.	Gardner v. The Collector Gardner v. Barney Sup Ct and Poltcl Questions 98-99	Mar 30, 1868	6 Wallace 499
303.	Union Insurance Co. v. United States Reconstruction 791	Mar 25, 1868	6 Wallace 759
304.	Armstrong's Foundry v. United States Reconstruction 791-792	Mar 25, 1868	6 Wallace 766
305.	St. Louis Street Foundry v. United States Reconstruction 792	Mar 25, 1868	6 Wallace 770

306. Bank of New York v. Board of   Jan 16, 1869   7 Wallace 26
         Supervisors of County of New
         York
     Monetary Decisions 70
     Reconstruction 710-711

307. "The China"   Jan 25, 1869   7 Wallace 53
     Steamship China v. Walsh
     *Cases Admiralty 69-72

308. Lane County v. Oregon   Feb 8, 1869   7 Wallace 71
     Reconstruction 701, 704

309. Bronson v. Rodes   Feb 15, 1869   7 Wallace 229
     Monetary Decisions 71
     Reconstruction 704-706

310. Butler v. Horwitz   Mar 1, 1869   7 Wallace 258
     Reconstruction 707-708

311. United States ex rel. Benbow v.   Jan 25, 1869   7 Wallace 313
         Mayor of Iowa City
     Reconstruction 951-956

312. Confiscation Cases   Mar 22, 1869   7 Wallace 454
     Reconstruction 793-796

313. United States v. Adams   Apr 12, 1869   7 Wallace 463
     Reconstruction 1441

314. United States v. Kirby   Apr 15, 1860   7 Wallace 482
     *Law Power 77-78

315. Ex parte McCardle   Apr 12, 1869   7 Wallace 506
     Am Consttn (Kelly) 452
     *Am Consttn (Lockhart) 33-34
     *Am Consttnl Law (Bartholomew) 129-130
     *Am Consttnl Law (Saye) 45-47
     Basic History 39-41
     CQ Guide 8, 667-668
     *Cases Consttnl Law (Cushman) 36-39
     *Cases Consttnl Law (Gunther) 48-50
     *Cases Consttnl Law (Rosenblum) 124-125
     *Cases Consttnl Rights 33-34
     *Cases Federal Courts 815-818
     *Cases Individual 50-52
     *Comparative 115-117
     Congress 38-41
     *Consttnl Law (Barrett) 555-557
     Consttnl Law (Barron) 39-41
     *Consttnl Law (Barron) 41-42
     *Consttnl Law (Freund) 141-142
     *Consttnl Law (Kauper) 102-104
     *Consttnl Law (Lockhart) 56-57
     *Consttnl Politics 281-283
     Consttnlity 7
     *Courts Judges 379-382
     Elements Judicial 193-195
     *Federal Courts 311-312

*Federal System 20-21
From Confederation 185-187
*Justices (Friedman) v. 2, 1129-1130
*Leading Consttnl Decisions 25-29
Petitioners 91
Power 35
Reconstruction 419-421, 437-440, 449-459, 467-481, 511-513
*Sup Ct and Consttn 177-178
This Honorable Court 181-182
PERIODICALS:
"Ex parte McCardle: judicial impotency?" Stanley I. Kutler. Am
Historical R 72: 835-851 Apr '67.

316. "The Alicia"   Jan 25, 1869   7 Wallace 571
     Schooner Alicia v. United States
     Reconstruction 1430

317. "The Floyd Acceptances"   Mar 1, 1869   7 Wallace 666
     Pierce v. United States
     Dover Five Cent Savings Bank v.
     United States
     Reconstruction 1437-1439

318. Texas v. White   Apr 12, 1869   7 Wallace 700
     Am Consttn (Kelly) 452-453
     *Am Consttnl Law (Mason) 171-174
     Basic History 38
     *CQ Guide 300
     *Documents History v. 1, 509-513
     *Federal System 280-282
     From Confederation 133-134, 166-168
     *Historic Decisions 75-80
     *Justices (Friedman) v. 2, 1131-1139
     *Liberty v. 1, 240-242
     Reconstruction 619, 628-662
     *Sup Ct and Consttn 179-182
     *Sup Ct Speaks 129-130

319. Thorington v. Smith   Nov 1, 1869   8 Wallace 1
     Reconstruction 852-853

320. Ex parte Yerger   Oct 25, 1869   8 Wallace 85
     Reconstruction 564-590
     Sup Ct Review 1962 163

321. Woodruff v. Parham   Nov 8, 1869   8 Wallace 123
     CQ Guide 330
     *Consttnl Law (Freund) 188-191
     Reconstruction 1404-1405
     Sup Ct and Commerce 43

322. Paul v. Virginia   Nov 1, 1869   8 Wallace 168
     *Consttnl Law (Barrett) 198-199
     Consttnl Law (Barrett) 587
     Great Reversals 143-144
     *Modern Business 69-70
     Reconstruction 1399-1402

323. Veazie Bank v. Fenno   Dec 13, 1869   8 Wallace 533
     *Am Consttnl Law (Saye) 154-156

    *Consttnl Law (Kauper) 194-196
    *Documentary v. 2, 1425-1440
    *Documents History v. 1, 508-509
    Monetary Decisions 49-50
    Perspectives (Black) 26
    Reconstruction 711-712

324. Willard v. Tayloe   Jan 24, 1870   8 Wallace 557
      Reconstruction 702

325. United States ex rel. Butz v. Mayor   Dec 20, 1869   8 Wallace 575
          of Muscatine
      Reconstruction 1000

326. Hepburn v. Griswold   Feb 7, 1870   8 Wallace 603
      "Legal Tender Case"
        Basic History 41-42
        CQ Guide 119-120
        Congress 41-42
        *Documentary v. 2, 1527-1552
        From Confederation 225-227
        Great Reversals 51-57
        *Justices (Friedman) v. 2, 1140-1149
        Monetary Decisions 71-76
        Reconstruction 702, 713-719
        Sup Ct and Commander in Chief 93-94
        *Sup Ct and Consttn 183-187
        This Honorable Court 183-184

327. McGlynn, Broderick's Executor v.   Feb 21, 1870   8 Wallace 639
          Magraw
      Reconstruction 701-702, 716

328. United States v. DeWitt   Feb 21, 1870   9 Wallace 41
      Reconstruction 1427-1429

329. United States v. Anderson   Feb 28, 1870   9 Wallace 56
      Reconstruction 840

330. The Justices of New York Supreme   Mar 14, 1870   9 Wallace 274
          Court v. United States ex rel
          Murray
      Reconstruction 1431-1434

331. Bigelow v. Forrest   Mar 28, 1870   9 Wallace 339
      Reconstruction 797-798

332. United States v. Padelford   Apr 30, 1870   9 Wallace 531
      Reconstruction 841-842

333. "The Blackwall"   Apr 30, 1870   10 Wallace 1
      Ship Blackwall v. Sancelito Water and
          Steam Tug Co.
        *Cases Admiralty 575-579

334. Ducat v. Chicago   Jan 9, 1871   10 Wallace 410
      Reconstruction 1402-1403

335. Gray v. Chicago, Iowa and   Dec 19, 1870   10 Wallace 454

Nebraska Railroad
"The Clinton Bridge"
Reconstruction 1407-1410

336. In re Paschal   Jan 23, 1871   10 Wallace 483
Texas v. White
Texas v. Russell
Reconstruction 662-667

337. Steamer Daniel Ball v. United States   Jan 23, 1871   10 Wallace 557
*Consttn (Mendelson) 91-92
*Consttnl Law (Barrett) 205-207
*Consttnl Law (Freund) 207-209
*Consttnl Law (Kauper) 124-127
Perspectives (Black) 23-24
Reconstruction 1405-1406

338. Marsh v. Fulton County Board of   Feb 13, 1871   10 Wallace 676
Supervisors
Reconstruction 1002-1008

339. New England Marine Insurance Co.   Mar 27, 1871   11 Wallace 1
v. Dunham
*Cases Admiralty 43-49

340. Virginia v. West Virginia   Mar 6, 1871   11 Wallace 39
Am Consttn (Kelly) 400
Reconstruction 619-627

341. Buffington, Collector of Internal   Apr 3, 1871   11 Wallace 113
Revenue v. Day
*Am Consttnl Law (Bartholomew) v. 1, 165-166
*Am Consttnl Law (Mason) 175-177
*Cases Consttnl Law (Cushman) 144-146
*Commerce 142-144
*Consttnl Law (Freund) 621-623
*Consttnl Law (Kauper) 457-461
*Documents History v. 1, 518-520
Reconstruction 1419-1420
Sup Ct in Free Society 85-86

342. Garnett v. United States   Mar 6, 1871   11 Wallace 256
Reconstruction 800

343. McVeigh v. United States   Mar 6, 1871   11 Wallace 259
Reconstruction 798-799, 823-827

344. Miller v. United States   Apr 3, 1871   11 Wallace 268
Page v. United States
Am Consttn (Kelly) 397-398
Reconstruction 800-807

345. Tyler v. Defrees   Apr 10, 1871   11 Wallace 331
Reconstruction 808-812

346. Missouri v. Kentucky   Mar 27, 1871   11 Wallace 395
Reconstruction 628

347. Stewart v. Kahn   Apr 10, 1871   11 Wallace 493
         Sup Ct and Commander in Chief 81-82

348. 207 Half Pound Papers of Smoking   May 1, 1871   11 Wallace 616
         Tobacco v. United States
         "The Cherokee Tobacco"
         *Am Indian v. 4, 2649-2654
         *Documents Indian 136
         *Law Indian 420-422

349. Hanauer v. Doane   Nov 27, 1871   12 Wallace 342
         Reconstruction 855-856

350. Ward v. Maryland   Dec 11, 1871   12 Wallace 418
         Reconstruction 1411-1412

351. Knox v. Lee   May 1, 1871   12 Wallace 457
      Parker v. Davis
      "Legal Tender Cases"
         *Am Consttnl Law (Bartholomew) v. 1, 189-191
         CQ Guide 120-122, 712
         *Documentary v. 2, 1553-1571
         *Documents History v. 1, 514-517
         Great Reversals 58-60
         *Handbook Politics v. 1 (1872): 53-62
         *Historic Decisions 81-84
         *Justices (Friedman) v. 2, 976-983, 1166-1178
         Monetary Decisions 77-80
         Reconstruction 754-755, 759-763
         *Sup Ct and Consttn 188-191
         *Sup Ct Speaks 116-123

352. Trebilcock v. Wilson   Jan 22, 1872   12 Wallace 687
         Great Reversals 60-61
         Reconstruction 764

353. Low v. Austin   Jan 29, 1872   13 Wallace 29
         CQ Guide 330

354. United States v. Klein   Jan 29, 1872   13 Wallace 128
         CQ Guide 226
         Consttnlity 7-8
         Quest 207
         Reconstruction 843-846

355. Klinger v. Missouri   Apr 1, 1872   13 Wallace 257
         Reconstruction 1445-1446

356. Chicago and Northwestern Railway   Feb 19, 1872   13 Wallace 270
         Co. v. Whitton's Administrator
         *Federal Courts 683-684

357. The President, Managers and Co.   Feb 26, 1872   13 Wallace 311
         of the Delaware and Hudson
         Canal Co. v. Clark
         *Copyright 267-271

358. Tarble's Case   Mar 4, 1872   13 Wallace 397

United States v. Tarble
*Federal Courts 423-427
Reconstruction 1421-1424

359. Blyew v. United States   Apr 1, 1872   13 Wallace 581
      "Insular Case"
      Basic History 48-49
      Dred Scott Case 585-587
      *Handbook Politics v. 1 (1872), 74-76
      Petitioners 88-89

360. White v. Hart   Apr 22, 1872   13 Wallace 646
      Reconstruction 858-859

361. Watson v. Jones   Apr 15, 1872   13 Wallace 679
      *Bill (Konvitz) 144-149
      Church and State 107-108
      Church State and Freedom 290-291
      *Civil Rights (Abernathy) 1977 346-349
      Expanding Liberties 4-5
      *First Amendment (Konvitz) 146-153
      *First Amendment (Marnell) 145-146
      Freedom and the Court 322
      Garden 80-87, 89-90
      Reconstruction 907-916
      Religion (Fellman) 61-62
      *Religious Freedom 96-98
      Sup Ct and Religion 34-35
      Sup Ct Review 1969 357-363

362. Delmas v. Merchants' Mutual Insur-   Nov 25, 1872   14 Wallace 661
         ance Co.
      Reconstruction 857

363. Brown v. Hiatts   Feb 10, 1873   15 Wallace 177
      Reconstruction 838-839

364. Philadelphia and Reading Railroad   Mar 3, 1873   15 Wallace 232
         Co. v. Pennsylvania
      "State Freight Tax Case"
      CQ Guide 331
      *Consttnl Law (Freund) 523-525
      Reconstruction 1412-1413
      Sup Ct and Commerce 36-37

365. Philadelphia and Reading Railroad   Mar 3, 1873   15 Wallace 284
         Co. v. Pennsylvania
      "State Tax on Railway Gross Receipts"
      CQ Guide 331
      *Consttnl Law (Freund) 525-528
      Reconstruction 1412-1413

366. Brown v. Kennedy   Mar 10, 1873   15 Wallace 591
      Reconstruction 838, 839

367. Butchers' Benevolent Association of   Apr 14, 1873   16 Wallace 36
         New Orleans v. Crescent City
         Live-Stock Landing and Slaughter-
         House Co.

Esteben v. Louisiana ex rel. Belden
Butchers' Benevolent Association of
     New Orleans v. Crescent City
     Live-Stock Landing and Slaughter-
     House Co.
"Slaughter House Cases"
  Am Consttn (Kelly) 474-477
  *Am Consttn (Lockhart) 356-359
  *Am Consttnl Law (Bartholomew) v. 2, 199-203
  *Am Consttnl Law (Mason) 395-401
  *Am Consttnl Law (Saye) 555-559
  *Am Consttnl Law (Shapiro) 301-306
  *Annals v. 10, 302-308
  Basic History 45
  Biography 305-308
  By What Right 188-204
  CQ Guide 27, 339-340
  *Cases Civil Liberties 20-25
  *Cases Consttnl Law (Cushman) 250-255
  *Cases Consttnl Law (Gunther) 464-473
  *Cases Consttnl Rights 116-119
  *Cases Individual 90-101
  *Civil Rights (Abernathy) 1977 28-32
  Civil Rights (Bardolph) 59-61
  *Civil Rights (Blaustein) 248-254
  Conceived 33
  Consttn (Konvitz) 31-36
  *Consttn (Mendelson) 245-251
  *Consttn (Pollak) 276-283
  *Consttnl Law (Barrett) 596-607
  *Consttnl Law (Barron) 402-412
  *Consttnl Law (Freund) 763-770
  *Consttnl Law (Grossman) 344-348
  *Consttnl Law (Kauper) 571-582
  *Consttnl Law (Lockhart) 428-432
  *Consttnl Law (Schmidhauser) 321-336
  *Consttnl Politics 421-428
  *Discrimination 12-18
  Dissent 79-80
  *Documents History v. 1, 521-525
  Equality (Berger) 63-64
  First Amendment (Marnell) 137-141
  *Free Enterprise 315-317
  Freedom and the Court 48-55
  From Brown 13-14
  From Confederation 227-230
  Government 37-38, 44-49
  *Government and Business 62-63
  *Handbook Politics v. 1 (1874), 40-49
  *Historic Decisions 85-88
  Judiciary (Abraham) 72-74
  *Justices (Friedman) v. 2, 1000-1003, 1025-1033
  *Leading Consttnl Decisions 164-175
  *Liberty v. 2, 266-268
  Morrison R. Waite 116-118
  Petitioners 102-109
  *Political Rights v. 2, 1013-1019
  Processes 712-716
  *Racial Equality 11-13

Quest 82-84
*Statutory History Civil Rights 335-340
Sup Ct (North) 44-45
*Sup Ct and American Economic Life 71-80
*Sup Ct and Consttn 225-241
Sup Ct and Electoral Process 47-48
Sup Ct in Crisis 121-122
Sup Ct in Free Society 218-219
Sup Ct Review 1978 57-61
Sup Ct Speaks 133-138
This Honorable Court 198-201
Warren (Carter) 54-55
PERIODICALS:
"Justice Field and inherent rights," Robert Goedecke.
    R of Poltcs   27: 198-207   Apr '65 (2).

368. Bradwell v. Illinois   Apr 15, 1873   16 Wallace 130
      CQ Guide 631
      Great Reversals 184-187
      *Handbook Politics v. 1 (1874), 49-51
      Quest 73-74
      Reconstruction 1364-1367
      *Sex Discrimination 1975 5-6
      *Sex Roles 42-44
      *Sup Ct Speaks 124-128
      *Text Consttnl Aspects 4-7
      *Text Sex-Based Discrimination 4-7
      *Woman 6-7
      PERIODICALS
      "ERA: losing battles, but winning the war," James J. Kilpatrick.
          Natns Bus   67: 15-16   Oct '79 (4).

369. Huntington and the First National Bank   Mar 3, 1873   16 Wallace 402
      of Washington v. Texas
      Reconstruction 650-653

370. Osborne v. Mobile   Apr 28, 1873   16 Wallace 479
      Reconstruction 1414-1415

371. Chicago, Burlington and Quincy Rail-   Mar 31, 1873   16 Wallace 667
      road v. County of Otoe
      Reconstruction 1017-1018

372. Olcott v. County Board of Supervisors, Mar 31, 1873   16 Wallace 678
      Fond du Lac County
      Reconstruction 1016-1021

373. Tyler v. Magwire   Mar 17, 1873   17 Wallace 253
      Elements Judicial 108-109

374. United States v. Baltimore and Ohio   Apr 7, 1873   17 Wallace 322
      Railroad
      Reconstruction 1435-1436

375. Adams v. Burks   Dec 8, 1873   17 Wallace 453
      *Cases Antitrust Law 582-583
      *Free Enterprise 1218-1221
      *Patent 667-671

376. Horn v. Lockhart   Nov 3, 1873   17 Wallace 570
      Reconstruction 863-865

377. Sioux City and Pacific Railroad   Jan 26, 1874 17 Wallace 657
      v. Stout
      *Cases Pleading 947-952

378. Bartemeyer v. Iowa   Mar 4, 1874   18 Wallace 129
      "Iowa Liquor Cases"
      *Handbook Politics v. 1 (1874), 51-53

379. Day v. Micou   Jan 19, 1874 18 Wallace 156
      Reconstruction 814-816

380. Ex parte Lange   Mar 2, 1874   18 Wallace 163
      Sup Ct Review 1978 107-108

381. Rees v. Watertown   Mar 2, 1874   19 Wallace 107
      Reconstruction 1040-1042

382. The Steamship Pennsylvania v. Troop   Mar 16, 1874 19 Wallace 125
      *Cases Admiralty 668-673

383. Head v. Curators of University of   Mar 23, 1874 19 Wallace 526
      Missouri
      Education (Lapati) 221

384. Pine Grove Township v. Talcott   May 4, 1874   19 Wallace 666
      Reconstruction 1021-1022

385. First National Bank of Washington   Apr 20, 1874 20 Wallace 72
      v. Texas
      Reconstruction 650, 653-658

386. United States v. Clarke   May 4, 1874   20 Wallace 92
      Confiscation Cases
      Reconstruction 816-819

387. Murdock v. Memphis   Jan 11, 1875 20 Wallace 590
      *Federal Courts 460-469
      *Materials Consttnl Law 9-22

388. Citizens' Savings and Loan Associa-   Feb 1, 1875   20 Wallace 655
      tion of Cleveland v. Topeka
      Am Consttn (Kelly) 483
      *Documents History v. 1, 526-528
      Freedom of Speech (Hudon) 39
      *Justices (Friedman) v. 2, 983-985
      Reconstruction 1101-1106

389. Vermilye v. Adams Express   Feb 22, 1875 21 Wallace 138
      Reconstruction 659-660

390. Minor v. Happersett   Mar 29, 1875 21 Wallace 162
      CQ Guide 477-478
      *Documents History v. 1, 534-536
      Equality (Berger) 64-65
      *Handbook Politics v. 1 (1876), 76-80
      *Liberty v. 2, 275-276
      Morrison R. Waite 119

Quest 74
Sex Discrimination 1975 11-14
*Sex Discrimination 1975 14-15
*Sex Roles 461-465
Sup Ct and Electoral Process 29-30
Sup Ct and Poltcl Questions 25-26
*Woman 15-17
PERIODICALS:
"Constitutional voting rights and early U. S. Supreme Court doctrine,"
Richard Claude. J Negro History 51: 114-124 Apr '66 (4).

391. Burke, Executor of Trist v. Child   Mar 22, 1875   21 Wallace 441
     *Materials Legislation 338-340
     *Sup Ct Speaks 145-149

392. Baltimore and Ohio Railroad v.   May 3, 1875   21 Wallace 456
     Maryland
     *Handbook Politics v. 1 (1876), 86

393. Rodd v. Heartt   May 3, 1875   21 Wallace 558
     The Lottawanna
     *Cases Admiralty 18-23

394. Texas v. White   Mar 29, 1875   22 Wallace 157
     In re Chiles
     Reconstruction 667-669

395. Semmes v. United States   Oct 25, 1875   91 U. S. 21
     Reconstruction 821-822

396. United States v. Union Pacific   Nov 29, 1875   91 U. S. 72
     Railroad
     *Handbook Politics v. 1 (1876), 81-86
     Morrison R. Waite 258

397. Welton v. Missouri   Jan 17, 1876   91 U. S. 275
     CQ Guide 332
     *Consttnl Law (Barrett) 202-203
     *Consttnl Law (Freund) 352-354

398. Union Pacific Railroad v. Hall   Feb 28, 1876   91 U. S. 343
     *Am Landmark v. 1, 215-224

399. Osborn v. United States   Feb 7, 1876   91 U. S. 474
     Reconstruction 832-836

400. Walker v. Sauvinet   Apr 24, 1876   92 U. S. 90
     Defendants 166
     Reconstruction 1374-1377

401. Totten v. United States   Apr 10, 1876   92 U. S. 105
     *Freedom vs National Security 156-157

402. Phillips v. Payne   Apr 17, 1876   92 U. S. 130
     Sup Ct and Poltcl Questions 99-100

403. Wallach v. Van Riswick   Jan 10, 1876   92 U. S. 202
     Reconstruction 848-850

404.   United States v. Reese   Mar 27, 1876   92 U.S. 214
          Consttn (Wilcox) 61-62
          Equality (Berger) 66
          *Handbook Politics v. 1 (1876), 66-69
          *Justices (Friedman) v. 2, 1230-1239
          *Liberty v. 2, 281
          Morrison R. Waite 120-134
          Petitioners 112, 150-153
          *Sup Ct and Consttn 197-199
       PERIODICALS:
          "Constitutional voting rights and early U.S. Supreme Court doctrine,"
             Richard Claude. J Negro History 51: 114-124 Apr '66 (4).

405.   Henderson v. Wickham, Mayor of   Mar 20, 1876   92 U.S. 259
          New York
       Commissioners of Immigration v. The
          North German Lloyd
          *Commerce 146-147

406.   Elmwood v. Marcy   May 8, 1876   92 U.S. 289
          Reconstruction 1051-1052

407.   Coloma v. Eaves   Mar 27, 1876   92 U.S. 484
          Reconstruction 1058-1060

408.   Venice v. Murdock   Mar 27, 1876   92 U.S. 494
          Reconstruction 1053-1058

409.   United States v. Cruikshank   Mar 27, 1876   92 U.S. 542
       "Grant Parish Case"
          Am Consttn (Kelly) 463-464
          CQ Guide 342, 478
          Civil Rights (Bardolph) 62
          *Civil Rights (Blaustein) 254-258
          Consttn (Konvitz) 36-37
          Equality (Berger) 65-66
          *Handbook Politics v. 1 (1876), 69-74
          *Justices (Friedman) v. 2, 1271-1277
          Morrison R. Waite 120-134
          Petitioners 109-110, 154
          *Political Rights v. 2, 1028-1031
          Quest 84-85
          Reconstruction 1378-1379
          Sup Ct and Electoral Process 53-56
          Sup Ct and Poltcl Questions 27
       PERIODICALS:
          "Constitutional voting rights and early U.S. Supreme Court doctrine,"
             Richard Claude. J Negro History 51: 114-124 Apr '66 (4).

410.   Harshman v. Bates County   May 8, 1876   92 U.S. 569
          Reconstruction 1050-1051, 1069-1074

411.   Town of Concord v. Portsmouth Savings Apr 10, 1876   92 U.S. 625
          Bank
          Reconstruction 1048-1050

412.   County of Moultrie v. Rockingham   Apr 10, 1876   92 U.S. 6311
          Savings Bank

Reconstruction 1061-1065

413. Windsor v. McVeigh   Dec 11, 1876   93 U.S. 274
      Reconstruction 826-828

414. Gregory v. McVeigh   Dec 11, 1876   93 U.S. 284
      Reconstruction 826-828

415. Munn v. Illinois   Mar 1, 1877   94 U.S. 113
      "Granger Case"
      Am Consttn (Kelly) 477-480
      *Am Consttnl Law (Bartholomew) v. 2, 207-209
      *Am Consttnl Law (Mason) 401-407
      *Am Consttnl Law (Shapiro) 307-312
      *Annals v. 10, 377-383
      CQ Guide 28
      *Cases Civil Liberties 27-31
      *Cases Consttnl Law (Cushman) 257-261
      Conceived 33-34
      Conservative 8-9
      *Consttn (Mendelson) 252-256
      *Consttn (Pollak) 285-286
      *Consttnl Law (Freund) 1078-1082
      *Consttnl Law (Grossman) 348-351
      Court and Consttn v. 1, 66-67
      Development 169-171
      *Documents History v. 1, 541-544
      First Amendment (Marnell) 141-142
      From Confederation 231-233
      *Govt and Business 306-309
      *Handbook Politics v. 2 (1878), 97-102
      Historic Decisions 89-91
      *Justices (Friedman) v. 2, 1090-1099, 1258-1265
      *Liberty v. 2, 288-290
      Morrison R. Waite 184-190
      Quarrels 109-127
      *Search for Meaning 187
      *Shaping 747-753
      *Sources American Republic v. 2, 67-70
      Sup Ct (Mendelson) 64-77
      Sup Ct (North) 46-47
      Sup Ct and Am Capitalism 52-53
      *Sup Ct and American Economic Life 80-87
      *Sup Ct and Consttn 242-246
      Sup Ct in Crisis 123-124
      Sup Ct in Free Society 219-220
      Sup Ct Review 1978 313-343
      This Honorable Court 202-204
      PERIODICALS:
      "Justice Field and inherent rights," Robert Goedecke. R Poltcs
          27: 198-207 Apr '65 (2).
      "Munn v. Illinois; a foot in the door," C. Peter Magrath. Am
          Heritage 15: 44-48, 88-92 Feb '64.

416. Cromwell v. County of Sac   Apr 16, 1877   94 U.S. 351
      *Cases Civil Procedure 962-965
      *Civil Procedure (Cound) 1065-1068
      *Elements Civil 1114-1116

417. McCready v. Virginia   Apr 30, 1877   94 U.S. 391
          Sup Ct Review 1979 86-89

418. United States v. Martin   Mar 13, 1877   94 U.S. 400
          *Handbook Politics v. 2 (1878), 108-109

419. The Steam-Tug Margaret v. Bliss   Mar 19, 1877   94 U.S. 494
      The Margaret
          *Cases Admiralty 700-702

420. Russell v. Place   Apr 16, 1877   94 U.S. 606
          *Civil Procedure (Cound) 1068-1070

421. Davis v. Indiana ex rel. Board of Com- May 7, 1877   94 U.S. 792
          missioners of Bartholomew County
          Digest 3

422. Cass County v. Johnston   Nov 12, 1877   95 U.S. 360
          Reconstruction 1077-1079

423. Hannibal and St. Joseph Railroad v.   Jan 7, 1878   95 U.S. 465
          Husen
      "Missouri Cattle Case"
          *Handbook Politics v. 2 (1878), 95-97

424. Hall v. DeCuir   Jan 14, 1878   95 U.S. 485
      "Louisiana Common Carrier Case"
          Civil Rights (Bardolph) 62-63
          *Civil Rights (Blaustein) 258-261
          *Consttn (Pollak) 261-263
          *Consttnl Law (Freund) 427-439
          Equality (Berger) 71-72
          *Handbook Politics v. 2 (1878), 106-100
          Morrison R. Waite 140-141
          Petitioners 166-167
          Sup Ct and Commerce 37
          *Sup Ct and Consttn 213-215

425. Pennoyer v. Neff   Jan 21, 1878   95 U.S. 714
          *Cases Civil Procedure 338-343
          *Cases Pleading 171-179
          *Civil Procedure (Carrington) 864-869
          *Civil Procedure (Cound) 59-65
          *Elements Civil 251-253
          Sup Ct Review 1965 241-288

426. Pensacola Telegraph Co. v. Western   Mar 25, 1878   96 U.S. 1
          Union Telegraph
      "Florida Telegraph Case"
          *Consttn (Mendelson) 92-93
          Development 144-145
          *Handbook Politics v. 2 (1878), 91-94

427. Meister v. Moore   Apr 29, 1878   96 U.S. 76
      Meister v. Bissell
          *Cases Domestic 129-130

428. Davidson v. New Orleans   Jan 7, 1878   96 U.S. 97
          Am Consttn (Kelly) 484

438. Smith v. Fort Scott, Humbolt   Apr 21, 1879   99 U.S. 398
        and Western Railroad Co.
     *Cases Civil Procedure 1008-1010

439. Central Pacific Railroad Co. v.   May 5, 1879   99 U.S. 727
        Gallatin
     "Sinking Fund Cases"
     *Justices (Friedman) v. 2, 1099-1109
     Morrison R. Waite 229-235
     *Sup Ct (Mendelson) 88-101

440. United States v. Steffens   Nov 17, 1879   100 U.S. 82
     United States v. Witteman
     United States v. Johnson
     "Trademark Cases"
     *Copyright 254-258

441. Tennessee v. Davis   Mar 1, 1880   100 U.S. 257
     *Federal Courts 420-422
     *Handbook Politics v. 2 (1880), 37-38

442. Strauder v. West Virginia   Mar 1, 1880   100 U.S. 303
     *Bill (Cohen) 598-601
     *Civil Rights (Abernathy) 1977 505-506
     Civil Rights (Bardolph) 63-64
     *Civil Rights (Blaustein) 261-268
     *Consttnl Law (Barrett) 764-765
     *Consttnl Law (Kauper) 701-705
     Desegregation (Wasby) 26
     Disaster 21-22
     Equality (Warsoff) 202-203
     *Freedom and Protection 36-38
     *Handbook Politics v. 2 (1880), 12 15
     *Justices (Friedman) v. 2, 1162-1166
     *Law Power 587-591
     Petitioners 122-123
     *Processes 436-439
     Quest 92-93

443. Ex parte Virginia   Mar 1, 1880   100 U.S. 313
     Virginia v. Rives
     Civil Rights (Bardolph) 65
     Equality (Warsoff) 203-204
     *Handbook Politics v. 2 (1880), 15-19
     Morrison R. Waite 147
     Petitioners 123-125
     Quest 93
     *Sup Ct and Consttn 209-212

444. Ex parte Virginia and Coles   May 1, 1880   100 U.S. 339
     Civil Rights (Bardolph) 64-65
     *Consttnl Law (Freund) 774-777
     *Consttnl Law (Kauper) 779-782
     Desegregation (Wasby) 26
     Equality (Warsoff) 204-205
     *Handbook Politics v. 2 (1880), 19-22
     Petitioners 126-128
     Quest 93-94
     *Sup Ct (Mendelson) 77-88

445. Ex parte Siebold   Mar 8, 1880   100 U.S. 371
      "Habeas Corpus Cases"
         Civil Rights (Bardolph) 66
         *Handbook Politics v. 2 (1880), 22-32
         *Statutory History Civil Rights v. 1, 578-587
         Sup Ct Review 1962 164

446. Ex parte Clarke   Mar 8, 1880   100 U.S. 399
      "Habeas Corpus Cases"
         *Handbook Politics v. 2 (1880), 32-37

447. Hauenstein v. Lynham   Jan 19, 1880   100 U.S. 483
         *Consttnl Law (Barrett) 266-267
         *Consttnl Law (Kauper) 270-272

448. Baker v. Selden   Jan 19, 1880   101 U.S. 99
         *Cases Copyright (Kaplan) 207-213
         *Cases Copyright (Nimmer) 96-101
         *Copyright 674-678
         *Legal Regulation 627-631

449. Stone v. Mississippi   May 10, 1880   101 U.S. 814
         *Am Consttnl Law (Bartholomew) v. 2, 196-197
         *Am Consttnl Law (Saye) 242-244
         CQ Guide 314
         Sup Ct in Free Society 205
         Sup Ct Review 1979 100

450. Shepherd v. The Schooner Clara   Nov 29, 1880   102 U.S. 200
      The Clara
         *Cases Admiralty 660-661

451. United States ex rel. Citizens' National Dec 20, 1880 102 U.S. 422
         Bank of Louisiana v. Knox
         *Handbook Politics v. 2 (1882), 85

452. Springer v. United States   Jan 24, 1881   102 U.S. 586
         Great Reversals 75
         *Handbook Politics v. 2 (1882), 85
         *Justices (Friedman) v. 2, 1003-1008

453. Tilghman v. Proctor   Jan 24, 1881   102 U.S. 707
         *Legal Regulation 805-809

454. Kilbourn v. Thompson   Jan 24, 1881   103 U.S. 168
         CQ Guide 158, 167-168
         *Comparative 118-121
         Congress versus 41-42
         Great Reversals 64-67
         *Handbook Politics v. 2 (1882), 85-86
         Law and Politics 51-52
         Watergate 23-25

455. Miles v. United States   Apr 4, 1881   103 U.S. 304
         *Handbook Politics v. 2 (1882), 86-90

456. Neal v. Delaware   May 2, 1881   103 U.S. 370
         *Handbook Politics v. 2 (1882), 90-91

Petitioners 128-129
*Sex Discrimination 1975 61-64

457. Egbert v. Lippman   Dec 12, 1881   104 U.S. 333
      *Legal Regulation 924-925

458. Ager v. Murray   Mar 6, 1882   105 U.S. 126
      *Cases Civil Procedure 1006-1008

459. Ex parte Mason   May 8, 1882   105 U.S. 696
      *Handbook Politics v. 2 (1882), 91-92

460. The North Star and the Ella Warley   Nov 6, 1882   106 U.S. 17
      Reynolds v. Vanderbilt
      Vanderbilt v. Reynolds
      *Cases Admiralty 106-108

461. United States v. Lee   Dec 4, 1882   106 U.S. 196
      Kaufman v. Lee
      "Arlington Case"
         CQ Guide 261
         *Handbook Politics v. 3 (1884), 78-79
         *Sup Ct Speaks 140-143

462. E. E. Bolles Wooden Ware Co. v.   Dec 18, 1882   106 U.S. 432
            United States
         *Cases Property (Casner) 204-207

463. Town of Elgin v. Marshall   Jan 8, 1883   106 U.S. 578
         *Cases Federal Courts 243-244

464. Pace v. Alabama   Jan 29, 1883   106 U.S. 583
         Civil Rights (Bardolph) 66-67

465. Albright v. Teas   Jan 22, 1883   106 U.S. 613
         *Cases Federal Courts 109-112

466. United States v. Harris   Jan 22, 1883   106 U.S. 629
         Civil Rights (Bardolph) 67
         Development 193
         *Justices (Friedman) v. 2, 1337-1342
         Morrison R. Waite 142
         Petitioners 113-114, 154-155
         Quest 86-87
         *Racial Equality 14

467. Burgess v. Seligman   Jan 29, 1883   107 U.S. 20
         Sup Ct Review 1972 119-120

468. Louisiana v. Jumel   Mar 5, 1883   107 U.S. 711
      Elliott v. Wiltz
      "Louisiana Bond Case"
         *Handbook Politics v. 3 (1884), 76-77

469. Antoni v. Greenhow   Mar 5, 1883   107 U.S. 769
         *Handbook Politics v. 3 (1884), 77

470. New Hampshire v. Louisiana   Mar 5, 1883   108 U.S. 76

New York v. Louisiana
*Handbook Politics v. 3, (1884), 77-78

471. United States v. Stanley   Oct 15, 1883   109 U.S. 3
      United States v. Ryan
      United States v. Nichols
      United States v. Singleton
      Robinson v. Memphis and Charleston Railroad Co.
      "Civil Rights Cases"
      *Am Consttnl Law (Bartholomew) v. 2, 310-312
      *Am Consttnl Law (Mason) 467-473
      *Am Consttnl Law (Saye) 259-263
      *Am Consttnl Law (Shapiro) 151-155
      *Am Landmark v. 1, 403-462
      *Annals v. 10, 577-583
      By What Right 203-206
      CQ Guide 340-341, 608
      *Cases Civil Liberties 413-416
      *Cases Consttnl Law (Cushman) 643-646
      *Cases Consttnl Law (Gunther) 978-983
      *Cases Consttnl Law (Rosenblum) 482-491
      *Cases Individual 504-511
      Century 102-123
      *Civil Liberties (Abernathy) 51-54
      *Civil Liberties (Sweet) 13-15
      *Civil Rights (Bardolph) 68-72
      *Civil Rights (Blaustein) 268-281
      Conceived 189-191
      Consttn (Konvitz) 8-28
      *Consttn (Mendelson) 536-541
      *Consttnl Cases 407-422
      *Consttnl Law (Barrett) 1042-1044
      *Consttnl Law (Barron) 989-995
      *Consttnl Law (Freund) 777-788
      *Consttnl Law (Grossman) 517-524
      *Consttnl Law (Kauper) 783-792
      *Desegregation (Ziegler) 43-49
      Development 193-196
      Discrimination 18-27
      Dissent 92-93
      *Documents History v. 1, 536-538
      Equality (Berger) 69-71
      Freedom and the Court 357-358
      From Brown 15-17
      Historic Decisions 92-95
      *Handbook Politics v. 3, (1884), 80-86
      *Liberty v. 2, 269-272
      Morrison R. Waite 142-146
      Petitioners 137-147
      *Political Rights v. 2, 1019-1028
      *Processes 609-616
      *Racial Equality 14-17
      Quarrels 128-144
      Quest 87-91
      *Statutory History Civil Rights v. 1, 780-788
      *Sup Ct and Consttn 200-208
      *Sup Ct Speaks 156-165
      This Honorable Court 193-194
      Warren (Carter) 55-56

PERIODICALS:
"Ride-in!" Alan F. Westin. <u>Am Heritage</u> 13: 57-64 Aug '62.

472. Feibelman v. Packard   Dec. 3, 1883   109 U.S. 421
      *Cases Federal Courts 112-114

473. Ex parte Kan-gi-Shun-ca (Otherwise   Dec 17, 1883   109 U.S. 556
           known as Crow Dog)
      *Am Indian v. 4, 2655-2666
      *Documents Indian 162-163
      *Law Indian 4-8

474. Julliard v. Greenman   Mar 3, 1884   110 U.S. 421
      "Legal Tender Cases"
      *Consttn (Mendelson) 191-193
      *Documentary v. 2, 1572-1600
      *Documents v. 1, 563-566
      *Government and Business 360-363
      *Handbook Politics v. 3 (1884), 86-92
      *Justices (Friedman) v. 2, 1390-1397
       Monetary Decisions 81-82
       Reconstruction 772-774

475. Hurtado v. California   Mar 3, 1884   110 U.S. 516
      *Am Consttnl Law (Bartholomew) v. 2, 234-236
      *Am Consttnl Law (Mason) 727-733
       CQ Guide 525
      *Cases Civil Liberties 43-46
      *Cases Consttnl Law (Cushman) 273-276
      *Consttn (Mendelson) 278-281
      *Consttnl Law (Kauper) 603-609
      *Criminal Justice (Way) 201-205
      *Due Process 3-5
       Freedom and the Court 56-57
      *Government and Business 32-33
      *Justices (Friedman) v. 2, 1366-1375
      *Leading Consttnl Decisions 189-195
      *Liberty v. 2, 277-278
       Power 363
      *Sup Ct and Consttn 193-196
       Sup Ct in Free Society 226, 288
       This Honorable Court 212-213

476. Ex parte Yarbrough   Mar 3, 1884   110 U.S. 651
      "The Ku-Klux Cases"
       CQ Guide 478-479
      *Cases Civil Liberties 394-397
       Cases Consttnl Law (Cushman) 624-627
      *Civil Rights (Bardolph) 145-146
      *Consttnl Law (Freund) 943-945
      *Discrimination 93-97
      *Documents History v. 1, 538-541
      *Handbook Politics v. 3 (1884), 92-96
      *Liberty v. 2, 281-282
       Petitioners 155-156
      *Political Rights v. 2, 1134-1138
      *Statutory History Civil Rights v. 1, 538-543
       Sup Ct and Electoral Process 30-31

PERIODICALS:
"Constitutional voting rights and early U. S. Supreme Court doctrine,"
Richard Claude. J Negro History 51: 114-124 Apr '68.

477. Burrow-Giles Lithographic Co. v.   Mar 17, 1884 111 U. S. 53
      Sarony
      *Cases Copyright (Kaplan) 161-164
      *Cases Copyright (Nimmer) 8-13

478. Mansfield, Coldwater and Lake Michigan Apr 21, 1884 111 U. S. 379
      Railway v. Swan
      *Federal Courts 833-835

479. Butchers' Union Slaughterhouse and   May 5, 1884   111 U. S. 746
      Livestock Landing Co. v. Cres-
      cent City Live-stock Landing and
      Slaughter-house Co.
      Reconstruction 1380-1386

480. Elk v. Wilkins   Nov 3, 1884   112 U. S. 94
      *Am Indian v. 4, 2667-2685
      Civil Rights (Konvitz) 134-135
      *Documents Indian 166-167
      *Handbook Politics v. 3 (1886), 59

481. Chew Heong v. United States   Dec 8, 1884   112 U. S. 536
      *Handbook Politics v. 3 (1886), 59

482. Barbier v. Connelly   1884   113 U. S. 27
      *Consttnl Law (Barrett) 765-766
      Equality (Warsoff) 175-177
      Quest 61-62

483. Morgan v. United States   Mar 2, 1885   113 U. S. 476
      United States v. Manhattan Savings
      Institution
      Von Hoffman v. United States
      Reconstruction 660-661

484. Erhardt v. Boaro   Mar 2, 1885   113 U. S. 537
      *Cases Civil Procedure 172-174

485. Soon Hing v. Crowley   Mar 16, 1885 113 U. S. 703
      Religion (Kurland) 98-99

486. Poindexter v. Greenhow   Apr 20, 1885 114 U. S. 270
      "Virginia Coupon Case"
      *Handbook Politics v. 3 (1886), 58

487. Ex parte Wilson   Mar 30, 1885 114 U. S. 417
      *Am Consttnl Law (Bartholomew) v. 2, 165
      *Criminal Law (Wells) 129-131

488. Brown v. Houston, State Tax   May 4, 1885   114 U. S. 622
      Collector
      *Am Consttnl Law (Mason) 225-226
      *Consttnl Law (Freund) 191-192
      Sup Ct and Commerce 43-44

489. New Orleans Gas-Light Co. v.   Dec 7, 1885   115 U.S. 650
          Louisiana Light and Heat Produc-
          ing and Manufacturing Co.
          *Commerce 148-149

490. Cannon v. United States   Dec 14, 1885   116 U.S. 55
          *Handbook Politics v. 3 (1886), 60-68

491. Presser v. Illinois   Jan 4, 1886   116 U.S. 252
          *Handbook Politics v. 3 (1886), 59-60
          *Justices (Friedman) v. 2, 1342-1347

492. Stone v. Farmers' Loan and Trust Co. Jan 4, 1886   116 U.S. 307
          "Railroad Commission Cases"
          Am Consttn (Kelly) 486
          Conservative 10-11
          *Handbook Politics v. 3 (1886), 60
          *Justices (Friedman) v. 2, 1265-1271
          Morrison R. Waite 198-200

493. Coe v. Errol   Jan 25, 1886   116 U.S. 517
          *Am Consttnl Law (Bartholomew) v. 1, 200-202
          *Consttnl Law (Barrett) 200-201
          *Govt and Business 102

494. Boyd v. United States   Feb 1, 1886   116 U.S. 616
          CQ Guide 541
          *Cases Civil Liberties 81-84
          *Cases Consttnl Law (Cushman) 311-314
          *Consttnl Criml Procedure (Scarboro) 36-43
          Defendants 261-262
          Exclusionary 14-17
          Freedom Spent 210-213
          Politics 229-230
          Privacy (Westin) 339-340
          *Rights (Shattuck) 7
          Search and Seizure 49-61
          Sup Ct Review 1979 182-184

495. Patch v. White   Mar 1, 1886   117 U.S. 210
          *Cases Law of Wills 127-134

496. Yick Wo v. Hopkins   May 10, 1886   118 U.S. 356
      Wo Le v. Hopkins
          *Am Consttnl Law (Mason) 477-478
          *Basic Business 49-51
          CQ Guide 625
          *Cases Consttnl Rights 897
          *Consttnl Law (Barrett) 766-768
          *Consttnl Law (Barron) 587-588
          *Consttnl Law (Freund) 869-871
          *Consttnl Law (Lockhart) 1279-1280
          Equality (Warsoff) 177-179
          *Justices (Friedman) v. 2, 1362-1366
          Least Dangerous 212-214
          *Public Planning 821-824
          Quest 95-96
          Reapportionment (McKay) 175-176

Sup Ct (Forte) 96-97
Sup Ct Review 1977 295

497. United States v. Kagama alias Pactah   May 10, 1886   118 U. S. 375
      Billy
      *Am Indian v. 4, 2686-2693
      *Documents Indian 168-169
      *Law Indian 12-15

498. Santa Clara County v. Southern Pacific   May 10, 1886   118 U. S. 394
      Railroad Co.
      Basic History 44
      Morrison R. Waite 222-224

499. Place v. Norwich and New York   May 10, 1886   118 U. S. 468
      Transportation Co.
      *Cases Admiralty 101-106

500. Wabash, St. Louis and Pacific   Oct 25, 1886   118 U. S. 557
      Railroad v. Illinois
      Am Consttn (Kelly) 517
      *Consttnl Law (Freund) 210-213
      *Documents History v. 1, 572-574
      *Justices (Friedman) v. 2, 1033-1041
      *Liberty v. 2, 290-291
      *Sup Ct and Consttn 247-250
      Sup Ct Review 1975 156-157

501. United States v. Jones   Dec 13, 1886   119 U. S. 477
      *Federal Courts 97-98

502. Cope v. Vallette Dry Dock   Jan 10, 1887   119 U. S. 625
      *Cases Admiralty 223-225

503. Robbins v. Shelby County Taxing   Mar 7, 1887   120 U. S. 489
      District
      *Am Consttnl Law (Bartholomew) v. 1, 227-229
      CQ Guide 333
      *Consttnl Law (Freund) 354-357
      *Justices (Friedman) v. 2, 1213-1217
      Sup Ct and Commerce 40-41

504. Ex parte Spies   Oct 24, 1887   123 U. S. 131
      "The Anarchists' Case"
      This Honorable Court 214

505. Ex parte Ayers   Dec 5, 1887   123 U. S. 443
      Ex parte Scott
      Ex parte McCabe
      "Virginia Coupon Cases"
      *Handbook Politics v. 4 (1890), 35

506. Des Moines Navigation and Railroad Co.   Dec 5, 1887   123 U. S. 552
      v. Iowa Homestead
      *Civil Procedure (Cound) 56-58

507. Mugler v. Kansas   Dec 5, 1887   123 U. S. 623
      Kansas ex rel. Tufts v. Ziebold
      *Am Consttnl Law (Mason) 407-410

       Conservative 29-31
       Consttnl Law (Barrett) 649
       *Handbook Politics v. 4 (1890), 36-37

508. Smith v. Alabama   Jan 30, 1888   124 U.S. 465
       Sup Ct Review 1975 157-158

509. Maynard v. Hill   Mar 19, 1888   125 U.S. 190
       *Family 773-774

510. United States v. San Jacinto Tin Co.   Mar 19, 1888   125 U.S. 273
       *Federal Courts 1295-1301

511. Bowman v. Chicago and Northwestern Mar 19, 1888   125 U.S. 465
       Railway
       *Handbook Politics v. 4 (1890), 37

512. Powell v. Pennsylvania   Apr 9, 1888   127 U.S. 678
       Conservative 31-32

513. Kidd v. Pearson   Oct 22, 1888   128 U.S. 1
       *Consttnl Law (Barrett) 199
       *Handbook Politics v. 4 (1890), 37-42

514. Ex parte Terry   Nov 12, 1888   128 U.S. 289
       Justice Rutledge 201

515. Morris v. Gilmer   Jan 28, 1889   129 U.S. 315
       *Cases Federal Courts 178-180

516. Amy v. Watertown (No. 1)   Apr 8, 1889   130 U.S. 301
       Reconstruction 1045

517. Amy v. Watertown (No. 2)   Apr 8, 1889   130 U.S. 320
       Reconstruction 1045-1046

518. Chae Chan Ping v. United States   May 13, 1889   130 U.S. 581
       "Chinese Exclusion Case"
       Civil Rights (Konvitz) 1-2

519. Pennsylvania Railroad v. Miller   Nov 11, 1889   132 U.S. 75
       *Handbook Politics v. 4 (1890), 42

520. Illinois Central Railroad Co. v.   Jan 20, 1890   133 U.S. 92
       Bosworth
       Reconstruction 850-852

521. DeGeofroy v. Riggs   Feb 3, 1890   133 U.S. 258
       Foreign Affairs 141

522. Davis v. Beason   Feb 3, 1890   133 U.S. 333
       Church and State 109 111
       Church State and Freedom 646-648
       *Family 381-382
       Freedom and the Court 252-253, 276
       *Handbook Politics v. 4 (1890), 42-45
       *Law Power 310-313
       Private Conscience 153-156
       Religion (Kauper) 28

Religion (Kurland) 22-25
*Religious Freedom (Pfeffer) 32-33
Religious Liberty 34-35
Sup Ct and Religion 41-42

523. Louisville, New Orleans and Texas   Mar 3, 1890   133 U. S. 587
     Railway v. Mississippi
     Civil Rights (Bardolph) 148-149
     Equality (Berger) 72-73
     Petitioners 167-168

524. Arndt v. Griggs   Mar 17, 1890   134 U. S. 316
     *Cases Pleading 180-184

525. In re Green   Mar 24, 1890   134 U. S. 377
     Fitzgerald v. Green
     Sup Ct and Electoral Process 232-233

526. Chicago, Milwaukee and St. Paul   Mar 24, 1890   134 U. S. 418
     Railway Co. v. Minnesota
     "Minnesota Rate Case"
     Am Consttn (Kelly) 486-488
     *Am Consttnl Law (Mason) 410-412
     Conservative 39-44
     Consttnl Law (Barrett) 649-650
     *Documents History v. 1, 582-583
     *Justices (Friedman) v. 2, 1415-1418
     Sup Ct (North) 47-48
     Sup Ct in Crisis 138-139

527. In re Neagle   Apr 14, 1890   135 U. S. 1
     Cunningham v. Neagle
     *Am Consttnl Law (Saye) 92-94
     *Cases Consttnl Law (Cushman) 83-86
     *Consttnl Aspects v. 4, 517-544
     *Federal System 89-91
     Growth v. 2, 1143-1148
     *Justices (Friedman) v. 2, 1456-1467
     Power 199

528. Leisy v. Hardin   Apr 28, 1890   135 U. S. 100
     *Am Consttn (Lockhart) 243-244
     *Am Consttnl Law (Bartholomew) v. 1, 219-221
     *Am Consttnl Law (Mason) 226-230
     *Am Consttnl Law (Saye) 176-177
     *Consttnl Law (Freund) 197-200
     *Consttnl Law (Kauper) 327-333
     *Consttnl Law (Lockhart) 283-285
     Sup Ct and Commerce 44-45

529. Late Corporation of the Church of Jesus May 19, 1890   136 U. S. 1
     Christ of Latter-Day Saints (Mor-
     mon Church) v. United States
     Church and State 111
     Dred Scott Case 583
     Freedom and the Court 276
     *Justices (Friedman) v. 2, 1201-1213
     Sup Ct and Religion 42-43

530. McCall v. California   May 19, 1890 136 U.S. 104
        *Justices (Friedman) v. 2, 1452-1455

531. Minnesota v. Barber   May 19, 1890 136 U.S. 313
        *Consttnl Law (Freund) 362-365
        Sup Ct and Commerce 41

532. York v. Texas   Nov 3, 1890   137 U.S. 15
        *Cases Civil Procedure 369-372
        *Elements Civil 259-261

533. Duncan v. McCall   Mar 30, 1891 139 U.S. 449
        Sup Ct and Poltcl Questions 101-102

534. Ross v. McIntyre   May 25, 1891 140 U.S. 453
     In re Ross
        *Consttnl Law (Freund) 709-711

535. Wilkerson v. Rahrer   May 25, 1891 140 U.S. 545
     In re Rahrer
        Commerce 35-36
        *Consttnl Law (Freund) 200-202
        *Consttnl Law (Kauper) 433-436
        Sup Ct and Commerce 45-46

536. Pullman's Palace Car Co. v.   May 11, 1891 141 U.S. 18
            Pennsylvania
        *Consttnl Law (Freund) 499-503

537. Union Pacific Railroad v. Botsford   May 25, 1891 141 U.S. 250
        *Right to Privacy 107-111
        *Teacher 34-35

538. Maine v. Grand Trunk Railway of   Dec 14, 1891 142 U.S. 217
            Canada
        *Consttnl Law (Freund) 489-492

539. District Township of Doon, Lyon   Jan 4, 1892   142 U.S. 366
            County, Iowa v. Cummins
        Digest 3-4

540. Counselman v. Hitchcock   Jan 11, 1892 142 U.S. 547
        Defendants 306-307
        Freedom Spent 365-366

541. Boyd v. Nebraska ex rel. Thayer   Feb 1, 1892   143 U.S. 135
        Sup Ct and Poltcl Questions 111-112

542. Horn Silver Mining Co. v. New York   Feb 29, 1892 143 U.S. 305
        *Consttnl Law (Freund) 492-493

543. Church of Holy Trinity v. United   Feb 29, 1892 143 U.S. 457
            States
        Church and State 111-112
        Expanding Liberties 9
        Freedom and the Court 280
        Religion (Kurland) 26-27
        Religious Freedom (Pfeffer) 26-27

544.   Budd v. New York   Feb 29, 1892   143 U.S. 517
       New York ex rel. Annan v. Walsh
       New York ex rel. Pinto v. Walsh
          Conservative 72-73
          *Justices (Friedman) v. 2, 1419-1428
          Sup Ct in Crisis 139-140

545.   United States v. Texas   Feb 29, 1892   143 U.S. 621
          *Cases Federal Courts 871-876
          *Federal Courts 244-248

546.   Field v. Clark   Feb 29, 1892   143 U.S. 649
       Boyd v. United States
       Sternbach v. United States
          Am Consttn (Kelly) 609-610
          Consttn (Barber) 59-63
          *Handbook Politics v. 4 (1892), 81-93
          Sup Ct and Poltcl Questions 100-101

547.   United States v. Ballin   Feb 29, 1892   144 U.S. 1
          *Handbook Politics v. 4 (1892), 93-96

548.   Logan v. United States   Apr 4, 1892   144 U.S. 263
          *Consttnl Law (Freund) 788-790

549.   Mutual Life Insurance Co. of New York   May 16, 1892   145 U.S. 285
             v. Hillmon
          *Cases Evidence 715-719
          *Principles Proof 179-183

550.   McPherson v. Blacker   Oct 17, 1892   146 U.S. 1
          Sup Ct and Electoral Process 233-234
          Sup Ct and Poltcl Questions 112-113

551.   Illinois Central Railroad Co. v. Illinois   Dec 5, 1892   146 U.S. 387
       Chicago v. Illinois Central Railroad Co.
          *Cases on Environmental Law (Hanks) 604-606

552.   Alexandre v. Machan   Jan 3, 1893   147 U.S. 72
       "The City of New York"
          *Cases Admiralty 666-668

553.   Noble v. Union River Logging Co.   Jan 9, 1893   147 U.S. 165
          *Govt and Business 635-636

554.   Virginia v. Tennessee   Apr 3, 1893   148 U.S. 503
          *Am Consttnl Law (Bartholomew) v. 1, 60-62
          Perspectives (Black) 52

555.   Atchison Board of Education v. DeKay   Apr 10, 1893   148 U.S. 591
          Digest 4-5

556.   Nix v. Hedden   May 10, 1893   149 U.S. 304
          *Legislative (Hetzel) 323-324

557.   California v. San Pueblo and Tulare   May 10, 1893   149 U.S. 308
             Railroad
          *Materials Consttnl Law 186-187

558.   Fong Yue Ting v. United States   May 15, 1893 149 U.S. 698
        Wong Quan v. United States
        Lee Joe v. United States
        *Cases Consttnl Law (Cushman) 120-122
        Civil Rights (Konvitz) 97-98

559.   Hicks v. United States   Nov 27, 1893 150 U.S. 442
        *Criminal Law (Kadish) 371-372

560.   In re Bonner   Jan 8, 1894   151 U.S. 242
        *Cases Criml Law (Hall) 24-26

561.   Tennessee v. Union and Planters' Bank   Mar 19, 1894 152 U.S. 454
        Tennessee v. Bank of Commerce
        *Cases Federal Courts 276-282

562.   Brass v. North Dakota ex rel. Stoeser   May 14, 1894 153 U.S. 391
        Conservative 175-176
        *Justices (Friedman) v. 2, 1593-1596
        Sup Ct in Crisis 140

563.   Mobile and Ohio Railroad v. Tennessee   May 14, 1894 153 U.S. 486
        *Justices (Friedman) v. 2, 1621-1630

564.   Reagen v. Farmer's Loan and Trust   May 26, 1894 154 U.S. 362
          Co.
        Conservative 176-178
        *Documents History v. 1, 585-586
        Sup Ct in Crisis 140-141

565.   Plumley v. Massachusetts   Dec 10, 1894 155 U.S. 461
        *Am Consttnl Law (Mason) 230-233

566.   Indiana ex rel. Stanton v. Glover   Jan 7, 1895   155 U.S. 513
        Digest 5-6

567.   United States v. E. C. Knight Co.   Jan 21, 1895 156 U.S. 1
        "Sugar Trust Case"
        Am Consttn (Kelly) 525-526
        *Am Consttnl Law (Bartholomew) v. 1, 246-248
        *Am Consttnl Law (Mason) 264-267
        *Am Consttnl Law (Shapiro) 261-265
        *Am Landmark v. 3, 385-430
        *Annals v. 12, 23-28
        Basic History 54
        CQ Guide 90-91
        *Cases Consttnl Law (Cushman) 192-195
        Changing 74-76
        *Commerce 36-37, 153-155
        *Competition 5-13
        Conservative 178-184
        *Consttn (Mendelson) 97-100
        Consttnl Law (Barrett) 216-217
        *Consttnl Law (Freund) 225-227
        Court and Consttn v. 1, 34-35
        Court Years 156-157
        Dissent 130-131
        *Documents History v. 1, 618-620
        *Govt and Business 224

*Liberty v. 2, 293-294
*Sup Ct and American Economic Life 123-129
Sup Ct and Commerce 60-61
*Sup Ct and Consttn 293-294
Sup Ct in Crisis 141-143
Sup Ct in Free Society 152-155
Sup Ct on Trial 154-156
This Honorable Court 229-230
PERIODICALS:
"Knight case revisited," Joe A. Fisher. Historian 35: 365-383
   May '73.
"Knight sugar decision of 1895 and the modernization of American
   corporation law, 1869-1903," Charles W. McCurdy. Bus History
   R 53: 304-342 Autumn '79.

568. Sparf and Hansen v. United States   Jan 21, 1895   156 U. S. 51
      *Law Power 651-654

569. Andrews v. Swartz   Feb 4, 1895   156 U. S. 272
      Petitioners 131-132

570. Grimm v. United States   Mar 4, 1895   156 U. S. 604
      *Obscenity (Bosmajian) 8-9

571. Ralli v. Troop   Apr 1, 1895   157 U. S. 386
      *Cases Admiralty 602-608

572. Pollock v. Farmers' Loan and Trust   Apr 8, 1895   157 U. S. 429
      Co.
      Am Consttn (Kelly) 532-537
      Biography 330-336
      CQ Guide 110
      Conservative 185-206
      Court and Consttn v. 1, 3-17
      Sup Ct in Crisis 143-147

573. Keeler v. Standard Folding Bed Co.   Apr 8, 1895   157 U. S. 659
      *Legal Regulation 1052-1056

574. Ellenwood v. Marietta Chair Co.   May 6, 1895   158 U. S. 105
      *Cases Civil Procedure 330-332

575. Beard v. United States   May 27, 1895   158 U. S. 550
      Criminal Law (Wells) 97-99
      *Criminal Law (Wells) 99

576. In re Debs   May 27, 1895   158 U. S. 564
      Am Consttn (Kelly) 529-531
      *Annals v. 12, 18-22
      *Cases Labor (Cox) 48-52
      Civil Rights (Fiss) 1-2
      *Consttnl Aspects v. 4, 545-555
      *Consttnl Law (Freund) 220-223
      Court and Consttn v. 1, 54-60
      Court Years 159-160
      *Documents History v. 1, 613-616
      *Injunctions 580-596
      *Justices (Friedman) v. 2, 1535-1546

Labor Relations (Taylor) 30, 47-48
*Liberty v. 2, 295-297
*Shaping 847-851
*Sup Ct and American Economic Life 119-123
*Sup Ct and Consttn 294-297
Sup Ct and Labor 11
Sup Ct in Crisis 147-149
This Honorable Court 215-216

577.   Pollock v. Farmers' Loan and Trust Co. May 20, 1895   158 U.S. 601
        Hyde v. Continental Trust Co. of New
            York
        Am Consttn (Kelly) 537-541
        *Am Consttnl Law (Bartholomew) v. 1, 148-150
        *Am Consttnl Law (Mason) 318-323
        *Am Consttnl Law (Shapiro) 265-269
        CQ Guide 110
        Conservative 207-214
        *Consttn (Mendelson) 129-133
        Court and Consttn v. 1, 3-17
        *Documents History v. 1, 605-609
        Great Reversals 77-80
        *Historic Decisions 96-99
        *Justices (Friedman) v. 2, 1302-1324, 1496-1506, 1570-1574, 1616-
            1621
        *Liberty v. 2, 297-299
        *Reapportionment (Baker) 141-144
        *Sup Ct and American Economic Life 129-134
        *Sup Ct and Consttn 304-308
        Sup Ct in Free Society 130-135
        Sup Ct Review 1970 217-218
        *Sup Ct Speaks 187-190
        This Honorable Court 219-222

578.   United States v. Gettysburg Electric   Jan 27, 1896   160 U.S. 668
            Railway Co.
        *Sup Ct Speaks 167-170

579.   Rosen v. United States   Jan 6, 1896   161 U.S. 29
        Law of Obscenity 223-224

580.   Swearingen v. United States   Mar 9, 1896   161 U.S. 446
        *Censorship Landmarks 46-47

581.   The Delaware   Mar 2, 1896   161 U.S. 459
        *Cases Admiralty 471-472

582.   Geer v. Connecticut   Mar 2, 1896   161 U.S. 519
        Sup Ct Review 1979 55-57

583.   Brown v. Walker   Mar 23, 1896   161 U.S. 501
        *Bill (Cohen) 553-556
        CQ Guide 556-557
        *Cases Civil Liberties 136-139
        *Cases Consttnl Law (Cushman) 366-369
        *Due Process 62-63
        Freedom Spent 367-370
        Justice Frankfurter 166-167

584. Texas and Pacific Railway v. Interstate Mar 30, 1896   162 U.S. 197
      Commerce Commission
      *Am Landmark v. 2, 533-574

585. Wong Wing v. United States   May 18, 1896   163 U.S. 228
      *Justices (Friedman) v. 2, 1596-1600

586. Hennington v. Georgia   May 18, 1896   163 U.S. 299
      Religion (Kurland) 98

587. Talton v. Mayes   May 18, 1896   163 U.S. 376
      *Am Indian v. 4, 2699-2704

588. Plessy v. Ferguson   May 18, 1896   163 U.S. 537
      *Am Consttn (Lockhart) 962-965
      *Am Consttnl Law (Bartholomew) v. 2, 298-300
      *Am Consttnl Law (Mason) 473-477
      *Am Consttnl Law (Saye) 435-437
      *Am Consttnl Law (Shapiro) 508-511
      *Annals v. 12, 92-100
      *Basic Cases 59-64
      Basic History 47-48
      *Bill (Cohen) 603-609
      Biography 347-349
      CQ Guide 608-609
      *Cases Civil Liberties 327-330
      *Cases Consttnl Law (Cushman) 557-560
      Cases Consttnl Law (Gunther) 754-757
      *Cases Consttnl Law (Rosenblum) 18-22
      *Cases Consttnl Rights 907-910
      *Civil Rights (Abernathy) 1977 506-508
      *Civil Rights (Bardolph) 149-152
      Civil Rights (Blaustein) 294-304
      *Civil Rights (Blaustein) 304-311
      *Civil Rights (Pious) 16-19
      Civil Rights (Schimmel) 184-186
      *Consttn (Hirschfield) 64-70
      *Consttn (Mendelson) 519-522
      *Consttn (Pollak) v. 2, 251-257
      *Consttnl Cases 447-452
      *Consttnl Decisions 162-166
      *Consttnl Law (Barrett) 810-813
      *Consttnl Law (Felkenes) 182-185
      *Consttnl Law (Freund) 881-884
      *Consttnl Law (Grossman) 429-435
      *Consttnl Law (Kauper) 706-713
      *Consttnl Law (Lockhart) 1265-1267
      *Consttnl Politics 462-469
      Court and Consttn v. 2, 260-261
      Decade 54-56
      Desegregation (Wasby) 27-28
      *Desegregation (Ziegler) 49-64
      Development 196-198
      Digest 76-77
      Disaster 22-23
      *Discrimination 159-163
      Dissent 139-140
      *Documents History v. 1, 628-630
      *Education (Hazard) 153-163

*Educational Policy 281-287
Equal Justice 57-58
Equality (Berger) 73-74
Freedom and the Court 13, 359-362
From Brown 17-19
Garden 125-129
Great Events American v. 2, 1261-1267
Great Reversals 158-162
*Historic Decisions 100-102
*Integration 13-22
Judiciary (Abraham) 128-129
Justice 50-59
*Justices (Friedman) v. 2, 1296-1301, 1564-1570
*Law Lawyers 130-141
*Leading Consttnl Decisions 408-414
*Liberty v. 2, 272-275
*Nature 962-967
*Negro (Franklin) 69-80
Petitioners 165-166, 168-174
*Political Rights v. 2, 1230-1234
Politics 159-162
*Processes 441-445
Prophets 22-53
*Prophets 197-206
Quarrels 145-158
Quest 98-102
*Racial Equality 24-27
School in the Legal Structure 57-58
*Sources American Republic v. 2, 37-40
*Struggle 29-34
*Sup Ct and Consttn 216-221
Sup Ct on Trial 9-10
*These Liberties 101-106
*Thin Disguise 108-121
This Honorable Court 194-196
Warren (Carter) 56
Warren (Hudgins) 14-16
PERIODICALS:
    "Case Law in Plessy v. Ferguson," Barton J. Bernstein. J Negro
        History 47: 192-198 July '62.
    "Courts in the saddle: school boards out," William R. Hazard.
        Phi Delta Kappan 56: 259-261 Dec '74 (5).
    "Ironies of School Desegregation," Faustus C. Jones. J Negro
        Eductn 47: 2-27 Winter '78 (7).
    "Litigation and education of Blacks: a look at the U.S. Supreme
        Court," Delores P. Aldridge. J Negro Eductn 47: 96-112
        Winter '78 (11).
    "Plessy v. Ferguson; the Birth of Jim Crow," C. Vann Woodward.
        Am Heritage 15: 52-55, 100-103 Apr '64.
    "Role of the Federal Courts in the changing status of Negroes since
        World War II," Daniel C. Thompson. 30· 94-101 Spring '01
        (2).

589. Acers v. United States   Nov 30, 1896   164 U.S. 388
        Criminal Law (Wells) 95

590. Gulf, Colorado and Santa Fe Railroad   Jan 18, 1897   165 U.S. 150
        Co. v. Ellis
        *Consttnl Law (Barrett) 769

591. Swaim v. United States   Mar 1, 1897   165 U.S. 553
      Sup Ct and Commander in Chief 106-108

592. Allgeyer v. Louisiana   Mar 1, 1897   165 U.S. 578
      *Basic History 129-131
      Conceived 34-35
      Consttnl Law (Barrett) 650
      *Consttnl Law (Kauper) 610-612
      Development 179-180
      *Justices (Friedman) v. 3, 1704-1709
      *Liberty v. 2, 337-338

593. Walker v. New Mexico and Southern   Mar 1, 1897   165 U.S. 593
      Pacific Railroad
      *Cases Civil Procedure 810-814

594. United States v. Trans-Missouri   Mar 22, 1897   166 U.S. 290
      Freight Association
      *Antitrust (Posner) 33-46
      *Cases Antitrust Law 117-123
      *Cases Trade 127-129
      *Competition 200-204
      Court and Consttn v. 1, 98-99
      *Govt Regulation 1-33
      *Judiciary (Roche) 110-111

595. In re Lennon   Apr 19, 1897   166 U.S. 548
      *Injunctions 632-635

596. In re Chapman   Apr 19, 1897   166 U.S. 661
      CQ Guide 159

597. Davis v. Massachusetts   May 10, 1897   167 U.S. 43
      Free Speech (Kurland) 126-127
      Negro (Kalven) 186-187
      Right of Assembly 110-111
      System 299-300

598. Stone v. United States   May 10, 1897   167 U.S. 178
      *Cases Civil Procedure 332-334

599. Interstate Commerce Commission v.   May 24, 1897   167 U.S. 479
      Cincinnati, New Orleans and
      Texas Pacific Railway
      "Maximum Rate Case"
      Am Consttn (Kelly) 520
      *Liberty v. 2, 291-292
      *Statutory History Economic v. 1, 580-584
      *Sup Ct and Consttn 258-260

600. Wight v. United States   May 24, 1897   167 U.S. 512
      *Free Enterprise 863-865

601. Interstate Commerce Commission v.   Nov 8, 1897   168 U.S. 144
      Alabama Midland Railway Co.
      *Statutory History Economic v. 1, 584-590

602. Underhill v. Hernandez   Nov 29, 1897   168 U.S. 250
      Sup Ct Review 1964 228-229

603. Holden v. Hardy   Feb 28, 1898   169 U.S. 366
        Am Consttn (Kelly) 494-495
        *Consttnl Law (Kauper) 612-616
        Development 185
        *Documents History v. 1, 630-631
        *Liberty v. 2, 340-341
        *Sup Ct and American Economic Life 87-93
        *Sup Ct Speaks 192-198

604. Smyth v. Ames   Mar 7, 1898   169 U.S. 466
      Smyth v. Smith
      Smyth v. Higginson
        *Cases Electronic 81-85
        Development 180-182
        *Documents History v. 1, 583-585
        *Historic Decisions 103-106
        Legacy 272-273
        *Liberty v. 2, 299-300
        *Sup Ct and Consttn 254-257

605. United States v. Wong Kim Ark   Mar 28, 1898   169 U.S. 649
        *Am Consttnl Law (Bartholomew) v. 2, 342-343
        CQ Guide 142-143
        *Civil Liberties (Sweet) 324-326
        *Civil Rights (Konvitz) 136
        *Consttnl Law (Freund) 734-738
        *Consttnl Law (Kauper) 533-538
        *Liberty v. 2, 279-280

606. The John G. Stevens   Apr 18, 1898   170 U.S. 113
        *Cases Admiralty 244-245, 257-258

607. Hawker v. New York   Apr 18, 1898   170 U.S. 189
        *US Prison Law v. 5, 183-198

608. Williams v. Mississippi   Apr 25, 1898   170 U.S. 213
        CQ Guide 479
        Civil Rights (Bardolph) 147-148
        Petitioners 159
        *Racial Equality 34-35
        Sup Ct and Electoral Process 73

609. Thompson v. Utah   Apr 25, 1898   170 U.S. 343
        *Criminal Law (Wells) 48-49

610. Vance v. Vandercook Co.   May 9, 1898   170 U.S. 468
        *Cases Federal Courts 224-226

611. The Carib Prince   May 23, 1898   170 U.S. 655
      Wupperman v. The Carib Prince
        *Cases Admiralty 477-479

612. Flint, Eddy and Co. v. Christall   May 31, 1898   171 U.S. 187
      The Irrawaddy
        *Cases Admiralty 624-626

613. Thompson v. Missouri   May 31, 1898   171 U.S. 380
        *Cases Criml (Perkins) 866-868

614. United States v. Joint-Traffic Association Oct 24, 1898   171 U. S. 505
      *Antitrust Analysis 261-263

615. The Elfrida   Dec 12, 1898   172 U. S. 186
      *Cases Admiralty 595-598

616. Ohio v. Thomas   Feb 27, 1899   173 U. S. 276
      *Consttnl Law (Freund) 643-644

617. Kirby v. United States   Apr 11, 1899   174 U. S. 47
      Defendants 94

618. Holmes v. Hurst   Apr 24, 1899   174 U. S. 82
      Communication (Hemmer) v. 2, 124
      *Copyright 190-194

619. Stephens v. Cherokee Nation   May 15, 1899   174 U. S. 445
      Choctaw Nation v. Robinson
      Johnson v. Creek Nation
      Chickasaw Nation v. Wiggs
      *Documents Indian 198-199

620. Addyston Pipe and Steel Co. v.   Dec 4, 1899   175 U. S. 211
      United States
      *Commerce 37-38
      *Competition 204-208
      *Selected Antitrust Cases 64-65

621. Bradfield v. Roberts   Dec 4, 1899   175 U. S. 291
      "Providence Hospital Case"
      Am Politics 52
      Church and State 113
      Expanding Liberties 10
      Freedom and the Court 322
      Religion (Kurland) 32-34
      *Religious Freedom (Pfeffer) 42-43
      Sup Ct and Religion 79
      *Teacher 129-132

622. Cumming v. Richmond County Board   Dec 18, 1899   175 U. S. 528
      of Education
      CQ Guide 591
      Desegregation (Wasby) 28-29
      Digest 77
      Disaster 23
      Education (Lapati) 268-269
      Education (Spurlock) 181-183
      Petitioners 213-214
      School in the Legal Structure 58
      Warren (Hudgins) 16-17

623. The Paquete Habana   Jan 8, 1900   175 U. S. 677
      The Lola
      Foreign Affairs 221

624. Maxwell v. Dow   Feb 26, 1900   176 U. S. 581
      *Cases Civil Liberties 25-27
      *Cases Consttnl Law (Cushman) 255-257

Freedom and the Court 57-58
Sup Ct (North) 93

625.   Petit v. Minnesota   Apr 9, 1900   177 U.S. 164
       Religion (Kurland) 98

626.   Ohio Oil Co. v. Indiana   Apr 9, 1900   177 U.S. 190
       *Cases Property (Donahue) 332-335

627.   Carter v. Texas   Apr 16, 1900   177 U.S. 44
       Civil Rights (Bardolph) 153

628.   Knowlton v. Moore   May 14, 1900   178 U.S. 41
       *Am Consttnl Law (Bartholomew) v. 1, 151-152

629.   Knott v. Botany Worsted Mills   Oct 22, 1900   179 U.S. 69
       *Cases Admiralty 474-477

630.   New Orleans v. Fisher   Jan 28, 1901   180 U.S. 185
       Digest 6

631.   International Navigation Co. v. Farr   Apr 22, 1901   181 U.S. 218
       and Bailey Manufacturing Co.
       *Cases Admiralty 480-482

632.   DeLima v. Bidwell   May 27, 1901   182 U.S. 1
       "Insular Case"
         Am Consttn (Kelly) 545-546
         CQ Guide 138-140
         Great Events American v. 2, 1318-1324
         This Honorable Court 232-233

633.   Downes v. Bidwell   May 27, 1901   182 U.S. 244
       "Insular Case"
         Am Consttn (Kelly) 545-546
         CQ Guide 138-140
         *Consttnl Law (Freund) 712-714
         *Documents History v. 2, 12-17
         Dred Scott Case 585-586
         *Liberty v. 2, 303-305
         This Honorable Court 232

634.   Homer Ramsdell Transportation Co.   May 27, 1901   182 U.S. 406
       v. La Compagnie Generale
       Transatlantique
       *Cases Admiralty 723-727

635.   Tucker v. Alexandroff   Jan 6, 1902   183 U.S. 424
       Executive Privilege 156-157

636.   American School of Magnetic Healing   Nov 17, 1902   187 U.S. 94
       v. McAnnulty
       *Cases Food 313-315

637.   Cherokee Nation v. Hitchcock   Dec 1, 1902   187 U.S. 294
       *Law Indian 422-425

638.   Lone Wolf v. Hitchcock   Jan 5, 1903   187 U.S. 553
       *Am Indian v. 4, 2705-2709

*Documents Indian 202-203
*Law Indian 425-429

639. Bleistein v. Donaldson Lithographing   Feb 2, 1903   188 U. S. 239
      Co.
      *Cases Copyright (Kaplan) 167-171
      *Cases Copyright (Nimmer) 2-6
      Communication (Hemmer) v. 2, 116-117
      *Copyright 634-638
      *Legal Regulation 636-638

640. Champion v. Ames   Feb 23, 1903   188 U. S. 321
      "Lottery Case"
      Am Consttn (Kelly) 553-555
      *Am Consttn (Lockhart) 132-133
      *Am Consttnl Law (Bartholomew) v. 1, 239-242
      *Am Consttnl Law (Mason) 268-272
      CQ Guide 95-96
      *Cases Consttnl Law (Gunther) 130-132
      Commerce 88-96
      *Commerce 97-102
      *Consttnl Law (Barron) 171-172
      *Consttnl Law (Freund) 230-233
      *Consttnl Law (Lockhart) 105-107
      *Consttnl Revolution 36-37
      *Documents History v. 2, 26-28
      *Justices (Friedman) v. 2, 1506-1511
      *Liberty v. 2, 332-333
      Sup Ct and Commerce 55-57
      *Sup Ct and Consttn 309-312
      Sup Ct in Crisis 151
      Sup Ct in Free Society 157-158
      Sup Ct on Trial 166-167

641. Hyatt v. New York (State) ex rel.   Feb 23, 1903   188 U. S. 691
      Corkran
      *Cases Criml (Perkins) 793-795

642. The Osceola   Mar 2, 1903   189 U. S. 158
      Sup Ct Review 1964 271-284

643. Giles v. Harris   Apr 27, 1903   189 U. S. 475
      Petitioners 159-162
      *Racial Equality 35-36
      Sup Ct Review 1961 202-203

644. James v. Bowman   May 4, 1903   190 U. S. 127
      Petitioners 157, 158

645. Hawaii v. Mankichi   June 1, 1903   190 U. S. 197
      Am Consttn (Kelly) 546
      *Law Indian 107-110
      *Liberty v. 2, 306-307

646. Mifflin v. White   June 1, 1903   190 U. S. 260
      Communication (Hemmer) v. 2, 124-125

647. Mifflin v. Dutton   June 1, 1903   190 U. S. 265
      Communication (Hemmer) v. 2, 125-126

648. Anglo-American Provision Co.   Nov 30, 1903 191 U.S. 373
          v. Davis Provision Co., No. 1
      Sup Ct Review 1964 119-120

649. South Dakota v. North Carolina   Feb 1, 1904   192 U.S. 286
      *Am Consttnl Law (Bartholomew) v. 1, 63-65
      *Cases Federal Courts 880-884

650. Buttfield v. Stranahan   Feb 23, 1904 192 U.S. 470
      Consttn (Barber) 73-75
      Consttnl Counterrevolution 610   .

651. Adams v. New York   Feb 23, 1904 192 U.S. 585
      Search and Seizure 62-63

652. W. W. Montague and Co. v. Lowry   Feb 23, 1904 193 U.S. 38
      *Govt Regulation 66-69

653. Northern Securities Co. v. United   Mar 14, 1904 193 U.S. 197
          States
      Am Consttn (Kelly) 566-568
      *Annals v. 12, 576-583
      *Antitrust (Posner) 321-330
      CQ Guide 91
      *Cases Antitrust Law 148-155
      Changing 86-87
      Commerce 159-161
      *Competition 18-21
      Court and Consttn v. 1, 94-96, 101-103
      Court Years 157
      Dissent 131-132
      *Documents History v. 2, 35-39
      *Govt Regulation 70-121
      Legacy 48-57
      *Liberty v. 2, 317-319
      Quarrels 159-175
      *Sup Ct and Consttn 271-275
      Sup Ct in Am History 91-107
      This Honorable Court 238-239
      PERIODICALS:
      "Speech that Validated the Sherman Antitrust Act of 1890; Philander
        Chase Knox's Address to the Supreme Court," Thomas A. Hop-
        kins. Quarterly J Speech 43: 51-58 Feb '62.

654. Tinker v. Colwell   Mar 21, 1904 193 U.S. 473
      *Family 396
      *Sex Roles 67-68

655. Bates and Guild Co. v. Payne   Apr 11, 1904 194 U.S. 106
      *Govt and Business 609-611

656. Hijo v. United States   May 16, 1904 194 U.S. 315
      Sup Ct and Commander in Chief 82

657. McCray v. United States   May 31, 1904 195 U.S. 27
      Am Consttn (Kelly) 555-556
      *Am Consttnl Law (Bartholomew) v. 1, 155-156
      *Am Consttnl Law (Mason) 323-325
      *Cases Consttnl Law (Cushman) 157-160

*Sup Ct and Consttn 312-317
Sup Ct in Free Society 138

658. Dorr v. United States   May 31, 1904   195 U. S. 138
      Am Consttn (Kelly) 546-547
      This Honorable Court 233-234

659. Swift and Co. v. United States   Jan 30, 1905   196 U. S. 375
      "Beef Trust Case"
      Am Consttn (Kelly) 568-569
      *Am Consttnl Law (Bartholomew) v. 1, 249-250
      CQ Guide 91-92
      Court and Consttn v. 1, 104-105
      Development 148-149
      *Govt Regulation 122-128
      *Liberty v. 2, 319-320
      Sup Ct and Commerce 52-53
      *Sup Ct and Consttn 275-277
      Sup Ct on Trial 156

660. Jacobson v. Massachusetts   Feb 20, 1905   197 U. S. 11
      Am Consttnl Law (Bartholomew) v. 2, 219-221
      Church and State 113-114
      *Comparative 370-372
      *Consttnl Law (Kauper) 617-622
      Digest 33-34
      *Liberty v. 2, 346-347
      Private Conscience 117-119
      *Rights (Shattuck) 95-96
      Sup Ct on Trial 177-178

661. Clyatt v. United States   Mar 13, 1905   197 U. S. 207
      Petitioners 190-191

662. Rassmussen v. United States   Apr 10, 1905   197 U. S. 516
      *Liberty v. 2, 308-310

663. Muhlker v. New York and Harlem   Apr 10, 1905   197 U. S. 544
      Railroad
      Sup Ct Review 1972 124-125

664. Lochner v. New York   Apr 17, 1905   198 U. S. 45
      Am Consttn (Kelly) 495-496
      *Am Consttn (Lockhart) 360-364
      *Am Consttnl Issues 425-431
      *Am Consttnl Law (Mason) 418-422
      *Am Consttnl Law (Saye) 412-414
      *Am Consttnl Law (Shapiro) 312-317
      *Am Primer 661-664
      *Annals v. 13, 8-15
      *Basic Cases 109-116
      Basic History 50-53
      *Basic History 136-138
      Biography 311-313
      CQ Guide 326
      *Cases Civil Liberties 35-39
      *Cases Consttnl Law (Cushman) 265-269
      *Cases Consttnl Law (Gunther) 511-516
      *Cases Consttnl Law (Rosenblum) 319-324

*Cases Consttnl Rights 120-124
*Cases Individual 155-162
 Changing 87
*Comparative 267-270
 Conceived 35-36
*Consttn (Mendelson) 256-261
*Consttn (Pollak) 293-298
*Consttnl Law (Barrett) 651-654
*Consttnl Law (Barron) 418-422
*Consttnl Law (Freund) 1083-1088
*Consttnl Law (Grossman) 351-355
*Consttnl Law (Klein) 106-114
*Consttnl Law (Lockhart) 435-439
*Consttnl Politics 440-446
*Consttnlism 60-64
 Development 186-187
 Dissent 101
*Documents History v. 2, 39-42
 Equality (Warsoff) 251-259
*Federal System 39-41
 Great Reversals 104-108
*Historic Decisions 107-111
*Introduction (Mashaw) 147-157
*Justices (Friedman) v. 3, 1709-1715
*Leading Consttnl Decisions 175-189
 Legacy 35-44
*Liberty v. 2, 341-343
*Processes 725-732
*Rights (Shattuck) 04-05
*Sex Discrimination 1975 20-23
*Sources American Republic v. 3, 115-120
 Sup Ct (Forte) 88-89
*Sup Ct (Mendelson) 101-100
 Sup Ct (North) 53-54
*Sup Ct and Am Capitalism 58-59
*Sup Ct and American Economic Life 94-101
*Sup Ct and Consttn 282-289
 Sup Ct in Crisis 152-153
 Sup Ct in Free Society 236
 Sup Ct on Trial 178-179
*Sup Ct Speaks 200-202
*Teaching Materials 21-24
 This Honorable Court 241-243

665. Harris v. Balk   May 8, 1905   198 U.S. 215
      *Cases Admiralty 314-317
      *Cases Civil Procedure 440-446
      *Cases Pleading 184-191
      *Civil Procedure (Carrington) 870-873
       Sup Ct Review 1965 278-279

666. Delaware, Lackawanna and Western   May 15, 1905   198 U.S. 341
          Railroad v. Pennsylvania
       Am Consttn (Kelly) 504

667. Clark v. Nash   May 15, 1905   198 U.S. 361
      *Am Land Planning v. 2, 1555-1561

668. Union Refrigerator Transit Co. v.   Nov 13, 1905   199 U.S. 194
          Kentucky

*Consttnl Law (Barrett) 372-374

669. Attorney General of Michigan ex rel.   Nov 13, 1905 199 U.S. 233
        Kies v. Lowrey
        Digest 6-7
        *Law and Public Education (Hamilton) 597-599
        *Law of Public Education 102-104
        *Principles School 123-124
        *Public School Law 184-186
        *School Law (Alexander) 160-162

670. South Carolina v. United States   Dec 4, 1905   199 U.S. 437
        *Cases Consttnl Law (Cushman) 149-150

671. Trono v. United States   Dec 4, 1905   199 U.S. 521
        Defendants 381
        Double (Sigler) 71
        Justice Frankfurter 162-164

672. Hale v. Henkel   Mar 12, 1906 201 U.S. 43
        Search and Seizure 80

673. Jay v. St. Louis   Apr 2, 1906   201 U.S. 332
        *Cases Federal Courts 114-116

674. United States v. Cornell Steamboat Co. May 14, 1906 202 U.S. 184
        *Cases Admiralty 587-589

675. Hodges v. United States   May 28, 1906 203 U.S. 1
        Petitioners 187-190
        Racial Equality 18-19

676. Guy v. Donald   Dec 3, 1906   203 U.S. 399
        *Cases Admiralty 727-730

677. Montana ex rel. Haire v. Rice   Jan 28, 1907 204 U.S. 291
        Digest 7-8

678. Texas and Pacific Railroad Co. v.   Feb 25, 1907 204 U.S. 426
        Abilene Cotton Oil Co.
        *Statutory History Economic v. 2, 995-1002

679. Patterson v. Colorado   Apr 15, 1907 205 U.S. 454
        Legacy 186-187
        Sup Ct Review 1978 254

680. Kansas v. Colorado   May 13, 1907 206 U.S. 46
        *Cases Consttnl Law (Cushman) 116-117
        *Consttnl Law (Felkenes) 50-52

681. Kessler v. Eldred   May 13, 1907 206 U.S. 285
        *Patent 889-894

682. Illinois Central Railroad Co. v.   May 27, 1907 206 U.S. 441
        Interstate Commerce Commission
        Am Consttn (Kelly) 575

683. American Tobacco Co. v. Werck-   Dec 2, 1907   207 U.S. 284
        meister

*Cases Copyright (Nimmer) 138-140

684. Howard v. Illinois Central Railroad Co.   Jan 6, 1908   207 U.S. 463
     Brooks v. Southern Pacific Co.
     "First Employer's Liability Cases"
        Am Consttn (Kelly) 564
        *Commerce 161-162
        Court and Consttn v. 1, 120-122
        *Justices (Friedman) v. 3, 1828-1844
        Sup Ct in Crisis 153-154

685. Winters v. United States   Jan 6, 1908   207 U.S. 564
        *Am Indian v. 4, 2726-2729
        *Law Indian 311-313

686. Adair v. United States   Jan 27, 1908   208 U.S. 161
        Am Consttn (Kelly) 499-500, 563-564
        Court and Consttn v. 1, 115-117
        *Documents History v. 2, 45-48
        *Labor Law (Herman) 85-89
        Legal Problems 244-245
        *Liberty v. 2, 325-326
        *Nature 874-881
        *Sup Ct (Mendelson) 124-132
        *Sup Ct and American Economic Life 134-137
        *Sup Ct and Consttn 300-303
        Sup Ct and Labor 12-13
        Sup Ct in Free Society 156-157

687. Loewe v. Lawlor   Feb 3, 1908   208 U.S. 274
     "Danbury Hatters Case"
        *Cases Labor (Oberer) 55-59
        Court and Consttn v. 1, 118-119
        *Labor Law (Herman) 45-47
        Labor Relations (Taylor) 48-50
        *Liberty v. 2, 323-324
        *Nature 845-849
        *Sup Ct and Consttn 297-300
        Sup Ct and Labor 13-14
        This Honorable Court 245-246

688. Muller v. Oregon   Feb 24, 1908   208 U.S. 412
        Am Consttn (Kelly) 496-498
        Am Land Planning v. 1, 96-106
        Consttnl Law (Barrett) 655-656
        Court and Consttn v. 1, 119-120
        Development 187
        *Documents History v. 2, 43-45
        Equality (Warsoff) 262-264
        Felix Frankfurter (Phillips) 96-97
        Great Events American v. 3, 1369-1373
        Great Reversals 108-109
        *Justices (Friedman) v. 2, 1546-1549
        Legacy 84-89
        Legal Problems 243-244
        *Materials Legislation 205
        Quarrels 176-190
        *Sex Discrimination 1975 30-32
        *Sex Roles 46-48

Sup Ct and Consttn 289-290
Sup Ct in Free Society 238-240
*Text Consttnl Aspects 10-15
*Text Sex Based Discrimination 10-15
US Sup Ct 34-36
*Woman 21-22
PERIODICALS:
"Advent of Forensic sociology, " A. John Dodds.   Social Studies
   61: 200-203 Oct '70.

689. White-Smith Music Co. v. Apollo   Feb 24, 1908   209 U.S. 1
      *Cases Copyright (Nimmer) 178-183

690. Ex parte Young   Mar 23, 1908   209 U.S. 123
      *Am Consttnl Law (Saye) 61-65
      *Cases Federal Courts 410-420
      Civil Rights (Fiss) 3
      *Consttnl Law (Barrett) 119-123

691. Hudson County Co. v. McCarter   Apr 6, 1908   209 U.S. 349
      Sup Ct Review 1979 90-91

692. Quick Bear v. Leupp   May 18, 1908   210 U.S. 50
      Church and State 114
      Education (Lapati) 163-164
      Education (Spurlock) 72-75
      Freedom and the Court 322
      *Law Indian 694-696
      School in the Legal Structure 61-62
      *Teacher 133-135
      *Two Swords 342-347
      PERIODICALS:
      "Concept of freedom in education, " William W. Brickman.   Eductnl
         Rec 45: 74-83 Winter '64 (5).

693. Old Dominion Copper Mining and   May 18, 1908   210 U.S. 206
         Smelting Co. v. Lewisohn
      *Basic Corporation 41-46

694. Galveston, Harrisburg and San   May 18, 1908   210 U.S. 217
         Antonio Railway v. Texas
      *Consttn (Mendelson) 216-218

695. St. Louis, Iron Mountain and Southern   May 18, 1908   210 U.S. 281
         Railway v. Taylor
      *Justices (Friedman) v. 3, 1823-1828

696. Londoner v. Denver   June 1, 1908   210 U.S. 373
      *Admin Law (Gellhorn) 152-153
      *Legislation (Linde) 56-62

697. Continental Paper Bag Co. v.   June 1, 1908   210 U.S. 405
         Eastern Paper Bag Co.
      *Patent 756-764

698. Berea College v. Kentucky   Nov 9, 1908   211 U.S. 45
      Civil Rights (Bardolph) 152
      Education (Lapati) 153-154

709. Siler v. Louisville and Nashville   Apr 5, 1909   213 U.S. 175
      Railroad Co.
      Consttnl Law (Barrett) 49-50

710. Leeds and Catlin Co. v. Victor   Apr 19, 1909   213 U.S. 325
      Talking Machine Co.
      *Antitrust (Posner) 579-583
      *Legal Regulation 1060-1065

711. American Banana Co. v. United   Apr 26, 1909   213 U.S. 347
      Fruit Co.
      *Cases Antitrust Law 1253-1256
      *Cases Regulation 26-29
      *Cases Trade 1149-1152
      *Govt Regulation 129-132

712. United States v. Delaware and Hudson   May 3, 1909   213 U.S. 366
      Co.
      *Commerce 162-164

713. Welch v. Swasey   May 17, 1909   214 U.S. 91
      *Legal Foundations 109-110

714. Peck v. Tribune   May 17, 1909   214 U.S. 185
      *Cases Copyright (Nimmer) 627-629

715. Fall v. Eastin   Nov 1, 1909   215 U.S. 1
      *Cases Equity 78-82

716. Interstate Commerce Commission v.   Jan 10, 1910   215 U.S. 452
      Illinois Central Railroad
      Am Consttn (Kelly) 575
      *Liberty v. 2, 314-316
      *Sup Ct and Consttn 261-263

717. Western Union Telegraph Co. v.   Jan 17, 1910   216 U.S. 1
      Kansas
      *Consttnl Law (Freund) 493-496

718. International Textbook Co. v. Pigg   Apr 4, 1910   217 U.S. 91
      Education (Lapati) 154-155
      Education (Spurlock) 33-35

719. Weems v. United States   May 2, 1910   217 U.S. 349
      Criminal Law (Wells) 64-65
      Defendants 398

720. Southern Railway v. King   May 16, 1910   217 U.S. 524
      "Blow Post Case"
      Sup Ct Review 1975 159-160

721. Chiles v. Chesapeake and Ohio   May 31, 1910   218 U.S. 71
      Railway Co.
      Petitioners 241-242

722. Franklin v. South Carolina   May 31, 1910   218 U.S. 161
      Petitioners 237-238

723. Ling Su Fun v. United States   Nov 14, 1910 218 U.S. 302
        Monetary Decisions 84-85, 86

724. Bailey v. Alabama   Jan 3, 1911   219 U.S. 219
        *Justices (Friedman) v. 3, 1934-1941
        Petitioners 193-194
        *Statutory History Civil Rights 172-178
        Sup Ct in Crisis 165-166
        This Honorable Court 251

725. Muskrat v. United States   Jan 23, 1911 219 U.S. 346
     Brown v. United States
        *Am Consttnl Law (Bartholomew) v. 1, 8-10
        *Cases Consttnl Law (Cushman) 9-13
        *Consttn (Mendelson) 10-12
        *Consttnl Law (Barron) 50-55
        Consttnl Law (Felkenes) 26-27
        *Consttnl Law (Freund) 49-54
        *Consttnl Law (Kauper) 9-16
        *Consttnl Law (Lockhart) 1625-1627
        *Federal Courts 120-124
        *Judiciary (Roche) 44-51

726. Hipolite Egg Co. v. United States   Mar 13, 1911 220 U.S. 45
        Am Consttn (Kelly) 560
        *Am Landmark v. 4, 359-374
        *Cases Food 592-594
        *Justices (Friedman) v. 3, 1737-1742

727. Lindsley v. Natural Carbonic Gas Co. Mar 13, 1911 220 U.S. 61
        *Am Consttnl Law (Sayc) 420-429

728. Flint v. Stone Tracy Co.   Mar 13, 1911 220 U.S. 107
        Court and Consttn v. 1, 149-150

729. Dr. Miles Medical Co. v. John D.   Apr 3, 1911   220 U.S. 373
        Park and Son Co.
        *Antitrust (Posner) 227-234
        *Antitrust Analysis 505-508
        *Cases Antitrust Law 513-518
        *Cases Trade 418-423
        *Competition 351-355
        *Govt Regulation 133-144
        Legacy 58-59
        Sup Ct Review 1977 179-180
        *Text Antitrust 76-79

730. United States v. Grimaud   May 1, 1911   220 U.S. 506
     United States v. Inda
        *Admin Law (Schwartz) 141-143
        Am Consttn (Kelly) 611
        *Cases Criml Law (Inbau) 46-50

731. Light v. United States   May 1, 1911   220 U.S. 523
        *Cases on Environmental Law (Hanks) 472-473

732. Standard Oil Co. of New Jersey v.   May 15, 1911 221 U.S. 1
        United States

*Am Testament 164-167
*Annals v. 13, 310-318
*Antitrust (Posner) 344-358
*Cases Antitrust Law 155-172
*Cases Trade 135-137, 311
*Competition 22-30
 Courts and Consttn v. 1, 150-153
*Documents History v. 2, 57-58
*Govt Regulation 145-177
*Judiciary (Roche) 116-127
*Justices (Friedman) v. 3, 1658-1681
*Legal Environment 258-260
*Liberty v. 2, 320-322
*Selected Antitrust Cases 10-16
*Sup Ct and Consttn 277-281

733. United States v. American Tobacco Co.   May 29, 1911 211 U.S. 106
     Court and Consttn v. 1, 153-154
     *Govt Regulation 178-199

734. West v. Kansas Natural Gas Co.   May 15, 1911 211 U.S. 229
     Sup Ct and Commerce 41

735. Gompers v. Buck's Stove and Range Co.   May 15, 1911 221 U.S. 418
     *Injunctions 714-720
     *Justices (Friedman) v. 3, 1990-1997
     Labor Relations (Taylor) 51-52

736. United States v. Johnson   May 29, 1911 221 U.S. 488
     *Cases Food 306-309
     *Competition 378-382
     *Materials Legislation 81-90

737. Coyle v. Smith   May 29, 1911 221 U.S. 559
     *Am Consttnl Law (Bartholomew) v. 1, 52-54
     *Cases Consttnl Law (Cushman) 134-138
     *Documents History v. 2, 89-97

738. Baltimore and Ohio Railroad v.   May 29, 1911 221 U.S. 612
     Interstate Commerce Commission
     Sup Ct in Crisis 161-162

739. Southern Railway Co. v. United States   Oct 30, 1911 222 U.S. 20
     *Am Consttnl Law (Bartholomew) v. 1, 251-252
     *Consttn (Pollak) 312-316
     *Consttnl Law (Kauper) 131-133

740. Southern Pacific v. Kentucky   Nov 13, 1911 222 U.S. 63
     Consttnl Law (Barrett) 375

741. Banker Brothers Co. v. Pennsylvania   Dec 4, 1911   222 U.S. 210
     *Consttnl Law (Freund) 564-565

742. Mondou v. New York, New Haven and   Jan 15, 1912 223 U.S. 1
     Hartford Railroad Co.
     "Second Employers' Liability Case"
     Am Consttn (Kelly) 565

743. Quong Wing v. Kirkendall   Jan 22, 1912 223 U.S. 59

Equality (Warsoff) 269-270
*Sex Discrimination 1975 92-93

744. Pacific States Telephone and Telegraph   Jan 19, 1912   223 U.S. 118
        v. Oregon
     Guarantee 264-268
     *Liberty v. 2, 348-349
     Sup Ct and Poltcl Questions 29-33

745. Ferris v. Frohman   Feb 19, 1912   223 U.S. 424
     *Cases Copyright (Kaplan) 64-69

746. Henry v. A. B. Dick Co.   Mar 11, 1912   224 U.S. 1
     *Antitrust (Posner) 583-587
     Great Reversals 92-93
     *Justices (Friedman) v. 3, 1864-1880

747. United States v. Terminal Railroad   Apr 22, 1912   224 U.S. 383
        Association
     *Antitrust (Posner) 556-563
     *Cases Antitrust Law 456-460
     *Govt Regulation 200-209
     *Justices (Friedman) v. 3, 1880-1889
     *Selected Antitrust Cases 236-242

748. Interstate Commerce Commission v.   Apr 29, 1912   224 U.S. 474
        United States ex rel. Humboldt
        Steamship Co.
     *Govt and Business 552-554

749. The Jason   May 13, 1912   225 U.S. 32
     *Cases Admiralty 626-631

750. Anderson v. Pacific Coast Steamship   May 27, 1912   225 U.S. 187
        Co.
     Jordan v. Pacific Coast Co.
     *Cases Admiralty 718-722

751. Johannessen v. United States   May 27, 1912   225 U.S. 227
     *Consttnl Law (Kauper) 540-544

752. United States v. Union Pacific Railroad   Dec 2, 1912   226 U.S. 61
     *Govt Regulation 210-219

753. 443 Cans of Frozen Egg Product v.   Dec 2, 1912   226 U.S. 172
        United States
     *Cases Food 655-657

754. Yazoo and Mississippi Valley Railroad   Dec 2, 1912   226 U.S. 217
        v. Jackson Vinegar Co.
     *Federal Courts 191-192

755. United States v. Winslow   Feb 3, 1913   227 U.S. 202
     *Govt Regulation 220-222

756. Home Telephone and Telegraph Co.   Feb 24, 1913   227 U.S. 278
        v. Los Angeles
     *Federal Courts 937-941

757. Hoke v. United States   Feb 24, 1913   227 U. S. 308
      Am Consttn (Kelly) 560
      *Commerce 103-105
      *Liberty v. 2, 334-335
      Sup Ct and Commerce 57-58

758. Marrone v. Washington Jockey Club of   Mar 10, 1913   227 U. S. 633
      District of Columbia
      *Cases Property (Casner) 1184

759. McDermott v. Wisconsin   Apr 7, 1913   228 U. S. 115
      Grady v. Wisconsin
      *Cases Food 787-792
      *Consttnl Law (Freund) 202-205

760. Slocum v. New York Life Insurance Co.   Apr 21, 1913   228 U. S. 364
      *Civil Procedure (Cound) 925-929

761. Degge v. Hitchcock   May 26, 1913   229 U. S. 162
      Maury v. Hitchcock
      *Admin Law (Schwartz) 626-628

762. Lewis Publishing Co. v. Morgan   June 10, 1913 229 U. S. 288
      Communication (Hemmer) v. 2, 200
      *Sup Ct on Freedom 182-183
      Sup Ct Review 1978 255-256

763. Nash v. United States   June 9, 1913   229 U. S. 373
      *Criminal Law (Kadish) 187-188

764. Butts v. Merchants and Mining Trans-   June 16, 1913 230 U. S. 126
      port Co.
      Petitioners 242

765. Simpson v. Shepard   June 9, 1913   230 U. S. 352
      Simpson v. Kennedy
      Simpson v. Shillaber
      "Minnesota Rate Cases"
      Am Consttn (Kelly) 577
      Commerce 156-157
      Sup Ct and Commerce 49

766. Gila Valley, Globe and Northern   Jan 5, 1914   232 U. S. 94
      Railway Co. v. Hall
      *Cases Civil Procedure 846-848

767. Patsone v. Pennsylvania   Jan 19, 1914   232 U. S. 138
      Equality (Warsoff) 270-271

768. Weeks v. United States   Feb 24, 1914   232 U. S. 383
      *Am Consttnl Law (Bartholomew) v. 2, 139-140
      CQ Guide 541, 548-549
      *Cases Civil Liberties 120-122
      *Cases Consttnl Law (Cushman) 350-352
      *Consttnl Criml Procedure (Scarboro) 49-51
      *Consttnl Law (Felkenes) 218-220
      *Consttnl Law (Klein) 52-59
      Criminal Law (Felkenes) 16-18
      Exclusionary 17-18

Freedom Spent 213-215, 218-219
Search and Seizure 63-66

769. United States v. Lexington Mill and   Feb 24, 1914 232 U.S. 399
         Elevator Co.
      *Cases Food 23-27
      *Materials Legislation 74-81

770. Browning v. Waycross   Apr 6, 1914   233 U.S. 16
      *Consttnl Law (Freund) 482-484

771. German Alliance Insurance Co. v.   Apr 20, 1914 233 U.S. 389
         Lewis
      Equality (Warsoff) 267-268

772. Gompers v. United States   May 11, 1914 233 U.S. 604
      Government 382

773. Port Richmond and Bergen Point   June 8, 1914 234 U.S. 317
         Ferry Co. v. Board of Chosen
         Freeholders of Hudson County
      *Consttnl Law (Barrett) 284-285

774. Houston, East and West Texas Railway   June 8, 1914 234 U.S. 342
         Co. v. United States
      "Shreveport Case"
      Am Consttn (Kelly) 577-579
      *Am Consttn (Lockhart) 134-137
      *Am Consttnl Law (Bartholomew) v. 1, 252-253
      *Am Consttnl Law (Mason) 272-274
      *Am Consttnl Law (Saye) 137-139
      *Cases Consttnl Law (Cushman) 195-197
      Commerce 157-158
      *Consttn (Mendelson) 100-101
      *Consttnl Law (Barrett) 211-213
      *Consttnl Law (Freund) 214-217
      *Consttnl Law (Lockhart) 109-111
      Development 150
      *Documents History v. 2, 95-96
      *Liberty v. 2, 316-317
      Sup Ct and Commerce 49-51
      *Sup Ct and Consttn 264-266
      Sup Ct in Crisis 164

775. Eastern States Retail Lumber Dealers'   June 22, 1914 234 U.S. 600
         Association v. United States
      McBride v. United States
      *Antitrust (Posner) 526-530
      *Antitrust Analysis 383-385
      *Govt Regulation 223-227

776. United States v. Reynolds   Nov 30, 1914 235 U.S. 133
      United States v. Broughton
      Petitioners 194-195

777. McCabe v. Atchison, Topeka and   Nov 30, 1914 235 U.S. 151
         Santa Fe Railway
      CQ Guide 609

Equality (Berger) 74
Petitioners 243

778. Lawlor v. Loewe   Jan 5, 1915   235 U. S. 522
      *Labor Law (Twomey) 19-21

779. Coppage v. Kansas   Jan 25, 1915   236 U. S. 1
      Am Consttn (Kelly) 500
      *Am Consttnl Law (Saye) 414-416
      *Cases Labor (Oberer) 50-54
      *Consttnl Law (Barrett) 656
      *Liberty v. 2, 338-340
      *Sup Ct and American Economic Life 101-105
      Sup Ct and Labor 17-18
      This Honorable Court 247

780. Burdick v. United States   Jan 25, 1915   236 U. S. 79
      CQ Guide 224
      *US Prison Law v. 5, 590-601

781. Mutual Film Corporation v. Industrial   Feb 23, 1915   236 U. S. 230
      Commission of Ohio
      *Censorship Landmarks 59-63
      Civil Liberties (Kauper) 75-76
      Communication (Hemmer) v. 1, 183-184
      Great Reversals 149-151
      Movies 10-16
      *Obscenity (Bosmajian) 151-153

782. Fox v. Washington   Feb 23, 1915   236 U. S. 273
      Legacy 189

783. United States v. Midwest Oil Co. Feb 23, 1915   236 U. S. 459
      CQ Guide 216
      *Cases on Environmental Law (Hanks) 474-478
      *Consttnl Politics 317-323

784. Northern Pacific Railway Co. v. North   Mar 8, 1915   236 U. S. 585
      Dakota
      Minneapolis, St. Paul and Sault Ste.
          Marie Railway Co. v. North Dakota
      *Free Enterprise 744-749

785. Sligh v. Kirkwood   Apr 5, 1915   237 U. S. 52
      *Govt and Business 298-300

786. Guffey v. Smith   Apr 5, 1915   237 U. S. 101
      *Federal Courts 719-721

787. Reinman v. Little Rock   Apr 5, 1915   237 U. S. 171
      *Cases Land 344-347

788. Rounds v. Cloverport Foundry and Apr 19, 1915   237 U. S. 303
      Machinery Co.
      *Cases Admiralty 68-69

789. Waugh v. Board of Trustees of   June 1, 1915   237 U. S. 589
      University of Mississippi
      Consttnl Right (Fellman) 36

Digest 34
Education (Lapati) 245
*Education (Spurlock) 157-159
Sup Ct Review 1961 102-103

790. Guinn and Beal v. United States   June 21, 1915 238 U.S. 347
     "Grandfather Clause Case"
     Black 17-18
     CQ Guide 480
     Civil Rights (Bardolph) 211-212
     Civil Rights (Blaustein) 328-333
     Equality (Berger) 77-78
     Least Dangerous 212
     Petitioners 219-220
     Private Pressure 14-15
     *Racial Equality 37
     Rise 71
     Sup Ct Review 1961 204-205
     Sup Ct Review 1969 382-383

791. United States v. Mosley   June 21, 1915 238 U.S. 383
     Petitioners 220-221
     Right of Assembly 147-148
     Sup Ct and Electoral Process 31

792. Truax v. Raich   Nov 1, 1915   239 U.S. 33
     *Am Consttnl Law (Bartholomew) v. 2, 316-317
     Reapportionment (McKay) 176-177
     Sup Ct Review 1077 295-296

793. Glenwood Light and Water Co. v.   Nov 15, 1915   239 U.S. 121
     Mutual Light Heat and Power Co.
     *Cases Federal Courts 230-232

794. Seaboard Air Line Railway v. Koen-   Dec 13, 1915   239 U.S. 352
     necke
     *Cases Civil Procedure 607-608

795. Hadacheck v. Sebastian   Dec 20, 1915   239 U.S. 394
     *Cases Land 506-511
     *Am Land Planning v. 1, 329-335

796. Bi-Metallic Investment Co. v. State   Dec 20, 1915   239 U.S. 441
     Board of Equalization of Colorado
     *Admin Law (Gellhorn) 154-155
     *Admin Law (Schwartz) 303-304
     *Legislation (Linde) 63-64

797. Seven Cases of Eckman's Alternative   Jan 10, 1916   239 U.S. 510
     v. United States
     *Cases Food 310-313

798. Mt. Vernon-Woodberry Cotton Duck Co.   Jan 24, 1916   240 U.S. 30
     v. Alabama Interstate Power Co.
     *Am Land Planning v. 2, 1561-1563

799. Hanover Star Milling Co. v. Metcalf   Mar 6, 1916   240 U.S. 403
     Allen and Wheeler Co. v. Hanover
     Star Milling Co.

*Cases Equity 746-750
*Legal Regulation 354-356

800. Pinel v. Pinel   Apr 3, 1916   240 U.S. 594
      *Cases Federal Courts 255-256

801. American Well Works Co. v. Layne   May 22, 1916   241 U.S. 257
      and Bowler Co.
      *Cases Federal Courts 152-153
      *Federal Courts 873-874
      *Materials Consttnl Law 108-110

802. United States v. Forty Barrels and   May 22, 1916   241 U.S. 265
      Twenty Kegs of Coca Cola
      *Cases Food 18-23

803. New York Life Insurance Co. v. Dun-   June 5, 1916   241 U.S. 518
      levy
      *Civil Procedure (Cound) 608-610
      *Elements Civil 319-320
      Sup Ct Review 1965 279-280

804. Ohio ex rel. Davis v. Hildebrant   June 12, 1916   241 U.S. 565
      Sup Ct and Poltcl Questions 33-34

805. Ex parte United States   Dec 4, 1916   242 U.S. 27
      *US Prison Law v. 1, 149-165

806. Clark Distilling Co. v. Western Mary-   Jan 8, 1917   242 U.S. 311
      land Railway Co.
      Clark Distilling Co. v. American Ex-
      press Co.
      *Am Consttnl Law (Bartholomew) v. 1, 222-223
      *Cases Consttnl Law (Cushman) 182-184
      *Consttnl Law (Freund) 603-606
      *Consttnl Law (Kauper) 437-441
      Sup Ct and Commerce 46-47
      Sup Ct in Crisis 163

807. Caminetti v. United States   Jan 15, 1917   242 U.S. 470
      Diggs v. United States
      Hays v. United States
      *Cases Criml Law (Inbau) 86-94
      *Consttnl Law (Kauper) 140-141
      *Courts Judges 557-560

808. Herbert v. the Shanley Co.   Jan 22, 1917   242 U.S. 591
      John Church Co. v. Hilliard Hotel Co.
      *Cases Copyright (Kaplan) 486-487
      *Cases Copyright (Nimmer) 209-211
      Communication (Hemmer) v. 2, 140
      *Copyright 680-681
      *Sup Ct Speaks 248

809. McDonald v. Mabee   Mar 6, 1917   243 U.S. 90
      *Cases Civil Procedure 354-355
      *Elements Civil 381-382

810. New York Central Railroad Co. v.   Mar 6, 1917   243 U. S. 188
     White
     Am Consttn (Kelly) 500
     *Cases Employment 36-45
     *Cases Workmen 55-62
     *Modern Social Legislation 153-160
     *Statutory History Income 44-56

811. Mountain Timber Co. v. Washington   Mar 6, 1917   243 U. S. 219
     Am Consttn (Kelly) 501

812. Pennington v. Fourth National Bank   Mar 6, 1917   243 U. S. 269
     of Cincinnati
     *Cases Civil Procedure 446-448
     *Elements Civil 318-319

813. Wilson v. New   Mar 19, 1917   243 U. S. 332
     Am Consttn (Kelly) 619-620
     *Documents History v. 2, 123-125
     *Liberty v. 2, 326-327
     Sup Ct in Crisis 162

814. Bunting v. Oregon   Apr 9, 1917   243 U. S. 426
     Am Consttn (Kelly) 498
     *Documents History v. 2, 134-135
     Felix Frankfurter (Phillips) 97-98
     Great Reversals 109
     *Sup Ct and American Economic Life 105-108
     *Sup Ct and Consttn 291-293

815. Motion Picture Patents Co. v. Universal Apr 9, 1917   243 U. S. 502
     Film Manufacturing Co.
     *Antitrust (Posner) 588-594
     *Antitrust Analysis 573-575
     *Govt Regulation 232-238
     Great Reversals 91-96
     *Patent 453-462

816. Marshall v. Gordon   Apr 23, 1917   243 U.S. 521
     CQ Guide 159

817. New York Central Railroad v. Win-   May 21, 1917   244 U. S. 147
     field
     *Consttnl Law (Freund) 457-465
     Court and Consttn v. 1, 215-216
     Legacy 96-99

818. Erie Railroad Co. v. Winfield   May 21, 1917   244 U. S. 170
     Court and Consttn v. 1, 215-216

819. South Pacific Railroad Co. v. Jensen   May 21, 1917   244 U. S. 205
     *Cases Admiralty 23-25
     Court and Consttn v. 1, 215-216

820. Seaboard Air Line Railway v. Blackwell June 4, 1917   244 U. S. 310
     "Blow Post Cases"
     Sup Ct Review 1975 159-160

821. Adams v. Tanner   June 11, 1917 244 U. S. 590
     Am Consttn (Kelly) 501-502
     Court and Consttn v. 1, 217
     Legacy 99-102
     This Honorable Court 259

822. Smith v. Interstate Commerce Com-   Nov 5, 1917   245 U. S. 33
     mission
     *Govt and Business 507-509

823. Buchanan v. Warley   Nov 5, 1917   245 U. S. 60
     *Am Land Planning v. 1, 763-772
     *Bill (Konvitz) 523-526
     CQ Guide 613
     *Civil Rights (Abernathy) 1977 509-510
     Civil Rights (Bardolph) 201-202
     Desegregation (Wasby) 34-35
     *Negro (Franklin) 442-445
     Petitioners 247-250
     *Public Planning 824-828
     *Racial Equality 40-42

824. Jones v. City of Portland   Dec 10, 1917 245 U. S. 217
     *Consttnl Law (Kauper) 1364-1366

825. Hitchman Coal and Coke Co. v.   Dec 10, 1917 245 U. S. 229
     Mitchell
     *Labor Law (Twomey) 14-17
     *Labor Relations (Group Trust) 5-18
     Labor Relations (Taylor) 38-41
     Legacy 119-120
     Sup Ct and Labor 19-21
     This Honorable Court 260

826. Crew Levick Co. v. Pennsylvania   Dec 10, 1917 245 U. S. 292
     *Consttnl Law (Freund) 544-545

827. Arver v. United States   Jan 7, 1918   245 U. S. 366
     Grahl v. United States
     Wangerin v. United States
     Kramer v. United States
     Graubard v. United States
     "Selective Draft Law Case"
     Am Consttn (Kelly) 624
     *Am Consttnl Law (Bartholomew) v. 1, 293-294
     Church and State 114-115
     Development 163-164
     *Liberty v. 2, 358-360
     Religion (Kurland) 37-38
     Sup Ct and Commander in Chief 95
     *Sup Ct and Consttn 321-323
     PERIODICALS:
     *"Selective draft law cases. " Current History 54: 359-363 June
       '68.
     "Supreme Court and conscription, " Carl Brent Swisher. Current
       History 54: 351-357, 365-366 June '68 (3).

828. Weeks v. United States   Feb 4, 1918   245 U. S. 618
     *Cases Food 128-130

829. Board of Trade of Chicago v.   Mar 4, 1918   246 U.S. 231
         United States
     *Antitrust (Posner) 188-192
     *Antitrust Analysis 343-347
     *Cases Antitrust Law 314-318
     *Cases Trade 310
     *Consttnl Law (Kauper) 217-221
     *Govt Regulation 240-243

830. Oetjen v. Central Leather Co.   Mar 11, 1918   246 U.S. 297
     *Freedom vs. National Security 23-26

831. Pendleton v. Benner Line   Mar 25, 1918   246 U.S. 353
     *Cases Admiralty 94-95

832. United States v. Schider   Apr 15, 1918   246 U.S. 519
     *Cases Food 265-266

833. York Manufacturing Co. v. Colley   May 20, 1918   247 U.S. 21
     *Consttnl Law (Freund) 485-486

834. United States v. United Shoe Ma-   May 20, 1918   247 U.S. 32
         chinery Co. of New Jersey
     *Competition 31-35
     *Govt Regulation 244-265

835. Hammer v. Dagenhart   June 3, 1918   247 U.S. 251
     Am Consttn (Kelly) 560-562
     *Am Consttn (Lockhart) 138-140
     *Am Consttnl Law (Bartholomew) v. 1, 254-256
     *Am Consttnl Law (Mason) 274-277
     *Am Consttnl Law (Saye) 139-141
     *Am Consttnl Law (Shapiro) 269-272
     Biography 320-322
     CQ Guide 96-97
     *Cases Consttnl Law (Cushman) 213-217
     *Cases Consttnl Law (Gunther) 135-139
     *Cases Consttnl Law (Rosenblum) 85-89
     Commerce 13-17
     *Comparative 271-274
     *Consttn (Mendelson) 102-106
     *Consttn (Pollak) 318-326
     *Consttnl Cases 211-220
     *Consttnl Law (Barrett) 217-218
     *Consttnl Law (Barron) 172-177
     *Consttnl Law (Freund) 233-237
     *Consttnl Law (Lockhart) 113-116
     *Consttnl Politics 389-394
     *Consttnlism 64-67
     Court and Consttn v. 1, 206-208
     *Documents History v. 2, 119-122
     *Federal System 230-234
     *Govt and Business 225-227
     Great Reversals 125-126
     Impact (Wasby) 107-109
     Justices (Friedman) v. 3, 1790-1794
     Legacy 111-117
     *Liberty v. 2, 335-336
     Perspectives (Black) 27-28

*Processes 300-304
*Sup Ct and American Economic Life 137-143
Sup Ct and Commerce 61-62
*Sup Ct and Consttn 337-340
Sup Ct in Crisis 162-163
Sup Ct in Free Society 158-159
Sup Ct on Trial 167-169
This Honorable Court 261-263

836. United States Glue Co. v. Town of   June 3, 1918   247 U. S. 321
      Oak Creek
      Consttnl Law (Barrett) 398
      *Consttnl Law (Freund) 545-548

837. Chelentis v. Luckenbach Steamship Co.   June 3, 1918   247 U. S. 372
      *Cases Admiralty 323-325
      Sup Ct Review 1964 286-288

838. Toledo Newspaper Co. v. United States   June 10, 1918   247 U. S. 402
      Communication (Hemmer) v. 2, 160
      Great Reversals 127-128
      Sup Ct Review 1978 256

839. United Drug Co. v. Rectanus Co.   Dec 9, 1918   248 U. S. 90
      *Copyright 331-337

840. Ruddy v. Rossi   Dec 9, 1918   248 U. S. 104
      *Am Landmark v. 1, 65-67

841. International News Service v. As-   Dec 23, 1918   248 U. S. 215
      sociated Press
      *Cases Copyright (Kaplan) 587-601
      *Cases Copyright (Nimmer) 539-557
      *Cases Equity 767-775
      Communication (Hemmer) v. 2, 130-131
      Law of Mass 240
      Legacy 266-267
      *Legal Regulation 18-33
      Mass Media (Francois) 567-568
      Sup Ct (Freund) 132-133
      *Sup Ct on Freedom 284-286

842. Nicholas and Co. v. United States   Mar 3, 1919   249 U. S. 34
      Shaw and Co. v. United States
      *Cases Regulation 464-466

843. Schenck v. United States   Mar 3, 1919   249 U. S. 47
      Baer v. United States
      Am Consttn (Kelly) 633
      *Am Consttn Law (Bartholomew) v. 2, 56
      *Am Consttnl Law (Mason) 553-554
      *Am Consttnl Law (Shapiro) 350-351
      *Basic Cases 165-167
      *Bill (Cohen) 49-50
      CQ Guide 397
      *Cases Civil Liberties 213-215
      *Cases Consttnl Law (Cushman) 443-445
      *Cases Consttnl Law (Gunther) 1119-1120
      *Cases Individual 653-655

Changing 91-92
*Civil Rights (Abernathy) 1977 381-382
Communication (Hemmer) v. 1, 16-17
*Consttn (Hirschfield) 94-96
*Consttn (Mendelson) 388-389
Consttnl Law (Barrett) 1128-1129
*Consttnl Law (Felkenes) 125-127
*Consttnl Law (Freund) 1131-1132
*Consttnl Law (Kauper) 1067-1068
*Consttnl Law (Klein) 478-480
*Consttnl Politics 525-527
Court and Consttn v. 1, 202-203
*Documents History v. 2, 146-147
First Amendment (Berns) 149-151
*Free Speech (Summers) 29-31
Freedom and the Court 228-229
Freedom of Speech (Haiman) 5
Freedom of Speech (Hudon) 59, 69-70
Freedom of Speech (Shapiro) 48-49, 50
*Freedom of the Press (Nelson) 60-66
Freedom Spent 75-76
*Freedom vs National Security 448-451
Handbook 11-13
Historic Decisions 112-115
Judiciary (Abraham) 109-110
*Law Power 461-463
Legacy 189-194
*Liberty v. 2, 360-361
*Mass Communications 10-12
*Mass Media (Devol) 5-7
*Political Rights 72-74
*Principles Freedom 127-130
Private Conscience 67-68
*Protest 36-38
Spirit 50-51
*Sup Ct and Am Govt 173-176
*Sup Ct and Consttn 324-326
Sup Ct and Uses 88-89
*Sup Ct on Freedom 17-18
Sup Ct Review 1978 256-257
Sup Ct in Crisis 166-167
System 64-65
This Honorable Court 264-265

844. United States v. Doremus   Mar 3, 1919   249 U.S. 86
Am Consttn (Kelly) 562
*Am Consttnl Law (Bartholomew) v. 1, 157
*Cases Consttnl Law (Cushman) 162-165
*Govt and Business 338-339

845. North Pacific Steamship Co. v. Hall   Mar 3, 1919   249 U.S. 119
Brothers Marine Railway and
Shipbuilding Co.
*Cases Admiralty 49-53

846. Frohwerk v. United States   Mar 10, 1919 249 U.S. 204
CQ Guide 397
*Cases Consttnl Law (Gunther) 1121-1122
*Cases Individual 655-657

Legacy 194-196
Sup Ct and Uses 88

847. Debs v. United States   Mar 10, 1919 249 U. S. 211
      Bill (Cohen) 51-53
      CQ Guide 397-398
      *Cases Consttnl Law (Gunther) 1122-1124
      *Cases Individual 657-659
      Communication (Hemmer) v. 1, 17
      First Amendment (Berns) 167-168
      Freedom of Speech (Hudon) 60
      Legacy 196-200
      This Honorable Court 266
      PERIODICALS:
      "Supreme Court and conscription," Carl Brent Swisher. Current
          History 54: 351-357 June '68 (3).

848. Houston v. St. Louis Independent   Apr 14, 1919 249 U. S. 479
      Packing Co.
      *Govt and Business 599-601

849. Northern Pacific Railway Co. v.   June 2, 1919 250 U. S. 135
      North Dakota
      Am Consttn (Kelly) 624-625
      *Liberty v. 2, 355-356

850. United States v. Colgate and Co.   June 2, 1919 250 U. S. 300
      *Antitrust (Posner) 237-239
      *Antitrust Analysis 554-555
      *Cases Antitrust Law 532-535
      *Cases Trade 455-459
      *Competition 356-357
      *Govt Regulation 266-269

851. American Manufacturing Co. v.   June 9, 1919 250 U. S. 459
      St. Louis
      Consttnl Law (Barrett) 410

852. Groesbeck v. Duluth South Shore   Nov 10, 1919 250 U. S. 607
      and Atlantic Railway
      *Free Enterprise 738-740

853. Abrams v. United States   Nov 10, 1919 250 U. S. 616
      Am Consttn (Kelly) 635-636
      *Am Consttn (Lockhart) 525-530
      *Am Primer 665-671
      *Annals v. 14, 244-247
      *By These Words 455-465
      CQ Guide 398-399
      *Cases Consttnl Law (Gunther) 1124-1131
      *Cases Consttnl Rights 324-329
      Changing 92-93
      Communication (Hemmer) v. 1, 17-19
      *Consttn (Morris) 157-159
      *Consttn (Pollak) v. 2, 9-11
      Consttnl Law (Barrett) 1129-1130
      *Consttnl Law (Barron) 734-736
      *Consttnl Law (Freund) 1133-1134
      *Consttnl Law (Lockhart) 659-663

  *Documents History v. 2, 148-149
  First Amendment (Berns) 151-155
  Freedom and the Court 230-232
  *Freedom of Speech (Haiman) 6-7
  Freedom of Speech (Hudon) 60-62, 71-73
  Freedom of Speech (Shapiro) 48-49, 50
  Freedom Spent 77
  Judiciary (Abraham) 110-111
  Justice Frankfurter 19-21
  *Justices (Friedman) v. 3, 1763-1766, 2088-2091
  *Law Power 463-468
  Legacy 202-210
  *Liberty v. 2, 361-365
  *Mass Communications 12-15
  Mass Media (Francois) 26
  Perspectives (Black) 84-85
  *Political Rights 11-12
  *Principles Freedom 131-142
  Private Conscience 68-69
  *Prophets 244-248
  *Protest 39-47
  *Sup Ct and Consttn 327-329
  Sup Ct and Uses 89-90
  Sup Ct in Crisis 167
  Sup Ct in Free Society 47
  *Sup Ct on Freedom 19-20
  *Sup Ct Speaks 211-212
  This Honorable Court 267-268

854. Hamilton v. Kentucky Distilleries Dec 15, 1919 215 U.S. 140
  Dryfoos v. Edwards
   *Am Consttnl Law (Bartholomew) v. 1, 291-292
   Sup Ct and Commander in Chief 82-85

855. Ruppert v. Caffey   Jan 5, 1920 251 U.S. 264
   Sup Ct and Commander in Chief 82-85

856. Silverthorne Lumber Co. v. United Jan 26, 1920 251 U.S. 385
   States
   *Consttnl Criml Procedure (Scarboro) 53-54
   Defendants 292-293
   Exclusionary 31
   Freedom Spent 216-217
   Search and Seizure 66-67

857. United States v. United States Steel Mar 1, 1920 251 U.S. 417
   Corporation
   *Annals v. 14, 258-265
   *Antitrust (Posner) 366-376
   *Cases Antitrust Law 175-185
   *Competition 36-42
   *Govt Regulation 270-281
   *Justices (Friedman) v. 3, 1742-1751, 1794-1798
   *Liberty v. 2, 375-376
   *Selected Antitrust Cases 16-24
   *Sources American Republic v. 2, 107-111

858. Schaefer v. United States Mar 1, 1920 251 U.S. 466
  Vogel v. United States

Werner v. United States
Darkow v. United States
Lemke v. United States
    CQ Guide 399
    Freedom of Speech (Hudon) 60-62, 117-118
    Legacy 210-213
    Sup Ct Review 1978 257-258
    This Honorable Court 266

859. Shaffer v. Carter   Mar 1, 1920   252 U.S. 37
      *Consttnl Law (Barrett) 376-377
      *School Law (Alexander) 771-775

860. Travis v. Yale and Towne Manufacturing Mar 1, 1920 252 U.S. 60
         Co.
      *Govt and Business 64-66

861. United States v. Schrader's Son, Inc. Mar 1, 1920   252 U.S. 85
      *Govt Regulation 282-284

862. Eisner v. Macomber   Mar 8, 1920   252 U.S. 189
      Court and Consttn v. 1, 208-210

863. Pierce v. United States   Mar 8, 1920   252 U.S. 239
      Am Consttn (Kelly) 634
      CQ Guide 399-400
      Freedom of Speech (Hudon) 60-62, 118
      Legacy 213-214
      Sup Ct in Crisis 167-168
      This Honorable Court 266-267

864. Missouri v. Holland   Apr 19, 1920   252 U.S. 416
      Am Consttn (Kelly) 642-644
      *Am Consttn (Lockhart) 202-204
      *Am Consttnl Issues 181-183
      *Am Consttnl Law (Bartholomew) v. 1, 114-115
      *Am Consttnl Law (Mason) 110-111
      *Am Consttnl Law (Shapiro) 140-142
      *Basic Cases 257-260
      CQ Guide 202-203
      *Cases Consttnl Law (Cushman) 227-229
      *Cases Consttnl Law (Gunther) 250-251
      *Comparative 219-221
      *Consttn (Mendelson) 179-181
      *Consttn (Pollak) 351-355
      *Consttnl Cases 141-144
      *Consttnl Law (Barrett) 267-270
      *Consttnl Law (Felkenes) 90-92
      *Consttnl Law (Freund) 695-697
      *Consttnl Law (Grossman) 1023-1024
      *Consttnl Law (Kauper) 274-276
      *Consttnl Law (Lockhart) 217-219
      *Consttnl Politics 350-353
      *Documents History v. 2, 163-164
      *Federal System 147-149
      Foreign Affairs 144-147
      Government 379-382
      *Liberty v. 2, 370-371
      *Sup Ct and Am Govt 77-81

Sup Ct in Crisis 168-169
Sup Ct Review 1975 77-122

865. Ward v. Love County Board of Com-   Apr 26, 1920   253 U.S. 17
        missioners
      *Federal Courts 517-521

866. Green v. Frazier   June 1, 1920   253 U.S. 233
        Am Consttn (Kelly) 507
      *Am Land Planning v. 2, 1573-1579
      *Documents History v. 2, 170-172
      *Govt and Business 352-356

867. Ohio Valley Water Co. v. Ben Avon   June 1, 1920   253 U.S. 287
        Borough
      *Govt and Business 646-648

868. Rhode Island v. Palmer   June 7, 1920   253 U.S. 350
      New Jersey v. Palmer
      Dempsey v. Boynton
      Kentucky Distilleries v. Gregory
      Feigenspan v. Bodine
      Sawyer v. Manitowoc Products
      St. Louis Brewing Association v. Moore
      "National Prohibition Cases"
        Am Consttn (Kelly) 638-639
        Court and Consttn v. 1, 254-255
      *Documents History v. 2, 156-157
      *Justices (Friedman) v. 3, 1954-1955
        Sup Ct and Poltcl Questions 103-104
        Sup Ct in Crisis 168

869. Federal Trade Commission v. Gratz   June 7, 1920   253 U.S. 421
        Am Consttn (Kelly) 678-679

870. Piedmont and Georges Creek Coal Co.   Oct 11, 1920   254 U.S. 1
        v. Seaboard Fisheries
      *Cases Admiralty 281-285

871. Johnson v. Maryland   Nov 8, 1920   254 U.S. 51
      *Am Consttn (Lockhart) 347
      *Consttn (Mendelson) 225-226
      *Consttnl Law (Freund) 644-645
      *Consttnl Law (Kauper) 489-490

872. Underwood Typewriter Co. v.   Nov 15, 1920   254 U.S. 113
        Chamberlain
      *Consttnl Law (Freund) 549-551

873. Thames Towboat Co. v. The Francis   Dec 6, 1920   254 U.S. 242
        McDonald
      *Cases Admiralty 222-223

874. United States v. Lehigh Valley Railroad   Dec 6, 1920   254 U.S. 255
      *Govt Regulation 296-302

875. Gilbert v. Minnesota   Dec 13, 1920   254 U.S. 325
        Freedom of Speech (Hudon) 63-64, 76-77
        Inquiring 41-54; reprinted from New Republic Jan 26, 1921

Legacy 215-218
Sup Ct in Free Society 289

876. Duplex Printing Press v. Deering   Jan 3, 1921   254 U.S. 443
      Am Consttn (Kelly) 653-654
      *Cases Labor (Cox) 59-69
      *Cases Labor (Oberer) 61-71
      Court and Consttn v. 1, 210-212
      *Documents History v. 2, 177-178
      *Labor Law (Herman) 48-51
      *Labor Law (Twomey) 23-29
      *Labor Relations (Getman) 6-13
      Labor Relations (Taylor) 57-58
      Legacy 122-127
      *Liberty v. 2, 379-380
      *Nature 856-865
      Sup Ct and Labor 15-16
      This Honorable Court 261

877. United States v. L. Cohen Grocery Co.   Feb 28, 1921   255 U.S. 81
      Am Consttn (Kelly) 625
      Sup Ct and Commander in Chief 96-97

878. Smith v. Kansas City Title and   Feb 28, 1921   255 U.S. 180
         Trust Co.
      *Federal Courts 879-882
      *Materials Consttnl Law 111-115

879. Gouled v. United States   Feb 28, 1921   255 U.S. 298
      CQ Guide 542
      *Rights (Shattuck) 9
      Search and Seizure 67-68
      Self-Inflicted Wound 214

880. United States ex rel. Milwaukee Social   Mar 7, 1921   255 U.S. 407
         Democratic Publishing Co. v.
         Burleson
      "Milwaukee Leader Case"
      Communication (Hemmer) v. 2, 195-196
      Federal Censorship 35-37
      Inquiring 55-61; reprinted from Nation Mar 23, 1921
      *Mass Communications 145-151
      *Sup Ct on Freedom 183-186

881. Block v. Hirsh   Apr 18, 1921   256 U.S. 135
      Am Consttn (Kelly) 659

882. Newberry v. United States   May 2, 1921   256 U.S. 232
      CQ Guide 171-172
      Sup Ct and Electoral Process 67-68

883. Brown v. United States   May 16, 1921   256 U.S. 335
      *Cases Criml (Perkins) 696-698

884. American Bank and Trust Co. v.   May 16, 1921   256 U.S. 350
         Federal Reserve Bank of Atlanta
      Monetary Decisions 58-59

885. Burdeau v. McDowell   June 1, 1921   256 U.S. 465

Arrest (Waddington) 159
Defendants 259-260
Exclusionary 18-19
Law of Arrest (Creamer) 341-346
Search and Seizure 68-70

886. American Steel Foundries v. Tri-   Dec 5, 1921   257 U.S. 184
City Central Trades Council
Labor Law (Twomey) 30-31
*Labor Relations (Group Trust) 29-35
Labor Relations (Taylor) 78-79
Right of Assembly 185-186
*Sup Ct Speaks 256-261

887. Dahnke-Walker Milling Co. v. Bondurant Dec 12, 1921   257 U.S. 282
*Federal Courts 631-637

888. Truax v. Corrigan   Dec 19, 1921   257 U.S. 312
Court and Consttn v. 1, 233-234
*Documents History v. 2, 174-177
Equality (Warsoff) 182-185
*Justices (Friedman) v. 3, 1766-1768, 2060-2071
Labor Relations (Taylor) 79-83
Legacy 129-136
*Liberty v. 2, 384-385
Quest 126
*Sup Ct and Consttn 344-347
This Honorable Court 273-274
William Howard Taft 237-242

889. American Column and Lumber Co. v.   Dec 19, 1921   257 U.S. 377
United States
*Antitrust (Posner) 193-204
*Antitrust Analysis 323-328
*Cases Antitrust Law 381-393
*Cases Trade 351-362
*Competition 226-231
*Free Enterprise 503-519
*Govt Regulation 303-313
*Justices (Friedman) v. 3, 2091-2100
Legacy 174-176
PERIODICALS:
"Supreme Court and American trade associations, 1921-1925, " M.
Browning Carrott. Bus History R 44: 320-338 Autumn '70
(4).

890. Federal Trade Commission v. Beech-   Jan 3, 1922   257 U.S. 441
Nut Packing Co.
*Govt Regulation 314-320

891. Terral v. Burke Construction Co.   Feb 27, 1922   257 U.S. 529
*Federal Courts 684-685

892. Railroad Commission of Wisconsin v.   Feb 27, 1922   257 U.S. 563
Chicago, Burlington and Quincy
Railroad
"Wisconsin Railroad Fares Case"
*Consttnl Law (Barrett) 213-214
*Consttnl Law (Kauper) 134-137

　　　*Documents History v. 2, 167-168
　　　*Liberty v. 2, 373-374
　　　Sup Ct in Crisis 181-182

893. Lemke v. Farmers Grain Co. of   Feb 27, 1922   258 U. S. 50
　　　Embden, N. D.
　　　Commerce 200-201

894. Leser v. Garnett   Feb 27, 1922   258 U. S. 130
　　　Sup Ct and Poltcl Questions 104-105

895. United States v. Balint   Mar 27, 1922   258 U. S. 250
　　　*Criminal Law (Dix) 281-282
　　　*Criminal Law (Kadish) 128-129
　　　Criminal Law (Wells) 110-111, 113
　　　Sup Ct Review 1962 113-114

896. United States v. Behrman   Mar 27, 1922   258 U. S. 280
　　　*Cases Drug 474-478
　　　Criminal Law (Wells) 110-111, 113

897. Balzac v. Porto Rico   Apr 10, 1922   258 U. S. 298
　　　*Documents History v. 2, 178-181

898. Standard Fashion Co. v. Magrane-   Apr 10, 1922   258 U. S. 346
　　　Houston Co.
　　　*Am Landmark v. 7, 734-736
　　　*Cases Antitrust Law 793-795
　　　*Cases Trade 543-546
　　　*Competition 334-337
　　　*Govt Regulation 321-323
　　　*Selected Antitrust Cases 316-322

899. United States v. Moreland   Apr 17, 1922   258 U. S. 433
　　　*Cases Criml (Perkins) 13-16

900. United Shoe Machinery Corporation v. Apr 17, 1922   258 U. S. 451
　　　United States
　　　*Competition 314-317
　　　*Govt Regulation 324-329

901. Federal Trade Commission v. Winsted   Apr 24, 1922   258 U. S. 483
　　　Hosiery Co.
　　　Communication (Hemmer) v. 2, 327-328

902. Stafford v. Wallace   May 1, 1922   258 U. S. 495
　　　Burton v. Clyne
　　　　Am Consttn (Kelly) 652
　　　*Am Consttnl Law (Mason) 278-279
　　　*Commerce 197-198
　　　*Govt and Business 231-232
　　　Sup Ct and Commerce 53-54
　　　Sup Ct and Consttn 359-362
　　　Sup Ct in Free Society 159-160
　　　Sup Ct on Trial 157-158
　　　*Sup Ct Speaks 251-254
　　　William Howard Taft 242-244

903. Bailey v. Drexel Furniture Co.   May 15, 1922   259 U. S. 20

"Child Labor Tax Case"
*Am Consttn (Lockhart) 141-143
*Am Consttnl Law (Bartholomew) v. 1, 158-159
*Am Consttnl Law (Mason) 325-327
*Am Consttnl Law (Saye) 156-157
Basic History 54-55
Biography 323-324
CQ Guide 114
*Cases Consttnl Law (Cushman) 160-162
*Cases Consttnl Law (Gunther) 213-217
*Commerce 105-106, 232-236
*Consttn (Mendelson) 133-136
*Consttnl Law (Barron) 226-228
*Consttnl Law (Felkenes) 78-81
*Consttnl Law (Freund) 237-240
*Consttnl Law (Kauper) 197-201
*Consttnl Law (Lockhart) 156-159
Court and Consttn v. 1, 235-236
*Documents History v. 2, 153-154
Impact (Wasby) 109
*Justices (Friedman) v. 3, 2122-2126
*Liberty v. 2, 380-381
Perspectives (Black) 28
*Processes 305-308
*Sup Ct and American Economic Life 144-148
*Sup Ct and Consttn 340-343
Sup Ct in Crisis 186-187
This Honorable Court 275-276
William Howard Taft 244-248

904. Hill v. Wallace   May 15, 1922 259 U.S. 44
        Elements Judicial 44-45, 131
        William Howard Taft 207

905. Union Tool Co. v. Wilson   May 15, 1922 259 U.S. 107
        *Injunctions 841-842

906. United States v. Southern Pacific Co. May 29, 1922 259 U.S. 214
        *Cases Antitrust Law 186-189
        *Govt Regulation 330-338

907. Carlisle Packing Co. v. Sandanger   Mar 20, 1922 259 U.S. 255
        Sup Ct Review 1964 305-306

908. United Mine Workers of America v.   June 5, 1922 259 U.S. 344
        Coronado Coal Co.
        *Materials Legislation 217-220
        William Howard Taft 202-203

909. Keogh v. Chicago and Northwestern   Nov 13, 1922 260 U.S. 156
        Railroad Co.
        *Cases Regulated 439-442

910. Zucht v. King   Nov 13, 1922 260 U.S. 174
        *Cases Federal Courts 840-842
        Digest 35
        Education (Spurlock) 160-162
        *Federal Courts 643-644

911. Kline v. Burke Construction Co.   Nov 20, 1922   260 U.S. 226
      *Cases Federal Courts 378-382

912. Heisler v. Thomas Colliery Co.   Nov 27, 1922   260 U.S. 245
      *Consttnl Law (Freund) 538-540

913. United States v. Lanza   Dec 11, 1922   260 U.S. 377
      *Am Consttnl Law (Bartholomew) v. 2, 159
      CQ Guide 571
      Double (Miller) 42-48
      Double (Sigler) 56-58
      *Govt and Business 11

914. Pennsylvania Coal Co. v. Mahon   Dec 11, 1922   260 U.S. 393
      *Am Consttn (Lockhart) 378-379
      *Cases Consttnl Law (Gunther) 546-549
      *Cases Consttnl Rights 138-139
      *Cases Individual 196-199
      *Consttnl Law (Barrett) 680-682
      *Consttnl Law (Kauper) 1348-1353
      *Land Ownership 614-618
      Legacy 267-270
      *Sup Ct Speaks 238-240

915. Osaka Shosen Kaisha v. Pacific Export   Jan 2, 1923   260 U.S. 490
      Lumber Co.
      The Saigon Mara
      *Cases Admiralty 235-237

916. Federal Trade Commission v. Curtis   Jan 8, 1923   260 U.S. 568
      Publishing Co.
      *Govt Regulation 339-343

917. Moore v. Dempsey   Feb 19, 1923   261 U.S. 86
      Civil Rights (Bardolph) 203-204
      *Civil Rights (Blaustein) 341-342
      *Consttn (Mendelson) 306-308
      *Consttnl Law (Kauper) 883-886
      Defendants 119-120
      *Due Process 114
      Petitioners 232-237
      Private Pressure 17
      This Honorable Court 281-282

918. Columbia Railway, Gas and Electric   Feb 19, 1923   261 U.S. 236
      Co. v. South Carolina
      *Consttnl Law (Kauper) 1369-1372

919. Federal Trade Commission v. Sin-   Apr 9, 1923   261 U.S. 463
      clair Refining Co.
      Federal Trade Commission v. Standard
      Oil Co. (New Jersey)
      Federal Trade Commission v. Gulf
      Refining Co.
      Federal Trade Commission v. Ma-
      loney Oil and Manufacturing
      Co.
      *Antitrust Analysis 584-585
      *Cases Antitrust Law 646-649

*Competition 338-339
*Govt Regulation 344-348

920. Adkins v. Children's Hospital of the   Apr 9, 1923   261 U.S. 525
         District of Columbia
      Adkins v. Lyons
         Am Consttn (Kelly) 656-658
         *Am Consttnl Law (Shapiro) 317-321
         *Annals v. 14, 391-399
         Biography 313-317
         CQ Guide 327
         *Cases Consttnl Law (Rosenblum) 89-97
         *Consttnl Law (Barrett) 657-658
         *Consttnl Law (Klein) 114-127
         *Consttnl Politics 449-453
         Court and Consttn v. 1, 240-243
         *Documents History v. 2, 187-191
         Equality (Warsoff) 277-279
         Franklin D. Roosevelt 74-79
         Great Reversals 110-113
         *Justices (Friedman) v. 3, 2126-2129, 2144-2153
         Legacy 142-149
         *Liberty v. 2, 382-383
         *Sex Discrimination 1975 42-47
         Sup Ct (North) 54-55
         *Sup Ct and American Economic Life 108-118
         *Sup Ct and Consttn 347-355
         Sup Ct in Crisis 184-185
         Sup Ct on Trial 179-180
         This Honorable Court 276-277
         William Howard Taft 248-250
      PERIODICALS:
         "Big switch: Justice Roberts and the minimum wage cases," John
            W. Chambers. Labor History 10: 44-73 Winter '69 (3).

921. Board of Trade of Chicago v. Olsen   Apr 16, 1923   262 U.S. 1
         *Commerce 198-199
         William Howard Taft 244

922. Oliver Iron Mining Co. v. Lord   May 7, 1923   262 U.S. 172
         *Consttnl Law (Barrett) 410-411

923. Missouri ex rel. Southwestern Bell   May 21, 1923   262 U.S. 276
         Telephone v. Public Service
         Commission of Missouri
         *Cases Regulated 86-96
         Legacy 274-278

924. United States v. American Linseed   June 4, 1923   262 U.S. 371
         Oil Co.
         *Competition 232-235
      PERIODICALS:
         "Supreme Court and American trade associations, 1921-1925," M.
            Browning Carrott. Bus History R   44: 320-338 Autumn '70
            (4).

925. Meyer v. Nebraska   June 4, 1923   262 U.S. 390
         *Am Consttnl Law (Mason) 631-633

*Bill (Konvitz) 90-94
Church and State 115
Communication (Hemmer) v. 1, 108-109
Conceived 52
*Consttn (Morris) 205-210
*Consttnl Law (Barrett) 697-698
*Consttnl Law (Kauper) 629-632
Digest 48
*Due Process 207-208
*Education (Hazard) 38-42
Education (Lapati) 155-156
*Education (Spurlock) 162-167
*Essentials 102-105
*Family 514-515
*First Amendment (Konvitz) 137-141
First Amendment (Marnell) 149-151
Garden 121-123
*Judicial Excerpts 41-42
*Justices (Friedman) v. 3, 2034-2037
Landmark Decisions 11-17
*Law and Public Education (Goldstein) 65-71
Legacy 258-261
*Principles School 187-190
*Public School Law 60-63
Public Schools 31-35
*Public Schools 36-40
*Rights (Shattuck) 97
School in the Legal Structure 69-70
*School Law (Alexander) 298-300
*School Law (Remmlein) 253-255
System 598-599
*Teacher 109-111
This Honorable Court 282
*Two Swords 256-259
PERIODICALS:
"Concept of freedom in education, " William W. Brickman.   Eductnl
    Rec 45: 74-83 Winter '64 (5).
"Education, Americanization and the Supreme Court: the 1920's, "
    Kenneth B. O'Brien.   Am Q 13: 161-171 Summer '61 (3).
"Education and parents' rights, " Bonnie Hume.   Religious Eductn
    60: 460-466, 472 Nov '65 (2).

926. Bartels v. Iowa   June 4, 1923   262 U.S. 404
      Bohning v. Ohio
      Pohl v. Ohio
      Digest 49

927. Massachusetts v. Mellon   June 4, 1923   262 U.S. 447
      Frothingham v. Mellon
      By What Right 274
      CQ Guide 291
      *Cases Consttnl Law (Cushman) 23-26
      Cases Consttnl Law (Gunther) 1617-1618
      *Cases Federal Courts 11-16
      *Consttnl Law (Barron) 59-63
      Consttnl Law (Felkenes) 27-30
      *Consttnl Law (Freund) 103-107
      *Consttnl Law (Kauper) 23-26
      *Consttnl Law (Klein) 442-447

*Federal System 53-54
Power 37
Sup Ct and Religion 95-96
Sup Ct in Crisis 187

928. Wolff Packing Co. v. Court of   June 11, 1923 262 U.S. 522
      Industrial Relations of Kansas
      Am Consttn (Kelly) 659-660
      *Documents History v. 2, 186-187
      *Govt and Business 258-259
      *Liberty v. 2, 385-387
      Sup Ct and Consttn 356-358
      Sup Ct in Free Society 243
      William Howard Taft 251-253

929. Pennsylvania v. West Virginia   June 11, 1923 262 U.S. 553
      Ohio v. West Virginia
      *Consttnl Law (Barrett) 335-337
      *Consttnl Law (Freund) 390-396

930. Farmers and Merchants Bank of   June 11, 1923 262 U.S. 649
      Monroe, N.C. v. Federal Reserve
      Bank of Richmond
      Monetary Decisions 59-60

931. Anderson, Warden, U.S. Penitentiary,   Nov 12, 1923   263 U.S. 193
      Leavenworth, Kansas v. Corall
      *US Prison Law v. 4, 361-365

932. Terrace v. Thompson   Nov 12, 1923   263 U.S. 197
      Equality (Warsoff) 277

933. Craig v. Hecht   Nov 19, 1923   263 U.S. 255
      William Howard Taft 144

934. National Association of Window Glass   Dec 10, 1923   263 U.S. 403
      Manufacturers v. United States
      *Cases Antitrust Law 318-319
      *Cases Trade 269-270
      *Govt Regulation 349-350

935. Dayton-Goose Creek Railway v.   Jan 7, 1924   263 U.S. 456
      United States
      *Documents History v. 2, 169-170

936. Federal Trade Commission v. Ray-   Jan 7, 1924   263 U.S. 565
      mond Brothers-Clark Co.
      *Antitrust Analysis 254
      *Cases Trade 473-476
      *Govt Regulation 351-353

937. Myers v. United States   Feb 18, 1924   264 U.S. 95
      *Injunctions 833-834

938. Federal Trade Commission v.   Mar 17, 1924   264 U.S. 298
      American Tobacco Co.
      Federal Trade Commission v. P.
      Lorillard Co.
      *Admin Law (Schwartz) 199-200

*Am Landmark v. 6, 605-614

939. Panama Railroad v. Johnson   Apr 7, 1924   264 U.S. 375
     *Cases Admiralty 326-329

940. First National Bank of Greeley v.   Apr 7, 1924   264 U.S. 450
     Weld County Board of Commissioners
     *Govt and Business 581-583

941. Burns Baking Co. v. Bryan   Apr 14, 1924   264 U.S. 504
     Legacy 153-155
     This Honorable Court 278

942. Chastleton Corporation v. Sinclair   Apr 21, 1924   264 U.S. 543
     *Consttnl Law (Freund) 334-336

943. Hester v. United States   May 7, 1924   265 U.S. 57
     Arrest (Waddington) 77-78

944. United States and Interstate Commerce May 26, 1924   265 U.S. 274
     Commission v. Abilene and
     Southern Railway Co.
     *Govt and Business 481-482

945. Asakura v. Seattle   May 26, 1924   265 U.S. 332
     Foreign Affairs 166

946. United States v. 95 Barrels (More   June 2, 1924   265 U.S. 438
     or Less) Alleged Apple Cider
     Vinegar
     *Cases Food 117-119

947. United Leather Workers International June 9, 1924   265 U.S. 457
     Union v. Herkert and Meisel
     Trunk Co.
     Labor Relations (Taylor) 62-64

948. William R. Warner and Co. v. Eli   June 9, 1924   265 U.S. 526
     Lilly and Co.
     *Copyright 82-86

949. Ziang Sung Wan v. United States   Oct 13, 1924   266 U.S. 1
     Inquiring 89-98; reprinted from New
     Republic Nov 12, 1924
     Sup Ct and Confessions 27-28

950. Michaelson v. United States ex rel.   Oct 20, 1924   266 U.S. 42
     Chicago, St. Paul, Minneapolis
     and Omaha Railway Co.
     *Cases Consttnl Law (Cushman) 39-41

951. Ex parte Grossman   Mar 2, 1925   267 U.S. 87
     "Contempt Pardon Case"
     *Am Consttnl Law (Bartholomew) v. 1, 131-132
     *Am Consttnl Law (Saye) 119-121
     *Injunctions 798-804

952. Carroll v. United States   Mar 2, 1925   267 U.S. 132
     *Am Consttnl Law (Bartholomew) v. 2, 137-138

    *Arrest (Waddington) 140-141
    CQ Guide 547
    *Consttnl Criml Procedure (Scarboro) 209-211
    Criminal Law (Felkenes) 60-62
    Defendants 281
    Law of Arrest (Markle) 125
    Search and Seizure 88-92

953. Buck v. Kuykendall   Mar 2, 1925   267 U.S. 307
    *Consttnl Law (Barrett) 287-289
    *Consttnl Law (Freund) 407-408
    *Consttnl Law (Kauper) 334-337

954. Mitchell v. United States   Mar 2, 1925   267 U.S. 341
    *Land Ownership 899-902

955. Brooks v. United States   Mar 9, 1925   267 U.S. 432
    Am Consttn (Kelly) 652

956. Coronado Coal Co. v. United Mine   May 25, 1925 268 U.S. 295
      Workers of America
    *Cases Labor (Oberer) 72-76
    Labor Relations (Taylor) 59-62

957. United States v. Dickey   May 25, 1925 268 U.S. 378
    Sup Ct Review 1978 259

958. Pierce v. Society of the Sisters of the June 1, 1925 268 U.S. 510
      Holy Names of Jesus and Mary
    Pierce v. Hill Military Academy
    *Am Consttnl Law (Saye) 204-205
    Authority 18, 139-140
    *Bill (Konvitz) 04-06
    Church and State 116
    Church State and Freedom 514-516, 629-630
    *Civil Rights (Abernathy) 1977 338-339
    Conceived 52
    *Consttn (Mendelson) 566-567
    *Consttn (Morris) 75-79
    Consttnl Law (Barrett) 698
    *Consttnl Law (Kauper) 632-633
    *Consttnl Rights (Kemerer) 57-59
    Digest 16
    *Documents History v. 2, 197-198
    Education (Lapati) 157-158
    Education (Spurlock) 169-170
    *Educational Policy 1-4
    Expanding Liberties 55-56, 60
    *First Amendment (Konvitz) 141-144
    First Amendment (Marnell) 151-154
    Freedom and the Court 325
    *Judicial Excerpts 10-11
    Landmark Decisions 19-26
    Law and Education 195
    *Law and Public Education (Goldstein) 33-36
    *Principles School 109-111
    Private Conscience 160-161
    Public Schools 40-47
    *Public Schools 47-48

Religion (Drinan) 122-126
Religion (Katz) 60-61
Religion (Kurland) 27-28
Religious Freedom (Arnold) 43
*Religious Freedom (Pfeffer) 153-155
Render 37-38
*Rights (Shattuck) 98-99
School Bus 33-35
School in the Legal Structure 62-63
*School Law (Alexander) 272-274
*School Law (Remmlein) 199-201
*Sup Ct and Education 3-5
System 599-600
*Teacher 136-138
This Honorable Court 283
*Two Swords 304-306
PERIODICALS:
   "Charter for private schools; Oregon's failure to suppress," Harold
      J. Noah.   Times Educatnl Supp 2546:   575   Mar 6 '64.
   "Concept of freedom in education," William W. Brickman.   Educatnl
      Rec 45:   74-83   Winter '64 (5).
   "Education and parents' rights," Bonnie Hume.   Religious Eductn
      60:   460-466, 472 Nov '65 (2).
   "Education, Americanization and the Supreme Court: the 1920's,"
      Kenneth B. O'Brien.   Am Q 13:   161-171 Summer '61 (3).
   "Look at the Oregon School Case after fifty years," C. Albert Koob.
      Religious Eductn 71:   164-170 Mar '76.
   "Religion in education," William B. Ball.   America 108:   528-530,
      532   Apr 20 '63.   Reaction: 108:   640-643   May 4 '63.   818
      June 8 '63.   109:   15   July 6 '63
   "Separation of school and state; Pierce reconsidered: First Amend-
      ment rights," Stephen Arons.   Harvard Eductnl R 46:   76-104
      Feb '76.

959. Maple Flooring Manufacturers Asso-   June 1, 1925   268 U.S. 563
         ciation v. United States
      *Antitrust (Posner) 205-212
      *Antitrust Analysis 328-332
      *Cases Antitrust Law 394-397
      *Competition 236-241
      *Free Enterprise 520-522
      *Govt Regulation 354-361
      *Liberty v. 2, 376-378
      PERIODICALS:
      "Supreme Court and American trade associations, 1921-1925," M.
         Browning Carrott.   Bus History R 44:   320-338 Autumn '70
         (4).

960. Cement Manufacturers Protection   June 1, 1925   268 U.S. 588
         Association v. United States
      *Antitrust Analysis 385-387
      *Competition 242-244
      *Govt Regulation 362-368
      PERIODICALS:
      See listing at 268 U.S. 563, entry no. 959.

961. Robertson v. Railroad Labor Board   June 8, 1925   268 U.S. 619
      *Federal Courts 1103-1106

962. Gitlow v. New York   June 8, 1925   268 U.S. 652
        Am Consttn (Kelly) 664
        *Am Consttnl Law (Bartholomew) v. 2, 58-60
        *Am Consttnl Law (Mason) 554-556
        *Annals v. 14, 476-480
        *Basic Cases 167-174
        Bill (Cohen) 59-61
        CQ Guide 344, 401, 404
        *Cases Civil Liberties 215-218
        *Cases Consttnl Law (Cushman) 445-448
        *Cases Consttnl Law (Gunther) 1137-1141
        *Cases Individual 673-679
        *Civil Liberties (Sweet) 80-81
        *Civil Rights (Abernathy) 1977 384-385
        Communication (Hemmer) v. 1, 19-20
        Conceived 43-47
        *Consttn (Mendelson) 392-395
        *Consttnl Law (Barrett) 1132-1136
        *Consttnl Law (Barron) 740-742
        *Consttnl Law (Freund) 1134-1137
        *Consttnl Law (Kauper) 1070-1076
        *Consttnl Law (Klein) 480-488
        *Consttnl Politics 530-535
        *Documents History v. 2, 198-201
        First Amendment (Berns) 155-159
        Freedom and the Court 60-61, 233-235
        *Freedom of Speech (Haiman) 8-9
        Freedom of Speech (Hudon) 64-65
        Freedom of Speech (Shapiro) 49
        *Freedom of the Press (Nelson) 78-87
        Freedom Spent 70-80
        Inquiring 99-107; reprinted from New Republic July 1, 1925
        Judiciary (Abraham) 112
        Justice Frankfurter 21-22
        *Justices (Friedman) v. 3, 2210-2218
        Law of Mass 36-37
        *Leading Consttnl Decisions 242-250
        Legacy 222-226
        *Liberty v. 2, 393-394
        *Mass Communications 18-20
        Mass Media (Francois) 26
        Movies 16-20
        *Political Rights 79-86
        Politics 23-25
        *Principles Freedom 145-157
        *Readings American 129-134
        *Sup Ct and Consttn 330-333
        Sup Ct in Free Society 289-290
        *Sup Ct on Freedom 21-23
        Sup Ct Review 1978 258
        *Sup Ct Speaks 214-215
        System 102-105
        This Honorable Court 283-284
      PERIODICALS:
        "From Gitlow to Near," Klaus H. Heberle. J Poltcs 34: 458-483
          May '72 (6).

963. Agnello v. United States   Oct 12, 1925   269 U.S. 20
        *Am Consttnl Law (Bartholomew) v. 2, 128-129

Search and Seizure 99
Sup Ct Review 1977 108

964. Central Union Telephone Co. v.   Nov 23, 1925   269 U.S. 190
      Edwardsville
      *Consttnl Law (Kauper) 96-97

965. Ex parte Gruber   Dec 14, 1925   269 U.S. 302
      *Federal Courts 288

966. Metcalf and Eddy v. Mitchell   Jan 11, 1926   269 U.S. 514
      *Cases Consttnl Law (Cushman) 147-149

967. Alexander Milburn Co. v. Davis-   Mar 8, 1926   270 U.S. 390
      Bournonville Co.
      *Legal Regulation 947-950

968. Weaver v. Palmer Brothers Co.   Mar 8, 1926   270 U.S. 402
      *Consttn (Mendelson) 261
      *Consttnl Law (Barrett) 658-659

969. Tutun v. United States   Apr 12, 1926   270 U.S. 568
      Neuberger v. United States
      *Federal Courts 93-95

970. Moore v. New York Cotton Exchange   Apr 12, 1926   270 U.S. 593
      *Cases Federal Courts 686-690

971. Corrigan v. Buckley   May 24, 1926   271 U.S. 323
      Desegregation (Wasby) 35-36
      Petitioners 252-254
      Sup Ct Review 1977 202

972. Raffel v. United States   June 1, 1926   271 U.S. 494
      Sup Ct Review 1977 142-143

973. Myers v. United States   Oct 25, 1926   272 U.S. 52
      Am Consttn (Kelly) 675-676
      *Am Consttnl Law (Bartholomew) v. 1, 101-104
      CQ Guide 212-214
      *Cases Consttnl Law (Cushman) 99-105
      *Cases Consttnl Law (Rosenblum) 355-361
      Consttn (Wilcox) 42
      *Consttnl Cases 96-105
      *Consttnl Law (Freund) 653
      *Consttnl Law (Grossman) 996-1003
      *Consttnl Politics 336-341
      Court and Consttn v. 1, 277-280
      *Documents History v. 2, 206-208
      Executive Privilege 55-57
      *Federal System 106-110
      Freedom and Reform 291-295
      *Historic Decisions 116-121
      Power 194-195
      Sup Ct and Uses 52-70
      Sup Ct in Crisis 187-188
      Sup Ct in Free Society 59-60
      Watergate 83-97
      William Howard Taft 225-226, 253-254

974. Dorchy v. Kansas   Oct 25, 1926   272 U. S. 306
     *Cases Labor (Cox) 688-689
     *Cases Labor (Handler) 581-583
     *Cases Labor (Oberer) 344-346
     *Labor Law (Meltzer) 395-396

975. Euclid v. Ambler Realty Co.   Nov 22, 1926   272 U. S. 365
     *Am Consttnl Law (Bartholomew) v. 2, 216-217
     *Am Land Planning v. 1, 336-350
     *Cases Land 521-529
     *Cases Property (Casner) 1192-1202
     *Cases Property (Donahue) 1200-1207
     *Consttnl Law (Barrett) 689-691
     *Consttnl Law (Freund) 1105-1109
     *Consttnl Law (Kauper) 1356-1363
     *Land Ownership 674-681
     *Land Use 194-203
     *Legal Foundations 76-80
     *Managing 638-645
     *Public Planning 386-393

976. United States v. General Electric Co. Nov 23, 1926   272 U. S. 476
     *Antitrust (Posner) 240-244, 284-286
     *Antitrust Analysis 451-454, 517-520
     *Cases Antitrust Law 344-352
     *Cases Trade 434-437, 885-887
     *Govt Regulation 369-375
     *Selected Antitrust Cases 414-416

977. Federal Trade Commission v. Western   Nov 23, 1926   272 U. S. 554
        Meat Co.
     Thatcher Manufacturing Co. v. Federal
        Trade Commission
     Swift and Co. v. Federal Trade Com-
        mission
     *Competition 87-90
     *Selected Antitrust Cases 128

978. Byars v. United States   Jan 3, 1927   273 U. S. 28
     Search and Seizure 70-71

979. DiSanto v. Pennsylvania   Jan 17, 1927   273 U. S. 34
     *Consttn (Mendelson) 208-209
     *Sup Ct (Mendelson) 132-135
     Sup Ct in Free Society 120

980. Mosler Safe Co. v. Ely-Norris   Jan 17, 1927   273 U. S. 132
        Safe Co.
     *Legal Regulation 77-78

981. McGrain v. Daugherty   Jan 17, 1927   273 U. S. 135
     Am Consttn (Kelly) 676-677
     *Am Consttnl Law (Bartholomew) v. 1, 72-73
     CQ Guide 159-160
     *Cases Consttnl Law (Cushman) 46-51
     *Congress Investigates v. 4, 2525-2541
     *Consttn (Mendelson) 427-430
     *Consttnl Aspects v. 3, 11-58
     *Criminal Law (Wells) 44-46

*Federal System 255-258
*First Amendment (Konvitz) 608-619
*Justices (Friedman) v. 3, 1956-1969
Law and Politics 52-53
*Liberty v. 2, 371-373
Watergate 25-27

982. DeForest Radio Telephone and Tele-   Feb 21, 1927 273 U. S. 236
      graph Co. v. United States
      *Patent 771-776

983. Farrington v. Tokushige   Feb 21, 1927 273 U. S. 284
      Authority 18-19
      Church State and Freedom 631
      Digest 77-78
      Education (Spurlock) 172
      *Educational Policy 32-35
      PERIODICALS:
      "Concept of freedom in education," William W. Brickman. Eductnl
      Rec 45: 74-83 Winter '64 (5).
      "Education, Americanization and the Supreme Court: the 1920's,"
      Kenneth B. O'Brien. Am Q 13: 161-171 Summer '61.

984. Eastman Kodak of New York v. Southern Feb 21, 1927 273 U. S. 359
      Photo Materials
      *Antitrust (Posner) 804-806
      *Antitrust Analysis 254-255

985. United States v. Trenton Potteries Co. Feb 21, 1927 273 U. S. 392
      *Antitrust (Posner) 63-65
      *Antitrust Analysis 267-268
      *Cases Antitrust Law 296-301
      *Competition 209-210
      *Consttnl Law (Kauper) 212-216
      *Govt Regulation 376-382
      *Selected Antitrust Cases 65-67
      *Text Antitrust 52-55

986. Tyson and Brother-United Theatre   Feb 28, 1927 273 U. S. 418
      Ticket Offices v. Banton
      Am Consttn (Kelly) 660
      Court and Consttn v. 1, 296-297
      *Documents History v. 2, 204-206
      *Justices (Friedman) v. 3, 1768-1769
      Legacy 158-162
      *Liberty v. 2, 387-388
      *Sup Ct Speaks 242-243
      This Honorable Court 278-279

987. Tumey v. Ohio   Mar 7, 1927   273 U. S. 510
      *Consttn (Mendelson) 305
      *Consttnl Law (Schmidhauser) 381-389
      Defendants 117
      *Due Process 108
      Impact (Wasby) 201-202

988. Nixon v. Herndon   Mar 7, 1927   273 U. S. 536
      Black 25-27
      Civil Rights (Bardolph) 212

Desegregation (Wasby) 30
*Documents History v. 2, 217-218
Freedom and the Court 396-397
Petitioners 222-223
Private Pressure 15
Rise 73-75
Sup Ct and Electoral Process 68
Sup Ct Review 1961 206

989.   Bedford Cut Stone Co. v. Journeymen   Apr 11, 1927   274 U.S. 37
            Stone Cutters' Association of North
            America
        Am Consttn (Kelly) 654
        Court and Consttn v. 1, 291
        Labor Relations (Taylor) 64-66
        Legacy 127-129
        This Honorable Court 279
        William Howard Taft 228-230

990.   Buck v. Bell   May 2, 1927   274 U.S. 200
        *Am Consttnl Issues 419-420
        *Comparative 389-390
        *Consttnl Law (Kauper) 633-635
        *Consttnl Politics 657-659
        *Documents History v. 2, 216-217
        Freedom and the Court 112-114
        *Liberty v. 2, 389-390
        Private Conscience 125-126
        US Sup Ct 107-108

991.   United States v. Sisal Sales Corporation May 16, 1927   274 U.S. 268
        *Cases Regulation 30-33
        *Cases Trade 1152-1155
        *Govt Regulation 383-385

992.   Burns v. United States   May 16, 1927   274 U.S. 328
        Freedom of Speech (Hudon) 65-66
        Inquiring 129-130

993.   Hess v. Pawloski   May 16, 1927   274 U.S. 352
        *Cases Civil Procedure 377-380
        *Civil Procedure (Carrington) 895-897
        *Civil Procedure (Cound) 67-69
        *Elements Civil 270-272

994.   Whitney v. California   May 16, 1927   274 U.S. 357
        *Am Consttn (Lockhart) 533-538
        *Am Consttnl Law (Mason) 557-561
        *Am Consttnl Law (Shapiro) 351-354
        *Bill (Cohen) 61-64
        CQ Guide 404
        Communication (Hemmer) v. 1, 20-21
        *Cases Consttnl Law (Gunther) 1143-1148
        *Cases Consttnl Rights 332-336
        *Cases Individual 680-685
        *Consttn (Mendelson) 390-392
        *Consttn (Morris) 159-160
        Consttnl Law (Barrett) 1136-1137
        *Consttnl Law (Barron) 743-747

*Consttnl Law (Freund) 1140-1143
*Consttnl Law (Kauper) 1077-1082
*Consttnl Law (Lockhart) 673-677
Court and Consttn v. 1, 246-247
First Amendment (Berns) 175-176
*First Amendment (Franklin) 76-78
*Freedom and Protection 97-99
Freedom and the Court 235-237
*Freedom of Speech (Haiman) 10-12
Freedom of Speech (Hudon) 65-66, 74-75
Freedom of Speech (Shapiro) 49-50
Inquiring 117-127, 131-133
Judiciary (Abraham) 112-113
Justice Frankfurter 22-25
Legacy 227-230
*Liberty v. 2, 395-397
*Mass Communications 21-25
Mass Media (Francois) 26
*Political Rights 12
*Principles Freedom 158-163
*Prophets 249-254
*Sup Ct (Mendelson) 109-124
*Sup Ct and Consttn 333-336
*Sup Ct on Freedom 23-25
*Sup Ct Speaks 219-223
System 105-107
PERIODICALS:
"From Gitlow to Near," Klaus H. Heberle. J Poltcs 34: 458-483 May '72 (6).

995. Fiske v. Kansas   May 16, 1927 274 U. S. 380
      CQ Guide 404-405
      *Federal Courts 574-577
      Inquiring 128-129
      System 107
      PERIODICALS:
      See listing at 274 U. S. 357, entry no. 994.

996. Biddle v. Perovich   May 31, 1927 274 U. S. 480
      CQ Guide 227

997. Merritt and Chapman Derrick and   May 31, 1927 274 U. S. 611
        Wrecking Co. v. United States
      *Cases Admiralty 582-583

998. Federal Trade Commission v. East- May 31, 1927 274 U. S. 619
        man Kodak Co.
      *Govt Regulation 386-390

999. United States v. International Har- June 6, 1927 274 U. S. 693
        vester Co.
      *Competition 43-46
      *Govt Regulation 391-397

1000. Gong Lum v. Rice   Nov 21, 1927 275 U. S. 78
       Desegregation (Wasby) 29
       Digest 78-79
       Disaster 23
       Education (Lapati) 269

*Education (Spurlock) 187-189
*Law Lawyers 156-160
Petitioners 215
Warren (Hudgins) 17-18

1001. Marron v. United States   Nov 21, 1927 275 U.S. 192
      Arrest (Waddington) 70
      *Consttnl Criml Procedure (Scarboro) 389-391
      Search and Seizure 100-101

1002. Robins Dry Dock and Repair v. Flint   Dec 12, 1927 275 U.S. 303
      *Cases Admiralty 409-410

1003. Gambino v. United States   Dec 12, 1927 275 U.S. 310
      Search and Seizure 71-72

1004. Miller v. Schoene   Feb 20, 1928 276 U.S. 272
      *Am Consttn (Lockhart) 379-380
      *Cases Consttnl Law (Gunther) 549-550
      *Cases Consttnl Rights 139-140
      *Cases Individual 199-200
      *Consttnl Law (Barrett) 682-683
      *Consttnl Law (Freund) 1095-1097
      *Consttnl Law (Kauper) 1355-1356
      *Public Planning 711-713

1005. Swift and Co. v. United States   Mar 19, 1928 276 U.S. 311
      *Cases Antitrust Law 1334-1339
      *Govt Regulation 398-404
      *Injunctions 349-354

1006. Hampton, J. W., Jr. and Co. v.   Apr 9, 1928 276 U.S. 394
      United States
      *Am Consttnl Law (Bartholomew) v. 1, 84-86, 154
      *Cases Consttnl Law (Cushman) 62-65
      *Commerce 186-188
      Consttn (Barber) 75-82

1007. Black and White Taxicab and Trans- Apr 9, 1928 276 U.S. 518
      fer Co. v. Brown and Yellow
      Taxicab and Transfer Co.
      Dissent 47-48

1008. Dugan v. Ohio   May 14, 1928 277 U.S. 61
      Defendants 117

1009. Plamals v. S.S. Pinar del Rio   May 14, 1928 277 U.S. 151
      Sup Ct Review 1964 306-307

1010. Nectow v. Cambridge   May 14, 1928 277 U.S. 183
      *Am Land Planning v. 1, 351-353
      *Cases Property (Casner) 1203-1206
      *Land Ownership 683-685
      *Land Use 205-207

1011. Willing v. Chicago Auditorium Asso- May 21, 1928 277 U.S. 274
      ciation
      Cases Consttnl Law (Gunther) 1611
      Felix Frankfurter (Mendelson) 20

1012.   Reed v. Delaware County, Pa.   May 28, 1928   277 U. S. 376
        County Commissioners
        CQ Guide 164

1013.   Quaker City Cab Co. v. Pennsylvania   May 28, 1928   277 U. S. 389
        Equality (Warsoff) 283-284
        Legacy 163-165

1014.   Olmstead v. United States   June 4, 1928   277 U. S. 438
        Green v. United States
        McInnis v. United States
        *Am Consttnl Law (Bartholomew) v. 2, 130-132
        *Am Consttnl Law (Mason) 689-693
        *Bill (Cohen) 519-523
        CQ Guide 550-551
        *Cases Civil Liberties 84-89
        *Cases Consttnl Law (Cushman) 314-319
        *Civil Liberties (Sweet) 234-236
        Communication (Hemmer) v. 1, 238-239
        *Consttnl Aspects v. 4, 343-365
        *Consttnl Criml Procedure (Scarboro) 707-714
        *Consttnl Law (Felkenes) 244-245
        Court and Consttn v. 1, 261-264
        Criminal Law (Felkenes) 128-131
        *Criminal Law (Kadish) 1063
        Defendants 285-286
        Freedom and the Court 161, 169
        Freedom Spent 217
        *Freedom Spent 242
        Great Reversals 182
        *Law Power 162-164
        *Leading Consttnl Cases 330-338
        *Liberty v. 2, 400-403
        Police 145-149
        Politics 244-245
        Privacy (Westin) 340-341
        Prophets 54-79
        *Prophets 207-217
        *Right to Privacy 35-40
        *Rights (Shattuck) 10-11
        Search and Seizure 200-206
        Sup Ct (Freund) 133-137
        Sup Ct Review 1962 218-228
        Sup Ct Review 1979 177-178
        *Sup Ct Speaks 225-229
        *These Liberties 267-276
        William Howard Taft 227, 255-259
        Wiretapping.
        *Wiretapping 104-122
        PERIODICALS:
        "Right to be let alone. " Economist 226: 28, 31 Jan '68 (2).

1015.   Foster-Fountain Packing Co. v.   Oct 15, 1928   278 U. S. 1
        Haydel
        Consttnl Law (Barrett) 337
        *Consttnl Law (Freund) 398-400

1016.   New York ex rel. Bryant v. Zim-   Nov 19, 1928   278 U. S. 63
        merman

        *Comparative 600-602
        *Consttnl Law (Freund) 1230-1232
        *Consttnl Law (Kauper) 99-101
        Consttnl Rights (Fellman) 71-73
        Free Speech (Kurland) 79-80
        Negro (Kalven) 91
        Sup Ct Review 1961 129-131

1017.   Louis K. Liggett Co. v. Baldridge   Nov 19, 1928   278 U.S. 105
        Legacy 170

1018.   Williams v. Standard Oil Co. of   Jan 2, 1929   278 U.S. 235
        Louisiana
        Williams v. Texas
        *Consttnl Law (Barrett) 659-660
        *Consttnl Law (Kauper) 53-55

1019.   George Van Camp and Sons Co. v.   Jan 2, 1929   278 U.S. 245
        American Can Co.
        *Competition 257-259

1020.   Frost v. Corporation Commission   Feb 18, 1929   278 U.S. 515
        of Oklahoma
        *Free Enterprise 394-402

1021.   Sinclair v. United States   Apr 8, 1929   279 U.S. 263
        *Congress Investigates v. 4, 2541-2550
        Law and Politics 53
        *Materials Legislation 486-489
        Watergate 25-27

1022.   Ex parte Bakelite Corporation   May 20, 1929   279 U.S. 438
        *Cases Consttnl Law (Cushman) 42-45
        *Consttnl Politics 285-290

1023.   St. Louis and O'Fallon Railway Co.   May 20, 1929   279 U.S. 461
        v. United States
        Am Consttn (Kelly) 679-680
        Legacy 278-279

1024.   United States v. California Cooperative May 20, 1929   279 U.S. 553
        Canneries
        *Injunctions 355-357

1025.   Barry v. United States ex rel. Cunning- May 27, 1929   279 U.S. 597
        ham
        CQ Guide 164

1026.   United States v. Schwimmer   May 27, 1929   279 U.S. 644
        *Conscience 187-192
        Freedom and the Court 276
        Justice 68-76
        Private Conscience 57-59
        Religion (Drinan) 17
        *Religious Freedom (Pfeffer) 110-113
        *Sup Ct Speaks 244-246

1027.   Okanogan Indians v. United States   May 27, 1929   279 U.S. 655
        "Pocket Veto Case"

*Am Consttnl Law (Bartholomew) v. 1, 126-128
CQ Guide 222-223
*Legislative (Hetzel) 792-796
PERIODICALS:
"Presidential pocket-veto power; a constitutional anachronism?"
   John W. Dumbrell and John D. Lees. Poltcl Studies 28: 109-
   116 Mar '80 (2).

1028. Gonzalez v. Roman Catholic Archbishop Oct 14, 1929   280 U. S. 1
       of Manila
       Sup Ct Review 1969 363-364

1029. Sanitary Refrigerator Co. v. Winters Oct 14, 1929   280 U. S. 30
       Winters v. Dent Hardware Co.
       *Patent 137-145

1030. United Railways and Electric Co.   Jan 6, 1930   280 U. S. 234
       of Baltimore v. West
       *Free Enterprise 665-676

1031. International Shoe Co. v. Federal   Jan 6, 1930   280 U. S. 291
       Trade Commission
       *Competition 95-98
       *Govt Regulation 405-410

1032. Kentucky v. Indiana   Apr 14, 1930   281 U. S. 163
       *Federal Courts 258-261

1033. Alexander Sprunt and Son v.   Apr 14, 1930   281 U. S. 249
       United States
       *Introduction (Mashaw) 809-812

1034. Patton v. United States   Apr 14, 1930   281 U. S. 276
       *Am Consttnl Law (Bartholomew) v. 2, 166-167
       Procedures 89-90

1035. Cochran v. Louisiana Board of   Apr 28, 1930   281 U. S. 370
       Education
       *Am Consttnl Law (Bartholomew) v. 2, 30-31
       Church and State 116-117
       Church State and Freedom 558-559
       Digest 16-17
       Education (Lapati) 165-168
       *Education (Spurlock) 76-77
       Expanding Liberties 11-12
       First Amendment (Marnell) 164-166
       Freedom and the Court 323
       Landmark Decisions 27-32
       Law and Education 278
       *Law and Public Education (Hamilton) 36-37
       *Public School Law 70-71
       Public Schools 84-86
       *Public Schools 86-87
       Religion (Kurland) 28-31
       School Bus 35-36
       *School Law (Alexander) 180-181
       *School Law (Remmlein) 251-252
       *Teacher 91-92
       *Two Swords 124-125

PERIODICALS:
"Federal aid to education and the religious controversy," Hurley
H. Doddy. J Negro Eductn 30: 83-86 Spring '61 (2).
"Public money for parochial schools?" E. Dale Doak. Eductnl
Leader 26: 246-249 Dec '68 (4).
"Sectarian schools court favors," Roy B. Allen and Robert Mar-
shall. Phi Delta Kappan 46: 426-430 May '65 (2).

1036. Eliason v. Wilborn   May 19, 1930 281 U.S. 457
      *Cases Property (Casner) 925-927

1037. Federal Radio Commission v. General May 19, 1930 281 U.S. 464
      Electric Co.
      *Consttn (Mendelson) 54-55

1038. Texas and New Orleans Railroad Co.   May 26, 1930 281 U.S. 548
      v. Brotherhood of Railway and
      Steamship Clerks
      *Cases Labor (Oberer) 98-105
      *Labor Law (Herman) 90-93
      *Labor Law (Meltzer) 140-147
      *Labor Relations (Group Trust) 38-44
      Sup Ct and Labor 23-24

1039. Baldwin v. Missouri   May 26, 1930 281 U.S. 586
      *Basic History 138-139

1040. Paramount Famous Lasky Corporation   Nov 24, 1930 282 U.S. 30
      v. United States
      *Antitrust Analysis 381-382
      *Cases Antitrust Law 440-443
      *Consttnl Law (Kauper) 277-281
      *Govt Regulation 411-413

1041. United States v. First National   Nov 24, 1930 282 U.S. 44
      Pictures
      *Antitrust Analysis 382-383

1042. O'Gorman and Young v. Hartford Fire   Jan 5, 1931   282 U.S. 251
      Insurance Co.
      O'Gorman and Young v. Phoenix As-
      surance Co.
      Equality (Warsoff) 282
      *Justices (Friedman) v. 3, 2071-2073

1043. Go-Bart Importing Co. v. United States Jan 5, 1931 282 U.S. 344
      Search and Seizure 101-102

1044. Alford v. United States   Feb 24, 1931 282 U.S. 687
      *Law of Evidence 259-263

1045. Husty v. United States   Feb 24, 1931 282 U.S. 694
      Law of Arrest (Markle) 127

1046. United States v. Sprague   Feb 24, 1931 282 U.S. 716
      Sup Ct and Poltcl Questions 105

1047. McBoyle v. United States   Mar 9, 1931   283 U.S. 25
      *Cases Criml Law (Hall) 44-45

*Law Power 79-80
*Nature 125-126

1048. Carbice Corporation of America v.   Mar 9, 1931   283 U. S. 27
       American Patents Development
       Corporation
       *Antitrust (Posner) 594-597
       *Govt Regulation 414-416
       *Patent 462-469

1049. Herron v. Southern Pacific Railroad   Apr 13, 1931   283 U. S. 91
       *Cases Federal Courts 637-639

1050. Standard Oil Co. (Indiana) v. United   Apr 13, 1931   283 U. S. 163
       States
       *Antitrust (Posner) 288-292
       *Cases Antitrust Law 365-373
       *Cases Trade 937-942
       *Consttn (Wilcox) 474-479
       *Govt Regulation 417-424

1051. Buck v. Jewell-Lasalle Realty Co.   Apr 13, 1931   283 U. S. 191
       *Cases Copyright (Nimmer) 215-220

1052. Aldridge v. United States   Apr 20, 1931   283 U. S. 308
       Civil Rights (Bardolph) 204-205

1053. Stromberg v. California   May 18, 1931   283 U. S. 359
       *Bill (Cohen) 358-359
       Communication (Hemmer) v. 1, 49-50
       Freedom and the Court 62
       Freedom of Speech (Hudon) 81
       *Liberty v. 2, 397-398
       Politics 34-35
       Sup Ct in Crisis 192-193
       This Honorable Court 291-292

1054. Arizona v. California   May 18, 1931   283 U. S. 423
       *Commerce 240-241

1055. New Jersey v. New York City   May 18, 1931   283 U. S. 473
       *Am Land Planning v. 1, 241-246

1056. Gasoline Products Co. v. Champlin   May 18, 1931   283 U. S. 494
       Refining Co.
       *Cases Civil Procedure 842-846
       *Elements Civil 989-992

1057. Baldwin v. Iowa State Traveling   May 18, 1931   283 U. S. 522
       Men's Association
       *Cases Civil Procedure 374-377
       *Cases Federal Courts 362-364
       *Cases Pleading 311-313

1058. Board of Tax Commissioners of   May 18, 1931   283 U. S. 527
       Indiana v. Jackson
       Equality (Warsoff) 284-285

1059. United States v. Macintosh   May 25, 1931   283 U. S. 605

Church and State 117-118
*Conscience 193-203
Freedom and the Court 276
Justice 89-97
Private Conscience 59-63
Religion (Drinan) 18
Religious Liberty 35-37
Sup Ct and Religion 57
Sup Ct in Crisis 193

1060. Federal Trade Commission v.   May 25, 1931   283 U.S. 643
       Raladam Co.
       Communication (Hemmer) v. 2, 328-329
       *Competition 383-386

1061. Near v. Minnesota ex rel. Olsen   June 1, 1931   283 U.S. 697
       Am Consttn (Kelly) 145-148
       *Am Consttn (Lockhart) 752-755
       *Am Consttnl Issues 235-241
       *Am Consttnl Law (Bartholomew) v. 2, 82-84
       *Am Consttnl Law (Mason) 584-587
       *Am Consttnl Law (Saye) 333-336
       *Bill (Konvitz) 329-334
       CQ Guide 425
       *Cases Civil Liberties 242-246
       *Cases Consttnl Law (Cushman) 472-476
       *Cases Consttnl Law (Gunther) 1505-1507
       *Cases Consttnl Rights 626-620
       *Cases Individual 919-923
       *Civil Liberties (Sweet) 118-119
       *Civil Rights (Abernathy) 1977 357-362
       Communication (Hemmer) v. 2, 196-197
       *Comparative 502-504
       Conceived 85-90
       *Consttn (Mendelson) 413-416
       *Consttnl Law (Barrett) 1225-1228
       *Consttnl Law (Freund) 1146-1149
       *Consttnl Law (Kauper) 1172-1180
       *Consttnl Law (Lockhart) 914-916
       *Consttnl Rights (Kemerer) 145-148
       *First Amendment (Konvitz) 278-285
       Freedom of Speech (Haiman) 43
       Freedom of Speech (Hudon) 81-82
       *Freedom of the Press (Nelson) 88-97
       Handbook 34-36
       Law of Mass 44-47
       *Leading Consttnl Decisions 266-274
       *Liberty v. 2, 398-400
       *Mass Communications 110-116
       Mass Media (Clark) 21-23
       *Mass Media (Devol) 35-38
       Mass Media (Francois) 37-39
       *Modern Consttnl Law 54-59
       Movies 20-24
       *Political Rights 674-679
       Power 229-230
       Sup Ct (North) 111-112
       *Sup Ct and Consttn 481-485
       Sup Ct and Uses 72-74

Sup Ct in Crisis 193-194
*Sup Ct on Freedom 43-48
Sup Ct Review 1978 260-261
System 504-506
This Honorable Court 292
PERIODICALS:
"From Gitlow to Near, " Klaus H. Heberle. J Poltcs 34: 458-
483 May '72 (6).

1062. United States v. Murdock   Nov 23, 1931 284 U.S. 141
       *Am Consttnl Law (Bartholomew) v. 2, 150

1063. Marine Transit Corporation v.   Jan 4, 1932 284 U.S. 263
       Dreyfus
       *Cases Admiralty 190-193

1064. Blockburger v. United States   Jan 4, 1932 284 U.S. 299
       *Criminal Justice (Way) 265-267

1065. Leman v. Krentler-Arnold Hinge   Feb 15, 1932 284 U.S. 448
       Last Co.
       *Cases Civil Procedure 995-1000
       *Injunctions 739-740

1066. Crowell v. Benson   Feb 23, 1932 285 U.S. 22
       *Admin Law (Schwartz) 678-685
       *Federal Courts 324-330
       *Govt and Business 637-645
       *Materials Consttnl Law 34-40
       Sup Ct in Free Society 38-39

1067. Packer Corporation v. Utah   Feb 23, 1932 285 U.S. 105
       Free Speech (Kurland) 377
       Sup Ct Review 1974 268

1068. New State Ice Co. v. Liebmann   Mar 21, 1932 285 U.S. 262
       *Annals v. 15, 140-148
       *Documents History v. 2, 229-232
       *Free Enterprise 317-336
       *Sup Ct and American Economic Life 151-155
       Sup Ct from Taft 177-180
       This Honorable Court 292-293

1069. Smiley v. Holm   Apr 11, 1932 285 U.S. 355
       Democratic 107-110
       Law and Politics 193-194
       Sup Ct and Electoral Process 207
       Sup Ct and Poltcl Questions 37-38

1070. Koenig v. Flynn   Apr 11, 1932 285 U.S. 375
       Sup Ct and Poltcl Questions 39

1071. Carroll v. Becker   Apr 11, 1932 285 U.S. 380
       Sup Ct and Poltcl Questions 39-40

1072. Burnet v. Coronado Oil and Gas Co.   Apr 11, 1932 285 U.S. 393
       *Sup Ct Speaks 231-233

1073. United States v. Lefkowitz   Apr 11, 1932 285 U.S. 452
       Search and Seizure 102

1074.   The Linseed King   Apr 11, 1932   285 U.S. 502
        Spencer Kellogg and Sons, Inc. v.
            Hicks
        Alexander v. Spencer Kellogg and
            Sons, Inc.
            *Cases Admiralty 95-97

1075.   United States v. Smith   May 2, 1932   286 U.S. 6
            Presidential Power 80-82; reprinted from J Politics 1: 17-61
            Feb '39

1076.   Nixon v. Condon   May 2, 1932   286 U.S. 73
            Black 28-31
            Desegregation (Wasby) 30
            Petitioners 223-225
            Sup Ct and Electoral Process 68-69

1077.   United States v. Swift and Co.   May 2, 1932   286 U.S. 106
        American Wholesale Grocers Associa-
            tion v. Swift and Co.
        National Wholesale Grocers Association
            v. Swift and Co.
            *Govt Regulation 425-430
            *Injunctions 359-366

1078.   Bradford Electric Light v. Clapper May 16, 1932   286 U.S. 145
            *Cases Workmen 540-545

1079.   Atlantic Cleaners and Dyers v.   May 23, 1932   286 U.S. 427
            United States
            Commerce 49-50

1080.   Wood v. Broom   Oct 18, 1932   287 U.S. 1
            Law and Politics 194
            Sup Ct and Electoral Process 208
            Sup Ct and Poltcl Questions 40-41

1081.   Powell v. Alabama   Nov 7, 1932   287 U.S. 45
        Patterson v. Alabama
        Weems v. Alabama
        "Scottsboro Cases"
            Am Consttn (Kelly) 665
            *Am Consttnl Law (Bartholomew) v. 2, 244-246
            *Am Consttnl Law (Mason) 719-722
            *Am Consttnl Law (Saye) 514-515
            CQ Guide 345, 565-566
            *Cases Civil Liberties 49-54
            *Cases Consttnl Law (Cushman) 279-284
            *Civil Rights (Abernathy) 1977 190-192
            *Civil Rights (Bardolph) 206-207
            *Consttn (Pollak) v. 2, 130-140
            *Consttnl Law (Felkenes) 304-306
            *Consttnl Law (Kauper) 894-895
            *Consttnl Law (Maddex) 39-43
            Criminal Law (Felkenes) 174-176
            Criminal Procedure (Wells) 5-6
            *Due Process 38-39
            Equality (Warsoff) 303-306
            Felix Frankfurter (Baker) 265-267

Freedom and the Court 63-64
Justice Rutledge 233
*Justices (Friedman) v. 3, 2169-2179
*Leading Consttnl Cases 408-416
*Leading Consttnl Decisions 196-205
*Negro (Franklin) 380-387
Petitioners 266-269
*Police 113-115
Procedures 109-111
Rationing 95-97
Scottsboro.
Sup Ct (North) 126-127
Sup Ct and Confessions 35
*Sup Ct and Criml Process 551-554
*These Liberties 22-28
This Honorable Court 337

1082.   United States v. Shreveport Grain   Nov 7, 1932   287 U. S. 77
        and Elevator Co.
        *Materials Legislation 90-93

1083.   Gebardi v. United States   Nov 7, 1932   287 U. S. 112
        *Cases Criml (Perkins) 319-322
        *Criminal Law (Kadish) 480-483

1084.   Sgro v. United States   Dec 5, 1932   287 U. S. 206
        Arrest (Waddington) 101

1085.   Reichelderfer v. Quinn   Dec 5, 1932   287 U. S. 315
        *Public Planning 718-719
        Sup Ct Review 1962 79

1086.   Sterling v. Constantin   Dec 12, 1932   287 U. S. 378
        Court Years 150
        Sup Ct and Commander in Chief 206
        Sup Ct in Free Society 63

1087.   Earle and Stoddart, Inc. v. Ellerman's Dec 12, 1932   287 U. S. 420
        Wilson Line
        The Galileo
        *Cases Admiralty 466-468

1088.   Sorrells v. United States   Dec 19, 1932   287 U. S. 435
        Criminal Law (Wells) 100-103

1089.   Wabash Valley Electric Co. v.   Jan 9, 1933   287 U. S. 488
        Young
        *Free Enterprise 736-738

1090.   Nashville Chattanooga and St. Louis   Feb 6, 1933   288 U. S. 249
        Railway v. Wallace
        *Consttnl Law (Kauper) 18-21

1091.   Appalachian Coals, Inc. v. United   Mar 13, 1933   288 U. S. 344
        States
        *Antitrust (Posner) 66-74
        *Antitrust Analysis 350-357
        *Cases Antitrust Law 320-331
        *Competition 212-216

*Consttnl Law (Kauper) 221-230
*Free Enterprise 442-453
*Govt Regulation 431-441
*Selected Antitrust Cases 68-72

1092. Louis K. Liggett Co. v. Leavy   Mar 13, 1933   288 U.S. 517
           Legacy 166-169

1093. Williams v. Mayor and City Council   Mar 13, 1933   289 U.S. 36
           of Baltimore
       Williams v. Mayor of Annapolis
       *Legislative (Hetzel) 381-383

1094. Board of Trustees University of   Mar 20, 1933   289 U.S. 48
           Illinois v. United States
       *Am Consttnl Law (Bartholomew) v. 1, 179
       *Cases Consttnl Law (Cushman) 156-157
       Commerce 50-51
       Education (Spurlock) 36-39

1095. Bradley v. Public Utilities Commis-   Apr 10, 1933   289 U.S. 92
           sion of Ohio
       *Consttnl Law (Barrett) 289-290
       *Consttnl Law (Freund) 408-410

1096. United States v. Flores   Apr 10, 1933   289 U.S. 137
       *Criminal Law (Wells) 146-147

1097. Hurn v. Oursler   Apr 17, 1933   289 U.S. 238
       *Materials Consttnl Law 136-140

1098. Federal Radio Commission v. Nelson   May 8, 1933   289 U.S. 266
           Brothers Bond and Mortgage Co.
           (Station WIBO)
       Federal Radio Commission v. North Shore
           Church (Station WPCC)
       *Consttn (Mendelson) 55-56

1099. Mintz v. Baldwin   May 8, 1933   289 U.S. 346
       *Consttnl Law (Freund) 366-367

1100. Quercia v. United States   May 29, 1933   289 U.S. 466
       *Cases Civil Procedure 779-783

1101. Minnesota v. Blasius   Nov 6, 1933   290 U.S. 1
       *Consttnl Law (Barrett) 384-387
       *Consttnl Law (Freund) 519-522

1102. Shepard v. United States   Nov 6, 1933   290 U.S. 96
       *Cases Evidence 722-725
       *Principles Proof 184-187

1103. Krauss Brothers Lumber v. Dimon   Nov 13, 1933   290 U.S. 117
           Steamship Co.
       The Pacific Cedar
       *Cases Admiralty 237-239

1104. Southern Railway v. Virginia ex   Dec 4, 1933   290 U.S. 190
           rel. Shirley

*Govt and Business 470-472

1105. Yarborough v. Yarborough   Dec 4, 1933   290 U. S. 202
       Sup Ct Review 1964 118

1106. May v. Hamburg-Amerikanische   Dec 4, 1933   290 U. S. 333
       Packetfahrt Aktiengesellschaft
       *Cases Admiralty 483-484

1107. Funk v. United States   Dec 11, 1933   290 U. S. 371
       *Law of Evidence 235-243

1108. Home Building and Loan Association Jan 8, 1934   290 U. S. 398
          v. Blaisdell
       "Minnesota Moratorium Case"
       Am Consttn (Kelly) 692
       *Am Consttn (Lockhart) 385-388
       *Am Consttnl Law (Bartholomew) v. 2, 191-195
       *Am Consttnl Law (Mason) 388-393
       *Am Consttnl Law (Saye) 244-247
       *Am Consttnl Law (Shapiro) 220-225
       CQ Guide 314
       *Cases Consttnl Law (Gunther) 557-560
       *Cases Consttnl Rights 145-148
       *Cases Individual 206-209
       *Consttnl Law (Barrett) 576-580
       *Consttnl Law (Freund) 1387-1393
       *Consttnl Law (Kauper) 1373-1383
       *Consttnlism 12-16
       Consttnlity 17-18
       Court and Consttn v. 2, 31-32
       *Courts Judges 589-595
       *Documents History v. 2, 296-298
       *Freedom vs National Security 26-28
       *Govt and Business 72-74
       *Historic Decisions 122-128
       *Processes 146-153
       *Social Forces 402-404
       *Sup Ct and American Economic Life 155-162
       *Sup Ct and Consttn 365-369
       Sup Ct and Uses 39-51
       Sup Ct from Taft 85-87
       Sup Ct in Crisis 196-198
       Sup Ct in Free Society 206-211
       *Sup Ct Speaks 268-273
       This Honorable Court 294

1109. First National Bank of Cincinnati v.   Jan 8, 1934   290 U. S. 504
       Flershem
       Arzt v. Flershem
       Clapier v. Flershem
       *Materials Reorganization 195-206

1110. Burroughs and Cannon v. United   Jan 8, 1934   290 U. S. 534
       States
       CQ Guide 172
       Sup Ct and Electoral Process 234-235

1111. Federal Trade Commission v.   Jan 8, 1934   291 U.S. 67
          Algoma Lumber
          *Legal Regulation 209-215

1112. Snyder v. Massachusetts   Jan 8, 1934   291 U.S. 97
          *Sup Ct Speaks 316-318

1113. Nebbia v. New York   Mar 5, 1934   291 U.S. 502
          Am Consttn (Kelly) 692-693
          *Am Consttn (Lockhart) 366-368
          *Am Consttnl Law (Bartholomew) v. 2, 210-212
          *Am Consttnl Law (Mason) 428-431
          *Am Consttnl Law (Shapiro) 321-323
          *Cases Civil Liberties 31-35
          *Cases Consttnl Law (Cushman) 261-265
          *Cases Consttnl Law (Gunther) 528-531
          *Cases Consttnl Rights 126-128
          *Cases Individual 174-178
          *Commerce 111-112
          *Consttn (Mendelson) 262-263
          *Consttnl Law (Barrett) 660-661
          *Consttnl Law (Barron) 428-430
          *Consttnl Law (Freund) 1089-1091
          *Consttnl Law (Kauper) 639-643
          *Consttnl Law (Lockhart) 441-444
          Court and Consttn v. 2, 32-33
          *Documents History v. 2, 298-301
          *Govt and Business 310-315
          *Liberty v. 2, 388-389
          *Sup Ct and American Economic Life 162-173
          *Sup Ct and Consttn 369-372
          Sup Ct from Taft 88
          Sup Ct in Free Society 247-248
          *Sup Ct Speaks 276-282
          This Honorable Court 293

1114. Arrow-Hart and Hegeman Electric Co. Mar 12, 1934   291 U.S. 587
          v. Federal Trade Commission
          *Competition 90-94
          Sup Ct in Free Society 38

1115. Local Loan Co. v. Hunt   Apr 30, 1934   292 U.S. 234
          *Materials Reorganization 250-252

1116. Healy v. Ratta   Apr 30, 1934   292 U.S. 263
          *Cases Federal Courts 244-249
          *Federal Courts 1149-1152

1117. Principality of Monaco v. Mississippi May 21, 1934   292 U.S. 313
          *Federal Courts 251-256

1118. The Thomas Barlum   Nov 5, 1934   293 U.S. 21
          The John J. Barlum
          Detroit Trust Co. v. Barlum Steam-
             ship Co.
          *Cases Admiralty 296-300

1119. Hamilton v. Regents of the Univer- Dec 3, 1934   293 U.S. 245
          sity of California

Church and State 118
Education (Lapati) 246
*Education (Spurlock) 96-99
Freedom and the Court 64, 276
Land Ownership 619-620
Private Conscience 73-75
Religion (Kurland) 38-41
*Religious Freedom (Pfeffer) 108-110
Sup Ct and Religion 57-58
*Two Swords 261-267

1120. Schnell v. The Vallescura   Dec 3, 1934   293 U. S. 296
       *Cases Admiralty 489-492

1121. Panama Refining Co. v. Ryan   Jan 7, 1935   293 U. S. 388
       Amazon Petroleum Co. v. Ryan
       "Hot Oil Case"
       *Admin Law (Schwartz) 78-84
       Am Consttn (Kelly) 694-695
       *Am Consttnl Law (Bartholomew) v. 1, 87-88
       CQ Guide 78
       Consttn (Barber) 82-87
       *Consttnl Cases 114-127
       Court and Consttn v. 2, 33
       Sup Ct in Crisis 199-200
       Sup Ct in Free Society 166
       This Honorable Court 296-297

1122. Gregory v. Helvering   Jan 7, 1935   293 U. S. 465
       Sup Ct Review 1961 143-145

1123. Dimick v. Schiedt   Jan 7, 1935   293 U. S. 474
       *Cases Civil Procedure 848-856

1124. Mooney v. Holohan   Jan 21, 1935   294 U. S. 103
       *Consttn (Mendelson) 380-382
       Criminal Evidence 41
       *Due Process 135-136
       Felix Frankfurter (Phillips) 130-135

1125. Norman v. Baltimore and Ohio Rail- Feb 18, 1935 294 U. S. 240
          road Co.
       Nortz v. United States   Feb 18, 1935   294 U. S. 317
       Perry v. United States   Feb 18, 1935   294 U. S. 330
       "Gold Clause Cases"
       Am Consttn (Kelly) 695, 696-697
       *Am Consttnl Law (Bartholomew) v. 1, 192-195
       CQ Guide 122
       *Consttnl Law (Barrett) 278-280, 317-322
       *Consttnl Law (Freund) 310-317
       Court and Consttn v. 2, 34-38
       *Documentary v. 4, 2841-2873
       *Documents History v. 2, 264-269
       *Govt and Business 344-346, 363-365
       *Justices (Friedman) v. 3, 2037-2040
       Monetary Decisions 90-93
       *Sup Ct and American Economic Life 173-174
       Sup Ct in Crisis 200-201
       Sup Ct Review 1962 77

Sup Ct Review 1979 106-107
This Honorable Court 297-298

1126. Aktieselskabet Cuzco v. The   Mar 4, 1935   294 U.S. 394
       Sucarseco
       The Toluma
       *Cases Admiralty 674-678

1127. Nashville, Chattanooga and St. Louis Mar 4, 1935   294 U.S. 405
       Railway v. Walters
       Sup Ct Review 1962 73-74

1128. Baldwin v. G.A.F. Seelig, Inc.   Mar 4, 1935   294 U.S. 511
       *Am Consttn (Lockhart) 256-258
       Am Consttnl Law (Bartholomew) v. 1, 238
       Cases Consttnl Law (Gunther) 298-300
       *Consttnl Law (Barrett) 324-326
       *Consttnl Law (Barron) 266-269
       *Consttnl Law (Freund) 381-385
       *Consttnl Law (Lockhart) 304-306
       *Govt and Business 295-298
       *Justices (Friedman) v. 3, 2312-2317

1129. Metropolitan Casualty Insurance of New Mar 18, 1935   294 U.S. 580
       York v. Brownell
       *Consttnl Law (Kauper) 697-699

1130. Norris v. Alabama   Apr 1, 1935   294 U.S. 507
       "Scottsboro Case"
       *Am Consttnl Law (Bartholomew) v. 2, 290-292
       *Cases Civil Liberties 320-323
       *Cases Consttnl Law (Cushman) 550-553
       *Civil Rights (Bardolph) 207-209
       *Civil Rights (Blaustein) 346-350
       Defendants 194-196
       *Federal Courts 595-601
       *Liberty v. 2, 403-404
       *Negro (Franklin) 387-391
       Petitioners 270-275
       Quest 111
       *Racial Equality 132-133

1131. Henry L. Doherty and Co. v. Good-   Apr 1, 1935   294 U.S. 623
       man
       *Cases Civil Procedure 385-388

1132. Continental Illinois National Bank   Apr 1, 1935   294 U.S. 648
       and Trust Co. of Chicago v.
       Chicago, Rock Island and Pacific
       Railway
       *Govt and Business 385-388
       *Social Forces 332-334

1133. Grovey v. Townsend   Apr 1, 1935   295 U.S. 45
       Black 34-36
       Desegregation (Wasby) 31
       Great Reversals 133-134
       Petitioners 225-229
       Private Pressure 29-30

Rise 75-76
Sup Ct and Electoral Process 69
Sup Ct Review 1961 207

1134. W. B. Worthen Co. ex rel. Board of   Apr 1, 1935   295 U. S. 56
       Commissioners of Street Improvement
       District No. 513 of Little Rock v.
       Kavanaugh
       *Consttnl Law (Barrett) 580-581

1135. Berger v. United States   Apr 15, 1935   295 U. S. 78
       *Criminal Justice (Kaplan) 267

1136. Doleman v. Levine   Apr 29, 1935   295 U. S. 221
       *Modern Social Legislation 426-429

1137. Railroad Retirement Board v. Alton   May 6, 1935   295 U. S. 330
       Railroad Co.
       *Commerce 107-111
       Court and Consttn v. 2, 41-42
       *Documents History v. 1, 305-308
       Sup Ct from Taft 88-89
       Sup Ct in Crisis 201-202
       Sup Ct in Free Society 167
       Sup Ct on Trial 160-161
       This Honorable Court 299-300

1138. Hollins v. Oklahoma   May 13, 1935   295 U. S. 394
       Private Pressure 17-18

1139. Herndon v. Georgia   May 20, 1935   295 U. S. 441
       *Cases Federal Courts 842-848
       *Federal Courts 526-531

1140. A. L. A. Schechter Poultry Corpora-   May 27, 1935   295 U. S. 495
       tion v. United States
       "Sick Chicken Case"
       *Admin Law (Schwartz) 89-93
       Am Consttn (Kelly) 699-701
       *Am Consttnl Law (Bartholomew) v. 1, 89-92
       *Am Consttnl Law (Mason) 280-285
       *Am Consttnl Law (Shapiro) 272-277
       *Am Testament 202-210
       *Annals v. 15, 301-309
       Biography 341-342
       CQ Guide 78, 98
       *Cases Consttnl Law (Cushman) 65-69, 197-200
       Cases Consttnl Law (Gunther) 142-145
       Changing 97-100
       Commerce 201-205
       Consttn (Barber) 87-95
       *Consttn (Barrett) 220-222
       *Consttn (Hirschfield) 34-39
       Consttnl Revolution 47-52
       Court and Consttn v. 2, 40-41, 42-43
       *Depression 185-193
       *Documents History v. 2, 278-283
       *Federal System 212-214, 234-238
       *Govt and Business 227-229

        *Historic Decisions 129-134
        *Liberty v. 2, 410-413
        Milestones 183-199
        Quarrels 191-209
        *Search for Meaning 391-393
        *Sources American Republic v. 2, 322-325
        Sup Ct (Mason) 125
        *Sup Ct and Consttn 373-377
        Sup Ct from Taft 90-91
        Sup Ct in Crisis 203-204
        Sup Ct in Free Society 167-169
        Sup Ct on Trial 159-160
        This Honorable Court 303-304

1141.   Louisville Joint Stock Land Bank v.   May 27, 1935 295 U.S. 555
           Radford
        *Am Consttnl Law (Bartholomew) v. 1, 298-299
        Court and Consttn v. 2, 43
        *Govt and Business 74-75
        Sup Ct in Crisis 202
        This Honorable Court 300-301

1142.   Humphrey's Executor (Rathbun) v.   May 27, 1935 295 U.S. 602
           United States
        *Am Consttnl Law (Bartholomew) v. 1, 104-106
        CQ Guide 214-215
        *Cases Consttnl Law (Cushman) 105-109
        *Consttnl Cases 105-113
        *Consttnl Decisions 80-84
        *Consttnl Politics 341-347
        *Documents History v. 2, 308-311
        *Federal System 110-112
        Freedom and Reform 276-312
        *Legislation (Linde) 658-665
        *Legislative (Hetzel) 882-888
        *Liberty v. 2, 441-443
        Presidential Power 104-106; reprinted from J Politics 1: 17-61
           Feb '39
        *Statutory History Economic v. 3, 1811-1818
        Sup Ct in Crisis 202-203
        This Honorable Court 301-302
        Watergate 95-97

1143.   Pacific States Box and Basket Co.   Nov 18, 1935 296 U.S. 176
           v. White
        *Introduction (Mashaw) 251-253

1144.   Fox Film Corporation v. Muller   Dec 9, 1935 296 U.S. 207
        *Federal Courts 471-473

1145.   Hopkins Federal Savings and Loan   Dec 9, 1935 296 U.S. 315
           Association v. Cleary
        *Consttnl Law (Freund) 324-326
        Perspectives (Black) 40-41

1146.   Colgate v. Harvey   Dec 16, 1935 296 U.S. 404
        Equality (Berger) 66
        Sup Ct (Mason) 131

1147.   United States v. Butler   Jan 6, 1936 297 U.S. 1

Am Consttn (Kelly) 702-704
*Am Consttn (Lockhart) 148-151
*Am Consttnl Issues 113-119
*Am Consttnl Law (Bartholomew) v. 1, 185-188
*Am Consttnl Law (Mason) 328-334
*Am Consttnl Law Reader 100-102
CQ Guide 117-118
*Cases Consttnl Law (Cushman) 117-120, 165-167
*Cases Consttnl Law (Gunther) 225-230
*Cases Consttnl Law (Rosenblum) 248-254
Changing 101-102
Commerce 242-248
*Consttn (Mendelson) 149-155
*Consttnl Law (Barrett) 252-255
*Consttnl Law (Barron) 235-236
*Consttnl Law (Freund) 253-259
*Consttnl Law (Grossman) 359-363
*Consttnl Law (Kauper) 203-216
*Consttnl Law (Lockhart) 162-166
Consttnl Revolution 58-64
Court and Consttn v. 2, 48-49
*Courts Judges 720-722
*Documents History v. 2, 246-255
*Federal System 41-42, 216-220
*Justices (Friedman) v. 3, 2245-2250, 2273-2283
*Leading Consttnl Decisions 84-89
*Liberty v. 2, 413-415
*Processes 309-313
*School Law (Alexander) 50-56
Sup Ct (Mason) 132-134
*Sup Ct and American Economic Life 184-192
*Sup Ct and Consttn 382-386
Sup Ct from Taft 94-95, 135-136
Sup Ct in Crisis 204
*Sup Ct Speaks 286-291
This Honorable Court 305-307

1148.   United States v. California   Feb 3, 1936   297 U.S. 175
        *Am Consttn (Lockhart) 345-346
        *Consttn (Mendelson) 128-129
        *Consttnl Law (Kauper) 493-495

1149.   Grosjean v. American Press Co.   Feb 10, 1936   297 U.S. 233
        *Am Consttnl Law (Bartholomew) v. 2, 119-120
        *Bill (Konvitz) 274-277
        CQ Guide 426
        Communication (Hemmer) v. 2, 199-200
        Consttnl Law (Barrett) 1341
        *Documents History v. 2, 311-313
        *First Amendment (Konvitz) 312-317
        *Freedom and Protection 109-111
        Freedom of Speech (Hudon) 82
        *Freedom of the Press (Nelson) 347-354
        Law of Mass 608-612
        *Liberty v. 2, 453-454
        *Mass Communications 157-161
        Sup Ct and Uses 75-78
        *Sup Ct on Freedom 76-81
        Sup Ct Review 1978 262
        System 418-419

1150.   Brown v. Mississippi   Feb 17, 1936   297 U.S. 278
        By What Right 146-149
        *Civil Liberties (Sweet) 248-251
        *Civil Rights (Abernathy) 1977 170-171
         Civil Rights (Bardolph) 209-210
        *Consttnl Law (Felkenes) 258-260
        *Consttnl Law (Maddex) 227-232
         Criminal Evidence 418-419
        *Criminal Justice (Kaplan) 178-182
        *Criminal Law (Felkenes) 214-217
         Defendants 342-343
        *Due Process 57
         Freedom Spent 377-378
        *Leading Consttnl Cases 468-473
         Petitioners 277-280
         Police 90-91
         Private Pressure 18
         Sup Ct and Confessions 43-50
        PERIODICALS:
         "Historic change in the Supreme Court," Anthony Lewis. N Y
           Times Mag 7, 36, 38-39 June 17 '62 (2).

1151.   Ashwander v. Tennessee Valley   Feb 17, 1936   297 U.S. 288
         Authority
        *Am Consttnl Law (Bartholomew) v. 1, 288-290
        *Am Landmark v. 5, 331-415
        *CQ Guide 288
        *Cases Consttnl Law (Rosenblum) 242-248
        *Civil Liberties (Sweet) 4-5
        *Consttn (Mendelson) 9-10
        *Consttnl Law (Barrett) 274-276
         Consttnl Law (Freund) 87-90
        *Consttnl Law (Freund) 91-99, 326-331
        *Consttnl Law (Kauper) 228-236
        *Contemporary Law 32-33
        *Documents History v. 2, 257-262
        *Govt and Business 425-429
        *Judiciary (Roche) 54
         Least Dangerous 119-120
        *Liberty v. 2, 408-410
        *Sup Ct and American Economic Life 21-23

1152.   Wine Railway Appliance Co. v.   Mar 2, 1936   297 U.S. 387
         Enterprise Railway Equipment Co.
        *Patent 883-886

1153.   Sugar Institute v. United States   Mar 30, 1936   297 U.S. 553
        *Antitrust (Posner) 213-217
        *Antitrust Analysis 333-336
        *Cases Antitrust Law 397-408
        *Competition 245-249
        *Govt Regulation 442-458

1154.   Jones v. Securities and Exchange   Apr 6, 1936   298 U.S. 1
         Commission
         Court and Consttn v. 2, 50-51
         Sup Ct in Crisis 206

1155.   St. Joseph's Stockyards v. United   Apr 27, 1936   298 U.S. 38
         States

Sup Ct in Free Society 39-40

1156. International Business Machines   Apr 27, 1936   298 U. S. 131
         Corporation v. United States
      *Antitrust (Posner) 605-609
      *Antitrust Analysis 585-588
      *Cases Trade 585-589
      *Competition 318-320
      *Govt Regulation 459-463

1157. Carter v. Carter Coal Co.   May 18, 1936   298 U. S. 238
      Helvering v. Carter
      R. C. Tway Coal Co. v. Glenn
      R. C. Tway Coal Co. v. Clark
      "Guffey Coal Case"
         Am Consttn (Kelly) 705-707
      *Am Consttn (Lockhart) 145-147
      *Am Consttnl Law (Bartholomew) v. 1, 256-259
      *Am Consttnl Law (Mason) 285-291
         CQ Guide 98-99
      *Cases Consttnl Law (Gunther) 146-149
      *Commerce 205-208
         Consttn (Barber) 95
      *Consttnl Law (Barrett) 222-224
      *Consttnl Law (Freund) 243-252
      *Consttnl Law (Lockhart) 119-122
         Consttnl Revolution 53-57
         Court and Consttn v. 2, 52
      *Documents History v. 2, 344-353
      *Govt and Business 230-231
      *Justices (Friedman) v. 3, 2153-2168
      *Legislative (Hetzel) 418-421
      *Liberty v. 2, 416-418
      *Processes 287-296
      *Sup Ct and American Economic Life 193-203
         Sup Ct and Commerce 62-64
      *Sup Ct and Consttn 378-381
         Sup Ct from Taft 91-94
         Sup Ct in Crisis 206-207
         Sup Ct in Free Society 169-171
         Sup Ct on Trial 160-161
      *Sup Ct Speaks 295-296
         This Honorable Court 308-309

1158. Morgan v. United States   May 25, 1936   298 U. S. 468
      *Admin Law (Gellhorn) 773-777
      *Admin Law (Schwartz) 491-493
      *Govt Regulation 482-484

1159. United States v. Elgin, Joliet and   May 25, 1936   298 U. S. 492
         Eastern Railway
      *Free Enterprise 950-952

1160. Ashton v. Cameron County Water   May 25, 1936   298 U. S. 513
         District
         Am Consttn (Kelly) 707-708
      *Am Consttnl Law (Bartholomew) v. 1, 300-301
         Court and Consttn v. 2, 53
         This Honorable Court 309

1161.   Morehead v. New York ex rel. Tipaldo   June 1, 1936   298 U.S. 587
        *Am Consttnl Law (Bartholomew) v. 2, 229-230
        CQ Guide 327
        Court and Consttn v. 2, 54
        *Justices (Friedman) v. 3, 2192-2199
        Legacy 150-151
        *Sup Ct and American Economic Life 203-211
        Sup Ct in Crisis 208
        Sup Ct in Free Society 248-249
        This Honorable Court 309-310
        US Sup Ct 39-40
        PERIODICALS:
        "Big switch: Justice Roberts and the minimum-wage cases,"
        John W. Chambers.   Labor History 10: 44-73 Winter '69
        (3).

1162.   State Board of Equalization of   Nov 9, 1936   299 U.S. 59
        California v. Young's Market
        *Consttnl Law (Freund) 378-380

1163.   Gully v. First National Bank in   Nov 9, 1936   299 U.S. 109
        Meridian
        *Cases Federal Courts 125-129
        *Materials Consttnl Law 116-120

1164.   Old Dearborn Distributing Co. v.   Dec 7, 1936   299 U.S. 183
        Seagram Distillers Corporation
        McNeil v. Joseph Triner Corporation
        *Competition 358-360

1165.   United States v. Curtiss-Wright Ex- Dec 21, 1936 299 U.S. 304
        port Corporation
        *Am Consttnl Law (Bartholomew) v. 1, 43-45, 287-288
        *Am Consttnl Law (Mason) 106-109
        *Am Consttnl Law (Saye) 102-104
        Am Consttnl Law (Shapiro) 182-185
        *Basic Cases 260-265
        CQ Guide 201-202
        *Cases Consttnl Law (Cushman) 69-72
        *Cases Consttnl Law (Gunther) 402-404
        *Comparative 222-224
        *Consttn (Mendelson) 176-179
        *Consttnl Cases 128-137
        *Consttnl Decisions 93-96
        *Consttnl Law (Barrett) 260-261
        *Consttnl Law (Barron) 359-363
        *Consttnl Law (Felkenes) 52-54
        *Consttnl Law (Freund) 697-700
        *Consttnl Law (Grossman) 1005-1008
        *Consttnl Law (Kauper) 264-269
        *Consttnl Politics 354-357
        *Documents History v. 2, 362-365
        Executive Privilege 100
        *Federal System 141-146
        Foreign Affairs 19-26
        *Freedom vs National Security 29-34
        Growth 1713-1717
        *Growth 1717-1730
        *Leading Consttnl Decisions 133-140

*Liberty v. 2, 443-445
*Processes 416-418
Quarrels 210-221
*Readings American 650-654
*Sup Ct and Am Govt 125-132

1166. Kentucky Whip and Collar Co. v.   Jan 4, 1937   299 U. S. 334
      Illinois Central Railroad
      *Am Consttnl Law (Bartholomew) v. 1, 224-226

1167. DeJonge v. Oregon   Jan 4, 1937   299 U. S. 353
      Am Consttn (Kelly) 765-766
      *Am Consttnl Law (Bartholomew) v. 2, 121-122
      *Bill (Konvitz) 344-349
      CQ Guide 405
      *Cases Consttnl Rights 337-339
      *Civil Liberties (Sweet) 177-179
      Communication (Hemmer) v. 1, 21-22
      *Consttn (Mendelson) 395-397
      *Consttnl Law (Barrett) 1138-1139
      *Consttnl Law (Freund) 1232-1235
      *Consttnl Law (Lockhart) 678-680
      *Documents History v. 2, 365-368
      *First Amendment (Konvitz) 154-159
      Free Speech (Kurland) 36
      *Freedom and Protection 118-119
      Freedom and the Court 65
      *Freedom of Speech (Haiman) 12-13
      Freedom of Speech (Hudon) 83
      Freedom Spent 80-81
      *Liberty v. 2, 455-456
      *Political Rights 90-93
      Politics 35-36
      Spirit 70-71
      *Sup Ct and Consttn 439-441
      System 108-109
      This Honorable Court 338

1168. City Bank and Farmers Trust Co. v.   Jan 4, 1937   299 U. S. 433
      Irving Trust Co.
      *Materials Reorganization 578-582

1169. Kuehner v. Irving Trust Co.   Jan 4, 1937   299 U. S. 445
      *Materials Reorganization 582-585

1170. Shoshone Tribe of Indians of the Wind Jan 4, 1937   299 U. S. 476
      River Reservation in Wyoming
      *Law Indian 450-453

1171. Thompson v. Consolidated Gas   Feb 1, 1937   300 U. S. 55
      Utilities Corp.
      Legacy 270-271

1172. Aetna Life Insurance Co. v. Haworth   Mar 1, 1937   300 U. S. 227
      *Cases Federal Courts 63-69
      *Elements Civil 122-127
      *Materials Consttnl Law 149-153

1173. Ingels v. Morf   Mar 1, 1937   300 U. S. 290
      Am Consttn (Kelly) 739

1174. New York ex rel. Cohn v. Graves   Mar 1, 1937   300 U.S. 308
       *Consttnl Law (Barrett) 377-378

1175. Phelps v. Board of Education of West   Mar 1, 1937   300 U.S. 319
           New York
       Askam v. Board of Education of West
           New York
           Digest 49-50
           Education (Lapati) 220-221
           Education (Spurlock) 43-46
           *Law and Public Education (Hamilton) 480-482
           *Law of Public Education 441-443
           *School Law (Remmlein) 53-54

1176. Holyoke Water Power Co. v. American   Mar 1, 1937   300 U.S. 324
           Writing Paper Co.
           Monetary Decisions 96-97

1177. West Coast Hotel v. Parrish   Mar 29, 1937   300 U.S. 379
           Am Consttn (Kelly) 718
           *Am Consttnl Law (Bartholomew) v. 2, 231-234
           *Am Consttnl Law (Mason) 432-435
           *Am Consttnl Law (Saye) 416-418
           *Am Consttnl Law (Shapiro) 324-326
           *Basic Cases 117-130
           Biography 317-319
           CQ Guide 327-328
           *Cases Civil Liberties 39-43
           *Cases Consttnl Law (Cushman) 269-273
           *Cases Consttnl Law (Gunther) 531-533
           *Cases Individual 178-180
           *Consttn (Mendelson) 263-265
           *Consttnl Decisions 117-121
           *Consttnl Law (Barrett) 662-663
           *Consttnl Law (Freund) 1091-1094
           *Consttnl Law (Kauper) 645-647
           *Consttnl Politics 455-457
           Court and Consttn v. 2, 74-75
           *Courts Judges 722-724
           *Documents History v. 2, 368-373
           *Franklin D. Roosevelt 79-82
           *Govt and Business 41-42
           Great Reversals 115-117
           *Justices (Friedman) v. 3, 1928-1934
           *Liberty v. 2, 422-424
           *Sex Discrimination 1975 50-53
           *Sup Ct and American Economic Life 211-217
           *Sup Ct and Consttn 387-393
           Sup Ct in Am History 108-125
           Sup Ct on Trial 180-181
           This Honorable Court 317
       PERIODICALS:
           "Big switch: Justice Roberts and the minimum-wage cases, "
           John W. Chambers. Labor History 10: 44-73 Winter '69
           (3).

1178. Wright v. Vinton Branch of the   Mar 29, 1937   300 U.S. 440
           Mountain Trust Bank of Roanoke
           *Materials Reorganization 268-275

1179. Sonzinsky v. United States   Mar 29, 1937   300 U. S. 506
       *Cases Criml Law (Inbau) 55-57
       *Consttnl Law (Barrett) 250-251

1180. Virginian Railway Co. v. System   Mar 29, 1937   300 U. S. 515
       Federation No. 40
       *Cases Labor (Oberer) 106-109
       Court and Consttn v. 2, 75
       *Labor Law (Twomey) 62-66
       *Statutory History Labor 147-160

1181. Henneford v. Silas Mason Co.   Mar 29, 1937   300 U. S. 577
       *Am Consttnl Law (Bartholomew) v. 1, 230-231
       *Am Consttnl Law (Saye) 195-197
       *Consttnl Law (Freund) 385-388
       Sup Ct and Commerce 320-321

1182. National Labor Relations Board v.   Apr 12, 1937   301 U. S. 1
       Jones and Laughlin Steel Co.
       Am Consttn (Kelly) 719
       *Am Consttn (Lockhart) 153-155
       *Am Consttnl Issues 130-138
       *Am Consttnl Law (Bartholomew) v. 1, 260-263
       *Am Consttnl Law (Mason) 292-296
       *Am Consttnl Law (Shapiro) 277-281
       *Am Consttnl Law Reader 69-79
       Basic History 60-61
       CQ Guide 100-101
       *Cases Consttnl Law (Cushman) 200-205
       *Cases Consttnl Law (Gunther) 153-157
       *Cases Labor (Cox) 99-101
       *Cases Labor (Oberer) 111-116
       *Cases Labor (Stern) 8-15
       *Consttn (Hirschfield) 48-53
       *Consttn (Mendelson) 109-112
       *Consttnl Cases 19-35
       *Consttnl Law (Barrett) 231-233
       *Consttnl Law (Felkenes) 82-83
       *Consttnl Law (Freund) 273-281
       *Consttnl Law (Grossman) 363-368
       *Consttnl Law (Kauper) 150-159
       *Consttnl Law (Lockhart) 123-127
       *Consttnl Politics 397-402
       Consttnl Revolution 65-69
       *Depression 206-215
       *Documents History v. 2, 318-324
       *Federal System 238-242
       Free Speech (Kurland) 58
       *Govt and Business 233-237
       *Historic Decisions 135-141
       *Justices (Friedman) v. 3, 1916-1927
       *Labor Law (Herman) 100-106
       *Labor Law (Twomey) 80-85
       *Labor Relations (Group Trust) 49-53
       Labor Relations (Taylor) 173-175
       *Liberty v. 2, 428-430
       *Nature 898-904
       *Readings American 562-568
       *Sources American Republic v. 2, 340-344

        *Statutory History Labor 348-365
        *Sup Ct and American Economic Life 217-227
        Sup Ct and Commerce 75-83
        *Sup Ct and Consttn 394-401
        Sup Ct and Labor 31-34
        Sup Ct from Taft 109-114
        Sup Ct in Crisis 214
        Sup Ct in Free Society 183-184
        Sup Ct on Trial 162-165
        *Sup Ct Speaks 296-303
        Wagner Act.

1183.   National Labor Relations Board v.   Apr 12, 1937   301 U.S. 49
            Fruehauf Trailer
        Wagner Act.

1184.   National Labor Relations Board v.   Apr 12, 1937   301 U.S. 58
            Friedman-Harry Marks Clothing
            Co.
        Am Consttn (Kelly) 719

1185.   Associated Press v. National Labor   Apr 12, 1937   301 U.S. 103
            Relations Board
        *Documents History v. 2, 324-325
        Mass Communications 721-722
        *Sup Ct on Freedom 276-281
        Wagner Act.
        PERIODICALS:
        "How the Constitution was violated; reprint, " D. Lawrence. US
        News 54: 124, 121-123 May 6 '63.

1186.   Herndon v. Lowry   Apr 26, 1037   301 U.S. 242
        Am Consttn (Kelly) 766
        CQ Guide 405-406
        *Cases Consttnl Rights 339-342
        *Cases Individual 689-693
        *Consttnl Law (Lockhart) 680-683
        *Documents History v. 2, 373-378
        Freedom of Speech (Hudon) 83-85
        *Justices (Friedman) v. 3, 2264-2273
        This Honorable Court 337-338

1187.   Ohio Bell Telephone v. Public Utilities Apr 26, 1937   301 U.S. 292
            Commission of Ohio
        *Admin Law (Gellhorn) 715-718

1188.   United States v. Belmont   May 3, 1937   301 U.S. 324
        *Am Consttn (Lockhart) 206-208
        *Am Consttnl Law (Bartholomew) v. 1, 111-113
        *Am Consttnl Law (Saye) 104-107
        CQ Guide 206
        *Cases Consttnl Law (Cushman) 98-99
        *Consttnl Law (Barrett) 272
        *Consttnl Law (Kauper) 280-284
        Executive Privilege 158-159
        Foreign Affairs 177-179, 184-185
        *Freedom vs National Security 34-38
        *Govt and Business 394-395
        Perspectives (Black) 69

Communications (Hemmer) v. 1, 239-240
*Consttnl Aspects v. 4, 367-373
*Police 150-151
Search and Seizure 206-208

1202. United States v. Raynor   Jan 3, 1938   302 U.S. 540
       United States v. Fowler
       *Legislative (Hetzel) 188-191

1203. Myers v. Bethlehem Steel Corporation Jan 31, 1938   303 U.S. 41
       Myers v. MacKenzie
       *Admin Law (Gellhorn) 997-999
       *Admin Law (Schwartz) 611-613
       *Govt and Business 542-544

1204. Adam v. Saenger   Jan 31, 1938   303 U.S. 59
       *Cases Pleading 290

1205. Connecticut General Life Insurance Jan 31, 1938   303 U.S. 77
       Co. v. Johnson
       Am Consttn (Kelly) 744
       Court Years 154-155
       *Documents History v. 2, 400-402

1206. Indiana ex rel. Anderson v. Brand   Jan 31, 1938   303 U.S. 95
       Digest 50-51
       Education (Lapati) 222-223
       *Education (Spurlock) 47-50
       *Essentials 109-111
       *Federal Courts 496-500
       *Principles School 202-204
       *School Law (Alexander) 580-583
       *School Law (Remmlein) 54-56

1207. South Carolina Highway Department v. Feb 14, 1938   303 U.S. 177
       Barnwell Brothers
       *Am Consttnl Law (Bartholomew) v. 1, 207-208
       *Am Consttnl Law (Saye) 180-181
       *Cases Consttnl Law (Cushman) 186-188
       *Cases Consttnl Law (Gunther) 275-279
       *Consttnl Law (Barrett) 293-297
       *Consttnl Law (Freund) 412-418
       *Processes 224-225
       Sup Ct and Commerce 236-238
       Sup Ct from Taft 177-178
       Sup Ct Review 1975 160-162

1208. Western Live Stock v. Bureau of   Feb 28, 1938   303 U.S. 250
       Revenue
       *Am Consttn (Lockhart) 295-297
       *Consttnl Law (Barrett) 412-413
       *Consttnl Law (Freund) 540-544
       *Consttnl Law (Lockhart) 365-366
       Sup Ct and Commerce 238-239

1209. National Labor Relations Board v.   Feb 28, 1938   303 U.S. 261
       Pennsylvania Greyhound Lines
       *Statutory History Labor 366-371

1210.   Lauf v. E. G. Shinner and Co.   Feb 28, 1938   303 U.S. 323
        Labor Relations (Taylor) 97-98

1211.   Electric Bond and Share Co. v.   Mar 28, 1938   303 U.S. 419
        Securities and Exchange Commission
        Am Consttn (Kelly) 731

1212.   Lovell v. Griffin   Mar 28, 1938   303 U.S. 444
        Am Consttn (Kelly) 761-762
        Am Consttnl Law (Saye) 337
        *Cases Consttnl Law (Gunther) 1201-1202
        *Cases Individual 747-748
        Church and State 118
        Communication (Hemmer) v. 1, 224-225
        Consttnl Law (Barrett) 1307-1308
        *Consttnl Law (Kauper) 1232-1233
        *First Amendment (Konvitz) 285-287
        First Amendment (Marnell) 156-157
        Freedom of Speech (Haiman) 60-61
        Freedom of the Press (Schmidt) 91
        Law of Mass 615-616
        Mass Communications 40-41
        *Mass Media (Devol) 39-40
        Movies 24-26
        O'er the Ramparts 99-106
        Religion (Kurland) 50-51
        Sup Ct and Religion 59-60
        *Sup Ct on Freedom 73-74
        System 346

1213.   Santa Cruz Fruit Packing Co. v.   Mar 28, 1938   303 U.S. 453
        National Labor Relations Board
        Am Consttn (Kelly) 722
        Sup Ct and Commerce 112-113

1214.   New Negro Alliance v. Sanitary   Mar 28, 1938   303 U.S. 552
        Grocery Co.
        *Cases Labor (Handler) 586-588
        *Labor Law (Meltzer) 366-368
        *Labor Law (Twomey) 32-35
        Labor Relations (Taylor) 98-99
        Petitioners 312-313
        *Statutory History Labor 248-251

1215.   Morgan v. United States   Apr 25, 1938   304 U.S. 1
        *Admin Law (Gellhorn) 777-780
        *Text Administrative Law 6-8

1216.   Erie Railroad Co. v. Tompkins   Apr 25, 1938   304 U.S. 64
        *Am Consttnl Law (Bartholomew) v. 1, 46-48
        *Am Consttnl Law (Saye) 50-53
        *Cases Civil Procedure 277-283
        *Cases Federal Courts 577-587
        *Cases Pleading 393-400
        *Civil Procedure (Carrington) 825-830
        *Civil Procedure (Cound) 277-283
        *Consttn (Mendelson) 45-48
        *Contemporary Law 213-216
        Dissent 48-49

*Elements Civil 388-392
*Federal Courts 702-706
Hugo Black (Dunne) 181-184
Justice Joseph Story 408-409
*Legal Environment 33-37
Milestones 217-229
This Honorable Court 323-324

1217.   United States v. Carolene Products Co. Apr 25, 1938   304 U.S. 144
By What Right 108-111
CQ Guide 45, 378
*CQ Guide 379
*Consttnl Law (Barrett) 663-666
*Courts Judges 724-725
*Documents History v. 2, 410
Equality (Berger) 90
*Federal System 44
Freedom and the Court 18-24
Freedom of Speech (Shapiro) 59
Government 275-277
Hugo Black (Dunne) 184-187
Sup Ct (Mason) 151-152, 155-157
Sup Ct (North) 134-135
This Honorable Court 340-342
PERIODICALS:
"Double standard of constitutional protection in the era of the wel-
fare state," Richard Funston. Poltcl Sci Q 90: 261-292
Summer '75 (3).

1218.   General Talking Pictures Corpora-   May 2, 1938   304 U.S. 175
tion v. Western Electric Co.
*Govt Regulation 464-471
*Legal Regulation 1057-1059

1219.   J.D. Adams Manufacturing Co. v.   May 16, 1938   304 U.S. 307
Storen
*Consttnl Law (Barrett) 413-415

1220.   National Labor Relations Board v.   May 16, 1938   304 U.S. 333
Mackay Radio and Telegraph Co.
Basic Text 328-329
*Cases Labor (Cox) 854-857
*Cases Labor (Leslie) 257-258
*Cases Labor (Oberer) 531
*Labor Law (Meltzer) 234-235
*Labor Relations (Group Trust) 255-258
*Statutory History Labor 371-377
Sup Ct and Labor 73-74

1221.   Helvering v. Gerhardt   May 23, 1938   304 U.S. 405
Helvering v. Wilson
Helvering v. Mulcahy
*Cases Consttnl Law (Gunther) 360-362
*Consttn (Mendelson) 142-145
*Consttnl Law (Barrett) 448-449
*Consttnl Law (Freund) 630-634
*Consttnl Law (Kauper) 463-469
*Documents History v. 2, 402-405
Hugo Black (Strickland) 173-176

1222. Allen v. Regents of University System   May 23, 1938   304 U.S. 439
          of Georgia
       *Education (Spurlock) 39-42

1223. Johnson v. Zerbst   May 23, 1938   304 U.S. 458
       *Am Consttnl Law (Bartholomew) v. 2, 175-176
        CQ Guide 566
        Hugo Black (Dunne) 200-201
        Hugo Black (Strickland) 102-103
        Law of Arrest (Markle) 253-256
       *One Man's Stand 51-55
        Rationing 97-98

1224. Polk Co. v. Glover   Nov 7, 1938   305 U.S. 5
       *Sup Ct (Mendelson) 145-151

1225. Kellogg Co. v. National Biscuit Co.   Nov 14, 1938   305 U.S. 111
       *Cases Copyright (Kaplan) 565-571
       *Legal Regulation 268-274

1226. General Talking Pictures v. Western   Nov 21, 1938   305 U.S. 124
          Electric Co.
       *Cases Antitrust Law 584-587
       *Cases Trade 897-901
       *Free Enterprise 1222-1226
       *Patent 597-602

1227. Consolidated Edison Co. of New York   Dec 12, 1938   305 U.S. 197
          v. National Labor Relations Board
       International Brotherhood of Electrical
          Workers v. National Labor Relations
          Board
        Sup Ct and Commerce 113-114

1228. Missouri ex rel. Gaines v. Canada   Dec 12, 1938   305 U.S. 337
        Am Consttn (Kelly) 859
       *By These Words 485-491
        CQ Guide 591-592
        Civil Rights (Bardolph) 271-272
       *Civil Rights (Blaustein) 407-410
       *Consttn (Hirschfield) 72-76
        Court and Consttn v. 2, 110
       *Courts 5-6
        Desegregation (Wasby) 50-52
        Disaster 24
        Education (Lapati) 269-270
        Education (Spurlock) 190-192
        Equality (Berger) 133
        Freedom and the Court 363-364
       *Liberty v. 2, 468-470
        Petitioners 333-334
        Private Pressure 21-22
        Quest 130-132
       *Racial Equality 50-51
        Sup Ct in Free Society 257-258
       PERIODICALS:
        "Litigation and education of Blacks: a look at the U.S. Supreme
          Court," Delores P. Aldridge. J Negro Eductn 47: 96-112
          Winter '78 (11).

1229.   Joseph S. Finch and Co. v.   Jan 3, 1939   305 U. S. 395
            McKittrick
        *Am Consttnl Law (Saye) 178-179

1230.   Gwin, White and Prince v. Henneford Jan 3, 1939   305 U. S. 434
        *Consttnl Law (Kauper) 403-407
        Sup Ct and Commerce 240-241

1231.   Currin v. Wallace   Jan 30, 1939   306 U. S. 1
        "Holding Company Case"
        Court and Consttn v. 2, 102-103

1232.   Washingtonian Publishing Co. v.   Jan 30, 1939   306 U. S. 30
            Pearson
        *Cases Copyright (Kaplan) 149-155
        *Cases Copyright (Nimmer) 167-171
        Communication (Hemmer) v. 2, 128-129
        *Copyright 614-619

1233.   Tennessee Electric Power Co. v.   Jan 30, 1939   306 U. S. 118
            Tennessee Valley Authority
        Sup Ct (Freund) 154-158

1234.   Interstate Circuit v. United States   Feb 13, 1939   306 U. S. 208
        Paramount Pictures Distributing Co.
            v. United States
        *Antitrust (Posner) 95-102
        *Antitrust Analysis 293-298
        *Cases Antitrust Law 410-418, 676-680
        *Cases Trade 384-390
        *Criminal Law (Kadish) 462-464
        *Free Enterprise 1226-1230
        *Govt Regulation 472-485
        *Text Antitrust 66-72

1235.   National Labor Relations Board v.   Feb 27, 1939   306 U. S. 240
            Fansteel Metallurgical Corporation
        *Cases Labor (Oberer) 134-141
        Expanding Liberties 308-309
        *Labor Law (Meltzer) 194-199
        Sup Ct and Labor 75-78

1236.   Taylor v. Standard Gas and Electric   Feb 27, 1939   306 U. S. 307
            Co.
        *Materials Reorganization 410-418

1237.   National Labor Relations Board v.   Feb 27, 1939   306 U. S. 332
            Sands Manufacturing Co.
        Sup Ct and Labor 82-83

1238.   Milk Control Board of Pennsylvania   Feb 27, 1939   306 U. S. 346
            v. Eisenberg Farm Products
        Cases Consttnl Law (Gunther) 317-318
        Consttnl Law (Barrett) 326
        *Consttnl Law (Freund) 388-390

1239.   Pierre v. Louisiana   Feb 27, 1939   306 U. S. 354
        *One Man's Stand 56-61
        Petitioners 287

1240. Hale v. Bimeo Trading, Inc.   Feb 27, 1939   306 U. S. 375
       Sup Ct and Commerce 321-322

1241. Keifer and Keifer v. Reconstruction   Feb 27, 1939   306 U. S. 381
         Finance Corporation and Regional
         Credit Corporation
       *Materials Legislation 220-224

1242. Texas v. Florida   Mar 13, 1939   306 U. S. 398
       Mr. Justice Frankfurter 20

1243. Lanzetta v. New Jersey   Mar 27, 1939   306 U. S. 451
       *Consttn (Mendelson) 292
       *Due Process 19

1244. Graves v. New York ex rel. O'Keefe   Mar 27, 1939   306 U. S. 466
       *Am Consttnl Law (Bartholomew) v. 1, 169-173
       *Am Consttnl Law (Mason) 178-180
       *Cases Consttnl Law (Cushman) 150-154
        Cases Consttnl Law (Gunther) 362-363
       *Consttn (Mendelson) 223-225
       *Consttnl Law (Barrett) 449-451
       *Documents History v. 2, 405-410
       *Liberty v. 2, 439-440
       *Mr. Justice Frankfurter 39-40

1245. National Labor Relations Board v.   Apr 17, 1939   306 U. S. 601
         Fainblatt
        Consttnl Law (Barrett) 233
        Hugo Black (Dunne) 198-199
        Sup Ct and Commerce 114-116

1246. Mulford v. Smith   Apr 17, 1939   307 U. S. 38
        Am Consttn (Kelly) 727-728
       *Am Consttnl Law (Bartholomew) v. 1, 271-273
       *Am Consttnl Law (Mason) 334-335
       *Readings American 600-604
        Sup Ct and Commerce 96-97

1247. Rochester Telephone Co. v. United   Apr 17, 1939   307 U. S. 125
         States
        Felix Frankfurter (Thomas) 298-299

1248. Federal Power Commission v. Pacific   Apr 17, 1939   307 U. S. 156
         Power and Light Co.
       *Govt and Business 586-588

1249. United States v. Miller   May 15, 1939   307 U. S. 174
       *Bill (Cohen) 707-708

1250. Electrical Fittings Corp. v. Thomas   May 22, 1939   307 U. S. 241
         and Betts Co.
       *Civil Procedure (Cound) 1005

1251. Lane v. Wilson   May 22, 1939   307 U. S. 268
       *Am Consttn (Lockhart) 958-959
        Black 18-19
       *Cases Consttnl Rights 903-904
        Desegregation (Wasby) 31-32

Petitioners 297-298
Sup Ct Review 1969 383-385

1252.   Newark Fire Insurance Co. v.   May 29, 1939   307 U.S. 313
            State Board of Tax Appeals
        Universal Insurance Co. v. State
            Board of Tax Appeals
        Mr. Justice Frankfurter 197

1253.   Coleman v. Miller   June 5, 1939   307 U.S. 433
        *Am Consttnl Issues 40-45
        *Am Consttnl Law (Bartholomew) v. 1, 25-28
        *Consttn (Mendelson) 16-19
        *Mr. Justice Frankfurter 61-64
        Sup Ct and Poltcl Questions 105-110

1254.   Hague v. Committee for Industrial   June 5, 1939   307 U.S. 496
            Organization
        Am Consttn (Kelly) 759
        CQ Guide 407-408
        Communication (Hemmer) v. 1, 72
        Consttn (Konvitz) 38
        *Consttnl Law (Freund) 857-859
        Consttnl Right (Fellman) 23-24
        Expanding Liberties 56
        *First Amendment (Konvitz) 160-163
        Free Speech (Kurland) 41-42, 126-129, 346-347
        *Freedom of Speech (Haiman) 61-62
        *Materials Consttnl Law 210-218
        Movies 27-29
        Negro (Kalven) 187-190
        Right of Assembly 115-124
        Spirit 69
        Sup Ct and Labor 42-43
        Sup Ct Review 1961 92-93
        Sup Ct Review 1974 237-238
        System 300-301, 312-313
        This Honorable Court 338-339

1255.   United States v. Rock Royal Co-op,   June 5, 1939   307 U.S. 533
            Inc.
        Noyes v. Rock Royal Co-op, Inc.
        Dairymen's League Co-op Association
            v. Rock Royal Co-op, Inc.
        Metropolitan Co-op Milk Producers Bargaining
            Agency v. Rock Royal Co-op, Inc.
        *Govt and Business 317-318, 452-453, 460-461
        *Justices (Friedman) v. 3, 2390-2396

1256.   Pittman v. Home Owners Loan Cor-   Nov 6, 1939   308 U.S. 21
            poration of Washington, D.C.
        Consttnl Law (Barrett) 461-462

1257.   Case v. Los Angeles Lumber   Nov 6, 1939   308 U.S. 106
            Products Co.
        *Materials Reorganization 382-389

1258.   Schneider v. New Jersey   Nov 22, 1939   308 U.S. 147
        Young v. California

        Snyder v. Milwaukee
        Nichols v. Massachusetts
            Am Consttn (Kelly) 762
            Church and State 119
            Consttnl Law (Barrett) 1251-1252
            Free Speech (Kurland) 130-132, 133, 348, 350
            Law of Mass 616-618
            Negro (Kalven) 191-194
            O'er the Ramparts 107-110
           *Sup Ct on Freedom 75-76
            Sup Ct Review 1965 16-18
            Sup Ct Review 1974 239-241
            Sup Ct Review 1976 49-51
            Sup Ct Review 1977 264-265
            System 346-347, 348-349

1259.   United States v. Borden Co.   Dec 4, 1939   308 U.S. 188
           *Govt Regulation 486-496

1260.   Cities Service Oil Co. v. Dunlap   Dec 4, 1939   308 U.S. 208
           *Cases Civil Procedure 705-706

1261.   United States v. Lowden   Dec 4, 1939   308 U.S. 225
            Court and Consttn v. 2, 103

1262.   Weiss v. United States   Dec 11, 1939   308 U.S. 321
           *Police 151

1263.   Ford Motor Co. v. Beauchamp   Dec 11, 1939   308 U.S. 331
           *Consttnl Law (Freund) 497-499

1264.   Nardone v. United States   Dec 11, 1939   308 U.S. 338
           *Police 152-153
            Search and Seizure 208-209

1265.   Chicot County Drainage District v.   Jan 2, 1940   308 U.S. 371
                Baxter State Bank
           *Am Consttnl Law (Bartholomew) v. 1, 22-23
           *Cases Federal Courts 365-369
           *Consttnl Law (Kauper) 49-52

1266.   American Federation of Labor v.   Jan 2, 1940   308 U.S. 401
                National Labor Relations Board
           *Cases Labor (Oberer) 126-131

1267.   Kalb v. Feuerstein   Jan 2, 1940   308 U.S. 433
        Kalb v. Luce
           *Cases Federal Courts 369-372

1268.   McGoldrick v. Berwind-White Coal   Jan 29, 1940   309 U.S. 33
                Mining Co.
           *Am Consttn (Lockhart) 303-307
           *Consttnl Law (Freund) 565-571
           *Consttnl Law (Kauper) 391-397
           *Consttnl Law (Lockhart) 385-388
            Sup Ct and Commerce 241-243

1269.   Madden v. Kentucky   Jan 29, 1940   309 U.S. 83
            Am Consttn (Kelly) 745-746

1270.   James Stewart and Co. v. Sadrakula   Jan 29, 1940   309 U.S. 94
           *Consttnl Law (Freund) 645-647

1271.   Federal Communications Commission   Jan 29, 1940   309 U.S. 134
              v. Pottsville Broadcasting Co.
           Felix Frankfurter (Mendelson) 208-211
           *Govt and Business 554-556
           *Sup Ct on Freedom 251-252

1272.   Illinois Central Railroad v. Minnesota   Jan 29, 1940   309 U.S. 157
           *Consttnl Law (Freund) 528-530

1273.   McCarroll v. Dixie Greyhound Lines,   Feb 12, 1940   309 U.S. 176
              Inc.
           Am Consttn (Kelly) 740-741
           *Consttnl Cases 247-255
           *Consttnl Law (Freund) 434-438

1274.   Chambers v. Florida   Feb 12, 1940   309 U.S. 227
           *Am Consttnl Law (Bartholomew) v. 2, 273-274
           *Am Consttnl Law (Mason) 735-737
            CQ Guide 559
            Civil Rights (Bardolph) 289
           *Consttnl Decisions 184-186
            Defendants 343
           *Documents History v. 2, 424-427
            Hugo Black (Dunne) 202-203, 259-260, 300-301
            Hugo Black (Strickland) 83-84
            Justice 107-114
           *Liberty v. 2, 465-466
           *One Man's Stand 62-69
            Petitioners 281
            Private Pressure 26
            Sup Ct and Confessions 50-55
           *These Liberties 18-22
         PERIODICALS:
            "Negro in the Supreme Court, 1940," Robert L. Gill. Negro
              History Bul 28: 194, 197-200 May '65 (4).

1275.   Federal Housing Administration v.   Feb 12, 1940   309 U.S. 242
              Burr
           *Consttnl Law (Kauper) 497-499

1276.   Amalgamated Utility Workers v. Con-   Feb 26, 1940   309 U.S. 261
              solidated Edison Co. of New York
           *Govt and Business 522-525

1277.   Minnesota ex rel. Pearson v. Probate   Feb 26, 1940   309 U.S. 270
              Court of Ramsey County, Minnesota
           *US Prison Law v. 1, 513-519

1278.   Sheldon v. Metro-Goldwyn Pictures   Mar 25, 1940   309 U.S. 390
              Corporation
           *Cases Copyright (Kaplan) 427-435
           *Cases Copyright (Nimmer) 449-457
            Communication (Hemmer) v. 2, 152-153

1279.   Ethyl Gasoline Corporation v. United   Mar 25, 1940   309 U.S. 436
              States

*Cases Antitrust Law 587-593
*Govt Regulation 497-506

1280. Federal Communications Commission   Mar 25, 1940   309 U.S. 470
              v. Sanders Brothers Radio Station
          *Cases Electronic 27-30
          Communication (Hemmer) v. 2, 287-288
          *Govt and Business 124-126, 569-570
          *Introduction (Mashaw) 816-818
          Sup Ct and Agencies 122-123

1281. Minnesota v. National Tea   Mar 25, 1940   309 U.S. 551
          *Federal Courts 473-478

1282. Maurer v. Hamilton   Apr 22, 1940   309 U.S. 598
          *Am Consttn (Lockhart) 280-283
          *Consttnl Law (Lockhart) 351-353

1283. Osborn v. Ozlin   Apr 22, 1940   310 U.S. 53
          *Consttnl Law (Freund) 441-444

1284. Thornhill v. Alabama   Apr 22, 1940   310 U.S. 88
          Am Consttn (Kelly) 757
          *Am Consttnl Law (Bartholomew) v. 1, 110-111
          *Cases Labor (Cox) 691-697
          *Cases Labor (Handler) 573-576
          *Cases Labor (Oberer) 347-352
          *Civil Liberties (Sweet) 99-101
          Communication (Hemmer) v. 1, 86
          Consttnl Law (Barrett) 1323
          *Consttnl Law (Freund) 1175-1178
          Freedom of Speech (Hudon) 87-88
          *Govt and Business 86-87
          Justice Frankfurter 36-37
          *Labor Law (Herman) 307-310
          *Labor Law (Meltzer) 373-378
          *Labor Law (Twomey) 246-250
          *Labor Relations (Group Trust) 275-280
          Labor Relations (Taylor) 504
          *Liberty v. 2, 456-458
          *Mass Communications 54-56
          Mr. Justice Murphy (Howard) 238-249
          *Mr. Justice Murphy (Norris) 109-116
          Movies 29-31
          *Nature 906-912
          Sup Ct and Uses 80-82
          System 436-438
          PERIODICALS:
          "Frank Murphy, the Thornhill decision, and picketing as free
              speech," Sidney Fine. Labor History 6: 99-120 Spring '65.

1285. Carlson v. California   Apr 22, 1940   310 U.S. 106
          *Mr. Justice Murphy (Norris) 116-118

1286. United States v. Socony-Vacuum   May 6, 1940   310 U.S. 150
              Oil Co.
          *Antitrust (Posner) 77-88
          *Antitrust Analysis 275-285
          *Cases Antitrust Law 301-312

*Cases Antitrust Policy 76-90
*Cases Trade 76-90
*Competition 217-223
*Documents History v. 2, 427-430
*Free Enterprise 460-467
*Govt Regulation 507-560
*Selected Antitrust Cases 72-78

1287. Dampskibsselkabet Dannebrog v. Signal May 20, 1940 310 U.S. 268
            Oil and Gas Co. of California
        The Stjerneborg
        *Cases Admiralty 285-288

1288. Cantwell v. Connecticut   May 20, 1940 310 U.S. 296
            Am Consttn (Kelly) 762-763
        *Am Consttnl Law (Bartholomew) v. 2, 12-14
        *Am Consttnl Law (Shapiro) 439-442
         By What Right 358
         CQ Guide 408
        *Cases Consttnl Law (Gunther) 1204-1206
        *Cases Individual 751-753
         Church and State 119-120
         Church State and Freedom 654-656
        *Civil Rights (Abernathy) 1977 341-344
         Communication (Hemmer) v. 1, 69
         Consttnl Law (Barrett) 1255-1256, 1475-1476
        *Consttnl Law (Freund) 1179-1183
        *Consttnl Law (Kauper) 1239-1244
         Expanding Liberties 290-291
         First Amendment (Marnell) 157-158
         Freedom and the Court 266-268, 280
        *Freedom of Speech (Hudon) 88-90, 91-92
         Garden 107-108
         Justice Frankfurter 84-85
        *Law Power 314-319
        *Mass Communications 41-42
         Movies 31-32
         O'er the Ramparts 111-116
         Private Conscience 82-83
         Religion (Kurland) 51-54
         Religious Freedom (Arnold) 39
        *Religious Freedom (Pfeffer) 135-139
         Render 38-39
         Sup Ct and Religion 60-64
         Sup Ct in Free Society 290
         Sup Ct Review 1977 263-264
         System 313-314
         This Honorable Court 347-348
         Warren (Carter) 72-73

1289. Nashville, Chattanooga and St. Louis   May 20, 1940 310 U.S. 362
            Railway v. Browning
         Consttnl Law (Barrett) 378-379
         Mr. Justice Frankfurter 15

1290. United States v. George S. Bush   May 20, 1940 310 U.S. 371
            and Co., Inc.
        *Govt and Business 602-604

1291. Sunshine Anthracite Coal Co.   May 20, 1940 310 U.S. 381
          v. Adkins
       Am Consttn (Kelly) 730

1292. Securities and Exchange Commission   May 27, 1940 310 U.S. 434
          v. United States Realty and Im-
          provement Co.
       *Materials Reorganization 221-230

1293. Apex Hosiery Co. v. Leader   May 27, 1940 310 U.S. 469
       *Cases Labor (Cox) 1222-1226
       *Cases Trade 139-140
       *Govt Regulation 561-589
        Hugo Black (Strickland) 203-204
       *Labor Law (Herman) 52-56
        Labor Relations (Taylor) 109-112
       *Liberty v. 2, 432-434

1294. White v. Texas   May 27, 1940 310 U.S. 530
        Court Years 218-219
       PERIODICALS:
        "Negro in the Supreme Court, 1940, " Robert L. Gill. Negro
        History Bul 28: 194, 197-200 May '65 (4).

1295. United States v. American Trucking   May 27, 1940 310 U.S. 534
          Association
       *Criminal Law (Wells) 50-51
       *Govt and Business 649-654

1296. Minersville School District v.   June 3, 1940   310 U.S. 586
          Gobitis
        Am Consttn (Kelly) 766-767
       *Am Consttnl Law (Mason) 608-613
        CQ Guide 457-458
        Church and State 120-121
        Church State and Freedom 635-638
        Civil Rights (Schimmel) 113-118
        Communication (Hemmer) v. 1, 110-111
        Court Years 44-45
        Digest 35-36
       *Documents History v. 2, 433-437
        Education (Lapati) 247-248
       *Education (Spurlock) 100-106
        Felix Frankfurter (Baker) 243-247
        Felix Frankfurter (Mendelson) 114-116
        Felix Frankfurter (Thomas) 45-52
        Freedom and the Court 25, 268-271, 277
        Freedom of Speech (Hudon) 93-94
        Great Reversals 137-138
       *Judicial Excerpts 51-52
        Justice Frankfurter 31-32
        Landmark Decisions 33-41
        Mr. Justice Murphy (Howard) 287-288
        O'er the Ramparts 34-54
        Private Conscience 164-166
        Prophets 108-130, 224-228
       *Prophets 224-228
        Public Schools 50-53
       *Public Schools 53-63

Quarrels 222-242
Religion (Fellman) 84-85
Religion (Kurland) 41-44
*Religious Freedom (Pfeffer) 127-128
Render 81-147
School in the Legal Structure 63-64
Spirit 41-42
Sup Ct (Mason) 159-160
Sup Ct and Religion 69-71
*Sup Ct on Freedom 206-207
Sup Ct Review 1977 260-263, 266-272
*Sup Ct Speaks 323-328
System 27-28
*These Liberties 183-191
This Honorable Court 348-349
*Two Swords 142-148
PERIODICALS:
"Courts in the saddle: school boards out," William R. Hazard.
Phi Delta Kappan 56: 259-261 Dec '74 (5).
"Student rights, legal principles and educational policy," Richard
L. Mandel. Intellect 103: 236-239 Jan '75 (2).

1297. Republic Steel Corporation v. National   Nov 11, 1940   311 U.S. 7
Labor Relations Board
*Govt and Business 682-686

1298. Hansberry v. Lee   Nov 12, 1940   311 U.S. 32
*Cases Pleading 674-680
*Civil Procedure (Cound) 573-576
*Elements Civil 509-515
*Injunctions 510-513
PERIODICALS:
"Negro in the Supreme Court, 1940," Robert L. Gill.   Negro
History Bul 28: 194, 197-200 May '65 (4).

1299. International Association of Machinists   Nov 12, 1940   311 U.S. 72
Tool and Die Makers v. National
Labor Relations Board
*Labor Law (Twomey) 96-99

1300. Smith v. Texas   Nov 25, 1940   311 U.S. 127
Civil Rights (Bardolph) 288
*One Man's Stand 70-73
PERIODICALS:
See listing at 311 U.S. 32, entry no. 1298.

1301. Fidelity Union Trust Co. v. Field   Dec 9, 1940   311 U.S. 169
*Cases Federal Courts 587-590

1302. United States v. Falcone   Dec 9, 1940   311 U.S. 205
*Cases Criml Law (Inbau) 871-874

1303. Montgomery Ward v. Duncan   Dec 9, 1940   311 U.S. 243
*Cases Civil Procedure 754-758

1304. Wright v. Union Central Life   Dec 9, 1940   311 U.S. 273
Insurance Co.
*Materials Reorganization 275-278

1305.   United States v. Harris   Dec 9, 1940   311 U.S. 292
        United States v. Kenny
        *Mr. Justice Murphy (Norris) 359-360

1306.   L. Singer and Sons v. Union Pacific Dec 16, 1940   311 U.S. 295
            Railroad Co.
        Kansas City v. L. Singer and Sons
        *Govt and Business 570-574

1307.   United States v. Appalachian Electric Dec 16, 1940 311 U.S. 377
            Power
        Am Consttn (Kelly) 735
        *Am Consttnl Law (Bartholomew) v. 1, 274-277

1308.   Wisconsin v. Penney Co.   Dec 16, 1940   311 U.S. 435
        *Consttnl Law (Lockhart) 369-371
        *Mr. Justice Frankfurter 199-200

1309.   Best and Co. v. Maxwell   Dec 23, 1940   311 U.S. 454
        *Am Consttnl Law (Saye) 193-194
        *Consttn (Mendelson) 215-216
        Sup Ct and Commerce 322

1310.   Milliken v. Meyer   Dec 23, 1940   311 U.S. 457
        *Cases Civil Procedure 350-352
        *Elements Civil 264-265

1311.   Palmer v. Connecticut Railway and   Jan 6, 1941   311 U.S. 544
            Lighting Co.
        *Materials Reorganization 595-601

1312.   Sibbach v. Wilson and Co.   Jan 13, 1941   312 U.S. 1
        *Cases Civil Procedure 269-273
        *Cases Federal Courts 643-648
        *Federal Courts 676-681

1313.   Gorin v. United States   Jan 13, 1941   312 U.S. 19
        Salich v. United States
        *Freedom vs National Security 262-267

1314.   Hines v. Davidowitz   Jan 20, 1941   312 U.S. 52
        *Am Consttn (Lockhart) 276-279
        *Consttnl Law (Lockhart) 347-350
        *Contemporary Law 188-191
        Foreign Affairs 243-244

1315.   United States v. Darby   Feb 3, 1941   312 U.S. 100
            Am Consttn (Kelly) 723
        *Am Consttn (Lockhart) 161-164
        *Am Consttnl Law (Bartholomew) v. 1, 265-268
        *Am Consttnl Law (Mason) 296-299
        *Am Consttnl Law (Saye) 142-144
        *Am Consttnl Law (Shapiro) 281-284
        *Basic Cases 42-46
        Basic History 62
        Biography 325-326
        CQ Guide 101-102
        *Cases Consttnl Law (Cushman) 217-220
        *Cases Consttnl Law (Gunther) 162-167

Am Consttn (Kelly) 758
*Cases Labor (Handler) 678-680
Felix Frankfurter (Thomas) 85
Hugo Black (Dunne) 205-206
Justice Frankfurter 103-104
*Labor Law (Meltzer) 392-395
*Labor Law (Twomey) 258-261
Labor Relations (Taylor) 508-509
Mr. Justice Murphy (Howard) 254-255
*One Man's Stand 74-82
*Sup Ct on Freedom 203-205
System 315-316

1320. American Federation of Labor   Feb 10, 1941   312 U.S. 321
           v. Swing
       Am Consttn (Kelly) 757
       Justice Frankfurter 101-102
       *Labor Law (Twomey) 264-266
       Labor Relations (Taylor) 505

1321. Federal Trade Commission v. Bunte   Feb 17, 1941   312 U.S. 349
           Brothers, Inc.
       *Consttn (Mendelson) 126-128

1322. Nelson v. Sears, Roebuck and Co.   Feb 17, 1941   312 U.S. 359
       *Consttnl Law (Freund) 572-574

1323. Fashion Originators' Guild of America   Mar 3, 1941   312 U.S. 457
           v. Federal Trade Commission
       *Antitrust (Posner) 532-536
       *Antitrust Analysis 389-393
       *Cases Antitrust Law 443-448
       *Consttnl Law (Kauper) 282-286
       *Free Enterprise 609-613
       *Govt Regulation 600-605
       Hugo Black (Strickland) 202-203
       Professional Sports 461

1324. Railroad Commission of Texas v.   Mar 3, 1941   312 U.S. 496
           Pullman Co.
       *Cases Federal Courts 463-466
       *Federal Courts 985-988

1325. Consolidated Rock Products Co.   Mar 3, 1941   312 U.S. 510
           v. Du Bois
       Badgley v. Du Bois
       *Materials Reorganization 392-400

1326. Ex parte Hull   Mar 3, 1941   312 U.S. 546
       *Consttnl Law (Felkenes) 399-401
       Criminal Procedure (Wells) 236-238
       *Mr. Justice Murphy (Norris) 401-404

1327. Cox v. New Hampshire   Mar 31, 1941   312 U.S. 569
       Am Consttn (Kelly) 760
       *Cases Consttnl Law (Gunther) 1202-1204
       *Cases Individual 748-751
       Church and State 121
       Communication (Hemmer) v. 1, 73-74

Consttnl Law (Barrett) 1308-1309
Free Speech (Kurland) 139-141, 350-352
Freedom and the Court 277
Mass Communications 45-46
Movies 33-36
Negro (Kalven) 204-207
Private Conscience 93-94
Religion (Kurland) 54
Right of Assembly 98-103
Sup Ct Review 1965 25-27
Sup Ct Review 1974 241
System 360

1328. Nye v. United States   Apr 14, 1941   313 U.S. 33
Communication (Hemmer) v. 2, 161
Court Years 141
*Douglas 71-74
Great Reversals 129

1329. Skiriotes v. Florida   Apr 28, 1941   313 U.S. 69
*Criminal Law (Wells) 153-154

1330. Mitchell v. United States   Apr 28, 1941   313 U.S. 80
Civil Rights (Bardolph) 283-285
*Depression 223-227
Desegregation (Wasby) 45
*Documents History v. 2, 457-459
Equality (Berger) 128-129
Petitioners 365-367
Private Pressure 41-42
Sup Ct and Commerce 198-199

1331. California v. Thompson   Apr 28, 1941   313 U.S. 109
*Cases Consttnl Law (Cushman) 184-186
*Consttn (Mendelson) 199-201

1332. Phelps-Dodge Corporation v. National Apr 28, 1941   313 U.S. 177
Labor Relations Board
*Cases Labor (Cox) 268-276
*Consttnl Law (Barrett) 669
Felix Frankfurter (Mendelson) 197-198
*Govt and Business 676-682
*Labor Law (Twomey) 118-120

1333. Gelfert v. National City Bank of   Apr 28, 1941   313 U.S. 221
of New York
*Govt and Business 75-76

1334. Olsen v. Nebraska ex rel. Western   Apr 28, 1941   313 U.S. 236
Reference and Bond Association
Consttnl Law (Barrett) 669-670

1335. United States v. Classic   May 26, 1941   313 U.S. 299
*Am Consttnl Law (Bartholomew) v. 2, 325-327
Black 38-41
CQ Guide 482
*Cases Civil Liberties 397-402
*Cases Consttnl Law (Cushman) 627-632
*Civil Rights (Abernathy) 1977 573-575

*Consttnl Law (Freund) 945-948
*Consttnl Law (Kauper) 591-594
Desegregation (Wasby) 32
*Documents History v. 2, 459-463
*Douglas 86-94
Modern Sup Ct 31-35
Quest 119, 126-127
Rise 78-79
Sup Ct and Electoral Process 32-36, 69

1336. United States v. Morgan   May 26, 1941   313 U.S. 409
        Sup Ct in Free Society 42

1337. Klaxon v. Stentor Electric Manu-   June 2, 1941   313 U.S. 487
          facturing Co.
        *Cases Federal Courts 591-594
        *Federal Courts 711-713

1338. Oklahoma ex rel. Phillips v. Atkinson   June 2, 1941   313 U.S. 508
        Am Consttn (Kelly) 735-736

1339. Indianapolis v. Chase National Bank   Nov 10, 1941   314 U.S. 63
          of New York City
        *Cases Federal Courts 210-220

1340. Cuno Engineering Corporation v.   Nov 10, 1941   314 U.S. 84
          Automatic Devices Corporation
        Sup Ct and Agencies 173-175

1341. Edwards v. California   Nov 24, 1941   314 U.S. 160
        Am Consttn (Kelly) 741-742
        *Am Consttn (Lockhart) 271-273
        *Am Consttnl Law (Bartholomew) v. 1, 235-236
        *Am Consttnl Law (Shapiro) 246-250
        *Cases Consttnl Law (Cushman) 188-192
        Consttn (Konvitz) 39-40
        *Consttnl Law (Freund) 341-345
        *Consttnl Politics 430-435
        Court and Consttn v. 2, 141-142
        *Dispassionate 249-254
        Dissent 71-72
        *Documents History v. 2, 463-464
        Great Reversals 131-133
        *Justices (Friedman) v. 4, 2537-2540
        *Legal Problems 5-8
        *Modern Social Legislation 730-733
        *Political Rights 908-915
        Sup Ct and Commerce 192-194

1342. Lisenba v. California   Dec 8, 1941   314 U.S. 219
        Modern Sup Ct 38-39
        Sup Ct and Confessions 57-61

1343. Bridges v. California   Dec 8, 1941   314 U.S. 252
        Times-Mirror Co. v. Superior Court
          of California
        Am Consttn (Kelly) 768
        *Am Consttnl Law (Bartholomew) v. 2, 80-81
        Argument 288-289

*Bill (Cohen) 191-196
Communication (Hemmer) v. 2, 161-163
Court Years 143-144
Felix Frankfurter (Thomas) 130-132
*First Amendment (Konvitz) 902-910
Freedom and the Court 178-179
Freedom of Speech (Hudon) 98-99
*Freedom of the Press (Nelson) 153-165
*Freedom Reader 133-135
Handbook 512-514
Hugo Black (Dunne) 206-207
Justice Frankfurter 71-76
Justice Hugo Black 114-115
Justices Black and Frankfurter 55
*Mass Media (Devol) 268-272
Modern Sup Ct 13-20
*One Man's Stand 83-92
*Sup Ct (Mendelson) 151-173
*Sup Ct on Freedom 91-94
Sup Ct Review 1978 268
System 451-453

1344.	United States v. Santa Fe Railroad *Am Indian v. 4, 2730-2738	Dec 8, 1941	314 U.S.	339
1345.	Duckworth v. Arkansas *Consttnl Law (Freund) 438-441 *Dispassionate 254-258	Dec 15, 1941	314 U.S.	390
1346.	Gray v. Powell Sup Ct in Free Society 41	Dec 15, 1941	314 U.S.	402
1347.	National Labor Relations Board v. Virginia Electric and Power Co. National Labor Relations Board v. Independent Organization of Employees of the Virginia Electric & Power Co. *Cases Labor (Cox) 170-173 *Cases Labor (Oberer) 272-277 *Labor Relations (Group Trust) 243-246 Mr. Justice Murphy (Howard) 256-260 *Mr. Justice Murphy (Norris) 118-123 *Statutory History Labor 378-383	Dec 22, 1941	314 U.S.	469
1348.	Morton Salt Co. v. G. S. Suppiger Co. *Cases Antitrust Law 680-683 *Cases Trade 902-905 *Free Enterprise 1233-1236 *Govt Regulation 606-609 *Patent 469-474	Jan 5, 1942	314 U.S.	488
1349.	B. B. Chemical Co. v. Ellis *Govt Regulation 610-612	Jan 5, 1942	314 U.S.	495
1350.	Taylor v. Georgia *Justices (Friedman) v. 4, 2535-2537	Jan 12, 1942	315 U.S.	25
1351.	Glasser v. United States	Jan 19, 1942	315 U.S.	60

Kretske v. United States
Roth v. United States
*Mr. Justice Murphy (Norris) 332-347

1352.   United States v. Wrightwood Dairy   Feb 2, 1942   315 U.S. 110
            Co.
        *Govt and Business 318-319

1353.   Exhibit Supply Co. v. Ace Patents   Feb 2, 1942   315 U.S. 126
            Corporation
        Genco, Inc. v. Ace Patents Corporation
        Chicago Coin Machine Co. v. Ace
            Patents Corporation
        *Patent 228-238

1354.   Cloverleaf Butter Co. v. Patterson   Feb 2, 1942   315 U.S. 148
            Am Consttn (Kelly) 742
            Sup Ct and Commerce 278-281

1355.   United States v. Pink   Feb 2, 1942   315 U.S. 203
            CQ Guide 206
            *Consttnl Law (Barrett) 272-273
            *Consttnl Law (Freund) 700-705
            *Contemporary Law 419-425
            Executive Privilege 159-160
            *Freedom vs National Security 38-48
            *Mr. Justice Frankfurter 56-58

1356.   Young v. United States   Feb 2, 1942   315 U.S. 257
            *Mr. Justice Murphy (Norris) 424-426

1357.   United States v. Bethlehem Steel Corp.   Feb 16, 1942   315 U.S. 289
        United States Shipping Board Merchant
            Fleet Corp. v. Bethlehem Ship-
            building Corp.
            Elements Judicial 129-130
            From the Diaries 330
            Mr. Justice Murphy (Howard) 278-279
            Sup Ct and Commander in Chief 96

1358.   Williams v. Jacksonville Terminal Co.   Mar 2, 1942   315 U.S. 386
        Pickett v. Union Terminal Co.
            *Modern Social Legislation 639-641

1359.   Hysler v. Florida   Mar 2, 1942   315 U.S. 411
            *Mr. Justice Frankfurter 169-170

1360.   United States v. New York   Mar 2, 1942   315 U.S. 510
            *Modern Social Legislation 64-66, 480-482

1361.   Chaplinsky v. New Hampshire   Mar 9, 1942   315 U.S. 568
            Am Consttn (Kelly) 760
            *Am Consttnl Law (Saye) 326-327
            *Bill (Cohn) 126-127
            CQ Guide 407
            Church and State 121-122
            Communication (Hemmer) v. 1, 30-31
            *Comparative 507-509
            Conceived 105-106

Sup Ct Review 1976 47-49
System 415-416
PERIODICALS:
"Advertising and the First Amendment," Dorothy Cohen. J Mar-
keting 42: 59-68 July '78 (4).
"Is national advertising still a step child of the first amendment?"
E. John Kottman. J Advertising 8: 6-12 Fall '79 (2).
"The new commercial speech doctrine," Michael B. Metzger and
Barry S. Roberts. MSU Bus Topics 27: 17-23 Spring '79
(3).

1369.   Goldstein v. United States   Apr 27, 1942   316 U.S. 114
Mr. Justice Murphy (Howard) 281-282
*Mr. Justice Murphy (Norris) 270-274
Search and Seizure 210-211
Sup Ct Review 1962 230

1370.   Goldman v. United States   Apr 27, 1942   316 U.S. 129
Shulman v. United States
*Consttnl Aspects v. 4, 375-383
Criminal Law (Felkenes) 132-134
Elements Judicial 68-73
Mr. Justice Murphy (Howard) 281-286
*Mr. Justice Murphy (Norris) 282-285
Modern Sup Ct 243
*Rights (Shattuck) 12-13
Search and Seizure 211-212
Sup Ct Review 1962 231-232

1371.   Federal Trade Commission v. Raladam Apr 27, 1942 316 U.S. 149
Communication (Hemmer) v. 2, 329

1372.   State Tax Commission of Utah v.   Apr 27, 1942   316 U.S. 174
Aldrich
*Mr. Justice Frankfurter 198

1373.   United States v. Masonite Corporation   May 11, 1942   316 U.S. 265
*Antitrust (Posner) 295-300
*Govt Regulation 613-623

1374.   Pence v. United States   May 11, 1942   316 U.S. 332
*Mr. Justice Murphy (Norris) 323-324

1375.   Betts v. Brady   June 1, 1942   316 U.S. 455
*Am Consttn (Lockhart) 453-455
*Am Consttnl Issues 402-407
*Basic Criminal 44-48
CQ Guide 566-567
*Cases Civil Liberties 56-61
*Cases Consttnl Law (Cushman) 286-291
*Cases Consttnl Rights 216-218
*Civil Liberties (Sweet) 264-266
Court and Consttn v. 2, 151
Criminal Law (Felkenes) 177-178
Defendants 213-214
*Due Process 39
Expanding Liberties 383-384
Freedom and the Court 76-77
Gideon's Trumpet.

Hugo Black (Strickland) 103-104
Justice Rutledge 232-233
*Leading Consttnl Cases 417-419
Mr. Justice Murphy (Howard) 428-430
Modern Sup Ct 41-42, 101-102
*One Man's Stand 93-96
Prophets 80-107
*Prophets 218-223
Rationing 98-101
Sup Ct (North) 127

1376.   Standard Oil Co. of California v.   June 1, 1942   316 U.S. 481
            Johnson
        *Federal Courts 483-485
        *Materials Consttnl Law 121-123

1377.   Kirschbaum v. Walling   June 1, 1942   316 U.S. 517
        Arsenal Building Corporation v.
            Walling
            Am Consttn (Kelly) 724
        *Am Consttnl Law (Bartholomew) v. 1, 268-270
        *Cases Employment 685-689
        Sup Ct and Commerce 121-123

1378.   Skinner v. Oklahoma ex rel. Williamson June 1, 1942   316 U.S. 535
        *Comparative 391-393
        Conceived 53
        Consttnl Law (Barrett) 699
        *Consttnl Law (Freund) 872-876
        *Family 494-495
        Freedom and the Court 114-117
        Quest 77
        *Rights (Shattuck) 99-100

1379.   Jones v. Opelika   June 8, 1942   316 U.S. 584
        Bowden v. Fort Smith
        Jobin v. Arizona
            Am Consttn (Kelly) 763
            Church and State 122
            Church State and Freedom 722-724
            Court and Consttn v. 2, 139-140
            Freedom and the Court 277
            Justice Rutledge 50-52
            Law of Mass 618-620
            Mr. Justice Murphy (Howard) 288-291
        *Mr. Justice Murphy (Norris) 179-181
            O'er the Ramparts 117-123
        *One Man's Stand 97-99
            Private Conscience 108
            Religion (Kurland) 57-60
            Render 197-201
            Sup Ct (North) 136-137
        *Sup Ct on Freedom 81-85

1380.   Walling v. A. H. Belo Corporation   June 8, 1942   316 U.S. 624
        *Modern Social Legislation 646-650

1381.   Ex parte Quirin   July 31, 1942   317 U.S. 1
        Ex parte Haupt

Ex parte Kerling
Ex parte Burger
Ex parte Heinek
Ex parte Thiel
Ex parte Neubauer
  Am Consttn (Kelly) 794-795
  CQ Guide 192
  *Cases Criml Law (Inbau) 185-194
  *Consttn (Mendelson) 171
  *Consttnl Law (Barrett) 548-549
  *Consttnl Law (Freund) 1054-1060
  *Contemporary Law 362-367
  Court Years 138-139
  Elements Judicial 48-49
  Hugo Black (Dunne) 209-210
  Presidential Power 117-119; reprinted from Am Poltcl Sci Rev
      37: 18-25 Feb '43
  Sup Ct and Commander in Chief 113-116

1382. Braverman v. United States
      Wainer v. United States   Nov 9, 1942   317 U.S. 49
        *Criminal Law (Kadish) 473-475

1383. Ex parte Kawoto   Nov 9, 1942   317 U.S. 69
        *One Man's Stand 100-103

1384. Warren-Bradshaw Drilling Co. v.   Nov 9, 1942   317 U.S. 88
         Hall
        Sup Ct and Commerce 123-124

1385. Wickard v. Filburn   Nov 4, 1942   317 U.S. 111
        Am Consttn (Kelly) 729-730
        *Am Consttn (Lockhart) 165-167
        *Am Consttnl Law (Mason) 299-302
        Am Consttnl Law (Shapiro) 284-286
        CQ Guide 103
        *Cases Consttnl Law (Gunther) 157-161
        *Comparative 181-183
        *Competition 13-16
        *Consttn (Hirschfield) 56-59
        *Consttn (Mendelson) 116-121
        *Consttn (Pollak) 339-342
        *Consttnl Cases 221-228
        *Consttnl Decisions 114-117
        *Consttnl Law (Barrett) 235-237
        *Consttnl Law (Barron) 190-193
        *Consttnl Law (Freund) 293-297
        *Consttnl Law (Kauper) 170-177
        *Consttnl Law (Lockhart) 135-138
        *Consttnl Politics 403-407
        *Contemporary Law 310-314
        *Federal System 246-249
        *Govt and Business 264-268
        *Liberty v. 2, 437-438
        *Social Forces 183-186
        Sup Ct (Forte) 31-32
        *Sup Ct and Am Govt 90-97
        Sup Ct and Commerce 97-101
        *Sup Ct and Consttn 406-412

Sup Ct in Free Society 98-99
*Sup Ct Speaks 409-415

1386. Sola Electric Co. v. Jefferson   Dec 7, 1942   317 U.S. 173
       Electric Co.
       *Cases Trade 931-933
       *Govt Regulation 624-626
       *Patent 795-799

1387. Ettelson v. Metropolitan Life   Dec 7, 1942   317 U.S. 188
       Insurance Co.
       *Cases Civil Procedure 1044-1046

1388. Garrett v. Moore-McCormack Co.   Dec 14, 1942   317 U.S. 239
       *Cases Admiralty 196-198

1389. Davis v. Department of Labor and   Dec 14, 1942   317 U.S. 249
       Industries of Washington
       *Mr. Justice Frankfurter 41-42

1390. Adams v. United States   Dec 21, 1942   317 U.S. 269
       *Mr. Justice Murphy (Norris) 316-317

1391. Williams v. North Carolina   Dec 21, 1942   317 U.S. 287
       *Dispassionate 258-267

1392. Parker v. Brown   Jan 4, 1943   317 U.S. 341
       *Am Consttn (Lockhart) 264-266
       *Am Consttnl Law (Mason) 233-236
       CQ Guide 361
       Cases Consttnl Law (Gunther) 318-319
       *Govt and Business 281-282
       *Govt Regulation 627-642
       *Selected Antitrust Cases 363-366
       Sup Ct and Commerce 243-245
       Sup Ct in Free Society 99-100, 121

1393. United States v. Miller   Jan 4, 1943   317 U.S. 369
       *Govt and Business 412-414
       Sup Ct Review 1962 93-94

1394. Natural Milk Producers Association   Jan 11, 1943   317 U.S. 423
       of California v. San Francisco
       From the Diaries 143

1395. United States v. Monia   Jan 11, 1943   317 U.S. 424
       From the Diaries 146
       *Mr. Justice Frankfurter 130-133

1396. Endicott Johnson Corporation v.   Jan 11, 1943   317 U.S. 501
       Perkins
       *Admin Law (Schwartz) 192-193
       *Govt and Business 497-501
       *Social Forces 552-554

1397. United States ex rel. Marcus v. Hess   Jan 18, 1943   317 U.S. 537
       *Dispassionate 234-237

1398. Walling v. Jacksonville Paper Co.   Jan 18, 1943   317 U.S. 564

*Cases Labor (Stern) 228-229
*Modern Social Legislation 611-615
Sup Ct and Commerce 124-126

1399.   Tileston v. Ullman   Feb 1, 1943   318 U.S. 44
        *Consttn (Mendelson) 14-15
        *Consttnl Law (Kauper) 31-32
        *Courts Judges 244-245
        *Federal Courts 150-151
        From the Diaries 157-158
        *Materials Consttnl Law 192-193
        *Nature 89-90

1400.   Tiller v. Atlantic Coast Line   Feb 1, 1943   318 U.S. 54
           Railroad Co.
        *Cases Workmen 26-36
        *Materials Law 474-485

1401.   Securities and Exchange Commission   Feb 1, 1943   318 U.S. 80
           v. Chenery Corporation
        Hugo Black (Dunne) 254-256
        Justice Rutledge 323-327

1402.   Jerome v. United States   Feb 1, 1943   318 U.S. 101
        Double (Miller) 51

1403.   Palmer v. Hoffman   Feb 1, 1943   318 U.S. 109
        *Cases Civil Procedure 706-709
        *Cases Evidence 658-661
        *Elements Civil 584-586
        *Principles Proof 343-246

1404.   Overstreet v. North Shore Corporation   Feb 1, 1943   318 U.S. 125
        Sup Ct and Commerce 127

1405.   C.J. Hendry Co. v. Moore   Feb 8, 1943   318 U.S. 133
        *Cases Admiralty 37-41
        From the Diaries 143

1406.   Johnson v. United States   Feb 15, 1943   318 U.S. 189
        From the Diaries 161, 177-184, 185
        *Principles Proof 652-659

1407.   United States v. Oklahoma Gas and   Feb 15, 1943   318 U.S. 206
           Electric Co.
        From the Diaries 142-143

1408.   Federal Security Administrator v.   Mar 1, 1943   318 U.S. 218
           Quaker Oats Co.
        *Cases Food 172-177
        *Legal Environment 167-169

1409.   McNabb v. United States   Mar 1, 1943   318 U.S. 332
        CQ Guide 558-559
        *Consttnl Politics 252-256
        Decade 167
        Defendants 340-342
        *Due Process 28-29
        Felix Frankfurter (Baker) 255-256
        Freedom Spent 379

*Justices (Friedman) v. 3, 2396-2398
*Mr. Justice Frankfurter 116-119
Modern Sup Ct 37
*Police 44-47, 92
Procedures 46
Sup Ct and Confessions 64-66

1410. Anderson v. United States   Mar 1, 1943   318 U.S. 350
        Sup Ct and Confessions 67

1411. Clearfield Trust Co. v. United States   Mar 1, 1943   318 U.S. 363
        *Cases Federal Courts 615-619
        *Federal Courts 756-759

1412. Helvering v. Griffiths   Mar 1, 1943   318 U.S. 371
        Justices Black and Frankfurter 32-33

1413. Jamison v. Texas   Mar 8, 1943   318 U.S. 413
        Church and State 126
        Free Speech (Kurland) 133-134, 348
        Freedom and the Court 281
        Negro (Kalven) 196-197
        O'er the Ramparts 127-129
        Private Conscience 97
        Religion (Kurland) 55-56
        Sup Ct Review 1965 19-20
        Sup Ct Review 1974 239

1414. Largent v. Texas   Mar 8, 1943   318 U.S. 418
        Negro (Kalven) 124-126
        Religion (Kurland) 56-57

1415. Group of Institutional Investors v.   Mar 15, 1943   318 U.S. 523
          Chicago, Milwaukee, St. Paul
          and Pacific Railroad Co.
        *Materials Reorganization 485-496

1416. Ex parte Republic of Peru   Apr 5, 1943   318 U.S. 578
        The Ucayali
        *Federal Courts 290-297
        *Mr. Justice Frankfurter 17-18

1417. Fred Fisher Music Co., Inc. v.   Apr 5, 1943   318 U.S. 643
          M. Witmark and Sons
        *Cases Copyright (Kaplan) 376-386
        *Cases Copyright (Nimmer) 262-270

1418. St. Pierre v. United States   May 3, 1943   319 U.S. 41
        *Materials Consttnl Law 188-189

1419. Jones v. Opelika   May 3, 1943   319 U.S. 103
        Church State and Freedom 725
        Freedom and the Court 280

1420. Murdock v. Pennsylvania   May 3, 1943   319 U.S. 105
        Am Consttn (Kelly) 763-764
        *Am Consttnl Law (Bartholomew) v. 2, 15-17
        *Cases Civil Liberties 282-285
        *Cases Consttnl Law (Cushman) 512-515

Church and State 122-123
Civil Rights (Fiss) 62-63
Communication (Hemmer) v. 1, 226
Dissent 205-206
*Douglas 132-140
Freedom and the Court 280
Great Reversals 140
Handbook 163-164
Justice Frankfurter 79-82
Justice Rutledge 52-53
*Liberty v. 2, 461-462
Modern Sup Ct 26-28
Private Conscience 109
Religion (Kurland) 60-63
Religious Freedom (Arnold) 39
*Religious Freedom (Pfeffer) 167-169
Render 203-204
Sup Ct and Uses 78-79
System 420-421

1421.   Martin v. City of Struthers   May 3, 1943   319 U.S. 141
Am Consttn (Kelly) 764
CQ Guide 420
*Cases Consttnl Law (Gunther) 1214-1215
Church and State 123-124
Communication (Hemmer) v. 1, 225-226
*Consttnl Law (Felkenes) 167-169
Free Speech (Kurland) 373-374
Freedom and the Court 281
From the Diaries 225-226
Handbook 141-142
Justice Rutledge 53-55, 368-373
Justices Black and Frankfurter 61-63
*Mr. Justice Frankfurter 75-76
Mr. Justice Murphy (Howard) 291-293
*Mr. Justice Murphy (Norris) 186-188
Negro (Kalven) 147-150
O'er the Ramparts 130-134
Private Conscience 131-135
Religion (Kurland) 63-64
Render 203-204
*Right to Privacy 93-98
Sup Ct and Religion 65-67
*Sup Ct on Freedom 192-194
Sup Ct Review 1974 264-265
System 349-350, 558

1422.   Douglas v. City of Jeanette   May 3, 1943   319 U.S. 157
Civil Rights (Fiss) 62-67
*Dispassionate 71-76
Dissent 206-207
Freedom and the Court 281
Religion (Kurland) 64-65
Render 203-206

1423.   Lockerty v. Phillips   May 10, 1943   319 U.S. 182
*Consttnl Law (Kauper) 79-81

1424.   National Broadcasting Co. v. United   May 10, 1943   319 U.S. 190
States

Columbia Broadcasting Co. v. United
   States
 *Cases Electronic 148-164
 Communication (Hemmer) v. 2, 262-264
 *First Amendment (Franklin) 487-492
 *Freedom of the Press (Schmidt) 131-132
 *Govt and Business 604-609
 *Mass Communications 755-763
 *Mass Media (Devol) 323-324
 Media and the First Amendment 121
 *Mr. Justice Murphy (Norris) 430-437
 *Statutory History Economic v. 4, 2529-2546
 *Sup Ct on Freedom 253-257
 System 656-657

1425. United States v. Johnson   May 24, 1943 319 U.S. 302
   *Consttnl Law (Freund) 54-56
   *Federal Courts 102-104

1426. Burford v. Sun Oil   May 24, 1943 319 U.S. 315
   *Cases Federal Courts 466-476

1427. Bailey v. Central Vermont Railroad May 24, 1943 319 U.S. 350
   From the Diaries 229-230

1428. Galloway v. United States   May 24, 1943 319 U.S. 372
   *Civil Procedure (Cound) 894-904
   *Elements Civil 1009-1030
   Justice Rutledge 327-331

1429. Freeman v. Bee Machine Co. June 1, 1943 319 U.S. 448
   *Federal Courts 1195-1199

1430. Tot v. United States   June 7, 1943 319 U.S. 463
   United States v. Delia
   *Am Consttnl Law (Bartholomew) v. 2, 177-179
   Defendants 106-107

1431. McLeod v. Threlkeld   June 7, 1943 319 U.S. 491
   *Cases Employment 676-679
   *Modern Social Legislation 615-620
   Sup Ct and Commerce 127-128

1432. Taylor v. Mississippi   June 14, 1943 319 U.S. 583
   Benoit v. Mississippi
   Cummings v. Mississippi
   Am Consttn (Kelly) 767-768
   Church and State 125-126
   Church State and Freedom 643
   *Consttnl Law (Klein) 489-491
   Digest 36
   Freedom and the Court 281
   System 67

1433. West Virginia Board of Education v. June 14, 1943 319 U.S. 624
   Barnette
   Am Consttn (Kelly) 767
   *Am Consttnl Issues 332-339
   *Am Consttnl Law (Bartholomew) v. 2, 26-29

*Am Consttnl Law (Mason) 616-618
*Am Consttnl Law (Saye) 286-287
*Am Consttnl Law (Shapiro) 442-447
*Annals v. 16, 148-158
Authority 23
*Bill (Konvitz) 198-210
CQ Guide 411, 458-459
*Cases Civil Liberties 286-290
*Cases Consttnl Law (Cushman) 516-520
Church and State 124-125
Church State and Freedom 640-643
*Civil Liberties (Sweet) 102-108
*Civil Rights (Abernathy) 1977 323-327
Civil Rights (Schimmel) 118-121
Communications (Hemmer) v. 1, 111-112
*Comparative 472-476
*Consttn (Mendelson) 567-572
*Consttn (Morris) 194-202
*Consttnl Cases 170-184
Consttnl Law (Barrett) 1476-1477
*Consttnl Law (Felkenes) 163-166
*Consttnl Law (Freund) 1345-1350
*Consttnl Law (Grossman) 180-183
*Consttnl Politics 569-578
*Consttnl Rights (Kemerer) 281-286
*Courts Judges 727-731
*Depression 215-223
Digest 36-37
*Dispassionate 34-39
Dissent 207-209
*Documents History v. 2, 437-442
*Education (Hazard) 81-87
Education (Lapati) 248-249
*Education (Spurlock) 107-115
*Educational Policy 105-111
Expanding Liberties 22-23
Felix Frankfurter (Baker) 268-270
Felix Frankfurter (Mendelson) 117-118
Felix Frankfurter (Thomas) 52-56
*First Amendment (Konvitz) 223-232
First Amendment (Marnell) 159-163
Freedom and the Court 4-5, 24-25, 272-274, 281
*Freedom of Speech (Haiman) 33-35
Freedom of Speech (Hudon) 94-96
Freedom of the Press (Schmidt) 33-34
From the Diaries 253-254
Garden 112-118
Great Reversals 141-143
Hugo Black (Dunne) 217-218
*Judicial Excerpts 52-54
*Judiciary (Roche) 98-107
Justice Frankfurter 48-51
*Justices (Friedman) v. 4, 2582-2590
Landmark Decisions 43-52
*Law and Public Education (Goldstein) 119-128
Law and Public Education (Hamilton) 136-144
*Law of Public Education 154-156
*Liberty v. 2, 462-465
Mr. Justice Frankfurter 5-7

Mr. Justice Jackson 37-38
Mr. Justice Murphy (Howard) 294-296
*Mr. Justice Murphy (Norris) 188-189
O'er the Ramparts 55-71
*One Man's Stand 104-106
Politics 41-42
Private Conscience 166-168
*Public School Law 558-566
Public Schools 64-66
*Public Schools 67-83
Quarrels 222-242
Religion (Fellman) 85-86
Religion (Kurland) 44-46
Religious Freedom (Arnold) 40
*Religious Freedom (Pfeffer) 129-133
Render 209-235
School in the Legal Structure 64
*School Law (Alexander) 250-252
*School Law (Remmlein) 217-225
Spirit 42-43
*Sup Ct (Mendelson) 173-194
*Sup Ct and Consttn 488-496
*Sup Ct and Education 32-47
Sup Ct and Religion 71-72
*Sup Ct on Freedom 207-208
*Sup Ct Speaks 332-348
System 28-29
*These Liberties 193-202
*Third Branch 38-44
This Honorable Court 349-350
*Two Swords 152-161
PERIODICALS:
"Courts in the saddle: school boards out," William R. Hazard.
   Phi Delta Kappan 56: 259-261 Dec '74 (5).
"Students rights, legal principles and educational policy," Richard
   L. Mandel. Intellect 103: 236-239 Jan '75 (2).

1434.   Interstate Commerce Commission v.   June 14, 1943 319 U.S. 671
        Inland Waterways Corporation
        From the Diaries 174

1435.   Marconi Wireless Telegraph Co. v.   June 21, 1943 320 U.S. 1
        United States
        Dissent 222-223

1436.   Hirabayashi v. United States   June 21, 1943 320 U.S. 81
        Am Consttn (Kelly) 788-789
        Court and Consttn v. 2, 146
        *Documents History v. 2, 465-470
        Elements Judicial 46-47
        *Freedom vs National Security 48-58
        From the Diaries 251-252
        Hugo Black (Dunne) 211-212
        Justice Rutledge 173-176, 356-360
        Mr. Justice Murphy (Howard) 301-309
        *Mr. Justice Murphy (Norris) 231-233
        Modern Sup Ct 46-47
        Prejudice 212, 215-216, 233-235
        Sovereign Prerogative 193-266
        Sup Ct and Commander in Chief 45-47

1437. Schneiderman v. United States   June 21, 1943 320 U.S. 118
         Am Consttn (Kelly) 800
         CQ Guide 143-144
         Felix Frankfurter (Baker) 289-291
         From the Diaries 208-209, 210-217, 248-249, 257-259
         Justice Rutledge 268-272
         Mr. Justice Murphy (Howard) 309-322
         *Mr. Justice Murphy (Norris) 133-151

1438. United States v. Dotterweich   Nov 22, 1943 320 U.S. 277
         *Cases Food 581-586
         *Criminal Law (Kadish) 133-136
         Criminal Law (Wells) 112
         *Materials Legislation 127-137
         Sup Ct Review 1962 116-119

1439. Cafeteria Employees Union v. Angelos Nov 22, 1943 320 U.S. 293
       Cafeteria Employees Union v. Tsakires
         Labor Relations (Taylor) 506-507

1440. Switchmen's Union of North America   Nov 22, 1943 320 U.S. 297
             v. National Mediation Board
         *Cases Labor (Handler) 156-160

1441. Magnolia Petroleum Co. v. Hunt   Dec 20, 1943 320 U.S. 430
         *Dispassionate 222-225

1442. Dobson v. Commissioner of Internal   Dec 20, 1943 320 U.S. 489
             Revenue
       Collins' Estate v. Commissioner of
             Internal Revenue
       Harwick v. Commissioner of Internal
             Revenue
         *Govt and Business 659-663

1443. United States v. Gaskin   Jan 3, 1944   320 U.S. 527
         *Mr. Justice Murphy (Norris) 360-361

1444. Falbo v. United States   Jan 3, 1944   320 U.S. 549
         Mr. Justice Murphy (Howard) 330-332
         *Mr. Justice Murphy (Norris) 351-354
         O'er the Ramparts 171-176

1445. Federal Power Commission v. Hope   Jan 3, 1944   320 U.S. 591
             Natural Gas Co.
       Cleveland v. Hope Natural Gas Co.
         *Cases Regulated 100-107
         *Free Enterprise 687-709
         Hugo Black (Dunne) 227
         Justice Rutledge 320-323, 373-377
         *Justices (Friedman) v. 4, 2478-2490

1446. Mercoid Corporation v. Mid-Continent Jan 3, 1944   320 U.S. 661
             Investment Co.
         *Antitrust (Posner) 598-601
         *Cases Antitrust Law 684-689
         *Cases Trade 905-909
         Court and Consttn v. 2, 130-131
         *Dispassionate 156-159

      *Govt Regulation 643-652
      *Legal Regulation 1065-1068
      *Patent 474-490

1447. Mercoid Corporation v. Minneapolis-   Jan 3, 1944   320 U. S. 680
      Honeywell Regulator Co.
      *Govt Regulation 653-656
      *Patent 491-494

1448. Snowden v. Hughes   Jan 17, 1944   321 U. S. 1
      Mr. Justice Frankfurter 68-69

1449. McLean Trucking Co. v. United   Jan 17, 1944   321 U. S. 67
      States
      *Cases Regulated 597-605
      *Free Enterprise 262-272

1450. Mahnich v. Southern Steamship Co.   Jan 31, 1944   321 U. S. 96
      Hugo Black (Dunne) 228-229
      Sup Ct Review 1964 307-308

1451. Prince v. Massachusetts   Jan 31, 1944   321 U. S. 158
      *Am Consttnl Law (Bartholomew) v. 2, 21-22
      Church and State 127-128
      Church State and Freedom 704-706
      *Consttnl Cases 395-406
      Freedom and the Court 277
      Justice Rutledge 55-61
      Mr. Justice Jackson 42
      Mr. Justice Murphy (Howard) 343-348
      *Mr. Justice Murphy (Norris) 189-193
      Private Conscience 156-159
      Religion (Fellman) 39-40
      Religion (Kurland) 65-66
      *Religious Freedom (Pfeffer) 150-153
      *Rights (Shattuck) 101
      *Sup Ct (Mendelson) 194-207

1452. Eastern Central Motor Carriers   Feb 7, 1944   321 U. S. 194
      Association v. United States
      *Cases Regulated 657-663

1453. Stark v. Wickard   Feb 28, 1944   321 U. S. 288
      *Admin Law (Schwartz) 546-550
      *Govt and Business 563-569

1454. Hecht Co. v. Bowles   Feb 28, 1944   321 U. S. 321
      *Injunctions 93-98

1455. J. I. Case Co. v. National Labor   Feb 28, 1944   321 U. S. 332
      Relations Board
      Basic Text 376-377
      *Cases Labor (Cox) 391-395
      *Cases Labor (Handler) 253-256
      *Cases Labor (Leslie) 58-61
      *Cases Labor (Oberer) 207-211
      *Labor Law (Meltzer) 633-636
      *Labor Relations (Group Trust) 70-74

*Nature 1106-1109
*Statutory History Labor 383-388

1456. Order of Railroad Telegraphers v.   Feb 28, 1944   321 U. S. 342
            Railway Express Agency
        *Cases Labor (Cox) 395-397
        *Cases Labor (Handler) 302-304

1457. Yakus v. United States   Mar 27, 1944   321 U. S. 414
        Rottenberg v. United States
            Am Consttn (Kelly) 784
        *Govt and Business 447-452, 532-535
        *Introduction (Cataldo) 55-58
        *Legal Environment 164-167
        *Liberty v. 2, 475-476
        *Sup Ct and American Economic Life 242-247
        *Sup Ct and Am Govt 83-86
        *Sup Ct and Consttn 429-432

1458. Bowles v. Willingham   Mar 27, 1944   321 U. S. 503
        *Admin Law (Gellhorn) 155-158
        *Govt and Business 478-479
        *Social Forces 560-562

1459. Follett v. McCormack   Mar 27, 1944   321 U. S. 573
            Justice Rutledge 61-62
        *Mr. Justice Murphy (Norris) 193
            O'er the Ramparts 139-143
            Private Conscience 109-110
            Religion (Kurland) 66-68
            Sup Ct and Patents 128
            System 420-421

1460. Tennessee Coal, Iron and Railroad Co. Mar 27, 1944   321 U. S. 590
            v. Muscoda Local No. 123
        Sloss-Sheffield Steel and Iron Co. v.
            Sloss Red Ore Local 109
        Republic Steel Corporation v. Raimund
            Local No. 121
            Hugo Black (Dunne) 233-235
        *Labor Relations (Group Trust) 488-497
            Mr. Justice Murphy (Howard) 387-390

1461. Sartor v. Arkansas Natural Gas   Mar 27, 1944   321 U. S. 620
            Corporation
        *Cases Civil Procedure 659-660

1462. Smith v. Allwright   Apr 3, 1944   321 U. S. 649
        *Am Consttnl Law (Bartholomew) v. 2, 329-330
        *Am Consttnl Law (Mason) 479-482
        *Am Consttnl Law (Shapiro) 536-539
            Black 41-46
            CQ Guide 482
        *Cases Civil Liberties 402-405
        *Cases Consttnl Law (Cushman) 632-635
            Civil Liberties (Kauper) 160-161
        *Civil Liberties (Sweet) 279-284
        *Civil Rights (Abernathy) 1977 575-576

*Civil Rights (Bardolph) 266-267
*Consttnl Decisions 128-132
*Consttnl Law (Freund) 948-953
*Consttnl Law (Grossman) 485-488
*Consttnl Law (Kauper) 796-801
*Consttnl Politics 473-478
Desegregation (Wasby) 32-33
Discrimination 73-78
*Documents History v. 2, 485-487
Equality (Berger) 93-94
Freedom and the Court 21, 398-399
Great Reversals 134-135
*Liberty v. 2, 467-468
Modern Sup Ct 33-35
Petitioners 294-295
*Political Rights v. 2, 1107-1113
Private Pressure 30-32
Quest 119-120
*Racial Equality 84
Rise 79-80
*Statutory History Civil Rights 435-439
*Sup Ct and Consttn 539-542
Sup Ct and Electoral Process 70-71
Sup Ct From Taft 191-192
*Sup Ct Speaks 234-235

1463. Franks Brothers Co. v. National   Apr 10, 1944   321 U.S. 702
           Labor Relations Board
           *Cases Labor (Cox) 291-293

1464. Pollock v. Williams   Apr 10, 1944   322 U.S. 4
           *Am Consttnl Law (Bartholomew) v. 2, 321-322
           Petitioners 311-312

1465. United States v. Mitchell   Apr 24, 1944   322 U.S. 65
           Sup Ct and Confessions 73-74

1466. United States v. Ballard   Apr 24, 1944   322 U.S. 78
           CQ Guide 454
           Church and State 126-127
           Church State and Freedom 690-694
           *Dispassionate 39-43
           Dissent 210-211
           First Amendment (Berns) 39-41
           Freedom and the Court 281
           Mr. Justice Jackson 40
           *Modern Consttnl Law 377-382
           *Political Rights 818-820
           Private Conscience 99-102
           Religion (Fellman) 25-29
           Religion (Kurland) 75-79
           *Religious Freedom (Pfeffer) 139-143
           Religious Liberty 37-43
           Right of Assembly 178-179
           Sup Ct and Religion 149-151
           *Sup Ct Speaks 350-352

1467. National Labor Relations Board v.   Apr 24, 1944   322 U.S. 111
           Hearst Publications, Inc.

National Labor Relations Board v.
  Stockholders Publishing Co.
National Labor Relations Board v.
  Times-Mirror Co.
  *Admin Law (Gellhorn) 298-307
  *Admin Law (Schwartz) 687-690
  *Cases Labor (Handler) 172-175
  *Labor Law (Meltzer) 579-582

1468.   Ashcraft v. Tennessee   May 1, 1944   322 U.S. 143
          Defendants 344
          *Due Process 57-58
          Mr. Justice Jackson 80-81
          *One Man's Stand 107-112
          Sup Ct and Confessions 91-93

1469.   Union Brokerage v. Jensen   May 8, 1944   322 U.S. 202
          Sup Ct and Commerce 260-261

1470.   Northwest Airlines v. Minnesota May 15, 1944   322 U.S. 292
          Sup Ct and Commerce 322-323

1471.   McLeod v. J. E. Dilworth Co.   May 15, 1944   322 U.S. 327
          *Am Consttn (Lockhart) 308-309
          *Consttnl Law (Barrett) 418-420
          *Consttnl Law (Freund) 574-576
          *Consttnl Law (Kauper) 398-402
          Sup Ct and Commerce 323

1472.   General Trading Co. v. State Tax May 15, 1944   322 U.S. 335
          Commission of Iowa
          *Consttnl Law (Barrett) 420-422
          *Consttnl Law (Freund) 576-578

1473.   International Harvester Co. v. Depart- May 15, 1944 322 U.S. 340
          ment of Treasury of Indiana
          *Consttnl Law (Freund) 578-583

1474.   Mortensen v. United States   May 15, 1944   322 U.S. 369
          *Courts Judges 561-563
          *Mr. Justice Murphy (Norris) 371-376

1476.   Arenas v. United States   May 22, 1944   322 U.S. 419
          *Law Indian 562-567

1475.   Steuart and Brothers v. Bowles   May 22, 1944   322 U.S. 398
          Am Consttn (Kelly) 785

1477.   Feldman v. United States   May 29, 1944   322 U.S. 487
          Justice Frankfurter 173-175

1478.   United States v. South-Eastern Under- June 5, 1944 322 U.S. 533
          writers Association
          Am Consttn (Kelly) 733-735
          *Am Consttnl Law (Bartholomew) v. 1, 278-282
          *Consttnl Law (Barrett) 234
          Hugo Black (Dunne) 224-225
          Justices Black and Frankfurter 32
          *Modern Business 71-74

*Sup Ct and American Economic Life 247-257
Sup Ct and Commerce 148-159
Sup Ct in Free Society 121-122

1479. Lyons v. Oklahoma   June 5, 1944   322 U.S. 596
       *Mr. Justice Murphy (Norris) 302-303
       Private Pressure 27-28
       Sup Ct and Confessions 93-96

1480. Polish National Alliance of the United June 5, 1944   322 U.S. 643
       States of North America v. Na-
       tional Labor Relations Board
       Sup Ct and Commerce 159-160

1481. Baumgartner v. United States   June 12, 1944 322 U.S. 665
       Am Consttn (Kelly) 800-801
       Justice Rutledge 272-273
       *Mr. Justice Murphy (Norris) 151-152
       *Sup Ct on Freedom 208-209

1482. Hartzel v. United States   June 12, 1944 322 U.S. 680
       Am Consttn (Kelly) 801
       CQ Guide 400
       *Mr. Justice Murphy (Norris) 152-157

1483. United States v. White   June 12, 1944 322 U.S. 694
       Mr. Justice Murphy (Howard) 383-384
       *Mr. Justice Murphy (Norris) 303-309

1484. Spector Motor Service v. McLaughlin Dec 4, 1944   323 U.S. 101
       *Consttn (Mendelson) 12-14
       *Consttnl Law (Kauper) 75-77

1485. Armour and Co. v. Wantock   Dec 4, 1944   323 U.S. 126
       *Cases Employment 739-742
       *Modern Social Legislation 620-623, 642-644

1486. Skidmore v. Swift and Co.   Dec 4, 1944   323 U.S. 134
       *Admin Law (Gellhorn) 324-328

1487. United States v. Crescent Amusement Dec 11, 1944   323 U.S. 173
       Co.
       *Govt Regulation 657-666

1488. Steele v. Louisville and Nashville   Dec 18, 1944   323 U.S. 192
       Railroad
       Basic Text 695-696
       *Cases Labor (Cox) 981-989
       *Cases Labor (Handler) 691-696
       *Cases Labor (Leslie) 462-465
       *Cases Labor (Oberer) 181-186
       *Cases Labor (Stern) 193-196
       Consttnl Law (Barrett) 1044
       *Discrimination 305-310
       Equality (Berger) 142-143
       *Labor Law (Meltzer) 888-893
       *Labor Relations (Group Trust) 74-79
       *Mr. Justice Murphy (Norris) 233-234
       Petitioners 314-315

1491.   Freeman v. Hewit   Dec 18, 1944   323 U.S. 249
        *Mr. Justice Frankfurter 209-212

1492.   United States v. Johnson   Dec 18, 1944   323 U.S. 273
        *Mr. Justice Murphy (Norris) 367-368

1493.   Ex parte Endo   Dec 18, 1944   323 U.S. 283
        Am Consttn (Kelly) 790-791
        *Douglas 37-43
        *Due Process 189-190
        *Freedom Reader 182-183
        *Freedom vs National Security 63-70
        Justice Rutledge 178-179
        *Mr. Justice Murphy (Norris) 239
        Prejudice 213-214, 252-254
        Sup Ct and Commander in Chief 47-48

1494.   Hartford-Empire Co. v. United   Jan 8, 1945   323 U.S. 386
            States
        *Govt Regulation 667-699
        Hugo Black (Strickland) 211
        *Selected Antitrust Cases 416-423

1495.   Western Union Telegraph Co. v.   Jan 8, 1945   323 U.S. 490
            Lenroot
        Mr. Justice Murphy (Howard) 386-387
        *Modern Social Legislation 629-631

1496.   Thomas v. Collins   Jan 8, 1945   323 U.S. 516
        Am Consttn (Kelly) 760-761
        *Am Consttnl Law (Bartholomew) v. 1, 108-110
        CQ Guide 410, 420
        Communications (Hemmer) v. 1, 70
        *Dispassionate 43-47
        Free Speech (Kurland) 37
        *Free Speech (Summers) 46-49
        *Freedom of Speech (Haiman) 66
        Freedom of Speech (Hudon) 101-103
        Justice Rutledge 118-122
        *Justices (Friedman) v. 4, 2602-2613
        Legacy 236-239
        *Liberty v. 2, 458-460
        Mass Communications 42-44
        Mr. Justice Jackson 39-40
        Modern Sup Ct 22-23
        Right of Assembly 188
        *Rights (Shattuck) 49-50
        Sup Ct (North) 137-138
        Sup Ct and Labor 47
        Sup Ct from Taft 159-160
        System 350-351

1497.   Tiller v. Atlantic Coast Line Rail- Jan 15, 1945   323 U.S. 574
            road Co.
        *Cases Pleading 806-807

1498.   Otis and Co. v. Securities and Ex- Jan 29, 1945   323 U.S. 624
            change Commission
        *Materials Reorganization 446-454

1499. Regal Knitwear Co. v. National   Jan 29, 1945   324 U.S. 9
           Labor Relations Board
       *Injunctions 692-695

1500. House v. Mayo   Feb 5, 1945   324 U.S. 42
           Sup Ct Review 1962 187

1501. Muschany v. United States   Feb 5, 1945   324 U.S. 49
       Andrews v. United States
           Mr. Justice Jackson 35-36

1502. Herb v. Pitcairn   Feb 5, 1945   324 U.S. 117
       Belcher v. Louisville and Nash-
           ville Railroad
       *Cases Federal Courts 848-855

1503. United States v. Beach   Feb 26, 1945   324 U.S. 193
       *Mr. Justice Murphy (Norris) 376-378

1504. Canadian Aviator, LTD v. United   Feb 26, 1945   324 U.S. 215
           States
       *Cases Admiralty 80-85

1505. United States v. Frankfort Distill-   Mar 5, 1945   324 U.S. 293
           eries, Inc.
       *Govt Regulation 713-718
           Hugo Black (Strickland) 205-206

1506. Northwestern Bands of Shoshone In-   Mar 12, 1945   324 U.S. 335
           dians v. United States
       *Dispassionate 142-146
       *Law Indian 459-463

1507. Special Equipment Co. v. Coe   Mar 26, 1945   324 U.S. 370
       *Cases Antitrust Law 273-280
       *Cases Trade 881-884
       *Govt Regulation 719-726

1508. Malinski v. New York   Mar 26, 1945   324 U.S. 401
       *Due Process 142-143
           Felix Frankfurter (Baker) 267-268
           Felix Frankfurter (Thomas) 156-158
           Justice Rutledge 210-214
       *Mr. Justice Murphy (Norris) 309-311

1509. Georgia v. Pennsylvania Railroad   Mar 26, 1945   324 U.S. 439
       *Cases Regulated 444-450

1510. Phillips Co. v. Walling   Mar 26, 1945   324 U.S. 490
       *Modern Social Legislation 631-634

1511. United States v. Willow River Power Co. Mar 26, 1945   324 U.S. 499
       *Cases Property (Casner) 1331-1339
       *Land Ownership 4-11
           Sup Ct Review 1962 79-80

1512. Market Street Railway v. Railroad   Mar 26, 1945   324 U.S. 548
           Commission
       *Admin Law (Schwartz) 482-484

1513. Hartford-Empire Co. v. United   Apr 2, 1945   324 U.S. 570
          States
       *Govt Regulation 700-706

1514. Brooklyn Savings Bank v. O'Neil   Apr 9, 1945   324 U.S. 697
       Dize v. Maddrix
       Arsenal Building Corporation v.
          Greenberg
       *Modern Social Legislation 657-662

1515. Corn Products Refining Co. v.   Apr 23, 1945   324 U.S. 726
          Federal Trade Commission
       *Cases Trade 998-999
       *Free Enterprise 940-947
       *Govt Regulation 727-736

1516. Federal Trade Commission v. A. E.   Apr 23, 1945   324 U.S. 746
          Staley Manufacturing Co. and
          Staley Sales Corporation
       *Antitrust Analysis 901-904
       *Cases Antitrust Law 1144-1152
       *Cases Trade 1060-1063
       *Competition 308-311
       *Govt Regulation 737-743
       *Text Antitrust 232-233

1517. Rice v. Olson   Apr 23, 1945   324 U.S. 786
       Justice Rutledge 236

1518. Republic Aviation Corporation v.   Apr 23, 1945   324 U.S. 793
          National Labor Relations Board
       National Labor Relations Board v. Le
          Tourneau Co. of Georgia
       Basic Text 329
       *Cases Labor (Cox) 145-150
       *Cases Labor (Handler) 8-13
       *Cases Labor (Leslie) 118-122
       *Cases Labor (Oberer) 249-254
       *Labor Law (Herman) 200-205
       *Labor Law (Meltzer) 124-128
       *Labor Relations (Group Trust) 228-233
       Sup Ct and Labor 51-52

1519. Precision Instrument Manufacturing Co. Apr 23, 1945   324 U.S. 806
          v. Automotive Maintenance Ma-
          chinery Co.
       *Injunctions 76-83
       *Patent 744-755

1520. Cramer v. United States   Apr 23, 1945   325 U.S. 1
       Am Consttn (Kelly) 797-798

1521. Screws v. United States   May 7, 1945   325 U.S. 91
       *Am Consttnl Law (Bartholomew) v. 2, 313-315
       Black 117-118
       Cases Consttnl Law (Gunther) 1041-1042
       *Cases Criml Law (Inbau) 99-117
       *Civil Rights (Abernathy) 1977 57-65
       *Civil Rights (Bardolph) 290-291

    *Civil Rights (Blaustein) 361-372
    Consttn (Konvitz) 48-72
    *Consttn (Mendelson) 549-552
    *Consttnl Law (Barrett) 1085-1086
    *Consttnl Law (Freund) 841-850
    *Consttnl Law (Kauper) 792-795
    Court and Consttn v. 2, 147-149
    *Discrimination 31-41
    Mr. Justice Murphy (Howard) 355-366
    *Mr. Justice Murphy (Norris) 255-257
    Modern Sup Ct 33
    Petitioners 284-286
    *Political Rights v. 2, 1036-1050
    Quest 127-128
    Right of Assembly 157-158
    Sup Ct Review 1962 122-123
    To Preserve 77-78
    PERIODICALS:
    "Screws case revisited," Woodford Howard and Cornelius Bushoven.
        J Poltcs 29: 617-636 Aug '67.

1522. Jewell Ridge Coal Corporation v.   May 7, 1945   325 U.S. 161
          Local No. 6167, United Mine
          Workers of America
       *Cases Labor (Handler) 548-551
       *Dispassionate 165-172
       Hugo Black (Dunne) 235-236
       Mr. Justice Murphy (Howard) 391-394

1523. Williams v. North Carolina   May 21, 1945   325 U.S. 226
       *Am Consttnl Issues 213-218
       *Am Consttnl Law (Bartholomew) v. 1, 57-58
       *Consttnl Cases 256-268
       *Family 307-310
       Justice Rutledge 296, 297-299

1524. Finn v. Meighan   May 21, 1945   325 U.S. 300
       *Materials Reorganization 586-588

1525. Chase Securities Corp. v. Donaldson   May 21, 1945   325 U.S. 304
       *Consttnl Law (Barrett) 670

1526. Bingham's Trust v. Commissioner of   June 4, 1945   325 U.S. 365
          Internal Revenue
       *Govt and Business 663-666

1527. American Power and Light Co. v.   June 4, 1945   325 U.S. 385
          Securities and Exchange Commission
       Securities and Exchange Commission v.
          Okin
       Mr. Justice Murphy (Howard) 406-407

1528. Akins v. Texas   June 4, 1945   325 U.S. 398
       *Mr. Justice Murphy (Norris) 317-318
       Petitioners 288
       Quest 113

1529. Walling v. Harnischfeger Corporation   June 4, 1945   325 U.S. 427
       *Labor Relations (Group Trust) 498-501

1530. Hill v. Florida ex rel. Watson   June 11, 1945 325 U.S. 538
         *Cases Labor (Handler) 201-202
         *Cases Labor (Oberer) 122-126
         Felix Frankfurter (Mendelson) 181
         Justices Black and Frankfurter 101-102
         Sup Ct and Labor 60

1531. In re Summers   June 11, 1945 325 U.S. 561
         Am Consttn (Kelly) 768
         Church and State 128-129
         Church State and Freedom 620-621
         *Conscience 207-209
         Freedom and the Court 277
         *One Man's Stand 120-124
         Private Conscience 75-77
         Religion (Kurland) 47-49

1532. 10 East 40th Street Building, Inc.   June 11, 1945 325 U.S. 578
           v. Callus
         *Sup Ct (Mendelson) 439-449
         Sup Ct and Commerce 129-130

1533. Borden Co. v. Borella   June 11, 1945 325 U.S. 679
         Sup Ct and Commerce 128-129

1534. Elgin, Joliet and Eastern Railway v.   June 11, 1945 325 U.S. 711
           Burley
         *Cases Labor (Handler) 359-363

1535. Southern Pacific Co. v. Arizona   June 18, 1945 325 U.S. 761
           ex rel. Sullivan
       "Arizona Train Limit Case"
         *Am Consttn (Lockhart) 250-254
         *Am Consttnl Issues 143-149
         *Am Consttnl Law (Bartholomew) v. 1, 209-211
         *Am Consttnl Law (Mason) 236-240
         *Am Consttnl Law (Shapiro) 241-246
         *Cases Consttnl Law (Gunther) 279-284
         *Consttn (Mendelson) 201-207
         *Consttnl Law (Barrett) 298-305
         *Consttnl Law (Barron) 259-262
         *Consttnl Law (Freund) 418-426
         *Consttnl Law (Kauper) 339-352
         *Consttnl Law (Lockhart) 293-297
         *Consttnl Politics 384-387
         *Federal System 333-338
         *Legal Environment 200-202
         *Processes 225-230
         *Sup Ct (Mendelson) 399-420
         Sup Ct and Commerce 245-246

1536. Allen Bradley Co. v. Local Union   June 18, 1945 325 U.S. 797
           No. 3, International Brotherhood
           of Electrical Workers
         *Cases Labor (Handler) 665-669
         *Cases Labor (Oberer) 1003-1008
         *Govt Regulation 777-788
         Hugo Black (Strickland) 204
         *Labor Law (Herman) 59-61

      *Labor Law (Meltzer) 502-507
      *Labor Law (Twomey) 43-49
      *Labor Relations (Group Trust) 730-737
      *Labor Relations (Taylor) 112-113
      Professional Sports 310-311

1537. Hunt v. Crumboch   June 18, 1945 325 U.S. 821
      Am Consttn (Kelly) 726
      *Cases Labor (Handler) 675-677
      *Cases Labor (Oberer) 145-147
      *Dispassionate 172-175
      *Govt Regulation 789-794

1538. Associated Press v. United States   June 18, 1945 326 U.S. 1
      Tribune Co. v. United States
      United States v. Associated Press
      *Antitrust (Posner) 565-571
      *Antitrust Analysis 401-405
      *Cases Antitrust Law 460-470
      *Cases Trade 292-298
      Communication (Hemmer) v. 2, 202-203
      *Documents History v. 2, 507-510
      *Free Enterprise 618-631
      *Freedom of the Press (Schmidt) 47, 229
      Freedom of the Press (Schmidt) 165, 248-250
      *Govt Regulation 795-822
      Law of Mass 573-577
      *Mass Communications 693-696
      Mass Media (Francois) 540-541
      *Mr. Justice Frankfurter 97-98
      *Sup Ct on Freedom 290-296
      Sup Ct Review 1978 266-267
      System 668-669

1539. Interstate Commerce Commission v.   June 18, 1945 326 U.S. 60
        Parker
      United States v. Parker
      *Cases Regulated 725-730

1540. Railway Mail Association v. Corsi   June 18, 1945 326 U.S. 88
      Century 172-174
      *Mr. Justice Frankfurter 201-202
      Petitioners 318-319

1541. Guaranty Trust Co. of New York v.   June 18, 1945 326 U.S. 99
        York
      *Cases Civil Procedure 284-288
      *Cases Federal Courts 594-599
      *Cases Pleading 404-409
      *Civil Procedure (Carrington) 832-836
      *Civil Procedure (Cound) 204-288
      *Elements Civil 394-396
      *Federal Courts 722-728

1542. Radio Station WOW v. Johnson   June 18, 1945 326 U.S. 120
      *Consttnl Law (Freund) 616-619

1543. Bridges v. Wixon   June 18, 1945 326 U.S. 135
      Civil Rights (Konvitz) 114-121

*Documents History v. 2, 496-498
Elements Judicial 188-192
Mr. Justice Murphy (Howard) 348-351
*Mr. Justice Murphy (Norris) 127-133
This Honorable Court 370-371

1544.   East New York Savings Bank v. Hahn   Nov 5, 1945   326 U.S. 230
*Govt and Business 77-79

1545.   Hawk v. Olson   Nov 13, 1945   326 U.S. 271
Justice Rutledge 236-238

1546.   International Shoe Co. v. Washington   Dec 3, 1945   326 U.S. 310
Office of Unemployment Compen-
sation and Placement
*Cases Civil Procedure 391-397
*Cases Pleading 194-202
*Civil Procedure (Carrington) 897-903
*Civil Procedure (Cound) 74-79
*Elements Civil 275-282
*Legal Environment 44-46
*Modern Social Legislation 539-542

1547.   Ashbacker Radio Corporation v. Fed-   Dec 3, 1945   326 U.S. 327
eral Communications Commission
*Admin Law (Schwartz) 401-403
Felix Frankfurter (Mendelson) 211-212

1548.   Markham v. Allen   Jan 7, 1946   326 U.S. 490
*Federal Courts 1183-1186

1549.   Marsh v. Alabama   Jan 7, 1946   326 U.S. 501
*Am Consttnl Law (Bartholomew) v. 2, 18-19
*Bill (Cohen) 298-301
CQ Guide 416
Church and State 129
Civil Liberties (Kauper) 160
Communication (Hemmer) v. 1, 228-229
*Consttn (Pollak) v. 2, 39-46
Consttnl Law (Barrett) 1044-1045
*Consttnl Law (Freund) 797-801
Equality (Berger) 116
Freedom and the Court 282
Freedom of the Press (Schmidt) 92-95
Handbook 104-105
Justice Hugo Black 164-165
*Law Indian 740-741
Negro (Kalven) 150-152
O'er the Ramparts 144-153
*One Man's Stand 125-128
*Processes 651-654
Religion (Kurland) 68-69
Sup Ct and Am Capitalism 147-148
System 308

1550.   Tucker v. Texas   Jan 7, 1946   326 U.S. 517
*First Amendment (Konvitz) 144-146
Religion (Kurland) 69-70

1551. New York v. United States   Jan 14, 1946   326 U.S. 572
        "New York Mineral Waters Case"
        *Am Consttn (Lockhart) 342-344
        *Am Consttnl Law (Bartholomew) v. 1, 174-176
        *Am Consttnl Law (Mason) 180-185
        *Cases Consttnl Law (Gunther) 363-366
        *Consttn (Mendelson) 145-149
        *Consttnl Law (Barrett) 466-470
        *Consttnl Law (Freund) 637-641
        *Consttnl Law (Kauper) 480-488
        *Consttnl Law (Lockhart) 173-177
        *Contemporary Law 234-238
        *Govt and Business 330-333
        *Processes 198-202
        Sup Ct in Free Society 87-89

1552. Roland Electric Co. v. Walling   Jan 28, 1946   326 U.S. 657
        Sup Ct and Commerce 130-131

1553. In re Yamashita   Feb 4, 1946   327 U.S. 1
        Yamashita v. Styer
        Am Consttn (Kelly) 796
        *Am Consttnl Law (Mason) 684-689
        *Consttnl Law (Felkenes) 114-117
        *Documents History v. 2, 522-525
        *Due Process 190-192
        Hugo Black (Dunne) 213-214
        Justice 135-149
        Justice Rutledge 180-192
        *Liberty v. 2, 478-479
        Mr. Justice Murphy (Howard) 367-377
        *Mr. Justice Murphy (Norris) 414-424
        *Teaching Materials 55-60

1554. Canizio v. New York   Feb 4, 1946   327 U.S. 82
        Justice Rutledge 248-250
        *Mr. Justice Murphy (Norris) 348-350

1555. Estep v. United States   Feb 4, 1946   327 U.S. 114
        Smith v. United States
        Defendants 156
        *Mr. Justice Murphy (Norris) 354-358
        O'er the Ramparts 176-185

1556. Hannigan v. Esquire   Feb 4, 1946   327 U.S. 146
        *Am Consttnl Law (Bartholomew) v. 1, 302-303
        *Bill (Konvitz) 370-373
        Communication (Hemmer) v. 1, 177; v. 2, 200-201
        Expanding Liberties 181-182
        *First Amendment (Konvitz) 775-779
        *Freedom Reader 109-110
        *Mass Communications 151-153
        *Mass Media (Devol) 81-84
        *Sup Ct on Freedom 186-188

1557. Mabee v. White Plains Publishing Co. Feb 11, 1946 327 U.S. 178
        Mass Communications 727
        *Modern Social Legislation 625-628

Sup Ct and Commerce 131-132
*Sup Ct on Freedom 281-282

1558. Oklahoma Press Publishing Co. v.   Feb 11, 1946   327 U.S. 186
         Walling
       News Printing Co., Inc. v. Walling
       *Admin Law (Schwartz) 193-197
       *Mass Communications 728-729
       *Mr. Justice Murphy (Norris) 437-438
       *Sup Ct on Freedom 282-283

1559. Bigelow v. RKO Radio Pictures, Inc.   Feb 25, 1946   327 U.S. 251
       *Cases Antitrust Law 1385-1391
       *Cases Trade 1248-1256
       *Govt Regulation 823-830

1560. Commissioner of Internal Revenue v.   Feb 25, 1946   327 U.S. 280
         Tower
       Hugo Black (Strickland) 183-185

1561. Duncan v. Kahanamoku   Feb 25, 1946   327 U.S. 304
       White v. Steer
         Am Consttn (Kelly) 792-794
         *Am Consttnl Law (Saye) 228-230
         *Cases Criml Law (Inbau) 122-136
         *Consttnl Law (Freund) 1061-1068
         *Freedom vs National Security 70-77
         *Liberty v. 2, 479-480
         Mr. Justice Murphy (Howard) 377-379
         *Mr. Justice Murphy (Norris) 407-414
         *One Man's Stand 129-134
         Sup Ct and Commander in Chief 58-59

1562. Social Security Board v. Nierotko   Feb 25, 1946   327 U.S. 358
       *Govt and Business 654-658
       *Labor Relations (Group Trust) 600-602
       *Modern Social Legislation 53-56

1563. Holmberg v. Armbrecht   Feb 25, 1946   327 U.S. 392
       *Federal Courts 822-825

1564. Nippert v. Richmond   Feb 25, 1946   327 U.S. 416
         Sup Ct and Commerce 324-325

1565. United States ex rel. Tennessee   Mar 25, 1946   327 U.S. 546
         Valley Authority v. Welch
         Sup Ct Review 1962 65-71

1566. American Federation of Labor v.   Mar 25, 1946   327 U.S. 582
         Watson
         *Mr. Justice Murphy (Norris) 438-439

1567. Jacob Siegel Co. v. Federal Trade   Mar 25, 1946   327 U.S. 608
         Commission
         *Admin Law (Gellhorn) 382-383

1568. M. Kraus and Brothers v. United   Mar 25, 1946   327 U.S. 614
         States
         *Govt and Business 531-532

1569. United States v. Carbone   Mar 25, 1946   327 U.S. 633
           *Mr. Justice Murphy (Norris) 362-367

1570. Lavender v. Kurn   Mar 25, 1946   327 U.S. 645
           *Civil Procedure (Cound) 46-50
           *Mr. Justice Murphy (Norris) 324-329

1571. Bell v. Hood   Apr 1, 1946   327 U.S. 678
           *Cases Federal Courts 143-147
           *Materials Consttnl Law 124-128

1572. North American Co. v. Securities   Apr 1, 1946   327 U.S. 686
           and Exchange Commission
           Am Consttn (Kelly) 731-732
           Mr. Justice Murphy (Howard) 406-407

1573. Girouard v. United States   Apr 22, 1946   328 U.S. 61
           *Am Consttnl Law (Bartholomew) v. 2, 23-25
           CQ Guide 143
           Church and State 129
           *Conscience 210-212
           *Douglas 118-125
           Freedom and the Court 282
           Justices Black and Frankfurter 30-31
           Private Conscience 63-65
           Religion (Drinan) 18-19
           *Religious Freedom (Pfeffer) 114-116

1574. Queenside Hills Realty Co. v. Saxl   Apr 22, 1946   328 U.S. 80
           *Am Land Planning v. 2, 1609-1611

1575. Seas Shipping Co. v. Sieracki   Apr 22, 1946   328 U.S. 85
           *Cases Admiralty 363-367

1576. D. A. Schulte, Inc. v. Gangi   Apr 29, 1946   328 U.S. 108
           Sup Ct and Commerce 132

1577. Reconstruction Finance Corporation v. May 13, 1946   328 U.S. 204
           Beaver County
           *Federal Courts 489-491

1578. Thiel v. Southern Pacific Co.   May 20, 1946   328 U.S. 217
           *Am Consttnl Law (Bartholomew) v. 2, 169-171
           *Civil Procedure (Carrington) 197-199
           *Civil Procedure (Cound) 825-828
           *Criminal Justice (Way) 361-363
           Defendants 184
           *Mr. Justice Murphy (Norris) 319-322
           *Modern Business 36-39

1579. United States v. Causby   May 27, 1946   328 U.S. 256
           *Cases Property (Casner) 1353-1364
           *Cases Property (Donahue) 364-370
           *Consttn (Mendelson) 271-272
           *Consttnl Law (Barrett) 683-686
           *Consttnl Law (Freund) 1097-1100
           *Consttnl Law (Kauper) 1337-1344
           *Douglas 436-440
           *Govt and Business 402-404
           Sup Ct Review 1962 82-84

1580. United States v. Lovett   June 3, 1946   328 U. S. 303
       United States v. Watson
       United States v. Dodd
         Am Consttn (Kelly) 769-770
         *Am Consttnl Law (Bartholomew) v. 2, 6-8
         *Am Consttnl Law (Saye) 231-232
         *Annals v. 16, 404-408
         *Bill (Konvitz) 637-640
          Consttnl Law (Barrett) 1190-1191
         *Consttnl Law (Freund) 1330-1334
          Defendants 87-88
         *Documents History v. 2, 510-512
          Felix Frankfurter (Mendelson) 3-8
          Felix Frankfurter (Thomas) 142-143
         *Liberty v. 2, 470-471
         *Mr. Justice Frankfurter 8-11
         *One Man's Stand 135-140
         *Processes 123-128

1581. Pennekamp v. Florida   June 3, 1946   328 U. S. 331
          Am Consttn (Kelly) 769
          Communication (Hemmer) v. 2, 163-164
          Freedom and the Court 179-180
          Freedom of Speech (Hudon) 99-100
          Handbook 514-515
          Justice Frankfurter 76-77
          Justice Rutledge 130-136
         *Mr. Justice Frankfurter 85-88
         *Mr. Justice Murphy (Norris) 158
         *Sup Ct on Freedom 95-100
          Sup Ct Review 1978 269
          System 453-454

1582. Morgan v. Virginia   June 3, 1946   328 U. S. 373
         *Am Consttnl Law (Bartholomew) v. 1, 213-214
          CQ Guide 609-610
          Civil Rights (Bardolph) 285-286
         *Consttnl Law (Freund) 429-432
          Desegregation (Wasby) 45-47
          Equality (Berger) 129
          Petitioners 367-368
          Private Pressure 42-43
         *Racial Equality 45-46
          Sup Ct (Mendelson) 430-439
          Sup Ct and Commerce 194-196

1583. Prudential Insurance Co. v. Benjamin   June 3, 1946   328 U. S. 408
         *Am Consttn (Lockhart) 285-287
         *Consttn (Mendelson) 229-233
          Justice Rutledge 291
          Sup Ct and Commerce 162-167

1584. Robertson v. California   June 3, 1946   328 U. S. 440
          Justice Rutledge 291
          Sup Ct and Commerce 167-168

1585. Fisher v. United States   June 10, 1946   328 U. S. 463
         *Cases Criml Law (Hall) 459-461

*Cases Criml Law (Inbau) 802-807
*Mr. Justice Murphy (Norris) 329-332

1586.   Reconstruction Finance Corporation v.   June 10, 1946 328 U.S. 495
        Denver and Rio Grande Western
        Railroad
        From the Diaries 266-268
        *Materials Reorganization 510-522

1587.   Colegrove v. Green   June 10, 1946 328 U.S. 549
        Am Consttn (Kelly) 942
        *Am Consttnl Law (Bartholomew) v. 1, 68-70; v. 2, 332-333
        CQ Guide 489-490
        *Cases Consttnl Law (Cushman) 16-18
        *Civil Liberties (Sweet) 284-287
        *Comparative 558-561
        *Consttnl Cases 186-195
        Consttnl Counterrevolution 94-95
        *Consttnl Law (Schmidhauser) 350-355
        *Consttnl Politics 210-213
        Court and Consttn v. 2, 149-150, 313
        *Courts Judges 252-254, 416
        Decade 90-91
        Democratic 111-112
        *Federal System 73-75
        Felix Frankfurter (Baker) 325-326
        Guarantee 272-275
        Impact (Washy) 117
        Justice Rutledge 300-301
        Law and Politics 185-191
        Least Dangerous 189-191
        *Mr. Justice Frankfurter 69-70
        Modern Sup Ct 122-123
        *One Man's Stand 141-146
        Political Thicket 43-46
        Politics 208-209
        Prophets 131-156
        *Prophets 229-234
        Reapportionment (Baker) 115-117
        Reapportionment (McKay) 66-68
        Rise 108-109
        Sup Ct and Electoral Process 150-151
        Sup Ct and Poltcl Questions 41-54
        Sup Ct from Taft 194-196
        Warren (Ball) 67-84
        PERIODICALS:
        "Reapportionment decisions: a return to dogma?" A. Spenser
            Hill. J Poltcs 31: 186-213 Feb '69 (4).

1588.   Davis v. United States   June 10, 1946 328 U.S. 582
        Justice Frankfurter 155-157
        *Mr. Justice Frankfurter 119-123
        Search and Seizure 81-82

1589.   Zap v. United States   June 10, 1946 328 U.S. 624
        Defendants 301
        Search and Seizure 81, 82

1590.   Pinkerton v. United States   June 10, 1946 328 U.S. 640

*Cases Criml Law (Hall) 723-728
*Cases Criml Law (Perkins) 324-326
*Criminal Law (Kadish) 429-431

1591.   Knauer v. United States   June 10, 1946 328 U. S. 654
        *Douglas 110-118
        Justice Rutledge 273-274

1592.   Anderson v. Mt. Clemens Pottery Co.   June 10, 1946 328 U. S. 680
        Court and Consttn v. 2, 162-163
        Impact (Wasby) 109-111
        *Third Branch 63-66

1593.   Kotteakos v. United States   June 10, 1946 328 U. S. 750
        Regenbogen v. United States
        *Criminal Law (Kadish) 468-470

1594.   American Tobacco Co. v. United   June 10, 1946 328 U. S. 781
            States
        Liggett & Myers Tobacco Co. v. United
            States
        R. J. Reynolds Tobacco Co. v. United
            States
        *Antitrust (Posner) 103-107
        *Competition 64-69
        *Govt Regulation 837-854
        *Selected Antitrust Cases 104-111

1595.   Halliburton Oil Well Cementing Co.   Nov 18, 1946   329 U. S. 1
            v. Walker
        *Legal Regulation 1026-1030

1596.   Cleveland v. United States   Nov 18, 1946   329 U. S. 14
        *Courts Judges 563-565
        *Mr. Justice Murphy (Norris) 378-381
        Religion (Fellman) 20

1597.   United States v. Alcea Band of Tilla- Nov 25, 1946   329 U. S. 40
            mooks
        *Am Indian v. 4, 2739-2750
        From the Diaries 304
        *Law Indian 465-467

1598.   American Power and Light Co. v.   Nov 25, 1946   329 U. S. 90
            Securities and Exchange Commission
        Electric Power and Light Corporation
            v. Securities and Exchange Com-
            mission
        Am Consttn (Kelly) 732-733
        *Govt and Business 168-170, 454-455, 674-676
        *Social Forces 565

1599.   Carter v. Illinois   Dec 9, 1946   329 U. S. 173
        Justice Rutledge 239-240
        Mr. Justice Frankfurter 152

1600.   Ballard v. United States   Dec 9, 1946   329 U. S. 187
        Defendants 185
        Mr. Justice Murphy (Howard) 445-447

1601.   Federal Communications Commis-   Dec 9, 1946   329 U.S. 223
            sion v. Woko, Inc.
        *First Amendment (Franklin) 551-554

1602.   Freeman v. Hewit   Dec 16, 1946   329 U.S. 249
        *Consttnl Law (Freund) 583-587
        Sup Ct and Commerce 325-326

1603.   MacGregor v. Westinghouse Electric   Jan 6, 1947   329 U.S. 402
            and Manufacturing Co.
        *Govt Regulation 855-857

1604.   Louisiana ex rel. Francis v. Resweber Jan 13, 1947 329 U.S. 459
        *Am Consttnl Law (Bartholomew) v. 2, 241-243
        Am Politics 44-48
        *Bill (Cohen) 728-731
        CQ Guide 575-576
        *Consttn (Pollak) v. 2, 162-169
        *Consttnl Law (Felkenes) 346-347
        Cruel 177-178
        Death 90-128
        Defendants 408
        *Due Process 161-162
        Felix Frankfurter (Baker) 281-286
        Felix Frankfurter (Thomas) 158-160
        Justice Frankfurter 193-194
        Justice Rutledge 353-356
        Mr. Justice Murphy (Howard) 438-439
        Sup Ct (North) 131-132
        *These Liberties 9-16
        *Third Branch 102-110

1605.   Hickman v. Taylor   Jan 13, 1947   329 U.S. 495
        *Cases Civil Procedure 626-637
        *Cases Pleading 818-826
        *Civil Procedure (Carrington) 460-466
        *Civil Procedure (Cound) 687-695
        *Elements Civil 798-807
        Mr. Justice Murphy (Howard) 408-410

1606.   Insurance Group Committee v. Denver   Feb 3, 1947   329 U.S. 607
            and Rio Grande Western Railroad
        From the Diaries 309-310
        *Materials Reorganization 525-527

1607.   Transparent-Wrap Machine Corporation   Feb 3, 1947   329 U.S. 637
            v. Stokes and Smith Co.
        *Cases Antitrust Law 690-694
        *Cases Trade 917-920
        *Govt Regulation 863-870
        *Patent 602 612

1608.   Everson v. Board of Education of   Feb 10, 1947   330 U.S. 1
            Ewing Township
        Am Consttn (Kelly) 849-850
        *Am Consttnl Law (Bartholomew) v. 2, 37-41
        *Am Consttnl Law (Saye) 297-299
        *Am Consttnl Law (Shapiro) 447-450
        *Bill (Cohen) 380-385

Religious Freedom (Arnold) 43-45
*Religious Freedom (Pfeffer) 44-47
School Bus 37-43
School in the Legal Structure 64-65
*School Law (Alexander) 182-185
*School Law (Remmlein) 235-242
School Prayers (Lauboch) 35-36
*Sup Ct and Consttn 497-501
*Sup Ct and Education 6-31
Sup Ct and Religion 90-93
Sup Ct in Crisis 232
Sup Ct Review 1973 60-61
*Sup Ct Speaks 360-372
*Teacher 112-114
This Honorable Court 380-381
*Two Swords 6-11
Wall (Oaks) 82-83
Wall (Sorauf) 19-20
PERIODICALS:
"Church and state in a public school system," S. A. Pleasants.
    Clearing House 34: 277-278 Jan '60 (3).
"Concept of freedom in education," William W. Brickman. Eductnl
    Rec 45: 74-83 Winter '64 (5).
"Constitution, the Supreme Court and religion," William A. Car-
    roll. Am Poltcl Sci R 61: 657-674 Sept '67.
"Editorial reaction to Supreme Court decisions on church and state,"
    Stuart Nagel and Robert Erikson. Public Opinion Q 30: 647-
    655 Winter '66/67 (4).
"Federal aid to education and the religious controversy," Hurley
    H. Doddy. J Negro Eductn 30: 83-86 Spring '61 (2).
"Public money for parochial schools?" E. Dale Doak. Eductnl
    Leader 26: 246-249 Dec '68 (4).
"Madison and the prayer case," Irving Brant. New Republic 147:
    18-20 July 30 '62 (2). Reaction: 147: 31 Sept 17 '62.
"Religion in education: a legal perspective," Bernard Schwartz.
    Teachers College Rec 64: 363-366 Feb '63.
"Religion in the school; a historical account of church and state in
    the public classroom," Samuel A. Pleasants. Clearing House
    37: 218-221 Dec '62 (2).
"Subsidizing private schools." New Republic 142: 6 June 27 '60.
    Reaction: 143: 22-23 July 18 '60. 143: 23 August 15 '60.

1609.   United Public Workers of America   Feb 10, 1947   330 U.S. 75
            v. Mitchell
        *Am Consttnl Law (Bartholomew) v. 2, 115-118
        Cases Consttnl Law (Gunther) 1656-1659
        *Consttnl Law (Barrett) 98-99
        *Consttnl Law (Barron) 103-104
        *Consttnl Law (Freund) 1260-1264
        *Federal Courts 133-140
        Justice Rutledge 141-146, 363-307
        *Labor Relations (Edwards) 840-845
        *One Man's Stand 157-161
        *Political Rights 524-530
        *Processes 1279-1284
        System 584-588

1610.   United States v. United Mine Work-   Mar 6, 1947   330 U.S. 258
            ers of America

United States v. Lewis
*Cases Equity 1112-1119
*Cases Federal Courts 352-361
Court and Consttn v. 2, 165-166
Court Years 139
Felix Frankfurter (Thomas) 83
*Injunctions 292-294, 720-738
Justice Rutledge 216-227
Mr. Justice Murphy (Howard) 413-416
*Nature 920-935
Sup Ct in Free Society 49

1611. Testa v. Katt   Mar 10, 1947   330 U.S. 386
       *Cases Federal Courts 373-377
       *Consttnl Law (Freund) 613-615
       *Federal Courts 431-434

1612. United Brotherhood of Carpenters and   Mar 10, 1947   330 U.S. 395
          Joiners of America v. United
          States
       Elements Judicial 45

1613. Joseph v. Carter and Weekes Steve-   Mar 10, 1947   330 U.S. 422
          doring Co.
       Joseph v. John T. Clark and Son
       *Am Consttn (Lockhart) 314-316
       *Consttnl Law (Barrett) 407-408
       *Consttnl Law (Freund) 531-534
       *Consttnl Law (Kauper) 409-412

1614. Aetna Casualty and Surety Co. v.   Mar 10, 1947   330 U.S. 464
          Flowers
       *Cases Federal Courts 249-251

1615. Cardillo v. Liberty Mutual Insurance   Mar 10, 1947   330 U.S. 469
          Co.
       *Modern Social Legislation 236-241

1616. Gulf Oil Corporation v. Gilbert   Mar 10, 1947   330 U.S. 501
       *Civil Procedure (Cound) 262-266
       *Elements Civil 366-370

1617. Interstate Commerce Commission v.   Mar 31, 1947   330 U.S. 567
          Mechling
       *Cases Regulated 618-624

1618. Penfield Co. v. Securities and   Mar 31, 1947   330 U.S. 585
          Exchange Commission
       *Injunctions 754-759

1619. New York ex rel. Halvey v. Halvey   Mar 31, 1947   330 U.S. 610
       Sup Ct Review 1964 112

1620. Industrial Commission of Wisconsin   Mar 31, 1947   330 U.S. 622
          v. McCartin
       *Cases Workmen 550-554
       *Justices (Friedman) v. 4, 2507-2510
       Sup Ct Review 1964 119

1621. Haupt v. United States   Mar 31, 1947   330 U.S. 631
         Am Consttn (Kelly) 798-799
         *Liberty v. 2, 481
         *Mr. Justice Murphy (Norris) 369-371

1622. Land v. Dollar   Apr 7, 1947   330 U.S. 731
         *Federal Courts 1356-1361

1623. Bethlehem Steel v. New York Labor   Apr 7, 1947   330 U.S. 767
           Relations Board
         Allegheny Ludlum Steel Corp. v. Kelley
         *Mr. Justice Frankfurter 213-216

1624. Fleming v. Rhodes   Apr 28, 1947   331 U.S. 100
         *Federal Courts 1574-1577

1625. Fleming v. Mohawk Wrecking and   Apr 28, 1947   331 U.S. 111
           Lumber Co.
         Raley v. Fleming
         Sup Ct and Commander in Chief 86

1626. Champion Spark Plug v. Sanders   Apr 28, 1947   331 U.S. 125
         *Legal Regulation 403-406

1627. Harris v. United States   May 5, 1947   331 U.S. 145
         *Am Consttnl Law (Bartholomew) v. 2, 124-126
          CQ Guide 544-545
          Court and Consttn v. 2, 179
          Defendants 278
          Felix Frankfurter (Thomas) 137
          Justice Frankfurter 157-158
          Mr. Justice Murphy (Howard) 435-437
         *Mr. Justice Murphy (Norris) 274-282
          Modern Sup Ct 60-61
          Police 205-206
          Politics 234
          Search and Seizure 103-105
          Self Inflicted Wound 207

1628. Rice v. Santa Fe Elevator Co.   May 5, 1947   331 U.S. 218
         Illinois Commerce Commission v.
           Santa Fe Elevator Corp.
         Sup Ct and Commerce 281-283

1629. Craig v. Harney   May 19, 1947   331 U.S. 367
         *Am Consttnl Law (Saye) 329-333
          Communication (Hemmer) v. 2, 164-165
         *Consttn (Mendelson) 472-478
         *Dispassionate 302-306
         *Douglas 78-84
         *First Amendment (Franklin) 255-261
          Freedom of Speech (Hudon) 100-101
          Handbook 515-516
          Justice Frankfurter 77-78
          Justice Rutledge 136-138
         *Mr. Justice Murphy (Norris) 157-158
         *Sup Ct on Freedom 100-102
          System 454

1630.   United States v. Walsh   May 19, 1947   331 U. S. 432
        *Cases Food 604-607

1631.   Clark v. Allen   June 9, 1947   331 U. S. 503
        *Consttnl Law (Barrett) 359-360

1632.   Rescue Army v. Municipal Court   June 9, 1947   331 U. S. 549
            of Los Angeles
        Cases Consttnl Law (Gunther) 1613-1614
        *Consttnl Law (Barron) 56-57
        Consttnl Law (Felkenes) 33-35
        *Federal Courts 649-655
        Perspectives (Black) 7
        *Processes 1223-1225

1633.   Interstate Natural Gas Co. v. Federal June 16, 1947   331 U. S. 682
            Power Commission
        Impact (Wasby) 113

1634.   United States v. Silk   June 16, 1947   331 U. S. 704
        Harrison v. Greyvan Lines
        *Cases Employment 801-804
        *Modern Social Legislation 27-33

1635.   Rutherford Food Corporation v.   June 16, 1947   331 U. S. 722
            McComb
        *Cases Employment 670-673
        *Modern Social Legislation 608-611

1636.   United States v. Petrillo   June 23, 1947   332 U. S. 1
        Sup Ct and Labor 152-153

1637.   United States v. California   June 23, 1947   332 U. S. 19
        *Am Consttnl Law (Bartholomew) v. 1, 49-51
        Court and Consttn v. 2, 172
        Impact (Wasby) 111-112
        *Liberty v. 2, 498-499

1638.   Adamson v. California   June 23, 1947   332 U. S. 46
        *Am Consttnl Issues 363-370
        *Am Consttnl Law (Bartholomew) v. 2, 259-261
        *Am Consttnl Law (Mason) 737-743
        *Am Consttnl Law (Saye) 254-258
        *Am Consttnl Law (Shapiro) 645-651
        *Am Consttnl Law Reader 133-143
        *Cases Individual 110-115
        *Consttn (Mendelson) 284-290
        *Consttnl Law (Barrett) 626-631
        *Consttnl Law (Barron) 437-445
        *Consttnl Law (Felkenes) 57-62
        *Consttnl Law (Kauper) 652-662
        *Consttnl Politics 601-605
        *Contemporary Law 466-473
        Court and Consttn v. 2, 206
        Criminal Law (Felkenes) 116-120
        *Criminal Procedure (Lewis) 26-28
        *Due Process 7-8
        *Family 547-555

Felix Frankfurter (Thomas) 160-162
*Freedom and Protection 55-59
Freedom and the Court 40-44
Hugo Black (Dunne) 261-264
Justice Frankfurter 194-197
*Leading Consttnl Cases 8-23
*Liberty v. 2, 563-566
*Mr. Justice Frankfurter 152-157
Mr. Justice Murphy (Howard) 439-442
*Mr. Justice Murphy (Norris) 311-312
*One Man's Stand 162-175
Self Inflicted Wound 42-44
*Statutory History Civil Rights 342-359
*Sup Ct (Mendelson) 207-225
Sup Ct (North) 95
*Sup Ct and Criml Process 103-106
Sup Ct Review 1965 132-134
*Teaching Materials 32-38

1639.   Foster v. Illinois   June 23, 1947 332 U.S. 134
Felix Frankfurter 166-167
Hugo Black (Strickland) 105-106
Justice Rutledge 251-252
*One Man's Stand 176-178

1640.   Gayes v. New York   June 23, 1947 332 U.S. 145
Justice Rutledge 253

1641.   Securities and Exchange Commis-   June 23, 1947 332 U.S. 194
sion v. Chenery Corporation
Securities and Exchange Commis-
sion v. Federal Water and Gas
Corporation
*Admin Law (Gellhorn) 213-222
*Dispassionate 195-201
Mr. Justice Murphy (Howard) 416-422

1642.   United States v. Yellow Cab Co.   June 23, 1947 332 U.S. 218
*Cases Antitrust Law 830-831
*Competition 70-73
*Govt and Business 134-135
*Govt Regulation 871-879

1643.   Fahey v. Mallone   June 23, 1947 332 U.S. 245
*Govt and Business 456-457

1644.   Fay v. New York   June 23, 1947 332 U.S. 261
Bove v. New York
*Am Consttnl Law (Bartholomew) v. 2, 258-259
CQ Guide 532-534
Justice Rutledge 200-210
Mr. Justice Jackson 78-79
*Mr. Justice Murphy (Norris) 312-315

1645.   Federal Crop Insurance Corporation   Nov 10, 1947 332 U.S. 380
v. Merrill
*Admin Law (Schwartz) 254-256
*Dispassionate 242-244

1646. International Salt Co., Inc. v.   Nov 10, 1947 332 U.S. 392
           United States
           *Antitrust (Posner) 609-611
           *Antitrust Analysis 581-583
           *Cases Antitrust Law 622-624
           *Cases Trade 591-593
           *Competition 321-323
           *Govt Regulation 880-888
           Law and Politics 283-284
           *Patent 571-575
           *Selected Antitrust Cases 424-425
           *Text Antitrust 115-117

1647. Cox v. United States   Nov 24, 1947 332 U.S. 442
           Thompson v. United States
           Roiaum v. United States
           *Mr. Justice Murphy (Norris) 361-362

1648. Patton v. Mississippi   Dec 8, 1947   332 U.S. 463
           Private Pressure 46

1649. Blumenthal v. United States   Dec 22, 1947 332 U.S. 539
           Goldsmith v. United States
           Weiss v. United States
           Feigenbaum v. United States
           *Criminal Law (Dix) 475-483
           Criminal Law (Kadish) 470-471

1650. Marino v. Ragen, Warden   Dec 22, 1947 332 U.S. 561
           Justice Rutledge 240-243

1651. Globe Liquor Co. v. San Roman   Jan 5, 1948   332 U.S. 571
           *Cases Civil Procedure 758-760

1652. United States v. Di Re   Jan 5, 1948   332 U.S. 581
           Police 54-55
           Search and Seizure 92-93

1653. Haley v. Ohio   Jan 12, 1948 332 U.S. 596
           *Courts Judges 362-364
           *Douglas 314-316
           Justice Frankfurter 197-198
           *Mr. Justice Frankfurter 143-146
           Sup Ct and Confessions 100

1654. Sipuel v. Board of Regents of Uni-   Jan 12, 1948 332 U.S. 631
           versity of Oklahoma
           Civil Rights (Bardolph) 272
           Desegregation (Wasby) 52-54
           Disaster 24-25
           Education (Lapati) 271
           Education (Spurlock) 198-199
           Expanding Liberties 246
           Justice Rutledge 331-332
           Petitioners 335
           Private Pressure 61-64
           This Honorable Court 388

1655. Oyama v. California   Jan 19, 1948 332 U.S. 633
           Am Consttn (Kelly) 814-815

*Am Consttnl Law (Bartholomew) v. 2, 318-320
<u>CQ Guide</u> 626-627
<u>From the Diaries</u> 340-341
*<u>Mr. Justice Murphy</u> (Norris) 239-251
*<u>One Man's Stand</u> 179-181
<u>Prejudice</u> 304-306

1656. United States v. Sullivan   Jan 19, 1948   332 U.S. 689
*<u>Cases Food</u> 608-614
*<u>Consttnl Law</u> (Felkenes) 86-88
*<u>Materials Legislation</u> 137-148
<u>Sup Ct and Commerce</u> 176

1657. Von Moltke v. Gillies   Jan 19, 1948   332 U.S. 708
<u>Justice Rutledge</u> 253-257

1658. Lee v. Mississippi   Jan 19, 1948   332 U.S. 742
<u>From the Diaries</u> 337-338
*<u>Mr. Justice Murphy</u> (Norris) 295-297

1659. Johnson v. United States   Feb 2, 1948   333 U.S. 10
*<u>Arrest</u> (Waddington) 7
*<u>Criminal Law</u> (Kadish) 837-839

1660. Bob-Lo Excursion Co. v. Michigan   Feb 2, 1948   333 U.S. 28
<u>Century</u> 174-176
<u>Private Pressure</u> 43-44
<u>Sup Ct and Commerce</u> 196-197

1661. Maggio v. Zeitz   Feb 9, 1948   333 U.S. 56
In re Luma Camera Service, Inc.
*<u>Dispassionate</u> 160-165

1662. Musser v. Utah   Feb 9, 1948   333 U.S. 95
<u>Justice Rutledge</u> 128-130

1663. Chicago and Southern Airlines v.   Feb 9, 1948   333 U.S. 103
       Waterman Steamship Corporation
Civil Aeronautics Board v. Waterman
       Steamship Corporation
<u>Consttn</u> (Wilcox) 14
*<u>Federal System</u> 146
*<u>Freedom vs National Security</u> 158-163
*<u>Govt and Business</u> 612-615
<u>Sup Ct and Am Capitalism</u> 189-190

1664. Funk Brothers Seed Co. v. Kalo   Feb 16, 1948   333 U.S. 127
       Inoculant
*<u>Legal Regulation</u> 818-822

1665. Woods v. Cloyd W. Miller Co.   Feb 16, 1948   333 U.S. 138
<u>Am Consttn</u> (Kelly) 810-811
*<u>Am Consttn</u> (Lockhart) 210-211
*<u>Am Consttnl Law</u> (Bartholomew) v. 1, 294-296
*<u>Cases Consttnl Law</u> (Gunther) 247-248
*<u>Consttn</u> (Mendelson) 160-162
*<u>Consttnl Law</u> (Barrett) 261-263
*<u>Consttnl Law</u> (Felkenes) 93-95
*<u>Consttnl Law</u> (Freund) 336-338
*<u>Consttnl Law</u> (Lockhart) 224-226

*Contemporary Law 385-388
*Govt and Business 392-393
*Liberty v. 2, 491-492
Sup Ct and Commander in Chief 86-87

1666. Fisher v. Hurst   Feb 16, 1948   333 U.S. 147
       Petitioners 335
       Private Pressure 64-65

1667. Cole v. Arkansas   Mar 8, 1948   333 U.S. 196
       *Civil Rights (Abernathy) 1977 106-107

1668. Illinois ex rel. McCollum v. Board of   Mar 8, 1948   333 U.S. 203
       Education of School District No. 71,
       Champaign County
       Am Consttn (Kelly) 850
       *Am Consttnl Law (Bartholomew) v. 2, 41-43
       *Am Consttnl Law (Mason) 618-622
       *Am Consttnl Law (Shapiro) 450-454
       Bible 172-178
       *Bill (Cohen) 433-437
       Bill (Cohen) 437-439
       *Bill (Konvitz) 39-41
       CQ Guide 462-463
       Church and State 131-133
       Church State and Freedom 401-414
       Civil Liberties (Kauper) 14-15
       *Civil Liberties (Sweet) 44-51
       *Civil Rights (Abernathy) 1977 292-295
       *Consttn (Morris) 331-333
       *Consttnl Cases 379-394
       *Consttnl Law (Kauper) 1256-1262
       *Contemporary Law 765-771
       Digest 18
       *Dispassionate 60-65
       *Documents History v. 2, 544-546
       Dynamics 47-48
       *Education (Hazard) 87-90
       Education (Lapati) 198-201
       *Education (Spurlock) 116-123
       Expanding Liberties 19-20
       Felix Frankfurter (Thomas) 60-62, 135-136
       *First Amendment (Konvitz) 28-43
       First Amendment (Marnell) 177-183
       *Freedom and Protection 25-26
       Freedom and the Court 297-299, 325
       From the Diaries 342-344
       Garden 139-141
       Impact (Wasby) 127-128
       *Judicial Excerpts 64-67
       Justice Frankfurter 43-45
       Justice Rutledge 73-74
       Landmark Decisions 65-72
       Law and Education 294
       *Law and Public Education (Hamilton) 62-71
       *Law of Public Education 39-40
       *Mr. Justice Frankfurter 113-114
       Mr. Justice Murphy (Howard) 451-452
       Modern Sup Ct 94-96

*One Man's Stand 182-187
One Woman's Fight.
*One Woman's Fight 220-257
*Political Rights 745-750, 772-779
*Principles School 159-161
Private Conscience 176-177
*Public School Law 108-110
Public Schools 110-111
*Public Schools 111-134
Religion (Drinan) 74-84
Religion (Felkenes) 86-89
Religion (Kurland) 86-89
Religion (School Admin) 15-16
Religious Freedom (Arnold) 49
*Religious Freedom (Pfeffer) 74-75
School Bus 43-47
School in the Legal Structure 65-66
*School Law (Alexander) 232-234
*School Law (Remmlein) 260-261
School Prayers (Lauboch) 36-38
Sup Ct (North) 115-116
*Sup Ct and Education 48-61
Sup Ct and Religion 126-129
Teacher 115-117
*Two Swords 35-44
Wall (Oaks) 83-84
PERIODICALS:
"Church and state in a public school system," S. A. Pleasants.
    Clearing House 34: 277-278 Jan '60 (3).
"Editorial reaction to Supreme Court decisions on church and
    state," Stuart Nagel and Robert Erikson. Public Opinion Q
    30: 647-655 Winter '66/67 (1).
"U.S. Supreme Court and religion in the schools," August W.
    Steinhilber. Theory into Practice 4: 8-13 Feb '65 (4).

1669. In re Oliver   Mar 8, 1948   333 U.S. 257
       *Bill (Konvitz) 696-702
       *Criminal Procedure (Lewis) 536-539
       *Due Process 107
       Justice Rutledge 199-202, 205-208
       *Sup Ct and Criml Process 694-696

1670. United States v. Line Material Co.   Mar 8, 1948   333 U.S. 287
       *Antitrust (Posner) 301-306
       *Antitrust Analysis 458-462
       *Cases Antitrust Law 352-365
       *Cases Trade 890-895
       *Govt Regulation 889-926

1671. Bakery Sales Drivers Union, Local 33   Mar 15, 1948   333 U.S. 437
           v. Wagshal
       *Cases Labor (Handler) 588-590
       *Labor Law (Meltzer) 369-372

1672. Winters v. New York   Mar 29, 1948   333 U.S. 507
       *Am Consttnl Law (Bartholomew) v. 2, 275-276
       Censorship 14-18
       *Censorship Landmarks 132-142
       *Criminal Law (Kadish) 182-185

      *Freedom Reader 113-114
      Justice Frankfurter 59-60
      Law of Obscenity 30-31
      Modern Sup Ct 90-91
      *Obscenity (Bosmajian) 30-39
      Sup Ct in Free Society 48
      Sup Ct Review 1968 158-159

1673. Connecticut Mutual Life Insurance   Mar 29, 1948 333 U. S. 541
      Co. v. Moore
      *Consttnl Law (Freund) 448-451

1674. Moore v. New York   Mar 29, 1948 333 U. S. 565
      *Mr. Justice Murphy (Norris) 315-316

1675. Commissioner of Internal Revenue   Apr 5, 1948   333 U. S. 591
      v. Sunnen
      *Civil Procedure (Cound) 1081-1084
      *Elements Civil 1164-1168

1676. Bute v. Illinois   Apr 19, 1948 333 U. S. 640
      Justice Rutledge 257-258

1677. Federal Trade Commission v.   Apr 26, 1948 333 U. S. 683
      Cement Institute
      *Admin Law (Schwartz) 430-433
      *Antitrust Analysis 309-314
      *Cases Antitrust Law 418-426
      *Competition 293-298
      *Free Enterprise 527-541
      *Selected Antitrust Cases 88-96

1678. Shelley v. Kraemer   May 3, 1948   334 U. S. 1
      McGhee v. Sipes
      *Am Consttn (Lockhart) 1035-1038
      *Am Consttnl Law (Bartholomew) v. 2, 294-295
      *Am Consttnl Law (Mason) 482-484
      *Am Consttnl Law (Saye) 263-264
      *Am Consttnl Law (Shapiro) 532-536
      *Am Land Planning v. 1, 309-321
      *Bill (Konvitz) 526-529
      By What Right 179-181
      CQ Guide 613-614
      *Cases Civil Liberties 323-327
      *Cases Consttnl Law (Cushman) 553-557
      *Cases Consttnl Law (Gunther) 999-1002
      *Cases Consttnl Law (Rosenblum) 23-28
      *Cases Consttnl Rights 987-989
      *Cases Individual 527-531
      *Cases Property (Casner) 987-991
      *Cases Property (Donahue) 163-168
      Century 142-144
      *Civil Liberties (Kauper) 146-148
      *Civil Liberties (Sweet) 190-191
      *Civil Rights (Abernathy) 1977 535-537
      *Civil Rights (Abernathy) 1980 85-86
      *Civil Rights (Bardolph) 281-283
      *Civil Rights (Blaustein) 389-395
      *Consttn (Mendelson) 546-549

          *Consttnl Law (Barrett) 1045-1050
          *Consttnl Law (Barron) 999-1001
          *Consttnl Law (Freund) 808-813
          *Consttnl Law (Grossman) 524-528
          *Consttnl Law (Kauper) 802-809
          *Consttnl Law (Lockhart) 1530-1532
          *Consttnl Politics 480-484
          *Contemporary Law 892-897
           Desegregation (Wasby) 37-43
          *Discrimination 359-366
           Freedom and the Court 417-418
          *Govt and Business 55-56
          *Legal Foundations 283-285
          *Liberty v. 2, 594-595
           Modern Sup Ct 110-112
          *Nature 991-996
          *Negro (Franklin) 445-449
           Petitioners 323-325
          *Political Rights v. 2, 1583-1591
           Politics 165-167
           Private Pressure 52-58
          *Processes 636-638
           Quest 116-117
          *Race 609-616
          *Racial Equality 43-44
           This Honorable Court 387-388

1679.   Hurd v. Hodge   May 3, 1948   334 U.S. 24
        Urciolo v. Hodge
          *Am Land Planning v. 1, 321-328
          *Consttnl Politics 484-486
           Modern Sup Ct 110-112
           Petitioners 323-324, 325-326
           Private Pressure 57-58

1680.   Federal Trade Commission v. Morton   May 3, 1948   334 U.S. 37
           Salt Co.
          *Antitrust (Posner) 748-755
          *Antitrust Analysis 867-871
          *Cases Antitrust Law 1086-1096
          *Cases Trade 1001-1006
          *Competition 264-268
          *Free Enterprise 834-847
          *Govt Regulation 927-940
          *Selected Antitrust Cases 258-262
          *Text Antitrust 215-219

1681.   United States v. Griffith   May 3, 1948   334 U.S. 100
          *Antitrust Analysis 153-157
          *Cases Antitrust Law 743-747
          *Cases Trade 651-655
          *Govt Regulation 967-972

1682.   Schine Chain Theaters v. United States May 3, 1948 334 U.S. 110
          *Govt Regulation 973-984

1683.   United States v. Paramount Pictures, May 3, 1948   334 U.S. 131
           Inc.

Loew's, Inc. v. United States
Paramount Pictures, Inc. v. United
  States
Columbia Pictures Corporation v.
  United States
United Artists Corporation v. United
  States
Universal Pictures Co., Inc. v.
  United States
American Theatres Association, Inc.
  v. United States
Allred v. United States
  *Competition 74-78
  *Govt Regulation 941-966
  Movies 45

1684. Mandeville Island Farms v. Amer-   May 10, 1948   334 U.S. 219
         ican Crystal Sugar Co.
         *Govt and Business 135-138
         Sup Ct and Commerce 169-173

1685. Price v. Johnston   May 24, 1948   334 U.S. 266
         *Mr. Justice Murphy (Norris) 381-395

1686. Sherrer v. Sherrer   June 7, 1948   334 U.S. 343
         *Cases Domestic 421-424
         *Family 310-311

1687. Toomer v. Witsell   June 7, 1948   334 U.S. 385
         *Am Consttn (Lockhart) 274-276
         *Am Consttnl Law (Bartholomew) v. 2, 346-348
         *Cases Consttnl Law (Gunther) 375-377
         *Consttnl Law (Barrett) 351-354

1688. Takahashi v. Fish and Game Com-   June 7, 1948   334 U.S. 410
         mission
         *Am Consttnl Law (Saye) 464-465
         CQ Guide 627
         *Consttn (Mendelson) 598-603
         *Mr. Justice Murphy (Norris) 251-255
         Poverty 306-307
         Sup Ct Review 1977 296-298

1689. United States v. Columbia Steel Co.   June 7, 1948   334 U.S. 495
         *Antitrust (Posner) 382-389, 688-691
         *Antitrust Analysis 692-696
         *Competition 99-106
         *Free Enterprise 132-134
         *Govt Regulation 985-1008
         US Sup Ct 75-76

1690. Estin v. Estin   June 7, 1948   334 U.S. 541
         *Dispassionate 267-269

1691. Saia v. New York   June 7, 1948   334 U.S. 558
         Am Consttn (Kelly) 846
         CQ Guide 409
         Communication (Hemmer) v. 1, 219-220
         *Dispassionate 76-79

      Dissent 439-440
      Freedom and the Court 189-190
    *Freedom of Speech (Haiman) 71-72
      Handbook 144
      Justice Frankfurter 85-88
      Justice Rutledge 122-124
      Mr. Justice Jackson 43
      Movies 36-38
      O'er the Ramparts 153-156
      Religion (Kurland) 70-71
    *Sup Ct on Freedom 209-211
      Sup Ct Review 1979 201

1692. United States v. John J. Felin and   June 14, 1948 334 U.S. 624
        Co.
      Sup Ct Review 1962 92-93

1693. Central Greyhound Lines of New York June 14, 1948 334 U.S. 653
        v. Mealey
      Consttnl Law (Barrett) 408-409

1694. Wade v. Mayo   June 14, 1948 334 U.S. 672
      Justice Rutledge 258-259
    *Mr. Justice Murphy (Norris) 395-401

1695. Trupiano v. United States   June 14, 1948 334 U.S. 699
      Mr. Justice Murphy (Howard) 437-438
    *Mr. Justice Murphy (Norris) 285-292
      Modern Sup Ct 99
      Search and Seizure 105-106
      Sup Ct Review 1962 237

1696. Townsend v. Burke   June 14, 1948 334 U.S. 736
      Justice Rutledge 259-260

1697. Lichter v. United States   June 14, 1948 334 U.S. 742
      Pownall v. United States
      Alexander Wool Combing Co. v. United
        States
    *Govt and Business 455-456
    *Liberty v. 2, 476-477

1698. Shapiro v. United States   June 21, 1948 335 U.S. 1
      Defendants 308-309
    *Govt and Business 514-515
    *Introduction (Mashaw) 601-606
    *Social Forces 557

1699. Memphis Natural Gas Co. v. Stone   June 21, 1948 335 U.S. 80
      From the Diaries 337

1700. United States v. Congress for Indus- June 21, 1948 335 U.S. 106
        trial Organization
      Justice Rutledge 146-149
      Right of Assembly 189-190
    PERIODICALS:
      "Corporations and labor unions in electoral politics," Edwin M.
        Epstein. Am Academy of Poltcl and Social Sci. Annals 425:
        33-58 May '76 (4).

1701. Ludecke v. Watkins   June 21, 1948 335 U. S. 160
           Am Consttn (Kelly) 811
           Felix Frankfurter (Thomas) 252-253
           *Mr. Justice Frankfurter 58-60
           *One Man's Stand 188-193
           Sup Ct and Commander in Chief 87-89

1702. Taylor v. Alabama   June 21, 1948 335 U. S. 252
           Mr. Justice Murphy (Norris) 297-301
           Private Pressure 47

1703. MacDougall v. Green   Oct 21, 1948   335 U. S. 281
           *Consttnl Cases 277-283
           Decade 91
           Law and Politics 198
           *Political Rights 990-993
           Political Thicket 74
           Right of Assembly 194-195
           Sup Ct and Electoral Process 238-239
           Sup Ct and Poltcl Questions 51-56

1704. Kordel v. United States   Nov 22, 1948   335 U. S. 345
           *Cases Food 105-108
           *Materials Legislation 119-124
           Significant Decisions 1969/70 18

1705. United States v. Urbuteit   Nov 22, 1948   335 U. S. 355
           *Cases Food 108-109
           *Materials Legislation 125-126

1706. Vermilya-Brown Co. v. Connell   Dec 6, 1948   335 U. S. 377
           Justices Black and Frankfurter 18-19

1707. Upshaw v. United States   Dec 13, 1948   335 U. S. 410
           Sup Ct and Confessions 75-77

1708. Uveges v. Pennsylvania   Dec 13, 1948   335 U. S. 437
           Justice Rutledge 261-262

1709. McDonald v. United States   Dec 13, 1948   335 U. S. 451
           *Arrest (Waddington) 152
           Search and Seizure 74, 107

1710. Goesaert v. Cleary   Dec 20, 1948   335 U. S. 464
           *Cases Consttnl Law (Rosenblum) 286-287
           *Consttnl Law (Freund) 877-878
           Quest 75-76
           *Sex Discrimination 1975 94-95
           *Sex Roles 469-471
           *Text Consttnl Aspects 17-19
           *Text Sex Based Discrimination 17-19

1711. Michelson v. United States   Dec 20, 1948   335 U. S. 469
           *Cases Evidence 945-955
           *Principles Proof 337-346

1712. Frazier v. United States   Dec 20, 1948   335 U. S. 497
           Defendants 190-191
           *Dispassionate 114-118

1713. Lincoln Federal Labor Union v.   Jan 3, 1949   335 U.S. 525
           Northwestern Iron Metal Co.
       Whitaker v. North Carolina
           *Am Consttnl Law (Bartholomew) v. 2, 213-215
           *Cases Labor (Handler) 418-422
           *Consttn (Mendelson) 265-267
           Consttnl Law (Barrett) 671
           *Labor Relations (Group Trust) 86-92
           *Liberty v. 2, 492-493

1714. American Federation of Labor v.   Jan 3, 1949   335 U.S. 538
           American Sash and Door Co.
           Dissent 462-463
           Felix Frankfurter (Baker) 286-288
           Felix Frankfurter (Thomas) 283
           Justice Rutledge 227-229
           *Mr. Justice Frankfurter 190-197

1715. Jungersen v. Ostby and Barton Co.   Jan 3, 1949   335 U.S. 560
           *Copyright 420-423
           *Dispassionate 159-160
           Sup Ct and Agencies 175-176

1716. Klappsott v. United States   Jan 17, 1949   335 U.S. 601
           Justice Rutledge 275-278

1717. Commissioner of Internal Revenue   Jan 17, 1949   335 U.S. 632
           v. Estate of Church
           Hugo Black (Strickland) 176-179

1718. Hirota v. MacArthur   Dec 6, 1948   335 U.S. 876
       Dohihara v. MacArthur
       Kido v. MacArthur
           *Dispassionate 306-311

1719. La Crosse Telephone Corporation v.   Jan 17, 1949   336 U.S. 18
           Wisconsin Employment Relations
           Board
       International Brotherhood of Electrical
           Workers v. Wisconsin Employment
           Relations Board
           *Cases Labor (Handler) 210-212

1720. Wilkerson v. McCarthy   Jan 31, 1949   336 U.S. 53
           *Cases Civil Procedure 728-737

1721. Kovacs v. Cooper   Jan 31, 1949   336 U.S. 77
           Am Consttn (Kelly) 846-847
           *Am Consttnl Law (Bartholomew) v. 2, 104-106
           Cases Consttnl Law (Gunther) 1210-1211
           Communication (Hemmer) v. 1, 220-221
           *Consttn (Mendelson) 461-464
           Consttnl Law (Barrett) 1252-1253
           *Consttnl Law (Freund) 1184-1189
           *Dispassionate 79-81
           Felix Frankfurter (Thomas) 232-234
           *First Amendment (Konvitz) 244-249
           *Free Speech (Summers) 50-51
           *Freedom of Speech (Haiman) 72-73

Handbook 144-147
Hugo Black (Dunne) 288
Justice Frankfurter 26-27, 89
Justice Rutledge 124-127
Mass Communications 28-33
*Mr. Justice Frankfurter 76-77
Movies 39-42
*One Man's Stand 194-199
Religion (Kurland) 71-72
*Sup Ct on Freedom 211-215
System 559

1722.   Railway Express Agency v. New York   Jan 31, 1949   336 U.S. 106
*Am Consttn (Lockhart) 370-372
*Cases Consttnl Law (Gunther) 681-684
*Cases Consttnl Rights 130-132
*Cases Individual 269-272
*Consttn (Mendelson) 274-276
*Consttnl Law (Barrett) 770-772
*Consttnl Law (Barron) 569-571
*Consttnl Law (Freund) 879-881
*Consttnl Law (Lockhart) 1247-1248
*Govt and Business 50-52
Least Dangerous 221-225
*Processes 553-555
*Sex Discrimination 1975 75-76

1723.   Fisher v. Pace   Feb 7, 1949   336 U.S. 155
*Cases Professional 544-550
*Courts Judges 340-343
Justice Rutledge 202-204
*Mr. Justice Murphy (Norris) 347-348

1724.   McComb v. Jacksonville Paper Co.   Feb 14, 1949   336 U.S. 187
*Injunctions 749-753

1725.   Lawson, Deputy Commissioner v.   Feb 14, 1949   336 U.S. 198
          Suwanee Fruit and Steamship Co.
*Cases Employment 405-409
*Cases Workmen 409-412
*Modern Social Legislation 308-312

1726.   Daniel v. Family Security Life   Feb 28, 1949   336 U.S. 220
          Insurance
*Consttnl Law (Barrett) 671-672

1727.   National Labor Relations Board v.   Feb 28, 1949   336 U.S. 226
          Stowe Spinning Co.
*Cases Labor (Cox) 150-159
*Mr. Justice Murphy (Norris) 123-127
Sup Ct and Labor 52-53

1728.   International Union, United Auto Work- Feb 28, 1949   336 U.S. 245
          ers v. Wisconsin Employment
          Relations Board
*Cases Labor (Handler) 212-215
*Labor Law (Meltzer) 597-602
*Labor Relations (Edwards) 496-499

1729. Stainback v. Mo Honk Ke Lok Po   Mar 14, 1949   336 U.S. 368
           Education (Spurlock) 173-174

1730. Black Diamond Steamship Corporation Mar 14, 1949   336 U.S. 386
           v. Robert Stewart and Sons, Ltd.
           United States v. Robert Stewart and Sons
           *Cases Admiralty 111-116

1731. Krulewitch v. United States   Mar 28, 1949   336 U.S. 440
           *Criminal Law (Kadish) 416-420
           Mr. Justice Jackson 54-55, 74

1732. United States v. Women's Sportswear Mar 28, 1949   336 U.S. 460
           Manufacturers Association
           Sup Ct and Commerce 174-175

1733. Giboney v. Empire Storage and Ice Co. Apr 4, 1949   336 U.S. 490
           *Am Consttnl Law (Bartholomew) v. 2, 112-113
           *Bill (Konvitz) 268-271
           Communication (Hemmer) v. 1, 86-87
           Consttnl Law (Barrett) 1157-1158
           *Freedom of Speech (Haiman) 70
           Justices Black and Frankfurter 59-60
           Labor Relations (Taylor) 510-511
           Law and Politics 78-79
           *Liberty v. 2, 530-531
           Sup Ct and Labor 44-45
           System 439-440

1734. Farrell v. United States   Apr 4, 1949   336 U.S. 511
           *Cases Admiralty 319-323

1735. H.P. Hood and Sons v. DuMond   Apr 4, 1949   336 U.S. 525
           *Am Consttn (Lockhart) 266-269
           *Am Consttnl Law (Bartholomew) v. 1, 218-219
           *Am Consttnl Law (Mason) 240-243
           *Am Consttnl Law (Saye) 182-185
           *Cases Consttnl Law (Gunther) 319-323
           *Consttnl Law (Barrett) 327-329
           *Consttnl Law (Barron) 273-278
           *Consttnl Law (Freund) 401-407
           *Consttnl Law (Lockhart) 319-322
           Sup Ct and Commerce 251-254
           Sup Ct in Free Society 124-126
           Sup Ct Review 1975 162-163

1736. Rice v. Rice   Apr 18, 1949   336 U.S. 674
           *Dispassionate 269-273

1737. Wade v. Hunter   Apr 25, 1949   336 U.S. 684
           Defendants 373-374
           *Mr. Justice Murphy (Norris) 301-302

1738. Griffin v. United States   Apr 25, 1949   336 U.S. 704
           *Mr. Justice Murphy (Norris) 405-407

1739. California v. Zook   Apr 25, 1949   336 U.S. 725
           Double (Miller) 51-54
           Sup Ct and Commerce 284-287

1744.   United States v. Cors   June 13, 1949 337 U.S. 325
            Sup Ct Review 1962 91-92

1745.   United States v. Interstate Commerce   June 20, 1949 337 U.S. 426
            Commission
            *Govt and Business 585-586

1746.   Aeronautical Industrial District Lodge   June 20, 1949 337 U.S. 521
            v. Campbell
            *Cases Labor (Handler) 499-502

1747.   Ragan v. Merchants Transfer and   June 20, 1949 337 U.S. 530
            Warehouse Co.
            *Cases Civil Procedure 288-290

1748.   Cohen v. Beneficial Industrial Loan   June 20, 1949 337 U.S. 541
            Corporation
            Beneficial Industrial Loan Corporation
            v. Smith
            *Basic Corporation 522-528
            Sup Ct Review 1979 283-284

1749.   Wheeling Steel Corporation v. Glander   June 20, 1949 337 U.S. 562
            National Distillers Products Corpora-
                tion v. Glander
            *Basic Corporation 59-63
            *Consttn (Pollak) 302-305
            *Douglas 272-275

1750.   National Mutual Insurance Co. v.   June 20, 1949 337 U.S. 582
            Tidewater Transfer Co.
            *Cases Federal Courts 73-88
            *Consttnl Law (Kauper) 63-69
            *Consttnl Politics 294-303
            *Federal Courts 400-415
            Justices Black and Frankfurter 88-90
            *Materials Consttnl Law 44-59
            *Mr. Justice Frankfurter 11-13

1751.   National Labor Relations Board v.   June 20, 1949 337 U.S. 656
            Pittsburgh Steamship Co.
            *Govt and Business 626-627
            *Social Forces 566-567

1752.   Larson v. Domestic and Foreign   June 27, 1949 337 U.S. 682
            Commerce Corporation
            *Admin Law (Gellhorn) 1056-1064
            *Civil Rights (Abernathy) 1980 376-381
            *Introduction (Mashaw) 660-666

1753.   Commissioner of Internal Revenue v.   June 27, 1949 337 U.S. 733
            Culbertson
            Hugo Black (Strickland) 185-186

1754.   Gibbs v. Burke   June 27, 1949 337 U.S. 773
            Justice Rutledge 262-263

1755.   Kimball Laundry Co. v. United States   June 27, 1949 338 U.S. 1
            Sup Ct Review 1962 97

1756. Wolf v. Colorado   June 27, 1949 338 U. S. 25
       *Am Consttn (Lockhart) 410-412
       *Am Consttnl Law (Bartholomew) v. 2, 262-264
       *Basic Criminal 172-174
       CQ Guide 548
       *Cases Civil Liberties 122-124
       *Cases Consttnl Law (Cushman) 352-355
       *Cases Consttnl Rights 170-172
       *Civil Liberties (Sweet) 237-238
       *Consttnl Criml Procedure (Scarboro) 54-59
       *Consttnl Law (Felkenes) 220-221
       *Consttnl Law (Freund) 1006-1008
       *Consttnl Law (Kauper) 910-913
       *Consttnl Politics 612-618
       Criminal Law (Felkenes) 18-20
       Defendants 294
       Dissent 299-300
       Exclusionary 19-21
       Freedom Spent 225-230
       Justice Frankfurter 199-200
       Justice Rutledge 154-158
       *Justices (Friedman) v. 4, 2510-2513
       *Leading Consttnl Cases 231-236
       Mr. Justice Murphy (Howard) 460-462
       *Mr. Justice Murphy (Norris) 292-295
       Modern Sup Ct 100-104, 244-246
       *One Man's Stand 200-202
       Search and Seizure 126-130
       *Sup Ct and Criml Process 190-192
       Sup Ct Review 1961 1-6
       *Teaching Materials 78-81

1757. Watts v. Indiana   June 27, 1949 338 U. S. 49
       Harris v. South Carolina
       Turner v. Pennsylvania
       *Consttn (Mendelson) 358-360
       *Consttnl Criml Procedure (Scarboro) 509-515
       *Dispassionate 130-133
       *Due Process 58
       *Police 116-118
       Private Pressure 47-48

1758. Lustig v. United States   June 27, 1949 338 U. S. 74
       Search and Seizure 72-73

1759. Christoffel v. United States   June 27, 1949 338 U. S. 84
       *Consttnl Politics 226-231
       *Mr. Justice Murphy (Norris) 426-429

1760. Securities and Exchange Commission   June 27, 1949 338 U. S. 96
          v. Central Illinois Securities
          Corporation
       *Materials Reorganization 456-461

1761. Brinegar v. United States   June 27, 1949 338 U. S. 160
       *Civil Rights (Abernathy) 1977 122-123
       Criminal Evidence 239
       Defendants 281-282
       *Dispassionate 107-114

         Law of Arrest (Markle) 126-127
         *Police 22-23
         *Principles Arrest 26-28
         Search and Seizure 93-96

1762. Eisler v. United States   June 27, 1949 338 U.S. 189
         Mr. Justice Murphy (Howard) 464-466
         *Mr. Justice Murphy (Norris) 368-369

1763. Hirota v. MacArthur   June 27, 1949 338 U.S. 197
         Dohihara v. MacArthur
         Kido v. MacArthur
         *Consttnl Law (Freund) 716-719
         Justice Rutledge 196-198, 360-363

1764. United States v. Spelar   Nov 7, 1949   338 U.S. 217
         *Dispassionate 225-227

1765. Graham v. Brotherhood of Loco-   Nov 7, 1949   338 U.S. 232
           motive Firemen and Enginemen
         Petitioners 316

1766. Reilly v. Pinkus   Nov 14, 1949 338 U.S. 269
         *Cases Food 324-326

1767. Brown v. Western Railway of Alabama   Nov 21, 1949 338 U.S. 294
         *Cases Civil Procedure 548-554

1768. Kingsland v. Dorsey   Nov 21, 1949 338 U.S. 318
         *Dispassionate 294-298

1769. United States v. Yellow Cab Co.   Dec 5, 1949   338 U.S. 338
         *Govt Regulation 1060-1063

1770. United States v. Aetna Casualty and   Dec 19, 1949 338 U.S. 366
           Surety Co.
         *Elements Civil 409-411

1771. Wilmette Park District v. Campbell   Dec 12, 1949 338 U.S. 411
         *Cases Consttnl Law (Cushman) 154-156

1772. United States v. Cumberland Public   Jan 9, 1950   338 U.S. 451
           Service Co.
         Hugo Black (Strickland) 181-182

1773. United States ex rel. Knauff v. Shaugh- Jan 16, 1950 338 U.S. 537
           nessy
         Civil Rights (Konvitz) 46-49
         *Dispassionate 202-206
         *Justices (Friedman) v. 4, 2714-2718
         Mr. Justice Jackson 51-52

1774. Secretary of Agriculture v. Central   Feb 6, 1950   338 U.S. 604
           Roig Refining Co.
         Porto Rican American Sugar Refinery,
           Inc. v. Central Roig Refining Co.
         Puerto Rico v. Secretary of Agriculture
         *Govt and Business 591-599

1775. United States v. Morton Salt Co.   Feb 6, 1950   338 U. S. 632
       United States v. International Salt Co.
       *Govt and Business 509-512
       *Introduction (Mashaw) 597-600
       *Social Forces 555-556

1776. United States v. Alpers   Feb 6, 1950   338 U. S. 680
       *One Man's Stand 203-205

1777. Maryland v. Baltimore Radio Show   Jan 9, 1950   338 U. S. 912
       *Cases Consttnl Rights 84
       *Consttnl Law (Lockhart) 69
       *Consttnl Politics 111-112
       *Contemporary Law 3-4
       *Courts Judges 93-95
       *Family 92
       *Sup Ct on Freedom 106-108

1778. District of Columbia v. Little   Feb 20, 1950   339 U. S. 1
       Search and Seizure 246-248

1779. Solesbee v. Balkcom   Feb 20, 1950   339 U. S. 9
       Justice Frankfurter 200-202
       *Mr. Justice Frankfurter 165-167

1780. Wong Yang Sung v. McGrath   Feb 20, 1950   399 U. S. 33
       *Admin Law (Gellhorn) 164-168
       Sup Ct in Free Society 44

1781. United States v. Rabinowitz   Feb 20, 1950   339 U. S. 56
       *Am Consttnl Law (Bartholomew) v. 2, 141-143
       *Consttn (Mendelson) 322-325
       *Consttnl Criml Procedure (Scarboro) 289-301
       *Criminal Law (Kadish) 840-841
       Felix Frankfurter (Thomas) 137-138
       Justice Rutledge 152-154
       *Justices (Friedman) v. 4, 2710-2714
       *Liberty v. 2, 567-568
       Modern Sup Ct 99-100
       *One Man's Stand 206-207
       *Rights (Shattuck) 25-27
       Search and Seizure 108-111
       Text Consttnl Aspects 231

1782. Dennis v. United States   Mar 27, 1950   339 U. S. 162
       Defendants 191
       *Dispassionate 119-122
       Felix Frankfurter (Thomas) 142
       *Mr. Justice Frankfurter 43-46

1783. South v. Peters   Apr 17, 1950   339 U. S. 276
       *Liberty v. 2, 613-614
       Sup Ct and Electoral Process 152
       Sup Ct and Poltcl Questions 76-77

1784. Cassell v. Texas   Apr 24, 1950   339 U. S. 282
       *Bill (Konvitz) 548-551
       *Freedom and Protection 45-46
       Petitioners 288-289

1785. Mullane v. Central Hanover Bank   Apr 24, 1950   339 U.S. 306
            and Trust Co.
        *Cases Pleading 203-212
        *Civil Procedure (Cound) 135-141
        *Due Process 227-228
        *Elements Civil 344-352
         Sup Ct Review 1965 275-276
         Sup Ct Review 1972 136-137
         Sup Ct Review 1974 110-115

1786. United States v. Bryan   May 8, 1950   339 U.S. 323
        *Consttnl Politics 231-236
        *Dispassionate 228-231

1787. American Communications Association   May 8, 1950   339 U.S. 382
            v. Douds
        United Steelworkers of America v. Na-
            tional Labor Relations Board
         Am Consttn (Kelly) 828-829
        *Am Consttnl Law (Bartholomew) v. 2, 70-74
         CQ Guide 510-511
         Court and Consttn v. 2, 174-175
        *Dispassionate 48-54
         Felix Frankfurter (Thomas) 203-204
        *First Amendment (Konvitz) 507-527
         Freedom of Speech (Hudon) 108-109
         Freedom of Speech (Shapiro) 62
        *Freedom Reader 66-60
         Freedom Spent 81-82
         Hugo Black (Strickland) 111-112
         Justice Frankfurter 37-38
        *Liberty v. 2, 540-543
        *Mass Communications 66-68
        *Mr. Justice Frankfurter 104-107
         Modern Sup Ct 75-77, 79
        *One Man's Stand 208-213
        *Political Rights 214-232
        *Rights (Shattuck) 61
         Sup Ct and Commerce 178
         System 32-35, 164-168
         This Honorable Court 364-366

1788. Hughes v. Superior Court of the   May 8, 1950   339 U.S. 460
            State of California for Contra
            Costa County
         Am Consttn (Kelly) 841
         Communication (Hemmer) v. 1, 87-88
        *First Amendment (Konvitz) 327-331
         Labor Relations (Taylor) 513
         Petitioners 313
         Sup Ct and Labor 45-46
         System 443-444

1789. International Brotherhood of Teamsters, May 8, 1950   339 U.S. 470
            Chauffeurs, Warehousemen and Helpers
            Union, Local 309 v. Hanke
        Automobile Drivers and Demonstrators Local
            Union No. 882 v. Cline
         Am Consttn (Kelly) 841
        *Nature 942-949

1790.   United States v. National Association   May 8, 1950   339 U.S. 485
            of Real Estate Boards
            *Govt and Business 197-198

1791.   Building Service Employees Union   May 8, 1950   339 U.S. 532
            v. Gazzam
            Labor Relations (Taylor) 512

1792.   Capitol Greyhound Lines v. Brice   May 15, 1950   339 U.S. 542
            *Consttnl Law (Kauper) 383-385

1793.   Ewing v. Mytinger and Casselberry,   May 29, 1950   399 U.S. 594
            Inc.
            *Cases Food 642-645

1794.   Graver Tank and Manufacturing Co.   May 29, 1950   339 U.S. 605
            v. Linde Air Products Co.
            *Criminal Procedure (Wells) 553-560
            *Patent 145-156

1795.   Sweatt v. Painter   June 5, 1950   339 U.S. 629
            Am Consttn (Kelly) 860-861
            *Am Consttnl Law (Bartholomew) v. 2, 301-302
            *Am Consttnl Law (Shapiro) 511-513
            CQ Guide 592
            *Cases Civil Liberties 330-333
            *Cases Consttnl Law (Cushman) 560-563
            *Civil Liberties (Sweet) 211-212
            *Civil Rights (Abernathy) 1977 513-514
            *Civil Rights (Bardolph) 273-275
            *Civil Rights (Blaustein) 410-414
            *Consttnl Law (Freund) 885-886
            *Courts 6-7
            Desegregation (Wasby) 54-57
            Digest 79
            Disaster 25
            Education (Lapati) 271-272
            *Education (Spurlock) 200-202
            Equality (Cohen) 63
            Expanding Liberties 247-250
            Felix Frankfurter (Baker) 313-314
            Freedom and the Court 365-366
            *Justices (Friedman) v. 4, 2659-2661
            *Law Lawyers 170-174
            Modern Sup Ct 116-117
            Petitioners 338-341
            Private Pressure 65-68
            *Public School Law 637-640
            Quest 133-136
            *Racial Equality 51-52
            *Sup Ct and Education 127-132
            Sup Ct in Free Society 259
            This Honorable Court 388-389
            US Sup Ct 48-50
        PERIODICALS:
            "Litigation and education of Blacks: a look at the U.S. Supreme
            Court," Delores P. Aldridge. J Negro Eductn 47: 96-112
            Winter '78 (11).

1796.   McLaurin v. Oklahoma State Re-   June 5, 1950   339 U.S. 637
           gents for Higher Education
        Am Consttn (Kelly) 861
        *Civil Rights (Bardolph) 275-276
        Courts 8
        Desegregation (Wasby) 54-57
        Digest 79-80
        Disaster 25
        Education (Lapati) 272-273
        *Education (Spurlock) 203-205
        Equality (Berger) 134-135
        Expanding Liberties 250-252
        Freedom and the Court 365, 367
        *Law Lawyers 174-176
        Petitioners 336-338
        Private Pressure 68-69
        Quest 136-138
        *Racial Equality 52-53
        This Honorable Court 389-390
        PERIODICALS:
        See listing at 339 U.S. 629, entry no. 1795.

1797.   Skelly Oil Co. v. Phillips Petroleum   June 5, 1950   339 U.S. 667
           Co.
        *Cases Federal Courts 156-160
        *Federal Courts 891-895
        *Materials Consttnl Law 130-133

1798.   Swift and Co. Packers v. Compania   June 5, 1950   339 U.S. 684
           Colombiana del Caribe
        *Cases Admiralty 73-76

1799.   United States v. Gerlach Live Stock   June 5, 1950   339 U.S. 725
           Co.
        *Dispassionate 146-150

1800.   Johnson v. Eisentrager   June 5, 1950   339 U.S. 763
        *Consttnl Law (Freund) 719-725

1801.   Henderson v. United States   June 5, 1950   339 U.S. 816
        Civil Rights (Bardolph) 287-288
        Desegregation (Wasby) 47-50
        Expanding Liberties 252-254
        *Justices (Friedman) v. 4, 2628-2632
        Petitioners 368-370
        *Racial Equality 46-47

1802.   Automatic Radio Manufacturing Co. v.   June 5, 1950   339 U.S. 827
           Hazeltine Research, Inc.
        *Cases Antitrust Law 695-701
        *Cases Trade 923-926
        *Govt Regulation 1064-1071
        *Patent 640-647

1803.   Great Atlantic and Pacific Tea v.   Dec 4, 1950   340 U.S. 147
           Supermarket Equipment Co.
        *Free Enterprise 1144-1149
        Sup Ct and Agencies 176

1804. Blau v. United States   Dec 11, 1950   340 U.S. 159
       *Liberty v. 2, 578-579

1805. McGrath v. Kristensen   Dec 11, 1950   340 U.S. 162
       *Dispassionate 312-314
       *Sup Ct Speaks 354-356

1806. Cities Service Gas Co. v. Peerless   Dec 11, 1950   340 U.S. 179
         Oil and Gas Co.
       Consttnl Law (Barrett) 338
       *Govt and Business 277-278

1807. Ackerman v. United States   Dec 11, 1950   340 U.S. 193
       *Cases Pleading 1108-1115

1808. Kiefer-Stewart Co. v. Joseph E.   Jan 2, 1951   340 U.S. 211
         Seagram and Sons
       *Antitrust (Posner) 537-538
       *Antitrust Analysis 286-288
       *Cases Antitrust Law 312-314
       *Consttnl Law (Kauper) 253-254
       *Govt Regulation 1091-1094

1809. Standard Oil Co. v. Federal Trade   Jan 8, 1951   340 U.S. 231
         Commission
       *Antitrust Analysis 896-899
       *Cases Antitrust Law 1152-1160
       *Cases Trade 1050-1054
       *Competition 276-280
       *Free Enterprise 867-876
       *Govt and Business 187-188
       *Govt Regulation 1072-1090
       *Legal Environment 300-303
       *Selected Antitrust Cases 262-266
       *Text Antitrust 228-232

1810. Niemotko v. Maryland   Jan 15, 1951   340 U.S. 268
       Kelley v. Maryland
         Church and State 133
         Communication (Hemmer) v. 1, 74-75
         Consttnl Right (Fellman) 27-28
       *First Amendment (Konvitz) 287-298
         Free Speech (Kurland) 45-46, 381-382
         Freedom and the Court 282
         Freedom of Speech (Hudon) 109-110
         Mr. Justice Frankfurter 94
         O'er the Ramparts 156-159
       *Political Rights 455-456
         Private Conscience 94-95
         Religion (Kurland) 72
         Right of Assembly 132-137
         Sup Ct (Freund) 69-70
         Sup Ct Review 1961 96
         Sup Ct Review 1974 272-273

1811. Kunz v. New York   Jan 15, 1951   340 U.S. 290
       *Am Consttnl Issues 246-251
       *Am Consttnl Law (Bartholomew) v. 2, 102-103
       *Bill (Konvitz) 337-338

CQ Guide 410
Cases Consttnl Law (Gunther) 1228
Church and State 133-134
Church State and Freedom 658-661
*Civil Rights (Abernathy) 1977 370-373
Communication (Hemmer) v. 1, 74
*Comparative 509-512
Consttnl Law (Barrett) 1309-1310
Consttnl Right (Fellman) 24-26
*Dispassionate 81-88
*First Amendment (Konvitz) 298-304
Free Speech (Kurland) 43-44
Freedom and the Court 191-192
*Freedom of Speech (Haiman) 64
Freedom of Speech (Hudon) 109-110
Handbook 119-121
Justice Frankfurter 89-91
*Mr. Justice Frankfurter 94-95
Mr. Justice Jackson 45-46
*Political Rights 483-490
Private Conscience 88-89
Religion (Kurland) 72-73
Right of Assembly 66-71
Sup Ct (Freund) 70-74
Sup Ct in Free Society 294
Sup Ct Review 1961 94-95
System 319

1812. Feiner v. New York   Jan 15, 1951   340 U.S. 315
Am Consttn (Kelly) 843-844
*Am Consttnl Law (Bartholomew) v. 2, 100-101
*Bill (Cohen) 284-289
*Bill (Konvitz) 225-230
CQ Guide 409-410
*Cases Consttnl Law (Gunther) 1222-1224
*Cases Individual 766-770
Communication (Hemmer) v. 1, 34-36
*Consttn (Mendelson) 464-466
*Consttnl Law (Barrett) 1257-1258
*Consttnl Law (Freund) 1189-1192
*Consttnl Law (Kauper) 1156-1159
*Consttnl Politics 537-542
Consttnl Right (Fellman) 30-32
Expanding Liberties 293-295
Felix Frankfurter (Thomas) 76
*First Amendment (Konvitz) 249-256
Free Speech (Kurland) 48-49
Freedom and the Court 192-194
*Freedom of Speech (Haiman) 94
Freedom of Speech (Hudon) 110
Handbook 84-86
Justice Frankfurter 95-99
*Liberty v. 2, 513-515
Mass Communications 37-38
*Mr. Justice Frankfurter 95-97
Modern Sup Ct 88-89
*One Man's Stand 214-218
*Political Rights 432-442
Politics 111-114

Private Conscience 86-88
Right of Assembly 74-77
Spirit 71-73
Sup Ct (Freund) 70
Sup Ct and Poltcl Freedom 105-106
Sup Ct in Free Society 295
Sup Ct Review 1961 99-100
*Sup Ct Speaks 396-400
System 317-319
*These Liberties 154-157

1813. Dean Milk Co. v. City of Madison   Jan 15, 1951   340 U.S. 349
        *Am Consttn (Lockhart) 259-261
        *Am Consttnl Law (Bartholomew) v. 1, 215-217
        *Cases Consttnl Law (Gunther) 303-306
        *Cases Food 798-802
        *Consttnl Law (Barrett) 318-322
        *Consttnl Law (Freund) 367-372
        *Consttnl Law (Lockhart) 306-308
        Justices Black and Frankfurter 109-111
        *Legal Environment 213-215
        *Sup Ct (Mendelson) 421-430
        Sup Ct and Commerce 257-259

1814. Rogers v. United States   Feb 26, 1951   340 U.S. 367
        Defendants 318-319
        *Materials Legislation 461-466
        *Principles Proof 659-664

1815. Amalgamated Association of Street,   Feb 26, 1951   340 U.S. 383
           Electric Railway and Motor Coach
           Employees v. Wisconsin Employment
           Relations Board
        United Gas, Coke & Chemical Workers of
           America v. Wisconsin Employment
           Relations Board
        *Cases Labor (Handler) 217-220

1816. United States ex rel. Touhy v. Ragen Feb 26, 1951   340 U.S. 462
        *Cases Evidence 1242-1245

1817. Universal Camera Corporation v.   Feb 26, 1951   340 U.S. 474
           National Labor Relations Board
        *Admin Law (Gellhorn) 258-265, 791-794
        *Admin Law (Schwartz) 659-665
        *Cases Labor (Oberer) 155-160
        *Cases Labor (Stern) 15-20
        *Govt and Business 627-631
        Sup Ct in Free Society 44-45

1818. Warren v. United States   Feb 26, 1951   340 U.S. 523
        The Anna Howard Shaw
        *Cases Admiralty 312-315

1819. Norton Co. v. Department of Revenue   Feb 26, 1951   340 U.S. 534
           of Illinois
        *Am Consttn (Lockhart) 310-311
        *Consttnl Law (Freund) 588-591

1820. Emich Motors Corporation v. General   Feb 26, 1951   340 U.S. 558
       Motors Corporation
       *Cases Trade 1290-1295
       *Govt Regulation 1095-1103

1821. Moore v. Chesapeake and Ohio Rail-   Feb 26, 1951   340 U.S. 573
       way Co.
       *Sup Ct (Mendelson) 449-455

1822. 62 Cases, More or Less, Each Con-   Mar 26, 1951   340 U.S. 593
       taining 6 Jars of Jam v. United
       States
       *Cases Food 266-268

1823. Spector Motor Service v. O'Connor   Mar 26, 1951   340 U.S. 602
       *Am Consttn (Lockhart) 317-319
       *Consttnl Law (Barrett) 401-402
       *Consttnl Law (Freund) 552-555
       *Consttnl Law (Kauper) 378-381

1824. American Fire and Casualty Co. v.   Apr 9, 1951   341 U.S. 6
       Finn
       *Cases Federal Courts 287-296
       *Federal Courts 1205-1211

1825. West Virginia ex rel. Dyer v. Sims   Apr 9, 1951   341 U.S. 22
       *Cases Consttnl Law (Gunther) 380-382
       *Cases Consttnl Law (Rosenblum) 327-329
       *Consttnl Law (Barrett) 494-498
       *Consttnl Law (Freund) 608-612
       Perspectives (Black) 51-52

1826. United States v. Alcea Band of Tilla- Apr 9, 1951   341 U.S. 48
       mooks
       *Am Indian v. 4, 2751

1827. Shepherd v. Florida   Apr 9, 1951   341 U.S. 50
       Communication (Hemmer) v. 2, 176-177
       *Dispassionate 133-137
       Mass Media (Francois) 272-273
       Mr. Justice Jackson 53-54
       US Sup Ct 79-80
       PERIODICALS:
       "Pretrial publicity and due process in criminal proceedings,"
       Caren Dubnoff. Poltcl Sci Q 92: 89-108 Spring '77 (8).

1828. Gerende v. Board of Supervisors of   Apr 12, 1951   341 U.S. 56
       Elections
       Free Speech (Kurland) 57
       *Political Rights 272-273
       System 202, 225-226

1829. United States v. Williams   Apr 23, 1951   341 U.S. 70
       Right of Assembly 148-151

1830. Williams v. United States   Apr 23, 1951   341 U.S. 97
       *Am Consttnl Law (Saye) 264-267
       To Preserve 78-79

1831. United States v. Pewee Coal Co.   Apr 30, 1951   341 U.S. 114
       *Govt and Business 404-407
       Presidential Power 130; reprinted from Columbia Law Rev 53: 53-
       66 (June '53)

1832. Joint Anti-Fascist Refugee Committee   Apr 30, 1951   341 U.S. 123
       v. McGrath
       National Council of American-Soviet
       Friendship, Inc., v. McGrath
       International Workers Order, Inc. v.
       McGrath
       Am Consttn (Kelly) 836
       CQ Guide 509
       *Civil Liberties (Sweet) 170-175
       *Douglas 301-308
       *Due Process 200-202
       Felix Frankfurter (Thomas) 204-205
       *First Amendment (Konvitz) 591-607
       *Freedom Reader 71-75
       Justice Frankfurter 129-130
       *Mr. Justice Frankfurter 28-36
       *One Man's Stand 219-222
       Right of Assembly 209-210
       *Rights (Shattuck) 56-57
       This Honorable Court 367

1833. National Labor Relations Board v.   May 14, 1951   341 U.S. 322
       Highland Park Manufacturing Co.
       *Admin Law (Gellhorn) 318-321

1834. Alabama Public Service Commission v.   May 21, 1951   341 U.S. 341
       Southern Railway
       Justices Black and Frankfurter 92

1835. Tenney v. Brandhove   May 21, 1951   341 U.S. 367
       CQ Guide 168
       *Consttnl Law (Freund) 1325-1330
       *Douglas 3-5
       System 701-702

1836. Schwegmann Brothers v. Calvert Dis-   May 21, 1951   341 U.S. 384
       tillers Corporation
       Schwegmann Brothers v. Seagram
       Distillers Corporation
       *Cases Antitrust Law 519-523
       *Cases Trade 490-494
       *Competition 361-363
       *Dispassionate 237-240

1837. Radio Corporation of America v.   May 28, 1951   341 U.S. 412
       United States
       Felix Frankfurter (Mendelson) 220-221

1838. Hoffman v. United States   May 28, 1951   341 U.S. 479
       *Consttn (Mendelson) 335-336

1839. Dennis v. United States   June 4, 1951   341 U.S. 494
       Am Consttn (Kelly) 829-830
       *Am Consttn (Lockhart) 559-569

1840. Timken Roller Bearing Co. v.   June 4, 1951   341 U.S. 593
           United States

1841. Breard v. Alexandria   June 4, 1951   341 U.S. 622

1842. Collins v. Hardyman   June 4, 1951   341 U.S. 651

1843. National Labor Relations Board v.   June 4, 1951   341 U.S. 665
           International Rice Milling Co.

1844. National Labor Relations Board v.   June 4, 1951   341 U.S. 675
           Denver Building and Construction
           Trades Council

*Cases Labor (Leslie) 295-298
*Cases Labor (Oberer) 430-434
*Labor Law (Herman) 291-293
*Labor Law (Meltzer) 434-438
Sup Ct and Commerce 117

1845. International Brotherhood of Electrical   June 4, 1951   341 U.S. 694
      Workers v. National Labor Rela-
      tions Board
    Sup Ct and Commerce 118

1846. United Brotherhood of Carpenters and   June 4, 1951   341 U.S. 707
      Joiners of America v. National
      Labor Relations Board
    Sup Ct and Commerce 118

1847. Garner v. Board of Public Works   June 4, 1951   341 U.S. 716
      of Los Angeles
    Am Consttn (Kelly) 838-839
    *Am Consttnl Law (Bartholomew) v. 2, 280-282
    CQ Guide 512
    Cases Consttnl Law (Gunther) 1446
    *Consttnl Law (Freund) 1334-1337
    Digest 51-52
    *Douglas 447-448
    *Felix Frankfurter (Phillips) 546-550
    Justice Frankfurter 130-131
    *One Man's Stand 229-230
    *Political Rights 329-336
    Politics 58-59
    Right of Assembly 211-213
    System 226-228

1848. Stack v. Boyle   Nov 5, 1951   342 U.S. 1
    *Cases Criml Justice 799-804
    *Consttnl Law (Felkenes) 341-343
    *Criminal Justice (Way) 215-216
    Criminal Law (Felkenes) 296-298
    *Criminal Law (Kadish) 1098-1101
    *Criminal Procedure (Lewis) 562-564
    Criminal Procedure (Wells) 30-31
    Defendants 58
    *Due Process 30-31
    *Elements Criminal 58-61
    *Leading Consttnl Cases 643-645
    *Sup Ct and Criml Process 954-957

1849. United States v. Jeffers   Nov 13, 1951   342 U.S. 48
    Search and Seizure 74-75

1850. Gallegos v. Nebraska   Nov 26, 1951   342 U.S. 55
    Sup Ct and Confessions 102-104

1851. Stefanelli v. Minard   Dec 3, 1951   342 U.S. 117
    Exclusionary 21-22
    Search and Seizure 145-146

1852. Lorain Journal Co. v. United States   Dec 11, 1951   342 U.S. 143
    *Antitrust (Posner) 806-809

*Antitrust Analysis 242-244
*Cases Antitrust Law 712-716
*Cases Trade 480-483
Communication (Hemmer) v. 2, 203-204
*Competition 370-373
Freedom of the Press (Schmidt) 48-50
*Govt Regulation 1120-1128
Law of Mass 577-580
*Mass Communications 698-699
*Sup Ct on Freedom 297-298

1853.   Rochin v. California   Jan 2, 1952   342 U.S. 165
Arrest (Waddington) 194
*Cases Civil Liberties 61-64
*Cases Consttnl Law (Cushman) 291-294
*Civil Liberties (Sweet) 239-242
*Civil Rights (Abernathy) 1977 182-184
*Comparative 380-382
*Consttnl Law (Felkenes) 62-64
*Consttnl Law (Freund) 999-1004
*Consttnl Law (Klein) 208-212
*Consttnl Law (Maddex) 86-89
*Courts Judges 732-735
Criminal Evidence 529-530
Criminal Law (Felkenes) 121-124
Criminal Procedure (Wells) 38-39
Defendants 346-347
Exclusionary 22-23
Felix Frankfurter (Thomas) 163
*Freedom and Protection 60-61
Freedom and the Court 118-123
*Freedom of the Press (Nelson) 670-674
Hugo Black (Dunne) 288-289
*Judiciary (Roche) 67-76
Justice Frankfurter 202-204
Justice Rutledge 158
*Law Power 166-169
*Leading Consttnl Cases 24-30
*Leading Consttnl Decisions 210-216
*Mr. Justice Frankfurter 157-161
Modern Sup Ct 103-104
*One Man's Stand 231-233
*Rights (Shattuck) 199-201
Search and Seizure 134-136
Spirit 86-88
Sup Ct Review 1961 7
*Teaching Materials 81-83

1854.   Kerotest Manufacturing Co. v.   Jan 2, 1952   342 U.S. 180
C-O-Two Fire Equipment Co.
*Federal Courts 1230-1232
*Patent 859-863

1855.   United States v. Hayman   Jan 7, 1952   342 U.S. 205
*Federal Courts 1514-1519

1856.   Carson v. Roane-Anderson Co.   Jan 7, 1952   342 U.S. 232
*Am Consttnl Law (Bartholomew) v. 1, 180-181

1857. International Longshoremen's and   Jan 7, 1952   342 U.S. 237
         Warehousemen's Union v.
         Juneau Spruce Corp.
         Sup Ct and Labor 158-159

1858. Morissette v. United States   Jan 7, 1952   342 U.S. 246
         *Cases Criml Law (Hall) 72-73, 532-540
         *Cases Criml Law (Inbau) 693-702
         *Cases Criml Law (Perkins) 461-467
         *Criminal Law (Dix) 283-290
         *Criminal Law (Kadish) 138-141
         *Criminal Law (Wells) 110
         *Dispassionate 123-129
         Mr. Justice Jackson 55
         Sup Ct Review 1962 119-120

1859. Halcyon Lines v. Haenn Ship Ceiling   Jan 14, 1952   342 U.S. 282
         and Refitting Co.
         *Cases Admiralty 392-394

1860. Georgia Railroad and Banking Co.   Jan 28, 1952   342 U.S. 299
         v. Redwine
         *Federal Courts 926-930

1861. Dice v. Akron, Canton and Youngs-   Feb 4, 1952   342 U.S. 359
         town Railroad
         *Civil Procedure (Cound) 320-324
         *Federal Courts 562-507

1862. Standard Oil Co. v. Peck   Feb 4, 1952   342 U.S. 382
         *Consttnl Law (Freund) 506-508

1863. Memphis Steam Laundry Cleaner, Inc.   Mar 3, 1952   342 U.S. 389
         v. Stone
         *Consttnl Law (Barrett) 437-438
         *Consttnl Law (Freund) 359-361

1864. Day-Brite Lighting v. Missouri   Mar 3, 1952   342 U.S. 421
         *Cases Individual 185-186
         *Consttn (Mendelson) 267-269

1865. Doremus v. Board of Education of   Mar 3, 1952   342 U.S. 429
         Borough of Hawthorne
         Bible 86-91
         Church State and Freedom 190
         *Consttnl Law (Freund) 108-111
         Education (Lapati) 207-208
         Education (Spurlock) 124-125
         Judicial Excerpts 57-58
         Religion (Drinan) 92-93
         Religion (Kurland) 34-35
         School in the Legal Structure 66-67
         School Prayers (Lauboch) 39

1866. Adler v. Board of Education of   Mar 3, 1952   342 U.S. 485
         City of New York
         Am Consttn (Kelly) 839
         *Am Consttnl Issues 297-301
         *Am Consttnl Law (Bartholomew) v. 2, 75-76

CQ Guide 512-513
Cases Consttnl Law (Gunther) 1659-1660
*Civil Liberties (Sweet) 192-193
Communication (Hemmer) v. 1, 117-118
Consttnl Law (Barrett) 99, 1195-1196
*Consttnl Law (Freund) 122-128
Digest 52-53
*Douglas 212-215
Education (Lapati) 234-236
*Education (Spurlock) 134-143
Expanding Liberties 86-89
*First Amendment (Konvitz) 550-556
Hugo Black (Strickland) 113
*Judicial Excerpts 164-168
Justices Black and Frankfurter 97-98
Landmark Decisions 81-88
*Law and Public Education (Hamilton) 427-430
Modern Sup Ct 67
*One Man's Stand 234-235
Right of Assembly 213-215
Rights of the People 124-126
School in the Legal Structure 70
*School Law (Remmlein) 64-65
System 228-230, 600-601

1867.   Frisbie v. Collins   Mar 10, 1952 342 U.S. 519
        *Cases Criml Law (Perkins) 803-804
        Criminal Law (Felkenes) 111-112
        *Leading Consttnl Cases 289-290
        *Teaching Materials 170-171

1868.   Carlson v. Landon   Mar 10, 1952 342 U.S. 524
        Butterfield v. Zydok
        Civil Rights (Konvitz) 98-100
        *Due Process 31-32
        Ransom 50-54
        This Honorable Court 371-372

1869.   Far East Conference v. United States Mar 10, 1952 342 U.S. 570
        *Admin Law (Gellhorn) 1049-1052
        *Admin Law (Schwartz) 592-594

1870.   Harisiades v. Shaughnessy   Mar 10, 1952 342 U.S. 580
        Mascitti v. McGrath
        Coleman v. McGrath
        *Civil Liberties (Sweet) 322-324
        Civil Rights (Konvitz) 100-102
        *Consttn (Mendelson) 597-598
        *Consttnl Law (Freund) 746-749
        *Consttnl Law (Kauper) 563-566
        Dissent 264-265
        *First Amendment (Konvitz) 764-773
        This Honorable Court 371-372

1871.   Sacher v. United States   Mar 10, 1952 343 U.S. 1
        *Consttnl Politics 638-648
        Justice Frankfurter 180-181
        *One Man's Stand 236-242

Sup Ct Review 1974 286-306
*Sup Ct Speaks 402-406
System 393-396

1879. Zorach v. Clauson   Apr 28, 1952   343 U. S. 306
       Am Consttn (Kelly) 850
       *Am Consttnl Issues 342-347
       *Am Consttnl Law (Bartholomew) v. 2, 44-48
       *Am Consttnl Law (Saye) 300-302
       *Am Consttnl Law (Shapiro) 454-457
       Am Poltcl System 262-270; reprinted from Am Poltcl Sci Rev
          53: 777-791 Sep '59
       Bible 179-186
       *Bill (Cohen) 440-444
       *Bill (Konvitz) 41-44
       CQ Guide 463
       *Cases Civil Liberties 295-299
       *Cases Consttnl Law (Cushman) 525-529
       *Cases Consttnl Law (Gunther) 1554-1557
       *Cases Individual 1062-1066
       Church and State 134
       Church State and Freedom 174-176, 414-435
       Civil Liberties (Kauper) 15-19
       *Civil Liberties (Sweet) 51-56
       *Civil Rights (Abernathy) 1977 295-299
       *Consttn (Mendelson) 576-580
       *Consttn (Morris) 333-340
       *Consttn (Pollak) v. 2, 76-85
       *Consttnl Law (Barrett) 1442-1445
       *Consttnl Law (Freund) 1359-1363
       *Consttnl Law (Kauper) 1262-1266
       *Consttnl Politics 585-591
       Digest 18-19
       *Dispassionate 65-68
       Dissent 214-215
       *Douglas 150-154
       Dynamics 49-50
       *Education (Hazard) 91-96
       Education (Lapati) 201-204
       *Education (Spurlock) 126-132
       Expanding Liberties 20-22
       *First Amendment (Konvitz) 44-52
       First Amendment (Marnell) 184-188
       Freedom and the Court 309-312, 323
       Impact (Wasby) 128-129
       *Judicial Excerpts 67-69
       Justice Frankfurter 45-46
       Justices Black and Frankfurter 63
       Landmark Decisions 73-80
       *Law and Public Education (Hamilton) 71-78
       *Law of Public Education 41-44
       *Leading Consttnl Decisions 328-336
       *Liberty v. 2, 509-511
       Modern Sup Ct 95-96, 296-298
       *One Man's Stand 250-254
       *Principles School 161-163
       Private Conscience 177-178
       *Public School Law 110-112
       *Public Schools 137-147

Religion (Drinan) 84-89
Religion (Fellman) 90-92
Religion (Kauper) 67-70
Religion (Kurland) 89-90
Religion (School Admin) 16-18
Religious Freedom (Arnold) 49-50
*Religious Freedom (Pfeffer) 27-28, 75-77
Rights of the People 42-44
School Bus 47-51
School in the Legal Structure 66
*School Law (Alexander) 235-237
*School Law (Remmlein) 262-265
School Prayers (Lauboch) 38-39
*Sup Ct and Consttn 502-504
*Sup Ct and Education 62-73
Sup Ct and Religion 129-131
*Sup Ct Speaks 375-382
*Teacher 118-119
*These Liberties 202-209
*Third Branch 140-145
This Honorable Court 383-384
*Two Swords 48-55
Wall (Oaks) 84
PERIODICALS:
"Church and state in a public school system," S. A. Pleasants.
   Clearing House 34: 277-278 Jan '60 (3).
"Editorial reaction to Supreme Court decisions on church and state,"
   Stuart Nagel and Robert Erikson. Public Opinion Q 30: 647-
   655 Winter '66/67 (4).
"U.S. Supreme Court and religion in the schools," August W.
   Steinhilber. Theory into Practice 4: 8-13 Feb '65 (4).

1880. United States v. Oregon Medical Society Apr 28, 1952   343 U.S. 326
      *Sup Ct (Mendelson) 455-467

1881. National Labor Relations Board v.   May 26, 1952   343 U.S. 395
         American National Insurance Co.
      Basic Text 505-506
      *Cases Labor (Cox) 460-468
      *Cases Labor (Handler) 290-294
      *Cases Labor (Oberer) 567-572
      *Labor Law (Meltzer) 638-643
      *Labor Relations (Group Trust) 434-439

1882. Besser Manufacturing Co. v. United   May 26, 1952   343 U.S. 444
         States
      *Govt Regulation 1129-1133

1883. Public Utilities Commission of District May 26, 1952   343 U.S. 451
         of Columbia v. Pollack
      Am Consttn (Kelly) 847
      *Bill (Konvitz) 210-214
      Communication (Hemmer) v. 1, 221-222
      *Consttnl Law (Schmidhauser) 344-347
      *Contemporary Law 715-719
      *Courts Judges 179-180
      *Douglas 231-234
      *First Amendment (Konvitz) 232-238
      Negro (Kalven) 156-158

1884. Federal Trade Commission v.   May 26, 1952   343 U. S. 470
       Ruberoid Co.

1885. Joseph Burstyn, Inc. v. Wilson   May 26, 1952   343 U. S. 495
       "Miracle Case"

1886. Youngstown Sheet and Tube Co. v.   June 2, 1952   343 U. S. 579
       Sawyer
       "Steel Seizure Case"

       *Consttn (Hirschfield) 171-184
       *Consttn (Mendelson) 58-66
       *Consttn (Pollak) 343-347
       *Consttnl Aspects v. 4, 557-633
       *Consttnl Cases 79-94
       *Consttnl Decisions 85-92
       *Consttnl Law (Barrett) 510-516
       *Consttnl Law (Barron) 320-329
       *Consttnl Law (Felkenes) 95-96
       *Consttnl Law (Freund) 659-668
       *Consttnl Law (Grossman) 1008-1016
       *Consttnl Law (Kauper) 301-307
       *Consttnl Law (Lockhart) 195-203
       *Consttnl Politics 324-334
       *Contemporary Law 409-414
       *Dispassionate 180-189
       *Documents History v. 2, 574-578
       *Douglas 32-37
       *Federal Courts 1390-1394
       *Federal System 91-98
       Felix Frankfurter (Mendelson) 16-19
       Felix Frankfurter (Thomas) 256-260
       *Freedom vs National Security 79-89
       *Growth v. 3, 2023-2035
       *Historic Decisions 147-150
       Hugo Black (Dunne) 290-292
       *Justices (Friedman) v. 3, 2348-2351; v. 4, 2572-2582
       Justices Black and Frankfurter 10-12
       *Labor Law (Herman) 327-333
       *Labor Law (Twomey) 330-332
       *Leading Consttnl Decisions 44-57
       *Legislation (Linde) 14-26
       *Legislative (Hetzel) 759-763
       *Liberty v. 2, 495-498
       *Mr. Justice Frankfurter 47-54
       *Modern Business 58-60
       Modern Sup Ct 125
       Perspectives 61-62
       Power 180-181
       Presidential Power 124-137; reprinted from Columbia Law Rev
          53: 53-66 June '53
       *Processes 393-404
       Sup Ct and Am Capitalism 100-103
       *Readings American 463-467
       *Sup Ct and American Economic Life 257-266
       *Sup Ct and Am Govt 117-124
       *Sup Ct and Consttn 419-422
       Sup Ct in Free Society 57-59
       Sup Ct Review 1974 59-60
       This Honorable Court 378-380
       Truman.
       Watergate 205-208

1887. Kawakita v. United States   June 2, 1952   343 U.S. 717
      Am Consttn (Kelly) 799

1888. On Lee v. United States   June 2, 1952   343 U.S. 747
      Criminal Law (Felkenes) 136-138
      *Douglas 332-337

　　　　　*Mr. Justice Frankfurter 124-127
　　　　　Police 159-160
　　　　　*Principles Arrest 365
　　　　　Search and Seizure 235-237
　　　　　*Sup Ct and Criml Process 359-360

1889.　Brotherhood of Railroad Trainmen　　June 9, 1952　343 U.S. 768
　　　　　　　v. Howard
　　　　　*Cases Labor (Handler) 715-718
　　　　　Equality (Berger) 143
　　　　　Petitioners 316-317

1890.　Leland v. Oregon　　　　　　　　　　June 9, 1952　343 U.S. 790
　　　　　*Mr. Justice Frankfurter 162-165

1891.　Gelling v. Texas　　　　　　　　　　June 2, 1952　343 U.S. 960
　　　　　Civil Liberties (Kauper) 78
　　　　　Movies 55-56

1892.　Brown v. Board of Education　　　　Oct 8, 1952　　344 U.S. 1
　　　　　Court Years 113

1893.　Johnson v. New York, New Haven　　Nov 17, 1952　344 U.S. 48
　　　　　　　and Hartford Railroad Co.
　　　　　*Cases Civil Procedure 761-766

1894.　Sweeney v. Woodall　　　　　　　　　Nov 17, 1952　344 U.S. 86
　　　　　Defendants 410-411
　　　　　*Douglas 419-420

1895.　Kedroff v. Saint Nicholas Cathedral　Nov 24, 1952　344 U.S. 94
　　　　　　　of Russian Orthodox Church in
　　　　　　　North America
　　　　　Church and State 135-136
　　　　　Church State and Freedom 295-299
　　　　　Freedom and the Court 326
　　　　　Religion (Fellman) 62-63
　　　　　*Religious Freedom (Pfeffer) 98-100
　　　　　Sup Ct Review 1969 365
　　　　　This Honorable Court 384-385

1896.　United States v. Caltex, Inc.　　　　Dec 8, 1952　　344 U.S. 149
　　　　　*Govt and Business 410-411
　　　　　*Social Forces 48-50
　　　　　Sup Ct Review 1962 77-78
　　　　　*Text Administrative Law 45-46

1897.　Lloyd Fry Roofing Co. v. Wood　　　Dec 8, 1952　　344 U.S. 157
　　　　　Sup Ct and Commerce 263-265

1898.　United States v. Cardiff　　　　　　Dec 8, 1952　　344 U.S. 174
　　　　　*Cases Food 711-712

1899.　Wieman v. Updegraff　　　　　　　　Dec 15, 1952　344 U.S. 183
　　　　　*Am Consttnl Law (Bartholomew) v. 2, 277-279
　　　　　Cases Consttnl Law (Gunther) 1447
　　　　　Civil Rights (Konvitz) 67-71
　　　　　Communication (Hemmer) v. 1, 118
　　　　　*Consttn (Mendelson) 450-452

       *Courts 68-71
       Digest 53
       Education (Lapati) 230-232
       Education (Spurlock) 143-146
       Expanding Liberties 89-91
       *First Amendment (Konvitz) 557-564
       *Freedom Reader 69-71
       Justice Frankfurter 130
       *Law and Public Education (Hamilton) 430-438
       Least Dangerous 40-41
       *Liberty v. 2, 553-555
       *Mr. Justice Frankfurter 101-104
       Modern Sup Ct 83-84
       *One Man's Stand 257-259
       Right of Assembly 215-217
       *Sup Ct and Education 175-180
       System 230-231, 601-602
       This Honorable Court 368
     PERIODICALS:
       "Supreme Court decisions: loyalty oaths." NEA Research Bul
          42: 76-78 Oct '64 (3).

1900.   Schwartz v. Texas   Dec 15, 1952   344 U.S. 199
       Communication (Hemmer) v. 1, 240
       *Police 153-154
       Search and Seizure 212-213
       Sup Ct Review 1961 14

1901.   F.W. Woolworth Co. v. Contemporary Dec 22, 1952   344 U.S. 228
       Arts, Inc.
       *Cases Copyright (Kaplan) 438-443
       *Cases Copyright (Nimmer) 458-462
       *Copyright 734-739

1902.   American Trucking Association v.   Jan 12, 1953   344 U.S. 298
       United States
       Eastern Motor Express v. United
       States
       Secretary of Agriculture v. United
       States
       *Govt and Business 457-459
       *Social Forces 550-551

1903.   Federal Trade Commission v. Motion Feb 2, 1953   344 U.S. 392
       Picture Advertising Service Co.
       *Antitrust Analysis 645-647
       *Cases Antitrust Law 807-809
       *Govt and Business 667-671
       *Govt Regulation 1134-1142
       *Social Forces 568-570
       *Text Antitrust 131-132

1904.   Brock v. North Carolina   Feb 2, 1953   344 U.S. 424
       Defendants 374

1905.   Brown v. Allen   Feb 9, 1953   344 U.S. 443
       Speller v. Allen
       Daniels v. Allen
       *Consttnl Politics 113-114

          *Dispassionate 277-284
          Quest 113-114

1906.   United States ex rel. Smith v. Baldi   Feb 9, 1953   344 U. S. 561
          Sup Ct Review 1970 161-162

1907.   Chicago v. Willett Co.   Feb 9, 1953   344 U. S. 574
          Sup Ct and Commerce 326-327

1908.   Lutwak v. United States   Feb 9, 1953   344 U. S. 604
          *Cases Evidence 1315-1316
          *Family 366-367

1909.   United States v. Reynolds   Mar 9, 1953   345 U. S. 1
          CQ Guide 231-232
          *Cases Evidence 1238-1242
          Communication (Hemmer) v. 2, 236-237
          Consttn (Wilcox) 14-15
          Criminal Evidence 171
          Executive Privilege 216-218
          *Freedom vs National Security 173-176
          *Law of Evidence 433-437
          Mass Media (Clark) 83-85
          *Principles Proof 770-774

1910.   Alstate Construction Co. v. Durkin   Mar 9, 1953   345 U. S. 13
          Sup Ct and Commerce 133-134

1911.   United States v. Kahriger   Mar 9, 1953   345 U. S. 22
          *Am Consttnl Issues 106-110
          *Am Consttnl Law (Bartholomew) v. 1, 160-162; v. 2, 153-155
          *Am Consttnl Law (Mason) 335-337
          *Cases Consttnl Law (Gunther) 219-223
          *Consttn (Mendelson) 136-141
          *Consttnl Decisions 73-78
          *Consttnl Law (Barron) 230-233
          *Federal System 214-216
          *Mr. Justice Frankfurter 13-14

1912.   United States v. Rumely   Mar 9, 1953   345 U. S. 41
          CQ Guide 160
          *Consttnl Cases 66-77
          Felix Frankfurter (Mendelson) 9-11
          *First Amendment (Konvitz) 620-624
          Least Dangerous 157
          *Legislation (Linde) 739-746
          *Mass Communications 669-670
          *Sup Ct and Am Govt 143-149
          Sup Ct in Free Society 46-47, 52
          *Sup Ct on Freedom 197-198
          Sup Ct Review 1978 271-272

1913.   Fowler v. Rhode Island   Mar 9, 1953   345 U. S. 67
          Church and State 136
          Freedom and the Court 282
          Private Conscience 95
          Religion (Kurland) 73-74
          Right of Assembly 126-128

1914.   National Labor Relations Board   Mar 9, 1953   345 U.S. 71
                v. Rockaway News Supply
             *Cases Labor (Handler) 327-330
             Sup Ct and Labor 84-85

1915.   American Newspaper Publishers As-   Mar 9, 1953   345 U.S. 100
                sociation v. National Labor Re-
                lations Board
             Basic Text 284-285
             *Cases Labor (Handler) 467-470
             *Cases Labor (Oberer) 503-509
             *Labor Law (Twomey) 242-244
             *Labor Relations (Group Trust) 677-681
             Sup Ct and Labor 153-154

1916.   National Labor Relations Board v.   Mar 9, 1953   345 U.S. 117
                Gamble Enterprises, Inc.
             Basic Text 284-285
             *Cases Labor (Cox) 839-842
             *Cases Labor (Handler) 470-473
             *Cases Labor (Leslie) 511-514
             *Labor Law (Meltzer) 559-562
             Sup Ct and Labor 154

1917.   Local Union No. 10, United Asso-   Mar 16, 1953   345 U.S. 192
                ciation of Journeymen Plumbers
                and Steamfitters in U.S. and
                Canada
             Sup Ct and Labor 46

1918.   Shaughnessy v. United States ex   Mar 16, 1953   345 U.S. 206
                rel Mezei
             *Dispassionate 206-212
             *Legal Foundations 40-41
             *One Man's Stand 260-262

1919.   In re Isserman   Apr 6, 1953   345 U.S. 286
             *Dispassionate 298-302

1920.   United States v. Public Utilities   Apr 6, 1953   345 U.S. 295
                Commission of California
          Mineral County, Nevada v. Public
                Utilities Commission of California
             *Dispassionate 240-242
             *Legislative (Hetzel) 212-213

1921.   Ford Motor Co. v. Huffman   Apr 4, 1953   345 U.S. 330
          International Union, United Automobile,
                Aircraft and Agricultural Implement
                Workers v. Huffman
             Basic Text 696-697

1922.   Poulos v. New Hampshire   Apr 27, 1953   345 U.S. 395
             Communication (Hemmer) v. 1, 75-76
             Consttnl Law (Barrett) 1310-1311
             Consttnl Right (Fellman) 28
             Free Speech (Kurland) 46
             *Freedom of Speech (Haiman) 66-67
             *Freedom Reader 131-132

Handbook 126-127
Justice Frankfurter 91-95
Mass Communications 46-48
Private Conscience 95-96
Religion (Kurland) 74
Sup Ct Review 1961 97
System 379-380

1923. Terry v. Adams   May 4, 1953   345 U. S. 461
       "Jaybird Party Case"
       CQ Guide 482
       *Cases Consttnl Law (Rosenblum) 491-498
       *Civil Rights (Blaustein) 397-406
       *Consttnl Cases 298-311
       Desegregation (Wasby) 33-34
       Discrimination 78-84
       Equality (Berger) 96
       Felix Frankfurter (Mendelson) 140-143
       Freedom of the Press (Schmidt) 94-95
       *Freedom Reader 184-185
       *Liberty v. 2, 612-613
       Mr. Justice Frankfurter 70-73
       *Negro (Franklin) 347-351
       Petitioners 296-297
       *Political Rights v. 2, 1113-1119
       Quest 121-122
       *Racial Equality 84-85

1924. May v. Anderson   May 18, 1953   345 U. S. 528
       *Family 320-322
       Sup Ct Review 1964 113-114

1925. Avery v. Georgia   May 25, 1953   345 U. S. 559
       Equality (Berger) 107-108
       Quest 112-113

1926. Times-Picayune Publishing Co. v.   May 25, 1953   345 U. S. 594
       United States
       *Antitrust (Posner) 632-636
       *Antitrust Analysis 589-593
       *Cases Trade 593-599
       Communication (Hemmer) v. 2, 204-206
       *Competition 324-329
       *Govt Regulation 1203-1222
       Law and Politics 284
       Law of Mass 580-583
       *Mass Communications 700-703
       Mass Media (Francois) 541
       *Sup Ct on Freedom 298-300

1927. United States v. W. T. Grant   May 25, 1953   345 U. S. 629
       *Injunctions 100-104

1928. Brown v. Board of Education of   June 8, 1953   345 U. S. 972
       Topeka, Kansas
       *Civil Rights (Blaustein) 418-420
       *Contemporary Law 862-863

1929.   Dalehite v. United States   June 8, 1953   346 U.S. 15
            *Dispassionate 150-156
            *Introduction (Mashaw) 689-697

1930.   Automatic Canteen Co. v. Federal   June 8, 1953   346 U.S. 61
            Trade Commission
            *Antitrust Analysis 962-971
            *Cases Antitrust Law 1210-1221
            *Cases Trade 1097-1105
            *Govt Regulation 1223-1236

1931.   Federal Communications Commission   June 8, 1953   346 U.S. 86
            v. RCA Communications
        Mackay Radio and Telegraph Co. v.
            RCA Communications
            *Cases Regulated 943-946
            *Govt and Business 671-673

1932.   Securities and Exchange Commission   June 8, 1953   346 U.S. 119
            v. Ralston Purina Co.
            *Basic Corporation 182-186
            *Legal Environment 363-365

1933.   New York, New Haven and Hartford   June 8, 1953   346 U.S. 128
            Railroad v. Nothnagle
            *Govt and Business 103

1934.   Burns v. Wilson   June 15, 1953 346 U.S. 137
            Defendants 155
            *Douglas 204-207
            *Federal Courts 1532-1537
            Private Pressure 87-93

1935.   Stein v. New York   June 15, 1953 346 U.S. 156
        Wissner v. New York
        Cooper v. New York
            Defendants 348
            *One Man's Stand 265-267
            Sup Ct and Confessions 108-112

1936.   Barrows v. Jackson   June 15, 1953 346 U.S. 249
            *Cases Consttnl Law (Rosenblum) 209-212
            *Cases Property (Casner) 991-994
            Civil Rights (Bardolph) 283
            Consttnl Law (Barrett) 1050-1051
            *Consttnl Law (Lockhart) 1663-1664
            Desegregation (Wasby) 43-44
            Petitioners 326-328
            Private Pressure 58-59
            Quest 117-118

1937.   Rosenberg v. United States   June 19, 1953 346 U.S. 273
            Court Years 78-82
            *Douglas 311-314

1938.   Olberding, doing business as Vess   Nov 9, 1953   346 U.S. 338
            Transfer Co. v. Illinois Cen-
            tral Railroad Co., Inc.
            *Cases Civil Procedure 381-385

1939.   Atchison Topeka and Santa Fe Rail-   Nov 9, 1953   346 U. S. 346
        way v. Public Utilities Commis-
        sion of California
        Sup Ct Review 1962 74

1940.   Toolson v. New York Yankees   Nov 9, 1953   346 U. S. 356
        Kowalski v. Chandler
        Corbett v. Chandler
        *Am Consttnl Law (Bartholomew) v. 1, 283-284
        Professional Sports 26-29

1941.   Dickinson v. United States   Nov 30, 1953   346 U. S. 389
        Defendants 156
        O'er the Ramparts 186-190

1942.   Pope and Talbot, Inc. v. Hawn   Dec 7, 1953   346 U. S. 406
        *Cases Admiralty 374-376

1943.   Wilko v. Swan   Dec 7, 1953   346 U. S. 427
        *Civil Procedure (Carrington) 246-249

1944.   National Labor Relations Board v.   Dec 7, 1953   346 U. S. 464
        Local 1229, International Brother-
        hood of Electrical Workers
        Basic Text 315-316
        *Cases Labor (Cox) 881-888
        *Cases Labor (Handler) 53-58
        *Cases Labor (Leslie) 239-246
        *Cases Labor (Oberer) 516-521
        *Labor Law (Meltzer) 181-187
        *Labor Law (Group Trust) 297-303
        Law and Politics 100-101
        Sup Ct and Labor 79

1945.   Howell Chevrolet v. National Labor   Dec 14, 1953   346 U. S. 482
        Relations Board
        Sup Ct and Commerce 119

1946.   Garner v. Teamsters, Chauffeurs and   Dec 14, 1953   346 U. S. 485
        Helpers, Local 776
        *Cases Labor (Leslie) 592-593
        *Labor Law (Group Trust) 356-359
        Law and Politics 85-86
        Sup Ct and Labor 60-61

1947.   Theatre Enterprises v. Paramount   Jan 4, 1954   346 U. S. 537
        Film Distributing Co.
        *Antitrust (Posner) 114-115
        *Antitrust Analysis 299-301
        *Cases Antitrust Law 426-428
        *Cases Trade 402-404
        *Govt and Business 132-133
        *Govt Regulation 1237-1241
        *Legal Environment 279-280
        *Modern Business 970-971
        *Selected Antitrust Cases 113-115
        *Text Antitrust 64-65

1948.   Madruga v. Superior Court of Cal-   Jan 18, 1954   346 U.S. 556
                ifornia for San Diego County
            *Cases Admiralty 213-216

1949.   Chicago, Rock Island and Pacific   Jan 18, 1954   346 U.S. 574
                Railroad v. Stude
            *Federal Courts 1172-1177

1950.   Superior Films v. Department   Jan 18, 1954   346 U.S. 587
                of Education of Ohio
            Commercial Pictures Corp. v.
                Regents of University of New York
            *Freedom of Speech (Haiman) 119
            Movies 61-62
            *Obscenity (Bosmajian) 153-154
            *Sup Ct on Freedom 226-227

1951.   Radio Officers Union of Commercial   Feb 1, 1954   347 U.S. 17
                Telegraphers v. National Labor
                Relations Board
            National Labor Relations Board v. Inter-
                national Brotherhood of Teamsters,
                Chauffeurs, Warehousemen and
                Helpers
            Gaynor News Service v. National Labor
                Relations Board
            Basic Text 329-330
            *Cases Labor (Handler) 07-73
            *Labor Law (Meltzer) 219-228
            Law and Politics 112-113
            *Materials Law 628-638

1952.   Walder v. United States   Feb 1, 1954   347 U.S. 62
            *Basic Criminal 721-723
            Sup Ct Review 1977 108-110

1953.   Kern-Limerick v. Scurlock   Feb 8, 1954   347 U.S. 110
            *Consttnl Law (Barrett) 453-456

1954.   Irvine v. California   Feb 8, 1954   347 U.S. 128
            *Cases Civil Liberties 64-66
            *Cases Consttnl Law (Cushman) 294-296
            Hugo Black (Strickland) 107-108
            Justice Frankfurter 204-206
            *Law Power 169-175
            *Leading Consttnl Decisions 216-221
            *Mr. Justice Frankfurter 171-172
            *One Man's Stand 268-272
            Search and Seizure 137-140
            Self Inflicted Wound 125
            Sup Ct Review 1961 7-10
            *Teaching Materials 83-88

1955.   Michigan-Wisconsin Pipe Line Co.   Feb 8, 1954   347 U.S. 157
                v. Calvert
            Panhandle Eastern Pipe Line Co. v.
                Calvert
            *Consttn (Mendelson) 219-220
            *Govt and Business 290-292

1956.   Mazer v. Stein   Mar 8, 1954   347 U. S. 201
        *Cases Copyright (Kaplan) 237-247
        *Cases Copyright (Nimmer) 53-65
        *Copyright 660-667
        *Legal Regulation 638-644

1957.   Federal Communications Commission   Apr 5, 1954   347 U. S. 284
            v. American Broadcasting Co.
        Federal Communications Commission
            v. National Broadcasting Co.
        Federal Communications Commission
            v. Columbia Broadcasting System
        Communication (Hemmer) v. 2, 274-275

1958.   Miller Brothers Co. v. Maryland   Apr 5, 1954   347 U. S. 340
        *Am Consttn (Lockhart) 312-313

1959.   Maryland Casualty Co. v. Cushing   Apr 12, 1954   347 U. S. 409
        *Cases Admiralty 120-122

1960.   Barsky v. Board of Regents of Uni-   Apr 26, 1954   347 U. S. 442
            versity of New York
        *One Man's Stand 273-278

1961.   Hernandez v. Texas   May 3, 1954   347 U. S. 475
        *Consttn (Mendelson) 312-314
        Defendants 197-198
        *Law Power 601-604
        Memoirs 299
        *Public Papers 129-134
        *Sex Discrimination 1975 81-82
        *Warren (Spaeth) 132-135

1962.   Brown v. Board of Education of   May 17, 1954   347 U. S. 483
            Topeka, Kansas
        Briggs v. Elliott
        Davis v. County School Board of
            Prince Edward County
        Gebhart v. Belton
            Am Consttn (Kelly) 862-863
        *Am Consttn (Lockhart) 965-969
        *Am Consttnl Issues 436-439
            Am Consttnl Law (Bartholomew) v. 2, 304-305
        *Am Consttnl Law (Mason) 484-489
        *Am Consttnl Law (Saye) 437-439
        *Am Consttnl Law (Shapiro) 513-516
        *Am Consttnl Law Reader 204-210
        *Am Govt 159-161
            Am Govt 551-559; reprinted from Memoirs of Earl Warren, 1977.
        *Am Primer 902-911
        *Am Spirit v. 2, 898-899
            Am Spirit v. 2, 899-901; reprinted from Congressional Record
                84 Cong., 2 sess, 4515-4516 Mar 12, 1956
        *Annals v. 17, 253-258
        *Anxiety 378-379
            Argument.
        *Argument 325-331
            Authority 39-41
        *Basic Business 55-58

PERIODICALS:
"Accommodation to undesired change; the case of the South,"
    James W. Vender Zanden. J Negro Edctn 31: 30-35 Winter
    '62.
"After twenty years: Brown: the noblest decision," James
    Caughey. Nation 218: 614-615 May 18 '74.
"After twenty years: reflections upon the constitutional significance
    of Brown v. Board of Education," A. Cox Civil Rights Dig 6:
    38-45 Summer '74.
"Birth control through desegregation," Sci News 114: 53 July
    22 '78.
"Black, white and Brown," David K. Cohen. New Repub 170:
    17-19 June 1 '74.
    Same: "What course desegregation now?" Current 164:
    16-21 July '74.
"Brown decade." Natl Rev 16: 433-434 June 2 '64.
"Brown revisited: from Topeka, Kansas to Boston, Mass.," Leon
    Jones. Phylon 37: 343-358 Dec '76 (3).
*"Brown v. Board of Education." Crisis 86: 149-150 May '79.
*"Brown vs Board of Education." Integ Edctn 12: 31-32 May
    '74.

*"Brown v. Board of education of Topeka; excerpts." <u>Current History</u> 57: 297-298, 302 Nov '69.
"Brown v. Board of education: twenty-five years later" (Symposium). <u>Crisis</u> 86: 189-273 June '79.
*"   ." <u>Crisis</u> 86: 195-197 June '79.
"Brown v. Board of education: the legal status of desegregation on the twenty-fifth anniversary; symposium." <u>NOLPE Sch Law</u> <u>J</u> 8 no. 2: 107-236 '79.
"Color-blind or color-conscious," Diane Ravitch. <u>New Republic</u> 180: 15-18, 20 May 5 '79.
"Courtrooms and classrooms," Eleanor P. Wolf. <u>Edctnl Forum</u> 41: 431-453 May '77 (2).
"Courts in the saddle: school boards out," William R. Hazard. <u>Phi Delta Kappan</u> 56: 259-261 Dec '74 (5).
"Curse of Brown on black," Derrick Bell. <u>First World</u> 2: 14-18 Spring '78.
"D-Day at the Supreme Court." <u>Ebony</u> 34: 180-182 May '79.
"Day race relations changed forever," Lerone Bennett, Jr. <u>Ebony</u> 32: 132-136, 138, 140-141 May '77.
"Desegregation and social reform since 1954," Leon Jones. <u>J</u> <u>Negro Eductn</u> 43: 155-171 Spring '74.
"Desegregation decision," Harry S. Ashmore. <u>Sat R</u> 47: 68-70, 90 May 16 '64.
"Desegregation--its inequities and paradoxes," Robert G. Newby. <u>Black Scholar</u> 11: 17-28, 67-68 Sep/Oct '79.
"Desegregation: where schools stand with the courts as the new year begins," H. C. Hudgins, Jr. <u>Am Sch Bd J</u> 156: 21-25 Jan '69 (7).
"Does California have segregated schools?" T. Roger Duncan. <u>CTA J</u> 61: 22-25 Mar '65.
"Dream deferred or a dream fulfilled; Brown v. Board of Education decision; special report." <u>Ebony</u> 34: 174-176, 178-179 May '79.
"Earl Warren and the Brown decision," S. Sidney Ulmer. <u>J</u> <u>Poltcs</u> 33: 689-702 Aug '71.
"The effects of the Brown decisions on black educators," James E. Haney. <u>J Negro Eductn</u> 47: 88-95 Winter '78.
"Eighteen years after Brown," Kenneth B. Clark. <u>Integ Eductn</u> 10: 7-15 Nov '72.
"Equal opportunity in educational and employment selection," Melvin R. Novick and Dorsey D. Ellis, Jr. <u>Am Psychologist</u> 32: 306-320 May '77 (20).
"Evolving nature of the Supreme Court since Brown v. Board of Education of Topeka, 1954 in retrospect and prospect," Robert L. Gill. <u>Negro Eductn R</u> 31: 17-34 Jan '80.
"Fertility reaction to a historical event," Ronald R. Rindfuss and others. <u>Science</u> 201: 178-180 July 14 '78.
"Fifteen years of deliberate speed," Kenneth B. Clark. <u>Sat R</u> 52: 59-61, 70 Dec 20 '69.
"The five who sued." <u>Sat R</u> 47: 71 May 16 '64.
"Florida and the school desegregation issue 1954-1959: a summary view," Joseph A. Tomberlin. <u>J Negro Eductn</u> 43: 457-467 Fall '74 (2).
"Forced schooling," B. Frank Brown. <u>Phi Delta Kappan</u> 54: 324 Jan '73 (3).
"Fragility of racial progress," Robert Lekachman. <u>Current</u> 182: 9-13 Apr '76; reprinted from <u>New Leader</u> p. 10-12 Feb 16 '74.

"Georgia Baptists and the 1954 Supreme Court desegregation decision," Len G. Cleveland. Ga Historical Q 59 (Suppl): 107-117 1975.

"Going the second mile," William Van Til. Phi Delta Kappan 56: 220-221 Nov '74.

"Human rights, law, and education," Wilson Record. J Negro Eductn 29: 453-457 Fall '60.

"Impact of the Brown decision; symposium," ed. by William J. Holloway. Negro Eductn R 30: 62-208 Apr/July '79.

"Impact of the 1954 Brown vs. Topeka Board of education decision on Black educators," Samuel B. Ethridge. Negro Eductn R 30: 217-232 Oct '79.

"   " (condensed). Eductn Dig 45: 24-27 Feb '80.

"Impact of the U.S. Supreme Court decisions on the lives of black people, 1950-1974," Robert L. Gill. Negro Eductn R 27: 92-112 Apr '76 (3).

"Implementing the promise of Brown," Julius L. Chambers. Eductnl Forum 41: 415-429 May '77.

"Inside the Supreme Court; the momentous school desegregation; excerpt from the Memoirs of Earl Warren," Earl Warren. Atlantic 239: 35-40 Apr '77.

"Ironies of school desegregation," Faustine C. Jones. J Negro Eductn 47: 2-27 Winter '78 (7).

"Is Brown Obsolete? yes!" Derrick A. Bell, Jr. Integ Eductn 14: 28, 30, 32, 34 May '76. Reply: Nathaniel R. Jones, 14: 29, 31, 33, 35-36 May '76.

"Judicial evolution of the law of school integration since Brown v. Board of education," Frank T. Read. Law and Contemporary Problems 39: 7-49 Winter '75 (6).

"Learning from the Brown experience," Derrick Bell. Black Scholar 11: 9-16 Sep/Oct '79.

"Linda Brown Smith: integration's unwitting pioneer," Michele Burgen. Ebony 34: 186, 188 May '79.

"Litigation and education of Blacks: a look at the U.S. Supreme Court," Delores P. Aldridge. J Negro Eductn 47: 96-112 Winter '78 (11).

"The many voices of the Burger Court and school desegregation," H. C. Hudgins. Phi Delta Kappan 60: 165-168 Nov '78 (2).

"March toward equality; excerpt from Portrait of a decade," Anthony Lewis Atlantic 214: 58-64 Sep '64.

"New educational decision; Is Detroit the end of the school bus line?" B. W. Young and G. B. Bress. Phi Delta Kappan 56: 515-520 Apr '75 (2).

"1954 revisited," Jack Slater. Ebony 29: 116-118, 120, 122, 124-127 May '74.

"Old business: from Brown to now," Kenneth B. Clark. Phi Delta Kappan 60: 194S-195S Nov '78.

"Polemics and the reversal of the separate but equal doctrine," David B. Strother. Q J Speech 49: 50-56 Feb '63. Reply: D. C. Simmons, Q J Speech 49: 444-446 Dec '63.

"Policy in search of law; the Warren Court from Brown to Miranda," Richard A. Maidment. J Am Studies 9: 301-320 '75 (4).

"Racial integration since 1954." Current 164: 3-21 July '74.

"Reassessment of racial balance remedies," Derrick A. Bell, Jr. Phi Delta Kappan 62: 177-179 Nov '80. Reaction: 62: 180-181 Nov '80.

"Reply to Herbert Wechsler's Holmes lecture--Toward neutral prin-

ciples of constitutional law," Robert G. Armstrong. <u>Phylon</u>
21: 211-224 Fall '60.

"Rhetoric of Brown v. Board of Education: paradigm for contemporary social protest," David M. Hunsaker. <u>Southern Speech</u>
<u>Communication J</u> 43: 91-109 Winter '78.

"The road from 'Brown,'" A. E. Dick Howard. <u>Wilson Q</u> 3:
96-107 Spring '79.

"The road since Brown: the Americanization of the race," William
Strickland. <u>Black Scholar</u> 11: 2-8 Sep/Oct '79.

"Role of the federal courts in the changing status of Negroes since
World War II," Daniel C. Thompson. <u>J Negro Eductn</u> 30: 94-
101 Spring '61 (2).

"School desegregation in retrospect and prospect," Leon Jones.
<u>J Negro Eductn</u> 47: 46-57 Winter '78.

"School desegregation--North, south, east, west: trends in court
decisions, 1849-1973," John Hogan. <u>Phi Delta Kappan</u> 55: 58-
63 Sept '73 (13).

"Since the Supreme Court spoke; decision on school desegregation,"
Anthony Lewis. <u>NY Times Mag</u> p. 9, 91-93 May 10 '64.

"Social science, segregation and the law," Robert B. McKay.
<u>Sch and Society</u> 89: 172-175 Apr 8 '61.

"Special Ebony poll: Have we moved with all deliberate speed in
ending segregation in public education?" <u>Ebony</u> 34: 183-185
May '79.

*"Supreme Court on school desegregation; excerpts." <u>Senior</u>
<u>Scholastic</u> 93: 14 Jan 10 '69.

"Ten tragic years," David Lawrence. <u>US News</u> 56: 120, 119
May 25 '64.

"Ten years of deliberate speed," Erwin Knoll. <u>Am Eductn</u> 1:
1-3 Dec '64/Jan '65.

"Thou shalt not feel inferior! reprint," David Lawrence. <u>US News</u>
55: 108 Sep 16 '63.

"Turning the clock back." <u>Progressive</u> 38: 11 May '74.

"Warren legacy; a very different constitution," James Jackson
Kilpatrick. <u>Natl R</u> 21: 794-800 Aug 12 '69 (2).

"When the Supreme Court ordered desegregation," Alfred H. Kelly.
<u>US News</u> 52: 86-88 Feb 5 '62.

"With all deliberate speed," Liva Baker. <u>Am Heritage</u> 24: 42-48
Feb '73.

"With all deliberate speed," Ernest Holsendolph. <u>Black Enterprise</u>
9: 17 July '79.

1963. Bolling v. Sharpe   May 17, 1954 347 U.S. 497
*<u>Am Consttn</u> (Lockhart) 971-972
*<u>Am Consttnl Issues</u> 440
*<u>Argument</u> 332-333
*<u>Cases Civil Liberties</u> 337-338
*<u>Cases Consttnl Law</u> (Cushman) 567-568
 <u>Cases Consttnl Law</u> (Gunther) 761
*<u>Cases Consttnl Rights</u> 917
*<u>Civil Rights</u> (Blaustein) 442-443
*<u>Consttn</u> (Morris) 719-720
*<u>Consttn</u> (Pollak) v. 2, 264-265
*<u>Consttnl Decisions</u> 170-171
*<u>Consttnl Law</u> (Barrett) 816-817
*<u>Consttnl Law</u> (Freund) 890-891
*<u>Consttnl Law</u> (Grossman) 444-445
*<u>Consttnl Politics</u> 500-501
*<u>Contemporary Law</u> 866-867

  *Desegregation (Blaustein) 306-308
  *Desegregation (Ziegler) 80-81
  Digest 81
  Education (Lapati) 274-277
  Education (Spurlock) 206-212
  *Education (Spurlock) 215-216
  *Law Lawyers 192-193
  *Leading Consttnl Decisions 424-425
  *Nature 1006-1007
  *Negro (Franklin) 280-282
  Petitioners 349
  *Political Rights v. 2, 1243-1245
  Private Pressure 82
  *Public Papers 143-145
  Quest 151-152
  *Sex Roles 571-572
  *Simple Justice 991-993
  Sup Ct on Trial 5-7
  Warren (Hudgins) 80-81

1964. Capital Service, Inc. v. National   May 17, 1954   347 U.S. 501
    Labor Relations Board
  *Cases Labor (Handler) 230-231

1965. United States v. Borden Co.   May 17, 1954   347 U.S. 514
  *Cases Trade 1234-1236

1966. Galvan v. Press   May 24, 1954   347 U.S. 522
  *Consttn (Mendelson) 596-597
  Felix Frankfurter (Thomas) 253-254
  *Mr. Justice Frankfurter 184-185
  *Sup Ct and Commander in Chief 279-281

1967. Leyra v. Denno   June 1, 1954   347 U.S. 556
  *Consttnl Politics 681-687
  Sup Ct and Confessions 113-114

1968. Braniff Airways, Inc. v. Nebraska   June 1, 1954   347 U.S. 590
    State Board of Equalization and
    Assessment
  *Am Consttn (Lockhart) 299-301
  *Am Consttnl Law (Saye) 199-201
  *Consttnl Law (Barrett) 394-396
  *Consttnl Law (Freund) 508-513
  *Consttnl Law (Lockhart) 381-383
  *Contemporary Law 264-267

1969. United States v. Harriss   June 7, 1954   347 U.S. 612
  CQ Guide 174
  *Cases Criml Law (Inbau) 31-41
  *Dispassionate 231-234
  *Legislation (Linde) 207-213
  *Legislative (Hetzel) 724-726
  *Materials Legislation 318-329
  *Political Rights 532-537
  System 640-642

1970. United Construction Workers, United   June 7, 1954   347 U.S. 656
    Mine Workers v. Laburnum Con-
    struction Corporation

1979. United States v. Shubert   Jan 31, 1955   348 U.S. 222
       Professional Sports 30-31

1980. United States v. International Boxing Jan 21, 1955   348 U.S. 236
       Club of New York
       Dissent 245-246
       Professional Sports 32-33

1981. Tee-Hit-Ton Indians v. United States   Feb 7, 1955   348 U.S. 272
       *Am Indian v. 4, 2752-2762
       *Law Indian 467-470

1982. Wilburn Boat Co. v. Firemen's Fund   Feb 28, 1955   348 U.S. 310
       Insurance Co.
       *Cases Admiralty 653-659

1983. Sicurella v. United States   Mar 14, 1955   348 U.S. 385
       *Religious Freedom (Pfeffer) 120-121

1984. Association of Westinghouse Salaried Mar 28, 1955   348 U.S. 437
       Employees v. Westinghouse Electric
       Corporation
       Labor Relations (Taylor) 416-417

1985. Weber v. Anheuser Busch, Inc.   Mar 28, 1955   348 U.S. 468
       Sup Ct and Labor 61-62

1986. Williamson v. Lee Optical of Okla-   Mar 28, 1955   348 U.S. 483
       homa
       *Cases Consttnl Law (Gunther) 538-539
       *Cases Individual 187-189
       *Consttn (Mendelson) 272-274
       *Consttnl Law (Barrett) 672-674
       *Contemporary Law 129-131
       *Introduction (Mashaw) 158-161
       *Processes 747-750
       Quest 67

1987. Amalgamated Clothing Workers of   Apr 4, 1955   348 U.S. 511
       America v. the Richman Brothers
       *Cases Federal Courts 383-391
       *Cases Labor (Handler) 231-235

1988. Shaughnessy v. Pedreiro   Apr 25, 1955   348 U.S. 48
       *Admin Law (Schwartz) 551-552

1989. Rice v. Sioux City Memorial Park   May 9, 1955   349 U.S. 70
       Cemetery
       Century 145-148
       *Contemporary Law 13-15
       Desegregation (Wasby) 132-137
       *Introduction (Cataldo) 621-624
       *One Man's Stand 282-283

1990. Bisso v. Inland Waterways Corporation May 16, 1955   349 U.S. 85
       *Cases Admiralty 705-711

1991. Boston Metals v. The Winding Gulf   May 16, 1955   349 U.S. 122
       *Cases Admiralty 711-714

1992. United States v. Nielson   May 16, 1955 349 U. S. 129
       *Cases Admiralty 730-731

1993. In re Murchison   May 16, 1955 349 U. S. 133
       *Consttnl Law (Kauper) 876-879
       *Consttnl Politics 649-652
       Defendants 118-119
       Justice Hugo Black 116

1994. Quinn v. United States   May 23, 1955 349 U. S. 155
       *Freedom Reader 87-88
       *Materials Legislation 452-459
       *Political Rights 401-404

1995. Emspak v. United States   May 23, 1955 349 U. S. 190
       Communication (Hemmer) v. 1, 212
       *Freedom and Protection 51-54

1996. Brown v. Board of Education of   May 31, 1955 349 U. S. 294
       Topeka, Kansas
       *Am Consttn (Lockhart) 972-973
       *Am Consttnl Issues 440-442
       *Am Consttnl Law (Mason) 489-490
       *Am Consttnl Law (Shapiro) 516-517
       *Am Consttnl Law Reader 210-213
       *Am Govt 162-163
       *Am Testament 230-235
       *Argument 533-535
       *Basic Documents 189-190
       Brethren 38
       *Cases Consttnl Law (Gunther) 764-765
       *Cases Consttnl Law (Rosenblum) 31-32
       *Cases Consttnl Rights 918-919
       *Cases Individual 317-318
       *Civil Liberties (Barker) 276-277
       *Civil Liberties (Sweet) 217-218
       *Civil Rights (Abernathy) 1977 519-520
       Civil Rights (Bardolph) 430-432
       *Civil Rights (Blaustein) 444-447
       *Civil Rights (Pious) 23-24
       Civil Rights (Schimmel) 189-190
       *Consttn (Hirschfield) 86-88
       *Consttn (Mendelson) 525-527
       *Consttn (Morris) 716-717
       *Consttnl Law (Barrett) 821-822
       *Consttnl Law (Barron) 603-605
       *Consttnl Law (Freund) 891-892
       *Consttnl Law (Grossman) 445-447
       *Consttnl Law (Kauper) 721-722
       *Consttnl Law (Lockhart) 1274-1275
       *Consttnl Law (Schmidhauser) 422-423
       *Contemporary Law 867-868
       Court Years 115
       *Desegregation (Blaustein) 309-312
       Desegregation (Wasby) 108-130
       Digest 81-82
       Disaster 33-37
       *Discrimination 177-178
       Dred Scott Case 582, 593

*Educational Policy 303-304
Felix Frankfurter (Baker) 319-321
Freedom and the Court 374-375
From Brown 62-68
*Great School Bus 44-46
*Integration 29-31
*It is so Ordered 146-149
Judiciary (Abraham) 133
*Law and Public Education (Hamilton) 540-542
*Law Lawyers 218-221
*Law of Public Education 644-646
*Law Sup Ct 423-427
Law Sup Ct 429-433
Memoirs 287-289
*Nature 1008-1009
*Negro (Franklin) 282-284
Petitioners 350
*Political Rights v. 2, 1252-1254
Private Pressure 84-87
*Public Papers 145-149
*Public School Law 645-647
School in the Legal Structure 60
*School Law (Remmlein) 208-209
*Sup Ct and Am Govt 185-187
*Sup Ct and Education 140-143
*Sup Ct Speaks 422-424
Warren (Hudgins) 81-82
*Warren (Spaeth) 121-124

1997. Marcello v. Bonds   May 31, 1955   349 U.S. 302
       *Douglas 444-445

1998. Peters v. Hobby   June 6, 1955   349 U.S. 331
       Congress versus 97, 99-101
       Earl Warren 185-186
       *Freedom Reader 77-79
       *One Man's Stand 284-286
       Warren (Lytle) 33-34

1999. Federal Communications Commission   June 6, 1955   349 U.S. 358
           v. Allentown Broadcasting Co.
       *Admin Law (Schwartz) 512-513

2000. Williams v. Georgia   June 6, 1955   349 U.S. 375
       *Courts Judges 390-392
       *Federal System 305-306
       Impact (Wasby) 198

2001. Carroll v. Lanza   June 6, 1955   349 U.S. 408
       *Cases Workmen 555-559

2002. Mitchell v. Vollmer   June 6, 1955   349 U.S. 427
       Sup Ct and Commerce 134-135

2003. Lucy v. Adams   Oct 10, 1955   350 U.S. 1
       Private Pressure 100-101

2004. United States ex rel. Toth v. Quarles   Nov 7, 1955   350 U.S. 11
       Am Consttn (Kelly) 819-820

*Am Consttnl Law (Bartholomew) v. 2, 181-183
*Civil Rights (Abernathy) 1977 263-265
Justice Frankfurter 183-184
*Sup Ct and Criml Process 1119-1122
This Honorable Court 398-399

2005. Reece v. Georgia   Dec 5, 1955   350 U. S. 85
       *Law Sup Ct 493-497

2006. Michel v. Louisiana   Dec 5, 1955   350 U. S. 91
       Poret v. Louisiana
       *Federal Courts 538-543
       *One Man's Stand 287-289

2007. Ryan Stevedoring Co. v. Pan-Atlantic   Jan 9, 1956   350 U. S. 124
       Steamship Corporation
       *Cases Admiralty 394-399

2008. Bernhardt v. Polygraphic Co. of   Jan 16, 1956   350 U. S. 198
       America
       *Materials Law 303-308

2009. Rea v. United States   Jan 16, 1956   350 U. S. 214
       Exclusionary 24
       Search and Seizure 145, 146-148
       Sup Ct Review 1961 12-13

2010. Steiner v. Mitchell   Jan 30, 1956   350 U. S. 247
       *Cases Employment 734-738

2011. Mastro Plastics Corporation v.   Feb 27, 1956   350 U. S. 270
       National Labor Relations Board
       *Cases Labor (Handler) 47-52
       *Cases Labor (Oberer) 716-721
       *Labor Law (Meltzer) 188-193
       *Labor Law (Twomey) 297-300
       *Labor Relations (Group Trust) 475-478
       Law and Politics 108

2012. United States v. Ryan   Feb 27, 1956   350 U. S. 299
       *Cases Labor (Handler) 749-751
       *Labor Law (Meltzer) 1185-1187

2013. Costello v. United States   Mar 5, 1956   350 U. S. 359
       *Cases Criml Justice 884-887
       *Criminal Law (Kadish) 1147-1149
       *Elements Criminal 3-6
       *Sup Ct and Criml Process 517-518

2014. Florida ex rel. Hawkins v. Board of   Mar 12, 1956   350 U. S. 413
       Control of Florida
       Education (Lapati) 278-279
       PERIODICALS:
       "Florida and the school desegregation issue 1954-1959: a sum-
           mary view," Joseph A. Tomberlin. J Negro Eductn 43: 457-
           467 Fall '74 (2).
       "Hawkins, the United States Supreme Court and justice," S. Seikow.
           J Negro Eductn 31: 97-101 Winter '62.

2015. United States v. Green   Mar 26, 1956 350 U.S. 415
       *Labor Law (Meltzer) 565-567
       *Labor Law (Twomey) 240-242

2016. Ullman v. United States   Mar 26, 1956 350 U.S. 422
       *Am Consttnl Issues 387-390
       *Am Consttnl Law (Bartholomew) v. 2, 146-148
       *Cases Criml Law (Perkins) 1003-1006
       Communication (Hemmer) v. 1, 214-215
       *Consttnl Law (Kauper) 979-983
       Defendants 330-331
       *Douglas 342-350
       *Due Process 63
       Freedom Spent 372
       Hugo Black (Hamilton) 16-19
       Justice Frankfurter 165-170
       *Liberty v. 2, 579-583
       *Materials Legislation 470-478
       *Mr. Justice Frankfurter 127-130

2017. General Stores Corporation v. Shlensky Mar 26, 1956 350 U.S. 462
       *Materials Reorganization 231-235

2018. Pennsylvania v. Nelson   Apr 2, 1956   350 U.S. 497
       Am Consttn (Kelly) 909-910
       *Am Consttnl Issues 202-208
       *Am Consttnl Law (Bartholomew) v. 1, 38-40
       *Am Consttnl Law (Mason) 186-107
       CQ Guide 513
       Congress 85-86
       Congress versus 72-81
       *Consttn (Mendelson) 227-229
       *Consttnl Law (Freund) 473-478
       *Contemporary Law 196-200
       Court and Consttn v. 2, 238
       Court Years 97
       Decade 25
       *Documents History v. 2, 614-617
       Double (Miller) 55-58
       *Federal System 285-288
       *Govt and Business 12-13
       Justice Frankfurter 133
       Justices Black and Frankfurter 102-103
       *Liberty v. 2, 555-556
       Modern Sup Ct 148-156
       *Political Rights 195-202
       *Public Papers 212-221
       Sup Ct (Freund) 181
       System 153
       This Honorable Court 396
       Warren (Carter) 76-77
       *Warren (Spaeth) 359-365

2019. Archawski v. Hanioti   Apr 9, 1956   350 U.S. 532
       *Cases Admiralty 168-170

2020. Slochower v. Board of Higher Edu- Apr 9, 1956   350 U.S. 551
       cation of City of New York
       Am Consttn (Kelly) 921
       *Am Consttnl Law (Bartholomew) v. 2, 283-284

CQ Guide 514
Cases Consttnl Law (Gunther) 1448-1449
Communication (Hemmer) v. 1, 115-116
*Contemporary Law 158-160
Court and Consttn v. 2, 239
Court Years 97-98
Courts 73-75
Defendants 313-315
Digest 54
Education (Lapati) 236
Justice Frankfurter 139
Modern Sup Ct 143-145
*School Law (Remmlein) 66-69
Warren (Hudgins) 122-123

2021. Souire v. Capoeman   Apr 23, 1956   351 U.S. 1
      *Am Indian v. 4, 2763-2767

2022. Griffin v. Illinois   Apr 23, 1956   351 U.S. 12
      *Am Consttnl Law (Saye) 487-490
      Basic History 77
      *Basic History 150-152
      CQ Guide 641
      Congress 82
      *Consttn (Mendelson) 376-379
      *Consttnl Law (Freund) 907-909
      *Consttnl Law (Schmidhauser) 14-17
      Court and Consttn v. 2, 238
      *Criminal Law (Kadish) 785-788
      *Criminal Procedure (Lewis) 76-78
      Democratic 144-145
      Dissent 236-238
      Expanding Liberties 382-383
      *Legal Problems 49-52
      *Mr. Justice Frankfurter 203-206
      *Poverty 45-49
      Quest 79-80
      *Sup Ct and Criml Process 133-136
      Sup Ct Review 1975 295-298

2023. National Labor Relations Board v.   Apr 30, 1956   351 U.S. 105
         Babcock and Wilcox Co.
      National Labor Relations Board v.
         Seamprufe, Inc.
      Ranco, Inc. v. National Labor Relations
         Board
      *Cases Labor (Leslie) 104-107
      *Cases Labor (Oberer) 254-257
      *Labor Law (Meltzer) 130-133
      *Labor Relations (Group Trust) 233-235
      Law and Politics 107-108
      Sup Ct and Labor 53-54

2024. Communist Party v. Subversive   Apr 30, 1956   351 U.S. 115
         Activities Control Board
      *Law Sup Ct 113-117
      Modern Sup Ct 145-146

2025. National Labor Relations Board v.   May 7, 1956   351 U.S. 149
         Truitt Manufacturing Co.

Basic Text 409
*Cases Labor (Cox) 409, 412-414
*Cases Labor (Handler) 288-290
*Cases Labor (Leslie) 372-374
*Cases Labor (Oberer) 601-604
*Labor Law (Herman) 275-278
*Labor Law (Meltzer) 697-700
Law and Politics 115-116
*Practice 510-514

2026. United States v. Storer Broadcasting   May 21, 1956 351 U.S. 192
    Co.
    *Cases Electronic 132-135

2027. Railway Employes' Department,   May 21, 1956 351 U.S. 225
    American Federation of Labor
    v. Hanson
    *Cases Labor (Handler) 422-428
    Court and Consttn v. 2, 239-240
    *Labor Relations (Group Trust) 965-972
    Labor Relations (Taylor) 366-367
    Law and Politics 132
    System 685

2028. United Automobile, Aircraft and   June 4, 1956 351 U.S. 266
    Agricultural Implement Workers
    v. Wisconsin Employment Relations
    Board
    *Cases Labor (Handler) 227-230

2029. Black v. Cutter Laboratories   June 4, 1956 351 U.S. 292
    Civil Liberties (Kauper) 149-150
    Congress 83

2030. United States v. McKesson and Rob-   June 11, 1956 351 U.S. 305
    bins, Inc.
    *Cases Trade 496-499
    *Free Enterprise 991-998

2031. Jay v. Boyd   June 11, 1956 351 U.S. 345
    Dissent 266-267
    Felix Frankfurter (Thomas) 255-256

2032. United States v. E. I. Du Pont de   June 11, 1956 351 U.S. 377
    Nemours and Co.
    *Antitrust Analysis 206-215
    *Cases Antitrust Law 192-210
    *Cases Antitrust Policy 14-33
    *Cases Trade 665-675
    *Competition 79-85
    *Govt and Business 139-141
    *Govt Regulation 1246-1275
    Hugo Black (Dunne) 342-343
    *Modern Business 960-962
    *Selected Antitrust Cases 41-54
    *Text Antitrust 34-39

2033. Sears, Roebuck and Co. v. Mackey   June 11, 1956 351 U.S. 427
    *Cases Federal Courts 786-794

*Civil Procedure (Cound) 972-977
*Elements Civil 1228-1234
*Federal Courts 1555-1561

2034. Kinsella v. Krueger   June 11, 1956   351 U. S. 470
       Am Consttn (Kelly) 820-821
       Felix Frankfurter (Thomas) 261-263
       Mr. Justice Frankfurter 18-19

2035. Reid v. Covert   June 11, 1956   351 U. S. 487
       Am Consttn (Kelly) 820-821

2036. Reed v. Pennsylvania Railroad   June 11, 1956   351 U. S. 502
       *Cases Employment 13-16
       *Cases Workmen 21-26

2037. Parr v. United States   June 11, 1956   351 U. S. 513
       Parr v. Rice
       Parr v. Allred
       Sup Ct Review 1979 282

2038. Czaplicki v. the Steamship Hoegh   June 11, 1956   351 U. S. 525
       Silvercloud
       *Cases Pleading 651-655

2039. Cole v. Young   June 11, 1956   351 U. S. 536
       Congress versus 97-100, 102-103
       Court and Consttn v. 2, 239
       Decade 24-25
       *Documents History v. 2, 613-614
       *Freedom vs National Security 518-524
       Modern Sup Ct 150-153
       This Honorable Court 397-398

2040. De Sylva v. Ballentine   June 11, 1956   351 U. S. 570
       *Cases Copyright (Nimmer) 256-261
       *Cases Federal Courts 620-624

2041. Mesaroch v. United States   Nov 5, 1956   352 U. S. 1
       *Public Papers 222-232

2042. Bank of America National Trust and   Nov 13, 1956   352 U. S. 29
       Savings Association v. Parnell
       *Civil Procedure (Cound) 312-314
       *Federal Courts 759-762

2043. United States v. Western Pacific Rail- Dec 3, 1956   352 U. S. 59
       road
       *Admin Law (Gellhorn) 1040-1043
       *Admin Law (Schwartz) 588-591

2044. Miller v. Arkansas   Dec 17, 1956   352 U. S. 187
       *Consttnl Law (Barrett) 471-472

2045. Fikes v. Alabama   Jan 14, 1957   352 U. S. 191
       *Consttn (Mendelson) 352-356
       Death 5-40
       Police 93-95
       Sup Ct and Confessions 115

2046.   United States v. Howard   Jan 14, 1957   352 U.S. 212
        *Govt and Business 444-445

2047.   La Buy v. Howes Leather Co.   Jan 14, 1957   352 U.S. 249
        *Cases Civil Procedure 1050-1054
        *Civil Procedure (Carrington) 235-240
        *Civil Procedure (Cound) 986-990
        *Elements Civil 1235-1238

2048.   National Labor Relations Board v.   Jan 22, 1957   352 U.S. 282
            Lion Oil Co.
        *Cases Labor (Handler) 268-272
        *Labor Law (Meltzer) 686-690
        *Labor Relations (Group Trust) 473-475
        Law and Politics 108-109

2049.   In re Groban   Feb 25, 1957   352 U.S. 330
        *Govt and Business 512-514

2050.   Butler v. Michigan   Feb 25, 1957   352 U.S. 380
        *Bill (Konvitz) 410-412
        Censorship 54-59
        *Censorship Landmarks 301-302
        Communication (Hemmer) v. 1, 197
        *Documents History v. 2, 619-620
        Expanding Liberties 175-176
        Federal Censorship 141-142
        *First Amendment (Konvitz) 844-846
        Freedom and the Court 215
        Justice Frankfurter 03
        Law of Obscenity 71-72, 156-157
        *Liberty v. 2, 525-526
        Literature 176
        *Mass Media (Devol) 95-96
        Movies 70
        *Obscenity (Bosmajian) 65-66
        Sup Ct Review 1960 5-7
        System 471
        PERIODICALS:
        "Pornographic and the obscene in legal and aesthetic contexts, "
            E. F. Kaelin. J Aesthetic Eductn 4: 69-84 July '70 (2).

2051.   Nilva v. United States   Feb 25, 1957   352 U.S. 385
        *One Man's Stand 290-296

2052.   United States v. Turley   Feb 25, 1957   352 U.S. 407
        *Cases Criml Law (Hall) 45-50
        *Cases Criml Law (Inbau) 680-683
        *Cases Criml Law (Perkins) 233-236

2053.   Federal Trade Commission v.   Feb 25, 1957   352 U.S. 419
            National Lead Co.
        *Competition 299-302

2054.   Breithaupt v. Abram   Feb 25, 1957   352 U.S. 432
        *Am Consttnl Law (Bartholomew) v. 2, 269-272
        *Civil Rights (Abernathy) 1977 185-187
        *Comparative 383-384
        *Consttn (Mendelson) 363-367

*Consttnl Politics 675-679
*Courts Judges 735-737
Criminal Evidence 523-524
Defendants 347
Felix Frankfurter (Thomas) 163-164
Freedom and the Court 123-126
Judiciary (Abraham) 81-82
Search and Seizure 141-143

2055. Radovich v. National Football   Feb 25, 1957   352 U.S. 445
         League
       *Govt and Business 99-100
       Law and Politics 283
       Professional Sports 33-37

2056. Rogers v. Missouri Pacific Rail-   Feb 25, 1957   352 U.S. 500
         road Co.
       *Cases Workmen 36-41
       *Civil Procedure (Cound) 912-914
       *Contemporary Law 4-5
       *Elements Civil 1246-1253
       *Evolution 224-229
       *Materials Law 487-492
       Sup Ct Review 1979 285-288
       *Warren (Spaeth) 63-67

2057. Ferguson v. Moore-McCormick Lines   Feb 25, 1957   352 U.S. 521
       Consttnl Politics 101-108
       *Contemporary Law 5-13
       *Materials Law 492-502

2058. United States v. International Union,   Mar 11, 1957   352 U.S. 567
         United Automobile, Aircraft and
         Agricultural Implement Workers
         of America
       *Cases Labor (Handler) 743-748
       *Consttnl Cases 284-297
       Dissent 465-466
       *Douglas 174-179
       *Labor Law (Meltzer) 1192-1197
       *Labor Relations (Group Trust) 128-137
       *Legislative (Hetzel) 206-210
       *Mr. Justice Frankfurter 36-38
       System 636-637

2059. Sheppard v. Ohio   Nov 13, 1956   352 U.S. 910
       *Consttnl Politics 112-113

2060. Guss v. Utah Labor Relations Board   Mar 25, 1957   353 U.S. 1
       *Am Consttnl Law (Saye) 186-188
       *Cases Labor (Handler) 224-227
       *Contemporary Law 205-207
       Labor Relations (Taylor) 251-252

2061. Amalgamated Meat Cutters and But-   Mar 25, 1957   353 U.S. 20
         cherWorkmen of North America
         v. Fairlawn Meats
       Sup Ct and Commerce 119

2062. Brotherhood of Railroad Trainmen   Mar 25, 1957   353 U.S. 30
       v. Chicago River and Indiana
       Railroad Co.
       *Cases Labor (Cox) 906-911
       *Cases Labor (Handler) 621-626
       *Statutory History Labor 251-257

2063. Roviaro v. United States   Mar 25, 1957   353 U.S. 53
       *Consttnl Law (Felkenes) 249-251
       Criminal Law (Felkenes) 167-170
       *Police 132-133
       *Principles Arrest 460-462
       *Principles Proof 784-789

2064. National Labor Relations Board v.   Apr 1, 1957   353 U.S. 87
       Truck Drivers Local 449, Inter-
       national Brotherhood of Teamsters,
       Chauffeurs, Warehousemen and
       Helpers of America
       *Cases Labor (Handler) 146-149
       *Cases Labor (Oberer) 224-227
       *Cases Labor (Stern) 72-75
       *Labor Law (Herman) 346-350
       *Labor Relations (Group Trust) 204-207
       Labor Relations (Taylor) 452
       Sup Ct and Labor 87-89

2065. United States v. Ohio Power Co.   Apr 1, 1957   353 U.S. 98
       *Elements Civil 1271-1275

2066. Automobile Club of Michigan v. Com-   Apr 22, 1957   353 U.S. 180
       missioner of Internal Revenue
       Law and Politics 148

2067. Fourco Glass Co. v. Transmirra   Apr 29, 1957   353 U.S. 222
       Products Corporation
       *Patent 833-839

2068. Pennsylvania, City of Philadelphia v.   Apr 29, 1957   353 U.S. 230
       The Board of Directors of City
       Trusts of City of Philadelphia
       "Girard College Case"
       *Am Consttnl Law (Saye) 268-269
       *Consttnl Law (Barrett) 1051-1052
       Court and Consttn v. 2, 242
       *Desegregation 81-82
       Warren (Hudgins) 82-83

2069. Schware v. Board of Bar Examiners   May 6, 1957   353 U.S. 232
       of New Mexico
       Am Consttn (Kelly) 921-922
       Congress 107
       Congress versus 107-110
       Court Years 98
       Justice Frankfurter 140-141
       *Mr. Justice Frankfurter 182-184
       Modern Sup Ct 166-173
       *US Prison Law v. 5, 234-252

2070. Konigsberg v. State Bar of California   May 6, 1957   353 U. S. 252
        Am Consttn (Kelly) 922
        *Am Consttnl Law (Bartholomew) v. 2, 285-286
        Congress 108
        Congress versus 110-112
        *Contemporary Law 177-182
        Court Years 98
        Modern Sup Ct 169-171, 233-235
        *One Man's Stand 297-307

2071. Office Employes International Union,   May 6, 1957   353 U. S. 313
        Local 11 v. National Labor Relations
        Board
        *Cases Labor (Handler) 167-169
        *Labor Law (Meltzer) 575-577

2072. Civil Aeronautics Board v. Hermann   May 6, 1957   353 U. S. 322
        *Admin Law (Schwartz) 204-205

2073. Kremen v. United States   May 13, 1957   353 U. S. 346
        Search and Seizure 111

2074. Arnold v. Panhandle and Sante   May 13, 1957   353 U. S. 360
        Fe Railway Co.
        *Cases Employment 26-28
        *Cases Workmen 47-48

2075. Libsom Shops v. Koehler   May 27, 1957   353 U. S. 382
        Law and Politics 145

2076. Grunewald v. United States   May 27, 1957   353 U. S. 391
        Halperin v. United States
        Bolich v. United States
        *Criminal Law (Wells) 155-156
        *Principles Proof 691-697

2077. Textile Workers Union of America   June 3, 1957   353 U. S. 448
        v. Lincoln Mills of Alabama
        *Arbitration 294-315
        Basic Text 544-545
        *Cases Federal Courts 161-174
        *Cases Labor (Cox) 603-610
        *Cases Labor (Handler) 304-307
        *Cases Labor (Leslie) 529-532
        *Cases Labor (Oberer) 667-672
        *Collective Bargaining 299-305
        *Federal Courts 779-785, 859-866
        Justices Black and Frankfurter 92-93
        *Labor Law (Meltzer) 793-798
        *Labor Law (Twomey) 324-327
        *Labor Relations (Group Trust) 848-854
        Labor Relations (Taylor) 417-418
        *Nature 1196-1200
        *Statutory History Labor 672-677

2078. California v. Taylor   June 3, 1957   353 U. S. 553
        *Cases Labor (Handler) 177-181
        Consttnl Law (Barrett) 480

2079. United States v. E. I. DuPont de   June 3, 1957   353 U.S. 586
       Nemours and Co.
       *Am Consttnl Law (Shapiro) 706-713
       *Antitrust (Posner) 691-703
       *Antitrust Analysis 707-711
       *Cases Antitrust Law 834-843
       *Cases Trade 710-715
       *Competition 107-113
       *Govt and Business 164-167
       *Govt Regulation 1285
       Hugo Black (Dunne) 343
       Law and Politics 275-283
       *Legal Environment 338-341
       *Modern Business 986-988
       *Social Forces 357-359
       *Text Antitrust 146-150

2080. Jencks v. United States   June 3, 1957   353 U.S. 657
       *Affair 237-242
       *Am Consttnl Law (Bartholomew) v. 2, 172-174
       Congress 99-100, 127-153
       Court and Consttn v. 2, 242
       Defendants 95-96
       Elements Judicial 125-126
       *Freedom vs National Security 178-180
       Hugo Black (Dunne) 339-340
       *Justices (Friedman) v. 4, 2693-2695
       *Law of Evidence 438-446
       *Law Sup Ct 322-331
       Modern Sup Ct 177-180
       This Honorable Court 402-403
       Warren (Lytle) 36-37
       *Warren (Spaeth) 216-222

2081. Reid v. Covert   June 10, 1957   354 U.S. 1
       Kinsella v. Kreuger
       Am Consttn (Kelly) 822
       *Am Consttn (Lockhart) 1231-1234
       *Am Consttnl Law (Bartholomew) v. 2, 183-186
       *Cases Consttnl Rights 1223-1226
       *Consttnl Law (Barrett) 270-272, 549-551
       *Consttnl Law (Felkenes) 100-104
       *Consttnl Law (Freund) 1069-1073
       *Consttnl Law (Kauper) 516-526
       *Contemporary Law 391-399
       *Evolution 252-259
       Justice Frankfurter 184-187
       Sup Ct and Commander in Chief 155-158

2082. Smith v. Sperling   June 10, 1957   354 U.S. 91
       *Cases Federal Courts 723-731

2083. Curcio v. United States   June 10, 1957   354 U.S. 118
       *Principles Proof 703-707

2084. Lake Tankers Corporation v. Henn   June 10, 1957   354 U.S. 147
       *Cases Admiralty 117-119

2085.   Watkins v. United States   June 17, 1957 354 U. S. 178
        Am Consttn (Kelly) 929-930
        *Am Consttnl Law (Bartholomew) v. 1, 75-80
        *Am Consttnl Law (Mason) 94-98
        *Am Consttnl Law Reader 192-201
        *Anxiety 338-344
        CQ Guide 160-161
        *Cases Consttnl Law (Cushman) 51-57
        Cases Consttnl Law (Gunther) 1487-1488
        *Civil Liberties (Sweet) 153-160
        Communication (Hemmer) v. 1, 212-213
        Congress 100-101
        Congress versus 42-58
        *Consttn (Mendelson) 430-438
        Consttnl Law (Barrett) 1179-1180
        *Consttnl Law (Felkenes) 154-155
        *Consttnl Law (Kauper) 247-256
        *Contemporary Law 335-342
        Court and Consttn v. 2, 243
        Court Years 99
        Decade 25-28
        Earl Warren 187-188
        *Federal System 258-263
        Felix Frankfurter (Mendelson) 129-131
        *First Amendment (Konvitz) 625-641
        Freedom of Speech (Hudon) 134-135
        *Historic Decisions 157-171
        In his own Image 65
        Judiciary (Abraham) 115
        Justice Frankfurter 136-138
        *Justices (Friedman) v. 4, 2686-2693
        Law and Politics 63-64
        *Law Sup Ct 174-180
        Least Dangerous 157-159
        *Liberty v. 2, 583-587
        *Materials Legislation 409-437
        Modern Sup Ct 171-177, 184-187
        *Political Rights 356-370
        Politics 62-66
        Power 155
        *Public Papers 232-257
        *Sup Ct and Consttn 455-463
        Sup Ct in Free Society 53-55
        System 257-258
        This Honorable Court 395
        Warren (Carter) 78-80
        *Warren (Spaeth) 223-236
        Watergate 29-30

2086.   Sweezy v. New Hampshire   June 17, 1957 354 U. S. 234
        Am Consttn (Kelly) 930
        Cases Consttnl Law (Gunther) 1489-1490
        Communication (Hemmer) v. 1, 147-148
        Congress 104-106
        Congress versus 44
        *Consttn (Morris) 165-174
        Court and Consttn v. 2, 243-244
        Court Years 98-99
        Courts 58-59

Education (Lapati) 237-238
Expanding Liberties 91-94
Felix Frankfurter (Baker) 297-298
*First Amendment (Konvitz) 667-682
Free Speech (Kurland) 53-54
Freedom of Speech (Hudon) 135-137
Justice Frankfurter 122-127
*Justices (Friedman) v. 3, 2439-2443
Justices Black and Frankfurter 55-57
Modern Sup Ct 174-177
*Public Papers 257-272
System 259-260, 602-603
This Honorable Court 395
Warren (Hudgins) 123-125
Warren (Lytle) 31

2087. International Brotherhood of Teamsters, June 17, 1957 354 U.S. 284
         Local 695 v. Vogt, Inc.
         Am Consttn (Kelly) 842
         *Cases Consttnl Law (Gunther) 1414-1417
         *Cases Consttnl Rights 767-770
         *Cases Individual 952-956
         *Cases Labor (Cox) 698-706
         *Cases Labor (Handler) 576-581
         *Cases Labor (Leslie) 203-209
         *Cases Labor (Oberer) 352-357
         *Consttn (Mendelson) 479-484
         *Consttnl Law (Barrett) 1323-1326
         *Freedom and Protection 147-150
         *Govt and Business 87-91
         Justice Frankfurter 105-107
         *Labor Law (Herman) 310-314
         *Labor Law (Meltzer) 378-384
         *Labor Relations (Group Trust) 280-283
         Labor Relations (Taylor) 505
         Law and Politics 79
         Sup Ct and Labor 46-47

2088. Yates v. United States   June 17, 1957 354 U.S. 298
         Schneiderman v. United States
         Richmond v. United States
         *Am Consttnl Law (Bartholomew) v. 2, 67-69
         *Am Consttnl Law (Mason) 569-571
         *Am Consttnl Law (Shapiro) 364-369
         Bill (Cohen) 77
         CQ Guide 504-505
         Cases Consttnl Law (Gunther) 1168-1170
         *Cases Consttnl Law (Rosenblum) 399-406
         *Civil Liberties (Sweet) 90-92
         Communication (Hemmer) v. 1, 26
         *Communism 44-50
         *Comparative 613-616
         Congress 102-104
         Congress versus 64-67
         *Consttn (Mendelson) 407-413
         *Consttnl Law (Barrett) 1144-1147
         *Consttnl Law (Freund) 1170-1172
         *Contemporary Law 556-565
         Court and Consttn v. 2, 244

Court Years 100-101
Decade 28-30
*Documents History v. 2, 625-626
*Evolution 173-181
Expanding Liberties 124-126
*First Amendment (Konvitz) 372-392
Freedom and the Court 203
*Freedom of Speech (Haiman) 18
Freedom of Speech (Hudon) 128-133
Freedom of Speech (Shapiro) 66
*Govt and Business 92-95
Handbook 22-23
Hugo Black (Strickland) 114-115
Judiciary (Abraham) 118-119
Justice Frankfurter 133-135
Law of Mass 40-41
*Law Sup Ct 117-127
*Liberty v. 2, 546-547
Mass Communications 82-83
Mass Media (Francois) 28
Modern Sup Ct 180-185
*One Man's Stand 308-313
*Political Rights 123-134
Politics 66-67
*Sup Ct and Consttn 448-454
Sup Ct from Taft 162-163
Sup Ct in Crisis 249
Sup Ct in Free Society 47, 297-299
*Sup Ct on Freedom 34-35
System 121-124
This Honorable Court 396-397
Warren (Lytle) 29-31
*Warren (Spaeth) 237-242
PERIODICALS:
   "Law, logic and revolution: the Smith act decisions," John Somer-
   ville. Western Poltcl Q 14: 839-849 Dec '61 (3).

2089. Service v. Dulles   June 17, 1957 354 U. S. 363
        Congress versus 98, 100-101
        Court and Consttn v. 2, 245
        Warren (Lytle) 33

2090. West Point Wholesale Grocery Co.   June 17, 1957 354 U. S. 390
           v. City of Opelika, Alabama
        *Legal Environment 240-241

2091. Vanderbilt v. Vanderbilt   June 17, 1957 354 U. S. 416
        *Family 617-620

2092. Kingsley Books v. Brown   June 24, 1957 354 U. S. 436
        *Affair 39-40
        *Am Consttn (Lockhart) 756-758
        *Cases Civil Liberties 248-252
        *Cases Consttnl Law (Cushman) 478-482
        Cases Consttnl Law (Gunther) 1378-1379
        *Cases Consttnl Rights 630-632
        Censorship 217
        *Censorship Landmarks 265-268
        *Civil Rights (Abernathy) 1977 362-364

Communication (Hemmer) v. 1, 188-189
*Consttn (Mendelson) 507-511
*Consttnl Law (Felkenes) 142-144
Federal Censorship 148-149
*First Amendment (Konvitz) 837-843
*Freedom of Speech (Haiman) 114-115
Freedom of Speech (Hudon) 128
Justice Frankfurter 64-66
Law of Obscenity 230
*Mass Media (Devol) 97-98
Movies 89-92
*Sup Ct on Freedom 52-54
System 507-508

2093. Mallory v. United States   June 24, 1957 354 U.S. 449
*Bill (Konvitz) 703-706
*Cases Criml Justice 576-579
*Congress Against 109-113
*Consttn (Mendelson) 360-361
Court and Consttn v. 2, 241
Decade 167
Freedom Spent 379
Hugo Black (Dunne) 341-342
*Law Sup Ct 244-249
*Nature 263-264
*Police 47-49, 92-93
Self Inflicted Wound 161-162
Sup Ct and Confessions 77-01
Sup Ct in Crisis 250-251
PERIODICALS:
"Why so much crime in the Nation's capital; Mallory rule," Robert
V. Murray, US News 55: 92 07 Oct 21 '63. Reaction: 55:
92-93 Nov 4 '63.

2094. Morey v. Doud   June 24, 1957 354 U.S. 457
*Am Consttn (Lockhart) 373-375
*Cases Consttnl Rights 133-135
*Consttnl Law (Barrett) 772-773
*Govt and Business 52-55
*Mr. Justice Frankfurter 206-207
Quest 67-68
Reapportionment (McKay) 171-172
*Sex Discrimination 1975 76-78

2095. Roth v. United States   June 24, 1957 354 U.S. 476
Alberts v. United States
*Affair 36-39
Am Consttn (Kelly) 967-968
*Am Consttn (Lockhart) 711-718
*Am Consttnl Issues 272-278
*Am Consttnl Law (Bartholomew) v. 2, 87-89
*Am Consttnl Law (Saye) 316-318
*Bill (Konvitz) 398-410
CQ Guide 428
*Cases Consttnl Law (Gunther) 1346-1350
*Cases Consttnl Law (Rosenblum) 291-299
*Cases Consttnl Rights 559-566
*Cases Individual 881-888
Censorship 21-30

System 471-474
*Warren (Spaeth) 158-163
PERIODICALS:
"Obscenity and the Supreme Court," G. Robert Blakey. America
115: 152-156 Aug 13 '66 (4).
"Obscenity: historical and behavioral perspectives," W. Barnett
Pearce and Dwight L. Teeter, Jr. Intellect 104: 166-170
Nov '75. Reaction: S. W. Briggs. 104: 480 Apr '76 (2).
"Pornographic and the obscene in legal and aesthetic contexts,"
E. F. Kaelin. J Aesthetic Eductn 4: 69-84 July '70 (2).
"What every teacher should know about the Supreme Court obscen-
ity decisions," Thomas L. Tedford. English J 63: 20-21
Oct '74 (2). Condensed in: Eductn Dig 40: 41-43 Jan '75.

2096. Wilson v. Girard   July 11, 1957 354 U.S. 524
       Am Consttn (Kelly) 823

2097. Ringhiser v. Chesapeake and Ohio   June 10, 1957 354 U.S. 901
       Railway Co.
       *Cases Workmen 44-46

2098. Alcorta v. Texas   Nov 12, 1957 355 U.S. 28
       *Consttn (Mendelson) 315-316

2099. Conley v. Gibson   Nov 18, 1957 355 U.S. 41
       *Cases Labor (Handler) 696-698
       *Cases Civil Procedure 490-493
       Equality (Borger) 143-144
       *Law Sup Ct 601-611

2100. Schaffer Transportation Co. v. United Dec 9, 1957 355 U.S. 83
       States and Interstate Commerce
       Commission
       *Cases Regulated 539-543
       *Free Enterprise 367-372
       *Govt and Business 116-117

2101. Benanti v. United States   Dec 9, 1957 355 U.S. 96
       *Am Consttnl Law (Bartholomew) v. 2, 134
       *Police 156-157
       Search and Seizure 214-215

2102. Rathbun v. United States   Dec 9, 1957 355 U.S. 107
       *Police 154-156
       Search and Seizure 216

2103. Rowoldt v. Perfetto   Dec 9, 1957 355 U.S. 115
       This Honorable Court 401-402

2104. Youngdahl v. Rainfair   Dec 9, 1957 355 U.S. 131
       *Am Consttnl Law (Bartholomew) v. 2, 114-115
       Law and Politics 89-90

2105. American Trucking Association v.   Dec 9, 1957 355 U.S. 141
       United States
       Railway Labor Executives' Association
       v. United States
       *Cases Regulated 731-734

318   U.S. Supreme Court Decisions

2106. Moore v. Michigan   Dec 9, 1957   355 U.S. 155
      *Consttnl Law (Klein) 507-511

2107. Green v. United States   Dec 16, 1957   355 U.S. 184
      *Civil Rights (Abernathy) 1977 214-216
      *Consttn (Mendelson) 370-373
      *Criminal Law (Kadish) 1411-1415
      Death 47-89
      Defendants 381
      Double (Sigler) 72
      Felix Frankfurter (Thomas) 179
      Justice Frankfurter 162-164
      *Mr. Justice Frankfurter 133-139

2108. McGee v. International Life Insurance Dec 16, 1957   355 U.S. 220
      Co.
      *Cases Civil Procedure 398-401
      *Elements Civil 285-286
      *Govt and Business 79-80

2109. Lambert v. California   Dec 16, 1957   355 U.S. 225
      *Cases Criml Law (Hall) 540-544
      *Cases Criml Law (Perkins) 598-601
      *Criminal Law (Dix) 267-271
      *Criminal Law (Kadish) 117-120
      *Due Process 19-20
      *Mr. Justice Frankfurter 180-181
      Sup Ct Review 1962 127-136
      *US Prison Law v. 5, 539-546

2110. United States v. Sharpnack   Jan 13, 1958   355 U.S. 286
      *Am Consttnl Issues 88-92
      *Cases Criml Law (Inbau) 58-61
      *Contemporary Law 227-229

2111. Staub v. Baxley   Jan 13, 1958   355 U.S. 313
      *Am Consttnl Law (Bartholomew) v. 2, 107-108
      *Bill (Konvitz) 189-191
      Communication (Hemmer) v. 1, 70-71
      *First Amendment (Konvitz) 163-166
      *Govt and Business 85
      *Justices (Friedman) v. 4, 2905-2910
      *Law Sup Ct 34-41

2112. Federal Trade Commission v. Standard Jan 27, 1958   355 U.S. 396
      Oil of Indiana
      *Selected Antitrust Cases 266-270

2113. Moog Industries v. Federal Trade   Jan 27, 1958   355 U.S. 411
      Commission
      Federal Trade Commission v. C. E.
      Nichoff and Co.
      *Introduction (Mashaw) 887-888

2114. Kernan v. American Dredging Co.   Feb 3, 1958   355 U.S. 426
      *Cases Admiralty 342-345
      *Cases Employment 29-34
      *Cases Workmen 49-53
      *Materials Law 506-520

2115. United States and Borg-Warner   Mar 3, 1958   355 U.S. 466
           Corporation v. Detroit
       *Consttnl Law (Kauper) 473-475
       *Govt and Business 333-335

2116. City of Detroit v. Murray Corpora-   Mar 3, 1958   355 U.S. 489
           tion of America
       *Am Consttnl Law (Bartholomew) v. 1, 177-178
       *Consttnl Law (Freund) 635-637
       *Contemporary Law 243-247

2117. Public Utilities Commission of Cal-   Mar 3, 1958   355 U.S. 534
           ifornia v. United States
       *Contemporary Law 253-255

2118. Harmon v. Brucker   Mar 3, 1958   355 U.S. 579
       Abramowitz v. Brucker
           This Honorable Court 399-400

2119. Northern Pacific Railway Co. v.   Mar 10, 1958   356 U.S. 1
           United States
       *Antitrust (Posner) 637-641
       *Antitrust Analysis 594-599
       *Cases Antitrust Law 625-633
       *Cases Trade 140-141, 599-604
       *Competition 330-333
       *Govt and Business 174-176
       *Govt Regulation 1324-1335
       *Modern Business 1018-1020
       *Selected Antitrust Cases 287-290
       *Text Antitrust 118-122

2120. Perez v. Brownell   Mar 31, 1958   356 U.S. 44
       *Annals v. 17, 499-500
        CQ Guide 145
       *Civil Liberties (Sweet) 327-329
       *Consttn (Mendelson) 172-175
       *Consttnl Cases 350-362
        Justice Rutledge 279-283
        Modern Sup Ct 211-215
       *Sup Ct and Public Policy 132-145
        Sup Ct Review 1963 341-342

2121. Trop v. Dulles   Mar 31, 1958   356 U.S. 86
       *Am Consttnl Issues 446-451
        CQ Guide 145
        Congress 186-187
       *Consttn (Mendelson) 175-176
       *Consttnl Politics 192-199
        Cruel 178-179
        Defendants 300
       *Due Process 162-163
        Felix Frankfurter (Thomas) 279-280
        Mr. Justice Frankfurter 8
        Modern Sup Ct 211-215
       *One Man's Stand 314-315
       *Public Papers 273-286
        Sup Ct Review 1963 342-343
        Sup Ct Review 1972 7-8
       *US Prison Law v. 5, 504-525

2122. Nishikawa v. Dulles   Mar 31, 1958 356 U. S. 129
       Modern Sup Ct 211
       Sup Ct Review 1963 340-341

2123. Brown v. United States   Mar 31, 1958 356 U. S. 148
       Justice Frankfurter 171-172
       Modern Sup Ct 198

2124. Green and Winston v. United States Mar 31, 1958 356 U. S. 165
       *Am Consttnl Issues 47-52
       Felix Frankfurter (Thomas) 179-180
       Justice Frankfurter 178-180
       Justice Hugo Black 118

2125. United States v. F & M Schaeffer   Apr 7, 1958   356 U. S. 227
       Brewing Co.
       *Civil Procedure (Cound) 1000-1003

2126. Grimes v. Raymond Concrete Pile   Apr 7, 1958   356 U. S. 252
       *Cases Admiralty 332-334

2127. National Labor Relations Board v. May 5, 1958   356 U. S. 342
       Wooster Division of Borg-
       Warner Corporation
       Basic Text 496-498
       *Cases Labor (Cox) 469-475
       *Cases Labor (Handler) 294-298
       *Cases Labor (Leslie) 382-384
       *Cases Labor (Oberer) 573-579
       *Labor Law (Herman) 260-266
       *Labor Law (Meltzer) 644-649
       *Labor Relations (Group Trust) 440-446
       *Nature 1124-1127
       *Practice 515-517

2128. Sherman v. United States   May 19, 1958 356 U. S. 369
       *Basic Criminal 478-484
       *Criminal Law (Dix) 666-675
       *Criminal Law (Kadish) 1081-1087
       *Criminal Law (Young) 280-285

2129. United States v. Cores   May 19, 1958 356 U. S. 405
       *Cases Criml Law (Perkins) 779-783

2130. Hoag v. New Jersey   May 19, 1958 356 U. S. 464
       Double (Miller) 6-8
       Double (Sigler) 52-53

2131. Federal Maritime Board v. Isbrandt- May 19, 1958 356 U. S. 481
       sen Co.
       Japan-Atlantic and Gulf Freight Con-
       ference v. United States
       *Free Enterprise 591-601

2132. Byrd v. Blue Ridge Rural Electric May 19, 1958 356 U. S. 525
       Cooperative
       *Cases Civil Procedure 292-299
       *Cases Federal Courts 600-604
       *Cases Pleading 415-420

        *Civil Procedure (Cound) 289-293
        *Elements Civil 874-876
        Justices Black and Frankfurter 83-85

2133. Payne v. Arkansas   May 19, 1958 356 U.S. 560
        *Police 96-97
        Sup Ct and Confessions 115-116

2134. Ciucci v. Illinois   May 19, 1958 356 U.S. 571
        *Consttn (Mendelson) 373-374
        Double (Miller) 8
        Double (Sigler) 53-54

2135. Eubanks v. Louisiana   May 26, 1958 356 U.S. 584
        Petitioners 287-288

2136. Kovacs v. Brewer   May 26, 1958 356 U.S. 604
        Sup Ct Review 1964 114-115

2137. International Association of Machinists May 26, 1958 356 U.S. 617
        v. Gonzales
        *Cases Labor (Cox) 1189-1192
        *Cases Labor (Handler) 242-244
        Felix Frankfurter (Mendelson) 182
        *Labor Law (Meltzer) 607-609

2138. International Union, United Automobile, May 26, 1958 356 U.S. 634
        Aircraft and Agricultural Imple-
        ment Workers v. Russell
        *Cases Labor (Handler) 238-242
        Law and Politics 87

2139. United States v. Procter and Gamble June 2, 1958 356 U.S. 677
        Co.
        *Cases Trade 1216-1220

2140. Chicago v. Atchison, Topeka and June 16, 1958 357 U.S. 77
        Santa Fe Railway
        Sup Ct and Commerce 288-289

2141. Local 1976, United Brotherhood of June 16, 1958 357 U.S. 93
        Carpenters and Joiners of America
        v. National Labor Relations Board
        National Labor Relations Board v. Gen-
        eral Drivers Union
        International Association of Machinists
        v. National Labor Relations Board
        *Labor Law (Herman) 294-298
        *Labor Relations (Group Trust) 317-327
        Law and Politics 105-106

2142. Kent v. Dulles   June 16, 1958 357 U.S. 116
        Am Consttn (Kelly) 917
        *Am Consttnl Law (Saye) 107-110
        Communication (Hemmer) v. 1, 246-247
        Congress versus 86-89
        Consttn (Barber) 97-98
        *Due Process 207
        *Freedom and Protection 122-123

*Freedom vs National Security 495-500
Justice Frankfurter 132-133
Least Dangerous 164-165
Modern Sup Ct 202-204
*Political Rights 919-923
System 198
This Honorable Court 400

2143. United States v. Central Eureka   June 16, 1958 357 U. S. 155
        Mining Co.
       *Consttnl Law (Freund) 1100-1102
       *Govt and Business 408-409
       *Social Forces 130-131
        Sup Ct Review 1962 77-79

2144. Societe Internationale pour Participa-   June 16, 1958 357 U. S. 197
        tions Industrielles et Commerciales,
        S. A. v. Rogers
       *Cases Civil Procedure 651-656
       *Elements Civil 837-840
       *Evolution 204-208

2145. Hanson v. Denckla   June 23, 1958 357 U. S. 235
        Lewis v. Hanson
       *Cases Civil Procedure 401-405
       *Cases Pleading 224-240
       *Elements Civil 358-360
        Sup Ct Review 1965 243-244

2146. McKinney v. Missouri-Kansas-Texas   June 23, 1958 357 U. S. 265
        Railroad Co.
       *Materials Law 417-421

2147. Miller v. United States   June 23, 1958 357 U. S. 301
       *Principles Arrest 412-416

2148. Wiener v. United States   June 30, 1958 357 U. S. 349
       *Am Consttnl Issues 173-176
       *Am Consttnl Law (Saye) 115-118
        CQ Guide 215-216
       *Cases Consttnl Law (Cushman) 109-111
       *Cases Consttnl Law (Rosenblum) 361-364
       *Consttn (Mendelson) 67-70
       *Contemporary Law 445-447
       *Mr. Justice Frankfurter 54-56
       *Text Administrative Law 101-103

2149. National Labor Relations Board v.   June 30, 1958 357 U. S. 357
        United Steelworkers of America
        and Nutone, Inc.
        National Labor Relations Board v.
        Avondale Mills
       *Cases Labor (Cox) 161-166
       *Cases Labor (Leslie) 123-126
       *Labor Law (Meltzer) 134-137

2150. Knapp v. Schweitzer   June 30, 1958 357 U. S. 371
       *Mr. Justice Frankfurter 176-180
       *Teaching Materials 15-17

2151.   Gore v. United States   June 30, 1958 357 U.S. 386
        *Criminal Law (Kadish) 1450-1453
        Justice Frankfurter 164
        *Mr. Justice Frankfurter 139-140

2152.   Beilan v. Board of Public Education June 30, 1958 357 U.S. 399
        of Philadelphia
        Am Consttn (Kelly) 922-923
        Communication (Hemmer) v. 1, 116-117
        Congress 189-192
        Congress versus 112-114
        Digest 54-55
        *Douglas 350-354
        *Education (Hazard) 435-439
        Education (Lapati) 238-239
        *Judicial Excerpts 177-179
        Justice Frankfurter 141-144
        *Justices (Friedman) v. 4, 2632-2636
        Landmark Decisions 105-110
        Modern Sup Ct 199-200
        *Public School Law 52-56
        School in the Legal Structure 71
        *School Law (Alexander) 559-562
        *School Law (Remmlein) 69-71
        *Sup Ct and Education 181-188
        System 231
        This Honorable Court 407-408
        Warren (Hudgins) 125-127

2153.   Crooker v. California   June 30, 1958 357 U.S. 433
        Death 167-257
        *Police 95-96
        Sup Ct and Confessions 116

2154.   National Association for the Advance- June 30, 1958 357 U.S. 449
        ment of Colored People v. Alabama
        ex rel. Patterson
        *Am Consttnl Law (Mason) 574-577
        *Am Consttnl Law (Saye) 365-368
        *Am Consttnl Law (Shapiro) 424-426
        *Bill (Cohen) 221-224
        *Bill (Konvitz) 191-197
        CQ Guide 402
        *Cases Consttnl Law (Gunther) 1455-1457
        *Cases Individual 989-991
        *Civil Liberties (Barker) 161-165
        *Civil Liberties (Sweet) 183-188
        Communication (Hemmer) v. 1, 60-61
        *Consttn (Mendelson) 447-449
        *Consttnl Law (Barrett) 1166 1168
        *Consttnl Law (Freund) 1235-1239
        *Consttnl Law (Kauper) 1106-1109
        Consttnl Right (Fellman) 64-66
        *Courts Judges 366-367
        Decade 39
        Desegregation (Wasby) 181-183
        *Documents History v. 2, 630-632
        Equality (Berger) 116-117
        *Evolution 135-139

Rupp v. Dickson
*Mr. Justice Frankfurter 167-168

2161. Cooper v. Aaron   Aug 28, 1958   358 U.S. 1
     Am Consttn (Kelly) 866-867
     Basic History 75-76
     *Basic History 159-161
     *Bill (Konvitz) 4-15
     CQ Guide 597
     *Civil Rights (Bardolph) 433-434
     *Civil Rights (Blaustein) 458-467
     *Comparative 183-185
     *Consttn (Mendelson) 527-530
     *Consttn (Pollak) v. 2, 274-279
     *Consttnl Decisions 53-62
     Consttnl Law (Barrett) 823-824
     *Consttnl Law (Felkenes) 188-191
     *Consttnl Law (Grossman) 121-125, 452-457
     *Consttnl Law (Kauper) 722-725
     *Consttnl Politics 503-510
     Court and Consttn v. 2, 229-230
     Decade 63-64
     Digest 82
     Disaster 39-40
     *Discrimination 180-187
     Dissent 326-327
     *Documents History v. 2, 633-636
     Education (Lapati) 281 282
     Equality (Berger) 139
     Expanding Liberties 281-282
     *Federal System 283-285
     Felix Frankfurter (Baker) 322 324
     From Brown 88-95
     Hugo Black (Dunne) 349-350
     *Integration 71-87
     *Judicial Excerpts 29-31
     Landmark Decisions 97-103
     *Law and Public Education (Hamilton) 542-552
     *Law Lawyers 242-253
     *Liberty v. 2, 600-601
     Memoirs 298-299
     Petitioners 356-358
     *Political Rights v. 2, 1257-1264
     Private Pressure 101-105
     *Public Papers 150-166
     *Public School Law 649-658
     *Racial Equality 61-62
     School in the Legal Structure 60-61
     *School Law (Remmlein) 210-215
     *Struggle 89-92
     *Sup Ct and Consttn 515-521
     *Sup Ct and Education 144-155
     Sup Ct in Free Society 264-265
     Sup Ct on Trial 78-79
     *These Liberties 114-122
     This Honorable Court 412-413
     Warren (Hudgins) 83-85
     *Warren (Spaeth) 124-127

PERIODICALS:
"Impact of Little Rock," James W. Vander Zanden.   J Eductnl
Sociology 35: 381-384 Apr '62.

2162. Moore v. Terminal Railroad Asso-   Oct 13, 1958   358 U.S. 31
        ciation of St. Louis
        Justices Black and Frankfurter 26-28

2163. Peurifoy v. Commissioner of Internal   Nov 10, 1958   358 U.S. 59
        Revenue
        Law and Politics 159-160
        PERIODICALS:
        "Tax expertise v. administrative law precedents," Michael Kamin-
        sky. Taxes 38: 283-292 Apr '60 (3).

2164. Hawkins v. United States   Nov 24, 1958   358 U.S. 74
        *Family 354-356

2165. Hotel Employees Local No. 255,   Nov 24, 1958   358 U.S. 99
        Hotel and Restaurant Employees
        and Bartenders International Union
        v. Leedom
        *Cases Labor (Handler) 170

2166. Shuttlesworth v. Birmingham Board of Nov 24, 1958   358 U.S. 101
        Education
        Disaster 40-41

2167. Leedom v. Kyne   Dec 15, 1958   358 U.S. 184
        *Cases Labor (Cox) 375-383
        *Cases Labor (Handler) 160-164
        *Cases Labor (Oberer) 230-233
        *Labor Law (Meltzer) 329-335
        *Labor Relations (Group Trust) 193-201

2168. Evers v. Dwyer   Dec 15, 1958   358 U.S. 202
        *Materials Consttnl Law 190-191
        Petitioners 372

2169. Mitchell v. Lublin, McGaughy and   Jan 12, 1959   358 U.S. 207
        Associates
        Sup Ct and Commerce 135

2170. Williams v. Lee   Jan 12, 1959   358 U.S. 217
        *Am Indian v. 4, 2785-2787
        *Law Indian 184-187

2171. Lee v. Madigan   Jan 12, 1959   358 U.S. 228
        *Douglas 256-259

2172. International Boxing Club of New   Jan 12, 1959   358 U.S. 242
        York v. United States
        *Govt Regulation 1389-1404

2173. Local 24, International Brotherhood   Jan 19, 1959   358 U.S. 283
        of Teamsters, Chauffeurs and
        Helpers of America v. Oliver
        *Cases Labor (Cox) 1193-1199
        *Cases Labor (Handler) 220-223

*Govt and Business 274-276
*Labor Law (Meltzer) 602-606
*Social Forces 49-52

2174. Draper v. United States   Jan 26, 1959   358 U.S. 307
       Arrest (Waddington) 96-97
       *Cases Criml Justice 55-62
       *Consttnl Criml Procedure (Scarboro) 135-143
       Criminal Evidence 235-236
       Law of Arrest (Markle) 27-30
       *Leading Consttnl Cases 81-84
       *Principles Arrest 471-474
       *Sup Ct and Criml Process 168-170
       Sup Ct Review 1960 68-69
       *Teaching Materials 142-146

2175. United States v. Radio Corporation   Feb 24, 1959   358 U.S. 334
       of America
       *Cases Electronic 139-145

2176. Romero v. International Terminal   Feb 24, 1959   358 U.S. 354
       Operating Co.
       *Cases Admiralty 124-131
       *Federal Courts 897-904

2177. Railway Express Agency v. Virginia   Feb 24, 1959   358 U.S. 434
       *Consttnl Law (Freund) 534-538

2178. Northwestern States Portland Co. v.   Feb 24, 1959   358 U.S. 450
       Minnesota
       Williams v. Stockham Valves and
       Fittings, Inc.
       *Am Consttn (Lockhart) 320-323
       *Consttnl Law (Barrett) 403-405
       *Consttnl Law (Freund) 555-560
       *Consttnl Law (Kauper) 414-420
       *Contemporary Law 273-277
       *Govt and Business 292-294
       Sup Ct and Commerce 327-329
       Sup Ct in Free Society 120
       *Warren (Spaeth) 51-55

2179. Cammarano v. United States   Feb 24, 1959   358 U.S. 498
       F. Strauss & Son, Inc. v. Commis-
           sioner of Internal Revenue
       Advertising 20
       Law and Politics 154-155
       Law of Mass 560-562
       *Sup Ct on Freedom 286-287
       PERIODICALS:
       See listing at 358 U.S. 59, entry no. 2163.

2180. Kelly v. Kosuga   Feb 24, 1959   358 U.S. 516
       *Govt Regulation 1405-1408
       Law and Politics 286

2181. Allied Stores of Ohio v. Bowers   Feb 24, 1959   358 U.S. 522
       *Am Consttnl Law (Bartholomew) v. 2, 288-289

2182. Youngstown Sheet and Tube Co. v.   Feb 24, 1959   358 U. S. 534
       Bowers
       United States Plywood Corporation v.
       Algoma
       *Am Consttn (Lockhart) 291-294
       *Contemporary Law 283-288
       *Mr. Justice Frankfurter 216-221

2183. Kermarec v. Compagnie Generale   Feb 24, 1959   358 U. S. 625
       Transatlantique
       *Cases Admiralty 198-201

2184. New York v. O'Neill   Mar 2, 1959   359 U. S. 1
       *Am Consttnl Law (Bartholomew) v. 2, 204-206

2185. United States v. Embassy Restaurant Mar 9, 1959   359 U. S. 29
       *Cases Labor (Handler) 568-571
       *Materials Law 600-605

2186. Bartkus v. Illinois   Mar 30, 1959   359 U. S. 121
       *Affair 242-247
       *Am Consttnl Issues 393-399
       *Am Consttnl Law (Bartholomew) v. 2, 161-163
       *Civil Rights (Abernathy) 1977 224-226
       *Criminal Law (Kadish) 1388-1391
       Defendants 366
       *Freedom and Protection 73-77
       *Mr. Justice Frankfurter 173-176
       *One Man's Stand 320-328
       *Warren (Spaeth) 316-323
       PERIODICALS:
       "Recent Supreme Court decisions; double jeopardy," Isidore Starr.
       Social Eductn 25: 185-188 Apr '61 (3).

2187. Abbate v. United States   Mar 30, 1959   359 U. S. 187
       *Criminal Law (Kadish) 1391-1393
       Defendants 367
       Double (Miller) 83-96
       PERIODICALS:
       See listing at 359 U. S. 121, entry no. 2186.

2188. Klors, Inc. v. Broadway-Hale Stores, Apr 6, 1959   359 U. S. 207
       Inc.
       *Antitrust (Posner) 540-541
       *Antitrust Analysis 394-396
       *Cases Antitrust Law 448-451
       *Cases Trade 286-289
       *Govt Regulation 1409-1414
       Hugo Black (Strickland) 206-207
       Law and Politics 287-289
       *Modern Business 1015-1016
       Professional Sports 462
       *Text Antitrust 92-94

2189. San Diego Building Trades Council   Apr 20, 1959   359 U. S. 236
       v. Garmon
       *Cases Labor (Cox) 1175-1184
       *Cases Labor (Handler) 244-251
       *Cases Labor (Leslie) 595-598

  *Cases Labor (Oberer) 358-366
  *Labor Law (Meltzer) 609-617
  *Labor Law (Twomey) 110-111
  Law and Politics 88-89, 92-94
  Sup Ct and Labor 62-63
  Warren (Spaeth) 68-71

2190. Melrose Distillers v. United States Apr 20, 1959 359 U.S. 271
  Law and Politics 285-286

2191. Herd and Co. v. Krawill Machinery Apr 20, 1959 359 U.S. 297
  Corporation
  *Cases Admiralty 508-512

2192. Frank v. Maryland May 4, 1959 359 U.S. 360
  *Am Consttnl Issues 376-382
  *Consttn (Mendelson) 331-334
  Criminal Law (Felkenes) 80-82
  Defendants 272
  Felix Frankfurter (Thomas) 166
  *Freedom and Protection 66-68
  Search and Seizure 248-253
  *Sup Ct (Mendelson) 225-232
  Sup Ct Review 1967 4-8

2193. Irvin v. Dowd May 4, 1959 359 U.S. 394
  *Mr. Justice Frankfurter 21-22

2194. Arroyo v. United States May 4, 1959 359 U.S. 419
  *Labor Law (Meltzer) 1187-1191

2195. TIME, Inc. v. United States May 18, 1959 359 U.S. 464
  Davidson Transfer and Storage Co.
   v. United States
  *Introduction (Blaustein) 1043-1051

2196. Beacon Theatres v. Westover May 25, 1959 359 U.S. 500
  *Cases Civil Procedure 681-691
  *Cases Equity 863-868
  *Civil Procedure (Carrington) 189-194
  *Civil Procedure (Cound) 782-787

2197. Bibb v. Navajo Freight Lines, Inc. May 25, 1959 359 U.S. 520
  *Am Consttn (Lockhart) 254-256
  *Cases Consttnl Law (Gunther) 286-290
  *Consttnl Law (Barrett) 307-311
  *Consttnl Law (Lockhart) 298-301
  *Contemporary Law 140-142
  *Federal System 338-341
  *Processes 232-233
  Sup Ct (Forte) 47-48
  Sup Ct and Commerce 265-266

2198. Vitarelli v. Seaton June 1, 1959 359 U.S. 535
  *Am Consttnl Law (Shapiro) 695-698
  Congress 232
  *Evolution 208-215
  *First Amendment (Konvitz) 585-590
  *Third Branch 225-229

2199. Louisiana Power and Light Co.   June 8, 1959   360 U.S. 25
            v. Thibodaux City
       *Cases Federal Courts 476-487
       *Consttnl Law (Schmidhauser) 148-149

2200. Lassiter v. Northampton County Board   June 8, 1959   360 U.S. 45
            of Elections
       *Consttn (Mendelson) 604-605
       Sup Ct and Electoral Process 75
       Sup Ct Review 1969 385-389

2201. Federal Trade Commission v. Sim-   June 8, 1959   360 U.S. 55
            plicity Pattern Co.
       *Antitrust Analysis 930-934
       *Cases Antitrust Law 1188-1194
       *Cases Trade 1091-1097
       *Free Enterprise 908-914
       *Govt Regulation 1415-1425

2202. Uphaus v. Wyman   June 8, 1959   360 U.S. 72
       *Affair 102-112
       Am Consttn (Kelly) 931
       Cases Consttnl Law (Gunther) 1493-1495
       Communication (Hemmer) v. 1, 215-216
       Congress 231
       Congress versus 53-57
       *Consttn (Mendelson) 443-446
       Consttnl Right (Fellman) 58-59
       Dissent 281-282
       *Documents History v. 2, 637-642
       Expanding Liberties 74-77, 82-85
       *First Amendment (Konvitz) 682-699
       Free Speech (Kurland) 70-71
       *Freedom and Protection 112-115
       Freedom of Speech (Hudon) 138-139
       *Readings American 68-74
       *Rights (Shattuck) 52-53
       Sup Ct Review 1961 121
       System 153, 263-264
       This Honorable Court 408-409
       *Warren (Spaeth) 256-259

2203. Barenblatt v. United States   June 8, 1959   360 U.S. 109
       Am Consttn (Kelly) 930-931
       *Am Consttn (Lockhart) 656-660
       *Am Consttnl Issues 96-102
       *Am Consttnl Law (Bartholomew) v. 1, 81-82
       *Am Consttnl Law (Mason) 98-102
       *Am Consttnl Law (Saye) 369-372
       *Am Consttnl Law (Shapiro) 369-375
       CQ Guide 161-162
       *Cases Consttnl Law (Cushman) 57-62
       *Cases Consttnl Law (Gunther) 1490-1493
       *Cases Consttnl Law (Rosenblum) 376-385
       *Cases Consttnl Rights 475-479
       *Cases Individual 1024-1027
       *Civil Liberties (Sweet) 161-168
       Communication (Hemmer) v. 1, 213-214
       *Comparative 121-125

Congress 229-230
Congress versus 48-53
*Consttn (Mendelson) 438-443
*Consttnl Cases 52-66
*Consttnl Decisions 64-73
*Consttnl Law (Barrett) 1180-1185
*Consttnl Law (Freund) 1317-1321
*Consttnl Law (Kauper) 1111-1115
*Consttnl Law (Lockhart) 812-816
*Contemporary Law 348-353
*Courts Judges 596-601
Decade 33, 35
*Documents History v. 2, 642-647
Education (Lapati) 239-240
*Evolution 147-153
Expanding Liberties 94-96
*Federal System 263-267
Felix Frankfurter (Mendelson) 137-139
*First Amendment (Konvitz) 641-667
*Freedom and Protection 100-102
Freedom of Speech (Haiman) 39
Freedom of Speech (Hudon) 139-141
Hugo Black (Strickland) 115-116
*Justices (Friedman) v. 3, 2356-2370
Law and Politics 64-66
*Leading Consttnl Decisions 30-43
*Materials Legislation 439-450, 479-485
Modern Sup Ct 224-225
*One Man's Stand 329-354
*Political Rights 372-386
Politics 70-72
*Rights (Shattuck) 53-54
*Sup Ct and Am Govt 99-114
*Sup Ct and Consttn 463-466
*Sup Ct and Education 220-229
*Sup Ct on Freedom 35-37
System 261-263, 603-604
This Honorable Court 408
Warren (Hudgins) 127-129
*Warren (Spaeth) 245-256

2204.   Harrison v. National Association   June 8, 1959   360 U.S. 167
           for the Advancement of Colored
           People
        *Consttnl Law (Schmidhauser) 150-157
        *Contemporary Law 222-224
         Negro (Kalven) 76-77
         Petitioners 384-387
         Private Pressure 108-109

2205.   National Labor Relations Board v.   June 8, 1959   360 U.S. 203
           Cabot Carbon Co.
        *Cases Labor (Handler) 74-77
        *Labor Relations (Getman) 124-126

2206.   National Association for the Advance-   June 8, 1959   360 U.S. 240
           ment of Colored People v. Alabama
           ex rel. Patterson

National Association for the Advance-
ment of Colored People v.
Livingston
*Courts Judges 367-369
Petitioners 379

2207. Ohio ex rel. Eaton v. Price   June 8, 1959   360 U.S. 246
       *Affair 343-346
       *Contemporary Law 16-18
       Search and Seizure 253-254
       *Sup Ct and Criml Process 31-32

2208. Burns v. Ohio   June 15, 1959   360 U.S. 252
       *Mr. Justice Frankfurter 22-24

2209. Napue v. Illinois   June 15, 1959   360 U.S. 264
       *Criminal Justice (Kaplan) 268-270
       Criminal Procedure (Wells) 16-17
       *Due Process 136

2210. Marshall v. United States   June 15, 1959   360 U.S. 310
       Communication (Hemmer) v. 2, 177

2211. Spano v. New York   June 22, 1959   360 U.S. 315
       *Consttnl Criml Procedure (Scarboro) 516-521
       Criminal Law (Felkenes) 218-220
       *Criminal Law (Kadish) 981-983
       Decade 168
       *Due Process 59
       *Leading Consttnl Cases 474-479
       Police 97-99

2212. Palermo v. United States   June 22, 1959   360 U.S. 343
       Congress 235

2213. Greene v. McElroy   June 29, 1959   360 U.S. 474
       Am Consttn (Kelly) 919-920
       CQ Guide 510
       Congress 232-234
       Congress versus 104-106
       Court and Consttn v. 2, 251-252
       *Due Process 242-243
       *Freedom vs National Security 525-534
       Least Dangerous 166
       *Political Rights 307-312
       *Public Papers 287-306
       *Rights (Shattuck) 151-152
       Warren (Lytle) 34-35

2214. Farmers Educational and Cooperative   June 29, 1959   360 U.S. 525
       Union v. WDAY, Inc.
       Communication (Hemmer) v. 2, 29-31, 301-303
       *Consttnl Cases 312-324
       Law of Mass 80-81
       *Mass Communications 283-285, 794-795
       *Sup Ct on Freedom 258-259

2215. Barr v. Matteo   June 29, 1959   360 U.S. 564
       *Admin Law (Gellhorn) 1078-1082

*Admin Law (Schwartz) 642-646
Communication (Hemmer) v. 2, 27-28
*Consttnl Law (Freund) 673-677
*Introduction (Mashaw) 706-713
Mass Media 72
System 704-705

2216. Kingsley International Pictures   June 29, 1959 360 U.S. 684
      Corporation v. Regents of the
      University of the State of New York
   "Lady Chatterley's Lover Case"
      Am Consttn (Kelly) 968
      *Am Consttnl Issues 280-286
      *Am Consttnl Law (Bartholomew) v. 2, 92-93
      *Bill (Cohen) 120-121
      *Bill (Konvitz) 457-459
      Cases Consttnl Law (Gunther) 1352-1353
      Censorship 181-185
      *Censorship Landmarks 326-333
      Civil Liberties (Kauper) 70, 79-80
      Communication (Hemmer) v. 1, 186
      *Consttn (Mendelson) 503-507
      Consttnl Counterrevolution 267-268
      *Consttnl Law (Freund) 1284-1285
      Expanding Liberties 194-195
      Federal Censorship 153-154
      *First Amendment (Konvitz) 869-881
      *Freedom of Speech (Haiman) 120
      Freedom of Speech (Hudon) 151-153
      Law of Obscenity 40-41, 157-158
      *Mass Media (Devol) 168-172
      Mass Media (Devol) 192-193; reprinted from "Morals and the Con-
         stitution; the sin of obscenity," Louis Henkin. Columbia Law R
         63: 391 Mar '63.
      *Mr. Justice Frankfurter 88-90
      Movies 96-100
      *Obscenity (Bosmajian) 164-171
      Obscenity (Clor) 44-51
      *Obscenity (Friedman) 87-88
      Obscenity (Sunderland) 51-52
      *One Man's Stand 355-358
      *Pornography 69-82
      *Sup Ct on Freedom 227-231
      Sup Ct Review 1960 28-34
      System 474-475

2217. United Steelworkers of America v.   Nov 7, 1959   361 U.S. 39
      United States
      *Cases Labor (Handler) 599-612
      *Cases Labor (Oberer) 1055-1066
      *Courts, Judges 332-335
      *Labor Law (Herman) 333-335
      *Labor Law (Meltzer) 976-987
      *Labor Relations (Group Trust) 689-699
      Labor Relations (Taylor) 531-533
      *Statutory History Labor 677-679

2218. Commissioner of Internal Revenue   Nov 16, 1959 361 U.S. 87

v. Acker
*Legislative (Hetzel) 210-211

2219. Henry v. United States   Nov 23, 1959   361 U. S. 98
       *Consttn (Mendelson) 293-296
       *Consttnl Criml Procedure (Scarboro) 193-196
       Police 21-22
       Sup Ct Review 1960 59-61
       *Teaching Materials 138-142

2220. Braen v. Pfeifer Oil Transportation Co. Dec 14, 1959   361 U. S. 129
       *Cases Admiralty 334-336

2221. Inman v. Baltimore and Ohio Railroad Dec 14, 1959   361 U. S. 138
       *Materials Law 520-525

2222. Smith v. California   Dec 14, 1959   361 U. S. 147
       *Affair 41-44
       *Cases Criml Law (Hall) 544-547
       *Cases Criml Law (Perkins) 459-460
       *Censorship Landmarks 318-325
       Communication (Hemmer) v. 1, 195
       Consttnl Counterrevolution 268-269
       Federal Censorship 155-156
       *First Amendment (Konvitz) 846-850
       *Law of Obscenity 425-429
       Literature 179
       *Mass Media (Devol) 116-118
       *Mr. Justice Frankfurter 90-93
       *One Man's Stand 359-362
       Sup Ct Review 1960 35-40
       PERIODICALS:
       "But can you do that?" Harriet F. Pilpel. Publishers Weekly
           179: 29-30 Mar 27 '61.

2223. Minneapolis and St. Louis Railway Co. Dec 14, 1959   361 U. S. 173
           v. United States
       South Dakota v. United States
       Minnesota v. United States
       Law and Politics 289-290

2224. Blackburn v. Alabama   Jan 11, 1960   361 U. S. 199
       *Criminal Procedure (Lewis) 360-362
       *Sup Ct and Criml Process 416-418

2225. Kinsella v. United States ex rel.   Jan 18, 1960   361 U. S. 234
           Singleton
       *Cases Criml Law (Inbau) 153-157
       *Justices (Friedman) v. 4, 2910-2918

2226. Mitchell v. Robert De Mario   Jan 18, 1960   361 U. S. 288
           Jewelry, Inc.
       *Cases Employment 757-759

2227. Lewis v. Benedict Coal Corporation   Feb 23, 1960   361 U. S. 459
       United Mine Workers of America v.
           Benedict Coal Corporation
       *Cases Labor (Handler) 562-568

2228. National Labor Relations Board v.   Feb 23, 1960   361 U.S. 477
           Insurance Agents International
           Union
        Basic Text 320
        *Cases Labor (Cox) 415-424
        *Cases Labor (Handler) 280-288
        *Cases Labor (Leslie) 371-372
        *Cases Labor (Oberer) 522-530
        *Labor Law (Meltzer) 700-707
        *Labor Law (Twomey) 226-230
        *Labor Relations (Getman) 166-170
        *Labor Relations (Group Trust) 404-413
        Law and Politics 97-98, 116-117
        *Materials Law 26-33
        *Practice 517-523
        Sup Ct and Labor 80-81
        *Warren (Spaeth) 56-62

2229. Bates v. Little Rock   Feb 23, 1960   361 U.S. 516
           Communication (Hemmer) v. 1, 61-62
        Consttnl Right (Fellman) 66-68
        Desegregation (Wasby) 186-187
        Expanding Liberties 66-67
        *First Amendment (Konvitz) 173-178
        Free Speech (Kurland) 75-76
        *Law Sup Ct 143-146
        Negro (Kalven) 95-97
        *One Man's Stand 363-364
        Petitioners 381-382
        Sup Ct Review 1961 136-127
        System 427-428

2230. Nelson v. Los Angeles   Feb 29, 1960   362 U.S. 1
           Affair 159-163
        Am Consttn (Kelly) 923-924
        Congress 240-241
        Congress versus 114-116
        *Consttn (Mendelson) 453-457
        Sup Ct (Freund) 182

2231. United States v. Raines   Feb 29, 1960   362 U.S. 17
           Black 207-209
        *Federal Courts 193-196
        Mr. Justice Frankfurter 41
        Petitioners 303-304
        *Processes 1256-1258
        Sup Ct and Electoral Process 89-90

2232. United States v. Parke Davis and Co.   Feb 29, 1960   362 U.S. 29
        *Antitrust (Posner) 542-547
        *Antitrust Analysis 555-559
        *Cases Antitrust Law 535-548
        *Cases Trade 424-433
        *Competition 367-370
        *Free Enterprise 965-978
        *Govt Regulation 1456-1472
        Law and Politics 290-296
        *Legal Environment 269-271
        Sup Ct Review 1960 258-326

*Text Antitrust 83-91
*Warren (Spaeth) 36-39

2233.   United States v. Thomas   Feb 29, 1960   362 U. S. 58
        Sup Ct and Electoral Process 90-91

2234.   Talley v. California   Mar 7, 1960   362 U. S. 60
        *Bill (Cohen) 218-220
        *Bill (Konvitz) 271-273
        Communication (Hemmer) v. 1, 218-219
        *First Amendment (Konvitz) 317-323
        Free Speech (Kurland) 134-135
        *Freedom of Speech (Haiman) 194-195
        *Mass Communications 168-170
        Negro (Kalven) 197-198
        *One Man's Stand 365-369
        *Political Rights 458-464
        *Rights (Shattuck) 66-67
        *Sup Ct on Freedom 198-201
        Sup Ct Review 1965 20-21
        System 352
        PERIODICALS:
        "Hidden persuaders." New Republic 142: 7 Mar 21 '60.

2235.   Florida Lime Growers v. Jacobsen   Mar 7, 1960   362 U. S. 73
        Mr. Justice Frankfurter 42-43

2236.   Federal Power Commission v.   Mar 7, 1960   362 U. S. 99
            Tuscarora Indian Nation
        Power Authority of New York v.
            Tuscarora Indian Nation
        *Am Indian v. 4, 2792-2811
        *Law Indian 441-443
        PERIODICALS:
        "Indians lose." Senior Scholastic 76: 18 Mar 23 '60.

2237.   Thompson v. Louisville   Mar 21 '60   362 U. S. 199
        *Bill (Konvitz) 706-709
        *Consttn (Mendelson) 367-369
        *Consttn (Pollak) v. 2, 180-183
        *Consttnl Law (Kauper) 995-997
        Defendants 105-106
        Desegregation (Wasby) 287-288, 298-300
        *Due Process 123
        Expanding Liberties 269-271
        *Federal Courts 610-614
        *Law Sup Ct 233-239
        *One Man's Stand 370-375
        Petitioners 396
        *These Liberties 84-86
        *Warren (Spaeth) 324-328
        PERIODICALS:
        "High court and 'shufflin' Sam, '" Joseph P. Blank. Readers Dig
            79: 94-98 Nov '61.
        "Shufflin' Sam's long step." Time 75: 15 Apr 4 '60.

2238.   Scripto v. Carson   Mar 21, 1960   362 U. S. 207
        *Consttnl Law (Freund) 591-593

*Legal Environment 237-239
Sup Ct and Commerce 330

2239.   Abel v. United States   Mar 28, 1960 362 U.S. 217
        *Admin Law (Schwartz) 152-157
        *Affair 187-190
        Congress 239-240
        Criminal Evidence 327
        *Criminal Procedure (Lewis) 290-291
        Defendants 275-276
        Law of Arrest (Markle) 88-89, 284-285
        Search and Seizure 111-112, 255-258
        Sup Ct Review 1962 242-243

2240.   Jones v. United States   Mar 28, 1960 362 U.S. 257
        *Consttnl Criml Procedure (Scarboro) 403-408
        *Criminal Law (Kadish) 842-843
        *Criminal Procedure (Lewis) 303-306
        Law of Arrest (Markle) 183-186
        *Leading Consttnl Cases 266-270
        Search and Seizure 75
        Self Inflicted Wound 216
        *Sup Ct and Criml Process 350-352
        Sup Ct Review 1960 69-70

2241.   National Labor Relations Board v. Mar 28, 1960 362 U.S. 274
        International Brotherhood of
        Teamsters, Chauffeurs Warehousemen
        and Helpers of America, Local 639
        *Cases Labor (Handler) 87-91
        *Cases Labor (Oberer) 169-174
        *Labor Law (Herman) 314-317
        *Labor Relations (Group Trust) 286-290
        Law and Politics 111
        PERIODICALS:
        "Significant decisions in labor cases." Monthly Labor R   83:
        507-508   May '60.

2242.   Mitchell v. Zachry Co.   Apr 4, 1960   362 U.S. 310
        Sup Ct and Commerce 136-137
        PERIODICALS:
        "Significant decisions in labor cases." Monthly Labor R   83: 623-
        627   June '60 (3).

2243.   Order of Railroad Telegraphers v. Apr 18, 1960 362 U.S. 330
        Chicago and North Western Rail-
        road Co.
        *Cases Labor (Handler) 260-264
        *Labor Law (Meltzer) 649-653
        *Labor Relations (Group Trust) 682-689
        Sup Ct Review 1960 113-157
        PERIODICALS:
        "High court backs strike, picketing." US News   48: 88-89
        May 2 '60.
        "Significant decisions in labor cases." Monthly Labor R   83:
        623-627   June '60 (3).

2244.   Dusky v. United States   Apr 18, 1960 362 U.S. 402

*Cases Criml Justice 931
*Reading Law 635

2245. International Association of Machinists   Apr 25, 1960   362 U. S. 411
       v. National Labor Relations Board
       *Cases Labor (Handler) 81-86
       PERIODICALS:
       "Significant decisions in labor cases. "   Monthly Labor R   83: 729-
       730   July '60.

2246. Huron Portland Cement Co. v. City   Apr 25, 1960   362 U. S. 440
       of Detroit, Michigan
       *Am Consttnl Issues 149-152
       *Consttnl Law (Barrett) 311-314
       *Consttnl Law (Freund) 468-473
       Sup Ct and Commerce 290-294

2247. United States v. Republic Steel Cor-   May 16, 1960   362 U. S. 482
       poration
       *Introduction (Mashaw) 17-28

2248. Wyatt v. United States   May 16, 1960   362 U. S. 525
       Criminal Evidence 164-165
       *Principles Proof 605-610
       *Sex Discrimination 1975 888-890

2249. Mitchell v. Trawler Racer, Inc.   May 16, 1960   362 U. S. 539
       *Cases Admiralty 350-354

2250. United States v. Alabama   May 16, 1960   362 U. S. 602
       Petitioners 305

2251. Local 24, International Brotherhood   May 16, 1960   362 U. S. 605
       of Teamsters, Chauffeurs, Ware-
       housemen and Helpers of America
       v. Oliver
       *Labor Law (Meltzer) 606

2252. Levine v. United States   May 23, 1960   362 U. S. 610
       Justice Hugo Black 118

2253. United States v. Louisiana   May 31, 1960   363 U. S. 1
       PERIODICALS:
       "Offshore oil claims settled. " Bus Wk p. 34   June 4 '60.
       "Supreme court as policy maker: the tidelands oil controversy, "
       Lucius J. Barker.   J Politics 24: 350-366   May '62.
       "Tidelands decision. " Time 75: 24   June 13 '60.

2254. De Veau v. Braisted   June 6, 1960   363 U. S. 144
       *Cases Labor (Handler) 203-210
       *US Prison Law v. 5, 91-112
       PERIODICALS:
       "Significant decisions in labor cases. " Monthly Labor R   83:
       853-856   Aug '60   (4).

2255. Federal Trade Commission v. Henry   June 6, 1960   363 U. S. 166
       Broch and Co.
       *Antitrust (Posner) 788-792
       *Antitrust Analysis 919-925

*Cases Antitrust Law 1173-1184
*Cases Trade 1071-1075
*Free Enterprise 894-904

2256. Kreshik v. St. Nicholas Cathedral of   June 6, 1960   363 U.S. 190
       the Russian Orthodox Church of
       North America
       Religion (Kurland) 91-96

2257. Commissioner of Internal Revenue   June 13, 1960   363 U.S. 278
       v. Duberstein
       Stanton v. United States
       *Cases Pleading 1025-1037
       *Consttnl Law (Freund) 316-321

2258. Hoffman v. Blaski   June 20, 1960   363 U.S. 335
       Sullivan v. Slawson
       *Civil Procedure (Cound) 268-273

2259. Hannah v. Larche   June 20, 1960   363 U.S. 420
       *Desegregation (Wasby) 251-252
       *Douglas 376-380
       *Judicial Excerpts 120-121
       *Mr. Justice Frankfurter 185-190
       Petitioners 305-306
       Sup Ct and Electoral Process 94-95
       Sup Ct on Trial 184-185
       PERIODICALS:
       "Judicial motives." New Republic 143: 8 July 11 '60.

2260. Brotherhood of Locomotive Engineers   June 20, 1960 363 U.S. 528
       v. Missouri-Kansas-Texas Railroad Co.
       PERIODICALS:
       "Significant decisions in labor cases." Monthly Labor R 83: 971-
       973 Sep '60 (2).

2261. Federal Trade Commission v.   June 20, 1960   363 U.S. 536
       Anheuser-Busch, Inc.
       *Cases Antitrust Law 1071-1076
       *Cases Trade 980-986
       *Govt Regulation 1475-1485

2262. United Steelworkers of America v.   June 20, 1960   363 U.S. 564
       American Manufacturing Co.
       *Arbitration 315-320
       Basic Text 551-552
       *Cases Labor (Cox) 614-617
       *Cases Labor (Handler) 338-340
       *Cases Labor (Leslie) 533-535
       *Cases Labor (Oberer) 673 675
       *Collective Bargaining 307-310
       *Labor Law (Meltzer) 799-802
       *Labor Relations (Getman) 335-336
       *Labor Relations (Group Trust) 855-857
       Labor Relations (Taylor) 419-420
       *Materials Law 358-363
       *Practice 526-528
       Sup Ct and Labor 110-112

PERIODICALS:
"Douglas doctrine; more power to arbitrators." Fortune 62: 271-
272 Oct '60 (3).
"Significant decisions in labor cases." Monthly Labor R 83: 853-
856 Aug '60 (4).
"Supreme court looks at arbitration." John J. McKew Mgt Rec
23: 17-22 Apr '61.
"Supreme Court upholds arbitrators," William E. Lissy. Supervision 23: 15 Apr '61.

2263. United Steelworkers of America v.   June 20, 1960 363 U.S. 574
Warrior and Gulf Navigation Co.
*Arbitration 320-329
Basic Text 552-553
*Cases Labor (Cox) 617-625
*Cases Labor (Handler) 340-348
*Cases Labor (Leslie) 535-541
*Cases Labor (Oberer) 675-683
*Collective Bargaining 310-319
*Labor Law (Meltzer) 802-810
*Labor Relations (Getman) 336-338
*Labor Relations (Group Trust) 858-865
Labor Relations (Taylor) 418-419
*Materials Law 347-357
*Practice 528-536
Sup Ct and Labor 112-113
PERIODICALS:
See listing at 363 U. S. 564, entry no. 2262.

2264. United Steelworkers of America v.   June 20, 1960 363 U.S. 593
Enterprise Wheel and Car Corporation
*Arbitration 329-334
Basic Text 555-556
*Cases Labor (Cox) 628-631
*Cases Labor (Handler) 348-353
*Cases Labor (Leslie) 545-548
*Cases Labor (Oberer) 684-687
*Collective Bargaining 339-342
*Labor Law (Meltzer) 811-813
*Labor Relations (Getman) 338-339
*Labor Relations (Group Trust) 867-871
Labor Relations (Taylor) 420
*Practice 536-542
Sup Ct and Labor 113
PERIODICALS:
See listing at 363 U. S. 564, entry no. 2262.

2265. Flemming v. Nestor   June 20, 1960 363 U.S. 603
*Cases Consttnl Law (Gunther) 239-243
*Cases Law and Poverty 51-59
*Cases Property (Donahue) 155-160
Consttnl Law (Barrett) 1223
Court and Consttn v. 2, 207
Dissent 269-270
*Douglas 448-450
*Labor Relations (Group Trust) 593-598
*Political Rights 257-263
*Poverty 549-554
System 193-194

2266. Continental Grain Co. v. The   June 27, 1960 364 U.S. 19
          Barge FBL-585
       *Cases Admiralty 53-58

2267. United States v. Dege   June 27, 1960 364 U.S. 51
       *Cases Consttnl Law (Rosenblum) 288-291
       *Cases Criml Law (Inbau) 851-854
       *Family 365-366
       *Sex Roles 262-266
       *Text Consttnl Aspects 20-24
       *Text Sex Based Discrimination 20-24

2268. United States v. Cannelton Sewer   June 27, 1960 364 U.S. 76
          Pipe Co.
       Law and Politics 164-165

2269. Hertz v. United States   June 27, 1960 364 U.S. 122
       Law and Politics 156-157

2270. Elkins v. United States   June 27, 1960 364 U.S. 206
       Exclusionary 24-26
       *Police 59-60
       Search and Seizure 149-157
       *Teaching Materials 89-91
       PERIODICALS:
       "Silver platter." New Republic 143: 6 July 18 '60.
       "States' evidence." Economist 196: 142 July 9 '60.

2271. Terrones Rios v. United States   June 27, 1960 364 U.S. 253
       Police 32-33
       *Police 60-62
       *Principles Arrest 28-30
       Sup Ct Review 1960 61-63

2272. Ohio ex rel. Eaton v. Price   June 27, 1960 364 U.S. 263
       *Contemporary Law 19
       Search and Seizure 254-255

2273. Gomillion v. Lightfoot   Nov 14, 1960   364 U.S. 339
       CQ Guide 483-484
       *Consttn (Pollak) v. 2, 346-350
       Consttnl Counterrevolution 96
       *Consttnl Law (Freund) 953-956
       Democratic 116-117
       Felix Frankfurter (Mendelson) 143-145
       Gomillion.
       *Gomillion 121-131
       Hugo Black (Dunne) 365-366
       Law and Politics 202-203
       *Law Sup Ct 450-454
       Least Dangerous 210-211
       *Liberty v. 2, 616-617
       *Managing 254-257
       *Mr. Justice Frankfurter 73-74
       Modern Sup Ct 249-251
       Petitioners 301-302
       *Political Rights 973-976
       Political Thicket 51-52
       *Race 158-161

Reapportionment (Baker) 119-120
Rise 83-84
Sup Ct and Electoral Process 83-84, 152-153
Sup Ct Review 1961 194-244
*These Liberties 229-232
PERIODICALS:
"Reporter at large," Bernard Taper. New Yorker 37: 39-40+
    June 17 '61.
"Tuskegee: in or out?" America 104: 284 Nov 26 '60.

2274. Knetsch v. United States   Nov 14, 1960   364 U.S. 361
      Law and Politics 144-145
      Sup Ct Review 1961 135-158

2275. Uphaus v. Wyman   Nov 14, 1960   364 U.S. 388
      *First Amendment (Konvitz) 700-708
      *One Man's Stand 376-384

2276. Boynton v. Virginia   Dec 5, 1960   364 U.S. 454
      Desegregation (Wasby) 288-292
      Modern Sup Ct 248
      Private Pressure 113
      Sup Ct and Commerce 198-200
      PERIODICALS:
      "Limited victory." Time 76: 18-19 Dec 19 '60.

2277. Shelton v. Tucker   Dec 12, 1960   364 U.S. 479
      Carr v. Young
      *Am Consttnl Issues 301-306
      CQ Guide 403
      *Cases Consttnl Law (Gunther) 1459-1462
      *Cases Individual 992-995
      *Cases Labor (Stern) 279-281
      Civil Liberties (Kauper) 101-102
      *Civil Liberties (Sweet) 193-196
      Communication (Hemmer) v. 1, 119
      *Consttn (Mendelson) 452-453
      Consttnl Right (Fellman) 68-69
      Digest 56
      *Documents History v. 2, 651-652
      Expanding Liberties 97-100
      *First Amendment (Konvitz) 178-184
      Free Speech (Kurland) 76-77
      *Justices (Friedman) v. 4, 2944-2947
      *Labor Relations (Edwards) 757-761
      Law and Education 182
      Modern Sup Ct 248
      Negro (Kalven) 99-105
      Petitioners 382
      Politics 95-98
      *Rights (Shattuck) 58-59
      *Sup Ct and Education 189-194
      Sup Ct Review 1961 127-128
      System 233-234
      Warren (Hudgins) 129-132
      *Warren (Spaeth) 172-177
      PERIODICALS:
      "Recent Supreme Court decisions: freedom of association for
          teachers," Isidore Starr. Socl Eductn 25: 357-360 Nov '61.

2278.   United States v. Louisiana   Dec 12, 1960   364 U.S. 502
        *Struggle 219-223

2279.   Reina v. United States   Dec 19, 1960   364 U.S. 507
        *Principles Proof 666-668

2280.   United States v. Mississippi Valley   Jan 9, 1961   364 U.S. 520
        Generating Co.
        Court Years 299-300

2281.   National Labor Relations Board v.   Jan 9, 1961   364 U.S. 573
        Radio and Television Broadcast
        Engineers Union
        "CBS Case"
        *Cases Labor (Cox) 815-822
        *Cases Labor (Handler) 770-775
        *Cases Labor (Leslie) 357-361
        *Labor Law (Herman) 239-244
        *Labor Law (Meltzer) 541-547
        *Labor Relations (Group Trust) 344-348
        Sup Ct and Labor 159-162
        PERIODICALS:
        "NLRB told to settle job feuds." Bus Wk p. 102 Jan 14 '61.
        "Significant decisions in labor cases." Monthly Labor R 84: 282-
        283 Mar '61.

2282.   Radiant Burners, Inc. v. Peoples Gas Jan 16, 1961   364 U.S. 656
        Light and Coke Co.
        *Cases Antitrust Law 451-452
        *Cases Trade 290-292
        *Govt Regulation 1498-1501
        Law and Politics 298

2283.   Federal Power Commission v. Trans-   Jan 25, 1961   365 U.S. 1
        continental Gas Pipe Line Corporation
        National Coal Association v. Trans-
        continental Gas Pipe Line Corporation
        *Warren (Spaeth) 46-50

2284.   Times Film Corporation v. Chicago   Jan 23, 1961   365 U.S. 43
        *Am Consttnl Issues 286-292
        *Bill (Konvitz) 459-463
        *Censorship Landmarks 347-358
        Civil Liberties (Kauper) 81-87
        Communication (Hemmer) v. 1, 181
        Federal Censorship 156-159
        *First Amendment (Konvitz) 881-901
        *Freedom and Protection 138-141
        *Freedom of Speech (Haiman) 120-123
        Freedom of Speech (Hudon) 153-155
        Law of Mass 393-394
        Law of Obscenity 230-231
        Least Dangerous 133-135, 138-142
        *Mass Media (Devol) 172-178
        Modern Sup Ct 235-237
        Movies 100-106, 107-108
        *Sup Ct on Freedom 232-241
        System 508-509

PERIODICALS:
"Free speech and movies." Commonweal 73: 495-496 Feb 10
    '61.
"Movie censorship upheld." America 104: 582 Feb 4 '61.
"Recent Supreme Court decisions: censorship of films," Isidore
    Starr. Socl Eductn 26: 19-22 Jan '62.
"Retreat from freedom." Christian Century 78: 163-164 Feb 8
    '61. Reaction: 78: 301 Mar 8 '61.
"Supreme Court's affirmation of official censorship," R. H. Smith.
    Pub Weekly 179: 68 Feb 6 '61.
"Who bans what." Newsweek 57: 89-90, 93 Feb 13 '61.

2285. Campbell v. United States   Jan 23, 1961   365 U.S. 85
       Criminal Law Revolution 5-6

2286. Eastern Railroad Presidents Confer-   Feb 20, 1961   365 U.S. 127
       ence v. Noerr Motor Freight, Inc.
       *Antitrust (Posner) 307-314
       *Antitrust Analysis 411-416
       *Cases Antitrust Law 483-491
       *Cases Trade 318-326
       Consttnl Right (Fellman) 10-11
       *Govt Regulation 1502-1512
       Hugo Black (Strickland) 214-215
       Law and Politics 297
       *Legislation (Linde) 233-237
       *Modern Business 149-153
       *Sup Ct on Freedom 301-304

2287. Monroe v. Pape   Feb 20, 1961   365 U.S. 167
       *Civil Rights (Abernathy) 1980 1-10
       Consttnl Law (Barrett) 1087
       *Discrimination 54-60
       *Introduction (Mashaw) 720-730
       *Law Sup Ct 251-254, 524-527
       Modern Sup Ct 253
       *Political Rights 1072-1078
       *Race 883-888
       *Sup Ct and Criml Process 808-810
       *Warren (Spaeth) 368-369
       PERIODICALS:
       "Schools and the law: Section 1983 suits against school districts:
       the Supreme Court speaks," Thomas J. Flygare. Phi Delta
       Kappan 60: 127-128 Oct '78 (3).

2288. Green v. United States   Feb 27, 1961   365 U.S. 301
       Criminal Law Revolution 9-10

2289. Tampa Electric Co. v. Nashville   Feb 27, 1961   365 U.S. 320
       Coal Co.
       *Antitrust (Posner) 720-725
       *Antitrust Analysis 648-650
       *Cases Antitrust Law 809-817
       *Cases Trade 562-569
       *Competition 346-349
       *Govt Regulation 1513-1522
       Law and Politics 299-302
       *Selected Antitrust Cases 322-328
       *Text Antitrust 133-137

2290. Aro Manufacturing Co. v. Convert-   Feb 27, 1961   365 U.S. 336
       ible Top Replacement Co.
       *Antitrust (Posner) 602-604
       *Free Enterprise 1189-1204
       *Legal Regulation 1068-1072
       *Patent 367-384

2291. Wilson v. Schnettler   Feb 27, 1961   365 U.S. 381
       Search and Seizure 157
       Sup Ct Review 1961 13

2292. Wilkinson v. United States   Feb 27, 1961   365 U.S. 399
       Civil Liberties (Kauper) 95
       *First Amendment (Konvitz) 708-722
       Freedom of Speech (Hudon) 142-143
       Law and Politics 66-67
       Modern Sup Ct 224-227
       *One Man's Stand 385-390
       *Sup Ct on Freedom 39
       System 264-265
       PERIODICALS:
       "Court and the Committee." Commonweal 73: 624-625 Mar 17
           '61.
       "High, wide and ugly." Christian Century 78: 315-317 Mar 15
           '61. Reaction: 78: 460 Apr 12 '61.
       "The Issue, Mr. Speaker." Nation 192: 226-227 Mar 18 '61.
           Reaction: Clement J. Zablocki. 192: inside cover Apr 1 '61.
       "Investigating power and Operation abolition." America 104: 745
           Mar 11 '61.
       "Un-American activities." New Republic 144: 5-6 Mar 13 '61.

2293. Braden v. United States   Feb 27, 1961   365 U.S. 431
       *First Amendment (Konvitz) 722-733
       Freedom of Speech (Hudon) 143-146
       Law and Politics 66-67
       Modern Sup Ct 224-227
       *One Man's Stand 391-396
       *Sup Ct on Freedom 37-39
       System 265-266
       PERIODICALS:
       "Southern conference educational fund, inc.: Braden decision."
           Negro History Bul 24: 187, 189 May '61.

2294. Pugach v. Dollinger   Feb 27, 1961   365 U.S. 458
       *Police 158

2295. Silverman v. United States   Mar 6, 1961   365 U.S. 505
       Criminal Law (Felkenes) 134-135
       Criminal Law Revolution 3-4
       *Rights (Shattuck) 14-15
       Search and Seizure 237-238
       Sup Ct Review 1962 232-233

2296. Rogers v. Richmond   Mar 20, 1961   365 U.S. 534
       Criminal Law Revolution 8
       Sup Ct and Confessions 117
       *Warren (Spaeth) 301-304

2297. Chapman v. United States   Apr 3, 1961   365 U.S. 610
       Search and Seizure 112-113

2298. Local 60, United Brotherhood of   Apr 17, 1961   365 U. S. 651
       Carpenters and Joiners of America
       v. National Labor Relations Board
       *Cases Labor (Handler) 404-407
       Sup Ct and Labor 166
       PERIODICALS:
       "Significant decisions in labor cases. "   Monthly Labor R   84:   641-
       645   June '61   (4).

2299. Local 357, International Brotherhood   Apr 17, 1961   365 U. S. 667
       of Teamsters, Chauffeurs, Ware-
       housemen and Helpers of America
       v. National Labor Relations Board
       *Cases Labor (Cox) 241-250
       *Cases Labor (Handler) 407-414
       *Cases Labor (Leslie) 518-525
       *Cases Labor (Oberer) 160-167
       *Labor Law (Herman) 226-231
       *Labor Law (Meltzer) 965-973
       *Labor Relations (Group Trust) 655-663
       Law and Politics 118
       Sup Ct and Labor 167-168
       PERIODICALS:
       "Significant decisions in labor cases. "   Monthly Labor R   84:   641-
       645   June '61   (4).

2300. National Labor Relations Board v.   Apr 17, 1961   365 U. S. 695
       News Syndicate Co.
       *Cases Labor (Handler) 414-418
       PERIODICALS:
       "NLRB policies under Landrum-Griffin and recent court rulings, "
       John H. Fanning.   Monthly Labor R   84: 960-965 Sept '61 (3).
       "Significant decisions in labor cases. "   Monthly Labor R   84:   641-
       645   June '61   (4).

2301. International Typographical Union,   Apr 17, 1961   365 U. S. 705
       Locals 38 and 165 v. National
       Labor Relations Board
       PERIODICALS:
       See listing under 365 U. S. 695, entry no. 2300.

2302. Burton v. Wilmington Parking Au-   Apr 17, 1961   365 U. S. 715
       thority
       *Am Consttn (Lockhart) 1030-1032
       By What Right 229
       *Cases Consttnl Law (Gunther) 1007-1010
       *Cases Consttnl Rights 980-983
       *Cases Individual 536-539
       Civil Liberties (Kauper) 144-145
       *Civil Rights (Abernathy) 1980 67-72
       *Consttn (Mendelson) 552-554
       Consttnl Counterrevolution 87-88
       *Consttnl Law (Barrett) 1053-1055
       *Consttnl Law (Barron) 1004-1007
       *Consttnl Law (Freund) 823-828
       *Consttnl Law (Grossman) 530-534
       *Consttnl Law (Kauper) 810-814
       *Consttnl Law (Lockhart) 1520-1523
       *Contemporary Law 901-906

Desegregation (Wasby) 293-298
Discrimination 407-411
Modern Sup Ct 248-249
Petitioners 329-331
*Political Rights v. 2, 1645-1649
*Processes 617-620
*Racial Equality 121-122
*Sup Ct and Consttn 522-525

2303. Kossick v. United Fruit Co.   Apr 17, 1961   365 U.S. 731
       *Cases Admiralty 201-205

2304. Konigsberg v. State Bar of Cali-   Apr 24, 1961   366 U.S. 36
       fornia
       Am Consttn (Kelly) 924
       Civil Liberties (Kauper) 95-96
       Communication (Hemmer) v. 1, 66
       *Consttn (Mendelson) 457-461
       Consttnl Law (Barrett) 1196-1197
       *Consttnl Law (Kauper) 1119-1126
       Court and Consttn v. 2, 201-202
       *First Amendment (Konvitz) 572-581
       Free Speech (Kurland) 4-8
       *One Man's Stand 397-407
       System 178-181

2305. In re Anastalpo   Apr 24, 1961   366 U.S. 82
       Modern Sup Ct 233-235
       *One Man's Stand 408-415
       System 181-182

2306. Cohen v. Hurley   Apr 24, 1961   366 U.S. 117
       *Affair 163-166

2307. Brotherhood of Maintenance of Way   May 1, 1961   366 U.S. 169
       Employes v. United States
       *Cases Labor (Handler) 477-481
       PERIODICALS:
       "Significant decisions in labor cases." Monthly Labor R 84:
       765-769 July '61 (2).

2308. Eli Lilly and Co. v. Sav-on-Drugs, Inc. May 22, 1961   366 U.S. 276
       Sup Ct and Commerce 261-263

2309. Louisiana ex rel. Gremillion v. Na-   May 22, 1961   366 U.S. 293
       tional Association for the Ad-
       vancement of Colored People
       Civil Liberties (Kauper) 96-98
       Negro (Kalven) 74-75, 97-99
       Petitioners 382-383

2310. United States v. E.I. Dupont de   May 22, 1961   366 U.S. 316
       Nemours and Co.
       Law and Politics 296-297

2311. McGowan v. Maryland   May 29, 1961   366 U.S. 420
       "Sunday Closing Cases"
       Am Consttn (Kelly) 973-974
       *Am Consttnl Issues 348-350

*Am Consttnl Law (Shapiro) 469-473
*Bill (Konvitz) 110-124
Cases Consttnl Law (Gunther) 1563-1564
Church and State 137-141
Church State and Freedom 281-287
Civil Liberties (Kauper) 19-25
*Civil Rights (Abernathy) 1977 311-316
*Consttn (Mendelson) 585-589
Consttnl Counterrevolution 240-241
*Consttnl Law (Kauper) 1281-1283
*Contemporary Law 787-798
Dissent 448-452
Expanding Liberties 40-43
*First Amendment (Konvitz) 93-110
Freedom and the Court 278, 284-287
Justice Rutledge 85
*Mr. Justice Frankfurter 108-112
Modern Sup Ct 238-241
*Political Rights 825-835
Private Conscience 136-142
Religion (Fellman) 34-37
Religion (Kurland) 99-101
*Religious Freedom (Pfeffer) 87-90
School Prayers (Lauboch) 40
Sup Ct and Religion 137-138
*Third Branch 294-301
*Warren (Spaeth) 179-186
PERIODICALS:
    "Blue laws and the Court." Christian Century 78: 867-868
        July 19 '61.
    "Blue law blues," Ralph Nader. Nation 192: 499-500, 508
        June 10 '61.
    "Sunday laws," Thomas J. O'Toole. Commonweal 74: 343-345
        June 30 '61.
    "Sunday laws and the first amendment," Robert F. Drinan.
        America 105: 627-630 Aug 19 '61.

2312. Two Guys from Harrison-Allentown   May 29, 1961 366 U.S. 582
            v. McGinley
       "Sunday Closing Cases"
            Church and State 137-141
            Church State and Freedom 281-287
           *Contemporary Law 798-799
           *First Amendment (Konvitz) 118-121
            Freedom and the Court 284-287
            Modern Sup Ct 238-241
           *Third Branch 294-301
       PERIODICALS:
            See listing at 366 U.S. 420, entry no. 2311.

2313. Braunfield v. Brown   May 29, 1961 366 U.S. 599
       "Sunday Closing Cases"
           *Affair 129-131
            Am Consttn (Kelly) 974
           *Am Consttnl Issues 350-355
           *Bill (Konvitz) 125-137
            CQ Guide 459
            Cases Consttnl Law (Gunther) 1585-1587
           *Cases Criml Law (Inbau) 298-307

*Cases Individual 1108-1112
Church and State 137-141
Church State and Freedom 281-287
*Civil Liberties (Sweet) 68-72
*Civil Rights (Abernathy) 1977 328-331
*Comparative 483-487
*Consttnl Law (Barron) 953-957
*Consttnl Law (Kauper) 1283-1289
*Contemporary Law 799-803
Dissent 452-454
*First Amendment (Konvitz) 121-136
Freedom and the Court 284-287
Modern Sup Ct 238-241
*Political Rights 836-840
Private Conscience 136-142
Religion (Kauper) 41
Religion (Kurland) 101-104
*Religious Freedom (Pfeffer) 161-163
*Third Branch 294-301
*Warren (Spaeth) 186-188
PERIODICALS:
See listing at 366 U.S. 420, entry no. 2311.

2314. Gallagher v. Crown Kosher Super   May 29, 1961 366 U.S. 617
Market of Massachusetts
"Sunday Closing Cases"
Church and State 137-141
Church State and Freedom 281-287
*Contemporary Law 803-804
*First Amendment (Konvitz) 110-118
Freedom and the Court 284-287
Modern Sup Ct 238-241
Private Conscience 136-142
Religion (Drinan) 206-217
Religion (Kurland) 101
*Third Branch 294-301

2315. Local 761, International Union of Elec- May 29, 1961 366 U.S. 667
trical Radio and Machine Workers,
AFL-CIO v. National Labor Rela-
tions Board
"General Electric Case"
*Cases Labor (Cox) 741-750
*Cases Labor (Handler) 635-642
*Cases Labor (Leslie) 304-311
*Cases Labor (Oberer) 434-440
*Labor Law (Meltzer) 438-445
*Labor Relations (Group Trust) 308-313
Labor Relations (Taylor) 484-485
Law and Politics 104-105
PERIODICALS:
"NLRB policies under Landrum-Griffin and recent court rulings,"
John H. Fanning. Monthly Labor R 84: 960-965 Sep '61
(3).
"Significant decisions in labor cases." Monthly Labor R 84:
878-881 Aug '61 (3).

2316. Irvin v. Dowd   June 5, 1961 366 U.S. 717
CQ Guide 441-442

Communication (Hemmer) v. 2, 178-179
*Consttn (Mendelson) 308-312
*Criminal Justice (Kaplan) 385-388
Criminal Procedure (Wells) 97
Dissent 181
*First Amendment (Franklin) 187-191
Handbook 523-524
Law of Mass 260-263
*Mass Communications 485-487
*Mass Media (Devol) 272-274
Mass Media (Francois) 273
Radio 37-38
*Sup Ct on Freedom 108-111
US Sup Ct 80-81

2317. International Ladies' Garment   June 5, 1961   366 U.S. 731
          Workers' Union v. National Labor
          Relations Board
       *Cases Labor (Cox) 288-291
       *Cases Labor (Handler) 77-81
       *Cases Labor (Leslie) 186-190
       *Cases Labor (Stern) 146-151
       *Labor Law (Meltzer) 166-170
       *Labor Relations (Group Trust) 216-221
       PERIODICALS:
          "Significant decisions in labor cases." Monthly Labor R   84:   878-
          881 Aug '61 (3).

2318. Communist Party of the United States   June 5, 1961   367 U.S. 1
          v. Subversive Activities Control
          Board
       Am Consttn (Kelly) 912-913
       *Am Consttnl Issues 33-38
       CQ Guide 506
       Cases Consttnl Law (Gunther) 1175
       Civil Liberties (Kauper) 90-93
       Communication (Hemmer) v. 1, 65-66
       *Communism 62-76
       *Consttn (Mendelson) 487-494
       *Consttnl Law (Barrett) 1169-1171
       Decade 37-38
       Expanding Liberties 142-149
       *First Amendment (Konvitz) 435-506
       Freedom and the Court 205
       Freedom of Speech (Hudon) 159-162
       Justice Hugo Black 35-36
       *Law Sup Ct 127-134
       Modern Sup Ct 224-229
       *One Man's Stand 416-430
       *Political Rights 163-177
       System 133-141
       *Warren (Spaeth) 273-281
       PERIODICALS:
          "Ban on communism." America 105: 458 June 24 '61.
          "Blows against communism." Time 77: 18 June 16 '61.
          "Communist cases; with editorial comment," Alexander M. Bickel.
             New Republic 144: 2, 15-16 June 19 '61.
          "Let the intellectuals take it from here." Natl R 10: 371-372
             June 17 '61.

"Made in Moscow." <u>Newsweek</u> 57: 28, 30 June 19 '61.
"Neither clear nor present." <u>Nation</u> 192: 509-510 June 17 '61.
"Security and civil rights." <u>Commonweal</u> 74: 316-317 June 23 '61.

2319. Scales v. United States   June 5, 1961   367 U.S. 203
Am Consttn (Kelly) 908-909
*Am Consttnl Issues 324-328
*Am Consttnl Law (Shapiro) 375-379
Bill (Cohen) 77-78
CQ Guide 505
Cases Consttnl Law (Gunther) 1171-1173
Civil Liberties (Kauper) 93-94
*Civil Liberties (Sweet) 92-98
*Civil Rights (Abernathy) 1977 404-408
Communication (Hemmer) v. 1, 26-27
*Communism 50-55
*Comparative 616-620
*Consttn (Mendelson) 484-487
*Consttnl Decisions 140-146
*Consttnl Law (Barrett) 1148-1152
Consttnl Right (Fellman) 60-61
Court Years 101-102
*Criminal Law (Kadish) 384-385
*Evolution 182-189
*First Amendment (Konvitz) 393-428
Free Speech (Kurland) 25
Freedom of Speech (Hudon) 156-159
Modern Sup Ct 229-232
*One Man's Stand 431-433
*Political Rights 136-145
Sup Ct Review 1961 76
System 127-129
*Warren (Spaeth) 261-272
PERIODICALS:
"Court's crackdown; death blow to reds?" <u>US News</u> 50: 42-44
June 19 '61 (2).
"Julius Scales," Laurent B. Frantz. <u>Nation</u> 193: 528-530 Dec 30 '61.
See also listing at 367 U.S. 1, entry no. 2318.

2320. Noto v. United States   June 5, 1961   367 U.S. 290
Communication (Hemmer) v. 1, 27-28
*Communism 56-59
Expanding Liberties 129
*First Amendment (Konvitz) 428-435
PERIODICALS:
"Court's crackdown: death blow to reds?" <u>US News</u> 50: 42-44
June 19 '61 (2).

2321. Horton v. Liberty Mutual Insurance   June 12, 1961 367 U.S. 348
Co.
*Cases Federal Courts 237-243
*Civil Procedure (Cound) 219-224
PERIODICALS:
"Significant decisions in labor cases." <u>Monthly Labor R</u> 84: 998-1005 Sep '61 (3).

2322. Gori v. United States   June 12, 1961   367 U. S. 364
     *Douglas 410-413
     Modern Criml Procedure 393

2323. Lott v. United States   June 12, 1961   367 U. S. 421
     Criminal Law Revolution 7-8

2324. Reck v. Pate   June 12, 1961   367 U. S. 433
     *Douglas 316-320
     *Police 99-101

2325. Deutch v. United States   June 12, 1961   367 U. S. 456
     *First Amendment (Konvitz) 733-744
     Freedom of Speech (Hudon) 162-163

2326. Torcasco v. Watkins   June 19, 1961   367 U. S. 488
     *Bill (Konvitz) 141-144
     *Civil Rights (Abernathy) 1977 334-335
     Church and State 141-142
     Communication (Hemmer) v. 1, 208-209
     *First Amendment (Phillips) 89-93
     Freedom and the Court 248, 282
     *One Man's Stand 434-438
     Private Conscience 142-143
     Religion (Blanchard) 82-83
     Religion (Kauper) 28-29
     Religion (Kurland) 107-108
     Religious Freedom (Arnold) 42
     *Religious Freedom (Pfeffer) 91-92
     Religious Liberty 56
     *Warren (Spaeth) 211-214
     PERIODICALS:
     "Atheist citizen." Commonweal 74: 388-389 July 14 '61.
     "End to religious tests," Thomas O. Hanley. Commonweal 74:
      419-420 July 28 '61.
     "Meaning of religion in the First amendment; the Torcasco case,"
      Milton R. Konvitz. Catholic World 197: 288-295 Aug '63.

2327. Poe v. Ullman   June 19, 1961   367 U. S. 497
     Doe v. Ullman
     Buxton v. Ullman
     *Am Consttn (Lockhart) 73-77
     *Am Consttnl Issues 27-33
     Cases Consttnl Law (Gunther) 1664-1665
     *Cases Consttnl Law (Rosenblum) 213-217
     *Cases Consttnl Rights 73-77
     Conceived 54
     Consttnl Law (Barrett) 100
     *Consttnl Law (Felkenes) 30-33
     *Consttnl Law (Lockhart) 1678-1682
     *Courts Judges 246-249
     Criminal Law Revolution 10-11
     *Evolution 88-102
     *Family 377-379
     *Federal System 64-66
     Felix Frankfurter (Mendelson) 21-23
     *First Amendment (Konvitz) 911-933
     Least Dangerous 145-148, 154-155
     *Mr. Justice Frankfurter 24-28

    *Nature 92-107
    *One Man's Stand 439-440
    *Rights (Shattuck) 103-104
    Sup Ct Review 1963 107-108
    PERIODICALS:
      "Bit of sleight-of-hand." New Republic 145: 7-8 July 3 '61 (2).

2328. Culombe v. Connecticut   June 19, 1961 367 U.S. 568
    *Civil Liberties (Sweet) 252-254
    Law of Arrest (Creamer) 373-376
    *Mr. Justice Frankfurter 146-152

2329. Mapp v. Ohio   June 19, 1961 367 U.S. 643
    *Am Consttn (Lockhart) 412-418
    *Am Consttnl Law (Bartholomew) v. 2, 265-267
    *Am Consttnl Law (Mason) 710-714
    *Am Consttnl Law (Saye) 508-510
    *Am Consttnl Law (Shapiro) 651-657
    Arrest (Waddington) 4-5
    *Basic Criminal 175-184
    *Bill (Konvitz) 641-648
    By What Right 161
    CQ Guide 549
    *Cases Civil Liberties 125-130
    *Cases Consttnl Law (Cushman) 355-361
    *Cases Consttnl Rights 172-179
    *Cases Criml Justice 64-75
    *Cases Individual 124-127
    *Civil Liberties (Barker) 199-204
    *Civil Liberties (Sweet) 242-247
    *Civil Rights (Abernathy) 1077 135-139
    Communication (Hemmer) v. 1, 232-233
    Conceived 149-150
    *Consttn (Mendelson) 326-331
    Consttnl Counterrevolution 142-143
    *Consttnl Criml (Marks) 276-281
    *Consttnl Criml (Scarboro) 61-67
    *Consttnl Decisions 174-184
    *Consttnl Law (Barron) 453-459
    *Consttnl Law (Felkenes) 240-243
    *Consttnl Law (Freund) 1008-1010
    *Consttnl Law (Grossman) 809-813
    *Consttnl Law (Kauper) 915-923
    *Consttnl Law (Klein) 212-221
    *Consttnl Law (Maddex) 89-98
    *Contemporary Law 480-492
    *Criminal Justice (Kaplan) 210-213
    *Criminal Justice (Way) 121-125
    Criminal Law (Felkenes) 101-104
    *Criminal Law (Kadish) 774-777, 937-938
    Criminal Law Revolution 1-3
    *Criminal Procedure (Lewis) 107-114
    Criminal Procedure (Wells) 294-296
    Dissent 302-304
    *Elements Criminal 233-244
    Exclusionary 26-31
    *Freedom and Protection 69-71
    Freedom and the Court 72-73
    Freedom Spent 230-233

Great Reversals 175-176
*Historic Decisions 172-175
Hugo Black (Dunne) 364-365
Impact (Wasby) 162-167
In His Own Image 40-41
Justice Rutledge 159-171
*Justices (Friedman) v. 4, 2678-2685
*Law Enforcement 33-37
Law of Arrest (Creamer) 346-348
*Law of Evidence 523-534
*Law Power 176-181
*Law Sup Ct 224-231
*Leading Consttnl Cases 237-250
*Liberty v. 2, 568-570
Milestones 283-293
*Modern Consttnl Law 131-136
Modern Sup Ct 244-246
*One Man's Stand 441-442
*Police 62-65
Politics 239-242
Power 267-268
*Principles Arrest 98-106
Rationing 12-18
*Rights (Shattuck) 39-40
Search and Seizure 158-164
Self Inflicted Wound 40-41, 46-48
Spirit 85-86
*Sup Ct and Consttn 565-567
*Sup Ct and Criml Process 193-197
*Sup Ct and Rights 133-140
Sup Ct as Policy Maker 1-26
Sup Ct Review 1961 1, 20-48
*Teaching Materials 92-97
Warren (Lytle) 77-78
*Warren (Spaeth) 291-298
PERIODICALS:
"Bit of Sleight-of-hand." New Republic 145: 7-8 July 3 '61.
"Court raps seizures in two obscenity trials." Pub Weekly 179:
59 June 26 '61.
"Is it wrong to handcuff the police?" William J. Dempsey.
Catholic World 204: 264-269 Feb '67 (3).
*"Mapp v. Ohio, 1961." Current History 61: 43-45 July '71.
"Reactions of state supreme courts to a U.S. Supreme Court civil
liberties decision," Bradley C. Canon. Law and Society R 8:
109-134 Fall '73.
"Retroactivity riddle." Time 85: 44, 47 June 18 '65 (2).
"The Role of the Supreme Court," Frank J. Remington. Current
History 60: 353-356, 369+ June '71.
"Supreme Court and law enforcement," Robert G. Caldwell. J
Police Sci and Administration 3: 222-237 June '75 (2).
"Supreme Court, defender of minorities," John B. Sheerin.
Catholic World 193: 275-279 Aug '61 (3).

2330. Marcus v. Search Warrants of   June 19, 1961 367 U.S. 717
Property at 104 East Tenth Street,
Kansas City, Missouri
*Affair 44-48
Communication (Hemmer) v. 1, 189-190
Handbook 709-710
Law of Obscenity 207-208, 215-216, 235-236

2331. International Association of Ma-   June 19, 1961 367 U.S. 740
      chinists v. Street
      *Cases Labor (Handler) 428-441
      Dissent 467-469
      Felix Frankfurter (Mendelson) 190
      *First Amendment (Konvitz) 184-198
      Freedom of the Press (Schmidt) 34-35
      *Labor Law (Meltzer) 1058-1073
      *Labor Relations (Group Trust) 973-988
      Law and Politics 137-139
      *Political Rights 870-883
      Sup Ct Review 1961 49-73
      System 685-688
      PERIODICALS:
      "Court on workers' rights." Fortune 64: 80, 82 Aug '61.
      "Significant decisions in labor cases." Monthly Labor R 84:
          998-1005 Sept '61 (3).
      "Union dues for political activity; what Court said and didn't say."
          US News 51: 82 July 3 '61.
      "Unions, dues and politics." Commonweal 74: 365 July 7 '61.
      "U.S. labor policy--recent Supreme Court decisions." Congres-
          sional Dig 44: 197-198, 224 Aug/Sept '65 (3).
      "Workers be damned." Natl R 11: 186 Sept 23 '61.

2332. Lathrop v. Donohue   June 19, 1961 367 U.S. 820
      *Cases Professional 68-87
      *Consttnl Law (Schmidhauser) 296-319
      Dissent 469-471
      *Evolution 154-162
      *First Amendment (Konvitz) 198-211
      System 688-691

2333. Cafeteria and Restaurant Workers   June 19, 1961 367 U.S. 886
      Union, Local 473, AFL-CIO v.
      McElroy
      *Admin Law (Gellhorn) 425-429
      *Affair 219-221
      *Due Process 202-203
      *Freedom vs National Security 534-540
      Least Dangerous 166-169
      Modern Sup Ct 251-252
      *Political Rights 312-316
      System 221-222
      *Warren (Spaeth) 283-287
      PERIODICALS:
      "Significant decisions in labor cases." Monthly Labor R 84: 998-
          1005 Sept '61 (3).

2334. Hamilton v. Alabama   Nov 13, 1961 368 U.S. 52
      *Consttnl Law (Felkenes) 309-310
      Criminal Law (Felkenes) 183-185
      *Douglas 360-364
      Private Pressure 109-110
      Rationing 105-106

2335. Hoyt v. Florida   Nov 20, 1961 368 U.S. 57
      CQ Guide 534
      Defendants 186
      *Sex Discrimination 1975 97-99

    *Sex Roles 74-79
    *Text Consttnl Aspects 26-30
    *Text Sex Based Discrimination 26-30
    *Women 23-24
    PERIODICALS:
      "Cases notes."   J Criml Law, Crimlgy and Police Sci   53:   227
      June '62.

2336.   Western Union Telegraph Co. v.   Dec 4, 1961   368 U. S.   71
       Pennsylvania
       *Cases Federal Courts 884-888
       *Civil Procedure (Carrington) 1141-1145
       *Consttnl Law (Freund) 451-455

2337.   Interstate Commerce Commission v.   Dec 4, 1961   368 U. S.   81
       J-T Transport Co.
       U. S. A. C. Transport, Inc. v. J-T
       Transport Co.
       Interstate Commerce Commission v.
       Reddish
       Arkansas-Best Freight System, Inc.
         v. Reddish
       *Cases Regulated 550-557
       *Free Enterprise 346-359

2338.   Garner v. Louisiana   Dec 11, 1961   368 U. S.   157
       Briscoe v. Louisiana
       Hoston v. Louisiana
         Communication (Hemmer) v. 1, 78-79
         Desegregation (Wasby) 298-301
         Dissent 330-332
         *Evolution 140-146
         Expanding Liberties 275-279
         Least Dangerous 175-180
         Negro (Kalven) 125-132
         Petitioners 395-398
         *Principles Freedom 212-217
         Private Pressure 115-116
       *Struggle 105-108
       PERIODICALS:
         "Long road to where?" Janette H. Harris.   Negro History Bul
         31:   16-17   Dec '68.
         "Sit-in decision."   America   106:   409-410   Dec 23 '61.

2339.   St. Regis Paper Co. v. United   Dec 11, 1961   368 U. S.   208
       States
       *Govt and Business 501-504
       PERIODICALS:
         "Confidential to whom?" Theodore G. Redman.   Controller   30:   67
         Feb '62.
         "FTC wins right to see secret census data."   Bus Wk   p. 32
         Dec 16 '61.

2340.   Killian v. United States   Dec 11, 1961   368 U. S.   231
       System 169-171

2341.   Cramp v. Board of Public Instruction   Dec 11, 1961   368 U. S.   278
       of Orange County, Florida
       Am Consttn (Kelly) 924-925

<u>Communication</u> (Hemmer) v. 1, 120
<u>Digest</u> 56-57
*<u>First Amendment</u> (Konvitz) 582-584
*<u>Liberty</u> v. 2, 557
*<u>Sup Ct</u> and Education 195-198
<u>System</u> 234
<u>Warren</u> (Hudgins) 140-142

2342. Campbell v. Hussy   Dec 18, 1961   368 U.S. 297
       Sup Ct and Commerce 294-298

2343. United States v. Drum   Jan 15, 1962   368 U.S. 370
       Regional Common Carrier Conference
       of American Trucking Associations v. Drum
       *<u>Cases Regulated</u> 521-526

2344. Blau v. Lehman   Jan 22, 1962   368 U.S. 403
       Sup Ct Review 1963 293-307

2345. Hill v. United States   Jan 22, 1962   368 U.S. 424
       *<u>One Man's Stand</u> 443-447

2346. Oyler v. Boles   Feb 19, 1962   368 U.S. 448
       Crabtree v. Boles
       *<u>Due Process</u> 159-160
       *<u>US Prison Law</u> v. 1, 544-559
       PERIODICALS:
       "Cases notes." <u>J Criml Law, Crimlgy and Police Sci</u> 53: 349
       Sept '62.

2347. Poller v. Columbia Broadcasting   Feb 19, 1962   368 U.S. 464
       System
       *<u>Cases Antitrust Law</u> 718-724
       <u>Law and Politics</u> 310-311

2348. Charles Dowd Box Co., Inc. v.   Feb 19, 1962   368 U.S. 502
       Courtney
       *<u>Cases Labor</u> (Handler) 307-310
       PERIODICALS:
       "Significant decisions in labor cases." <u>Monthly Labor R</u> 85: 423-
       424 Apr '62 (2).

2349. Bailey v. Patterson   Feb 26, 1962   369 U.S. 31
       *<u>Cases Federal Courts</u> 441-442
       *<u>Warren</u> (Spaeth) 136-137

2350. Organized Village of Kake v. Egan   Mar 5, 1962   369 U.S. 60
       *<u>Am Indian</u> v. 4, 2826-2838
       *<u>Law Indian</u> 189-192

2351. Griggs v. Allegheny County,   Mar 5, 1962   369 U.S. 84
       Pennsylvania
       Sup Ct Review 1962 72, 76, 84-87
       *<u>Text Legislation</u> 129-131
       PERIODICALS:
       "Age of noise." <u>Time</u> 79: 65-66 Mar 16 '62.
       "New controversy, many suits due after airport noise ruling."
       <u>Aviation Wk</u> 76: 319 Mar 12 '62.
       "What price noise?" <u>Newsweek</u> 59: 36 Mar 19 '62.

2352. Local 174, Teamsters, Chauffeurs,   Mar 5, 1962   369 U. S. 95
       Warehousemen and Helpers of
       America v. Lucas Flour Co.
       Basic Text 546
       *Cases Labor (Cox) 610-613
       *Cases Labor (Handler) 310-313
       *Cases Labor (Oberer) 690-694
       *Labor Law (Meltzer) 842-844
       *Labor Relations (Group Trust) 873-875
       PERIODICALS:
       "Binding arbitration bars strike, Court says." Bus Wk p. 120
       Mar 10 '62.
       "New strike curb upheld by Court." US News 52: 79 Mar 19
       '62.
       "Significant decisions in labor cases." Monthly Labor R 85: 546
       May '62.

2353. Public Affairs Associates, Inc. v.   Mar 5, 1962   369 U. S. 111
       Rickover
       Communication (Hemmer) v. 2, 145
       *Materials Consttnl Law 154-158

2354. Di Bella v. United States   Mar 19, 1962   369 U. S. 121
       United States v. Koenig
       Criminal Law Revolution 14-15
       PERIODICALS:
       "Cases notes." J Criml Law, Crimlgy and Police Sci 53: 353
       Sept '62.

2355. Fong Foo v. United States   Mar 19, 1962   369 U. S. 141
       Standard Coil Products Co., Inc.
       v. United States
       *Cases Criml Justice 1197-1200
       *Criminal Law (Kadish) 1399-1400
       Sup Ct Review 1978 149-150

2356. Baker v. Carr   Mar 26, 1962   369 U. S. 186
       *Affair 284-308
       Am Consttn (Kelly) 942-944
       *Am Consttn (Lockhart) 88-99
       *Am Consttnl Issues 62-76
       *Am Consttnl Law (Bartholomew) v. 1, 17-22; v. 2, 334-339
       *Am Consttnl Law (Mason) 54-59
       *Am Consttnl Law (Shapiro) 89-103
       *Am Govt 193-205
       *Annals v. 18, 130-135
       *Anxiety 41-50
       Apportionment.
       *Bill (Konvitz) 612-622
       Biography 353-354
       By What Right 132-136
       CQ Guide 490-491
       *Cases Consttnl Law (Cushman) 18-23
       *Cases Consttnl Law (Gunther) 1698-1703
       *Cases Consttnl Law (Rosenblum) 33-48
       *Cases Consttnl Rights 88-99
       *Cases Federal Courts 35-43
       *Cases Individual 1226-1233
       Changing 172-173

Rise 111-128
*Rise 203-204
*Sup Ct (Mendelson) 264-291
*Sup Ct and Am Govt 28-38
*Sup Ct and Consttn 549-559
Sup Ct and Electoral Process 154-159, 210-211
Sup Ct and News 96-98
Sup Ct and Poltcl Questions 59-72
Sup Ct and Uses 120-125
Sup Ct from Taft 239-240
Sup Ct in Am History 162-179
Sup Ct Review 1962 252-327
Sup Ct Review 1964 2-3
Sup Ct Review 1973 7, 38-39
This Honorable Court 418-419
Warren (Ball) 88-135
Warren (Cox) 115-117
*Warren (Saylor) 170-186
*Warren (Spaeth) 74-86
PERIODICALS:
"Apportionment facts," William J. D. Boyd. Natl Civic R 53:
     530-534, 544 Nov '64 (2).
"Baker v. Carr." Commonweal 76: 52-53 Apr 13 '62.
"Battle over state reapportionment; pro and con discussion."
     Senior Scholastic 85: 12-13, 30 Oct 28 '64.
"Bigger voice for big cities." Newsweek 59: 29-30, 32-34
     Apr 9 '62.
"Congress and the Supreme Court." Senior Scholastic 86: 10-11,
     36 Feb 18 '65.
"Court and state politics," Howard Penniman. America 107: 40
     Apr 14 '62.
"Court reversal on cities' rights." Senior Scholastic 80: 20-21
     Apr 11 '62.
"Court steps in." Sat Evening Post 235: 92 May 5 '62.
"Court unafraid," Kenneth Crawford. Newsweek 59: 39 May 14
     '62.
"Court's decision," Max Ascoli. Reporter 26: 12, 14 Apr 12
     '62.
"Either Court or Constitution is wrong on election rules," Felix
     Morley. Natns Bus 51: 27-28 May '63.
"Fragmented Bench." Time 79: 15-16 Apr 6 '62.
"Great apportionment case; with editorial comment," Alexander
     Bickel. New Republic 146: 8, 13-14 Apr 9 62.
"Great dissent," Raymond Moley. Newsweek 59: 116 Apr 16 '62.
"High court gives boost to cities' power." Bus Wk p. 32 Mar
     31 '62.
"Legislative apportionment and the federal Constitution," Robert
     G. Dixon, Jr. Law and Contemporary Problems 27: 329-389
     Summer '62.
"One man, one vote? Baker v. Carr," Walter D. Burnham.
     Commonweal 76: 145-148 May 4 '62.
"Politics, not as usual." Commonweal 76: 339-340 June 29 '62.
"Quiet revolution in state government." Senior Scholastic 83: 13-
     15, 24 Nov 22 '63.
"Reapportionment decision applied," Howard Penniman. America
     107: 609 Aug 18 '62.
"Reapportionment riddle," James E. Clayton. Reporter 30: 34-
     37 Feb 27 '64.

"Reapportionment; rhubarb in the political thicket; with chart, "
Senior Scholastic 85: 8-11, 19 Oct 14 '64.
"Rights of majorities and of minorities in the 1961 term of the
Supreme Court, " Benjamin F. Wright. Am Poltcl Sci R 57:
98-115 Mar '63 (2).
"Shame of the states, " Karl E. Meyer. New Statesman 63: 478
Apr 6 '62.
"Silent gerrymander slain ... and why. " America 107: 36 Apr
14 '62.
"Story of the recent court decisions. " Congressional Dig 44: 1-
32 Jan '65.
"Supreme Court jumps into another big battle, " US News 52: 53-
54 Apr 9 '62.
"Tennessee case; notes on the Supreme Court's decision to open
apportionment to judicial review, " Howard Margolis. Science
136: 30-32 Apr 6 '62.
"Warren legacy; a very different constitution, " James Jackson
Kilpatrick. Natl R 21: 794-800 Aug 12 '69 (3).
"What can't be conserved. " Fortune 65: 100 May '62.
"Where we stand; the revolt against rural rule, " John R. Moskin.
Look 27: 58-61 Jan 15 '63.
"Your vote; Supreme Court may put a new value on it. " US News
51: 101 Nov 6 '61.

2357. Rusk v. Cort   Apr 2, 1962   369 U.S. 367
Sup Ct Review 1963 325-356

2358. National Labor Relations Board v.   Apr 9, 1962   369 U.S. 404
Walton Manufacturing Co.
National Labor Relations Board v.
Florida Citrus Canners Cooperative
*Labor Law (Meltzer) 207-209

2359. Coppedge v. United States   Apr 30, 1962   369 U.S. 438
Criminal Law Revolution 15-16

2360. Dairy Queen v. Wood   Apr 30, 1962   369 U.S. 469
*Cases Civil Procedure 691-697
*Cases Equity 868-873
*Cases Federal Courts 754-759
*Elements Civil 859-863
*Introduction (Cataldo) 251-253

2361. California v. Federal Power Com-   Apr 30, 1962   369 U.S. 482
mission
*Cases Regulated 357-360
Law and Politics 302-304

2362. Carnley v. Cochran   Apr 30, 1962   369 U.S. 506
*One Man's Stand 448-450
PERIODICALS:
"Cases Notes. " J Criml Law, Crimlgy and Police Sci 53: 499
Dec '62.

2363. Vaughan v. Atkinson   May 14, 1962   369 U.S. 527
*Cases Admiralty 315-318

2364. Beck v. Washington   May 14, 1962   369 U.S. 541
Criminal Law Revolution 18-19

PERIODICALS:
"Case notes." J Criml Law Crimlgy and Police Sci 53: 497
Dec '62.

2365. Goldblatt v. Town of Hempstead   May 14, 1962 369 U.S. 590
       *Cases Land 348-351
       *Consttnl Law (Barrett) 686-688
       *Managing 648-652

2366. Free v. Bland   May 21, 1962 369 U.S. 663
       *Social Forces 50-51

2367. In re Green   May 21, 1962 369 U.S. 689
       Criminal Law Revolution 21-22
       PERIODICALS:
       "Significant decisions in labor cases." Monthly Labor R 85: 793
       July '62 (3).

2368. Lynch v. Overholser   May 21, 1962 369 U.S. 705
       Criminal Law Revolution 16-17
       *Evolution 215-222
       PERIODICALS:
       "Case notes." J Criml Law, Crimlgy and Police Sci 53: 496 Dec '62.

2369. National Labor Relations Board v.   May 21, 1962 369 U.S. 736
       Katz
       Basic Text 439-440
       *Cases Labor (Cox) 424-429
       *Cases Labor (Handler) 273-276
       *Cases Labor (Leslie) 374-377
       *Cases Labor (Oberer) 548-552
       *Labor Law (Meltzer) 713-716
       *Labor Relations (Group Trust) 447-451
       Law and Politics 117
       *Nature 1119-1123
       PERIODICALS:
       "Significant decisions in labor cases." Monthly Labor R 85: 793
       July '62 (3).

2370. Russell v. United States   May 21, 1962 369 U.S. 749
       Shelton v. United States
       Whitman v. United States
       Liveright v. United States
       Price v. United States
       Gojack v. United States
       Am Consttn (Kelly) 933-935
       Criminal Law Revolution 19-21
       *First Amendment (Konvitz) 744-752

2371. National Labor Relations Board v.   May 28, 1962 370 U.S. 9
       Washington Aluminum Co.
       *Cases Labor (Handler) 40-45
       *Cases Labor (Oberer) 511-515
       *Labor Relations (Group Trust) 270-273
       Sup Ct and Labor 83-84
       PERIODICALS:
       "Significant decisions in labor cases." Monthly Labor R 85: 793
       July '62 (3).

2372. Sunkist Growers v. Winckler and   May 28, 1962   370 U.S. 19
      Smith Citrus Products
      Law and Politics 309-310

2373. Gallegos v. Colorado   June 4, 1962   370 U.S. 49
      Police 101-102

2374. Calbeck v. Travelers Insurance Co.   June 4, 1962   370 U.S. 114
      Donovan v. Avondale Shipyards, Inc.
      *Cases Workmen 559-568

2375. Lanza v. New York   June 4, 1962   370 U.S. 139
      Criminal Law Revolution 17-18
      PERIODICALS:
      "Case notes." J Criml Law, Crimlgy and Police Sci 53: 493
      Dec '62.

2376. Taylor v. Louisiana   June 4, 1962   370 U.S. 154
      Expanding Liberties 280
      Petitioners 398
      *Woman 24-25

2377. Morales v. Galveston   June 11, 1962 370 U.S. 165
      Sup Ct Review 1964 253-254

2378. Marine Engineer's Beneficial As-   June 11, 1962 370 U.S. 173
      sociation v. Interlake Steamship Co.
      Law and Politics 95
      PERIODICALS:
      "Significant decisions in labor cases." Monthly Labor R 85: 903-
      906 Aug '62.

2379. Sinclair Refining Co. v. Atkinson   June 18, 1962 370 U.S. 195
      *Cases Labor (Cox) 914-922
      *Cases Labor (Handler) 313-322
      *Labor Law (Meltzer) 844-852
      *Labor Relations (Group Trust) 882-888
      *Practice 548-557
      PERIODICALS:
      "Significant decisions in labor cases." Monthly Labor R 85:
      903-906 Aug '62 (3).

2380. In re McConnell   June 18, 1962 370 U.S. 230
      Criminal Law Revolution 21

2381. Atkinson v. Sinclair Refining Co.   June 18, 1962 370 U.S. 238
      *Labor Law (Meltzer) 853-857
      *Labor Law (Group Trust) 876-880
      PERIODICALS:
      "Significant decisions in labor cases." Monthly Labor R 05: 903-
      906 Aug '62 (3).

2382. Drake Bakeries, Inc. v. Local 50,   June 18, 1962 370 U.S. 254
      American Bakery and Confectionery
      Workers International, AFL-CIO
      *Cases Labor (Handler) 353-358
      *Cases Labor (Oberer) 721-725
      *Labor Law (Meltzer) 823-828

PERIODICALS:
"Significant decisions in labor cases. " Monthly Labor R 85:
903-906 Aug '62.

2383. Brown Shoe Co. v. United States   June 25, 1962 370 U. S. 294
    *Antitrust (Posner) 390-396, 725-729
    *Antitrust Analysis 712-721, 727-732
    *Cases Antitrust Law 843-866
    *Cases Trade 716-738
    *Competition 116-127
    *Free Enterprise 165-182
    *Govt Regulation 1587-1636
    Law and Politics 304-309
    *Modern Business 977-981
    *Selected Antitrust Cases 129-143
    *Text Antitrust 150-166
    *Warren (Spaeth) 40-44
    PERIODICALS:
    "Blight on business marriages. " Bus Wk p. 52 July 7 '62.
    "Less room than ever for mergers. " Bus Wk p. 98 June 30 '62.
    "Shoe didn't fit. " Newsweek 60: 65-66 July 9 '62.

2384. Wood v. Georgia   June 25, 1962 370 U. S. 375
    *Am Consttn (Lockhart) 685-689
    *Cases Consttnl Law (Gunther) 1407-1412
    *Cases Consttnl Rights 506-510
    *Cases Individual 944-951
    Communication (Hemmer) v. 2, 166-167
    Criminal Law Revolution 23
    Freedom of Speech (Hudon) 164-166
    Handbook 516
    *Sup Ct on Freedom 103-104
    System 455-456
    PERIODICALS:
    "Cases notes. " J Criml Law, Crimlgy and Police Sci 53: 494
    Dec '62.

2385. United States v. Wise   June 25, 1962 370 U. S. 405
    Law and Politics 302

2386. Engel v. Vitale   June 25, 1962 370 U. S. 421
    Am Consttn (Kelly) 975
    *Am Consttnl Law (Bartholomew) v. 2, 48-51
    *Am Consttnl Law (Shapiro) 458-463
    *Am Govt 150-156
    Bible 186-200
    *Bill (Cohen) 445-451
    *Bill (Konvitz) 44-50
    CQ Guide 464
    Cases Consttnl Law (Gunther) 1558-1560
    *Cases Individual 1068-1071
    Church and State 142-144
    Church State and Freedom 460-469
    *Civil Liberties (Sweet) 56-60
    Communication (Hemmer) v. 1, 112-113
    *Consttn (Mendelson) 580-584
    *Consttn (Morris) 341-346
    *Consttn (Pollak) v. 2, 86-89
    Consttnl Counterrevolution 237-239

Sup Ct Review 1963 1-33
*Teacher 120-123
*These Liberties 209-216
This Honorable Court 421
*Two Swords 69-74
Wall (Oaks) 84-85, 147-150, 153-158
Warren (Hudgins) 27-29
Warren (Lytle) 47-48
*Warren (Spaeth) 189-196
PERIODICALS:
"After June 25, 1962; Regent's prayer." America 107: 483-484
    July 14 '62.
"Anise and cummin," Gerald W. Johnson. New Republic 147: 8
    July 9 '62.
"Back to school; stratagems to bypass prayer-banning decision."
    Newsweek 60: 69 Sept 10 '62.
"Ban on public school prayer," John B. Sheerin. Catholic World
    195: 261-265 Aug '62.
"Black Monday decision." America 107: 456 July 7 '62.
"Court decision and the school prayer furor." Newsweek 60: 43-
    45 July 9 '62.
"Court on prayer; New York school prayer case." Commonweal
    76: 387-388 July 13 '62. Reaction: Journet Kahn. 77: 257-
    259 Nov 30 '62.
"Engel v. Vitale." New Republic 147: 3-5 July 9 '62.
"Facts about prayer in schools," Louis Carrels. US News 68:
    96 Mar 23 '70 (2).
"Forbidden prayer," William B. Ball. Commonweal 76: 419-422
    July 27 '62. Reaction: 77: 74-76 Oct 12 '62.
"Furor over School prayers; latest in a growing debate." US
    News 56: 72-74 May 11 '64.
"God, man and liberty," Raymond R. Moley. Newsweek 60: 76
    July 23 '62.
"God save this honorable court." Natl R 13: 10-12 July 17 '62.
"Has the Supreme Court outlawed religious observance in the
    schools? debate," William J. Butler, James A. Pike. Readers
    Dig 81: 78-85 Oct '62.
"Impact of the Supreme court decisions on religion in public
    schools," R. B. Dierenfield. Religious Eductn 62: 445-451
    Sept '67 (2).
"Individual liberty and the common good," Brendan F. Brown.
    Vital Speeches 40: 756-761 Oct 1 '74 (4).
"Keeping public schools secular," Charles Bunyan Smith. Eductnl
    Forum 29: 71-77 Nov '64 (2).
"Law, religion, and public education; excerpts from Law and public
    school operation," L. Peterson and others. Sch and Society
    96: 466-471 Dec 7 '68 (2).
"Laws respecting an establishment of religion," Jon Ligtenberg.
    Am Teacher Mag 47: 5-6 Feb '63.
*"Majority decision in Engel v. Vitale." Overview 3: 60-62
    Aug '62.
"Nation chooses sides in fight over prayer." US News 56: 63-64
    May 18 '64.
"New prayer ruling." New York State Eductn 50: 12 Oct '62.
"New York state honors spirit of law." Christian Century 79:
    1249-1250 Oct 17 '62.
"Not too far! dissenting from editorials on the Supreme court
    prayer decision," Francis P. Foote. Christian Century 79:
    1419 Nov 21 '62.

"Now I lay me down to sleep; Court's anti-prayer decision," Russel Kirk. Natl R 13: 230 Sept 25 '62.

"Of schema, hotheads, theology, and smoke," William B. Ball. Teachers College Rec 64: 355-362 Feb '68.

"On praying in school." America 107: 715 Sept 15 '62.

"On second thought." Time 80: 40 Aug 24 '62.

"Open letter to the Supreme Court," Robert T. Reilly. America 107: 623 Aug 18 '62.

"Paradoxes in legal logic." Life 53: 4 July 13 '62.

"Politics and prayer," Kenneth Crawford. Newsweek 63: 36 May 25 '64.

"Politics of prayer stir the nation." Christian Century 79: 856 July 11 '62.

"Popular perceptions of Supreme court rulings," Gregory Casey. Am Poltcs Q 4: 3-46 Jan '76 (4).

"Prayer amendment." America 107: 685 Sept 8 '62.

"Prayer and Hysteria." Nation 195: 2 July 14 '62.

"Prayer and the Court," John Cogley. Commonweal 76: 447-448 Aug 10 '62.

"Prayer barred: what it means," L. O. Garber. Natns Schools 70: 54-55, 76 Aug '62.

"Prayer debate," Kenneth Crawford. Newsweek 60: 28 July 16 '62.

"Prayer still legal in public schools." Christian Century 79: 832-833 July 4 '62.

"Prayer, the Bible and the public schools," H. C. Hudgins, Jr. and Robert A. Nelson. Eductn Dig 32: 22-25 Dec '66; reprinted from: North Carolina Eductn 33: 12-13, 43-45 Oct '66 (2).

"Prayers in the public schools; address, June 28, 1962," Strom Thurmond. Vital Speeches 28: 642-645 Aug 15 '62.

"Prayers in the public schools; address, July 28, 1962," Francis Conklin. Vital Speeches 28: 645-649 Aug 15 '62.

"Public reverence; challenge to the democracy," Robert G. Howes. NCEA Bul 64: 60-65 Feb '68.

"The public school's responsibility toward moral and spiritual values," Ethan B. Janova. Ill Eductn 53: 305-308 Mar '65 (2).

"Reaction to Court decision," Charles D. Kean. Christian Century 79: 896-897 July 18 '62.

"Reaction of Congress to the ruling on school prayer," Elaine Exton. Am Sch Bd J 145: 66-70 Sept '62.

"Recent Supreme Court decisions: separation of church and state," Isidore Starr. Socl Eductn 26: 439-444 Dec '62.

"Regents prayer decision; an analysis of the Supreme Court ruling," John E. Glenn. New York State Eductn 50: 20-21 Oct '62.

"Religion and citizenship," John Ciardi. Sat R 45: 14 Sept 22 '62. Reaction: 45:25 Oct 27 '62.

"Religion and the Court," Leo Pfeffer. Commonweal 76: 417-419 July 27 '62. Reaction: 76: 495-497 Sept 7 '62.

"Religion cases appealed to Supreme Court." Christian Century 79: 767 June 20 '62.

"Religion in public schools." Ohio Sch 42: 12-20 Dec '64 (2).

"Religious symbols in public life," Will Herberg. Natl R 13: 145, 162 Aug 28 '62.

"Restating the hard lesson." Christian Century 79: 881-882 July 18 '62.

"Rights of majorities and of minorities in the 1961 term of the

Supreme Court, " Benjamin F. Wright. Am Poltcl Sci R 57:
98-115 Mar '63.
"Roundup on prayer case. " America 107: 541-542 July 28 '62.
Reaction: 107: 575 Aug 11 '62.
"School prayer battle, " Theodore Powell. Sat R 46: 62-64, 77-
78 Apr 20 '63. Reaction: 46: 62-63 May 18 '63.
"School prayers and religious warfare, " Walter Berns. Natl R
14: 315-318 Apr 23 '63. Reaction: 14: 421 May 21 '63.
14: 473 June 4 '63.
"School prayers and the founding fathers, " Leonard Levy. Com-
mentary 34: 225-230 Sept '62.
"Should we revise amendment one?" Christian Century 79: 1088-
1089 Sept 12 '62.
"Supreme Court and public policy; the school prayer cases, "
Donald R. Reich. Phi Delta Kappan 48: 29-32 Sept '66 (2).
"Supreme Court and school prayer. " Pa Sch J 111: 48 Sept '62.
"Supreme Court decision on government-sponsored prayer, " August
W. Steinhilber. Sch Life 44: 8-9 July '62. Condensed in:
Eductn Dig 28: 35-37 Dec '62.
"Supreme court prayer decision; questions and answers. " NEA J
51: 38 Oct '62.
"Supreme Court ruling on school prayer, " Sam Duker. Eductnl
Forum 27: 71-77 Nov '62.
"Supreme Court's decision on prayer. " Senior Scholastic 81: 1T,
4T-6T Sept 19 '62.
"Supreme Court's new frontier between religion and the public
schools, " George R. La Noue. Phi Delta Kappan 45: 123-
127 Dec '63 (2).
"Survey research on judicial decisions; the prayer and Bible read-
ing cases, " H. Frank Way. Western Poltcl Q 21: 189-205
June '68 (2).
"T. R. B. from Washington: God and the court. " New Republic
147: 2 July 9 '62.
"Take a vote, gentlemen, " William F. Buckley, Jr. Natl R 13:
177 Sept 11 '62.
"Teaching about religion: when and where to begin, " Bert S.
Gerard. Religious Eductn 63: 215-218 May '68 (2).
"This month's feature: Congress and the school prayer decisions. "
Congressional Dig 43: 257-288 Nov '64 (2).
"Thou shalt not pray. " Natl R 13: 51-52 July 31 '62.
"To pray or not to pray: is that the question?" Frank Greenberg.
PTA Mag 58: 22-25, 34 Feb '64 (2).
"To stand as a guarantee. " Time 80: 7-9 July 6 '62.
"True piety and the Regents' prayer, " Edward O. Miller. Chris-
tian Century 79: 934-936 Aug 1 '62. Reaction: 79: 1037-
1039 Aug 29 '62; 79: 1298 Oct 24 '62.
"U. S. Supreme Court decisions. " Congressional Dig 59: 292-
293, 314 Dec '80 (2).
"Uproar over school prayer, and the aftermath. " US News 53:
42-44 July 9 '62.
"We must permit prayer in the schools; school administrators
opinion poll findings. " Natns Sch 70: 101, 121-122 Sept '62.
"What's happening in education? Supreme court rule on the prayer
case, " William D. Boutwell. PTA Mag 57: 11 Nov '62.
"While most believe in God. " Newsweek 60: 11-12 July 9 '62.
"Why clergymen are against school prayer, " Arlene Eisenberg and
Howard Eisenberg. Redbook 124: 38-39, 95-98, 104-105
Jan '65 (2).

2387.   State Board of Insurance v. Todd   June 25, 1962 370 U. S. 451
        Shipyards Corporation
        *Consttnl Law (Freund) 444-447

2388.   United States v. Borden Co.   June 25, 1962 370 U. S. 460
        *Antitrust Analysis 888-892
        *Cases Antitrust Law 1129-1134
        *Cases Trade 1042-1046
        *Free Enterprise 887-893
        *Govt Regulation 1577-1586
        *Text Antitrust 233-239

2389.   Manual Enterprises v. Day   June 25, 1962 370 U. S. 478
        Am Consttn (Kelly) 969
        *Bill (Konvitz) 378-384
        Censorship 212-214
        *Censorship Landmarks 361-375
        Communication (Hemmer) v. 1, 178-179
        Consttnl Counterrevolution 269
        Dissent 405-406
        Expanding Liberties 205-208
        *First Amendment (Konvitz) 785-793
        Freedom of Speech (Hudon) 163-164
        Law of Mass 361
        Law of Obscenity 41-42
        Mass Media (Clark) 285-286
        Obscenity (Clor) 60-69
        *Obscenity (Friedman) 141-142
        Obscenity (Sunderland) 52-53
        Sup Ct Review 1966 14-17

2390.   Glidden Co. v. Zdanok   June 25, 1962 370 U. S. 530
        Lurk v. United States
        *Federal Courts 375-395
        *Materials Consttnl Law 60-81

2391.   Central Railroad Co. of Pennsylvania   June 25, 1962 370 U. S. 607
        v. Pennsylvania
        *Consttnl Law (Barrett) 375-376
        *Consttnl Law (Freund) 513-518
        *Consttnl Law (Kauper) 386-391

2392.   Link v. Wabash Railroad   June 25, 1962 370 U. S. 626
        *Cases Professional 473-477
        Hugo Black (Strickland) 226-230, 235-244

2393.   Robinson v. California   June 25, 1962 370 U. S. 660
        *Cases Criml Law (Inbau) 351-361
        *Cases Drug 249-253
        *Consttnl Law (Felkenes) 348-349
        *Criminal Law (Dix) 146-150
        Criminal Law (Felkenes) 357-359
        *Criminal Law (Kadish) 637-640
        Criminal Law (Wells) 50
        *Criminal Law (Wells) 60-61
        Criminal Law Revolution 13-14
        Defendants 402
        Dissent 393-394
        *Douglas 421-425

Expanding Liberties 164-165
Freedom and the Court 74-75
*Law Sup Ct 336-341
*Readings American 734-736
Sup Ct (North) 132-133
*Sup Ct and Criml Process 862-864
*Sup Ct and Rights 364-368
*Warren (Spaeth) 342-348
*Woman 116-117
PERIODICALS:
"Case notes." J Criml Law, Crimlgy and Police Sci 53: 492 Dec '62.

2394. Continental Ore Co. v. Union Carbide   June 25, 1962   370 U. S. 690
        and Carbon Corporation
        *Cases Antitrust Law 1266-1271
        *Cases Regulation 33-36
        *Cases Trade 1161-1165

2395. Meredith v. Fair   Sep 10, 1962   371 U. S. 19
        Hugo Black (Dunne) 376-377
        *One Man's Stand 462-464

2396. United States v. Loew's Inc.   Nov 5, 1962   371 U. S. 38
        Loew's Inc. v. United States
        C & C Super Corporation v. United States
        *Antitrust (Posner) 642-645
        *Antitrust Analysis 601-605
        *Cases Antitrust Law 634-638
        *Cases Trade 604-607
        *Govt Regulation 1662-1673
        Making 82-84
        Sup Ct Review 1963 152-157
        PERIODICALS:
        "Final curtain falls on block booking." Broadcasting 63: 62-63
            Nov 12 '62.
        "High court hits block booking of television films." Adv Age 33:
            10 Nov 12 '62.
        "How Goldberg views the late show." Bus Wk p. 142 Nov 10 '62.

2397. Southern Construction Co. v. Pickard   Nov 5, 1962   371 U. S. 57
        *Civil Procedure (Cound) 510-511

2398. Los Angeles Meat and Provision   Nov 19, 1962   371 U. S. 94
        Drivers Union v. United States
        *Cases Labor (Handler) 669-675
        *Govt and Business 147-149
        *Govt Regulation 1674-1684
        PERIODICALS:
        "Significant decisions in labor cases." Monthly Labor R 86: 61-
            62 Jan '63.

2399. Burlington Truck Lines, Inc.   Dec 3, 1962   371 U. S. 156
        v. United States
        General Drivers and Helpers Union,
            Local 554 v. United States
        *Govt and Business 621-625

2400. Foman v. Davis   Dec 3, 1962   371 U. S. 178
        *Cases Civil Procedure 1055-1058

2401.   Ford v. Ford   Dec 10, 1962   371 U.S. 187
        *Family 324
        Sup Ct Review 1964 109-112

2402.   Smith v. Evening News Association   Dec 10, 1962   371 U.S. 195
        *Cases Labor (Handler) 323-327
        *Cases Labor (Oberer) 776-780
        *Labor Relations (Group Trust) 904-907
        Law and Politics 129-130
        PERIODICALS:
            "Significant decisions in labor cases." Monthly Labor R   86:   174-
            175 Feb '63.

2403.   Schroeder v. New York City   Dec 17, 1962   371 U.S. 208
        *Civil Procedure (Carrington) 942-945
        *Text Legislation 45-46

2404.   National Labor Relations Board v.   Jan 7, 1963   371 U.S. 224
            Reliance Fuel Oil Corporation
        Sup Ct and Commerce 119-120
        PERIODICALS:
            "Significant decisions in labor cases." Monthly Labor R   86:   307
            Mar '63.

2405.   Jones v. Cunningham, Penitentiary   Jan 14, 1963   371 U.S. 236
            Superintendent
        Criminal Law Revolution 30
        Defendants 138-139
        *US Prison Law v. 4, 250-258

2406.   Paul v. United States   Jan 14, 1963   371 U.S. 245
        PERIODICALS:
            "The milkman rings twice," John R. Donnelly.   Law and Contem-
            porary Problems   29:   347-360 Sept '64.

2407.   Pan American World Airways v.   Jan 14, 1963   371 U.S. 296
            United States
        *Cases Regulated 1136-1143
        Law and Politics 316-318

2408.   Shotwell Manufacturing Co. v. United   Jan 14, 1963   371 U.S. 341
            States
        Making 112-114

2409.   Cleary v. Bolger   Jan 14, 1963   371 U.S. 392
        Criminal Law Revolution 33-34

2410.   National Association for the Advance- Jan 14, 1963   371 U.S. 415
            ment of Colored People v. Button
        *Affair 112-119
        By What Right 220-222
        CQ Guide 403
        *Cases Consttnl Law (Gunther) 1418-1423
        *Cases Consttnl Law (Rosenblum) 423-430
        *Cases Individual 966-972
        *Civil Liberties (Sweet) 197-203
        *Civil Rights (Blaustein) 489-496
        *Consttnl Law (Freund) 1241-1246
        *Courts Judges 280-283

Desegregation (Wasby) 191-192
Dissent 354-355
*Evolution 163-172
Expanding Liberties 67-69
*First Amendment (Konvitz) 211-222
*Law Lawyers 302-318
*Law Sup Ct 152-157
*Legal Problems 530-534
Making 107-108
Negro (Kalven) 75-76, 80-90
*Political Rights 510-515
System 429-430

2411. Wong Sun v. United States   Jan 14, 1963   371 U. S. 471
        *Affair 191-194
        Arrest (Waddington) 169, 173
        *Cases Criml Justice 75-85
        *Cases Criml Law (Perkins) 1008-1012
        *Consttnl Criml (Marks) 339-345
        *Consttnl Criml (Scarboro) 451-452
        Criminal Evidence 258-259
        Criminal Law (Felkenes) 107-111
        *Criminal Law (Kadish) 960-963
        Criminal Law Revolution 34
        *Criminal Procedure (Lewis) 292-298
        Exclusionary 32
        *Leading Consttnl Cases 272-277
        Making 72-75, 109-112
        Police 20-21
        *Principles Arrest 106-117
        *Sup Ct and Criml Process 343-346
        *Teaching Materials 99-105
        PERIODICALS:
        "Case notes." J Criml Law, Crimlgy and Police Sci 54: 189
            June '63.

2412. Federal Trade Commission v. Sun   Jan 14, 1963   371 U. S. 505
        Oil Co.
        *Antitrust Analysis 908-912
        *Competition 280-285
        *Free Enterprise 880-887
        *Govt Regulation 1697-1711
        Making 106-107
        PERIODICALS:
        "New guidelines for oil marketers" NPN 55: 83-88 Feb '63.
        *"   ." NPN 55: 86-88 Feb '63.
        "Nightmare for oil marketers." Bus Wk p. 66 Jan 19 '63.

2413. Local No. 438, Construction and   Jan 21, 1963   371 U. S. 542
        General Laborers' Union, AFL-
        CIO v. Curry
        *Federal Courts 620-624

2414. McCulloch v. Sociedad Nacional   Feb 18, 1963   372 U. S. 10
        de Marineros de Honduras
        McLeod v. Empresa Hondurena de
        Vapores, S. A.
        National Maritime Union of America
        v. Empresa Hondurena de
        Vapores, S. A.

Making 173-176
Sup Ct Review 1963 34-100

2415.   Incres Steamship Co. v. International   Feb 18, 1963   372 U.S. 24
      Maritime Workers Union
      Sup Ct Review 1963 34-100

2416.   United States v. National Dairy   Feb 18, 1963   372 U.S. 29
      Products Corporation
      *Cases Antitrust Law 1239-1243
      *Cases Trade 1127-1129
      *Govt Regulation 1712-1718

2417.   Bantam Books, Inc. v. Sullivan   Feb 18, 1963   372 U.S. 58
      *Affair 48-52
      *Cases Consttnl Rights 640-642
      *Censorship Landmarks 413-420
      Communication (Hemmer) v. 1, 186-187
      Expanding Liberties 210-212
      *First Amendment (Konvitz) 856-862
      Free Speech (Kurland) 436-439
      *Mass Media (Devol) 119-121
      Mass Media (Francois) 41-42
      Movies 109-113
      *Sup Ct on Freedom 57-59
      Sup Ct Review 1963 108-109
      Sup Ct Review 1974 327-331
      PERIODICALS:
      "R. I. censors' activities ruled unconstitutional, with editorial
        comment." Pub Weekly 183: 42-43, 49 Mar 4 '63.
      "US Supreme Court overrules Rhode Island censors' group."
        Library J 88: 1736 Apr 15 '63.

2418.   Gallick v. Baltimore and Ohio   Feb 18, 1963   372 U.S. 108
      Railroad Co.
      *Civil Procedure (Carrington) 375-381
      Making 171-172

2419.   Kennedy v. Mendoza-Martinez   Feb 18, 1963   372 U.S. 144
      Rusk v. Cort
      *Civil Liberties (Sweet) 329-336
      *Freedom vs National Security 487-493
      Justice Rutledge 283-285
      Making 60, 164-169
      Sup Ct Review 1963 325-356
      PERIODICALS:
      "Citizenship and other cases." Time 81: 20-21 Mar 1 '63.
      "Expatriation decisions," John P. Roche. Am Poltcl Sci R 58:
        72-80 Mar '64.
      "The security of citizenship." Socl Eductn 30: 433-444 Oct '66.

2420.   Schneider v. Rusk   Feb 1963   372 U.S. 224
      Making 169

2421.   Edwards v. South Carolina   Feb 25, 1963   372 U.S. 229
      *Am Consttn (Lockhart) 805-807
      Am Politics 81-82
      *Bill (Cohen) 289-292
      *Bill (Konvitz) 186-189

By What Right 222
CQ Guide 413, 415
*Cases Consttnl Rights 686-688
*Civil Liberties (Sweet) 179-182
*Civil Rights (Abernathy) 1977 428-431
Civil Rights (Bardolph) 521-522
Communication (Hemmer) v. 1, 92-93
*Consttn (Mendelson) 466-471
Consttnl Law (Barrett) 1258-1259
*Consttnl Law (Kauper) 1160-1162
*Consttnl Law (Lockhart) 1044-1046
*Consttnl Law (Maddex) 418-422
Decade 210-213
Desegregation (Wasby) 343-345
Expanding Liberties 267-268
*First Amendment (Konvitz) 323-327
Free Speech (Kurland) 118-124
*Free Speech (Summers) 111-115
*Freedom of Speech (Haiman) 95-96
*Judicial Crises 270-274
*Judicial Excerpts 84-86
*Law Sup Ct 27-34
*Liberty v. 2, 605-606
Negro (Kalven) 141-147
Politics 115-116
*Principles Freedom 218-226
*Protest 188-196
Sup Ct Review 1965 4-5, 6-7, 176-178
System 320-321
*These Liberties 158-161

2422.   White Motor Co. v. United States   Mar 4, 1963   372 U. S. 253
        *Antitrust (Posner) 261-266
        *Antitrust Analysis 531-537
        *Cases Antitrust Law 552-564
        *Cases Trade 301-302, 516-525
        *Govt Regulation 1719-1735
        Law and Politics 312-313
        Sup Ct Review 1977 177-178
        PERIODICALS:
        "Supreme Court delays ruling on territorial franchise restrictions, "
        Sidney A. Diamond. Adv Age 34: 82, 84 Apr 15 '63.

2423.   Townsend v. Sain   Mar 18, 1963   372 U. S. 293
        *Criminal Law (Kadish) 1544-1549
        Criminal Law Revolution 29-30
        *Federal Courts 1494-1503
        Making 80-81, 231-232
        PERIODICALS:
        "Case notes. " J Criml Law, Crimlgy and Police Sci 54: 335-
        336 Sept '63.

2424.   Gideon v. Wainright   Mar 18, 1963   372 U. S. 335
        *Am Consttn (Lockhart) 456-458
        *Am Consttnl Law (Bartholomew) v. 2, 248-249
        *Am Consttnl Law (Shapiro) 664-666
        *Am Govt 129-135
        *Basic Cases 217-226
        *Basic Criminal 49-52

*Sup Ct (Mendelson) 232-239
Sup Ct (North) 127-128
*Sup Ct and Consttn 572-576
*Sup Ct and Criml Process 554-556
*Sup Ct and Public Policy 166-172
*Sup Ct and Rights 8-14
Sup Ct Review 1963 211-272
Warren (Lytle) 78-79
*Warren (Sayler) 240-250
*Warren (Spaeth) 328-334
PERIODICALS:
   "Annals of law; Gideon case," Anthony Lewis. New Yorker 40:
      144, 146, 149-152, 154-169 Apr 25 '64; 108+ ending p. 175
      May 2 '64; 150+ ending p. 190 May 9 '64.
   "Case notes." J Criml Law, Crimlgy and Police Sci 54: 193
      June '63.
   "Court keeps in step." Economist 207: 1356 June 29 '63.
   "Dissenter Harlan critical of fellow justices." US News 55: 26
      Oct 28 '63.
   "Ex-con overturns the law," with report by Michael Durham.
      Life 56: 83-84, 86, 89 June 12 '64.
   "Facing up to Gideon," David G. Temple. Natl Civic R 54: 354-
      356, 386 July '65.
   "Gideon's impact." Time 86: 39 Dec 17 '65.
   "Is it wrong to handcuff the police?" William J. Dempsey. Cath-
      olic World 204: 264-269 Feb '67 (3).
   "Justice for the poor." Socl Service R 37: 321-322 Sept '63.
   "Justice for the poor; the banner of Gideon," Robert G. Sherrill.
      Nation 198: 367-372 Apr 13 '64.
   "The right to legal counsel." Socl Eductn 30: 101-112 Feb '66.
   "Supreme Court hands down major rulings." Senior Scholastic
      82: 17 Apr 3 '63 (3).

2425. Douglas v. California   Mar 18, 1963 372 U.S. 353
      *Am Consttn (Lockhart) 464-466
      *Basic Criminal 71-77
      *Cases Consttnl Law (Gunther) 941-943
      *Cases Consttnl Rights 230-233
      *Cases Criml Law (Perkins) 987-990
      *Cases Individual 410-413
      *Consttnl Law (Barron) 658-659
      *Consttnl Law (Kauper) 1015-1021
      Court and Consttn v. 2, 303
      Criminal Law (Felkenes) 186-188
      *Criminal Law (Kadish) 789-792
      Criminal Law Revolution 26-27
      Criminal Procedure 205-206
      *Due Process 48-49
      *Elements Criminal 84-87
      *Evolution 13-18
      *Law Sup Ct 264-268
      *Leading Consttnl Cases 424-429
      Making 227-228
      *Police 122-123
      *Poverty 168-172
      *Processes 830-834

2426. Gray v. Sanders   Mar 18, 1963 372 U.S. 368
      Am Consttn (Kelly) 945

CQ Guide 492
*Civil Liberties (Sweet) 296-300
Consttnl Counterrevolution 99-100
Court and Consttn v. 2, 319-320, 321-322
Decade 94
Democratic 172-177, 179-182
Making 141-151, 228-229
Reapportionment (Baker) 124-125
Reapportionment (McKay) 83-89
Rights of the People 140-141
*Social Forces 119-124
Sup Ct and Electoral Process 163-165
Sup Ct and Poltcl Questions 79-83
Sup Ct Review 1964 4
Warren (Ball) 139-159
PERIODICALS:
"Crime and reapportionment," Alexander M. Bickel. New Republic 148: 5 Apr 6 '63 (2).
"Equality in representation; congressional districts." Christian Century 81: 291-292 Mar 4 '64.
"Supreme Court hands down major rulings." Senior Scholastic 82: 17 Apr 3 '63 (3).
"Where High court put federal standards on state rules." US News 54: 30 Apr 1 '63.

2427. Fay v. Noia   Mar 18, 1963 372 U.S. 391
*Affair 221-231
By What Right 282-288
*Cases Criml Law (Hall) 1209-1210
*Cases Federal Courts 551-572
*Civil Rights (Abernathy) 1977 258-262
*Consttnl Criml (Scarboro) 785-801
*Criminal Law (Kadish) 1532-1543
Criminal Law Revolution 28-29
Criminal Procedure (Wells) 203-204
Dissent 359-360
*Due Process 193-194
*Evolution 46-57
*Federal Courts 1436-1464
*Law Sup Ct 347-355
Making 124-131, 223-227
Sup Ct Review 1979 258
PERIODICALS:
"Case notes." J Criml Law, Crimlgy and Police Sci 54: 334-355 Sept '63.
"Crime and reapportionment," Alexander M. Bickel. New Republic 148: 5 Apr 6 '63 (2).
"Supreme Court hands down major rulings." Senior Scholastic 82: 17 Apr 3 '63 (3).

2428. Lane v. Brown   Mar 18, 1963 372 U.S. 477
Criminal Law Revolution 27
Making 222-223

2429. Draper v. Washington   Mar 18, 1963 372 U.S. 487
Criminal Law Revolution 27-28
Making 221-222

2430. Lynum v. Illinois   Mar 25, 1963 372 U.S. 528

Criminal Law Revolution 35-36
Police 106-107

2431.   Gibson v. Florida Legislative   Mar 25, 1963   372 U. S. 539
        Investigation Committee
        Am Consttn (Kelly) 934
        *Am Consttn (Lockhart) 663-668
        *Am Consttnl Law (Shapiro) 380-385
        *Bill (Cohen) 228-233
        By What Right 224
        CQ Guide 403
        *Cases Consttnl Law (Gunther) 1495-1500
        *Cases Consttnl Rights 481-487
        *Cases Individual 1028-1034
        Communication (Hemmer) v. 1, 62-63
        *Consttn (Mendelson) 446-447
        Consttnl Law (Barrett) 1187-1188
        *Consttnl Law (Freund) 1322-1325
        *Consttnl Law (Lockhart) 819-824
        Decade 45
        Expanding Liberties 80-82
        *First Amendment (Konvitz) 752-763
        Making 288-289
        Negro (Kalven) 105-119
        Petitioners 388-389
        *Political Rights 389-400
        Politics 99-104
        *Rights (Shattuck) 59-60
        System 267-269

2432.   Wolf v. Weinstein   Apr 15, 1963   372 U. S. 633
        *Materials Reorganization 620-627
        Sup Ct Review 1963 277-291

2433.   Arrow Transportation Co. v. Southern   Apr 15, 1963   372 U. S. 658
        Railway Co.
        *Govt and Business 544-550

2434.   Colorado Anti-Discrimination Com-   Apr 22, 1963   372 U. S. 714
        mission v. Continental Air Lines
        Green v. Continental Air Lines, Inc.
        *Law Sup Ct 611-618
        Sup Ct and Commerce 200
        *Warren (Spaeth) 366-368
        PERIODICALS:
        "Significant decisions in labor cases." Monthly Labor R   86:   826-
        827 July '63.

2435.   Ferguson v. Skrupa   Apr 22, 1963   372 U. S. 726
        *Am Consttn (Lockhart) 375-376
        *Am Consttnl Law (Mason) 435-437
        *Basic Cases 130-132
        *Cases Consttnl Rights 135-136
        *Comparative 276-277
        *Consttnl Law (Kauper) 671-673
        *Consttnlism 73-75
        *Federal System 43-44
        *Sup Ct and Consttn 422-424

Teaching Materials 25-28
This Honorable Court 322

2436. Downum v. United States   Apr 22, 1963   372 U.S. 734
       *Consttnl Law (Kauper) 1010-1012
       *Criminal Law (Kadish) 1394-1397
       *Sup Ct and Criml Process 406-407
       PERIODICALS:
       "Case notes." J Criml Law, Crimlgy and Police Sci 54: 494
       Dec '63.

2437. Interstate Commerce Commission v.   Apr 22, 1963   372 U.S. 744
       New York, New Haven and
       Hartford Railroad
       *Cases Regulated 689-699

2438. Sanders v. United States   Apr 29, 1963   373 U.S. 1
       *Criminal Law (Kadish) 1549-1552
       *Evolution 235-241

2439. White v. Maryland   Apr 29, 1963   373 U.S. 59
       Justice Rutledge 250
       Police 123-124
       Rationing 106

2440. Johnson v. Virginia   Apr 29, 1963   373 U.S. 61
       *Discrimination 299-300
       *Political Rights v. 2, 1425-1426

2441. Brady v. Maryland   May 13, 1963   373 U.S. 83
       Criminal Evidence 40-41
       *Due Process 136-137
       Law of Arrest (Creamer) 476-477
       PERIODICALS:
       "Case notes." J Criml Law, Crimlgy and Police Sci 54: 494-
       495 Dec '63.

2442. Brotherhood of Railway and Steam-   May 13, 1963   373 U.S. 113
       ship Clerks, Freight Handlers,
       Express and Station Employees v.
       Allen
       *Labor Relations (Group Trust) 989-997
       PERIODICALS:
       "Blow at unions' political power?" US News 54: 101 May 27 '63.
       "Significant decisions in labor cases." Monthly Labor R 86: 825
       July '63.
       "U.S. labor policy--recent major Supreme Court decisions." Con-
       gressional Dig 44: 197-198, 224 Aug/Sept '65 (3).

2443. Florida Lime and Avocado Growers   May 13, 1963   373 U.S. 132
       v. Paul
       "Avocado Pear Case"
       *Cases Food 792-797
       *Consttnl Law (Kauper) 422-428
       *Govt and Business 283-289
       Sup Ct and Commerce 298-304

2444. Gutierrez v. Waterman Steamship   May 13, 1963   373 U.S. 206
       Corporation

Sup Ct Review 1964 250-256

2445. National Labor Relations Board v.   May 13, 1963   373 U.S. 221
       Erie Resistor Co.
       Basic Text 331-332
       *Cases Labor (Cox) 859-863
       *Cases Labor (Leslie) 258-262
       *Cases Labor (Oberer) 533-538
       *Labor Law (Meltzer) 236-242
       *Labor Relations 260-264
       Law and Politics 118-121
       PERIODICALS:
       "Significant decisions in labor cases." Monthly Labor R 86: 824-
       825 July '63.

2446. Peterson v. City of Greenville   May 20, 1963   373 U.S. 244
       CQ Guide 611
       Communication (Hemmer) v. 1, 79-80
       *Consttnl Decisions 171-174
       Equality (Berger) 123
       Expanding Liberties 316-317
       *Liberty v. 2, 602-604
       Making 239-245
       Petitioners 399
       Protest 270-272
       *Racial Equality 123
       *Struggle 131-133
       Sup Ct Review 1963 101-151
       PERIODICALS:
       "Civil rights boil-up," Alexander M. Bickel. New Republic 148:
       10-14 June 8 '63.
       "Civil rights decisions." Commonweal 78: 292-293 June 7 '63.
       "In High Court, a blanket rule against segregation?" US News
       54: 65 June 3 '63.
       "Letter from Washington," Richard H. Rovere. New Yorker 39:
       101-104, 107-108 June 1 '63.
       "Mental urges of the mob," David Lawrence. US News 54: 112
       June 17 '63.
       "Warren again." Natl R 14: 436-437 June 4 '63.

2447. Shuttlesworth v. Birmingham   May 20, 1963   373 U.S. 262
       *Protest 272-274

2448. Lombard v. Louisiana   May 20, 1963   373 U.S. 267
       Communication (Hemmer) v. 1, 80-81
       Decade 202-203, 205-206
       Making 245
       Petitioners 399-400
       *Protest 274-280
       *Racial Equality 123-124

2449. Wright v. Georgia   May 20, 1963   373 U.S. 284
       *Bill (Konvitz) 584-586
       Communication (Hemmer) v. 1, 81
       Expanding Liberties 280
       *Struggle 127-131

2450. Silver v. New York Stock Exchange   May 20, 1963   373 U.S. 341
       *Antitrust (Posner) 572-578

           *Antitrust Analysis 399-400
           *Cases Antitrust Law 470-478
           *Govt and Business 143-147
           *Govt Regulation 1751-1770
           Professional Sports 462-463
           *Social Forces 290-294
           PERIODICALS:
           "New cop on Big board beat." Bus Wk p. 28 May 25 '63.

2451. Sperry v. Florida ex rel Florida Bar   May 27, 1963 373 U.S. 379
        *Cases Professional 127-131

2452. Reed v. The Steamship Yaka   May 27, 1963 373 U.S. 410
        Sup Ct Review 1964 257-258

2453. Lopez v. United States   May 27, 1963 373 U.S. 427
        *Affair 194-202
        *Cases Criml Law (Perkins) 1015-1019
        Criminal Evidence 566-567
        Criminal Law (Felkenes) 138-140
        Criminal Law Revolution 32-33
        *Police 160-161
        *Principles Arrest 364
        Privacy (Westin) 356-359
        Search and Seizure 238-243
        Self Inflicted Wound 260-261
        *These Liberties 278-283
        PERIODICALS:
        "Cases notes." J Criml Law, Crimlgy and Police Sci 54: 495-
          496 Dec '63.

2454. Haynes v. Washington   May 27, 1963 373 U.S. 503
        Am Consttn (Kelly) 955
        *Due Process 59
        Police 107-109
        Sup Ct and Confessions 123-125
        PERIODICALS:
        "Case notes." J Criml Law, Crimlgy and Police Sci 54: 490
        Dec '63.

2455. Watson v. Memphis   May 27, 1963 373 U.S. 526
        *Bill (Konvitz) 586-592
        Communication (Hemmer) v. 1, 81-82
        *Consttn (Pollak) v. 2, 287-289
        Desegregation (Wasby) 278-281
        Expanding Liberties 283-284
        PERIODICALS:
        "In the courts: action for faster integration." US News 54: 10
        June 10 '63.

2456. Arizona v. California   June 3, 1963   373 U.S. 546
        *Law Indian 313-316
        Making 57-59, 251-254
        Sup Ct Review 1963 158-205
        PERIODICALS:
        "West's water fight is far from over." Bus Wk p. 26 June 8
        '63.

2457. Wheeldin v. Wheeler   June 3, 1963   373 U.S. 647
        *Federal Courts 907-913

2458. McNeese v. Board of Education for   June 3, 1963   373 U. S. 668
       School District 187, Cahokia, Ill.
       Education (Lapati) 282-283
       Warren (Hudgins) 85-86

2459. Goss v. Board of Education of   June 3, 1963   373 U. S. 683
       Knoxville, Tennessee
       *Bill (Konvitz) 555-558
       *Consttn (Mendelson) 530-532
       Decade 67-68
       Desegregation (Wasby) 199-202
       Digest 82-83
       Disaster 42
       Education (Lapati) 283
       From Brown 95-96
       Obscenity (Bosmajian) 85-86
       PERIODICALS:
       "Supreme Court on school desegregation, 1963." NEA Research
       Bul 41: 75-76 Oct '63 (2).

2460. Local 100 of United Association of   June 3, 1963   373 U. S. 690
       Journeymen and Apprentices v.
       Borden
       *Labor Relations (Group Trust) 367-372
       PERIODICALS:
       "Significant decisions in labor cases." Monthly Labor R 86: 954-
       956 Aug '63.

2461. Rideau v. Louisiana   June 3, 1963   373 U. S. 723
       Communication (Hemmer) v. 2, 179-180
       Criminal Law (Wells) 142-143
       Handbook 525-526
       *Justices (Friedman) v. 4, 2942-2944
       Law of Mass 263-264
       Mass Media (Devol) 297-299
       Mass Media (Francois) 273
       Procedures 102-103
       Radio 10-12
       *Sup Ct on Freedom 111-113
       PERIODICALS:
       "Case notes." J Criml Law, Crimlgy and Police Sci 54: 500
       Dec '63.

2462. National Labor Relations Board v.   June 3, 1963   373 U. S. 734
       General Motors Corporation
       *Cases Labor (Cox) 1052-1057
       *Cases Labor (Handler) 397-401
       *Cases Labor (Leslie) 514-517
       *Cases Labor (Oberer) 808-812
       *Labor Law (Meltzer) 956-960
       *Labor Relations (Group Trust) 637-639
       PERIODICALS:
       "From the High Court: a boost and a setback for unions." US
       News 54: 87-88 June 17 '63 (2).
       "Significant decisions in labor cases." Monthly Labor R 86: 953-
       954 Aug '63.

2463. Retail Clerks International Union   June 3, 1963   373 U. S. 746
       v. Schermerhorn

Basic Text 662-663
*Cases Labor (Handler) 401-404
*Labor Law (Meltzer) 962-964
*Labor Relations (Group Trust) 665-667
PERIODICALS:
"From the High Court; a boost and a setback for unions. " US
    News 54: 87-88 June 17 '63 (2).
"Significant decisions in labor cases. " Monthly Labor R 86: 953-
    954 Aug '63.
"Significant decisions in labor cases. " Monthly Labor R 87: 65
    Jan '64.

2464. Ker v. California   June 10, 1963 374 U.S. 23
      *Affair 202-208
      Arrest (Waddington) 5
      *Cases Criml Justice 135-146
      Communication (Hemmer) v. 1, 233
      Criminal Evidence 335-336
      Criminal Law (Felkenes) 25-28
      *Criminal Law (Kadish) 932-934
      Criminal Law Revolution 31-32
      Exclusionary 33-34
      Justice Without Trial 221-224
      Law of Arrest (Markle) 105-106
      *Police 24, 67-69
      *Principles Arrest 179-187
      Search and Seizure 113, 165-167
      PERIODICALS:
      "Case notes. " J Criml Law, Crimlgy and Police Sci 54: 488-
          489 Dec '63.

2465. Amalgamated Association of Street,   June 10, 1963 374 U.S. 74
          Electric Railway and Motor
          Coach Employees v. Missouri
      *Cases Labor (Oberer) 1069-1071
      *Govt and Business 255-256
      *Labor Relations (Group Trust) 704-707
      PERIODICALS:
      "Significant decisions in labor cases. " Monthly Labor R 86:
          1071 Sept '63.

2466. Yellin v. United States   June 17, 1963 374 U.S. 109
      Am Consttn (Kelly) 934-935
      Making 285-286
      *Materials Legislation 494-511

2467. United States v. Muniz   June 17, 1963 374 U.S. 150
      Criminal Law (Felkenes) 411-413
      Making 290-291

2468. United States v. Singer Manufacturing   June 17, 1963 374 U.S. 174
          Co.
      *Antitrust (Posner) 859-870
      *Antitrust Analysis 483-485
      *Corporal 1578-1579
      *Free Enterprise 1136-1138
      *Govt and Business 179-181
      Law and Politics 322-324

2469. School District of Abington Township   June 17, 1963 374 U. S. 203
       v. Schempp
   Murray v. Curlett
   *Affair 135-152
   Am Consttn (Kelly) 975-976
   *Am Consttn (Lockhart) 876-883
   *Am Consttnl Law (Bartholomew) v. 2, 52-54
   *Am Consttnl Law (Mason) 622-628
   *Am Consttnl Law (Shapiro) 302-304, 463-469
   Bible 99-107, 132-154, 288-292
   *Bill (Cohen) 451-462
   *Bill (Konvitz) 50-57
   CQ Guide 464-466
   *Cases Civil Liberties 299-302
   *Cases Consttnl Law (Cushman) 529-532
   Cases Consttnl Law (Gunther) 1560-1563
   *Cases Consttnl Law (Rosenblum) 407-422
   *Cases Consttnl Rights 802-809
   Church and State 144-147
   Church State and Freedom 469-476
   *Civil Liberties (Barker) 36-42
   *Civil Liberties (Sweet) 60-67
   *Civil Rights (Abernathy) 1977 301-308
   Civil Rights (Schimmel) 121-124
   Communication (Hemmer) v. 1, 113-115
   *Consttn (Morris) 346-350
   *Consttn (Pollak) v. 2, 96-105
   Consttnl Counterrevolution 239-240
   *Consttnl Decisions 146-156
   *Consttnl Law (Barrett) 1448-1454
   *Consttnl Law (Barron) 967-971
   *Consttnl Law (Freund) 1370-1375
   *Consttnl Law (Kauper) 1267-1278
   *Consttnl Law (Lockhart) 1173-1179
   *Contemporary Law 818-835
   Decade 127-134
   Digest 19-20
   Dissent 218-220
   *Documents History v. 2, 678-680
   Dynamics 52-55, 79-84
   Earl Warren 211-212
   *Education (Hazard) 105-116
   Education (Lapati) 208-214
   *Educational Policy 94-101
   *Essentials 168-181
   Expanding Liberties 25-27
   First Amendment (Berns) 60-61
   *First Amendment (Konvitz) 52-62
   First Amendment (Marnell) 195-201
   Freedom and the Court 302-305, 326
   Great Events Worldwide v. 2, 949-954
   Impact (Becker) 25-34, 106-114
   Impact (Wasby) 132-135
   *Judicial Excerpts 58-60
   Justice Rutledge 86-89
   *Justices (Friedman) v. 4, 2939-2942
   Landmark Decisions 121-129
   Law and Education 289-290
   *Law and Public Education (Goldstein) 136-143

PERIODICALS:
"ABC's on prayers in school." US News 55: 41 July 1 '63.
"All others are invited." America 109: 34 July 13 '63.
"Are we violating the Constitution?" Donald Meints. Music Ed-
    ucators J 51: 62, 67 Jan '65.
"Behind the fight against school prayer; Christian view," H. B.
    Sissel. Look 27: 25-9 June 18 '63. Reply: America 108:
    874 June 22 '63.
"Bible; better in school than in Court." Life 54:4 Mar 15 '63.
    Reaction: Life 54: 63-64, 68A Apr 12 '63.
"Bible in the English program," Robert F. Hogan. English J
    54: 488-494 Sept '65.
"Bible reading and prayer in public schools," Isidore Starr. Socl
    Edctn 29: 361-372 Oct '65.
"Bible reading in the public schools," August W. Steinhilber.
    Sch Life 46: 13-16 Oct '63.

"Bible reading, prayers, and public schools," William W. Brickman. Sch & Society 91: 272 Oct 5 '63.
"Church and state." Newsweek 62: 48 July 1 '63.
"Confusion on church and state," Robert L. Gildea. Christian Century 80: 1381-1382 Nov 6 '63.
"Court bars Bible reading, but finds place for religion in schools," Lee O. Garber Natns Schools 72: 50-51 Aug '63.
"Court: complete separation of the spheres." Michigan Edctn J 41: 10-11 Dec '63.
"Court decides wisely; school prayer." Christian Century 80: 851 July 3 '63.
"Court on prayer" Commonweal 78: 388-389 July 5 '63.
"Decision on the Lord's prayer and Bible reading," J. B. Sheerin. Catholic World 197: 276-279 Aug '63.
"Dialogue with Mrs. O'Hair; interview," Niels C. Nielsen, Jr. Christian Century 83: 615-618 May 11 '66.
"Do court decisions give minority rule?" Dale Doak. Phi Delta Kappan 45: 20-24 Oct '63.
"Facts about prayer in schools," Louis Cassels. US News 68: 96 Mar 23 '70 (2).
"God banished from the classroom twice," Howard D. Hamilton. Teachers Col J 35: 174-177 Mar '64.
"God go home." Natl R 14: 521 July 2 '63.
"Impact of the Supreme Court decisions on religion in public schools," R. B. Dierenfield. Religious Edctn 62: 445-451 Sept '67 (2).
"In God we trust." Nation 197: 2 July 6 '63.
"Individual liberty and the common good," Brendan F. Brown. Vital Speeches 40: 756-761 Oct 1 '74 (4).
"Keeping public schools secular," Charles Bunyan Smith. Edctnl Forum 29: 71-77 Nov '64 (2).
"Law, religion and public education; excerpts from Law and public school operation," L. Peterson and others. Sch & Society 96: 466-471 Dec 7 '68 (2).
"Loss to make up for." Time 81: 13-14 June 28 '63.
"Moral heritage and the law." Life 54: 4 June 28 '63.
"Morality and religion in public education; a dialogue," Robert T. Hall. Religious Edctn 72: 273-292 May/June '77.
"Popular perceptions of Supreme Court rulings," Gregory Casey. Am Politics Q 4: 3-46 Jan '76 (4).
"Prayer amendment," William F. Buckley, Jr. Natl R 23: 1375 Dec 3 '71.
"Prayer amendments; a Catholic lawyer's view," William B. Ball. Catholic World 199: 345-351 Sep '64.
"Prayer and the schools; Bible-reading decision." America 108: 898 June 29 '63.
"Prayer or pluralism in the schools?" James Cass. Sat R 47: 41 July 18 '64.
"Prayer, the Bible, and the public schools," H. C. Hudgins and Robert A. Nelson. North Carolina Edctn 33: 12-13, 43-45 Oct '66 (2). Reprinted in: Ed Dig 32: 22-25 Dec '66.
"Prayers, Bibles and schools; in Maryland and Pennsylvania." Christian Century 79: 1279-1280 Oct 24 '62.
"The public school's responsibility toward moral and religious values," Ethan B. Janova. Illinois Edctn 53: 305-308 Mar '65 (2).
"Religion and public life," Will Herberg. Natl R 15: 61 July 30 '63.

"Religion and the Court," James O'Gara. Commonweal 78: 391
    July 5 '63.
"Religion expelled." Economist 207: 1252, 1255 June 22 '63.
"Religion in public schools," Ohio Sch 42: 12-20 Dec '64 (2).
"Religion in the public schools; symposium," Religious Edctn 59:
    443-479, 504 Nov '64.
"Religion in the school: what are the alternatives?" Charles C.
    Chandler. Edctnl Leadership 23: 369-372 Feb '66.
"Religious freedom; the Court expands a concept," Thomas G.
    Sanders. Nation 197: 25-28 July 13 '63.
"Religious neutrality," John J. Regan. America 110: 74-76
    Jan 18 '64 (2).
"Religious scholarship and the Court," Clyde Holbrook. Christian
    Century 80: 1076-1078 Sep 4 '63. Reaction: Sidney E.
    Mead. 80: 1342-1343 Oct 30 '63.
"Right to pray," David Lawrence. US News 56: 96 Mar 2 '64.
"Room for objections and doubts." Time 82: 54 Oct 25 '63.
"Saving our children from God," L. Brent Bozell. Natl R 15:
    19-22, 34 July 16 '63. Reaction: 15: 119-120 Aug 13 '63.
"School prayers decision." Senior Scholastic 83: 9-11 Sep 13
    '63.
"Schoolrooms and prayers." Emmet John Hughes. Newsweek
    62: 15 July 1 '63.
"Schools and religion; court rulings on the Bible and prayer,"
    Samuel A. Pleasants. Clearing House 38: 268-270 Jan '64.
"Schools react to Court decision." Christian Century 80: 1228-
    1229 Oct 9 '63.
"Second Bible ruling." Senior Scholastic 83: 4T Sep 13 '63.
"Secular purpose." America 109: 127 Aug 10 '63.
"Shall we pray." New Republic 148: 4-6 June 29 '63.
"Should what is rendered to God be commanded by Caesar?"
    Marshall J. Tyree. Phi Delta Kappan 44: 74-76 Nov '62.
"Supreme Court and public policy: the school prayer cases,"
    Donald R. Reich. Phi Delta Kappan 48: 29-32 Sep '66 (2).
"Supreme Court Bible decision stirs both legal and philosophical
    discussions." Pennsylvania Sch J 112: 68 Oct '63.
"Supreme Court decision on Bible reading and prayer recitation."
    NEA J 52: 55-56 Sep '63.
"Supreme Court decision on religion in public schools," Lucile
    Lindberg and Jeannette Veatch. Instructor 73: 43-44, 87
    Oct '63.
"Supreme Court to hear Bible reading cases; Maryland and Penn-
    sylvania." Christian Century 80: 198 Feb 13 '63.
"Supreme Court's new frontier between religion and the public
    schools," George R. La Noue. Phi Delta Kappan 45: 123-127
    Dec '63 (2).
"Survey research on judicial decision: the prayer and Bible read-
    ing cases," H. Frank Way. Western Poltcl Q 21: 189-205
    June '68 (2).
"Teaching about religion: when and where to begin," Bert S.
    Gerard. Religious Edctn 63: 215-218 May '68 (2).
"This month's feature: Congress and the school prayer decisions,"
    Congressional Dig 43: 257-288 Nov '64 (2).
"To pray or not to pray: is that the question?" Frank Greenberg.
    PTA Mag 58: 22-25, 34 Feb '64 (2).
"To prevent hysteria: Lord's prayer and Bible readings in Mary-
    land and Pennsylvania." Christian Century 80: 485-486 Apr
    17 '63. Reaction: 80: 750 June 5 '63.

"Unconstitutional prayers; letters to the editor." Natl R 15: 163
  Aug 27 '63.
"U. S. Supreme Court and religion in the schools," August W.
  Steinhilber. TIP 4: 8-13 Feb '65 (4).
"U. S. Supreme Court decisions." Congressional Dig 59: 292-293,
  314 Dec '80 (2).
"Where are we with the Supreme Court." Religious Edctn 59:
  313-329, 337 July '64.
"Why clergymen are against school prayer," Arlene Eisenberg and
  Howard Eisenberg. Redbook 124: 38-39, 95-98, 104-105
  Jan '65 (2).

2470. United States v. Philadelphia   June 17, 1963 374 U. S. 321
         National Bank
       *Antitrust (Posner) 398-404
       *Antitrust Analysis 746-755
       *Cases Antitrust Law 877-890
       *Cases Trade 739-750
       *Competition 146-155
       *Free Enterprise 142-162
        Law and Politics 318-322
        Making 181-190, 263-265
       *Selected Antitrust Cases 367-383
       *Text Antitrust 175-183
       PERIODICALS:
       "Bigger stick" Newsweek 62: 54 July 1 '63
       "Supreme Court, Congress, and bank mergers," William T. Lif-
         land. Law & Contemporary Problems 32: 15-39 Winter '67
         (3).
       "Thunderbolt for bank mergers" Bus Wk p. 80, 82 June 22 '63.

2471. Sherbert v. Verner   June 17, 1963 374 U. S. 398
       *Affair 131-135
       *Bill (Cohen) 401-406
       *Bill (Konvitz) 137-140
        By What Right 268-269
        CQ Guide 460
       *Cases Consttnl Law (Gunther) 1587-1592
       *Cases Individual 1112-1117
       *Cases Law and Poverty 70-77
        Church and State 147-148
       *Civil Liberties (Sweet) 73-76
       *Consttn (Mendelson) 590-594
        Consttnl Counterrevolution 241-243
       *Consttnl Law (Barrett) 1482-1486
       *Consttnl Law (Barron) 957-961
       *Consttnl Law (Freund) 1367-1369
       *Consttnl Law (Kauper) 1289-1296
       *Evolution 107-111
        Freedom and the Court 283, 287-290
        Justice Rutledge 89-93
        Making 281-283
        Religion (Fellman) 37-38
        Religion (Katz) 98-100
        Religion (Kauper) 20, 41-43
       *Religious Freedom (Pfeffer) 164-166
        Religious Liberty 74-75
        Sup Ct and Religion 147-149
       *Warren (Spaeth) 204-210

PERIODICALS:
"Court upholds Sabbatarian. " Christian Century 80: 854 July 3
'63.
"Matter of principle. " America 109: 127 Aug 10 '63.
"Religious neutrality, " John J. Regan. America 110: 74-76
Jan 18 '64 (2).

2472. Head v. New Mexico Board of   June 17, 1963 374 U.S. 424
Examiners in Optometry
*Govt and Business 278-280
Sup Ct and Commerce 304-306
*Warren (Spaeth) 350-354

2473. Rosenberg v. Fleuti   June 17, 1963 374 U.S. 449
Making 260-262

2474. Fahy v. Connecticut   Dec 2, 1963   375 U.S. 85
Criminal Evidence 259-260
Criminal Law (Felkenes) 99-101
Criminal Law Revolution 46
*Principles Arrest 117-120

2475. Retail Clerks International Associa-   Dec 2, 1963   375 U.S. 96
tion v. Schermerhorn
*Labor Relations (Group Trust) 668-670

2476. Durfee v. Duke   Dec 2, 1963   375 U.S. 106
*Civil Procedure (Carrington) 995-998
Sup Ct Review 1964 103-109

2477. Securities and Exchange Commission   Dec 9, 1963   375 U.S. 180
v. Capital Gains Research Bureau
*Govt and Business 215-217
*Social Forces 78-79
PERIODICALS:
"Court to rule on scalping. " US News 54: 84 Feb 4 '63.

2478. Eiekel v. New York Central Railroad   Dec 16, 1963 375 U.S. 253
Co.
*Civil Procedure (Carrington) 420-422

2479. Carey v. Westinghouse Electric Co.   Jan 6, 1964   375 U.S. 261
Basic Text 569, 731
*Cases Labor (Cox) 656-661
*Labor Law (Meltzer) 871-876
*Labor Relations (Group Trust) 907-912
Sup Ct and Labor 114-116
PERIODICALS:
"Significant decisions in labor cases. " Monthly Labor R 87: 187-
188 Feb '64.

2480. National Equipment Rental, Ltd.   Jan 6, 1964   375 U.S. 311
v. Szukhent
*Cases Civil Procedure 356-361
*Cases Federal Courts 664-668
*Cases Pleading 290-295
*Civil Procedure (Carrington) 884-889
*Civil Procedure (Cound) 165-168
*Elements Civil 267-269

2481.   Humphrey v. Moore   Jan 6, 1964   375 U. S. 335
        General Drivers, Warehousemen and
            Helpers, Local Union No. 89
            v. Moore
        *Labor Relations (Group Trust) 920-923
        PERIODICALS:
        "Significant decisions in labor cases. " Monthly Labor R 87: 316-
            317 Mar '64.

2482.   Polar Ice Cream and Creamery Co. Jan 6, 1964   375 U. S. 361
            v. Andrews
        *Consttnl Law (Kauper) 353-358
        *Govt and Business 335-337
        Sup Ct and Commerce 259-260

2483.   Griffin v. County School Board of Jan 6, 1964   375 U. S. 391
            Prince Edward County
        Desegregation (Wasby) 204-208
        This Honorable Court 413
        PERIODICALS:
        "Prince Edward County, Virginia, " J. Rupert Picott and Edward
            H. Peeples, Jr.   Phi Delta Kappan 45: 393-397 May '64.

2484.   Anderson v. Martin   Jan 13, 1964   375 U. S. 399
        *Struggle 217-219
        Sup Ct and Electoral Process 62-63

2485.   National Labor Relations Board v. Jan 13, 1964   375 U. S. 405
            Exchange Parts Co.
        *Cases Labor (Cox) 207-210
        *Cases Labor (Leslie) 163-164
        *Cases Labor (Oberer) 293-295
        *Labor Law (Meltzer) 120-122
        PERIODICALS:
        "Significant decisions in labor cases. " Monthly Labor R 87: 316
            Mar '64.

2486.   England v. Louisiana Board of   Jan 13, 1964   375 U. S. 411
            Medical Examiners
        *Cases Federal Courts 488-495
        *Civil Procedure (Carrington) 795-800

2487.   Rudolph v. Alabama   Oct 21, 1963   375 U. S. 889
        *Consttn (Mendelson) 382-383
        Cruel 28-29

2488.   Wesberry v. Sanders   Feb 17, 1964   376 U. S. 1
        Am Consttn (Kelly) 946
        *Am Consttnl Law (Shapiro) 103-110
        *Am Govt 206-211
        CQ Guide 492
        Changing 173-174
        *Consttn (Mendelson) 606-615
        Consttnl Counterrevolution 100
        *Consttnl Decisions 35-46
        *Consttnl Law (Felkenes) 211-212
        *Consttnl Law (Grossman) 701-703
        Democratic 182-195
        Dissent 426-427

*Evolution 265-272
*Federal System 189-191
*Law Sup Ct 459-463
Reapportionment (Baker) 11, 127-129
*Reapportionment (Baker) 175-183
Reapportionment (McKay) 89-97
Rights of the People 141-143
Sup Ct (North) 25-27
Sup Ct and Electoral Process 212-213
Sup Ct and Poltcl Questions 84-87
Sup Ct and Uses 128-135
Sup Ct Review 1964 4-8
Sup Ct Review 1965 135-136
Sup Ct Review 1973 6
*These Liberties 245-252
This Honorable Court 419
*Warren (Spaeth) 87-96
PERIODICALS:
"Congressional districting; a landmark decision of the Supreme
    Court," Howard D. Hamilton. Socl Eductn 29: 23-26 Jan '65.
"Congressional reapportionment," Richard Perry.   Socl Eductn
    29: 541-552 Dec '65.
"Court backs voter equity." Senior Scholastic 84: 21-22 Mar
    6 '64.
"Court says all votes must weigh the same." Bus Wk p. 27
    Feb 22 '64.
"Georgia redraws its political map." Bus Wk p. 34 Feb 29 '64.
"Illegal Congress?" US News 56: 31-34 Mar 2 '64.
"One voter, one vote," Walter Dean Burnham. Commonweal 80:
    12-15 Mar 27 '64.
"Principles and heresies; Court challenges the Congress," Frank
    S. Meyer. Natl R 16: 233 Mar 24 '64.
"Reapportionment and revenge," Theodore O. Cron. Am Sch and
    University 36: 51 Apr '64.
"Redistricting order." Senior Scholastic 84: 18 Mar 20 '64.
"Ship of state." Nation 198: 206 Mar 2 '64.
"Supreme Court draws the line." Newsweek 63: 15-16 Mar 2
    '64.
"Uhuru." Natl R 16: 182-183 Mar 10 '64.

2489. Wright v. Rockefeller   Feb 17, 1964   376 U.S. 52
        Consttnl Counterrevolution 116-117
        Decade 98
        Democratic 464-470
        *Political Rights 976-988
        *Race 161-167
        Reapportionment (McKay) 256-257

2490. United States v. Wiesenfeld Ware-   Feb 17, 1964   376 U.S. 86
        house Co.
        *Cases Food 614-615
        *Materials Legislation 100-103

2491. Sears, Roebuck and Co. v. Stiffel   Mar 9, 1964   376 U.S. 225
        *Cases Copyright (Kaplan) 603-608
        *Cases Copyright (Nimmer) 469-474
        *Cases Equity 761-764
        *Cases Trade 867-870
        *Copyright 137-141

*Free Enterprise 1183-1187
*Govt and Business 210-212
*Legal Regulation 39-43
Modern Business 1111
*Social Forces 132-133
Sup Ct Review 1974 81-95
PERIODICALS:
"Knocking down the pole. " Time 83: 86 Mar 20 '64.

2492. Compco Corporation v. Day-Brite   Mar 9, 1964   376 U. S. 234
Lighting, Inc.
*Cases Copyright (Kaplan) 608-611
*Cases Copyright (Nimmer) 474-476
*Cases Equity 764-765
*Cases Trade 870
*Copyright 141-144
*Legal Regulation 43-47
Sup Ct Review 1974 81-95

2494. Local Union No. 721, United Packing- Mar 9, 1964   376 U. S. 247
house Food and Allied Workers
v. Needham Packing Co.
PERIODICALS:
"Significant decisions in labor cases. " Monthly Labor R 87: 563-
564 May '64.

2495. New York Times v. Sullivan   Mar 9, 1964   376 U. S. 254
Abernathy v. Sullivan
Advertising 21
*Affair 68-80
*Am Consttn (Kelly) 960-961
*Am Consttn (Lockhart) 693-697
*Am Consttnl Law (Mason) 587-593
*Am Consttnl Law (Saye) 324-326
*Am Consttnl Law (Shapiro) 420-424
*Bill (Konvitz) 315-328
By What Right 225
CQ Guide 433-434
*Cases Consttnl Law (Gunther) 1330-1333
*Cases Consttnl Law (Rosenblum) 430-440
*Cases Consttnl Rights 516-523
*Cases Copyright (Nimmer) 664-673
*Cases Individual 861-867
*Civil Liberties (Barker) 148-156
*Civil Liberties (Sweet) 119-127
*Civil Rights (Abernathy) 1977 456-460
Communication (Hemmer) v. 2, 44-47
*Comparative 532-535
*Consttn (Mendelson) 418-427
*Consttnl Decisions 132-139
*Consttnl Law (Barrett) 1160-1165
*Consttnl Law (Barron) 841-847
*Consttnl Law (Felkenes) 149-152
*Consttnl Law (Freund) 1215-1222
*Consttnl Law (Grossman) 1143-1148
*Consttnl Law (Kauper) 1193-1197
*Consttnl Law (Lockhart) 850-855
*Contemporary Law 603-616
Court and Consttn v. 2, 294-295

PERIODICALS:
  "Another landmark decision." Nation 198: 283 Mar 23 '64.
  "Broadcasting and the law of defamation," Milan D. Meeske. J
      Broadcasting 15: 331-346 Summer '71.
  "Charter of liberty for news." Broadcasting 66: 76-78 Mar 16
      '64.
  "Court gives editorial ads immunity of first amendment in 'Times'
      decision." Adv Age 35: 116 Mar 16 '64.
  "Criticism of officials; what new ruling means." US News 56:
      15 Mar 23 '64.
  "Go ahead and say it!" Time 83: 78 Mar 20 '64.
  "Immunity from criticism." New Republic 150: 7-8 Mar 21 '64.
  "Important victory for a free press, a free nation," R. H. Smith.
      Pub Weekly 185: 33 Mar 16 '64.
  "Libel landmark." Newsweek 63: 74 Mar 23 '64.
  "New York Times's vital victory; Alabama libel case," Richard L.
      Tobin. Sat R 47: 69-70 Apr 11 '64. Reaction: 47: 61
      May 9 '64; 47: 52 June 13 '64.
  "Right to criticism upheld." Senior Scholastic 84: 30 Apr 3 '64.
  "Speak up, everybody." Natl R 16: 222 Mar 24 '64.
  "Strange case of libel; be careful how you say it," Samuel G.
      Blackman. Sat R 54: 48-49, 56 Apr 10 '71 (2).
  "Supreme Court places limit on officials' libel claims." Editor
      and Pub 97: 9, 13 Mar 14 '64.

*"Supreme Court's opinion on libel. " Editor and Pub 97: 10-13
   Mar 14 '64.
"Victory for a free press. " Sat Evening Post 237: 78 Apr 4
   '64.

2496. Italia Societa par Azioni di   Mar 9, 1964   376 U. S. 315
           Navigazione v. Oregon Stevedoring Co.
        Sup Ct Review 1964 258-259

2497. United States v. Ward Baking Co.   Mar 9, 1964   376 U. S. 327
        *Cases Trade 1224-1228

2498. Preston v. United States   Mar 23, 1964   376 U. S. 364
        *Consttnl Law (Felkenes) 228-230
        Criminal Law (Felkenes) 62-64
        *Law of Arrest (Markle) 119-120
        Police 72-75
        *Principles Arrest 223-225

2499. Banco Nacional de Cuba v.   Mar 23, 1964   376 U. S. 398
           Sabbatino
        *Cases Consttnl Law (Rosenblum) 125-135
        *Evolution 272-281
        Foreign Affairs 217-220
        Sup Ct and Am Capitalism 187-189
        Sup Ct Review 1964 223-247
        PERIODICALS:
        "Contested cargo. " Time 83: 71-72 Apr 3 '64.
        "Courts can't bar seizures; suit by Banco nacional de Cuba against
           U. S. firm. " Senior Scholastic 84: 20, 22 Apr 10 '64.
        "Thieves' market? Only Congress can prevent the U. S. from
           turning into one, " Alice Widener. Barrons 45: 9, 16 June
           28 '65.

2500. Boire v. Greyhound Corporation   Mar 23, 1964   376 U. S. 473
        *Govt and Business 631-634
        PERIODICALS:
        "Significant decisions in labor cases. " Monthly Labor R 87: 562
           May '64.

2501. Stoner v. California   Mar 23, 1964   376 U. S. 483
        *Consttnl Criml (Scarboro) 430-433
        Criminal Law (Felkenes) 31-32
        Criminal Law Revolution 46
        Law of Arrest (Markle) 268
        *Leading Consttnl Cases 182-184
        PERIODICALS:
        "Case notes. " J Criml Law, Crimlgy and Police Sci 55: 387
           Sept '64.

2502. United Steelworkers of America v.   Mar 23, 1964   376 U. S. 492
           National Labor Relations Board
        *Cases Labor (Leslie) 313-316
        *Labor Law (Twomey) 277-280
        PERIODICALS:
        "Significant decisions in labor cases. " Monthly Labor R 87: 562-
           563 May '64.

2503. Rugendorf v. United States   Mar 30, 1964   376 U. S. 528

```
     *Cases Evidence 1250-1254
     Criminal Law (Felkenes) 159-161
     Criminal Law Revolution 47
     Law of Arrest (Markle) 186-192
     PERIODICALS:
     "Case notes. " J Criml Law, Crimlgy and Police Sci  55:  380-
     381  Sept '64.
```

2504. John Wiley and Sons v.   Mar 30, 1964 376 U.S. 543
      Livingston
      Basic Text 575-577
      *Cases Labor (Cox) 639-647
      *Cases Labor (Leslie) 566-571
      *Cases Labor (Oberer) 725-732
      *Collective Bargaining 323-329
      *Labor Law (Meltzer) 829-835
      Sup Ct and Labor 113-114, 139-141
      PERIODICALS:
      "Significant decisions in labor cases. " Monthly Labor R 87: 564
      May '64.
      "Union's arbitration demand upheld in merger situation. " Pub
      Weekly 185: 31-32 Apr 13 '64.

2505. Ungar v. Sarafite   Mar 30, 1964 376 U.S. 575
      Criminal Law Revolution 45

2506. Van Dusen v. Barrack   Mar 30, 1964 376 U.S. 612
      *Cases Federal Courts 341-351
      *Cases Pleading 451-473
      *Civil Procedure (Carrington) 980-987

2507. United States v. El Paso Natural   Apr 6, 1964 376 U.S. 651
      Gas Co.
      *Antitrust (Posner) 452-456
      *Competition 169-172
      *Selected Antitrust Cases 384-389
      Sup Ct Review 1964 171-189
      PERIODICALS:
      "Justice gets some sharper teeth. " Bus Wk p. 29-30 Apr 11
      '64 (2).

2508. United States v. First National Bank   Apr 6, 1964 376 U.S. 665
      and Trust Co. of Lexington
      *Antitrust (Posner) 469-472
      *Cases Antitrust Law 1018-1022
      *Cases Trade 704-709
      PERIODICALS:
      "Justice gets some sharper teeth. " Bus Wk p. 29-30 Apr 11
      '64 (2).
      "Mergers and monopolies, " Richard J. Barber. New Republic
      150: 9 June 13 '64.

2509. United States v. Barnett   Apr 6, 1964 376 U.S. 681
      *Am Consttnl Law (Saye) 532-534
      *Cases Equity 1126-1130
      Criminal Law Revolution 44
      Frontiers 233-242
      Sup Ct Review 1964 123-136

PERIODICALS:
"Cool on contempt." Time 83: 57 Apr 17 '64.
"Jury trial barred." Senior Scholastic 84: 15-16 Apr 24 '64.
"Trial without jury." New Republic 150: 5-6 Apr 18 '64.

2510. Arnold v. North Carolina   Apr 6, 1964   376 U. S. 773
        Criminal Law Revolution 45

2511. Brotherhood of Railway Trainmen v.   Apr 20, 1964   377 U. S. 1
        Virginia ex rel. Virginia State Bar
        Cases Consttnl Law (Gunther) 1423-1424
        *Consttnl Law (Barrett) 1328-1331
        PERIODICALS:
        "Legal Blue cross?" Time 83: 76, 78 May 1 '64.
        "Significant decisions in labor cases," Monthly Labor R 87: 689
            June '64.

2512. Simpson v. Union Oil Co.   Apr 20, 1964   377 U. S. 13
        *Antitrust (Posner) 245-251
        *Antitrust Analysis 521-525
        *Cases Antitrust Law 597-604
        *Cases Trade 437-443
        *Govt and Business 194-197
        *Legal Environment 271-273
        *Social Forces 210-212
        *Text Antitrust 95-99
        PERIODICALS:
        "Supreme court decision strikes at consignment system." NPN
            56: 59 May '64.
        "Supreme court's ruling on Union oil seen marketing-pricing bench-
            mark," Stanley E. Cohen. Adv Age 35: 62 Apr 27 '64.

2513. Federal Power Commission v.   Apr 20, 1964   377 U. S. 33
        Texaco, Inc.
        *Govt and Business 475-477

2514. National Labor Relations Board v.   Apr 20, 1964   377 U. S. 46
        Servette, Inc.
        *Cases Labor (Cox) 764-769
        *Cases Labor (Oberer) 446-450
        *Labor Law (Meltzer) 457-460
        *Labor Relations (Group Trust) 332-335
        Sup Ct and Labor 98-99
        PERIODICALS:
        "Significant decisions in labor cases." Monthly Labor R 87: 686-
            687 June '64.

2515. National Labor Relations Board v.   Apr 20, 1964   377 U. S. 58
        Fruit and Vegetable Packers,
            Local 760
        "Tree Fruits Case"
        Basic Text 258-259
        *Cases Labor (Cox) 770-784
        *Cases Labor (Leslie) 325-333
        *Cases Labor (Oberer) 450-462
        *Cases Labor (Stern) 83-99
        *Labor Law (Meltzer) 460-471
        *Labor Law (Twomey) 281-285
        *Labor Relations (Group Trust) 335-342
        Labor Relations (Taylor) 489-490

Sup Ct and Labor 99-104
System 441-443
PERIODICALS:
"Significant decisions in labor cases. " Monthly Labor R   87:
687-688   June '64.

2516.   Coleman v. Alabama   May 4, 1964   377 U.S. 129
Criminal Law Revolution 45-46
Cruel 16-18
CQ Guide 144-145
*Civil Liberties (Sweet) 336-340
*Consttnl Law (Barrett) 610-612
*Consttnl Law (Kauper) 557-560
*Douglas 125-130
PERIODICALS:
"Now 40, 000 ex-Americans can be citizens again. " US News   56:
13   June 1 '64.
"Welcome home. " Time   83:   57 May 29 '64.

2517.   Schneider v. Rusk   May 18, 1964   377 U.S. 163

2518.   Clay v. Sun Insurance Office, Ltd.   May 18, 1964   377 U.S. 179
Sup Ct Review 1964 91-99

2519.   Parden v. Terminal Railway of the   May 18, 1964   377 U.S. 184
Alabama State Docks Department
*Govt and Business 432-435

2520.   Massiah v. United States   May 18, 1964   377 U.S. 201
*Cases Criml Justice 405-488
*Consttnl Criml (Scarboro) 526-533
*Consttnl Law (Felkenes) 260-262
Criminal Evidence 467-468, 471
Criminal Law (Felkenes) 220-222
*Criminal Law (Kadish) 995-996
Criminal Law Revolution 38-40
*Criminal Procedure (Lewis) 363-364
Freedom and the Court 134-137
Law of Arrest (Creamer) 565-569
*Leading Consttnl Cases 480-482
*Police 124-126
Police 161-162
*Principles Arrest 135-137
Self Inflicted Wound 163-164
*Teaching Materials 425-428
Warren (Lytle) 79-80
PERIODICALS:
"Case notes. " J Criml Law, Crimlgy and Police Sci 55: 494 Dec '64.
*"Massiah v. United States. " Current History 53: 43-45 July '67.

2521.   Griffin v. County School Board of   May 25, 1964   377 U.S. 218
Prince Edward County
Am Consttn (Kelly) 871
*Bill (Konvitz) 558-562
CQ Guide 599
Civil Rights (Bardolph) 440-441
*Consttn (Mendelson) 532-534
*Consttn (Pollak) 292-294
*Consttnl Law (Barrett) 824-825

*Consttnl Law (Freund) 893-897
Desegregation (Wasby) 204-208
Digest 83
Disaster 43
*Discrimination 190-194
Education (Lapati) 284-286
*Educational Policy 312-316
From Brown 97-101
*Law Lawyers 265-272
*Liberty v. 2, 601-602
Petitioners 361-363
*Political Rights v. 2, 1268-1273
*Public School Law 658-665
*School Law (Alexander) 470-475
*Sup Ct and Education 156-163
*These Liberties 123-126
Warren (Hudgins) 88-90
*Warren (Spaeth) 128-131

2522. Local 20, Teamsters, Chauffeurs and   May 25, 1964   377 U. S. 252
        Helpers Union v. Morton
        *Cases Labor (Cox) 1185-1189
        *Cases Labor (Leslie) 599-601
        *Social Forces 454-477
        PERIODICALS:
        "Significant decisions in labor cases."   Monthly Labor R   87:
        808-809   July '64.

2523. Calhoun v. Latimer   May 25, 1964   377 U. S. 263
        Education (Lapati) 283-284

2524. United States v. Aluminum Company   June 1, 1964   377 U. S. 271
        of America
        *Antitrust (Posner) 434-436
        *Antitrust Analysis 760-765
        *Cases Antitrust Law 890-895
        *Cases Trade 750-759
        *Competition 128-131
        PERIODICALS:
        "New powers for trustbusters."   Time   84:   77   July 3 '64.

2525. National Association for the Advance-   June 1, 1964   377 U. S. 288
        ment of Colored People v. Alabama
        ex rel. Flowers
        *Cases Federal Courts 859-863
        *Civil Liberties (Sweet) 189
        *Courts Judges 369-372
        Desegregation (Wasby) 184-185
        Equality (Berger) 118
        *Federal System 307-310
        *Law Sup Ct 147-151
        Petitioners 380-381
        System 430-431

2526. Hostetter v. Idlewild Bon Voyage   June 1, 1964   377 U. S. 324
        Liquor Corporation
        *Consttnl Law (Barrett) 354-357

2527. Department of Revenue v. James B.   June 1, 1964   377 U. S. 341
        Beam Distilling Co.

*Consttnl Law (Freund) 380-381

2528. Baggett v. Bullitt   June 1, 1964   377 U.S. 360
       Am Consttn (Kelly) 925-926
       Communication (Hemmer) v. 1, 121
       *Courts 71-73
       *Courts Judges 543-547
       Decade 45-46
       Digest 57-58
       *Political Rights 340-344
       System 234-235
       Warren (Hudgins) 142-143
       PERIODICALS:
       "Rhode Island report; teacher's pledge of loyalty abolished, " Ken-
         neth F. Lewalski. AAUP Bul 51: 34-37 Mar '65.
       "University of Washington loyalty oath case, " Arval A. Morris.
         AAUP Bul 50: 221-231 Sept '64.

2529. Chamberlin v. Dade County Board   June 1, 1964   377 U.S. 402
       of Public Instruction
       Digest 20
       Warren (Hudgins) 35-37

2530. Donovan v. Dallas   June 8, 1964   377 U.S. 408
       *Cases Equity 123-129
       *Cases Federal Courts 399-404

2531. Wilbur-Ellis Co. v. Kuther   June 8, 1964   377 U.S. 422
       *Copyright 507-509
       *Patent 365-367

2532. J. I. Case Co. v. Borak   June 8, 1964   377 U.S. 426
       *Basic Corporation 435-438
       *Introduction (Mashaw) 962-966
       *Materials Consttnl Law 143-147

2533. General Motors Corporation v.   June 8, 1964   377 U.S. 436
       Washington
       *Am Consttn (Lockhart) 325-330
       *Consttnl Law (Freund) 593-601
       Sup Ct and Commerce 331-334

2534. United States v. Tateo   June 8, 1964   377 U.S. 463
       *Criminal Law (Kadish) 1397-1399
       Criminal Law Revolution 48
       *Sup Ct and Criml Process 374-376
       PERIODICALS:
       "Case notes. " J Criml Law, Crimlgy and Police Sci 55: 492-
         493 Dec '64.

2535. Aro Manufacturing Co. v. Convertible June 8, 1964   377 U.S. 476
       Top Replacement Co.
       *Legal Regulation 1072-1081
       *Patent 384-420

2536. Reynolds v. Sims   June 15, 1964 377 U.S. 533
       Vann v. Baggett
       McConnell v. Baggett
       Am Consttn (Kelly) 946

Sup Ct and Uses 135-138
Sup Ct Review 1965 136-137
*These Liberties 253-265
Warren (Ball) 165-199
*Warren (Spaeth) 95-105
PERIODICALS:
"Apportionment facts, " William J. D. Boyd.   Natl Civic R   53:
    530-534, 544   Nov '64   (2).
"Democracy and the Court, " Walter Dean Burnham.   Commonweal
    80:   499-503   July 24 '64.
"Fair challenge to redistricting. "   Life   57:   4   Aug 21 '64.
"Landmark I: equal votes. "   Life   56:   4   June 26 '64.
"Let the people decide!   Court decision on reapportionment. "
    Farm J   89:   150   Feb '65.
"New charter for state legislatures. "   Time   83:   22-23   June
    26 '64.
"Non-violent revolution. "   Natl R   16:   519   June 30 '64.
"Not so sovereign states. "   Economist   211: 1368 June 20 '64   (2).
"One man, one vote. "   Commonweal   80:   441   July 3 '64.
"One man, one vote, yes or no?"   Andrew Hacker.   New York
    Times Mag   p. 31, 131-132 Nov 8 '64.
"Reapportionment and the courts, " Alexander Bickel.   New Re-
    public   150:   7   June 27 '64.
"Reapportionment: shall the Court or the people decide?" Holman
    Harvey and Kenneth O. Gilmore.   Readers Dig   86:   111-116
    Mar '65.
"Reapportionment: what impact on the elections, and after?"
    Senior Scholastic   89:   11-13, 29 Sept 30 '66   (3).
"Shakeup in states. "   Senior Scholastic   85:   21, 24 Sept 16 '64.
"Spur for the states, " Jefferson B. Fordham.   Natl Civic R   53:
    474-478, 502   Oct '64.
"Supreme court vs. farmer legislatures. "   Am City   79:   7   July
    '64.
"Sweeping decision. "   Newsweek   63:   22, 25 June 29 '64.
"Upheaval in state capitols. "   Bus Wk   p. 94-96, 100 Aug 22 '64.
"What can happen when courts step into state elections. "   US News
    57:   39   Sept 21 '64.
"What the courts are ordering states to do. "   US News   57:   40-
    41   Aug 24 '64.
"What the Supreme Court did to your vote, " Claude W. Gifford.
    Farm J   88:   19, 37   Aug '64.

2537.   WMCA, Inc. v. Lomenzo   June 15, 1964 377 U.S. 633
        *Consttn (Mendelson) 639-648
        *Contemporary Law 989
        Democratic 201-209, 275-276
        *Sup Ct (Mendelson) 340-357

2538.   Maryland Committee for Fair   June 15, 1964 377 U.S. 656
          Representation v. Tawes
        *Contemporary Law 990-991
        Democratic 217-226

2539.   Davis v. Mann   June 15, 1964 377 U.S. 678
        *Contemporary Law 992-993
        Democratic 227-229, 275-276

2540.   Roman v. Sincock   June 15, 1964 377 U.S. 695

*Contemporary Law 993-994
Democratic 229-233

2541. Lucas v. 44th General Assembly   June 15, 1964 377 U. S. 713
of Colorado
Am Consttn (Kelly) 947
Consttnl Counterrevolution 107-109
*Consttnl Law (Freund) 962-970
*Contemporary Law 995-999
Democratic 234-250, 274-275
Reapportionment (Baker) 131-132
*Reapportionment (Baker) 195-203
*Warren (Spaeth) 106-112

2542. Malloy v. Hogan   June 15, 1964 378 U. S. 1
*Affair 166-173
*Am Consttnl Law (Bartholomew) v. 2, 151-153
*Am Consttnl Law (Shapiro) 658-664
CQ Guide 557-558
*Cases Civil Liberties 150-156
*Cases Consttnl Law (Cushman) 380-386
*Cases Evidence 1146-1161
*Civil Liberties (Sweet) 255-261
*Consttn (Mendelson) 337-348
*Consttn (Pollak) v. 2, 174-176
Consttnl Counterrevolution 145
*Consttnl Law (Felkenes) 262-264
*Consttnl Law (Freund) 1012-1015
*Consttnl Law (Grossman) 770-774
*Consttnl Law (Kauper) 940-949
*Criminal Justice (Way) 168-170
Criminal Law (Felkenes) 222-224
Criminal Law Revolution 41-43
Decade 168
Dissent 120-121
*Due Process 63-64
*Elements Criminal 206-210
Freedom and the Court 78-79
*Legal Environment 99-100
*Police 79-80
*Principles Proof 637-644
*Sup Ct (Mendelson) 239-264
Sup Ct (North) 123-124
*Sup Ct and Consttn 568-571
*Sup Ct and Criml Process 418-419
*Sup Ct and Rights 20-26
*Teaching Materials 444-446
*These Liberties 40-46
*Warren (Spaeth) 304-315
PERIODICALS:
"Case notes." J Criml Law, Crimlgy and Police Sci 55: 496-
497 Dec '64.
"Extending the Fifth: to state courts." Time 83: 43 June 26
'64.
"Freedom of non-speech." Newsweek 63: 21-22 June 29 '64.
"Not so sovereign states." Economist 211: 1368 June 20 '64
(2).
"Privilege against self-incrimination." Socl Eductn 30: 261-272
Apr '66.

2543. Murphy v. Waterfront Commis-   June 15, 1964 378 U. S. 52
       sion of New York Harbor
       Against 177-178
       CQ Guide 558
       *Cases Civil Liberties 156-162
       *Cases Consttnl Law (Cushman) 386-392
       *Civil Rights (Abernathy) 1977 164-167
       *Consttn (Mendelson) 348-352
       Criminal Law (Felkenes) 224-226
       Criminal Law Revolution 43-44
       Due Process 56, 64-65
       Equal Justice 80
       Freedom and the Court 79-80
       Freedom Spent 381-382
       *Liberty v. 2, 575-578
       *Police 78-79
       *Principles Proof 669-673
       Sup Ct (North) 124-125
       *Sup Ct and Criml Process 467-468
       PERIODICALS:
       "Case notes. " J Criml Law, Crimlgy and Police Sci 55: 497-
       498 Dec '64.

2544. Aguilar v. Texas   June 15, 1964 378 U. S. 108
       Arrest (Waddington) 89-90
       Communication (Hemmer) v. 1, 233-234
       *Consttn (Mendelson) 317-322
       Criminal Law (Felkenes) 28-30
       Criminal Law Revolution 47-48
       Dissent 313-314
       Law of Arrest (Creamer) 122-124
       Law of Arrest (Markle) 181-182
       Police 247
       *Principles Arrest 324-327
       *Rights (Shattuck) 27-28
       PERIODICALS:
       "Case notes. " J Criml Law, Crimlgy and Police Sci 55: 495
       Dec '64.

2545. Griffin v. Maryland   June 22, 1964 378 U. S. 130
       Sup Ct Review 1964 138-139

2546. Barr v. City of Columbia   June 22, 1964 378 U. S. 146
       Expanding Liberties 319
       Sup Ct Review 1964 141-142

2547. Robinson v. Florida   June 22, 1964 378 U. S. 153
       Expanding Liberties 319-320
       Sup Ct Review 1964 139-140

2548. United States v. Penn-Olin Chemical June 22, 1964 378 U. S. 158
       Co.
       *Antitrust (Posner) 499-505
       *Antitrust Analysis 781-787
       *Cases Antitrust Law 928-941
       *Cases Trade 825-835
       *Competition 190-198
       *Free Enterprise 219-232

*Selected Antitrust Cases 242-253
Sup Ct Review 1964 171-189
PERIODICALS:
"New powers for trustbusters." Time 84: 77 July 3 '64 (3).
"Putting the squeeze on mergers." Chemical Wk 95: 17 July
    4 '64.

2549. Jacobellis v. Ohio   June 22, 1964 378 U.S. 184
        *Affair 52-56
        Am Consttn (Kelly) 969-970
        *Bill (Konvitz) 463-471
        *Censorship Landmarks 423-429
        *Civil Liberties (Sweet) 135-138
        Communication (Hemmer) v. 1, 166-167
        *Consttn (Mendelson) 495-502
        Consttnl Counterrevolution 269-270
        Dissent 408-410
        Expanding Liberties 216-220
        *Freedom of Speech (Haiman) 135-136
        Law of Obscenity 42, 118-120
        Mass Media (Clark) 286
        Mass Media (Francois) 361
        Movies 86-89
        *Obscenity (Bosmajian) 171-176
        Obscenity (Clor) 69-74
        *Obscenity (Friedman) 172-176
        Obscenity (Sunderland) 53-55
        *Political Rights 634-640
        *Pornography 97-105
        Rights of the People 112-113
        *Sup Ct on Freedom 241-245
        Sup Ct Review 1966 17-21
        System 475-476
        *These Liberties 162-167
        Tropic 236-245
        PERIODICALS:
        "ALA as amicus curiae: Tropic of Cancer before the U.S. Su-
            preme Court; excerpts from brief." ALA Bul 58: 290-298
            Apr '64.
        "Case notes." J Criml Law, Crimlgy and Police Sci 55: 493
            Dec '64.
        "Chaos in the Court." America 111:83-84 July 25 '64.
        "Supreme court decision limits censorship." Pub Weekly 186:
            48-49 July 6 '64.
        "Supreme Court, obscenity and censorship," John J. Regan.
            Catholic World 200: 142-143, 148 Dec '64 (2).

2550. A Quantity of Copies of Books   June 22, 1964 378 U.S. 205
            v. Kansas
        *Censorship Landmarks 502-507
        Communication (Hemmer) v. 1, 190
        Law of Obscenity 208-209
        Movies 114-116

2551. Bell v. Maryland   June 22, 1964 378 U.S. 226
        *Affair 261-266
        Am Consttn (Kelly) 879-880
        *Am Consttnl Law (Saye) 269-273
        *Basic Corporation 66-71

*Cases Property (Donahue) 171-194
*Civil Rights (Abernathy) 1977 542-546
*Civil Rights (Blaustein) 511-523
*Consttn (Mendelson) 555-563
*Consttn (Pollak) v. 2, 234-237
Consttnl Law (Barrett) 1057
Decade 207-209
Desegregation (Wasby) 311-313, 315-316, 318-320
Discrimination 411-422
*Documents History v. 2, 686-687
*Douglas 287-294
Expanding Liberties 320-326
Hugo Black (Dunne) 391-392
Hugo Black (Strickland) 87-91
*Justices (Friedman) v. 4, 2991-3005
*Law Sup Ct 529-537
*Nature 1042-1051
Negro (Kalven) 166-172
*Political Rights v. 2, 1649-1662
*Racial Equality 124-126
*Sup Ct (Mendelson) 357-373
Sup Ct and Uses 100-118
Sup Ct in Free Society 326
Sup Ct Review 1964 142-145
Sup Ct Review 1965 145-149
*Warren (Spaeth) 138-144

2552. Bouie v. Columbia   June 22, 1964 378 U.S. 347
       *Affair 257-261
       *Cases Criml Law (Perkins) 871-872
       Expanding Liberties 317-319
       Negro (Kalven) 163-166
       Petitioners 404-409
       Sup Ct Review 1964 140-141

2553. Jackson v. Denno   June 22, 1964 378 U.S. 368
       *Cases Criml Justice 1050-1056
       *Cases Criml Law (Perkins) 993-999
       *Consttn (Mendelson) 356-357
       *Consttnl Law (Felkenes) 272-274
       Criminal Law (Felkenes) 233-235
       Criminal Law Revolution 40-41
       Decade 169-170
       Defendants 349-350
       *Due Process 83-84
       Law of Arrest (Creamer) 569-575
       *Social Forces 268-275
       PERIODICALS:
       "Case notes." J Criml Law, Crimlgy and Police Sci 55: 490-491
           Dec '64.

2554. United States v. Continental   June 22, 1964 378 U.S. 441
           Can Co.
       *Antitrust (Posner) 475-483
       *Cases Trade 759-773
       *Competition 132-137
       *Evolution 244-251
       *Govt and Business 157-162
       *Selected Antitrust Cases 143-156

Sup Ct Review 1964 171-189
PERIODICALS:
"Court narrows road to corporate growth. " Bus Wk   p. 30-31
    June 27 '64.
"Supreme Court vs. corporate mergers, " Milton Handler and Stan-
    ley D. Robinson. Fortune 71: 164-165, 174, 176, 178 Jan
    '65 (4).

2555. Escobedo v. Illinois   June 22, 1964 378 U. S. 478
        Am Consttn (Kelly) 955
       *Am Consttnl Law (Bartholomew) v. 2, 249-252
       *Basic Criminal 523-530
        CQ Guide 560
        Changing 168-169
       *Civil Liberties (Sweet) 269-273
        Communication (Hemmer) v. 1, 216-217
        Consttnl Counterrevolution 162-164
       *Consttnl Criml (Marks) 222-227
       *Consttnl Criml (Scarboro) 534-538
       *Consttnl Law (Felkenes) 264-266
       *Consttnl Law (Freund) 1021-1024
        Consttnl Law (Grossman) 860-862, 875-876
       *Consttnl Law (Maddex) 63-70
        Court and Consttn v. 2, 304-305
        Criminal Law (Felkenes) 226-228
       *Criminal Law (Kadish) 997-999
        Criminal Law Revolution 37-38
        Decade 162-165
        Defendants 220
        Dissent 364-366
       *Documents History v. 2, 684-685
        Earl Warren 266-267
        Equal Justice 11-12
        Freedom and the Court 137-144
        Great Reversals 178-180
        Impact (Wasby) 155
       *Justices (Friedman) v. 4, 3005-3011
       *Law Enforcement 20-21
        Law of Arrest (Creamer) 418-421
       *Law Sup Ct 275-283
       *Leading Consttnl Cases 491-500
       *Legal Environment 89-93
       *Police 104-105, 128-131
        Politics 260-261
        Procedures 115-116
        Rights of the People 67-71
        Self Inflicted Wound 154-155, 164-166
        Spirit 97-100
        Sup Ct (North) 129-130
        Sup Ct and Confessions 125-128
       *Sup Ct and Rights 84-90
        Sup Ct in Free Society 330-331
       *Teaching Materials 446-454
       *These Liberties 34-40
        Warren (Lytle) 80-81
PERIODICALS:
"Case notes. " J Criml Law, Crimlgy and Police Sci 55: 493-
    494 Dec '64.

"Concern about confessions. " Time 87: 52-54, 57-58, 60-61
    Apr 29 '66.
"Confessions from suspects. " Time 84: 51 July 3 '64.
"Criminal justice; after Escobedo. " Time 85: 74-75 Feb 12 '65.
"Rising storm over crime and the courts. " Senior Scholastic
    88: 6-10 Mar 18 '66.
"Revolution in criminal justice; Time essay. " Time 86: 22-23
    July 16 '65 (4).
"Story of Danny Escobedo. " Senior Scholastic 106: 6-8 Apr
    24 '75.
"The Supreme Court and the police: 1968?" James R. Thompson.
    J Criml Law, Crimlgy and Police Sci 57: 419-425 Nov '66.

2556.   Aptheker v. Secretary of State   June 22, 1964 378 U.S. 500
        Am Consttn (Kelly) 918
        *Bill (Konvitz) 516-522
        *Civil Liberties (Sweet) 204-210
        Communication (Hemmer) v. 1, 247
        Conceived 53-54
        *Consttnl Law (Barrett) 1222-1223
        *Consttnl Law (Felkenes) 207-208
        *Consttnl Law (Kauper) 1128-1135
        Decade 41-42
        *Freedom vs National Security 501-508
        *Political Rights 926-936
        Rights of the People 129-131
        System 198-199
        PERIODICALS:
        "Passport for Communists. " Time 84: 51 July 3 '64.
        "Relief for Communists. " Economist 211: 1481 June 27 '64.

2557.   Aldrich v. Aldrich   June 22, 1964 378 U.S. 540
        Sup Ct Review 1964 100-103

2558.   Cooper v. Pate   June 22, 1964 378 U.S. 546
        *Law Sup Ct 101-106
        *US Prison Law v. 3, 111

2559.   National Labor Relations Board v.   Nov 9, 1964   379 U.S. 21
            Burnup and Sims, Inc.
        *Cases Labor (Oberer) 243-245
        PERIODICALS:
        "Significant decisions in labor cases. " Monthly Labor R 88: 70
            Jan '65.

2560.   Brulotte v. Thys Co.   Nov 16, 1964   379 U.S. 29
        *Cases Trade 926-930
        *Legal Regulation 563-568
        *Patent 676-684

2561.   Garrison v. Louisiana   Nov 23, 1964   379 U.S. 64
        *Affair 80-87
        Communication (Hemmer) v. 2, 47-49
        Criminal Law Revolution 56-57
        *Freedom of Speech (Haiman) 28-29
        Handbook 301-302
        Individual 104
        Law of Mass 313-314
        *Mass Communications 252-255

*Mass Media (Devol) 208-211
Mass Media (Francois) 90-91
*Protest 167-173
*Statutory History Economic 627-630
*Sup Ct on Freedom 141-146
System 524-525
PERIODICALS:
"Supreme Court decision about criminal libel," Harriet F. Pilpel.
Pub Weekly 186: 41-42 Dec 28 '64.

2562. Beck v. Ohio   Nov 23, 1964   379 U.S. 89
        *Cases Criml Justice 166-168
        Criminal Law Revolution 53-54
        *Criminal Procedure (Lewis) 136-139
        *Law of Arrest (Markle) 31-33
        Police 24-25

2563. Schlagenhauf v. Holder   Nov 23, 1964   379 U.S. 104
        *Civil Procedure (Carrington) 430-437
        *Civil Procedure (Cound) 666-672

2564. Calhoon v. Harvey   Dec 7, 1964   379 U.S. 134
        *Cases Labor (Cox) 1127-1133
        *Cases Labor (Leslie) 710-714
        *Cases Labor (Oberer) 900-906
        *Labor Law (Meltzer) 1112-1117
        *Labor Relations (Group Trust) 1060-1065
        *Statutory History Labor 789-792
        PERIODICALS:
        "Significant decisions in labor cases." Monthly Labor R 88: 191-
        192 Feb '65.

2565. Gillespie v. United States Steel Dec 7, 1964   379 U.S. 148
        Corporation
        *Cases Federal Courts 807-812
        *Civil Procedure (Cound) 981-983

2566. American Federation of Musicians Dec 7, 1964   379 U.S. 171
        v. Wittstein
        *Labor Relations (Group Trust) 1076-1082
        *Statutory History Labor 784-789
        PERIODICALS:
        "Significant decisions in labor cases." Monthly Labor R 88: 192-
        193 Feb '65.

2567. McLaughlin v. Florida   Dec 7, 1964   379 U.S. 184
        *Cases Criml Law (Inbau) 424-429
        Desegregation (Wasby) 141-144
        *Race 275-278
        *Sex Discrimination 1975 82-83
        *US Prison Law v. 1, 372-386
        PERIODICALS:
        "Bedroom issues." Newsweek 64: 21 Dec 21 '64.
        "Interracial cohabitation." New Republic 151: 5 Dec 19 '64.
        "Race, sex and the Supreme Court," Anthony Lewis. NY Times
        Mag p. 30, 130, 132, 134 Nov 22 '64.
        "Strict caution on miscegenation; case of McLaughlin v. Florida."
        Time 84: 43-44 Dec 18 '64.

"Will High Court O. K. mixed marriages?" <u>US News</u> 57: 10
Oct 26 '64.
"Will High court rule on mixed marriages?" <u>US News</u> 57: 14
May 11 '64.

2568. Fibreboard Paper Products Corporation Dec 14, 1964 379 U. S. 203
v. National Labor Relations Board
Basic Text 509-512
*<u>Cases Labor</u> (Cox) 480-493
*<u>Cases Labor</u> (Leslie) 386-390
*<u>Cases Labor</u> (Oberer) 581-589
*<u>Competition</u> 654-662
*<u>Labor Law</u> (Herman) 266-273
*<u>Labor Law</u> (Twomey) 212-218
*<u>Labor Relations</u> (Group Trust) 451-459
*<u>Labor Relations</u> (Taylor) 384-385
<u>Sup Ct and Labor</u> 129-133
PERIODICALS:
"Rights of management." <u>Economist</u> 214: 33 Jan 2 '65 (3).
"Seeking silver linings." <u>Chem Wk</u> 96: 103 Jan 9 '65.
"Significant decisions in labor cases." <u>Monthly Labor R</u> 88: 191
Feb '65.

2569. Farmer v. Arabian American Dec 14, 1964 379 U. S. 227
Oil Co.
Arabian American Oil Co. v. Farmer
*<u>Civil Procedure</u> (Carrington) 673-678

2570. Heart of Atlanta Motel, Inc. v. Dec 14, 1964 379 U. S. 241
United States
<u>Am Consttn</u> (Kelly) 893
*<u>Am Consttn</u> (Lockhart) 169-172
*<u>Am Consttnl Law</u> (Bartholomew) v. 1, 243-245
*<u>Am Consttnl Law</u> (Mason) 302-303
*<u>Am Consttnl Law</u> (Saye) 146-151
*<u>Am Consttnl Law</u> (Shapiro) 286-289
*<u>Basic Cases</u> 46-51
*<u>Bill</u> (Konvitz) 597-607
<u>CQ</u> Guide 611-612
*<u>Cases Consttnl Law</u> (Cushman) 205-210
*<u>Cases Consttnl Law</u> (Gunther) 204-206
*<u>Cases Consttnl Law</u> (Rosenblum) 171-177
*<u>Civil Liberties</u> (Sweet) 221-228
*<u>Civil Rights</u> (Abernathy) 1977 548-550
*<u>Civil Rights</u> (Abernathy) 1980 432-437
*<u>Civil Rights</u> (Bardolph) 512-513
*<u>Civil Rights</u> (Blaustein) 552-558
*<u>Consttn</u> (Mendelson) 121-124
*<u>Consttn</u> (Pollak) v. 2, 326-337
<u>Consttnl Counterrevolution</u> 80-81
*<u>Consttnl Law</u> (Barrett) 237-240
*<u>Consttnl Law</u> (Barron) 200-204
*<u>Consttnl Law</u> (Felkenes) 84-86
*<u>Consttnl Law</u> (Freund) 300-304
*<u>Consttnl Law</u> (Grossman) 539-545
*<u>Consttnl Law</u> (Kauper) 182-186
*<u>Consttnl Law</u> (Lockhart) 147-150
*<u>Consttnlism</u> 162-166

*Contemporary Law 321-325
Court and Consttn v. 2, 278
Decade 228-230
Desegregation (Wasby) 325-328, 332-334
*Discrimination 436-444
Expanding Liberties 331-333
*Federal System 249-252
*Law Sup Ct 538-542
*Leading Consttnl Decisions 117-128
Petitioners 410-416
*Political Rights v. 2, 1686-1692
*Race 209-214
*Racial Equality 127-128
*Statutory History Civil Rights 1456-1466
Sup Ct and Commerce 215-217
*Sup Ct and Consttn 526-531
Sup Ct Review 1965 160
*Text Administrative Law 46-50
PERIODICALS:
"Beyond a doubt." Time 84: 13-14 Dec 25 '64.
"Civil disobedience: an imprimatur." Natl R 16: 1134-1135
   Dec 29 '64.
"Following the returns," Raymond Moley. Newsweek 64: 60
   Dec 28 '64.
"Government's big stick for enforcing civil rights." US News 57:
   40-42 Dec 28 '64.
"Public accommodations on trial." Time 84: 69 Oct 16 '64.
"Rights bill upheld." Senior Scholastic 85: 17-18 Jan 7 '65.
"Supreme Court weathers the storm," John B. Sheerin. Catholic
   World 200: 329-332 Mar '65.
"Upholding Title II." Newsweek 64: 16, 19 Dec 28 '64.

2571.   Katzenbach v. McClung   Dec 14, 1964   379 U.S. 294
         Am Consttn (Kelly) 893-894
         *Am Consttn (Lockhart) 172-175
         *Am Consttnl Law (Mason) 303-305
         *Cases Consttnl Law (Cushman) 210-213
         *Cases Consttnl Law (Gunther) 206-210
         *Civil Liberties (Sweet) 228-231
         *Civil Rights (Abernathy) 1980 437-440
         Civil Rights (Bardolph) 513-514
         *Consttn (Mendelson) 124-126
         Consttnl Counterrevolution 81
         *Consttnl Law (Barrett) 240-243
         *Consttnl Law (Barron) 204-209
         *Consttnl Law (Freund) 304-308
         *Consttnl Law (Kauper) 186-191
         *Consttnl Law (Lockhart) 150-154
         *Contemporary Law 325-327
         Court and Consttn v. 2, 278-279
         Desegregation (Wasby) 328-330
         *Discrimination 444-448
         *Leading Consttnl Decisions 128-133
         *Modern Business 75-78
         Petitioners 410-416
         *Political Rights v. 2, 1692-1696
         *Processes 326-331
         Sup Ct and Commerce 217-220

*Sup Ct and Consttn 425-428
Sup Ct Review 1965 160-164

2572. Hamm v. Rock Hill   Dec 14, 1964   379 U.S. 306
       Lupper v. Arkansas
       Am Consttn (Kelly) 894-895
       Desegregation (Wasby) 335-340
       Expanding Liberties 333-334
       Sup Ct Review 1965 164-167

2573. All States Freight, Inc. v. New York,   Dec 14, 1964   379 U.S. 343
       New Haven and Hartford Railroad
       Co.
       *Cases Regulated 672-676

2574. United States v. First National City   Jan 18, 1965   379 U.S. 378
       Bank
       Sup Ct Review 1965 284-285

2575. Fortson v. Dorsey   Jan 18, 1965   379 U.S. 433
       *Affair 309-312
       Consttnl Counterrevolution 117-118
       Democratic 476-478
       Sup Ct and Electoral Process 185-186
       Warren (Ball) 200-202

2576. Henry v. Mississippi   Jan 18, 1965   379 U.S. 443
       *Basic Criminal 735-742
       *Cases Federal Courts 864-869
       *Consttnl Criml (Scarboro) 804-807
       *Consttnl Law (Barrett) 45-48
       *Consttnl Law (Freund) 44-46
       Criminal Law Revolution 54-55
       Decade 171
       *Evolution 57-62
       *Federal Courts 548-557
       Sup Ct Review 1965 187-239

2577. Stanford v. Texas   Jan 18, 1965   379 U.S. 476
       *Criminal Procedure (Lewis) 144-147

2578. Jankovich v. Indiana Toll Road   Jan 18, 1965   379 U.S. 487
       Commission
       *Cases Federal Courts 855-858
       *Cases Land 826-827

2579. El Paso v. Simmons   Jan 18, 1965   379 U.S. 497
       *Cases Individual 210-213
       *Consttnl Law (Barrett) 582-585

2580. Cox v. Louisiana   Jan 18, 1965   379 U.S. 536
       CQ Guide 415
       *Cases Consttnl Law (Gunther) 1262-1265
       *Cases Individual 786-791
       Communication (Hemmer) v. 1, 93-95
       Conceived 116-118
       Consttnl Law (Barrett) 1253-1254
       *Consttnl Law (Barrett) 1259-1261

*Consttnl Law (Freund) 1192-1199
*Consttnl Law (Grossman) 1204-1211
Court and Consttn v. 2, 281
*Criminal Law (Young) 75-82
Desegregation (Wasby) 345-347
*Federal Courts 577-590
Free Speech (Kurland) 118-124, 135-137, 143, 144-146
*Freedom of Speech (Haiman) 74-75
*Judicial Crises 275-290
*Political Rights 443-452
Politics 116-117
*Protest 196-215
*Sup Ct and Consttn 425-428
Sup Ct Review 1965 1-32, 178-184
Sup Ct Review 1974 242-243
System 295-296, 301-302, 321-322, 361-362
Warren (Cox) 105-106
PERIODICALS:
"Mobs vs. the law; what High court says." US News 58: 16
   Feb 1 '65.
"New limits for an old conflict." Time 85: 39 Jan 29 '65.

2581. Cox v. Louisiana   Jan 18, 1965   379 U.S. 559
        CQ Guide 415
        *Cases Consttnl Law (Gunther) 1265-1268
        *Cases Individual 792-796
        Conceived 119
        Consttnl Law (Barrett) 1265-1266
        *Political Rights 464-468
        System 295, 354-356, 369

2582. Securities and Exchange Commission v. Jan 18, 1965   379 U.S. 594
        American Trailer Rentals Co.
        *Materials Reorganization 236-244

2583. Republic Steel Corporation v. Maddox   Jan 25, 1965   379 U.S. 650
        *Labor Relations (Group Trust) 951-959
        PERIODICALS:
        "Significant decisions in labor cases." Monthly Labor R 88: 315-
        316 Mar '65.

2584. Texas v. New Jersey   Feb 1, 1965   379 U.S. 674
        *Am Consttnl Law (Saye) 53-55

2585. Udall v. Tallman   Mar 1, 1965   380 U.S. 1
        *Cases Environmental Law (Hanks) 512-518

2586. Singer v. United States   Mar 1, 1965   380 U.S. 24
        Criminal Law Revolution 57-58
        *Due Process 122
        Procedures 92
        PERIODICALS:
        "Compulsory jury trial." Time 85: 72 Mar 12 '65.

2587. Freedman v. Maryland   Mar 1, 1965   380 U.S. 51
        *Am Consttn (Lockhart) 760-762
        *Bill (Konvitz) 471-475
        *Cases Civil Liberties 252-255
        *Cases Consttnl Law (Cushman) 482-485

```
        *Cases Consttnl Law (Gunther) 1375-1377
        *Cases Consttnl Rights 636-638
        *Cases Individual 937-940
        *Censorship Landmarks 515-518
        *Civil Liberties (Sweet) 127-128
        *Civil Rights (Abernathy) 1977 375-377
         Communication (Hemmer) v. 1, 181-182
        *Consttnl Law (Barrett) 1237-1239
        *Consttnl Law (Kauper) 1224-1227
         Freedom of Speech (Shapiro) 156-157
         Handbook 57-60
         Law of Mass 395
         Law of Obscenity 231-232
        *Mass Communications 556-558
        *Mass Media (Devol) 179-182
         Movies 117-122
        *Obscenity (Friedman) 200-202
        *Political Rights 680-686
        *Sup Ct on Freedom 245-249
         System 510-511
      PERIODICALS:
      "Censoring the censors." Time   85:   72-73  Mar 12 '65.
```

2588.   United States v. Gainey   Mar 1, 1965   380 U.S. 63
        Criminal Law Revolution 57
      PERIODICALS:
      "The moonshine war." Time   85: 72 Mar 12 '65.

2589.   Carrington v. Rash   Mar 1, 1965   380 U.S. 89
        Sup Ct and Electoral Process 6-8

2590.   United States v. Ventresca   Mar 1, 1965   380 U.S. 102
        Criminal Law (Felkenes) 33-35
        Criminal Law Revolution 53
        Law of Arrest (Creamer) 124-129
        Law of Arrest (Markle) 192-200
        *Law of Evidence 535-540
        Police 25-26

2591.   United States v. Mississippi   Mar 8, 1965   380 U.S. 128
        Frontiers 317-330
        *Law Sup Ct 467-475
        Petitioners 307-308
        Sup Ct and Electoral Process 103-105

2592.   Louisiana v. United States   Mar 8, 1965   380 U.S. 145
        *Consttnl Law (Kauper) 739-740
        Petitioners 308
        Sup Ct and Electoral Process 103-104
        Sup Ct Review 1969 390-402

2593.   United States v. Seeger   Mar 8, 1965   380 U.S. 163
        United States v. Jakobson
        Peter v. United States
        *Bill (Konvitz) 149-160
        Cases Consttnl Law (Gunther) 1600
        Conflict 46-54
        *Conscience 260-270
        *Documents History v. 2, 706-708

First Amendment (Berns) 46
Freedom and the Court 255-257, 283
*Judicial Crises 208-213
*Law Sup Ct 83-89
*Political Rights 845-851
Private Conscience 26
Religious Freedom (Arnold) 40-41
*Religious Freedom (Pfeffer) 117-120
Religious Liberty 88-98
Spirit 44-46
Sup Ct and Religion 167-169
Sup Ct Review 1971 39-40
PERIODICALS:
"Any God will do." Time 85: 74 Mar 19 '65.
"Conscience and religion." America 111: 771 Dec 12 '64.
"Test for believers; rights of conscientious objectors." Newsweek
    65: 64 Mar 22 '65.

2594. Swain v. Alabama   Mar 8, 1965   380 U.S. 202
        *Consttnl Law (Felkenes) 193-196
        Criminal Law (Felkenes) 308-310
        *Criminal Law (Kadish) 1343-1347
        *Discrimination 284-293
        Dissent 343-344
        *Elements Criminal 165-173
        *Law Power 605-625
        *Leading Consttnl Cases 673-678
        Petitioners 291-292
        *Political Rights v. 2, 1406-1416
        *Race 950-965
        *Racial Equality 134-135
        *Sup Ct and Criml Process 624-627

2595. Textile Workers of America v.   Mar 29, 1965   380 U.S. 263
            Darlington Manufacturing Co.
        National Labor Relations Board v. Dar-
            lington Manufacturing Co.
        Basic Text 145-147
        *Cases Labor (Cox) 257-263
        *Cases Labor (Leslie) 192-197
        *Cases Labor (Oberer) 296-300
        *Cases Labor (Stern) 60-65
        *Labor Law (Herman) 211-217
        *Labor Law (Meltzer) 229-234
        *Labor Law (Twomey) 199-203
        *Legal Environment 442-444
        *Statutory History Labor 388-393
        Sup Ct and Labor 133-137
PERIODICALS:
"High court upsets NLRB rulings; but decisions do little to boost
    management's right to manage," R. W. Crosby. Iron Age
    195: 26-27 Apr 8 '65.
"Limits on labor and management." Time 85: 66-67 Apr 9 '65.
"New rules for employers from the Supreme Court." US News
    58: 101-104 Apr 12 '65.
"Significant decisions in labor cases." Monthly Labor R 88: 566-
    567 May '65.
"Supreme Court upholds employer rights," William E. Lissy.
    Supervision 27: 15 July '65.

"Supreme Court's Darlington mills opinion, " Robert A. Bedolis
Conference Bd Rec   2:   49-53   June '65.

2596.   National Labor Relations Board   Mar 29, 1965   380 U.S. 278
            v. Brown
        *Cases Labor (Leslie) 267-274
        *Labor Law (Meltzer) 253-256
        *Labor Law (Twomey) 195-198
        *Labor Relations (Group Trust) 207-211
        Sup Ct and Labor 89-91
        Sup Ct Review 1965 105-111
        PERIODICALS:
        "Multiemployer bargaining and the balancing of power, " Monthly
            Labor R   88:   III-IV   Apr '65.
        "Significant decisions in labor cases, " Monthly Labor R   88:   568-
            569   May '65.
        "Supreme court upholds employer rights, " William E. Lissy.   Su-
            pervision   27:   15   July '65   (3).

2597.   American Shipbuilding Co. v.   Mar 29, 1965   380 U.S. 300
            National Labor Relations Board
        Basic Text 334-335
        *Cases Labor (Cox) 864-874
        *Cases Labor (Leslie) 274-283
        *Cases Labor (Oberer) 539-546
        *Labor Law (Herman) 342-346
        *Labor Law (Meltzer) 243-252
        *Labor Relations (Group Trust) 413-423
        Sup Ct and Labor 91-93
        Sup Ct Review 1965 96-105
        PERIODICALS:
        "High court strengthens right to lockout. "   Engineering News-Rec
            174:   213-214   Apr 8 '65   (2).
        "Significant decisions in labor cases. "   Monthly Labor R   88:   567-
            568   May '65.
        "Strike vs. lockout. "   Newsweek   65:   82   Apr 12 '65.
        "Supreme Court upholds employer rights, " William E. Lissy.   Su-
            pervision   27:   15   July '65   (3).

2598.   O'Keeffe v. Smith, Hinchman and   Mar 29, 1965   380 U.S. 359
            Grylls Associates
        *Admin Law (Schwartz) 694-698
        *Evolution 229-234

2599.   Federal Trade Commission v.   Apr 5, 1965   380 U.S. 374
            Colgate-Palmolive Co.
        *Cases Food 833-841
        Communication (Hemmer) v. 2, 335-336
        *Competition 393-398
        Dissent 490-491
        Law of Mass 513-516
        *Legal Regulation 217-222
        Mass Media (Clark) 354-359
        Mass Media (Francois) 394
        PERIODICALS:
        "Agencies see sandpaper decision as anti-climactic. "   Sponsor   19:
            22   Apr 12 '65.
        "Court backs FTC in ruling on Rapid shave. "   Adv Age   36:   1,
            62, 64   Apr 12 '65.

"Deceptive TV advertising," Malcolm L. Searle. <u>Socl Eductn</u> 31:
703-714 Dec '67.
"Marketing and the United States Supreme Court," Ray O. Werner.
<u>J Marketing</u> 31: 4-8 Jan '67 (4).
"Pulling the props out." <u>Newsweek</u> 65: 81-82 Apr 19 '65.
"Rule on reality in advertising, Supreme Court affirming sandpaper
case." Broadcasting 68: 28, 30, 33 Apr 12 '65.
"Supreme Court says TV no place for fake ads." <u>Editor and Pub</u>
98: 60 Apr 10 '65.
"Supreme Court's Rapid shave decision bucks up consumer pro-
tection folk," Stanley E. Cohen. <u>Adv Age</u> 36: 44 Apr 12 '65.

2600. Pointer v. Texas   Apr 5, 1965   380 U. S. 400
       Against 337-339
       *Cases Criml (Perkins) 1053-1056
       *Cases Evidence 563-568
       *Civil Liberties (Sweet) 274-277
       *Consttnl Law (Felkenes) 318-319
       *Consttnl Law (Kauper) 667-670, 986-988
       *Consttnl Law (Maddex) 328-331
       *Criminal Justice (Way) 444-448
       Criminal Law (Felkenes) 321-323
       *Criminal Law (Kadish) 1355
       Criminal Law Revolution 50-51
       Defendants 96
       *Due Process 127
       *Elements Criminal 264-266
       Freedom and the Court 80-83
       *Law of Evidence 265-269
       *Law Sup Ct 332-334
       *Leading Consttnl Cases 744-747
       *Sup Ct and Criml Process 675-678
       *Sup Ct and Rights 26-30
       PERIODICALS:
       "Now comes the Sixth amendment," <u>Time</u> 85: 46 Apr 16 '65.

2601. Douglas v. Alabama   Apr 5, 1965   380 U. S. 415
       Criminal Evidence 114
       Criminal Law Revolution 51

2602. National Labor Relations Board v.   Apr 5, 1965   380 U. S. 438
           Metropolitan Life Insurance Co.
       *Cases Labor (Cox) 346-348
       PERIODICALS:
       "Significant decisions in labor cases." <u>Monthly Labor R</u> 88: 688-
       689 June '65.

2603. Hanna v. Plumer   Apr 26, 1965   380 U. S. 460
       *Cases Civil Procedure 299-310
       *Cases Federal Courts 604-613
       *Cases Pleading 420-432
       *Civil Procedure (Carrington) 839-843
       *Civil Procedure (Cound) 295-303
       *Elements Civil 399-404
       *Federal Courts 739-746

2604. Dombrowski v. Pfister   Apr 26, 1965   380 U. S. 479
       *Affair 119-124
       *Cases Equity 130-137

Consttnl Law (Felkenes) 36-37
*Courts Judges 105-107
*Federal Courts 1013-1020
*Federal System 315-317
Freedom Spent 172-173
*Injunctions 29-40
*Law Sup Ct 161-170
*Political Rights 205-210
Self Inflicted Wound 147-148
Sup Ct Review 1979 260-261
System 157-159

2605. Harman v. Forssenius   Apr 27, 1965   380 U.S. 528
      *Civil Liberties (Sweet) 316-318
      *Political Rights v. 2, 1122-1125
      Sup Ct and Electoral Process 79-81

2606. General Motors Corporation v.   Apr 27, 1965   380 U.S. 553
      District of Columbia
      *Consttnl Law (Barrett) 400-401

2607. Federal Trade Commission v.   Apr 28, 1965   380 U.S. 592
      Consolidated Foods Corporation
      *Antitrust (Posner) 662-664
      *Antitrust Analysis 817-820
      *Cases Antitrust Law 1008-1012
      *Competition 174-177
      *Free Enterprise 214-218
      *Selected Antitrust Cases 214-219
      *Text Antitrust 196-200
      PERIODICALS:
      "Marketing and the United States Supreme Court," Ray O. Werner.
         J Marketing 31: 4-8 Jan '67 (4).
      "Mergers and reciprocity," Betty Bock. Conference Bd Rec 2:
         27-36 July '65.

2608. Griffin v. California   Apr 28, 1965   380 U.S. 609
      *Cases Criml Justice 1289-1292
      *Cases Criml Law (Perkins) 999-1002
      *Civil Liberties (Sweet) 261-263
      *Consttnl Criml (Scarboro) 488-493
      *Consttnl Law (Felkenes) 64-66
      *Consttnl Law (Kauper) 972-976
      Criminal Law (Felkenes) 350-352
      Criminal Law Revolution 55-56
      Decade 170-171
      Defendants 321
      Dissent 121-122
      *Due Process 68
      *Elements Criminal 210-215
      *Law Sup Ct 292-295
      *Police 80-81
      Principles Proof 697-702
      Procedures 182-183
      Sup Ct Review 1977 142, 146-147

2609. Brotherhood of Railway and Steam-   Apr 28, 1965   380 U.S. 650
      ship Clerks, Freight Handlers,
      Express and Station Employees v.

Association for the Benefit of
Non-Contract Employees
United Air Lines, Inc. v. National
  Mediation Board
National Mediation Board v. Associ-
  ation for the Benefit of Non-
  Contract Employees
PERIODICALS:
  "Significant decisions in labor cases. "   Monthly Labor R   88:   690
  June '65.

2610.   Warren Trading Post Co. v. Arizona   Apr 29, 1965   380 U.S.   685
        Tax Commission
        *Am Indian v. 4, 2851-2858
        *Law Indian 193-195

2611.   Zemel v. Rusk, Secretary of State   May 3, 1965   381 U.S.   1
        *Bill (Cohen) 373-377
        Communication (Hemmer) v. 1, 247-248
        *Contemporary Law 433-440
        Dissent 287-288
        Hugo Black (Strickland) 117-118
        *Political Rights 937-944
        System 199-200

2612.   Jaben v. United States   May 17, 1965   381 U.S.   214
        Consttnl Criml (Scarboro) 132-133

2613.   Lamont v. Postmaster General of   May 24, 1965   381 U.S.   301
        United States
        Fixa v. Heilberg
        Am Consttn (Kelly) 919
        *Am Consttnl Law (Saye) 313-315
        *Civil Liberties (Sweet) 139-143
        Communication (Hemmer) v. 2, 201-202
        *Consttnlism 116-118
        *Contemporary Law 592-595
        *Freedom of Speech (Haiman) 45-46
        Frontiers 117-130
        *Mass Communications 154-157
        Mass Media (Clark) 346-347
        *Mass Media (Devol) 86-87
        *Rights (Shattuck) 67
        PERIODICALS:
        "Free mail and free speech. "   Time   85:   52   June 4 '65.

2614.   Minnesota Mining and Manufacturing Co.   May 24, 1965   381 U.S.   311
        v. New Jersey Wood Finishing
        Co.
        *Cases Trade 1277-1284
        PERIODICALS:
        "Chemical trade's latest worry: Antitrust damage suits in wake
        of statute of limitations ruling. "   Oil Paint and Drug Rep   137:
        3, 42   May 31 '65.
        See also listing at 380 U.S. 592, entry no. 2607.

2615.   Case v. Nebraska   May 24, 1965   381 U.S.   336
        *Criminal Law (Kadish) 1568-1572
        Criminal Procedure (Wells) 197

2616. Atlantic Refining Co. v. Federal   June 1, 1965   381 U.S. 357
       Trade Commission
Goodyear Tire and Rubber Co. v.
       Federal Trade Commission
       *Cases Antitrust Law 654-662
       *Legal Environment 313-316
       PERIODICALS:
       "Marketing and the United States Supreme Court," Ray O. Werner.
       J Marketing 31: 4-8 Jan '67 (4).
       "Supreme Court decision in Atlantic case could be dynamite for
       TBA marketers." NPN 57: 71-72 July '65.
       "Supreme Court upholds FTC ban on Goodyear-Atlantic TBA ar-
       rangement." Adv Age 36: 1, 136 June 7 '65.

2617. United States v. Brown   June 7, 1965   381 U.S. 437
       Am Consttn (Kelly) 915
       *Am Consttnl Law (Mason) 572-574
       CQ Guide 511
       *Cases Civil Liberties 4-11
       *Cases Consttnl Law (Cushman) 234-241
       *Cases Consttnl Rights 438-443
       *Cases Labor (Oberer) 938-949
       Consttnl Law (Barrett) 1191-1194
       *Consttnl Law (Kauper) 1026-1032
       *Contemporary Law 573-582
       Decade 42-43
       *Legislation (Linde) 30-39
       *Political Rights 237-243
       *Processes 129-138
       Sup Ct and Commerce 179-180
       System 172-173
       PERIODICALS:
       "Significant decisions in labor cases." Monthly Labor R 88:
       1108-1109 Sept '65.

2618. Griswold v. Connecticut   June 7, 1965   381 U.S. 479
       "Connecticut Anti-Contraception Case"
       Am Consttn (Kelly) 963-964
       *Am Consttn (Lockhart) 1104-1115
       *Am Consttnl Law (Mason) 633-638
       *Am Consttnl Law (Saye) 419-421
       *Am Consttnl Law (Shapiro) 719-722
       Am Politics 62
       *Bill (Cohen) 566-574
       *Bill (Konvitz) 480-488
       Biography 360-361
       By What Right 339-340
       *Cases Civil Liberties 71-74
       *Cases Consttnl Law (Cushman) 301-304
       *Cases Consttnl Law (Gunther) 573-586
       *Cases Consttnl Law (Rosenblum) 440-452
       *Cases Consttnl Rights 1073-1084
       *Cases Criml Law (Inbau) 317-325
       *Cases Domestic 15-19
       *Cases Individual 217-233
       *Civil Liberties (Barker) 344-350
       *Civil Liberties (Sweet) 143-150
       Communication (Hemmer) v. 1, 249
       *Comparative 394-398

"Life, liberty and privacy." Life 59: 4 July 2 '65.
"Now legal family planning," Harland G. Lewis. Christian Century
82: 970 Aug 4 '65.
"Population control takes a forward step." Bus Wk p. 108 June
19 '65.
"Privacies of life," Paul Bender. Harper's Mag 248: 36, 40-42,
44-45 Apr '74 (3).
"Supreme court, defender of minorities," John B. Sheerin. Cath-
olic World 193: 275-279 Aug '61 (3).
"Supreme Court reverses birth control law." Christian Century
82: 796 June 23 '65.
"Test for an ancient law." Time 84: 44 Dec 18 '64.

2619.   Estes v. Texas   June 7, 1965   381 U.S. 532
     *Civil Liberties (Sweet) 19-31
     Communication (Hemmer) v. 2, 185-187
     *Consttnl Law (Kauper) 888-893
     *Criminal Justice (Kaplan) 391-397
     Criminal Law (Felkenes) 336-339
     *Criminal Law (Kadish) 1313-1316
     Criminal Law Revolution 49-50
     *Criminal Procedure (Lewis) 483-489
     Dissent 381-384
     *Due Process 115-116
     *Evolution 3-10
     Freedom and the Court 183
     Frontiers 245-255
     Handbook 534-540
     Law of Mass 267-272
     *Mass Communications 530-534
     *Mass Media (Devol) 300-312
     Mass Media (Devol) 313-316; reprinted from Judicature 59: 60
       Aug/Sept '74.
     *Political Rights 540-552
     *Procedure 99-101
     *Radio 192-250
     Self Inflicted Wound 26-28
     *Sup Ct on Freedom 259-273
     *These Liberties 60-69
   PERIODICALS:
     "Crack in Canon 35," Herbert Brucker. Sat R 48: 43-49 July
       10 '65. Reaction: 48: 50-51 Aug 14 '65.
     "End of term decisions." New Republic 152: 7-8 June 19 '65
       (2).
     "Free trial vs. free press." Socl Eductn 30: 633-644 Dec '66.
     "Freedom of the press." Senior Scholastic 107: 6-10 Jan 13
       '76 (3).
     "Sigma delta chi examines access to news." Broadcasting 69:
       68 Nov 1 '65.
     "Television and fair trial." Time 85: 44 June 18 '65.
     "What the Estes decision means." Broadcasting 68: 50-54, 56,
       58, 62-63, 66 June 14 '65.

2620.   Linkletter v. Walker   June 7, 1965   381 U.S. 618
     By What Right 77-79
     Consttnl Counterrevolution 216-219
     *Courts Judges 435-438
     Criminal Law Revolution 52-53
     *Criminal Procedure (Lewis) 680-682

Dissent 395-397
Exclusionary 34-35
*Police 69-70
*Processes 1130-1135
*Sup Ct and Am Govt 20-26
*Sup Ct and Rights 142-148
PERIODICALS:
"Retroactivity riddle." Time 85: 44, 47 June 18 '65 (2).

2521. Angelet v. Fay   June 7, 1965   381 U.S. 654
        Police 70-71

2522. United Mine Workers of America   June 7, 1965   381 U.S. 657
        v. Pennington
        Basic Text 629-631
        *Cases Labor (Cox) 1228-1234
        *Cases Labor (Leslie) 436-443
        *Cases Labor (Oberer) 1008-1014
        *Labor Law (Meltzer) 508-514
        *Labor Law (Twomey) 49-55
        Labor Relations (Taylor) 117-118
        PERIODICALS:
        "Antitrust law moves into bargaining room." Bus Wk p. 139-140
          June 12 '65.
        "Labor and antitrust: new worry for unions." US News 58: 101,
          104-105 June 21 '65.
        *"Recent U.S. Supreme Court decision on antitrust law and labor
          unions; opinion and dissent." Congressional Dig 44: 216-223
          Aug '65.
        "Significant decisions in labor cases." Monthly Labor R 88:
          1105-1108 Sept '65.
        "Unions suffer disastrous defeat," R. W. Crosby. Iron Age 195:
          28-29 June 17 '65 (2).
        "US Labor policy--recent major Supreme Court decisions." Con-
          gressional Dig 44: 197-198, 224 Aug/Sept '65 (3).
        "Wage rates as a barrier to entry: the Pennington case in per-
          spective," Oliver E. Williamson. Q J Economics 82: 85-
          116 Feb '68.
        "Will Supreme Court ruling hit pattern bargaining?" Steel 156:
          27-28 June 21 '65.

2623. Local Union No. 189, Amalgamated   June 7, 1965   381 U.S. 676
        Meat Cutters and Butcher Workmen
        of North America v. Jewel Tea Co.
        Basic Text 631-632
        *Cases Labor (Cox) 1235-1246
        *Cases Labor (Leslie) 443-451
        *Cases Labor (Oberer) 1014-1032
        *Labor Law (Twomey) 55-57
        Labor Relations (Taylor) 116-117
        Professional Sports 307-310
        PERIODICALS:
        "Rights of management." Economist 214: 33 Jan 2 '65 (3).
        "Significant decisions in labor cases." Monthly Labor R 88: 1105-
          1108 Sept '65.
        "Unions suffer disastrous defeat," R. W. Crosby. Iron Age 195:
          28-29 June 17 '65.

2624. WMCA v. Lomenzo   Oct 11, 1965   382 U.S. 4

Democratic 485-486
PERIODICALS:
"A+B+C+D=NY^2, " Meg Greenfield. Reporter 33: 32-35 Dec 2
'65.

2625. Gondeck v. Pan American World   Oct 18, 1965   382 U.S. 25
Airways
*Federal Courts 1594-1596

2626. Federal Trade Commission v.   Nov 8, 1965   382 U.S. 46
Mary Carter Paint Co.
*Legal Environment 518-519
*Legal Regulation 223-227

2627. Albertson v. Subversive Activities   Nov 15, 1965   382 U.S. 70
Control Board
Am Consttn (Kelly) 913-914
Decade 43-44
Freedom and the Court 206-207
Sup Ct Review 1966 103-166
Sup Ct Review 1967 199-200
Sup Ct Review 1971 7-8
PERIODICALS:
"Going public. " Newsweek 66: 25 Nov 29 '65.
"Reds' registration overruled. " Senior Scholastic 87: 14 Dec
2 '65.
"Up from the underground. " Time 86· 26 Nov 26 '65.

2628. Shuttlesworth v. City of Birmingham   Nov 15, 1965   382 U.S. 87
Criminal Law Revolution 71-72

2029. Bradley v. School Board of City of   Nov 15, 1965   382 U.S. 103
Richmond, Va.
Gilliam v. School Board of City of
Hopewell, Va.
Digest 84
PERIODICALS:
"Impact of U.S. Supreme Court decisions on the lives of black
people, 1950-1974, " Robert L. Gill. Negro Eductn R 27: 92-
122 Apr '76 (3).

2630. Swift and Co. , Inc. v. Wickham   Nov 22, 1965   382 U.S. 111
*Cases Federal Courts 446-455

2631. United States v. Romano   Nov 22, 1965   382 U.S. 136
Criminal Law Revolution 79

2632. United Steelworkers of America,   Nov 22, 1965   382 U.S. 145
AFL-CIO v. R. H. Bouligny, Inc.
*Cases Federal Courts 185-189
*Federal Courts 1089-1092
Sup Ct Review 1966 254-255, 265-269

2633. Seaboard Air Line Railroad Co.   Nov 22, 1965   382 U.S. 154
v. United States
Interstate Commerce Commission v.
Florida East Coast Railroad Co.
*Cases Trade 839-840
*Selected Antitrust Cases 389-390

2634. Harris v. United States   Dec 6, 1965   382 U. S. 162
       Criminal Law Revolution 76-77
       *Douglas 75-78
       Justice Hugo Black 116-117

2635. Walker Process Equipment, Inc.   Dec 6, 1965   382 U. S. 172
       v. Food Machinery and Chemical
       Corporation
       *Antitrust (Posner) 871-873
       *Antitrust Analysis 247-249
       *Cases Trade 876-879
       *Patent 685-691

2636. Hanna Mining Co. v. District 2,   Dec 6, 1965   382 U. S. 181
       Marine Engineers Beneficial
       Association
       *Cases Labor (Cox) 1210-1218
       *Labor Law (Meltzer) 625-630
       Sup Ct Review 1966 269-279
       PERIODICALS:
       "Significant decisions in labor cases. "   Monthly Labor R   89:   186-
       187 Feb '66 (2).

2637. Rogers v. Paul   Dec 6, 1965   382 U. S. 198
       Digest 84-85
       Warren (Hudgins) 90
       PERIODICALS:
       "Desegregation: where schools stand with the courts as the new
       year begins, " H. C. Hudgins. Am Sch Bd J 156: 21-25
       Jan '69 (7).

2638. International Union, United Automobile,   Dec 7, 1965   382 U. S. 205
       Aerospace and Agricultural Imple-
       ment Workers of America,
       AFL-CIO Local 283 v. Scofield
       PERIODICALS:
       "Significant decisions in labor cases. "   Monthly Labor R   89:
       186-187 Feb '66.

2639. Hazeltine Research, Inc. v. Brenner,   Dec 8, 1965   382 U. S. 252
       Commissioner of Patents
       *Legal Regulation 950-952

2640. Evans v. Newton   Jan 17, 1966   382 U. S. 296
       *Consttnl Law (Barrett) 1057-1061
       *Consttnl Law (Barron) 1012-1014
       *Consttnl Law (Freund) 832-835
       Court and Consttn v. 2, 279
       Desegregation (Wasby) 152-157
       *Discrimination 424-429
       Dissent 356-358
       *Federal Courts 506-512
       Freedom and the Court 428-429
       *Political Rights v. 2, 1667-1672
       Private Pressure 136-137
       Warren (Cox) 41-43

2641. Katchen v. Landy   Jan 17, 1966   382 U. S. 323
       *Cases Civil Procedure 697-700

2642. United States v. Yazell   Jan 17, 1966   382 U.S. 341
       *Cases Federal Courts 624-629
       *Sex Roles 199-204

2643. Giaccio v. Pennsylvania   Jan 19, 1966   382 U.S. 399
       Criminal Law Revolution 80

2644. Tehan v. United States ex rel Shott   Jan 19, 1966   382 U.S. 406
       Criminal Law Revolution 64

2645. Simmons v. Union News Co.   Oct 18, 1965   382 U.S. 884
       *Labor Law (Meltzer) 936-938

2646. Graham v. John Deere Co.   Feb 21, 1966   383 U.S. 1
       Calmar, Inc. v. Cook Chemical Co.
       Colgate-Palmolive Co. v. Cook Chem-
         ical Co.
       *Cases Antitrust Law 261-271
       *Cases Trade 857-866
       *Copyright 410-420, 544-549
       *Legal Regulation 860-876
       Sup Ct and Agencies 221-225
       Sup Ct Review 1966 293-346
       PERIODICALS:
       "Chemical makers can expect harder time in patent office on heels
         of US court decision." Oil Paint and Drug Rep 189: 5, 34
         Feb 28 '66.

2647. United States v. Adams   Feb 21, 1966   383 U.S. 39
       *Legal Regulation 877-885
       Sup Ct and Agencies 221-225
       Sup Ct Review 1966 328-330

2648. Linn v. United Plant Guard Workers   Feb 21, 1966   383 U.S. 53
         of America
       *Cases Labor (Cox) 1200-1210
       *Labor Law (Meltzer) 618-624
       Sup Ct Review 1966 279-291
       PERIODICALS:
       "Significant decisions in labor cases." Monthly Labor R 89: 532-
         533 May '66.

2649. Rosenblatt v. Baer   Feb 21, 1966   383 U.S. 75
       *Affair 88-91
       CQ Guide 435-436
       Communication (Hemmer) v. 2, 58-60
       Handbook 272-273
       Law of Mass 98
       Mass Media (Clark) 239-242
       Politics 104-105
       Sup Ct Review 1978 278
       System 525-526
       PERIODICALS:
       "Recent libel decision expands Times case doctrine," Harriet F.
         Pilpel. Pub Weekly 189: 43-45 May 9 '66.

2650. Baxstrom v. Herold   Feb 23, 1966   383 U.S. 107
       *Consttnl Law (Felkenes) 404-405
       Criminal Law Revolution 66

*Readings Law 681-684
*U. S. Prison Law v. 3, 431-438
PERIODICALS:
"Constitutional requirements in the commitment of the mentally
ill in the USA: rights to liberty and therapy," Franklin N.
Flaschorer. Intl J Offender Therapy 18 no 3: 283-301 '74
(2).

2651. United States v. Ewell   Feb 23, 1966   383 U. S. 116
      Criminal Law Revolution 68-69
      PERIODICALS:
      "Case notes." J Criml Law, Crimlgy and Police Sci   57: 335-336
      Sept '66.

2652. Brown v. Louisiana   Feb 23, 1966   383 U. S. 131
      *Am Consttnl Law (Mason) 577-580
      *Bill (Konvitz) 289-300
      Cases Consttnl Law (Gunther) 1278-1280
      *Cases Individual 805-809
      Communication (Hemmer) v. 1, 82-84
      *Consttnl Law (Kauper) 1166-1169
      *Contemporary Law 909-915
      Criminal Law Revolution 70-71
      Decade 216-218
      Desegregation (Wasby) 349-350
      Equality (Berger) 126-127
      Free Speech (Kurland) 355-356
      *Freedom of Speech (Haiman) 76-77
      Hugo Black (Dunne) 392-393
      Hugo Black (Strickland) 92-93
      Justice Hugo Black 165-166
      Politics 118-121
      Sup Ct and Poltcl Freedom 137-138
      Sup Ct Review 1974 246-247
      Warren (Cox) 109
      PERIODICALS:
      "From songs to sedition." Newsweek 67: 27 Mar 7 '66.
      "Negro protests upheld by Supreme Court." Library J 91: 1374
      Mar 15 '66.
      "Word to the wise." Time 87: 61 Mar 4 '66.

2653. United States v. Johnson   Feb 24, 1966   383 U. S. 169
      CQ Guide 169-170
      Criminal Law Revolution 75
      System 703-704

2654. Idaho Sheet Metal Works, Inc. v.   Feb 24, 1966   383 U. S. 190
      Wirtz, Secretary of Labor
      Wirtz v. Steepleton General Tire Co.
      Sup Ct and Commerce 137-138

2655. Accardi v. Pennsylvania Railroad Co.   Feb 28, 1966   383 U. S. 225
      PERIODICALS:
      "Significant decisions in labor cases." Monthly Labor R 89: 417-
      418 Apr '66.

2656. Hicks v. District of Columbia   Feb 28, 1966   383 U. S. 252
      *Legal Problems 10-11

2657. Hopson v. Texaco   Feb 28, 1966   383 U.S. 262
       *Cases Admiralty 346-347

2658. South Carolina v. Katzenbach   Mar 7, 1966   383 U.S. 301
       Am Consttn (Kelly) 898-899
       *Am Consttnl Law (Shapiro) 539-542
       *Bill (Konvitz) 622-636
       CQ Guide 486
       *Cases Civil Liberties 420-425
       *Cases Consttnl Law (Cushman) 650-655
       *Cases Federal Courts 16-18
       *Civil Liberties (Barker) 294-301
       *Civil Rights (Abernathy) 1977 592-593
       *Civil Rights (Abernathy) 1980 587-600
       *Civil Rights (Bardolph) 499-501
       *Civil Rights (Blaustein) 573-582
       *Comparative 552-555
       *Consttnl Law (Freund) 974-980
       *Consttnl Law (Grossman) 492-497
       *Contemporary Issues 19-28
       *Contemporary Law 932-942
       Desegregation (Wasby) 252-260
       *Discrimination 120-135
       Dissent 347-348
       *Documents History v. 2, 711-713
       *Federal System 350-354
       Hugo Black (Dunne) 403
       *Law Sup Ct 479-484
       *Liberty v. 2, 623-626
       *Political Rights v. 2, 1191-1205
       Private Pressure 138-140
       *Processes 1034-1045
       *Race 144-152
       *Racial Equality 87-92
       *Statutory History Civil Rights 1612-1625
       *Struggle 223-230
       *Sup Ct and Am Govt 151-158
       *Sup Ct and Consttn 543-548
       Sup Ct and Electoral Process 124-127
       Sup Ct Review 1966 80-93
       *These Liberties 233-240
       Warren (Cox) 55-57
       PERIODICALS:
         "Challenge from the South." Time 87: 18-19 Jan 28 '66.
         "Some needed nudges." Time 87: 29-29A Mar 18 '66.
         "Voting act upheld." Senior Scholastic 88: 7-8 Mar 25 '66.

2659. Surowitz v. Hilton Hotels Corporation   Mar 7, 1966   383 U.S. 363
       *Civil Procedure (Carrington) 710-714
       *Civil Procedure (Cound) 412-415
       PERIODICALS:
         "Stitch in time." Time 87: 67 Mar 18 '66.

2660. Pate v. Robinson   Mar 7, 1966   383 U.S. 375
       *Cases Criml Justice 925-931
       Criminal Law Revolution 66-67
       *Readings Law 635-639

2661. Perry v. Commerce Loan Co.   Mar 7, 1966   383 U.S. 392
       *Materials Reorganization 252-257

2662. A Book named "John Cleland's Memoirs Mar 21, 1966   383 U.S. 413
       of a Woman of Pleasure" v. At-
       torney General of Massachusetts
       "Fanny Hill Case"
       Am Consttn (Kelly) 972
       *Bill (Konvitz) 417-426
       By What Right 322-323
       *Cases Consttnl Rights 574-578
       *Censorship Landmarks 521-535
       Communication (Hemmer) v. 1, 167-168
       *Consttnl Law (Barron) 908-909
       *Consttnl Law (Freund) 1291-1293
       Criminal Law Revolution 74
       Dissent 411-412
       *Freedom of Speech (Haiman) 137
       Law of Mass 363-364
       Law of Obscenity 42-43
       Literature 218-219
       *Mass Communications 562-563
       Mass Media (Clark) 298-299
       *Mass Media (Devol) 122-124
       Mass Media (Francois) 362-364
       *Obscenity (Bosmajian) 90-103
       Obscenity (Clor) 77-78
       *Obscenity (Friedman) 275-277
       Obscenity (Sunderland) 55-57
       *Pornography 106-127
       Rights of the People 114-115
       *Sex Roles 606-609
       *Sup Ct and Consttn 472-477
       Sup Ct Review 1966 41-56
       Sup Ct Review 1976 69
       System 477-478
       PERIODICALS:
       "Bad news for smut peddlers." Time 87: 56, 58 Apr 1 '66.
       "Confusion on obscenity." America 114: 430 Apr 2 '66.
       "Court stirs a hornet's nest." Christian Century 83: 451-452
           Apr 13 '66.
       *"Decisions, decisions: what's smut, what isn't? opinions in Ginz-
           burg case and Fanny Hill case; excerpts." Newsweek 67: 20
           Apr 4 '66.
       "How not to read a dirty book." America 114: 614 Apr 30 '66.
       "May it please the Court," Andrew Kopkind. New Republic 153:
           9-10 Dec 18 '65.
       "Obscenity and the Supreme Court," G. Robert Blakey. America
           115: 152-156 Aug 13 '66 (4).
       "Obscenity business," Jason Epstein. Atlantic 218: 56-60 Aug
           '66. Reprinted: Library J 91: 4566-4571 Oct 1 '66.
       "Obscenity chore." Time 86: 36, 39 Dec 17 '66.
       "Obscenity muddle," Paul Bender. Harper's Mag 246: 46, 50-52
           Feb '73. Reaction: Raymond P. Gauer. 246: 20 Apr '73.
       "Obscenity test--a legal poser." Newsweek 67: 19, 21-22 Apr
           4 '66.
       "Society's lack of confidence in itself," R. H. Smith. Pub Weekly
           189: 41 Apr 4 '66.

"Spring harvest festival, " Ervin J. Gaines. ALA Bul 60: 551-552 June '66.

"Supreme Court OK's Fanny Hill. " Library J 91: 2020 Apr 15 '66.

"Supreme Court rulings on obscenity cases. " Wilson Library Bul 40: 795, 797 May '66.

"Supreme Court to review Mass. Fanny Hill ruling. " Pub Weekly 188: 73 Nov 15 '65.

"Titillation's a crime. " Library J 91: 2016 Apr 15 '66.

"U.S. Supreme Court reexamines precedents in hearings on three book censorship cases. " Pub Weekly 188: 61-66 Dec 27 '65.

"U.S. Supreme Court rules pro-censorship in 2 of 3 cases involving books. " Pub Weekly 189: 43-44 Mar 28 '66.

"Warren Court and whither obscenity, " Harriet F. Pilpel and Kenneth P. Norwick. Pub Weekly 196: 46-48 July 7 '69 (5).

2663. Ginzburg v. United States   Mar 21, 1966   383 U.S. 463
*Affair 56-50
Am Consttn (Kelly) 970-971
*Annals v. 18, 350-356
*Bill (Konvitz) 426-432
*Cases Consttnl Law (Rosenblum) 299-305
*Censorship Landmarks 485-493, 566-569
Communication (Hemmer) v. 1, 196-197
Consttnl Counterrevolution 270-271
*Consttnl Law (Barron) 909-912
*Consttnl Law (Freund) 1293-1295
Dissent 412-414
*Evolution 120-123
Freedom and the Court 218-219
*Freedom of Speech (Haiman) 137-139
Great Events Worldwide 106-107
Handbook 164-165, 627-631
*Judicial Crises 354-359
Law of Mass 365-367
Law of Obscenity 80-84
*Law of Obscenity 410-417
*Mass Communications 564-565
Mass Media (Clark) 300-301, 443-444
*Mass Media (Devol) 125-130
Mass Media (Francois) 361-362
*Modern Consttnl Law 305-316
*Obscenity (Bosmajian) 103-114
Obscenity (Clor) 79-83
*Obscenity (Friedman) 267-273
*Principles Freedom 278-299
Rights of the People 115-118
*Sup Ct on Freedom 61-68
Sup Ct Review 1966 25-37
Sup Ct Review 1968 162-163
Sup Ct Review 1976 69-71
System 478-479
*These Liberties 167-174
PERIODICALS:
"Demeaning the Court. " Nation 202: 379-380 Apr 4 '66.
"Dissent to the High court's harsh verdict, " Loudon Wainwright. Life 60: 26 Apr 22 '66.

"Ginzburg decision and the law," Leon Friedman. <u>Am Scholar</u>
   36: 71-91 Winter '66-67.
"Ginzburg petitions for rehearing." <u>Library J</u> 91: 2440, 2442
   May 15 '66.
"High court rulings on Borden, Eros seen as in direct conflict."
   <u>Adv Age</u> 37: 3, 136 June 6 '66.
"Implications of the Ginzburg affair; address, April 20, 1966,"
   K. Molz. <u>Wilson Library Bul</u> 40: 941-947 June '66.
"Obscenity and the law." <u>New Republic</u> 154: 5-6 Apr 2 '66.
   Reaction: S. Kipperman 154: 28 Apr 23 '66.
"Obscenity cases," Alexander M. Bickel. <u>New Republic</u> 156: 15-
   17 May 27 '67 (2).
"Pornography problem; Ginzburg case." <u>Sat Evening Post</u> 239:
   98 May 7 '66.
"Ralph Ginzburg begins term for 1963 porno conviction." <u>Library J</u>
   97: 1650, 1652-1654 May 1 '72.
See also listing at 383 U.S. 413, entry no. 2662.

2664. Mishkin v. New York   Mar 21, 1966 383 U.S. 502
        Am Consttn (Kelly) 971-972
        *Censorship Landmarks 560-565
        Communication (Hemmer) v. 1, 168-169
        Consttnl Counterrevolution 271
        Handbook 652-653
        *Judicial Crises 351-353
        Law of Mass 364-365
        Law of Obscenity 77-79
        *Law of Obscenity 417-424
        Mass Media (Clark) 299-300
        Mass Media (Francois) 362
        *Obscenity (Bosmajian) 114-119
        *Obscenity (Friedman) 273-275
        Sup Ct Review 1966 37-40
        System 479-480
        PERIODICALS:
        See listing at 383 U.S. 413, entry no. 2662.

2665. Brenner v. Manson   Mar 21, 1966 383 U.S. 519
        *Cases Trade 853-856
        *Copyright 448-454
        *Legal Regulation 847-854

2666. Kent v. United States   Mar 21, 1966 383 U.S. 541
        *Cases Criml Law (Perkins) 511-516
        *Consttnl Law (Felkenes) 358-360
        Criminal Law (Felkenes) 389-391
        Criminal Law Revolution 81
        Sup Ct Review 1966 176-183

2667. Federal Trade Commission v. Borden   Mar 23, 1966 383 U.S. 637
        Co.
        *Antitrust Analysis 761-762
        *Cases Antitrust Law 1111-1121
        *Cases Trade 967-975
        *Legal Environment 296-298
        *Selected Antitrust Cases 270-277
        PERIODICALS:
        "Ads don't raise value of goods." <u>Adv Age</u> 37: 1, 30 Mar 28
        '66.

"The Borden case--a legal basis for private brand price discrimination," Morris L. Mayer. MSU Bus Topics 18: 56-63 Winter '70.
"Borden decision spells change, but changes already in wind, AA learns." Adv Age 37: 2, 120 Apr 4 '66.
"FTC gains high court support in private label territory." Merchandising Wk 98: 3 Mar 28 '66.
"High court rulings on Borden, Eros seen as in direct conflict." Adv Age 37: 3, 136 June 6 '66 (2).
"Private brands; the Borden case is not over yet," Sidney Diamond. Adv Age 37: 80, 82 Apr 18 '66.
*"Supreme Court decision upholding Federal Trade Commission in Borden milk case." Adv Age 37: 82, 84, 87-88 Apr 4 '66.
"Supreme Court to review Borden, Sealy, Brown Shoe Co." Adv Age 36: 60 Oct 18 '65 (3).

2668.   Harper v. Virginia State Board of   Mar 24, 1966 383 U.S. 663
        Elections
Butts v. Harrison
   Am Consttn (Kelly) 899-900
   *Am Consttnl Law (Saye) 477
   *Cases Consttnl Law (Gunther) 924-927
   *Cases Individual 387-393
   *Consttnl Law (Barrett) 947-950
   *Consttnl Law (Barron) 665-668
   *Consttnl Law (Freund) 981-984
   *Consttnl Law (Grossman) 498-500
   *Consttnl Law (Kauper) 758-762
   *Contemporary Law 924-930
   Desegregation (Wasby) 261-263
   *Discrimination 88-93
   Dissent 348-351
   *Evolution 79-83
   *Federal System 348-350
   Hugo Black (Strickland) 91-92
   *Judicial Crises 104-108
   *Legal Problems 71-73
   *Political Rights v. 2, 1125-1130
   *Poverty 227-232
   Private Pressure 142-143
   *Processes 810-815
   Sup Ct and Electoral Process 81-82
   Sup Ct from Taft 264-265
   Sup Ct Review 1966 93-95
   *These Liberties 241-245
   Warren (Cox) 125-126
PERIODICALS:
   "Dead as the poll tax." Economist 219: 40 Apr 2 '66.
   "The poll tax case." Socl Eductn 31: 313-314 Apr '67.
   "R.I.P." Time 87: 25B Apr 1 '66.

2669.   Commissioner of Internal Revenue v.   Mar 24, 1966 383 U.S. 687
        Tellier
PERIODICALS:
   "How IRS adapts its practice to adverse Supreme Court decisions," Lester R. Uretz. J Taxation 26: 290-293 May '67 (4).
   "Tellier decision of the Supreme Court," Earl C. Crouter. Taxes 44: 612-616 Sept '66.

2670. United Mine Workers of America   Mar 28, 1966   383 U.S. 715
           v. Gibbs
       *Cases Federal Courts 147-151
       *Civil Procedure (Cound) 227-231
       *Civil Rights (Abernathy) 1980 218-222
       *Federal Courts 917-921
       PERIODICALS:
       "Significant decisions in labor cases." Monthly Labor R 89: 776-
       779 July '66 (2).

2671. United States v. Guest   Mar 28, 1966   383 U.S. 745
       *Affair 266-273
       *Am Consttn (Lockhart) 1193-1199
        By What Right 236
       *Cases Civil Liberties 416-419
       *Cases Consttnl Law (Cushman) 646-649
       *Cases Consttnl Law (Gunther) 1031-1038
       *Cases Consttnl Rights 1181-1188
       *Cases Individual 562-571
       *Civil Rights (Abernathy) 1977 78-82
       *Civil Rights (Abernathy) 1980 297-304
       *Civil Rights (Friedman) v. 1, 791-799
        Conceived 209-210
       *Consttnl Law (Barrett) 1087-1088
       *Consttnl Law (Barron) 1066-1073
       *Consttnl Law (Felkenes) 177-179
       *Consttnl Law (Freund) 851-857
       *Consttnl Law (Kauper) 851-858
       *Consttnl Law (Lockhart) 1588-1593
       *Discrimination 41-47
        Equality (Berger) 113-114
       *Political Rights v. 2, 1056-1063
        Private Pressure 135-136
       *Race 868-873
        Sup Ct and Electoral Process 59-61
        Warren 60-69

2672. United States v. Price   Mar 28, 1966   383 U.S. 787
       *Cases Consttnl Law (Gunther) 1038-1040
       *Civil Rights (Abernathy) 1977 82-85
       *Civil Rights (Blaustein) 584-589
        Criminal Law Revolution 69-70
        Equality (Berger) 112-114
       *Law Sup Ct 504-515
       *Political Rights v. 2, 1050-1056
        Private Pressure 134-135
       *Race 858-868
        Sup Ct and Electoral Process 58-59
        To Preserve 79-80

2673. De Gregory v. Attorney General of   Apr 4, 1966   383 U.S. 825
           New Hampshire
        Am Consttn (Kelly) 935
        Criminal Law Revolution 76
       *Law Sup Ct 181-184

2674. Brookhart v. Janis   Apr 18, 1966   384 U.S. 1
        Criminal Law Revolution 67

2675. Elfbrandt v. Russell   Apr 18, 1966   384 U.S. 11
          Am Consttn (Kelly) 926
          CQ Guide 514, 516
          *Cases Consttnl Law (Gunther) 1464-1466
          *Cases Individual 999-1001
          Communication (Hemmer) v. 1, 209
          *Consttnl Law (Barrett) 1199-1201
          Consttnl Law (Cortner) 105-131, 135-137
          *Consttnl Law (Cortner) 132-135
          Decade 46
          Digest 58
          *Douglas 208-211
          Education (Lapati) 233
          Free Speech (Kurland) 147-206
          *Judicial Excerpts 168-170
          Landmark Decisions 131-135
          *Law Sup Ct 193-200
          *Political Rights v. 1, 345-348
          Rights of the People 126-127
          School in the Legal Structure 71-72
          Sup Ct Review 1966 193-252
          System 235-237
          Warren (Hudgins) 143-144
      PERIODICALS:
          "The Elfbrandt case." Socl Eductn 31: 125-136 Feb '67.
          "Teach-in in Tucson." Newsweek 67: 21 May 2 '66.

2676. Burns v. Richardson   Apr 25, 1966   384 U.S. 73
          Cravalho v. Richardson
          Abe v. Richardson
          Consttnl Counterrevolution 110
          Democratic 478-480
          Sup Ct and Electoral Process 186-188
          Warren (Ball) 202-204

2677. National Association for the Advance-   Apr 27, 1966   384 U.S. 118
              ment of Colored People v. Over-
              street
          *Race 320-324

2678. United States v. General Motors   Apr 28, 1966   384 U.S. 127
              Corporation
          *Antitrust (Posner) 547-554
          *Competition 373-376
          *Legal Environment 274-277
          *Selected Antitrust Cases 329-336

2679. Westbrook v. Arizona   May 2, 1966   384 U.S. 150
          *Cases Criml Justice 933

2680. Ashton v. Kentucky   May 16, 1966   384 U.S. 195
          Communication (Hemmer) v. 2, 68-69
          Conceived 101-102
          Criminal Law Revolution 73
      PERIODICALS:
          "Right to speak or write inciting words," H. F. Pilpel. Pub
              Weekly 189: 70 June 27 '66.

2681. Pure Oil Co. v. Suarez   May 16, 1966   384 U.S. 202
       *Cases Admiralty 348-349

2682. Mills v. Alabama   May 23, 1966   384 U.S. 214
       Communication (Hemmer) v. 2, 211-212
       *Mass Communications 672-673
       Mass Media (Clark) 454-455
       *Mass Media (Devol) 41-42
       *Sup Ct on Freedom 68-71
       System 638
       PERIODICALS:
       "A crime to publish an editorial on election day, " Harriet F. Pil-
       pel. Pub Weekly 189: 71 June 27 '66.
       "Law that muzzles press on election day voided. " Editor and Pub
       99: 11, 52 May 28 '66.

2683. United States v. Standard Oil Co.   May 23, 1966   384 U.S. 224
       *Introduction (Mashaw) 34-41
       *Text Legislation 109-110

2684. United States v. Blue   May 23, 1966   384 U.S. 251
       Criminal Law Revolution 80-81

2685. United States v. Von's Grocery Co.   May 31, 1966   384 U.S. 270
       Antitrust (Posner) 405-413
       *Antitrust (Posner) 413-416
       *Antitrust Analysis 769-772
       *Cases Antitrust Law 900-914
       *Cases Trade 778-788
       *Competition 143-145
       Hugo Black (Dunne) 399-400
       Hugo Black (Strickland) 208-209
       *Legal Environment 325-330
       *Selected Antitrust Cases 156-167
       *Social Forces 280-286
       *Text Antitrust 183-186
       PERIODICALS:
       "Antitrust: a tough new line. " Newsweek 67: 81 June 13 '66.
       "Antitrust in a coonskin cap. " Fortune 74: 65-66, 68 July 1 '66.
       "High court bars merger of rivals. " Bus Wk p. 36 June 4 '66.
       "Now a 'little' merger is ruled illegal. " US News 60: 58 June
       13 '66.
       "Supreme court decision; merger-minded retailers beware. " Mer-
       chandising Wk 98: 3 June 6 '66.

2686. Rinaldi v. Yeager   May 31, 1966   384 U.S. 305
       Criminal Law Revolution 80

2687. Federal Trade Commission v.   June 6, 1966   384 U.S. 316
       Brown Shoe Co.
       *Antitrust (Posner) 730-733
       *Cases Antitrust Law 817-819
       *Cases Trade 579-582
       *Legal Environment 310-312
       *Text Antitrust 138-140
       PERIODICALS:
       "Federal Trade Commission v. Brown Shoe Co. , " John L. Peter-
       man. J of Law and Economics 18: 361-419 Oct '75.

"More and more power for the trustbusters." US News 60: 15
    June 20 '66.
"Supreme Court hits Brown shoe franchise setup." Adv Age 37:
    70 June 13 '66.
"Supreme Court to review Borden, Sealy, Brown shoe Co." Adv
    Age 36: 60 Oct 18 '65 (3).

2688. Sheppard v. Maxwell   June 6, 1966   384 U.S. 333
        *Am Consttnl Law (Saye) 536-539
        *Annals 18: 402-406
        Argument 274-276
        *Bill (Konvitz) 709-723
        CQ Guide 442
        *Cases Consttnl Rights 280-283
        *Civil Rights (Abernathy) 1977 449-451
        Communication (Hemmer) v. 2, 180-183
        Communications Law 57-58
        *Consttnl Law (Freund) 1305-1308
        *Consttnl Law (Grossman) 902-907
        *Consttnl Law (Klein) 144-158
        *Contemporary Law 657-662
        Court Years 142-143
        Criminal Law (Felkenes) 340-343
        *Criminal Law (Kadish) 1298-1303
        Criminal Law Revolution 67-68
        *Due Process 116-117
        *First Amendment (Franklin) 192-196
        Freedom and the Court 183-184
        Handbook 544-548, 552-554
        Law of Mass 273-279
        *Law Sup Ct 300-309
        *Leading Consttnl Cases 728-743
        *Mass Communications 492-500
        *Mass Media (Devol) 274-290
        Procedures 101-102, 159
        *Sup Ct on Freedom 114-127
        *These Liberties 69-82
        PERIODICALS:
        "Advice to the press," Hans Linde. Center Mag 12: 2-6 Jan
            '79. Reaction: Richard Salant. 12: 32-33 May '79.
        "Press v. the accused." Time 87: 66-67 June 17 '66.
        *"Sheppard v. Maxwell 1966." Current History 61: 106-110, 115
            Aug '71.
        "Supreme Court says judge should stifle publicity." Editor and
            Pub 99: 11, 76 June 11 '66.
        "Word from the top to all courts; cut out carnival coverage."
            Broadcasting 70: 72 June 13 '66.

2689. Shillitani v. United States   June 6, 1966   384 U.S. 364
        Pappadio v. United States
        Criminal Law Revolution 78

2690. Cheff v. Schnackenburg, U.S.   June 6, 1966   384 U.S. 373
        Circuit Judge
        Criminal Law Revolution 77
        Justice Hugo Black 119

2691. Miranda v. Arizona   June 13, 1966   384 U.S. 436
        Vignera v. New York

*Criminal Procedure (Lewis) 365-373
Decade 173-177
Defendants 220-221, 338-340
Dissent 366-375
*Documents History v. 2, 713-717
*Due Process 44-45, 55, 59-61
Earl Warren 267-270
*Elements Criminal 218-232
*Evolution 37-45
Freedom and the Court 144-147
Freedom Spent 380-381
Great Reversals 180-181
Impact (Becker) 149-175
Impact (Wasby) 155-162
In His own Image 48-49, 68-69
*Judicial Crises 12-26
*Justices (Friedman) v. 4, 2774-2800, 2837-2846
Law of Arrest (Creamer) 377-382
*Law of Evidence 548-576
*Law Sup Ct 283-291
*Leading Consttnl Cases 501-529
*Leading Consttnl Decisions 369-385
*Liberty v. 2, 572-575
Memoirs 316-317
Milestones 325-343
*Modern Consttnl Law 180-194
*Nature 273-278
New Dimensions 234-241
Perspectives (Black) 106-107
Police 110-111
Politics 261-266
*Principles Arrest 137-140
*Principles Proof 736-741
*Readings American 139-152
Rights of the People 72-79
Self Inflicted Wound 153-160, 178-184, 188-193
Spirit 100-102
Sup Ct (Forte) 83, 85
*Sup Ct and Am Govt 205-217
Sup Ct and Confessions 129-139
*Sup Ct and Consttn 577-581
*Sup Ct and Criml Process 423-429
Sup Ct and Criml Process 443-446; reprint of "Participating Mi-
    randa," Peter W. Lewis and Harry E. Allen. Crime and De-
    linquency Jan '77.
Sup Ct and News 99-101
*Sup Ct and Rights 93-110
Sup Ct Review 1969 123-131
Sup Ct Review 1976 520-524
Sup Ct Review 1977 99-169
*Teaching Materials 455-472
*These Liberties 46-59
Warren (Cox) 83-87
Warren (Lytle) 82-88
PERIODICALS:
    "Case notes." J Criml Law, Crimlgy and Police Sci 57: 335
        Sept '66.
    "Confession debate continues," Irving R. Kaufman. New York Times

Mag p. 36-37, 47, 50, 52, 54, 57, 60, 62, 64, 72, 74, 87
Oct 2 '66.
"Crime, confessions and the Court; excerpts from the Crime War,"
Robert M. Cipes. Atlantic 218: 51-58 Sept '66. Reaction:
218: 46-48 Dec '66 (2).
"Crime, confessions and the Supreme Court," Gary L. Chamber-
lain. America 117: 32-34 July 8 '67.
"Don't say a word, Mac." Natl R 18: 606-608 June 28 '66.
"Is it wrong to handcuff the police?" William J. Dempsey. Catho-
lic World 204: 264-269 Feb '67 (3).
"Is the court handcuffing the cops?" James Vorenberg and James
Q. Wilson. New York Times Mag 32-33, 134-136, 139-140
May 11 '69.
"Key arguments from recent Supreme Court decisions." Senior
Scholastic 94: 14-15 Mar 28 '69 (3).
"Law and order," Nicholas deB. Katzenbach. Look 32: 27-29
Oct 29 '68.
"Let's have justice for non-criminals, too!" Eugene H. Methvin.
Readers Dig 89: 53-60 Dec '66 (2).
"Miranda v. Arizona discussed." Am City 82: 52 June '67.
*"Miranda v. Arizona; excerpts." Current History 52: 359-362,
367-368 June '67.
"Miranda's fate in the Burger Court," Ronald K. L. Collins and
Robert Welsh. Center Mag 13: 43-52 Sept/Oct '80 (2).
"More criminals to go free? Effect of High court's ruling."
US News 60: 32-34 June 27 '66.
"New rules for police rooms." Time 87: 53-54 June 24 '66.
"Other voices, other rooms." Newsweek 68: 26-27 Aug 1 '66.
"Policy in search of law: the Warren Court from Brown to Mi-
randa," Richard A. Maidment. J Am Studies (Great Britain)
9 no3: 301-320 '75 (4).
"Popular perceptions of Supreme Court rulings," Gregory Casey.
Am Politics Q 4: 3-46 Jan '76 (4).
*"Pro and Con: Here's what the justices said." US News 60: 34-
36 June 27 '66.
"Question of questioning." Reporter 34: 8-9 June 30 '66.
"Rewriting the rules." Newsweek 67: 21-22 June 27 '66.
"Station house confessions." New Republic 154: 8-9 June 25
'66.
"Supreme Court and crime; justice or lawlessness; address,"
Michael A. Musmanno. Vital Speeches 34: 666-668 Aug 15
'68. Excerpts: US News 65: 71-72 Sept 2 '68 (3).
"Supreme Court and law enforcement," Robert G. Caldwell. J
Police Sci and Administration 3: 222-237 June '75 (2).
"Supreme Court says Miranda warnings do not apply to non-custodial
interviews," Donald L. Herskovitz. J Taxation 45: 5-7 July
'76 (2).
"Under review by Supreme Court: just what rights do suspects
have? US News 59: 10 Dec 6 '65.
"Where are they now? Gideon, Escobedo, and Miranda." Newsweek 74: 8 Aug 11 '69 (3).
"Witness for the court," John Galloway. Christian Century 85:
1473-1474 Nov 20 '68 (3).

2692.   United States v. Pabst Brewing Co.   June 13, 1966 384 U.S. 546
        Antitrust (Posner) 441-446
        *Antitrust (Posner) 447-448
        *Cases Antitrust Law 895-900
        *Cases Trade 788-794

*Competition 138-142
Dissent 481-483
Hugo Black (Strickland) 209-210
PERIODICALS:
"High court tightens the antitrust reins." Bus Wk p. 40-41 June
18 '66.

2693.   United States v. Grinnell Corporation   June 13, 1966 384 U.S. 563
Grinnell Corporation v. United States
American District Telegraph v. United
States
Holmes Electric Protective Co. v.
United States
Automatic Fire Alarm Co. v. United
States
*Cases Antitrust Law 216-231
*Cases Trade 676-687
*Courts Judges 177-179
*Modern Business 965-967
*Selected Antitrust Cases 54-62
*Text Antitrust 40-45

2694.   Katzenbach v. Morgan   June 13, 1966 384 U.S. 641
New York City Board of Elections
v. Morgan
*Affair 273-278
Am Consttn (Kelly) 899
*Am Consttn (Lockhart) 1201-1206
*Am Consttnl Law (Saye) 161-163
*Cases Consttnl Law (Gunther) 1078-1000
*Cases Consttnl Rights 1190-1195
*Cases Individual 605-614
*Civil Liberties (Sweet) 319-320
*Civil Rights (Abernathy) 1980 602-610
*Consttnl Law (Barrett) 1106-1112
*Consttnl Law (Barron) 1085-1091
*Consttnl Law (Freund) 902-906
*Consttnl Law (Kauper) 840-847
*Consttnl Law (Lockhart) 1596-1601
Consttnlity 9-12
*Contemporary Law 946-954
*Discrimination 140-145
Dissent 434-438
*Evolution 260-264
*Justices (Friedman) v. 4, 2882-2889
*Political Rights v. 2, 1208-1213
Private Pressure 140-142
*Processes 1047-1056
*Sup Ct and Am Govt 56-67
Sup Ct and Electoral Process 128-130
Sup Ct Review 1966 95-101
Sup Ct Review 1969 82-84, 97, 101-106, 127-134
Warren (Cox) 57-60, 127-130

2695.   Cardona v. Power   June 13, 1966 384 U.S. 672
*Contemporary Law 955-956
*Discrimination 145-150
*Political Rights v. 2, 1214-1219
Sup Ct and Electoral Process 128

2696. Gojack v. United States   June 13, 1966 384 U.S. 702
       Criminal Law Revolution 75-76
       *Legislative (Hetzel) 665-669

2697. Johnson v. New Jersey   June 20, 1966 384 U.S. 719
       Consttnl Counterrevolution 220-222
       *Consttnl Law (Freund) 1032-1034
       Criminal Law Revolution 63
       Self Inflicted Wound 191
       Sup Ct and Confessions 146-147
       *Sup Ct and Rights 112-116
       Sup Ct Review 1977 116

2698. Davis v. North Carolina   June 20, 1966 384 U.S. 737
       Sup Ct and Confessions 147-148

2699. Schmerber v. California   June 20, 1966 384 U.S. 757
       *Affair 176-179, 208-212
       *Bill (Cohen) 559-562
       *Cases Criml Justice 47-54
       Consttnl Counterrevolution 188-191
       *Consttnl Criml (Scarboro) 614-624
       *Consttnl Law (Felkenes) 278-281
       *Consttnl Law (Klein) 309-315
       Criminal Evidence 334-335, 524-525
       Criminal Law (Felkenes) 239-241
       *Criminal Law (Kadish) 1016-1020
       Criminal Law Revolution 65-66
       *Criminal Procedure (Lewis) 195-197, 391-394
       *Due Process 69-70, 71
       Freedom and the Court 126-128
       *Judicial Crises 31-36
       Law of Arrest (Creamer) 283-286
       *Leading Consttnl Cases 558-566
       *Police 84-86
       *Principles Arrest 173-179
       *Principles Proof 750-754
       *Right to Privacy 118-122
       Self Inflicted Wound 233-234
       *Social Forces 57-62
       *Sup Ct and Criml Process 264-266, 487-490
       *Sup Ct and Rights 187-192
       *Teaching Materials 519-525
       PERIODICALS:
       "Sample of blood is not self-incriminating testimony." Time 88:
       65-66 July 1 '66.

2700. Georgia v. Rachel   June 20, 1966 384 U.S. 780
       Criminal Law Revolution 72
       Desegregation (Wasby) 361-364
       *Federal Courts 1218-1225
       *Political Rights v. 2, 1441-1452

2701. City of Greenwood v. Peacock   June 20, 1966 384 U.S. 808
       *Courts, Judges 118-121
       Criminal Law Revolution 72-73
       Desegregation (Wasby) 361-362, 364-366, 369-372
       *Federal System 312-314
       *Political Rights v. 2, 1452-1465

PERIODICALS:
"No easy transfers to federal courts." Time 88: 66, 68 July 1 '66.

2702. Dennis v. United States   June 20, 1966 384 U.S. 855
Criminal Law Revolution 78-79
PERIODICALS:
"Significant decisions in labor cases." Monthly Labor R 89: 892-893 Aug '66.

2703. Switzerland Cheese Association v.   Nov 7, 1966 385 U.S. 23
E. Horne's Market, Inc.
*Civil Procedure (Carrington) 570-571
*Injunctions 196

2704. Pittsburgh Towing Co. v. Mississippi Nov 7, 1966 385 U.S. 32
Valley Barge Line
*Elements Civil 1187-1189

2705. Adderley v. Florida   Nov 14, 1966 385 U.S. 39
*Am Consttn (Lockhart) 829-832
*Am Consttnl Law (Shapiro) 392-396
Am Politics 82
*Bill (Cohen) 250-254
*Bill (Konvitz) 300-305
CQ Guide 415-416
*Cases Civil Liberties 227-233
*Cases Consttnl Law (Cushman) 457-463
*Cases Consttnl Law (Gunther) 1281-1284
*Cases Consttnl Rights 710-713
*Cases Individual 810-814
*Civil Liberties (Barker) 116-121
*Civil Rights (Abernathy) 1977 433-435
Communication (Hemmer) v. 1, 96-97
*Consttnl Law (Barrett) 1266-1268
*Consttnl Law (Barron) 808-813
*Consttnl Law (Felkenes) 145-147
*Consttnl Law (Freund) 1199-1203
*Consttnl Law (Kauper) 1169-1171
*Consttnl Law (Lockhart) 1083-1086
Decade 218-219
Desegregation (Wasby) 351-353
Free Speech (Kurland) 356-358
*Free Speech (Summers) 116-122
*Freedom of Speech (Haiman) 75-76
Handbook 97-99
Hugo Black (Strickland) 93-95
*Justices (Friedman) v. 4, 2472-2478
*Modern Consttnl Law 246-253
Politics 122-125
*Principles Freedom 227-237
*Protest 216-225
Sup Ct Review 1974 247-249
System 302-303
Warren (Cox) 110
PERIODICALS:
"Delicate balance." Newsweek 68: 29-30 Nov 28 '66.
"Speech without assembly? the court and the demonstrators,"
Thomas I. Emerson. Nation 203: 704-708 Dec 26 '66.

"Supreme Court temporizes." Christian Century 83: 1463-1464
   Nov 30 '66.
"Test that wasn't a test." Time 88: 55 Nov 25 '66.

2706. Bond v. Floyd   Dec 5, 1966   385 U.S. 116
       Cases Consttnl Law (Gunther) 1183-1184
       Communication (Hemmer) v. 1, 28-30
       *Conscience 300-312
       *Law Sup Ct 41-47
       *Legislative (Hetzel) 498-502
       *Protest 94-103
       Sup Ct and Poltcl questions 116-117
       System 68-69
       PERIODICALS:
       "Bond's word." Newsweek 68: 27 Dec 19 '66.
       "High court's ruling against a state legislature." US News 61:
          8 Dec 19 '66.
       "Right to speak." Time 88: 31 Dec 16 '66.
       "Supreme Court rules on Julian Bond." Christian Century 83:
          1560-1561 Dec 21 '66.

2707. United States v. Demko   Dec 5, 1966   385 U.S. 149
       *US Prison Law v. 2, 371-374

2708. Transportation-Communication Em- Dec 5, 1966   385 U.S. 157
       ployees Union v. Union Pacific
       Railroad
       *Labor Law (Meltzer) 877-881
       PERIODICALS:
       "Significant decisions in labor cases." Monthly Labor R 90: 59-
          60 Feb '67.

2709. Walker v. Southern Railway Co.   Dec 5, 1966   385 U.S. 196
       PERIODICALS:
       "Significant decisions in labor cases." Monthly Labor R 90: 60
          Feb '67.

2710. Lewis v. United States   Dec 12, 1966 385 U.S. 206
       *Consttnl Criml (Scarboro) 740-742
       Criminal Evidence 367-368
       Criminal Law (Felkenes) 165-166
       Criminal Law Revolution 90-91
       Law of Arrest (Markle) 148-149
       *Leading Consttnl Cases 339-341
       *Principles Arrest 469-471
       Sup Ct Review 1968 143-145
       PERIODICALS:
       "Case notes." J Criml Law, Crimlgy and Police Sci 58: 558
          Dec '67.

2711. Fortson v. Morris   Dec 12, 1966 385 U.S. 231
       *Douglas 94-98
       *Justices (Friedman) v. 4, 3028-3032
       Sup Ct and Electoral Process 188-189
       Warren (Cox) 130-133

2712. United States v. Fabrizio   Dec 12, 1966 385 U.S. 263
       Criminal Law Revolution 114-115

2713. Hoffa v. United States   Dec 12, 1966   385 U.S. 293
       Parks v. United States
       Campbell v. United States
       King v. United States
         *Am Consttnl Law (Shapiro) 672-674
         *Cases Criml Justice 489-497
         *Consttnl Criml (Scarboro) 747-755
          Criminal Law (Felkenes) 161-164
         *Criminal Law (Kadish) 1048-1053
          Criminal Law Revolution 87-90
          Dissent 319-320
          Law of Arrest (Creamer) 150-156
          Law of Arrest (Markle) 149-150
         *Leading Consttnl Cases 342-351
         *Principles Arrest 466-469
          Private Pressure 145-149
         *Sup Ct and Rights 265-271
          Sup Ct Review 1968 148-151
       PERIODICALS:
          "Case notes." J Criml Law, Crimlgy and Police Sci 58: 555
          Dec '67.
          "Hoffa decision." Nation 204: 5-6 Jan 2 '67.
          "Pragmatic view of privacy." Time 88: 36, 38 Dec 23 '66.

2714. Osborn v. United States   Dec 12, 1966   385 U.S. 323
         *Criminal Law (Kadish) 1053-1054
          Criminal Law Revolution 86-87
          Law of Arrest (Creamer) 491-497
         *Principles Arrest 463-466
          Self Inflicted Wound 263-265
          Sup Ct Review 1968 145-148
       PERIODICALS:
          "Case notes." J Criml Law, Crimlgy and Police Sci 58: 554
          Dec '67.

2715. Parker v. Gladden   Dec 12, 1966   385 U.S. 363
          Defendants 97
       PERIODICALS:
          "Harassment for juries." Time 88: 38 Dec 23 '66.

2716. Time, Inc. v. Hill   Jan 9, 1967   385 U.S. 374
          Am Consttn (Kelly) 964-966
         *Bill (Konvitz) 488-497
          CQ Guide 437
          Cases Consttnl Law (Gunther) 1341-1342
         *Cases Copyright (Nimmer) 821-836
          Communication (Hemmer) v. 2, 100-102
          Crisis 218-219
          Earl Warren 266
         *Evolution 124-129
          Free Speech (Kurland) 210-249
          Handbook 376-384
          Individual 57-65, 106-107
          Justice Hugo Black 87-88
          Law of Mass 105, 201-208
         *Mass Communications 317-320
          Mass Media (Clark) 215-216, 219-223
         *Mass Media (Devol) 251-256
          Mass Media (Francois) 171-172

Politics 137
Privacy (Pember) 210-218
*Right to Privacy 212-221
*Sup Ct on Freedom 169-179
Sup Ct Review 1967 267-309
Sup Ct Review 1979 206-207
System 551-556
Warren (Cox) 97-102
PERIODICALS:
"Supreme Court extends press freedoms in overruling 'Desperate
hours' verdict." Pub Weekly 191: 221 Jan 23 '67.
"Top court broadens defense for libel," Luther A. Huston. Edi-
tor and Pub 100: 11 Jan 14 '67.
"Vote for the press over privacy." Time 89: 56 Jan 20 '67.

2717. National Labor Relations Board v.   Jan 9, 1967   385 U.S. 421
       C & C Plywood Corporation
       Basic Text 732-733
       *Cases Labor (Cox) 662-666
       *Cases Labor (Leslie) 410-413
       *Cases Labor (Oberer) 752-756
       *Collective Bargaining 441-445
       *Labor Law (Herman) 279-283
       *Labor Law (Meltzer) 868-871
       PERIODICALS:
       "Significant decisions in labor cases." Monthly Labor R 90: 53
       Mar '67.

2718. National Labor Relations Board v.   Jan 9, 1967   385 U.S. 432
       Acme Industrial Co.
       *Cases Labor (Oberer) 756-759
       PERIODICALS:
       "Significant decisions in labor cases." Monthly Labor R 90: 53-
       54 Mar '67.

2719. Swann v. Adams   Jan 9, 1967   385 U.S. 440
       CQ Guide 495
       Democratic 444-446
       Sup Ct and Electoral Process 182-183
       Sup Ct Review 1973 13
       Warren (Ball) 211

2720. Lassen v. Arizona ex rel. Arizona   Jan 10, 1967   385 U.S. 458
       Highway Department
       PERIODICALS:
       "Public land not free for roads." Eng News 178: 51 Feb 2 '67.

2721. Garrity v. New Jersey   Jan 16, 1967   385 U.S. 493
       *Consttnl Law (Felkenes) 281-283
       Criminal Evidence 425-426
       Criminal Law (Felkenes) 241-242
       *Criminal Law (Kadish) 987-989
       Criminal Law Revolution 106-107
       *Labor Relations (Edwards) 752-754
       Law of Arrest (Creamer) 441-442
       *Leading Consttnl Cases 577-582
       *Sup Ct and Criml Process 835-837
       Sup Ct Review 1967 200-204

PERIODICALS:
"Case notes. " J Criml Law, Crimlgy and Police Sci 58: 550-551
   Dec '67.

2722. Spevack v. Klein   Jan 16, 1967   385 U.S. 511
       *Cases Professional 43-48
       *Consttnl Criml (Scarboro) 598-605
       *Consttnl Law (Felkenes) 283-285
       Criminal Law (Felkenes) 246-248
       Criminal Law Revolution 107-108
       Sup Ct Review 1967 200-204
       PERIODICALS:
       "Case notes. " J Criml Law, Crimlgy and Police Sci 58: 555-
       556 Dec '67.

2723. Sims v. Georgia   Jan 23, 1967   385 U.S. 538
       Equality (Berger) 109

2724. Whitus v. Georgia   Jan 23, 1967   385 U.S. 545
       Criminal Law Revolution 114

2725. Spencer v. Texas   Jan 23, 1967   385 U.S. 554
       Bell v. Texas
       Reed v. Beto
       Defendants 93
       *Due Process 160
       PERIODICALS:
       "Case notes. " J Criml Law, Crimlgy and Police Sci 58: 560-
       561 Dec '67.

2726. Keyishian v. Board of Regents of   Jan 23, 1967   385 U.S. 589
       tho University of the State of
       New York
       Am Consttn (Kelly) 927-928
       *Am Consttn (Lockhart) 599-602
       *Am Consttnl Law (Bartholomew) v. 2, 77-79
       *Am Consttnl Law (Shapiro) 385-392
       CQ Guide 516
       *Cases Consttnl Law (Gunther) 1466-1469
       *Cases Consttnl Rights 407-410
       *Cases Individual 1002-1005
       Communication (Hemmer) v. 1, 121-122
       *Consttn (Morris) 176-184
       Consttnl Law (Barrett) 1197
       *Consttnl Law (Freund) 1339-1343
       *Consttnl Law (Lockhart) 742-746
       Digest 58-59
       Education (Lapati) 240-242
       *Freedom of Speech (Haiman) 36-37
       *Judicial Excerpts 171-174
       Landmark Decisions 137-143
       *Law of Public Education 449-455
       Rights of the People 127-129
       School in the Legal Structure 72-73
       *School Law (Alexander) 549-556
       *Sup Ct and Education 199-209
       System 237-239, 604
       *Teacher 170-172

*These Liberties 175-181
Warren (Hudgins) 145-148
PERIODICALS:
"Angelic vision of the Warren Court." Natl R 19: 122 Feb 7
'67.
"Feinberg law." America 116: 200-201 Feb 11 '67.
"Loyalty laws: Supreme Court upholds academic freedom,"
Luther J. Carter. Science 155: 987 Feb 24 '67.
"On the cutting edge of the law: the expansion of teacher's rights,"
David Schimmel and Louis Fischer. Sch R 82: 261-279 Feb
'74 (2).
"Self-reversal." Time 89: 47 Feb 3 '67.

2727. Miller v. Pate   Feb 13, 1967   386 U. S. 1
        *Cases Evidence 108-111
        Criminal Evidence 42
        Criminal Law Revolution 108-109

2728. Chapman v. California   Feb 20, 1967   386 U. S. 18
        *Basic Criminal 687-692
        Criminal Law Revolution 104-105
        *Criminal Procedure (Lewis) 674-677
        Criminal Procedure (Wells) 207-208
        PERIODICALS:
        "Case notes." J Criml Law, Crimlgy and Police Sci 58: 561
        Dec '67.

2729. Cooper v. California   Feb 20, 1967   386 U. S. 58
        Arrest (Berry) 129-131
        Criminal Evidence 287-288
        Criminal Law (Felkenes) 67-69
        Criminal Law Revolution 95-96
        PERIODICALS:
        "Case notes." J Criml Law, Crimlgy and Police Sci 58: 559-
        560 Dec '67.

2730. Giles v. Maryland   Feb 20, 1967   386 U. S. 66
        Criminal Evidence 41
        Criminal Law Revolution 109-110
        *Due Process 137-138
        *Justices (Friedman) v. 4, 3032-3034
        PERIODICALS:
        "Case notes." J Criml Law, Crimlgy and Police Sci 58: 556-558
        Dec '67.

2731. Kilgarlin v. Hill, Secretary of   Feb 20, 1967   386 U. S. 120
        State of Texas
        Democratic 447-448

2732. Cascade National Gas Corporation Feb 27, 1967   386 U. S. 129
        v. El Paso National Gas Co.
        California v. El Paso Natural Gas Co.
        Southern California Edison Co. v.
        El Paso Natural Gas Co.
        Antitrust (Posner) 460-469

2733. Vaca v. Sipes   Feb 27, 1967   386 U. S. 171
        Basic Text 392-393
        *Cases Labor (Cox) 1004-1024

*Cases Labor (Leslie) 583-588
*Cases Labor (Oberer) 789-799
*Collective Bargaining 393-404
*Labor Law (Meltzer) 938-952
Sup Ct Review 1967 81-126
PERIODICALS:
"Significant decisions in labor cases."   Monthly Labor R   90:   54
May '67.

2734.   Klopfer v. North Carolina   Mar 13, 1967   386 U.S.   213
*Consttnl Law (Felkenes) 321-323
Criminal Law (Felkenes) 255-257
*Criminal Law (Kadish) 1195-1197
Criminal Law Revolution 101
Criminal Procedure (Wells) 105-106
Defendants 114
*Due Process 105
Freedom and the Court 89-90
PERIODICALS:
"Case notes."   J Criml Law, Crimlgy and Police Sci   58:   561
Dec '67.

2735.   Federal Trade Commission v. Jantzen,   Mar 13, 1967   386 U.S.   228
Inc.
PERIODICALS:
"High court rules Jantzen can't evade FTC price complaint."   Adv
Age 38: 102   Mar 27 '67.

2736.   McCray v. Illinois   Mar 20, 1967   386 U.S.   300
*Arrest (Waddington) 93-94
*Cases Criml Justice 106-111
*Cases Drug 329-336
*Cases Evidence 1254-1260
Criminal Evidence 235
Criminal Law (Felkenes) 170-172
*Criminal Law (Kadish) 857-859
Criminal Law Revolution 91-93
*Douglas 325-328
Law of Arrest (Creamer) 156-161
Law of Arrest (Markle) 19-21
*Principles Arrest 474-479
*Principles Proof 789-795
Self Inflicted Wound 211-212
PERIODICALS:
"Vital informers."   Time   83:   73   Mar 31 '67.

2738.   Neely v. Martin K. Eby Construction   Mar 20, 1967   386 U.S.   317
Co., Inc.
*Civil Procedure (Carrington) 348-352
*Civil Procedure (Cound) 931-935
*Elements Civil 1046-1051

2738.   Railway Transfer Service Co. v.   Mar 27, 1967   386 U.S.   351
Chicago
Sup Ct and Commerce 289-290

2739.   United States v. First National   Mar 27, 1967   386 U.S.   361
City Bank of Houston

United States v. Provident National
   Bank
PERIODICALS:
"Blow to bank mergers." Bus Wk p. 23 Apr 1 '67.
"Congressional comments on the merger decision." Banking 59:
   40-42, 128 May '67.
"Supreme Court and the Bank merger act of 1966," William T.
   Lifland. Bankers Mag 150: 20-25 Autumn '67.
"Supreme Court, Congress, and bank mergers," William T. Lifland.
   Law & Contemporary Problems 32: 15-39 Winter '67 (3).
*"Supreme Court's latest bank merger decision." Banking 59: 38-
   39 May '67.
"What they thought they were doing." Banking 59: 39, 133 May
   '67.

2740. State Farm Fire and Casualty Co.   Apr 10, 1967   386 U. S. 523
          v. Tashire
       *Cases Federal Courts 680-686
       *Cases Pleading 604-612
       *Civil Procedure (Carrington) 1150-1155
       *Civil Procedure (Cound) 618-622
       *Elements Civil 213-215, 494-498
       *Materials Consttnl Law 238-242

2741. Pierson v. Ray   Apr 11, 1967   386 U. S. 547
       *Cases Criml Justice 747-752
       *Civil Rights (Abernathy) 1980 46-50
       Criminal Law Revolution 115-116
       *Douglas 64-71
       *Introduction (Mashaw) 738-745
       *Law Sup Ct 523-528

2742. Federal Trade Commission v.   Apr 10, 1967   386 U. S. 568
          Procter and Gamble Co.
       *Antitrust (Posner) 488-496
       *Competition 178-182
       *Free Enterprise 192-213
       *Legal Environment 331-334
       *Modern Business 990-992
       *Selected Antitrust Cases 180-192
       *Text Antitrust 189-195
       PERIODICALS:
       "Clorox case; a washday miracle." Consumer Rep 32: 360-363
          July '67.
       "High court backs FTC; orders Procter and Gamble to drop Clorox."
          Adv Age 38: 1, 73 Apr 17 '67.
       *(Decision text:) Adv Age 38: 3, 165-168, 170 Apr 17 '67.
       "High court dissolves a sudsy conglomerate." Bus Wk p. 40-41
          Apr 15 '67.
       "Mergers make FTC feathers fly." Bus Wk p. 124, 126 May 6
          '67.
       "New court ruling may open attack on conglomerates." Iron Age
          199: 19 Apr 20 '67.
       "Supreme Court versus corporate efficiency," Robert H. Bork.
          Fortune 76: 92-93, 155-156, 158 Aug '67.

2743. Specht v. Patterson   Apr 11, 1967   386 U. S. 605
       Criminal Law Revolution 112-113
       *Reading Law 770-772

PERIODICALS:
"Case notes. " J Criml Law, Crimlgy and Police Sci 58: 561-
562 Dec '67.

2744. National Woodwork Manufacturers   Apr 17, 1967 386 U.S. 612
Association v. National Labor
Relations Board
*Cases Labor (Cox) 790-806
*Cases Labor (Leslie) 342-349
*Cases Labor (Oberer) 462-471
*Labor Law (Meltzer) 472-486
*Labor Law (Twomey) 290-293
PERIODICALS:
"Significant decisions in labor cases. " Monthly Labor R 90: 65-
66 June '67.
"Will boycott rule put brake on technology?" Bus Wk p. 104,
108 Apr 29 '67.

2745. Utah Pie Co. v. Continental Baking   Apr 24, 1967 386 U.S. 685
Co.
*Antitrust (Posner) 738-746
*Antitrust Analysis 856-860
*Cases Antitrust Law 1061-1071
*Competition 269-275
*Free Enterprise 851-860
*Modern Business 1030-1033
*Selected Antitrust Cases 277-285
*Text Antitrust 219-228
PERIODICALS:
"Court raps price cuts. " Bus Wk p. 50 Apr 29 '67.
"Utah pie case may bring shifts in thinking on ads, trust regula-
tion, " Stanley E. Cohen. Adv Age 38: 4, 26 May 22 '67.

2746. Clevis v. Texas   Apr 24, 1967 386 U.S. 707
Criminal Law Revolution 105-106

2747. Fleischmann Distilling Corporation   May 8, 1967 386 U.S. 714
v. Maier Brewing Co.
*Copyright 372-375

2748. Anders v. California   May 8, 1967 386 U.S. 738
*Basic Criminal 80-82
*Cases Professional 442-444
Criminal Law Revolution 102-103
*Elements Criminal 87-89
*Poverty 172-175
PERIODICALS:
"Case notes. " J Criml Law, Crimlgy and Police Sci 58: 551
Dec '67.

2749. National Bellas Hess, Inc. v.   May 8, 1967 386 U.S. 753
Department of Revenue of Illionis
*Consttnl Law (Barrett) 427-430
*Legal Environment 241-243
Sup Ct and Commerce 335-337
PERIODICALS:
"High court hits Illinois tax law in Bellas Hess case." Adv Age
38: 43 May 22 '67.

2750. Redrup v. New York   May 8, 1967   386 U.S. 767
       Austin v. Kentucky
       Gent v. Arkansas
         Cases Environmental Law (Gray) 192-193
         *Censorship Landmarks 596-598
         Communication (Hemmer) v. 1, 169-170
         Criminal Law Revolution 113-114
         *Federal Courts 1597-1599
         Law of Mass 369-370
         Law of Obscenity 44
         Literature 196-197
         *Obscenity (Bosmajian) 119-120
         Obscenity (Clor) 83
       PERIODICALS:
         "Case notes." J Criml Law, Crimlgy and Police Sci 58: 551-552
           Dec '67.
         "High court reverses 3 obscenity convictions." Pub Weekly 191:
           41-42   May 22 '67.
         "Re obscenity and the Supreme Court." Wilson Library Bul 41:
           997 June '67.

2751. In re Gault   May 15, 1967   387 U.S. 1
         Against 299-300
         *Bill (Konvitz) 723-743
         *Cases Criml Law (Hall) 1217-1225
         *Cases Criml Law (Perkins) 516-522
         *Cases Modern 13-14, 62-91, 417-427, 607-609, 660-665
         *Civil Rights (Abernathy) 1977 207-209
         Consttnl Law (Cortner) 57-78, 103-104
         *Consttnl Law (Cortner) 78-103
         *Consttnl Law (Felkenes) 360-365
         *Consttnl Law (Grossman) 925-930
         *Consttnl Law (Kauper) 1214-1216
         *Consttnl Rights (Kemerer) 324-329
         Criminal Law (Felkenes) 391-393
         *Criminal Law (Kadish) 1427-1438
         Criminal Law Revolution 111-112
         Criminal Procedure (Wells) 212-214
         Defendants 89-90
         Digest 37-38
         Dissent 377
         *Due Process 41, 103
         *Education (Hazard) 231-239
         *Evolution 18-26
         Frontiers 213-230
         Impact (Wasby) 152-153
         *Judicial Excerpts 121-123, 125-126
         *Justices (Friedman) v. 4, 3035-3059
         Juvenile Offender.
         *Juvenile Offender 157-237
         Law and Education 236-237
         Law Enforcement 93-96
         Law of Arrest (Creamer) 479-486
         *Law Sup Ct 360-368
         Milestones 345-353
         Rights of the People 85-90
         Spirit 121-122
         *Sup Ct and Criml Process 704-710
         *Sup Ct and Rights 408-421

Sup Ct Review 1966 184-189
Sup Ct Review 1967 233-266
Sup Ct Review 1979 305-307, 345-349
*These Liberties 87-99
PERIODICALS:
"Children under the law," Hillary Rodham. Harvard Eductnl R
    43: 487-514 Nov '73 (5).
"Children's hour in the Supreme Court. " Socl Service R 41:
    304-306 Sept '67.
"Court intervention in pupil discipline; implications and comment, "
    William R. Hazard. Am Behavioral Scientist 23: 169-205
    Nov '79 (4).
"Due process and the juvenile court; the Gault case, " William F.
    Eagan and Michael P. Litka. Socl Eductn 32: 469-480 May
    '68.
*"In the matter of Gault. " Current History 53: 112-113, 117
    Aug '67.
"Juvenile courts and the Gault decision, " Howard G. Brown and
    William T. Downs. Children 15: 86-96 May '68. Reaction:
    M. K. Rosenheim. Children 15: 168 July '68.
"Juvenile courts; the legacy of Gault, " Monrad G. Paulsen. PTA
    Mag 62: 6-8 Feb '68; 62: 12-14 Mar '68.
"Juveniles and the right to trial by jury, " Keith Beavan. Times
    Eductnl Supp 2928: 15 July 2 '71.
"Student and juvenile rights and responsibilities. " Senior Scholas-
    tic 106: 8-10, 18 May 8 '75 (3).
"Supreme Court rules; treat juvenile offenders like adults. " US
    News 62: 12 May 29 '67.

2752. Dombrowski v. Eastland   May 15, 1967 387 U.S. 82
        CQ Guide 168
        *Legislative (Hetzel) 523-525

2753. Sailors v. Board of Education of   May 22, 1967 387 U.S. 105
        County of Kent
        Consttnl Counterrevolution 121-122
        Democratic 547-548
        Digest 8
        *Law of Public Education 718-720
        *School Law (Alexander) 141-143
        Warren (Ball) 204-205

2754. Dusch v. Davis   May 22, 1967 387 U.S. 112
        Democratic 548-551
        Warren (Ball) 205-206
        PERIODICALS:
        "One man, one vote: it means school boards too; Hadley decision, "
        August W. Steinhilber and Russel A. Burnham. Am Sch Bd J
        157: 36-37 June '70 (2).

2755. Boutclier v. Immigration and   May 22, 1967 387 U.S. 118
        Naturalization Service
        *Douglas 308-311

2756. Abbott Laboratories v. Gardner,   May 22, 1967 387 U.S. 136
        Secretary of Health, Education
        and Welfare
        *Admin Law (Gellhorn) 1010-1021
        *Admin Law (Schwartz) 619-623

*Cases Food 232-237
*Contemporary Law 41-45
*Introduction (Mashaw) 910-917
*Materials Consttnl Law 167-172

2757. Toilet Goods Association v. Gardner,   May 22, 1967 387 U. S. 158
       Secretary of Health, Education and
       Welfare
       *Cases Food 237-239
       *Contemporary Law 45-47
       *Introduction 917-923
       *Materials Consttnl Law 172-174
       PERIODICALS:
       "Drug men may get pre-enforcement review of FDA rules: High
          Court. " Adv Age 38: 1, 96 May 29 '67.
       "Supreme Court drug ruling is seen as civil rights move for
          business, " Stanley E. Cohen. Adv Age 38: 4, 95 May 29
          '67.

2758. Gardner v. Toilet Goods Association   May 22, 1967 387 U. S. 167
       *Cases Food 239-245
       *Contemporary Law 47-53
       *Materials Consttnl Law 174-185

2759. Federal Trade Commission v. Uni-   May 29, 1967 387 U. S. 244
       versal-Rundle Corporation
       *Admin Law (Gellhorn) 388-391

2760. Afroyim v. Rusk   May 29, 1967 387 U. S. 253
       *Am Consttnl Law (Saye) 553-554
       *Am Consttnl Law (Shapiro) 200-205
       CQ Guide 146
       *Consttnl Law (Barrett) 612-615
       *Consttnl Law (Freund) 741-742
       *Consttnl Law (Kauper) 548-555
       *Documents History v. 2, 719-720
       *Sup Ct and Public Policy 145-157
       PERIODICALS:
       "Approving dual citizenship. " Time 89: 76 June 9 '67.

2761. Warden, Maryland Penitentiary v.   May 29, 1967 387 U. S. 294
       Hayden
       *Basic Criminal 218-221
       CQ Guide 542-543
       *Cases Criml Justice 396-397
       *Civil Rights (Abernathy) 1977 109-110
       *Consttnl Criml (Scarboro) 633-641
       *Consttnl Law (Maddex) 183-186
       Criminal Evidence 332-333
       Criminal Law (Felkenes) 36-38
       *Criminal Law (Kadish) 879-882
       Criminal Law Revolution 93-95
       *Criminal Procedure (Lewis) 198-201
       Defendants 264-265
       Law of Arrest (Creamer) 221-225
       Law of Arrest (Markle) 55-58
       *Leading Consttnl Cases 169-181
       *Principles Arrest 187-197
       Self Inflicted Wound 215

*Sup Ct and Criml Process 262-264
*Sup Ct and Rights 194-197
PERIODICALS:
"Helping prosecutors." Time 89: 75-76 June 9 '67.

2762. Reitman v. Mulkey   May 29, 1967 387 U.S. 369
Am Consttn (Kelly) 901
*Am Consttn (Lockhart) 1043-1048
By What Right 229-230
CQ Guide 614-615
*Cases Consttnl Law (Gunther) 1015-1020
*Cases Consttnl Law (Rosenblum) 96-101
*Cases Consttnl Rights 1001-1006
*Cases Individual 545-551
*Civil Rights (Abernathy) 1977 538-540
*Civil Rights (Abernathy) 1980 87-92
*Consttnl Law (Barrett) 1061-1065
*Consttnl Law (Barron) 1015-1022
*Consttnl Law (Freund) 837-840
*Consttnl Law (Kauper) 819-825
*Consttnl Law (Lockhart) 1543-1548
Desegregation (Wasby) 235-243
*Discrimination 373-382
First Amendment (Franklin) 167-168
*Justices (Friedman) v. 4, 2969-2974
*Law Sup Ct 547-554
*Legal Foundations 286-288
Private Pressure 137-138
*Processes 642-650
*Race 618-623
*Racial Equality 114-115
*Sup Ct and Public Policy 157-166
Sup Ct Review 1967 39-80
*These Liberties 133-141
Warren (Cox) 43-50
PERIODICALS:
"Mr. Jones goes to Washington," John Galloway. Commonweal.
   87: 374-375 Dec 22 '67.
"Open issue." Newsweek 69: 30, 33 June 12 '67.
"Say no to Proposition 14." Time 89: 75 June 9 '67.

2763. American Trucking Association v.   May 29, 1967 387 U.S. 397
Atchison, Topeka and Sante Fe
Railway Co.
*Cases Regulated 627-639

2764. Commissioner of Internal Revenue   June 5, 1967 387 U.S. 456
v. Estate of Bosch
Second National Bank of New Haven
v. United States
*Cases Federal Courts 629-633
PERIODICALS:
"Supreme Court rules on when state court decisions will bind fed-
   eral courts," John A. Clark. J Taxation 27: 82-85 Aug '67.

2765. Camara v. Municipal Court of San   June 5, 1967 387 U.S. 523
Francisco
*Admin Law (Schwartz) 168-174
Arrest (Waddington) 166

*Cases Criml Justice 306-309
*Cases Food 720-721
*Civil Rights (Abernathy) 1977 128-131
*Consttnl Criml (Scarboro) 245-253
*Consttnl Law (Felkenes) 236-237
Criminal Law (Felkenes) 82-84
Defendants 273-274
*In His Own Image 360-363
*Introduction (Mashaw) 565-571
*Justices (Friedman) v. 4, 2962-2969
Law of Arrest (Creamer) 191-196
Legal Foundations 31-32
*Legislation (Linde) 787-790
*Public Planning 628-633
*Rights (Shattuck) 31-32
Sup Ct Review 1967 9-38
PERIODICALS:
    "Case notes." J Criml Law, Crimlgy and Police Sci   58:   558-
    559 Dec '67.
    "Get a warrant." Time   89:   48   June 16 '67.
    "The right to privacy." Socl Eductn   31:   497-508   Oct '67.

2766.   See v. City of Seattle   June 5, 1967   387 U. S.   541
        *Cases Criml Justice 309-314
        *Cases Food 721
        Frontiers 258-267
        *Introduction (Mashaw) 571-576
        *Sup Ct and Am Capitalism 790-797
        Sup Ct Review 1967 9-38
        *Text Legal Regulation 32-33

2767.   Denver and Rio Grande Western   June 5, 1967   387 U. S.   556
        Railroad Co. v. Brotherhood
        of Railroad Trainmen
        *Cases Federal Courts 336-340

2768.   Loving v. Virginia   June 12, 1967   388 U. S.   1
        *Am Consttnl Law (Saye) 461-462
        *Bill (Cohen) 649-651
        *Bill (Konvitz) 538-543
        *Cases Consttnl Law (Gunther) 748-751
        *Cases Consttnl Rights 920-921
        *Cases Domestic 20-24
        *Cases Individual 300-303
        *Civil Rights (Abernathy) 1977 557-559
        Civil Rights (Bardolph) 518-519
        Consttnl Law (Barrett) 705
        *Consttnl Law (Barrett) 778-782
        *Consttnl Law (Barron) 575-578
        *Consttnl Law (Felkenes) 179-180
        *Consttnl Law (Lockhart) 1276-1278
        Criminal Law Revolution 116
        *Criminal Procedure (Lewis) 81-83
        Desegregation (Wasby) 144-149
        *Discrimination 475-477
        *Judicial Crises 101-103
        *Law Sup Ct 568-573
        *Race 278-283
        *Rights (Shattuck) 112-113

*These Liberties 142-147
PERIODICALS:
"Anti-miscegenation statutes: repugnant indeed." Time 89: 45-46 June 23 '67.
"Good court gets better." Christian Century 84: 827-828 June 28 '67 (2).

2769. Washington v. Texas   June 12, 1967 388 U.S. 14
*Cases Criml Justice 1284-1289
*Cases Criml Law (Hall) 1094-1095
*Cases Evidence 230-235
*Consttnl Law (Maddex) 341-343
*Criminal Justice (Way) 441-444
Criminal Law (Felkenes) 330-332
*Criminal Procedure (Lewis) 518-520
Defendants 98
*Due Process 131
*Sup Ct and Criml Process 687-688
*Sup Ct and Rights 34-38

2770. National Labor Relations Board v.   June 12, 1967 388 U.S. 26
Great Dane Trailers, Inc.
Basic Text 335-336, 362-363
*Cases Labor (Cox) 875-880
*Cases Labor (Oberer) 556-561
*Labor Law (Meltzer) 257-261
*Labor Law (Twomey) 205-209
Sup Ct and Labor 94-96
PERIODICALS:
"Significant decisions in labor cases." Monthly Labor R 90: 59-60 Aug '67.

2771. Berger v. New York   June 12, 1967 388 U.S. 41
*Basic Criminal 432-440
*Cases Criml Justice 406-416
*Civil Rights (Abernathy) 1977 145-148
Communication (Hemmer) v. 1, 241-242
*Consttnl Aspects v. 4, 385-416
Consttnl Counterrevolution 195-196
*Consttnl Law (Maddex) 198-200
Criminal Law (Felkenes) 140-144
*Criminal Law (Kadish) 1056-1063
Criminal Law Revolution 83-86
*Criminal Procedure (Lewis) 331-335
Dissent 163-165
Great Reversals 183
Hugo Black (Dunne) 424
*Judicial Crises 61-66
Justice Hugo Black 83
*Justices (Friedman) v. 5, 186-191
Law of Arrest (Creamer) 297-303
Police 254-258
Politics 246-247
Self Inflicted Wound 266-267
*Sup Ct and Criml Process 356-358
*Sup Ct and Rights 202-214
Warren (Cox) 77-83
PERIODICALS:
"Case notes." J Criml Law, Crimlgy and Police Sci 58: 553-554 Dec '67.

"Eavesdropping legislation: down--but not out?" Time 89: 45
    June 23 '67.

2772. Curtis Publishing Co. v. Butts   June 12, 1967 388 U.S. 130
        Associated Press v. Walker
        Am Consttn (Kelly) 961-962
        CQ Guide 436, 438
        Communication (Hemmer) v. 2, 49-52
        *Contemporary Law 628-640
        Court and Consttn v. 2, 295-296
        *Evolution 129-134
        Free Speech (Kurland) 213-249
        Freedom of the Press (Schmidt) 76
        Individual 105-106
        Justice Hugo Black 76-77
        Law of Mass 100-104
        *Mass Communications 257-258
        *Mass Media (Devol) 212-221
        Mass Media (Francois) 92-94
        *Sup Ct on Freedom 148-157
        Sup Ct Review 1967 267-309
        Sup Ct Review 1978 278-279
        System 526-528
        PERIODICALS:
        "Libel liability: test for public figures." Time 89: 46, 48 June
            23 '67.
        "Limits of libel." Newsweek 69: 76-77 June 26 '67.
        "SEP must pay Butts $460,000, high court says." Adv Age 38:
            6 June 19 '67.
        "Strange case of libel; be careful how you say it," Samuel G.
            Blackman. Sat R 54: 48-49, 56 Apr 10 '71 (2).
        "Toward free and responsible speech." Natl R 19: 673-674
            June 27 '67.

2773. National Labor Relations Board v.   June 12, 1967 388 U.S. 175
        Allis-Chalmers Manufacturing Co.
        Basic Text 678
        *Cases Labor (Cox) 1065-1078
        *Cases Labor (Leslie) 672-679
        *Cases Labor (Oberer) 814-821
        *Labor Law (Meltzer) 1080-1092
        Labor Relations (Taylor) 460-461
        PERIODICALS:
        "Significant decisions in labor cases." Monthly Labor R 90: 58
            Aug '67.

2774. United States v. Wade   June 12, 1967 388 U.S. 218
        *Basic Criminal 599-613
        *Cases Criml Justice 681-694
        *Cases Criml Law (Hall) 895-897
        *Congress Against 140-160
        *Consttnl Criml (Marks) 332-335
        *Consttnl Law (Felkenes) 314-315
        *Consttnl Law (Klein) 356-366
        Criminal Law (Felkenes) 198-201
        *Criminal Law (Kadish) 1031-1035
        Criminal Law Revolution 97-100
        *Criminal Procedure (Lewis) 463-468
        Criminal Procedure (Wells) 43-44

*Due Process 46-47
*Judicial Crises 37-43
Law of Arrest (Creamer) 457-462
*Leading Consttnl Cases 595-609
*Principles Proof 754-760
Self Inflicted Wound 229-232, 234-236
*Sup Ct and Criml Process 490-495
*Sup Ct and Rights 304-314
*Teaching Materials 498-507
PERIODICALS:
"Case notes." J Criml Law, Crimlgy and Police Sci 58: 552
    Dec '67.
"Witness for the court," John Galloway. Christian Century 85:
    1473-1474 Nov 20 '68 (3).

2775. Gilbert v. California   June 12, 1967 388 U.S. 263
*Basic Criminal 613-617
*Criminal Law (Kadish) 1035-1036
Criminal Law Revolution 100-101
*Teaching Materials 525-527
PERIODICALS:
"Case notes." J Criml Law, Crimlgy and Police Sci 58: 552-553
    Dec '67.
"Witness for the court," John Galloway. Christian Century 85:
    1473-1474 Nov 20 '68.

2776. Stovall v. Denno   June 12, 1067 390 U.S. 293
*Basic Criminal 618-619
Consttnl Counterrevolution 222-223
Criminal Evidence 489-490
*Criminal Procedure (Lewis) 469-470
*Sup Ct and Criml Process 498-500
*Sup Ct and Rights 316-321
PERIODICALS:
"Case notes." J Criml Law, Crimlgy and Police Sci 58: 553
    Dec '67.

2777. Walker v. Birmingham   June 12, 1967 388 U.S. 307
*Bill (Cohen) 274-280
Cases Civil Liberties 233-238
*Cases Consttnl Law (Cushman) 463-468
*Civil Procedure (Carrington) 72-83
Civil Rights (Fiss) 29-30
Communication (Hemmer) v. 1, 99-100
*Comparative 521-523
*Consttnl Law (Barron) 814-816
*Consttnl Law (Grossman) 1211-1214
*Courts Judges 336-338
Criminal Law Revolution 116
Desegregation (Wasby) 354 356
*Federal System 24-25
*Freedom of Speech (Haiman) 68
Handbook 127-130
*Injunctions 303-321
*Judicial Crises 291-299
*Leading Consttnl Decisions 298-312
Mass Communications 48-50
*Protest 230-249
Sup Ct Review 1967 181-192

System 380-383
PERIODICALS:
"Court v. King." Time 89: 20 June 23 '67.
"Good court gets better." Christian Century 84: 827-828 June
28 '67 (2).

2778. United States v. Sealy, Inc.   June 12, 1967 388 U.S. 350
*Antitrust (Posner) 222-225
*Antitrust Analysis 368-370
*Cases Antitrust Law 1403-1420
PERIODICALS:
"High court hits Sealy, Schwinn franchise plans." Adv Age 38:
1, 48 June 19 '67 (2).
"Supreme Court to review Borden, Sealy, Brown Shoe Co." Adv
Age 36: 60 Oct 18 '65 (3).

2779. United States v. Arnold, Schwinn   June 12, 1967 388 U.S. 365
and Co.
Antitrust (Posner) 266-272
*Antitrust (Posner) 273-281
*Antitrust Analysis 542-548
*Free Enterprise 1009-1024
*Selected Antitrust Cases 336-346
Sup Ct Review 1977 178-179
*Text Antitrust 100-108
PERIODICALS:
"High court hits Sealy, Schwinn franchise plans." Adv Age 38:
1, 48 June 19 '67 (2).
"Schwinn case: a landmark decision," S. Powell Bridges. Bus
Horizons 11: 77-85 Aug '68.
"When bicycle maker peddles alone." Bus Wk p. 39-40 July 1
'67.

2780. Jacobs v. New York   June 12, 1967 388 U.S. 431
*Censorship Landmarks 599-601

2781. Roberts v. United States   Oct 16, 1967   389 U.S. 18
Criminal Law Revolution 129

2782. Beecher v. Alabama   Oct 23, 1967   389 U.S. 35
Sup Ct and Confessions 149-150

2783. Whitehill v. Elkins   Nov 6, 1967   389 U.S. 54
Am Consttn (Kelly) 928
Communication (Hemmer) v. 1, 122-123
Digest 59
Education (Lapati) 233-234
System 239
Warren (Hudgins) 144-145

2784. International Longshoremen's Asso-   Nov 6, 1967   389 U.S. 64
ciation, Local 1291 v. Philadelphia
Marine Trade Association
PERIODICALS:
"Significant decisions in labor cases." Monthly Labor R 91: 65-
66 Jan '68.

2785. Will v. United States   Nov 13, 1967   389 U.S. 90
Criminal Law Revolution 147
*Federal Courts 1565-1570

2786. Burgett v. Texas   Nov 13, 1967   389 U.S. 109
       Criminal Law Revolution 159-160
       PERIODICALS:
       "Case notes." J Criml Law, Crimlgy and Police Sci 59: 271-
       272 June '68.

2787. Mempa v. Rhay   Nov 13, 1967   389 U.S. 128
       Walkling v. Washington State Board
         of Prison Terms and Paroles
       *Basic Criminal 99-102
       *Consttnl Law (Felkenes) 310-311
       Criminal Law (Felkenes) 191-193
       *Criminal Law (Kadish) 1478-1481
       *Sup Ct and Criml Process 740-742
       PERIODICALS:
       "Case notes." J Criml Law, Crimlgy and Police Sci 59: 270-
       271 June '68.

2788. Whitney v. Florida   Nov 13, 1967   389 U.S. 138
       Criminal Law Revolution 146-147

2789. Hackin v. Arizona   Nov 13, 1967   389 U.S. 143
       Criminal Law Revolution 160

2790. United Mine Workers of America v.   Dec 5, 1967   389 U.S. 217
         Illinois State Bar Association
       *Elements Civil 61-65
       *Law Sup Ct 157-161
       PERIODICALS:
       "Significant decisions in labor cases." Monthly Labor R 91: 67
       Feb '68.

2791. Nash v. Florida Industrial Commis-   Dec 5, 1967   389 U.S. 235
         sion
       PERIODICALS:
       "Significant decisions in labor cases." Monthly Labor R 91: 67-
       68 Feb '68.

2792. Zwickler v. Koota   Dec 5, 1967   389 U.S. 241
       Criminal Law Revolution 164-165
       *Materials Consttnl Law 242-251
       PERIODICALS:
       "Case notes." J Criml Law, Crimlgy and Police Sci 59: 269-270
       June '68.

2793. United States v. Robel   Dec 11, 1967   389 U.S. 258
       Am Consttn (Kelly) 916
       CQ Guide 508
       *Cases Civil Liberties 223-227
       *Cases Consttnl Law (Cushman) 453-457
       *Cases Criml Law (Inbau) 249-256
       Communication (Hemmer) v. 1, 67-68
       Consttnl Law (Barrett) 1198
       *Freedom vs National Security 540-543
       *Leading Consttnl Decisions 260-266
       *Legal Environment 80-81
       *Protest 104-117
       *Rights (Shattuck) 62-63
       System 186-189

PERIODICALS:
"Case notes. " J Criml Law, Crimlgy and Police Sci 59: 270
   June '68.
"Right to associate" America 118: 2-3 Jan 6 '68.

2794. United States v. Correll   Dec 11, 1967 389 U. S. 299
        *Business 727-728
        *Legal Environment 227-229

2795. DuBois Clubs of America v. Clark   Dec 11, 1967 389 U. S. 309
        System 143-144

2796. Eagar v. Magma Copper Co.   Dec 11, 1967 389 U. S. 323
        PERIODICALS:
        "Significant decisions in labor cases. " Monthly Labor R 91: 109-
           110 Mar '68.

2797. Katz v. United States   Dec 18, 1967 389 U. S. 347
        *Am Consttn (Lockhart) 441-442
        *Am Consttnl Law (Bartholomew) v. 2, 135-137
        *Am Consttnl Law (Mason) 693-699
        *Am Consttnl Law (Shapiro) 674-676
         Arrest (Waddington) 78
        *Arrest (Waddington) 181-184
        *Basic Criminal 203-209
        *Bill (Cohen) 526-531
         By What Right 73-75
        *Cases Civil Liberties 89-93
        *Cases Consttnl Law (Cushman) 319-323
        *Cases Consttnl Rights 204-206
        *Cases Criml Justice 62-64, 416-421
        *Cases Criml Law 823-824
        *Cases Evidence 1198-1206
        *Cases Property (Donahue) 716-725
        *Civil Rights (Abernathy) 1977 148-150
         Communication (Hemmer) v. 1, 242
        *Consttnl Aspects v. 4, 417-433
         Consttnl Counterrevolution 192-195
        *Consttnl Criml (Marks) 270-272
        *Consttnl Law (Felkenes) 246-248
        *Consttnl Law (Grossman) 841-847
        *Consttnl Law (Kauper) 932-936
        *Consttnl Law (Klein) 221-225
        *Consttnl Rights (Kemerer) 629-633
         Criminal Law (Felkenes) 144-146
        *Criminal Law (Kadish) 1063-1068
         Criminal Law Revolution 126-127
        *Criminal Procedure (Lewis) 325-330
         Equal Justice 15-16
        *Freedom vs National Security 325-326
        *Judicial Crises 67-71
         Law of Arrest (Creamer) 306-312
        *Leading Consttnl Cases 352-357
        *Police 250-254
         Politics 247-252
        *Principles Arrest 359-364
        *Right to Privacy 40-46
        *Rights (Shattuck) 15-17
         Self Inflicted Wound 267-268

*Social Forces 263-268
Spirit 79
*Sup Ct and Criml Process 159-163
*Sup Ct and Rights 216-223
Sup Ct Review 1968 133-152
Sup Ct Review 1969 188-190
*Teaching Materials 191-195
PERIODICALS:
"The right to be left alone." America 118: 3 Jan 6 '68.
"Right to be let alone." Economist 226: 28, 31 Jan 6 '68 (2).
"Unconstitutional bugging." New Republic 158: 11-12 Jan 6 '68.
"Unplugging bugging." Time 90: 43 Dec 29 '67.

2798. National Labor Relations Board v.   Dec 18, 1967   389 U.S. 375
      Fleetwood Trailer Co.
      Basic Text 337
      *Cases Labor (Oberer) 561-563
      *Labor Law (Twomey) 301-304
      Sup Ct and Labor 96-97
      PERIODICALS:
      "Significant decisions in labor cases." Monthly Labor R 96: 67-
      68 June '73.
      "Significant decisions in labor cases." Monthly Labor R 94: 70-
      71 Mar '71.

2799. Brooks v. Florida   Dec 18, 1967   389 U.S. 413
      Sup Ct and Confessions 150

2800. Zschernig v. Miller   Jan 15, 1968   389 U.S. 430
      Consttnl Law (Barrett) 360
      Foreign Affairs 238-241

2801. Wirtz v. Local 125, Laborers' Interna- Jan 15, 1968   389 U.S. 477
      tional Union
      PERIODICALS:
      "Significant decisions in labor cases." Monthly Labor R 91: 109
      Mar '68.

2802. Penn-Central Merger and N & W   Jan 15, 1968   389 U.S. 486
      Inclusion Cases
      *Materials Reorganization 549-553

2803. Mora v. McNamara   Nov 6, 1967   389 U.S. 934
      *Conscience 316-320
      *Consttnl Law (Barrett) 504-506

2804. Snohomish County v. Seattle Disposal   Dec 18, 1967   389 U.S. 1016
      Co.
      *Law Indian 280-281

2805. Schneider v. Smith, Commandant,   Jan 16, 1968   390 U.S. 17
      U.S. Coast Guard
      System 36-37, 190-191

2806. Marchetti v. United States   Jan 29, 1968   390 U.S. 39
      *Am Consttnl Law (Bartholomew) v. 1, 163-164; v. 2, 157-158
      *Cases Civil Liberties 144-150
      *Cases Consttnl Law (Cushman) 374-380
      Criminal Law Revolution 132-133

*Evolution 196-203
*Introduction (Mashaw) 608-611
*Sup Ct and Am Govt 69-75
Sup Ct Review 1971 8-11
PERIODICALS:
"Case notes." J Criml Law, Crimlgy and Police Sci 59: 267-268
June '68 (3).
"[Deleted]," Jerrold K. Footlick and Diane Camper. Newsweek
85: 66 June 9 '75.

2807. Grosso v. United States   Jan 29, 1968   390 U.S. 62
Criminal Law Revolution 133-134
PERIODICALS:
"Case notes." J Criml Law, Crimlgy and Police Sci 59: 267-
268 June '68 (3).

2808. Haynes v. United States   Jan 29, 1968   390 U.S. 85
PERIODICALS:
"Case notes." J Criml Law, Crimlgy and Police Sci 59: 267-268
June '68 (3).

2809. Provident Tradesmens Bank and   Jan 29, 1968   390 U.S. 102
Trust Co. v. Patterson
*Cases Federal Courts 671-680
*Civil Procedure (Carrington) 1102-1110
*Civil Procedure (Cound) 543-550
*Elements Civil 463-469

2810. Smith v. Illinois   Jan 29, 1968   390 U.S. 129
Police 248-249
*Principles Arrest 479-481
PERIODICALS:
"Case notes." J Criml Law, Crimlgy and Police Sci 59: 268-269
June '68.

2811. Teitel Film Corporation v. Cusack   Jan 29, 1968   390 U.S. 139
*Censorship Landmarks 604-605
Law of Obscenity 232-233

2812. Albrecht v. Herald Co.   Mar 4, 1968   390 U.S. 145
*Antitrust (Posner) 256-260
*Antitrust Analysis 511-515, 563-567
*Legal Environment 263-265
PERIODICALS:
"Circulation price action held illegal." Editor and Pub 101: 11
Mar 9 '68.
"Newspaper problems arise from decision on pricing." Editor and
Pub 101: 9, 54 Mar 16 '68.

2813. United States v. Third National Bank   Mar 4, 1968   390 U.S. 171
in Nashville
*Competition 156-161

2814. Harris v. United States   Mar 5, 1968   390 U.S. 234
Criminal Evidence 286-287
*Criminal Justice (Way) 116-117
Criminal Law (Felkenes) 44-45
Criminal Law Revolution 131
Law of Arrest (Creamer) 201-202

Law of Arrest (Markle) 136-137
*Sup Ct and Criml Process 250-251
PERIODICALS:
"Case notes." J Criml Law, Crimlgy and Police Sci 59:   402
Sept '68.

2815.   National Labor Relations Board v.   Mar 6, 1968   390 U.S. 254
United Insurance Co. of America
Insurance Workers International Union
v. National Labor Relations Board
*Labor Law (Meltzer) 584-586
PERIODICALS:
"Significant decisions in labor cases." Monthly Labor R   91:   53
May '68.

2816.   Lee v. Washington   Mar 11, 1968   390 U.S. 333
*Consttnl Law (Felkenes) 403-404
*US Prison Law v. 3, 138-139

2817.   Federal Trade Commission v.   Mar 18, 1968   390 U.S. 341
Fred Meyer, Inc.
*Antitrust (Posner) 779-784
*Antitrust Analysis 946-951

2818.   Simmons v. United States   Mar 18, 1968   390 U.S. 377
*Cases Criml Justice 1056-1059
*Consttnl Criml (Scarboro) 411-414
Criminal Evidence 487
Criminal Law (Felkenes) 204-207
*Criminal Law (Kadish) 958-960
Criminal Law Revolution 130
Dissent 127-128
*Evolution 192-196
Law of Arrest (Creamer) 348-351
*Leading Consttnl Cases 615-621
Principles Proof 510-515; reprinted from "Displaying robbery sur-
veillance photographs," Larry Rissler. FBI Law Enforcement
Bul Dec '75.
Self Inflicted Wound 239-240
*Sup Ct and Rights 330-334
PERIODICALS:
"Case notes." J Criml Law, Crimlgy and Police Sci 59:   397-
398 Sept '68.

2819.   Newman v. Piggie Park Enter-   Mar 18, 1968   390 U.S. 400
prises, Inc.
*Nature 1102-1104

2820.   Protective Committee for Independent   Mar 25, 1968   390 U.S. 414
Stockholders of TMT Trailer
Ferry, Inc. v. Anderson
*Materials Reorganization 373-377
Sup Ct Review 1968 77-87

2821.   Avery v. Midland County   Apr 1, 1968   390 U.S. 474
Cases Property (Donahue) 122
Consttnl Counterrevolution 122-124
*Consttnl Law (Grossman) 713-716
Democratic 554-557

Dissent 432-433
*Evolution 74-79
*Legislation (Linde) 73-80
*Sup Ct and Electoral Process 192-196
Warren (Ball) 206-210
PERIODICALS:
"Counting heads." Senior Scholastic 92: 19-20 May 2 '68.

2822. Johnson v. Massachusetts   Apr 1, 1968   390 U.S. 511
        Criminal Law Revolution 144

2823. Greenwald v. Wisconsin   Apr 1, 1968   390 U.S. 519
        *Cases Criml Justice 567-568

2824. Avco Corporation v. Aero Lodge No.   Apr 8, 1968   390 U.S. 557
        735, International Association of
        Machinists and Aerospace Workers
        *Cases Labor (Cox) 930-933
        *Labor Law (Meltzer) 857-859
        Sup Ct and Labor 120
        PERIODICALS:
        "Significant decisions in labor cases." Monthly Labor R 91: 58-
        59 July '68.

2825. United States v. Johnson   Apr 8, 1968   390 U.S. 563
        Criminal Law Revolution 163-164

2826. United States v. Jackson   Apr 8, 1968   390 U.S. 570
        By What Right 298
        Criminal Law (Felkenes) 359-362
        *Criminal Law (Kadish) 1321-1322
        Criminal Law Revolution 148-149
        Cruel 115-118
        Defendants 163-164
        *Due Process 166
        *Legislative (Hetzel) 416-417
        Police 229-230
        Sup Ct and Confessions 154
        PERIODICALS:
        "Case notes." J Criml Law, Crimlgy and Police Sci 59: 404
        Sept '68.

2827. Stern v. South Chester Tube Co.   Apr 22, 1968   390 U.S. 606
        *Materials Consttnl Law 40-43

2828. Cameron v. Johnson   Apr 22, 1968   390 U.S. 611
        Communication (Hemmer) v. 1, 88
        Criminal Law Revolution 164
        Sup Ct Review 1974 243-244
        Sup Ct Review 1977 205-206
        System 357-358, 376-377

2829. Ginsberg v. New York   Apr 22, 1968   390 U.S. 629
        *Am Consttn (Lockhart) 723-726
        *Bill (Konvitz) 432-436
        *Cases Consttnl Rights 582-585
        *Censorship Landmarks 610-622
        Communication (Hemmer) v. 1, 198
        Consttnl Counterrevolution 278-280

*Consttnl Law (Freund) 1295-1298
Freedom and the Court 220-221
Freedom of the Press (Barron) 281
*Judicial Crises 360-364
Law of Mass 367-368
Law of Obscenity 88-99
*Law of Obscenity 400-410
*Mass Media (Devol) 131-134
Mass Media (Francois) 364
*New Dimensions 87-92
*Obscenity (Bosmajian) 120-133
Obscenity (Clor) 83-85
*Obscenity (Friedman) 304-307
*Pornography 127-135
Sup Ct Review 1968 169-170, 176-185
System 481-483
PERIODICALS:
"Case notes." J Criml Law, Crimlgy and Police Sci 59: 403-
404 Sept '68 (2).
"Censorship double standard approved by Supreme Court." Library
J 93: 1949 May 15 '68.
"Controlling candor." Newsweek 71: 31-32 May 6 '68.
"Minor obscenity." Time 91: 60 May 3 '68.
"States right upheld to censor for minors." Pub Weekly 193: 58-
59 Apr 29 '68.
"Supreme Court approves variable obscenity law," Harriet F. Pil-
pel and Kenneth P. Norwick. Pub Weekly 193: 32 May 27 '68.
"Supreme Court backs censorship double standard." Library J
93: 3103 Sept 15 '68.

2830.   Interstate Circuit, Inc. v. Dallas   Apr 22, 1968   390 U.S. 676
United Artists Corporation v. Dallas
*Censorship Landmarks 623-630
Communication (Hemmer) v. 1, 192-193
Consttnl Counterrevolution 275-276
Law of Mass 395-396
Law of Obscenity 90, 162-163
Private Pressure 159-160
Sup Ct Review 1968 170-175, 185-187
PERIODICALS:
"Case notes." J Criml Law, Crimlgy and Police Sci 59: 403-404
Sept '68 (2).

2831.   Barber v. Page   Apr 23, 1968   390 U.S. 719
Against 338-339
*Cases Evidence 569-572
Criminal Law (Felkenes) 323-326
Criminal Procedure (Wells) 134-135
Private Pressure 161-162
PERIODICALS:
"Case notes." J Criml Law, Crimlgy and Police Sci 59: 410-411
Sept '68.

2832.   St. Amant v. Thompson   Apr 29, 1968   390 U.S. 727
Communication (Hemmer) v. 2, 52-54
Law of Mass 123-124
PERIODICALS:
"Serious doubts needed for actual malice," Harriet F. Pilpel and
Kenneth P. Norwick. Pub Weekly 193: 33 May 27 '68.

2833.   Mathis v. United States   May 6, 1968   391 U. S. 1
        Criminal Evidence 430
        Criminal Law Revolution 139-140
        Sup Ct and Confessions 145-146
        Sup Ct Review 1977 138
        PERIODICALS:
        "Case notes. " J Criml Law, Crimlgy and Police Sci 59: 599
           Dec '68.
        "Supreme Court's decision in Mathis likely to have very limited
           effect, " Paul P. Lipton. J Taxation 19: 32-34 July '68.

2834.   Peyton v. Rowe   May 20, 1968   391 U. S. 54
        Criminal Law Revolution 144-145

2835.   Levy v. Louisiana   May 20, 1968   391 U. S. 68
        Cases Consttnl Law (Gunther) 898-899
        *Douglas 275-277
        *Evolution 84-87
        Frontiers 393-404
        Law Sup Ct 573-578
        PERIODICALS:
        "Justice for black Americans 200 years after independence: the
           Afro-American before the Burger court, 1969-1976, " Robert
           L. Gill. Negro Education R 27: 271-317 July '76 (9).

2836.   American Federation of Musicians   May 20, 1968   391 U. S. 99
             v. Carroll
        *Cases Labor (Cox) 1247-1260
        *Cases Labor (Oberer) 1033-1042
        *Labor Law (Meltzer) 531-540
        PERIODICALS:
        "Significant decisions in labor cases. " Monthly Labor R 91: 57-
           58 Aug '68.

2837.   Bruton v. United States   May 20, 1968 391 U. S. 123
        Arrest (Waddington) 189
        Criminal Evidence 115
        *Criminal Law (Kadish) 1360-1362
        Criminal Law Revolution 137-139
        *Criminal Procedure (Lewis) 508-510
        Criminal Procedure (Wells) 77-78
        *Sup Ct and Criml Process 681-684

2838.   Duncan v. Louisiana   May 20, 1968 391 U. S. 145
        Am Consttn (Kelly) 957
        *Am Consttnl Law (Mason) 743-750
        *Cases Civil Liberties 198-203
        *Cases Consttnl Law (Cushman) 428-433
        *Cases Consttnl Law (Gunther) 489-497
        *Cases Criml Justice 1226-1231
        *Cases Individual 130-139
        *Civil Rights (Abernathy) 1977 229-230
        *Consttn (Morris) 51-53
        Consttnl Counterrevolution 147-149
        *Consttnl Criml (Marks) 215-222
        *Consttnl Law (Barrett) 632-642
        *Consttnl Law (Barron) 472-479
        *Consttnl Law (Felkenes) 325-328
        *Consttnl Law (Freund) 1035-1038

*Consttnl Law (Grossman) 775-779
*Consttnl Law (Maddex) 312-318
*Criminal Justice (Way) 356-359
Criminal Law (Felkenes) 305-308
*Criminal Law (Kadish) 764-773
Criminal Law Revolution 153-156
*Criminal Procedure (Lewis) 29-37
Defendants 162
*Due Process 120
*Elements Criminal 136-143
*Evolution 26-36
Freedom and the Court 90-93
*Law Power 585-587
*Leading Consttnl Cases 45-65
*Modcrn Business 103-104
*Sup Ct and Criml Process 107-112
*Sup Ct and Rights 41-59
Sup Ct Review 1979 302-305
PERIODICALS:
"Case notes." J Criml Law, Crimlgy and Police Sci   59:   601-
602   Dec '68.

2839.   Bloom v. Illinois   May 20, 1968   391 U.S. 194
Criminal Law Revolution 156-158
*Injunctions 848-857
Justice Hugo Black 119-120

2840.   Dyke v. Taylor Implement Manu-   May 20, 1968   391 U.S. 216
facturing Co.
Arrest (Berry) 137-139
*Arrest (Waddington) 142
Criminal Law Revolution 158-159
Law of Arrest (Markle) 127-129

2841.   Carafas v. LaVallee   May 20, 1968   391 U.S. 234
Criminal Law Revolution 145-146
Defendants 139

2842.   United States v. United Shoe   May 20, 1968   391 U.S. 244
Machinery Corporation
*Injunctions 400-404

2843.   Amalgamated Food Employees v.   May 20, 1968   391 U.S. 308
Logan Valley Plaza
Basic Text 188
*Bill (Cohen) 301-306
CQ Guide 416
Cases Consttnl Law (Gunther) 1297-1298
Communication (Hemmer) v. 1, 89-90
*Consttnl Law (Barron) 1028-1031
Handbook 105-106
Justice Hugo Black 163-164
*Justices (Friedman) v. 4, 3093-3100
*Labor Law (Meltzer) 385-392
Labor Relations (Taylor) 514
Mass Media (Francois) 28
Private Pressure 160
*Protest 287-299
*Social Forces 163-174

Sup Ct and Labor 47-51
Sup Ct Review 1974 244
System 297, 308-309
PERIODICALS:
"Court and farm workers." New Republic 158: 10 June 29 '68.
"First, Fifth and Fourteenth Amendment rights: the shopping cen-
ter as a public forum," J. B. Mason. J Retailing 51: 21-30
Summer '75.
"Significant decisions in labor cases." Monthly Labor R 91: 56-
57 Aug '68.

2844. United States v. O'Brien   May 27, 1968 391 U.S. 367
*Am Consttn (Lockhart) 844-848
*Bill (Cohen) 345-351
*Bill (Konvitz) 242-249
CQ Guide 412
*Cases Consttnl Law (Gunther) 1306-1309
*Cases Consttnl Rights 725-729
*Cases Criml Law (Inbau) 219-223
*Cases Individual 833-838
Communication (Hemmer) v. 1, 44-45
*Consttnl Law (Barrett) 1301-1302
*Consttnl Law (Barron) 818-822
*Consttnl Law (Freund) 1205-1207
*Consttnl Law (Grossman) 68-73
*Consttnl Law (Kauper) 1141-1148
*Consttnl Law (Lockhart) 1101-1105
*Contemporary Issues 67-76
Criminal Law Revolution 162-163
Free Speech (Kurland) 251, 256-276, 287-292, 294-301
*Freedom of Speech (Haiman) 48
Freedom of the Press (Barron) 118
*Freedom vs National Security 451-458
Handbook 195-198
*Judicial Crises 300-306
*Law Power 504-509
*Mass Communications 99-101
Mass Media (Francois) 28
Politics 138-139
*Principles Freedom 249-263
Private Conscience 69-71
*Processes 94-99
*Protest 48-56
Sup Ct Review 1968 1-52
System 82-86
PERIODICALS:
*"Draft cardburning case, 1968; excerpts." Current History 55:
112-113 Aug '68.
"Symbolic speech: the draft card burners," Peter W. Martin.
Nation 207: 42-45 July 22 '68.
"Will government be tougher now in draft cases?" US News 64:
16 June 10 '68.

2845. Puyallup Tribe v. Department of   May 27, 1968 391 U.S. 392
Game of Washington
Kautz v. Department of Game of
Washington
*Am Indian v. 4, 2878-2882
*Law Indian 301-303

2846. Menominee Tribe of Indians v.   May 27, 1968   391 U.S. 404
       United States
       *Am Indian v. 4, 2883-2887

2847. National Labor Relations Board v.   May 27, 1968   391 U.S. 418
       Industrial Union of Marine and
       Shipbuilding Workers
       Basic Text 678-679
       *Cases Labor (Oberer) 896-900
       PERIODICALS:
       "Significant decisions in labor cases." Monthly Labor R 91: 58-
       59 Aug '68.

2848. Green v. County School Board of   May 27, 1968   391 U.S. 430
       New Kent County, Virginia
       Am Consttn (Kelly) 873
       *Bill (Konvitz) 562-567
       Busing 10-11
       CQ Guide 599-600
       *Civil Rights (Abernathy) 1977 522-524
       Civil Rights (Schimmel) 192-194
       *Consttn (Morris) 721-725
       Consttnl Law (Barrett) 826-827
       *Consttnl Law (Grossman) 452-457
       Consttnlity 15
       Desegregation (Wasby) 383-384
       Digest 85
       Disaster 67-89
       *Discrimination 221-225
       *Education (Hanard) 174-179
       Education (Lapati) 287-289
       *Educational Policy 347-352
       From Brown 115-118
       *Law and Public Education (Goldstein) 553-560
       *Law Lawyers 290-296
       *Processes 499-501
       *Public School Law 699-705
       *Race 462-466
       *Racial Equality 66-67
       School in the Legal Structure 75-76
       *School Law (Alexander) 475-478
       *Sup Ct and Education 164-171
       Warren (Hudgins) 90-91
       PERIODICALS:
       "Court edict." US News 64: 15 June 10 '68.
       "Desegregation: where schools stand with the courts as the new
         year begins," H. C. Hudgins. Am Sch Bd J 156: 21-25 Jan
         '69 (7).
       "Judicial evolution of the law of school integration since Brown v.
         Board of Education," Frank T. Read. Law and Contemporary
         Problems 39: 7-49 Winter '75 (6).

2849. Raney v. Board of Education of Gould   May 27, 1968   391 U.S. 443
       School District
       Disaster 74
       Warren (Hudgins) 92

2850. Monroe v. Board of Commissioners,   May 27, 1968   391 U.S. 450
       Jackson, Tennessee

Digest 85-86
Disaster 74
Education (Lapati) 289-290
Warren (Hudgins) 92-93

2851. Wirtz v. Hotel, Motel and Club   June 3, 1968   391 U.S. 492
         Employees Union, Local 6
       *Cases Labor (Cox) 1133-1141
       *Cases Labor (Oberer) 907-914
       *Labor Law (Meltzer) 1101-1108
       PERIODICALS:
       "Significant decisions in labor cases." Monthly Labor R 91: 58-
         59 Sept '68.

2852. Witherspoon v. Illinois   June 3, 1968   391 U.S. 510
         Criminal Law (Felkenes) 353-355
       *Criminal Law (Kadish) 1347-1349
         Criminal Law Revolution 149-153
         Cruel 118-125
         Defendants 192-193
       *Due Process 166-167
         Law Sup Ct 312-318
         Procedures 160-161
       *Sup Ct and Rights 397-405
       PERIODICALS:
       "Concern about high court--why Dirksen switched in Fortas case."
         US News 65: 22 Oct 14 '68.
       "Doomed penalty." Time 91: 78 June 14 '68.
       "An end to all death sentences?" US News 64: 15 June 17 '68.
       "Role of the social sciences in determining the constitutionality of
         capital punishment," Welsh S. White. Am J Orthopsychiatry
         45: 581-595 July '75 (3).

2853. Bumper v. North Carolina   June 3, 1968   391 U.S. 543
         Arrest (Waddington) 133
         Criminal Law (Felkenes) 39-40
         Criminal Law Revolution 130-131
       *Leading Consttnl Cases 185-186
       PERIODICALS:
       "Case notes." J Criml Law, Crimlgy and Police Sci 59: 599-600
         Dec '68.
       "Consent to search in response to police threats to seek or to ob-
         tain a search warrant: some alternatives," Thomas G. Gard-
         iner. J Criml Law and Crimlgy 71: 163-172 Summer '80.
       "Rights of children," Charles A. Hollister, M. Chester Nolte,
         M. A. McGhehey. Am Sch Bd J 156: 8-16 June '69. Ex-
         cerpts: Eductn Dig 35: 16-19 Oct '69 (2).
       "Supreme Court and crime; justice or lawlessness; address,"
         Michael A. Musmanno. Vital Speeches 34: 666-668 Aug 15
         '68. Excerpts: US News 65: 71-72 Sept 2 '68 (3).

2854. Pickering v. Board of Education of   June 3, 1968   391 U.S. 563
         Township High School District
         205, Will County
         Communication (Hemmer) v. 1, 148-150
       *Consttn (Morris) 597-604
         Digest 60
       *Education (Hazard) 440-449
         Education (Lapati) 242-243

*Educational Policy 220-224
Freedom Spent 93
*Judicial Excerpts 221-223
*Labor Relations (Edwards) 762-766
Landmark Decisions 145-151
Law and Education 189
*Law and Public Education (Goldstein) 364-372
*Law of Public Education 515-518
Private Pressure 160-161
*Protest 130-136
*Public School Law 46-50
School in the Legal Structure 74
*School Law (Alexander) 533-537
*Sup Ct and Education 210-219
System 578-581
Warren (Hudgins) 132-133
PERIODICALS:
"On the cutting edge of the law: the expansion of teachers' rights, "
David Schimmel and Louis Fischer. Sch R 82: 261-279
Feb '74 (2).
"Schools and the law--the free speech rights of teachers: public
v. private expression, " Thomas J. Flygare. Phi Delta Kappan
60: 242-243 Nov '78 (2).
"To speak out freely: do teachers have the right?" David Schim-
mel. Phi Delta Kappan 54: 258-260 Dec '72.

2855. Sabbath v. United States   June 3, 1968   391 U.S. 585
Criminal Law Revolution 131-132
Law of Arrest (Creamer) 196-200
*Principles Arrest 417-419
PERIODICALS:
"Case notes. " J Criml Law, Crimlgy and Police Sci 59: 601
Dec '68.

2856. Terry v. Ohio   June 10, 1968   392 U.S. 1
Arrest (Berry) 25-27
Arrest (Waddington) 12-13, 14, 15, 28
*Arrest (Waddington) 27
*Basic Criminal 374-384
*Cases Civil Liberties 99-104
*Cases Consttnl Law (Cushman) 329-334
*Cases Criml Justice 208-226, 735-737
*Cases Criml Law (Perkins) 923-926
*Civil Liberties 204-210
Communication (Hemmer) v. 1, 235
Consttnl Counterrevolution 201-203
*Consttnl Criml (Marks) 313-327
*Consttnl Criml (Scarboro) 212-228
*Consttnl Law (Felkenes) 233-235
*Consttnl Law (Grossman) 795-799
*Consttnl Law (Klein) 59-70
*Consttnl Law (Maddex) 127-133
*Criminal Evidence 227-228
Criminal Evidence 348
*Criminal Justice (Way) 101-107
Criminal Law (Felkenes) 87-90
*Criminal Law (Kadish) 903-910
Criminal Law Revolution 117-120
*Criminal Procedure 248-253

Defendants 280-281
*Due Process 24-25
*Judicial Crises 47-54
 Law of Arrest (Creamer) 181-187
*Law of Arrest (Markle) 58-62
*Leading Consttnl Cases 291-304
 Police 188-190
*Police 190-194
 Politics 232
*Principles Arrest 251-262
*Rights (Shattuck) 30-31
*Sup Ct and Criml Process 332-338
*Sup Ct and Rights 160-171
 Sup Ct Review 1969 166-167
 Sup Ct Review 1974 132, 146-149
*Teaching Materials 349-358
PERIODICALS:
"Approval to 'stop and frisk.'" Time 91: 39-40 June 21 '68.
"Case notes." J Criml Law, Crimlgy and Police Sci 59: 600-
    601 Dec '68.
"'Frisking' ruling, boon to police." US News 64: 12 June 24 '68.
"Rule of reason." Newsweek 71: 38 June 24 '68.
"Stop and frisk; eroding the fourth amendment," Isidore Silver.
    Commonweal 88: 455-456 July 12 '68 (2).

2857. Sibron v. New York   June 10, 1968 392 U.S. 40
        Peters v. New York
        Arrest (Waddington) 29, 41-42
       *Arrest (Waddington) 47-50
       *Cases Criml Justice 226-235
        Communication (Hemmer) v. 1, 235-236
        Criminal Law (Felkenes) 91-93
       *Criminal Law (Kadish) 910-911
        Criminal Law Revolution 120-124
       *Federal Courts 114-118
        Law of Arrest (Creamer) 187-191
        Law of Arrest (Markle) 12-13, 62-64
       *Law of Arrest (Markle) 64-65
        Police 186-187
        Politics 233
       *Principles Arrest 262-273
       *Sup Ct and Rights 173-180
PERIODICALS:
"Stop and frisk; eroding the fourth amendment," Isidore Silver.
    Commonweal 88: 455-456 July 12 '68 (2).

2858. Flast v. Cohen   June 10, 1968 392 U.S. 83
       *Am Consttn (Lockhart) 44-52
        CQ Guide 291-292
       *Cases Consttnl Law (Cushman) 26-31
        Cases Consttnl Law (Gunther) 1619-1622
       *Cases Consttnl Rights 44-52
       *Cases Federal Courts 18-35
       *Consttnl Law (Barrett) 63-65, 67-72
       *Consttnl Law (Barron) 64-78
       *Consttnl Law (Freund) 111-118
       *Consttnl Law (Grossman) 141-147
       *Consttnl Law (Klein) 448-458
       *Consttnl Law (Lockhart) 1635-1641

*Contemporary Law 67-77
Digest 114-115
*Federal Courts 161-177
*Federal System 54-57
Power 37
*Public School Law 14-18
Sup Ct and Religion 96-100
Warren (Hudgins) 40-41
PERIODICALS:
"Establishment clause; requiem or rebirth?" George R. La Noue.
    Phi Delta Kappan 50: 85-89 Oct '68 (2).
"Impact of court decisions on educational strategies," Edgar Fuller.
    Eductnl Leader 26: 227-231 Dec '68 (2).
"Legal challenges now OK on government spending," Lee O. Gar-
    ber. Nations Schools 82: 72 Nov '68.
"School aid decisions," William B. Ball. Commonweal 88: 431-
    432 June 28 '68 (2).
"Supreme Court rulings." Socl Service R 42: 362-364 Sept '68
    (3).
"Tax bramble bush; Flast v. Cohen; expanded basis for taxpayers'
    suits--is Pandora's box open, shut or ajar?" Kermit G. Cudd
    and Arthur D. Lynn, Jr. Natl Tax J 21: 358-361 Sept '68.
"Three pence and parochial schools." Time 91: 39 June 21 '68.

2859. Perma Life Mufflers, Inc. v.   June 10, 1968 392 U.S. 134
        International Parts Corporation
    *Antitrust (Posner) 252-255
PERIODICALS:
"High court muffles Midas." Bus Wk p. 44 June 15 '68.

2860. United States v. Southwestern   June 10, 1968 392 U.S. 157
        Cable Co.
    Midwest Television, Inc. v. South-
        western Cable Co.
    *Cases Electronic 370-378
    Communication (Hemmer) v. 2, 266-267
    *Free Enterprise 377-387
    *Mass Communications 955-959

2861. Maryland v. Wirtz   June 10, 1968 392 U.S. 183
    *Cases Employment 663-669
    *Cases Labor (Stern) 230-232
    Digest 60-61
PERIODICALS:
"Next finger in the collective bargaining pie may be on a federal
    hand," M. Chester Nolte. Am Sch Bd J 156: 24-25 Feb '69.
"Significant decisions in labor cases." Monthly Labor R 91: 57-
    58 Sept '68.

2862. Harrison v. United States   June 10, 1962 392 U.S. 219
    *Criminal Law (Kadish) 967-970
    Criminal Law Revolution 140-142

2863. Board of Education of Central School June 10, 1968 392 U.S. 236
        District No. 1 v. Allen
    Am Consttn (Kelly) 979-980
    *Bill (Konvitz) 57-67
    CQ Guide 467
    *Cases Civil Liberties 290-295

*Cases Consttnl Law (Cushman) 520-525
*Cases Individual 1080-1084
*Civil Rights (Abernathy) 1977 279-280
*Consttn (Morris) 375-385
*Consttnl Law (Kauper) 1305-1311
Digest 20-21
*Douglas 155-160
Education (Lapati) 168-170
Freedom and the Court 312-315, 323
*Law of Public Education 49-51
*Public School Law 98-103
Religious Freedom (Arnold) 46-47
*Religious Freedom (Pfeffer) 47-49
School in the Legal Structure 76-77
*School Law (Alexander) 187-192
*Sup Ct and Education 101-111
Sup Ct and Religion 100-103
Sup Ct Review 1973 62-63
Warren (Hudgins) 37-39
PERIODICALS:
"Aid to private schools: legal and economic implications." Mo-
    mentum 2: 4-9 Feb '71 (2).
"Catholic view of textbook decision," C. A. Koeb. Sch and So-
    ciety 96: 327-328 Oct 12 '68.
"Constitution and American education." America 118: 786 June
    22 '68.
"Establishment clause: requiem or rebirth?" George R. La Noue.
    Phi Delta Kappan 50: 85-89 Oct '68 (2).
"Impact of court decisions on educational strategies," Edgar Fuller.
    Eductnl Leader 26: 227-231 Dec '68 (2).
"NEA support for federal aid." Sch and Society 96: 328-329
    Oct 12 '68.
"Nonsectarian public parochial school," Philip Jacobson. Christian
    Century 86: 769-774 June 4 '69.
"School aid decisions," William B. Ball. Commonweal 88: 431-
    432 June 28 '68 (2).
"Secular education: Catholic schools and the Supreme Court,"
    Charles M. Whelan. NCEA Bul 65: 8-12 Nov '68.
"Supreme Court upholds N. Y. textbook aid law." Pub Weekly
    193: 45 June 17 '68.
"Textbooks and the taxpayers; future of the First Amendment,"
    Charles M. Whelan. America 119: 8-11 July 6 '68.
"Why Supreme Court judges OK'd N. Y. textbook loans," Lee O.
    Garber. Nations Sch 82: 32, 44 Aug '68.

2864. Gardner v. Broderick   June 10, 1968 392 U. S. 273
        *Cases Civil Liberties 163-164
        *Cases Consttnl Law (Cushman) 393-394
        Criminal Evidence 426
        Criminal Law (Felkenes) 243-244
        Criminal Law Revolution 134-135
        *Leading Consttnl Cases 583-585

2865. Uniformed Sanitation Men's   June 10, 1968 392 U. S. 280
        Association v. Commissioner of
        Sanitation of City of New York
        Criminal Law (Felkenes) 244-246
        Criminal Law Revolution 135

2866. George Campbell Painting Cor-   June 10, 1968 392 U.S. 286
       poration v. Reid
       Criminal Law Revolution 135-136

2867. King v. Smith   June 17, 1968 392 U.S. 309
       *Cases Law and Poverty 140-151
       *Consttnl Law (Grossman) 656-660
       *Legal Problems 604-613
       *Poverty 579-588
       Rights of the People 151-160
       *Sex Discrimination 1975 761-768
       *Sex Roles 675-683
       *Statutory History Income 858-872
       PERIODICALS:
       *"Evolving welfare system," Earl Warren. Current 98: 21-25
         Aug '68.
       "Open housing: Congress and the court." America 118: 805
         June 29 '68 (2).
       "Victory for 400,000 children; the case of Mrs. Sylvester Smith,"
         Walter Goodman. N Y Times Mag p. 28-29, 62, 67, 69, 70,
         72 Aug 25 '68.
       "Welfare policy and the Supreme Court." Public Welfare 30:
         16-27 Spring '72 (8).

2868. Mancusi v. De Forte   June 17, 1968 392 U.S. 364
       *Criminal Law (Kadish) 953-956
       Criminal Law Revolution 129-130
       *Text Legal Regulation 33-35

2869. Lee v. Florida   June 17, 1968 392 U.S. 378
       Communication (Hemmer) v. 1, 240-241
       Criminal Law (Felkenes) 147-148
       Criminal Law Revolution 128-129
       PERIODICALS:
       "Case notes." J Criml Law, Crimlgy and Police Sci 6: 69
         Mar '69.

2870. Fortnightly Corporation v. United   June 17, 1968 392 U.S. 390
       Artists Television, Inc.
       *Cases Copyright (Kaplan) 491-500
       *Cases Copyright (Nimmer) 221-229
       Communication (Hemmer) v. 2, 147-148
       *Copyright 684-690
       *Free Enterprise 1209-1213
       Legal Aspects 21-22
       PERIODICALS:
       "CATV and fairness cases in high court," L. A. Huston. Editor
         and Pub 100: 13 Dec 9 '68 (2).
       "High court to rule on new CATV case and fairness issue." Adv
         Age 38: 99 Dec 11 '67.

2871. Jones v. Alfred H. Mayer Co.   June 17, 1968 392 U.S. 409
       Am Consttn (Kelly) 902-903
       *Am Consttn (Lockhart) 1222-1225
       *Am Consttnl Law (Saye) 164-167
       *Am Consttnl Law (Shapiro) 155-157
       *Bill (Konvitz) 529-538
       CQ Guide 616

*Cases Civil Liberties 425-429
*Cases Consttnl Law (Cushman) 655-659
*Cases Consttnl Law (Gunther) 1052-1055
*Cases Consttnl Rights 1211-1214
*Cases Employment 869-873
*Cases Individual 587-592
*Cases Property (Donahue) 203-209
*Civil Rights (Abernathy) 1977 87-88
*Civil Rights (Abernathy) 1980 238-248
Conceived 211
*Consttnl Law (Barrett) 1091-1094
*Consttnl Law (Barron) 1102-1106
*Consttnl Law (Freund) 814-822
*Consttnl Law (Grossman) 549-553
*Consttnl Law (Kauper) 859-864
*Consttnl Law (Lockhart) 1618-1621
Desegregation (Wasby) 244-249
*Discrimination 395-401
*Documents History v. 2, 720-721
From Confederation 192-194
*Justices (Friedman) v. 5, 306-320
*Land Ownership 28-37
*Law Sup Ct 555-560
*Legal Foundations 296-299
*Processes 665-673
*Race 626-637
*Racial Equality 115-116
Reconstruction 1207-1259
*Statutory History Civil Rights 1816-1837
Sup Ct Review 1968 89-132
PERIODICALS:
   "Housing and the Negro," William B. Ball. America 119: 11-13
      July 6 '68.
   "Open housing: Congress and the court." America 118: 805
      June 29 '68 (2).

2872. Hanover Shoe Co. v. United Shoe   June 17, 1968 392 U.S. 481
           Machinery Corporation
        *Antitrust (Posner) 143-146
        PERIODICALS:
           "Antitrusters acquire a hefty fist." Bus Wk p. 39 May 25 '68.

2873. Powell v. Texas   June 17, 1968 392 U.S. 514
        *Am Consttnl Law (Mason) 750-756
        *Cases Criml Law (Perkins) 576-583
        *Cases Drug 253-267
        *Consttnl Law (Felkenes) 350-351
        *Criminal Law (Dix) 151-162, 181-183
        Criminal Law (Felkenes) 362-364
        *Criminal Law (Kadish) 640-650
        Criminal Law Revolution 161-162
        Defendants 403-404
        *Due Process 163-164
        *Justices (Friedman) v. 4, 3100-3108
        Private Pressure 161, 162
        *Readings Law 755-760
        *Sup Ct and Criml Process 865-871
        *Sup Ct and Rights 369-378

PERIODICALS:
"Case notes." J Criml Law, Crimlgy and Police Sci 59: 602-604
Dec '68.

2874. American Commercial Lines v.   June 17, 1968 392 U.S. 571
Louisville and Nashville Railroad
American Trucking Association, Inc. v.
Louisville and Nashville Railroad
American Waterways Operators v. Louis-
ville and Nashville Railroad
Interstate Commerce Commission v.
Louisville and Nashville Railroad
"Ingot Molds Case"
*Cases Regulated 706-714
*Free Enterprise 753-762

2875. Wainwright v. New Orleans   June 17, 1968 392 U.S. 598
*Criminal Law Revolution 124-126
Law of Arrest (Creamer) 173-178
PERIODICALS:
"Cop's right (?) to stop and frisk; decisions the Supreme Court
must make," Fred P. Graham. NY Times Mag p. 44-45, 142,
144-145, 147, 150-153 Dec 10 '67.

2876. Lee Art Theatre, Inc. v. Virginia   June 17, 1968 392 U.S. 636
Law of Obscenity 210

2877. Houghton v. Shafer   June 17, 1968 392 U.S. 639
*US Prison Law v. 3, 83-85

2878. Williams v. Rhodes   Oct 15, 1968   393 U.S. 23
Socialist Labor Party v. Rhodes
Am Politics 110-115
Sup Ct and Electoral Process 240-242
Sup Ct Review 1969 279-285
Sup Ct Review 1973 224-225
PERIODICALS:
"Quantitative analysis of the presidential ballot case," Werner F.
Greenbaum. J Politics 34: 223-243 Feb '72.

2879. Epperson v. Arkansas   Nov 12, 1968   393 U.S. 97
"Monkey Law Case"
Authority 20-21, 24
*Bill (Cohen) 466-471
*Bill (Konvitz) 86-90
Cases Consttnl Law (Gunther) 1564-1565
Communication (Hemmer) v. 1, 109-110
*Consttn (Morris) 211-215
Consttnl Law (Barrett) 1454-1455
*Consttnl Law (Freund) 1376 1380
*Consttnl Rights (Kemerer) 240-245
Digest 61
Education (Lapati) 216-218
*Educational Policy 210-214
Freedom and the Court 336
*Judicial Excerpts 42-44
Landmark Decisions 153-159
*Law and Public Education (Goldstein) 71-80
*Law of Public Education 150-152

*Law Sup Ct 96-101
*Religious Freedom (Pfeffer) 85-86
*Sup Ct and Education 112-124
School in the Legal Structure 74-75
*School Law (Alexander) 301-303
System 605-607
*Teacher 93-95
Warren (Hudgins) 41-42
PERIODICALS:
"Change without violence; teaching the theory of evolution." Mary
E. Hawkins. Sci Teacher 36: 19 Feb '69.
"Court rules in a Scopes case." US News 65: 16 Nov 25 '68.
"Evolution revolution in Arkansas," Susan McBee and John Neary.
Life 65: 89 Nov 22 '68.
"Making Darwin legal." Time 92: 41 Nov 22 '68.
"Monkey law out." Senior Scholastic 93: 22 Dec 6 '68.
"Monkey trial 1968." Newsweek 72: 36-37 Nov 25 '68.
"Supreme Court voids anti-evolution law." Sch and Society 97:
132-133 Mar '69.

2880. Brotherhood of Locomotive Fire-   Nov 18, 1968   393 U.S. 129
men and Enginemen v. Chicago,
Rock Island and Pacific Railroad Co.
PERIODICALS:
"Significant decisions in labor cases." Monthly Labor R 92: 70-
71 Feb '69.

2881. Grunenthal v. Long Island Railroad Co. Nov 18, 1968   393 U.S. 156
*Elements Civil 997-1001

2882. Carroll v. President and Commis-   Nov 19, 1968   393 U.S. 175
sioners of Princess Anne County,
Maryland
*Civil Procedure (Carrington) 67-71
Communication (Hemmer) v. 1, 101-102
Consttnl Law (Barrett) 1312-1313
*Injunctions 156-161
Mass Communications 50-51
System 322-323

2883. Federal Trade Commission v.   Dec 16, 1968   393 U.S. 223
Texaco, Inc.
*Antitrust Analysis 631-633

2884. Oestereich v. Selective Service   Dec 16, 1968   393 U.S. 233
System Board No. 11, Cheyenne,
Wyoming
Communication (Hemmer) v. 1, 42-43
Criminal Law Revolution 204-205
*Judicial Crises 214-215
*Law Sup Ct 370-377
Private Conscience 50
Protest 66-71

2885. United States v. Nardello   Jan 13, 1969   393 U.S. 286
Criminal Law Revolution 208-209

2886. United States v. Donruss   Jan 13, 1969   393 U.S. 297

PERIODICALS:
"Supreme Court's Donruss decision calls for a shift in tactics in
531 area," David Altman and Allan B. Muchin. J Taxation 30:
202-206 Apr '69.

2887. Glover v. St. Louis-San Francisco   Jan 14, 1969   393 U.S. 324
Railroad
*Race 736-739
PERIODICALS:
"Significant decisions in labor cases." Monthly Labor R 92: 71-
72 Apr '69.

2888. United States v. Container Corporation Jan 14, 1969 393 U.S. 333
of America
*Antitrust (Posner) 218-220
*Antitrust Analysis 336-341
*Free Enterprise 525-527
*Legal Environment 277-279
*Selected Antitrust Cases 78-83

2889. National Labor Relations Board v.   Jan 15, 1969   393 U.S. 357
Strong dba Strong Roofing and
Insulating Co.
*Collective Dargaining 446-449

2890. Smith v. Hooey   Jan 20, 1969   393 U.S. 374
*Cases Criml Law (Perkins) 1021-1026
Criminal Law (Felkenes) 258-260
Criminal Law Revolution 191-192
Procedures 83-84
*US Prison Law v. 4, 412-422

2891. Hunter v. Erikson   Jan 20, 1969   393 U.S. 385
Am Consttn (Kelly) 903-904
Freedom and the Court 421-422
*Processes 550-552

2892. Spinelli v. United States   Jan 29, 1969   393 U.S. 410
Arrest (Waddington) 91
*Basic Criminal 231-238
*Cases Criml Justice 89-97
*Cases Criml Law (Perkins) 881-886
*Consttnl Criml (Scarboro) 143-152
Criminal Law (Felkenes) 50-52
*Criminal Law (Kadish) 844-849
Criminal Law Revolution 172-175
*Criminal Procedure (Lewis) 148-152
Law of Arrest (Creamer) 129-133
Law of Arrest (Markle) 205-210
*Leading Consttnl Cases 89-96
*Principles Arrest 327-331
*Sup Ct and Criml Process 176-179
Sup Ct Review 1969 158-162
*Teaching Materials 225-231
PERIODICALS:
"Case notes." J Criml Law, Crimlgy and Police Sci 60: 374-
375 Sept '69.
"New irritant." Time 93: 35-36 Feb 7 '69.

2893. Presbyterian Church in U. S. v.   Jan 27, 1969   393 U. S. 440
       Mary Elizabeth Blue Hull Me-
       morial Presbyterian Church
       Freedom and the Court 326
       *Religious Freedom (Pfeffer) 100-102
       Sup Ct Review 1969 347-378
       PERIODICALS:
       "Church property rights." Christianity Today 14: 26-27 Feb
           13 '70.
       "Landmark property hearing." Christianity Today 13: 32-33
           Jan 3 '69.
       "Seceding churches win property." Christianity Today 14: 36
           Feb 13 '70.
       "Secular courts must avoid doctrinal disputes." Christianity To-
           day 13: 42, 44 Feb 14 '69.
       "Setback in court for breakaway church groups." US News 66:
           11 Feb 10 '69.
       "Supreme Court and ecumenism." America 120: 154 Feb 8
           '69.
       "Supreme Court weighs churches' stand." Christianity Today 12:
           42-43 July 5 '68.

2894. Johnson v. Avery   Feb 24, 1969   393 U. S. 483
       *Basic Criminal 110-116
       *Cases Professional 133-136
       *Consttnl Law (Felkenes) 401-403
       *Consttnl Rights (Palmer) 431-434
       Criminal Law (Felkenes) 408-409
       Criminal Law Revolution 209-210
       *Due Process 194-195
       *US Prison Law v. 3, 27-46
       PERIODICALS:
       "Case notes." J Criml Law, Crimlgy and Police Sci 60: 378-
           379 Sept '69.

2895. Tinker v. Des Moines Independent   Feb 24, 1969   393 U. S. 503
       Community School District
       *Am Consttnl Law (Mason) 580-583
       *Am Consttnl Law (Shapiro) 418-420
       Authority 28
       *Bill (Cohen) 351-356
       *Bill (Konvitz) 249-258
       *Cases Consttnl Law (Gunther) 1309-1312
       *Cases Consttnl Law (Rosenblum) 541-547
       *Cases Consttnl Rights 737-742
       *Cases Individual 838-843
       *Civil Liberties (Barker) 128-134
       *Civil Rights (Abernathy) 1977 438-441
       Civil Rights (Schimmel) 18-26
       *Civil Rights (Schimmel) 310-328
       Communication (Hemmer) v. 1, 51-52, 131
       *Consttn (Morris) 254-263
       *Consttnl Law (Barrett) 1268-1272
       *Consttnl Law (Barron) 823-826
       *Consttnl Law (Freund) 1207-1209
       *Consttnl Law (Grossman) 60-68
       *Consttnl Law (Klein) 159-164
       *Consttnl Law (Lockhart) 1110-1115
       *Consttnl Rights (Kemerer) 114-121

PERIODICALS:
"After Tinker: the students' right to free expression," Eileen
Sullivan. Wilson Library Bul 51: 168-171 Oct '76.
"Are secondary school principals ignoring Tinker?" M. G. Kirsch.
Phi Delta Kappan 56: 286 Dec '74.
"Black armband case stirs debate by Supreme Court," Lee O.
Garber. Natns Sch 83: 72, 74 June '69.
"Court intervention in pupil discipline; implications and comment,"
William R. Hazard. Am Behavioral Scientist 23: 169-205
Nov '79 (4).
*"Courts and the child." Library J 95: 216-217 Jan 15 '70.
"Demonstrations, not disruptions." Time 93: 47 Mar 7 '69.
"Forced schooling," B. Frank Brown. Phi Delta Kappan 54:
324 Jan '73.
"Free to speak out--with limits." Senior Scholastic 94: 14
Mar 14 '69.
"Freedom and rights in schools; towards just entitlements for the
young," Romulo F. Magsino. Eductnl Theory 29: 171-185
Summer '79.
"Freedom of speech for students," Kent Greenawalt. Seventeen
28: 54, 66 May '69.
"High court uses picketing to tinker with Tinker," Laurence W.
Knowles. Natns Sch 90: 17 Nov '72 (3).
"How the Tinker decision has affected student rights," David
Schimmel. Eductn Dig 46: 40-43 Oct '80.
"Is treason permissible as merely 'free speech?'" David Lawr-
ence. US News 66: 108 Mar 10 '69.
"John Tinker: still an idealist," Thomas J. Flygare. Phi Delta
Kappan 61: 210-212 Nov '79.

"Not for adults alone: children begin pressing for expansion of
their constitutional rights. " Civil Rights Dig 11: 12-22 Winter '79 (3).
"Role of the federal judiciary in directing student-authority inter-
action, " Henry S. Bangrer. Eductn and Urban Society 8: 267-
306 May '76 (3).
"School protest: is it a right?" US News 66: 12 Mar 10 '69.
"Student and juvenile rights and responsibilities. " Senior Scholas-
tic 106: 8-10, 18 May 8 '75 (3).
"Students in court: free speech and the functions of schooling in
America, " Richard L. Berkman. Harvard Eductnl R 40:
567-595 Nov '70.
"Ten years of tumult in school law and their lessons; Tinker case, "
M. Chester Nolte. Am Sch Bd J 161: 48-51 Jan '74.
"Tinker and the administrator, " Ronald K. Olson. Sch and So-
ciety 100: 86-89 Feb '72.
"Tinker case: a principal's view two years later, " Richard P.
Klahn. Natl Assoc of Secondary Sch Principals Bul 55: 69-
73 Feb '71.
"Using negotiation for teaching civil liberties and avoiding liabil-
ity, " John De Cecco and Arlene Richards. Phi Delta Kappan
57: 23-25 Sept '75 (3).

2896. Dunbar-Stanley Studios v. Alabama   Feb 25, 1969   393 U.S. 537
PERIODICALS:
"Three recent Supreme Court actions may have repercussions in
state taxation. " J Taxation 30: 376-377 June '69.

2897. Allen v. Virginia State Board of   Mar 3, 1969   393 U.S. 544
Elections
Fairley v. Patterson
Bunton v. Patterson
Whitley v. Williams
Sup Ct and Electoral Process 131-133

2898. United States v. Louisiana   Mar 3, 1969   394 U.S. 1
Impact (Wasby) 112

2899. Golden v. Zwickler   Mar 3, 1969   394 U.S. 103
*Cases Federal Courts 69-72
*Consttnl Law (Barrett) 101-102

2900. Gregory v. Chicago   Mar 10, 1969   394 U.S. 111
*Civil Rights (Abernathy) 1977 435-437
Communication (Hemmer) v. 1, 95-96
Criminal Law Revolution 201-202
*Freedom of Speech (Haiman) 97
*Law Sup Ct 71-80
*Protest 250-260
*Race 373-378
System 323

2901. Citizen Publishing Co. v. United   Mar 10, 1969   394 U.S. 131
States
*Antitrust Analysis 739-744
Communication (Hemmer) v. 2, 208-210
*Free Enterprise 232-237
Law of Mass 591-596

*Mass Communications 711-713
Mass Media (Francois) 544

2902. Shuttlesworth v. Birmingham   Mar 10, 1969 394 U.S. 147
       *Am Consttn (Lockhart) 775-779
       *Bill (Cohen) 269-271
       *Bill (Konvitz) 305-309
       *Cases Civil Liberties 238-242
       *Cases Consttnl Law (Cushman) 468-472
       *Cases Consttnl Rights 656-660
       Communication (Hemmer) v. 1, 100-101
       *Consttnl Law (Lockhart) 1017-1020
       Criminal Law Revolution 199-201
       Handbook 117-118, 125-126
       *Leading Consttnl Decisions 312-318
       Mass Communications 51-54

2903. Alderman v. United States   Mar 10, 1969 394 U.S. 165
       Ivanov v. United States
       Butenko v. United States
       *Basic Criminal 672-682
       *Consttnl Criml (Scarboro) 419-429
       Court Years 258-259
       Criminal Law (Felkenes) 149-151
       Criminal Law Revolution 176-179
       *Leading Consttnl Cases 367-380
       *Sup Ct and Rights 227-246
       Sup Ct Review 1969 162-163
       PERIODICALS:
       "Did John Mitchell hear the justices?" Robert Shogan. New Re-
          public 160: 11-13 Apr 26 '69.

2904. Kaufman v. United States   Mar 24, 1969 394 U.S. 217
       *Consttnl Criml (Scarboro) 808-815
       *Criminal Law (Kadish) 1553-1557
       Criminal Law Revolution 206-207
       *Federal Courts 1519-1526

2905. Desist v. United States   Mar 24, 1969 394 U.S. 244
       *Basic Criminal 653-665
       *Cases Consttnl Rights 305-312
       Criminal Law Revolution 180-181

2906. Kaiser v. New York   Mar 24, 1969 394 U.S. 280
       Criminal Law Revolution 180

2907. Harris v. Nelson   Mar 24, 1969 394 U.S. 286
       Criminal Law Revolution 207-208

2908. Giordano v. United States   Mar 24, 1969 394 U.S. 310
       Criminal Law Revolution 179-180
       *Freedom vs National Security 327-328
       Sup Ct Review 1969 163-164

2909. Orozco v. Texas   Mar 25, 1969 394 U.S. 324
       *Contemporary Law 22-25
       Criminal Evidence 430-431
       Criminal Law (Felkenes) 237-239
       Criminal Law Revolution 186-188

*Leading Consttnl Cases 530-533
*Sup Ct and Rights 117-121
PERIODICALS:
"Amplification of Miranda. " Time   93: 55 Apr 4 '69.

2910. Snyder v. Harris   Mar 25, 1969 394 U. S. 332
       Gas Service Co. v. Coburn
       *Federal Courts 1162-1169

2911. Hadnott v. Amos   Mar 25, 1969 394 U. S. 358
       Injunctions 676-682
       *Injunctions 682-686
       Sup Ct and Electoral Process 133-134

2912. Brotherhood of Railroad Trainmen   Mar 25, 1969 394 U. S. 369
       v. Jacksonville Terminal Co.
       PERIODICALS:
       "Significant decisions in labor cases. " Monthly Labor R 92: 62-
       64 June '69.

2913. In re Herndon   Mar 25, 1969 394 U. S. 399
       *Injunctions 686-687

2914. Scofield v. National Labor Relations Apr 1, 1969   394 U. S. 423
       Board
       Basic Text 679-680
       *Cases Labor (Cox) 1079-1085
       *Labor Law (Twomey) 345-349
       PERIODICALS:
       "Significant decisions in labor cases. " Monthly Labor R 92:
       64-65 June '69.

2915. Foster v. California   Apr 1, 1969   394 U. S. 440
       Criminal Law (Felkenes) 207-209
       Criminal Law Revolution 195-196
       *Leading Consttnl Cases 622-623
       *Sup Ct and Criml Process 500-501
       Sup Ct Review 1969 195

2916. McCarthy v. United States   Apr 2, 1969   394 U. S. 459
       Cases Criml Justice 1079-1085
       *Criminal Law (Kadish) 1211-1213
       Criminal Law Revolution 189-190
       Sup Ct Review 1969 174-177

2917. Boulden v. Holman   Apr 2, 1969   394 U. S. 478
       Criminal Law Revolution 194-195
       Sup Ct and Confessions 148-149

2918. Gregg v. United States   Apr 2, 1969   394 U. S. 489
       Criminal Law Revolution 209

2919. Fortner Enterprises, Inc. v. United Apr 7, 1969   394 U. S. 495
       States Steel Corporation
       *Antitrust (Posner) 646-651
       *Antitrust Analysis 617-629
       *Free Enterprise 1088-1099
       *Selected Antitrust Cases 302-314
       Sup Ct Review 1969 1-40

PERIODICALS:
"High court forecloses on loans," K. A. Kaufman. Iron Age 203:
98 Apr 17 '69.

2920. Kirkpatrick v. Preisler   Apr 7, 1969   394 U.S. 526
Heinkel v. Preisler
CQ Guide 494
*Consttnl Law (Grossman) 717-721
Sup Ct and Electoral Process 217-219
Sup Ct Review 1973 8-9
Warren (Ball) 211-213
PERIODICALS:
"New shake-up of voting districts?" US News 66: 39-40 Apr 21
'69.
"Slide rule for legislators." Time 93: 65-66 Apr 18 '69.

2921. Wells v. Rockefeller   Apr 7, 1969   394 U.S. 542
Sup Ct and Electoral Process 221

2922. Stanley v. Georgia   Apr 7, 1969   394 U.S. 557
*Am Consttn (Lockhart) 726-728
*Bill (Konvitz) 437-439
*Cases Consttnl Law (Gunther) 1353-1354
*Cases Consttnl Law (Rosenblum) 305-308
*Cases Consttnl Rights 589-591
*Cases Criml Justice 132-134
*Cases Criml Law (Inbau) 288-291
*Cases Drug 244-245
*Civil Rights (Abernathy) 1977 480-481
Communication (Hemmer) v. 1, 198-199
Consttnl Counterrevolution 283-285
*Consttnl Law (Barrett) 719-721
*Consttnl Law (Barron) 915-918
*Consttnl Law (Grossman) 1242-1244
*Consttnl Law (Kauper) 1218-1220
Criminal Law (Wells) 57
*Criminal Law (Wells) 173-174
Criminal Law Revolution 198-199
Freedom and the Court 221
*Freedom of Speech (Haiman) 139-140
*Judicial Crises 365-367
Law of Mass 371-372
Law of Obscenity 64-67
*Mass Media (Devol) 135-136
Mass Media (Francois) 365
*Obscenity (Bosmajian) 181-185
*Obscenity (Friedman) 332-334
Obscenity (Sunderland) 58-68
Private Pressure 163-164
*Right to Privacy 57-00
*Rights (Shattuck) 117
*Sup Ct and Criml Process 1062-1065
Sup Ct Review 1969 203-217
Sup Ct Review 1979 200
System 484-485
PERIODICALS:
"Home movies." Time 93: 66 Apr 18 '69.
"Home movies, anybody?" Newsweek 73: 36 Apr 21 '69.

"Privacies of life," Paul Bender. Harpers Mag 248: 36, 40-42,
    44-45 Apr '74.
"Restricting Stanley and Freedom of speech," Haig Bosmajian.
    Midwest Q 20: 228-240 Spring '79.
"Supreme Court rules obscenity in home legal." Pub Weekly 195:
    68 Apr 14 '69.

2923. Street v. New York   Apr 21, 1969   394 U. S. 576
        *Bill (Cohen) 361-362
        *Bill (Konvitz) 258-268
        *Cases Consttnl Law (Gunther) 1312-1317
        *Cases Individual 843-848
         Communication (Hemmer) v. 1, 45-47
        *Consttnl Law (Maddex) 410-417
         Handbook 204-205
        *Protest 137-150
        *Race 358-359
         Sup Ct Review 1979 261
         System 87-88

2924. Shapiro v. Thompson   Apr 21, 1969   394 U. S. 618
        Washington v. Legrant
        Reynolds v. Smith
        *Am Consttn (Lockhart) 1130-1136
        *Am Consttnl Law (Mason) 502-508
        *Am Consttnl Law (Saye) 490-494
        *Am Consttnl Law (Shapiro) 564-570
        *Bill (Konvitz) 501-507
         By What Right 251-252
        *Cases Consttnl Law (Gunther) 949-956
        *Cases Consttnl Rights 1100-1106
        *Cases Individual 422-430
        *Cases Law and Poverty 115-127
        *Civil Rights (Abernathy) 1977 496-498
         Consttnl Counterrevolution 57-59
        *Consttnl Law (Barrett) 927-933
        *Consttnl Law (Barron) 677-682
        *Consttnl Law (Felkenes) 209-211
        *Consttnl Law (Freund) 346-351
        *Consttnl Law (Grossman) 660-666
        *Consttnl Law (Kauper) 765-788
        *Consttnl Law (Lockhart) 1461-1466
        *Judicial Crises 155-165
        *Law Sup Ct 587-596
        *Legal Problems 671-681
        *Processes 264-274
        *Statutory History Income 875-884
         Sup Ct Review 1969 303-346
         Sup Ct Review 1972 55-56
         Sup Ct Review 1975 316-318
        PERIODICALS:
        "Breakthrough on welfare." Newsweek 73: 33-34 May 5 '69.
        "Constitutionality of durational residence requirements," M. K.
            Rosenheim. Socl Service R 44: 82-93 Mar '70.
        "Implications of recent U. S. Supreme Court decisions on residence
            requirements," Norman V. Lourie and Stanley J. Brody. Public
            Welfare 28: 45-51 Jan '70.
        "Now it's instant welfare: impact across the U. S." US News 66:
            32-33 May 5 '69.

"Welfare and the Court," Ernest Van Den Haag.   Natl R   21:   805
Aug 12 '69.

2925.   United States v. Skelly Oil Co.   Apr 21, 1969   394 U.S. 678
PERIODICALS:
"Oral argument of a tax case before US Supreme Court," Richard
D. Hobbet.   J Taxation 30:   146-149 Mar '69.
"Supreme Court raises more questions than it answers in Skelly
oil decision," Larry McLane.   J Taxation   31:   66-69   Aug
'69.

2926.   Watts v. United States   Apr 21, 1969   394 U.S. 705
*Bill (Konvitz) 239-242
Communication (Hemmer) v. 1, 36-37

2927.   Davis v. Mississippi   Apr 22, 1969   394 U.S. 721
*Cases Criml Justice 246-249
*Consttnl Law (Felkenes) 238-239
Criminal Evidence 540
Criminal Law (Felkenes) 74-75
*Criminal Law (Kadish) 917-919
Criminal Law Revolution 175-176
*Due Process 26
*Judicial Crises 44-46
*Leading Consttnl Cases 313-316
*Principles Arrest 46-48
Sup Ct Review 1969 169-171
*Teaching Materials 381-385
PERIODICALS:
"Dragnet arrests--court says 'no.'"   US News   66:   12   May 5
'69.
"Dooming the dragnet." Time 93:   76, 78 May 2 '69.

2928.   Frazier v. Cupp   Apr 22, 1969   394 U.S. 731
*Cases Criml Justice 572-573
Criminal Law Revolution 193-194

2929.   Bingler v. Johnson   Apr 23, 1969   394 U.S. 741
PERIODICALS:
"Supreme Court in unenlightening decision holds scholarship tax-
able," John H. Myers.   J Taxation   31:   20-23   July '69.

2930.   National Labor Relations Board v. Apr 23, 1969   394 U.S. 759
Wyman-Gordon Co.
*Admin Law (Gellhorn) 223-230
*Admin Law (Schwartz) 282-290
*Cases Labor (Leslie) 129-133
*Cases Labor (Oberer) 285-292
*Introduction (Mashaw) 441-448
*Labor Law (Meltzer) 144-153
*Legislation (Linde) 888-898
PERIODICALS:
"Significant decisions in labor cases." Monthly Labor R   92:
73-75   July '69.

2931.   United States v. An Article of   Apr 28, 1969   394 U.S. 784
Drug ... Bacto-Unidisk
*Cases Food 302-305

2932. Moore v. Ogilvie   May 5, 1969   394 U.S. 814
       Sup Ct and Electoral Process 239

2933. Kramer v. Caribbean Mills, Inc.   May 5, 1969   394 U.S. 823
       *Cases Federal Courts 195-199
       *Federal Courts 1094-1097

2934. Halliday v. United States   May 5, 1969   394 U.S. 831
       *Legal Environment 144-145

2935. Leary v. United States   May 19, 1969   395 U.S. 6
       *Cases Consttnl Law (Rosenblum) 268-274
       Criminal Evidence 144
       Criminal Law Revolution 184-186
       *Principles Proof 890-904
       PERIODICALS:
       "Key ruling on marijuana." US News 66: 11 June 2 '69.

2936. Zenith Radio Corporation v. Hazeltine May 19, 1969 395 U.S. 100
       Research, Inc.
       *Antitrust (Posner) 618-625
       *Free Enterprise 1241-1249

2937. Frank v. United States   May 19, 1969   395 U.S. 147
       Criminal Law Revolution 196-197

2938. McKart v. United States   May 26, 1969   395 U.S. 185
       *Introduction (Cataldo) 61-64
       *Introduction (Mashaw) 927-931
       *Text Legal Regulation 64-66

2939. Jenkins v. Delaware   June 2, 1969   395 U.S. 213
       Criminal Law Revolution 188-189

2940. United States v. Montgomery County   June 2, 1969   395 U.S. 225
       Board of Education
       Carr v. Montgomery County Board
       of Education
       Digest 86-87
       Disaster 90-92
       From Brown 118
       *Injunctions 476-481
       School in the Legal Structure 78-79
       Warren (Hudgins) 93-94

2941. Boykin v. Alabama   June 2, 1969   395 U.S. 238
       *Cases Criml Justice 1085-1088
       *Criminal Justice (Kaplan) 429-431
       *Criminal Law (Kadish) 1213-1214
       Criminal Law Revolution 190-191
       *Criminal Procedure (Lewis) 543-544
       Cruel 168-170, 181-185
       *Elements Criminal 318-320
       *Sup Ct and Criml Process 978-981
       Sup Ct Review 1969 172-173

2942. Harrington v. California   June 2, 1969   395 U.S. 250
       *Consttnl Law (Felkenes) 320-321
       Criminal Evidence 131-132

Criminal Law (Felkenes) 326-328
Criminal Law Revolution 192-193
Sup Ct Review 1969 197-200

2943. O'Callahan v. Parker   June 2, 1969   395 U.S. 258
       *Cases Criml Law (Inbau) 158-167
       *Civil Rights (Abernathy) 1977 265-266
       *Consttnl Law (Barrett) 551-552
       *Consttnl Law (Felkenes) 104-107
       Criminal Law Revolution 203-204
       Defendants 164-165
       *Douglas 259-264
       *Federal System 168-170
       *Sup Ct and Criml Process 1123-1125
       PERIODICALS:
          "Curbing courts-martial." Time 93: 66 June 13 '69.

2944. Gaston County v. United States   June 2, 1969   395 U.S. 285
       Sup Ct and Electoral Process 130-131
       Sup Ct Review 1969 408-426

2945. Daniel v. Paul   June 2, 1969   395 U.S. 298
       *Bill (Konvitz) 607-611
       Civil Rights (Bardolph) 516-517
       *Judicial Crises 112-115
       *Racial Equality 129

2946. United States v. Grace Estate   June 2, 1969   395 U.S. 316
       PERIODICALS:
          "Supreme Court's Estate of Grace decision: what does it mean?"
          James A. Turley, Jr. J Taxation 31: 130-134 Sept '69.

2947. Sniadach v. Family Finance   June 9, 1969   395 U.S. 337
          Corporation of Bay View
       *Civil Procedure (Carrington) 23-26
       *Due Process 213-214
       *Elements Civil 153-156
       *Law Sup Ct 581-587
       *Legal Problems 59-61
       *Poverty 84-87
       Sup Ct Review 1972 137-138
       PERIODICALS:
          "Individuals triumphant." Time 93: 61 June 20 '69 (3).
          "Significant decisions in labor cases." Monthly Labor R 92: 66-
          68 Aug '69.
          "Supreme Court cases affecting the rights of debtors and creditors,"
          Albert F. Reisman. Credit and Financial Management 74:
          16-17, 40 Nov '72 (4).

2948. Red Lion Broadcasting Co. v.   June 9, 1969   395 U.S. 367
          Federal Communications Com-
          mission
       United States v. Radio Television
          News Directors Association
       Cases Consttnl Law (Gunther) 1302
       *Cases Electronic 214-227
       Communication (Hemmer) v. 2, 310-313
       *Consttnl Law (Barron) 869-871
       *Consttnl Law (Freund) 1247-1251

*Consttnl Law (Grossman) 1175-1179
Crisis 228-230
*First Amendment (Franklin) 495-507
*Freedom of Speech (Haiman) 174-176
Freedom of the Press (Barron) 135-149
Freedom of the Press (Schmidt) 8, 12-13, 158, 161-163, 165-166,
    169, 174, 176-177, 181, 186-188, 194-215, 225, 228-230, 239,
    241-245
Good Guys 3-77
Law of Mass 484-486
*Mass Communications 798-806
*Mass Media (Devol) 325-327
Mass Media (Francois) 484-486
Media Access 10-13,
*Sex Roles 614-625
System 658-660
PERIODICALS:
"CATV and fairness cases in high court," L. A. Huston.   Editor
    and Pub 100: 13 Dec 9 '67 (2).
"Case of the Red Lion," Robert L. Shayon.   Sat R 52: 55-56
    July 12 '69.
"Individuals triumphant." Time 93: 61 June 20 '69 (3).
"Media access; romance and reality," William Francois.   America
    129: 186-188 Sept 22 '73 (2).

2949. Brandenburg v. Ohio   June 9, 1969 395 U. S. 444
    *Am Consttn (Lockhart) 583-585
    *Am Consttnl Law (Shapiro) 396-397
    *Bill (Cohen) 79-83
    *Bill (Konvitz) 364-369
    CQ Guide 406
    *Cases Consttnl Law (Gunther) 1179-1181
    *Cases Consttnl Rights 391-393
    *Cases Criml Law (Inbau) 205-211
    *Cases Individual 722-726
    Civil Rights (Abernathy) 1977 437
    Communication (Hemmer) v. 1, 22-24
    *Consttnl Law (Barrett) 1152-1155
    *Consttnl Law (Barron) 771-773
    *Consttnl Law (Felkenes) 130-131
    *Consttnl Law (Freund) 1173-1175
    *Consttnl Law (Kauper) 1103-1106
    *Consttnl Law (Lockhart) 725-728
    *Consttnl Rights (Kemerer) 108-111
    Criminal Law Revolution 198
    *Douglas 205-208
    *Freedom of Speech (Haiman) 21-23
    *Freedom vs National Security 460-462
    Handbook 24-26
    *Mass Communications 83-85
    Mass Communications 85-89
    *Protest 118-124
    Sup Ct Review 1969 42-43
    System 156-157
PERIODICALS:
    "Individuals triumphant." Time 93: 61 June 20 '69 (3).

2950. Utah Public Service Commission   June 16, 1969 395 U. S. 464
    v. El Paso Natural Gas Co.

Brethren 79-85
Court Years 167, 233

2951. Powell v. McCormack   June 16, 1969 395 U.S. 486
       Adam.
       *Adam 253-280
       Am Politics 132-137
       Brethren 24-25
       By What Right 139-144
       CQ Guide 165-166
       *Cases Consttnl Law (Gunther) 451-454
       *Cases Consttnl Law (Rosenblum) 385-393
       *Comparative 132-136
       *Consttnl Law (Barrett) 109-112
       *Consttnl Law (Barron) 133-136
       *Consttnl Law (Freund) 71-80
       *Consttnl Law (Grossman) 174-179
       Court Years 150-151
       *Douglas 13-18
       *Federal System 191-195
       Impeachment 104-107
       In His own Image 89-91
       *Legislation (Linde) 99-111
       *Legislative (Hetzel) 503-513
       Memoirs 317-318
       *Processes 1147-1156
       Rise 139
       Sup Ct (Forte) 40
       Sup Ct and Electoral Process 39-40
       Sup Ct and Poltcl Questions 117-129
       PERIODICALS:
          "Challenge to Congress." Time 93: 17-18 June 27 '69.
          "Earl Warren vs Warren Earl." New Republic 160: 10 June
             28 '69.
          "Powell decision." Newsweek 73: 45-46 June 30 '69.
          "Unanswered questions in the Powell case," David Lawrence. US
             News 66: 88 June 30 '69.
          "Warren court vs Congress." US News 66: 23-24 June 30 '69.

2952. National Labor Relations Board v.   June 16, 1969 395 U.S. 575
          Gissel Packing Co., Inc.
       Food Store Employees Union v. Gissel
          Packing Co.
       Sinclair Co. v. National Labor
          Relations Board
       Basic Text 94-96
       *Cases Labor (Cox) 295-313
       *Cases Labor (Leslie) 149-153, 166-179
       *Cases Labor (Oberer) 309-322
       *Labor Law (Meltzer) 343-357
       *Labor Law (Twomey) 157-161, 164-171
       *Labor Relations (Getman) 79-82
       Labor Relations (Taylor) 296-297
       PERIODICALS:
          "Card-bargaining policy upheld." US News 66: 63-64 June 30
             '69.
          "Remedial actions of the NLRB in representation cases; an analysis
             of the Gissel bargaining order," Max X. Wortman, Jr. and
             Nathaniel Jones. Labor Law J 30: 281-288 May '79.

"Significant decisions in labor cases. " Monthly Labor R 92: 50-
52 Sept '69.

2953.   Kramer v. Union Free School   June 16, 1969 395 U. S. 621
District
*Am Consttn (Lockhart) 1091-1094
*Am Consttnl Law (Saye) 484-486
Authority 144-145
*Cases Civil Liberties 315-320
*Cases Consttnl Law (Cushman) 545-550
*Cases Consttnl Law (Gunther) 928-930
*Cases Consttnl Rights 1053-1056
*Cases Individual 396-400
*Consttnl Law (Barron) 670-671
*Consttnl Law (Lockhart) 1446-1448
Digest 9-10
*Poverty 236-240
*Processes 818-823
*School Law (Alexander) 138-141

2954.   Perkins v. Standard Oil Co. of   June 16, 1969 395 U. S. 642
California
*Antitrust (Posner) 785-788
*Legal Environment 294-295

2955.   Lear, Inc. v. Adkins   June 16, 1969 395 U. S. 653
*Copyright 587-593
*Free Enterprise 1167-1175
Legal Aspects 42-43
*Legal Regulation 568-573

2956.   North Carolina v. Pearce   June 23, 1969 396 U. S. 711
Simpson v. Rice
CQ Guide 572
*Cases Criml Law (Perkins) 838-842
Criminal Law (Felkenes) 375-376
*Criminal Law (Kadish) 1418-1424
Criminal Law Revolution 183-184
*Criminal Procedure (Lewis) 617-621
Defendants 357-358
*Douglas 413-418
*Due Process 184-186
*Sup Ct and Criml Process 1011-1016
Sup Ct Review 1978 108-110
*US Prison Law v. 1, 388-427

2957.   Chimel v. California   June 23, 1969 395 U. S. 752
*Am Consttnl Law (Bartholomew) v. 2, 144-146
*Am Consttnl Law (Mason) 703-706
*Am Consttnl Law (Shapiro) 676-682
Arrest (Waddington) 121-123
*Basic Criminal 266-274
*Cases Criml Justice 176-186
*Cases Criml Law (Hall) 799-801
*Cases Criml Law (Perkins) 919-922
*Civil Rights (Abernathy) 1977 113-116
Communication (Hemmer) v. 1, 231-232
Consttnl Counterrevolution 186-188
*Consttnl Criml (Marks) 209-214

*Consttnl Criml (Scarboro) 313-320
*Consttnl Law (Felkenes) 223-226
*Consttnl Law (Klein) 225-232
*Consttnl Law (Maddex) 150-153
Criminal Evidence 318-319
*Criminal Justice (Way) 83-88
Criminal Law (Felkenes) 46-49
*Criminal Law (Kadish) 867-871
Criminal Law Revolution 169-172
*Criminal Procedure (Lewis) 173-179
Criminal Procedure (Wells) 37-38
Defendants 278-279
*Judicial Crises 55-60
Law of Arrest (Creamer) 234-237
Law of Arrest (Markle) 75-77
*Leading Consttnl Cases 112-124
Police 205
Politics 235-236
*Principles Arrest 215-220
*Rights (Shattuck) 29-30
Self Inflicted Wound 207-208
*Sup Ct and Criml Process 218-222
*Sup Ct and Rights 150-157
Sup Ct Review 1974 133-134
*Teaching Materials 263-268

2958. Benton v. Maryland   June 23, 1969 395 U.S. 784
*Cases Consttnl Law (Rosenblum) 452-456
*Cases Criml Law (Perkins) 834-837
*Civil Rights (Abernathy) 1977 216-218
*Consttnl Law (Felkenes) 290-292
*Consttnl Law (Klein) 492-498
Criminal Law (Felkenes) 372-374
*Criminal Law (Kadish) 1382-1383
Criminal Law Revolution 181-183
Criminal Procedure (Wells) 70-71
Defendants 355-356
Freedom and the Court 94-95
*Sup Ct and Criml Process 113-115
*Sup Ct and Rights 75-78
*Teaching Materials 38-42

2959. Alexander v. Holmes County Board   Oct 29, 1969   396 U.S. 19
          of Education
Brethren 36-56
Busing 11
Civil Rights (Bardolph) 465-471
*Consttn (Morris) 726-727
*Consttnl Law (Kauper) 727
Desegregation (Wasby) 399-407
Digest 87
Disaster 92-94
Education (Lapati) 291
*Racial Equality 67
*School Law (Alexander) 478
Significant Decisions 1969/70 3-4
PERIODICALS:
   "'At once,' at last." Christian Century 86: 1442 Nov 12 '69.

"Court says: integrate now!" Senior Scholastic 95: School
    Teach 1 Dec 1 '69.
"Court, the schools and the southern strategy," Gary Orfield.
    Sat R 52: 62, 71-72 Dec 20 '69.
"Desegregate now; but how to do it?" US News 67: 45-46 Nov
    10 '69.
"Desegregate now." Senior Scholastic 95: 21-22, 24 Nov 17 '69.
"Historic Supreme Court decision; desegregation in Mississippi
    schools." Integrated Eductn 8: 12-13 Jan '70.
"Immediate compliance for school integration." Library J 94:
    4565 Dec 15 '69.
"Integration now." Time 94: 19-20 Nov 7 '69.
"Judicial evolution of the law of school integration since Brown v.
    Board of Education," Frank T. Read. Law and Contemporary
    Problems 39: 7-49 Winter '75 (6).
"Supreme Court rebuffs Nixon," Victoria Brittain. New Statesman
    78: 645 Nov 7 '69.
*"U.S. Supreme Court ruling on school desegregation, 1969." Cur-
    rent History 58: 40-41 Jan '70.
"What the Court said." New Republic 161: 12 Nov 15 '69.
"White flight from desegregation in Mississippi," Luther Munford.
    Integrated Eductn 11: 12-26 May '73.
"Yes Virginia, there is a Constitution." Newsweek 74: 35-37
    Nov 10 '69.

2960. Hall v. Beals   Nov 24, 1969   396 U.S. 45
       *Federal Courts 107-110

2961. United States v. Knox   Dec 8, 1969   396 U.S. 77
       Criminal Law Revolution 243
       Significant Decisions 1969/70   18

2962. Minor v. United States   Dec 8, 1969   396 U.S. 87
       Buie v. United States
       Criminal Law Revolution 239-241

2963. Morales v. New York (State)   Dec 8, 1969   396 U.S. 102
       Criminal Law Revolution 247-248
       *Principles Arrest 44-46
       Significant Decisions 1969/70 9

2964. Sullivan v. Little Hunting Park, Inc. Dec 15, 1969   396 U.S. 229
       *Civil Rights (Abernathy) 1980 250-254
       *Elements Civil 140-144
       *Judicial Crises 116-119
       *Public Planning 908-910
       *Race 644-646
       Significant Decisions 1969/70 3
       PERIODICALS:
       "Court's ruling on a suburban swimming pool." US News 67: 19
           Dec 29 '69.

2965. National Labor Relations Board v.   Dec 15, 1969   396 U.S. 258
           Rutter-Rex Manufacturing Co.
       Significant Decisions 1969/70 14-15

2966. Dowell v. Board of Education of   Dec 15, 1969   396 U.S. 269
           Oklahoma City Public Schools
       Digest 87-88

2967. Wade v. Wilson   Jan 13, 1970   396 U.S. 282
       Criminal Law Revolution 252

2968. Carter v. West Feliciana Parish   Jan 14, 1970   396 U.S. 290
          School Board
       Singleton v. Jackson Municipal Separate
          School District
       Digest 88
       Disaster 94-97
       Editorials 1970 15-25
       In His Own Image 126-128
       PERIODICALS:
       "After 15 years; 17 days to desegregate." US News   68:   53
          Jan 26 '70.

2969. Gutknecht v. United States   Jan 19, 1970   396 U.S. 295
       Criminal Law Revolution 254-256
       Editorials 1970 97-103
       *Judicial Crises 216-219
       *Protest 72-79
       PERIODICALS:
       "Curbing the boards." Time   95: 11-12   Feb 2 '70.
       "Draft is not for punishing." Senior Scholastic 96: 13   Feb 16
          '70.
       "End to draft as punishment." US News   68: 9   Feb 2 '70.
       "Supreme Court Review (1970)." J Criml Law, Crimlgy and
          Police Sci 61: 495-500 Dec '70 (3).

2970. Carter v. Jury Commission of   Jan 19, 1970   396 U.S. 320
          Greene County
       Significant Decisions 1969/70 4

2971. Turner v. Fouche   Jan 19, 1970   396 U.S. 346
       Digest 10-11
       Significant Decisions 1969/70 5

2972. Mills v. Electric Auto-Lite Co.   Jan 20, 1970   396 U.S. 375
       *Basic Corporation 438-441, 517-520
       Significant Decisions 1969/70 6

2973. Turner v. United States   Jan 20, 1970   396 U.S. 398
       *Cases Evidence 31-44
       Criminal Law Revolution 241-242

2974. Evans v. Abney   Jan 26, 1970   396 U.S. 435
       *Am Consttnl Law (Saye) 274-276
       Brethren 59-61
       Consttnl Counterrevolution 83-84
       *Consttnl Law (Barron) 1024-1026
       Desegregation (Wasby) 158-159
       Significant Decisions 1969/70 4-5
       Sup Ct Review 1972 51-52

2975. Breen v. Selective Service Local   Jan 26, 1970   396 U.S. 460
          Board
       *Criminal Law Revolution 256-257
       *Judicial Crises 220-222
       Significant Decisions 1969/70 17

PERIODICALS:
"Supreme Court Review (1970)." J Criml Law, Crimlgy and Police
Sci 61: 495-500 Dec '70 (2).

2976. United States v. Interstate Com-   Feb 2, 1970   396 U.S. 491
      merce Commission
      Brundage v. United States
      Auburn v. United Sates
      Livingston Anti-Merger Commission v.
      Interstate Commerce Commission
      *Antitrust (Posner) 335-343
      *Cases Regulated 483-491
      *Free Enterprise 274-276

2977. Ross v. Bernhard   Feb 2, 1970   396 U.S. 531
      *Basic Corporation 482-487
      *Cases Federal Courts 759-769
      *Cases Pleading 882-891
      Significant Decisions 1969/70 5

2978. Byrne v. Karalexis   Dec 15, 1969   396 U.S. 976
      *Douglas 225-227

2979. United States v. Kordel   Feb 24, 1970   397 U.S. 1
      Criminal Law Revolution 242-243
      Police 224-226
      PERIODICALS:
      "Supreme Court Review (1970)." J Criml Law, Crimlgy and Police
      Sci 61: 530-534 Dec '70.

2980. United States v. Reynolds   Feb 24, 1970   397 U.S. 14
      *Public Planning 731-733

2981. Hadley v. Junior College District   Feb 25, 1970   397 U.S. 50
      of Metropolitan Kansas City,
      Missouri
      *Consttnl Law (Barrett) 994-997
      Digest 11-12
      *Law of Public Education 721-724
      *School Law (Alexander) 143-145
      Significant Decisions 1969/70 12
      PERIODICALS:
      "One man, one vote: it means school boards too; Hadley decision,"
      August W. Steinhilber and Russell A. Burnham. Am Sch Bd J
      157: 36-37 June '70 (2).

2982. Colonnade Catering Corporation v.   Feb 25, 1970   397 U.S. 72
      United States
      Criminal Law (Felkenes) 84-87
      Criminal Law Revolution 246-247
      Defendants 276
      Significant Decisions 1969/70 15-16

2983. Reetz v. Bozanich   Feb 25, 1970   397 U.S. 82
      *Cases Federal Courts 495-498

2984. H. K. Porter Co. v. National   Mar 2, 1970   397 U.S. 99
      Labor Relations Board
      Basic Text 535-536

*Cases Labor (Leslie) 419-422
*Cases Labor (Oberer) 642-646
*Labor Law (Twomey) 120-124
*Labor Relations (Getman) 161-163
Significant Decisions 1969/70 14
PERIODICALS:
"Court cases lost by unions." US News 68: 55-56 Mar 16 '70.
"Significant decisions in labor cases." Monthly Labor R 93: 71-72 May '70.

2985. Toussie v. United States   Mar 2, 1970   397 U.S. 112
Criminal Law Revolution 259
*Judicial Crises 230-233
Significant Decisions 1969/70 17
PERIODICALS:
"Supreme Court Review (1970)." J Criml Law, Crimlgy and Police
Sci 61: 500-504 Dec '70.

2986. Pike v. Bruce Church, Inc.   Mar 2, 1970   397 U.S. 137
*Consttnl Law (Barrett) 338-340
*Consttnl Law (Lockhart) 324-326
Sup Ct Review 1979 63-64

2987. Association of Data Processing   Mar 3, 1970   397 U.S. 150
Service Organizations v. Camp
*Admin Law (Gellhorn) 966-969
*Admin Law (Schwartz) 567-571
*Cases Consttnl Law (Rosenblum) 217-220
*Cases Federal Courts 44-49
*Introduction (Mashaw) 821-824
Significant Decisions 1969/70 12

2988. Barlow v. Collins   Mar 3, 1970   397 U.S. 159
*Admin Law (Gellhorn) 969-974
*Admin Law (Schwartz) 571-577
*Cases Consttnl Law (Rosenblum) 220-224
*Introduction (Mashaw) 824-828
PERIODICALS:
"New Supreme Court rulings on the right to sue," William B.
Widnall. Banking 62: 41-42, 102 May '70.

2989. Northcross v. Board of Education   Mar 9, 1970   397 U.S. 235
of Memphis
Disaster 97-100

2990. United States v. Van Leeuwen   Mar 23, 1970 397 U.S. 249
Criminal Law Revolution 246
Significant Decisions 1969/70 16

2991. Goldberg v. Kelley   Mar 23, 1970 397 U.S. 254
*Admin Law (Gellhorn) 434-444
*Admin Law (Schwartz) 335-338, 370-372
*Am Consttnl Law (Shapiro) 699-701
*Bill (Cohen) 754-758, 771-772
*Cases Consttnl Law (Rosenblum) 525-532
*Cases Law and Poverty 59-70
*Civil Rights (Pious) 57-60
*Consttnl Law (Barron) 489-497
*Consttnl Law (Grossman) 666-671

  *Consttnl Law (Kauper) 1052-1059
  *Due Process 203, 231-232, 236-238
  *Introduction (Mashaw) 328-337
  *Judicial Crises 166-171
  *Legal Problems 64-69
  *Legislation (Linde) 836-840
  *Poverty 737-747
  *Processes 680-687
  Significant Decisions 1969/70 10-11
  Sup Ct Review 1970 161-214

2992. Wheeler v. Montgomery   Mar 23, 1970 397 U.S. 280
   Sup Ct Review 1970 161-214

2993. United States v. Davis   Mar 23, 1970 397 U.S. 301
   PERIODICALS:
   "Supreme Court's Davis decision: does it do away with the
    302(b)(1) redemption?" Joseph E. McAndrews. J Taxation
    32: 328-331 June '70.

2994. Illinois v. Allen   Mar 31, 1970 397 U.S. 337
   Brethren 62-63
   Cases Consttnl Law (Rosenblum) 547-553
   *Cases Criml Justice 1253-1258
   *Cases Criml Law (Hall) 1087-1089
   *Cases Criml Law (Perkins) 1027-1031
   *Civil Rights (Abernathy) 1977 202-203
   *Consttnl Law (Felkenes) 331-333
   *Consttnl Law (Grossman) 919-922
   Criminal Law (Felkenes) 333-335
   *Criminal Law (Kadish) 1356-1357
   Criminal Law Revolution 222-224
   *Criminal Procedure (Lewis) 511-515
   Criminal Procedure (Wells) 89-90
   *Due Process 129-130
   Editorials 1970 403-409
   *Judicial Crises 315-319
   *Leading Consttnl Cases 718-723
   Police 263-264
   Procedures 105-109
   *Protest 158-166
   Significant Decisions 1969/70 6
   *Sup Ct and Criml Process 678-681
   PERIODICALS:
   "New ruling: 'order in the court' means what it says." US News
    68: 63 Apr 13 '70.
   "Order in the courtroom." Time 95: 51 Apr 13 '70.
   "Point of order; ruling in the Allen case." Newsweek 75: 21-22
    Apr 13 '70.
   "Supreme Court Review (1970)." J Criml Law, Crimlgy and
    Police Sci 61: 518-521 Dec '70.

2995. In re Winship   Mar 31, 1970 397 U.S. 358
   Against 301-302
   *Cases Evidence 1030-1034
   *Cases Modern 93-105
   *Consttnl Law (Barrett) 645
   *Consttnl Law (Felkenes) 365-366
   *Criminal Justice (Way) 435-437

Criminal Law (Felkenes) 394-396
*Criminal Law (Kadish) 1370-1372
Criminal Law Revolution 230-231
*Criminal Procedure (Lewis) 64-66
Criminal Procedure (Wells) 214
Defendants 90-91
*Due Process 123-124
Significant Decisions 1969/70 10
*Sup Ct and Criml Process 711-714
*Sup Ct and Rights 422-424

2996. Waller v. Florida   Apr 6, 1970   397 U.S. 387
       *Cases Criml Law (Hall) 222-223
       *Criminal Justice (Way) 278-281
       Significant Decisions 1969/70 9-10
       *Sup Ct and Criml Process 376-377

2997. Rosado v. Wyman   Apr 6, 1970   397 U.S. 397
       *Cases Law and Poverty 260-264, 335-343
       *Legal Problems 799-807
       *Poverty 686-691
       PERIODICALS:
       "Welfare policy and the Supreme Court." Public Welfare 30: 16-
          27 Spring '72 (8).

2998. Ashe v. Swenson   Apr 6, 1970   397 U.S. 436
       Brethren 72-74
       *Cases Criml Justice 1040-1048
       *Cases Criml Law (Perkins) 851-856
       *Civil Rights (Abernathy) 1977 221-222
       *Consttnl Law (Felkenes) 293-294
       *Criminal Justice (Way) 270-273
       Criminal Law (Felkenes) 377-379
       *Criminal Law (Kadish) 1383-1387
       Criminal Law Revolution 235-237
       *Criminal Procedure (Lewis) 350-353
       Criminal Procedure (Wells) 71-72
       Defendants 377-378
       *Leading Consttnl Cases 776-783
       Police 268
       Significant Decisions 1969/70 9
       *Sup Ct and Criml Process 395-400
       PERIODICALS:
       "Supreme Court Review (1970)." J Criml Law, Crimlgy and
          Police Sci 61: 508-514 Dec '70.

2999. Dandridge v. Williams   Apr 6, 1970   397 U.S. 471
       *Am Consttnl Law (Shapiro) 570-575
       *Cases Consttnl Law (Rosenblum) 532-541
       *Cases Environmental Law (Hanks) 173-178
       *Cases Law and Poverty 77-94
       *Civil Rights (Pious) 60-64
       Consttnl Counterrevolution 60-62
       *Consttnl Law (Barrett) 933-935
       *Consttnl Law (Barron) 690-692
       *Consttnl Law (Freund) 912-914
       *Consttnl Law (Grossman) 671-676
       *Judicial Crises 178-182
       *Legal Problems 75-79

        Politics 204-205
        *Poverty 691-707
        *Sex Discrimination 1975 79-80
        Significant Decisions 1969/70 11
        PERIODICALS:
        See listing at 397 U.S. 397, entry no. 2997.

3000. Lewis v. Martin   Apr 20, 1970   397 U.S. 552
        *Cases Law and Poverty 293-296
        *Legal Problems 617-619

3001. Bachellar v. Maryland   Apr 20, 1970   397 U.S. 564
        Communication (Hemmer) v. 1, 37-38
        Criminal Law Revolution 253
        *Judicial Crises 312-314
        Significant Decisions 1969/70 13

3002. Walz v. Tax Commission of New   May 4, 1970   397 U.S. 664
        York City
        Am Consttn (Kelly) 996
        *Bill (Konvitz) 179-185
        *Cases Civil Liberties 302-306
        *Cases Consttnl Law (Cushman) 532-536
        *Cases Consttnl Law (Rosenblum) 135-143
        *Cases Consttnl Rights 817-822
        *Civil Liberties (Barker) 49-53
        *Civil Rights (Abernathy) 1977 280-282
        Consttnl Counterrevolution 246-251
        *Consttnl Law (Barrett) 1456-1457
        *Consttnl Law (Kauper) 1311-1318
        Digest 21
        Editorials 1970 538-540
        Freedom and the Court 323
        *Leading Consttnl Decisions 318-328
        Religious Freedom (Arnold) 42
        *Religious Freedom (Pfeffer) 40-42
        Significant Decisions 1969/70 15
        Sup Ct and Religion 105-107
        Sup Ct Review 1970 93-107
        Sup Ct Review 1973 64-66
        Wall (Sorauf) 136-137
        PERIODICALS:
        "Benevolent neutrality." Newsweek 75: 77 May 18 '70.
        "Supreme Court weighs churches' tax exemption," Robert E.
           Friedrich. Christianity Today 13: 38 July 18 '69.
        "Tax churches? what the Supreme Court says." US News 68:
           105 May 18 '70.
        "Tax exemptions: race and religion." America 122: 576 May
           30 '70.
        "Walz case," Charles M. Whelan. America 122: 518-519 May
           16 '70.

3003. Rowan v. United States Post Office   May 4, 1970   397 U.S. 728
        Department
        *Bill (Konvitz) 384-390
        Communication (Hemmer) v. 1, 179-180
        *Consttnl Law (Barrett) 1282-1284
        *Freedom of Speech (Haiman) 153-154
        Handbook 149-151

*Judicial Crises 368-370
*Mass Media (Devol) 88-91
Significant Decisions 1969/70 13-14
PERIODICALS:
"Supreme Court upholds bar to erotic mail," Susan Wagner. Pub
Weekly 197: 18 May 18 '70.

3004. Brady v. United States   May 4, 1970   397 U.S. 742
Against 211-215
*Cases Criml Justice 1115-1129
*Consttnl Law (Felkenes) 377-379
*Criminal Justice (Way) 230-233
Criminal Law (Felkenes) 282-286
*Criminal Law (Kadish) 1225-1231
Criminal Law Revolution 216-217
*Criminal Procedure (Lewis) 545-549
Criminal Procedure (Wells) 60-62
*Due Process 91-93
*Elements Criminal 305-310
*Leading Consttnl Cases 660-667
Police 231-232
Procedures 133-134
Significant Decisions 1969/70 6-7
Sup Ct and Confessions 156
*Sup Ct and Criml Process 984-988
PERIODICALS:
"Supreme Court Review (1970). " J Criminl Law, Crimlgy and
Police Sci 61: 521-526 Dec '70 (3).

3005. McMann v. Richardson   May 4, 1970   397 U.S. 759
Against 202-206
*Cases Criml Justice 1129-1132
Criminal Law (Felkenes) 289-292
*Criminal Law (Kadish) 1220-1222
Criminal Law Revolution 213-216
*Due Process 93
Police 233-234
Significant Decisions 8
Sup Ct and Confessions 155-156
*Sup Ct and Rights 441-443
PERIODICALS:
"Supreme Court Review (1970). " J Criml Law, Crimlgy and
Police Sci 61: 521-526 Dec '70 (3).

3006. Parker v. North Carolina   May 4, 1970   397 U.S. 790
Criminal Law Revolution 217-218
Police 234-236
Significant Decisions 1969/70 8
Sup Ct and Confessions 156
PERIODICALS:
"Supreme Court Review (1970). " J Criml Law, Crimlgy and
Police Sci 61: 521-526 Dec '70 (3).

3007. Greenbelt Cooperative Publishing   May 18, 1970 398 U.S. 6
Association v. Bresler
Communication (Hemmer) v. 2, 57-58
Significant Decisions 1969/70 13

3008. Dickey v. Florida   May 25, 1970   398 U. S. 30
        Against 368-372
        Criminal Law (Felkenes) 261-263
        Criminal Law Revolution 231-232
        Significant Decisions 1969/70 7

3009. Schacht v. United States   May 25, 1970   398 U. S. 58
        Communication (Hemmer) v. 1, 52-53
        Criminal Law Revolution 252-253
        *Federal Courts 1589-1592
        Freedom of Speech (Haiman) 152-153
        Significant Decisions 1969/70 12-13
        PERIODICALS:
        "Supreme Court Review (1970)." J Criml Law, Crimlgy and
          Police Sci 61: 534-538 Dec '70.

3010. Chandler v. Judicial Council of   June 1, 1970   398 U. S. 74
          Tenth Circuit of United States
        *Civil Procedure (Carrington) 139-144
        *Courts Judges 193-198
        *Douglas 58-64

3011. Adickes v. S. H. Kress and Co.   June 1, 1970   398 U. S. 144
        *Cases Consttnl Law (Rosenblum) 498-509
        *Cases Pleading 786-796
        *Civil Rights (Abernathy) 1980 95-102
        Consttnl Law (Barrett) 1066
        Significant Decisions 1969/70 5

3012. Boys Markets v. Retail Clerks Union,   June 1, 1970   398 U. S. 235
          Local 770
        Basic Text 610-611
        *Cases Labor (Leslie) 558-564
        *Cases Labor (Oberer) 694-703
        *Collective Bargaining 363-372
        *Courts Judges 329-332
        *Labor Law (Twomey) 36-41
        Labor Relations (Taylor) 425-426
        Significant Decisions 1969/70 14
        Sup Ct and Labor 121-125
        Sup Ct Review 1970 215-268
        PERIODICALS:
        "Blow to unions." Time 95: 60-61 June 15 '70.
        "No-strike pacts now mean what they say." Bus Wk p. 25
          June 6 '70.
        "No-strike reversal by Supreme Court." US News 68: 52-53
          June 15 '70.
        "Significant decisions in labor cases." Monthly Labor R 93: 70-
          72 Aug '70.

3013. Maxwell v. Bishop   June 1, 1970   398 U. S. 262
        Brethren 205-206
        Criminal Law Revolution 254
        Cruel 94-105, 158-167, 186-187, 197-213, 227-228

3014. Atlantic Coast Line Railroad Co. v.   June 8, 1970   398 U. S. 281
          Brotherhood of Locomotive Engineers
        *Federal Courts 1239-1245

3015. Hellenic Lines LTD v. Rhoditis   June 8, 1970   398 U.S. 306
       *Cases Admiralty 337-341

3016. Price v. Georgia   June 15, 1970 398 U.S. 323
       Criminal Law Revolution 238-239
       Significant Decisions 1969/70 10-11
       *Sup Ct and Criml Process 388-389
       PERIODICALS:
       "Supreme Court Review (1970)." J Criml Law, Crimlgy and
           Police Sci 61: 514-518 Dec '70.

3017. Welsh v. United States   June 15, 1970 398 U.S. 333
       *Bill (Konvitz) 160-164
       Cases Consttnl Law (Gunther) 1600-1601
       *Cases Consttnl Law (Rosenblum) 569-575
       *Consttnl Law (Grossman) 1307-1311
       Criminal Law Revolution 258-259
       Editorials 1970 649-656
       First Amendment (Berns) 46-47
       Freedom and the Court 259-261, 383
       *Judicial Crises 234-240
       Private Conscience 27-29
       *Race 407-413
       Religious Freedom (Arnold) 41
       Significant Decisions 1969/70 16-17
       Spirit 46-47
       Sup Ct and Religion 169-171
       Sup Ct Review 1971 41-42
       PERIODICALS:
       "CO riddle." Newsweek 75: 19-20 June 29 '70.
       "Conscientious objection." New Republic 163: 10 July 18 '70.
       "Conscription, Conscience and the Court." Christian Century 87:
           908-909 July 29 '70.
       "Defining conscientious objectors." Christianity Today 14: 21
           July 17 '70.
       "How court ruling changes draft." US News 68: 17-19 June 29
           '70.
       "Reinterpreting the draft law." Christianity Today 14: 31 July
           3 '70.
       "Selective objectors and the Court." America 123: 6 July 11
           '70.
       "Supreme Court Review (1970)." J Criml Law, Crimlgy and
           Police Sci 61: 491-495 Dec '70.
       "Who's sincere." Time 95: 40 June 29 '70.

3018. Moragne v. States Marine Lines, Inc.   June 15, 1970 398 U.S. 375
       *Cases Admiralty 377-385
       *Federal Courts 809-817
       *Introduction (Mashaw) 937-947

3019. Mulloy v. United States   June 15, 1970 398 U.S. 410
       Criminal Law Revolution 257
       Significant Decisions 1969/70 18

3020. Evans v. Cornman   June 15, 1970 398 U.S. 419
       Private Pressure 167
       Significant Decisions 1969/70 11

3021. Coleman v. Alabama   June 22, 1970 399 U. S. 1
       Against 28-29, 31-32, 228-230
       *Basic Criminal 92-98
       Brethren 69-71
       By What Right 68-69
       *Cases Criml Justice 874-879
       Criminal Law (Felkenes) 189-191
       *Criminal Law (Kadish) 800-801
       Criminal Law Revolution 228-230
       Criminal Procedure (Wells) 50-51
       *Due Process 48
       *Leading Consttnl Cases 628-632
       Significant Decisions 1969/70 8-9

3022. Vale v. Louisiana   June 22, 1970 399 U. S. 30
       Against 75-77
       Arrest (Waddington) 120-121
       *Consttnl Criml (Scarboro) 346-350
       Criminal Law (Felkenes) 58-60
       Criminal Law Revolution 245-246
       Law of Arrest (Creamer) 202-206
       *Leading Consttnl Cases 125-129
       Police 197-199
       *Principles Arrest 221-223
       PERIODICALS:
       "Supreme Court Review (1970)." J Criml Law, Crimlgy and
          Police Sci 61: 504-508 Dec '70 (2).

3023. Chambers v. Maroney   June 22, 1970 399 U. S. 42
       Against 77-78, 225-226
       Arrest (Berry) 139-142
       Arrest (Waddington) 145-146, 147, 150
       *Basic Criminal 293-298
       *Cases Criml Justice 319-325
       *Consttnl Criml (Scarboro) 351-355
       *Consttnl Law (Felkenes) 230-232
       Criminal Evidence 345-346
       Criminal Law (Felkenes) 64-67
       *Criminal Law (Kadish) 886-890
       Criminal Law Revolution 244-245
       *Criminal Procedure (Lewis) 227-231
       Law of Arrest (Creamer) 245-250
       Law of Arrest (Markle) 131-135
       *Leading Consttnl Cases 130-135
       Police 199-202
       *Principles Arrest 234-238
       Significant Decisions 1969/70 16
       *Sup Ct and Criml Process 273-276
       *Teaching Materials 298-303
       PERIODICALS:
       "Supreme Court Review (1970)." J Criml Law, Crimlgy and
          Police Sci 61: 504-508 Dec '70 (2).

3024. Baldwin v. New York   June 22, 1970 399 U. S. 66
       Against 260-266
       *Cases Criml Law (Perkins) 1035-1037
       *Criminal Justice (Way) 359-361
       Criminal Law Revolution 222

Defendants 163
*Due Process 120-121
Significant Decisions 1969/70 8

3025. Williams v. Florida   June 22, 1970 399 U.S. 78
        Against 141-148, 264-276
        *Basic Business 35-37
        CQ Guide 530
        *Cases Civil Liberties 203-206
        *Cases Consttnl Law (Cushman) 433-436
        *Cases Criml Justice 955-963
        *Civil Rights (Abernathy) 1977 230-231
        *Consttnl Law (Barrett) 642-644
        *Consttnl Law (Felkenes) 329-331
        *Consttnl Law (Maddex) 324-325
        *Criminal Justice (Way) 368-371
        Criminal Law (Felkenes) 311-313
        *Criminal Law (Kadish) 1279-1281, 1324-1325
        Criminal Law Revolution 218-222
        Defendants 166-167
        *Due Process 121-122, 132-133
        *Leading Consttnl Cases 683-699
        *Procedures 94-95
        Procedures 124
        *Processes 103-112
        Significant Decisions 1969/70 7-8
        Sup Ct (Forte) 61-63
        *Sup Ct and Criml Process 594-598
        *Sup Ct and Rights 60-65
        Sup Ct Review 1978 193-195, 197-203
        Sup Ct Review 1979 277-278
        PERIODICALS:
        "Supreme Court Review (1970)." J Criml Law, Crimlgy and
            Police Sci 61: 526-530 Dec '70.

3026. California v. Green   June 23, 1970 399 U.S. 149
        Against 341-347
        *Cases Evidence 813-831
        *Criminal Law (Kadish) 1363-1366
        Criminal Law Revolution 224-228
        *Principles Proof 305-314
        Significant Decisions 1969/70 8

3027. Phoenix v. Kolodziejski   June 23, 1970 399 U.S. 204
        Significant Decisions 1969/70 12

3028. Nelson v. George   June 29, 1970 399 U.S. 224
        Criminal Law Revolution 251-252

3029. Williams v. Illinois   June 29, 1970 399 U.S. 235
        *Consttnl Law (Felkenes) 197-199
        Criminal Law (Felkenes) 384-385
        Criminal Law Revolution 233-234
        *Leading Consttnl Cases 808-812
        Procedures 234-235
        Significant Decisions 1969/70 12
        *Sup Ct and Criml Process 970-972
        Sup Ct Review 1975 299-302

3030.   United States v. Sisson   June 29, 1970   399 U. S. 267
        Criminal Law Revolution 248-250

3031.   United States v. Phillipsburg   June 29, 1970   399 U. S. 350
        National Bank and Trust
        *Competition 161-168

3032.   Gunn v. University Committee to   June 29, 1970   399 U. S. 383
        End the War in Vietnam
        Criminal Law Revolution 250-251

3033.   North Carolina v. Alford   Nov 23, 1970   400 U. S. 25
        Against 215-216
        *Cases Criml Justice 1137-1141
        *Consttnl Law (Barrett) 432-435
        *Consttnl Law (Felkenes) 379-381
        *Consttnl Law (Klein) 511-516
        *Consttnl Law (Maddex) 279-281
        Criminal Law (Felkenes) 293-295
        *Criminal Law (Kadish) 1218-1220
        Criminal Law Revolution 287-289
        *Criminal Procedure (Lewis) 551-554
        Criminal Procedure (Wells) 62-64
        *Due Process 93-94
        *Elements Criminal 311-313
        In His Own Image 173-174
        *Leading Consttnl Cases 668-672
        *Police 236-238
        Significant Decisions 1970/71 16
        Sup Ct and Confessions 156-157
        *Sup Ct and Criml Process 990-994
        *Sup Ct and Rights 438-441
        PERIODICALS:
        "Recognizing reality." Time 96: 68 Dec 7 '70.
        "Supreme Court Review." J Criml Law, Crimlgy and Police
        Sci 62: 504-509 Dec '71.

3034.   Port of Boston Marine Terminal   Dec 8, 1970   400 U. S. 62
        Association v. Rederiaktiebolaget
        Transatlantic
        *Text Administrative Law 249-252

3035.   Dutton v. Evans   Dec 15, 1970   400 U. S. 74
        Against 347-355
        *Cases Criml Justice 1259-1274
        *Cases Evidence 842-857
        *Due Process 128-129
        Private Pressure 171
        Significant Decisions 1970/71 17-18
        PERIODICALS:
        "New 5 to 4 majority." Time 96: 46-47 Dec 28 '70.
        "Supreme Court Review." J Criml Law, Crimlgy and Police Sci
        62: 516-520 Dec '71.

3036.   Oregon v. Mitchell   Dec 21, 1970   400 U. S. 112
        Texas v. Mitchell
        United States v. Arizona
        United States v. Idaho
        Am Consttn (Kelly) 1011-1012

*Am Consttn (Lockhart) 1210-1220
*Cases Consttnl Law (Gunther) 1087-1096
*Cases Consttnl Law (Rosenblum) 329-346
*Cases Consttnl Rights 1199-1209
*Cases Individual 616-631
*Civil Rights (Abernathy) 1977 596-599
*Consttnl Law (Barrett) 1112-1114
*Consttnl Law (Freund) 987-992
*Consttnl Law (Grossman) 500-506
*Consttnl Law (Lockhart) 1605-1615
*Douglas 99-104
Editorials 1970 1371-1383
Government 90-98
Hugo Black (Dunne) 427-429
Power 442-443
Private Pressure 169-170
*Processes 1057-1075
Rise 144
Significant Decisions 1970/71 9-10
Sup Ct Review 1971 276-278
Sup Ct Review 1979 280-281
PERIODICALS:
"Big vote to come." Time 97: 24 Jan 4 '71.
"Sometime 18 year old vote." Nathan Lewin. New Republic
    164: 21-22 Jan 2 '71.
"Vote for 18 year olds." US News 70: 88-89 Jan 25 '71.

3037. National Labor Relations Board v.   Jan 12, 1971   400 U.S. 297
        International Union of Operating
        Engineers
    Burns & Roe, Inc. v. International
        Union of Operating Engineers
    *Labor Law (Twomey) 286-288
    Significant Decisions 1970/71 30-31

3038. Wyman v. James   Jan 12, 1971   400 U.S. 309
    *Am Consttnl Law (Mason) 699-703
    Brethren 120-121
    *Cases Law and Poverty 319-335
    *Civil Rights (Abernathy) 1977 131-133
    Consttnl Counterrevolution 64-65
    *Consttnl Law (Grossman) 676-683
    *Consttnl Law (Klein) 232-240
    Defendants 274-275
    *Douglas 328-332
    *Introduction (Mashaw) 581-593
    *Judicial Crises 183-192
    *Legal Problems 645-656
    *Poverty 767-780
    *Rights (Shattuck) 32-33
    Significant Decisions 1970/71 11-12
    Sup Ct Review 1979 333-334
    PERIODICALS:
    "Good of the child versus the rights of the parent; the Supreme
        Court upholds the welfare home-visit," Nanette Dembitz.
        Poltcl Sci Q 86: 389-405 Sept '71.
    See also listing at 397 U.S. 397, entry no. 2997.

3039.   United States Bulk Carriers   Jan 13, 1971   400 U. S. 351
        v. Arguelles
        PERIODICALS:
        "Significant decisions in labor cases. " Monthly Labor R   94: 67-
        68 May '71.

3040.   Perkins v. Matthews, Mayor of the   Jan 14, 1971   400 U. S. 379
        City of Canton
        *Civil Rights (Abernathy) 1977 594-596
        Sup Ct Review 1971 279-280

3041.   Blount v. Rizzi   Jan 14, 1971   400 U. S. 410
        Blount v. The Mail Box
        United States v. The Book Bin
        *Bill (Konvitz) 390-394
        Communication (Hemmer) v. 1, 180
        Significant Decisions 1970/71 26
        PERIODICALS:
        "Supreme Court considers basic obscenity statutes. " Pub Weekly
        199: 45-46 Feb 1 '71.
        "Supreme Court Review. " J Criml Law, Crimlgy and Police Sci
        62: 520-525 Dec '71 (3).

3042.   Kennerly v. District Court of   Jan 18, 1971   400 U. S. 423
        Ninth Judicial District of Montana
        *Law Indian 203-209

3043.   Wisconsin v. Contantineau   Jan 19, 1971   400 U. S. 433
        Communication (Hemmer) v. 1, 255
        *Due Process 211
        *Rights (Shattuck) 154-155
        Significant Decisions 1970/71 19
        PERIODICALS:
        "Public employment and the Supreme Court's 1976-77 term, " Carl
        F. Goodman. Public Personnel Management 6: 283-293
        Sept '77 (9).

3044.   Procunier v. Atchley   Jan 19, 1971   400 U. S. 446
        Criminal Law Revolution 300
        *Police 239-240
        Significant Decisions 1970/71 15

3045.   Mayberry v. Pennsylvania   Jan 20, 1971   400 U. S. 455
        *Cases Consttnl Law (Rosenblum) 553-560
        *Civil Procedure (Carrington) 163-165
        *Courts Judges 344-346
        Criminal Law Revolution 298
        *Due Process 110-111
        *Federal System 26-28
        Significant Decisions 1970/71 22
        PERIODICALS:
        "Supreme Court Review. " J Criml Law, Crimlgy and Police Sci
        62: 525-530 Dec '71.

3046.   United States v. Jorn   Jan 25, 1971   400 U. S. 470
        Criminal Law (Felkenes) 379-383
        *Criminal Law (Kadish) 1402-1405
        Criminal Law Revolution 294-295
        Significant Decisions 1970/71 10-11

3047. Groppi v. Wisconsin   Jan 25, 1971   400 U.S. 505
      Criminal Law Revolution 293-294
      Criminal Procedure (Wells) 99-100
      Significant Decisions 1970/71 20-21

3048. Phillips v. Martin Marietta Cor-   Jan 25, 1971   400 U.S. 542
      poration
      Brethren 123
      *Collective Bargaining 908-909
      *Processes 592-594
      *Sex Discrimination 1975 245
      *Sex Roles 315-317
      Significant Decisions 1970/71 8
      *Text Sex Based Discrimination 623-624
      PERIODICALS:
      "ERA: losing battles but winning the war," James Kilpatrick.
      Natns Bus 67: 15-16 Oct '79 (4).

3049. Piccirillo v. New York   Jan 25, 1971   400 U.S. 548
      Criminal Law Revolution 279

3050. Baird v. Arizona State Bar   Feb 23, 1971   401 U.S. 1
      Cases Consttnl Law (Gunther) 1472-1473
      Communication (Hemmer) v. 1, 66-67
      *Consttnl Law (Barrett) 1202-1204
      *Rights (Shattuck) 64
      Significant Decisions 1970/71 23-24

3051. In re Stolar   Feb 23, 1971   401 U.S. 23
      Cases Consttnl Law (Gunther) 1474
      Consttnl Law (Barrett) 1205 1206

3052. Younger, District Attorney of Los Feb 23, 1971   401 U.S. 37
      Angeles County v. Harris
      *Cases Consttnl Law (Gunther) 1681-1683
      *Cases Federal Courts 506-518
      *Civil Rights (Abernathy) 1980 164-170
      *Consttnl Law (Barrett) 102-103
      *Consttnl Law (Grossman) 156-160
      *Consttnl Law (Lockhart) 1695-1698
      *Courts Judges 107-110
      Criminal Law Revolution 302-304
      *Federal Courts 1021-1029
      *Federal System 317-320
      *Injunctions 41-51
      Significant Decisions 1970/71 18
      Sup Ct Review 1971 294-295
      Sup Ct Review 1977 194-199, 224-228
      PERIODICALS:
      "Supreme Court Review." J Criml Law, Crimlgy and Police Sci
      62: 509-516 Dec '71.

3053. Samuels v. Mackell, District   Feb 23, 1971   401 U.S. 66
      Attorney of Queens County
      Fernandez v. Mackell
      Cases Consttnl Law (Gunther) 1683-1684
      *Cases Federal Courts 519-522
      Criminal Law Revolution 305

*Federal Courts 1030-1033
*Injunctions 53-56

3054. Boyle v. Landry   Feb 23, 1971   401 U.S. 77
       Criminal Law Revolution 304-305

3055. Perez v. Ledesma   Feb 23, 1971   401 U.S. 82
       Criminal Law Revolution 305-306
       *Federal Courts 1033-1042
       *Injunctions 56-71

3056. Sanks v. Georgia   Feb 23, 1971   401 U.S. 144
       Brethren 90

3057. Law Students Civil Rights Research   Feb 23, 1971   401 U.S. 154
            Council, Inc. v. Wadmond
       Cases Consttnl Law (Gunther) 1475-1478
       *Cases Professional 86-96
       *Consttnl Law (Barrett) 1206-1211
       Private Pressure 171-172
       Significant Decisions 1970/71 24

3058. Dyson, Chief of Police of Dallas   Feb 23, 1971   401 U.S. 200
            v. Stein
       Criminal Law Revolution 306-307
       Law of Mass 375

3059. Byrne v. Karalexis   Feb 23, 1971   401 U.S. 216
       Criminal Law Revolution 307
       Law of Mass 372-373

3060. Harris v. New York   Feb 24, 1971   401 U.S. 222
       Against 149-162
       Am Consttn (Kelly) 987
       *Basic Criminal 724-726
       *Cases Criml Justice 649-654
       *Civil Rights (Abernathy) 1977 180-182
       *Consttnl Law (Felkenes) 275-276
       *Consttnl Law (Maddex) 262-265
       *Criminal Justice (Galloway) 93-96
       *Criminal Justice (Way) 186-187
       Criminal Law (Felkenes) 235-237
       *Criminal Law (Kadish) 970-972
       Criminal Law Revolution 277-278
       *Due Process 45-46
       In His Own Image 157-159
       *Judicial Crises 27-30
       *Leading Consttnl Cases 540-544
       Police 243-244
       *Principles Proof 743-749
       Significant Decisions 1970/71 14-15
       Sup Ct and Confessions 159-163
       *Sup Ct and Criml Process 455-457
       *Sup Ct and Rights 122-126
       Sup Ct Review 1971 301-302
       Sup Ct Review 1977 106-115
       PERIODICALS:
       "Right from Miranda." Economist 238: 60 Mar 6 '71.

"Right turn." Time 97: 38 Mar 8 '71.
"Supreme Court Review." J Criml Law, Crimlgy and Police Sci
62: 473-480 Dec '71.

3061. International Brotherhood of Boiler-   Feb 24, 1971 401 U.S. 233
       makers, Iron Shipbuilders, Black-
       smiths, Forgers and Helpers,
       AFL-CIO v. Hardeman
       *Cases Labor (Leslie) 695-701
       *Cases Labor (Oberer) 864-870
       *Labor Law (Twomey) 338-343
       *Legal Environment 469-471
       PERIODICALS:
       "Significant decisions in labor cases." Monthly Labor R 94: 81-
       83 June '71.

3062. United States v. Weller   Feb 24, 1971 401 U.S. 254
       Criminal Law Revolution 313

3063. Monitor Patriot Co. v. Roy   Feb 24, 1971 401 U.S. 265
       Communication (Hemmer) v. 2, 60

3064. Time, Inc. v. Pape   Feb 24, 1971 401 U.S. 279
       Communication (Hemmer) v. 2, 56-57
       PERIODICALS:
       "Court defends media in libel decisions." Broadcasting 80: 33-
       34 Mar 1 '71.

3065. Ocala Star-Banner Co. v. Damron   Feb 24, 1971 401 U.S. 295
       Communication (Hemmer) v. 2, 61

3066. Ramsey dba Leon Nunley Coal Co. v. Feb 24, 1971 401 U.S. 302
       United Mine Workers of America
       Labor Relations (Taylor) 119-120
       Significant Decisions 1970/71 29

3067. Zenith Radio Corporation v.   Feb 24, 1971 401 U.S. 321
       Hazeltine Research, Inc.
       *Antitrust (Posner) 627-632

3068. Relford v. Commandant, U. S.   Feb 24, 1971 401 U.S. 355
       Disciplinary Barracks, Fort
       Leavenworth
       *Consttnl Law (Barrett) 552-554
       Criminal Law Revolution 313-314
       Significant Decisions 1970/71 18
       *Sup Ct and Criml Process 1125-1128

3069. Boddie v. Connecticut   Mar 2, 1971 401 U.S. 371
       Brethren 90
       *Cases Domestic 352-356
       *Cases Law and Poverty 456-460
       *Consttnl Law (Barron) 686
       *Due Process 250-251
       Editorials 1971 255, 257, 259-260
       *Elements Civil 44-50
       *Judicial Crises 172-177
       *Justices (Friedman) v. 5, 231-236
       *Legal Problems 53-57

    *Poverty 126-133
    *Processes 839-844
    Significant Decisions 1970/71 21
    Sup Ct Review 1975 308-315

3070. Tate v. Short   Mar 2, 1971   401 U. S. 395
    Criminal Law (Felkenes) 386-387
    Criminal Law Revolution 287
    *Criminal Procedure (Lewis) 565-567
    Editorials 1971 255-261
    Significant Decisions 1970/71 9
    *Sup Ct and Criml Process 139-140
    *US Prison Law v. 1, 257-263
    PERIODICALS:
    "Supreme Court Review." J Criml Law, Crimlgy and Police Sci
    62: 493-497 Dec '71.

3071. Citizens to Preserve Overton   Mar 2, 1971   401 U. S. 402
    Park, Inc. v. Volpe, Secretary
    of Transportation
    *Admin Law (Gellhorn) 332-337
    *Admin Law (Schwartz) 532-536, 561-563, 668-670
    *Am Consttnl Law (Shapiro) 701-706
    *Cases Environmental Law (Hanks) 233-239
    *Cases Property (Donahue) 1395-1402
    *Environmental 674-678
    *Text Legal Regulation 186-189

3072. Griggs v. Duke Power Co.   Mar 8, 1971   401 U. S. 424
    *Bill (Konvitz) 544-548
    Brethren 122-123
    CQ Guide 619
    *Cases Employment 905-911
    *Cases Labor (Leslie) 490-494
    *Cases Labor (Stern) 197-201
    *Cases Law and Poverty 883-889
    Civil Liberties (Wasby) 72-75
    *Civil Rights (Abernathy) 1977 552-554
    *Civil Rights (Abernathy) 1980 443-448
    *Collective Bargaining 809-814
    *Consttnl Law (Grossman) 564-566
    Digest 88-89
    *Judicial Crises 109-111
    *Labor Law (Twomey) 376-379
    Law and Education 156-157
    *Legal Environment 401-404
    *Modern Business 1074-1075
    *Nature 1147-1153
    *Race 756-760
    *Racial Equality 101-103
    *School Law (Alexander) 515-517
    *Sex Discrimination 1975 332-335
    Significant Decisions 1970/71 7
    Sup Ct Review 1976 263-316
    Sup Ct Review 1979 17-24
    *Text Sex Based Discrimination 720-727
    *US Prison Law v. 5, 164-175
    PERIODICALS:
    "Assessment center in the post-Griggs era," Donald J. Willis

and Jared H. Becker. Personnel and Guidance J 55: 201-205
Dec '76. Reaction: Robert L. Williams. 55: 277-278 Jan
'77.
"Beyond Griggs v. Duke Power Co.: Title VII of Washington v.
Davis," James D. Portwood and Stuart M. Schmidt. Labor
Law J 28: 174-181 Mar '77 (3).
"Court craft and competence: a reexamination of 'teacher evalua-
tion' procedures," Henry C. Johnson, Jr. Phi Delta Kappan
57: 606 May '76.
"Court's new rule on job testing." US News 70: 82-83 Apr 12
'71.
"Credentialing by tests or by degrees; title VII of the Civil Rights
Act and Griggs v. Duke Power Company," Sheila Huff. Harvard
Eductnl R 44: 246-299 May '74.
"Impact of Duke Power on testing," Donald J. Petersen. Person-
nel 51: 30-37 Mar '74.
"Justice for black American 200 years after independence: the
Afro-American before the Burger court, 1969-1976," Robert L.
Gill. Negro Eductn R 27: 271-317 July '76 (9).
"More of the same." Natl R 23: 352 Apr 6 '71.
"A new vision of equality: testing the effects of gate-keeping cri-
teria," Donald W. Jackson. Policy Studies J 4: 122-126
Winter '75 (2).
"Onward and upward." Natl R 23: 302-303 Mar 23 '71 (3).
"Significant decisions in labor cases." Monthly Labor R 94: 79-
80 June '71.
"Stricter standards for personnel tests." Bus Wk p. 34 Mar
20 '71.
"Testing: educational goals and change; federal court decision in
the Griggs case," Bruce G. Beezer. Intellect 102: 114-115
Nov '73.
"They just changed the rules on how to get ahead," Peter Koenig.
Psychology Today 8: 87-92, 94, 96, 100, 102-103 June '74.

3073. Gillette v. United States   Mar 8, 1971   401 U.S. 437
Negre v. Larsen
  *Am Consttn (Lockhart) 927-931
  *Bill (Konvitz) 164-179
  Cases Consttnl Law (Gunther) 1602
  *Cases Consttnl Rights 866-870
  *Civil Rights (Pious) 25-33
  *Consttnl Law (Barrett) 1487-1489
  *Consttnl Law (Lockhart) 1236-1240
  *Consttnl Law (Grossman) 1311-1314
  Criminal Law Revolution 308-309
  *Documents History v. 2, 753-756
  *Douglas 245-249
  Editorials 1971 246-255
  First Amendment (Berns) 36-37
  Freedom and the Court 279
  *Judicial Crises 241-249
  Private Conscience 40-42, 49
  Private Pressure 169
  *Race 417-419
  Religious Freedom (Arnold) 41
  *Religious Freedom (Pfeffer) 121-126
  Significant Decisions 1970/71 33
  Sup Ct and Religion 175-176
  Sup Ct Review 1971 31-34, 68-91

PERIODICALS:
"All or nothing for CO's." Time 97: 52 Mar 22 '71.
"Conscientious Objection." New Republic 164: 7 Mar 27 '71.
"The court and conscience; selective CO--Pandora's box or neces-
sary freedom?" Dean M. Kelley. Christianity and Crisis 31:
68-74 Apr 19 '71.
"Great disappointment." Christian Century 88: 363 Mar 24 '71.
"Just-war theology; rejected by the Court," Peter Monkres.
Christian Century 92: 547-549 May 28 '75.
"Onward and upward." Natl R 23: 302-303 Mar 23 '71 (3).
"Parting shots." Life 70: 62-64 Feb 5 '71 (4).
"Selective conscientious objectors decision." America 124: 278
Mar 20 '71.
"Viet objectors overruled." Senior Scholastic 98: 12 Mar 22
'71.

3074. Askew, Governor of Florida v.   Mar 8, 1971   401 U.S. 476
       Hargrave
       *Cases Federal Courts 498-500
       *Civil Rights (Abernathy) 1980 162-163
       Digest 12

3075. Schlanger v. Seamans, Secretary   Mar 23, 1971 401 U.S. 487
       of the Air Force
       Criminal Law Revolution 314-315

3076. Ohio v. Wyandotte Chemicals   Mar 23, 1971 401 U.S. 493
       Corporation
       *Cases Federal Courts 889-895
       *Federal Courts 277-284
       *Text Legal Regulation 73-76

3077. Labine v. Vincent   Mar 29, 1971 401 U.S. 532
       *Cases Consttnl Law (Gunther) 899
       PERIODICALS:
       "Legal rights of unmarried fathers; the impact of recent court de-
       cisions," Rita Dukette and Nicholas Stevenson. Socl Service R
       47: 1-15 Mar '73 (2).

3078. Whiteley v. Warden, Wyoming   Mar 29, 1971 401 U.S. 560
       State Penitentiary
       Against 78-81
       *Cases Criml Justice 102-106
       *Cases Criml Law (Hall) 747-751
       Criminal Evidence 223-224
       Criminal Law Revolution 270-272
       Law of Arrest (Creamer) 166-169
       *Law of Arrest (Markle) 30-31
       Law of Arrest (Markle) 34-36
       Significant Decisions 1970/71 12

3079. United Transportation Union v.   Apr 5, 1971   401 U.S. 576
       State Bar of Michigan
       *Cases Professional 238-243
       Significant Decisions 1970/71 22-23
       PERIODICALS:
       "Significant decisions in labor cases." Monthly Labor R 94: 58-
       59 July '71.

3080. United States v. Freed   Apr 5, 1971   401 U.S. 601
      *Criminal Law (Kadish) 142
      Criminal Law Revolution 281
      Police 226
      Significant Decisions 1970/71 15

3081. Investment Company Institute v.   Apr 5, 1971   401 U.S. 617
      Camp, Comptroller of the Currency
      National Association of Securities Dealers,
      Inc. v. Securities and Exchange
      Commission
      Significant Decisions 1970/71 29

3082. Williams v. United States   Apr 5, 1971   401 U.S. 646
      Elkanich v. United States
      *Consttnl Criml (Scarboro) 840-855
      *Courts Judges 438-440
      Criminal Law Revolution 275-276

3083. Mackey v. United States   Apr 5, 1971   401 U.S. 667
      Criminal Law Revolution 282

3084. United States v. United States Coin   Apr 5, 1971   401 U.S. 715
      and Currency
      Criminal Law Revolution 283
      Significant Decisions 1970/71 14

3085. United States v. White   Apr 5, 1971   401 U.S. 745
      Against 120-129
      *Arrest (Waddington) 184-186
      *Basic Criminal 459-465
      *Cases Criml Justice 497-508
      *Civil Liberties (Barker) 356-360
      *Consttnl Criml (Scarboro) 759-779
      Criminal Evidence 566
      Criminal Law (Felkenes) 156-158
      *Criminal Law (Kadish) 1070-1074
      Criminal Law Revolution 272-273
      *Criminal Procedure (Lewis) 336-339
      Law of Arrest (Creamer) 313-318
      *Leading Consttnl Cases 358-366
      Police 259-261
      *Principles Arrest 365-366
      *Right to Privacy 47-53
      *Rights (Shattuck) 22-23
      Significant Decisions 1970/71 11
      *Sup Ct and Criml Process 360-363
      *Sup Ct and Rights 274-287
      *Teaching Materials 401-405
      PERIODICALS:
      "Privacy and the third party bug," Nathan Lewin.   New Republic
      164: 12-17 Apr 17 '71.
      "Supreme Court Review." J Criml Law, Crimlgy and Police Sci
      62: 489-493 Dec '71.

3086. Hill v. California   Apr 5, 1971   401 U.S. 797
      Criminal Evidence 317-318
      Criminal Law Revolution 276-277

Law of Arrest (Markle) 22-24
Significant Decisions 1970/71 11

3087. Rewis v. United States   Apr 5, 1971   401 U. S. 808
       *Cases Criml Law (Inbau) 83-86
       Sup Ct Review 1974 45

3088. Rogers v. Bellei   Apr 5, 1971   401 U. S. 815
       CQ Guide 146-147
       *Consttnl Law (Barrett) 616-617
       In His Own Image 159-161
       *Legal Environment 140-142

3089. Swann v. Charlotte-Mecklenburg Board   Apr 20, 1971   402 U. S. 1
       of Education
       Charlotte-Mecklenburg Board of Edu-
          cation v. Swann
       Am Consttn (Kelly) 1003-1004
       *Am Consttn (Lockhart) 978-982
       *Am Consttnl Law (Shapiro) 517-521
       *Am Govt 165-171
       *Bill (Konvitz) 567-580
       Brethren 96-112, 154-155
       Busing 15-20
       CQ Guide 601
       Cases Civil Liberties 338-340
       *Cases Consttnl Law (Cushman) 568-570
       *Cases Consttnl Law (Gunther) 769-773
       *Cases Consttnl Rights 925-930
       *Cases Individual 324-328
       *Civil Rights (Abernathy) 1977 524-527
       Civil Rights (Schimmel) 194-197
       Conceived 182-183
       *Consttn (Morris) 733-741
       Consttnl Counterrevolution 41-42
       *Consttnl Law (Barrett) 827-835
       *Consttnl Law (Barron) 612-617
       *Consttnl Law (Grossman) 457-464
       *Consttnl Law (Kauper) 728-738
       *Consttnl Law (Lockhart) 1300-1304
       *Consttnl Rights (Kemerer) 551-555
       Consttnlity 14-15
       Digest 90-91
       Disaster 104-132
       *Documents History v. 2, 756-760
       Editorials 1971 471-494
       Education (Lapati) 292-295
       *Educational Policy 354-364
       Equality (Cohen) 156-166
       Freedom and the Court 379-381
       From Brown 134, 137-139
       God 203-204
       *Great School Bus 47-64
       *Judicial Crises 92-100
       *Judicial Excerpts 31-33
       Judiciary (Abraham) 137-138
       Landmark Decisions 179-188
       Law and Education 208-209
       *Law and Public Education (Goldstein) 586-601

PERIODICALS:
"Brown revisited: from Topeka, Kansas to Boston, Mass.," Leon
  Jones. Phylon 37: 343-358 Dec '76 (3).
"Busing." New Republic 164: 11-12 May 1 '71.
"Busing decision," John Beckler. Sch Mgt 15: 8 June '71.
"Busing: the court rules." Newsweek 77: 26-27 May 3 '71.
"Busing the South." Senior Scholastic 98: 16 May 17 '71.
"Constitutional precipice," Stewart Alsop. Newsweek 79: 88
  Apr 3 '72.
*"Far reaching school decisions." US News 70: 40-42 May 3
  '71.
"Green light for busing." Sat R 54: 68 May 22 '71.
"High court's desegregation ruling needs explanation," Edwin R.
  Render. Natns Sch 88: 40 July '71.
"Judicial evolution of the law of school integration since Brown v.
  Board of Education," Frank T. Read. Law and Contemporary
  Problems 39: 7-49 Winter '75 (6).
"Legitimizing segregation: the Supreme Court's recent school de-
  segregation decisions," John Bannon. Civil Rights Dig 9: 12-
  17 Summer '77 (3).
"The many voices of the Burger Court and school desegregation,"
  H. C. Hudgins, Jr. Phi Delta Kappan 60: 165-168 Nov '78
  (2).
"Notes and comment." New Yorker 48: 27-29 Mar 11 '72.
"Now Supreme Court sets rules for busing students." US News
  70: 12-14 May 3 '71.
"Question before high court: how much integration?" US News
  69: 37-38 Oct 26 '70.
"Racial balance in every school is not required." US News 71:
  23 Sept 13 '71.
"School desegregation and the courts," William L. Taylor. Socl
  Policy 6: 32-41 Jan '76 (3).
"School desegregation: the court, the Congress and the President,"
  Michael B. Wise. Sch R 82: 159-182 Feb '74 (3).
"Southern editors size up busing decision." US News 70: 49-50
  May 10 '71.
"Supreme Court ruling applied in California," Stanley A. Weigel.
  Integrated Eductn 9: 29-33 July '71.
"Supreme Court yes to busing." Time 97: 13-14 May 3 '71.
"Supreme Court's abuse of power," Lino A. Graglia. Natl R
  30: 892-896 July 21 '78 (2).
"Will the Court settle the question of school segregation?" John
  Beckler. Sch Mgt 14: 4-5 Dec '70.

3090. Davis v. Board of School Commis-   Apr 20, 1971 402 U.S. 33
        sioners of Mobile County

3091. McDaniel v. Barresi   Apr 20, 1971   402 U.S. 39
       Digest 92
       Significant Decisions 1970/71 5

3092. North Carolina State Board of   Apr 20, 1971   402 U.S. 43
       Education v. Swann
       *Bill (Konvitz) 582-584
       Consttnlity 15-16
       *Racial Equality 73
       Significant Decisions 1970/71 5-6

3093. United States v. Vuitch   Apr 21, 1971   402 U.S. 62
       Criminal Law Revolution 299-300
       Significant Decisions 1970/71 20
       PERIODICALS:
       "Parting shots." Life 70: 62-64 Feb 5 '71 (4).
       "Supreme Court and abortion." America 124: 443 May 1 '71.

3094. Ehlert v. United States   Apr 21, 1971   402 U.S. 99
       Criminal Law Revolution 309-311
       *Government 250-253
       Private Conscience 51-52
       Significant Decisions 1970/71 33-34

3095. California Department of Human Re-   Apr 26, 1971   402 U.S. 121
       sources Development v. Java
       PERIODICALS:
       "Significant decisions in labor cases." Monthly Labor R   94: 67-
       68 Aug '71.

3096. James v. Valtierra   Apr 26, 1971   402 U.S. 137
       Shaffer v. Valtierra
       *Am Consttnl Law (Mason) 508-509
       *Am Consttnl Law (Shapiro) 575-576
       *Am Land Planning v. 2, 968-974
       *Cases Law and Poverty 830-834
       Consttnl Counterrevolution 62-63
       *Consttnl Law (Barron) 661-663
       *Consttnl Law (Grossman) 683-686
       Editorials 1971 495-500
       *Judicial Crises 193-195
       *Land Use 899-902
       *Legal Foundations 289-293
       *Legal Problems 93-95
       *Poverty 264-268
       Private Pressure 172
       *Public Planning 869-873
       *Race 691-694
       Significant Decisions 1970/71 71
       PERIODICALS:
       "Gauntlet for the poor." Nation 212: 611-612 May 17 '71.
       "Higher wall around suburbia." Bus Wk p. 24 May 1 '71.
       "Neighborhood veto--a ruling on housing." US News 70: 38
       May 10 '71.
       "Supreme Court and the rights of poor." America 124: 477
       May 8 '71.
       "Votes against the poor." Time 97: 16-17 May 10 '71.

3097. Perez v. United States   Apr 26, 1971   402 U.S. 146
       *Cases Consttnl Law (Rosenblum) 346-349
       *Cases Criml Law (Inbau) 64-71
       *Consttnl Law (Barrett) 244-247
       *Consttnl Law (Barron) 220-222
       *Consttnl Law (Grossman) 374-378
       *Legal Environment 196-199

3098. McGautha v. California   May 3, 1971   402 U.S. 183
       Crampton v. Ohio
       Against 383-389
       Criminal Law Revolution 284-287
       Criminal Procedure (Wells) 172-174
       Cruel 228-231, 240-245
       Defendants 389
       *Douglas 397-402
       *Due Process 143-144, 167
       Editorials 1971 553-564
       Significant Decisions 1970/71 16-17
       *Sup Ct and Rights 381-395
       Sup Ct Review 1972 4-5
       PERIODICALS:
       "Fatal decision." Time 97: 64 May 17 '71.
       *"McGautha v. California, May '71." Current History 61: 40-42,
       51 July '71.
       "Question of life or death." Newsweek 77: 30-32 May 17 '71.
       "Ultimate question." Nation 212: 610-611 May 17 '71.

3099. Blonder-Tongue Laboratories, Inc.   May 3, 1971   402 U.S. 313
       v. University of Illinois Foundation
       *Copyright 572 586

3100. United States v. Reidel   May 3, 1971   402 U.S. 351
       *Bill (Konvitz) 445-451
       *Cases Consttnl Law (Gunther) 1354-1355
       Civil Rights (Abernathy) 1977 481
       Communication (Hemmer) v. 1, 200
       *Consttnl Law (Barron) 919-920
       Criminal Law Revolution 295-296
       *Judicial Crises 371-376
       Law of Mass 373-374
       *Mass Media (Devol) 137-139
       Mass Media (Francois) 365-366
       *Obscenity (Bosmajian) 135-138
       Significant Decisions 1970/71 26
       PERIODICALS:
       "Blow to the smut trade." Christianity Today 15: 22 June 4
       '71 (2).
       "Supreme Court Review." J Criml Law, Crimlgy and Police Sci
       62: 520-525 Dec '71 (3).

3101. United States v. Thirty-seven   May 3, 1971   402 U.S. 363
       Photographs
       *Bill (Konvitz) 439-445
       *Cases Consttnl Law (Rosenblum) 308-314
       Communication (Hemmer) v. 1, 199-200
       Criminal Law Revolution 296-297
       Hugo Black (Dunne) 424-425
       Law of Obscenity 233

520   U. S. Supreme Court Decisions

*Obscenity (Bosmajian) 188-195
Significant Decisions 1970/71 26-27
PERIODICALS:
See listing at 402 U. S. 351, entry no. 3100.

3102. Richardson v. Perales   May 3, 1971   402 U. S. 389
       *Admin Law (Gellhorn) 734-742
       *Admin Law (Schwartz) 461-468
       PERIODICALS:
       "U. S. Supreme Court renders decision on disability insurance
       case." Natl Underwriter (Property ed) 75: 36 May 21 '71.

3103. Organization for a Better Austin   May 17, 1971   402 U. S. 415
          v. Keefe
       *Bill (Konvitz) 334-337
       Brethren 123-124
       Communication (Hemmer) v. 1, 229-230
       *Injunctions 127-131
       Mass Media (Francois) 42-43
       Significant Decisions 1970/71 23

3104. California v. Byers   May 17, 1971   402 U. S. 424
       Against 165-173
       *Am Consttnl Law (Saye) 525-528
       By What Right 333-334
       *Cases Evidence 1163-1168
       *Consttnl Criml (Scarboro) 581-594, 629-632
       *Criminal Justice 187-190
       Criminal Law Revolution 279-281
       *Legal Environment 85-86
       Significant Decisions 1970/71 16
       Sup Ct Review 1971 2-4, 15-28

3105. McGee v. United States   May 17, 1971   402 U. S. 479
       Criminal Law Revolution 312-313
       Private Conscience 51
       Significant Decisions 1970/71 32-33

3106. Bell v. Burson   May 24, 1971   402 U. S. 535
       Significant Decisions 1970/71 19-20

3107. Palmer v. Euclid, Ohio   May 24, 1971   402 U. S. 544
       *Cases Criml Justice 245-246
       *Cases Criml Law (Perkins) 2-4
       Significant Decisions 1970/71 21

3108. United States v. International Minerals   June 1, 1971   402 U. S. 558
          and Chemical Corporation
       *Criminal Law (Dix) 271-275
       *Text Legal Regulation 6-7

3109. Chicago and North Western Railway   June 1, 1971   402 U. S. 570
          v. United Transportation Union
       *Labor Law (Twomey) 70-74
       Significant Decisions 1970/71 30
       PERIODICALS:
       "Significant decisions in labor cases." Monthly Labor R 94:
       67-68 Oct '71.

3110. National Labor Relations Board   June 1, 1971   402 U.S. 600
       v. Natural Gas Utility District
       of Hawkins County, Tennessee
       *Labor Relations (Edwards) 40-44
       Significant Decisions 1970/71 29-30
       PERIODICALS:
       "Significant decisions in labor cases." Monthly Labor R 94: 75-
       76 Dec '71.

3111. Coates v. Cincinnati   June 1, 1971   402 U.S. 611
       *Cases Criml Law (Inbau) 406-410
       *Consttnl Law (Barrett) 1313-1317
       *Federal Courts 201-204
       Significant Decisions 1970/71 21-22

3112. Nelson v. O'Neill   June 1, 1971   402 U.S. 622
       Against 357-359
       *Cases Evidence 831-836
       Criminal Law Revolution 292-293
       *Principles Proof 318-321
       Significant Decisions 1970/71 17

3113. Perez v. Campbell   June 1, 1971   402 U.S. 637
       *Legal Environment 70-72
       *Sex Roles 220-224

3114. United States v. Armour and Co.   June 1, 1971   402 U.S. 673
       *Injunctions 394-398

3115. Gordon v. Lance   June 7, 1971   403 U.S. 1
       Consttnl Law (Barrett) 998-999
       Digest 13
       *Poverty 259-261
       Sup Ct Review 1971 280-281
       PERIODICALS:
       "One man, one vote doesn't apply in education," R. B. Marshall
          and R. M. Ritchie. Phi Delta Kappan 53: 248-249 Dec '71.

3116. Cohen v. California   June 7, 1971   403 U.S. 15
       Am Consttn (Kelly) 1001
       *Am Consttn (Lockhart) 810-814
       Am Politics 74-79
       *Bill (Cohen) 128-132
       *Bill (Konvitz) 219-224
       Brethren 129-133
       CQ Guide 407
       *Cases Consttnl Law (Gunther) 1230-1235
       *Cases Consttnl Rights 691-695
       *Cases Criml Law (Inbau) 212-217
       *Cases Individual 775-781
       *Civil Rights (Abernathy) 1977 424-425
       Communication (Hemmer) v. 1, 38-39
       *Consttnl Law (Barrett) 1262-1265
       *Consttnl Law (Grossman) 1217-1221
       *Consttnl Law (Lockhart) 1050-1053
       First Amendment (Berns) 188-190
       Free Speech (Kurland) 422-423, 424-425
       *Freedom of Speech (Haiman) 98-101
       God 198-199

Handbook 78-79
Justice Hugo Black 167-168
*Justices (Friedman) v. 5, 225-230
*Mass Communications 94-98
*Obscenity (Bosmajian) 269-272
Significant Decisions 1970/71 24-25
*Sup Ct and Criml Process 1073-1075
Sup Ct Review 1974 313-317
Sup Ct Review 1979 204-205

3117. Rosenbloom v. Metromedia, Inc.   June 7, 1971   403 U.S. 29
        CQ Guide 438
        Communication (Hemmer) v. 2, 61-64
        *Communications Law 441-499
        Crisis 211-212
        Freedom of the Press (Barron) 341-342
        Freedom of the Press (Schmidt) 77-79
        Handbook 235-238
        Individual 107
        *Justices (Friedman) v. 5, 275-288
        Law of Mass 106
        *Mass Communications 264-267
        *Mass Media (Devol) 223-225
        Mass Media (Francois) 95-97
        Significant Decisions 1970/71 25-26
        Sup Ct Review 1978 282
        PERIODICALS:
        "Justice White and the first amendment," Deckle McLean.
        Journalism Q 56: 305-310 Summer '79 (2).

3118. Griffin v. Breckenridge   June 7, 1971   403 U.S. 88
        By What Right 237
        *Cases Consttnl Law (Rosenblum) 509-515
        *Civil Rights (Abernathy) 1980 305-313
        *Consttnl Law (Barrett) 1094-1097
        *Consttnl Law (Freund) 864-866
        *Consttnl Law (Grossman) 553-557
        Great Events Worldwide 210-211
        Significant Decisions 1970/71 7-8

3119. Whitcomb v. Chavis   June 7, 1971   403 U.S. 124
        *Cases Consttnl Rights 1038-1042
        *Civil Rights (Abernathy) 1977 619-621
        Consttnl Counterrevolution 118-120
        *Consttnl Law (Grossman) 721-726
        *Processes 1205-1208
        *Race 179-190
        *Racial Equality 94-95
        Significant Decisions 1970/71 9
        Sup Ct Review 1973 25-26

3120. Abate v. Mundt   June 7, 1971   403 U.S. 182
        Consttnl Counterrevolution 125
        Sup Ct Review 1973 13-14

3121. United States v. Mitchell   June 7, 1971   403 U.S. 190
        *Land Ownership 274-281
        *Text Sex Based Discrimination 149-157

PERIODICALS:
"Supreme Court holds wife liable in Mitchell: a too harsh adher-
ance to precedence?" J. Chrys Dougherty. J Taxation 35:
296-298 Nov '71.

3122. Connell v. Higginbotham   June 7, 1971   403 U.S. 207
       *Bill (Konvitz) 309-311
       Communication (Hemmer) v. 1, 209-210
       Digest 62
       *Labor Relations (Edwards) 747-748
       *School Law (Alexander) 557

3123. Johnson v. Mississippi   June 7, 1971   403 U.S. 212
       *Cases Criml Justice 1022-1024
       Criminal Law Revolution 298-299

3124. Palmer v. Thompson   June 14, 1971   403 U.S. 217
       *Bill (Konvitz) 592-597
       Cases Consttnl Law (Gunther) 710-711
       *Cases Consttnl Law (Rosenblum) 177-186
       *Civil Rights (Abernathy) 1977 560-561
       *Consttnl Law (Barron) 583-585
       *Douglas 284-287
       Freedom and the Court 430
       *Judicial Crises 120-133
       *Justices (Friedman) v. 5, 195-198
       Private Pressure 172-173
       *Processes 1019-1027
       *Race 221-227
       Significant Decisions 1970/71 6
       Sup Ct Review 1071 06 146
       PERIODICALS:
       "Everybody out of the pool." Newsweek 77: 36 June 28 '71.
       "Swimming pools: black and white." America 124: 645 June
       26 '71.

3125. Amalgamated Association of Street,   June 14, 1971   403 U.S. 274
       Electric Railway and Motor Coach
       Employees v. Lockridge
       *Cases Labor (Leslie) 602-611
       *Cases Labor (Oberer) 367-377
       Significant Decisions 1970/71 31
       Sup Ct and Labor 64-68
       *Text Administrative Law 253-257

3126. Hodgson v. United Steelworkers   June 14, 1971   403 U.S. 333
       of America
       Significant Decisions 1970/71 31-32

3127. Commissioner of Internal Revenue v.   June 14, 1971   403 U.S. 345
       Lincoln Savings and Loan Association
       Significant Decisions 1970/71 34

3128. Graham v. Richardson   June 14, 1971   403 U.S. 365
       Sailor v. Leger
       *Am Consttn (Lockhart) 941-942
       *Cases Consttnl Rights 881-882
       *Consttnl Law (Barrett) 867-871
       *Consttnl Law (Kauper) 775-777

*Processes 577-581
Significant Decisions 1970/71 8-9
Sup Ct Review 1977 275, 294, 307-308

3129. Bivens v. Six Unknown Named Agents   June 21, 1971 403 U. S. 388
        of Federal Bureau of Narcotics
        Against 67-68, 70-74
        Brethren 68-69
        By What Right 293-294
        *Cases Criml Justice 753-763
        *Civil Liberties (Barker) 210-214
        *Civil Procedure (Carrington) 771-779
        *Civil Procedure (Cound) 190-195
        *Civil Rights (Abernathy) 1980 357-364
        *Consttnl Law (Freund) 867-868
        *Criminal Justice (Galloway) 127-133
        Criminal Law (Felkenes) 104-106
        *Criminal Law (Kadish) 945-948
        Criminal Law Revolution 273-275
        *Criminal Procedure (Lewis) 115-120
        *Elements Criminal 255-264
        Exclusionary 35-36
        *Exclusionary 97-105
        *Federal Courts 787-797
        Freedom Spent 236-238
        *Freedom vs National Security 571-575
        God 196-197
        *Introduction (Mashaw) 753-763
        *Justices (Friedman) v. 5, 474-481
        Law of Arrest (Creamer) 486-491
        *Law Power 184-193
        Law Power 193-197
        Self Inflicted Wound 124-129
        Significant Decisions 1970/71 12-13
        *Sup Ct and Criml Process 812-814
        *Teaching Materials 118-123
        PERIODICALS:
        "Supreme Court Review." J Criml Law, Crimlgy and Police Sci
        62: 480-485 Dec '71 (2).

3130. Jenness v. Fortson   June 21, 1971 403 U. S. 431
        Significant Decisions 1970/71 22

3131. Coolidge v. New Hampshire   June 21, 1971 403 U. S. 443
        Against 87-94
        *Arrest (Waddington) 143-144
        Arrest (Waddington) 148
        *Basic Criminal 298-308
        Brethren 116-119
        *Cases Civil Liberties 104-113
        *Cases Consttnl Law (Cushman) 334-343
        *Cases Criml Justice 325-336
        *Cases Criml Law (Hall) 778-781
        *Cases Electronic 893-899
        Communication (Hemmer) v. 1, 234
        *Consttnl Criml (Scarboro) 392-399
        *Consttnl Law (Klein) 71-88
        Criminal Law Revolution 262-267
        *Criminal Procedure (Lewis) 241-247

*Justices (Friedman) v. 5, 320-341
Law of Arrest (Creamer) 115-122
*Law of Arrest (Markle) 102-103
Law of Arrest (Markle) 135-136
*Leading Consttnl Cases 207-230
Police 202-205
Significant Decisions 1970/71 13
*Sup Ct and Criml Process 252-257
*Teaching Materials 319-332
PERIODICALS:
"Supreme Court Review. " J Criml Law, Crimlgy and Police Sci
   62: 480-485 Dec '71 (2).

3132. McKeiver v. Pennsylvania   June 21, 1971 403 U.S. 528
In re Burrus
Against 298-299
*Cases Civil Liberties 66-71
*Cases Consttnl Law (Cushman) 296-301
*Cases Criml Law (Perkins) 517-531
*Cases Law and Poverty 497-506
*Cases Modern 106-131
*Consttnl Law (Felkenes) 367-369
Criminal Law (Felkenes) 396-398
*Criminal Law (Kadish) 1438-1441
Criminal Law Revolution 289-291
Criminal Procedure (Wells) 214-215
Significant Decisions 1970/71 19
*Sup Ct and Criml Process 717-722
*Sup Ct and Rights 426-435
PERIODICALS:
"Children under the law," Hillary Rodham. Harvard Eductnl R
   43: 487-514 Nov '73 (5).
"From Burger: a call for action to stop freeing the guilty. "
   US News 71: 33 July 5 '71.
"Supreme Court Review. " J Criml Law, Crimlgy and Police Sci
   62: 497-504 Dec '71.

3133. United States v. Harris   June 28, 1971 403 U.S. 573
Against 84-87
Arrest (Waddington) 95-96
*Basic Criminal 238-243
*Cases Criml Justice 97-102
*Cases Criml Law (Hall) 770-774
*Criminal Evidence 237-238
Criminal Law (Felkenes) 55-58
*Criminal Law (Kadish) 849-854
Criminal Law Revolution 267-270
Law of Arrest (Creamer) 165-166
Law of Arrest (Markle) 212-217
*Leading Consttnl Cases 97-111
*Principles Arrest 331-333
Significant Decisions 1970/71 14
*Sup Ct and Criml Process 179-183
*Teaching Materials 231-236
PERIODICALS:
"Supreme Court Review. " J Criml Law, Crimlgy and Police Sci
   62: 485-488 Dec '71.

3134. Lemon v. Kurtzman   June 28, 1971 403 U.S. 602

Earley v. DiCenso
Robinson v. DiCenso
  Am Consttn (Kelly) 996-997
  *Am Consttn (Lockhart) 891-895
  *Bill (Konvitz) 66-76
  CQ Guide 467-468
  *Cases Consttnl Law (Rosenblum) 101-115
  *Cases Consttnl Rights 825-829
  *Cases Individual 1087-1091
  *Civil Liberties (Barker) 42-49
  *Civil Rights (Abernathy) 1977 282-284
  *Consttn (Morris) 388-402
  Consttnl Counterrevolution 252-253
  Consttnl Law (Barrett) 1458
  *Consttnl Law (Barron) 974-984
  *Consttnl Law (Freund) 1380-1385
  *Consttnl Law (Grossman) 1296-1302
  *Consttnl Law (Kauper) 1318-1327
  *Consttnl Law (Lockhart) 1191-1194
  Digest 21-23
  Education (Lapati) 178-183, 190-191
  Editorials 1971 857-865
  Freedom and the Court 315-316, 327
  Landmark Decisions 171-178
  Law and Education 284-285
  *Law and Public Education (Goldstein) 875-889
  *Law of Public Education 52-59
  Religious Freedom (Arnold) 47-48
  *Religious Freedom (Pfeffer) 29-31, 50-54
  School in the Legal Structure 81-82
  *School Law (Alexander) 195-204
  Significant Decisions 1970/71 27
  Sup Ct and Religion 110-112
  Sup Ct Review 1971 147-200
  Sup Ct Review 1973 67-68
PERIODICALS:
  "Aid to private schools," Michael P. Litka. Momentum 2: 4-9
    Feb '71.
  "Church in court." Economist 240: 55-56 July 10 '71.
  "Court considers aid to private schools," John Beckler. Sch Mgt
    15: 4-5 May '71.
  "Federal aid to parochial schools? and if so, how?" John Beckler.
    Sch Mgt 15: 4, 6 Nov '71.
  "First amendment is not for sale," Patrick S. Duffy. Phi Delta
    Kappan 52: 55-58 Sept '71.
  "Joker in private school aid," Stephen Arons. Sat R 54: 45-47,
    56 Jan 16 '71.
  "Lessons from the school aid decisions," Charles M. Whelan.
    America 125: 32-33 July 24 '71.
  "Parochaid decision," Leo Pfeffer. Todays Eductn 60: 63-64,
    79 Sept '71.
  "Parochiaid: more legal turmoil ahead." Natn's Sch 88: 9-10
    Aug '71. Reprint: Eductn Dig 37: 23-25 Nov '71.
  "Parochial opinion." Newsweek 78: 55 July 12 '71.
  "Parochial school tangle." Sat R 54: 48-49 Aug 21 '71.
  "Parochial school aid." New Republic 165: 7 July 10 '71.
  "School aid decisions," Charles M. Whelan. America 125: 8-11
    July 10 '71.

"Supreme Court cases: questions and answers, " Charles M.
Whelan. America 124: 372-375 Apr 10 '71.
"Supreme court considers problems of education, " John Beckler.
Sch Mgt 14: 6, 8 Oct '70.
"U.S. Supreme Court as prophet, " William W. Brickman. Sch
and Society 99: 330-331 Oct '71.

3135. Tilton v. Richardson   June 28, 1971 403 U.S. 672
        *Am Consttn (Lockhart) 895-901
        *Bill (Konvitz) 76-86
        CQ Guide 469-470
        *Cases Consttnl Rights 829-835
        *Cases Individual 1092-1096
        Consttnl Counterrevolution 253-255
        *Consttnl Law (Lockhart) 1195-1200
        *Consttnl Rights (Kemerer) 251-257
        *Douglas 160-165
        Education (Lapati) 175-178
        Freedom and the Court 324
        *Law and Public Education (Goldstein) 890-900
        Private Pressure 173
        Religious Freedom (Arnold) 50
        *Religious Freedom (Pfeffer) 69-73
        Significant Decisions 1970/71 27-28
        Sup Ct and Religion 108-110
        Sup Ct Review 1973 82-84
        Wall (Sorauf) 135-136
    PERIODICALS:
        "Church college and the scramble for public funds; Supreme Court
        ruling, " Judy Weldman. Christian Century 93: 883-885 Oct
        20 '76 (3).
        "Future of church-related colleges: implications of Tilton v. Rich-
        ardson, " E. D. Farwell. Liberal Eductn 58: 280-285 May
        '72.
        "Win one, lose one, " William C. McInnes. America 125: 170-
        173 Sept 18 '71.
        See also listing at 403 U.S. 602, entry no. 3134.

3136. Cassius Clay (Muhammad Ali) v.   June 28, 1971 403 U.S. 698
        United States
        Brethren 136-138
        *Cases Consttnl Law (Rosenblum) 575-580
        Criminal Law Revolution 311-312
        Editorials 1971 866-872
        Private Conscience 31
        *Race 414-417
        Significant Decisions 1970/71 32
    PERIODICALS:
        "Decision for Allah. " Newsweek 78: 61, 63 July 12 '71.
        "Don't call me champ. " Nation 213: 37 July 19 '71.

3137. New York Times Co. v. United   June 30, 1971 403 U.S. 713
        States
    United States v. Washington Post Co.
    "Pentagon Papers Case"
        Am Consttn (Kelly) 1026-1027
        *Am Consttn (Lockhart) 763-768
        *Am Consttnl Law (Bartholomew) v. 2, 97-99
        *Am Consttnl Law (Mason) 593-602

*Am Consttnl Law (Saye) 338-339
*Am Consttnl Law (Shapiro) 191-193
*Bill (Konvitz) 338-343
Brethren 140-150
CQ Guide 431-433
*Cases Civil Liberties 266-275
*Cases Consttnl Law (Cushman) 496-505
*Cases Consttnl Law (Gunther) 1507-1515
*Cases Consttnl Law (Rosenblum) 456-470
*Cases Consttnl Rights 643-649
*Cases Individual 924-935
*Civil Rights (Abernathy) 364-369
Communication (Hemmer) v. 2, 198-199
*Communications Law 373-423
Conceived 99-100
Consttn (Wilcox) 35-36
*Consttnl Aspects v. 4, 635-676
*Consttnl Law (Barrett) 1230-1237
Consttnl Law (Barron) 751-759
*Consttnl Law (Felkenes) 170-171
*Consttnl Law (Freund) 1149-1157
*Consttnl Law (Grossman) 1069-1083
*Consttnl Law (Kauper) 1183-1189
*Consttnl Law (Lockhart) 928-933
*Consttnl Rights (Kemerer) 149-153
Crisis 87, 127-129
*Documents History v. 2, 760-764
Douglas 215-219
Editorials 1971 798-844
*Federal System 99-103
*First Amendment (Franklin) 379-393
Freedom and the Court 186-188
*Freedom vs National Security 180-197
God 209-210
Handbook 43-50
Hugo Black (Dunne) 429-432
In His Own Image 180-214
*Injunctions 131-154
Justice Hugo Black 29-30
Law of Mass 47-53
*Law Power 479-496
*Leading Consttnl Decisions 274-285
*Mass Communications 120-137
*Mass Media (Devol) 43-52
Mass Media (Devol) 61-68; reprinted from "Free at last, at least,"
    Jack London. The Quill 59: 7+ Aug '71.
Mass Media (Francois) 39-41, 43-48
Media and the First Amendment 45-47
Papers.
*Pentagon Papers 101-128
Perspectives (Rembar) 131-147
Power 230-231
Press Freedoms 133-193
Role (Cox) 37-38
Significant Decisions 1970/71 25-26
Spirit 60
Sup Ct (Forte) 74
Sup Ct and Commander in Chief 181-188
Sup Ct Review 1971 285-289

Sup Ct Review 1972 319-321
Sup Ct Review 1974 61-62
Sup Ct Review 1978 284-285
PERIODICALS:
"The case of the Pentagon papers." America 125: 6-7 July
10 '71.
"Court allows publication of Pentagon study." Pub Weekly 200:
51 July 12 '71.
"Court ruling on secrets--where will it lead?" US News 71: 22-
24 July 12 '71.
"Freedom of the press." Senior Scholastic 107: 6-10 Jan 13 '76
(3).
"The great cases that made great law; right to publish," Nathan
Lewin. New Republic 165: 11-13 July 10 '71.
"Just one cheer." Nation 213: 35-36 July 19 '71.
"No censorship by government," R. H. Smith. Pub Weekly 200:
57 July 12 '71.
"Paper victory," Charles Rembar. Atlantic 228: 61-66 Nov '71.
Reaction: A. M. Rosenthal. 228: 46, 48 Dec '71.
"Press wins and presses roll." Time 98: 10-12 July 12 '71.
"Secrets and security; postscript to the Pentagon Papers." Com-
monweal 94: 399-402 Aug 6 '71.
*"Texts of Supreme Court opinions on publishing Viet War docu-
mentary." Editor and Pub 104: 11-19 July 10 '71.
*"Three points of view from the Court." Time 98: 10-11 July
12 '71.
"Toward the legal showdown; Pentagon papers." Time 98: 13
July 5 '71.
"Victory for the press." Newsweek 78: 16-17, 19 July 12 '71;
⁺78: 18 July 12 '71.
"You can do that." Publishers Weekly 200: 37 Aug 2 '71 (3).

3138. Arciniega v. Freeman   Oct 26, 1971   404 U.S. 4
      *US Prison Law v. 4, 239

3139. Superintendent of Insurance of   Nov 8, 1971   404 U.S. 6
      New York v. Bankers Life and
      Casualty Co.
      Significant Decisions 1971/72 57-58

3140. Reed v. Reed   Nov 22, 1971   404 U.S. 71
      *Bill (Cohen) 681-682
      *Bill (Konvitz) 498-501
      CQ Guide 632
      *Civil Rights (Abernathy) 1977 564-565
      *Civil Rights (Pious) 116-118
      *Consttnl Law (Barrett) 877-879
      *Consttnl Law (Grossman) 615-618
      *Consttnl Law (Klein) 557-560
      Editorials 1071 1513-1517
      Great Reversals 184, 189-191
      *Sex Discrimination 1975 109-111
      *Sex Roles 514-517
      Significant Decisions 1971/72 30-31
      Sup Ct Review 1972 157-160, 162, 250-251
      *Text Consttnl Aspects 60-66
      *Text Sex Based Discrimination 60-66
      *Woman 26-27

PERIODICALS:
"ERA: losing battles, but winning the war," James J. Kilpatrick.
Natns Bus 67: 15-16 Oct '79 (4).
"First no to sex bias." Time 98: 71 Dec 6 '71.
"Ladies day." Newsweek 78: 23-24 Dec 6 '71.
"Woman's place in the Constitution: the Supreme Court and gender
discrimination," Betsey Levin. High Sch J 59: 31-45 Oct '75
(3).

3141.   Richardson v. Belcher   Nov 22, 1971   404 U.S. 78
        Sup Ct Review 1972 257-258

3142.   Chevron Oil Co. v. Huson   Dec 6, 1971   404 U.S. 97
        *Consttnl Law (Barrett) 37-38

3143.   National Labor Relations Board v.   Dec 6, 1971   404 U.S. 116
          Plasterers' Local Union No. 79
        Texas State Tile and Terrazzo Co. v.
          Plasterers' Local Union
        *Cases Labor (Oberer) 497-502
        *Labor Law (Twomey) 232-237
        Significant Decisions 1971/72 56
        Sup Ct and Labor 162-164
        PERIODICALS:
        "Significant decisions in labor cases." Monthly Labor R 95: 58-
        59 Mar '72.

3144.   National Labor Relations Board v.   Dec 8, 1971   404 U.S. 138
          Nash-Finch Co. dba Jack and
          Jill Stores
        Significant Decisions 1971/72 44-45

3145.   Allied Chemical and Alkali Workers   Dec 8, 1971   404 U.S. 157
          of America v. Pittsburgh Plate
          Glass Co.
        National Labor Relations Board v.
          Pittsburgh Plate Glass Co.
        *Cases Labor (Leslie) 406-410
        *Collective Bargaining 49-55
        Significant Decisions 1971/72 55-56
        PERIODICALS:
        "Significant decisions in labor cases." Monthly Labor R 95:
        56-58 Mar '72.

3146.   Mayer v. City of Chicago   Dec 13, 1971   404 U.S. 189
        *Poverty 61-65
        Significant Decisions 1971/72 10
        PERIODICALS:
        "Supreme Court review." J Criml Law, Crimlgy and Police Sci
        63: 513-517 Dec '72 (2).

3147.   Britt v. North Carolina   Dec 13, 1971   404 U.S. 226
        Significant Decisions 1971/72 10-11
        PERIODICALS:
        See listing at 404 U.S. 189, entry no. 3146.

3148.   Wilwording v. Swenson   Dec 14, 1971   404 U.S. 249
        *Civil Rights (Abernathy) 1980 144-145

Criminal Law (Felkenes) 410-411
*US Prison Law v. 2, 444-448

3149. Santobello v. New York   Dec 20, 1971 404 U.S. 257
       *Cases Criml Justice 1163-1167
       *Cases Criml Law (Hall) 995-998
       *Civil Rights (Abernathy) 1977 241-243
       *Consttnl Law (Felkenes) 381-382
       *Consttnl Law (Klein) 516-519
       Criminal Law (Felkenes) 286-289
       *Criminal Procedure (Lewis) 555-557
       Defendants 232-233
       Significant Decisions 1971/72 16-17
       *Sup Ct and Criml Process 994-997
       Sup Ct Review 1972 303
       *US Prison Law v. 1, 13-25

3150. Picard v. Connor   Dec 20, 1971 404 U.S. 270
       Significant Decisions 1971/72 22

3151. Townsend v. Swank   Dec 20, 1971 404 U.S. 282
       Alexander v. Swank
       *Cases Law and Poverty 159-164
       *Legal Problems 634-637
       Significant Decisions 1971/72 61
       Sup Ct Review 1972 256-257

3152. United States v. Campos-Serrano   Dec 20, 1971 404 U.S. 293
       *Legislative (Hetzel) 331-335

3153. United States v. Marion   Dec 20, 1971 404 U.S. 307
       Against 373-374
       Criminal Law (Felkenes) 263-266
       *Criminal Law (Kadish) 1204-1206
       *Criminal Procedure (Lewis) 524-527
       Defendants 115-116
       *Douglas 381-387
       *Due Process 105
       *Leading Consttnl Cases 646-650
       Significant Decisions 1971/72 19-20
       *Sup Ct and Criml Process 661-663
       Sup Ct Review 1972 279-280
       *Text Social Issues 26-29

3154. United States v. Bass   Dec 20, 1971 404 U.S. 336
       *Law Power 99-107
       Sup Ct Review 1974 46

3155. Schilb v. Kuebel   Dec 20, 1971 404 U.S. 357
       *Consttnl Law (Felkenes) 343-345
       *Consttnl Law (Klein) 393-399
       Criminal Law (Felkenes) 299-302
       Significant Decisions 1971/72 20-21
       *Sup Ct and Criml Process 957-963
       Sup Ct Review 1972 277-278

3156. Reliance Electric Co. v. Emerson Jan 11, 1972 404 U.S. 418
           Electric Co.
       Significant Decisions 1971/72 58-59

3157. Lego v. Twomey   Jan 12, 1972   404 U.S. 477
       Against 164-165
       *Basic Criminal 755-763
       *Due Process 84
       Police 240-241
       *Principles Proof 164-170
       Significant Decisions 1971/72 16
       Sup Ct Review 1972 289-290
       *US Prison Law 1093-1100
       PERIODICALS:
       "Supreme Court review." J Criml Law, Crimlgy and Police Sci
       63: 509-513 Dec '72.

3158. Groppi v. Leslie   Jan 13, 1972   404 U.S. 496
       *Legislation (Linde) 121-126
       *Legislative (Hetzel) 672-676
       Significant Decisions 1971/72 27

3159. California Motor Transport Co. v. Jan 13, 1972   404 U.S. 508
       Trucking Unlimited
       *Antitrust (Posner) 314-318
       *Antitrust Analysis 417-420
       *Modern Business 153-155
       Significant Decisions 1971/72 52

3160. Haines v. Kerner   Jan 13, 1972   404 U.S. 519
       Civil Procedure (Carrington) 545-546
       *Elements Civil 602-603
       *US Prison Law v. 2, 149-150

3161. Love v. Pullman Co.   Jan 17, 1972   404 U.S. 522
       United States v. Pullman Co.
       *Cases Employment 926-929
       Sup Ct Review 1972 197-198

3162. University of Texas System Board Jan 24, 1972   404 U.S. 541
       of Regents v. New Left Education
       Project
       Sup Ct Review 1972 234-235

3163. Lee v. Runge   Oct 19, 1971   404 U.S. 887
       *Cases Copyright (Kaplan) 180-184
       *Cases Copyright (Nimmer) 21-25

3164. Spencer v. Kugler   Jan 17, 1972   404 U.S. 1027
       Disaster 161
       Education (Lapati) 305

3165. Winston-Salem/Forsyth County Board Aug 31, 1971 404 U.S. 1221
       of Education v. Scott
       Disaster 137-141

3166. Harris v. United States   Aug 31, 1971   404 U.S. 1232
       *Douglas 388-390

3167. Roudebush v. Hartke   Feb 23, 1972   405 U.S. 15
       CQ Guide 173
       *Douglas 9-12
       Significant Decisions 1971/72 46-47

3168. Parisi v. Davidson   Feb 23, 1972   405 U.S. 34
      *Text Administrative Law 143-145

3169. Lindsey v. Normet   Feb 23, 1972   405 U.S. 56
      *Cases Property (Donahue) 771-777
      Consttnl Law (Barrett) 924-925
      *Legal Problems 383-389
      *Poverty 103-109
      Significant Decisions 1971/72 32-33
      Sup Ct Review 1972 310-311
      PERIODICALS:
      "Supreme Court tells tenants: you can't withhold rent for lack of
      repairs." House and Home 41: 47 Apr '72.

3170. United States v. Generes   Feb 23, 1972   405 U.S. 93
      Significant Decisions 1971/72 60-61

3171. National Labor Relations Board v.   Feb 23, 1972   405 U.S. 117
      Scrivener dba AA Electric Co.
      *Legal Environment 445-447
      Significant Decisions 1971/72 57
      PERIODICALS:
      "Significant decisions in labor cases." Monthly Labor R 95: 58-
      59 May '72.

3172. Duncan v. Tennessee   Feb 23, 1972   405 U.S. 127
      Sup Ct Review 1972 269

3173. Bullock v. Carter   Feb 24, 1972   405 U.S. 134
      *Civil Rights (Abernathy) 1977 584-586
      Consttnl Law (Barrett) 954
      *Poverty 248-252
      Significant Decisions 1971/72 35
      PERIODICALS:
      "Supreme Court and school finance: some possibilities," H. L.
      Preston. Phi Delta Kappan 54: 120-123 Oct '72 (5).

3174. Papachristou v. City of Jacksonville   Feb 24, 1972   405 U.S. 156
      *Bill (Konvitz) 19-25
      *Cases Criml Law (Hall) 50-55
      *Cases Criml Law (Inbau) 400-406
      *Criminal Justice 31-35
      *Criminal Law (Dix) 163-167
      *Criminal Law (Kadish) 194-198
      *Criminal Law (Wells) 62
      *Historic Documents 1972 207-211
      *Introduction (Mashaw) 225-229
      Significant Decisions 1971/72 22
      Sup Ct Review 1972 286-287
      PERIODICALS:
      "Supreme Court review." J Criml Law, Crimlgy and Police Sci
      63: 496-499 Dec '72.

3175. D. H. Overmyer Co., Inc.   Feb 24, 1972   405 U.S. 174
      v. Frick Co.
      *Civil Procedure (Carrington) 53-58
      Significant Decisions 1971/72 24
      Sup Ct Review 1972 311-312

534   U.S. Supreme Court Decisions

PERIODICALS:
"Supreme Court cases affecting the rights of debtors and creditors,"
Albert F. Reisman. Credit and Financial Management 74: 16-
17, 40 Nov '72 (4).

3176. Swarb v. Lennox   Feb 24, 1972   405 U.S. 191
       Significant Decisions 1971/72 25
       PERIODICALS:
       See listing at 405 U.S. 174, entry no. 3175.

3177. Federal Trade Commission v. Sperry   Mar 1, 1972   405 U.S. 233
       and Hutchinson Co.
       *Cases Food 847-849
       Mass Media (Francois) 395
       *Modern Business 1035-1037
       Significant Decisions 1971/72 53
       PERIODICALS:
       "High court's decision on S&H supports FTC." Adv Age   43: 8
       Mar 6 '72.

3178. Hawaii v. Standard Oil Co.   Mar 1, 1972   405 U.S. 251
       v. California
       *Antitrust (Posner) 153-159
       *Civil Procedure (Carrington) 1193-1198
       Significant Decisions 1971/72 52-53

3179. Adams v. Illinois   Mar 6, 1972   405 U.S. 278
       Significant Decisions 1971/72 9
       Sup Ct Review 1972 271-272

3180. Rabe v. Washington   Mar 20, 1972 405 U.S. 313
       Communication (Hemmer) v. 1, 201-202
       *Obscenity (Bosmajian) 195-196
       Sup Ct Review 1972 225-226

3181. Cruz v. Beto   Mar 20, 1972 405 U.S. 319
       *Bill (Konvitz) 507-510
       *Criminal Justice (Way) 526
       *Religious Freedom (Pfeffer) 143-144
       *US Prison Law v. 3, 112-117

3182. Dunn v. Blumstein   Mar 21, 1972 405 U.S. 330
       *Am Consttnl Law (Saye) 480-482
       By What Right 262-263
       *Cases Civil Liberties 405-412
       *Cases Consttnl Law (Cushman) 635-643
       *Civil Rights (Abernathy) 1977 581-583
       *Consttnl Law (Barrett) 935-936, 950-951
       *Historic Documents 1972 283-290
       Rise 152-153
       *Sex Discrimination 1975 84-86
       Significant Decisions 1971/72 34-35
       Sup Ct Review 1972 206-209
       Sup Ct Review 1973 29-30
       PERIODICALS:
       See listing at 405 U.S. 134, entry no. 3173.

3183. Fein v. Selective Service System Mar 21, 1972 405 U.S. 365
       *Judicial Crises 223-229

Significant Decisions 1971/72 59
*Text Administrative Law 146-149

3184. Commissioner of Internal Revenue v.   Mar 21, 1972   405 U.S. 394
First Security Bank of Utah
Significant Decisions 1971/72 59-60
PERIODICALS:
"First Security Bank of Utah taxpayer disability and the Supreme
Court," Paul A. Teschner. Taxes 50: 260-273 May '72.
"Supreme Court's decisions in 482 case is not as limited as first
appeared," Leon M. Nad and Charles T. Crawford. J Taxation
37: 226-230 Oct '72.

3185. Schneble v. Florida   Mar 21, 1972   405 U.S. 427
Against 359-361
Sup Ct Review 1972 288

3186. Eisenstadt v. Baird   Mar 22, 1972   405 U.S. 438
Brethren 175-176
*Cases Domestic 311-318
*Cases Environmental Law (Hanks) 150-154
*Cases Individual 474-478
Communication (Hemmer) v. 1, 249-250
*Consttnl Law (Barron) 709-712
*Douglas 236-240
*Patent 85-88
*Processes 566-572
*Rights (Shattuck) 113-114
*Sex Roles 122-130
Significant Decisions 1971/72 31-32
Sup Ct Review 1972 247-249
Sup Ct Review 1979 197-198
*Text Sex Based Discrimination 335-344
*Woman 183

3187. Loper v. Beto   Mar 22, 1972   405 U.S. 473
Significant Decisions 1971/72 9-10
Sup Ct Review 1972 272-273

3188. Gooding v. Wilson   Mar 23, 1972   405 U.S. 518
*Bill (Cohen) 133-135
*Bill (Konvitz) 214-219
*Cases Criml Law (Inbau) 412-416
*Civil Rights (Abernathy) 1977 426-427
Communication (Hemmer) v. 1, 31-32
*Processes 1262-1265
PERIODICALS:
"Supreme Court Review." J Criml Law, Crimlgy and Police Sci
63: 492-496 Dec '72.

3189. Lynch v. Household Finance   Mar 23, 1972   405 U.S. 538
Corporation
*Cases Federal Courts 261-266
*Due Process 204
*Federal Courts 951-956
Significant Decisions 1971/72 43-44
Sup Ct Review 1972 313-314

3190. Ford v. United States   Mar 29, 1972   405 U.S. 562

PERIODICALS:
"Ford starts Motorcraft push in wake of high court move." Adv
   Age 43: 8 Apr 3 '72.
"Justice wins two and files three." Bus Wk p. 28 Apr 1 '72
   (2).

3191. United States v. Topco Associates, Inc. Mar 29, 1972 405 U.S. 596
      *Antitrust Analysis 370-375
      *Modern Business 1003-1007
      *Selected Antitrust Cases 346-355
      Significant Decisions 1971/72 51
      PERIODICALS:
      "Congress must OK closed area pacts for private brands." Adv
         Age 43: 2, 67 Apr 3 '72.
      "Justice wins two and files three." Bus Wk p. 28 Apr 1 '72
         (2).

3192. Alexander v. Louisiana   Apr 3, 1972   405 U.S. 625
      *Consttnl Law (Felkenes) 191-193
      *Criminal Justice (Way) 363-365
      *Criminal Procedure (Lewis) 423-426
      *Douglas 277-284
      *Law Power 632-635
      *Sex Discrimination 1975 99-100
      *Sex Roles 83-88
      Significant Decisions 1971/72 23
      *Sup Ct and Criml Process 525-528
      Sup Ct Review 1972 282-284

3193. Stanley v. Illinois   Apr 3, 1972   405 U.S. 645
      By What Right 301-302
      *Cases Domestic 722-731
      *Cases Law and Poverty 465-468
      *Due Process 208, 249
      *Sex Roles 288-298
      Significant Decisions 1971/72 26
      Sup Ct Review 1972 157-160, 162, 252-253
      Text Consttnl Aspects appendix 1-10
      *Text Sex Based Discrimination 299-308
      *Woman 172-174
      PERIODICALS:
      "Legal rights of unmarried fathers," Rita Dukette and Nicholas
         Stevenson. Socl Service R 47: 1-15 Mar '73 (2).
      "Unmarried father revisited," Reuben Pannor and Byron W. Evans.
         J Sch Health 45: 286-291 May '75.

3194. Carter v. Stanton   Apr 3, 1972   405 U.S. 669
      *Civil Rights (Abernathy) 1980 137-138

3195. Cole v. Richardson   Apr 18, 1972   405 U.S. 676
      *Am Consttn (Lockhart) 610-613
      *Bill (Konvitz) 311-315
      Cases Consttnl Law (Gunther) 1469-1470
      *Cases Consttnl Rights 418-421
      Communication (Hemmer) v. 1, 210-211
      Consttnl Law (Barrett) 1201-1202
      *Consttnl Law (Barron) 788-792
      *Consttnl Law (Lockhart) 752-754
      Digest 62-63

Editorials 1972 573-575
*Labor Relations (Edwards) 748-751
Significant Decisions 1971/72 38-39
Sup Ct Review 1972 240
*Text Social Issues 95-98

3196. Evansville-Vanderburgh Airport   Apr 19, 1972   405 U.S. 707
       Authority District v. Delta Airlines, Inc.
       Northeast Airlines, Inc. v. New Hampshire
       Aeronautics Commission
       *Consttnl Law (Barrett) 438-442
       *Consttnl Law (Barron) 301-306
       Significant Decisions 1971/72 47

3197. Sierra Club v. Morton   Apr 19, 1972   405 U.S. 727
       Brethren 163-165
       *Cases Consttnl Law (Rosenblum) 224-233
       *Cases Environmental Law (Hanks) 88-92, 205-213
       *Cases Property (Donahue) 430-437
       *Environmental 625-634
       In His Own Image 281
       *Introduction (Mashaw) 832-838
       *Legal Environment 172-174
       Power 37-38
       Significant Deicisions 1971/72 45-46
       Sup Ct Review 1972 308-310
       PERIODICALS:
       "Commentary: California's Mineral King valley," Peter Browning.
            Harper's Mag 245: 102-103 Aug '72.
       "Disputing Disney." Time 99: 62 May 1 '72.
       *"Mr. Justice Douglas, dissenting," William O. Douglas. Living
            Wilderness 36: 19-29 Summer '72.
       *"Nature's constitutional rights," William O. Douglas. North
            American R 258: 11-14 Spring '73.
       "Sierra Club foiled in High Court," C. Holden. Science 176:
            494 May 5 '72.
       "Supreme Court and Mickey Mouse," Jeanne Nienaber. Am
            Forests 78: 28-31, 40-43 July '72.

3198. Addonizio v. United States   Feb 22, 1972   405 U.S. 936
       *Douglas 404-408

3199. Joseph v. United States   Mar 27, 1972   405 U.S. 1006
       *Race 404-407

3200. S & E Contractors, Inc. v.   Apr 24, 1972   406 U.S. 1
       United States
       Significant Decisions 1971/72 61-62

3201. Illinois v. City of Milwaukee,   Apr 24, 1972   406 U.S. 91
       Wisconsin
       *Cases Environmental Law (Hanks) 814-820
       Significant Decisions 1971/72 43

3202. Weber v. Aetna Casualty and   Apr 24, 1972   406 U.S. 164
       Surety Co.
       *Am Consttnl Law (Saye) 466-468
       *Am Consttnl Law (Shapiro) 590-593
       *Bill (Konvitz) 510-516

*Cases Law and Poverty 461-465
*Comparative 355-358
*Consttnl Law (Barron) 716-718
*Courts Judges 504-509
Significant Decisions 1971/72 31
Sup Ct Review 1972 253-255
*Text Sex Based Discrimination 280-288
PERIODICALS:
"Justice for black Americans 200 years after independence: the
Afro-American before the Burger court, 1969-1976," Robert
L. Gill. Negro Eductn R 27: 271-317 July '76 (9).

3203. Sixty-seventh Minnesota Senate   Apr 29, 1972   406 U.S. 187
       v. Beens
       Sup Ct Review 1972 202-203

3204. Wisconsin v. Yoder   May 15, 1972   406 U.S. 205
       "Amish School Case"
       *Am Consttn (Lockhart) 916-921
       *Am Consttnl Law (Saye) 288-290
       *Bill (Cohen) 413-420
       *Bill (Konvitz) 96-100
       CQ Guide 460
       *Cases Consttnl Law (Gunther) 1592-1597
       *Cases Consttnl Rights 853-858
       *Cases Domestic 769-772
       *Cases Individual 1117-1123
       *Cases Law and Poverty 529-531
       *Civil Liberties (Barker) 54-60
       Civil Rights (Schimmel) 129-135
       *Comparative 479-483
       Compulsory 99-148
       *Compulsory 149-181
       *Consttn (Morris) 82-99
       *Consttnl Law (Barrett) 1489-1494
       *Consttnl Law (Barron) 940-945
       *Consttnl Law (Grossman) 1292-1297
       *Consttnl Law (Lockhart) 1223-1227
       *Consttnl Rights (Kemerer) 292-299
       Digest 24
       *Douglas 140-146
       Editorials 1972 703-706
       Education (Lapati) 159-162
       *Educational Policy 10-25
       First Amendment (Berns) 37-38
       Freedom and the Court 283
       *Judicial Excerpts 13-15
       *Justices (Friedman) v. 5, 209-212
       Landmark Decisions 189-198
       Law and Education 196
       *Law and Public Education (Goldstein) 37-57
       *Law of Public Education 561-567
       *Law Power 330-339
       Private Conscience 169-171
       *Religious Freedom (Pfeffer) 155-161
       *School in the Legal Structure 34
       *School Law (Alexander) 277-285
       Significant Decisions 1971/72 41
       Sup Ct (Forte) 79-80

*Sup Ct and Criml Process 1087-1091
Sup Ct and Religion 160-161
Sup Ct Review 1972 215-219
Sup Ct Review 1979 335
*Text Social Issues 207-213
PERIODICALS:
"Agony of the Amish, exodus from America?" Sch and Society
   100: 281-282 Summer '72.
"Amish and the Supreme Court," Joe Wittmer.   Phi Delta Kappan
   54: 50-52 Sept '72.
"Amish case," Russell Kirk.   Natl R   24:   747   July 7 '72.
"Amish ruling and religious liberty." Eductn Dig 38: 36-37 Dec
   '72. Condensed from: Church and State 25: 6-7 July/Aug '72.
"Catholics and the Amish," Jim Castelli.   Commonweal 96: 331-
   332 June 16 '72. Reaction: W. C. Lindholm.   96: 419, 437
   Aug 11 '72.
"Children under the law," Hillary Rodham.   Harvard Eductnl R
   43: 487-514 Nov '73 (5).
"Compulsory education: the plain people resist," Stephen Arons.
   Sat R 55: 52-57 Jan 15 '72.
"Court finds for the Amish." America 126: 554 May 27 '72.
"Court upholds Amish exemption from compulsory school laws."
   Christian Century 89: 627 May 31 '72.
"Forced schooling," B. Frank Brown.   Phi Delta Kappan 54:
   324 Jan '73.
"Ratiocinations; religion and exemption from a law; the Amish,"
   Walter Berns. Harper's Mag 246: 36, 40, 42 Mar '73.
   Reaction: Paul Marcus 246: 113 May '73.
"Right to be different." Time 99: 67 May 29 '72.
"SR education update; the Amish." Sat R 55: 49 June 24 '72.
"Victory for the Amish." Newsweek 79: 89 May 29 '72.
*"Wisconsin v. Yoder." Current History 63: 82 Aug '72
"Yoder and free exercise," Peter J. Riza. J Law and Eductn
   6: 449-472 Oct '77.

3205. Dukes v. Warden, Connecticut   Mar 15, 1972 406 U.S. 250
       State Prison
       Against 226-227
       Significant Decisions 1971/72 17

3206. National Labor Relations Board v.   May 15, 1972 406 U.S. 272
       Burns International Security
       Services, Inc.
       Basic Text 120-124
       *Cases Labor (Leslie) 571-580
       *Cases Labor (Oberer) 732-743
       *Collective Bargaining 417-428
       Significant Decisions 1971/72 54-55
       Sup Ct and Labor 141-147
       PERIODICALS:
       "Court clarifies bargaining rule." US News 72: 75 May 29 '72.
       "Significant decisions in labor cases." Monthly Labor R 95: 65-
          66 Sept '72.
       "Significant decisions in labor cases." Monthly Labor R 96: 67-
          68 Jan '73.

3207. United States v. Biswell   May 15, 1972 406 U.S. 311
       *Admin Law (Schwartz) 176-178
       *Cases Criml Justice 314-319

*Cases Food 722-724
*Consttnl Criml (Scarboro) 255-258
Defendants 276-277
Significant Decisions 1971/72 13

3208. Johnson v. Louisiana   May 22, 1972   406 U. S. 356
      Against 277-288
      CQ Guide 531
      Criminal Law (Felkenes) 313-316
      *Criminal Law (Kadish) 1325-1326
      *Criminal Procedure (Lewis) 38-48
      *Documents History v. 2, 769-772
      *Douglas 392-397
      *Due Process 12-13, 124-125
      Editorials 1972 697-703
      *Historic Documents 1972 423
      *Leading Consttnl Cases 700-713
      Police 269-270
      Procedures 199
      Significant Decisions 1971/72 6-7
      *Sup Ct and Criml Process 598-603
      *Sup Ct and Rights 66-76
      Sup Ct Review 1978 204-208
      PERIODICALS:
      "Annals of law: trial by jury," Richard Harris. New Yorker 48:
          117-125 Dec 16 '72 (2).
      "Backward run backward." Natl R 24: 629 June 9 '72.
      "Jury decision models and the Supreme Court," Bernard Grofman.
          Policy Studies J 8: 749-772 Spring '80 (4).
      "Law and order cases; Powell's day," Alexander M. Bickel. New
          Republic 166: 11-12 June 10 '72. Reaction: Robert L. Bard.
          167: 32-33 Sept 9 '72 (3).
      "Nixon radicals." Time 99: 65 June 5 '72 (2).
      "Nixon way." Newsweek 79: 39 June 5 '72 (2).
      "Supreme Court review." J Criml Law, Crimlgy and Police Sci
          63: 500-505 Dec '72 (2).

3209. Apodaca v. Oregon   May 22, 1972   406 U. S. 404
      Against 276-277, 288-298
      Brethren 222-223
      *Cases Civil Liberties 206-212
      *Cases Consttnl Law (Cushman) 436-442
      *Cases Criml Justice 1240-1253
      *Civil Rights (Abernathy) 1977 232-235
      *Consttnl Law (Freund) 1038-1040
      *Criminal Justice (Way) 375-378
      Criminal Law (Felkenes) 316-318
      *Criminal Law (Kadish) 1327-1330
      *Elements Criminal 143-151
      *Leading Consttnl Cases 714-717
      *Procedures 200-202
      Significant Decisions 1971/72 7
      Sup Ct (Forte) 63
      Sup Ct Review 1972 284-285
      Sup Ct Review 1978 204-208
      *Teaching Materials 43-50
      PERIODICALS:
      "Annals of law: trial by jury," Richard Harris. New Yorker
          48: 117-125 Dec 16 '72 (2).

"Jury decision models and the Supreme Court," Bernard Grofman.
Policy Studies J 8: 749-772 Spring '80 (4).

3210. Kastigar v. United States   May 22, 1972 406 U.S. 441
Against 173-174, 181-187
*Cases Civil Liberties 139-144
*Cases Consttnl Law (Cushman) 369-374
*Cases Criml Justice 1299-1309
*Cases Evidence 1169-1188
*Civil Rights (Abernathy) 1977 160-163
*Criminal Justice (Way) 170-174
Criminal Law (Felkenes) 248-250
*Criminal Law (Kadish) 1013-1014
*Criminal Procedure (Lewis) 404-409
Defendants 327-328
*Due Process 65-66
Freedom Spent 387-388
*Leading Consttnl Cases 586-594
Police 227-228
*Principles Proof 673-691
Significant Decisions 1971/72 14
*Sup Ct and Criml Process 468-472
Sup Ct Review 1972 298-301
PERIODICALS:
"Law and order cases; Powell's day," Alexander M. Bickel. New
Republic 166: 11-12 June 10 '72. Reaction: Robert L.
Bard. 167: 32-33 Sept 9 '72 (3).
"Nixon radicals." Time 99: 65 June 5 '72 (2).
"Nixon way." Newsweek 79: 39 June 5 '72 (2).
"Supreme Court review." J Criml Law, Crimlgy and Police Sci
63: 505-509 Dec '72.

3211. Zicarelli v. New Jersey State Com-   May 22, 1972 406 U.S. 472
mission of Investigation
*Consttnl Law (Felkenes) 286-288
Criminal Law (Felkenes) 251-252
Significant Decisions 1971/72 15
*Text Administrative Law 236-238
PERIODICALS:
"Law and order cases; Powell's day," Alexander M. Bickel. New
Republic 166: 11-12 June 10 '72. Reaction: Robert L. Bard.
167: 32-33 Sept 9 '72 (3).

3212. International Union of Operating   May 30, 1972 406 U.S. 487
Engineers, Local 150 v. Flair
Builders, Inc.
Significant Decisions 1971/72 56-57

3213. Lake Carriers' Association v.   May 30, 1972 406 U.S. 498
MacMullan
*Civil Rights (Abernathy) 1980 157-160
Significant Decisions 1971/72 42-43

3214. Deepsouth Packing Co. v. Laitram   May 30, 1972 406 U.S. 518
Corporation
*Legal Regulation 1046-1051

3215. Jefferson v. Hackney   May 30, 1972 406 U.S. 535
*Cases Law and Poverty 268-279

*Consttnl Law (Barrett) 782-784
*Legal Problems 693-697, 823-834
*Poverty 707-720
Significant Decisions 1971/72 36
Sup Ct Review 1972 258-260

3216. Socialist Labor Party v. Gilligan   May 30, 1972   406 U.S. 583
        *Consttnl Law (Barron) 106-108

3217. Carleson v. Remillard   June 7, 1972   406 U.S. 598
        *Cases Law and Poverty 174-177
        *Legal Problems 637-640

3218. Brooks v. Tennessee   June 7, 1972   406 U.S. 605
        Against 313-314
        Significant Decisions 1971/72 15-16

3219. United States v. Midwest Video   June 7, 1972   406 U.S. 649
        Corporation
        Communication (Hemmer) v. 2, 267-268
        *Mass Communications 960-966
        PERIODICALS:
        "High court gives FCC firmer grip on cables." Broadcasting 82:
            19-20 June 12 '72.
        "TV, CATV factions split on court ruling," J. Revett. Adv Age
            43: 2, 77 June 12 '72.

3220. Kirby v. Illinois   June 7, 1972   406 U.S. 682
        Against 242-252
        *Basic Criminal 626-629
        *Cases Criml Justice 697-702
        *Cases Criml Law (Hall) 891-893
        Consttnl Counterrevolution 180-181
        *Consttnl Criml (Marks) 272-275
        *Consttnl Law (Felkenes) 315-317
        Criminal Evidence 487-488
        *Criminal Justice (Galloway) 175-180
        Criminal Law (Felkenes) 202-204
        *Criminal Law (Kadish) 1036-1038
        *Leading Consttnl Cases 610-614
        Police 245
        *Principles Arrest 152-153
        Significant Decisions 1971/72 8
        *Sup Ct and Rights 323-329
        Sup Ct Review 1972 273-275
        *Teaching Materials 507-510
        PERIODICALS:
        "Supreme Court Review." J Criml Law, Crimlgy and Police
            Sci 63: 478-483 Dec '72.

3221. Jackson v. Indiana   June 7, 1972   406 U.S. 715
        *Cases Criml Justice 934
        *Cases Criml Law (Hall) 1107-1115
        *Consttnl Law (Felkenes) 410-412
        Criminal Law (Felkenes) 404-407
        *Reading Law 639-642
        Significant Decisions 1971/72 34
        Sup Ct Review 1972 275-276

PERIODICALS:
"Constitutional requirements in the commitment of the mentally ill
in the USA: rights to liberty and therapy," Franklin N. Fles-
chorer. Intl J Offender Therapy 18 no 3: 283-301 '74 (2).

3222. United States v. Allegheny-Ludlum   June 7, 1972   406 U.S. 742
        Steel Corporation
        *Text Administrative Law 160-164

3223. First National City Bank v. Banco   June 7, 1972   406 U.S. 759
        Nacional de Cuba
        Foreign Affairs 62-63

3224. Laird v. Nelms   June 7, 1972   406 U.S. 797
        *Admin Law (Schwartz) 648-652
        Significant Decisions 1971/72 53-54

3225. Bremen v. Zapata Off-Shore Co.   June 12, 1972 407 U.S. 1
        *Cases Admiralty 164-167
        *Cases Pleading 295-307

3226. Argersinger v. Hamlin   June 12, 1972 407 U.S. 25
        Against 230-242
        *Bill (Konvitz) 673-677
        *Cases Consttnl Law (Rosenblum) 275-283
        *Cases Criml Justice 1311-1316
        *Cases Criml Law (Hall) 1064-1066
        Civil Liberties (Wasby) 204-208
        *Civil Rights (Abernathy) 1977 196-199
        *Consttnl Criml (Marks) 197-202
        *Consttnl Law (Felkenes) 312-313
        *Consttnl Law (Grossman) 895-897
        *Criminal Justice (Kaplan) 296-306
        *Criminal Justice (Way) 319-321
        Criminal Law (Felkenes) 194-196
        *Criminal Law (Kadish) 795-799
        *Criminal Procedure (Lewis) 438-439
        Defendants 216-217
        *Douglas 368-374
        *Due Process 42
        Editorials 1972 780, 781
        In His Own Image 254-255
        *Leading Consttnl Cases 430-443
        *Modern Business 105-107
        Police 244-245
        Procedures 111-112
        *Processes 996-1002
        Right to Counsel.
        *Right to Counsel 669-692
        Significant Decisions 1971/72 7-8
        Spirit 102-103
        *Sup Ct and Criml Process 557-559
        Sup Ct Review 1972 269-271
PERIODICALS:
        "Gideon's encore." Newsweek 79: 24 June 26 '72.
        "Impact of Argersinger--one year later," Barton L. Ingraham.
        Law and Society R 8: 615-644 Summer '74.
        "No lawyer, no jail." Time 99: 73 June 26 '72.

"Supreme Court review."   J Criml Law, Crimlgy and Police Sci
63: 473-478 Dec '72.

3227. Fuentes v. Shevin   June 12, 1972 407 U.S. 67
       Parham v. Cortese
       *Cases Pleading 123-143
       *Civil Procedure (Cound) 142-152
       *Consttnl Law (Barrett) 742-746
       *Consttnl Law (Barron) 502-507
       *Due Process 215-216, 232-233
       *Legal Problems 61-63, 1086-1091
       *Poverty 89-97
       Significant Decisions 1971/72 25-26
       Sup Ct Review 1972 137-138, 314-315
       PERIODICALS:
       "Supreme Court cases affecting the rights of debtors and creditors,"
       Albert F. Reisman. Credit and Financial Management 74: 16-
       17, 40 Nov '72 (4).

3228. Colton v. Kentucky   June 12, 1972 407 U.S. 104
       *Am Consttnl Law (Saye) 394-397
       Criminal Procedure (Wells) 194-195
       *Sup Ct and Criml Process 1016-1021
       Sup Ct Review 1972 268-269

3229. James v. Strange   June 12, 1972 407 U.S. 128
       Significant Decisions 1971/72 33

3230. Adams v. Williams   June 12, 1972 407 U.S. 143
       Against 106-108
       *Am Consttnl Law (Saye) 510-512
       *Am Consttnl Law (Shapiro) 682-685
       Arrest (Berry) 29-31
       Arrest (Waddington) 13, 24
       *Basic Criminal 389-393
       *Cases Criml Justice 235-241
       *Cases Criml Law (Hall) 785-788
       Consttnl Counterrevolution 203-205
       *Consttnl Criml (Scarboro) 236-242
       Criminal Evidence 240-241
       *Criminal Justice (Way) 107-109
       Criminal Law (Felkenes) 93-95
       *Criminal Law (Kadish) 911-915
       *Criminal Procedure (Lewis) 254-256
       *Introduction (Cataldo) 307-310
       Law of Arrest (Creamer) 161-163
       *Law of Arrest (Markle) 68-72
       *Leading Consttnl Cases 305-312
       Police 194-197
       *Principles Arrest 481-483
       Significant Decisions 1971/72 12
       *Sup Ct and Criml Process 338-339
       Sup Ct and Rights 183-184
       Sup Ct Review 1972 264-265
       PERIODICALS:
       "Other decisions." Time 99: 73 June 26 '72 (2).
       "Supreme Court review." J Criml Law, Crimlgy and Police Sci
       63: 525-528 Dec '72.

3231. Moose Lodge No. 107 v. Irvis   June 12, 1972 407 U. S. 163
       *Am Consttn (Lockhart) 1050-1053
       *Am Consttnl Law (Mason) 497-502
       *Cases Consttnl Law (Rosenblum) 515-520
       *Cases Consttnl Rights 1009-1012
       *Civil Rights (Abernathy) 1977 69-74
       Consttnl Counterrevolution 85-90
       *Consttnl Law (Barrett) 1067-1072
       *Consttnl Law (Barron) 1042-1047
       *Consttnl Law (Grossman) 534-539
       *Consttnl Law (Lockhart) 1550-1553
       Editorials 1972 781-783
       Freedom and the Court 433-435
       God 278-279
       *Judicial Crises 134-139
       Judiciary (Abraham) 154-155
       *Race 227-235
       *Sex Discrimination 1975 1048-1055
       Significant Decisions 1971/72 29-30
       Sup Ct Review 1972 187-190
       PERIODICALS:
       "From Supreme Court: a key ruling on private clubs." US News
           72: 28 June 26 '72.
       "Gideon's encore." Newsweek   79: 24 June 26 '72 (2).
       "Justice for black American 200 years after independence," Robert
           L. Gill. Negro Eductn R 27: 271-317 July '76 (9).
       "Other decisions." Time 99: 73 June 26 '72 (2).

3232. Flower v. United States   June 12, 1972 407 U. S. 197
       Communication (Hemmer) v. 1, 84
       Sup Ct Review 1972 239

3233. Mitchum dba Book Mart v. Foster   June 19, 1972 407 U. S. 225
       Brethren 169
       *Cases Federal Courts 391-398
       Significant Decisions 1971/72 44

3234. McNeil v. Patuxent Institution Director June 19, 1972 407 U. S. 245
       *Readings Law 783-784

3235. Flood v. Kuhn   June 19, 1972 407 U. S. 258
       Brethren 189-192
       *Courts Judges 548-556
       Professional Sports 57-65, 312-314
       Significant Decisions 1971/72 50
       PERIODICALS:
       "Loss for Curt Flood." Newsweek 80: 67 July 3 '72.
       "Reserve clause anomaly." Natl R 24: 731 July 7 '72.
       "Safe, kind of." Time 100: 30-31 July 3 '72.

3236. United States v. United States   June 19, 1972 407 U. S. 297
       District Court for the Eastern
       District of Michigan
       Against 130-135
       Am Consttn (Kelly) 1027-1028
       *Am Consttnl Law (Mason) 706-710
       *Basic Cases 243-255
       *Cases Civil Liberties 93-99
       *Cases Consttnl Law (Cushman) 323-329

*Cases Consttnl Law (Rosenblum) 471-478
*Civil Rights (Abernathy) 1977 151-156
*Civil Rights (Pious) 220-232
*Consttnl Aspects v. 4, 435-482
*Consttnl Law (Grossman) 848-854
 Criminal Law (Felkenes) 151-154
*Criminal Law (Kadish) 1076-1077
*Documents History v. 2, 779-782
 Editorials 1972 801, 803, 805-810
*Freedom vs National Security 328-338
*Historic Documents 1972 485-489
 In His Own Image 255-257
*Judicial Crises 72-78
*Leading Consttnl Decisions 353-368
*Rights (Shattuck) 34-35
 Significant Decisions 1971/72 11-12
 Sup Ct and Commander in Chief 171-178
*Sup Ct and Rights 251-263
 Sup Ct from Taft 313
 Sup Ct Review 1972 265-266
 Sup Ct Review 1974 62-63
*Text Administrative Law 231-235
PERIODICALS:
   "Listen here, John Mitchell." New Republic 167: 5-6 July 8
      '72.
   "Not a syllable is there," Edward Glynn. America 128: 483
      May 26 '73.
   "Supreme Court review." J Criml Law, Crimlgy and Police Sci
      63: 518-525 Dec '72.
   "Untapped." Newsweek 80: 17-18 July 3 '72.

3237. Shadwick v. City of Tampa   June 19, 1972 407 U.S. 345
       Significant Decisions 1971/72 12-13

3238. Milton v. Wainwright   June 22, 1972 407 U.S. 371
       Against 314-317
       Sup Ct Review 1972 290-291

3239. Pipefitters Local Union No. 562 v. June 22, 1972 407 U.S. 385
       United States
       Labor Relations (Taylor) 235-236
       Significant Decisions 1971/72 54
       Sup Ct Review 1972 210-212
       PERIODICALS:
       "Significant decisions in labor cases." Monthly Labor R 95: 63-
          65 Sept '72.
       "Union get ruling on political funds." US News 73: 69-70 July
          3 '72.

3240. Wright v. Council of the City of   June 22, 1972 407 U.S. 451
       Emporia
       Am Consttn (Kelly) 1004-1005
       CQ Guide 600
       *Cases Consttnl Law (Rosenblum) 580-589
       *Consttnl Law (Barrett) 848-849
       Digest 94-95
       Disaster 146-152
       Editorials 1972 814-816
       Education (Lapati) 305-306

*Educational Policy 433-443
God 279-280
Landmark Decisions 199-207
*Race 486-494
Significant Decisions 1971/72 30
Sup Ct Review 1972 193-197
PERIODICALS:
"Justice for black Americans 200 years after independence,"
Robert L. Gill. Negro Eductn R 27: 271-317 July '76 (9).
"School desegregation: the Court, the Congress, and the President," Michael B. Wise. Sch R 82: 159-182 Feb '74 (3).

3241. United States v. Scotland Neck   June 22, 1972 407 U.S. 484
        City Board of Education
        Cotton v. Scotland Neck City Board
        of Education
        *Cases Consttnl Law (Rosenblum) 589-592
        Digest 95
        Disaster 152-155
        Education (Lapati) 306

3242. Peters v. Kiff   June 22, 1972 407 U.S. 493
        *Due Process 117
        *Law Power 640-642
        *Racial Equality 137-138
        Sup Ct Review 1972 191-193

3243. Barker v. Wingo   June 22, 1972 407 U.S. 514
        Against 374-382
        *Bill (Konvitz) 677-685
        CQ Guide 535
        *Cases Criml Justice 903-914
        *Cases Criml Law (Hall) 1071-1077
        *Consttnl Criml (Marks) 203-209
        *Consttnl Law (Felkenes) 323-325
        *Criminal Justice (Way) 421-428
        Criminal Law (Felkenes) 266-269
        *Criminal Law (Kadish) 1198-1204
        *Criminal Procedure (Lewis) 528-535
        *Due Process 106
        *Leading Consttnl Cases 651-659
        *Procedures 80-83
        Significant Decisions 1971/72 20
        *Sup Ct and Criml Process 666-672
        Sup Ct Review 1972 280-282
        *Text Social Issues 21-26

3244. Central Hardware Co. v. National   June 22, 1972 407 U.S. 539
        Labor Relations Board
        *Cases Labor (Oberer) 359-362
        *Labor Law (Twomey) 251-256
        Sup Ct and Labor 54-56
        Sup Ct Review 1972 238-239

3245. Lloyd Corporation v. Tanner   June 22, 1972 407 U.S. 551
        *Bill (Cohen) 306-312
        Brethren 178-181
        CQ Guide 417
        Cases Consttnl Law (Gunther) 1298-1299

Communication (Hemmer) v. 1, 90-91
*Consttnl Law (Barron) 1038-1041
*Consttnl Law (Freund) 801-807
*Documents History v. 2, 776-779
Freedom of the Press (Barron) 104-107
*Legal Environment 78-79
*Race 380-393
Significant Decisions 1971/72 39-40
Sup Ct and Labor 56-58
*Text Social Issues 143-146

3246. Laird v. Tatum   June 26, 1972 408 U. S. 1
Against 136
*Am Consttn (Lockhart) 68-71
Cases Consttnl Law (Gunther) 1666
*Cases Consttnl Rights 68-71
*Cases Criml Justice 509-511
Communication (Hemmer) v. 1, 244-245
*Consttnl Law (Barrett) 103-106
*Consttnl Law (Barron) 109-114
*Consttnl Law (Lockhart) 1674-1676
*Douglas 50-58
Editorials 1972 812-813
*Federal System 59-62
*Freedom of Speech (Haiman) 42
*Freedom vs National Security 576-581
Power 40-41
*Rights (Shattuck) 77-78
Sup Ct Review 1972 230-234
*Text Social Issues 98-100

3247. Gelbard v. United States   June 26, 1972 408 U. S. 41
Against 136-137
Criminal Law (Felkenes) 154-155
Significant Decisions 1971/72 13-14

3248. Police Department of Chicago v.   June 26, 1972 408 U. S. 92
Mosley
Communication (Hemmer) v. 1, 97-98
*Consttnl Law (Barrett) 1247-1251
*Consttnl Law (Freund) 1203-1205
Digest 38-39
Free Speech (Kurland) 382-384
Handbook 134-136
Sup Ct Review 1972 235-236
Sup Ct Review 1974 273-275
PERIODICALS:
"High court uses picketing to tinker with Tinker," Laurence W.
Knowles. Natns Sch 90: 17 Nov '72.

3249. Grayned v. Rockford   June 26, 1972 408 U. S. 104
Cases Consttnl Law (Gunther) 1286-1287
Civil Rights (Schimmel) 99-100
Communication (Hemmer) v. 1, 98
*Consttn (Morris) 314-320
*Consttnl Law (Barrett) 1272-1273
*Consttnl Rights (Kemerer) 205-208
Digest 39-40
Free Speech (Kurland) 360-361

*Race 363-370
Sup Ct Review 1972 236-237
Sup Ct Review 1974 250-252
*Text Social Issues 139-143

3250. Byrum v. United States   June 26, 1972 408 U.S. 125
PERIODICALS:
"Supreme Court rules on grantor's retaining certain rights over
property transferred to trust," Peter C. Aslanides. Taxes 51:
157-162 Mar '73.
"Supreme Court says grantor may retain voting control of stock
placed in trust," John A. Clark. J Taxation 37: 138-140
Sept '72.
"Transfers of corporate securities by persons in control of cor-
porate policy: Byrum revisited," Lawrence Newman and Albert
Kalter. Trusts and Estates 111: 710-711, 745 Sept '72.

3251. Healy v. James   June 29, 1972 408 U.S. 169
*Am Consttnl Law (Saye) 349-353
*Bill (Konvitz) 278-289
*Cases Consttnl Law (Rosenblum) 560-569
Civil Rights (Schimmel) 88-96
Communication (Hemmer) v. 1, 138-140
*Consttn (Morris) 297-307
*Consttnl Rights (Kemerer) 210-215
Digest 41
Education (Lapati) 254-256
*Educational Policy 168-173
*Freedom of Speech (Haiman) 84
Handbook 121-123
Significant Decisions 1971/72 39
*Sup Ct and Criml Process 1096-1099
*Sup Ct and Education 251-259
Sup Ct Review 1972 224-225
PERIODICALS:
"Recognition of gay liberation on the state-supported campus,"
Annette Gibbs and Arthur C. McFarland. J Col Student Person-
nel 15: 5-7 Jan '74.

3252. Mancusi v. Stubbs   June 26, 1972 408 U.S. 204
Against 361-362
Sup Ct Review 1972 288-289

3253. Kois v. Wisconsin   June 26, 1972 408 U.S. 229
Brethren 200

3254. Furman v. Georgia   June 29, 1972 408 U.S. 238
Jackson v. Georgia
Branch v. Texas
Against 389-420
Am Consttn (Kelly) 990-992
*Bill (Konvitz) 686-696
Brethren 211-220
CQ Guide 576, 578
*Cases Consttnl Law (Rosenblum) 594-625
*Comparative 431-438
Conceived 161-162
*Consttnl Criml (Marks) 227-248
*Consttnl Law (Grossman) 183-185, 934-944

*Courts Judges 364-365
*Criminal Justice (Galloway) 15-36
Criminal Law (Felkenes) 365-368
Criminal Law (Wells) 63-64
Cruel 246-258, 267-279, 289-305
Defendants 390-393
*Documents History v. 2, 788-792
*Douglas 425-434
*Due Process 168-173
Editorials 1972 874-883
*Federal System 47-49
Great Events Worldwide v. 3, 1279-1286
*Historic Documents 1972 499-505
In His Own Image 268, 272-275
*Justices (Friedman) v. 5, 403-428
*Law Enforcement 123-127
*Leading Consttnl Decisions 385-407
Power 269-270
Processes 895-903
Significant Decisions 1971/72 5-6
*Sup Ct and Rights 339-362
Sup Ct Review 1972 1-40, 294-297
PERIODICALS:
"Bringing back death," Robert A. Prigsley. Commonweal 103:
    518-519 Aug 13 '76.
"Capital punishment--cruel and unusual?" Morton S. Enslin. Re-
    ligion in Life 41: 254-258 Summer '72.
"Closing death row." Time 100: 37 July 10 '72.
"Controversy over the question of capital punishment in the United
    States." Congressional Dig 52: 1-32 Jan '73.
"Court on the death penalty." Newsweek 80: 20 July 20 '72.
"End to Death row?" US News 73: 25-27 July 10 '72.
"Issues, the High Court and the Constitution." Senior Scholastic
    106: 14-15 Apr 24 '75 (3).
"Justice for black Americans 200 years after independence,"
    Robert L. Gill. Negro Eductn R 27: 271-317 July '76 (9).
"Mixed reviews." New Republic 167: 7-8 July 15 '72 (3).
"The problem of capital punishment," Hugo Adam Bedau. Current
    History 71: 14-18, 34-35 July/Aug '76.
"Role of the social sciences in determining the constitutionality of
    capital punishment," Welsh S. White. Am J Orthopsychiatry 45:
    581-595 July '75 (3).
"Supreme Court review." J Criml Law, Crimlgy and Police Sci
    63: 484-492 Dec '72.
"Two perspectives on structuring discretion: Justices Stewart and
    White on the death penalty," Larry I. Palmer. J Criml Law
    and Crimlgy 70: 194-213 Summ '79.

3255. Morrissey v. Brewer   June 29, 1972 408 U. S. 471
    *Consttnl Law (Felkenes) 406-407
    *Consttnl Rights (Palmer) 480-496
    *Criminal Justice (Way) 502-507
    Criminal Law (Felkenes) 399-401
    *Criminal Law (Kadish) 1481-1485
    Criminal Procedure (Wells) 238-240
    *Due Process 157-158, 159, 205, 226-227
    *Procedures 230-231, 232-233
    Significant Decisions 1971/72 21
    *Sup Ct and Criml Process 742-746

Sup Ct Review 1972 305-307
*US Prison Law v. 4, 168-182
PERIODICALS:
"Legal issues facing parole," Eugene N. Barkin. Crime and De-
    linquency 25: 219-235 Apr '79.
"Parole and probation revocation procedures after Morrissey and
    Gagnon," H. Richmond Fisher. J Criml Law and Crimlgy 65:
    46-61 Mar '74 (2).

3256. United States v. Brewster   June 29, 1972 408 U.S. 501
        CQ Guide 170
        *Federal System 198-201
        *Legislative (Hetzel) 515-516
        *Legislation (Linde) 483-492
        *Processes 370-378
        Significant Decisions 1971/72 17-18
        Sup Ct Review 1972 316-319

3257. Board of Regents of State Colleges   June 29, 1972 408 U.S. 564
        v. Roth
        *Admin Law (Gellhorn) 451-459
        *Am Consttn (Lockhart) 1164-1168
        Bill (Cohen) 759-763
        Cases Consttnl Law (Gunther) 649-654
        *Cases Consttnl Rights 1138-1142
        Communication (Hemmer) v. 1, 154-155
        *Consttnl Law (Barrett) 747-752
        *Consttnl Law (Barron) 513-520
        *Consttnl Law (Freund) 1041-1043
        Digest 63-64
        *Due Process 216-218, 225-226
        *Education (Hazard) 449-457
        Education (Lapati) 225-226
        *Educational Policy 236-244
        *Labor Relations (Edwards) 797-804
        *Law of Public Education 407-411
        *School Law (Alexander) 611-616
        Significant Decisions 1971/72 26-27
        *Sup Ct and Education 230-238
        Sup Ct Review 1972 221-223
PERIODICALS:
"Evaluation and due process: legal aspects," J. Everett DeVaughn.
    Natl Elementary Principal 52: 88-91 Feb '73.
"High court rulings key factor in contract cases," Philip Semas.
    Chronicle of Higher Eductn 11: 1, 8-9 Feb 2 '76. Reaction:
    12: 19 Apr 19 '76 (2).
"Public employment and the Supreme Court's 1976-77 term," Carl
    F. Goodman. Public Personnel Management 6: 283-293
    Sept '77 (9).
"Reprise: due process and the nontenured teacher," John C.
    Walden. Natl Elementary Principal 52: 78-80 Jan '73 (2).
"Roth and Sindermann: nontenured rights may be constitutional,"
    John P. Linn. Natns Sch 91: 36 Mar '73 (2).
"Supreme Court rules on rights of students, nontenured teachers."
    Col and University Bus 53: 24 Sept '72 (3).
"Supreme Court speaks to the untenured: a comment on Board of
    Regents v. Roth and Perry v. Sindermann," William Van Alstyne.
    AAUP Bul 58: 267-270 Sept '72 (2). *AAUP Bul 58: 271-
    276 Sept '72.

"U.S. Supreme Court supports teachers' due process rights." Today's Eductn 61: 37-39 Sept '72 (2).

3258. Perry v. Sindermann   June 29, 1972 408 U.S. 593
       *Admin Law (Gellhorn) 459-464
       *Bill (Cohen) 764-765
       Communication (Hemmer) v. 1, 155-157
       *Consttn (Morris) 625-629
       *Consttnl Law (Barron) 521-525
       Digest 64-65
       Education (Lapati) 226-228
       *Educational Policy 244-249
       *Labor Relations (Edwards) 804-808
       *Law of Public Education 411-415
       *School Law (Alexander) 617-621
       Sup Ct Review 1972 220-221
       PERIODICALS:
       *AAUP Bul 58: 276-278 Sept '72.
       See also listing at 408 U.S. 564, entry no. 3257.

3259. Gravel v. United States   June 29, 1972 408 U.S. 606
       CQ Guide 168
       *Douglas 5-9
       *Federal System 195-198
       In His Own Image 266-267
       *Legislative (Hetzel) 527-535
       Significant Decisions 1971/72 18-19
       PERIODICALS:
       "Will United States prosecute Beacon after high court decision?"
       Susan Wagner. Pub Weekly 202: 29-30 July 10 '72.

3260. Branzburg v. Hayes   June 29, 1972 408 U.S. 665
       In re Pappas
       United States v. Caldwell
       *Am Consttn (Lockhart) 670-682
       *Am Consttnl Law (Shapiro) 405-410
       *Bill (Cohen) 235-244
       Brethren 223
       CQ Guide 445-448
       *Cases Consttnl Law (Gunther) 1522-1530
       *Cases Consttnl Rights 489-502
       *Cases Individual 1036-1049
       *Civil Liberties (Barker) 139-147
       *Civil Rights (Abernathy) 1977 452-456
       Communication (Hemmer) v. 2, 215-220
       *Communications Law 189-276
       *Consttnl Law (Barrett) 1374-1379
       *Consttnl Law (Felkenes) 172-173
       *Consttnl Law (Freund) 1310-1314
       *Consttnl Law (Grossman) 1179-1185
       *Consttnl Law (Lockhart) 956-965
       Criminal Evidence 169-170
       Crisis 206-207
       Defendants 334-335
       *Documents History v. 2, 782-788
       *Douglas 189-198
       *Due Process 77-78
       Editorials 1972 884-889
       *First Amendment (Franklin) 127-138

Handbook 425-438
*Historic Documents 1972 507-519
In His Own Image 266-267
Justice Hugo Black 132-159
Law of Mass 327-330
Media and the First Amendment 210-216
*Mass Communications 373-391
*Mass Media (Devol) 16-23
Mass Media (Francois) 329-336
Role (Cox) 42
Significant Decisions 1971/72 37-38
*Sup Ct and Criml Process 523-525
Sup Ct Review 1972 241-246
Sup Ct Review 1978 285-288
Watergate 72-73
PERIODICALS:
"Branzburg revisited: the struggle to define newsman's privilege
  goes on," G. M. Killenberg. Journalism Q 55: 703-710
  Winter '78.
"Freedom, the courts and the media; symposium." Center Mag
  12: 28-45 Mar '79.
"Freedom of the press." Senior Scholastic 107: 6-10 Jan 13
  '76 (3).
"General spirit of the people," Helen K. Copley. Vital Speeches
  46: 169-172 Jan 1 '80 (4).
"Justice & the journalist," Vince Blasi. Nation 215: 198-199
  Sept 18 '72.
"New obstacles for journalists; interview with legal correspondent
  for CBS News," Fred Graham. Center Mag 12: 37-44 July
  '79.
"No immunity." Newsweek 80: 62-63 July 10 '72.
"Notes and comment." New Yorker 49: 27 Mar 3 '73.
"Prosecutor and the researcher; present and prospective variations
  on the Supreme Court's Branzburg decision," Paul Nejelski and
  Kurt Finsterbusch. Socl Problems 21: 3-21 Summer '73.
"Rehnquist recuse: judging your own case," John MacKenzie.
  Washington Monthly 6: 54-61 May '74 (2).
"Shielding the press," Joseph A. Califano. New Republic 168:
  21-23 May 5 '73.
"Shielding the press," Patrick Maines. Natl R 25: 574-576
  May 25 '73.
"Supreme Court requires newsmen to testify," L. A. Huston.
  Editor and Pub 105: 14 July 1 '72.
"Supreme Court rules against newsmen's privilege." Broadcasting
  83: 26-27 July 3 '72.

3261. Kleindienst v. Mandel   June 29, 1972 408 U.S. 753
        Communication (Hemmer) v. 1, 248
        *Consttnl Law (Barrett) 280-281
        Significant Decisions 1971/72 40-41
        Sup Ct Review 1972 249-250
        PERIODICALS:
        "New US Supreme Court philosophy on advertising faces opposition,"
          Denise M. Trauth and John L. Huffman. Journalism Q 56:
          540-545 Autumn '79 (3).

3262. Moore v. Illinois   June 29, 1972 408 U.S. 786
        Against 318-320
        Brethren 224-225

*Cases Criml Justice 942-954
*Cases Professional 490-499
*Consttnl Law (Felkenes) 334-336
Criminal Law (Felkenes) 347-350
*Elements Criminal 107-115
*Leading Consttnl Cases 757-768
Sup Ct Review 1972 291-292

3263. Rosenfeld v. New Jersey   June 26, 1972   408 U.S. 901
First Amendment (Berns) 199
*Freedom of Speech (Haiman) 102
*Obscenity (Bosmajian) 272-276

3264. O'Brien v. Brown   July 7, 1972   409 U.S. 1
Keane v. National Democratic Party
Editorials 1972 850-852
Sup Ct Review 1972 199-201

3265. Robinson v. Hanrahan   Oct 24, 1972   409 U.S. 38
Due Process 228-229
Significant Decisions 1972/73 11-12

3266. Murch v. Mottram   Nov 6, 1972   409 U.S. 41
Significant Decisions 1972/73 63-64
PERIODICALS:
"Supreme Court Review."   J Criml Law and Crimlgy   64:   438-
439   Dec '73.

3267. National Labor Relations Board v.   Nov 17, 1972   409 U.S. 48
International Van Lines
*Cases Labor (Stern) 76-78
Significant Decisions 1972/73 112-113
PERIODICALS:
"Significant decision in labor cases."   Monthly Labor R   96:   68-
69   Jan '73.

3268. Ward v. Monroeville   Nov 14, 1972   409 U.S. 57
*Cases Criml Justice 1019-1022
*Consttnl Law (Klein) 399-401
Defendants 117
*Due Process 109
Significant Decisions 1972/73 53-54

3269. Gottschalk v. Benson   Nov 20, 1972   409 U.S. 63
*Cases Copyright (Kaplan) 232-235
*Copyright 893-900
Significant Decisions 1972/73 115

3270. Johnson v. New York State   Nov 20, 1972   409 U.S. 75
Education Department
*Consttn (Morris) 976-977

3271. Webb v. Texas   Dec 4, 1972   409 U.S. 95
*Criminal Procedure (Lewis) 521-523
*Sup Ct and Criml Process 688-690

3272. Cool v. United States   Dec 4, 1972   409 U.S. 100
Defendants 104
*Sup Ct and Criml Process 690-692

3273. California v. LaRue   Dec 5, 1972   409 U.S. 109
       *Bill (Konvitz) 475-479
       *Obscenity (Bosmajian) 259-267
       Significant Decisions 1972/73 30-31
       PERIODICALS:
       "Porno on the rocks." Newsweek 80: 23 Dec 18 '72.

3274. Neil v. Biggers   Dec 6, 1972   409 U.S. 188
       *Basic Criminal 643-647
       *Cases Criml Justice 716-721
       Criminal Law (Felkenes) 209-211
       *Criminal Law (Kadish) 1042-1045
       *Criminal Procedure (Lewis) 471-474
       *Leading Consttnl Cases 624-627
       Significant Decisions 1972/73 66-67
       *Sup Ct and Criml Process 501-504

3275. Trafficante v. Metropolitan Life   Dec 7, 1972   409 U.S. 205
       Insurance Co.
       Significant Decisions 1972/73 98-99

3276. National Labor Relations Board v.   Dec 7, 1972   409 U.S. 213
       Granite State Joint Board,
       Textile Workers Union
       Significant Decisions 1972/73 110-111
       PERIODICALS:
       "Significant decisions in labor cases." Monthly Labor R 96: 56-
       57 Feb '73.

3277. Swanson v. Stidham   Dec 7, 1972   409 U.S. 224
       Significant Decisions 1972/73 64

3278. One Lot Emerald Cut Stones v.   Dec 11, 1972   409 U.S. 232
       United States
       Significant Decisions 1972/73 71-72

3279. Executive Jet Aviation, Inc.   Dec 18, 1972   409 U.S. 249
       v. Cleveland
       *Cases Admiralty 135-142

3280. Heublein v. South Carolina Tax   Dec 18, 1972   409 U.S. 275
       Commission
       Consttnl Law (Barrett) 406-407
       Significant Decisions 1972/73 128-129

3281. Ricci v. Chicago Mercantile Exchange   Jan 9, 1973   409 U.S. 289
       *Admin Law (Schwartz) 595-602
       Significant Decisions 1972/73 92-93

3282. Couch v. United States   Jan 0, 1973   409 U.S. 322
       Against 188-190
       *Cases Evidence 1221-1237
       *Douglas 355-359
       *Legal Environment 87-88
       *Principles Proof 715-719
       Significant Decisions 1972/73 44-45
       PERIODICALS:
       "Supreme Court's Couch decision signals new directions in guard-

ing client's records," Melvin A. Coffee. J Taxation 38: 258-
261 May '73.
"_____." CPA J 43: 603-608 July '73.

3283. Bronston v. United States   Jan 10, 1973   409 U.S. 352
       Significant Decisions 1972/73 75

3284. Hughes Tool Co. v. Trans World   Jan 10, 1973   409 U.S. 363
       Airlines, Inc.
       Significant Decisions 1972/73 89-90

3285. Philpott v. Essex County Welfare   Jan 10, 1973   409 U.S. 413
       Board
       *Cases Law and Poverty 281-283
       Significant Decisions 1972/73 122

3286. District of Columbia v. Carter   Jan 10, 1973   409 U.S. 418
       *Civil Rights (Abernathy) 1980 351-355
       Significant Decisions 1972/73 99-100

3287. United States v. Kras   Jan 10, 1973   409 U.S. 434
       *Civil Procedure (Carrington) 661-672
       *Consttnl Law (Barrett) 922-924
       *Due Process 251-253
       *Elements Civil 51-58
       *Processes 844-848
       Significant Decisions 1972/73 27-28
       PERIODICALS:
       "Blackmun's cake," Marvin Karpatkin.   Nation 216: 227-228
       Feb 19 '73.

3288. Almota Farmers Elevator and Ware-   Jan 16, 1973   409 U.S. 470
       house v. United States
       *Land Use 710-715
       Significant Decisions 1972/73 126

3289. United States v. Fuller   Jan 16, 1973   409 U.S. 488
       *Consttnl Law (Freund) 1103-1105
       *Land Use 715-718
       Significant Decisions 1972/73 127

3290. Robinson v. Neil   Jan 16, 1973   409 U.S. 505
       Significant Decisions 1972/73 69-70

3291. Goosby v. Osser   Jan 17, 1973   409 U.S. 512
       Significant Decisions 1972/73 81-82

3292. Ham v. South Carolina   Jan 17, 1973   409 U.S. 524
       Criminal Law (Felkenes) 318-319
       *Criminal Law (Kadish) 1350-1351
       *Due Process 118-119
       *Legal Environment 55-56
       Significant Decisions 1972/73 57-58
       PERIODICALS:
       "Supreme Court review." J Criml Law and Crimlgy 64: 449-453
       Dec '73.

3293. Gomez v. Perez   Jan 17, 1973   409 U.S. 535
       *Cases Domestic 711-713
       Significant Decisions 1972/73 25

3294. Laird v. Tatum   Oct 10, 1972   409 U.S. 824
       *Courts Judges 181-184
       *Due Process 109-110
       *Introduction (Mashaw) 405-410

3295. Aberdeen and Rockfish Railroad Co.   July 19, 1972   409 U.S. 1207
       v. Students Challenging Regulatory
       Agency Procedures (SCRAP)
       Interstate Commerce Commission v.
       Students Challenging Regulatory
       Agency Procedures
       *Cases Regulated 371-386
       *Public Planning 1000-1002

3296. United States v. Dionisio   Jan 22, 1973   410 U.S. 1
       *Cases Criml Justice 249-255
       *Consttnl Criml (Scarboro) 684-699
       Criminal Law (Felkenes) 78-80
       *Criminal Law (Kadish) 1143-1147
       *Due Process 70
       Law of Arrest (Creamer) 290-295
       *Leading Consttnl Cases 317-329
       Significant Decisions 1972/73 45-46
       PERIODICALS:
       "Supreme Court review (1973)."   J Criml Law and Crimlgy   64:
       414-418 Dec '73 (2).

3297. United States v. Mara   Jan 22, 1973   410 U.S. 19
       *Cases Criml Justice 255-262
       Criminal Evidence 285-286
       *Due Process 70
       Law of Arrest (Creamer) 295-296
       Significant Decisions 1972/73 46-47
       PERIODICALS:
       See listing at 410 U.S. 1, entry no. 3296.

3298. United States v. Gloxo Group, LTD   Jan 22, 1973   410 U.S. 52
       Significant Decisions 1972/73 94-95

3299. Environmental Protection Agency   Jan 22, 1973   410 U.S. 73
       v. Mink
       *Admin Law (Schwartz) 222-225
       Communication (Hemmer) v. 2, 239-241
       Consttn (Wilcox) 30-31
       *Douglas 27-32
       *Freedom vs National Security 205-211
       *Introduction (Mashaw) 637-645
       Mass Media (Francois) 234-235
       Significant Decisions 1972/73 84-85

3300. Roe v. Wade   Jan 22, 1973   410 U.S. 113
       Am Consttn (Kelly) 993-995
       *Am Consttn (Lockhart) 1118-1121
       *Am Consttnl Law (Bartholomew) v. 2, 222-228
       *Am Consttnl Law (Mason) 638-646
       *Am Consttnl Law (Shapiro) 723-732
       *Basic Cases 133-149
       *Bill (Cohen) 577-587
       Biography 357-359

PERIODICALS:
    "Abortion." America 128: 506-507 June 2 '73. Same with title:
        "Contemporary Catholic view of Abortion." Current 154: 31-
        34 Sept '73.
    "Abortion." New Republic 168: 9 Feb 10 '73. Reply: Meade
        P. O'Boyle. 168: 32 Mar 24 '73.
    "Abortion." Sci News 103: 54 Jan 27 '73.
    "Abortion: a year later." Time 103: 60-61 Feb 4 '74.
    "Abortion and the Court." Christianity Today 17: 32-33 Feb
        16 '73.
    "Abortion decision," Commonweal 97: 435-436 Feb 16 '73. Re-
        action: 98: 133-135 Apr 13 '73; 98: 251, 271 May 18 '73.

"Abortion decision," Robert F. Drinan. Commonweal 97: 438-
440 Feb 16 '73. Reaction: 98: 75, 94-95 Mar 30 '73.
"Abortion decision." Scientific Am 228: 44-45 Mar '73.
"Abortion decision; a balancing of rights," J. Claude Evans.
Christian Century 90: 195-197 Feb 14 '73.
"Abortion decision; a death blow?" Christianity Today 17: 48
Feb 16 '73.
"Abortion decision: a year later." America 130: 22 Jan 19
'74.
"Abortion: legal questions and legislative alternatives," Richard
J. Orloski. America 131: 50-51 Aug 10 '74.
"Abortion revolution." Newsweek 81: 27-28 Feb 5 '73.
"Capable of meaningful life, anyone?" Christianity Today 18:
29 Mar 29 '74.
"Confusion at the highest level," J. Robert Nelson. Christian
Century 90: 254-255 Feb 28 '73.
"Death of pluralism?" Natl R 25: 193 Feb 16 '73.
"The decision blow by blow." Time 101: 51 Feb 5 '73.
"The doctor as abortion ally," Judith Mears. Civil Liberties R
1: 134-136 Summer '74.
"For American Catholics: end of an illusion," Timothy E. O'Con-
nell. America 128: 514-517 June 2 '73.
"Goodbye to the Judeo-Christian era in law," Robert M. Byrn.
America 128: 511-514 June 2 '73.
"Issues, the High Court and the Constitution." Senior Scholastic
106: 14-15 Apr 24 '75 (3).
"Jane Roe and Mary Doe." Nation 216: 165 Feb 5 '73.
"Media agendas and human rights: the Supreme Court decision
on abortion," John C. Pollock and others. Journalism Q 55:
544-548, 561 Autumn '78.
"Pro-life amendments and due process," James J. Diamond.
America 130: 27-29 Jan 19 '74. Reaction: 130: 121
Feb 23 '74.
"Protecting the unborn," Paul Ramsey. Commonweal 100: 308-
314 May 31 '74.
"Raw judicial power," John T. Noonan. Natl R 25: 260-264
Mar 2 '73.
"Rethinking abortion?" Christianity Today 21: 48 Mar 4 '77.
"State implementation of Supreme Court decisions: abortion rates
since Roe v. Wade," Susan B. Hansen. J Poltcs 42: 372-395
May '80.
"Stunning Approval for Abortion." Time 101: 50-51 Feb 5 '73.
"Supreme Court and abortion." Society 13: 6-9 Mar '76.
"Supreme Court eases rules on abortion." US News 74: 36
Feb 5 '73.
"Supreme Court on abortion." America 128: 81 Feb 3 '73.
"Supreme Court review (1973)." J Criml Law and Crimlgy 64:
393-399 Dec '73.
"The Supreme Court's abortion decisions and public opinion in the
United States," Judith Blake. Population and Development R
3: 45-62 Mar/June '77.
"Supreme Court's abortion rulings and social change," David W.
Brady and Kathleen Kemp. Socl Sci Q 57: 535-546 Dec '76.
"Supreme Court's slow but certain impact on abortion." Sat R
Society 1: 35 Apr '73.
"This much, at least: the Court," James J. Kilpatrick. Natl R
25: 1047-1052 Sept 28 '73 (3).
"What the Supreme Court ruled on abortion laws." US News 76:
44 Mar 4 '74.

3301. Doe v. Bolton   Jan 22, 1973   410 U.S. 179
       Am Consttn (Kelly) 993-995
       *Am Consttn (Lockhart) 1121-1127
       *Cases Consttnl Rights 1090-1096
       *Cases Environmental Law (Hanks) 132-137
       Civil Liberties (Wasby) 101-103
       Communication (Hemmer) v. 1, 251
       *Consttnl Law (Barrett) 88-89, 718-725
       *Consttnl Law (Lockhart) 530-535
       *Douglas 240-244
       Editorials 1973 112-121
       Role (Cox) 51-55
       *Sex Discrimination 1975 960-975
       Significant Decisions 1972/73 7-9
       Sup Ct Review 1973 165
       Sup Ct Review 1974 337-360
       *Text Sex Based Discrimination 365-377

3302. United States v. Florida East   Jan 22, 1973   410 U.S. 224
          Coast Railway
       *Admin Law (Gellhorn) 178-187
       *Admin Law (Schwartz) 267-274
       *Introduction (Mashaw) 282-288
       *Legislation (Linde) 816-821
       Significant Decisions 1972/73 85-86

3303. United States v. Chandler   Jan 22, 1973   410 U.S. 257
       Significant Decisions 1972/73 120-121

3304. McGinnis v. Royster   Feb 21, 1973   410 U.S. 263
       Significant Decisions 1972/73 72-73
       *Sup Ct and Criml Process 1021-1025
       *US Prison Law v. 4, 375-385

3305. Chambers v. Mississippi   Feb 21, 1973   410 U.S. 284
       Against 355-357
       *Cases Criml Justice 1274-1284
       Criminal Evidence 102-103
       Criminal Law (Felkenes) 344-347
       *Criminal Law (Kadish) 1368-1369
       *Due Process 131-132
       *Elements Criminal 268-278
       *Leading Consttnl Cases 748-756
       *Principles Proof 322-332
       Significant Decisions 1972-73 54
       PERIODICALS:
       "Supreme Court Review." J Criml Law and Crimlgy 64: 453-458
          Dec '73.

3306. Mahan v. Howell   Feb 21, 1973   410 U.S. 315
       City of Virginia Beach v. Howell
       Weinberg v. Prichard
       *Am Consttn (Lockhart) 1072-1077
       CQ Guide 495-496
       *Cases Consttnl Rights 1031-1036
       *Civil Rights (Abernathy) 1977 613-615
       Comparative 575-578
       Consttnl Counterrevolution 126-127
       *Consttnl Law (Barrett) 965-966

*Consttnl Law (Grossman) 727-730
*Historic Documents 1973 277-289
Significant Decisions 1972/73 18-20
Sup Ct Review 1973 14-17

3307. Tacon v. Arizona   Feb 21, 1973   410 U.S. 351
        *Douglas 408-410

3308. Lehnhausen v. Lake Shore   Feb 22, 1973   410 U.S. 356
        Auto Parts Co.
        *Am Consttnl Law (Saye) 430-431
        Significant Decisions 1972/73 29

3309. Otter Tail Power Co. v. United   Feb 22, 1973   410 U.S. 366
        States
        *Antitrust Analysis 179-185
        *Selected Antitrust Cases 396-404
        Significant Decisions 1972/73 91-92
        Sup Ct Review 1973 100-101, 115
        PERIODICALS:
        "Otter tail decision raises possibility of new legislation." Public
        Utilities Fortnightly 91: 52 Mar 29 '73.

3310. United States v. Enmons   Feb 22, 1973   410 U.S. 396
        *Consttnl Law (Barrett) 248
        Significant Decisions 1972/73 75-76

3311. Tillman v. Wheaton-Haven Recreation   Feb 27, 1973   410 U.S. 431
        Association
        Significant Decisions 1972/73 97-98
        PERIODICALS:
        "Justice for black Americans 200 years after independence,"
        Robert L. Gill. Negro Eductn R 27: 271-317 July '76 (9).

3312. United States v. Basye   Feb 27, 1973   410 U.S. 441
        Significant Decisions 1972/73 117-118
        PERIODICALS:
        "Basye decision one year later: judging its effect upon related
        areas," Larry E. Shapiro. J Taxation 39: 376-379 Dec '73.
        "Basye projected: fringe benefits and the Supreme Court," Paul
        A. Teschner. Taxes 51: 324-354 June '73.
        "Supreme Court in Basye taxes partnership on plan payments made
        for it by corporation," Andrew H. Cox. J Taxation 38: 270-
        273 May '73.

3313. Illinois v. Somerville   Feb 27, 1973   410 U.S. 458
        *Cases Criml Justice 1033-1040
        *Cases Criml Law (Perkins) 830-834
        *Criminal Law (Kadish) 1405-1409
        *Leading Consttnl Cases 790-799
        Significant Decisions 1972/73 70-71
        *Sup Ct and Criml Process 407-411
        Sup Ct Review 1978 92-94
        PERIODICALS:
        "Supreme Court review." J Criml Law and Crimlgy 64: 445-448
        Dec '73.

3314. Braden v. Thirtieth Judicial   Feb 28, 1973   410 U.S. 484
        Circuit Court of Kentucky

Criminal Procedure (Wells) 241
Significant Decisions 1972/73 58-59

3315.   Brennan v. Arnheim and Neely, Inc.   Feb 28, 1973   410 U. S. 512
        Significant Decisions 1972/73 113

3316.   United States v. Falstaff Brewing Co.   Feb 28, 1973   410 U. S. 526
        *Antitrust (Posner) 506-509
        *Antitrust Analysis 805-814
        *Selected Antitrust Cases 203-213
        Significant Decisions 1972/73 93-94
        PERIODICALS:
        "High court shifts on antitrust." Bus Wk   p. 64-65 Mar 24 '73.

3317.   Hurtado v. United States   Mar 5, 1973   410 U. S. 578
        Significant Decisions 1972/73 73

3318.   Linda R. S. v. Richard D.   Mar 5, 1973   410 U. S. 614
        *Courts Judges 294-297
        Significant Decisions 1972/73 77

3319.   United Air Lines v. Mahin   Mar 5, 1973   410 U. S. 623
        Significant Decisions 1972/73 129

3320.   Ortwein v. Schwab   Mar 5, 1973   410 U. S. 656
        *Admin Law (Schwartz) 554-556
        Consttnl Law (Barrett) 924
        Significant Decisions 1972/73 28-29

3321.   Papish v. University of Missouri   Mar 19, 1973   410 U. S. 667
        Curators
        Communication (Hemmer) v. 1, 137-138
        *Consttn (Morris) 266-269
        *Consttnl Rights (Kemerer) 196-200
        Digest 42
        First Amendment (Berns) 197
        *Obscenity (Bosmajian) 276-279
        Significant Decisions 1972/1973 34-35

3322.   Marston v. Lewis   Mar 19, 1973   410 U. S. 679
        Consttnl Law (Barrett) 952
        Significant Decisions 1972/73 23-24

3323.   La Vallee v. Delle Rose   Mar 19, 1973   410 U. S. 690
        Police 241-242
        Significant Decisions 1972/73 65-66
        PERIODICALS:
        "Supreme Court review." J Criml Law and Crimlgy 64: 440-
        442 Dec '73.

3324.   Texas v. Louisiana   Mar 20, 1973   410 U. S. 702
        PERIODICALS:
        "Texas-Louisiana boundary dispute," Alexander Melamid. Geo-
        graphical R 65: 268-270 Apr '75.

3325.   Sayler Land Co. v. Tulare Lake   Mar 20, 1973   410 U. S. 719
        Basin Water Storage District
        *Consttnl Law (Barrett) 997-998

Court Years 165-166
Significant Decisions 1972/73 22-23

3326. Associated Enterprises v. Toltec   Mar 20, 1973   410 U.S. 743
        Watershed Improvement District
        Significant Decisions 1972/73 23

3327. Rosario v. Rockefeller   Mar 21, 1973   410 U.S. 752
        Significant Decisions 1972/73 24-25

3328. San Antonio Independent School District   Mar 21, 1973   411 U.S. 1
        v. Rodriguez
        *Am Consttn (Lockhart) 1145-1159
        *Am Consttnl Law (Saye) 431-435
        *Am Consttnl Law (Shapiro) 576-590
        *Annals v. 19, 313-320
        Authority 101-102
        *Basic Cases 70-85
        Brethren 258-259
        CQ Guide 643-646
        *Cases Civil Liberties 366-373
        *Cases Consttnl Law (Cushman) 596-603
        *Cases Consttnl Law (Gunther) 910-924
        *Cases Consttnl Rights 1118-1132
        *Cases Individual 448-468
        *Cases Law and Poverty 97-106
        *Civil Liberties (Barker) 360-371
        *Civil Rights (Abernathy) 1977 499-504
        *Comparative 322-329
        Consttnl Counterrevolution 66-70
        *Consttn (Morris) 947-972
        *Consttnl Law (Barrett) 999-1012
        *Consttnl Law (Barron) 696-705
        *Consttnl Law (Freund) 916-922
        *Consttnl Law (Grossman) 686-694
        *Consttnl Law (Lockhart) 1480-1494
        *Consttnl Rights (Kemerer) 531-539
        Digest 13-14
        Editorials 1973 406-415
        *Education (Hazard) 505-515
        Education (Lapati) 143-145
        *Educational Policy 583-606
        *Historic Documents 1973 361-377
        *Justices (Friedman) v. 5, 428-457
        Law and Education 126-127
        *Law and Public Education (Goldstein) 646-686
        *Law of Public Education 212-223
        *Legal Problems 80-93
        *Poverty 405-434
        Power 514
        *Processes 856-874
        *School Law (Alexander) 794-805
        Significant Decisions 1972/73 15-17
        *Sup Ct and Education 283-298
        Sup Ct Review 1973 36-55
        *Teacher 40-42
        PERIODICALS:
        "About the complicated and oh so important Rodriguez decision,"
          Michael A. Resnick. Am Sch Bd J 160: 23-24, 52 May '73.

"Children under the law," Hillary Rodham. Harvard Eductnl R
43: 487-514 Nov '73 (5).
"Commentary on school finance and the Supreme Court." Phi
Delta Kappan 54: 77 Sept '72.
"Confusion over school finance," Hope Justus. Compact 7: 17
May/June '73.
"Court rules property tax can finance public schools." Library J
98: 1621 May 15 '73.
"Courts in the saddle; school boards out," William R. Hazard.
Phi Delta Kappan 56: 259-261 Dec '74 (5).
"Financing public schools after Rodriguez," John E. Coons. Sat
R World 1: 44-47 Oct 9 '73.
"From the states ... Rodriguez: reactions." Compact 7: 18-23
May/June '73.
"In a manner restrained," John E. Coons. Nation 216: 556
Apr 30 '73.
"Legal challenges to public school finance," Arthur E. Wise.
Sch R 82: 1-25 Nov '73.
"Major groups file on Rodriguez." Phi Delta Kappan 54: 138
Oct '72.
"Paying for schools." Time 101: 59 Apr 2 '73.
"The real issue: need for tax reform," David Hall. Compact 7:
24-26 May/June '73.
"Recent adventures of state school finance: a saga of rocket ships
and glider planes," Joel S. Berke. Sch R 82: 183-206 Feb
'74.
"Rodriguez: a dream shattered or a call for finance reform?"
Thomas A. Shannon. Phi Delta Kappan 54: 587-588, 640-641
May '73.
"Rodriguez ruling fails to halt finance reform," George Neill.
Phi Delta Kappan 54: 637-638 May '73.
*"Rodriguez, the decision." Compact 7: 3-8 May/June '73.
*"Rodriguez, the dissent." Compact 7: 10-16 May/June '73.
"Ruckus over Rodriguez and how most of the media goofed."
Natns Sch 91: 14-15 May '73.
"School taxes." Newsweek 81: 97-98 Apr 2 '73.
"Schooling not a fundamental right," Alison Wolf. Times Eductnl
Supp 3019: 19 Apr 6 '73.
"Supreme Court and school finance: some possibilities," H.
L. Preston. Phi Delta Kappan 54: 120-123 Oct '72
(5).
"Supreme Court ponders momentous Texas case." Phi Delta Kap
pan 54: 288 Dec '72.
"This much, at least: the Court," James J. Kilpatrick. Natl R
25: 1047-1052 Sept 28 '73. Reaction: 25: 1084 Oct 12 '73
(3).
"Two fateful decisions," Robert M. Hutchins. Center Mag 8: 7-
13 Jan '75. Condensed in: Eductn Dig 40: 17-20 Apr '75
(2).
"What did the Supreme Court say in deciding Rodriguez?" Earl
Hoffman. Sch Mgt 17: 9, 12-13 May '73.
"Why some kids have a right to bilingual education." Compact
9: 16-19 Aug '75 (2).

3329.   Camp v. Pitts   Mar 26, 1973   411 U.S. 138
        *Admin Law (Gellhorn) 338-341
        Significant Decisions 1972/73   87-88

3330. Mescalero Apache Tribe v. Jones   Mar 27, 1973   411 U.S. 145
       Significant Decisions 1972/73 130-131

3331. McClanahan v. Arizona State Tax   Mar 27, 1973   411 U.S. 164
       Commission
       *Am Indian v. 4, 3018-3026
       *Consttnl Law (Barrett) 463-465
       Significant Decisions 1972/73 130

3332. Butz v. Glover Livestock Commis-   Mar 28, 1973   411 U.S. 183
       sion Co.
       *Legal Environment 176-178
       Significant Decisions 1972/73 88-89
       *Text Administrative Law 158-160

3333. Lemon v. Kurtzman   Apr 2, 1973   411 U.S. 193
       Digest 24-25
       School in the Legal Structure 81-82
       Significant Decisions 1972/73 37-38
       Sup Ct Review 1973 70-71

3334. Fontaine v. United States   Apr 2, 1973   411 U.S. 213
       *Cases Criml Justice 1114-1115
       Significant Decisions 1972/73 57

3335. Brown v. United States   Apr 17, 1973   411 U.S. 223
       *Cases Criml Law (Hall) 1010-1012
       *Criminal Procedure (Lewis) 307-310
       Significant Decisions 1972/73 51
       *Sup Ct and Criml Process 352-354

3336. Davis v. United States   Apr 17, 1973   411 U.S. 233
       *Consttnl Criml (Scarboro) 816-821
       *Criminal Law (Kadish) 1558-1562
       Modern Criml Procedure 454-455
       Significant Decisions 1972/73 62-63
       PERIODICALS:
       "Supreme Court review (1973)."   J Criml Law and Crimlgy 64:
       434-438 Dec '73.

3337. Tollett v. Henderson   Apr 17, 1973   411 U.S. 258
       Against 221-225
       *Criminal Law (Kadish) 1223-1225
       Significant Decisions 1972/73 61-62

3338. Employees of Department of Public   Apr 18, 1973   411 U.S. 279
       Health and Welfare v. Department
       of Public Health and Welfare of
       Missouri
       Significant Decisions 1972/73 113-114

3339. Askew v. American Waterways   Apr 18, 1973   411 U.S. 325
       Operators, Inc.
       *Cases Admiralty 741-750
       Significant Decisions 1972/73 105-106

3340. Hensley v. Municipal Court, San   Apr 18, 1973   411 U.S. 345
       Jose-Milpitas Judicial District
       Significant Decisions 1972/73 60

3341. Mourning v. Family Public   Apr 24, 1973   411 U. S. 356
          Services, Inc.
       *Introduction (Cataldo) 58-61
       *Legal Environment 532-535
       *Legal Problems 1033-1037
        Significant Decisions 1972/73 103
       *Text Social Issues 306-310

3342. Palmore v. United States   Apr 24, 1973   411 U. S. 389
       *Cases Federal Courts 89-100
       *Consttnl Law (Barrett) 542-544
        Significant Decisions 1972/73 80-81

3343. United States v. Russell   Apr 24, 1973   411 U. S. 423
          Against 323-333
          Arrest (Waddington) 103
       *Basic Criminal 484-490
       *Cases Criml Justice 460-474
       *Cases Criml Law (Hall) 842-848
       *Cases Criml Law (Perkins) 730-736
       *Cases Drug 341-348
       *Consttnl Law (Klein) 530-536
       *Criminal Law (Dix) 675-683
       *Criminal Law (Kadish) 1091-1095
       *Criminal Procedure (Lewis) 414-418
       *Due Process 139-140
        Law of Arrest (Creamer) 498-504
       *Leading Consttnl Cases 395-407
        Police 265-267
       *Principles Arrest 428-436
        Significant Decisions 1972/73 51-52
       *Sup Ct and Criml Process 477-480
       *Teaching Materials 409-416
       *Text Social Issues 9-12
       PERIODICALS:
          "Enmeshed in entrapment." Time 101: 103 May 7 '73.
          "Supreme Court review (1973)." J Criml Law and Crimlgy 64:
             407-413 Dec '73.

3344. Preiser v. Rodriguez   May 7, 1973   411 U. S. 475
       *Civil Rights (Abernathy) 1980 146-154
       *Legislative (Hetzel) 291-293
        Significant Decisions 1972/73 60-61

3345. Georgia v. United States   May 7, 1973   411 U. S. 526
       *Civil Rights (Abernathy) 1980 614-620
        Significant Decisions 1972/73 96-97

3346. United States v. Cartwright   May 7, 1973   411 U. S. 546
        Significant Decisions 1972/73 117

3347. Gibson v. Berryhill   May 7, 1973   411 U. S. 564
       *Admin Law (Schwartz) 428-429
       *Introduction (Mashaw) 401-404
        Significant Decisions 1972/73 12-13

3348. Kern County Land Co. v. Occidental   May 7, 1973   411 U. S. 582
          Petroleum Corporation
        Significant Decisions 1972/73 115-116

3349. New Jersey Welfare Rights   May 7, 1973   411 U.S. 619
         Organization v. Cahill
         Significant Decisions 1972/73 25-26
         *Text Sex Based Discrimination 288-290

3350. Burbank v. Lockheed Air Terminal   May 14, 1973   411 U.S. 624
         Inc.
         Consttnl Law (Barrett) 362-363
         *Consttnl Law (Barron) 283-285
         *Federal System 341-344
         *Legal Environment 203-204
         Significant Decisions 1972/73 106-107
         PERIODICALS:
         "Court voids Burbank curfew: FAA airlines uncertain of scope."
         Aviation Wk 98: 26 May 21 '73.

3351. United States v. Pennsylvania   May 14, 1973   411 U.S. 655
         Industrial Chemical Corporation
         *Introduction (Mashaw) 49-55
         Significant Decisions 1972/73 104-105

3352. Frontiero v. Richardson   May 14, 1973   411 U.S. 677
         *Am Consttn (Lockhart) 947-949
         *Am Consttnl Law (Mason) 509-514
         *Am Consttnl Law (Saye) 469-470
         *Am Consttnl Law (Shapiro) 593-595
         Brethren 253-255
         CQ Guide 633
         *Cases Consttnl Law (Gunther) 867-870
         *Cases Consttnl Rights 888-890
         *Cases Individual 362-367
         *Civil Liberties (Barker) 340-344
         *Civil Rights (Abernathy) 1977 566-568
         *Comparative 343-345
         *Consttnl Law (Barrett) 880-884
         *Consttnl Law (Barron) 648-653
         *Consttnl Law (Freund) 930-934
         *Consttnl Law (Grossman) 618-621
         *Consttnl Rights (Kemerer) 519-522
         *Legal Problems 707-712
         *Processes 583-589
         *Sex Discrimination 1975 111-116
         Significant Decisions 1972/73 13-14
         Sup Ct Review 1979 374-375
         *Text Consttnl Aspects 80-89
         *Text Sex Based Discrimination 80-89
         *Woman 29-31
         PERIODICALS:
         "Sex equality: impact of a key decision." US News 74: 69
         May 28 '73.

3353. Moor v. Alameda County   May 14, 1973   411 U.S. 693
         *Elements Civil 242-245
         Significant Decisions 1972/73 100-101

3354. Federal Maritime Commission v.   May 14, 1973   411 U.S. 726
         Seatrain Lines, Inc.
         Significant Decisions 1972/73 90-91

3355. Gulf States Utilities Co. v.   May 14, 1973   411 U.S. 747
       Federal Power Commission
       Significant Decisions 1972/73 95-96

3356. Gagnon v. Scarpelli   May 14, 1973   411 U.S. 778
       *Basic Criminal 104-108
       *Cases Criml Law (Hall) 1153-1158
       *Consttnl Law (Felkenes) 408-409
       *Consttnl Rights (Palmer) 496-502
       *Criminal Justice (Way) 498-502
       *Criminal Law (Kadish) 1486-1489
       *Due Process 240-242
       *Poverty 163-166
       Significant Decisions 1972/73 56-57
       *Sup Ct and Criml Process 747-749
       *Text Administrative Law 124-128
       *US Prison Law v. 4, 313-319
       PERIODICALS:
       "Parole and probation revocation procedures after Morrissey and
       Gagnon," H. Richmond Fisher. J Criml Law and Crimlgy 65:
       46-61 Mar '74.

3357. McDonnell Douglas Corporation   May 14, 1973   411 U.S. 792
       v. Green
       *Civil Rights (Abernathy) 1980 464-468
       *Collective Bargaining 841-847
       *Racial Equality 103-104
       *Sex Discrimination 1975 400-404
       Significant Decisions 1972/73 101-102

3358. Hall v. Cole   May 21, 1973   412 U.S. 1
       Significant Decisions 1972/73 79-80
       PERIODICALS:
       "Significant decisions in labor cases." Monthly Labor R 96: 81-
       83 Aug '73.

3359. Chaffin v. Stynchcombe   May 21, 1973   412 U.S. 17
       Defendants 359-360
       Significant Decisions 1972/73 68-69

3360. Michigan v. Payne   May 21, 1973   412 U.S. 47
       Significant Decisions 1972/73 68

3361. National Labor Relations Board v.   May 21, 1973   412 U.S. 67
       Boeing Co.
       *Cases Labor (Leslie) 683-685
       *Cases Labor (Oberer) 822-829
       Significant Decisions 1972/73 111-112
       PERIODICALS:
       "Significant decisions in labor cases." Monthly Labor R 96: 79-
       80 Aug '73.

3362. Booster Lodge, International Asso-   May 21, 1973   412 U.S. 84
       ciation of Machinists and Aerospace
       Workers v. National Labor Relations
       Board
       *Labor Law (Twomey) 349-351
       Significant Decisions 1972/73 111

PERIODICALS:
"Significant decisions in labor cases. " Monthly Labor R 96: 80-81 Aug '73.

3363. School Board of Richmond v. Virginia   May 21, 1973   412 U.S. 92
Board of Education
Bradley v. Virginia Board of Education
Disaster 155-159
PERIODICALS:
"Merge city-suburban schools. " US News 74: 53 June 4 '73.
"Schools in limbo. " Economist 247: 55-56 May 26 '73.
"A step sideways. " Newsweek 81: 62 June 4 '73.
"Supreme Court agrees to hear Richmond's desegregation case. "
Phi Delta Kappan 54: 506 Mar '73.
"Supreme Court backs Nixon on integration issue, " Jack McCurdy.
Times Eductnl Supp 3028: 14 June 8 '73.

3364. Columbia Broadcasting System, Inc.   May 29, 1973   412 U.S. 94
v. Democratic National Committee
Federal Communications Commission v.
Business Executives' Move for
Vietnam Peace
Post-Newsweek Stations, Capital area,
Inc. v. Business Executives' Move
for Vietnam Peace
American Broadcasting Co. v. Democratic
National Committee
*Am Consttnl Law (Saye) 340-342
*Bill (Cohen) 315-329
CQ Guide 446-447
Cases Consttnl Law (Gunther) 1303-1304
*Cases Electronic 265-275
Communication (Hemmer) v. 2, 313-316, 354
*Communications Law 307-365
*Consttnl Law (Barrett) 1360-1372
*Consttnl Law (Barron) 872-877
*Freedom of Speech (Haiman) 179-182
Freedom of the Press (Schmidt) 175, 176-182
Good Guys 121-141
Law of Mass 548, 551-559
*Mass Communications 816-823
*Mass Media (Devol) 328-334
Mass Media (Francois) 522-526
Significant Decisions 1972/73 42-43
PERIODICALS:
"Limited access. " Newsweek 81: 73-74 June 11 '73.
"Media access; romance and reality, " William Francois. America
129: 186-188 Sept 22 '73 (2).

3365. Keeble v. United States   May 29, 1973   412 U.S. 205
Significant Decisions 1972/73 74-75

3366. Schneckloth v. Bustamonte   May 29, 1973   412 U.S. 218
Against 99-102
*Basic Criminal 340-349
*Cases Criml Justice 283-299
*Cases Criml Law (Hall) 813-818
Criminal Evidence 362-363
*Criminal Justice (Galloway) 148-155

Criminal Law (Felkenes) 40-43
*Criminal Law (Kadish) 923-929, 1562-1566
*Criminal Procedure (Lewis) 216-222
*Leading Consttnl Cases 187-202
Police 207-208
Significant Decisions 1972/73 50-51
*Sup Ct and Criml Process 293-297
PERIODICALS:
"Schneckloth v. Bustamonte: the question of noncustodial and cus-
todial consent searches," J. Vegosen. J Criml Law and
Crimlgy 66: 286-305 Sept '75.
"Supreme Court review (1973)." J Criml Law and Crimlgy 64:
418-424 Dec '73.

3367.	Cupp v. Murphy				May 29, 1973 412 U.S. 291
Against 98-99
*Cases Criml Justice 262-268
*Cases Criml Law (Hall) 797-799
*Consttnl Law (Maddex) 176-178
*Criminal Evidence 328-329
Criminal Evidence 549-550
Criminal Law (Felkenes) 76-77
*Criminal Procedure (Lewis) 202-204
*Introduction (Cataldo) 310-312
Law of Arrest (Creamer) 287-290
Law of Arrest (Markle) 48-50
*Leading Consttnl Cases 166-168
Police 209-211
Significant Decisions 1972/73 47
*Sup Ct and Criml Process 223-226

3368.	Doe v. McMillan				May 29, 1973 412 U.S. 306
Communication (Hemmer) v. 1, 256-257
Significant Decisions 1972/73 123-125

3369.	United States v. Bishop			May 29, 1973 412 U.S. 346
Significant Decisions 1972/73 74

3370.	United States v. Mississippi Tax		June 4, 1973 412 U.S. 363
Commission
*Consttnl Law (Barrett) 477-478
Significant Decisions 1972/73 131-132

3371.	United States v. Chicago, Burlington	June 4, 1973 412 U.S. 401
and Quincy Railroad
Significant Decisions 1972/73 119
PERIODICALS:
"What constitutes contribution to capital is still unclear--can it be
treated as gift?" A. Jan Behrsin. J Taxation 44: 270-275
May '76.

3372.	Northcross v. Memphis Board of		June 4, 1973 412 U.S. 427
Education
Busing 13-14
Significant Decisions 1972/73 102

3373.	Douglas v. Buder				June 4, 1973 412 U.S. 430
Significant Decisions 1972/73 55-56

3374. Strunk v. United States   June 11, 1973 412 U.S. 434
       Criminal Law (Felkenes) 270-272
       Significant Decisions 1972/73 58
       PERIODICALS:
       "Supreme Court review (1973)." J Criml Law and Crimlgy 64:
       442-444 Dec '73.

3375. Vlandis v. Kline   June 11, 1973 412 U.S. 441
       *Am Consttn (Lockhart) 1174-1178
       *Cases Consttnl Rights 1154-1158
       *Consttnl Law (Barrett) 1028-1031
       Education (Lapati) 258-259
       *Introduction (Cataldo) 255-258
       Rise 160-161
       Significant Decisions 1972/73 9-10
       Sup Ct Review 1975 318-320
       PERIODICALS:
       "Out-of-state tuition and the Connecticut case," Raymond Leisy.
           J College Student Personnel 14: 468-470 Nov '73.
       "Public college tuition flap," Robert F. Carbone. Sat R 2: 49-
           50 Feb 8 '75.
       "Supreme Court decides out of state tuition case." Phi Delta Kap-
           pan 55: 86-87 Sept '73.
       "Supreme Court decision regarding out-of-state tuition," Raymond
           Leisy. J Col Student Personnel 15: 3 Jan '74.

3376. Wardius v. Oregon   June 11, 1973 412 U.S. 470
       *Criminal Law (Kadish) 1281
       Criminal Procedure (Wells) 34
       *Due Process 133-134
       Significant Decisions 1972/73 52-53

3377. Kenosha v. Bruno   June 11, 1973 412 U.S. 507
       Significant Decisions 1972/73 100

3378. Logue v. United States   June 11, 1973 412 U.S. 521
       Significant Decisions 1972/73 107

3379. Dean v. Gadsden Times Publishing   June 11, 1973 412 U.S. 543
       Corporation
       Significant Decisions 1972/73 13
       PERIODICALS:
       "Significant decisions in labor cases." Monthly Labor R 96: 66
       Nov '73.

3380. Goldstein v. California   June 18, 1973 412 U.S. 546
       *Cases Copyright (Kaplan) 713-734
       *Cases Copyright (Nimmer) 477-494
       *Consttnl Law (Barrett) 357-359
       *Copyright 867-891
       *Legal Regulation 491-502
       *Processes 216-219
       Significant Decisions 1972/73 125-126
       Sup Ct Review 1975 147-187

3381. United States v. Little Lake   June 18, 1973 412 U.S. 580
       Misere Land Co.
       Significant Decisions 1972/73 82

3382. Weinberger v. Hynson, Wescott   June 18, 1973 412 U.S. 609
       and Dunning, Inc.
       *Cases Food 471-480
       *Introduction (Mashaw) 508-515
       Significant Decisions 1972/73 108
       PERIODICALS:
       "Supreme Court rule on ineffective drugs gives FDA sweeping reg-
          ulatory powers," Judy Gardner. Natl J 5: 963 June 30 '73.
       "Toward a new era in consumer protection: the Supreme Court
          rulings on drug effectiveness," Wallace F. Janssen. FDA Con-
          sumer 7: 19-27 Oct '73.

3383. Weinberger v. Bentex Pharmaceuticals, June 18, 1973 412 U.S. 645
       Inc.
       *Cases Food 481-483
       *Introduction (Mashaw) 515-517
       Significant Decisions 1972/73 109-110
       PERIODICALS:
       "Supreme Court will decide outcome in FDA, industry drug effec-
          tiveness battle," Judy Gardner. Natl J 5: 519-526 Apr 14
          '73.
       "Toward a new era in consumer protection; the Supreme Court
          rulings on drug effectiveness," Wallace F. Janssen. FDA
          Consumer 7: 19-27 Oct '73 (4).

3384. USV Pharmaceutical Corporation v.   June 18, 1973 412 U.S. 655
       Weinberger
       *Cases Food 483-487
       Significant Decisions 1972/73 109
       PERIODICALS:
       See listing at 412 U.S. 645, entry no. 3383.

3385. United States v. Students Challenging   June 18, 1973 412 U.S. 669
       Regulatory Agency Procedures
       Aberdeen & Rockfish Railroad Co. v.
       Students Challenging Regulatory Agency
          Procedures (SCRAP)
       *Admin Law (Gellhorn) 977-982
       *Admin Law (Schwartz) 581-586
       *Courts Judges 283-286
       *Elements Civil 176-183
       *Environmental 636-639
       *Federal System 58-59
       *Processes 1243-1247
       Significant Decisions 1972/73 83-84
       PERIODICALS:
       "Door to courts opens wider," Arnold W. Reitze, Jr. and Glenn
          L. Reitze. Environment 15: 2-3 Oct '73.

3386. Gaffney v. Cummings   June 18, 1973 412 U.S. 735
       *Consttnl Law (Barrett) 967-971
       Significant Decisions 1972/73 20-21
       Sup Ct Review 1973 17-24

3387. White v. Regester   June 18, 1973 412 U.S. 755
       *Consttnl Law (Barrett) 971-974
       *Processes 1208-1210
       *Racial Equality 95-96

Significant Decisions 1972/73 21
Sup Ct Review 1973 26-28

3388. White v. Weiser   June 18, 1973 412 U.S. 783
        *Civil Rights (Abernathy) 1977 616-619
        Consttnl Law (Barrett) 974-975
        Significant Decisions 1972/73 123
        Sup Ct Review 1973 9-12

3389. Atchison, Topeka and Santa Fe Rail-   June 18, 1973 412 U.S. 800
        way v. Wichita Board of Trade
        Interstate Commerce Commission v.
        Wichita Board of Trade
        Significant Decisions 1972/73 86-87
        *Text Administrative Law 9-11

3390. Barnes v. United States   June 18, 1973 412 U.S. 837
        Against 321-323
        *Cases Criml Law (Inbau) 661-669
        *Criminal Evidence 145-146
        *Criminal Justice 437-441
        *Criminal Law (Kadish) 1373-1375
        *Elements Criminal 201-204
        Significant Decisions 1972/73 54-55

3391. Gilligan v. Morgan   June 21, 1973 413 U.S. 1
        *Consttnl Law (Barrett) 113
        Significant Decisions 1972/73 77-78

3392. Miller v. California   June 21, 1973 413 U.S. 15
        Am Consttn (Kelly) 999
        *Am Consttn (Lockhart) 730-734
        *Am Consttnl Law (Bartholomew) v. 2, 94-96
        *Am Consttnl Law (Mason) 602-608
        *Am Consttnl Law (Saye) 319-322
        *Am Consttnl Law (Shapiro) 410-417
        *Bill (Cohen) 97-101
        CQ Guide 429
        *Cases Civil Liberties 255-260
        *Cases Consttnl Law (Cushman) 485-491
        *Cases Consttnl Law (Gunther) 1356-1360
        *Cases Consttnl Rights 595-600
        *Cases Criml Law (Inbau) 275-287
        *Cases Individual 897-903
        Civil Liberties (Wasby) 172-174
        *Civil Rights (Abernathy) 1977 482-486
        Civil Rights (Schimmel) 59-60
        Communication (Hemmer) v. 1, 170-171
        Conceived 109-111
        *Consttnl Law (Barrett) 1416-1422
        *Consttnl Law (Barron) 921-925
        *Consttnl Law (Felkenes) 138-142
        *Consttnl Law (Freund) 1300-1302
        *Consttnl Law (Lockhart) 888-892
        *Consttnl Law (Maddex) 426-430
        *Consttnl Rights (Kemerer) 188-193
        *Courts Judges 1244-1250
        Crisis 240-243

*Documents History v. 2, 801-804
Editorials 1973 838-845
*First Amendment (Franklin) 400-408
Freedom and the Court 222-224
*Freedom of Speech (Haiman) 144-145
Great Events Worldwide v. 3, 1174-1181
Handbook 615-621
*Historic Documents 1973 611-621
Law of Mass 375-382
Law of Obscenity 45-48, 120-124, 139-143, 164-167
*Law of Obscenity 333-345
Literature 230-234
*Mass Communications 571-574
*Mass Media (Devol) 140-143
Mass Media (Devol) 144-145; reprinted from "The Obscenity Quag-
    mire," Burt Pines. California State Bar J 49: 509 Nov/Dec
    '74.
Mass Media (Francois) 366-370
*Obscenity (Bosmajian) 138-147
Obscenity (Sunderland) 8-17
*Pornography 135-151
Significant Decisions 1972/73 31-32
Sup Ct (Forte) 72
*Sup Ct and Criml Process 1065-1069
*Sup Ct Obscenity 91-124
PERIODICALS:
    "Behind the fig leaf; a legal analysis," Charles M. Whelan.
        America 129: 84-87 Aug 18 '73 (5).
    "Conservatives v. conservatism; the question of obscenity," R.
        Shnayerson. Harper's Mag 247: 57 Sept '73.
    "Court and obscenity," William F. Fore. Christian Century 91:
        717-718 July 17 '74 (2).
    "Court ruling: let states decide what is obscene." US News 75:
        35-36 July 2 '73.
    "Dealing with obscenity: kid porn v. the Burger five," John
        Leonard. Current 154: 19-21 Sept '73.
    "Dealing with obscenity: what community standards?" Max Lerner.
        Current 154: 17-19 Sept '73 (2).
    "Freedom from filth," William W. Brickman. Intellect 102: 149
        Dec '73. Reaction: E. M. Oboler. 103: 263-264 Jan '75.
    "Giant step backward." Nation 217: 37-38 July 16 '73.
    "Green light to combat smut," Charles H. Keating. Readers Dig
        104: 147-150 Jan '74.
    "Hardnosed about hard-core." Time 102: 42, 45 July 2 '73.
    "Industry brief sees chaos following high court obscenity ruling,"
        Susan Wagner. Pub Weekly 204: 48 July 23 '73.
    "Last tango in Paris, et al. v. the Supreme Court: the current
        state of obscenity law," J. Donald Ragsdale. Q J Speech 61:
        279-289 Oct '75 (2).
    "Librarians ask reconsideration of latest obscenity decisions."
        Phi Delta Kappan 55: 84 Sept '73.
    "Media coalition says high court is way behind." Pub Weekly
        204: 90 July 16 '73.
    "Obscenity and the constitution," Harriet F. Pilpel. Pub Weekly
        204: 24-27 Dec 10 '73. Reaction: Charles Rembar. 205:
        77-79 Jan 14 '74.
    "Obscenity guidelines threaten widespread confusion over local
        standards," Susan Wagner. Pub Weekly 204: 53-54 July 2
        '73.

"Obscenity: historical and behavioral perspectives, " W. Barnett
Pearce and Dwight L. Teeter, Jr. Intellect 104: 166-170
Nov '75. Reaction: 104: 480 Apr '76 (2).
"Obscenity: redistributing the risk. " America 129: 5 July 7
'73.
"Porn: the vice goes on ice. " Newsweek 82: 44-45, 47 July
23 '73.
"Pornography and Court presupposition. " Christian Century 90:
747-748 July 18 '73. Reaction: 90: 901 Sept 12 '73.
"Pornography, community, law, " Gary North. Natl R 25: 943-
944 Aug 31 '73.
"Sex at high noon in Times Square, " Nathan Lewis. New Republic
169: 19-21 July 7 '73. Same with title: "What new guidelines?"
Current 154: 12-17 Sept '73.
"Supreme Court hands down pornography decision. " Am Libraries
4: 462 Sept '73.
"Supreme Court review (1973). " J Criml Law and Crimlgy 64:
399-407 Dec '73 (5).
"Turn of the tide. " Newsweek 82: 18, 21 July 2 '73.
"Will fig leaves blossom again?" Richard A. Blake. America
129: 82-84 Aug 18 '73.

3393.   Paris Adult Theatre I v. Slaton   June 21, 1973 413 U.S. 49
Am Consttn (Kelly) 999-1000
*Am Consttn (Lockhart) 734-741
*Bill (Cohen) 95-96, 124-125
Brethren 244-245, 247-253
*Cases Civil Liberties 261-266
*Cases Consttnl Law (Cushman) 491-496
*Cases Consttnl Law (Gunther) 1360-1367
*Cases Consttnl Rights 600-609
*Cases Individual 903-914
Communication (Hemmer) v. 1, 171-172
Communications Law 369-370
*Consttnl Law (Barrett) 735-736, 1422-1431
*Consttnl Law (Barron) 926-933
*Consttnl Law (Freund) 1302-1304
*Consttnl Law (Grossman) 1250-1256
*Consttnl Law (Lockhart) 892-899
*Douglas 227-230
*First Amendment (Franklin) 408-420
Freedom and the Court 222-224
*Freedom of Speech (Haiman) 145-147
*Historic Documents 1973 621-628
*Justices (Friedman) v. 5, 256-275
Law of Obscenity 67
*Law of Obscenity 345-356
*Leading Consttnl Decisions 285-297
Literature 235-238
*Mass Communications 574-581
*Mass Media (Devol) 183-187
*Obscenity (Bosmajian) 203-221
Obscenity (Sunderland) 17-26
*Processes 791-797
*Rights (Shattuck) 118-119
Significant Decisions 1972/73 32-33
*Sup Ct Obscenity 23-90
PERIODICALS:
"Behind the fig leaf; a legal analysis, " Charles M. Whelan. Amer-
ica 129: 84-87 Aug 18 '73 (5).

576   U.S. Supreme Court Decisions

"Dealing with obscenity: what community standards?" Max Lerner.
Current 154: 17-19 Sept '73 (2).
"Supreme Court review (1973)." J Criml Law and Crimlgy 64:
399-407 Dec '73 (5).
"Will fig leaves blossom again?" Richard A. Blake. America
129: 82-84 Aug 18 '73 (5).
See also listing at 413 U.S. 15, entry no. 3392.

3394. Kaplan v. California   June 21, 1973 413 U.S. 115
Brethren 245-253
Communication (Hemmer) v. 1, 172
Literature 238-240
*Obscenity (Bosmajian) 148-150
Obscenity (Sunderland) 26-28
Significant Decisions 1972/73 34
Sup Ct Obscenity 125-133
PERIODICALS:
See listing at 413 U.S. 49, entry no. 3393.

3395. United States v. Twelve 200 Foot   June 21, 1973 413 U.S. 123
Reels of Super 8mm Film
Brethren 196, 200-204, 246-253
Communication (Hemmer) v. 1, 201
*Obscenity (Bosmajian) 224-228
Obscenity (Sunderland) 28-32
Significant Decisions 1972/73 33
*Sup Ct Obscenity 135-152
PERIODICALS:
See listing at 413 U.S. 49, entry no. 3393.

3396. United States v. Orito   June 21, 1973 413 U.S. 139
Brethren 196, 200-204, 246-253
Communication (Hemmer) v. 1, 200-201
*Consttnl Law (Barrett) 1431-1433
*Obscenity (Bosmajian) 221-224
Obscenity (Sunderland) 32-33
Significant Decisions 1972/73 33-34
*Sup Ct Obscenity 153-162
PERIODICALS:
See listing at 413 U.S. 49, entry no. 3393

3397. Colgrove v. Batten   June 21, 1973 413 U.S. 149
*Civil Procedure (Carrington) 220-230
*Due Process 254-255
*Legal Environment 27-28
Significant Decisions 1972/73 78-79
PERIODICALS:
"Jury decision models and the Supreme Court," Bernard Grofman.
Policy Studies J 8: 749-772 Spring '80 (4).

3398. Keyes v. Denver School District   June 21, 1973 413 U.S. 189
No. 1
Am Consttn (Kelly) 1005-1006
Brethren 260-267, 268
Busing 32-37
CQ Guide 598
Cases Consttnl Law (Gunther) 774-776
*Civil Rights (Abernathy) 1977 528-533
Conceived 183-184

*Consttn (Morris) 754-764
Consttnl Counterrevolution 50-51
*Consttnl Law (Barrett) 836-840
*Consttnl Law (Barron) 622-626
Digest 96-97
Disaster 160-202
Editorials 1973 846-851
Education (Lapati) 300-302
*Educational Policy 410-426
Freedom and the Court 381
From Brown 164-165, 195-200
*Great School Bus 65-77
*Law and Public Education (Goldstein) 604-635
*Law of Public Education 657-662
*Processes 506-513, 524-529
*Racial Equality 74-75
*School Law (Alexander) 480-486
Schools (Hogan) 37-55
Significant Decisions 1972/73 17-18
PERIODICALS:
"Desegregation: the justices look northward. " Am Sch Bd J
    160: 11 Aug '73.
"Denver decision: death knoll for de facto segregation?" Thomas
    A. Shannon. Phi Delta Kappan 55: 6-9 Sept '73.
"Judicial evolution of the law of school integration since Brown v.
    Board of Education," Frank T. Read. Law and Contemporary
    Problems 39: 7-49 Winter '75 (6).
"Legitimizing segregation: the Supreme Court's recent school de-
    segregation decisions," John Bannon. Civil Rights Dig 9: 12-
    17 Summer '77 (3).
"School desegregation and the courts," William L. Taylor. Socl
    Policy 6: 32-41 Jan '76 (3).
"School desegregation: the court, the Congress and the President,"
    Michael B. Wise. Sch R 82: 159-182 Feb '74 (3).
"Supreme Court faces questions raised by northern segregation,"
    John Beckler. Sch Mgt 16: 4-5 Dec '73.
"Supreme Court's abuse of power," Lino A. Graglia. Natl R 30:
    892-896 July 21 '78.

3399. Almeida-Sanchez v. United States   June 21, 1973 413 U.S. 266
    Against 97-98
    Brethren 259-260
    *Cases Criml Justice 367-377
    *Consttnl Law (Maddex) 214-216
    *Criminal Law (Kadish) 899-903
    *Criminal Procedure (Lewis) 261-266
    Defendants 282-283
    *Legislation (Linde) 797-800
    Police 208-209
    Significant Decisions 1972/73 48
    *Sup Ct and Criml Process 307-310
    PERIODICALS:
    "Supreme Court review (1973). " J Criml Law and Crimlgy 64:
        428-434 Dec '73.

3400. United States v. Ash   June 21, 1973 413 U.S. 300
    Against 252-256
    *Basic Criminal 632-642
    *Cases Criml Justice 702-716

*Cases Criml Law (Hall) 899-905
*Criminal Justice (Galloway) 180-189
*Criminal Law (Kadish) 1039-1042
Law of Arrest (Creamer) 463-468
Significant Decisions 1972/73 44
PERIODICALS:
"Supreme Court review (1973)." J Criml Law and Crimlgy 64:
424-428 Dec '73.

3401. National Association for the Ad-   June 21, 1973 413 U.S. 345
vancement of Colored People v.
New York
Significant Decisions 1972/73 79

3402. Pittsburgh Press Co. v. Pittsburgh   June 21, 1973 413 U.S. 376
Commission on Human Relations
Advertising 21-22
*Am Consttn (Lockhart) 750-752
*Bill (Cohen) 336-341
CQ Guide 427
*Cases Consttnl Rights 622-625
Communication (Hemmer) v. 2, 324-325
*Communications Law 289-304
Consttnl Law (Barrett) 1229
*Consttnl Law (Barrett) 1342-1344
*Consttnl Law (Barron) 835-839
Freedom of the Press (Schmidt) 250-251
Handbook 38-41, 160-161, 165
Law of Mass 563-564
*Mass Communications 173-177
Mass Media (Francois) 401-402
Significant Decisions 1972/73 41
Sup Ct Review 1976 65-68
*Text Sex Based Discrimination 695-711
PERIODICALS:
"First Amendment right of advertiser upheld." Editor and Pub
112: 13 June 23 '79.
"Significant decisions in labor cases." Monthly Labor R 96: 81-
83 Sept '73.

3403. New York State Department of   June 21, 1973 413 U.S. 405
Social Services v. Dublino
Onondaga County Department of Social
Services v. Dublino
*Cases Law and Poverty 194-203
*Legal Problems 747-756
*Legislative (Hetzel) 248-254
*Poverty 673-681
Significant Decisions 1972/73 121

3404. Cady v. Dombrowski   June 21, 1973 413 U.S. 433
Against 95-97
*Cases Criml Justice 337-346
*Cases Criml Law (Hall) 803-806
*Consttnl Criml (Scarboro) 359-368
Criminal Evidence 288
Criminal Law (Felkenes) 69-73
*Criminal Law (Kadish) 890-893

Law of Arrest (Markle) 140-147
Significant Decisions 1972/73 47-48

3405. Norwood v. Harrison   June 25, 1973 413 U.S. 455
CQ Guide 602
*Consttn (Morris) 804-808
Consttnl Law (Barrett) 1072-1073, 1460
Digest 97-98
Education (Lapati) 287
*Law and Public Education (Goldstein) 928-937
*Processes 622-625
Significant Decisions 1972/73 18

3406. Levitt and Nyquist v. Committee for   June 25, 1973 413 U.S. 472
Public Education and Religious
Liberty
Anderson v. Committee for Public Education
and Religious Liberty
Cathedral Academy v. Committee for Public
Education and Religious Liberty
*Consttn (Morris) 404-405
Consttnl Law (Barrett) 1459
Digest 25-26
Education (Lapati) 189-190
Freedom and the Court 327
*Historic Documents 1973 641-656
*Religious Freedom (Pfeffer) 55-56
Significant Decisions 1972/73 36
Sup Ct Review 1973 71-75
PERIODICALS:
"Supreme Court and the sectarian school," William W. Brickman.
Intellect 102: 82-84 Nov '73 (4).

3407. Heller v. New York   June 25, 1973 413 U.S. 483
Communication (Hemmer) v. 1, 190-191
Law of Obscenity 211-215
*Law of Obscenity 356-361
Significant Decisions 1972/73 49-50

3408. Roaden v. Kentucky   June 25, 1973 413 U.S. 496
Communication (Hemmer) v. 1, 191-192
Law of Obscenity 216-218
*Law of Obscenity 362-367
Significant Decisions 1972/73 48-49

3409. United States Department of Agriculture June 25, 1973 413 U.S. 508
v. Murry
*Consttnl Law (Freund) 939-941
*Introduction (Mashaw) 180-186
Significant Decisions 1972/73 10-11

3410. United States Department of Agriculture June 25, 1973 413 U.S. 528
v. Moreno
*Legal Problems 698-703
Significant Decisions 1972/73 11

3411. United States Civil Service Com-   June 25, 1973 413 U.S. 548
mission v. National Association
of Letter Carriers

*Am Consttnl Law (Saye) 353-355
*Comparative 594-596
*Consttnl Law (Barrett) 1213-1214
*Douglas 170-174
*Labor Relations (Edwards) 847-856
Significant Decisions 1972/73 39-40
PERIODICALS:
  "Hatch Act in court; some recent developments," P. L. Martin.
    Public Admin R 33: 443-447 Sept '73.
  "Significant decisions in labor cases." Monthly Labor R 96: 58-
    59 Oct '73.

3412. Broadrick v. Oklahoma   June 25, 1973 413 U.S. 601
        *Am Consttn (Lockhart) 620-624
        Cases Consttnl Law (Gunther) 1190-1194
        *Cases Consttnl Rights 428-432
        *Consttnl Law (Barrett) 1317-1319
        *Consttnl Law (Lockhart) 759-764
        Significant Decisions 1972/73 40-41

3413. Sugarman v. Dougall   June 25, 1973 413 U.S. 634
        Consttnl Law (Barrett) 871
        Significant Decisions 1972/73 26
        PERIODICALS:
          "Public employment and the Supreme Court's 1975-76 term," Carl
            F. Goodman. Public Personnel Mgt 5: 287-302 Sept '76
            (12).
          "Significant decisions in labor cases." Monthly Labor R 96: 59-
            60 Oct '73.

3414. Gosa v. Mayden   June 25, 1973 413 U.S. 665
        Warner v. Flemings
        Significant Decisions 1972/73 67
        PERIODICALS:
          "Supreme Court spurns the GI," Marvin M. Karpatkin. Nation
            217: 328-331 Oct 8 '73.

3415. In re Griffiths   June 25, 1973 413 U.S. 717
        Brethren 256-257
        *Civil Rights (Abernathy) 1977 494-495
        Consttnl Law (Barrett) 871-872
        *Consttnl Law (Freund) 923-925
        Significant Decisions 1972/73 26-27

3416. Hunt v. McNair   June 25, 1973 413 U.S. 734
        *Consttn (Morris) 405-406
        Consttnl Law (Barrett) 1460
        Education (Lapati) 186-187
        Freedom and the Court 324
        Significant Decisions 1972/73 38-39
        PERIODICALS:
          "Church colleges and the scramble for public funds; Supreme Court
            ruling," Judy Weidman. Christian Century 93: 883-885 Oct
            20 '76 (3).
          "School aid decisions," Charles M. Whelan. America 129: 6-8
            July 7 '73 (2).

3417. Committee for Public Education and   June 25, 1973 413 U.S. 756
          Religious Liberty v. Nyquist

Anderson v. Committee for Public
Education and Religious Liberty
Nyquist v. Committee for Public Ed-
ucation and Religious Liberty
Cherry v. Committee for Public Ed-
ucation and Religious Liberty
Am Consttn (Kelly) 998
*Am Consttnl Law (Bartholomew) v. 2, 32-36
*Am Consttnl Law (Saye) 304-308
*Am Consttnl Law (Shapiro) 473-483
*Cases Civil Liberties 306-314
*Cases Consttnl Law (Cushman) 536-544
*Civil Rights (Abernathy) 1977 285-289
*Consttn (Morris) 403-404
Consttnl Counterrevolution 256-258
Consttnl Law (Barrett) 1458-1459
Digest 26-27
Education (Lapati) 187-189
*Educational Policy 70-80
*Law and Public Education (Goldstein) 901-917
*Law of Public Education 61-66
Religious Freedom (Arnold) 48
*Religious Freedom (Pfeffer) 56-62
*School Law (Alexander) 204-213
Significant Decisions 1972/73 35-36
PERIODICALS:
"Aid to church-related schools; the Supreme Court says no!"
Robert L. Jacobson. Compact 7: 10-13 Sept '73.
"Aid to parochial schools coming to a halt?" US News 75: 27-
28 July 9 '73.
"Church, state and school." Newsweek 82: 64 July 9 '73.
"Dead end with the courts," William F. Buckley, Jr. Natl R
25: 806-807 July 20 '73.
"No to church-school aid." Time 102: 35 July 9 '73.
"Parochiaid: end of the line?" Stephen J. Pollak. Today's Eductn
62: 77-79, 96 Nov '73 (2).
"Supreme Court and the sectarian school," William W. Brickman.
Intellect 102: 82-84 Nov '73 (4).
"Tax credits and the tests of establishment," Dean M. Kelley.
Christian Century 90: 1024-1028 Oct 17 '73.

3418. Sloan v. Lemon   June 25, 1973 413 U.S. 825
Crouter v. Lemon
Consttnl Law (Barrett) 1459
Digest 27
*Historic Documents 1973 656-658
*Law and Public Education (Goldstein) 918-927
*School Law (Alexander) 214-216
Significant Decisions 1972/73 36-37
Sup Ct Review 1973 76
PERIODICALS:
"Court raps parochaid again." Phi Delta Kappan 55: 84 Sept
'73.
"Parochiaid: end of the line?" Stephen J. Pollak. Today's Eductn
62: 77-79, 96 Nov '73 (2).
"Supreme Court and the sectarian school," William W. Brickman.
Intellect 102: 82-84 Nov '73 (4).

3419. Fausner v. Commissioner of   June 25, 1973 413 U.S. 838

582   U. S. Supreme Court Decisions

Internal Revenue
Significant Decisions 1972/73 119-120

3420. Taylor v. United States   Nov 5, 1973   414 U.S. 17
       *Criminal Justice (Way) 420-421

3421. Wainwright v. Stone   Nov 5, 1973   414 U.S. 21
       *Readings Law 768

3422. Berry v. Cincinnati   Nov 5, 1973   414 U.S. 29
       Significant Decisions 1973/74 38

3423. Kasper v. Pontikes   Nov 19, 1973   414 U.S. 51
       *Am Consttnl Law (Saye) 483-484
       Significant Decisions 1973/74 89-90

3424. Lefkowitz v. Turley   Nov 19, 1973   414 U.S. 70
       Consttnl Law (Barrett) 1211-1212
       *Due Process 246-247
       Significant Decisions 1973/74 34-35

3425. Espinoza v. Farah Manufacturing Co. Nov 19, 1973 414 U.S. 86
       Significant Decisions 1973/74 133
       PERIODICALS:
       "Alien discrimination; the case of a Mexican seamstress," Marvin
       M. Karpatkin. Nation 218: 179-180 Feb 9 '74.
       "Beyond Griggs v. Duke Power Co.: Title VII after Washington
       v. Davis," James D. Portwood and Stuart M. Schmidt. Labor
       Law J 28: 174-181 Mar '77 (3).
       "Significant decisions in labor cases." Monthly Labor R 97: 68-
       69 Feb '74.

3426. Hess v. Indiana   Nov 19, 1973   414 U.S. 105
       Communication (Hemmer) v. 1, 39-40
       Conceived 103-104

3427. North Dakota State Board of Pharmacy Dec 5, 1973 414 U.S. 156
       v. Snyder's Drug Stores, Inc.
       *Consttnl Law (Barrett) 675
       *Consttnl Law (Grossman) 355-358
       *Legal Environment 217-219

3428. Golden State Bottling Co. v. National Dec 5, 1973 414 U.S. 168
       Labor Relations Board
       Basic Text 140-141
       Significant Decisions 1973/74 129-130
       Sup Ct and Labor 138
       PERIODICALS:
       *"Significant decisions in labor cases." Monthly Labor R 97:
       68-69 Apr '74.

3429. Falk v. Brennan   Dec 5, 1973   414 U.S. 190
       Significant Decisions 1973/74 128-129
       PERIODICALS:
       "Significant decisions in labor cases." Monthly Labor R 97: 50-
       51 Mar '74.

3430. United States v. Robinson   Dec 11, 1973   414 U.S. 218
       Against 109-117

*Basic Criminal 319-329
*Cases Civil Liberties 113-120
*Cases Consttnl Law (Cushman) 343-350
*Cases Criml Justice 186-198
*Cases Criml Law (Hall) 792-796
*Civil Rights (Abernathy) 1977 117-121
*Consttnl Criml (Marks) 327-331
*Consttnl Criml (Scarboro) 325-342
*Consttnl Law (Grossman) 799-804
*Criminal Evidence 323-324
*Criminal Justice (Galloway) 155-161
*Criminal Justice (Way) 97-101
 Criminal Law (Felkenes) 95-98
*Criminal Law (Kadish) 871-876
*Criminal Procedure (Lewis) 180-184
 Criminal Procedure (Wells) 36-37
 Defendants 283
*Documents History v. 2, 337-353
 Law of Arrest (Creamer) 250-255
*Law of Arrest (Markle) 43-45
*Law of Evidence 540-547
*Leading Consttnl Cases 143-153
 Police 214-216
*Rights (Shattuck) 35-36
 Significant Decisions 1973/74 16-17
*Sup Ct and Criml Process 232-238
 Sup Ct Review 1974 128-131, 135-136, 150-162, 185 216, 231
*Teaching Materials 270-278
PERIODICALS:
"Key ruling on police power." US News 75: 55 Dec 24 '73.
"Police search without a warrant," Frank Carrington and Lloyd
    Weinreb. Current 162: 28-31 May '74.
*"Search and seizure: a new horizon," Thurgood Marshall. Con-
    temporary Drug Problems 3: 21-44 Spring '74.
"Supreme Court review (1974)." J Criml Law and Crimlgy 65:
    448-453 Dec '74 (2).

3431.   Gustafson v. Florida   Dec 11, 1973   414 U.S. 260
        Criminal Evidence 324-325
        Law of Arrest (Markle) 45-47
        Police 216-218
        Sup Ct Review 1974 130-131, 161
        PERIODICALS:
        "Supreme Court review (1974)." J Criml Law and Crimlgy 65:
            448-453 Dec '74 (2).

3432.   National Labor Relations Board v.   Dec 17, 1973   414 U.S. 270
        Savair Manufacturing Co.
        *Cases Labor (Oberer) 334-341
        *Legal Environment 448-450
        Significant Decisions 1973/74 126-127
        PERIODICALS:
        "Significant decisions in labor cases." Monthly Labor R 97: 49-
            50 Mar '74.

3433.   Zahn v. International Paper Co.   Dec 17, 1973   414 U.S. 291
        *Cases Environmental Law (Gray) 585-593
        *Cases Federal Courts 713-723
        *Civil Procedure (Carrington) 1209-1213

*Civil Procedure (Cound) 566-571
Significant Decisions 1973/74 99-100
PERIODICALS:
"Class action chill." Time 102: 49 Dec 31 '73.
"Supreme Court's ruling inhibits class action, slows up consumer-
    ists." Adv Age 44: 3 Dec 24 '73.

3434. United States v. Calandra   Jan 8, 1974   414 U.S. 338
       Against 423-426
       *Cases Criml Justice 890-902
       *Cases Criml Law (Hall) 833-836, 974-976
       *Civil Liberties (Barker) 214-217
       *Consttnl Law (Grossman) 822-825
       Criminal Law (Felkenes) 113-115
       *Criminal Law (Kadish) 939-943
       *Criminal Procedure (Lewis) 121-126
       Defendants 297
       *Due Process 78-79
       *Elements Criminal 245-255
       Exclusionary 37-38
       Freedom Spent 239-242, 309-310
       Law of Arrest (Creamer) 359-366
       *Leading Consttnl Cases 278-288
       *Police 219-221
       Significant Decisions 1973/74 15-16
       *Sup Ct and Criml Process 518-523
       PERIODICALS:
       "Pulling teeth." Newsweek 83: 72 Jan 21 '74.
       "Supreme Court review (1974)." J Criml Law and Crimlgy 65:
           460-465 Dec '74.

3435. Gateway Coal Co. v. United Mine   Jan 8, 1974   414 U.S. 368
           Workers of America
       Labor Relations (Taylor) 421
       Significant Decisions 1973/74 122-123
       PERIODICALS:
       "Significant decisions in labor cases." Monthly Labor R 97: 67-
           68 Apr '74.

3436. Marshall v. United States   Jan 9, 1974   414 U.S. 417
       Significant Decisions 1973/74 43
       *Text Social Issues 86-89

3437. Communist Party of Indiana v.   Jan 9, 1974   414 U.S. 441
           Whitcomb
       Communication (Hemmer) v. 1, 68
       Consttnl Law (Barrett) 1223-1225
       Significant Decisions 1973/74 90-91

3438. National Railroad Passenger Cor-   Jan 9, 1974   414 U.S. 453
           poration v. National Association
           of Railroad Passengers
       *Introduction (Mashaw) 1005-1012

3439. O'Shea v. Littleton   Jan 15, 1974   414 U.S. 488
       Cases Consttnl Law (Gunther) 1663-1664
       *Consttnl Law (Grossman) 136-140
       Significant Decisions 1973/74 105-106

3440.   O'Brien v. Skinner   Jan 16, 1974   414 U.S. 524
        Significant Decisions 1973/74 51-52
        *US Prison Law v. 5, 479-485

3441.   Lau v. Nichols   Jan 21, 1974   414 U.S. 563
        Authority 53
        *Civil Rights (Abernathy) 1980 403-407
        *Consttn (Morris) 900-903
        Digest 98
        *Education (Hazard) 228-231
        Education (Lapati) 261-263
        Law and Education 220-221
        *Law and Public Education (Goldstein) 694-698
        *School Law (Alexander) 313-315
        Significant Decisions 1973/74 58-59
        *Text Social Issues 271-273
        PERIODICALS:
        "Bilingual education and state legislatures," Bruce Beezer.
           Eductnl Forum 40: 537-541 May '76.
        "The bilingual education mandate: it says schools must 'do some-
           thing,' must do it soon--and probably must find the money to
           get it done," Barbara Deane and Perry A. Zirkel. Am Sch Bd
           J 163: 29-32 July '76.
        "Bilingual education should gain from San Francisco ruling." Phi
           Delta Kappan 55: 582 Apr '74.
        "Bilingual education: the legal mandate," Herbert Teitelbaum and
           Richard H. Hiller. Harvard Eductnl R 47: 138-170 May '77.
        "Colorado Springs wrestles with Lau: a case study in federal in-
           tervention," Elaine Yaffe. Phi Delta Kappan 60: 51-55 Sept
           '78.
        "HEW asks help of 26 states to end language discrimination." Phi
           Delta Kappan 56: 504 Mar '75.
        "Integrity, promise and language planning," Glendon F. Drake.
           Language Learning 25: 267-279 Dec '75.
        "Lau decision and higher education," Todd A. Demitchell. Col
           Student J 11: 344-345 Winter '77.
        "Lingualism: the real implications of Lau v. Nichols," Ronald K.
           S. Macaulay. Claremont Reading Conference Yearbook (Center
           for Developmental Studies in Education) 41: 86-93 '77.
        "School rules." Time 103: 79-80 Feb 4 '74 (2).
        "Suit for bilingual education may be year's most important." Phi
           Delta Kappan 55: 430 Feb '74.
        *"Supreme Court ruling on Chinese children." Integrated Eductn
           12: 33-35 Jan '74.
        "Supreme Court: San Francisco neglects Chinese-speaking kids."
           Phi Delta Kappan 55: 501 Mar '74.
        "Washington's message to school boards: find a way to educate
           non English-speaking students or lose federal funds." Am Sch
           Bd J 163: 32-34 July '76.
        "Your stake, Mr. (or Ms) administrator, in three 1974 Supreme
           Court decisions," Thomas A. Shannon. Phi Delta Kappan
           55: 460-461 Mar '74 (2).

3442.   Sea Land Services, Inc. v. Gaudet   Jan 21, 1974   414 U.S. 573
        *Cases Admiralty 386-391

3443.   Cleveland Board of Education v.   Jan 21, 1974   414 U.S. 632
        LaFleur

Cohen v. Chesterfield County
    School Board
*Am Consttnl Law (Saye) 422-425
 CQ Guide 635
*Cases Individual 479-486
*Consttn (Morris) 586-594
*Consttnl Law (Barrett) 1031-1035
*Consttnl Law (Barron) 721-724
 Digest 98-99
*Education (Hazard) 239-250
 Education (Lapati) 228-230
*Labor Relations (Edwards) 882-888
*Labor Law (Twomey) 411-415
*Law of Public Education 398-404
*Processes 877-888
*Rights (Shattuck) 130-132
*School Law (Alexander) 624-629
*Sex Discrimination 1978 267-279
 Sex Litigation 107-110
 Significant Decisions 1973/74 109-110
*Text Social Issues 50-54
PERIODICALS:
    "Mrs. Cohen's gift to working wives," Norman Lobsenz.   Good
        Housekeeping 179: 16, 18, 22, 24, 27 July '74.
    "Public employment and the Supreme Court," Carl F. Goodman.
        Civil Service J 15: 18-22 July '74 (4).
    "School rules." Time 103: 79-80 Feb 4, '74 (2).
    "Significant decisions in labor cases." Monthly Labor R 97: 65-
        67 Apr '74.
    "Teacher maternity cases coming." Phi Delta Kappan 55: 84
        Sept '73.
    "Unpaid maternity leaves ruled unconstitutional." Phi Delta Kap-
        pan 55: 501-502 Mar '74.
    "Your stake, Mr. (or Ms) administrator, in three 1974 Supreme
        Court decisions," Thomas A. Shannon. Phi Delta Kappan 55:
        460-461 Mar '74 (2).

3444. Holtzman v. Schlesinger   Aug 1, 1973   414 U. S. 1304
        Court Years 235-236
        *Douglas 43-50
        *Federal System 161-166

3445. Alexander v. Gardner-Denver Co. Feb 19, 1974   415 U. S. 36
        *Cases Labor (Leslie) 482-488
        *Cases Labor (Oberer) 953-961
        *Civil Rights (Abernathy) 1980 519-524
        *Collective Bargaining 473-481
        *Labor Relations (Getman) 395-400
        PERIODICALS:
        "Deferral to arbitration awards in Title VII actions," Jay S. Siegel.
            Labor Law J 25: 398-403 July '74.
        "Significant decisions in labor cases." Monthly Labor R 98: 69-
            70 Apr '75.

3446. Phillips Petroleum Co. v. Texaco Feb 19, 1974   415 U. S. 125
        *Cases Federal Courts 130-132

3447. Lewis v. New Orleans   Feb 20, 1974   415 U. S. 130
        Communications (Hemmer) v. 1, 32-33
        *Consttnl Law (Barrett) 1319-1322

3448. United States v. Kahn   Feb 20, 1974   415 U.S. 143
       *Cases Criml Justice 440-446
       Police 261-262
       Significant Decisions 1973/74 27-28

3449. United States v. Matlock   Feb 20, 1974   415 U.S. 164
       *Cases Criml Justice 299-306
       *Consttnl Criml (Scarboro) 439-448
       *Criminal Procedure (Lewis) 224-226
       Law of Arrest (Creamer) 229-233
       Law of Arrest (Markle) 286-288
       *Leading Consttnl Cases 203-206
       Police 221-223
       Significant Decisions 1973/74 19-20
       *Sup Ct and Criml Process 297-299
       Sup Ct Review 1974 217-231, 232
       PERIODICALS:
       "Supreme Court review (1974)." J Criml Law and Crimlgy 65:
          453-459 Dec '74 (3).

3450. Curtis v. Loether   Feb 20, 1974   415 U.S. 189
       *Civil Procedure (Carrington) 183-188
       *Civil Procedure (Cound) 801-804
       *Due Process 253-254
       *Racial Equality 117
       Significant Decisions 1973/74 104-105

3451. Morton, Secretary of the Interior   Feb 20, 1974   415 U.S. 199
          v. Ruiz
       *Admin Law (Gellhorn) 235-239
       *Legislation (Linde) 325-332

3452. United States v. Kahan   Feb 25, 1974   415 U.S. 239
       *Cases Criml Justice 1060-1062

3453. Memorial Hospital v. Maricopa   Feb 26, 1974   415 U.S. 250
          County
       Cases Consttnl Law (Gunther) 957-959
       *Consttnl Law (Barrett) 936-939
       *Legal Environment 101-104
       Significant Decisions 1973/74 116-117
       Sup Ct Review 1975 322-324

3454. Davis v. Alaska   Feb 27, 1974   415 U.S. 308
       *Cases Criml Law (Perkins) 531-533
       *Due Process 128
       Significant Decisions 1973/74 35

3455. National Labor Relations Board v.   Feb 27, 1974   415 U.S. 322
          Magnavox Co. of Tennessee
       *Cases Labor (Leslie) 128-129
       *Labor Law (Twomey) 161-163
       Significant Decisions 1973/74 131
       PERIODICALS:
       "Significant decisions in labor cases." Monthly Labor R 97: 61-
          62 June '74.

3456. National Cable Television Association   Mar 4, 1974   415 U.S. 336
          v. United States

*Admin Law (Gellhorn) 70-74
PERIODICALS:
"Supreme Court sends FCC fees back to square one." Broadcast-
ing 86: 23-24 Mar 11 '74.

3457. Johnson, Administrator of Veterans'   Mar 4, 1974   415 U.S. 361
        Affairs v. Robison
        *Admin Law (Schwartz) 557-560
        *Douglas 253-256
        Freedom and the Court 279
        *Introduction (Mashaw) 849-852
        Significant Decisions 1973/74 117-118

3458. Teleprompter Corporation v. Columbia Mar 4, 1974   415 U.S. 394
        Broadcasting System
        Communication (Hemmer) v. 2, 149-150
        *Mass Communications 744-747
        Significant Decisions 1973/74 145-146
        PERIODICALS:
        "High court acts to free cable from copyright fees," Penny Girard.
        Electronic News 19: 12 Mar 11 '74.
        "Supreme Court CATV ruling." Am Libraries 5: 227 May '74.

3459. Steffel v. Thompson   Mar 19, 1974   415 U.S. 452
        Cases Consttnl Law (Gunther) 1684-1686
        *Cases Federal Courts 523-533
        *Civil Rights (Abernathy) 1980 174-182
        *Consttnl Law (Barrett) 138-145
        *Consttnl Law (Lockhart) 1700-1702
        *Processes 1308-1310
        Significant Decisions 1973/74 100-101
        PERIODICALS:
        "Supreme Court review (1974)." J Criml Law and Crimlgy 65:
        483-492 Dec '74.

3460. United States v. General Dynamics   Mar 19, 1974   415 U.S. 486
        Corporation
        *Antitrust (Posner) 425-433
        *Antitrust Analysis 1035-1051
        *Modern Business 981-985
        *Selected Antitrust Cases 167-178
        Significant Decisions 1973/74 139-141

3461. Hagans v. Lavine, Commissioner,   Mar 25, 1974   415 U.S. 528
        New York Department of Social
        Services
        *Civil Rights (Abernathy) 1980 225-230
        Significant Decisions 1973/74 102-103

3462. Smith, Sheriff v. Goguen   Mar 25, 1974   415 U.S. 566
        *Am Consttnl Law (Saye) 383-386
        Communication (Hemmer) v. 1, 47-48
        *Freedom of Speech (Haiman) 52-54
        Handbook 205-206
        Significant Decisions 1973/74 30-31
        *Text Social Issues 127-130

3463. Mayor of Philadelphia v. Educa-   Mar 25, 1974   415 U.S. 605
        tional Equality League

Digest 99-100
*Legislation (Linde) 657-658
Significant Decisions 1973/74 62-63

3464. Edelman, Director Department of   Mar 25, 1974 415 U.S. 651
       Public Aid of Illinois v. Jordan
       *Cases Federal Courts 427-438
       *Civil Rights (Abernathy) 1980 203-209
       *Consttnl Law (Barrett) 124-128
       *Consttnl Law (Grossman) 125-130
       Significant Decisions 1973/74 115-116

3465. Eaton v. Tulsa   Mar 25, 1974 415 U.S. 697
       *Courts Judges 338-340

3466. Lubin v. Panish, Registrar-Recorder   Mar 26, 1974 415 U.S. 709
       of County of Los Angeles
       *Am Consttnl Law (Saye) 477-479
       Consttnl Law (Barrett) 954-955
       *Poverty 252-256
       Significant Decisions 1973/74 88-89
       PERIODICALS:
       "Filing fees and poor candidates, " Jim McClellan and David E.
       Anderson. Progressive 38: 10 Aug '74.

3467. Storer v. Brown, Secretary of   Mar 26, 1974 415 U.S. 724
       State of California
       *Consttnl Law (Barrett) 955-959
       Significant Decisions 1973/74 86-88

3468. American Party of Texas v. White,   Mar 26, 1974 415 U.S. 767
       Secretary of State of Texas
       Hainsworth v. White
       *Douglas 104-108
       Significant Decisions 1973/74 84-86

3469. United States v. Edwards   Mar 26, 1974 415 U.S. 800
       *Cases Criml Justice 200-206
       *Consttnl Law (Maddex) 154-156
       *Criminal Evidence 326
       *Criminal Justice (Galloway) 161-166
       Criminal Law (Felkenes) 53-55
       *Criminal Procedure (Lewis) 185-189
       Law of Arrest (Creamer) 279-282
       *Law of Arrest (Markle) 96-101
       *Leading Consttnl Cases 161-165
       Significant Decisions 1973/74 18-19
       *Sup Ct and Criml Process 228-231
       PERIODICALS:
       "Supreme Court review (1974). " J Criml Law and Crimlgy 65:
       453-459 Dec '74 (3).

3470. Belle Terre v. Boraas   Apr 1, 1974   416 U.S. 1
       *Am Land Planning v. 2, 974-986
       *Cases Environmental Law (Gray) 428-433
       *Cases Land 737-742
       *Consttnl Law (Barrett) 691-695
       *Consttnl Law (Freund) 1109-1111
       *Land Use 1049-1056

*Legal Foundation 203-206
*Processes 802-805
*Rights (Shattuck) 139-140
Significant Decisions 1973/74 77
*Text Social Issues 54-55
PERIODICALS:
"New conservative rulings by Court." US News 76: 37 Apr 15
'74 (2).
"New privacy problems." Time 103: 104 Apr 15 '74 (2).
"Shifting sands of land use in the U.S. Supreme Court," Randall
Scott. Mortgage Banker 37: 74, 76, 78, 80 May '77 (5).
"Supreme Court fails to recognize new zoning trends." Norman
Williams. Am City 89: 104 Sept '74.
"Verdicts." Newsweek 83: 105-106 Apr 15 '74 (2).

3471. California Bankers Association v.   Apr 1, 1974   416 U.S. 21
Shultz
*Douglas 337-341
Significant Decisions 1973/74 74-77
PERIODICALS:
"Checking on checking accounts," Carrie Johnson. Progressive
38: 9 Aug '74.
"New conservative rulings by Court." US News 76: 37 Apr
15 '74 (2).
"New privacy problems." Time 103: 104 Apr 15 '74 (2).
"Verdicts." Newsweek 83: 105-106 Apr 15 '74 (2).

3472. Super Tire Engineering Co. v.   Apr 16, 1974   416 U.S. 115
McCorkle
Significant Decisions 1973/74 101-102

3473. Arnett, Director, Office of Economic   Apr 16, 1974   416 U.S. 134
Opportunity v. Kennedy
*Admin Law (Gellhorn) 466-476
*Admin Law (Schwartz) 350-358
Communication (Hemmer) v. 1, 40-41
*Due Process 218-219, 234-236
*Introduction (Mashaw) 351-365
*Labor Relations (Edwards) 808-826
*Land Ownership 68-78
Significant Decisions 1973/74 72-74
*Text Social Issues 115-119
PERIODICALS:
"Public employment and the Supreme Court," Carl F. Goodman.
Civil Service J 15: 18-22 July '74 (4).

3474. Scheuer, Administratix v. Rhodes,   Apr 17, 1974   416 U.S. 232
Governor of Ohio
Krause v. Rhodes
*Am Consttnl Law (Saye) 68-71
Consttnl Law (Barrett) 133
*Consttnl Rights (Palmer) 649-657
*Historic Documents 1974 265-270
Sup Ct and Commander in Chief 207-208

3475. Shea, Executive Director, Department   Apr 23, 1974   416 U.S. 251
of Social Services of Colorado v.
Vialpando
*Poverty 614-619

3476. National Labor Relations Board v.   Apr 23, 1974   416 U.S. 267
        Bell Aerospace Co., Division
        of Textron, Inc.
      *Admin Law (Schwartz) 277-281
      *Introduction (Mashaw) 450-456
       Significant Decisions 1973/74 123-125
      PERIODICALS:
      "Are buyers managers? the Supreme Court's view, " M. Manente.
        J Purchasing and Materials Mgt 11: 49-51 Sept '75.
      "Significant decisions in labor cases." Monthly Labor R 97: 62-
        64 July '74.

3477. De Funis v. Odegaard   Apr 23, 1974   416 U.S. 312
       Am Consttn (Kelly) 1009-1010
       Bakke (Sindler).
      *Bill (Cohen) 656-663
       Brethren 282
       By What Right 314-315
      *Consttnl Law (Barrett) 94-97
      *Consttnl Law (Barron) 96-101, 641-644
       Consttnl Law (Barron) 638-641
       Court Years 119
      *Defunis v. 3, 1349-1393
       Disaster 261-262
       Discriminating.
      *Discriminating 221-257
      *Douglas 294-300
       Editorials 1974 484-489
      *Elements Civil 199-204
       Equality (Cohen) 63-83; reprinted from "The De Funis case: the
        right to go to law school" Donald Dworkin. NY Review of
        Books 23: 29-33 Feb 5 '76
       Equality (Cohen) 157-166
      *Processes 1269-1273
      *Racial Equality 142
       Reverse 184-197
      *Reverse 198-207
       Significant Decisions 1972/73 57-58
       Sup Ct (Forte) 3-9
       Sup Ct Review 1974 1-32
       Taking 223-239
      *Woman 43-44
      PERIODICALS:
      "Affirmative action." Today's Eductn 64: 89-92, 94 Mar '75.
      "Ameliorative racial preference and the Fourteenth Amendment:
        some constitutional problems," Ralph A. Rossum. J Poltcs
        38: 346-366 '76.
      "Bias against whites." US News 76: 60 May 6 '74.
      "The case against preferential racial quotas; Justice Douglas's dis-
        sent in the De Funis case," Fred M. Hechinger. Sat R World
        1: 51-52, 56 July 27 '74.
      *"Court's majority opinion and dissent in De Funis case." Chronicle
        of Higher Eductn 8: 6-8 Apr 29 '74.
      "Decision not to decide." Newsweek 83: 50 May 6 '74.
      "De Funis case; race and the Constitution," Carl Cohen. Nation
        220: 135-145 Feb 8 '75.
      "De Funis reconsidered: a comparative analysis of alternative ad-
        missions strategies," Hunter M. Breland and Gail H. Ironson.
        J Eductnl Measurement 13: 89-99 '76.

"DeFunis revisited," William J. Hilton. J Natl Assoc of Col Admissions Counselors 19: 8-9 Mar '75.
"Discriminating to end discrimination," Nina Totenburg. NY Times
Mag p. 8-9, 36-37, 39, 41, 43 Apr 14 '74.
"Discrimination in reverse? now that Marco DeFunis has his law
degree," Warren Weaver. Compact 8: 5-7 July '74; *Compact
8: 8 July '74. Condensed: Eductn Dig 40: 50-52 Nov '74.
"High court avoids ruling on preference to minorities in law school
admissions," Cheryl M. Fields. Chronicle of Higher Eductn
8: 1 Apr 29 '74.
"Hints on reverse bias." Time 103: 65 May 6 '74.
"Justice for black Americans 200 years after independence,"
Robert L. Gill. Negro Eductn R 27: 271-317 July '76 (9).
"Public employment and the Supreme Court," Carl F. Goodman.
Civil Service J 15: 18-22 July '74 (4).
"Racism in reverse," Jerrold K. Footlick. Newsweek 83: 61-62
Mar 11 '74.
"Reverse racism: the great white hoax," Celia Zitron. Freedom-
ways 15 no. 3: 188-95 '75.
"Supreme Court and quotas," J. S. Fuerst and Roy Petty. Chris-
tian Century 94: 948-952 Oct 19 '77 (5).
"Which man's burden?" Nathan Lewis. New Republic 170: 8-9
May 4 '74. Reaction: Jane Jordan. 170: 8-9 May 18 '74.

3478. Kahn v. Shevin, Attorney General   Apr 24, 1974 416 U.S. 351
of Florida
*Bill (Cohen) 685-687
*Consttnl Law (Barrett) 885-888
*Processes 596-599
*Sex Discrimination 1975 116-120
Significant Decisions 1973/74 112
Sup Ct Review 1975 4-6
*Woman 38-40
PERIODICALS:
"Woman's place in the Constitution: the Supreme Court and gender
discrimination," Betsy Levin. High Sch J 59: 31-45 Oct
'75 (3).

3479. Pernell v. Southall Realty   Apr 24, 1974 416 U.S. 363
*Civil Procedure (Carrington) 181-183
Significant Decisions 1973/74 103-104
*Text Social Issues 357-360

3480. Lehman Brothers v. Schein   Apr 29, 1974 416 U.S. 386
Simon v. Schein
Investors Diversified Services, Inc.
v. Schein
*Cases Federal Courts 500-505

3481. Procunier, Corrections Director   Apr 29, 1974 416 U.S. 396
v. Martinez
*Am Consttnl Law (Saye) 363-364
CQ Guide 444
Consttnl Law (Barrett) 1277-1278
*Consttnl Rights (Palmer) 261-268
*Criminal Justice (Way) 526-530
Significant Decisions 1973/74 46-48
*Sup Ct and Criml Process 756-759

*Text Social Issues 224-229
*US Prison Law v. 2, 14-29

3482. Gooding v. United States   Apr 29, 1974   416 U.S. 430
        Law of Arrest (Creamer) 333-337

3483. Kewanee Oil Co. v. Bicron   May 13, 1974   416 U.S. 470
        Corporation
        Legal Aspects 43-44
        *Legal Regulation 576-586
        Significant Decisions 1973/74 146-148
        Sup Ct Review 1974 81-95

3484. United States v. Giordano   May 13, 1974   416 U.S. 505
        Editorials 1974 633-635
        *Historic Documents 1974 391-399
        Significant Decisions 1973/74 23-25
        PERIODICALS:
        "Mitchell's 60-case mistake." Time 103: 57 May 27 '74.

3485. United States v. Chavez   May 13, 1974   416 U.S. 562
        *Historic Documents 1974 400-405
        Significant Decisions 1973/74 25-27

3486. Mitchell v. W. T. Grant Co.   May 13, 1974   416 U.S. 600
        *Civil Procedure (Carrington) 27-35
        *Consttnl Law (Barron) 509-512
        *Poverty 113-120
        Significant Decisions 1973/74 70-72
        Sup Ct Review 1075 203-267
        *Text Social Issues 322-327

3487. Beasley v. Food Fair of North   May 15, 1974   416 U.S. 653
        Carolina
        *Cases Labor (Oberer) 401-405
        Significant Decisions 1973/74 125-126

3488. Calero-Toledo v. Pearson Yacht   May 15, 1974   416 U.S. 663
        Leasing
        *Due Process 233-234
        Significant Decisions 1973/74 22-23

3489. Bradley v. School Board of the   May 15, 1974   416 U.S. 696
        City of Richmond
        Am Consttn (Kelly) 1005
        Digest 100-101
        Disaster 155-159
        Significant Decisions 1973/74 59-60

3490. Bob Jones University v. Simon,   May 15, 1974   416 U.S. 725
        Secretary of Treasury
        Significant Decisions 1973/74 135-136

3491. Alexander, Commissioner of Internal   May 15, 1974   416 U.S. 752
        Revenue v. "Americans United," Inc.
        Significant Decisions 1973/74 136-138

3492. Allee v. Medrano   May 20, 1974   416 U.S. 802

*Courts Judges 324-326
Significant Decisions 1973/74 80-83

3493. Air Pollution Variance Board of   May 20, 1974   416 U.S. 861
      Colorado v. Western Alfalfa
      Corporation
      *Cases Environmental Law (Gray) 309-310
      Significant Decisions 1973/74 20
      PERIODICALS:
      "Open for inspection." Chemical Wk 114: 16 May 29 '74.

3494. National Labor Relations Board v.   May 20, 1974   417 U.S. 1
      Food Store Employees Union, Local
      347, Amalgamated Meat Cutters and
      Butcher Workmen of North America
      *Cases Labor (Oberer) 662-666
      *Labor Law (Twomey) 129-130

3495. William E. Arnold Co. v. Carpenters   May 20, 1974   417 U.S. 12
      District Council of Jacksonville
      and vicinity
      Significant Decisions 1973/74 127-128

3496. Blackledge, Warden v. Perry   May 20, 1974   417 U.S. 21
      *Cases Criml Justice 1132-1135
      *Criminal Procedure (Lewis) 643-646
      Defendants 358-359
      *Modern Criml Procedure 421-426
      Significant Decisions 1973/74 32-34

3497. Fuller v. Oregon   May 20, 1974   417 U.S. 40
      *Modern Criml Procedure 31-34
      Poverty 182-188
      Significant Decisions 1973/74 40-41
      *Sup Ct and Criml Process 141-143
      PERIODICALS:
      "Supreme court review (1974)." J Criml Law and Crimlgy 65:
      493-498 Dec '74.

3498. Kosydar, Tax Commissioner of   May 20, 1974   417 U.S. 62
      Ohio v. National Cash Register Co.
      *Legal Environment 244-246
      Significant Decisions 1973/74 138

3499. Bellis v. United States   May 28, 1974   417 U.S. 85
      Law of Arrest (Creamer) 538-543
      Significant Decisions 1973/74 41-42

3500. Eisen v. Carlisle and Jacquelin   May 28, 1974   417 U.S. 156
      *Cases Federal Courts 699-713
      *Cases Pleading 698-709
      *Civil Procedure (Carrington) 1202-1208
      *Civil Procedure (Cound) 584-590
      *Courts Judges 298
      Courts Judges 299-301
      Editorials 1974 690-692
      *Elements Civil 1206-1207
      *Federal System 68-69
      *Historic Documents 1974 427-433

*Modern Business 132-136
Significant Decisions 1973/74 97-99
Sup Ct Review 1974 98-126
*Text Social Issues 302-306
PERIODICALS:
"Class actions." New Republic 171: 7-8 Sept 14 '74.
"Consumers take a knock." Economist 251: 45 June 8 '74.
"Setback for class suits." Chemical Wk 114: 14 June 5 '74.
"Supreme Court rules notice must be given class action litigants."
    Natl Underwriter (Property ed) 78: 19 June 7 '74.
"Taking mass from class." Time 103: 79 June 10 '74.
"Will class action suits be crimped?" Bus Wk p. 61, 63 May
    11 '74.

3501. Corning Glass Works v. Brennan   June 3, 1974   417 U.S. 188
        *Collective Bargaining 1022-1028
        *Labor Law (Twomey) 399-404
        *Sex Discrimination 1978 151-159
        Significant Decisions 1973/74 110-112
        PERIODICALS:
        "ERA: Losing battles, but winning the war," James J. Kilpatrick"
            Natns Bus 67: 15-16 Oct '79 (4).
        "Significant decisions in labor cases." Monthly Labor R 97: 79-
            81 Aug '74.

3502. Howard Johnson, Inc. v. Detroit Local June 3, 1974   417 U.S. 249
        Joint Executive Board, Hotel and
        Restaurant Employees and Bartenders
        International Union
        Basic Text 580-583
        *Cases Labor (Oberer) 743-751
        *Collective Bargaining 429-435
        Significant Decisions 1973/74 120-122
        Sup Ct and Labor 147-149
        PERIODICALS:
        "Significant decisions in labor cases." Monthly Labor R 97: 81-
            83 Aug '74.

3503. Pittsburgh v. Alco Parking Corporation June 10, 1974 417 U.S. 369
        *Business 726-727
        *Legal Environment 224-225
        Significant Decisions 1973/74 138-139

3504. Federal Power Commission v.   June 10, 1974 417 U.S. 380
            Texaco, Inc.
        Dougherty v. Texaco, Inc.
        Significant Decisions 1973/74 144-145

3505. Wheeler v. Barrera   June 10, 1974 417 U.S. 402
        Digest 27-28
        *Douglas 165-168
        Education (Lapati) 193-196
        *School Law (Alexander) 65-70
        Significant Decisions 1973/74 63-64
        PERIODICALS:
        "Barrera: hope for the children," Charles M. Whelan. America.
            130: 514-516 June 29 '74.

3506. Michigan v. Tucker   June 10, 1974 417 U.S. 433

*Cases Criml Justice 655-666
*Cases Criml Law (Hall) 869-875
Consttnl Counterrevolution 178-179
*Consttnl Criml (Scarboro) 570-577
*Consttnl Law (Grossman) 882-887
Criminal Evidence 447-448
*Douglas 365-368
Editorials 1974 756-758
*Historic Documents 1974 473-485
Law of Arrest (Creamer) 388-394
*Leading Consttnl Cases 549-557
Significant Decisions 1973/74 20-22
Sup Ct Review 1977 115-125
PERIODICALS:
"Supreme Court review (1974)." J Criml Law and Crimlgy 65:
    466-475 Dec '74.
"Testing the Burger Court." Newsweek 83: 46-47 Jan 7 '74.
"Trimming Miranda." Time 103: 64-65 June 24 '74.

3507. Geduldig, Director, Department of   June 17, 1974 417 U.S. 484
        Human Resources Development
        v. Aiello
        CQ Guide 635-636
        *Cases Civil Liberties 378-382
        *Cases Consttnl Law (Cushman) 607-613
        *Consttnl Law (Barrett) 888-890
        Digest 65
        *Sex Discrimination 1978 49-56
        Significant Decisions 1973/74 112-113
        Sup Ct Review 1975 7-11
        Sup Ct Review 1979 381-382
        *Woman 66-68
        PERIODICALS:
        "High court rules ban on pregnancy benefits is not discriminatory."
            Natl Underwriter (Property ed) 78: 37 June 21 '74.
        "Significant decisions in labor cases." Monthly Labor R 97: 69-
            71 Sept '74.
        "Supreme Court rules pregnancy benefits not compulsory in state
            benefit plans." Natl Underwriter (Life ed) 78: 1, 8 June
            22 '74.
        "Woman's place in the Constitution: the Supreme Court and gender
            discrimination," Betsy Levin. High Sch J 59: 31-45 Oct '75
            (3).

3508. Scherk v. Alberto-Culver Co.   June 17, 1974 417 U.S. 506
        Significant Decisions 1973/74 106-107
        PERIODICALS:
        "Greater certainty in international transactions through choices of
            forum?" Edward L. Kling. Am J International Law 69: 366-
            374 Apr '75.

3509. Morton, Secretary of the Interior   June 17, 1974 417 U.S. 535
        v. Mancari
        *Consttnl Law (Barrett) 865-867
        *Racial Equality 145
        Significant Decisions 1973/74 118-119

3510. Gilmore v. City of Montgomery,   June 17, 1974 417 U.S. 556
        Alabama

CQ Guide 602-603
Consttnl Law (Barrett) 1074
Digest 101-102
Significant Decisions 1973/74 60-62

3511. Cardwell, Warden v. Lewis   June 17, 1974 417 U.S. 583
*Cases Criml Justice 346-353
Criminal Evidence 284-285
*Criminal Procedure (Lewis) 232-236
Law of Arrest (Creamer) 256-260
*Law of Arrest (Markle) 289-295
Significant Decisions 1973/74 17-18
*Sup Ct and Criml Process 276-279
*Text Social Issues 186-189
PERIODICALS:
"Chipping away." Newsweek 84: 61-62 July 1 '74 (3).
"Supreme Court review (1974)." J Criml Law and Crimlgy 65:
453-459 Dec '74 (3).

3512. Ross v. Moffitt   June 17, 1974 417 U.S. 600
*Cases Consttnl Law (Gunther) 943-944
*Cases Criml Law (Hall) 1196-1202
*Criminal Law (Kadish) 793-794
*Criminal Procedure (Lewis) 638-642
Criminal Procedure (Wells) 229-231
*Due Process 49-50, 182-183
*Leading Consttnl Cases 444-453
*Modern Criml Procedure 34-39
*Poverty 177-181
Significant Decisions 1973/74 38-40
*Sup Ct and Criml Process 559-564
*Text Social Issues 338-342
PERIODICALS:
"Chipping away." Newsweek 84: 61-62 July 1 '74 (3).

3513. Jimenez v. Weinberger, Secretary of   June 19, 1974 417 U.S. 628
Health, Education and Welfare
Significant Decisions 1973/74 114-115
PERIODICALS:
"Significant decisions in labor cases." Monthly Labor R 97: 68-
69 Sept '74.

3514. Bangor Punta Operations, Inc. v.   June 19, 1974 417 U.S. 703
Bangor and Aroostook Railroad Co.
Significant Decisions 1973/74 95-96

3515. Parker, Warden v. Levy   June 19, 1974 417 U.S. 733
*Am Consttnl Law (Saye) 360-362
Consttnl Law (Barrett) 1322
Defendants 78-79
*Douglas 267-271
Editorials 1974 768-770
*Federal System 170-174
Significant Decisions 1973/74 31-32
*Sup Ct and Criml Process 1130-1133
*Text Social Issues 130-134
PERIODICALS:
"Chipping away." Newsweek 84: 61-62 July 1 '74 (3).

"Supreme Court review (1974)." J Criml Law and Crimlgy 65: 505-513 Dec '74.
"What's happening to free speech?" Nathan Lewin. New Republic 171: 13-17 July 27 '74 (3).

3516. Florida Power and Light Co. v.   June 24, 1974 417 U.S. 790
       International Brotherhood of
       Electrical Workers, Local 641
       Basic Text 692-693
       *Cases Labor (Leslie) 685-688
       Significant Decisions 1973/74 130-131
       Sup Ct and Labor 169-171
       PERIODICALS:
       "Significant decisions in labor cases." Monthly Labor R 97: 57-
       58 Sept '74.

3517. Pell v. Procunier, Corrections   June 24, 1974 417 U.S. 817
       Director
       Procunier v. Hillery
       CQ Guide 433-444
       Cases Consttnl Law (Gunther) 1533-1534
       Communication (Hemmer) v. 2, 231-232
       *Consttnl Law (Barrett) 1380-1383
       *Consttnl Rights (Palmer) 249-256
       *Criminal Justice (Way) 530-533
       Handbook 486-489
       *Mass Communications 424-427
       Significant Decisions 1973/74 45-46
       *Sup Ct and Criml Process 759-762
       Sup Ct Review 1978 288-289
       *US Prison Law v. 3, 194-203

3518. Saxbe, Attorney General v.   June 24, 1974 417 U.S. 843
       Washington Post Co.
       CQ Guide 443-444
       Cases Consttnl Law (Gunther) 1533-1534
       Communication (Hemmer) v. 2, 231-232
       *Consttnl Rights (Palmer) 256-260
       Handbook 490-492
       Sup Ct Review 1978 289-290
       *US Prison Law v. 3, 204-219
       PERIODICALS:
       "Court, convicts and the press," Ben H. Bagdikian. Nation 219:
       145-146 Aug 31 '74.
       "High court rules on access and accountability cases." Editor and
       Pub 107: 9, 37, 38 June 29 '74 (3).

3519. Richardson, County Clerk and Registrar June 24, 1974 418 U.S. 24
       of Voters of Mendocino County
       v. Ramirez
       *Criminal Justice (Way) 496-498
       *Processes 166-169
       Significant Decisions 1973/74 52-53
       *Sup Ct and Criml Process 800-803
       *Text Social Issues 289-292
       *US Prison Law v. 5, 449-478

3520. Hamling v. United States   June 24, 1974 418 U.S. 87
       Communication (Hemmer) v. 1, 173-174

Consttnl Law (Barrett) 1433-1434
*Criminal Law (Kadish) 1351-1352
*Historic Documents 1974 520-522
Law of Mass 384-387
Law of Obscenity 124-125
*Law of Obscenity 367-396
Mass Media (Francois) 370-371
Obscenity (Sunderland) 107-110
*Text Social Issues 168-174
PERIODICALS:
    "Supreme Court review (1974)."   J Criml Law and Crimlgy   65:
        499-504   Dec '74   (2).

3521.   Jenkins v. Georgia   June 24, 1974 418 U.S. 153
*Bill (Cohen) 106-110
Brethren 280-282
Communication (Hemmer) v. 1, 172-173
Consttnl Counterrevolution 293
*Consttnl Law (Barrett) 1434-1437
*Consttnl Law (Grossman) 1256-1259
Editorials 1974 764-767
*Freedom of Speech (Haiman) 148
*Historic Documents 1974 514-520
Law of Mass 383-384
Law of Obscenity 114-115
*Law of Obscenity 396-400
Literature 241-243
*Mass Media (Devol) 188-189
Mass Media (Francois) 373
Obscenity (Sunderland) 111-114
Significant Decisions 1973/74 69-70
PERIODICALS:
    "Clearing the calendar."   Time   104: 57-58 July 8 '74   (2).
    "Effect of High court rulings on obscenity, press, freedom."   US
        News   77: 25 July 8 '74.
    "Last tango in Paris, et al. v. the Supreme Court," J. Donald
        Ragsdale. Q J Speech 61: 279-289 Oct '75 (2).
    "Obscenity amici questioned." Wilson Library Bul   48:   530-531
        Mar '74.
    "Obscenity: balancing act." Newsweek 84: 78-79 July 8 '74.
    "Supreme Court review (1974)." J Criml Law and Crimlgy 65:
        499-504 Dec '74 (2).
    "Supreme Court reviews Carnal Knowledge case," Susan Wagner.
        Pub Weekly 205: 19 Apr 29 '74.

3522.   United States v. Richardson   June 25, 1974 418 U.S. 166
*Cases Consttnl Law (Cushman) 31-35
Cases Consttnl Law (Gunther) 1622-1628
*Cases Federal Courts 49-62
*Cases Individual 1150-1161
*Consttnl Law (Barrett) 72-73
*Consttnl Law (Grossman) 147-154
*Courts Judges 236-244
*Douglas 23-27
*Freedom vs National Security 583-588
*Justices (Friedman) v. 5, 84-91
*Processes 1231-1242
Significant Decisions 1973/74 92-93

3523. Schlesinger, Secretary of Defense   June 25, 1974 418 U. S. 208
           v. Reservists Committee to
         Stop the War
       *Am Consttn (Lockhart) 59-62
        Cases Consttnl Law (Gunther) 1628-1629
       *Cases Consttnl Rights 59-62
       *Consttnl Law (Barrett) 74-76
       *Consttnl Law (Barron) 87-92
       *Consttnl Law (Lockhart) 1648-1651
       *Douglas 18-23
        Significant Decisions 1973/74 93-95

3524. Miami Herald Publishing Co.   June 25, 1974 418 U. S. 241
           v. Tornillo
       *Bill (Cohen) 332-336
        CQ Guide 427
       *Civil Liberties (Barker) 156-161
        Communication (Hemmer) v. 2, 213-214
       *Consttnl Law (Barrett) 1354-1360
       *Consttnl Law (Barron) 881-886
       *Consttnl Law (Grossman) 1172-1175
        Crisis 237-240
        Editorials 1974 759-763
       *First Amendment (Franklin) 359-369
       *Freedom of Speech (Haiman) 185
        Freedom of the Press (Schmidt) 12-14, 127-248
        Good Guys 192-198
       *Historic Documents 1974 523-528
        Law of Mass 12-14
       *Mass Communications 613-621
       *Mass Media (Devol) 341-344
        Mass Media (Francois) 510-512
        Significant Decisions 1973/74 66-67
       *Text Social Issues 153-156
       PERIODICALS:
       *"Excerpts from ruling on 'right of assembly.'"   Editor and Pub
          107: 10-11 June 29 '74.
        "Freedom of the press." Newsweek 84: 77-78 July 8 '74 (3).
        "High court rules on access and accountability cases." Editor and
          Pub 107: 9, 37, 38 June 29 '74 (3).
        "High court rulings weaken advertisers' access demands." Adv
          Age 45: 3, 58 July 1 '74 (2).

3525. Old Dominion Branch No. 496,   June 25, 1974 418 U. S. 264
         National Association of Letter
         Carriers, AFL-CIO v. Austin
        Mass Media (Francois) 100-101
        Significant Decisions 1973/74 132-133
       PERIODICALS:
        "Significant decisions in labor cases." Monthly Labor R 97: 58-
          59 Sept '74.
        "When is a libel not a libel?" Harriet F. Pilpel and Alan U.
          Schwartz. Pub Weekly 206: 29-30 Dec 16 '74 (2).

3526. Lehman v. City of Shaker Heights   June 25, 1974 418 U. S. 298
       *Am Consttn (Lockhart) 836-840
       *Bill (Cohen) 259-265
       *Cases Consttnl Law (Gunther) 1287-1291
       *Cases Consttnl Rights 717-721

*Cases Individual 815-821
Communication (Hemmer) v. 2, 347-348
*Consttnl Law (Barrett) 1274-1277
*Consttnl Law (Lockhart) 1090-1093
Free Speech (Kurland) 343-344, 361, 384-389
*Freedom of Speech (Haiman) 78-79
Freedom of the Press (Schmidt) 113-117
Handbook 100-102, 138-139
*Mass Media (Devol) 335-337
Mass Media (Francois) 507-508
Significant Decisions 1973/74 78
Sup Ct Review 1974 234-235, 252-253, 275-280
Sup Ct Review 1976 73-77
PERIODICALS:
"High court rulings weaken advertisers' access demands." Adv
   Age 45: 3, 58 July 1 '74 (2).

3527. Gertz v. Robert Welch, Inc.   June 25, 1974 418 U.S. 323
*Am Consttn (Lockhart) 705-710
*Bill (Cohen) 160-169
CQ Guide 438-439
Cases Consttnl Law (Gunther) 1338-1341
*Cases Consttnl Rights 541-554
*Cases Copyright (Nimmer) 680-696
*Civil Rights (Abernathy) 1977 463-464
Communication (Hemmer) v. 2, 64-66
Conceived 102-103
*Consttnl Law (Barrett) 1397-1409
*Consttnl Law (Barron) 858-866
*Consttnl Law (Freund) 1223-1228
*Consttnl Law (Grossman) 1148-1155
*Consttnl Law (Lockhart) 860-867
*Douglas 185-189
*First Amendment (Franklin) 303-318
*Freedom of Speech (Haiman) 31
Freedom of the Press (Schmidt) 79-84
Handbook 239-249
Individual 107-108, 114-117
*Justices (Friedman) v. 5, 205-208
Law of Mass 107-113
*Mass Communications 216-224
Mass Media (Devol) 226-231
Mass Media (Devol) 237-241; reprinted from "The selective impact
   of libel law," David A. Anderson. Columbia Journalism R 14:
   38+ May/June '75.
Mass Media (Francois) 109-112
Role (Cox) 39-40
Significant Decisions 1973/74 67-69
Sup Ct Review 1978 282-284
Text Social Issues 110-114
PERIODICALS:
"Clearing the calendar." Time 104: 57-58 July 8 '74 (2).
"Freedom of the press." Newsweek 84: 77-78 July 8 '74 (3).
"How state courts have responded to Gertz in setting standards of
   fault," W. O. McCarthy. Journalism Q 56: 531-539, 693
   Autumn '79.
"Justice White and the first amendment," Deckle McLean. Jour-
   nalism Q 56: 305-310 Summer '79 (2).
"Libel, advertising and freedom of the press," Harriet F. Pilpel

and Laurie R. Rockett. Pub Weekly 209: 46-48 Mar 1 '76
(2).
"New shift in the libel law," Edwin L. Gasperini. Public Rela-
tions J 30: 6-9 Dec '74.
"Term private in libel ruling stumps attorneys." Editor and Pub
107: 15 Aug 31 '74.
"When is a libel not a libel?" Harriet F. Pilpel and Alan U.
Schwartz. Pub Weekly 206: 29-30 Dec 16 '74 (2).

3528. Spence v. Washington   June 25, 1974 418 U. S. 405
       *Bill (Cohen) 363-368
       *Cases Consttnl Law (Gunther) 1319-1324
       *Cases Criml Law (Inbau) 223-231
       *Cases Individual 851-857
       Communication (Hemmer) v. 1, 48-49
       *Consttnl Law (Barrett) 1303-1307
       *Freedom of Speech (Haiman) 55-56
       *Freedom vs National Security 474-478
       Handbook 206-212
       Significant Decisions 1973/74 80
       *Sup Ct and Criml Process 1076-1080

3529. Wingo, Warden v. Wedding   June 26, 1974 418 U. S. 461
       Significant Decisions 1973/74 53-54

3530. Taylor v. Hayes, Judge   June 26, 1974 418 U. S. 488
       Significant Decisions 1973/74 35-37

3531. Codispoti v. Pennsylvania   June 26, 1974 418 U. S. 506
       *Cases Criml Law (Hall) 1082-1084
       *Civil Procedure (Carrington) 169-172
       Significant Decisions 1973/74 37-38

3532. Wolff, Warden v. McDonnell   June 26, 1974 418 U. S. 539
       *Cases Criml Law (Hall) 1168-1177
       *Civil Liberties (Barker) 240-248
       *Civil Rights (Abernathy) 1977 268-271
       *Consttnl Law (Grossman) 960-967
       *Consttnl Law (Maddex) 395-399
       *Consttnl Rights (Palmer) 268-277, 473-479
       *Criminal Justice (Way) 512-519
       *Due Process 206, 231, 238, 245-246
       *Justices (Friedman) v. 5, 357-374
       Significant Decisions 1973/74 48-51
       *US Prison Law v. 2, 276-305
       PERIODICALS:
       "Supreme Court review (1974)." J Criml Law and Crimlgy 65:
       476-482 Dec '74.

3533. United States v. Marine Bancor-   Jan 26, 1974 418 U. S. 602
       poration, Inc.
       Significant Decisions 1973/74 141-143
       PERIODICALS:
       "High court finally rules on merger cases," Stan Strachan. Bur-
       rough Clearing House 58: 29 Aug '74.
       "More permissive view." Time 104: 46, 48 July 8 '74.

3534. United States v. Connecticut   June 26, 1974 418 U. S. 656
       National Bank

*Legal Environment 323-325
Significant Decisions 1973/74 143-144

3535.   United States v. Nixon   July 24, 1974 418 U.S. 683
        *Admin Law (Schwartz) 248-251
        Am Consttn (Kelly) 1036
        *Am Consttn (Lockhart) 216-224
        *Am Consttnl Law (Bartholomew) v. 1, 136-140
        Am Consttnl Law (Mason) 119-122
        *Am Consttnl Law (Mason) 122-125
        *Am Consttnl Law (Saye) 97-101
        *Am Consttnl Law (Shapiro) 193-200
        *Am Govt 419-427
        Am Politics 154-161
        *Annals v. 20, 4-16
        *Basic Business 51-55
        *Basic Cases 279-286
        Biography 287-288
        Brethren 289-347
        By What Right 315-316
        CQ Guide 232-233
        *Cases Consttnl Law (Cushman) 91-97
        *Cases Consttnl Law (Gunther) 437-443
        *Cases Criml Law (Hall) 1037-1040
        Communication (Hemmer) v. 2, 245-246
        *Comparative 154-157
        *Congress Investigates v. 5, 4032-4049
        Consttn (Wilcox) 10-14
        *Consttnl Aspects v. 3, 705-738
        *Consttnl Law (Barrett) 527-537
        *Consttnl Law (Barron) 340-348
        *Consttnl Law (Felkenes) 96-98
        *Consttnl Law (Freund) 679-689
        *Consttnl Law (Grossman) 81, 1083-1088
        *Consttnl Law (Lockhart) 238-245
        Court Years 139-140
        *Due Process 101-102
        Editorials 1974 806, 808-811, 877-884
        *Elements Civil 190-194, 1221-1222
        *Federal System 128-132
        *Freedom vs National Security 214-226
        *Growth v. 3, 2256-2274
        *Historic Documents 1974 621-638
        *Justices (Friedman) v. 5, 481-494
        Law of Arrest (Creamer) 519-525
        *Leading Consttnl Decisions 57-69
        *Legislation (Linde) 428-435
        *Legislative (Hetzel) 623-628
        Milestones 372-395
        *Modern Business 61-64
        Power 192-193
        *Principles Proof 775-783
        *Processes 382-390
        Significant Decisions 1973/74 10-13
        Sup Ct and Commander in Chief 189-196
        Sup Ct Decisionmaking 201-203
        Sup Ct from Taft 314-315
        US v. Nixon.
        *US v. Nixon 598-619

Watergate 64-67
PERIODICALS:
"Behind the 8 ball." New Republic 171: 8-9 Aug 10 '74.
"Court and the tapes." Newsweek 84: 21, 23-24 July 15 '74.
"Court gets a C." Time 104: 96 Nov 4 '74.
"Court's historic ruling narrowing president's power." US News
    77: 16-17 Aug 5 '74.
"Historic debate before Supreme Court." US News 77: 72-75
    July 22 '74.
"Man proposes but the court disposes." Natl R 26: 904, 906-
    907 Aug 16 '74 (2).
"Mild magistracy of the law: U.S. v. Richard Nixon," D. Grier
    Stephenson, Jr. Intellect 103: 288-292 Feb '75.
"President's day in court," Anthony Lewis. New Republic 171:
    10-11 July 20 '74.
"Showdown before the justices." Time 104: 13-14 July 15 '74.
"Supreme Court and the Watergate tapes." Nathan Lewin. New
    Republic 170: 13-16 June 22 '74.
"Unanimous no to Nixon." Time 104: 20, 24 Aug 5 '74.
"U.S. v. Richard M. Nixon." Time 104: 10-12, 15-17 July
    22 '74.
"United States of America v. Richard Nixon." Economist 252:
    45 July 13 '74.
"Very definitive decision." Newsweek 84: 23-26 Aug 5 '74.

3536.   Milliken v. Bradley   July 25, 1974   418 U.S.   717
        Allen Park Public Schools v. Bradley
        Grosse Pointe Public School System
            v. Bradley
        Am Consttn (Kelly) 1006-1007
        *Am Consttnl Law (Bartholomew) v. 2, 307-310
        *Am Consttnl Law (Mason) 490-497
        Busing 39-42
        CQ Guide 606
        Cases Civil Liberties 340-351
        *Cases Consttnl Law (Cushman) 570-581
        Cases Consttnl Law (Gunther) 781-784
        *Civil Liberties (Barker) 277-284
        *Comparative 317-322
        *Consttn (Morris) 786-795
        Consttnl Counterrevolution 48-49
        Consttnl Law (Barrett) 849-854
        *Consttnl Law (Barron) 629-634
        *Consttnl Law (Grossman) 465-473
        *Consttnl Rights (Kemerer) 568-575
        Digest 102-103
        Disaster 203-257
        Editorials 1974 890-897
        *Education (Hazard) 187-201
        From Brown 218-232
        *Historic Documents 1974 639-654
        Law and Education 209-210
        *Law of Public Education 662-668
        *Leading Consttnl Decisions 426-446
        Poverty 456-474
        Power 260
        *Processes 514-524
        *Racial Equality 75-77
        Role (Cox) 81-86

*School Law (Alexander) 499-504
Significant Decisions 1973/74 56-57
*Sup Ct and Education 311-323
*Text Social Issues 267-271
PERIODICALS:
"Ban on busing: was there a choice?" Am Sch Bd J 161: 15-
16 Sept '74.
"Big-city desegregation since Detroit," Eugene E. Eubanks and
Daniel U. Levine. Phi Delta Kappan 56: 521-522, 550 Apr
'75.
"Brown revisited: from Topeka, Kansas to Boston, Mass.," Leon
Jones. Phylon 37: 343-358 Dec '76 (3).
"Busing and balancing," William W. Brickman. Intellect 103:
333 Feb '75.
"Busing is stopped at the city line," John Mathews. Compact 8:
14-18 Sept '74.
"Case of Detroit," Warren Button. Urban Eductn 9: 211-212
Oct '74.
"City/suburban school desegregation; the Supreme Court speaks
out," Betty E. Sinowitz. Today's Eductn 63: 47, 49 Nov
'74.
"Court stops the bus," Newsweek 84: 38-39 Aug 5 '74.
"Courtrooms and classrooms," Eleanor P. Wolf. Eductnl Forum
41: 431-453 May '77 (2).
"Curb on racial busing--impact of 'Detroit decision.'" US News
77: 23-24 Aug 5 '74.
"Desegregation: a historic reversal." Time 104: 55-56 Aug
5 '74.
"Dred Scott revived." Progressive 38: 6-7 Sept '74.
"Integration and education: the Supreme Court's view of Detroit,"
Wolfgang Pindur. Education 96: 245-250 Spring '76.
"Integration and the Burger court: the new boundaries of school
desegregation." Intellect 103: 387-390 Mar '75.
"Judicial evolution of the law of school integration since Brown v.
Board of Education," Frank T. Read. Law and Contemporary
Problems 39: 7-49 Winter '75 (6).
"Legitimizing segregation: the Supreme Court's recent school de-
segregation decisions," John Bannon. Civil Rights Dig 9: 12-
17 Summer '77 (3).
"Major changes in school integration litigation, 1954-1979," Frank
Brown. Eductnl Admin Q 15: 76-97 Spring '79 (3).
"Man proposes but the court disposes." Natl R 26: 904, 906-907
Aug 16 '74 (2).
"New educational decision: is Detroit the end of the school bus
line?" B. W. Young and G. B. Bress. Phi Delta Kappan 56:
515-520 Apr '75 (2).
"School desegregation and the courts," William L. Taylor. Socl
Policy 6: 32-41 Jan '76 (3).
"Step backward." Newsweek 84: 39 Aug 5 '74.
"Supreme Court calls a halt to busing." Times Eductnl Supp
3088: 8 Aug 2 '74.
"Two fateful decisions," Robert M. Hutchins. Center Mag 8: 7-
13 Jan '75. Condensed in: Eductn Dig 40: 17-20 Apr '75
(2).

3537. United States v. American Friends   Oct 29, 1974   419 U.S. 7
        Service Committee
        *Douglas 146-150

3538. Allenberg Cotton Co. v. Pittman   Nov 19, 1974   419 U.S. 20
       *Consttnl Law (Barrett) 344-347
       Significant Decisions 1974/75 120-121

3539. Saxbe v. Bustos   Nov 25, 1974   419 U.S. 65
       Cardona v. Saxbe
       Significant Decisions 1974/75 136
       *Text Social Issues 250-254
       PERIODICALS:
       "Permanent resident status redefined," Austen T. Frazomen, Jr.
       International Migration R 9: 63-68 Spring '75.

3540. Gonzalez v. Automatic Employees   Dec 10, 1974   419 U.S. 90
       Credit Union
       *Elements Civil 1223-1227
       Significant Decisions 1974/75 88-89

3541. Regional Rail Reorganization Act   Dec 16, 1974   419 U.S. 102
       Cases
       Blanchette, Trustees of property of Penn
       Central Transportation Co. v. Con-
       necticut General Insurance Corp.
       Smith, Trustee of property of New York,
       New Haven and Hartford Railroad
       v. United States
       U.S. Railway Association v. Connecticut
       General Insurance Corp.
       United States v. Connecticut General
       Insurance Corporation
       Significant Decisions 1974/75 125-127
       PERIODICALS:
       "Rail act upheld," R. M. McConnell. Railway Age 175: 12
       Dec 30 '74.

3542. Gulf Oil Corporation v. Copp   Dec 17, 1974   419 U.S. 186
       Paving Co.
       *Legal Environment 289-291
       PERIODICALS:
       "Court turns against antitrust." Bus Wk p. 52 July 14 '75 (5).

3543. American Radio Association v.   Dec 17, 1974   419 U.S. 215
       Mobile Steamship Association
       Communication (Hemmer) v. 1, 88-89
       *Consttnl Law (Barrett) 1326-1328

3544. Cantrell v. Forest City Publishing Co. Dec 18, 1974   419 U.S. 245
       Communication (Hemmer) v. 2, 104-105
       Crisis 219
       Law of Mass 191-192
       *Mass Media (Devol) 257-260
       Mass Media (Francois) 174-175
       *Right to Privacy 221-224
       Significant Decisions 1974/75 68-69
       PERIODICALS:
       "The latest battle of Point Pleasant; law and the writer," Bill
       Francois. Writers Dig 55: 17 July '75.
       "Newspaper must pay award for invasion of privacy," I. William
       Hill. Editor and Pub 107: 13 Dec 28 '74.

3545. Schick v. Reed, Chairman,   Dec 23, 1974   419 U.S. 256
       U.S. Board of Parole
       CQ Guide 227-228
       *Cases Criml Law (Hall) 1213-1216
       Consttnl Law (Barrett) 524
       *Consttnl Law (Lockhart) 273-275
       Significant Decisions 1974/75 38-39

3546. Bowman Transportation, Inc. v.   Dec 23, 1974   419 U.S. 281
       Arkansas-Best Freight System
       Johnson Motor Lines, Inc. v. Arkansas-
       Best Freight System
       Red Ball Motor Freight, Inc. v. Arkansas-
       Best Freight System
       Lorch-Westway Corporation v. Arkansas-
       Best Freight System
       United States v. Arkansas-Best Freight
       System
       *Cases Regulated 558-562
       PERIODICALS:
       "Court pushes more truck competition."   Fleet Owner   70: 29
       Feb '75.

3547. Linden Lumber Division, Summer   Dec 23, 1974   419 U.S. 301
       and Co. v. National Labor Relations
       Board
       National Labor Relations Board v. Truck
       Drivers Union Local No. 413
       *Cases Labor (Oberer) 323-326
       *Legal Environment 456-458
       PERIODICALS:
       "Significant decisions in labor cases."   Monthly Labor R   98: 65-
       66 Mar '75.

3548. Jackson v. Metropolitan Edison Co.   Dec 23, 1974   419 U.S. 345
       *Bill (Cohen) 767-770
       *Cases Consttnl Law (Gunther) 1021-1026
       *Cases Individual 552-559
       *Civil Rights (Abernathy) 1980 77-83
       *Consttnl Law (Barrett) 1074-1078
       *Consttnl Law (Lockhart) 1558-1563
       *Legal Environment 96-97
       *Processes 628-633
       *Sex Discrimination 1978 304-310
       Significant Decisions 1974/75 54-55
       PERIODICALS:
       "Pay up or shut off."   Time   105: 75 Jan 6 '75.

3549. Sosna v. Iowa   Jan 14, 1975   419 U.S. 393
       Cases Consttnl Law (Gunther) 959-960
       *Cases Domestic 427-433
       *Consttnl Law (Barrett) 939-943
       *Federal System 289-292
       Significant Decisions 1974/75 55-58

3550. Maness v. Meyer, Judge   Jan 15, 1975   419 U.S. 449
       Law of Arrest (Creamer) 529-533
       Significant Decisions 1974/75 18-19
       Sup Ct Review 1977 158-159

3551. Cousins v. Wigoda   Jan 15, 1975   419 U.S. 477
       Significant Decisions 1974/75 71-72

3552. Schlesinger, Secretary of Defense   Jan 15, 1975   419 U.S. 498
       v. Ballard
       Consttnl Law (Barrett) 890-891
       Significant Decisions 1974/75 98-99
       Sup Ct Review 1975 7
       *Woman 41
       PERIODICALS:
       "Significant decisions in labor cases. " Monthly Labor R 98: 72-
       73 Apr '75.

3553. Taylor v. Louisiana   Jan 21, 1975   419 U.S. 522
       *Cases Criml Justice 1233-1238
       *Civil Rights (Abernathy) 1977 236-238
       *Criminal Justice (Way) 366-368
       *Criminal Law (Kadish) 1349-1350
       Criminal Procedure (Wells) 95-97
       *Due Process 117-118
       Editorials 1975 153-155
       *Historic Documents 1975 55-66
       *Modern Criml Procedure 349-354
       Significant Decisions 1974/75 95-97
       Sup Ct Review 1975 14-16
       PERIODICALS:
       "Supreme Court surprises. " Time 105: 59 Feb 3 '75 (2).

3554. United States v. Mazurie   Jan 21, 1975   419 U.S. 544
       *Consttnl Law (Barrett) 283-284
       *Legislation (Linde) 572-573

3555. Standard Press Steel Co. v.   Jan 22, 1975   419 U.S. 560
       Washington Department of Revenue
       *Consttnl Law (Barrett) 424-426
       *Legal Environment 234-236
       PERIODICALS:
       "Supreme Court hands down many important new decisions in state
       and local tax area, " James H. Peters. J Taxation 43: 174-
       176 Sept '75 (5).

3556. Goss v. Lopez   Jan 22, 1975   419 U.S. 565
       *Admin Law (Schwartz) 341-346
       Authority 149-150
       *Bill (Cohen) 773-775
       *Civil Rights (Abernathy) 1977 210-213
       Communication (Hemmer) v. 1, 140
       *Consttn (Morris) 513-519
       *Consttnl Law (Barrett) 753-757
       *Consttnl Law (Barron) 530-534
       *Consttnl Rights (Kemerer) 357-364
       Consttnl Rights (Kemerer) 409-498
       Digest 42-43
       *Due Process 221-222, 229-230
       *Education (Hazard) 299-308
       *Historic Documents 1975 67-80
       *Judicial Excerpts 143-146
       Law and Education 237-238
       Law of Arrest (Creamer) 534-538

*Law of Public Education 615-620
*School Law (Alexander) 351-358
Significant Decisions 1974/75 43-45
*Sup Ct and Education 260-271
Sup Ct Review 1975 25-75
PERIODICALS:
"Are students 'persons' under the Constitution?" M. Chester Nolte.
Law in Am Society 5: 9-15 Feb '76. Condensed in: Eductn
Dig 41: 43-46 May '76.
"Boost or a blow to school discipline?" Senior Scholastic 106:
TE1 Apr 10 '75.
"Coping with suspension and the Supreme Court." NASSP Bul 61:
68-76 Mar '77.
"Courts as intervenors," Joel Grossman. Eductn and Urban So-
ciety 11: 567-571 Aug '79 (2).
"Court intervention in pupil discipline; implications and comment,"
William R. Hazard. Am Behavioral Scientist 23: 169-205
Nov '79 (3).
"Discipline and due process in the schools," David Schimmel and
Louis Fischer. Eductn Dig 43: 5-8 Jan '78 (2). Condensed
from: Update on Law Related Eductn 1: 4-6, 34-36 Fall '77
(2).
"Due process for the unruly student," Fred M. Hechinger. Sat R
2: 44-45 Apr 5 '75.
"Due process in school disciplinary proceedings," Stephen R. Gold-
stein. Eductnl Horizons 54: 4-9 Fall '75.
"Due process rights of students: limitations on Goss v. Lopez--a
retreat out of the thicket," Michael A. Mass. J Law and
Eductn 9: 449-462 Oct '80 (3).
"Education; pupil power," Economist 255 [254]: 46 Feb 1 '75.
"Educator's response to Goss and Wood," Ronald J. Anson. Phi
Delta Kappan 57: 16-19 Sept '75.
"Impact of the Goss decision: a state survey," Robert E. Draba
and others. Viewpoints 52: 1-19 Sept '76.
"Legal breakthrough on student rights," John Mathews. Compact
9: 18-20 Apr '75.
"Let's set the record straight on student rights; Goss decision,"
Today's Eductn 64: 69-70 Sept '75.
"Not for adults alone: children begin pressing for expansion of
their constitutional rights." Civil Rights Dig 11: 12-22
Winter '79 (3).
"The nuts and bolts of procedural due process," Richard MacFeeley.
Phi Delta Kappan 57: 26 Sept '75.
"Perilous precedent?" Natns Sch and Col 2: 51-52 Mar '75.
"Pupils get legal safeguards against suspension," Francis Hill.
Times Eductnl Supp 3115: 18 Feb 7 '75.
"Right to education: from Rodriguez to Goss," Martha M. Mc-
Carthy. Eductnl Leadership 33: 519-521 Apr '76 (2).
"The role of the federal judiciary in directing student-authority
interaction," Henry S. Bangrer. Eductn and Urban Society 8:
267-306 May '76 (3).
"Rules for schools." Newsweek 85: 50 Feb 3 '75.
"Student and juvenile rights and responsibilities." Senior Scholastic
106: 8-10, 18 May 8 '75 (3).
"Supreme Court on students' rights," John Mathews. New Republic
172: 16-17 Mar 29 '75 (2).
"Supreme Court surprises." Time 105: 59 Feb 3 '75 (2).
"Supreme Court's new rules for due process," M. Chester Nolte.

Am Sch Bd J 162: 47-49 Mar '75. Condensed in: Eductn
Dig 40: 40-42 May '75.
"Two suspension cases the Supreme Court must decide," Thomas
J. Flygare. Phi Delta Kappan 56: 257-258 Dec '74.
"U.S. Supreme Court outlaws suspensions without hearings." Phi
Delta Kappan 56: 504 Mar '75.
"Using negotiation for teaching civil liberties and avoiding liability,"
John DeCecco and Arlene Richards. Phi Delta Kappan 57:
23-25 Sept '75 (3).

3557. North Georgia Finishing, Inc.   Jan 22, 1975   419 U.S. 601
        v. Di-Chem, Inc.
        *Cases Consttnl Rights 1148-1151
        *Cases Pleading 143-148
        *Civil Procedure (Carrington) 35-38
        Consttnl Law (Barrett) 746-747
        *Legal Environment 94-96
        *Poverty 120-124
        Significant Decisions 1974/75 58-59
        *Text Social Issues 327-329

3558. Chapman v. Meier   Jan 27, 1975   420 U.S. 1
        *Civil Rights (Abernathy) 1977 621-622
        Consttnl Law (Barrett) 975-976
        Significant Decisions 1974/75 72-73
        *Text Social Issues 284-288

3559. Train v. New York City   Feb 18, 1975   420 U.S. 35
        Am Consttn (Kelly) 1021-1022
        *Cases Environmental Law (Gray) 327-331
        *Consttnl Law (Grossman) 1105-1107
        Editorials 1975 193-197
        *Historic Documents 1975 135-140
        *Legislation (Linde) 355-359
        *Legislative (Hetzel) 830-833
        Significant Decisions 1974/75 137
        PERIODICALS:
        "Feud at the top." Senior Scholastic 106: 17 Mar 20 '75.

3560. Emporium Capwell Co. v. Western   Feb 18, 1975   420 U.S. 50
        Addition Community Organization
        National Labor Relations Board v. Western
        Addition Community Organization
        Basic Text 390, 392
        *Cases Labor (Leslie) 62-69
        *Cases Labor (Oberer) 188-197
        Significant Decisions 1974/75 112-113
        PERIODICALS:
        "Significant decisions in labor cases." Monthly Labor R 98: 63-
        65 May '75.

3561. Harris County Commissioners Court   Feb 18, 1975   420 U.S. 77
        v. Moore
        *Consttnl Law (Barrett) 149-151

3562. Gerstein v. Pugh   Feb 18, 1975   420 U.S. 103
        *Cases Criml Justice 786-798
        *Cases Criml Law (Hall) 950-954
        *Consttnl Criml (Marks) 249-253

*Criminal Law (Kadish) 854-856
*Due Process 29-30
*Elements Criminal 27-34
*Leading Consttnl Cases 633-642
*Modern Criml Procedure 84-92
Significant Decisions 1974/75 30-31

3563. Board of School Commissioners of   Feb 18, 1975   420 U.S. 128
       Indianapolis v. Jacobs
       PERIODICALS:
       "Gutter language case pondered by high court." Phi Delta Kappan
       56: 437   Feb '75.
       "Supreme Court ducked some hard decisions in February." Phi
       Delta Kappan 56: 576 Apr '75.

3564. United States v. Bisceglia   Feb 18, 1975   420 U.S. 141
       Significant Decisions 1974/75 32

3565. Drope v. Missouri   Feb 18, 1975   420 U.S. 162
       *Cases Criml Law (Hall) 1103-1107
       *Sup Ct and Criml Process 118-120

3566. National Labor Relations Board v.   Feb 19, 1975   420 U.S. 251
       Weingarten, Inc.
       Basic Text 298-299, 396
       *Cases Labor (Leslie) 251-256
       *Labor Law (Twomey) 185-188
       *Legal Environment 433-437
       Significant Decisions 1974/75 111-112
       PERIODICALS:
       "Significant decisions in labor cases." Monthly Labor R 98:
       62-63 May '75.

3567. Lefkowitz v. Newsome   Feb 19, 1975   420 U.S. 283
       *Modern Criml Procedure 312-313

3568. Wood v. Strickland   Feb 25, 1975   420 U.S. 308
       *Civil Rights (Abernathy) 1980 51-56
       Communication (Hemmer) v. 1, 140-142
       *Consttnl Rights (Palmer) 658-667
       Digest 43-44
       *Education (Hazard) 308-319
       *Judicial Excerpts 146-148
       *Law of Public Education 301-305
       *School Law (Alexander) 443-448
       Significant Decisions 1974/75 45-47
       *Sup Ct and Education 272-279
       PERIODICALS:
       "Administrators' liability in pupil discipline cases," John C. Walden.
       Natl Elementary Principal 54: 104 106 July '75.
       "Coping with suspension and the Supreme Court," Robert C. Von-
       Brock. NASSP Bul 61: 68-76 Mar '77 (2).
       "Court intervention in pupil discipline; implications and comment,"
       William R. Hazard. Am Behavioral Scientist 23: 169-205
       Nov '79.
       "Defensive education." Intellect 105: 297 Mar '77.
       "Educator's response to Goss and Wood," Ronald J. Anson. Phi
       Delta Kappan 57: 16-19 Sept '75 (2).
       "How to survive the Supreme Court's momentous new strictures

on school people," M. Chester Nolte. Am Sch Bd J 162: 50-
53 May '75. Condensed in: Eductn Dig 41: 22-25 Sept '75.
"Legal breakthrough on student rights," John Mathews. Compact
9: 18-20 Apr '75 (2).
"The role of the federal judiciary in directing student-authority
interaction," Henry S. Bangrer. Eductn and Urban Society 8:
267-306 May '76 (3).
"School boards: your authority has just been restricted; school
board members: your security has just been threatened," M.
Chester Nolte. Am Sch Bd J 162: 33-35 Apr '75.
"Schooling and the law; reflections on social change," William R.
Hazard. Eductn and Urban Society 8: 307 May '76.
"Students rights supported by Supreme Court ruling." Phi Delta
Kappan 56: 574 Apr '75.
"Supreme Court on students' rights," John Mathews. New Republic
172: 16-17 Mar 29 '75 (2).
"Supreme Court upholds students' civil rights." SLJ 21: 10
Apr '75.
"Two suspension cases the Supreme Court must decide," Thomas
J. Flygare. Phi Delta Kappan 56: 257-258 Dec '74 (2).
"Using negotiation for teaching civil liberties and avoiding liability."
Phi Delta Kappan 57: 23-25 Sept '75 (3).

3569. United States v. Wilson   Feb 25, 1975   420 U.S. 332
       *Cases Criml Justice 1024-1032
       *Cases Criml Law (Hall) 1040-1044
       *Criminal Law (Kadish) 1409-1410
       *Leading Consttnl Cases 784-789
       Significant Decisions 1974/75 20-21
       PERIODICALS:
       "Supreme Court review (1975)." J Criml Law and Crimlgy 66:
       428-435 Dec '75 (3).

3570. United States v. Jenkins   Feb 25, 1975   420 U.S. 358
       *Criminal Law (Kadish) 1410-1411
       Significant Decisions 1974/75 21-22
       Sup Ct Review 1978 141-142
       PERIODICALS:
       See listing at 420 U.S. 332, entry no. 3569.

3571. Serfass v. United States   Mar 3, 1975   420 U.S. 377
       Significant Decisions 1974/75 22-23
       Sup Ct Review 1978 139-140
       PERIODICALS:
       See listing at 420 U.S. 332, entry no. 3569.

3572. Chemehuevi Tribe of Indians v.   Mar 3, 1975   420 U.S. 395
       Federal Power Commission
       *Cases Environmental Law (Gray) 519-526

3573. Cox Broadcasting Corporation   Mar 3, 1975   420 U.S. 469
       v. Cohn
       Cases Consttnl Law (Gunther) 1343
       *Cases Copyright (Nimmer) 780-789
       *Cases Federal Courts 826-840
       *Cases Pleading 1074-1081
       Communication (Hemmer) v. 2, 95-96
       *Consttnl Law (Barrett) 1410-1414
       Crisis 216

*First Amendment (Franklin) 337-342
Handbook 337-340, 388-390
Law of Mass 177-180
*Mass Communications 331-334
*Mass Media (Devol) 54-58
Significant Decisions 1974/75 50-51
Sup Ct Review 1978 290-291
Sup Ct Review 1979 207-208
*Text Social Issues 157-159
PERIODICALS:
"High court backs naming of rape victims in news." Editor and
Pub 108: 11, 38 Mar 8 '75.

3574. United States v. Maine   Mar 17, 1975 420 U.S. 515
*Cases Environmental Law (Gray) 186-190
Editorials 1975 324-328
*Historic Documents 1975 167-175
Significant Decisions 1974/75 137-138
PERIODICALS:
"Court decision will spur offshore and onshore oil and gas develop-
ment." Engineering News 194: 10 Mar 27 '75.
"Feds win; life with father." Time 105: 84 Mar 31 '75 (2).
"Offshore oil: Supreme Court ruling intensifies debate," D. Shap-
ley. Science 188: 135, 177 Apr 11 '75.
"Oil battle at home: U.S. Government wins a big one." Senior
Scholastic 106: 23-24 Apr 17 '75.

3575. Estelle v. Dorrough   Mar 17, 1975 420 U.S. 534
*Sup Ct and Criml Process 144-146

3576. Southeastern Promotions, LTD   Mar 18, 1975 420 U.S. 540
v. Conrad
Cases Consttnl Law (Gunther) 1292
Communication (Hemmer) v. 1, 182-183
*Consttnl Law (Barrett) 1239-1244
Law of Obscenity 233-234
Significant Decisions 1974/75 62-63
*Text Social Issues 174-177
PERIODICALS:
"Letting the sun shine in." Newsweek 85: 37 Mar 31 '75 (2).

3577. Burns v. Alcala   Mar 18, 1975 420 U.S. 575
*Modern Business 90-94
Significant Decisions 1974/75 132-133

3578. Huffman v. Pursue, LTD   Mar 18, 1975 420 U.S. 592
*Cases Federal Courts 533-543
*Civil Procedure (Carrington) 785-794
*Civil Rights (Abernathy) 1980 193-198
Significant Decisions 1974/75 83 84

3579. Weinberger v. Wiesenfeld   Mar 19, 1975 420 U.S. 636
*Bill (Cohen) 689-692
Consttnl Law (Barrett) 891
*Consttnl Law (Grossman) 621-624
Editorials 1975 384-387
*Obscenity (Bosmajian) 177-185
*Sex Discrimination 1978 8-13
Significant Decisions 1974/75 97-98

Sup Ct Review 1975 16-18
*Woman 32-34
PERIODICALS:
"Letting the sun shine in." Newsweek 85: 37 Mar 31 '75.

3580. Austin v. New Hampshire   Mar 19, 1975 420 U.S. 656
      *Consttnl Law (Barrett) 380-383
      *Legal Environment 246-248
      Significant Decisions 1974/75 65-66
      PERIODICALS:
      "Supreme Court hands down many important new decisions in
      state and local tax area," James H. Peters. J Taxation 43:
      174-176 Sept '75 (5).

3581. Oregon v. Hass   Mar 19, 1975 420 U.S. 714
      *Consttnl Law (Maddex) 265-269
      Criminal Evidence 473-474
      *Criminal Procedure (Lewis) 382-386
      Law of Arrest (Creamer) 403-405
      *Modern Criml Procedure 232-233
      Significant Decisions 1974/75 16-17
      *Sup Ct and Criml Process 457-459
      Sup Ct Review 1977 125-129
      PERIODICALS:
      "Supreme Court review (1975)." J Criml Law and Crimlgy 66:
      419-427 Dec '75 (2).

3582. Schlesinger v. Councilman   Mar 25, 1975 420 U.S. 738
      Significant Decisions 1974/75 85-87

3583. Iannelli v. United States   Mar 25, 1975 420 U.S. 770
      *Cases Criml Law (Inbau) 855-861
      Law of Arrest (Creamer) 549-553
      Sup Ct Review 1978 118-120

3584. MTM, Inc. v. Baxley   Mar 25, 1975 420 U.S. 799
      *Cases Federal Courts 455-461
      Significant Decisions 1974/75 87-88
      PERIODICALS:
      "Supreme Court review (1975)." J Criml Law and Crimlgy 66:
      464-469 Dec '75.

3585. Stanton v. Stanton   Apr 15, 1975 421 U.S. 7
      *Consttnl Law (Barrett) 895-896
      *Sex Discrimination 1978 13-17
      Significant Decisions 1974/75 99-100
      Sup Ct Review 1975 18-19
      *Woman 34-35

3586. McLucas v. DeChamplain   Apr 15, 1975 421 U.S. 21
      *Cases Federal Courts 819-823

3587. Withrow v. Larkin   Apr 16, 1975 421 U.S. 35
      *Admin Law (Gellhorn) 859-863
      *Admin Law (Schwartz) 437-443
      *Due Process 247-248
      *Legislation (Linde) 823-826
      Significant Decisions 1974/75 63-65

3588. Train v. Natural Resources   Apr 16, 1975   421 U.S. 60
       Defense Council
       *Cases Environmental Law (Gray) 250-261

3589. Colonial Pipeline Co. v. Traigle   Apr 28, 1975   421 U.S. 100
       *Legal Environment 231-233
       Significant Decisions 1974/75 119-120
       PERIODICALS:
       See listing at 420 U.S. 656, entry no. 3580.

3590. Kugler v. Helfant   Apr 28, 1975   421 U.S. 117
       Helfant v. Kugler
       Significant Decisions 1974/75 84-85

3591. National Labor Relations Board v.   Apr 28, 1975   421 U.S. 132
       Sears, Roebuck and Co.
       *Admin Law (Gellhorn) 586-592
       Mass Media (Francois) 244
       Significant Decisions 1974/75 128-130
       PERIODICALS:
       "Significant decisions in labor cases." Monthly Labor R 98: 50-
       51 July '75.

3592. Renegotiation Board v. Grumman   Apr 28, 1975   421 U.S. 168
       Aircraft Engineering Corporation
       Significant Decisions 1974/75 130-131

3593. Johnson v. Mississippi   May 12, 1975   421 U.S. 213
       Significant Decisions 1974/75 92-94

3594. Alyeska Pipeline Service Co. v.   May 12, 1975   421 U.S. 240
       Wilderness Society
       *Cases Environmental Law (Gray) 98-107
       *Civil Procedure (Carrington) 685-695
       *Elements Civil 132-139
       *Environmental 823-829
       Signficant Decisions 1974/75 91-92
       PERIODICALS:
       "Fee gloom." Time 105: 42 May 26 '75.
       "Has the Supreme Court abandoned the Constitution?" Laughlin
       McDonald. Sat R 4: 10-12, 14 May 28 '77.
       Same article with title: "Supreme Court today." Current 194:
       32-39 July '77.
       "People's advocates." Nation 220: 644-645 May 31 '75.

3595. Hill v. Stone   May 12, 1975   421 U.S. 289
       *Consttnl Law (Barrett) 952-953
       *Poverty 240-246
       Significant Decisions 1974/75 74
       PERIODICALS:
       "All ballots count." Engineering News 194: 50 June 5 '75.

3596. Meek v. Pittenger   May 19, 1975   421 U.S. 349
       *Bill (Cohen) 475-486
       *Consttn (Morris) 406-407
       *Consttnl Law (Barrett) 1461-1467
       *Consttnl Law (Grossman) 1302-1306
       Digest 28-29
       Editorials 1975 577-580

*Education (Hazard) 117-129
Freedom and the Court 324, 327
*Law of Public Education 66-71
*Religious Freedom (Pfeffer) 62-68
*School Law (Alexander) 216-221
Significant Decisions 1974/75 41-43
*Sup Ct and Education 301-310
*Text Social Issues 202-207
PERIODICALS:
"Arguments, attitudes and 'aid,'" Russell Shaw. Momentum 6:
    34-37 Dec '75.
"Books, buses, maps, mousetraps." America 132: 410 May
    31 '75.
"Church-state decision in Supreme Court threatens ESEA program."
    Am Libraries 6: 404, 406 July '65.
"Schools and the law--state aid to parochial schools: diminished
    alternatives," Thomas J. Flygare. Phi Delta Kappan 57: 205-
    206 Nov '75.
"Supreme Court acts on sectarian aid," Hugh Wamble. Today's
    Eductn 64: 63 Nov '75.
"Textbooks, auxiliary services and parochial pupils," William W.
    Brickman. Intellect 104: 113 Sept '75.

3597. United States v. Reliable Transfer Co. May 19, 1975 421 U. S. 397
        Significant Decisions 1974/75 122-123
        PERIODICALS:
        "U. S. scraps equal-damage maritime law." Natl Underwriter
        (Property ed) 79: 1, 32 May 23 '75.

3598. Johnson v. Railway Express Agency,   May 19, 1975 421 U. S. 454
        Inc.
        *Racial Equality 104-105

3599. Eastland v. U. S. Servicemen's Fund   May 27, 1975 421 U. S. 491
        *Consttnl Law (Barrett) 538-541
        *Legislation (Linde) 768-775
        *Legislative (Hetzel) 683-688
        Significant Decisions 1974/75 59-60

3600. Breed v. Jones   May 27, 1975 421 U. S. 519
        *Cases Criml Law (Hall) 1225-1232
        Significant Decisions 1974/75 23-24
        *Sup Ct and Criml Process 723-727
        PERIODICALS:
        "Supreme Court review (1975)." J Criml Law and Crimlgy 66:
        408-418 Dec '75.

3601. Fry v. United States   May 27, 1975 421 U. S. 542
        Significant Decisions 1974/75 121-122
        PERIODICALS:
        "Significant decisions in labor cases." Monthly Labor R 98: 43
        Aug '75.

3602. Connell Construction Co. v.   June 2, 1975 421 U. S. 616
        Plumbers and Steamfitters
        Local Union No. 100
        Basic Text 272-273, 633-635
        Brethren 377-378
        *Cases Labor (Leslie) 453-460

*Cases Labor (Oberer) 1043-1053
Significant Decisions 1974/75 106-108
PERIODICALS:
"Significant decisions in labor cases." Monthly Labor R 98: 57-
58 Sept '75.

3603. United States v. Park   June 9, 1975   421 U.S. 658
*Cases Criml Law (Hall) 640-645
*Cases Criml Law (Inbau) 702-713
*Modern Business 738-741
Significant Decisions 1974/75 36-38
PERIODICALS:
"Growing criminal liability of executives; J. R. Park case," Tony
McAdams and Robert C. Miljus. Harvard Bus R 55: 36-37,
40, 164, 166 Mar '77.
"Supreme Court review (1975)." J Criml Law and Crimlgy 66:
456-463 Dec '75.

3604. Mullaney v. Wilbur   June 9, 1975   421 U.S. 684
*Cases Criml Justice 1212-1224
Defendants 104-105
*Elements Criminal 180-189
Significant Decisions 1974/75 32-34

3605. Philbrook v. Glodgett   June 9, 1975   421 U.S. 707
Weinberger v. Glodgett
*Poverty 644-647
Significant Decisions 1974/75 133-134
*Text Social Issues 378-380

3606. Blue Chip Stamps v. Manor   June 9, 1975   421 U.S. 723
Drug Stores
*Basic Corporation 610-621

3607. Goldfarb v. Virginia State Bar   June 16, 1975   421 U.S. 773
*Cases Professional 254-262
Editorials 1975 702-705
*Legal Environment 265-269
*Problems 75-80
Significant Decisions 1974/75 108-109
PERIODICALS:
"Classic case of fixing." Time 105: 53 June 30 '75.
"Discount lawyers?" Jerrold K. Footlick and Diane Camper.
Newsweek 85: 39 June 30 '75.
"High court rulings affect land-use suits, co-ops, legal fees,"
Daniel Moskowitz. House and Home 47 [48]: 12 Aug '75
(3).
"Lawyers' fees; Goldfarb case," Peter H. Schuck. New Republic
173: 6-8 Oct 11 '75.

3608. Murphy v. Florida   June 16, 1975   421 U.S. 794
*Cases Criml Justice 1011-1016
*Cases Criml Law (Hall) 1095-1098
Communication (Hemmer) v. 2, 183-185
*Consttnl Law (Klein) 164-168
*Criminal Procedure (Lewis) 478-482
Handbook 526-529
*Leading Consttnl Cases 679-682
*Modern Criml Procedure 359-360

Significant Decisions 1974/75 35
*Sup Ct and Criml Process 634-638
PERIODICALS:
"Pretrial publicity and due process in criminal proceedings,"
Caren Dubnoff. Poltcl Sci Q 92: 89-108 Spring '77 (8).

3609. Bigelow v. Virginia   June 16, 1975 421 U.S. 809
Advertising 22-24
*Cases Criml Law (Inbau) 257-266
Communication (Hemmer) v. 2, 325-326
Consttnl Law (Barrett) 1344-1345
*Consttnl Law (Freund) 1254-1257
*Freedom of Speech (Haiman) 189-190
Handbook 167-168
Law of Mass 564-566
*Mass Communications 179-180
*Mass Media (Devol) 338-339
Mass Media (Francois) 402-403
Significant Decisions 1974/75 51-52
Sup Ct Review 1976 78-87
PERIODICALS:
"Abortion ad is protected by First Amendment, high court says."
Broadcasting 88: 41 June 23 '75.
"Advertising and the First Amendment," Dorothy Cohen. J Mark-
eting 42: 59-68 July '78 (4).
"High court rules against state, group ad limits." Adv Age 46:
67 June 23 '75 (2).
"Libel, advertising and freedom of the press," Harriet F. Pilpel
and Laurie R. Rockett. Pub Weekly 209: 46-48 Mar 1 '76
(2).
"The new commercial speech doctrine," Michael B. Metzger and
Barry S. Roberts. MSU Bus Topics 27: 17-23 Spring '79
(3).
"New US Supreme Court philosophy on advertising faces opposition,"
Denise M. Trauth and John L. Huffman. Journalism Q 56:
540-546 Autumn '79 (3).
"Supreme Court rules: commercial ads protected by First Amendment," I. William Hill. Editor and Pub 108: 11 June 21 '75.

3610. United Housing foundation, Inc.   June 16, 1975 421 U.S. 837
v. Forman
New York v. Forman
Significant Decisions 1974/75 123-125
PERIODICALS:
"High court rulings affect land-use suits, co-ops, legal fees,"
David Moskowitz. House and Home 47 [48]: 12 Aug '75 (3).

3611. Cort v. Ash   June 17, 1975 422 U.S. 66
Significant Decisions 1974/75 75-76

3612. United States v. Citizens and   June 17, 1975 422 U.S. 86
Southern National Bank
Significant Decisions 1974/75 103-106
PERIODICALS:
"Court turns against antitrust." Bus Wk p. 52 July 14 '75 (5).

3613. Twentieth Century Music Corporation June 17, 1975 422 U.S. 151
v. Aiken
*Cases Copyright (Nimmer) 230-236

Significant Decisions 1974/75 118-119
PERIODICALS:
"ASCAP loses out on high court ruling on restaurant radio. "
Broadcasting 88: 45 June 23 '75.

3614. United States v. Hale   June 23, 1975 422 U.S. 171
       *Criminal Evidence 474-475
       *Due Process 69
       *Principles Proof 473-478
       PERIODICALS:
       "Supreme Court review (1975). " J Criml Law and Crimlgy 66:
       419-427 Dec '75 (2).

3615. Erznoznik v. Jacksonville   June 23, 1975 422 U.S. 205
       Brethren 363-365
       Cases Consttnl Law (Gunther) 1238-1243
       Communication (Hemmer) v. 1, 202-203
       *Consttnl Law (Barrett) 1286-1291
       *Consttnl Law (Grossman) 1259-1262
       *Freedom of Speech (Haiman) 158-160
       Handbook 137-138, 698-699
       *Right to Privacy 81-85
       *Rights (Shattuck) 121-122
       Significant Decisions 1974/75 61-62
       Sup Ct Review 1979 202-204

3616. United States v. Nobles   June 23, 1975 422 U.S. 225
       *Cases Criml Justice 963-972
       Significant Decisions 1974/75 35-36

3617. Administrator, Federal Aviation   June 24, 1975 422 U.S. 255
       Administration v. Robertson
       Communication (Hemmer) v. 2, 242-243
       *Legal Environment 568-570
       Mass Media (Francois) 244-245
       Significant Decisions 1974/75 131-132

3618. United States v. American Building   June 24, 1975 422 U.S. 271
       Maintenance Industries
       Significant Decisions 1974/75 110

3619. Hicks v. Miranda   June 24, 1975 422 U.S. 332
       *Civil Rights (Abernathy) 1980 185-189
       *Consttnl Law (Barrett) 145-146
       *Justices (Friedman) v. 5, 374-382
       Significant Decisions 1974/75 81-82

3620. Richmond v. United States   June 24, 1975 422 U.S. 358
       *Civil Rights (Abernathy) 1980 621-628
       Significant Decisions 1074/75 76-77

3621. Preiser v. Newkirk   June 25, 1975 422 U.S. 395
       *US Prison Law v. 6, 285-289

3622. Albemarle Paper Co. v. Moody   June 25, 1975 422 U.S. 405
       Halifax Local No. 425, United
       Papermakers and Paperworkers
       v. Moody

CQ Guide 620
*Civil Rights (Abernathy) 1980 450-458, 527-534
*Collective Bargaining 896-907
*Labor Law (Twomey) 388-392
Significant Decisions 1974/75 66-68
Sup Ct Review 1976 263-316
PERIODICALS:
   "Albemarle v. Moody: where it all began," W. H. Warren. Labor
      Law J 27: 609-613 Oct '76.
   "A new vision of equality," Donald W. Jackson. Policy Studies J
      4: 122-126 Winter '75 (2).
   "Significant decisions in labor cases." Monthly Labor R 98: 57-
      58 Oct '75.

3623. Muniz v. Hoffman   June 25, 1975 422 U.S. 454
      Modern Criml Procedure 347
      Significant Decisions 1974/75 114-115
      PERIODICALS:
         "Significant decisions in labor cases." Monthly Labor R 98: 58
            Sept '75.

3624. Warth v. Seldin   June 25, 1974 422 U.S. 490
      *Admin Law (Gellhorn) 983-986
      Brethren 366-367
      *Cases Consttnl Law (Gunther) 1629-1639
      *Cases Pleading 632-647
      *Consttnl Law (Barrett) 76-84
      *Consttnl Law (Lockhart) 1653-1660
      *Courts Judges 287-291
      *Federal System 62-64
      Significant Decisions 1974/75 89-91
      PERIODICALS:
         "High court rulings affect land-use suits, co-ops, legal fees,"
            Daniel Moskowitz. House and Home 47 [48]: 12 Aug '75
            (3).
         "Shifting sands of land use in the U.S. Supreme Court," Randall
            Scott. Mortgage Banker 37: 74, 76, 78, 80 May '77 (5).

3625. United States v. Peltier   June 25, 1975 422 U.S. 531
      Brethren 383-384
      *Cases Civil Liberties 131-136
      *Cases Consttnl Law (Cushman) 361-366
      *Criminal Justice (Galloway) 133-136
      *Criminal Procedure (Lewis) 133-135
      Significant Decisions 1974/75 26-27
      *Teaching Materials 108-118
      PERIODICALS:
         "Supreme Court review (1975)." J Criml Law and Crimlgy 66:
            436-446 Dec '75 (4).

3626. O'Connor v. Donaldson   June 26, 1975 422 U.S. 563
      Brethren 369-377, 378-382
      Courts Judges 228-230
      *Due Process 204-205
      Editorials 1975 834-838
      *Historic Documents 1975 469-480
      Right to Treatment 121-123
      *Right to Treatment 211-236
      Significant Decisions 1974/75 52-54

*Text Social Issues 229-232
PERIODICALS:
"Amicus curiae brief in the Donaldson case." Am J Psychiatry
    132: 109-115 Jan '75.
"Commentary: O'Connor v. Donaldson," Richard C. Allen. MH
    59: 2 Fall '75.
"Kenneth Donaldson's fight for freedom," Rena Steinzor. Pro-
    gressive 41: 48-50 Apr '77.
"Law: decision in O'Connor vs Donaldson case." MH 59: 35
    Summer '75.
"Opening the asylums." Time 106: 44 July 7 '75.
"Review of major implications of the O'Connor v. Donaldson de-
    cision," Louis E. Kopolow. Am J Psychiatry 133: 379-383
    Apr '76.
"Significance for psychology of O'Connor v. Donaldson," J. L.
    Bernard. Am Psychologist 32: 1085-1088 Dec '77. Reaction:
    33: 858-861 Sept '78. 34: 280-282 Mar '79.
"Supreme Court; decisions." Economist 256: 58 July 12 '75.
"Supreme Court review (1975)." J Criml Law and Crimlgy 66:
    447-455 Dec '75.
"Freeing mental patients," Jean Seligmann and Diane Camper.
    Newsweek 86: 45 July 7 '75.

3027. Brown v. Illinois   June 26, 1975 422 U.S. 590
       *Cases Criml Justice 668-679
       *Cases Criml Law (Hall) 884-889
       *Consttnl Criml (Scarboro) 455-463
       *Criminal Evidence 260-261
       Criminal Evidence 472
       Criminal Evidence 266-272; reprinted from "Miranda and the deriv-
          ative evidence rule--Brown v. Illinois," Donald McLaughlin.
          FBI Law Enforcement Bul Jan '76.
       *Criminal Procedure (Lewis) 299-302
       Law of Arrest (Creamer) 509-515
       *Modern Criml Procedure 220-223
       Significant Decisions 1974/75 17-18
       *Sup Ct and Criml Process 346-348

3628. Ivan Allen Co. v. United States   June 26, 1975 422 U.S. 617
       PERIODICALS:
       "Supreme Court tax decisions focuses on realistic financial con-
          dition." CPA J 45: 9-10 Oct '75.
       "Supreme Court's Ivan Allen holding based on economic reality
          may cause 531 problems," Neal D. Borden and Robert K.
          Briskin. J Taxation 43: 130-134 Sept '75.

3629. Gordon v. New York Stock Exchange   June 26, 1975 422 U.S. 659
       *Selected Antitrust Cases 404-410
       PERIODICALS:
       "Court turns against antitrust." Bus Wk p. 52 July 14 '75 (5).

3630. United States v. National Association June 26, 1975 422 U.S. 694
          of Securities Dealers
       Significant Decisions 1974/75 102-103

3631. Weinberger v. Salfi   June 26, 1975 422 U.S. 749
       *Consttnl Law (Barrett) 1035-1039
       *Consttnl Law (Lockhart) 1506-1510
       Significant Decisions 1974/75 134-135

3632. Faretta v. California   June 30, 1975 422 U.S. 806
        *Cases Civil Liberties 179-186
        *Cases Consttnl Law (Cushman) 409-416
        *Cases Criml Justice 1338-1351
        *Cases Criml Law (Hall) 1066-1068
        *Consttnl Law (Grossman) 899-902
        *Consttnl Law (Maddex) 51-56
        *Criminal Procedure (Lewis) 440-444
        *Due Process 43
        *Elements Criminal 92-105
        *Leading Consttnl Cases 454-467
        *Modern Criml Procedure 12-15
        Procedures 112-113
        Significant Decisions 1974/75 25
        *Sup Ct and Criml Process 564-568
        *Text Social Issues 343-346
        PERIODICALS:
        "Rights of defendants in criminal cases." Intellect 104: 282
            Jan '76.
        "Supreme Court review (1975)." J Criml Law and Crimlgy 66:
            400-407 Dec '75.

3633. Herring v. New York   June 30, 1975 422 U.S. 853
        *Due Process 134-135
        Significant Decisions 1974/75 26

3634. United States v. Brignoni-Ponce   June 30, 1975 422 U.S. 873
        *Cases Criml Justice 378-385
        Law of Arrest (Creamer) 263-270
        Significant Decisions 1974/75 28-29
        PERIODICALS:
        "Liberty at bay; Supreme Court and search and seizure," Norman
            Abrams. Center Mag 10: 16-20 Jan '77 (8).
        "Supreme Court review (1975)." J Criml Law and Crimlgy 66:
            436-446 Dec '75 (4).

3635. United States v. Ortiz   June 30, 1975 442 U.S. 891
        Significant Decisions 1974/75 27-28
        PERIODICALS:
        See listing at 422 U.S. 873, entry no. 3634.

3636. Bowen v. United States   June 30, 1975 422 U.S. 916
        PERIODICALS:
        See listing at 422 U.S. 873, entry no. 3634.

3637. Doran v. Salem Inn, Inc.   June 30, 1975 422 U.S. 922
        *Consttnl Law (Barrett) 146
        *Freedom of Speech (Haiman) 151-152
        Sup Ct Review 1977 206-207

3638. Day and Zimmermann v. Challoner   Nov 3, 1975   423 U.S. 3
        *Cases Federal Courts 614-615

3639. Turner v. Department of Employ-   Nov 17, 1975   423 U.S. 44
            ment Security
        *Sex Discrimination 1978 279-281
        PERIODICALS:
        "Significant decisions in labor cases." Monthly Labor R 99: 64-
            65 Jan '76.

3640. Rose v. Locke   Nov 17, 1975   423 U.S. 48
       *Cases Criml Law (Inbau) 416-423
       *Criminal Procedure (Lewis) 50-53
       *Due Process 22
       *Sup Ct and Criml Process 97-98

3641. Menna v. New York   Nov 17, 1975   423 U.S. 61
       *Cases Criml Justice 1135-1136

3642. Dillingham v. United States   Dec 1, 1975   423 U.S. 64
       *Modern Criml Procedure 297-299

3643. Texas v. White   Dec 1, 1975   423 U.S. 67
       *Criminal Evidence 346-347
       *Sup Ct and Criml Process 287

3644. Michigan v. Mosley   Dec 9, 1975   423 U.S. 96
       *Cases Criml Justice 632-638
       *Cases Criml Law (Hall) 863-866
       *Civil Liberties (Barker) 230-234
       *Consttnl Law (Maddex) 252-259
       Criminal Evidence 460-461
       *Criminal Justice (Galloway) 96-102
       *Criminal Justice (Way) 181-184
       Editorials 1975 1588-1591
       Law of Arrest (Creamer) 397-402
       *Modern Criml Procedure 159-165
       Significant Decisions 1975/76 30-31
       *Sup Ct and Criml Process 447-450
       Sup Ct Review 1977 129-137
       PERIODICALS:
       "Supreme Court review (1976)." J Criml Law and Crimlgy 67:
          397-407 Dec '76 (2).

3645. Weinstein v. Bradford   Dec 10, 1975   423 U.S. 147
       *US Prison Law v. 4, 103-105

3646. Foremost-McKesson, Inc. v.   Jan 13, 1976   423 U.S. 232
          Provident Securities Co.
       Significant Decisions 1975/76 161-162

3647. Mathews v. Weber   Jan 14, 1976   423 U.S. 261
       Significant Decisions 1975/76 115-117
       Sup Ct Review 1976 190-191

3648. Michelin Tire Corporation v. Wages Jan 14, 1976 423 U.S. 276
       *Consttnl Law (Barrett) 387-392
       *Consttnl Law (Freund) 192-197
       Significant Decisions 1975/76 182-183
       Sup Ct Review 1976 99-133
       PERIODICALS:
       "Supreme Court sets new test for local taxation of imports in
          Michelin Tire," James H. Peters. J Taxation 44: 244-245
          Apr '76.

3649. Thermtron Products, Inc. v.   Jan 20, 1976   423 U.S. 336
          Hermansdorfer
       *Cases Federal Courts 317-327
       *Civil Procedure (Carrington) 812-819

Significant Decisions 1975/76 121-122
Sup Ct Review 1976 191-192

3650. Rizzo v. Goode   Jan 21, 1976   423 U.S. 362
       Brethren 416-417
       *Civil Rights (Abernathy) 1980 122-127
       *Consttnl Law (Klein) 576-584
       *Courts Judges 101-104
       *Federal System 320-323
       Significant Decisions 1975/76 45-46
       PERIODICALS:
       "Blow against liberty," Louis B. Schwartz. Progressive 40: 9-
          10 Mar '76.
       "Supreme Court and the cities," Sarah C. Casey. Natns Cities
          14: 10-16 Oct '76 (3).

3651. National Independent Coal Operators' Jan 26, 1976   423 U.S. 388
          Association v. Kleppe
       *Admin Law (Schwartz) 308-310
       PERIODICALS:
       "Significant decisions in labor cases." Monthly Labor R 99: 49-
          50 Apr '76.

3652. United States v. Watson   Jan 26, 1976   423 U.S. 411
       *Cases Criml Justice 150-166
       *Consttnl Criml (Marks) 335-339
       *Consttnl Law (Felkenes) 222-223
       *Consttnl Law (Klein) 240-245
       *Consttnl Law (Maddex) 141-144
       Criminal Evidence 364
       *Criminal Justice (Way) 94-97
       *Criminal Procedure (Lewis) 140-143, 223
       *Due Process 23-24
       Law of Arrest (Creamer) 240-244
       *Law of Evidence 577-582
       *Leading Consttnl Cases 85-88
       *Modern Criml Procedure 77-84
       Significant Decisions 1975/76 28-29
       *Sup Ct and Criml Process 170-173, 299-301

3653. Buckley v. Valeo   Jan 30, 1976   424 U.S. 1
       *Admin Law (Schwartz) 21-26
       *Am Consttnl Law (Shapiro) 397-405
       Am Politics 92-97
       *Basic Cases 198-216
       Brethren 395-396, 398-400
       CQ Guide 172-173
       *Cases Consttnl Law (Cushman) 111-115
       *Cases Consttnl Law (Gunther) 1425-1438, 1481-1485
       *Comparative 587-594
       *Consttnl Law (Barrett) 258-259, 519-524, 1172-1177, 1331-1337
       *Consttnl Law (Freund) 1265-1283
       *Consttnl Law (Lockhart) 1146-1156
       Editorials 1976 122-131
       *Federal System 103-106
       *Historic Documents 1976 71-111
       *Legislative (Hetzel) 713-717, 873-875
       *Mass Communications 682-688
       *Rights (Shattuck) 68-69

Significant Decisions 1975/76 73-83
Sup Ct Review 1976 1-43
Sup Ct Review 1978 281-282
Ultimate Tyranny 47-89
Watergate 99-102, 184-188
PERIODICALS:
"Bull market in politicians," Frank Mankiewicz. Harper's Mag
    252: 14, 18-19 Apr '76.
"Constitution and campaign finance regulation after Buckley v.
    Valeo," Albert J. Rosenthal. Am Academy of Poltcl and Socl
    Sci Annals 425: 124-133 May '76.
"Court has ruled 'long live chaos,'" W. F. Buckley, Jr. Natl R
    28: 230-231 Mar 5 '76.
"Hard cases make bad law." Economist 258: 31-32 Feb 7 '76.
"Infanticide." Nation 222: 162 Feb 14 '76.
"Lifting the lid on campaign spending," Nathan Lewin. New Re-
    public 174: 11-14 Feb 14 '76.
"Money and politics--impact of Supreme Court ruling." US News
    80: 16-17 Feb 9 '76.
"Money game: changing the rules; what it means to the candidate."
    Time 107: 10-14 Feb 9 '76.
"New money rules; decision on campaign spending," David M. Al-
    pern and others. Newsweek 87: 14-16 Feb 9 '76.
"Ninety-fourth Congress action on House and Senate campaign fi-
    nancing." Congressional Dig 56: 74-75 Mar '76.
"Public financing after the Supreme Court decision," George E.
    Agree. Am Academy of Poltcl and Socl Sci Annals 425: 134-
    142 May '76.
"Rethinking election reform," Herbert E. Alexander. Am Academy
    of Poltcl and Socl Sci Annals 425: 1-16 May '76.
"Significant decisions in labor cases." Monthly Labor R 99: 48
    49 Apr '76.
"Supreme Court's ruling on election law causes confusion," Michael
    J. Malbin. Natl J 8: 167-168 Feb 7 '76.
"Transfusion." Newsweek 87: 13 Jan 5 '76.
"U.S. government; countdown to convention '76." Senior Scholastic
    108: 29 Mar 23 '76.
"Unworkable and inequitable: the Court clips election reform,"
    Maurice deG. Ford. Nation 222: 231-234 Feb 28 '76.

3654. Mathews v. Eldridge   Feb 24, 1976 424 U.S. 319
        *Admin Law (Gellhorn) 499-508
        *Admin Law (Schwartz) 360-369
        Significant Decisions 1975/76 179-181
        PERIODICALS:
        "Significant decisions in labor cases." Monthly Labor R 99: 44-
            45 May '76.

3655. DeCanas v. Bica   Feb 25, 1976 424 U.S. 351
        *Consttnl Law (Barrett) 363-366
        Significant Decisions 1975/76 141-142
        PERIODICALS:
        "Significant decisions in labor cases." Monthly Labor R 99: 45-
            46 May '76.

3656. Great Atlantic and Pacific Tea Co. Feb 25, 1976 424 U.S. 366
            v. Cottrell
        *Consttnl Law (Barrett) 329-334
        Significant Decisions 1975/76 169-170

3657. United States v. Testan   Mar 2, 1976   424 U.S. 392
       PERIODICALS:
       "Public employment and the Supreme Court's 1975-76 term," Carl
         F. Goodman. Public Personnel Mgt 5: 287-302 Sept '76
         (12).
       "Significant decisions in labor cases." Monthly Labor R 99: 47
         May '76.

3658. Imbler v. Pachtman   Mar 2, 1976   424 U.S. 409
       *Civil Rights (Abernathy) 1980 58-65
       Law of Arrest (Creamer) 525-529
       Significant Decisions 1975/76 43-45
       *Sup Ct and Criml Process 821-824

3659. Time, Inc. v. Firestone   Mar 2, 1976   424 U.S. 448
       CQ Guide 439-440
       *Cases Copyright (Nimmer) 697-715
       Communication (Hemmer) v. 2, 66-68
       Consttnl Law (Barrett) 1414-1415
       *Consttnl Law (Grossman) 1155-1157
       Crisis 212-213
       Handbook 282-286, 341-343
       Law of Mass 117-118
       *Mass Communications 226-231
       *Mass Media (Devol) 233-236
       Mass Media (Francois) 112-116
       Significant Decisions 1975/76 92-93
       PERIODICALS:
       "Danger: pendulum swinging: using the courts to muzzle the
         press," Alan U. Schwartz. Atlantic 239: 29-34 Feb '77.
       "Demise of the public figure doctrine," John J. Watkins. J Com-
         munication 27: 47-53 Summer '77.
       "Private lives," Harry F. Waters and Diane Camper. Newsweek
         87: 66 Mar 15 '76.
       "Supreme Court libel ruling in Firestone case is a new danger to
         press freedom," Harriet F. Pilpel and Laurie R. Rockett.
         Pub Weekly 209: 39-40 Mar 29 '76.
       "Who is a public figure?" Time 107: 66 Mar 15 '76.

3660. Hudgens v. National Labor Relations   Mar 3, 1976   424 U.S. 507
       Board
       Basic Text 188-189
       CQ Guide 417
       Cases Consttnl Law (Gunther) 1299-1300
       *Cases Labor (Leslie) 108-116
       *Cases Labor (Oberer) 263-270
       *Civil Liberties (Barker) 121-128
       Communication (Hemmer) v. 1, 91-92
       *Consttnl Law (Barrett) 1296-1301
       *Consttnl Law (Lockhart) 1554-1557
       *Freedom of Speech (Haiman) 81
       Labor Law (Twomey) 256-257
       *Mass Communications 60-63
       Significant Decisions 1975/76 87-88
       Sup Ct Review 1976 224-227
       PERIODICALS:
       "Nixon's last laugh: the Constitution in retreat," Arthur S. Miller.
         Nation 222: 422-423 Apr 10 '76.

"Significant decisions in labor cases." Monthly Labor R 99: 46-47 May '76.

3661. Hines v. Anchor Motor Freight, Inc.   Mar 3, 1976   424 U.S. 554
*Cases Labor (Oberer) 800-807
*Collective Bargaining 404-413
*Labor Law (Twomey) 335-338
Labor Relations (Taylor) 422-423
PERIODICALS:
"Significant decisions in labor cases." Monthly Labor R 99: 47
May '76.

3662. Lavine v. Milne   Mar 3, 1976   424 U.S. 577
PERIODICALS:
"Significant decisions in labor cases." Monthly Labor R 99: 45
May '76.

3663. Ristaino v. Ross   Mar 3, 1976   424 U.S. 589
Significant Decisions 1975/76 62-63
*Sup Ct and Criml Process 627-630

3664. United States v. Dinitz   Mar 8, 1976   424 U.S. 600
*Criminal Justice (Way) 274-278
*Modern Criml Procedure 396-399
Significant Decisions 1975/76 58-59
*Sup Ct and Criml Process 411-414

3665. Commissioner of Internal Revenue   Mar 8, 1976   424 U.S. 614
v. Shapiro
Sup Ct Review 1976 206-207
PERIODICALS:
"Supreme Court's Shapiro decision restricts use of jeopardy as-
sessments," John M. Bray. J Taxation 44: 264-266 May
'76.

3666. McCarthy v. Philadelphia Civil   Mar 22, 1976   424 U.S. 645
Service Commission
Consttnl Law (Barrett) 943
Digest 66
Significant Decisions 1975/76 123
PERIODICALS:
"Supreme Court rules on residency requirements," Andrij Bilyk.
Natns Cities 14: 37 Apr '76.

3667. Garner v. United States   Mar 23, 1976   424 U.S. 648
Law of Arrest (Creamer) 436-440
Significant Decisions 1975/76 37-39
Sup Ct Review 1977 156-158
PERIODICALS:
"Supreme Court's Garner decision puts illegal income earners in
a bind," Michael I. Saltzman. J Taxation 44: 334-337 June
'76.

3668. McKinney v. Alabama   Mar 23, 1976   424 U.S. 669
Consttnl Law (Barrett) 1244-1245
Handbook 690
PERIODICALS:
"Court strikes down civil obscenity conviction," W. D. Nelson.
Wilson Library Bul 50: 683-684 May '76.

3669. Paul v. Davis   Mar 23, 1976   424 U. S. 693
       *Admin Law (Gellhorn) 489-496
       *Am Consttnl Law (Saye) 403-408
       Brethren 403-405
       Cases Consttnl Law (Gunther) 662-664
       Communication (Hemmer) v. 1, 255-256
       *Courts Judges 230-235
       *Due Process 212-213
       *Justices (Friedman) v. 5, 132-140
       *Rights (Shattuck) 161-163
       Significant Decisions 1975/76 42-43
       *Sup Ct and Criml Process 815-821
       PERIODICALS:
       "Constitutional rights in retreat." Progressive 40: 7 June '76.
       "He that filches ... my good name: the Supreme Court on defa-
         mation," Louis Fisher. Nation 223: 485-487 Nov 13 '76.
       "Police upheld on criminal records use." Editor and Pub 109:
         12 Mar 27 '76.

3670. Franks v. Bowman Transportation Co. Mar 24, 1976   424 U. S. 747
       CQ Guide 621
       *Cases Labor (Oberer) 980-990
       *Civil Liberties (Stone) 122-125
       *Civil Rights (Abernathy) 1980 536-546
       *Collective Bargaining 965-981
       *Racial Equality 107-108
       Significant Decisions 1975/76 106-107
       Sup Ct Review 1976 187-190
       PERIODICALS:
       "More seniority for the victims." Time 107: 65 Apr 5 '76.
       "Seniority rights of blacks ruled retroactive." Chronicle of Higher
         Eductn 12: 8 Apr 5 '76.
       "Significant decisions in labor cases." Monthly Labor R 99: 51-
         52 June '76.
       "Supreme Court and quotas," J. S. Fuerst and Roy Petty. Chris-
         tian Century 94: 948-952 Oct 19 '77 (5).
       "Supreme Court's seniority ruling leaves questions." Industry Wk
         189: 13-14 Apr 5 '76.

3671. Colorado River Water Conservation   Mar 24, 1976   424 U. S. 800
         District v. United States
       Akin v. United States
       Sup Ct Review 1976 213-214

3672. Greer v. Spock   Mar 24, 1976   424 U. S. 828
       Cases Consttnl Law (Gunther) 1293-1296
       Communication (Hemmer) v. 1, 84-85
       *Consttnl Law (Barrett) 1278-1280
       *Consttnl Law (Grossman) 1214-1217
       Significant Decisions 1975/76 93-95

3673. Abbott Laboratories v. Portland   Mar 24, 1976   425 U. S. 1
         Retail Druggists Association
       *Am Druggist 173: 24-25 May '76.
       PERIODICALS:
       "Supreme Court puts strict curbs on hospitals' use of drugs bought
         at preferential prices." Am Druggist 173: 20, 24-25 May
         '76.

3674.   Middendorf v. Henry   Mar 24, 1976   425 U.S. 25
        Significant Decisions 1975/76 61-62
        *Sup Ct and Criml Process 1134-1138

3675.   Goldberg v. United States   Mar 30, 1976   425 U.S. 94
        Significant Decisions 1975/76 55
        PERIODICALS:
        "Supreme Court review (1976)." J Criml Law and Crimlgy 67:
        416-421 Dec '76.

3676.   Beer v. United States   Mar 30, 1976   425 U.S. 130
        Significant Decisions 1975/76 103-104

3677.   United States v. United Continental   Mar 30, 1976 425 U.S. 164
        Tuna Corporation
        Sup Ct Review 1976 198-201

3678.   Ernst and Ernst v. Hochfelder   Mar 30, 1976   425 U.S. 185
        *Legal Environment 369-373
        Significant Decisions 1975/76 160-161
        PERIODICALS:
        "American accountants; deceived but relieved." Economist 259:
        126 Apr 10 '76.
        "Hochfelder decision: how it will effect future malpractice suits
        against accountants," Michael Schlesinger. Practical Accountant
        9: 77-81 Sept '76.
        "Significance of the Hochfelder decision," Allan Kramer. CPA J
        46: 11-14 Aug '76.
        "Supreme Court and the new fraud," Arthur Fleischer, Jr. Insti-
        tutional Investor 10: 13 July '76.
        "Supreme Court decision backs Hochfelder case on intent, sustains
        AICPA amicus brief." J Accountancy 150: 7 July '80 (2).

3679.   Kelley v. Johnson   Apr 5, 1976   425 U.S. 238
        Cases Consttnl Law (Gunther) 643-644
        Communication (Hemmer) v. 1, 258
        *Due Process 210
        *Labor Relations (Edwards) 793-796
        *Rights (Shattuck) 136-138
        Significant Decisions 1975/76 125-126
        *Sup Ct and Criml Process 837-842
        PERIODICALS:
        *"Significant decisions in labor cases." Monthly Labor R 99: 53-
        54 June '76.

3680.   Diamond National Corporation v. Apr 19, 1976   425 U.S. 268
        State Board of Equalization
        PERIODICALS:
        "Supreme Court says California sales tax is subject to federal im-
        munity," James H. Peters. J Taxation 45: 116-117 Aug '76.

3681.   Hills v. Gautreaux   Apr 20, 1976   425 U.S. 284
        CQ Guide 616-618
        *Civil Liberties (Barker) 290-294
        Consttnl Law (Barrett) 854-855
        Editorials 1976 492-501
        *Historic Documents 1976 223-233
        *Land Use 911-913

*Racial Equality 118-120
Significant Decisions 1975/76 104-106
Sup Ct Review 1976 252-254
PERIODICALS:
"Courts and desegregated housing: the meaning (if any) of the
Gautreaux case," Irvine Welfeld. Public Interest 45: 123-135
Fall '76.
"Court's ruling on opening white suburbs: less than meets the
eye." House and Home 49: 16 June '76.
"Cracking suburbs for blacks." US News 80: 69 May 3 '76.
"Ethnic purity runs into the Constitution." Economist 259: 29
Apr 24 '76.
"Hills v. Gautreaux: implications for education," Robert L. Crow-
son. Phi Delta Kappan 58: 550-552 Mar '77.
"Shifting sands of land use in the U.S. Supreme Court," Randall
Scott. Mortgage Banker 37: 74, 76, 78, 80 May '77 (5).
"Supreme Court orders HUD to disperse public housing," Sylvia
Lewis. Planning 42: 8-10 June '76.
"TRB from Washington; blacks and whites." New Republic 174:
2 Apr 10 '76.
"Very small suburban wedge." Time 107: 10-11 May 3 '76.

3682. Baxter v. Palmigiano   Apr 20, 1976 425 U.S. 308
        Enomoto v. Clutchette
        *Consttnl Criml (Scarboro) 606-611
        *Consttnl Rights (Palmer) 470-473
        *Criminal Justice (Way) 519-522
        Significant Decisions 1975/76 148-149
        *Sup Ct and Criml Process 762-767
        Sup Ct Review 1977 138-141
        *US Prison Law v. 6, 342-357
        PERIODICALS:
        "Supreme Court says Miranda warnings do not apply to non-
        custodial interviews," Donald L. Herskovitz. J Taxation
        45: 5-7 July '76 (2).

3683. Beckwith v. United States   Apr 21, 1976 425 U.S. 341
        *Consttnl Law (Felkenes) 269-270
        *Criminal Evidence 431-432
        *Criminal Justice (Galloway) 102-105
        *Criminal Procedure (Lewis) 374-377
        Law of Arrest (Creamer) 413-417
        *Leading Consttnl Cases 537-539
        Modern Criml Procedure 166
        Significant Decisions 1975/76 41-42
        *Sup Ct and Criml Process 450-452
        Sup Ct Review 1977 147-150

3684. Department of Air Force v. Rose   Apr 21, 1976 425 U.S. 352
        *Admin Law (Gellhorn) 618-621
        Mass Media (Francois) 242-243
        *Rights (Shattuck) 169-171
        Significant Decisions 1975/76 187-188
        PERIODICALS:
        "Significant decisions in labor cases." Monthly Labor R 99: 53-
        54 July '76.

3685. Fisher v. United States   Apr 21, 1976 425 U.S. 391
        United States v. Kasmir

*Consttnl Criml (Scarboro) 653-674
*Modern Criml Procedure 260-266
Significant Decisions 1975/76 35-37
PERIODICALS:
"Accountants' work papers given attorney, not privileged. " CPA
J 46: 41-42 Nov '76.
"Supreme Court on accountants' work papers." CPA J 46: 6-8
Aug '76.
"Supreme Court narrows Fifth Amendment privilege for records
held by third party, " Ira L. Tilzer. J Taxation 45: 2-4
July '76.
"Supreme Court review (1976). " J Criml Law and Crimlgy 67:
373-388 Dec '76 (2).
"Supreme Court's decisions in Fisher requires greater alertness
in handling tax fraud cases, " Marvin J. Garbis and L. Paige
Marvel. Practical Accountant 9: 35-38 July '76.

3686.   United States v. Miller   Apr 21, 1976   425 U.S. 435
Editorials 1976 596-599
*Rights (Shattuck) 190-192
Significant Decisions 1975/76 35
PERIODICALS:
"Supreme Court: fourth Amendment does not bar subpoena of tax-
payer's bank records, " Terry P. Segal. J Taxation 45: 80-
81 Aug '76.
"Supreme Court review (1976). " J Criml Law and Crimlgy 67:
373-388 Dec '76.

3687.   Hampton v. United States   Apr 27, 1976   425 U.S. 484
*Consttnl Law (Klein) 536-539
*Criminal Procedure (Lewis) 419-422
*Due Process 140
Law of Arrest (Creamer) 504-508
*Modern Criml Procedure 152-154
Significant Decisions 1975/76 46
*Sup Ct and Criml Process 480-484
PERIODICALS:
"Supreme Court review (1976). " J Criml Law and Crimlgy 67:
422-429 Dec '76.

3688.   Estelle v. Williams   May 3, 1976   425 U.S. 501
*Criminal Procedure (Lewis) 496-500
*Leading Consttnl Cases 724-727
Modern Criml Procedure 457-459
Significant Decisions 1975/76 146
*Sup Ct and Criml Process 630-634
*US Prison Law v. 6, 358-373

3689.   Francis v. Henderson   May 3, 1976   425 U.S. 536
Modern Criml Procedure 456-457
Significant Decisions 1975/76 149-150

3690.   United States v. Mandujano   May 3, 1976   425 U.S. 564
*Criminal Procedure (Lewis) 427-433
*Modern Criml Procedure 266-276
Significant Decisions 1975/76 40-41
*Sup Ct and Criml Process 528-533
Sup Ct Review 1977 154-156, 158-163

3691. Hynes v. Mayor and Council of   May 19, 1976 425 U. S. 610
      Borough of Oradell
      Cases Consttnl Law (Gunther) 1215-1216
      Communication (Hemmer) v. 1, 227-228
      Consttnl Law (Barrett) 1284-1286
      Significant Decisions 1975/76 90-91
      Sup Ct Review 1976 185

3692. National Association for the Advance- May 19, 1976 425 U. S. 662
      ment of Colored People v. Federal
      Power Commission
      Significant Decisions 1975/76 168-169

3693. Alfred Dunhill of London, Inc. v.   May 24, 1976 425 U. S. 682
      Republic of Cuba
      Significant Decisions 1975/76 165-167

3694. Hospital Building Co. v. Trustees   May 24, 1976 425 U. S. 738
      of Rex Hospital
      *Modern Business 923-925

3695. Virginia State Board of Pharmacy v.   May 24, 1976 425 U. S. 748
      Virginia Citizens Consumer Council, Inc.
      *Cases Consttnl Law (Gunther) 1382-1388
      Communication (Hemmer) v. 2, 355-356
      *Consttnl Law (Barrett) 1345-1354
      *Consttnl Law (Grossman) 1190-1195
      *Consttnl Law (Lockhart) 826-831
      Editorials 1976 737-742
      *First Amendment (Franklin) 431-439
      *Freedom of Speech (Haiman) 191-193
      Handbook 169-173, 180-182
      *Historic Documents 1976 351-363
      Law of Mass 566-567
      *Legal Regulation 54-65
      *Mass Communications 180
      Mass Media (Francois) 403-405
      *Modern Business 926-929
      Significant Decisions 1975/76 85-87
      Sup Ct Review 1976 88-97
   PERIODICALS:
      "Advertisers win a free speech case," Jethro K. Lieberman. Bus
         Wk p. 26 Jun 7 '76.
      "Advertising and the First Amendment," Dorothy Cohen. J Mark-
         eting 42: 59-68 July '78 (4).
      "Balm for drug buyers." Time 107: 50 July 7 '76.
      "Commercial activity on campus: where does it end?" Annette Gibbs
         and Miriam Jernigan. NASPA J 18: 28-32 Summer '80 (3).
      "Cure for Rx prices," Glenn White. Good Housekeeping 183: 82,
         84, 86, 88 Nov '76.
      *"Excerpts from Supreme Court decision." Am Druggist 174: 26,
         30-31 July '76.
      "Is national advertising still a step child of the first amendment?"
         E. John Kottman. J Adv 8: 6-12 Fall '79 (2).
      "The new commercial speech doctrine," Michael B. Metzger and
         Barry S. Roberts. MSU Bus Topics 27: 17-23 Spring '79 (3).
      "New US Supreme Court philosophy on advertising faces opposition,"
         Denise M. Trauth and John L. Huffman. Journalism Q 56:
         540-545 Autumn '79 (3).
      "Prescription price advertising; is there a loophole in Supreme

Court's landmark decision," Dan Kushner. <u>Am Druggist</u> 174:
24, 26, 30 July '76.
"Rx for drug prices?" Tom Nicholson and Diane Camper. <u>News-
week</u> 87: 75-76 June 7 '76.
"SCOOP drug retailer goes under; victim of court decision," John
J. O'Connor. <u>Adv Age</u> 47: 10 July 19 '76.
"Supreme Court adds broad protection of advertising," Stakley E.
Cohen. <u>Adv Age</u> 47: 1, 57 May 31 '76.
*"Supreme Court decision in drug price advertising case." <u>Adv Age</u>
47: 2B-3, 62A-62B May 31 '76.
"Supreme Court rules 7 to 1 that states may no longer bar com-
petitive advertising of drug prices by pharmacies." <u>Retirement
Living</u> 16: 11-12 July '76.
"Supreme Court strikes down bans on Rx advertising." <u>Consumer
Rep</u> 41: 374-375 July '76.
"Virginia v. North Dakota: was the court inconsistent?" <u>Am Drug-
gist</u> 174: 24, 32, 36 July '76 (2).

3696.   South Prairie Construction Co. v.   May 24, 1976   425 U.S. 800
International Union of Operating Engineers
National Labor Relations Board v.
International Union of Operating Engineers
*Cases Labor (Leslie) 199-201

3697.   Brown v. General Services Ad-   June 1, 1976   425 U.S. 820
ministration
*Civil Rights (Abernathy) 1980 512-516
PERIODICALS:
"Significant decisions in labor cases." <u>Monthly Labor R</u> 99: 42-
43 Aug '76 (2).

3698.   Chandler v. Roudebush   June 1, 1976   425 U.S. 840
Brethren 419-420
PERIODICALS:
See listing at 425 U.S. 820, entry no. 3697.

3699.   Train v. Colorado Public Interest   June 1, 1976   426 U.S. 1
Research Group, Inc.
*Cases Environmental Law (Gray) 346-349
PERIODICALS:
"Supreme Court draws nuclear regulatory lines." <u>Electrical
World</u> 186: 25 July 1 '76.

3700.   Simon v. Eastern Kentucky Welfare   June 1, 1976   426 U.S. 26
Rights Organization
Cases Consttnl Law (Gunther) 1639-1642
Significant Decisions 1975/76 119-121
Sup Ct Review 1976 183-185
PERIODICALS:
"Supreme Court severely limits third party's right to contest
exempt status," Stuart A. Sheldon and George H. Bostick.
J Taxation 45: 140-143 Sept '76.

3701.   Mathews v. Diaz   June 1, 1976   426 U.S. 67
*Consttnl Law (Barrett) 872-875
Significant Decisions 1975/76 140-141
Sup Ct Review 1977 282-294, 316-317
PERIODICALS:
"Significant decisions in labor cases." <u>Monthly Labor R</u> 99: 43-
44 Aug '76 (2).

3702. Hampton v. Mow Sun Wong   June 1, 1976   426 U.S. 88
       Brethren 402
       Cases Consttnl Law (Gunther) 894-896
       *Consttnl Law (Barrett) 875-877
       Editorials 1976 825-831
       *Justices (Friedman) v. 5, 163-175
       *Labor Relations (Edwards) 894-903
       Significant Decisions 1975/76 135-138
       Sup Ct Review 1977 278-282
       PERIODICALS:
       See listing at 426 U.S. 67, entry no. 3701.

3703. Radzanower v. Touche Ross and Co.   June 7, 1976   426 U.S. 148
       *Cases Pleading 439-447
       Sup Ct Review 1976 215-216

3704. Hancock v. Train   June 7, 1976   426 U.S. 167
       *Cases Environmental Law (Gray) 300-309
       Consttnl Law (Barrett) 473-474

3705. Environmental Protection Agency v.   June 7, 1976   426 U.S. 200
       California ex rel State Water Re-
       sources Control Board
       *Cases Environmental Law (Gray) 350-357

3706. Washington v. Davis   June 7, 1976   426 U.S. 229
       *Am Consttnl Law (Shapiro) 543-545
       CQ Guide 620
       *Cases Consttnl Law (Gunther) 714-719
       *Civil Liberties (Barker) 307-313
       *Collective Bargaining 825-834
       Conceived 218-219
       *Consttnl Law (Barrett) 784-793
       *Consttnl Law (Grossman) 567-571
       *Consttnl Law (Lockhart) 1283-1288
       Digest 104
       Editorials 1976 825-831
       *Labor Relations (Edwards) 872-878
       *Racial Equality 106
       Significant Decisions 1975/76 110-111
       Sup Ct Review 1976 263-316
       Sup Ct Review 1979 24-25, 28-29
       PERIODICALS:
       "Beyond Griggs v. Duke Power Co.: Title VII after Washington
         v. Davis," James D. Portwood and Stuart M. Schmidt. Labor
         Law J 28: 174-181 Mar '77 (3).
       "Public employment and the Supreme Court's 1975-76 term," Carl
         F. Goodman. Public Personnel Mgt 5: 287-302 Sept '76
         (12).
       "Recent developments in equal employment opportunity law and
         their effect on teacher credentialling practices," Michael A.
         Rebell. Am Association of Colleges for Teacher Eductn Year-
         book 69-81 '77.
       "Schools and the law--Austin and Indianapolis: a new approach to
         desegregation?" Thomas Flygare. Phi Delta Kappan 58: 709-
         710 May '77 (2).
       "Significant decisions in labor cases." Monthly Labor R 99: 41-
         42 Aug '76.

"Supreme Court and quotas, " J. S. Fuerst and Roy Petty.   Christian Century   94:   948-952   Oct 19 '77   (5).

3707. Federal Power Commission v. Conway   June 7, 1976   426 U.S. 271
        Corporation
        PERIODICALS:
        "Conway price-squeeze issue, " Jack L. Weiss.   Public Utilities
        Fortnightly   101:   22-26   Mar 30 '78.
        "Price squeeze allegations now heard separately. "   Public Utilities
        Fortnightly   104:   62-64   Dec 6 '79.

3708. Charlotte v. Local 660, International   June 7, 1976   426 U.S. 283
        Association of Firefighters
        *Labor Relations (Edwards) 454-456
        PERIODICALS:
        "Significant decisions in labor cases. "   Monthly Labor R   99:   45
        Oct '76.

3709. Nader v. Allegheny Airlines, Inc.   June 7, 1976   426 U.S. 290
        *Admin Law (Schwartz) 602-608
        PERIODICALS:
        "A big bump for bumping. "   Time   107:   48   June 21 '76.

3710. United States v. MacCollom   June 10, 1976   426 U.S. 317
        *Modern Criml Procedure 39-41
        Significant Decisions 1975/76 150-151

3711. Bishop v. Wood   June 10, 1976   426 U.S. 341
        *Admin Law (Gellhorn) 477-482
        *Cases Consttnl Law (Gunther) 655-661
        *Consttnl Law (Barrett) 757-762
        Digest 66 67
        *Labor Relations (Edwards) 826-831
        Law and Education 153-155
        *Rights (Shattuck) 165-167
        Significant Decisions 1975/76 123-125
        *Sup Ct and Criml Process 843-847
        PERIODICALS:
        "Due process rights of students: limitations on Goss v. Lopez; a
        retreat out of the thicket, " Michael A. Mass.   J Law and
        Eductn   9:   449-462   Oct '80   (3).
        "Recent Supreme Court rulings. "   Today's Eductn   65:   18, 20
        Nov '76   (3).
        "Significant decisions in labor cases. "   Monthly Labor R   99:   46
        Oct '76.

3712. Kerr v. U.S. District Court for   June 14, 1976   426 U.S. 394
        Northern District of California
        *Cases Pleading 1068-1073

3713. Oil, Chemical and Atomic Workers   June 14, 1976   426 U.S. 407
        v. Mobil Oil Corporation
        PERIODICALS:
        "Significant decisions in labor cases. "   Monthly Labor R   99:   52
        Sept '76.

3714. TSC Industries v. Northway, Inc.   June 14, 1976   426 U.S. 438
        *Basic Corporation 736-739
        Significant Decisions 1975/76 162-163

3715. Burrell v. McCray   June 14, 1976 426 U.S. 471
       Brethren 423-425
       *Consttnl Law (Barrett) 58-59

3716. Hortonville Joint School District v.   June 17, 1976 426 U.S. 482
       Hortonville Education Association
       *Consttn (Morris) 690-695
       Digest 67
       *Education (Hazard) 457-465
       *Labor Relations (Edwards) 550-556
       Significant Decisions 1975/76 127-128
       PERIODICALS:
       "Hear this: school boards, not teacher unions, are in charge of
          schools." Am Sch Bd J 163: 39-41 Aug '76. Condensed in:
          Eductn Dig 42: 12-14 Nov '76.
       "Schools and the law--Supreme Court upholds boards' right to fire
          striking teachers," Thomas Flygare. Phi Delta Kappan 58:
          206-207 Oct '76.
       "Significant decisions in labor cases." Monthly Labor R 99: 46
          Oct '76.
       "Striking teachers may be fired, Court says," Philip W. Semas.
          Chronicle of Higher Eductn 12: 3 June 28 '76.

3717. United States v. Chesapeake and   June 17, 1976 426 U.S. 500
       Ohio Railroad Co.
       PERIODICALS:
       "Court upholds ICC in ex parte 305." Railway Age 177: 14
          July 4 '76.

3718. Kleppe v. New Mexico   June 17, 1976 426 U.S. 529
       *Consttnl Law (Barrett) 276-278, 479-480

3719. Federal Energy Administration v.   June 17, 1976 426 U.S. 548
       Algonquin SNG, Inc.
       Significant Decisions 1975/76 185-186

3720. Examining Board of Engineers, Archi- June 17, 1976 426 U.S. 572
       tects and Surveyors v. Flores De
       Otero
       Significant Decisions 1975/76 138-140
       Sup Ct Review 1976 203-205

3721. Doyle v. Ohio   June 17, 1976 426 U.S. 610
       Wood v. Ohio
       *Consttnl Law (Felkenes) 270-271
       *Consttnl Law (Maddex) 269-272
       Criminal Evidence 475-476
       *Criminal Procedure (Lewis) 387-388
       Law of Arrest (Creamer) 430-436
       *Leading Consttnl Cases 545-548
       Significant Decisions 1975/76 54-55
       *Sup Ct and Criml Process 460-463
       Sup Ct Review 1977 141-142, 144-147
       PERIODICALS:
       "Supreme Court review (1976)." J Criml Law and Crimlgy 67:
          397-407 Dec '76 (2).

3722. Henderson v. Morgan   June 17, 1976 426 U.S. 637
       *Consttnl Law (Klein) 519-523

Procedures 58-59
Significant Decisions 1975/76 53-54
*Sup Ct and Criml Process 998-1002

3723. Pennsylvania v. New Jersey   June 17, 1976 426 U.S. 660
        Maine v. New Hampshire
        *Consttnl Law (Barrett) 93
        Significant Decisions 1975/76 184-185

3724. Eastlake v. Forest City Enter-   June 21, 1976 426 U.S. 668
        prises, Inc.
        *Legal Foundations 293-296
        Significant Decisions 1975/76 164-165
        PERIODICALS:
        "Legal scene; will the Supreme Court turn the rezoning process
        into a popularity contest?" Lenard L. Wolffe and Douglas G.
        Linn. House and Home 49: 40 Mar '76.
        "Supreme Court's Eastlake ruling seen as new setback for build-
        ers." House and Home 50: 24 Aug '76.

3725. Serbian Eastern Orthodox Diocese   June 21, 1976 426 U.S. 696
        v. Milivojevich
        Significant Decisions 1975/76 132-134

3726. Roemer v. Board of Public Works   June 21, 1976 426 U.S. 736
        of Maryland
        *Am Consttnl Law (Mason) 628-630
        Conceived 124-125
        *Consttnl Law (Barrett) 1467-1474
        Digest 29-30
        Editorials 1976 881-886
        Freedom and the Court 324
        Religious Freedom (Arnold) 50-51
        Significant Decisions 1975/76 130-132
        PERIODICALS:
        "Aid to church colleges ruled constitutional." Chronicle of Higher
        Eductn 12: 3 June 28 '76.
        "Aid to private colleges upheld." America 135: 2-3 July 10 '76.
        "Church colleges and the scramble for public funds," Judy Weid-
        man. Christian Century 93: 883-885 Oct 20 '76 (3).
        "Ruling on aid to colleges provokes mixed reaction." Christian
        Century 93: 726 Sept 1 '76.
        "Rulings that penalize private schools," James J. Kilpatrick.
        Natns Bus 64: 19-20 Sept '76.

3727. Flint Ridge Development Co. v.   June 24, 1976 426 U.S. 776
        Scenic Rivers Association of Oklahoma
        Hills v. Scenic Rivers Association of
        Oklahoma
        Significant Decisions 1975/76 150-158

3728. Hughes v. Alexandria Scrap   June 24, 1976 426 U.S. 794
        Corporation
        *Consttnl Law (Barrett) 340-343
        Significant Decisions 1975/76 99-101

3729. National League of Cities v. Usery   June 24, 1976 426 U.S. 833
        California v. Usery
        *Am Consttnl Law (Mason) 187-193

*Am Consttnl Law (Saye) 214-218
Am Consttnl Law (Shapiro) 142-151
*Basic Cases 51-57
Brethren 406-410
CQ Guide 105-106
*Cases Consttnl Law (Cushman) 220-226
*Cases Consttnl Law (Gunther) 186-195
*Consttnl Law (Barrett) 480-492
*Consttnl Law (Freund) 286-292
*Consttnl Law (Grossman) 378-387
*Consttnl Law (Lockhart) 180-188
*Courts Judges 510-518
Digest 68
Editorials 1976 893-896
*Federal System 292-297
*Historic Documents 1976 377-389
*Labor Law (Twomey) 443-447
*Labor Relations (Edwards) 47-59
*Legal Environment 193-196
*School Law (Alexander) 58-62
Significant Decisions 1975/76 97-99
Sup Ct (Forte) 50-51
Sup Ct Review 1976 161-182
PERIODICALS:
"Anatomy of a Supreme Court decision," Andrij Bilyk. Natns
    Cities 14: 17-18 Sept '76.
"Can a federal collective bargaining statute for public employees
    meet the requirements of the National League of Cities v. Us-
    ery? symposium." J Law and Eductn 6: 491-526 Oct '77.
"Constitutional issue on wages." Bus Wk p. 27, 30 July 12 '76.
"Court found that Congress exceeded its power," Sarah C. Carey.
    Natns Cities 14: 19-24 Sept '76.
"Federal law on bargaining for public employees ruled out," Philip
    W. Semas. Chronicle of Higher Eductn 12: 3 July 6 '76.
"Possible federal mandate: the present picture," Felix A. Nigro.
    State Government 49: 202-206 Autumn '76 (2).
"Significant decisions in labor cases." Monthly Labor R 99: 50-
    51 Sept '76 and Dec '76.
"Supreme Court grants NLC plea for FLSA stay." Natns Cities
    13: 9-10, 12 Jan '75.
"We may be spared a federal collective bargaining law, thanks to
    the Supreme Court," August W. Steinhilber. Am Sch Bd J
    163: 40-41 Sept '76.
"What the Supreme Court is really telling business," Walter Guz-
    zardi, Jr. Fortune 95: 147-154 Jan '77.

3730. Aldinger v. Howard, Treasurer of   June 24, 1976 427 U.S. 1
            Spokane County
        *Cases Pleading 367-378
        Significant Decisions 1975/76 117-119
        Sup Ct Review 1976 197

3731. United States v. Santana   June 24, 1976 427 U.S. 38
        *Consttnl Law (Klein) 245-248
        *Consttnl Law (Maddex) 145-147
        Criminal Evidence 333
        *Criminal Justice (Way) 88-90
        Law of Arrest (Creamer) 225-228

Significant Decisions 1975/76 29-30
*Sup Ct and Criml Process 267-269

3732. Young, Mayor of Detroit v.   June 24, 1976 427 U.S. 50
American Mini Theatres
*Cases Consttnl Law (Gunther) 1243-1248
*Civil Liberties (Barker) 165-169
Communication (Hemmer) v. 1, 203-204
*Consttnl Law (Barrett) 1291-1296
*Consttnl Law (Grossman) 1262-1267
*Consttnl Law (Lockhart) 907-912
Editorials 1976 977-981
Handbook 701-708
Law of Mass 410
*Legal Foundations 168-174
Significant Decisions 1975/76 88-90
PERIODICALS:
"New court member no libertarian on obscenity," W. Dale Nelson.
Wilson Library Bul 51: 16 Sept '76.
"Two payments for freedom; freedom of speech vs pornography,"
James M. Wall. Christian Century 93: 619 July 7 '76.
"Young v. American Mini Theatres, Inc.: the war on neighbor-
hood deterioration leaves first amendment casualty," Carol R.
Kirshick. Environmental Affairs 6 no. 1: 101-125 '77.
"Zone defense against porn." America 135: 3 July 10 '76.

3733. United States v. Agurs   June 24, 1976 427 U.S. 97
*Consttnl Law (Felkenes) 336-338
Criminal Evidence 42-43
*Leading Consttnl Cases 769-775
*Modern Criml Procedure 334-341
Significant Decisions 1975/76 60-61
*Sup Ct and Criml Process 606-609
PERIODICALS:
"Supreme Court review (1976)." J Criml Law and Crimlgy 67:
408-415 Dec '76.

3734. Lodge 76, International Association   June 25, 1976 427 U.S. 132
of Machinists and Aerospace Workers
v. Wisconsin Employment Relations
Commission
*Cases Labor (Leslie) 621-625
Significant Decisions 1975/76 171
PERIODICALS:
"Significant decisions in labor cases." Monthly Labor R 99: 51-
52 Sept '76.

3735. Runyon et ux., dba Bobbe's School   June 25, 1976 427 U.S. 160
v. McCrary
Fairfax-Brewster School v. Gonzales
Southern Independent School Association
v. McCrary
CQ Guide 603
*Civil Rights (Abernathy) 1980 277-285
Conceived 184-185
*Consttn (Morris) 744-751
*Consttnl Law (Barrett) 1098-1106
*Consttnl Law (Grossman) 557-564

Digest 105
Editorials 1976 971-976
Freedom and the Court 436-438
*Historic Documents 1976 391-404
Judiciary (Abraham) 155-156
*Racial Equality 78-80
Significant Decisions 1975/76 107-108
PERIODICALS:
"The Court and white academies." America 135: 3-4 July 10
'76.
"Mr. Justice Stevens and the Zeitgeist," Arthur Shenfield. Modern
Age 23: 130-139 Spring '79.
"Supreme Court: private schools can't bar blacks." US News
81: 18 July 5 '76.
"Schools and the law--the Supreme Court ruling on exclusion by
private schools," Thomas J. Flygare. Phi Delta Kappan 58:
279-280 Nov '76.

3736.   Meachum, Correctional Superintendent   June 25, 1976 427 U.S. 215
        v. Fano
        *Consttnl Rights (Palmer) 688-695
        *Criminal Justice (Way) 507-512
        Significant Decisions 1975/76 147-148
        *Sup Ct and Criml Process 767-770
        *US Prison Law v. 6, 270-279

3737.   Montanye, Correctional Superintendent   June 25, 1976 427 U.S. 236
        v. Haymes
        *Consttnl Rights (Palmer) 685-688
        *US Prison Law v. 6, 280-284

3738.   Union Electric Co. v. Environmental   June 25, 1976 427 U.S. 246
        Protection Agency
        *Cases Environmental Law (Gray) 263-270
        *Environmental 390-397
        Significant Decisions 1975/76 158-159
        PERIODICALS:
        "Supreme Court ruling may hike power rates," Daniel Gottlieb.
        Purchasing 81: 19 Aug 17 '76.

3739.   McDonald v. Santa Fe Trail   June 26, 1976 427 U.S. 273
        Transportation Co.
        *Civil Rights (Abernathy) 1980 287-291
        *Collective Bargaining 820-824
        Conceived 212
        *Consttnl Law (Barrett) 862-865
        *Historic Documents 1976 405-411
        Significant Decisions 1975/76 109
        PERIODICALS:
        "Job-bias ruling in favor of white males." Bus Wk p. 30, 32
        July 12 '76.
        "Significant decisions in labor cases." Monthly Labor R 99: 53
        Nov '76.

3740.   New Orleans v. Dukes dba   June 25, 1976 427 U.S. 297
        Louisiana Concessions
        *Consttnl Law (Barrett) 1025-1027
        *Consttnl Law (Lockhart) 1249-1250

Significant Decisions 1975/76 167-168
Sup Ct Review 1976 192-193
PERIODICALS:
"Significant decisions in labor cases." Monthly Labor R 99: 45
Oct '76.

3741. Massachusetts Board of Retirement   June 25, 1976 427 U.S. 307
v. Murgia
*Am Consttnl Law (Shapiro) 596-599
*Cases Consttnl Law (Gunther) 697-701
*Consttnl Law (Barrett) 1019-1025
*Consttnl Law (Maddex) 444-446
*Criminal Procedure (Lewis) 84-90
Digest 68-69
*Labor Law (Twomey) 416-417
*Labor Relations (Edwards) 890-893
Significant Decisions 1975/76 126-127
*Sup Ct and Criml Process 848-852
PERIODICALS:
"Significant decisions in labor cases." Monthly Labor R 99: 44
Oct '76.
"Supreme Court rules on mandatory retirement case." Aging
263: 3 Sept '76.

3742. North v. Russell   June 28, 1976 427 U.S. 328
*Courts Judges 159-161
*Criminal Procedure (Lewis) 501-507
*Due Process 112
Significant Decisions 1975/76 56-57
*Sup Ct and Criml Process 612-617

3743. Elrod, Sheriff v. Burns   June 28, 1976 427 U.S. 347
*Am Consttnl Law (Saye) 355-357
*Consttnl Law (Barrett) 1215-1220
Editorials 1976 982-986
Significant Decisions 1975/76 95-97
*Sup Ct and Criml Process 1101-1106
PERIODICALS:
"Significant decisions in labor cases." Monthly Labor R 99: 46-
47 Oct '76.

3744. Kleppe, Secretary of the Interior   June 28, 1976 427 U.S. 390
v. Sierra Club
American Electric Power System
v. Sierra Club
*Cases Environmental Law (Gray) 38-48
Significant Decisions 1975/76 155-156

3745. Pasadena City Board of Education   June 28, 1976 427 U.S. 424
v. Spangler
CQ Guide 607
Conceived 185-186
*Consttnl Law (Barrett) 840-844
*Consttnl Law (Grossman) 473-480
Digest 105-106
From Brown 245-246
*Historic Documents 1976 413-423
Significant Decisions 1975/76 112-113

PERIODICALS:
"Two key decisions that limit busing." US News 81: 63 July
12 '76.

3746. Fitzpatrick v. Bitzer, Chairman,   June 28, 1976 427 U.S. 445
State Employees' Retirement Commission
Bitzer v. Matthews
*Civil Rights (Abernathy) 1980 505-510
*Consttnl Law (Barrett) 130-132
Significant Decisions 1975/76 129
Sup Ct Review 1976 201-202
PERIODICALS:
"Recent Supreme Court rulings." Today's Eductn 65: 18 Nov
'76.
"Significant decisions in labor cases." Monthly Labor R 99: 51
Sept '76.

3747. Andresen v. Maryland   June 29, 1976 427 U.S. 463
*Consttnl Criml (Scarboro) 674-682
*Consttnl Law (Felkenes) 276-277
Criminal Evidence 657-658
*Criminal Procedure 395-398
Law of Arrest (Creamer) 543-549
*Leading Consttnl Cases 567-576
*Modern Criml Procedure 66-69
Significant Decisions 1975/76 39-40
PERIODICALS:
"Liberty at bay; Supreme Court and search and seizure," Norman
Abrams. Center Mag 10: 16-20 Jan '77 (8).
"Supreme Court Review (1976)." J Criml Law and Crimlgy 67:
389-396 Dec '76.

3748. Mathews v. Lucas   June 29, 1976 427 U.S. 495
Cases Consttnl Law (Gunther) 899-900
Consttnl Law (Barrett) 913-920
*Consttnl Law (Lockhart) 1393-1396
*Justices (Friedman) v. 5, 175-178
Significant Decisions 1975/76 177-179

3749. Nebraska Press Association v.   June 30, 1976 427 U.S. 539
Stuart
Argument 294-298
Brethren 420-423
CQ Guide 443
*Cases Civil Liberties 275-282
*Cases Consttnl Law (Cushman) 505-512
Cases Consttnl Law (Gunther) 1517-1520
*Civil Liberties (Barker) 134-139
Communication (Hemmer) v. 2, 174-175
Consttnl Criml (Marks) 292-303
*Consttnl Law (Barrett) 1383-1397
*Consttnl Law (Grossman) 907-911
*Criminal Justice (Way) 428-435
Editorials 1976 873-880
*First Amendment (Franklin) 234-251
Handbook 51-55, 554-568
*Historic Documents 1976 463-479
Law of Mass 296-300
Mass Communications 512-515

*Mass Communications 515-518
*Mass Media (Devol) 59-60
Mass Media (Francois) 56
*Modern Criml Procedure 365-369
Significant Decisions 1975/76 83-85
Sup Ct and Criml Process 638-641
*Sup Ct and Criml Process 641-649
Sup Ct Review 1978 291-292
PERIODICALS:
"Can judges stop the presses?" D. Grier Stephenson. Intellect
    105: 171-173 Dec '76.
"Conflict over gap." Time 107: 44 May 3 '76.
"Editorials approve gag order ruling." Editor and Pub 109: 9
    July 10 '76.
"Excerpts from the gag order arguments: proceedings in the Su-
    preme Court of the United States." Editor and Pub 109: 46A-
    46D, 54A-54D May 1 '76.
"Free press vs fair trial: a classic collision," Patrick R. Oster.
    US News 80: 44-45 Feb 23 '76.
"Gag order in Nebraska held unconstitutional," I. William Hill.
    Editor and Pub 109: 9, 11 July 3 '76.
"Judges are told: you can't gag the press." US News 81: 69
    July 12 '76.
"Newsmen praise unanimity of top court's gag ruling." Editor and
    Pub 109: 11 July 3 '76.
*"Partial test of majority opinion by Justice Burger." Editor and
    Pub 109: 10 July 3 '76.
*"Supreme Court of the United States; Nebraska Press Association
    et al. v. Stuart, judge, et al." Editor and Pub 109: 27-28,
    33-47 July 17 '76.
"Supreme Court review (1976)." J Criml Law and Crimlgy 67:
    430-436 Dec '76.
"Untying the gag," Susan Fraher and Diane Camper. Newsweek
    88: 15 July 12 '76.

3750. Ludwig v. Massachusetts   June 30, 1976 427 U.S. 618
        Modern Criml Procedure 348-349
        Significant Decisions 1975/76 57-58
        *Sup Ct and Criml Process 617-621

3751. Usery, Secretary of Labor v. Turner   July 1, 1976   428 U.S. 1
        Elkhorn Mining Co.
        *Consttnl Law (Barrett) 676-678, 1039
        Significant Decisions 1975/76 173-176
        PERIODICALS:
        "Significant decisions in labor cases." Monthly Labor R 99: 44-
            45 Oct '76.
        "Top court upholds black lung benefits." Natl Underwriter (Life
            ed) 80: 2 July 10 '76.

3752. Planned Parenthood of Central Mis-   July 1, 1976   428 U.S. 52
        souri v. Danforth, Attorney
        General of Missouri
        Brethren 414-416
        Cases Consttnl Law (Gunther) 610-612
        *Cases Domestic 672-680
        Communication (Hemmer) v. 1, 251-252
        *Consttnl Law (Barrett) 725-733
        Editorials 1976 965-970

*Historic Documents 1976 483-488
Religious Freedom (Arnold) 78-79, 85
*Sex Discrimination 1978 224-236
Significant Decisions 1975/76 65-68
Sup Ct Review 1979 336
*Woman 188-190
PERIODICALS:
"Abortion: no adjustment." Christianity Today 20: 21 Aug 27
   '76.
"Abortion; the woman's choice." Economist 260: 35-36 July
   10 '76.
"Butt out, your honors." Natl R 28: 832 Aug 6 '76.
"High court forbids parental, spouse veto over abortions." Family
   Planning Perspectives 8: 177-178 July/Aug '76.
"More on abortion," Susan Fraher and Diane Camper. Newsweek
   88: 15 July 12 '76.
"Opportunity, out of this world," Malachi B. Martin. Natl R 28:
   1124 Oct 15 '76.
"Supreme Court: life, death and the law." America 135: 21
   July 24 '76.
"Teenagers and pregnancy," Eve W. Paul and Harriet F. Pilpel.
   Family Planning Perspectives 11: 297-302 Sept/Oct '79 (4).

3753. Singleton, Chief, Bureau of Medical   July 1, 1976   428 U.S. 106
        Services, Department of Health
        and Welfare of Missouri v. Wulff
        Brethren 414-416
        Significant Decisions 1975/76 68-70
        Sup Ct Review 1976 186-187

3754. Bellotti, Attorney General of Massa-   July 1, 1976   428 U.S. 132
        chusetts v. Baird
        Hunerwadel v. Baird
        Brethren 414-416
        PERIODICALS:
        "Teenagers and pregnancy," Eve W. Paul and Harriet F. Pilpel.
           Family Planning Perspectives 11: 297-302 Sept/Oct '79 (4).

3755. Gregg v. Georgia   July 2, 1976   428 U.S. 153
        *Am Consttnl Law (Mason) 756-761
        Brethren 430-441
        CQ Guide 578-579
        *Cases Civil Liberties 186-197
        *Cases Consttnl Law (Cushman) 416-427
        *Cases Criml Law (Inbau) 363-378
        *Cases Criml Law (Perkins) 6-13
        *Civil Liberties (Barker) 234-240
        *Civil Rights (Abernathy) 1977 246-255
        *Comparative 439-442
        Conceived 162-164
        *Consttnl Criml (Marks) 258-270
        *Consttnl Law (Felkenes) 351-354
        *Consttnl Law (Grossman) 945-953
        *Consttnl Law (Klein) 401-421
        *Consttnl Rights (Palmer) 574-604
        *Criminal Justice (Galloway) 36-55
        *Criminal Justice (Way) 464-472
        Criminal Procedure (Lewis) 568-580
        *Criminal Procedure (Lewis) 581-591

*Due Process 174-177
Editorials 1976 887-892
*Historic Documents 1976 489-507
*Leading Consttnl Cases 813-838
Procedures 244-245
Significant Decisions 1975/76 47-51
*Sup Ct and Criml Process 882-895
Sup Ct and Criml Process 881
Sup Ct Review 1979 337
PERIODICALS:
   "Death delayed." Progressive 40: 8-9 Sept '76.
   "Death ends its holiday." Economist 260: 25-26 July 10 '76.
   "Death penalty revived." Time 108: 35-37 July 12 '76.
   "Execution eve?" Natl R 28: 1167 Oct 29 '76.
   "New life for the death penalty," Hugo A. Bedau. Nation 223:
      144-148 Aug 28 '76.
   "Reviving the death penalty," Susan Fraker and Diane Camper.
      Newsweek 88: 14-15 July 12 '76.
   "Spreading impact of a historic court decision." US News 81:
      49-51 July 12 '76.
   "Supreme Court review (1976)." J Criml Law and Crimlgy 67:
      437-449 Dec '76.
*"The Supreme Court rulings on capital punishment, 1976." Current
   History 71: 30-31 July/Aug '76.

3756. Proffitt v. Florida   July 2, 1976   428 U.S. 242
           Brethren 430-441
           *Consttnl Rights (Palmer) 605-611
           Significant Decisions 1975/76 50
           Sup Ct and Criml Process 881-882
           *Sup Ct and Criml Process 895-899
       PERIODICALS:
           "Death and confusion at the Court." Time 108: 85 Dec 13 '76.
           See also listing at 428 U.S. 153, entry no. 3755.

3757. Jurek v. Texas   July 2, 1976   428 U.S. 262
           Brethren 430-441
           *Consttnl Rights (Palmer) 611-617
           Justice Frankfurter 873-879
           *Justice Frankfurter 899-902
       PERIODICALS:
           See listing at 428 U.S. 153, entry no. 3755.

3758. Woodson v. North Carolina   July 2, 1976   428 U.S. 280
           Brethren 430-441
           *Consttnl Rights (Palmer) 617-634
           *Criminal Justice (Galloway) 55-62
           *Criminal Justice (Way) 472-477
           *Due Process 177-179
           Significant Decisions 1975/76 51-53
           Sup Ct and Criml Process 879-880
           *Sup Ct and Criml Process 922-927
       PERIODICALS:
           See listing at 428 U.S. 153, entry no. 3755.

3759. Roberts v. Louisiana   July 2, 1976   428 U.S. 325
           Brethren 430-441
           *Consttnl Rights (Palmer) 634-648
           *Criminal Justice (Galloway) 68-69

*Due Process 179
*Sup Ct and Criml Process 932-934
PERIODICALS:
"Death and confusion at the Court. " Time 108: 85 Dec 13 '76.
See also listing at 428 U. S. 153, entry no. 3755.

3760.   South Dakota v. Opperman   July 6, 1976   428 U. S. 364
        *Consttnl Criml (Scarboro) 369-382
        *Consttnl Law (Maddex) 167-170
        *Criminal Evidence 342-343
        Criminal Evidence 369-370
        *Criminal Justice (Way) 117-121
        *Criminal Procedure (Lewis) 237-240
        Law of Arrest (Creamer) 260-263
        *Leading Consttnl Cases 136-142
        *Modern Criml Procedure 94-102
        Significant Decisions 1975/76 33-34
        *Sup Ct and Criml Process 279-286

3761.   Buffalo Forge Co. v. United   July 6, 1976   428 U. S. 397
        Steelworkers of America
        *Cases Labor (Oberer) 706-714
        *Collective Bargaining 373-384
        Labor Relations (Taylor) 427
        Significant Decisions 1975/76 172-173
        PERIODICALS:
        "Courtroom snarl over wildcat strikes. " Bus Wk   p. 26   Aug 30
            '76.
        "Significant decisions in labor cases. " Monthly Labor R   99: 52-
            53 Nov '76.

3762.   United States v. Janis   July 6, 1976   428 U. S. 433
        Conceived 150-152
        Criminal Evidence 283
        Significant Decisions 1975/76 27-28
        *Sup Ct and Criml Process 214-215
        PERIODICALS:
        "Liberty at bay, " Norman Abrams. Center Mag   10: 16-20 Jan
            '77.

3763.   Stone, Warden v. Powell   July 6, 1976   428 U. S. 465
        Wolff v. Rice
        *Am Consttnl Law (Mason) 714-718
        Brethren 429-430
        *Consttnl Criml (Marks) 303-313
        *Consttnl Criml (Scarboro) 84-111
        *Consttnl Law (Felkenes) 227-228
        *Consttnl Law (Grossman) 825-831
        *Consttnl Law (Klein) 254-264
        *Consttnl Law (Maddex) 112-116
        *Courts Judges 110-113
        *Criminal Justice (Galloway) 136-140
        Criminal Justice (Galloway) 215-219
        *Criminal Justice (Way) 478-483
        *Criminal Procedure (Lewis) 127-132, 661-669
        *Due Process 195-197
        Editorials 1976 959-964
        Exclusionary 38-40
        *Federal System 324-326

*Historic Documents 1976 521-536
Law of Arrest (Creamer) 356-358
*Leading Consttnl Cases 251-265
*Modern Criml Procedure 432-442
*Rights (Shattuck) 41-43
Significant Decisions 1975/76 144-145
Sup Ct and Criml Process 197-202
*Sup Ct and Criml Process 202-210
Sup Ct Review 1976 195-197
PERIODICALS:
"Curbs on habeas corpus." Newsweek 88: 58 July 19 '76.
"Reconsidering suspects' rights." Time 107: 44-45 Mar 8 '76.
See listing at 428 U.S. 433, entry no. 3762.

3764. United States v. Martinez-Fuerte   July 6, 1976   428 U.S. 543
       Sifuentes v. United States
       Communication (Hemmer) v. 1, 237-238
       *Consttnl Criml (Scarboro) 265-283
       Law of Arrest (Creamer) 270-274
       *Modern Criml Procedure 117-121
       Significant Decisions 1975/76 31-33
       *Sup Ct and Criml Process 310-317

3765. Cantor dba Selden Drugs Co. v.   July 6, 1976   428 U.S. 579
       Detroit Edison Co.
       Significant Decisions 1975/76 159-160
       PERIODICALS:
       "RPh defuses utility in Supreme Court case." Am Druggist 177:
       46, 50 Feb '78.

3766. United States v. Morrison   Oct 12, 1976   429 U.S. 1
       *Sup Ct and Criml Process 390-392
       PERIODICALS:
       "Supreme Court review (1977)." J Criml Law and Crimlgy 68:
       555-570 Dec '77 (6).

3767. United States v. Sanford   Oct 12, 1976   429 U.S. 14
       *Sup Ct and Criml Process 392, 394
       Sup Ct Review 1978 144-145
       PERIODICALS:
       See listing at 429 U.S. 1, entry no. 3766.

3768. Hutto, Arkansas Department of   Nov 1, 1976   429 U.S. 28
       Correction Commissioner v. Ross
       *Consttnl Law (Klein) 523-524

3769. United States v. Foster Lumber Co.   Nov 2, 1976   429 U.S. 32
       PERIODICALS:
       "Analysis of the loss-wastage problem in view of Supreme Court's
       Foster lumber decision," Jerry M. Hamovit and Joel Z. Silver.
       J Taxation 46: 100-103 Feb '77.

3770. Moody v. Daggett   Nov 15, 1976   429 U.S. 78
       *Consttnl Rights (Palmer) 696-701
       Significant Decisions 1976/77 120-121
       *US Prison Law v. 6, 569-577

3771. Estelle, Corrections Director v.   Nov 30, 1976   429 U.S. 97
       Gamble

*Impact (Becker) 701-706
Significant Decisions 1976/77 116-117
*Sup Ct and Criml Process 770-773
*US Prison Law v. 6, 433-443
PERIODICALS:
"Supreme Court review (1977)." J Criml Law and Crimlgy 68:
591-600 Dec '77 (3).

3772. Davis v. Georgia   Dec 6, 1976   429 U.S. 122
*Sup Ct and Criml Process 936
PERIODICALS:
"Supreme Court review (1977)." J Criml Law and Crimlgy 68:
601-612 Dec '77 (5).

3773. General Electric Co. v. Gilbert   Dec 7, 1976   429 U.S. 125
CQ Guide 636
*Civil Rights (Abernathy) 1980 483-493
*Collective Bargaining 921-935
Conceived 221-222
*Consttnl Law (Grossman) 630-635
*Court Judges 566-573
Editorials 1976 1591-1594
*Historic Documents 1976 891-905
*Labor Law (Twomey) 371-374
*Modern Business 1087-1093
*Sex Discrimination 1978 78-92, 138-141
Significant Decisions 1976/77 100-102
PERIODICALS:
"All things being equal: General Electric v. Gilbert: an analysis,"
Larry L. French. J Law and Eductn 7: 21-30 Jan '78.
"Pregnancy ruling that could cost $1.6 billion." Bus Wk p. 41
Nov 29 '76.
"Pregnancy sick pay." US News 81: 31 Dec 20 '76.
"Pregnant decisions," Jerrold K. Footlick and Lucy Howard.
Newsweek 88: 59 Dec 20 '76.
"Supreme Court KOs maternity sick pay," Mary Jane Fisher.
Natl Underwriter (Property ed) 80: 13 Dec 17 '76.
"Significant decisions in labor cases." Monthly Labor R 100: 73-
74 Mar '77.
"Top court KOs maternity sick pay," Mary Jane Fisher. Natl
Underwriter (Life ed) 80: 1, 5 Dec 11 '76.

3774. City of Madison Joint School District   Dec 8, 1976   429 U.S. 167
No. 8 v. Wisconsin Employment
Relations Commission
*Cases Labor (Oberer) 1149-1155
Communication (Hemmer) v. 1, 151-153
*Consttn (Morris) 677-681
Digest 69-70
*Labor Relations (Edwards) 423-428
*School Law (Alexander) 685-688
Significant Decisions 1976/77 62-63
PERIODICALS:
"Rights of the exclusive bargaining representative versus the rights
of the individual; symposium." J Law and Education 6: 349-
372 July '77.
"Schools and the law: Supreme Court says nonunion teacher can
address board on issue under negotiation," Thomas J. Flygare.
Phi Delta Kappan 58: 573-574 Mar '77.

"Significant decisions in labor cases. " Monthly Labor R 100: 79-80 Apr '77.

3775. Mathews, Secretary of Health, Dec 13, 1976 429 U.S. 181
Education and Welfare v. DeCastro
*Cases Domestic 522-527
Significant Decisions 1976/77 99

3776. Craig v. Boren Dec 20, 1976 429 U.S. 190
*Cases Consttnl Law (Gunther) 871-879
*Consttnl Law (Barrett) 89-93, 898-911
*Consttnl Law (Grossman) 626-630
*Criminal Procedure (Lewis) 91-97
*Sex Discrimination 1978 19-30
Significant Decisions 1976/77 96-98
Sup Ct (Forte) 94

3777. International Brotherhood of Electrical Dec 20, 1976 429 U.S. 229
Radio & Machine Workers v. Robbins
and Myers, Inc.
Guy v. Robbins and Myers, Inc.
*Cases Labor (Oberer) 962-968

3778. Connally v. Georgia Jan 10, 1977 429 U.S. 245
*Criminal Procedure (Lewis) 153-154

3779. Village of Arlington Heights v. Jan 11, 1977 429 U.S. 252
Metropolitan Housing Development
Corporation
*Am Consttnl Law (Shapiro) 546
CQ Guide 616
Cases Consttnl Law (Gunther) 720-721
*Civil Rights (Abernathy) 1980 37-41
Conceived 220-221
*Consttnl Law (Barrett) 84-86, 793-799
Digest 106-107
Editorials 1977 105-112
*Historic Documents 1977 35-44
*Legal Foundations 302-309
Significant Decisions 1976/77 89-91
PERIODICALS:
"Arlington Heights case." America 136: 90-91 Feb 5 '77.
"Common sense on race, " George F. Will. Newsweek 89: 80
Jan 24 '77.
"Deviating into sense." Natl R 29: 136 Feb 4 '77.
"Equal protection clause and the Fair housing act: Judicial alter-
natives for exclusionary zoning challenges after Arlington
Heights, " Carol R. Cohen. Environmental Affairs 6 no. 1:
63-99 '77.
"Intent not impact. " Time 109; 52 Jan 24 '77.
"Major zoning rule. " Engineering News 198: 32 Jan 20 '77.
"Right to refuse, " Jerrold K. Footlick. Newsweek 89: 77 Jan 27 '77.
"Schools and the law--Austin and Indianapolis: a new approach to
desegregation?" Thomas Flygare. Phi Delta Kappan 58: 709-
710 May '77 (2).
"Setback in Arlington Heights, " Jerry DeMuth. America 136:
167-168 Feb 26 '77.
"Shifting sands of land use in the U. S. Supreme Court, " Randall
Scott. Mortgage Banker 37: 74, 76, 78, 80 May '77 (5).

"Suburban iron curtain." Commonweal 104: 99-100 Feb 18 '77.
"Supreme Court considers discriminatory land-use cases," Dan
    Moskowitz. Architectural Rec 159: 37 Feb '76.
"Supreme Court zoning decision," Tamila C. Jensen. Bus Hori-
    zons 20: 72-75 Aug '77.
"Zoning out low-income families in suburbia," J. S. Fuerst.
    Christian Century 94: 77-78 Feb 2 '77.

3780. Mt. Healthy City School District   Jan 11, 1977   429 U.S. 274
        Board of Education v. Doyle
        *Am Consttnl Law (Saye) 358-360
        Communication (Hemmer) v. 1, 153-154
        *Consttn (Morris) 632-636
        *Consttnl Law (Barrett) 129, 752-753
        Digest 70-71
        *Labor Relations (Edwards) 771-775
        *School Law (Alexander) 538-542
        Significant Decisions 1976/77 68-69
    PERIODICALS:
        "Schools and the law: Supreme Court clarifies first amendment
        rights of teachers," Thomas Flygare. Phi Delta Kappan 58:
        645-646 Apr '77.
        "Significant decisions in labor cases." Monthly Labor R 100:
        75-76 Mar '77.

3781. Bayride Enterprises v. National   Jan 11, 1977   429 U.S. 298
        Labor Relations Board
        *Labor Law (Twomey) 105-107

3782. Local 3489, United Steelworkers of   Jan 12, 1977   429 U.S. 305
        America, AFL-CIO v. Usery,
        Secretary of Labor
        *Cases Labor (Leslie) 703-709
        *Labor Law (Twomey) 354-355
        Significant Decisions 1976/77 127-128
    PERIODICALS:
        "Significant decisions in labor cases." Monthly Labor R 100:
        80 Apr '77.

3783. Boston Stock Exchange v. State   Jan 12, 1977   429 U.S. 318
        Tax Commission of New York
        *Consttnl Law (Barrett) 423-424
        *Consttnl Law (Lockhart) 358-361
        Significant Decisions 1976/77 146-147

3784. G. M. Leasing Corporation v. United   Jan 12, 1977   429 U.S. 338
        States
        Significant Decisions 1976/77 26-27
    PERIODICALS:
        "Supreme Court in G. M. Leasing, restricts IRS property seizures
        without search warrants," Harry D. Shapiro and Robert K.
        Briskin. J Taxation 45: 218-221 Apr '77.
        "Supreme Court Review (1977)." J Criml Law and Crimlgy 68:
        493-504 Dec '77 (4).

3785. United States v. Donovan   Jan 18, 1977   429 U.S. 413
        *Modern Criml Procedure 143-146
        Significant Decisions 1976/77 23-25

PERIODICALS:
"Supreme Court review (1977)." J Criml Law and Crimlgy 68:
505-516 Dec '77.

3786. United States v. County of Fresno   Jan 25, 1977   429 U.S. 452
      United States v. County of Tuolumne
      *Consttnl Law (Barrett) 456-461
      Significant Decisions 1976/77 143-144

3787. Brunswick Corporation v. Pueblo   Jan 25, 1977   429 U.S. 477
      Bowl-O-Mat, Inc.
      Significant Decisions 1976/77 132-134

3788. Oregon v. Mathiason   Jan 25, 1977   429 U.S. 492
      Criminal Evidence 434-435
      *Criminal Justice (Way) 184-186
      *Criminal Procedure (Lewis) 378-381
      *Leading Consttnl Cases 534-536
      *Modern Criml Procedure 168-169
      Significant Decisions 1976/77 19-20
      *Sup Ct and Criml Process 437-439
      Sup Ct Review 1977 150-154
      *US Prison Law v. 6, 564-568
      PERIODICALS:
      "Supreme Court review (1977)." J Criml Law and Crimlgy 68:
      517-525 Dec '77 (2).

3789. National Labor Relations Board v.   Feb 22, 1977   429 U.S. 507
      Enterprise Association of Steam,
      Hot Water, Hydraulic Sprinkler, Pneumatic
      Tube, Ice Machine and General Pipefitters
      of New York and Vicinity, Local Union No. 638
      *Cases Labor (Leslie) 349-354
      *Cases Labor (Oberer) 473-486
      Significant Decisions 1976/77 123-124
      PERIODICALS:
      "Significant decisions in labor cases." Monthly Labor R 100: 57-
      58 June '77.
      "Supreme Court rulings during the 1976-7 term; some good news,
      some bad news and some maybe's," Arthur T. Kornblut.
      Architectural Rec 162: 63 Aug '77 (3).

3790. Weatherford, Agent of the South   Feb 22, 1977   429 U.S. 545
      Carolina Law Enforcement Division
      v. Bursey
      Law of Arrest (Creamer) 169-173
      *Modern Criml Procedure 125-128
      Significant Decisions 1976/77 42-44

3791. Whalen, Commissioner of Health of   Feb 22, 1977   429 U.S. 589
      New York v. Roe
      Cases Consttnl Law (Gunther) 644-646
      *Consttnl Law (Barrett) 738-740
      Significant Decisions 1976/77 77-79
      PERIODICALS:
      "Coming about." Time 105: 43 June 2 '75.
      "Schedule II drugs: Supreme Court upholds patient identification."
      Drug Topics 121: 12 Apr 1 '77.

3792. United States Steel Corporation   Feb 22, 1977   429 U. S. 610
           v. Fortner Enterprises
        Significant Decisions 1976/77 134
        PERIODICALS:
        "Settle or fight? U. S. Steel's 14-year case." Bus Wk p. 81, 84,
           86 Oct 11 '76.

3793. Codd, Police Commissioner, City   Feb 22, 1977   429 U. S. 624
           of New York v. Velger
        Digest 71
        *Labor Relations (Edwards) 831-836
        Significant Decisions 1976/77 80

3794. Karen v. California   Oct 18, 1976   429 U. S. 900
        *US Prison Law v. 6, 374-376

3795. Piper Aircraft Corporation v. Chris-   Feb 23, 1977   430 U. S. 1
           Craft Industries, Inc.
        First Boston Corporation v. Chris-
           Craft Industries
        Bangor Punta Corporation v. Chris-
           Craft Industries
        Significant Decisions 1976/77 135-136

3796. Califano, Secretary of Health,   Feb 23, 1977   430 U. S. 99
           Education and Welfare v. Sanders
        *Admin Law (Schwartz) 631-634

3797. E. I. DuPont de Nemours and Co. v.   Feb 23, 1977   430 U. S. 112
           Train, Administrator, Environmental
           Protection Agency
        *Cases Environmental Law (Gray) 339-346
        *Historic Documents 1977 131-141
        Significant Decisions 1976/77 138-139
        Sup Ct Review 1977 40, 45-48, 58

3798. United Jewish Organizations of   Mar 1, 1977   430 U. S. 144
           Williamsburgh, Inc. v. Carey,
           Governor of New York
        *Civil Rights (Abernathy) 1980 631-646
        *Consttnl Law (Barrett) 976-993
        *Consttnl Law (Grossman) 509-517
        *Historic Documents 1977 151-167
        Significant Decisions 1976/77 82-83
        PERIODICALS:
        "Court docket," Jerrold K. Footlick. Newsweek 89: 97-98
           Mar 14 '77.
        "Supreme Court and quotas," J. S. Fuerst and Roy Petty.
           Christian Century 94: 948-952 Oct 19 '77.

3799. Marks v. United States   Mar 1, 1977   430 U. S. 188
        *Consttnl Law (Barrett) 39
        Significant Decisions 1976/77 44-45
        PERIODICALS:
        "Judicial thicket: the Supreme Court and obscenity," Mel Fried-
           man. Nation 225: 110-113 Aug 6 '77 (4).
        "Obscenity: new High Court ruling, AAP on Flynt," Susan Wagner.
           Pub Weekly 211: 41-42 Mar 14 '77.

"Supreme Court review (1977)." J Criml Law and Crimlgy 68:
613-623 Dec '77 (4).

3800. Califano, Secretary of Health,   Mar 2, 1977   430 U.S. 199
Education and Welfare v. Goldfarb
*Am Govt 187-191
*Consttnl Law (Barrett) 891-895
*Historic Documents 1977 169-181
*Sex Discrimination 1978 30-40
Significant Decisions 1976/77 100
PERIODICALS:
"Administration readies to comply with Social Security bias ruling."
National Underwriter (Life ed) 81: 1, 7-8 Mar 12 '77.
"In the works: a fairer but costlier social security." US News
82: 85-86 Mar 21 '77.
"Supreme Court cases social security rules." Aging 274: 27
Aug '77.
"Significant decisions in labor cases." Monthly Labor R 100:
51-52 May '77.
"Supreme Court strikes down a social security dependency require-
ment for widowers." Retirement Living 17: 13-14 Apr '77.

3801. Nolde Brothers, Inc. v. Local No.   Mar 7, 1977   430 U.S. 243
358, Bakery and Confectionary
Workers Union
*Collective Bargaining 332-337
*Labor Law (Twomey) 321-324
Labor Relations (Taylor) 422
PERIODICALS:
"Significant decisions in labor cases." Monthly Labor R 100: 46-
47 July '77.

3802. Town of Lockport, N.Y. v. Citizens   Mar 7, 1977   430 U.S. 259
for Community Action at the
Local Level
Consttnl Law (Barrett) 997
Significant Decisions 1976/77 83-84

3803. Complete Auto Transit, Inc. v.   Mar 7, 1977   430 U.S. 274
Brady, Chairman, Mississippi
Tax Commission
*Consttnl Law (Barrett) 431-436
*Consttnl Law (Lockhart) 374-377
Significant Decisions 1976/77 142

3804. Farmer, Special Administrator v.   Mar 7, 1977   430 U.S. 290
United Brotherhood of Carpenters
and Joiners of America, Local 25
*Cases Labor (Leslie) 611-618
*Cases Labor (Oberer) 377-384
PERIODICALS:
"Significant decisions in labor cases." Monthly Labor R 100:
47-48 July '77.

3805. Oklahoma Publishing Co. v. District   Mar 7, 1977   430 U.S. 308
Court in and for Oklahoma County,
Oklahoma
*Sup Ct and Criml Process 655-657

3806. Califano, Secretary of Health,   Mar 21, 1977   430 U.S. 313
       Education and Welfare v. Webster
       *Cases Consttnl Law (Gunther) 794-797
       *Consttnl Law (Lockhart) 1406-1407
       *Sex Discrimination 1978 40-43
       Significant Decisions 1976/77 98

3807. Juidice, Judge v. Vail   Mar 22, 1977   430 U.S. 327
       *Consttnl Law (Barrett) 147-148
       Significant Decisions 1976/77 108-109

3808. Gardner v. Florida   Mar 22, 1977   430 U.S. 349
       *Criminal Justice (Galloway) 62-68
       *Criminal Procedure (Lewis) 622-626
       Significant Decisions 1976/77 33-34
       Sup Ct and Criml Process 1025-1028
       *Sup Ct and Criml Process 1028-1033

3809. Swain, Reformatory Superintendent   Mar 22, 1977   430 U.S. 372
       v. Pressley
       PERIODICALS:
       "Supreme Court review (1977)." J Criml Law and Crimlgy   68:
       571-582   Dec '77   (3).

3810. Brewer v. Williams   Mar 23, 1977   430 U.S. 387
       Criminal Evidence 469-471
       *Criminal Justice (Galloway) 105-117
       *Criminal Justice (Way) 321-326
       Criminal Procedure (Lewis) 445-448
       *Criminal Procedure (Lewis) 449-460
       Editorials 1977 429-436
       *Historic Documents 1977 219-235
       Law of Arrest (Creamer) 394-397
       *Leading Consttnl Cases 483-490
       *Modern Criml Procedure 176-191
       Significant Decisions 1976/77 41-42
       Sup Ct and Criml Process 568-571
       *Sup Ct and Criml Process 571-582
       PERIODICALS:
       "Supreme Court review (1977)." J Criml Law and Crimlgy   68:
       517-525   Dec '77   (2).

3811. Atlas Roofing Co., Inc. v. Occu-   Mar 23, 1977   430 U.S. 442
       pational Safety and Health Review
       Commission
       *Admin Law (Gellhorn) 100-102
       *Admin Law (Schwartz) 128-134
       *Cases Pleading 892-900
       Significant Decisions 1976/77 111-112

3812. Santa Fe Industries, Inc. v. Green   Mar 23, 1977   430 U.S. 462
       *Basic Corporation 752-756
       Significant Decisions 1976/77 136-138

3813. Casteneda v. Partida   Mar 23, 1977   430 U.S. 482
       *Consttnl Law (Barrett) 799-809
       Significant Decisions 1976/77 87-89
       PERIODICALS:
       "Supreme Court review (1977)." J Criml Law and Crimlgy   68:
       533-542   Dec '77.

3814. Jones, Director, Department of   Mar 29, 1977   430 U.S. 519
      Weights and Measures, Riverside
      County v. Rath Packing Co.
    Jones v. General Mills, Inc.
      Significant Decisions 1976/77 150-151

3815. National Geographic Society v.   Apr 4, 1977   430 U.S. 551
      California Board of Equalization
      Consttnl Law (Barrett) 430-431
      Significant Decisions 1976/77 141-142
    PERIODICALS:
      "Nexus for use taxes and National Geographic," John F. Due.
        Natl Tax J 30: 213-217 June '77.

3816. United States v. Martin Linen   Apr 4, 1977   430 U.S. 564
      Supply Co.
      *Criminal Procedure (Lewis) 647-650
      Significant Decisions 1976/77 37
      Sup Ct Review 1978 151-154
    PERIODICALS:
      "Supreme Court review (1977)." J Criml Law and Crimlgy 68:
        555-570 Dec '77.

3817. Ingraham v. Wright   Apr 19, 1977   430 U.S. 651
      *Cases Criml Law (Inbau) 394-399
      *Consttn (Morris) 534-543
      *Consttnl Rights (Kemerer) 377 384
      Corporal 91-106, 169-172, 173-193, 196-206, 207-215, 329-333,
        394-403
      Digest 46
      Editorials 1977 598-606
      *Education (Hazard) 559-572
      *Historic Documents 1977 293-309
      Law and Education 228, 230-231
      *School Law (Alexander) 333-340
      Significant Decisions 1976/77 73-75
      *Sup Ct and Criml Process 728-735
      Sup Ct Review 1979 341-342
    PERIODICALS:
      "Corporal punishment foes strike out," Karen Schaar. Children
        Today 6: 16, 24-25 Sept/Oct '77.
      "Corporal punishment is not yet dead as a constitutional issue,"
        Thomas J. Flygare. Phi Delta Kappan 62: 53 Sept '80.
      "Corporal punishment: legalized battery," Daniel V. Davidson.
        Eductnl Forum 45: 95-105 Nov '80 (2).
      "Court: don't spare the rod." Time 109: 58 May 2 '77.
      "Courts as intervenors," Joel Grossman. Eductn and Urban
        Society 11: 567-571 Aug '79.
      "The Court's corporal punishment mandate to parents, local au-
        thorities and the profession," Meryl E. Englander. Phi Delta
        Kappan 59: 529-532 Apr '78 (2).
      "Dark side of the discipline picture; new laws don't change unfair-
        ness." Phi Delta Kappan 60: 468 Feb '79.
      "Discipline and due process in the schools," David Schimmel and
        Louis Fischer. Eductn Dig 43: 5-8 Jan '78 (2). Condensed
        from: Update on Law Related Eductn 1: 4-6, 34-36 Fall '77.
      "Full speed backward," Fred M. Hechinger. Sat R 4: 14 May
        28 '77.

"Ingraham v. Wright: the continuing debate over corporal punishment," J. Patrick Mahon. J Law and Eductn 6: 473-479 Oct '77.

"License to beat children." Progressive 41: 8 June '77.

"Neither corporal punishment cruel nor due process due," Philip K. Piele. J Law and Education 7: 1-19 Jan '78.

"Notes and comment." New Yorker 53: 27 May 30 '77.

"Paddling, punishing and force: where do we go from here?" Irwin A. Hyman. Children Today 6: 17-23 Sept/Oct '77.

"Press coverage of the Supreme Court: a troubling question," William R. Dahms. Intellect 106: 299-301 Feb '78.

"Remarkable decision," Donald Brieland. Socl Work 22: 258 July '77.

"Ruling on the rod," Merrill Sheils and Frederick V. Boyd. Newsweek 89: 65-66 May 2 '77.

"Schools and the law: The Supreme Court approves corporal punishment," Thomas Flygare. Phi Delta Kappan 59: 347-348 Jan '78.

"Spare the rod and spoil the child revisited," Jane Knitzer. Am J Orthopsychiatry 47: 372-373 July '77.

"Supreme Court and corporal punishment," Charles R. Lemley. Eductn 98: 228-231 Winter '77 (2).

"Supreme Court on spanking: upholding discipline or abuse?" Edward Zigler and Susan Hunsinger. Young Children 32: 14-15 Sept '77.

"Supreme Court rules: carry on beating." Times Eductnl Supp 3231: 13 May 6 '77.

"Supreme Court review (1977)." J Criml Law and Crimlgy 68: 634-642 Dec '77.

3818. Wooley, Chief of Police of Lebanon   Apr 20, 1977   430 U.S. 705
       v. Maynard
       *Cases Criml Law (Inbau) 292-298
       Communication (Hemmer) v. 1, 53-54
       *Consttnl Law (Grossman) 1221-1223
       *Mass Communications 191-193
       Significant Decisions 1976/77 63-64
       Sup Ct Review 1977 212-214
       PERIODICALS:
       "Right not to speak," Carey McWilliams. Nation 225: 69-70 July 23 '77.
       "Supreme Court review (1977)." J Criml Law and Crimlgy 68: 583-590 Dec '77.

3819. United States v. Consumer Life   Apr 26, 1977   430 U.S. 725
       Insurance Co.
       First Railroad and Banking Co. of
       Georgia v. United States
       United States v. Penn Security Life
       Insurance Co.
       PERIODICALS:
       "Supreme Court holds reinsurance agreements effective to produce life insurance co. status," John L. Snyder. CLU J 32: 58-63 Jan '78.
       "Supreme Court in Consumer Life Insurance Co. resolves the credit life issue," Gerald I. Lenrow and others. Best's R (Life ed) 78: 50, 52, 54 July '77.
       "Supreme Court settles conflict involving life insurance company

qualification," Francis M. Gregory and Carolyn P. Chiechi.
J Taxation   47: 40-41   July '77.

3820.   Trimble v. Gordon   Apr 26, 1977   430 U.S. 762
        Cases Consttnl Law (Gunther) 900-903
        *Cases Domestic 713-722
        *Justices (Friedman) v. 5, 141-145
        Significant Decisions 1976/77 72-73
        Watergate 168-169

3821.   Fiallo, a minor, by Rodriquez   Apr 26, 1977   430 U.S. 787
        v. Bell, Attorney General
        *Sex Discrimination 1978 43-48
        Significant Decisions 1976/77 104-105

3822.   Bounds, Correction Commissioner   Apr 27, 1977   430 U.S. 817
        v. Smith
        *Consttnl Rights (Palmer) 706-713
        *Modern Criml Procedure 42-45
        Significant Decisions 1976/77 117-118
        Sup Ct and Criml Process 774-776
        *Sup Ct and Criml Process 776-781
        *US Prison Law v. 6, 323-336
        PERIODICALS:
        "High court hears arguments on prison law libraries," W. D.
           Nelson. Wilson Library Bul 51: 286-287 Dec '76.
        "High court reaffirms need for prison law libraries," W. Dale
           Nelson. Wilson Library Bul 51: 857-858 June '77.
        "Supreme Court review (1977)." J Criml Law and Crimlgy 68:
           591-600 Dec '77 (3).

3823.   U.S. Trust Co. of New York,   Apr 27, 1977   431 U.S. 1
        trustee v. New Jersey
        *Legal Foundations 16-25
        Significant Decisions 1976/77 144-146
        Sup Ct Review 1979 102-105, 108-109

3824.   Linmark Associates, Inc. v.   May 2, 1977   431 U.S. 85
        Township of Willingboro
        Communication (Hemmer) v. 2, 358-359
        Handbook 177-178
        *Historic Documents 1977 313-320
        *Mass Communications 187-189
        Significant Decisions 1976/77 59-60
        PERIODICALS:
        "For sale signs may not be prohibited." Real Estate Appraiser
           43: 16 July '77.
        "Supreme Court kills for-sale sign ban," Dan Moskowitz. House
           and Home 52: 18 July '77.

3825.   Environmental Protection Agency v.   May 2, 1977   431 U.S. 99
        Brown, Governor of California
        *Cases Environmental Law (Gray) 285-286

3826.   Dixon, Secretary of State of   May 16, 1977   431 U.S. 105
        Illinois v. Love
        Significant Decisions 1976/77 79
        *US Prison Law v. 6, 644-654

3827. Henderson, Correctional Superintendent   May 16, 1977   431 U. S. 145
      v. Kibbe
      PERIODICALS:
      "Supreme Court review (1977)."   J Criml Law and Crimlgy   68:
      571-582   Dec '77   (3).

3828. United States v. Wong   May 23, 1977   431 U. S. 174
      *Sup Ct and Criml Process 533-535
      Sup Ct Review 1977 163-164

3829. United States v. Washington   May 23, 1977   431 U. S. 181
      Modern Criml Procedure 276-277
      Significant Decisions 1976/77 40-41
      *Sup Ct and Criml Process 536-538
      Sup Ct Review 1977 164-167

3830. Abood v. Detroit Board of Education   May 23, 1977   431 U. S. 209
      *Am Consttnl Law (Saye) 374-379
      *Cases Labor (Leslie) 642-655
      *Cases Labor (Oberer) 838-850
      Digest 72
      *Labor Relations (Edwards) 461-475
      *Mass Communications 190-191
      *School Law (Alexander) 675-681
      Significant Decisions 1976/77 60-62
      PERIODICALS:
      "Mandatory union fees upheld for public employees, " Philip W.
        Semas.   Chronicle of Higher Eductn   14:   11   May 31 '77.
      "Significant decisions in labor cases. "   Monthly Labor R   100:
        46-47   Aug '77.
      "Teacher and the law, " Betty E. Sinowitz.   Today's Eductn   66:
        18, 23   Sept '73.

3831. Douglas, Commissioner, Virginia   May 23, 1977   431 U. S. 265
      Marine Resources Commission
      v. Seacoast Products, Inc.
      Significant Decisions 1976/77 149-150
      Sup Ct Review 1977 239-241

3832. Smith dba Intrigue v. United States   May 23, 1977   431 U. S. 291
      Communication (Hemmer) v. 1, 193-194
      *Consttnl Law (Grossman) 1267-1269
      Significant Decisions 1976/77 45-46
      PERIODICALS:
      "High court upholds criminal conviction of Smith for intrastate
        mailing, " Susan Wagner.   Pub Weekly   211:   42   June 6 '77.
      ".'Judicial thicket: the Supreme Court and obscenity, " Mel Fried-
        man.   Nation   225:   110-113   Aug 6 '77   (4).
      "Media coalition challenges obscenity law in High Court, " Susan
        Wagner.   Pub Weekly   210:   20, 22   Sept 27 '76.
      "Supreme Court review (1977). "   J Criml Law and Crimlgy   68:
        613-623   Dec '77   (4).

3833. Massachusetts v. Westcott   May 23, 1977   431 U. S. 322
      Sup Ct Review 1977 241-242

3834. International Brotherhood of Teamsters   May 31, 1977   431 U. S. 324
      v. United States
      T. I. M. E. -D. C. , Inc. v. U. S.

CQ Guide 621
*Cases Labor (Leslie) 468-482
*Cases Labor (Oberer) 990-1001
*Civil Rights (Abernathy) 1980 471-475
*Collective Bargaining 847-881
Digest 72-73
Editorials 1977 785-788
*Historic Documents 1977 383-393
*Labor Law (Twomey) 383-387
*Modern Business 1077-1082
Significant Decisions 1976/77 92-94
PERIODICALS:
"Affect of the Supreme Court's seniority decisions," Stephen C.
Swanson. Personnel J 56: 625-627 Dec '77 (2).
"Court strikes a blow for seniority." Time 109: 60 June 13 '77.
"EEOC retreats after a seniority ruling." Bus Wk p. 28, 30
June 20 '77.
"Significant decisions in labor cases." Monthly Labor R 100: 48-
49 Aug '77.
"Supreme Court upholds seniority systems." Industry Wk 193:
18 June 20 '77.

3835. Connor v. Finch, Governor of   May 31, 1977   431 U.S. 407
Mississippi
Finch v. Connor
United States v. Finch
Significant Decisions 1976/77 85-86

3836. Trainor, Director, Illinois Department May 31, 1977   431 U.S. 434
of Public Aid v. Hernandez
*Cases Pleading 380-388
Significant Decisions 1976/77 109-111

3837. Ohio Bureau of Employment Services   May 31, 1977   431 U.S. 471
v. Hodory
Significant Decisions 1976/77 124-125
PERIODICALS:
"Significant decisions in labor cases." Monthly Labor R 100: 40-
41 Sept '77.

3838. Moore v. City of East Cleveland,   May 31, 1977   431 U.S. 494
Ohio
Cases Consttnl Law (Gunther) 630-633
Significant Decisions 1976/77 71-72
Sup Ct Review 1979 388-391
PERIODICALS:
"Zoning and land use; Supreme Court bails grandma out of local
jail," Victor J. Yannacone. Natl Real Estate Investor 19: 32-
33 Dec '77.

3839. United Air Lines, Inc. v. Evans   May 31, 1977   431 U.S. 553
*Collective Bargaining 881-884
PERIODICALS:
"Affect of the Supreme Court's seniority decisions," Stephen C.
Swanson. Personnel J 56: 625-627 Dec '77 (2).
"Blow to minorities; seniority system decision," H. Hill. Com-
monweal 104: 552-555 Sept 2 '77.

3840. Alabama Power Co. v. Davis   June 6, 1977   431 U.S. 581

PERIODICALS:
"Significant decisions in labor cases." Monthly Labor R 100: 71
Oct '77.

3841. Splawn v. California   June 6, 1977   431 U.S. 595
Handbook 631-633
PERIODICALS:
"Judicial thicket: the Supreme Court and obscenity," Mel Friedman.
Nation 225: 110-113 Aug 6 '77 (4).

3842. United States v. Ramsey   June 6, 1977   431 U.S. 606
Communication (Hemmer) v. 1, 236-237
*Criminal Procedure (Lewis) 267-270
Significant Decisions 1976/77 21-22
Sup Ct and Criml Process 317-320
*Sup Ct and Criml Process 320-324
PERIODICALS:
"Supreme Court review (1977)." J Criml Law and Crimlgy 68:
493-504 Dec '77 (4).

3843. Roberts v. Louisiana   June 6, 1977   431 U.S. 633
*Criminal Justice (Galloway) 69-73
*Criminal Procedure (Lewis) 592-594
*Historic Documents 1977 397-405
Sup Ct and Criml Process 927-929
*Sup Ct and Criml Process 929-932
PERIODICALS:
"Supreme Court review (1977)." J Criml Law and Crimlgy 68:
601-612 Dec '77 (5).

3844. Abney v. United States   June 9, 1977   431 U.S. 651
Modern Criml Procedure 427-429

3845. Stencel Aero Engineering Corporation June 9, 1977   431 U.S. 666
v. United States
PERIODICALS:
"Ejection seat case goes to High court." Aviation Wk 105: 20
Nov 22 '76.

3846. Carey v. Population Services Inter-   June 9, 1977   431 U.S. 678
national
Cases Consttnl Law (Gunther) 626-629
Communication (Hemmer) v. 2, 359-360
Significant Decisions 1976/77 51-53
PERIODICALS:
"First Amendment rights of ads get strong high court support."
Adv Age 48: 2, 93 June 13 '77.
"High court outlaws curbs on contraceptive sales, displays, ads."
Drug Topics 121: 7, 16 July 1 '77.
"Not for adults alone: children begin pressing for expansion of
their constitutional rights." Civil Rights Dig 11: 12-22
Winter '79 (3).
"Teenagers and pregnancy: the law in 1979," Eve W. Paul and
Harriet F. Pilpel. Family Planning Perspectives 11: 297-302
Sept/Oct '79 (4).

3847. Illinois Brick Co. v. Illinois   June 9, 1977   431 U.S. 720
*Modern Business 916-921
Significant Decisions 1976/77 131-132

PERIODICALS:
"Consumer and antitrust law." Congressional Dig 59: 33-64
Feb '80; *59: 38-43 Feb '80.

3848. Ward v. Illinois   June 9, 1977   431 U.S. 767
Communication (Hemmer) v. 1, 174-175
Handbook 624-625
PERIODICALS:
"Judicial thicket: the Supreme Court and obscenity," Mel Fried-
man. Nation 225: 110-113 Aug 6 '77 (4).

3849. United States v. Lovasco   June 9, 1977   431 U.S. 783
Significant Decisions 1976/77 22-23
*Sup Ct and Criml Process 663-666
PERIODICALS:
"Supreme Court review (1977)." J Criml Law and Crimlgy 68:
543-554 Dec '77.

3850. Lefkowitz, Attorney General of   June 13, 1977 431 U.S. 801
New York v. Cunningham
*Criminal Procedure (Lewis) 410-413
Significant Decisions 1976/77 39-40
*Sup Ct and Criml Process 472-475

3851. Smith v. Organization of Foster   June 13, 1977 431 U.S. 816
Families for Equality and Reform
Shapiro v. Organization of Foster Families ...
Rodriguez v. Organization of Foster Families ...
Gandy v. Organization of Foster Families ...
*Cases Domestic 868-883
Significant Decisions 1976/77 75-77

3852. Nyquist v. Mauclet   June 13, 1977 432 U.S. 1
Significant Decisions 1976/77 105-106
PERIODICALS:
"Supreme Court ruling opens up public funds for student aliens."
Times Higher Eductn Supp 297: 14 July 1 '77.

3853. Lee v. United States   June 13, 1977 432 U.S. 23
Significant Decisions 1976/77 38
PERIODICALS:
"Supreme Court review (1977)." J Criml Law and Crimlgy 68:
555-570 Dec '77 (6).

3854. National Socialist Party of America June 14, 1977 432 U.S. 43
v. Village of Skokie
Communication (Hemmer) v. 1, 102-103
Handbook 60
PERIODICALS:
"Marching through Skokie," Hadley Arkes. Natl R 30: 588-593
May 12 '78.

3855. TransWorld Airlines v. Hardison   June 16, 1977 432 U.S. 63
International Association of Machinists
and Aerospace Workers v. Hardison
*Collective Bargaining 943-954
*Modern Business 1096-1099
Significant Decisions 1976/77 122-123

PERIODICALS:
"Sabbatarians and the courts: court decisions over the years leave
religious questions unresolved, " Leo Pfeffer.   Civil Rights Dig
11: 28-33   Spring '79.
"Supreme Court eases employers' religious discrimination obliga-
tion, " William E. Lissy.   Supervision 39: 13 Oct '77.
"Significant decisions in labor cases. "   Monthly Labor R 100: 39-
40 Sept '77.
"Working on the Sabbath. "   Time 109: 50-51   June 27 '77.

3856.   Manson v. Brathwaite   June 16, 1977 432 U.S. 98
*Consttnl Law (Klein) 366-375
*Criminal Evidence 498-500
*Criminal Procedure (Lewis) 475-477
Law of Arrest (Creamer) 468-471
*Modern Criml Procedure 199-207
Significant Decisions 1976/77 20-21
Sup Ct and Criml Process 504-507
*Sup Ct and Criml Process 507-514
PERIODICALS:
"Supreme Court review (1977). "   J Criml Law and Crimlgy 68:
526-532 Dec '77.

3857.   Jeffers v. United States   June 16, 1977 432 U.S. 137
*Cases Criml Law (Inbau) 861-869
Significant Decisions 1976/77 38-39
Sup Ct Review 1978 120-122
PERIODICALS:
See listing at 432 U.S. 23, entry no. 3853.

3858.   Brown v. Ohio   June 16, 1977 432 U.S. 161
*Criminal Justice (Way) 267-270
*Criminal Law (Dix) 242-247
*Criminal Procedure (Lewis) 345-349
*Modern Criml Procedure 289-292
Significant Decisions 1976/77 36-37
Sup Ct and Criml Process 377-380
*Sup Ct and Criml Process 380-384
Sup Ct Review 1978 156-163
PERIODICALS:
See listing at 432 U.S. 23, entry no. 3853.

3859.   Patterson v. New York   June 17, 1977 432 U.S. 197
*Cases Criml Law (Inbau) 468-477
*Criminal Law (Dix) 25-33
Significant Decisions 1976/77 18-19

3860.   Dobbert v. Florida   June 17, 1977 432 U.S. 282
*Consttnl Law (Klein) 427-436
*Criminal Justice (Way) 26-30
Significant Decisions 1976/77 34-36
*Sup Ct and Criml Process 916-922
PERIODICALS:
"Supreme Court Review (1977). "   J Criml Law and Crimlgy 68:
601-612 Dec '77 (5).

3861.   Hunt v. Washington State Apple   June 20, 1977 432 U.S. 333
Advertising Commission

Cases Consttnl Law (Gunther) 311-313
Significant Decisions 1976/77 147-149

3862.   Batterton v. Francis   June 20, 1977 432 U.S. 416
        Significant Decisions 1976/77 126-127
        PERIODICALS:
        "Significant decisions in labor cases." Monthly Labor R 100: 41-
            42 Sept '77.

3863.   Beal v. Doe   June 20, 1977 432 U.S. 438
        Cases Consttnl Law (Gunther) 617-621
        Editorials 1977 828-835
        *Historic Documents 1977 407-430
        Significant Decisions 1976/77 49-50
        PERIODICALS:
        "Abortion and the Supreme Court: anti-abortion view," Sidney
            Callahan. Current 198: 21-23 Dec '71. Reprinted from:
            Hastings Center Report p. 7-8 Aug '77.
        "Abortion and the Supreme Court: egalitarian view," Mary C.
            Segers. Current 198: 17-21 Dec '77. Reprinted from:
            Hastings Center Report p. 5-6 Aug '77.
        "Abortion and fairness; medicaid funds." Progressive 41: 9
            Sept '77.
        "Abortion funding where it stands now." US News 83: 22 July
            11 '77.
        "Abortion: who pays?" Susan Fraker and others. Newsweek 90:
            12-13 July 4 '77.
        "High Court's abortion rulings: what they mean." US News 83:
            66 July 4 '77.
        "New abortion debate: decision on medicaid funding." Common-
            weal 104: 451-452 July 22 '77.
        "New abortion rulings (What they really mean)," Lucie Prinz.
            McCalls 105: 111 Oct '77.
        "Of abortion and the unfairness of life; Time essay," Lance Mor-
            row. Time 110: 49 Aug 1 '77.
        "Supreme Court ignites a fiery abortion debate." Time 110: 6-8
            July 4 '77.
        "Unborn and the born again; Supreme Court decision on use of
            state funds to cover abortion costs." New Republic 177: 5-6,
            8 July 2 '77.

3864.   Maher v. Roe   June 20, 1977 432 U.S. 464
        *Basic Cases 149-164
        *Cases Civil Liberties 373-378
        *Cases Consttnl Law (Cushman) 603-607
        *Courts Judges 622-635
        Editorials 1977 828-835
        Significant Decisions 1976/77 50-51

3865.   Poelker v. Doe   June 20, 1977 432 U.S. 519
        Editorials 1977 828-835

3866.   United States v. Chadwick   June 21, 1977 433 U.S. 1
        *Consttnl Law (Maddex) 157-160
        *Criminal Evidence 403-405
        *Criminal Justice (Galloway) 166-169
        *Criminal Procedure (Lewis) 190-194
        Law of Arrest (Creamer) 237-240

*Leading Consttnl Cases 154-160
*Modern Criml Procedure 103-111
Significant Decisions 1976/77 25-26
*Sup Ct and Criml Process 242-246
PERIODICALS:
"Supreme Court review (1977)." J Criml Law and Crimlgy 68:
493-504 Dec '77 (4).

3867. Continental TV, Inc. v. GTE Sylvania, June 23, 1977 433 U. S. 36
Inc.
*Modern Business 1008-1014
Significant Decisions 1976/77 129-131
Sup Ct Review 1977 171-177, 182-192
PERIODICALS:
"Franchiser case strengthened." Adv Age 48: 65 Aug 1 '77.
"Supreme Court OK's location clauses; impact not clear yet, " Bill
Streeter. Industrial Distributor 67: 43-44 Aug '77.
"Supreme Court tags dealers in second round," Russell Decker.
Purchasing 84: 75-76 Apr 26 '78.

3868. Wainwright v. Sykes   June 23, 1977 433 U. S. 72
*Criminal Procedure (Lewis) 670-673
*Leading Consttnl Cases 840-858
*Modern Criml Procedure 459-468
Significant Decisions 1976/77 118-120
Sup Ct and Criml Process 1045-1048
*Sup Ct and Criml Process 1048-1054

3869. Jones v. North Carolina Prisoners'   June 23, 1977 433 U. S. 119
Labor Union, Inc.
*Consttnl Rights (Palmer) 713-723
*Criminal Justice (Way) 533-538
Significant Decisions 1976/77 114-116
Sup Ct and Criml Process 781-785
*Sup Ct and Criml Process 785-789
*US Prison Law v. 6, 110-124
PERIODICALS:
"Prisoner representative organizations, prison reform and Jones
v. North Carolina prisoners' labor union," Bradley B. Falkof.
J Criml Law and Crimlgy 70: 42-56 Spring '79.
"Supreme Court review (1977)." J Criml Law and Crimlgy 68:
591-600 Dec '77 (3).

3870. Commissioner of Internal Revenue   June 23, 1977 433 U. S. 148
v. Standard Life and Accident
Insurance Co.
PERIODICALS:
"Supreme Court decides key case on insurance taxation of deferred
and uncollected premiums, " Francis M. Gregory and Carolyn
P. Chiechi. J Taxation 47: 170-172 Sept '77.
"Supreme Court decides the loading issue," Gerald I. Lenrow and
others. Best R (life ed) 78: 64, 66-68 Aug '77.

3871. Shaffer v. Heitner   June 24, 1977 433 U. S. 186
*Cases Pleading 241-263
*Civil Procedure (Cound) 119-130
Significant Decisions 1976/77 151-152

3872. Wolman v. Walter   June 24, 1977 433 U. S. 229

*Consttn (Morris) 407-419
*Consttnl Rights (Kemerer) 265-272
Digest 30-31
Editorials 1977 849-853
*Historic Documents 1977 431-445
Law and Education 287-288
*School Law (Alexander) 222-231
Significant Decisions 1976/77 65-67
PERIODICALS:
"Aid to nonpublic education." America 137: 2-3 July 2 '77.
"Parochial decision." Newsweek 90: 59 July 4 '77.
"Public aid to religious schools: what the Supreme Court said
and didn't say," M. Chester Nolte. Am Sch Bd J 165: 35,
45 Jan '78. Condensed in: Eductn Dig 43: 20-21 Apr '78.
"Schools and the law--finally, a partial victory for parochial
schools," Thomas J. Flygare. Phi Delta Kappan 59: 51-53
Sept '77 (2).

3873. Milliken v. Bradley   June 27, 1977 433 U.S. 267
Brethren 283-285
*Civil Rights (Abernathy) 1980 129-133
*Consttn (Morris) 139-146
Digest 108-109
Editorials 1977 842 848
Education (Lapati) 303-304
Significant Decisions 1976/77 91-92

3874. Hazelwood School District v.   June 27, 1977 433 U.S. 299
United States
*Collective Bargaining 885 804
Digest 109-110
*School Law (Alexander) 526-530
PERIODICALS:
"Significant decisions in labor cases." Monthly Labor R 100: 51-
52 Nov '77.

3875. Dothard v. Rawlinson   June 27, 1977 433 U.S. 321
CQ Guide 637-638
*Cases Labor (Leslie) 497-503
*Collective Bargaining 909-921
*Sex Discrimination 1978 116-123, 127-131
Significant Decisions 1976/77 102-103
*Sup Ct and Criml Process 828-834
Sup Ct Review 1979 34-36
PERIODICALS:
"Significant decisions in labor cases." Monthly Labor R 100: 70-
71 Oct '77.

3876. Bates v. State Bar of Arizona   June 27, 1977 433 U.S. 350
Cases Consttnl Law (Gunther) 1390-1392
Communication (Hemmer) v. 2, 356-357
*Consttnl Law (Grossman) 1195-1202
Editorials 1977 854-858
Handbook 173-177
*Justices (Friedman) v. 5, 45-60
*Mass Communications 182-186
Mass Media (Francois) 405
Significant Decisions 1976/77 56-59

PERIODICALS:
"Advertisers-at-law, " Jerrold K. Footlick and Lucy Howard.
Newsweek 90: 47-48 July 11 '77.
"Advertising and the First Amendment, " Dorothy Cohen. J Mar-
keting 42: 59-68 July '78 (4).
"Bar's blushing maidens; decision allowing lawyers to advertise, "
Nathan Lewin. New Republic 177: 17-19 Sept 17 '77.
"Commercial activity on campus; where does it end?" Annette
Gibbs and Miriam Jernigan. NASPA J 18: 28-32 Summer
'80.
"Farewell barrage from the Court. " Time 110: 62-63 July 11
'77 (5).
"Lawyer price ads begin as court eases ban. " Adv Age 48: 1,
51 July 4 '77.
"Now that lawyers can advertise.... " US News 83: 21 July 11
'77.
"Supreme Court review (1977). " J Criml Law and Crimlgy 68:
624-633 Dec '77.
"Supreme Court rules that attorneys may advertise, and specula-
tion flourishes among the other professions, " William Hickman.
Architectural Rec 162: 34 Aug '77.

3877.   Dayton Board of Education v.   June 27, 1977 433 U.S. 406
        Brinkman
        CQ Guide 606-607
        *Civil Rights (Abernathy) 1980 134-136
        Digest 110-111
        Editorials 1977 842-848
        From Brown 246
        *Historic Documents 1977 447-464
        Sup Ct Review 1979 6-9
        PERIODICALS:
        "Conflicting signals; decision in case of NAACP against the Dayton
        Board of Education, " Jonathan Miller. New Republic 177: 10-
        11 July 23 '77.
        "Schools and the law--Rehnquist's Dayton decision and systemwide
        desegregation plans, " Thomas Flygare. Phi Delta Kappan 59:
        126-127 Oct '77.
        "Tale of two cities; decisions on the proper role of federal judges
        in school desegregation cases, " Merril Sheils and others. News-
        week 90: 54 July 11 '77.

3878.   Nixon v. Administrator of   June 28, 1977 433 U.S. 425
        General Services
        CQ Guide 233-234
        Communication (Hemmer) v. 2, 247-249
        *Courts Judges 474-476
        Editorials 1977 836-841
        *Federal System 132-137
        *Historic Documents 1977 465-516
        Mass Media (Francois) 225
        Significant Decisions 1976/77 154-158
        PERIODICALS:
        "Farewell barrage from the court. " Time 110: 62-63 July 11
        '77 (5).
        "Nixon documents: More court fights ahead. " US News 83: 22
        July 11 '77.
        "Nixon's tapes someday. " Newsweek 90: 17 July 11 '77.

3879. Zacchini v. Scripps-Howard   June 28, 1977 433 U.S. 562
         Broadcasting Co.
         CQ Guide 436
         *Cases Copyright (Nimmer) 888-903
         Handbook 400-402
         *Legal Regulation 610-618
         *Mass Communications 355-358
         Mass Media (Francois) 179-181
         Significant Decisions 1976/77 64-65
       PERIODICALS:
         "Farewell barrage from the Court." Time 110: 62-63 July 11
         '77 (5).

3880. Coker v. Georgia   June 29, 1977 433 U.S. 584
         *Am Consttnl Law (Shapiro) 685-687
         *Consttnl Law (Klein) 421-427
         *Criminal Justice (Galloway) 73-86
         *Criminal Procedure (Lewis) 595-601
         Editorials 1977 905-910
         *Historic Documents 1977 517-528
         *Procedures 246-249
         Significant Decisions 1976/77 32-33
         Sup Ct and Criml Process 905-908
         *Sup Ct and Criml Process 908-915
       PERIODICALS:
         "Arguing about death for rape." Time 109: 80 Apr 11 '77.
         "Death penalty for rape?" Deborah Leavy. Ms 6: 20 July '77.
         "Farewell barrage from the Court." Time 110: 62-63 July 11
         '77 (5).
         "Rape and death." Newsweek 90: 48 July 11 '77.
         "Supreme Court review (1977)." J Criml Law and Crimlgy 68:
         601-612 Dec '77 (5)

3881. Commissioner of Internal Revenue   Nov 29, 1977 434 U.S. 77
         v. Kowalski
       PERIODICALS:
         "Cash meal allowances paid to state troopers taxable says Supreme
         Court." J Taxation 48: 105-106 Feb '78.

3882. Pennsylvania v. Mimms   Dec 5, 1977   434 U.S. 106
         *Consttnl Law (Maddex) 136-140
         *Criminal Procedure (Lewis) 257-260
         Law of Arrest (Creamer) 179-180
         Significant Decisions 1977/78 37-38
       PERIODICALS:
         "Supreme Court review (1978)." J Criml Law and Crimlgy 69:
         464-473 Dec '78.

3883. New York v. Cathedral Academy   Dec 6, 1977   434 U.S. 125
         Significant Decisions 1977/78 69-70
         Sup Ct Review 1978 171, 174-182

3884. Nashville Gas Co. v. Satty   Dec 6, 1977   434 U.S. 136
         CQ Guide 636-637
         *Historic Documents 1977 871-881
         Significant Decisions 1977/78 97-98
       PERIODICALS:
         "Schools and the law--a legal embarrassment: paid sick leave for

pregnant teachers, " Thomas Flygare. Phi Delta Kappan 59:
558-559 Apr '78 (2).
"Significant decisions in labor cases. " Monthly Labor R 101: 58
Feb '78.

3885. United States v. New York   Dec 7, 1977   434 U. S. 159
Telephone Co.
*Consttnl Law (Klein) 248-254
*Historic Documents 1977 883-896
Significant Decisions 1977/78 40-41
PERIODICALS:
"Supreme Court review (1978). " J Criml Law and Crimlgy 69:
493-504 Dec '78 (2).

3886. United Air Lines, Inc. v. McMann   Dec 12, 1977   434 U. S. 192
Significant Decisions 1977/78 99-100
PERIODICALS:
"Supreme Court OKs early forced retirement. " Bus Insurance 11:
8 Dec 26 '77.
"U. S. Supreme Court backs airline's age-60 pre 1967 mandatory
retirement plan. " Retirement Living 18: 47 Feb '78.
"Significant decisions in labor cases. " Monthly Labor R 101: 57
Feb '78.

3887. Moore v. Illinois   Dec 12, 1977   434 U. S. 220
*Consttnl Law (Klein) 375-381
*Modern Criml Procedure 197-199
PERIODICALS:
"Supreme Court review (1978). " J Criml Law and Crimlgy 69:
538-543 Dec '78.

3888. Quillion v. Walcott   Jan 10, 1978   434 U. S. 246
*Cases Domestic 1058-1064
Significant Decisions 1977/78 105-106

3889. Adamo Wrecking Co. v. United States Jan 10, 1978   434 U. S. 275
PERIODICALS:
"Restricted judicial review provisions of the Clean air act--denial
of due process or indispensable to efficient administration?"
Mary P. Squiers. Boston Col Environmental Affairs Law R
8 no. 1: 119-151 '79.

3890. Pfizer v. India   Jan 11, 1978   434 U. S. 308
Significant Decisions 1977/78 126-127

3891. National Labor Relations Board v.   Jan 17, 1978   434 U. S. 335
International Association of Bridge
Structural and Ornamental Iron Workers,
A FL-CIO
PERIODICALS:
"Significant decisions in labor cases. " Monthly Labor R 101: 48
Mar '78.

3892. Bordenkircher v. Hayes   Jan 18, 1978   434 U. S. 357
*Consttnl Law (Maddex) 337-340
*Criminal Justice (Way) 234-236
*Criminal Procedure (Lewis) 558-561
*Modern Criml Procedure 301-308
Significant Decisions 1977/78 42-43

*US Prison Law v. 6, 8-16
PERIODICALS:
"Supreme Court review (1978)." J Criml Law and Crimlgy 69:
484-492 Dec '78.

3893. Zablocki v. Redhail   Jan 18, 1978   434 U.S. 374
Cases Consttnl Law (Gunther) 636-640
*Cases Domestic 224-233
Significant Decisions 1977/78 103-105

3894. Christiansburg Garment Co. v. Equal Jan 23, 1978   434 U.S. 412
Employment Opportunity Commission
PERIODICALS:
"Significant decisions in labor cases." Monthly Labor R 101:
49-50 Mar '78.

3895. Raymond Motor Transportation, Inc.   Feb 21, 1978   434 U.S. 429
v. Rice
*Cases Consttnl Law (Gunther) 290-294
Significant Decisions 1977/78 145-146

3896. United States Steel Corporation v.   Feb 21, 1978   434 U.S. 452
Multistate Tax Commission
Significant Decisions 1977/78 151-152
PERIODICALS:
"Analysis of the Supreme Court's US Steel decision upholding Multi-
state Tax Compact," William D. Dexter. J Taxation 48: 368
371 June '78.

3897. Arizona v. Washington   Feb 21, 1978   434 U.S. 497
*Criminal Procedure (Lewis) 340-344
Modern Criml Procedure 390-393
Significant Decisions 1977/78 28-29
Sup Ct Review 1978 95-96
PERIODICALS:
"Developments in the manifest necessity rule," T. W. Dressler.
J Criml Law and Crimlgy 70: 63-67 Spring '79.
"Supreme Court review (1978)." J Criml Law and Crimlgy 69:
563-573 Dec '78 (2).

3898. Fulman v. United States   Feb 22, 1978   434 U.S. 528
PERIODICALS:
"Supreme Court limits dividends paid deduction to adjusted basis of
distributed property," Michael E. Fox. J Taxation 48: 266-
268 May '78.

3899. Procunier v. Navarette   Feb 22, 1978   434 U.S. 555
*Labor Relations (Edwards) 922-927
Significant Decisions 1977/78 89-90
US Prison Law v. 6, 393-402
PERIODICALS:
"Supreme Court review (1978)." J Criml Law and Crimlgy 69:
588-596 Dec '78.

3900. Lorillard, Division of Loew's   Feb 22, 1978   434 U.S. 575
Theatres, Inc. v. Pons
PERIODICALS:
"Significant decisions in labor cases." Monthly Labor R 101: 51
Apr '78.

670 U.S. Supreme Court Decisions

3901. Central Illinois Public Service Co.   Feb 28, 1978   435 U.S. 21
      v. United States
      PERIODICALS:
      "Impact of Supreme Court decision limiting withholding on em-
      ployees' meal allowances," Mark H. Kovey.   J Taxation   48:
      276-279   May '78.
      "Supreme Court decides against withholding on lunch reimburse-
      ments," Glenn I. Lenrow and Ralph Milo.   Bests R   (Life ed)
      79: 48, 50, 52 May '78.   Same in: Bests R (Property ed)
      79: 68+ May '78.

3902. Board of Curators of University of   Mar 1, 1978   435 U.S. 78
      Missouri v. Horowitz
      *Consttnl Rights (Kemerer) 398-403
      Significant Decisions 1977/78 94-95
      PERIODICALS:
      *"Academic dismissals: the Supreme Court's opinion." Chronicle
      of Higher Eductn 16: 13-14 Mar 6 '78.
      "The dismissal of Charlotte Horowitz," Cheryl M. Fields.   Chron-
      icle of Higher Eductn 15: 1, 8 Nov 14 '77.
      "Due process rights of students; limitations on Goss v. Lopez--a
      retreat out of the thicket," Michael A. Mass   J Law and Eductn
      9: 449-462 Oct '80 (3).
      "School and the law--the Horowitz case," Thomas Flygare.   Phi
      Delta Kappan 59: 626-627 May '78.
      "Student who fails academically needn't get dismissal hearing,"
      Cheryl M. Fields.   Chronicle of Higher Eductn 16: 1, 13
      Mar 6 '78.
      "Supreme Court rules on expulsion rights," Clive Cookson.   Times
      Higher Eductn Supp 332: 5 Mar 17 '78.

3903. Ray v. Atlantic Richfield Co.   Mar 6, 1978   435 U.S. 151
      Editorials 1978 427-433

3904. Ballew v. Georgia   Mar 21, 1978   435 U.S. 223
      *Criminal Justice (Way) 371-375
      *Criminal Procedure (Lewis) 490-495
      Procedures 95
      Significant Decisions 1977/78 45-46
      Sup Ct Review 1978 191-224
      PERIODICALS:
      "Getting off a slippery slope," Elizabeth D. Tanke and Tony J.
      Tanke.   Am Psychologist 34: 1130-1138 Dec '79.
      "Supreme Court review (1978)." J Criml Law and Crimlgy 69:
      516-527 Dec '78.

3905. Carey v. Piphus   Mar 21, 1978   435 U.S. 247
      *Civil Rights (Abernathy) 1980 108-114
      *School Law (Alexander) 448-454
      Significant Decisions 1977/78 90-91
      PERIODICALS:
      "Schools and the law: Section 1983 suits against school districts,"
      Thomas J. Flygare.   Phi Delta Kappan 60: 127-128 Oct '78
      (3).

3906. United States v. Ceccolini   Mar 21, 1978   435 U.S. 268
      *Consttnl Law (Maddex) 101-109
      Law of Arrest (Creamer) 515-518

*Modern Criml Procedure 227-232
Significant Decisions 1977/78 38-40
PERIODICALS:
"Supreme Court review (1978)." J Criml Law and Crimlgy 69:
583-587 Dec '78.

3907. Folie v. Connelie   Mar 22, 1978 435 U.S. 291
*Criminal Procedure (Lewis) 98-103
*Labor Relations (Edwards) 903-907
Significant Decisions 1977/78 101-102
PERIODICALS:
"Agents of the state," John W. Donohue. America 140: 453
June 2 '79 (2).
"Significant decisions in labor cases." Monthly Labor R 101: 52
June '78.

3908. Lakeside v. Oregon   Mar 22, 1978 435 U.S. 333
Significant Decisions 1977/78 51-52

3909. Stump v. Sparkman   Mar 28, 1978 435 U.S. 349
*Courts Judges 208-214
Editorials 1978 440-446
*Historic Documents 1978 259-268
Significant Decisions 1977/78 87-89

3910. Lafayette v. Louisiana Power   Mar 29, 1978 435 U.S. 389
and Light Co.
Significant Decisions 1977/78 125-126

3911. Holloway v. Arkansas   Apr 3, 1978 435 U.S. 475
*Modern Criml Procedure 24-31
Significant Decisions 1077/78 49-50
PERIODICALS:
"Supreme Court review (1978)." J Criml Law and Crimlgy 69:
574-582 Dec '78.

3912. Vermont Yankee Nuclear Power   Apr 3, 1979 435 U.S. 519
Corporation v. Natural Resources
Defense Council
*Admin Law (Gellhorn) 192-201
*Consttnl Law (Grossman) 400-407
Editorials 1978 434-439
Significant Decisions 1977/78 133-135
Sup Ct Review 1978 345-409
PERIODICALS:
"Judges, stay out," Jerrold K. Footlick and Mary Lord. News-
week 91: 122 Apr 17 '78.
"Liability limits of nuclear power plants upheld by US Supreme
Court," Mary Jane Fisher. Natl Underwriter (Property ed)
82: 46 June 30 '78.
"Nuclear law; the battle over atomic power in the courts," Sidney
Bernstein. Trial 16: 28-32, 61 Apr '80 (2).
"Supreme Court: getting out of politics." Economist 267: 52
Apr 15 '78.
"Vermont Yankee in King Burger's court," James F. Raymond.
Boston Col Environmental Affairs Law R 7 no. 4: 629-664
'79.

3913. Frank Lyon Co. v. United States   Apr 18, 1978 435 U.S. 561

PERIODICALS:
"Sale-leaseback arrangement held valid by Supreme Court."
J Taxation 48: 353-354 June '78.
"Supreme Court's sale-leaseback decision in Lyon lists multiple
criteria," Stanton H. Zarrow and David E. Gordon. J Taxation
49: 42-47 July '78.

3914. Nixon v. Warner Communications, Inc. Apr 18, 1978 435 U.S. 589
Communication (Hemmer) v. 2, 249-250
Editorials 1978 495-499
Significant Decisions 1977/78 63-65
Sup Ct Review 1978 230-232
PERIODICALS:
"Nixon wins one," Don Holt and Diane Camper. Newsweek 91:
29 May 1 '78.
"Tape tie-up; Nixon wins a delay." Time 111: 72 May 1 '78.

3915. McDaniel v. Paty   Apr 19, 1978 435 U.S. 618
Significant Decisions 1977/78 70-71
Sup Ct Review 1978 171, 183-190

3916. Elkins v. Moreno   Apr 19, 1978 435 U.S. 647
Significant Decisions 1977/78 119-120
PERIODICALS:
"Challenge to out-of-state tuition sent back to Md. by High court,"
Ellen K. Coughlin. Chronicle of Higher Eductn 16: 2 Apr
24 '78.
"High court hears challenge to out of state tuition," Ellen Cough-
lin. Chronicle of Higher Eductn 16: 9 Feb 27, 1978.

3917. National Society of Professional   Apr 25, 1978 435 U.S. 679
Engineers v. United States
Significant Decisions 1977/78 124-125
PERIODICALS:
"Collision between professional ethics and antitrust," Charles M.
Hewitt. Bus Horizons 22: 73-74 Feb '79.
"Supreme Court ruling against NSPE; allows engineers to bid on
jobs," William Hickman. Architectural Rec 163: 34 June
'78.
"Supreme Court strikes down NSPE's ethical ban on bidding."
Engineering News 200: 11-12 May 4 '78.

3918. Los Angeles, Department of Water   Apr 25, 1978 435 U.S. 702
and Power v. Manhart
CQ Guide 638
*Civil Rights (Abernathy) 1980 497-504
*Collective Bargaining 936-943
Editorials 1978 593-596
*Historic Documents 1978 293-306
Significant Decisions 1977/78 98-99
PERIODICALS:
"Benefit front: bias ruling could force major pension overhaul,"
Jerry Geisel. Bus Insurance 12: 1, 33 May 15 '78.
"High court's ruling on pensions is wrong," Alfred I. Jaffe. Natl
Underwriter (Life ed) 82: 14, 20-21 May 20 '78. Same: Natl
Underwriter. (Property ed) 82: 48 May 26 '78.
"Higher pension costs for women barred by Supreme Court,"
Cheryl Fields. Chronicle of Higher Eductn 16: 1, 10 May
1, 1978.

"Making liars out of Senators," Daniel Seligman.   Fortune   97:
  100   June 5 '78.
"Outlaw pension bias against women," Mary Jane Fisher.   Natl
  Underwriter   (Life ed) 82: 1, 30 Apr 29 '78.
"Pension plans can't require women to pay more Supreme Court
  decides."   Bus Insurance   12: 2 May 1 '78.
"Schools and the law--the aftermath of Manhart," Thomas Flygare.
  Phi Delta Kappan   60: 310 Dec '78.
"Sex-bias threat to pension funding."   Bus Wk   p. 40-41   May 8
  '78.
"Significant decisions in labor cases."   Monthly Labor R   101:   39
  July '78.
"Unisex, TIAA, and post-Manhart litigation," David M. Rabban.
  Academe   66: 160-163 Apr '80.
"U.S. Supreme Court strikes down pension plans favoring women."
  Retirement Living   18: 48 June '78.

3919. Washington Department of Revenue v.   Apr 26, 1978   435 U.S. 734
       Association of Washington
       Stevedoring Co.
       Significant Decisions 1977/78 149-151

3920. First National Bank of Boston   Apr 26, 1978   435 U.S. 765
          v. Bellotti
       *Am Consttnl Law (Saye) 346-349
       Cases Consttnl Law (Gunther) 1439-1443
       Editorials 1978 579-586
       *Historic Documents 1978 307-324
       *Justices (Friedman) v. 5, 92-105
       *Mass Communications 162-166, 674-679
       Significant Decisions 1977/78 59-60
       Sup Ct Review 1978 232-234
       PERIODICALS:
       "Burger's blast; free speech ruling stirs a row."   Time   111:   68
         May 8 '78.
       "First Amendment rights and the corporation," John H. Brebbia.
         Public Relations J   35: 16-20 Dec '79.
       "Free speech for corporations," Arthur S. Miller.   Progressive
         42: 8 July '78.
       "Government control: business strikes back," William R. Boulton.
         Bus Horizons   22: 61-66 Aug '79.
       "High court adds more protection to advertising."   Broadcasting
         94: 30 May 1 '78.
       "More leeway for companies to sway public."   US News   84: 91
         May 8 '78.
       "Supreme Court review (1978)."   J Criml Law and Crimlgy   69:
         544-551 Dec '78.
       "You and I and corporate management," Melvin Wulf.   Nation   226:
         589-590 May 20 '78.

3921. Landmark Communications, Inc.   May 1, 1978   435 U.S. 829
          v. Virginia
       Cases Consttnl Law (Gunther) 1167-1168
       *Cases Criml Law (Inbau) 266-275
       Editorials 1978 587-592
       Handbook 517-520
       Significant Decisions 1977/78 68-69
       Sup Ct Review 1978 235-237

3922.   United States v. MacDonald   May 1, 1978   435 U.S. 850
         Modern Criml Procedure 429-430

3923.   Memphis Light, Gas and   May 1, 1978   436 U.S. 1
           Water Division v. Craft
         *Am Consttnl Law (Saye) 408-410
         Significant Decisions 1977/78 92-94

3924.   Santa Clara Pueblo v. Martinez   May 15, 1978   436 U.S. 49
         *Am Consttnl Law (Saye) 73-75

3925.   Kulko v. Superior Court of California May 15, 1978 436 U.S. 84
           in and for San Francisco
         *Cases Pleading 263-273
         Significant Decisions 1977/78 106-107

3926.   Scott v. United States   May 15, 1978   436 U.S. 128
         *Modern Criml Procedure 147-149
         Significant Decisions 1977/78 41-42
         PERIODICALS:
         See listing at 434 U.S. 159, entry no. 3885.

3927.   Flagg Brothers, Inc. v. Brooks   May 15, 1978   436 U.S. 149
         Cases Consttnl Law (Gunther) 1026-1028
         *Consttnl Law (Lockhart) 1566-1572
         *Modern Business 675-680
         Significant Decisions 1977/78 95-96

3928.   Sears, Roebuck and Co. v. San Diego May 15, 1978 436 U.S. 180
           County District Council of Carpenters
         *Cases Labor (Leslie) 625-636
         *Cases Labor (Oberer) 385-400
         *Labor Law (Twomey) 112-116
         Significant Decisions 1977/78 111-112
         PERIODICALS:
         "Significant decisions in labor cases." Monthly Labor R 101: 46-
           47 Aug '78.

3929.   Slodov v. United States   May 22, 1978   436 U.S. 238
         PERIODICALS:
         "Failure to collect and pay over withholding taxes in bankruptcies."
           CPA J 48: 61-64 Nov '78 (2).
         "Liability under section 6672 of the Internal Revenue Code," Roy
           E. Lachman. Taxes 57: 593-596 Sept '79.

3930.   Pinkus dba Rosslyn News Co.   May 23, 1978   436 U.S. 293
           v. United States
         PERIODICALS:
         "Court removes children from obscenity definition," Susan Wagner.
           Pub Weekly 213: 17 June 5 '78.
         "Supreme Court review (1978)." J Criml Law and Crimlgy 69:
           474-483 Dec '78.

3931.   Marshall v. Barlow's, Inc.   May 23, 1978   436 U.S. 307
         *Admin Law (Gellhorn) 533-540
         Criminal Procedure (Lewis) 271-275
         *Criminal Procedure (Lewis) 275-279
         Editorials 1978 700-706
         *Historic Documents 1978 339-353

*Labor Law (Twomey) 460-463
*Modern Business 1063-1067
Significant Decisions 1977/78 36-37
PERIODICALS:
  "Barlow decision, " Jeff Ball. Job Safety and Health 6: 15-17
    June '78.
  "Bill vindicated, inspectors may need warrants. " Time 111: 16
    June 5 '78.
  "Blow for freedom?" Patrick P. McCurdy. Chemical Wk 122: 5
    June 7 '78.
  "Dust on the Constitution. " Nation 226: 684 June 10 '78.
  "Man from OSHA must have warrant. " Fleet Owner 73: 20
    July '78.
  "OSHA must get warrants. " Chronicle of Higher Eductn 16: 12
    May 30 '78.
  "OSHA needs warrant for inspections. " Professional Builder and
    Apartment Bus 43: 86 July '78.
  "Significant decisions in labor cases. " Monthly Labor R 101:
    38-39 July '78.
  "Supreme Court review (1978). " J Criml Law and Crimlgy 69:
    552-562 Dec '78 (2).

3932. United States v. Mauro   May 23, 1978 436 U.S. 340
       United States v. Ford
       *US Prison Law v. 6, 588-602

3933. Baldwin v. Montana Fish and Game   May 23, 1978 436 U.S. 371
       Commission
       *Consttnl Law (Lockhart) 341-345
       Significant Decisions 1977/78 153-154
       PERIODICALS:
         "License gouge, " Richard Starnes. Outdoor Life 162: 8, 10, 12
           Sept '78.

3934. In re Primus   May 30, 1978 436 U.S. 412
       Cases Consttnl Law (Gunther) 1392-1394
       Significant Decisions 1977/78 57-59
       PERIODICALS:
         "Major changes in school integration litigation, 1954-1979, " Frank
           Brown. Eductnl Admin Q 15: 76-97 Spring '79 (3).
         "Sterile justice in South Carolina?" Milton Jordan. Black Enter-
           prise 8: 11-12 Mar '78.
         "Supreme Court review (1978). " J Criml Law and Crimlgy 69:
           505-515 Dec '78 (2).

3935. Ohralick v. Ohio State Bar Association May 30, 1978 436 U.S. 447
       Cases Consttnl Law (Gunther) 1392-1394
       Communication (Hemmer) v. 2, 357-358
       Significant Decisions 1977/78 55-57
       PERIODICALS:
         "Commercial activity on campus; where will it end?" Annette
           Gibbs and Miriam Jernigan. NASPA J 18: 28-32 Summer
           '80 (3).
         "Supreme Court review (1978). " J Criml Law and Crimlgy 69:
           505-515 Dec '78 (2).

3936. Taylor v. Kentucky   May 30, 1978 436 U.S. 478
       Criminal Procedure (Lewis) 67-70
       *Criminal Procedure (Lewis) 71-75

3937. Michigan v. Tyler and Tompkins   May 30, 1978   436 U.S. 499
*Consttnl Law (Grossman) 804-809
Criminal Procedure (Lewis) 280-284
*Criminal Procedure (Lewis) 284-289
Law of Arrest (Creamer) 212-215
Significant Decisions 1977/78 34-36
PERIODICALS:
"Supreme Court Review (1978)." J Criml Law and Crimlgy 69:
552-562 Dec '78 (2).

3938. California v. Southland Royalty Co.   May 31, 1978   436 U.S. 519
El Paso Natural Gas Co. v. Southland
Royalty Co.
Federal Energy Regulatory Commission
v. Southland Royalty Co.
PERIODICALS:
"Permanent dedication upheld by high court." Oil and Gas J   76:
43 June 5 '78.
"Supreme Court speaks on gas service abandonment." Public Util-
ities 104: 46-49 Aug 2 '79 (3).
"US upheld in natural gas case by Supreme Court." Chemical
Marketing Reporter 213: 3, 65 June 5 '78.

3939. Zurcher v. Stanford Daily   May 31, 1978   436 U.S. 547
Bergna v. Stanford Daily
CQ Guide 448, 543-544
Cases Consttnl Law (Gunther) 1531-1532
*Consttnl Law (Maddex) 186-194
*Criminal Procedure (Lewis) 155-162
Editorials 1978 690-699
Handbook 478-485
*Historic Documents 1978 355-372
Law of Arrest (Creamer) 141-144
Law of Mass 641-647
*Mass Communications 395-399
*Modern Criml Procedure 69-74
Significant Decisions 1977/78 60-62
Sup Ct from Taft 308-309
Sup Ct Review 1978 237-241
PERIODICALS:
"Anti-press backlash in courts?" US News 84: 40 June 12 '78.
"Bill to protect the press," Robert F. Drinan. Nation 227: 102-
103 Aug 5 '78.
"Blow to freedom," Arthur S. Miller. Progressive 42: 8-9
Aug '78.
"Carter v. common sense." Natl R 31: 76, 80 Jan 19 '79.
"Constitutionality of congressional legislation to overrule Zurcher
v. Stanford daily," Michael E. Solimine. J Criml Law and
Crimlgy 71: 147-162 Summer '80.
"Editorials lambast court's search ruling." Editor and Pub 111:
7 June 10 '78.
*"Excerpts from opinions on newsroom search." Editor and Pub
111: 38, 47 June 10 '78.
"General spirit of the people," Helen K. Copley. Vital Speeches
46: 169-172 Jan 1 '80 (4).
"High court shoots holes in first and fourth amendments." Editor
and Pub 111: 6 June 10 '78.
"How the Supreme Court zaps the press," Sidney Zion. New York
11: 10-11 June 19 '78.

"Impact of the U.S. Supreme Court's decision in Zurcher v. the
Stanford Daily," Jerry W. Friedheim. Vital Speeches 44:
722-724 Sept 15 '78.
"Press and the courts: is news gathering shielded by the first
amendment?" Columbia Journalism R 17: 43-50 Nov '78.
"Press freedom's tarnished hero," Nathan Lewin. New Republic
180: 12-15 Jan 6 '79.
"Publishers seek remedial action on search ruling." Editor and
Pub 111: 9 June 10 '78.
"A right to rummage: police can frisk newsrooms, says the court."
Time 111: 101 June 12 '78.
"Searching for evidence." America 138: 476-477 June 17 '78.
"Searching the press," Jerrold Footlick and Lucy Howard. News-
week 91: 105-106 June 12 '78.
"Sleuths in the newsroom." Economist 267: 16-17 June 10 '78.
"Snooping about in the files." Nation 226: 748 June 24 '78.
"Supreme Court review (1978)." J Criml Law and Crimlgy 69:
528-537 Dec '78.
"Supreme Court upholds right of police with a warrant to search
newsrooms." Broadcasting 94: 56-57 June 5 '78.
"Supreme Court upholds search of Stanford newspaper's offices,"
Anne C. Roark. Chronicle of Higher Eductn 16: 12 June 19
'78.
"Supreme Court vs. the press," Gilda Morse. Graduate Woman
74: 27-29, 49 Jan/Feb '80 (3).
"Two bills introduced to protect news files," Miriam Ottenberg.
Editor and Pub 111: 9 June 10 '78.
"Zurcher: judicial dangers and legislative action," Charles M.
Mathias, Jr. Trial 15: 40-43 Jan '79.

3940. Robertson v. Wegmann   May 31, 1978 436 U.S. 584
       Significant Decisions 1977/78 91-92

3941. Monell v. Department of Social   June 6, 1978 436 U.S. 658
          Services of New York City
       *Civil Rights (Abernathy) 1980 12-18
       *Consttnl Law (Klein) 560-576
       *Labor Relations (Edwards) 916-922
       *Legislative (Hetzel) 297-305
       Significant Decisions 1977/78 84-86
       PERIODICALS:
       "Significant decisions in labor cases." Monthly Labor R 101: 53
       Oct '78.
       See also listing at 435 U.S. 247, entry no. 3905.

3942. Federal Communications Commission   June 12, 1978 436 U.S. 775
          v. National Citizens Committee
          for Broadcasting
       Channel Two Television v. National
          Citizens Committee ...
       National Association of Broadcasters v.
          Federal Communications Commission
       American Newspaper Publishers Association
          v. National Citizens Committee for
          Broadcasting
       Illinois Broadcasting Co., Inc. v. National
          Citizens Committee ...
       Post Co. v. National Citizens Committee ...
       CQ Guide 447

   *Cases Electronic 108-124
   Communication (Hemmer) v. 2, 291-292
   *Historic Documents 1978 419-432
   *Mass Communications 941-952
   Significant Decisions 1977/78 65-66
   Sup Ct Review 1978 1-37, 241-242
   PERIODICALS:
    "Crossowners win claim on crossownership." Broadcasting 94:
    27-28 June 19 '78.
    "Legal fallout from decision on crossownership." Broadcasting
    95: 35 July 17 '78.

3943. Burks v. United States   June 14, 1978 437 U.S. 1
   Modern Criml Procedure 418-419
   Significant Decisions 1977/78 29-30
   Sup Ct Review 1978 145-147, 150
   PERIODICALS:
    "Developments in the attachment of jeopardy," R. Foglia. J Criml
    Law and Crimlgy 70: 68-72 Spring '79 (3).

3944. Crist v. Bretz   June 14, 1978 437 U.S. 28
   *Criminal Justice (Way) 281-284
   *Criminal Procedure (Lewis) 354-359
   Modern Criml Procedure 388-389
   Significant Decisions 1977/78 31-32

3945. Sanabria v. United States   June 14, 1978 437 U.S. 54
   Significant Decisions 1977/78 30-31
   Sup Ct Review 1978 163-168

3946. United States v. Scott   June 14, 1978 437 U.S. 82
   *Am Consttnl Law (Saye) 541-545
   *Criminal Procedure (Lewis) 652-660
   *Modern Criml Procedure 401-409
   Significant Decisions 1977/78 26-27
   Sup Ct Review 1978 142-144
   PERIODICALS:
    "Developments in the attachment of jeopardy," R. Foglia. J Criml
    Law and Crimlgy 70: 68-72 Spring '79 (3).

3947. Exxon Corporation v. Governor June 14, 1978 437 U.S. 117
   of Maryland
   Shell Oil Co. v. Governor of Maryland
   Continental Oil Co. v. Governor of Maryland
   Gulf Oil Co. v. Governor of Maryland
   Ashland Oil, Inc. v. Governor of Maryland
   Cases Consttnl Law (Gunther) 313-316
   Significant Decisions 1977/78 146-148
   PERIODICALS:
    "Thinning out the pumps," David Pauly. Newsweek 91: 56 June
    26 '78.

3948. Tennessee Valley Authority v. Hill June 15, 1978 437 U.S. 153
   Editorials 1978 770-777
   *Historic Documents 1978 433-452
   *Legislative (Hetzel) 860-871
   Significant Decisions 1977/78 135-137
   PERIODICALS:
    "Ask not for whom Griffin Bell tolls--it's the snail darter," Bob
    Drogin. New Times 10: 24 May 15 '78.

"Fish vindicated. " New Republic 179: 5 July 1 '78.
"Fish wins. " Newsweek 91: 99 June 26 '78.
"Lessons to be learned from a bad law, " James J. Kilpatrick.
Nations Bus 66: 11-12 Aug '78.
"Mr. Bell argues his case. " Time 111: 72 May 1 '78.
"Snail darter halts dam--for now. " Sci News 113: 403 June 24
'78.
"Tellico Dam Case, " Ross Sandler. Environment 20: 4-5, 42-43
July '78.

3949. National Labor Relations Board   June 15, 1978 437 U.S. 214
v. Robbins Tire and Rubber Co.
Significant Decisions 1977/78 112-113
PERIODICALS:
"Significant decisions in labor cases. " Monthly Labor R 101: 41-
42 Nov '78.

3950. Moorman Manufacturing Co. v. Bair   June 15, 1978 437 U.S. 267
*Am Consttnl Law (Saye) 202-204
Significant Decisions 1977/78 152-153
PERIODICALS:
"Single factor sales formula and the Moorman Manufacturing Co.
decision, " J. Nelson Young. Taxes 56: 659-665 Nov '78.

3951. Oppenheimer Fund, Inc. v. Sanders   June 19, 1978 437 U.S. 340
Significant Decisions 1977/78 117-118
PERIODICALS:
"High court denies 3 class action pleas, " Steve Long. Electronic
News 24 [23]: 18 June 26 '78.

3952. Owen Equipment and Erection Co. v.   June 21, 1978 437 U.S. 365
Kroger
*Civil Procedure (Cound) 235-241
Significant Decisions 1977/78 118-119

3953. Mincey v. Arizona   June 21, 1978 437 U.S. 385
*Consttnl Law (Maddex) 160-164, 272-275
Criminal Procedure (Lewis) 205-209
*Criminal Procedure (Lewis) 209-215, 399-403
Significant Decisions 1977/78 33-34

3954. American Broadcasting Co. v. Writers   June 21, 1978 437 U.S. 411
Guild of America, West, Inc.
Association of Motion Picture and Television
Producers, Inc. v. Writers Guild of
America, West, Inc.
National Labor Relations Board v. Writers
Guild of America, West, Inc.
PERIODICALS:
"Hyphenates win at High Court. " Broadcasting 94: 64 June 20
'78.
"Significant decisions in labor cases. " Monthly Labor R 101: 60-
61 Sept '78.

3955. Zenith Radio Corporation v.   June 21, 1978 437 U.S. 443
United States
Editorials 1978 912-915
Significant Decisions 1977/78 129-131
Sup Ct Review 1978 297-312

PERIODICALS:
"Supreme Court rules against Zenith in Japanese television imports case." Merchandising 3: 121 July '78.
"Top court rule rebates in Japan not subsidies, " S. Long. Electronic News 24 [23]: 1, 24 June 26 '78.
"Zenith decisions settles a vital export subsidy issue. " Commerce America 3: inside front cover July 3 '78.

3956. Coopers and Lybrand v. Livesay   June 21, 1978 437 U. S. 463
        *Cases Pleading 1058-1067
        Significant Decisions 1977/78 115-116

3957. Gardner v. Westinghouse Broad-   June 21, 1978 437 U. S. 478
        casting Co.
        Significant Decisions 1977/78 116-117
        PERIODICALS:
        "High court denies three class action pleas, " Steve Long. Electronic News 24 [23]: 18 June 26 '78.
        "Significant decisions in labor cases. " Monthly Labor R 101: 61 Sept '78.

3958. Beth Israel Hospital v. National   June 22, 1978 437 U. S. 483
        Labor Relations Board
        Labor Relations (Taylor) 261
        Significant Decisions 1977/78 110
        PERIODICALS:
        "Significant decisions in labor cases. " Monthly Labor R 101: 40 Nov '78 (2).

3959. Hicklin v. Orbeck   June 22, 1978 437 U. S. 518
        Significant Decisions 1977/78 100-101
        Sup Ct Review 1979 79-81
        PERIODICALS:
        "Significant decisions in labor cases. " Monthly Labor R 101: 53-54 Oct '78.

3960. Eastex, Inc. v. National Labor   June 22, 1978 437 U. S. 556
        Relations Board
        Significant Decisions 1977/78 109
        PERIODICALS:
        "Significant decisions in labor cases. " Monthly Labor R 101: 40 Nov '78 (2).

3961. Parker v. Flook   June 22, 1978 437 U. S. 584
        *Legal Regulation 836-846
        Significant Decisions 1977/78 137

3962. Philadelphia v. New Jersey   June 23, 1978 437 U. S. 617
        Cases Consttnl Law (Gunther) 339-341
        *Consttnl Law (Lockhart) 328-330

3963. Will v. Calvert Fire Insurance Co.   June 23, 1978 437 U. S. 655
        Significant Decisions 1977/78 120-121

3964. Hutto v. Finney   June 23, 1978 437 U. S. 678
        *Civil Rights (Abernathy) 1980 211-216
        *Criminal Justice (Way) 522-525
        Significant Decisions 1977/78 86-87
        *US Prison Law v. 6, 238-258, 467-487

3965. Houchins v. KQED, Inc.   June 26, 1978 438 U.S. 1
      CQ Guide 444-445
      Cases Consttnl Law (Gunther) 1534-1536
      Communication (Hemmer) v. 2, 232-233
      Editorials 1978 916-920
      Handbook 496-504
      *Mass Communications 427-429
      Significant Decisions 1977/78 62-63
      Sup Ct Review 1978 242-247
      *US Prison Law v. 6, 411-430
      PERIODICALS:
      "Keep out; another rebuff for newsmen." Time 112: 73 July 10
          '78.
      "News media lose another in high court." Broadcasting 95: 64
          July 3 '78.

3966. United States v. Grayson   June 26, 1978 438 U.S. 41
      Criminal Procedure (Lewis) 627-630
      *Criminal Procedure (Lewis) 631-637
      *Leading Consttnl Cases 800-807
      Modern Criml Procedure 300
      Significant Decisions 1977/78 50-51
      *US Prison Law v. 6, 35-44

3967. Duke Power Co. v. Carolina   June 26, 1978 438 U.S. 51
          Environmental Study Group, Inc.
      U.S. Nuclear Regulatory Commission v.
          Carolina Environmental Study Group, Inc.
      *Admin Law (Gellhorn) 990-996
      Cases Consttnl Law (Gunther) 1642-1644
      Significant Decisions 1977/78 131-133
      PERIODICALS:
      "Nuclear law" the battle over atomic power in the courts," Sidney
          Bernstein. Trial 16: 28-32, 61 Apr '80 (2).

3968. Penn Central Transportation Co.   June 26, 1978 438 U.S. 104
          v. New York (City)
      *Consttnl Law (Lockhart) 455-464
      Editorials 1978 925-928
      *Historic Documents 1978 453-465
      Significant Decisions 1977/78 148-149
      PERIODICALS:
      "Saving a station; Grand Central wins in court." Time 112: 26
          July 10 '78.
      "Supreme Court validates landmark laws as community tools for
          building conservation," William Hickman. Architectural Record
          164: 34 Aug '78.

3969. Franks v. Delaware   June 26, 1978 438 U.S. 154
      *Consttnl Law (Maddex) 123-126
      Criminal Procedure (Lewis) 163-166
      *Criminal Procedure (Lewis) 166-172
      Law of Arrest (Creamer) 134-138
      Significant Decisions 1977/78 48-49

3970. Swisher v. Brady   June 28, 1978 438 U.S. 204
      Significant Decisions 1977/78 32-33
      PERIODICALS:
      "Supreme Court review (1978)." J Criml Law and Crimlgy 69:
          563-573 Dec '78 (2).

3971. Allied Structural Steel Co. v.   June 28, 1978 438 U.S. 234
        Spannaus
        *Consttnl Law (Lockhart) 467-475
        Significant Decisions 1977/78 143-144
        Sup Ct Review 1979 110-113
        PERIODICALS:
        "Significant decisions in labor cases." Monthly Labor R 101: 40-
        41 Nov '78.

3972. Regents of University of California   June 28, 1978 438 U.S. 265
        v. Bakke
        *Am Consttnl Law (Saye) 446-458
        *Am Consttnl Law (Shapiro) 599-614
        *Basic Cases 86-108
        Bakke (Dreyfuss).
        Bakke (Sindler).
        CQ Guide 604-605
        *Cases Civil Liberties 351-366
        *Cases Consttnl Law (Cushman) 581-595
        *Cases Consttnl Law (Gunther) 804-834
        Consttnl Law (Grossman) 578-584
        *Consttnl Law (Grossman) 584-600
        *Consttnl Law (Lockhart) 1335-1362
        *Consttnl Rights (Kemerer) 585-599
        *Courts Judges 635-652
        Editorials 1977 1214-1223
        Editorials 1978 818-837
        From Brown 253-306
        *Historic Documents 1978 467-492
        Judiciary (Abraham) 144-146
        Labor Relations (Edwards) 880-882
        Law and Education 211-212
        *Legislative (Hetzel) 191-200
        Significant Decisions 1977/78 78-82
        Sup Ct (Forte) 98, 101-102
        Sup Ct from Taft 297-300
        PERIODICALS:
        "After caution comes red: the Bakke decision and its threat to
           black educational institutions," R. Jean Simms-Brown. Crisis
           86: 67-69 Feb '79.
        "Aftermath of Bakke decision." USA Today 107: 6-7 Feb '79.
        "Bakke battle," Jerrold K. Footlick and Diane Camper. Newsweek
           90: 45-46 Oct 24 '77.
        "Bakke brief," Jerrold K. Footlick and Diane Camper. Newsweek
           90: 97 Sept 19 '77.
        "Bakke brief," Nathan Lewin. New Republic 177: 17-18 Oct 1
           '77.
        "Bakke case," B. Jeanne Fisher. J Col Student Personnel Pt. I:
           the issues 19: 174-179 Mar '78; Pt. II: an analysis and
           implications 20: 264-271 May '79.
        "Bakke case: affirmative distractions," Stephanie A. Cleverdon.
           Progressive 41: 26-29 Dec '77.
        "Bakke case: are racial quotas defensible?" Charles Lawrence,
           3rd. Sat R 5: 10-16 Oct 15 '77. Same: Current 198: 3-
           11 Dec '77. Reaction: Sat R 5: 5 Dec 10 '77.
        "Bakke case: how to argue about reverse discrimination," Stan
           Pottinger. Ms 6: 59-60 Jan '78.
        "Bakke case; just the beginning," Norman Cousins. Sat R 5: 4
           Nov 26 '77.

"Bakke case: question of special minority admissions programs, " John Walsh. Science 197: 25-27 July 1 '77. Reaction: 197: 514 Aug 5 '77.

"Bakke case: testing the liberal alliance, " Paul Delaney. Nation 225: 498-499 Nov 12 '77.

"Bakke conundrum. " Nation 225: 322-324 Oct 8 '77.

"Bakke decision doesn't bar expansion of affirmative action, HEW concludes, " Lorenzo Middleton. Chronicle of Higher Education 19: 11 Oct 15 '79.

"The Bakke decision: illusion and reality in the Supreme Court, " Herbert Shapiro. Crisis 86: 62-66 Feb '79.

"Bakke decision: implications for Black educational and professional opportunities, " Thaddeus H. Spratlen. J Negro Eductn 48: 449-456 Fall '79.

"The Bakke decision: mixed signals from the court, " William Hazard. Phi Delta Kappan 60: 16-19 Sept '78.

"Bakke in perspective: an exercise in judicial wisdom, " G. M. Kendrigan. Trial 15: 48-50 Aug '79.

"Bakke in the press--justice was done, " Bernard Bard. Editor and Pub 111: 17 Nov 18 '78; 111: 14, 16, 24 Nov 25 '78.

"Bakke: pro and con. " Phi Delta Kappan 59: 447-455 Mar '78 (National Education Association amicus curiae brief pp. 447-450; American Federation of Teachers amicus curiae brief pp. 451-455).

"Bakke ruling seen having little effect, " Lorenzo Middleton. Chronicle of Higher Eductn 18: 1, 13 July 30 '79.

"Bakke: some changes, " Susan Fraker, Newsweek 92: 29-30 July 17 '78.

"Bakke: some views. " Civil Rights Dig 10: 10-19 Summer '78.

"Bakke: spelling out the rules. " Newsweek 94: 83 Oct 22 '79.

"Bakke v. University of California, " John H. Bunzel. Commentary 63: 59-64 Mar '77. Reaction: 64: 8, 10-12 July '77.

"Campuses given little guidance on Bakke rulings, " Cheryl M. Fields. Chronicle of Higher Eductn 17: 1, 12-13 Sept 18 '78.

"Conflicting reactions to the Bakke decision. " Chronicle of Higher Eductn 16: 12 July 3 '78.

"Courts v. self-government, " Paul H. Connolly. Nat R 29: 1225-1228 Oct 28 '77.

"Disadvantaged groups, individual rights. " New Republic 177: 5-9 Oct 15 '77. Reprinted in: Current 198: 11-16 Dec '77.

"Efforts in Bakke case called less than competent, " Beverly T. Watkins. Chronicle of Higher Eductn 14: 1, 4 Apr 4 '77.

"Essay on the unfairness of life, " Lance Morrow. Horizon 20: 34-37 Dec '77.

"Fateful court test. " US News 83: 21-22, 94-96, 112 Oct 24 '77.

"Furor over reverse discrimination, " Jerrold K. Footlick and others. Newsweek 90: 52-55, 57-58 Sept 26 '77.

"The good news of Bakke, " John M. Stevens. Phi Delta Kappan 59: 23-26 Sept '77.

"The government decides to walk a legal tightrope, " Cheryl M. Fields. Chronicle of Higher Eductn 15: 1, 3-4 Sept 19, '77.

"High court turns to landmark race-quota case. " US News 83: 39 Sept 26 '77.

"How to resolve the Bakke case, " Meg Greenfield. Newsweek 90: 128 Oct 24 '77.

"In Bakke's victory, no death knell for affirmative action," Cheryl M. Fields. Chronicle of Higher Eductn 16: 1, 12 July 3, '78.

"In the wake of Bakke," Denton L. Watson. Crisis 86: 51-52, 54-61 Feb '79.

"Is a Bakke compromise possible?" Phi Delta Kappan 59: 225, 270 Dec '77.

"Issue before the court: who gets ahead in America?" McGeorge Bundy. Atlantic 240: 41-50, 53-54 Nov '77. Reaction: 241: 75-80 Jan '78.

"Justice department plans to back U. of California in reverse-bias suit." Chronicle of Higher Eductn 14: 10 July 25 '77.

*"Justice Thurgood Marshall's opinion in the Bakke case." Crisis 86: 45-50 Feb '79.

"MBE funding in the construction industry: a constitutional question of reverse discrimination," Peter G. Kilgore. Labor Law J 30: 289-294 May '79.

"Major changes in school integration litigation, 1954-1979," Frank Brown. Eductnl Admin Q 15: 76-97 Spring '79 (3).

"Minority-admissions programs after Bakke," John Sexton. Harvard Eductnl R 49: 313-339 Aug '79.

"Must principles collide?" America 137: 121 Sept 10 '77.

"NAACP statement on implications of the Bakke decision." Crisis 86: 41-43 Feb '79.

"Opening shots fired in legal challenge to special minority admissions programs," Cheryl M. Fields. Chronicle of Higher Eductn 14: 7 July 5 '77.

"Parable of the talents," Ben L. Martin. Harper's Mag 256: 12, 18, 21-24 Jan '78.

"Parties in Bakke case submit new briefs requested by court," Cheryl M. Fields. Chronicle of Higher Eductn 15: 11 Nov 21 '77.

"Preliminary report on the Bakke case," William Van Alstyne. AAUP Bul 64: 286-297 Dec '78. Reaction: Academe 65: 49-59 Feb '79.

"Professional education after Bakke," W. Todd Furniss. Eductnl Rec 60: 137-145 Spring '79.

"Pros and cons of the Bakke case: who deserves to become a doctor?" Karl Neumann. Am Druggist 177: 50 Feb '78.

"Question of quotas." Economist 264: 52, 55 Sept 24 '77.

"Race and class: the basic issue of the Bakke case," Robert Gahringer. Ethics 90: 97-114 Oct '79.

"Racial quota at med school," William F. Buckley, Jr. Natl R 29: 904-905 Aug 5 '77.

"Reflections on Bakke and beyond," Richard J. Regan. Thought 54: 58-66 Mar '79.

"Reverse discrimination," Jerrold K. Footlick. Newsweek 89: 66 Mar 7 '77.

"Schools and the law--Bakke: implications for federal affirmative action," Thomas Flygare. Phi Delta Kappan 59: 418-419 Feb '78.

"Semantics of the Bakke decision," Gertrude Block. ETC 35: 348-353 Winter '78.

"Significant decisions in labor cases." Monthly Labor R 101: 46 Aug '78.

"Some thoughts on the Powell opinion in Bakke," Matthew W. Finkin. Academe 65: 192-196 Apr '79.

"Student Bakke: tough going," Eileen Keerdoja and others. Newsweek 93: 18 Apr 30 '79.

"Supreme Court and quotas," J. S. Fuerst and Roy Petty. Christian Century 94: 52 Oct 19 '77 (5).
"Supreme Court at Delphi," Robert Shrum. New Times 11: 46-48, 50 Aug 7 '78.
"Supreme Court calls for additional briefs in reverse-bias case," Cheryl M. Fields. Chronicle of Higher Eductn 15: 14 Oct 25 '77.
"Supreme Court: setback for affirmative action." Black Enterprise 9: 30 Mar '79.
"Supreme Court will review allege 'reverse bias' in admissions," Anne C. Roark. Chronicle of Higher Eductn 14: 1 Feb 28 '77.
"Text of HEW's interpretation of Bakke." Chronicle of Higher Eductn 19: 11-12 Oct 15 '79.
"Text of Justice Department's brief in Bakke case." Chronicle of Higher Eductn 15: 9-12 Sept 26 '77.
"Top court to rule on anti-white bias," Michael Binyon. Times Eductnl Supp 3222: 14 Mar 4 '77.
"Unequal but fair; the morality of justice by quota," Daniel C. Maguire. Commonweal 104: 647-652 Oct 14 '77. Reaction 105: 29, 31 Jan 6 '78.
"United States urges Supreme Court to send Bakke case back to California," Cheryl M. Fields. Chronicle of Higher Eductn 15: 9 Sept 26 '77.
"Wait begins for ruling on Bakke case," Cheryl M. Fields. Chronicle of Higher Eductn 15: 5 Oct 17 '77.
"What rights for whites?" Time 110: 95, 97-98 Oct 24 '77.
"What the Court said in two 5-to-4 rulings on the Bakke case." Chronicle of Higher Eductn 16: 3-12 July 3 '78.
"White/Caucasian--and rejected," Robert Lindsey. NY Times Mag p. 42-47, 95 Apr 3 '77.
"Would-be doctor." Time 108: 51 Nov 29 '76.

3973. United States v. United States   June 29, 1978 438 U.S. 422
        Gypsum Co.
        *Criminal Law (Dix) 504-512
        Significant Decisions 1977/78 127-128

3974. Butz v. Economou   June 29, 1978 438 U.S. 478
        *Admin Law (Gellhorn) 1091-1101
        *Am Consttnl Law (Saye) 77-84
        *Labor Relations (Edwards) 927-935
        Significant Decisions 1977/78 82-84

3975. Furnco Construction Corporation   June 29, 1978 438 U.S. 567
        v. Waters
        *Consttnl Law (Grossman) 571-575
        Sup Ct Review 1979 30

3976. Lockett v. Ohio   July 3, 1978   438 U.S. 586
        *Am Consttnl Law (Saye) 546-549
        *Consttnl Law (Grossman) 953-958
        *Criminal Law (Dix) 62-74
        *Criminal Procedure (Lewis) 602-614
        Editorials 1978 921-924
        *Historic Documents 1978 495-514
        Significant Decisions 1977/78 46-47
        PERIODICALS:
        "Death row dilemma," Jerrold C. Footlick and Diane Camper.
        Newsweek 92: 36 July 17 '78.

3977. Bell v. Ohio   July 3, 1978   438 U.S. 637
       Editorials 1978 921-924

3978. Federal Communications Commission   July 3, 1978   438 U.S. 726
          v. Pacifica Foundation
       CQ Guide 447
       *Cases Consttnl Law (Gunther) 1248-1258
       *Cases Electronic 302-319
        Communication (Hemmer) v. 2, 283-285
       *Consttnl Law (Grossman) 1269-1275
       *Consttnl Law (Lockhart) 1058-1071
        Editorials 1978 904-911
       *Historic Documents 1978 515-531
       *Mass Communications 889-900
        Mass Media (Francois) 455-457
       *Pornography 151-175
        Significant Decisions 1977/78 66-68
        Sup Ct Review 1978 248-250
       PERIODICALS:
       "Dollars for decency." Rolling Stones p. 17 Sept 7 '78.
       "Filthy words decision." America 139: 44-45 July 29 '78.
       "Seven dirty words: Supreme Court ruling raises fear of censor-
          ship," Susan Wagner. Pub Weekly 214: 84-85 July 17 '78.
       "Supreme Court review (1978)." J Criml Law and Crimlgy 69:
          474-483 Dec '78 (2).
       "WBAI ruling: Supreme Court saves the worst for the last."
          Broadcasting 95: 20-22 July 10 '78.
       "Which way the wind blows at the FCC after WBAI." Broadcasting
          95: 31-32 July 24 '78.

3979. Dougherty County Board of Education   Nov 28, 1978   439 U.S. 32
          v. White
       Significant Decisions 1978/79 96-97
       PERIODICALS:
       "Significant decisions in labor cases." Monthly Labor R 102: 61
          Apr '79.

3980. Holt Civic Club v. Tuscaloosa   Nov 28, 1978   439 U.S. 60
       Significant Decisions 1978/79 95-96

3981. New Motor Vehicle Board v. Orrin   Dec 5, 1978   439 U.S. 96
          W. Fox Co.
       Northern California Motor Car Dealers
          Association v. Orrin W. Fox Co.
       Significant Decisions 1978/79 159-160

3982. Rakas v. Illinois   Dec 5, 1978   439 U.S. 128
       CQ Guide 547
       *Criminal Justice (Way) 125-132
        Criminal Procedure (Lewis) 311-314
       *Criminal Procedure (Lewis) 315-324
       *Historic Documents 1978 753-764
        Law of Arrest (Creamer) 351-355
       *Modern Criml Procedure 210-219
        Significant Decisions 1978/79 28-29
       PERIODICALS:
       "Supreme Court review." J Criml Law and Crimlgy 70: 498-509
          Dec '79.

3983. Califano v. Aznavorian   Dec 11, 1978   439 U.S. 170
       Significant Decisions 1978/79 128-129

3984. Corbitt v. New Jersey   Dec 11, 1978   439 U.S. 212
       *Modern Criml Procedure 308-310
       Significant Decisions 1978/79 45-46
       PERIODICALS:
       "Supreme Court review." J Criml Law and Crimlgy 70: 474-481
       Dec '79.

3985. Lalli v. Lalli   Dec 11, 1978   439 U.S. 259
       *Cases Consttnl Law (Gunther) 903-908
       Significant Decisions 1978/79 120-121

3986. Michigan v. Doran   Dec 18, 1978   439 U.S. 282
       Significant Decisions 1978/79 46-47

3987. Parklane Hosiery Co. v. Shore   Jan 9, 1979   439 U.S. 322
       *Cases Pleading 505-521
       *Civil Procedure (Cound) 1102-1109
       Significant Decisions 1978/79 146-148

3988. Duren v. Missouri   Jan 9, 1979   439 U.S. 357
       Significant Decisions 1978/79 53-54
       PERIODICALS:
       "Supreme Court review." J Criml Law and Crimlgy 70: 490-
       497 Dec '79 (2).

3989. Colautti v. Franklin   Jan 9, 1979   439 U.S. 379
       Cases Consttnl Law (Gunther) 614-617
       Significant Decisions 1978/79 137-138

3990. Givhan v. Western Line Consolidated   Jan 9, 1979   439 U.S. 410
       School District
       *Consttn (Morris) 605-607
       *Labor Relations (Edwards) 776-778
       *School Law (Alexander) 542-544
       Significant Decisions 1978/79 91-92
       Sup Ct Review 1979 217-249
       PERIODICALS:
       "Private communications protected, court rules." Chronicle of
       Higher Eductn 17 [18]: 17 Jan 15 '79.
       "Schools and the law--teachers' private expression: constitutional-
       ity protected, but with a limitation," Thomas J. Flygare. Phi
       Delta Kappan 60: 602-603 Apr '79.
       "Schools and the law--The free speech rights of teachers: public
       and private expression," Thomas J. Flygare. Phi Delta Kappan
       60: 242-243 Nov '78 (2).
       "Significant decisions in labor cases." Monthly Labor R 102:
       61-62 Apr '79.

3991. Leis v. Flynt   Jan 15, 1979   439 U.S. 438
       Significant Decisions 1978/79 118
       PERIODICALS:
       "Traveling bar; decision against right to use out-of-state lawyers."
       Nation 228: 228 May 3 '79.

3992. Federal Energy Regulatory   Jan 16, 1979   439 U.S. 508
       Commission v. Pennzoil Producing Co.

PERIODICALS:
"FERC's special rate relief authority upheld." Oil and Gas J   77:
34   Jan 22 '79.
"Supreme Court speaks on gas service abandonment." Public Utilities   104:   46-49   Aug 2 '79 (3).

3993.   Thor Power Tool Co. v. Commis-   Jan 16, 1979   439 U.S. 522
sioner of Internal Revenue
PERIODICALS:
"Can GAAP still support inventory valuation after Thor?" John H.
Dasburg and C. Richard Morehead.   J Accountancy   148:   68-
76   Oct '79.
"Cash flow and inventory write-downs: the Supreme Court changes
the rules," John F. Benedik.   Pub Weekly   215:   75   Apr 9 '79.
"High court upholds IRS in inventory valuation case," Roberta
Wyper.   Electronic News   25:   supp 3   Feb 5 '79.
"IRS ruling is seen threatening supplies of many scholarly and pro-
fessional books," Ellen K. Coughlin.   Chronicle of Higher Edu-
ctn   21:   1, 22   Sept 29 '80.
"IRS' tough new rules under Thor Power: how they work; what
they mean; how to cope," J. N. Bush and others.   J Taxation
52:   194-201   Apr '80.
"Inventory valuation after Thor Power Tool; analyzing the Supreme
Court decision and its impact," John H. Dasburg and others.
J Taxation 50:   200-205   Apr '79.
"Inventory write-downs and Thor Power Tool," Joseph B. Mihalov.
Taxes   57:   384-388   June '79.
"Inventory write-downs; can you write off obsolete stock?"   Indus-
trial Distributor   69:   83-84, 86, 88   Oct '79.
"Inventory write-downs: why some formulas won't work."   Indus-
trial Distributor   69:   73-74, 77   Sept '79.
"Thor decision puts squeeze on cash flow," Neal J. Menachem and
Howard B. Lucas.   Credit and Financial Mgt   82:   30-31   Sept
'80.
"Thor's sledgehammer blow against books--the case for repealing
a tax law," Daniel N. Fischel.   Pub Weekly   218:   17-18   Aug
1 '80.

3994.   International Brotherhood of Teamsters, Jan 16, 1979   439 U.S. 551
Chauffeurs, Warehousemen and
Helpers v. Daniel
Significant Decisions 1978/79   168-169
PERIODICALS:
"John Daniel's pension troubles are over," Bernie Swart.   Fleet
Owner   74:   181   Mar '79.
"Pensions decision."   Bests R (Life ed)   79:   76   Feb '79.
"Regulatory threat hanging over pensions."   Bus Wk   p. 46   Oct
9 '78.
"Significant decisions in labor cases."   Monthly Labor R   102:
62-63   Mar '79.
"Supreme Court in Daniel leaves open possibility that some plans
may be subject to securities laws," Lawrence J. Hass.   J
Taxation 50:   263-267   May '79.
"Supreme Court's decision on the Daniel case: implications for
pension regulations," Susan M. Phillips.   J Risk and Insurance
47:   157-164   Mar '80.

3995.   Friedman v. Rogers   Feb 21, 1979   440 U.S. 1

Rogers v. Friedman
Texas Optometric Association
 v. Rogers
Cases Consttnl Law (Gunther) 1394-1395
Significant Decisions 1978/79 92-93

3996. Director, Office of Workers' Com- Feb 21, 1979 440 U.S. 29
   pensation Programs v. Rasmussen
   General Control, Inc. v. Rasmussen
   PERIODICALS:
   "Court ruling could hike shipper work comp bills," Jerry Geisel.
    Bus Insurance 13: 6 Mar 5 '79.

3997. Great Atlantic and Pacific Tea Co. Feb 22, 1979 440 U.S. 69
   v. Federal Trade Commission
   Significant Decisions 1978/79 165-167
   PERIODICALS:
   "A & P wins showdown at Supreme Court corral," L. E. Densford.
    Progressive Grocer 58: 31 May '79.
   "Supreme Court shields buyers from liability." Purchasing 86:
    19 May 19 '79.

3998. Vance v. Bradley Feb 22, 1979 440 U.S. 93
   Cases Consttnl Law (Gunther) 701-703
   Significant Decisions 1978/79 66-67
   PERIODICALS:
   "Significant decisions in labor cases." Monthly Labor R 102: 53
    May '79.

3999. Montana v. United States Feb 22, 1979 440 U.S. 147
   Significant Decisions 1978/79 148-150

4000. Illinois State Board of Elections Feb 22, 1979 440 U.S. 173
   v. Socialist Workers Party
   Significant Decisions 1978/79 98

4001. Harrah Independent School District Feb 26, 1979 440 U.S. 194
   v. Martin
   *Consttn (Morris) 667-670
   PERIODICALS:
   "Mandatory continuing education and teachers," David Lisman.
    Phi Delta Kappan 62: 125-126 Oct '80.

4002. Group Life and Health Insurance Co. Feb 27, 1979 440 U.S. 205
   aka Blue Shield of Texas v.
   Royal Drug Co., dba Royal Pharmacy
   of Castle Hills
   Significant Decisions 1978/79 164-165
   PERIODICALS:
   "Marty Rubin--man of the decade," James G. Dickinson. Drug
    Topics 123: 31-34, 50 July 2 '79.
   "Rule against Blues in pharmacy case," Mary Jane Fisher. Natl
    Underwriter (Life ed) 83: 1, 22 Mar 3 '79. Same: Natl
    Underwriter (Property ed) 83: 28-29 Mar 9 '79.
   "Supreme Court OKs suit against service contract," Jerry Geisel.
    Bus Insurance 13: 6 Mar 19 '79.
   "Supreme Court ruling may bring switch by 3rd parties to usual-
    &-customary." Am Druggist 179: 7, 79, 81 Apr '79.
   "Top court draws insurer blood again." Natl Underwriter (Property
    ed) 83: 1, 8 Mar 9 '79.

4003.   Aronson v. Quick Point Pencil Co.   Feb 28, 1979   440 U.S. 257
        *Legal Regulation 587-593
        Significant Decisions 1978/79 167-168

4004.   Orr v. Orr   Mar 5, 1979   440 U.S. 268
        *Consttnl Law (Lockhart) 1408-1409
        Editorials 1979 270-274
        *Historic Documents 1979 193-206
        Significant Decisions 1978/79 71-72
        PERIODICALS:
        "Equalimony," Tom Morganthau and Diane Camper.   Newsweek
        93: 40 Mar 19 '79.

4005.   Detroit Edison Co. v. National   Mar 5, 1979   440 U.S. 301
        Labor Relations Board
        Sup Ct Review 1979 47-48
        PERIODICALS:
        "DECo. v. NLRB, and the consequences of open testing in industry,"
        William L. Roskind.   Personnel Psychology 33: 3-9 Spring
        '80.
        "Significant decisions in labor cases." Monthly Labor R 102: 44
        June '79.
        "War on testing: Detroit Edison in perspective," Barbara Lerner.
        Personnel Psychology 33: 11-16 Spring '80.

4006.   Quern v. Jordan   Mar 5, 1979   440 U.S. 332
        Significant Decisions 1978/79 101-102

4007.   Scott v. Illinois   Mar 5, 1979   440 U.S. 367
        *Historic Documents 1979 207-214
        *Modern Criml Procedure 8-10
        Significant Decisions 1978/79 59

4008.   Lake Country Estates, Inc. v.   Mar 5, 1979   440 U.S. 391
        Tahoe Regional Planning Agency
        Significant Decisions 1978/79 102-103

4009.   Nevada v. Hall   Mar 5, 1979   440 U.S. 410
        Significant Decisions 1978/79 103-105

4010.   New Jersey v. Portash   Mar 20, 1979   440 U.S. 450
        Law of Arrest (Creamer) 426-430
        Significant Decisions 1978/79 56
        PERIODICALS:
        "Supreme Court review." J Criml Law and Crimlgy 70: 424-432
        Dec '79.

4011.   National Muffler Dealers Association   Mar 20, 1979   440 U.S. 472
        v. United States
        PERIODICALS:
        "Supreme Court's holding in National Muffler precludes exemption
        for franchises associations," Robert R. Statham and Richard W.
        Buek. J Taxation 51: 80-82 Aug '79.

4012.   National Labor Relations Board v.   Mar 21, 1979   440 U.S. 490
        Catholic Bishop of Chicago
        Significant Decisions 1978/79 154-155
        PERIODICALS:
        "Catholic schools and teachers' unions," Douglas Laycock. Amer-
        ica 140: 406-408 May 19 '79.

"If you want us to teach: Catholic teacher unionization without the
NLRB," Harold J. T. Isenberg. America 141: 260-262 Nov
3 '79.
"NLRB: back to the bishops." America 140: 268-269 Apr 7
'79.
"Schools and the law--teacher unions not required at parochial
schools," Thomas J. Flygare. Phi Delta Kappan 60: 747-748
June '79.
"Significant decisions in labor cases." Monthly Labor R 102: 52-
53 May '79.
"Supreme Court limits labor's relations." Christianity Today 23:
41 Apr 20 '79.

4013. New York Telephone Co. v. New   Mar 21, 1979 440 U.S. 519
York State Department of Labor
Significant Decisions 1978/79 153-154
PERIODICALS:
"High court gives approval to jobless pay for strikers." Engineer-
ing News 202: 14 Mar 29 '79.
"Should strikers receive unemployment insurance benefits?" Harry
H. Rains. Labor Law J 30: 700-708 Nov '79.
"Significant decisions in labor cases." Monthly Labor R 102: 52
May '79.

4014. New York City Transit Authority   Mar.21, 1979 440 U.S. 568
v. Beazer
Cases Consttnl Law (Gunther) 703-704
*Civil Rights (Abernathy) 1980 459-463
Significant Decisions 1978/79 67-69
+US Prison Law v. 6, 618-639
PERIODICALS:
"Significant decisions in labor cases." Monthly Labor R 102: 53-
54 May '79.

4015. County of Los Angeles v. Davis   Mar 27, 1979 440 U.S. 625
PERIODICALS:
"Significant decisions in labor cases." Monthly Labor R 102: 43
June '79.

4016. Delaware v. Prouse   Mar 27, 1979 440 U.S. 648
*Criminal Justice (Way) 112-116
Editorials 1979 392-396
Law of Arrest (Creamer) 274-279
Significant Decisions 1978/79 36-37
PERIODICALS:
"Curbing random traffic checks; outlawing spot traffic searches."
Newsweek 93: 70 Apr 9 '79.
"Highway privacy." Time 113: 74 Apr 9 '79.
"Supreme Court review." J Criml Law and Crimlgy 70: 498-509
Dec '79.

4017. Federal Communications Commis-   Apr 2, 1979   440 U.S. 689
sion v. Midwest Video Corporation
American Civil Liberties Union v.
Federal Communications Commission
National Black Media Coalition v. Midwest
Video Corporation
*Cases Electronic 441-451

PERIODICALS:
"Cable and broadcasters win one at Supreme Court." Broadcasting
96: 59-60 Apr 9 '79.

4018. United States v. Caceres   Apr 2, 1979   440 U.S. 741
Law of Arrest (Creamer) 318-322
Significant Decisions 1978/79 42-43

4019. Broadcast Music, Inc. v. Columbia   Apr 17, 1979   441 U.S. 1
Broadcasting System
American Society of Composers and
Publishers v. Columbia Broadcasting
System
Significant Decisions 1978/79 162-164

4020. Ambach v. Norwick   Mar 17, 1979   441 U.S. 68
*Cases Consttnl Law (Gunther) 891-894
*Consttnl Law (Lockhart) 1384-1388
*School Law (Alexander) 572-575
Significant Decisions 1978/79 65
PERIODICALS:
"Agents of the state," John W. Donohue. America 140: 453
June 2 '79 (2).
"Impact of High Court's latest rulings." US News 86: 62 Apr
30 '79.
"Significant decisions in labor cases." Monthly Labor R 102: 40-
41 July '79.

4021. Gladstone, Realtors v. Bellwood   Apr 17, 1979   441 U.S. 91
Significant Decisions 1978/79 144-146

4022. Burch v. Louisiana   Apr 17, 1979   441 U.S. 130
*Criminal Justice (Way) 378-380
*Historic Documents 1979 263-268
Significant Decisions 1978/79 55
PERIODICALS:
"Supreme Court review." J Criml Law and Crimlgy 70: 490-497
Dec '79.

4023. Herbert v. Lando   Apr 18, 1979   441 U.S. 153
CQ Guide 435
*Consttnl Law (Grossman) 1157-1164
Editorials 1979 437-446
*Historic Documents 1979 285-318
*Mass Communications 296-309
Significant Decisions 1978/79 85-87
PERIODICALS:
"Chilling effect; libel law and the Supreme Court," Cynthia Bolbach.
Christian Century 96: 729-733 July 18 '79.
"Code duello," Murray Kempton. Natl R 31: 754-756 June 8
'79 (2).
"Condensed version of court's opinions in Herbert v. Lando and
CBS libel case." Editor and Pub 112: 44, 46, 52, 54, 56,
58, 60, 62 Apr 28 '79.
"Crying wolf!" George F. Will. Newsweek 93: 104 Apr 30 '79.
"General spirit of the people," Helen K. Copley. Vital Speeches
46: 169-172 Jan 1 '80 (4).
"High court opens the minds of journalists to investigation."
Broadcasting 96: 25-27 Apr 23 '79.

"How editors feel about Lando ruling. " Editor and Pub 112: 24
May 5 '79.
"Impact of High Court's latest rulings. " US News 86: 62 Apr
30 '79.
"Journalists' privilege, " Michael Kinsley. New Republic 180: 12-
14 May 12 '79.
"Justices rule, 6 to 3, to open editing process. " Editor and Pub
112: 102 Apr 21 '79.
"Malicious minds, " A. Neier. Nation 228: 485-486 May 5 '79.
"Mind of a journalist. " Time 113: 53-54 Apr 30 '79.
"No quarter from this court, " Bruce W. Sanford. Columbia
Journalism R 18: 59-63 Sept '79 (4).
"Not free to libel. " Economist 271: 62 Apr 21 '79.
"Press and its critics, " William G. Mullen. Public Relations Q
24: 30-31 Summer '79.
"Probing a newsman's mind, " David Gelman and Diane Camper.
Newsweek 93: 77 Apr 30 '79.
"Question of motives. " America 140: 365 May 5 '79.
"Supreme Court vs. the press, " Gilda Morse. Graduate Woman
74: 27-29, 49 Jan/Feb '80 (3).
"60 Minutes on trial, " Michael Kramer. New York 12: 10 May
7 '79.

4024. Douglas Oil Co. v. Petrol Stops   Apr 18, 1979   441 U.S. 211
Northwest
Significant Decisions 1978/79 150-151
PERIODICALS:
"Supreme Court review. " J Criml Law and Crimlgy 70: 424-432
Dec '79.

4025. Dalia v. United States   Apr 18, 1979   441 U.S. 238
*Consttnl Law (Grossman) 856-860
*Historic Documents 1979 269-284
Law of Arrest (Creamer) 328-332
*Modern Criml Procedure 134-136
Significant Decisions 1978/79 29-31

4026. Chrysler Corporation v. Brown   Apr 18, 1979   441 U.S. 281
*Admin Law (Gellhorn) 608-617
Significant Decisions 1978/79 171-173
Sup Ct Review 1979 52-53, 84-85

4027. Hughes v. Oklahoma   Apr 24, 1979   441 U.S. 322
*Cases Consttnl Law (Gunther) 328-332
Significant Decisions 1978/79 156-157

4028. Parham v. Hughes   Apr 24, 1979   441 U.S. 347
Significant Decisions 1978/79 73-75

4029. North Carolina v. Butler   Apr 24, 1979   441 U.S. 309
*Criminal Justice (Way) 326-329
Law of Arrest (Creamer) 421-426
Modern Criml Procedure 159
Significant Decisions 1978/79 41-42

4030. Caban v. Mohammed   Apr 24, 1979   441 U.S. 380
Significant Decisions 1978/79 72-73

4031. Addington v. Texas   Apr 30, 1979   441 U.S. 418

*Historic Documents 1979 335-344
Significant Decisions 1978/79 118-120

4032.   Japan Line, Ltd. v. County of   Apr 30, 1979   441 U. S. 434
        Los Angeles
        Significant Decisions 1978/79 157-159
        PERIODICALS:
        "State's power to tax foreign commerce dominates Supreme Court's
        1978 agenda," Walter Hellerstein.   J Taxation   51: 106-111
        Aug '79.

4033.   Smith v. Arkansas State Highway   Apr 30, 1979   441 U. S. 463
        Employees
        *Labor Relations (Edwards) 103-104
        PERIODICALS:
        "Significant decisions in labor cases."   Monthly Labor R   102: 41
        July '79.

4034.   Ford Motor Co. (Chicago Stamping   May 14, 1979   441 U. S. 488
        Plant) v. National Labor Relations Board
        PERIODICALS:
        "Significant decisions in labor cases."   Monthly Labor R   102: 58
        Sept '79.

4035.   Bell v. Wolfish   May 14, 1979   441 U. S. 520
        *Consttnl Law (Grossman) 968-977
        Law of Arrest (Creamer) 337-341
        Significant Decisions 1978/79 123-126
        *US Prison Law v. 6, 139-179
        PERIODICALS:
        "Supreme Court review."   J Criml Law and Crimlgy   70: 482-489
        Dec '79.

4036.   Cannon v. University of Chicago   May 15, 1979   441 U. S. 677
        *Civil Rights (Abernathy) 1980 414-421
        Significant Decisions 1978/79 79-80
        PERIODICALS:
        "Getting in."   Time   113: 57 May 28 '79.
        "High court rules individuals may sue colleges to enforce anti-sex-
        bias law," Cheryl M. Fields.   Chronicle of Higher Eductn   18:
        1, 8 May 21 '79.
        "The issue: can an individual file private suit under sex-bias law?"
        Ellen K. Coughlin.   Chronicle of Higher Eductn   17 [18]: 17
        Jan 15 '79.
        "She, too, can sue," Aric Press and Diane Camper.   Newsweek
        93: 98 May 28 '79.
        *"Text of majority opinion on anti-sex-bias lawsuits."   Chronicle
        of Higher Eductn   18: 8-10 May 21 '79.

4037.   Oscar Mayer & Co. v. Evans   May 21, 1979   441 U. S. 750
        PERIODICALS:
        "Significant decisions in labor cases."   Monthly Labor R   102: 59
        Sept '79.

4038.   Greenholtz v. Inmates of Nebraska   May 29, 1979   442 U. S. 1
        Penal and Correctional Complex
        Significant Decisions 1978/79 111-113
        *US Prison Law v. 6, 523-542

PERIODICALS:
"Supreme Court review." J Criml Law and Crimlgy 70: 466-473
Dec '79.

4039. International Brotherhood of Elec- May 29, 1979 442 U.S. 42
trical Workers v. Foust
PERIODICALS:
"Significant decisions in labor cases." Monthly Labor R 102: 59
Sept '79.

4040. Parker v. Randolph May 29, 1979 442 U.S. 62
Law of Arrest (Creamer) 471-475
*Modern Criml Procedure 295-296
Significant Decisions 1978/79 59-60
PERIODICALS:
"Supreme Court review." J Criml Law and Crimlgy 70: 439-
445 Dec '79.

4041. United States v. Batchelder June 4, 1979 442 U.S. 114
*Modern Criml Procedure 249-251

4042. County Court of Ulster County June 4, 1979 442 U.S. 140
v. Allen
*Criminal Law (Dix) 757-764
Significant Decisions 1978/79 58-59

4043. United States v. Addonizio June 4, 1979 442 U.S. 178
*US Prison Law v. 6, 550-555

4044. Dunaway v. New York June 5, 1979 442 U.S. 200
Law of Arrest (Creamer) 406-413
*Modern Criml Procedure 122-124
Significant Decisions 1978/79 37-39
PERIODICALS:
"Supreme Court review." J Criml Law and Crimlgy 70: 446-457
Dec '79.

4045. Davis v. Passman June 5, 1979 442 U.S. 228
*Civil Rights (Abernathy) 1980 366-373
*Historic Documents 1979 399-411
Significant Decisions 1978/79 78-79
PERIODICALS:
"Capitol Hill sexists beware." Newsweek 93: 52 June 18 '79.
"Court to Congress: obey your own laws." US News 86: 6
June 18 '79.
"Significant decisions in labor cases." Monthly Labor R 102: 58
Aug '79.

4046. Personnel Administrator of Massa- June 5, 1979 442 U.S. 256
chusetts v. Feeney
*Cases Consttnl Law (Gunther) 722-728
*Consttnl Law (Grossman) 635-642
Editorials 1979 646-650
Significant Decisions 1978/79 76-78
PERIODICALS:
"New victory for veterans," Aric Press and Diane Camper.
Newsweek 93: 52 June 18 '79.
"Other 99%." Time 113: 78 June 18 '79.

"Significant decisions in labor cases." Monthly Labor R 102:
57-58 Aug '79.
"Women vs veterans," Kenneth Labich. Newsweek 93: 59 Mar
5 '79.

4047. Babbitt v. United Farm Workers   June 5, 1979 442 U.S. 289
National Union
Significant Decisions 1978/79 142-144
PERIODICALS:
"Significant decisions in labor cases." Monthly Labor R 102:
54-55 Nov '79.

4048. Lo-Ji Sales, Inc. v. New York   June 11, 1979 442 U.S. 319
Law of Arrest (Creamer) 144-150
Significant Decisions 1978/79 32-33
PERIODICALS:
"Six groups file Supreme Court brief on massive seizure from
Bookstore." Pub Weekly 215: 36 Feb 5 '79.
"Supreme Court decides bookstore search and seizure case." Pub
Weekly 215: 34 June 25 '79.

4049. Reiter v. Sonotone Corporation   June 11, 1979 442 U.S. 330
PERIODICALS:
"Court to rule on consumer injury in antitrust cases," Roberta
Wyper. Electronic News 25: supp 16 Jan 22 '79.

4050. Andrus v. Sierra Club   June 11, 1979 442 U.S. 347
Significant Decisions 1978/79 171

4051. Great American Federal Savings and   June 11, 1979 442 U.S. 366
Loan Association v. Novotny
*Civil Rights (Abernathy) 1980 344-348

4052. Southeastern Community College v.   June 11, 1979 442 U.S. 397
Davis
Editorials 1979 755, 756
Significant Decisions 1978/79 129-130
PERIODICALS:
"High court clarifies colleges' obligations to the handicapped,"
Cheryl M. Fields. Chronicle of Higher Eductn 18: 1, 15
June 18 '79.
"Higher hurdles for the handicapped." US News 86: 10 June
25 '79.
"Judicial reasoning or attitudinal barriers?" John H. Gavin.
America 141: 366-369 Dec 9 '79.
"Nondiscrimination and the otherwise qualified handicapped student,"
Eileen S. Nelson and William R. Nelson. College Student J
14: 288-292 Fall '80.
"Shutting out the handicapped," Linda Marie Delloff. Christian
Century 96: 752-753 Aug 1 '79.
"Significant decisions in labor cases." Monthly Labor R 102:
70 Oct '79.
"Supreme Court holds that section 504 does not require affirmative
action," Thomas J. Flygare. Phi Delta Kappan 61: 63-64
Sept '79.
"Supreme Court to hear case of deaf nurse," Constance Holden.
Science 204: 158-159 Apr 13 '79.
*"Text of high court's ruling on admitting the handicapped."
Chronicle of Higher Eductn 18: 15-16 June 18 '79.

"Twenty-five states ask the Supreme Court to decide issues involving handicapped students," Thomas J. Flygare. Phi Delta Kappan 60: 456-457 Feb '79.
"What must colleges do to avoid bias against handicapped?" Cheryl M. Fields. Chronicle of Higher Eductn 18: 5 Apr 30 '79.

4053. Moore v. Sims   June 11, 1979 442 U.S. 415
       Significant Decisions 1978/79 140-142

4054. Torres v. Puerto Rico   June 18, 1979 442 U.S. 465
       Significant Decisions 1978/79 33-34

4055. United States v. Helstoski   June 18, 1979 442 U.S. 477
       *Historic Documents 1979 467-478
       *Legislative (Hetzel) 517-523
       Significant Decisions 1978/79 100-101
       PERIODICALS:
       "Of kids, Congressmen and cancer." Time 114: 50 July 2 '79
       (3).

4056. Helstoski v. Meanor   June 18, 1979 442 U.S. 500
       Significant Decisions 1978/79 152

4057. Sandstrom v. Montana   June 18, 1979 442 U.S. 510
       Significant Decisions 1978/79 56-57

4058. United States v. Rutherford   June 18, 1979 442 U.S. 544
       Editorials 1979 753, 754
       PERIODICALS:
       "Courts, terminal patients, and unapproved drugs," Wallace Janssen. FDA Consumer 13: 4-7 Nov '79.
       "Of kids, Congressmen and cancer." Time 114: 50 July 2 '79
       (3).
       "Yes, Washington can ban laetrile." US News 87: 5 July 2 '79
       (3).

4059. Touche Ross & Co. v. Redington   June 18, 1979 442 U.S. 560
       Significant Decisions 1978/79 169-171

4060. Parham v. J. L., a minor   June 20, 1979 442 U.S. 584
       Cases Consttnl Law (Gunther) 633-635
       Editorials 1979 750-752
       Significant Decisions 1978/79 108-111
       Sup Ct Review 1979 330-333
       PERIODICALS:
       "Children's rights after the Supreme Court's decision on Parham v. J. L. and J. R.," Carol C. Frank. Child Welfare 59: 375-380 June '80.
       "Court backs parental rights," Aric Press and others. Newsweek 94: 64 July 2 '79.
       "Laetrile's day in court," Eliot Marshall. Science 203: 528 Feb 9 '79.
       "Of kids, Congressmen and cancer." Time 114: 50 July 2 '79
       (3).
       "Parents, children and the Supreme Court," Maurice DeG. Ford. Commonweal 106: 462-465 Aug 31 '79.
       "Yes, Washington can ban laetrile." US News 87: 5 July 2 '79 (3).

4061.   Califano v. Yamasaki   June 20, 1979 442 U. S. 682
        Significant Decisions 1978/79 117

4062.   Fare v. Michael C.   June 20, 1979 442 U. S. 707
        Law of Arrest (Creamer) 443-449
        *Modern Criml Procedure 157-159
        Significant Decisions 1978/79 40-41
        PERIODICALS:
        "Supreme Court review." J Criml Law and Crimlgy 70: 458-
        465 Dec '79.

4063.   Smith v. Maryland   June 20, 1979 442 U. S. 735
        Law of Arrest (Creamer) 323-328
        Significant Decisions 1978/79 27-28
        PERIODICALS:
        "Supreme Court review." J Criml Law and Crimlgy 70: 433-438
        Dec '79.

4064.   Arkansas v. Sanders   June 20, 1979 442 U. S. 753
        *Criminal Justice (Way) 90-94
        Law of Arrest (Creamer) 553-558
        Significant Decisions 1978/79 34-35

4065.   National Labor Relations Board v.   June 20, 1979 442 U. S. 773
        Baptist Hospital, Inc.
        PERIODICALS:
        "Significant decisions in labor cases." Monthly Labor R 102: 54
        Nov '79.

4066.   Mackey v. Montrym   June 25, 1979 443 U. S. 1
        Significant Decisions 1978/79 113-115

4067.   Michigan v. DeFillippo   June 25, 1979 443 U. S. 31
        Law of Arrest (Creamer) 561-565
        Significant Decisions 1978/79 39-40

4068.   Brown v. Texas   June 25, 1979 443 U. S. 47
        *Criminal Justice 110-112
        Law of Arrest (Creamer) 558-561
        Significant Decisions 1978/79 31-32

4069.   Barry v. Barchi   June 25, 1979 443 U. S. 55
        Significant Decisions 1978/79 115-116

4070.   Califano v. Westcott   June 25, 1979 443 U. S. 76
        Pratt v. Westcott
        Significant Decisions 1978/79 75-76
        PERIODICALS:
        "Significant decisions in labor cases." Monthly Labor R 102:
        69 Oct '79.

4071.   Smith v. Daily Mail Publishing Co.   June 26, 1979 443 U. S. 97
        Modern Criml Procedure 370
        Significant Decisions 1978/79 90-91
        PERIODICALS:
        "Law protecting juvenile criminals held unconstitutional." Broad-
        casting 97: 76 July 2 '79.
        "Top court rules on prior restraint law," I. William Hill. Editor
        and Pub 112: 11 June 30 '79.

4072.   Hutchinson v. Proxmire   June 26, 1979   443 U.S. 111
     *Consttnl Law (Grossman) 1164-1169
     Editorials 1979 745-747
     Historic Documents 1979 479-491
     *Legislative (Hetzel) 543-552
     Significant Decisions 1978/79 88-90
     PERIODICALS:
     "Brief of American Psychological Association and American Asso-
       ciation for the Advancement of Science as Amici Curiae." Am
       Psychologist 35: 750-758 Aug '80.
     "High court eases libel curb in public figure cases," Malcolm
       Oliver. Pub Weekly 216: 12 July 9 '79 (2).
     "Hutchinson versus Proxmire," Charles A. Kiesler and Robert P.
       Lowman. Am Psychologist 35: 689-690 Aug '80.
     "Justices rule Proxmire may be sued for libel by scientist," Ellen
       Coughlin. Chronicle of Higher Eductn 18: 1, 11 July 2 '79.
     "No quarter from this court," Bruce W. Sanford. Columbia Jour-
       nalism Q 18: 59-63 Sept '79 (4).
     "Public-figure libel defense is reduced by Supreme Court." Broad-
       casting 97: 74-75 July 2 '79 (2).
     "Private people." Time 114: 62 July 9 '79.
     "Proxmire decision, a caution to Congress," John Walsh. Science
       205: 170-171 July 13 '79.
     "Public or private lives," Arlic Schardt and others. Newsweek
       94: 50 July 9 '79 (2).
     "Supreme Court: bag of surprises," Economist 272: 47-48 July
       7 '79 (3).
     "Supreme Court to hear two public figure libel cases," Susan Wag-
       ner. Pub Weekly 215: 45, 48 Feb 12 '79 (2).
     "Supreme Court's Golden Fleece ruling supports researchers,"
       Peter Gwynne. Industrial Research/Development 21: 46 Aug
       '79.
     "Taste of his own fleece," William H. Gregory. Aviation Wk and
       Space Technology 112: 13 Mar 31 '80.
     "Yes Washington can ban laetrile." US News 87: 5 July 2 '79
       (3).

4073.   Baker v. McCollan   June 26, 1979   443 U.S. 137
     Significant Decisions 1978/79 43-45

4074.   Wolston v. Reader's Digest Association June 26, 1979   443 U.S. 157
     Editorials 1979 745-747
     Significant Decisions 1978/79 87-88
     PERIODICALS:
     "Court narrows libel shield and broadens private rights." Editor
       and Pub 112: 11-12 June 30 '79.
     "High court eases libel curb in public figure cases," Malcolm Ol-
       iver. Pub Weekly 216: 12 July 9 '79 (2).
     "No quarter from this court," Bruce W. Sanford. Columbia
       Journalism R 18: 59-63 Sept '79 (4).
     "Public-figure libel defense is reduced by Supreme Court." Broad-
       casting 97: 74-75 July 2 '79 (2).
     "Public or private lives," Arlic Schardt and others. Newsweek
       94: 50 July 9 '79 (2).
     "Supreme Court: bag of surprises." Economist 272: 47-48
       July 7 '78 (3).
     "Supreme Court to hear two public figure libel cases," Susan Wag-
       ner. Pub Weekly 215: 45, 48 Feb 12 '79 (2).

4075.   United Steelworkers of America   June 27, 1979 443 U.S. 193
         v. Weber
        Kaiser Aluminum and Chemical
          Corporation v. Weber
        United States v. Weber
          CQ Guide 605
          Cases Consttnl Law (Gunther) 835-837
          *Civil Rights (Abernathy) 1980 565-584
          *Consttnl Law (Grossman) 600-608
          Editorials 1979 722-732
          *Historic Documents 1979 493-507
          Judiciary (Abraham) 147-148
          *Legislative (Hetzel) 222-237
          *Nature 1171-1192
          Significant Decisions 1978/79 63-65
          Sup Ct Review 1979 2-6, 45
        PERIODICALS:
          "Affirmed," Joel Dreyfuss. Black Enterprise 10: 18 Aug '79.
          "Allan Bakke's blue-collar cousin," Richard Regan. America 140:
            106-109 Feb 17 '79.
          "As the Supreme Court weighs reverse discrimination in jobs."
            US News 86: 77-78 Apr 9 '79.
          "Bakke case moves to the factory," Steven V. Roberts. NY Times
            Mag p. 36-38, 84, 86, 100-101 Feb 25 '79.
          "Bakke in a blue collar." Natl R 31: 16-17 Jan 5 '79.
          "Bakke to Weber to--?" Isidore Silver. Commonweal 106: 420
            Aug 3 '79.
          "Bakke revisited," Peter Bonventre and Diane Camper. Newsweek
            93: 70 Apr 9 '79.
          "Bigger than Bakke? B. Weber's charges of reverse discrimination
            against Kaiser Aluminum and Chemical Corporation." Time
            112: 44 Dec 25 '78.
          "The catch-22 case," Rick Harris and Jack Hartog. Civil Rights
            Dig 11: 3-11 Winter '79.
          "Death sentence for affirmative action?" Isidore Silver. Common-
            weal 106: 171-175 Mar 30 '79. Reaction: 106: 322, 350-
            351 June 8 '79.
          "Double thought," William F. Buckley, Jr. Natl R 31: 990
            Aug 3 '79.
          "Goldwater wins." Natl R 31: 899 July 20 '79.
          "Hard hats, hard case: the Supreme Court's abuse of legislative
            history," Richard J. Regan. America 141: 229-231 Oct 27
            '79.
          "High court backs Kaiser's affirmative action plan." Chemical
            Wk 125: 21 July 4 '79.
          "High court okays preference by race in voluntary affirmative
            action plans." Phi Delta Kappan 61: 76 Sept '79.
          "High court upholds affirmative action in employment," Lorenzo
            Middleton. Chronicle of Higher Eductn 18: 1, 12 July 2 '79.
          "How to read the Civil Rights Act," Ronald Dworkin. NY Review
            of Books 26: 37-43 Dec 20 '79.
          "Justice debased: the Weber decision," Carl Cohen. Commentary
            68: 43-53 Sept '79.
          "Match for Houdini," Daniel Seligman. Fortune 100: 49-50
            July 30 '79.
          "Narrow approach to regulatory issues." Bus Wk p. 21-22 July
            9 '79.
          "Paradoxes of equal opportunity: voluntary racial preferences and

the Weber case," Michael J. Phillips. Bus Horizons 23: 41-47 Aug '80.

"Quotas, again." Time 113: 28 Apr 9 '79.

"Race quotas for jobs; impact of Court ruling." US News 87: 70-71 July 9 '79.

"Significant decisions in labor cases." Monthly Labor R 102: 56-57 Aug '79.

"Steelworkers: a hex on Weber," Steve Askin. Black Enterprise 9: 12 July '79.

"Supreme Court accepts affirmative-action case," Cheryl M. Fields. Chronicle of Higher Eductn 17 [16]: 9 Dec 18 '79.

"Supreme Court backs affirmative action." Chemical and Engineering News 57: 6 July 2 '79.

"Supreme Court: setback for affirmative action." Black Enterprise 9: 30 Mar '79 (2).

"Supreme Court upholds affirmative action." Engineering News 203: 60-61 July 5 '79.

*"Text of Supreme Court's majority opinion on legality of affirmative action in jobs." Chronicle of Higher Eductn 18: 12-13 July 2 '79.

"Victory for quotas," Aric Press and Diane Camper. Newsweek 94: 77-78 July 9 '79.

"Voluntary quotas," Nathan Lewin. New Republic 181: 16-18 July 21 '79.

"Weber: a small step forward." America 141: 4-5 July 7 '79.

"Weber and beyond," E. Richard Larson. Nation 229: 69-70 July 28 '79.

"Weber case affirms affirmative action," Brian S. Moskal. Industry Wk 202: 21, 23 July 9 '79.

"Weber case: another step Bakke-wards," Herman Schwartz. Nation 228: 585, 602-604 May 26 '79.

"Weber: now I know it's over." Newsweek 94: 24 Oct 22 '79.

"Weber versus affirmative action?" Neil D. McFeeley. Personnel 57: 38-51 Jan '80.

"What the Weber ruling does." Time 114: 48-49 July 9 '79.

"When are racial quotas permissible?" R. Bruce Douglass. Christian Century 96: 1076-1078 Nov 7 '79.

"Why racial preference is illegal and immoral," Carl Cohen. Commentary 67: 40-52 June '79.

4076. Edmonds v. Compagnie Generale   June 27, 1979 443 U.S. 256
        Transatlantique
    PERIODICALS:
    "Shipowners lose chance to cut costs of loaders' injuries." Bus Insurance 13: 10 July 23 '79.

4077. Califano v. Boles   June 27, 1979 443 U.S. 282
        Significant Decisions 1978/79 122-123
    PERIODICALS:
    "Significant decisions in labor cases." Monthly Labor R 102: 70 Oct '79.

4078. Jackson v. Virginia   June 28, 1979 443 U.S. 307
        Modern Criml Procedure 445-447
        Significant Decisions 1978/79 50-51

4079. Federal Open Market Committee of   June 28, 1979 443 U.S. 340
        Federal Reserve System v. Merrill
        Significant Decisions 1978/79 173-175

4080.   Gannett v. DePasquale   July 2, 1979   443 U.S. 368
          Cases Consttnl Law (Gunther) 1536-1540
          *Consttnl Law (Grossman) 911-918
          Editorials 1979 738-744
          *Historic Documents 1979 511-533
          *Modern Criml Procedure 370-379
          Significant Decisions 1978/79 84-85
        PERIODICALS:
          "Battle joined at Supreme Court over Gannett." Broadcasting
            97:   90   Sept 10 '79.
          "Blackmun speaks out on Gannett decision," I. William Hill.
            Editor and Pub   112:   22   Sept 1 '79.
          "Burger says courtroom closure rule applies only in pretrial
            hearings." Editor and Pub   112:   8   Aug 18 '79.
          "Confusion in the courts." Time   114:   82   Sept 17 '79.
          "Court vs. the press," Aric Press and Diane Camper. Newsweek
            94:   60, 63   July 16 '79.
          "Disorder in court," Economist   272:   42-43   Sept 15 '79.
          *"Excerpts from Gannett-DePasquale decision." Editor and Pub
            112:   48-56   July 14 '79.
          "Ganging up against Gannett decision." Broadcasting   97:   21-23
            Aug 27 '79.
          "General spirit of the people," Helen K. Copley. Vital Speeches
            46:   169-172   Jan 1 '80   (4).
          "High court gives judges broad freedom to bar public and press
            from courtroom." Editor and Pub   112:   9-10   July 7 '79.
          "High court rules defendant rights supersede those of press, pub-
            lic." Broadcasting   97:   46-47   July 9 '79.
          "Judge Wachtler writes sequel to his DePasquale decision." Editor
            and Pub   112:   12   Dec 1 '79.
          "Judge quick to slam courtroom doors." US News   87:   7   Aug
            20 '79.
          "Judge Stevens discounts fears of secret trials," I. W. Hill.
            Editor and Pub   112:   9-10, 48   Sept 15 '79.
          "No quarter from this court," Bruce W. Sanford. Columbia
            Journalism R   18:   59-63   Sept '79   (4).
          "160 take part in forum of DePasquale rule." Editor and Pub
            113:   32   Jan 5 '80.
          "Open and shut cases," Aric Press and others. Newsweek   94:
            69   Aug 27 '79.
          "Slamming the courtroom doors." Time   114:   66, 71   July 16
            '79.
          "Supreme Court vs. the press," Gilda Morse. Graduate Woman
            74:   27-29, 49   Jan/Feb '80   (3).
          "What do you do when the Supreme Court is wrong," Daniel P.
            Moynihan. Public Interest   no. 57:   3-24   Fall '79.

4081.   Columbus Board of Education v.   July 2, 1979   443 U.S. 449
          Penick
          Cases Consttnl Law (Gunther) 776-777
          *Consttn (Morris) 765-782
          *Consttnl Law (Lockhart) 1309-1318
          Editorials 1979 733-737
          *Historic Documents 1979 535-552
          Significant Decisions 1978/79 131-132
          Sup Ct Review 1979 6-9
        PERIODICALS:
          "Busing wins another round," Sharon Begley and Lucy Howard.
            Newsweek   94:   63   July 16 '79.

4082. Dayton Board of Education v.   July 2, 1979   443 U.S. 526
       Brinkman
       Cases Consttnl Law (Gunther) 778-781
       *Consttnl Law (Lockhart) 1318-1324
       Editorials 1979 733-737
       Significant Decisions 1978/79 132-133
       PERIODICALS:
       "Dayton II: school desegregation on a roller coaster," Thomas J.
       Flygare. Phi Delta Kappan 61: 124-125 Oct '79.
       See also listing at 443 U.S. 449, entry no. 4081.

4083. Rose v. Mitchell   July 2, 1979   443 U.S. 545
       *Modern Criml Procedure 255-256
       Modern Criml Procedure 447-450
       Significant Decisions 1978/79 51-53

4084. Jones v. Wolf   July 2, 1979   443 U.S. 595
       Significant Decisions 1978/79 127-128
       PERIODICALS:
       "Connectional denomination try retying their property slipknots,"
       John Maust. Christianity Today 23: 50, 52 Sept 21 '79.

4085. Bellotti v. Baird   July 2, 1979   443 U.S. 622
       Hunerwadel v. Baird
       Cases Consttnl Law (Gunther) 612-614
       Editorials 1979 750-752
       Significant Decisions 1978/79 135-137
       PERIODICALS:
       "Split decision on abortions," Sharon Begley and L. Howard.
       Newsweek 94: 63-64 July 16 '79.
       "Teenagers and pregnancy: the law in 1979," Eve W. Paul and
       Harriet F. Pilpel. Family Planning Perspectives 11: 297-
       302 Sept/Oct '79 (4).

4086. P. C. Pfeiffer Co. v. Ford   Nov 27, 1979   444 U.S. 69
       PERIODICALS:
       "Significant decisions in labor cases." Monthly Labor R 103:
       51-52 Mar '80.

4087. Ybarra v. Illinois   Nov 28, 1979   444 U.S. 85
       PERIODICALS:
       "Supreme Court review." J Criml Law and Crimlgy 71: 558-
       566 Winter '80.

4088. Board of Education of the City School Nov 28, 1979   444 U.S. 130
       District of New York v. Harris, Secretary
       of Health, Education and Welfare
       PERIODICALS:
       "Significant decisions in labor cases." Monthly Labor R 103:
       52 Mar '80.

4089. Ferri v. Ackman   Dec 4, 1979   444 U.S. 193
       PERIODICALS:
       "Liability of government-appointed attorneys in state tort actions,"
       Patricia B. Carlson. J Criml Law and Crimlgy 71: 136-146
       Summer '80.

4090. Carbon Fuel Co. v. United Mine   Dec 10, 1979   444 U.S. 212
       Workers of America

PERIODICALS:
"Significant decisions in labor cases. " Monthly Labor R 103: 51
Mar '80

4091. Stryker's Bay Neighborhood Council   Jan 7, 1980   444 U. S. 223
v. Karlen
City of New York v. Karlen
Secretary of Housing and Urban
Development v. Karlen
PERIODICALS:
"Shrinking NEPA, " Ross Sandler. Environment 22: 43-44 Apr
'80.

4092. United States v. Bailey   Jan 21, 1980   444 U. S. 394
United States v. Cogdell
*US Prison Law v. 6, 196-216

4093. Norfolk and Western Railway Co.   Feb 19, 1980   444 U. S. 490
v. Liepelt, Administratrix
PERIODICALS:
"Significant decisions in labor cases. " Monthly Labor R 103:
52 June '80.

4094. Snepp v. United States   Feb 19, 1980   444 U. S. 507
PERIODICALS:
"CIA's case against Snepp, " George A. Carver, Jr. Newsweek
95: 21 Mar 17 '80.
"First show your book to Uncle Sam. " Economist 274: 47-48
Feb 23 '80.
"Good soldier system, " Thomas Powers. Commonweal 107: 261-
262 May 9 '80.
"Government won't use Snepp ruling against publishers, " H. Fields.
Pub Weekly 218: 16-17 Aug 15 '80.
"High court ends Snepp's fight to keep royalties, " Howard Fields.
Pub Weekly 217: 18, 23 Apr 25 '80.
"High court hexes free speech, " Nathan Lewin. New Republic
182: 18-21 Mar 22 '80.
"High court hits tellers of secrets, " Aric Press and Diane Camper.
Newsweek 95: 50-51 Mar 3 '80 (2).
"Indecent haste. " Nation 230: 257 Mar 8 '80.
"Is the press losing the First Amendment?" Ronald Dworkin. NY
Review of Books 27: 49-57 Dec 4 '80.
"Royalties to the Treasury, " Herbert Mitgang. NY Times Bk R
85: 23 Aug 31 '80.
"Snepp fallout. " Nation 230: 323 Mar 22 '80.
"Snepp to U. S. Supreme Court, " Malcolm Oliver. Pub Weekly
216: 80 July 23 '79.
"Supreme Court says Snepp violated CIA contracts, " Stella Dong.
Pub Weekly 217: 12, 18 Mar 7 '80.
"Wages of faithlessness. " Time 115: 48-49 Mar 3 '80.

4095. California Brewers Association v.   Feb 20, 1980   444 U. S. 598
Bryant
PERIODICALS:
"High court to rule in 45-week seniority system, " Roberta Wyper.
Electronic News 25: supp 8S June 18 '79.
"Significant decisions in labor cases. " Monthly Labor R 103: 51-
52 June '80.

4096. Village of Schaumburg v. Citizens   Feb 20, 1980   444 U.S. 620
       for a Better Environment
       Cases Consttnl Law (Gunther) 1216-1219

4097. Committee for Public Education and   Feb 20, 1980   444 U.S. 646
       Religious Liberty v. Regan,
       Comptroller of New York
       *Cases Consttnl Law (Gunther) 1569-1580

4098. National Labor Relations Board v.   Feb 20, 1980   444 U.S. 672
       Yeshiva University
       Yeshiva University Faculty Association
       v. Yeshiva University
       PERIODICALS:
       "AAUP to fight Yeshiva ruling," Beverly T. Watkins. Chronicle
         of Higher Eductn 20: 4 June 30 '80.
       "Are professionals managers?" Bus Wk p. 59-60, 62 Apr 14 '80.
       "Chill for campus unions." America 142: 182 Mar 8 '80.
       "Faculty union bid dealt severe blow." Times Higher Eductn Supp
         384: 5 Feb 29 '80.
       "Faculty union ruling hits campus pay negotiations." Times Higher
         Eductn Supp 387: 5 Mar 21 '80.
       "Fallout from the Yeshiva ruling," Beverly T. Watkins. Chronicle
         of Higher Eductn 20: 3-4 June 9 '80.
       "High court calls Yeshiva faculty managers, not subject to National
         Labor Relations Act," Beverly T. Watkins. Chronicle of Higher
         Eductn 19: 1, 7 Feb 25 '80.
       "High court hears arguments in Yeshiva case that may shape future
         of faculty bargaining," Beverly Watkins. Chronicle of Higher
         Eductn 19: 1, 12 Oct 15 '79.
       "High court hits tellers of secrets," Aric Press and Diane Camper.
         Newsweek 95: 50-51 Mar 3 '80 (2).
       "NLRB v. Yeshiva University; symposium," ed. by Hugh D. Jas-
         court. J Law and Eductn 9: 463-488 Oct '80.
       "Practical implications of the Yeshiva decision," K. J. Daponte.
         J College and University Personnel Association 31: 45-50
         Summer '80.
       "Significant decisions in labor cases." Monthly Labor R 103: 57-
         58 Apr '80.
       "Supreme Court considers future of faculty unionization," Robin M.
         Henig. Bioscience 29: 719-722, 762 Dec '79.
       "Supreme Court squelches faculty unions," Susan Walton. Bio-
         science 30: 228 Apr '80.
       "Supreme Court's Yeshiva decision produces uncertainty, disappoint-
         ment," Beverly T. Watkins. Chronicle of Higher Eductn 20:
         8 Mar 3 '80.
       "Taking stock after Yeshiva," Gene I. Maeroff. Eductnl Rec 61:
         14-18 Summer '80.
       *"Text of Brennan's dissent on Yeshiva." Chronicle of Higher
         Eductn 19: 8-9 Feb 25 '80.
       *"Text of the majority opinion on Yeshiva." Chronicle of Higher
         Eductn 19: 7-8 Feb 25 '80.
       "Wages of faithlessness." Time 115: 48-49 Mar 3 '80 (2).
       "Yeshiva: a legal analysis," D. H. Roots and I. M. Shepard.
         J College and University Personnel Association 31: 51-55
         Summer '80.
       "Yeshiva: an end to faculty unions?" Edward J. Burke. Change
         12: 15-16 Apr '80.

"The Yeshiva decision," Robert A. Gorman. Academe 66: 188-
197 May '80; *Academe 66: 190-197 May '80.
"Yeshiva decision," Barbara Stein. Todays Eductn 69: 10GE
Nov/Dec '80.
"Yeshiva University: implications for the future of college collective bargaining," Thomas J. Flygare. Phi Delta Kappan 61:
639-640 May '80.

4099. United States v. Euge   Feb 20, 1980   444 U.S. 707
       PERIODICALS:
       "IRS power to summons handwriting; analyzing the Supreme Court's
       Euge decision," John M. Bray and David J. Curtin. J Taxation
       52: 290-292 May '80.

4100. Whirlpool Corporation v. Marshall,   Feb 26, 1980   445 U.S. 1
       Secretary of Labor
       PERIODICALS:
       "Employees can refuse to perform hazardous jobs," William E.
       Lissy. Supervision 42: 19-20 Aug '80.
       "OSHA protects refusal to work, court rules." Engineering News
       204: 76 Mar 6 '80.
       "Significant decisions in labor cases." Monthly Labor R 103: 57
       Apr '80.
       "Unsafe: workers can refuse tasks." Bus Insurance 14: 1, 29
       Mar 3 '80.
       "Who decides when a job's too dangerous?" Daniel D. Cook.
       Industry Wk 204: 23-25 Mar 17 '80.

4101. United States v. Clark, guardian   Feb 26, 1980   445 U.S. 23
       PERIODICALS:
       "Significant decisions in labor cases." Monthly Labor R 103:
       53 June '80.

4102. Trammel v. United States   Feb 27, 1980   445 U.S. 40
       PERIODICALS:
       "Mate vs. mate." Time 115: 49 Mar 10 '80.
       "Supreme Court review." J Criml Law and Crimlgy 71: 593-600
       Winter '80 (2).

4103. Kissinger v. Reporters Committee   Mar 3, 1980   445 U.S. 136
       for Freedom of the Press
       PERIODICALS:
       "High court limits scholars' use of Information act," Cheryl M.
       Fields. Chronicle of Higher Eductn 20: 1, 12 Mar 10 '80.
       "Kissinger transcripts," Aric Press and Diane Camper. Newsweek
       95: 60 Mar 17 '80.
       "State secrets." Time 115: 51 Mar 17 '80.
       "Supreme Court upholds Kissinger over transcripts," M. Reuter.
       Pub Weekly 217: 19-20 Mar 21 '80.
       "Top court limits media access to government papers," I. William
       Hill. Editor and Pub 113: 8 Mar 8 '80.

4104. Forsham v. Harris, Secretary of   Mar 3, 1980   445 U.S. 169
       Health, Education and Welfare
       PERIODICALS:
       "Court upholds confidentiality of research records/data," David
       Florio. Eductnl Researcher 9: 19-20 May '80.

4105. Chiarella v. United States   Mar 18, 1980   445 U.S. 222

PERIODICALS:
"Strict views of the law," Aric Press and Diane Camper.
Newsweek 95: 49 Mar 31 '80 (2).
"Supreme Court review." J Criml Law and Crimlgy 71: 474-487
Winter '80.

4106. Rummel v. Estelle, Corrections   Mar 18, 1980   445 U.S. 263
      Director
      *US Prison Law v. 6, 683-706
      PERIODICALS:
      "Cruel as usual." Nation 230: 387-388 Apr 5 '80.
      "Law: Collect $230 and go to jail," Maurice deG. Ford. Atlantic
      246: 14, 16, 18 July '80.
      "Petty crimes, severe sentence," Ronald Goetz. Christian Cen-
      tury 97: 428-429 Apr 16 '80.
      "Strict views of the law," Aric Press and Diane Camper. News-
      week 95: 49 Mar 31 '80 (2).

4107. Mobil Oil Corporation v. Commis-   Mar 19, 1980   445 U.S. 425
      sioner of Taxes of Vermont
      PERIODICALS:
      "Another view of the Mobil Oil case." CPA J 50: 67-68 Sept
      '80.
      "Corporate taxes: ounce of flesh for American states." Econo-
      mist 274: 110 Mar 29 '80.
      "State taxation of foreign source dividend income." CPA J 50:
      64-67 Sept '80.
      "State wins on foreign source dividend." CPA J 50: 46-47
      June '80.
      "Unitary tax: the Supreme Court says pay." Economist 275: 84
      June 21 '80.

4108. United States v. Crews   Mar 25, 1980   445 U.S. 463
      PERIODICALS:
      "Supreme Court review." J Criml Law and Crimlgy 71: 488-498
      Winter '80.

4109. Vitek, Correctional Director v.   Mar 25, 1980   445 U.S. 480
      Jones
      PERIODICALS:
      "Supreme Court review." J Criml Law and Crimlgy 71: 578-592
      Winter '80.

4110. Branti v. Finkel   Mar 31, 1980   445 U.S. 507
      Cases Consttnl Law (Gunther) 1479-1481
      PERIODICALS:
      "Blow against political patronage." Newsweek 95: 30 Apr 14
      '80.
      "Court throws wrench in machine politics." US News 88: 7
      Apr 14 '80.
      "Significant decisions in labor cases." Monthly Labor R 103:
      44-45 Aug '80.
      "System spoiled." Time 115: 71 Apr 14 '80.
      "Zbig for life," Robert Laus. Washington Monthly 12: 25-32
      June '80.

4111. Payton v. New York   Apr 15, 1980   445 U.S. 573
      PERIODICALS:
      "Supreme Court review." J Criml Law and Crimlgy 71: 518-
      528 Winter '80.

4112.   Owen v. City of Independence,   Apr 15, 1980   445 U.S. 622
        Missouri
        PERIODICALS:
        "Civil rights: an American's home is his castle." Economist
            275: 24   Apr 26 '80.
        "Court guards the door," Jerry Adler and Diane Camper. News-
            week   95: 81   Apr 28 '80.
        "House arrests." Time 115: 65   Apr 28 '80.

4113.   City of Mobile, Ala v. Bolden   Apr 22, 1980   446 U.S. 55
        *Cases Consttnl Law (Gunther) 728-745
        *Consttnl Law (Lockhart) 1435-1443
        PERIODICALS:
        "Another blow for the blacks," William Lowther. Macleans 93:
            31-32   May 26 '80.
        "Right to vote, not a right to win," Aric Press and Diane Camper.
            Newsweek 95: 99   May 5 '80.

4114.   Wengler v. Druggists Mutual   Apr 22, 1980   446 U.S. 142
        Insurance Co.
        *Cases Consttnl Law (Gunther) 797-801
        PERIODICALS:
        "Significant decisions in labor cases." Monthly Labor R 103: 45
            Aug '80.

4115.   Rome v. United States   Apr 22, 1980   446 U.S. 156
        *Cases Consttnl Law (Gunther) 1066-1078

4116.   Marshall, Secretary of Labor v.   Apr 28, 1980   446 U.S. 238
        Jerrico, Inc.
        PERIODICALS:
        "Significant decisions in labor cases." Monthly Labor R 103: 52-
            53   June '80.

4117.   Rhode Island v. Innis   May 12, 1980   446 U.S. 291
        PERIODICALS:
        "Feel free." Economist 275: 32   June 7 '80.
        "God forbid excuse for the cops," Aric Press and Diane Camper.
            Newsweek 95: 93   May 26 '80.
        "Miranda's fate in the Burger Court," Ronald K. L. Collins and
            Robert Welsh. Center Mag 13: 43-52   Sept/Oct ' 80   (2).
        "Rights ruling." Time 115: 59   May 26 '80.
        "Supreme Court review." J Criml Law and Crimlgy 71: 466-
            473   Winter '80.

4118.   General Telephone Company of the   May 12, 1980   446 U.S. 318
        Northwest, Inc. v. Equal Employ-
        ment Opportunity Commission
        PERIODICALS:
        "Significant decisions in labor cases." Monthly Labor R 103: 46
            Aug '80.

4119.   Nachman Corporation v. Pension   May 12, 1980   446 U.S. 359
        Benefit Guaranty Corporation
        PERIODICALS:
        "Significant decisions in labor cases." Monthly Labor R 103: 56
            Sept '80.
        "Supreme Court rules in pension case," Mary Jane Fisher. Natl

Underwriter (Life ed) 84: 1 May 17 '80.   Same: Natl Underwriter (Property ed) 84: 56 May 23 '80.

4120. United States v. Mendenhall   May 27, 1980 446 U.S. 544
        PERIODICALS:
        "Score for the crooks, " Daniel Seligman.   Fortune 102: 45-46
        June 30 '80.

4121. Catalino, Inc. v. Target Sales, Inc.   May 27, 1980 446 U.S. 643
        PERIODICALS:
        "Supreme Court decision illustrates dangers of competitor coopera-
        tion. " Industrial Distributor 70: 18 Sept '80.
        "Supreme Court rules on trade credit case, " William Parsons.
        Credit and Financial Mgt 82: 32-33 Sept '80.

4122. Pruneyard Shopping Center v. Robins   June 9, 1980   447 U.S. 74
        Cases Consttnl Law (Gunther) 1300-1301
        PERIODICALS:
        "First Amendment rights upheld by high court, " Editor and Pub
        113: 20A June 21 '80.
        "There's still life in states' rights, " Aric Press and Diane Camper.
        Newsweek 95: 88 June 23 '80.

4123. Coffy v. Republic Steel Corporation   June 10, 1980 447 U.S. 191
        PERIODICALS:
        "Significant decisions in labor cases. " Monthly Labor R 103: 48
        Nov '80.

4124. Agins v. City of Tiburon   June 10, 1980 447 U.S. 255
        PERIODICALS:
        "Supreme Court victory for land use and open space preservation. "
        Natl Parks and Conservation Mag 54: 28 Aug '80.

4125. United States v. Henry   June 16, 1980 447 U.S. 264
        PERIODICALS:
        "Cheap water for a lush valley. " Time 115: 51 June 30 '80.
        "Supreme Court review. " J Criml Law and Crimlgy 71: 601-
        609 Winter '80.

4126. Diamond, Commissioner of Patents and June 16, 1980 447 U.S. 303
        Trademarks v. Chakrabarty
        PERIODICALS:
        "Adding life to patent law. " Sci News 117: 387 June 21 '80.
        "Court decision spurs genetic research, " Peter Gwynne. Industrial
        Research/Development 22: 45-46 Aug '80.
        "Court says lab-made life can be patented, " Nicholas Wade. Sci-
        ence 208: 1445 June 27 '80.
        "End justifies the genes, " William Lowther. Macleans 93: 35
        June 30 '80.
        *"Excerpts from opinions in high court's patent ruling. " Chronicle
        of Higher Eductn 20: 11-12 June 23 '80.
        "Genetic engineers await patent office go-ahead. " Times Higher
        Eductn Supp 400: 5 June 27 '80.
        "Genetic patents: less than meets the eye. " Bus Wk p. 48 June
        30 '80.
        "Illinois biochemist wins a crucial patent fight, " G. Breu. People
        14: 37-38 July 14 '80.
        "Life: patent pending ... implications for research, " William

Lasser and E. R. Shell. Technology R 82: 85-86 Aug/Sept
'80.
"New life forms; a clear road ahead?" US News 88: 34-35
June 30 '80.
"Out of the bottle." Progressive 44: 8 Aug '80.
"Patent of life." Economist 275: 18 June 21 '80.
"Patenting germs." Nation 230: 772 June 28 '80.
"Patenting life; split perspectives." Sci News 118: 71 Aug 2
'80.
"Right to patent life," Aric Press and others. Newsweek 95:
74-75 June 30 '80.
"Science policy: the Chakrabarty decision," C. Larry O'Rourke.
Environment 22: 4-5, 42 July/Aug '80.
"Supreme Court hears argument on patenting life forms," Nicholas
Wade. Science 208: 31-32 Apr 4 '80.
"Supreme Court lets scientists patent new forms of life," Cheryl
M. Fields. Chronicle of Higher Eductn 20: 1, 11 June 23
'80.
"Supreme Court rules life forms patentable." Chemical and En-
gineering News 58: 10 June 23 '80.
"Supreme Court rules on life form patents." Research Mgt 23:
2-3 Sept '80.
"Supreme Court to say if life is patentable," Nicholas Wade.
Science 206: 664 Nov 9 '79.
"Test-tube life; reg. U.S. Pat. Off.: the Supreme Court protects
the genetic engineers," John S. DeMott and Evan Thomas.
Time 115: 52-53 June 30 '80.

4127. Bryant v. Yellen   June 16, 1980 447 U.S. 352
California v. Yellen
Imperial Irrigation District v. Yellen
PERIODICALS:
"Cheap water for a lush valley." Time 115: 51 June 30 '80
(2).
"Empire built on water." Newsweek 95: 75 June 30 '80.

4128. National Labor Relations Board   June 20, 1980 447 U.S. 490
v. International Longshoremen's
Association, AFL-CIO
PERIODICALS:
"Significant decisions in labor cases." Monthly Labor R 103:
46-47 Nov '80.

4129. Consolidated Edison Company of   June 20, 1980 447 U.S. 530
New York v. Public Service
Commission of New York
PERIODICALS:
"Corporate free speech rights upheld." Editor and Pub 113: 27
June 28 '80 (2).
"Utilities win free-speech cases at Supreme Court." Broadcasting
98: 66-67 June 30 '80 (2).
"Utility free speech." Public Utilities Fortnightly 106: 48-51
Aug 14 '80 (2).

4130. Central Hudson Gas and Electric   June 20, 1980 447 U.S. 557
Corporation v. Public Service
Commission of New York
* Cases Consttnl Law (Gunther) 1398-1406

PERIODICALS:
See listing at 447 U.S. 530, entry no. 4129.

4131.   National Labor Relations Board v.   June 20, 1980 447 U.S. 607
        Retail Store Employees Union,
        Local 1001, Retail Clerks International
        Association
        PERIODICALS:
        "Significant decisions in labor cases."   Monthly Labor R   103: 47-
        48 Nov '80.

4132.   Maine v. Thiboutot   June 25, 1980 448 U.S. 1
        PERIODICALS:
        "Open season on state governments."   US News   89: 8 July 7
        '80.
        "Suing a state." Time 116: 72 July 7 '80.

4133.   Adams v. Texas   June 25, 1980 448 U.S. 38
        PERIODICALS:
        "Supreme Court review."   J Criml Law and Crimlgy   71: 538-546
        Winter '80 (3).

4134.   United States v. Salvucci   June 25, 1980 448 U.S. 83
        PERIODICALS:
        "Supreme Court review."   J Criml Law and Crimlgy   71: 567-
        578 Winter '80 (3).

4135.   Rawlings v. Kentucky   June 25, 1980 448 U.S. 98
        PERIODICALS:
        See listing at 448 U.S. 83, entry no. 4134.

4136.   Dawson Chemical Co. v. Rohm and   June 27, 1980 448 U.S. 176
        Haas Co.
        PERIODICALS:
        "American patents; dog in the manger."   Economist   276: 71 July
        5 '80.
        "Rulings from the High Court: benzene, patents for unpatentable
        chemicals, the Hyde Amendment."   Sci News   118: 20-21
        July 12 '80 (3).

4137.   United States v. Ward dba L. O.   June 27, 1980 448 U.S. 242
        Ward Oil and Gas Operations
        PERIODICALS:
        "Supreme Court review."   J Criml Law and Crimlgy   71: 610-
        621 Winter '80 (2).

4138.   Harris, Secretary of Health and   June 30, 1980 448 U.S. 297
        Human Services v. McRae
        Cases Consttnl Law (Gunther) 622-625
        Editorials 1980 261-263, 762-771
        PERIODICALS:
        "Abortion and the constitution."   America   143: 24 July 19-26
        '80.
        "Court continues its bamboozlement."   Economist   276: 21-22
        July 5 '80.
        "Courts and elective abortions under Medicaid," June E. Mendelson
        and Serena Domolky.   Socl Service R   54: 124-134 Mar '80.
        "Dissent of four just men."   Ms   9: 24 Sept '80.
        "Edges of life."   Commonweal   107: 421 Aug 1 '80.

"Four big decisions: high court rules on abortions, race quotas, open trials, safety rules," George J. Church and Evan Thomas. Time 116: 10-13 July 14 '80 (4).
"High court's grand finale," Aric Press and Diane Camper. Newsweek 96: 22-25 July 14 '80 (3).
"Hyde Amendment." America 142: 181 Mar 8 '80.
"Hyde and hysteria," Richard J. Neuhaus. Christian Century 97: 849-852 Sept 10-17 '80. Reaction: 97: 1066-1068 Nov 5 '80.
"Legal blow to abortion," Catherine Fox. Macleans 93: 33-34 July 14 '80.
"Let them eat cake, says the Supreme Court." Christian Century 97: 820-824 Aug 27/Sept 3 '80.
"Not free to choose." Nation 231: 33 July 12 '80.
"Rulings from the High Court: benzene, patents for unpatentable chemicals, the Hyde Amendment." Sci News 118: 20-21 July 12 '80 (3).
"Two Princeton scholars cast a cold eye on the Supreme Court's abortion ruling: nobody wins," James Trussell, Jane Menken. People 14: 77-78, 81, 83 July 21 '80.
"Where abortion fight goes from here." US News 89: 42 July 14 '80.

4139.   United States v. Sioux Nation   June 30, 1980 448 U.S. 371
        of Indians
        PERIODICALS:
        "Black Hills whitewash," Jill Norgren and Petra T. Shattuck. Nation 230: 557-560 May 10 '80.

4140.   Reid v. Georgia   June 30, 1980 448 U.S. 438
        PERIODICALS:
        "Supreme Court review." J Criml Law and Crimlgy 71: 499-517 Winter '80 (2).

4141.   Fullilove v. Klutznick, Secretary   July 2, 1980   448 U.S. 448
        of Commerce
        *Cases Consttnl Law (Gunther) 838-862
        Editorials 1980 772-777
        PERIODICALS:
        "Court finds MBE set-aside legal." Engineering News 204 [205]: 12-13 July 10 '80.
        "Four big decisions: high court rules on abortion, race quotas, open trials, safety rules," George J. Church and Evan Thomas. Time 116: 10-13 July 14 '80 (4).
        "High court's grand finale," Aric Press and Diane Camper. Newsweek 96: 22-25 July 14 '80 (3).
        "New hope for Blacks to reach the zenith," Clive Cookson. Times Higher Eductn Supp 403: 4 July 18 '80.
        "Significant decisions in labor cases." Monthly Labor R 103: 54-56 Sept '80.

4142.   Richmond Newspapers, Inc. v.   July 2, 1980   448 U.S. 555
        Virginia
        Cases Consttnl Law (Gunther) 1540-1545
        *Consttnl Law (Lockhart) 982-990
        Editorials 1980 778-781
        PERIODICALS:
        "Access to information: affirming the press's right," Cynthia J. Bolbach. Christian Century 97: 879-883 Sept 24 '80.

"Closed trials ruled out by US Supreme Court, " I. William Hill.
Editor and Pub 113: 10 July 5 '80.
"Four big decisions: high Court rules on abortions, race quotas,
open trials, safety rules, " George J. Church and Evan Thomas.
Time 116: 10-13 July 14 '80 (4).
"High court bars trials in secret. " Broadcasting 99: 27-28
July 7 '80.
"High court's grand finale, " Aric Press and Diane Camper. News-
week 96: 22-25 July 14 '80 (3).
"Maybe court will decide right to gather news. " Editor and Pub
113: 28 Apr 26 '80.
"Powell absents himself from gag order hearing, " I. William Hill.
Editor and Pub 113: 27 Mar 1 '80.
"Press leaders laud Richmond ruling, " Bill Gloede. Editor and
Pub 113: 12 July 12 '80.
"Press seeks clearcut guidance from high court, " I. William Hill.
Editor and Pub 112: 10 Sept 1 '79.
"Supreme Court gets a chance to explain. " Broadcasting 97: 76
Oct 15 '79 (2).
"Supreme Court may clarify closed courtroom ruling, " I. William
Hill. Editor and Pub 112: 13, 66 Oct 13 '79.
"Supreme Court review. " J Criml Law and Crimlgy 71: 547-557
Winter '80.
*"Text of Richmond v. Virginia decision. " Editor and Pub 113:
18-20, 48-49, 52-53 July 12 '80.

4143.   Industrial Union Department, AFL-CIO July 2, 1980   448 U.S. 607
        v. American Petroleum Institute
        Marshall, Secretary of Labor v. American
        Petroleum Institute
        PERIODICALS:
        "Court leaves OSHA hanging. " Bus Wk p. 07-08 July 21 '80.
        "Deregulation fever hits the Supreme Court, " Edward H. Greer.
        Nation 231: 666-668 Dec 20 '80.
        "Dispute over cancer risk quantification; Supreme Court to review
        OSHA's proposed benzene standard case, " Luther J. Carter.
        Science 203: 1324-1325 Mar 30 '79.
        "Four big decisions: high court rules on abortions, race quotas,
        open trials, safety rules, " George J. Church and Evan Thomas.
        Time 116: 10-13 July 14 '80 (4).
        "High court hears benzene arguments. " Chemical Wk 125: 53
        Oct 17 '79.
        "High court overturns OSHA benzene rule. " Chemical and Engineer-
        ing News 58: 4-5 July 7 '80.
        "Hot regulation case lands in the high court. " Bus Wk p. 35-36
        Oct 8 '79.
        "Light rein falls on OSHA, " R. Jeffrey Smith. Science 209: 567-
        568 Aug 1 '80.
        "OSHA standard found unjustified. " Engineering News-Rec 204
        [205]: 73 July 10 '80.
        "Significant decisions in labor cases. " Monthly Labor R 103:
        53-54 Sept '80.
        "Supreme Court becomes red tape battleground, " Edwin W. Bowers.
        Iron Age 223: 22-23 Aug 11 '80.
        "Supreme Court rules against OSHA on its benzene standard. "
        Chemical Market Rep 218: 3, 53 July 7 '80.

4144.   Stone v. Graham, Superintendent of   Nov 17, 1980   449 U.S. 39
        Public Instruction of Kentucky

Editorials 1980 1357-1363
PERIODICALS:
"Carols get green light, Ten Commandments get red." Christianity
   Today 24: 59-60 Dec 12 '80.
"Church-state commandments." Time 116: 74 Dec 1 '80.
"First amendment fight to take place in schools," Clive Cookson.
   Times Eductnl Supp 3364: 10 Dec 12 '80.

4145. Environmental Protection Agency v.   Dec 2, 1980   449 U.S. 64
          National Crushed Stone Association
       Costle, Administrator, Environmental Protection
          Agency v. Consolidation Coal Co.
       Editorials 1980 1408-1410

4146. United States v. DiFrancesco   Dec 9, 1980   449 U.S. 117
       Editorials 1980 1490-1494
       PERIODICALS:
       "Toward more uniform sentences." Time 116: 74 Dec 22 '80.

4147. United States v. Will   Dec 15, 1980   449 U.S. 200
       Editorials 1980 1495-1498

4148. Chandler v. Florida   Jan 26, 1981   449 U.S. 560
       PERIODICALS:
       "Cameras in the courtroom issue goes to court." Broadcasting
          99: 65-67 Nov 17 '80.
       "Media joins state in dispute over courtroom photos." Editor
          and Pub 113: 38 Aug 23 '80.

Board of Supervisors of County of
New York; Bank of New York
v. 306
Board of Supervisors of Elections
of Baltimore; Gerende v. 1828
Board of Tax Commissioners of
Indiana v. Jackson 1058
Board of Trade of Chicago v.
Olsen 921
___ v. United States 829
Board of Trustees of University
of Illinois v. United States
1094
Board of Trustees of University
of Mississippi; Waugh v. 789
Board of Trustees of Vincennes
University v. Indiana 220
Board of Wardens of Port of
Philadelphia; Cooley v. 208
Boardman; Hope Insurance Co.
of Providence v. 47
Boaro; Erhardt v. 484
Bob Jones University v. Simon,
Secretary of Treasury 3490
Bob-Lo Excursion Co. v. Michi-
gan 1660
Bobbe's School, Runyon dba, v.
McCrary 3735
Boddie v. Connecticut 3069
Bodine; Feigenspan v. 868
Bodinger; Baltimore Contractors
v. 1978
Boeing Co.; National Labor Rela-
tions Board v. 3361
Bogart v. The Steamboat John Jay
231
Bohning v. Ohio 926
Boire v. Greyhound Corp. 2500
Bolden; Mobile, Ala. v. 4113
Boles; Califano v. 4077
___; Crabtree v. 2346
___; Oyler v. 2346
Bolger; Cleary v. 2409
Bolich v. United States 2076
Bolles (E. E.) Wooden-Ware Co.
v. United States 462
Bolling v. Sharpe 1963
Bollman, ex parte 43
Bolton; Doe v. 3301
Bond v. Floyd 2706
Bonds; Marcello v. 1997
Bondurant; Deknke-Walker Milling
Co. v. 887
Bonner, In re 560
Book Bin; United States v. 3041
Book Mart, Mitchum dba, v.
Foster 3233
Book named "John Cleland's
Memoirs of a Woman of Pleas-

ure" v. Attorney General of
Massachusetts 2662
Booster Lodge, International Asso-
ciation of Machinists and Aero-
space Workers v. National Labor
Relations Board 3362
Booth; Ableman v. 246
___; United States v. 246
Boraas; Belle Terre v. 3470
Borak; J. I. Case Co. v. 2532
Borden; Local 100 of United Associa-
tion of Journeymen and Appren-
tices v. 2460
___; Luther v. 188
Borden Co. v. Borella 1533
___; Federal Trade Commission v.
2667
___; United States v. 1259, 1965,
2388
Bordenkircher v. Hayes 3892
Borella; Borden Co. v. 1533
Boren; Craig v. 3776
Borg-Warner Corp., Wooster Divi-
sion; National Labor Relations
Board v. 2127
Bosch Estate; Commissioner of In-
ternal Revenue v. 2764
Boston; Norris v. 190
Boston Marine Terminal Association
Port v. Rederiaktiebolaget Trans-
atlantic 3034
Boston Metals v. The Winding Gulf
1991
Boston Stock Exchange v. State Tax
Commission of New York 3783
Bosworth; Illinois Central Railroad
Co. v. 520
Botany Worsted Mills; Knott v. 629
Botsford; Union Pacific Railroad v.
537
Bouie v. Columbia 2552
Boulden v. Holman 2917
Bouligny (R. H.), Inc.; United Steel-
workers of America, AFL-CIO v.
2632
Bounds, Correction Commissioner v.
Smith 3822
Boutelier v. Immigration and Natur-
alization Service 2755
Bove v. New York 1644
Bowden v. Fort Smith 1379
Bowen v. United States 3636
Bowerbank; Hodgson and Thompson
v. 50
Bowers; Allied Stores of Ohio v.
2181
___; Youngstown Sheet and Tube Co.
v. 2182
Bowles; Hecht Co. v. 1454

Cantwell v. Connecticut 1288
Capital Gains Research Bureau;
Securities and Exchange Com-
mission v. 2477
Capital Service, Inc. v. National
Labor Relations Board 1964
Capitol Greyhound Lines v. Brice
1792
Capoeman; Squire v. 2021
Capron v. Van Noorden 33
Carafas v. LaVallee 2841
Carbice Corp. of America v.
American Patents Development
Corp. 1048
Carbon Fuel Co. v. United Mine
Workers of America 4090
Carbone; United States v. 1569
Cardiff; United States v. 1898
Cardillo v. Liberty Mutual Insur-
ance Co. 1615
Cardona v. Power 2695
____ v. Saxbe 3539
Cardwell, Warden v. Lewis 3511
Carey v. Piphus 3905
____ v. Population Services Inter-
national 3846
____ v. Westinghouse Electric Co.
2479
Carey, Governor of New York;
United Jewish Organizations of
Williamsburgh, Inc. v. 3798
Cargo of the Brig Aurora Burnside
v. United States 59
Carib Prince; Wupperman v. 611
Caribbean Mills, Inc.; Kramer v.
2933
Caritavtivo v. California 2160
Carleson v. Remillard 3217
Carlisle and Jacquelin; Eisen v.
3500
Carlisle Packing Co. v. Sandanger
907
Carlson v. California 1285
____ v. Landon 1868
Carmichael v. Gulf States Paper
Corp. 1192
____ v. Southern Coal Co. 1192
Carnley v. Cochran 2362
Carolina Environmental Study
Group, Inc.; Duke Power Co.
v. 3967
____; U.S. Nuclear Regulatory
Commission v. 3967
Caroline Products Co.; United
States v. 1217
Carpenters and Joiners Union of
America v. Ritter's Cafe 1364
Carpenters District Council of

Jacksonville and vicinity;
William E. Arnold Co. v. 3495
Carr; Baker v. 2356
____ v. Montgomery County Board
of Education 2940
____ v. Young 2277
Carrington v. Rash 2589
Carroll; American Federation of Musicians v. 2836
____ v. Becker 1071
____ v. Lanza 2001
____ v. President and Commissioners
of Princess Anne County, Mary-
land 2882
____ v. United States 952
Carson v. Roane-Anderson Co. 1856
____; Scripto v. 2238
Carter; Bullock v. 3173
____ v. Carter Coal Co. 1157
____; District of Columbia v. 3286
____ v. Illinois 1599
____ v. Jury Commissioners of
Greene County 2970
____; Shaffer v. 859
____ v. Stanton 3194
____ v. Texas 627
____ v. West Feliciana Parish School
Board 2968
Carter and Weekes Stevedoring Co.;
Joseph v. 1613
Carter Coal Co.; Carter v. 1157
Carter (Mary) Paint Co.; Federal
Trade Commission v. 2626
Cartwright; United States v. 3346
Cary v. Curtis 171
Cascade Natural Gas Corp. v. El
Paso Natural Gas Co. 2732
Case v. Los Angeles Lumber Prod-
ucts 1257
____ v. Nebraska 2615
Case (J.I.) Co. v. Borak 2532
____ v. National Labor Relations
Board 1455
Casey; Lerner v. 2155
Cass County v. Johnston 422
Cassell v. Texas 1784
Casteneda v. Partida 3813
Castle v. Hayes Freight Lines, Inc.
1975
Catalino, Inc. v. Target Sales, Inc.
4121
Cathedral Academy v. Committee
for Public Education and Religious
Liberty 3406
____; New York v. 3883
Catholic Bishop of Chicago; National
Labor Relations Board v. 4012
Causby; United States v. 1579

Damron; Ocala Star-Banner Co. v. 3065

"Danbury Hatters Case" 687

Dandridge; President, Directors and Co. of the Bank of United States v. 107

_____ v. Williams 2999

Danforth, Attorney General of Missouri; Planned Parenthood of Central Missouri v. 3752

Daniel v. Family Security Life Insurance Co. 1726

_____; International Brotherhood of Teamsters, Chauffeurs, Warehousemen and Helpers v. 3994

_____ v. Paul 2945

_____; Wilson v. 22

Daniel Ball (Steamer) v. United States 337

Daniels v. Allen 1905

_____ v. Chicago and Rock Island Railroad Co. 280

Darby; United States v. 1315

Darkow v. United States 858

Darlington Manufacturing Co.; National Labor Relations Board v. 2595

_____; Textile Workers of America v. 2595

Darnall; LeGrand v. 122

Dartmouth College v. Woodward 82

Dauchy; Wiscart v. 16

Daugherty; McGrain v. 981

Davidowitz; Hines v. 1314

Davidson v. New Orleans 428

Davidson; Parisi v. 3168

Davidson Transfer and Storage Co. v. United States 2195

Davis; Alabama Power Co. v. 3840

_____ v. Alaska 3454

_____ v. Beason 522

_____ v. Board of School Commissioners of Mobile County 3090

_____; County of Los Angeles v. 4015

_____ v. County School Board of Prince Edward County 1962

_____ v. Department of Labor and Industries of Washington 1389

_____; Dusch v. 2754

_____; Foman v. 2400

_____ v. Georgia 3772

_____; Helvering v. 1194

_____ v. Indiana ex rel. Board of Commissioner of Bartholomew County 421

_____ v. Mann 2539

_____ v. Massachusetts 597

_____ v. Mississippi 2927

_____ v. North Carolina 2698

_____; Parker v. 351

_____ v. Passman 4045

_____; Paul v. 3669

_____; Southeastern Community College v. 4052

_____; Steward Machine Co. v. 1193

_____; Tennessee v. 441

_____ v. United States 1588, 3336

_____; United States v. 2993

_____; Washington v. 3706

_____; Wood v. 57

Davis-Bournonville Co.; Alexander-Milburn Co. v. 967

Davis, Ohio ex rel., v. Hildebrant 804

Davis Provision Co., No. 1; Anglo-American Provision Co. v. 648

Dawson Chemical Co. v. Rohm and Haas Co. 4136

Day; Buffington, Collector of Internal Revenue v. 341

_____; Manual Enterprises v. 2389

_____ v. Micou 379

Day and Zimmerman v. Challoner 3638

Day-Brite Lighting, Inc.; Compco Corp. v. 2492

_____ v. Missouri 1864

Dayton Board of Education v. Brinkman 3877, 4082

Dayton-Goose Creek Railway v. United States 935

Dean v. Gadsden Times Publishing Corp. 3379

Dean Milk Co. v. City of Madison 1813

Debolt; Ohio Life Insurance and Trust Co. v. 227

Debs, In re 576

_____ v. United States 847

DeCanas v. Bica 3655

DeCastro; Mathews, Secretary of Health Education and Welfare v. 3775

Decatur v. Paulding 150

Dechamplain; McLucas v. 3586

DeCuir; Hall v. 424

Deepsouth Packing Co. v. Laitram Corp. 3214

Deere (John) Co.; Graham v. 2646

Deering; Duplex Printing Press v. 876

DeFillippo; Michigan v. 4067

DeForest Radio Telephone and Telegraph Co. v. United States 982

Doon District Township, Lyon
County, Iowa v. Cummins   539
Doran; Michigan v.   3986
_____ v. Salem Inn, Inc.   3637
Dorchy v. Kansas   974
Doremus v. Board of Education
of Borough of Hawthorne   1865
_____; United States v.   844
Dorr, Ex parte   168
_____ v. United States   658
Dorrough; Estelle v.   3575
Dorsey; Fortson v.   2575
_____; Kingsland v.   1768
Dothard v. Rawlinson   3875
Dotterweich; United States v.   1438
Doud; Morey v.   2094
Douds; American Communications
Association v.   1787
Dougall; Sugarman v.   3413
Dougherty v. Texaco, Inc.   3504
Dougherty County Board of Educa-
tion v. White   3979
Douglas v. Alabama   2601
_____ v. Buder   3373
_____ v. California   2425
_____ v. City of Jeanette   1422
Douglas, Commissioner, Virginia
Marine Resources Commission
v. Seacoast Products, Inc.
3831
Douglas Oil Co. v. Petrol Stops
Northwest   4024
Douglass; Huidekoper's Lessee v.
38
Dover Five Cent Savings Bank v.
United States   317
Dow; Maxwell v.   624
Dowd; Irvin v.   2193, 2316
Dowell v. Board of Education of
Oklahoma City Public Schools
2966
Downes v. Bidwell   633
Downum v. United States   2436
Doyle; Mt. Healthy City School
District Board of Education v.
3780
_____ v. Ohio   3721
Drake Bakeries v. American Bak-
ery and Confectionary Workers
International   2382
Draper v. United States   2174
_____ v. Washington   2429
Dravo Contracting Co.; James v.
1197
Dred Scott v. Sanford   239
Drexel Furniture Co.; Bailey v.
903
Dreyfus; Marine Transit Corp. v.
1063

Drope v. Missouri   3565
Druggists Mutual Insurance Co.;
Wengler v.   4114
Drum; Regional Common Carrier
Conference of American Trucking
Associations v.   2343
_____; United States v.   2343
Drury v. Foster   269
Dryfoos v. Edwards   854
Duberstein; Commissioner of Internal
Revenue v.   2257
Dublino; New York State Department
of Social Services v.   3403
_____; Onondago County Department
of Social Services v.   3403
DuBois; Badgely v.   1325
_____; Consolidated Rock Products v.
1325
DuBois Clubs of America v. Clark
2795
Dubuque; Gelpcke v.   262
Ducat v. Chicago   334
Duckworth v. Arkansas   1345
Dugan, Ex parte   270
_____ v. Ohio   1008
Duke; Durfee v.   2476
Duke Power Co. v. Carolina En-
vironmental Study Group, Inc.
3967
_____; Griggs v.   3072
Dukes v. Warden, Connecticut State
Prison   3205
Dukes dba Louisiana Concessions;
New Orleans v.   3740
Dulles; Kent v.   2142
_____; Nishikawa v.   2122
_____; Service v.   2089
_____; Trop v.   2121
Duluth South Shore and Atlantic Rail-
way; Groesbeck v.   852
DuMond; H. P. Hood and Sons v.
1735
Dunaway v. New York   4044
Dunbar-Stanley Studios v. Alabama
2896
Duncan v. Kahanamoku   1561
_____ v. Louisiana   2838
_____ v. McCall   533
_____; Montgomery Ward v.   1303
_____ v. Tennessee   3172
Dunham; New England Marine In-
surance Co. v.   339
Dunhill (Alfred) of London, Inc. v.
Republic of Cuba   3692
Dunlap; Cities Service Oil Co. v.
1260
Dunlevy; New York Life Insurance
Co. v.   803
Dunn; Anderson v.   91

____ v. Blumstein 3182
Duplex Printing Press v. Deering 876
DuPont (E. I.) de Nemours and Co.
v. Train, Administrator, Environmental Protection Agency 3797
____; United States v. 2032, 2079, 2310
Duren v. Missouri 3988
Durfee v. Duke 2476
Durkin; Alstate Construction Co. v. 1910
Dusch v. Davis 2754
Dusky v. United States 2244
Dutton v. Evans 3035
____; Mifflin v. 647
Dwyer; Evers v. 2168
Dyer, West Virginia ex rel., v. Sims 1825
Dyke v. Taylor Implement Manufacturing Co. 2840
Dynes v. Hoover 240
Dyson, Chief of Police of Dallas v. Stein 3058

E. C. Knight Co. ; United States v. 567
E. E. Bolles Wooden-Ware Co. v. United States 462
E. G. Shinner and Co. ; Lauf v. 1210
E. Horne's Market, Inc. ; Switzerland Cheese Association v. 2703
E. I. DuPont de Nemours and Co. v. Train 3797
____; United States v. 2032, 2079, 2310
Eagar v. Magma Copper Co. 2796
Earle; Bank of Augusta v. 147
____; New Orleans and Carrollton Railroad Co. v. 147
Earle and Stoddart, Inc. v. Ellerman's Wilson Line 1087
Earley v. DiCenso 3134
East Cleveland, Ohio; Moore v. 3838
East New York Savings Bank v. Hahn 1544
Eastern Central Motor Carriers Association v. United States 1452
Eastern Kentucky Welfare Rights Organization; Simon v. 3700
Eastern Motor Express v. United States 1902
Eastern Paper Bag Co. ; Continental Paper Bag Co. v. 697

Eastern Railroad Presidents Conference v. Noerr Motor Freight Inc. 2286
Eastern State Retail Lumber Dealers' Association v. United States 775
Eastex, Inc. v. National Labor Relations Board 3960
Eastin; Fall v. 715
Eastlake v. Forest City Enterprises, Inc. 3724
Eastland; Dombrowski v. 2752
____ v. US Servicemen's Fund 3599
Eastman Kodak Co. ; Federal Trade Commission v. 998
Eastman Kodak of New York v. Southern Photo Materials Co. 984
Eaton v. Tulsa 3465
Eaton, Ohio ex rel., v. Price 2207, 2272
Eaves; Coloma v. 407
Eby (Martin K.) Construction Co., Inc. ; Neely v. 2737
Economou; Butz v. 3974
Edelman, Director Department of Public Aid of Illinois v. Jordan 3464
Edmonds v. Compagnie Generale Transatlantique 4076
Educational Equality League; Mayor of Philadelphia v. 3463
Edwards v. California 1341
____ v. Dryfoos 854
____ v. South Carolina 2421
____; United States v. 3469
Edwardsville; Central Union Telephone Co. v. 964
Egan; Organized Village of Kake v. 2350
Egbert v. Lippmann 457
Ehlert v. United States 3094
Eikel v. New York Central Railroad Co. 2478
Eisen v. Carlisle and Jacquelin 3500
Eisenberg Farm Products; Milk Control Board of Pennsylvania v. 1238
Eisenstadt v. Baird 3186
Eisentrager; Johnson v. 1800
Eisler v. United States 1762
Eisner v. Macomber 862
El Paso v. Simmons 2579
El Paso Natural Gas Co. ; California v. 2632
____; Cascade Natural Gas Corp. v. 2732
____; Southern California Edison Co. v. 2632

770

L. O. Ward Oil and Gas Operations,
Ward dba; United States v.
4137
L. Singer and Sons; Kansas City
v. 1306
___ v. Union Pacific Railroad
Co. 1306
Labine v. Vincent 3077
Laborers' International Union;
Wirtz v. 2801
Laburnum Construction Corp.;
United Construction Workers,
United Mine Workers v. 1970
LaBuy v. Howes Leather Co.
2047
La Crosse Telephone Corp. v.
Wisconsin Employment Rela-
tions Board 1719
"Lady Chatterley's Lover Case"
2216
Lafayette v. Louisiana Power
and Light Co. 3910
LaFleur; Cleveland Board of Ed-
ucation v. 3443
LaGay; Cicenia v. 2157
Laird v. Nelms 3224
___; Stuart v. 32
___ v. Tatum 3246, 3294
Laitram Corp.; Deepsouth Packing
Co. v. 3214
Lake Carriers' Association v.
MacMullan 3213
Lake Country Estates, Inc. v.
Tahoe Regional Planning
Agency 4008
Lake Shore Auto Parts; Lehnhausen
v. 3308
Lake Tankers Corp. v. Henn 2084
Lakeside v. Oregon 3908
Lalli v. Lalli 3985
Lambert v. California 2109
Lamont v. Postmaster General
of United States 2613
Lancaster; United States v. 89
Lance; Gorden v. 3115
Land v. Dollar 1622
Landmark Communications, Inc.
v. Virginia 3921
Lando; Herbert v. 4023
Landon; Carlson v. 1868
Landry; Boyle v. 3054
Landy; Katchen v. 2641
Lane v. Brown 2428
___ v. Wilson 1251
Lane County v. Oregon 308
Lange, Ex Parte 380
Langer, North Dakota ex rel.;
Northern Pacific Railway Co.
v. 849

Lanza; Carroll v. 2001
___ v. New York 2375
___; United States v. 913
Lanzetta v. New Jersey 1243
Larche; Hannah v. 2259
Largent v. Texas 1414
Larkin; Withrow v. 3587
Larsen; Negre v. 3073
Larson v. Domestic and Foreign
Commerce Corp. 1752
LaRue; California v. 3273
Lassen v. Arizona ex rel. Arizona
Highway Department 2720
Lassiter v. Northampton County
Board of Elections 2200
Late Corporation of the Church of
Jesus Christ of Latter-Day Saints
(Mormon Church) v. United States
529
Lathrop v. Donohue 2332
Latimer; Calhoun v. 2523
Lau v. Nichols 3441
Lauf v. E. G. Shinner and Co. 1210
LaVallee; Carafas v. 2841
___ v. Delle Rose 3323
Lavender v. Kurn 1570
Lavine v. Milne 3662
Lavine, Commissioner, New York
Department of Social Services;
Hagans v. 3461
Law Students Civil Rights Research
Council, Inc. v. Wadmond 3057
Lawlor; Loewe v. 687
___ v. Loewe 778
Lawson v. Suwanee Fruit and Steam-
ship Co. 1725
Layne and Bowler Co.; American
Well Works Co. v. 801
Leader; Apex Hosiery Co. v. 1293
Lear, Inc. v. Adkins 2955
Leary v. United States 2935
Leavy; Louis K. Liggett Co. v.
1092
Ledesma; Perez v. 3055
Lee v. Florida 2869
___; Hansberry v. 1298
___; Kaufman v. 461
___; Knox v. 351
___ v. Madigan 2171
___ v. Mississippi 1658
___ v. Runge 3163
___; United States v. 461
___ v. United States 3853
___ v. Washington 2816
___; Williams v. 2170
Lee Art Theatre, Inc. v. Virginia
2876
Lee Joe v. United States 558

Marine Engineer's Beneficial Association v. Interlake Steamship Co. 2378
Marine Transit Corp. v. Dreyfus 1063
Marino v. Ragen 1650
Marion; United States v. 3153
Market Street Railway v. Railroad Commission of California 1512
Markham v. Allen 1548
Marks v. United States 3799
Maroney; Chambers v. 3023
Marron v. United States 1001
Marrone v. Washington Jockey Club of District of Columbia 758
Marsh v. Alabama 1549
___ v. Fulton County Board of Supervisors 338
Marshall v. Baltimore and Ohio Railroad 225
___ v. Barlow's, Inc. 3931
___; Elgin v. 463
___ v. Gordon 816
___ v. Jerrico, Inc. 4116
___ v. United States 2210, 3436
___; Whirlpool Corp. v. 4100
Marshall, Secretary of Labor v. American Petroleum Institute 4143
Marston v. Lewis 3322
Marietta (Martin) Corp.; Phillips v. 3048
Martin; Anderson v. 2484
___; Harrah Independent School District v. 4001
___ v. Hunter's Lessee 71
___; Lewis v. 3000
___ v. Mott 106
___ v. Struthers (City) 1421
___; United States v. 418
Martin K. Eby Construction Co., Inc.; Neely v. 2737
Martin Linen Supply Co.; United States v. 3816
Martin Marietta Corp.; Phillips v. 3048
Martinez; Procunier, Corrections Director v. 3481
___; Santa Clara Pueblo v. 3924
Martinez-Fuerte; United States v. 3764
Mary Carter Paint Co.; Federal Trade Commission v. 2626
Mary Elizabeth Blue Hull Memorial Presbyterian Church; Presbyterian Church in United States v. 2893
Maryland; Andresen v. 3747

___; Bachellar v. 3001
___; Baltimore and Ohio Railroad v. 392
___ v. Baltimore Radio Show 1777
___; Bell v. 2551
___; Benton v. 2958
___; Brady v. 2441
___; Brown v. 110
___; Frank v. 2192
___; Freedman v. 2587
___; Giles v. 2730
___; Griffin v. 2545
___; Johnson v. 871
___; Kelley v. 1810
___; M'Culloch v. 80
___; McGowan v. 2311
___; Miller Brothers Co. v. 1958
___; Niemotko v. 1810
___; Smith v. 4063
___; Ward v. 350
___; White v. 2439
___ v. Wirtz 2861
Maryland Board of Public Works; Roemer v. 3726
Maryland Casualty Co. v. Cushing 1959
Maryland Committee for Fair Representation v. Tawes 2538
Maryland Penitentiary, Warden v. Hayden 2761
Mascitti v. McGrath 1870
Mason, Ex parte 459
___; Brashear v. 182
___ v. Haile 109
___; Wilson v. 28
Mason (Silas) Co.; Henneford v. 1181
Masonite Corp.; United States v. 1373
Massachusetts; Davis v. 597
___; Jacobson v. 660
___; Johnson v. 2822
___; Ludwig v. 3750
___ v. Mellon 927
___; Nichols v. 1259
___; Plumley v. 565
___; Prince v. 1451
___; Rhode Island v. 144, 149, 174
___; Snyder v. 1112
___; Thurlow v. 181
___ v. Westcott 3833
Massachusetts Attorney General; Book named "John Cleland's Memoirs of a Woman of Pleasure" 2662
Massachusetts Board of Retirement v. Murgia 3741

796   U. S. Supreme Court Decisions

Association; National Labor Relations Board v. 4131
Rewis v. United States 3087
Rex Hospital Trustees; Hospital Building Co. v. 3694
Reynolds v. Sims 2536
___ v. Smith 2924
___ v. United States 436
___; United States v. 776, 1909, 2980
___; Vanderbilt v. 460
Reynolds (R. J.) Tobacco Co. v. United States 1594
Rhay; Mempa v. 2787
Rhode Island; Fletcher v. 181
___; Fowler v. 1913
___ v. Innis 4117
___ v. Palmer 868
___ v. Massachusetts 144, 149, 174
Rhodes; Fleming v. 1624
___; Krause v. 3474
___; Socialist Labor Party v. 2878
___; Williams v. 2878
Rhodes, Governor of Ohio; Scheuer, Administratix v. 3474
Rhoditis; Hellenic Lines LTD v. 3015
Ricci v. Chicago Mercantile Exchange 3281
Rice; Gong Lum v. 1000
___; Montana ex rel. Haire v. 677
___ v. Olson 1517
___; Parr v. 2037
___; Raymond Motor Transportation v. 3895
___ v. Rice 1736
___ v. Santa Fe Elevator Co. 1628
___; Simpson v. 2956
___ v. Sioux City Memorial Park Cemetery 1989
___; Wolff v. 3763
Richard D.; Linda R.S. v. 3318
Richardson; Abe v. 2676
___ v. Belcher 3141
___; Burns v. 2676
___; Cole v. 3195
___; Cravalho v. 2676
___; Frontiero v. 3352
___ v. Goddard 250
___; Graham v. 3128
___; McMann v. 3005
___ v. Perales 3102
___; Tilton v. 3135

___; United States v. 3522
Richardson, County Clerk and Registrar of Voters of Mendocino County v. Ramirez 3519
Richmond; Nippert v. 1564
___; Rogers v. 2296
___ v. United States 2088, 3620
Richmond Brothers; Amalgamated Clothing Workers of America v. 1987
Richmond, Fredericksburg and Potomac Railroad Co. v. Louisa Railroad Co. 213
Richmond Newspapers, Inc. v. Virginia 4142
Richmond City School Board; Bradley v. 2629, 3489
Richmond County Board of Education; Cumming v. 622
Richmond School Board v. Virginia Board of Education 3363
Rickover; Public Affairs Associates, Inc. v. 2353
Riddle and Co.; Mandeville and Jameson v. 31
Rideau v. Louisiana 2461
Riggs; De Geofroy v. 521
___ v. Lindsay 61
___; Thompson v. 297
Rinaldi v. Yeager 2686
Ringhiser v. Chesapeake and Ohio Railway 2097
Ristaino v. Ross 3663
Ritchie; Merchants' Insurance Co. v. 296
Ritter's Cafe; Carpenters and Joiners Union of America v. 1364
Rives; Virginia v. 443
Rizzi; Blount v. 3041
Rizzo v. Goode 3650
Roaden v. Kentucky 3408
Roane-Anderson Co.; Carson v. 1856
Robbins v. Shelby County Taxing District 503
Robbins and Myers, Inc.; Guy v. 3777
___; International Brotherhood of Electrical, Radio and Machine Workers v. 3777
Robbins Tire and Rubber Co.; National Labor Relations Board v. 3949
Robel; United States v. 2793
Robert De Marco Jewelry, Inc.; Mitchell v. 2226
Robert Stewart and Sons, LTD; Black Diamond Steamship Corp. v. 1730

tional Brotherhood of Teamsters, Chauffeurs, Warehousemen and Helpers of America; National Labor Relations Board v. 2064
Truck Drivers Union Local No. 413; National Labor Relations Board v. 3547
Trucking Unlimited; California Motor Transport Co. v. 3159
Truitt Manufacturing Co.; National Labor Relations Board v. 2025
Trupiano v. United States 1695
Trustees of Rex Hospital; Hospital Building Co. v. 3694
Tucker v. Alexandroff 635
___; Michigan v. 3506
___; Shelton v. 2277
___ v. Texas 1550
Tufts, Kansas ex rel., v. Ziebold 507
Tulare Lake Basin Water Storage District; Sayler Land Co. v. 3325
Tulsa; Eaton v. 3465
Tumey v. Ohio 987
Tunstall v. Brotherhood of Locomotive Firemen and Enginemen, Ocean Lodge No. 76 1489
Tuolumne County; United States v. 3786
Turley; Lefkowitz v. 3424
___; United States v. 2052
Turner v. Bank of North America 24
___ v. Department of Employment Security of Utah 3639
___ v. Fouche 2971
___; Smith v. 190
___ v. United States 2973
Turner Elkhorn Mining Co.; Usery, Secretary of Labor v. 3751
Tuscaloosa; Holt Civic Club v. 3980
Tuscarora Indian Nation; Federal Power Commission v. 2236
___; Power Authority of New York v. 2236
Tutun v. United States 969
Twelve 200-Foot Reels of Super 8mm Film; United States v. 3395
Twentieth Century Music Corp. v. Aiken 3613
Twining v. New Jersey 699
Two Guys from Harrison-Allentown v. McGinley 2312
207 half pound papers of smoking tobacco v. United States 348

Twomey; Lego v. 3157
Tyler v. Defrees 345
___ v. Magwire 373
___; Michigan v. 3937
Tyson; Swift v. 157
Tyson and Brother--United Theatre Ticket Office v. Banton 986
Tzakires; Cafeteria Employees Union v. 1439

U. S. A. C. Transport, Inc. v. J-T Transport Co. 2337
USV Pharmaceutical Corp. v. Weinberger 3384
Ucayali, The 1416
Udall v. Tallman 2585
Ullman; Buxton v. 2327
___; Doe v. 2327
___; Poe v. 2327
___; Tileston v. 1399
___ v. United States 708, 2016
Ulster County Court v. Allen 4042
Underhill v. Hernandez 602
Underwood Typewriter Co. v. Chamberlain 872
Ungar v. Sarafite 2505
Uniformed Sanitation Men's Association v. Commissioner of Sanitation of City of New York 2865
Union and Planters' Bank; Tennessee v. 561
Union Brokerage v. Jensen 1469
Union Carbide and Carbon Corp.; Continental Ore v. 2394
Union Central Life Insurance Co.; Wright v. 1304
Union Electric Co. v. Environmental Protection Agency 3738
Union Free School District; Kramer v. 2953
Union Insurance Co. v. United States 303
Union News Co.; Simmons v. 2645
Union Oil Co.; Simpson v. 2512
Union Pacific Railroad v. Botsford 537
___ v. Hall 398
___; L. Singer and Sons v. 1306
___; Transportation Communications Employees Union v. 2708
___; United States v. 396, 752
Union Refrigerator Transit Co. v. Kentucky 668
Union River Logging Co.; Noble v. 553
Union Terminal Co.; Pickett v. 1358
Union Tool Co. v. Wilson 905

v. Florida 2788
Whitton's Administrator; Chicago and Northwestern Railway Co. v. 356
Whitus v. Georgia 2724
Wichita Board of Trade; Atchison, Topeka and Santa Fe Railway v. 3389
___; Interstate Commerce Commission v. 3389
Wickard v. Filburn 1385
___; Stark v. 1453
Wickham; Swift and Co., Inc. v. 2630
Wickham, Mayor of New York; Henderson v. 405
Wieman v. Updegraff 1899
Wiener v. United States 2148
Wiesenfeld; Weinberger v. 3579
Wiesenfeld Warehouse Co.; United States v. 2490
Wiggs; Chickasaw Nation v. 619
Wight v. United States 600
Wigoda; Cousins v. 3551
Wilborn; Eliason v. 1036
Wilbur; Mullaney v. 3604
Wilbur-Ellis Co. v. Kuther 2531
Wilburn Boat Co. v. Firemen's Fund Insurance Co. 1982
Wilcox v. Jackson ex dem M'Connel 146
Wilder; Gayler v. 203
Wilderness Society; Alyeska Pipeline Service Co. v. 3594
Wiley (John) and Sons v. Livingston 2504
Wilkerson v. McCarthy 1720
___ v. Rahrer 535
Wilkins; Elk v. 480
Wilkinson v. Leland 121
___ v. United States 2292
Wilko v. Swan 1943
Will v. Calvert Fire Insurance Co. 3963
___ v. United States 2785
___; United States v. 4147
Will County Board of Education of Township High School District 205; Pickering v. 2854
Willard v. Tayloe 324
Willett Co.; Chicago v. 1907
William E. Arnold Co. v. Carpenters District Council of Jacksonville and vicinity 3495
William R. Warner and Co. v. Eli Lilly and Co. 948
Williams; Adams v. 3230
___; Brewer v. 3810

___; Clementson v. 63
___; Dandridge v. 2999
___; Estelle v. 3688
___ v. Florida 3025
___ v. Georgia 2000
___ v. Illinois 3029
___ v. Jacksonville Terminal Co. 1358
___ v. Lee 2170
___ v. Mayor of Annapolis 1093
___ v. Mayor of Baltimore 1093
___ v. Mississippi 608
___ v. New York 1742
___ v. Nolan 283
___ v. North Carolina 1391, 1523
___; Pollock v. 1464
___ v. Rhodes 2878
___ v. Standard Oil Co. of Louisiana 1018
___ v. Stockham Valves and Fittings, Inc. 2178
___ v. Texaco Co. 1018
___; United States v. 1829
___ v. United States 1830, 3082
___; Whitley v. 2897
Williams and Arnest v. Bruffy 429
Williamson v. Lee Optical of Oklahoma 1986
___; Suydam v. 254
Williamson, Oklahoma ex rel.; Skinner v. 1378
Willing v. Chicago Auditorium Association 1011
Willingboro Township; Linmark Associates, Inc. v. 3824
Willingham; Bowles v. 1458
Willow River Power Co.; United States v. 1511
Wilmette Park District v. Campbell 1771
Wilmington Parking Authority; Burton v. 2302
Wilson, Ex parte 487
___ v. Black Bird Creek Marsh Co. 117
___; Burns v. 1934
___ v. Daniel 22
___ v. Girard 2096
___; Gooding v. 3188
___; Helvering v. 1221
___; Joseph Burstyn, Inc. v. 1885
___; Lane v. 1251
___ v. Mason 28
___ v. New 813
___; New Jersey v. 56
___ v. Schnettler 2291
___; Trebilcock v. 352
___; United States v. 132, 3569

ABORTION 3093, 3300, 3301, 3754
  advertisement 3609
  consent of parent or spouse 3752, 4085
  lifesaving measures for fetus 3989
  Medicaid 3753, 3863, 3864, 4138
  public hospitals 3865
ABSTENTION DOCTRINE 2486
ADMINISTRATIVE AGENCIES 154, 415, 655, 682, 867, 944, 1332, 1442,
    1476, 1499, 1663, 1931, 2046, 2072, 2513, 2758, 2988, 3200, 3811
  building and loans association regulation 1643
  conservation regulation 730
  enforcement of decisions 1158, 1276, 1568, 1617
  food regulation see Food Regulation
  foreign trade regulation 1290, 1869
  injunctions 1203, 2433
  investigations 703, 822, 1396, 1698, 1775, 2049, 2339
  judicial power to review 748, 848, 940, 1199, 1247, 1248, 1280, 1306,
    1453, 1467, 1746, 1774, 2113, 2215, 2756, 2757
  jurisdiction 553, 702, 1295
  livestock regulation 1336, 3332
  mine regulation 1346
  natural gas regulation 1362, 1633, 1806, 1971, 3504
  rate fixing 1155, 1215
  rent control 1458
  telephone regulation 1187
  See also Atomic Energy Commission; Central Intelligence Agency; Equal
    Employment Opportunity Commission; Federal Communications Com-
    mission; Federal Maritime Commission; Federal Power Commission;
    Internal Revenue Service; Occupational Safety and Health Administra-
    tion; Search warrant for administrative agency officials; Securities
    and Exchange Commission; and specific agencies listed in "Case
    Name Index"
ADMIRALTY LAW 18, 81, 104, 184, 231, 382, 611, 612, 642, 939, 2019,
    3039
  jurisdiction 76, 103, 112, 142, 180, 209, 210, 233, 241, 290, 788,
    845, 873, 1096, 1948, 3279
  piracy 5, 17, 65, 85
  prize 5, 6, 12, 29, 623; see also Civil War Blockade
  salvage 27, 333, 502, 615, 674, 997
  ship collision 307, 450, 460, 499, 552, 581, 606, 1126, 1859, 1877,
    1991, 2084, 3597, 3677
  ship neutrality 34
  tug boats 419, 1959, 1990, 1992
  See also Maritime Law; Shipping
Adoption see Children, Illegitimate--parent veto of adoption

ANTITRUST LAW (cont.)
  cleaning industry 1079
  concrete blocks 1882
  electric utilities 3765, 3910
  exclusive dealing arrangements 898, 919, 1156, 1646, 1744, 1903,
    2289, 2422
  futures market 2180
  gas burners 2282
  gas stations 2883
  glass 1513
  highway carriers 3159
  hospitals 3694
  insurance 4002
  janitorial services 3618
  labor see Labor Law--Antitrust
  meat packers 3114
  medical association 1880
  mergers 755, 829, 977, 1031, 1114, 1261, 1449, 1689, 2383, 2470,
    2507, 2508, 2524, 2554, 2607, 2685, 2692, 2742, 2813, 2972, 3316,
    3460, 3812, 3987
  monopoly 479, 2693, 3309
  motion pictures 1040, 1041, 1487, 1559, 1681, 1682, 1683, 1947
  natural gas 2361, 2732, 2950
  news communications 1538
  newspapers 1852, 1926
  price discrimination 600, 1019, 1159, 1515, 1680, 1809, 1884, 1930,
    1977, 2112, 2201, 2255, 2261, 2388, 2412, 2667, 2745, 2759, 3673,
    3997
  price fixing 620, 934, 960, 985, 1018, 1091, 1113, 1286, 1373, 1505,
    1790, 1808, 1836, 2497, 2778, 2812, 2888, 2901, 2954, 3607, 3630,
    3973, 4121
  railroads 614, 752, 906, 909, 2119
  resale prices 729, 861, 890, 1164, 1516, 2030, 2053, 2232
  "Rule of Reason" 594, 732, 733, 857
  sewing machines 2468
  suit for treble damages 711, 2859, 2872, 3787, 3847, 3890, 4049
  television 2175, 2347
  theater bookings 1979
  tobacco 1594
  trade associations 652, 889, 924, 959, 1153, 1677, 1732
  trading stamps 3177
  tying arrangements 2919, 3792
  wholesalers 775
  See also Patents--antitrust
APPORTIONMENT 1070, 1071, 1080, 2537, 2538, 2539, 2540, 2575, 2624,
    2676, 2711, 2719, 2731, 3798
  city council 2754, 3676
  college board of trustees 2981
  Congressional districts 1069, 2488, 2920, 2921, 3388
  county district 3120
  local government 2821
  "political thicket" 1587
  school board 2753
  state legislature 2356, 2489, 2426, 2536, 3203, 3306, 3345, 3386,
    3387, 3558, 3835
  state referendum 804, 2541
Arbitration see Labor Law--Arbitration

ARMED FORCES MEMBERS 158, 214, 1428, 1753, 2096, 2118, 2655,
     2796, 3075
  See also Free Speech--Military bases; Military Draft
ARMED FORCES RESERVE 3523
ARREST 1571, 1761, 1867, 2219, 2271, 2875, 2963, 3562, 4073
  mail carrier 314
  warrants 3237
  without warrant 2291, 2855, 4111, 4112
  See also Searches and seizures, unreasonable--incident to arrest
ATOMIC ENERGY COMMISSION 3200
AUTOMOBILES
  abandoned 3728
  accident liability 2809
  drivers license 3106, 3826
  forfeiture 3265
  stolen 955, 2052
  traffic regulation 1722
  See also Air Pollution--vehicle pollution control; Antitrust Law--auto-
     mobiles; Searches and seizures, unreasonable--automobiles

Bankruptcy see Business and Government--bankruptcy
BANKS AND BANKING 71, 99, 100, 107, 123, 140, 166, 183, 228, 236,
     272, 323, 451, 878, 930, 1145, 1402, 1785, 2094, 3081, 3127, 3184,
     3329, 3612, 3703
  federal reserve bank 884
  mergers 2470, 2739, 2813, 3031, 3533, 3535
  notes 201
  taxation 227, 283
Baseball see Antitrust Law--baseball
Bible reading see Education--Bible reading
BILL OF ATTANDER 607, 1580, 2617
Bill of Rights see Constitution--Bill of Rights
Birth Control see Abortion; Contraceptives; Sterilization
BITUMINOUS COAL CONSERVATION ACT OF 1935 1157, 1291
BLACK LUNG BENEFITS 3751
BONDS 369, 385, 394, 2042
  Confederate 349, 376
  mass transit 3823
  municipal railroad construction bonds 262, 247, 261, 264, 265, 294,
     311, 338, 371, 372, 381, 384, 406, 407, 408, 410, 411, 412, 422,
     430, 516, 517
  negotiable securities 434
  school bonds 555
  township bonds 566
  Treasury bonds 483
Boycott see Labor Law--Boycott
BUSINESS AND GOVERNMENT 1697, 1902, 3917, 3927
  advertising 901, 1067, 2472, 2599, 3178, 3695, 3876
  bankruptcy 36, 78, 79, 108, 162, 167, 178, 185, 191, 472, 1115, 1132,
     1168, 1178, 1267, 1292, 1311, 1360, 1524, 1661, 2017, 2432, 2582,
     2661, 3113, 3287
  commercial paper 1411
  franchise 3867, 3981
  holding companies 1211, 1527, 1598
  insurance 760, 771, 1042, 1374, 1584, 1726, 1771, 1974, 2108, 2518
  liability for quality 2496
  licensing 496, 1020, 1154

COURT JURISDICTION (cont.)
    824, 911, 1011, 1097, 1163, 1339, 1387, 1426, 1429, 1521, 1541,
    1548, 1616, 1748, 1769, 1797, 1938, 2047, 2392, 2400, 2740, 3162,
    3446, 3464, 3590, 3638, 3952
    political issues 1783
    state courts 52, 72, 84
Courts see also Congress--power over courts
COURTS, CONSTITUTIONAL 2390
COURTS, LEGISLATIVE 1022
"CRIMES AGAINST NATURE"--VAGUENESS 3421, 3640
CUMBERLAND ROAD 169
CURRENCY
    Confederate 319
    counterfeit 198, 1202
    gold 1125, 1176
    Greenbacks 306, 352
    legal tender 297, 308, 309, 310, 324, 326, 327, 351, 474

DAM CONSTRUCTION--FEDERAL GOVERNMENT 1054, 1338
    Tellico Dam 3948
DAMAGE CLAIMS 19, 401, 537
DEATH PENALTY 77, 1604, 1906, 2160, 2826, 3098, 3254, 3262, 3545,
    3755, 3756, 3757, 3808, 3860, 3976, 3977
    for rape 2487, 3880
    mandatory 3758, 3759, 3843
DEBTS 22, 25, 35, 61, 63, 89, 206, 317, 803, 809, 1464, 2397, 2435,
    2584, 2642, 3170, 3176, 3486
    credit term disclosure 3341
    imprisonment 109
    installment note 3175
    loan shark 3097
    mortgage 363, 366
    notes payable 389
    promissory note 24, 31
    suit for payment 197
    See also Corporations--debts; States--debts
"DEEP THROAT" 3619
DENTISTRY 1492
Discrimination see Age Discrimination; Race Discrimination; Sex Discrim-
    ination
DISTRICT OF COLUMBIA 37, 86, 1585, 1738, 3286, 3809
    boundary 402
    courts 1750, 3342
    rent control 881
DIVORCE 248, 509, 812, 1523, 1686, 1690, 1736, 2091
    alimony 2557
    children 1105
        custody 1619, 1924, 2136, 2401
        support 3925
    fees as restriction for poor 3069
    residency requirement 3549
    See also Marriage
DOUBLE JEOPARDY 671, 913, 2107, 2131, 2186, 2187, 2355, 2436, 2534,
    2651, 2956, 2958, 2996, 2998, 3016, 3046, 3278, 3290, 3313, 3496,
    3569, 3570, 3571, 3600, 3766, 3816, 3844, 3853, 3857, 3858, 3943,
    3944, 3945, 3946, 3970
    appeal for stiffer sentence 4146

INTERSTATE COMMERCE (cont.)
    bridge construction 237
    carriers 754, 1539, 1897, 2343, 3895
    federal regulation 190, 335, 599, 601, 739, 774, 785, 892, 921, 1217,
        1352, 1478, 1623, 2337
    rate regulation 1023, 1138, 1434, 1452, 2195
    state regulation 110, 117, 139, 208, 276, 350, 397, 423, 424, 508,
        531, 542, 586, 592, 717, 734, 806, 893, 953, 1015, 1095, 1099,
        1101, 1162, 1181, 1207, 1230, 1238, 1273, 1282, 1283, 1309, 1331,
        1341, 1345, 1354, 1535, 1673, 1735, 1813, 1862, 1975, 2336, 2387,
        2391, 3656, 3861, 4027
    telegraph 426
    waterways 96, 1307
    See also Business and Government

Japanese Americans see Citizenship--Japanese Americans
Jehovah's Witnesses see Freedom of Religion--Jehovah's Witnesses
JIM CROW LAWS 1582
JUDICIAL PROCEDURE 74, 88, 244, 506, 798, 995, 1024, 1057, 1064,
        1139, 1172, 1204, 1301, 1312, 1342, 1425, 1622, 1640, 1662, 1824,
        1893, 1935, 2006, 2013, 2208, 2258, 2323, 2354, 2359, 2447, 3439
    access to records 1605
    appeal 2428, 2704, 3575
    award for court costs 2569, 2643
    award for lawyer's costs 13, 2819, 3358, 3489
    bail 1848, 3155, 3166
    co-defendant 1351, 2601, 2781, 3112, 3911, 4040
    criminal intent 895, 896
    determination of legislative intent 1082, 1397, 1440, 1656, 2490
    discovery 2205
    embezzlement 1858
    entrapment 2128, 2714
    extradition 176, 219, 252, 641, 1894, 3986
    guilt by association 1543, 1899
    guilt by presence 2588, 2631
    habitual offenders 2346, 2725
    indigent's attorney 4089
    indigent's free transcripts 2429, 2686, 2967, 3146, 3147, 3710
    indigent's legal fees repayment 3229
    indigent's sentencing 3029
    motion for a new trial 766, 1056, 1123
    narcotics violation 2151
    perjury 1305, 3283
    physical examination 2563
    presentencing report 2918
    pretrial publicity 2316
    race segregation 2440
    self defense 575, 589
    service of summons 425, 993, 1131, 2603
    transfer of case 2506
    trial judge 1049, 1100
    two tier court system 3228, 3750
    writ of error 504
    See also Arrest; Confessions; Contempt proceedings; Double Jeopardy;
        Due Process; Evidence; Grand Jury; Guilty Plea; Habeas Corpus;
        Parole and Probation; Plea Bargaining; Right to Counsel; Rights of
        the Accused; Search Warrant; Searches and seizures, unreasonable;
        Self incrimination; Sentencing; Trial; Witness

LABOR LAW (cont.)
      Catholic teachers   4012
      College faculty   4098
      contracts   1175, 3257, 4001
      pensions   1195
      strikes   3716
      tenure   1206
      untenured faculty rights   3258
   unemployment compensation   1193, 2791, 3095, 3639, 3837, 4013
   unfair labor practices   1480, 1751, 1970, 2638, 2718, 3494
      by employer   1220, 1347, 1518, 1727, 1817, 1951, 2064, 2149,
         2485, 2559, 2595, 2597, 2798, 3171, 3267, 3428, 3455, 3566,
         4065
      by union   1843, 1857, 1916, 2281, 2299, 2317, 2515, 2744, 2773,
         2847, 3276, 3362, 3495, 3516, 3734, 3789, 3891
   workmen's compensation   810, 811, 817, 818, 819, 1066, 1078, 1136,
      1363, 1389, 1400, 1441, 1546, 1614, 1615, 1620, 1723, 1725, 1767,
      1821, 2001, 2007, 2036, 2038, 2057, 2074, 2097, 2114, 2126, 2133,
      2321, 2374, 2598, 2657, 2790, 3141, 3202
   See also Fair Labor Standards Act; Pensions; Prisoners--labor union;
      Wages
LABOR ORGANIZATION   1180, 1182, 1266, 1496, 1534, 2062, 2217, 2331,
      2500, 3143, 3244, 3958, 3960
   closed shop   1299, 1566, 1713, 2298, 2462
   Company union   1209, 2205, 2246
   election   1455, 2564, 2566, 2801, 2851, 2930, 3126, 3782
   Farm workers   3492, 4047
   individual and union   1540, 2254, 2402, 2460, 2583, 3061, 3804, 4039
   internal affairs   1183, 2012, 2058, 2185, 2194, 2227, 2914, 3125, 3708
   union liability for labor violence   2670
   union liability for wildcat strikes   4000
   union shop   2027, 2442
   yellow dog contract   686, 779
   See also Free Speech--labor unions; Searches and seizures, unreason-
      able--labor union files
LAETRILE   4058
LAND   67, 93, 121, 126, 127, 715, 1085, 1304, 2720
   church property   see   Freedom of religion--church property disputes
   eminent domain   186, 667, 914, 954, 1030, 1393, 1511, 1565, 1579,
      1745, 1755, 1799, 1831, 1896, 1949, 1973, 2143, 2199, 2365, 2980,
      3288
   off-shore   1329, 2253, 2898, 3574
   public   151, 462, 510, 578, 598, 2585, 3718
      Chicago   189
      homesteading   840
      livestock grazing   3289
      military posts   1501
      mineral rights   3381
      See also President--control over public lands
   state claims and disputes   119, 144, 2476
      boundaries   149, 174, 192, 278, 346, 545, 3324
      Florida   130, 131, 135
      Georgia   251
      Kentucky   94
   title   15, 28, 54, 62, 131, 135, 136, 137, 146, 153, 193, 254, 300,
      524, 673, 1036, 1260
   trespassing   758
   zoning   975, 1010, 2578, 3470, 3724, 3779
   See also Indians--land

PATENTS (cont.)
    chemical process 4136
    computer program 3269
    discoveries of nature 1664
    human-made organisms 4126
    mathematical formula 3961
    telegraph 222
    trade secrets 3483
PENSIONS 150, 1137, 3840, 3971, 3994, 4119
    See also Labor Law--Teachers--pensions
PENTAGON PAPERS 3137, 3259
PERSONAL SECURITY 1842
PETROLEUM IMPORTS 3719
PHYSICIAN'S LICENSE 1960, 2210, 3347, 3587
    See also Antitrust Law--Medical Association
Picketing see Free Speech--picketing; Labor Law--picketing
Piracy see Admiralty Law--Piracy
PLEA BARGAINING 3149, 3768, 3892
Police see City--Police misconduct; Due Process--police ...; Labor Law--
    police; Suits--police immunity
Pollution see Air Pollution; Noise Pollution; Water Pollution
Polygamy see Marriage--polygamy
POOR--rights 2022, 3070
    See also Divorce--fees ...; Judicial Procedure--indigents ...
Pornography see Censorship of Obscene Materials
POST OFFICE DEPARTMENT 143, 761
    See also Censorship of Obscene Materials--Post Office control of mail;
    Free Press--Postal regulation; International Mail; Search Warrants--
    first class mail
Prayer see Education--school prayer
PRESIDENT
    control over public lands 783
    electors 525, 550, 1875, 1876
    impoundment of funds 3559
    pardon 235, 780, 996
    power of removal 230, 973, 1142, 2148
    powers 106, 1886
    veto 1027
    war powers 849, 942, 1625
    See also Free Speech--threats against the President
PRISONERS 3344
    access to courts 2894, 3715
    access to legal materials 2877
    access to the press 3517, 3518, 3965
    compensation 2707
    disciplinary procedures 3532, 3682
    labor union 3869
    libraries 3822
    medical care 3771
    race segregation 2816
    rights 2467
        mail censorship 3481
        religious liberty 2558, 3181
        right to register and vote 3440
    suicide 3378
    transfer process 3621, 3736, 3737
    See also Parole and Probation
PRIVATE DETECTIVES 1830

SEARCH WARRANTS FOR ADMINISTRATIVE AGENCY OFFICIALS
     drug enforcement agent 4140
     federal agent 1758
     health inspector 1778, 2765, 3493
     Immigration and Naturalization Service   2239
     Internal Revenue Service 3784
     Occupational Safety and Health Administration inspector 3931
SEARCHES AND SEIZURES, UNREASONABLE   75, 494, 768, 1003, 1014,
     1621, 1627, 1659, 1756, 1781, 2073, 2147, 2156, 2174, 2192, 2207,
     2240, 2272, 2287, 2297, 2411, 2464, 2474, 2498, 2501, 2544, 2562,
     2590, 2612, 2620, 2699, 2710, 2729, 2736, 2761, 2766, 2771, 2857,
     2892, 2904, 2982, 3086, 3227, 3343, 3366, 3367, 3469, 3488, 3906,
     4087, 4120, 4135
     arson evidence 3837
     automobiles 952, 1045, 1652, 2814, 2840, 3023, 3130, 3131, 3404,
          3511, 3643, 3652, 3760, 3882, 3982, 4016
     automobiles by border patrol 3317, 3399, 3625, 3634, 3635, 3636, 3764
     business 856, 1589
          attorney files 3747
          firearms dealer 3207
     co-conspirators 3335
     consent, involuntary 2853
     consent, third party 3449
     emergency 1709
     incident to arrest 963, 2957, 3022, 3082, 3430, 3431
     labor union files 2868
     narcotics 1849, 1952, 2009
     "open fields" doctrine 943
     scene of homicide 3953
     "stop and frisk" 2856
     suit for damages 3129
     See also Evidence, Illegal
SECURITIES AND EXCHANGE COMMISSION 1401
SEDITION 992
     See also States--sedition act
SELECTIVE TRAINING AND SERVICE ACT 1647
SELF INCRIMINATION 583, 879, 1150, 1406, 1410, 1508, 1588, 1638,
     1804, 2020, 2328, 2542, 2543, 2608, 2627, 2684, 2721, 2722, 2728,
     2807, 2864, 2909, 2962, 2979, 3025, 3084, 3104, 3210, 3211, 3218,
     3296, 3424, 3506, 3616, 3627, 3644, 3908, 4010, 4062, 4125
     blood test 2054
     gambling 2806
     handwriting 2775
     law firm records 3499
     oil discharge into navigable waters 4137
     political party official 3850
     recording of conversation 3044
     registration of sawed off shotgun 2808
     tax records 3282, 3667
     union officials 1483, 2183
     See also Grand Jury Witness--self incrimination
Seniority see Labor Law--seniority; Race Discrimination in Employment--
     seniority system
SENTENCING 1696, 1743, 2743, 3359, 3360, 3966, 4041, 4043
     right to speak 2288, 2345
"SEPARATE BUT EQUAL" DOCTRINE   588, 777, 1795, 1962
SEQUOIA NATIONAL FOREST 3197
SEX DISCRIMINATION
     alimony 4004